Carl Maria Reinhold

SOCIAL PSYCHOLOGY IN THE 80s

THIRD EDITION

SOCIAL PSYCHOLOGY IN THE 80S

THIRD EDITION

Lawrence S. Wrightsman

UNIVERSITY OF KANSAS

Kay Deaux

PURDUE UNIVERSITY

*In collaboration with
Carol K. Sigelman, Mark Snyder,
and Eric Sundstrom*

Brooks/Cole Publishing Company

MONTEREY, CALIFORNIA

To our students and colleagues

Brooks/Cole Publishing Company
A Division of Wadsworth, Inc.

Printed in the United States of America

10 9 8 7 6 5 4 3 2 1

Library of Congress Cataloging in Publication Data:

Wrightsman, Lawrence Samuel.
    Social psychology in the eighties.

    Second ed. published in 1977 under title: Social
psychology.
    Bibliography: p.
    Includes indexes.
    1.   Social psychology.   I.   Deaux, Kay, joint
author.   II.   Title.
HM251.W78   1981   302   80-23440
ISBN   0-8185-0415-3

Acquisition Editor: Claire Verduin
Production Coordinator: Sally Schuman
Production Assistant: Jennifer Young
Manuscript Editors: Staff
Coordinating Production Artist: Jamie Sue Brooks
Photoresearch: Lyndsay Kefauver
Technical Illustrations: Florence Fujimoto
Interior Design: Albert Burkhardt
Cover Design: Stanley Rice
Typesetting: Graphic Typesetting Service, Los Angeles,
    California

Cover photo and frontispiece photo © Stanley Rice

Quote p. 208 from "Sweeney Todd" © 1979 Revelation
Music Publishing Company and Rilting Music, Inc. A
Tommy Valando Publication. From "Sweeney Todd"
by Stephen Sondheim. Lyric reprinted by special
permission.

Preface

Revising a textbook is much like attending a family reunion. One has the pleasure of seeing old friends and acquaintances (or old topics), some of whom have become more prominent or less prominent in the overall dynamics of the family (or the field) while others have remained unchanged. Yet, as new faces and new generations appear at the family reunion, so do new topics, issues, and research present themselves to the author who undertakes a revision. And in the case of this book, even one of the authors has grown up in the interim—from the author of a single chapter in the last edition to coauthor of the present edition.

Social Psychology in the Eighties is a comprehensive text that integrates the development of constructs and methodology with our needs as social beings to understand the phenomena around us. In it we have tried to combine the best of the old and the new. Topics that are traditional in social-psychological research—social perception, attitudes and attitude change, aggression, prejudice, prosocial behaviors, conformity, leadership, and group dynamics—are fully covered. As we survey these issues, we again relate them to the basic theoretical orientations of the field. Chapter 1 introduces five important theories and shows how each theoretical orientation generates different constructs and approaches to a problem. In this edition, the example we use to make

our comparison of theories is a new one, and we look more closely at how theories generate research questions rather than at how they explain events after the fact. Similarly, in Chapter 2, we discuss the process of formulating questions as well as the methods for answering them.

We have made a great many other changes in this edition as well, leading several prepublication reviewers to describe the revision as a major one. Many new areas of research have opened up since the second edition was published, and this activity is reflected in *Social Psychology in the Eighties*. As an illustration, approximately 1000 references are new to this edition.

Two entirely new chapters reflect new emphases in the field. Chapter 5 deals with communication, including both verbal and nonverbal aspects, and considers the interaction process that communication implies. Chapter 16 developed out of the extensive work that social psychologists have done with individual-difference variables; the general issues of personality and of person/situation interaction are discussed, and four specific examples of personality variables that relate to social behavior (authoritarianism, achievement, androgyny, and uniqueness) are chosen for emphasis.

Many other chapters have been substantially revised and reorganized. Chapter 4 not only deals with the topic of impression management but is framed more generally in terms of theories and concepts of self. In Chapter 14 we go beyond our earlier treatment of conformity and obedience and take a more general look at the process of social influence, including some of the newest work on perception of control. Chapter 11 has broadened its focus from the coverage of racism to include sexism and Canadian separatism. Chapter 15 combines earlier material on sex, race, and social class with issues of age and culture, stressing general issues in the use of demographic factors in social-psychological research.

We have given substantially greater coverage in this edition to topics such as attribution theory and social cognition, the attitude/behavior relationship, principles of equity and justice, research in energy and health-related topics, sexual behavior and erotica, the effects of environmental factors on aggression, and many more. Nonlaboratory research data in areas such as love, aggression, and group behavior are woven throughout the text. This list of new topics is, of course, only a partial one. The reader who is familiar with earlier editions will note many other areas of expansion and change.

We believe that Chapter 20, "Social Psychology and Society," is a fitting conclusion for the textbook. Drawing on the principles and concepts that we have introduced throughout the book, we look carefully at how social psychology can and does contribute to society. We expand our previous discussions of action research to include methods of evaluation research. Using the areas of health and energy as our focus, we demonstrate how extensive the social psychologist's contribution can be. And, as is appropriate for a text entitled *Social Psychology in the Eighties*, we also look beyond what has been done to the field of futuristics—acknowledging the responsibility of social psychologists to predict as well as to explain and describe.

Readers who are familiar with the second edition may notice that there is no longer a separate chapter on sex roles. This change in no way means that we assign less importance to the topic than we did before; on the contrary, we believe that its importance is greater than a single chapter, and critical issues relating to sex and gender are discussed throughout the book, from the opening quotations through the final summaries. We have also tried to deal more directly with issues pertaining to Canada. We avoid inappropriate generalizations beyond U.S. data, and we frequently cite Canadian examples to illustrate general principles of social behavior.

The content of social psychology can be organized in many ways. *Social Psychology in the Eighties* moves from theories and methods through individual and group processes to more applied topics, an organization that we find very satisfactory. At the same time, however, each chapter stands as an independent unit, and instructors who have used previous editions report using the chapters in a variety of orders with success. Cross-referencing of topics and a detailed index will aid those who choose to cover the chapters in a different order.

We believe that the most important benefit of a textbook is that it facilitates the learning process, and, with each new edition of this book, we have tried to make that process more effective. As in the second edition, each chapter opens with a chapter outline and closes with a summary. Important terms in each chapter are boldfaced when they first appear and are defined in the glossary, which follows Chapter 20. (In addition, a list of glossary terms, without definitions, appears at the end of each chapter.) This edition also contains interest boxes, which elaborate on material presented in the text through the use of real-life examples, humorous anecdotes, research findings, art, cartoons, and so on.

A Study Guide and an Instructor's Manual accompany this text. The instructor's manual provides multiple-choice and discussion questions for each text chapter, as well as extensive suggestions for further reading, classroom discussion, demonstration, and individual-involvement exercises. The study guide includes the following for each chapter: a chapter preview; a list of basic terms, concepts, and theories; a set of completion items; and sample multiple-choice and short-answer questions. Prepared by T. Edward Hannah, this workbook provides an efficient means for students to identify and evaluate their understanding of material presented in the text.

It is our firm belief that, as textbook authors, our responsibility to instructors and students does not end with the preparation of this book. Rather, the book is only the instigator or facilitator of a never-ending search for understanding. We continue our search, and we hope that *Social Psychology in the Eighties* and the accompanying aids will help you in yours.

Lawrence S. Wrightsman
Kay Deaux

Acknowledgments

For this edition

Many people have made valuable contributions to this text, from the initial planning stages through the final production process. As we began to plan the third edition, we asked a number of social psychologists in psychology, sociology, and the behavioral-sciences departments in colleges and universities in the United States and Canada for their advice and criticism. The following people, who had used earlier editions, offered their suggestions for the new edition: Norma Baker, Belmont College; Terry J. Prociuk, Royal Military College; Katherine Garner, New York University; Frederick D. Miller, New York University; B. McRae, Carleton University; Navin C. Jain, Memorial University of Newfoundland; Malcolm J. Grant, Memorial University of Newfoundland; D. F. Soltz, University of Northern Colorado; Steve Slane, Cleveland State University; Danny E. Blanchard, University of Alabama at Huntsville; Thomas K. Saville, Denver Metropolitan State College; Hugh McGinley, University of Wyoming; Michael Wolff, Brooklyn College; Steven Ranish, George Peabody College for Teachers; Eric Sundstrom, University of Tennessee; Anthony J. Smith, University of Kansas; Stuart Fischoff, California State University at Los Angeles; Harry Tiemann, Mesa College; Barbara Strudler Wallston, George Peabody College for Teachers; Harry G. Schrickel, La Verne College; John Peterson, Claremont Men's College; David J. Senn, Clemson University; Miriam Rothman, Southwestern College; Joseph R. Heller, California State University at Sacramento; Keith A. Holly, Point Loma College; and Rosemary H. Lowe, Clemson University.

As our plans for the third edition became clearer, we asked a number of colleagues to provide thorough reviews of the second edition and to comment on our proposed changes for the third edition. The following people made very helpful comments and suggestions: Katherine Garner, New York University; Elizabeth Rice Allgeier, State University of New York College at Fredonia; T. Edward Hannah, Memorial University of Newfoundland; Thomas W. Milburn, The Ohio State University; Robert F. Bales, Harvard University; Raymond F. Paloutzian, University of Idaho; Richard M. Rozelle, University of Houston; Richard Noel, California State College at Bakersfield; Stuart Fischoff, California State University at Los Angeles; James G. Stemler, University of Portland; Stan Sadava, Brock University; and Eric Sundstrom, University of Tennessee.

Drafts of individual chapters were read and criticized by the following persons. *Chapter 1*: Katherine Garner, New York University. *Chapter 2*: Jacob Jacoby, Purdue University. *Chapter 3*: John Harvey,

Vanderbilt University. *Chapter 4*: William J. Ickes, University of Missouri at St. Louis. *Chapter 5*: Clara Mayo, Boston University; Irwin Altman, University of Utah; Linda Putnam, Purdue University; and Lisa Demian, Purdue University. *Chapter 6*: L. Anne Peplau, University of California, Los Angeles. *Chapter 7*: Elizabeth Rice Allgeier, State University of New York College at Fredonia, and Paul R. Abramson, University of California, Los Angeles. *Chapter 9*: Russell D. Clark III, Florida State University. *Chapter 10*: Brendan Gail Rule, University of Alberta. *Chapters 11, 12, and 13*: James Jaccard, Purdue University. *Chapter 14*: Jack Brehm, University of Kansas. *Chapter 15*: Carl Jorgenson, University of California at Davis. *Chapter 16*: C. R. Snyder, University of Kansas. *Chapter 17*: Rick Crandall, Texas Christian University. *Chapter 18*: Robert W. Rice, State University of New York at Buffalo. *Chapter 19*: Andrew Bawn, U.S. University School of Medicine, and Paul A. Bell, Colorado State University. *Chapter 20*: Leonard Bickman, Loyola University of Chicago.

The complete manuscript for this edition was read by a number of instructors of social-psychology courses who made many suggestions that were incorporated into the final draft. These persons were the following: Richard L. Moreland, University of Pittsburgh; Steve Slane, Cleveland State University; Frederick D. Miller, New York University; Linda Holcomb, University of Central Arkansas; T. Edward Hannah, Memorial University of Newfoundland; Ross Loomis, Colorado State University; Ross Connor, University of California, Irvine; and Daniel L. Johnson, Radford University.

The contributions of the staff at Brooks/Cole have been enormous. Their dedication to making this book the best possible was an inspiration when the authors' own spirits occasionally flagged. Claire Verduin combined praise with nudges in an appropriate blend. The review process and many other preproduction tasks were expertly handled by Loraine Brownlee. Sally Schuman oversaw the book's production with grace and concern. The contributions of coordinating production artist Jamie Brooks and photoresearcher Lyndsay Kefauver have added greatly to the appearance of the book. Other people too numerous to mention, both at Brooks/Cole and beyond, have contributed their efforts and enthusiasm to the production of this book. We would like to single out Barbara Hearn Jacobs and thank her for proofreading the entire book. Finally, mention of the Brooks/Cole staff would not be complete without an acknowledgment of the people who originally got the present authors involved. Charles T. Hendrix got the Wrightsman book-writing machine started nearly 15 years ago, and, at roughly the same time, a book representative named Jean-Francois Vilain introduced Brooks/Cole to Deaux. We both have found the intervening years of association to be rewarding, and we hope that the pleasures of those associations are manifested in the quality of this book.

Brief Contents

Contents

SOCIAL PSYCHOLOGY IN THE 80s

THIRD EDITION

I do not say it is good; I do not say it is bad; I say it is the way it is.
TALLEYRAND

Truth emerges more easily from error than from confusion. FRANCIS BACON

1

Theories as Explanations of Social Behavior

Juan Corona was on trial for murder. During the four-month trial, the prosecution sought to prove that 25 men, all skid-row bums and winos who had no real homes or families, had been savagely murdered by Corona. The defense denied the charges. While the jury deliberated the case, supporters of Corona demonstrated outside the courtroom. Members of his family—his wife and mother, children and brothers—stood outside the courtroom, too, positioning themselves near the television cameras each day and watching the jurors go to and from the court (see Figure 1-1).

The jury consisted of ten men and two women, ranging in age from 26 to 66 years, all citizens of Fairfield, California. Ernie, the foreman, was a retired Air Force sergeant; the jury also included other retired military personnel, a teacher, a grocer, a welder, a janitor, and a machinist. Over a period of four months, they heard the testimony of 117 witnesses and saw 980 exhibits, and, when the time came for their deliberations, they were sequestered to avoid contact with the media. On the eighth day of deliberations, the jury reached its verdict.

At the time—1972—this case represented the largest mass murder charged to a single person in history. Since then, there have been worse. Yet this particular trial, documented in Victor Villaseñor's (1977) vivid account of the jury deliberations, provides us with an intriguing opportunity to look at social behavior and, in turn, at the principles of social psychology (see Box 1-1).

The goal of social psychology is to understand, explain, and predict the multitude of human social behaviors—certainly a broad

a.

d.

Figure 1-1. The trial of Juan Corona. (a) Supporters of Juan Corona pray outside the courthouse. (b) The jury is out. (c) Juan Corona is led from the courthouse after his conviction of murder. (d) Mrs. Juan Corona, supported by a friend, leaves the courthouse after her husband was found guilty. (Photos © Wide World Photos [a,b] and United Press International [c,d].)

c.

Box 1-1. The People versus Juan Corona.

Consider the following comments made by the jury during its deliberations:

"Corona is nice-looking and his clothes are neat—and a killer, to have killed twenty-five men in the manner that these were killed, wouldn't look or act like Corona looks and acts . . . would he?" [p. 113]

Frank said to himself that he agreed with them, but he didn't like the way they were talking, so he pushed his chair away from the table and covered his ears, not hearing any more. [p. 115]

"A man, if he's a man, doesn't cause outbursts like that. Especially toward women." [p. 116]

"I bet you didn't hear half the evidence and half of that didn't register and you think he's guilty because you hate Mexicans!" [p. 120]

"I still can't bridge within my soul from thinking he's guilty to saying and voting that, yes, he's guilty." [p. 129]

"Mexicans are basically no different than any other people. There are smart ones, dumb ones, good ones, lazy ones. . . ." [p. 132]

In these and many other statements that were written or that we could imagine, we see facets of human social behavior. We see attitudes, beliefs, and stereotypes about what Mexicans are like or what killers are like. We see assumptions about appropriate role behavior for males and for females. We can see or infer that communication is occurring, both verbal and nonverbal. We see the difficulties of translating attitudes into action. And we see the effects of social pressure by some members of the group on others. Such events, and many others, comprise the subject matter of social psychology.

and rich field of study. One social psychologist, Gordon Allport (1968), defined the science of social psychology in his statement that "social psychologists regard their discipline as an attempt to understand how the *thought*, *feeling*, and *behavior* of individuals are influenced by the *actual, imagined* or *implied* presence of others" (p. 3; italics in original). In this useful definition, the term *implied presence* refers to the fact that, in their actions, people often reflect an awareness that they belong to specific cultural, occupational, or social groups. Furthermore, even when we are alone, our behavior may be influenced by our awareness that we are performing a role in a complex social structure, thus reflecting the implied presence of others. If we fail at our job, if our physical appearance changes, or if we get arrested, our reactions are affected by an awareness of others and our relationships to them.

The ramifications of Allport's definition are thought provoking. Just how far does the concern of social psychology extend? Clearly within the domain of social psychology is the behavior of a young man sitting on a crowded bus as a frail old woman stands wearily in the aisle beside him. Does he offer her his seat? Or does he pretend to be engrossed in a book or in the passing scenery? Does he feel any concern about what she thinks of him? About what others are thinking? When a young woman enters a doctor's office for an eye examination, her actions also may be affected by the presence of others. The ophthalmologist asks her to look at the eye chart, trying first one lens and then another. The young woman's task is a straightforward one of determining and reporting which lens gives a clearer image, but she may be thinking "Am I giving the right answer? What if I really can't tell the difference? Does the doctor know if I'm making a mistake?" Such questions reflect her concern about the impression she is making; certainly they demonstrate that many responses in such a situation are social behavior.

Not all activities carried out by humans are social behaviors. For example, if you pick an apricot off a tree, eat it, immediately get sick, and thereafter avoid eating apricots (at least those straight off the tree), your reactions occur whether other people are present or not and probably do not reflect an awareness of others. Reflex actions, such as removing your hand from a hot stove, are nonsocial; the immediate physical response is the same regardless of the presence or the awareness of others. However, your oral response to touching a hot stove may well be colored by the presence of others. Certain internal responses—glandular, digestive, excretory —are generally considered to be beyond the realm of social psychology. On the other hand, nausea, constipation, or other physical responses may result from feelings associated with the actions or presence of other people. Even the time of dying may be a response to social considerations. David Phillips (1970, 1972) has suggested that Jews "postpone" the date of dying until after significant events, such as Yom Kippur, the Day of Atonement. In Jewish populations in both New York City and Budapest, he found a "death dip"—a significant decrease in death rates—during the months prior to Yom Kippur.

Thus, a great deal—perhaps more than you first realized—of any person's behavior is social. In an effort to understand, explain, and predict this behavior, social psychologists have developed numerous theories, several of which we will present here.

I. Theories in Social Psychology

Anyone who offers an explanation of why a social relationship exists or how it functions is, at one level, reflecting a theory of social behavior. The history of such human theorizing is extensive and examples are numerous. Thus some people may postulate a connection between phases of the moon and social behavior (see Figure 1-2); others, as we shall discuss in Chapter 3, may formulate implicit theories of personality to explain why certain people behave the way they do. In this sense, we are all theorists forming explanations for the events that occur around us, although our theories may be vague, idiosyncratic, and not verifiable (see Figure 1-3 for a humorous instance of such theorizing).

Figure 1-2. Lunacy and the moon. Throughout history, people have speculated that there was a connection between the phase of the moon and human behavior. Aristotle, for example, suggested that menstruation begins when the moon is waning. Others have hypothesized that the moon's phases are related to sexual prowess, birth, death, and mental disturbance. Scientists David E. Campbell and John L. Beets (1978), however, have shown that, at least in the case of lunacy, this theory has little basis in fact. These investigators reviewed a number of studies and found no support for the hypothesized relationship between the moon's phases and increased incidence of mental disturbance (as reflected by rates of admission to mental hospitals and by suicide and homicide rates). Their conclusion must be qualified, however, by the period of investigation. Electric lighting may cause the effect of the moon to be diminished, and hence in recent times no effect can be seen. It is interesting to speculate on whether, in places where the moon is more prominent in people's lives, lunacy and the moon may bear some relationship to each other. (Rufino Tamayo, *The Window*, 1932. Oil on canvas, 19½" × 23½". San Francisco Museum of Modern Art. Gift of Howard Putzel.)

Within science, the term *theory* is used more specifically, and theories are considered essential to the scientific enterprise (Kaufmann, 1973). Generally speaking, we can consider a theory to be a set of conventions created as a way of representing reality (Hall & Lindzey, 1978). A more formal definition of theory is the following: "A theory is a

Figure 1-3. (© 1977 by United Feature Syndicate, Inc. Reprinted by permission.)

set of interrelated hypotheses or propositions concerning a phenomenon or set of phenomena" (Shaw & Costanzo, 1970, p. 4).

Every theory makes a rather arbitrary set of assumptions about the nature of the behavior it seeks to describe and explain. It also contains a set of empirical definitions and **constructs.**[1] Theories developed by different groups of scientists vary in their assumptions, constructs, and emphases; yet all theories serve common purposes. One of these purposes is to organize and explicate the relationship between diverse bits of knowledge about social phenomena (Hendrick & Jones, 1972). Every person has a tremendous accumulation of knowledge about human behavior. Some of this knowledge is based on personal experience; some

is based on recent public events; and some is based on what we glean from books, movies, or the accounts of friends. Similarly, the scientists of human social behavior have an extensive set of observations and empirical data, and theory provides a convenient way of organizing them (Shaw & Costanzo, 1970). In short, a theory integrates known empirical findings within a logically consistent and reasonably simple framework (Hall & Lindzey, 1978).

Another vital function of any theory in social psychology is to indicate gaps in knowledge, so that further research can lead to a more comprehensive understanding of social phenomena. Theory guides future investigations; it provides a source of **hypotheses** to test predictions about the world. Theory may also anticipate kinds of events that we can expect to occur, even if the particular conditions have not yet been encoun-

[1] Terms printed in **boldface** are listed in the "Glossary Terms" section at the end of each chapter and are defined in the Glossary, which follows Chapter 20.

tered (Shaw & Costanzo, 1970). For example, in the physical sciences, theoretically derived hypotheses that were made decades ago by Albert Einstein about the relation between space and time have been tested only recently, since the advent of supersonic travel. In the social sciences, too, we can make predictions about events that have yet to occur (see our discussion of futuristics in Chapter 20).

Data generated by a theory may not always be supportive of the original theoretical framework—the research may, in fact, show that the theory itself has to be revised or even ultimately rejected. A theory is simply a model of behavior, and as such it may have a limited life span. Without the use of some theory, however, the task of understanding the variety of social behavior would be tremendously difficult.

Which theory should be used? Every social scientist must consider—and finally answer—this important question. No one theory adequately accounts for all social phenomena, just as no single theory in the physical sciences can account for all observations (Kaufmann, 1973). At present, social psychology uses several basic theoretical approaches. Sometimes two or more of these approaches may be useful in explaining the same event, perhaps with varying degrees of success or perhaps with equal accuracy. In other cases, theories may be applicable to totally different domains of behavior and thus cannot be compared.

Judging the ultimate validity or "goodness" of any theory is not particularly easy and often requires the accumulation of considerable data. Shaw and Costanzo (1970) have suggested three necessary characteristics of a good theory: (1) The propositions of a theory must be logically consistent among themselves; (2) the theory must agree with known facts and data; and (3) the theory must be able to be tested in order to determine its usefulness. Other desirable characteristics of a theory noted by Shaw and Costanzo include simplicity, ease of relating to real-world observations, and usefulness in generating further research.

In this chapter, we shall describe five broad theories of social psychology:

psychoanalytic theory, role theory, stimulus-response theory, Gestalt theory, and field theory. Each of these theories has a different orientation, set of assumptions, and set of constructs, and each can be evaluated in terms of the criteria specified above. Within each of these general theoretical approaches, it is also possible to develop more limited models (sometimes called "minitheories") that attempt to explain a much narrower range of human behavior. Many of these more limited theories will be discussed here and in subsequent chapters.

Our purpose at this point, then, is to demonstrate how the theoretical approach that an investigator adopts will lead that investigator to ask certain kinds of questions about the behavior he or she is researching. Depending on the basic assumptions of the theory he or she is using, an investigator will focus on the individual or on the environment, on past learning or on present circumstances, on limited behaviors or on global events. To show how theory can influence the kinds of questions that are asked, and in turn the kinds of answers that are obtained, we have chosen to focus on the jury situation.

We could have chosen any number of settings to examine. Social psychology is concerned with the full range of human behavior, and the jury represents only one limited set of those behaviors. Yet the jury setting has the advantage of highlighting both individual judgments and reactions to others as well as the group-interaction process. Furthermore, the jury trial is a "real-life" setting; occurring outside the confines of the psychological laboratory, it reminds us how relevant the theories of social psychology can be to events that we read about and experience every day.

The choice of the Juan Corona trial was a somewhat arbitrary one. There have been many murder trials throughout history—some more recent, some more famous, and many less shocking and less well known. Yet, for the Corona trial, we have a detailed account of the jury process itself, and these notes and observations can help to illustrate many of the basic theoretical principles of social psychology. Thus we will begin our consideration of each theory by taking a look at some of the events that occurred during the Corona jury deliberations, as recorded in *Jury: The People vs. Juan Corona* (Villaseñor, 1977). With these excerpts as a framework, we will discuss the principles of each theory and their contributions to social psychology. Finally, we will consider what kinds of questions an investigator might ask if she or he were operating out of that particular theoretical model. The focus of interest will be the same in each case—human social behavior in a jury context—but, as we shall see, the questions to be considered will differ markedly from theory to theory.

II. Psychoanalytic Theory

A. *Basic Assumptions and Concepts*

Psychoanalytic theory, which was developed by Sigmund Freud and his followers, is essentially a theory of personality that developed as part of an approach to psychotherapy. Yet it also has considerable applicability to social behavior (see Box 1-2). One reason for this is that Freud postulated a basic conflict between satisfying individual desires and needs and providing a society that meets the needs of all.

According to psychoanalytic theory, the personality of an adult is primarily the result of what happens to that person in childhood. During the early formative years (ages 1 through 6), each stage of psychological development is assumed to be related to the child's preoccupation with a different part of the body. Infants, for example, are oriented toward their mouths; in this **oral stage,** the child has oral needs (sucking and biting) that are either satisfied or not satisfied. According to psychoanalytic theory, all children move through the same series of stages as they grow older—the oral, the **anal,** the **phallic,** and the **genital** stages (see Chapter 8 for further discussion of these stages). If the relevant needs of a given stage are not satisfied, some degree of *fixation* may result, causing **libido,** or psychic energy, to remain committed to that need

rather than be available to meet the needs at the next stage of development. Many adults, according to this theory, never reach fully mature psychological development (the genital stage) because much of their psychic energy remains invested in earlier stages.

In conceptualizing the structure of personality, Freud posited three sets of forces—called the **ego,** the **id,** and the **superego**—that are constantly in conflict over the control of behavior (we will examine these forces in greater detail in Chapters 8 and 16). According to Freud, when the ego has control over the other two sets of forces in the personality, the person has made a rational adjustment to his or her environment. Even though unconscious id forces such as aggressive and sexual urges will continue to seek discharge, these will be released in healthful, socially acceptable ways if the ego is in control. Dreams and slips of the tongue, for example, are means by which such unconscious urges express themselves. The ego uses a number of devices, called **defense mechanisms,** that deny reality and operate at an unconscious level. By using these defense mechanisms, the ego can reduce tensions that might otherwise erupt from the id and the superego (Shaw & Costanzo, 1970).

B. *Contributions to Social Psychology*

Psychoanalytic theory had a major impact on some of the early work in social psychology. Although current investigators rely less explicitly on the psychoanalytic model, its contributions to social-psychological thought in general have nonetheless been pervasive. Hall and Lindzey (1968) suggest five major areas of contribution: socialization of the individual, group psychology, family structure and dynamics, the origin of society, and the nature of culture and society.

Some of these contributions are anthropological in nature and thus are not of immediate interest to most social psychologists. In discussing the origin of society and the relationship between culture and society, for example, Freud applied his ideas of

Box 1-2. Psychoanalytic Theory.

Matt smiled, pulling at his beard. All through history these people with the security of religion had proved to be the most fanatic and zealous of soldiers once they figured they were in the right. Hell, no group had ever done more killing and slaughtering in the name of truth than the Christians. These do-gooders would jump for guilty once they cleansed their conscience and saw that finding Corona guilty was in the name of truth. [pp. 107–108]

Then Naomi said, "Look, what I can't understand is how can a man with such a nice family have done all those awful things with dirty old men?" [p. 209]

Victor added that it was like Fahey had said—ten psychiatrists could work ten years and never agree about what went on in the mind of anyone who had killed and buried so many men. [Villaseñor, 1977, p. 178]

If a psychoanalytic theorist approached the jury setting, what kinds of observations would he or she make? In general, the focus would probably be on each individual's psychological history. As illustrated in the quotes above, some of the jurors themselves seemed to be re-flecting this theoretical approach. For example, Naomi's statement reflects a belief that a person who has an apparently normal family life cannot be capable of immoral acts. Matt seems to believe that religious beliefs go hand in hand with the possibility of persecution.

The psychoanalyst might derive similar models of personality to account for the behavior of Juan Corona; or he or she might try to explain why particular jurors might be more or less likely to vote for conviction.

Courtesy of Clark University

individual functioning to the broader framework. In *Totem and Taboo* (1913) and in *Moses and Monotheism* (1939), Freud offered his explanation of how societies evolved. In the beginning of human society, people lived in small groups under the control of a strong, autocratic, male ruler. When this ruler chose one of his sons to be his successor, the other sons were driven from the tribe; they then banded together to seek the overthrow and destruction of their father. Thus a *social contract* among individuals developed—first, to combine forces to defeat a common enemy who could not otherwise be defeated and, second, to prevent the self-destruction that could result from aggression among brothers. The notion of a social contract as a means of forming society did not, of course, originate with Freud. But what he added was an emphasis on using family relations to control aggressive and other instinctual impulses. Society, according to Freud, serves to restrain people from expressing unacceptable instinctual impulses. As society becomes more complex, it must establish more prohibitions and more severe punishments for expression of natural impulses. Hence, as Freud saw it, civilization was necessarily repressive and authoritarian.

Although these ideas are interesting, they are probably not subject to empirical testing. Nor are they the central focus of much current work in social psychology. More direct influences of psychoanalytic thought can be seen, however, in Freud's discussion of the socialization process, of group psychology, and of family structure and dynamics.

Socialization, or the process of acquiring behaviors that are considered appropriate by society, is a basic concern of psychoanalytic theory. For example, how does a child learn to be a responsible, moral person? According to Freud, the superego develops as a result of early socialization processes. The substance of the superego is distilled from the teachings and admonitions of parents, teachers, other authorities, and peers. Eventually these messages become internalized as *conscience.* Freud's analysis of the stages of personality development outlines the path to responsible adulthood, and his conceptualizations have been elaborated on by others (see, for example, Peck & Havighurst, 1960), who are specifically concerned with moral development. Chapter 8 presents these elaborations in detail.

Freud's theory of groups assumed that a system of libidinal ties existed among members of the group (Hall & Lindzey, 1968); when each group member has accepted the group leader as his or her ideal, an identity is formed among all group members. Although academic social psychologists have not been greatly influenced by this concept of group functioning, practitioners dealing with work groups and experiential groups (see Chapter 18) have often used psychoanalytic ideas (Bennis & Shepard, 1956; Bion, 1959). Writings of popular social critics such as Eric Hoffer (1951, 1964) seem also to reflect Freud's speculations; Hoffer has described the existence of the "true believer," a person who needs to affiliate with some movement and does so regardless of the particular movement's goals or ideology.

The nature of the family is a final area to which psychoanalytic theory has made contributions. Hall and Lindzey (1968) call Freud's analysis of the structure and dynamics of the family "one of his greatest achievements and his most notable contribution to social psychology" (p. 273). At each stage of personality development, a central concern is the relationship of the child toward the parents. Libido, or psychic energy, is invested first in the mother; later, for the boy, this investment transfers to the father. These shifts in identification, according to Freud, lay the foundation for future social behavior. The impact of the child's orientation toward the parents on that child's subsequent adult behavior is reflected in the writings of Karen Horney (1937, 1939). Horney is classified as a **neo-Freudian;** that is, she shares Freud's basic psychoanalytic approach but includes some qualifications and variations in emphasis. According to Horney, a child learns early in life to develop a particular type of response to other people—either moving toward others (affiliation, dependence), moving against others (hostility, rigidity), or moving away from others (isolation, autonomy). A child's characteristic style of response to the parents, according to such an analysis, will also serve later in life as his or her characteristic style of response to other people.

C. *Applications to the Jury*

We have touched on some of the general contributions of psychoanalytic theory to social psychology—the functioning of groups, the development of leaders, the importance of the family, and more general questions of the relationship between culture and the individual. Now let us look more specifically at our jury situation. What kinds of questions might an investigator who was working from a psychoanalytic perspective want to consider about the jury setting?

One natural question would be to consider the jury as a group. For example, how do the dynamics of group interaction reflect each individual's emotional needs? According to Freud, the effects of a group are to intensify individual emotions and to inhibit intellectual functioning (Hall & Lindzey, 1968). Thus an investigator might wish to compare the emotional and intellectual behavior of an individual when alone to his or her behavior when a member of a group (such as a jury), predicting less effective behavior in the latter situation. Studies of groups have often considered such questions (for more on groups, see Chapter 17).

A more personality-oriented approach to the jury situation would be to explore the reasons for aggressive behavior—in effect, to determine why an alleged killer like Juan Corona might have committed the crimes. Unfortunately, attempts to predict violent behavior have been notably unsuccessful (Megargee, 1974; Monahan, 1975), and even postdiction—explaining the violence after the fact—has been subject to considerable error. As the jurors in the Corona trial suggested, ten psychiatrists might work ten years without reaching agreement.

Still another approach is to look at the personality characteristics of the jury members themselves and to attempt to determine whether their judgments of innocence or guilt can be predicted on the basis of specific personality traits. The concept of authoritarianism (which will be discussed in greater detail in Chapter 16) was derived directly from psychoanalytic theory. Highly authoritarian people are believed to have a strong superego combined with a weak ego. As a result, it is assumed that they will be particularly deferent to authority and punitive in their judgments. In a case such as the Juan Corona trial, it might therefore be predicted that highly authoritarian jurors would respond very favorably to the prosecution arguments and be more likely than others to assign guilt to the alleged murderer.

In an investigation of the link between authoritarianism and jury decisions, Bray and Noble (1978) presented subjects with a 30-minute audio recording of a murder trial, based on a case in Illinois in which two male defendants purportedly murdered a woman who had rebuffed their advances earlier in the evening. As shown in Figure 1-4, both judgments of guilt and recommended punishment varied as a function of the personalities of the mock jurors. Subjects with a high level of authoritarianism were more likely to vote guilt and recommended more severe punishment for the crime.

Many other experiments could be cited here that reflect psychoanalytic theory. The important point, however, is that adopting psychoanalytic theory, or portions of that theory, *will lead the investigator to ask certain kinds of questions and to ignore others.* For psychoanalytic theory, the questions are framed primarily in terms of personality characteristics—either of the defendant or of the juror—and situational factors are disregarded. The locus of the explanation of a given behavior lies within the individual, and the individual is considered to be a product of past experiences (generally those that occurred in childhood). For this reason we say that psychoanalytic theory relies on *historical causation;* of all the approaches, it is the most extreme in this regard.

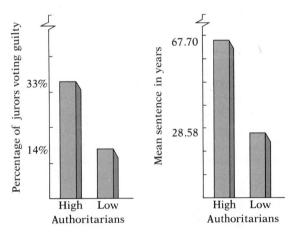

Figure 1-4. Judgments of jurors following deliberation. (Data from "Authoritarianism and Decisions of Mock Juries: Evidence of Jury Bias and Group Polarization," by R. M. Bray and A. M. Noble, *Journal of Personality and Social Psychology,* 1978, *36,* 1424–1430. Copyright 1978 by the American Psychological Association. Used by permission.)

III. Role Theory

A. *Basic Assumptions and Concepts*

Role theory as an explanation of social behavior stands out in several respects from the other theories considered in this chapter. First, it is less formalized than any other approach considered here and consists of a loosely linked network of hypotheses and a set of rather broad constructs (Neiman & Hughes, 1951; Shaw & Costanzo, 1970). Second, in contrast to psychoanalytic theory, role theory does not consider individualized, within-the-person determinants of social behavior. Rarely, if ever, does it consider concepts such as *personality, attitudes*, and *motivation*. Instead, behavior is explained primarily in terms of the roles, role expectations and demands, role skills, and reference groups operating on the participants in a social interaction (see Box 1-3). A humorous introduction to the flavor of role theory is shown in Figure 1-5.

Last, role theory is the most sociological of the five approaches considered here; that is, it gives more attention to larger social networks and organizations than the other theories do.

The term **role** is usually defined as the set of behaviors or functions associated with a particular position within a particular social context (Biddle & Thomas, 1966; Shaw & Costanzo, 1970). Gloria McWilliams, as a student, performs certain behaviors—she attends classes, prepares assignments, makes an application for graduation, and so on. When interacting with Gloria McWilliams in her role as a student, other people assume that she will act in certain ways; their assumptions about her behavior are called *role expectations*. For example, professors expect their students to attend class with some regularity and to show some concern about grades; some faculty may expect a certain amount of deference from their students, whereas others may not. **Norms** are more general expectations about behaviors that are deemed appropriate for all persons in a social context, regardless of the position they hold. For example, both students and professors are expected to be on time for class (a norm), but the professor is expected to call the class to order (a role expectation).

Role conflict results when a person holds several positions that have incompatible demands *(interrole conflict)* or when a single role has expectations that are incompatible *(intrarole conflict)*. Of course, we all fill a number of different roles every day. For example, while studying for an important final exam, Gloria McWilliams may receive a call from the local kindergarten teacher reporting that her son is ill and must be taken home from school. At the

---

Box 1-3. Role Theory.

"Well," said Ernie, "I guess the first thing we do is elect a foreman." "And you're it!" bellowed Matt in a thundering voice. "I second it!" yelled Rick. "Here's Hawk's chair," continued bellowing Matt. "It's the biggest one. So sit right down, Ernie, and this spot will now officially become known as the foreman's place." [p. 6]

Ernie stood up and said: "All right, I'm going to talk before anyone else talks, so put your hands down." Faye made a resentful face. "Go ahead, make faces," continued Ernie, "but you elected me foreman and I'm going to serve as I see fit for the jury as a whole." [pp. 85–86]

"Why has it only started bothering you now?" asked Rogers. Ernie smiled. "Because I'm the foreman and foremen do things like this." [p. 205]

Matt laughed. "You know, Ernie, you're beginning to sound better every day. I think if this deliberation goes on for another thirty days or so we'll all be wanting to run you for President of the United States." [Villaseñor, 1977, p. 170]

The role theorist who looked at the jury setting would be particularly interested in the quotes above. For this theorist, the major questions are framed in terms of how a role or position affects people's behavior. As illustrated here, being a foreman influences Ernie's own behavior as well as the ways that the other jurors react to him.

Figure 1-5. A person holding one role can be seen from many perspectives. Block (1952) interviewed 23 persons who interacted with the same individual. An analysis of these interactions revealed five different roles for this person in these interactions; for each there was a different set of role expectations.

Here's how I really am, but I look like this . . .

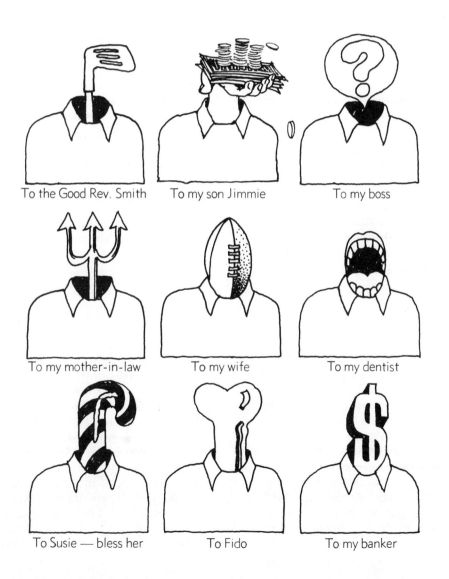

same time, her husband may come home and announce that his boss is coming over for dinner. In this example, the roles of student, mother, and wife cannot be satisfied at the same time, and interrole conflict is produced. On the other hand, Gloria would experience *intrarole* conflict if she had to choose between studying for a history exam the next day and typing a psychology term paper that was due the next day.

To say that people "perform a series of roles" does not mean that people are pretending; nor does it mean that they necessarily are being deceitful or deceptive (Sarbin & Allen, 1968). To a significant extent, we behave in ways that are in agreement with the settings we are in and the positions we hold (Barker, 1960). It is true that there is some latitude in what behaviors are considered acceptable in a particular setting; even an occasional sleeper may be tolerated in some large classes if he or she does not snore too loudly! But the role defines the limits of what is appropriate in the setting.

B. *Contributions to Social Psychology*

The concept of role has been used often in social psychology: terms such as *role model, role playing,* and *role taking* appear frequently in the literature. Yet, as Shaw and Costanzo (1970) have noted, "Despite the ubiquity of the concept of role, it is nevertheless a rather ephemeral concept" (p. 344). In other words, the concept has proved a convenient one, but rarely is it linked specifically to a set of hypotheses and definitions. A somewhat more systematic use of the concept *role* can be seen in the work of Erving Goffman (1959, 1967). Goffman points out that role enactment facilitates and "smoothes" social interaction. Many of Goffman's provocative ideas will be discussed in more detail in Chapter 4.

A vivid demonstration of the effect of roles is seen in Lieberman's (1965) study of the attitudes of factory workers. In an initial testing phase, Lieberman assessed the attitudes of virtually every worker in a Midwestern home-appliance factory toward union and management policies. Approximately a year later, he went back to the same factory and again assessed workers' attitudes—this time selecting two specific groups of workers. Members of the first group had been promoted to the position of foreman in the intervening year, a position that should ally them more closely to the position of management. A second group of workers had been elected stewards, a union position. Did the attitudes of these workers change as a function of their new roles in the organization? In both cases, the answer is yes, when the responses were compared to those of a control group of workers who remained in the same position. Workers who became foremen expressed more positive attitudes toward management officers and became more favorable toward the incentive system, a policy that paid workers according to what they produced. In contrast, those workers who had been elected union stewards became more positive in their attitudes toward union officers and favored the seniority policy over ability criteria. In each case, attitudes shifted according to the new role the worker occupied.

Eighteen months later, the researchers returned to the factory again. By this time, some of the foremen had been returned to nonsupervisory jobs, and some of the stewards had also returned to their original positions. Once again, shifts in attitudes were detected. The former foremen once again became less positive toward management, and the former stewards became somewhat less strongly in favor of union officers. Thus, this study serves as a striking illustration of the influence of roles on our attitudes and beliefs.

We learn about ourselves from our roles, too. In fact, we may develop attitudes about ourselves on the basis of the other people's attitudes toward us. Charles H. Cooley (1922) and George Herbert Mead (1934), two of the founders of the *symbolic-interactionist* approach, noted that a person's self-concept is a social phenomenon; it develops from the variety of roles the person takes on in social interaction. In other words, the self reflects the responses of others, as colored by the person's own interpretation of what others see (Cameron, 1950; Sarbin & Allen, 1968). Charles H.

Cooley called the self-concept a "looking-glass self," because it contains our beliefs about how we appear to others and our expectations of how others judge our behavior and appearance. More discussion of these issues can be found in Chapter 4.

C. *Applications to the Jury*

A role theorist who was interested in the courtroom as a setting for research would—to use a sports analogy—look at the positions rather than at the specific players. Unlike psychoanalytic theorists, who would focus their attention on the personality characteristics of defendants, jurors, or lawyers, the role theorist would focus on the role of defendant, juror, or lawyer. How does the role of the prosecuting attorney differ from the role of the defense lawyer? For example, how might the same person, occupying those two roles on different occasions, alter his or her style of presentation, the substance of arguments, or the use of objections and procedural blocks according to the constraints of the role? How does being placed in the role of juror affect an individual's behavior? The individuals differ because of their own past experiences, but how are all jurors alike because of the common role expectations that are held for them? These are the kinds of questions that a role theorist would ask.

One very specific role in the jury situation is the role of foreman, and, as the quotations in Box 1-3 suggest, Ernie behaved in certain ways *because* he was the foreman. In turn, others acted in specific ways toward him for the same reason; they responded to his role as well as to his individual characteristics. Although a number of investigators have considered the process of *selecting* a foreman (Davis, Bray, & Holt, 1976), relatively little attention has been paid to the behavior of the individual once he or she occupies the role of foreman. One exception is the work of Strodtbeck and his colleagues (R. James, 1959; Strodtbeck, James, & Hawkins, 1957), who recorded the participation rates of all members of the jury during the deliberation process. They found that the foreman was responsible for

approximately 25% to 30% of the verbalizations, obviously a much greater share than would be expected by chance. More work in this area, analyzing specific statements made by the jury foreman, would be a natural line of research for the role theorist. In a related vein, research on the behavior of people in the more general role of leader will be discussed in Chapter 18.

Other role-related questions in the jury context have focused on the research methodology itself. Investigators have asked, for example, whether making the role of the juror a realistic one for subjects will affect decisions, as compared to the less involved subject whose decisions have only hypothetical consequences. It has been found that, when the juror role is more realistic, subjects recall more evidence and reach more guilty verdicts (Wilson & Donnerstein, 1977).

For the role theorist, then, the jury would be viewed as a set of positions, role expectations, and role enactments. Individual characteristics are incidental, and the current demands of the roles are paramount.

IV. Stimulus-Response and Social-Learning Theories

Basic Assumptions and Concepts

A third approach to social behavior, stimulus-response theory (abbreviated S-R theory), proposes that social behavior can be understood by studying the associations between stimuli and responses (see Box 1-4). This approach concentrates on the analysis of these specific units. A **stimulus** is an external or internal event that brings about an alteration in a person's behavior (Kimble, 1961). This alteration in behavior is called a **response**. If a response leads to a favorable outcome for the person, a state of **reinforcement** then exists; that is, the person has been rewarded for his or her response. The degree of reinforcement associated with the response is important in determining whether the same response will be made

Box 1-4. S-R and Social-Learning Theories.

"I didn't speak up," said Rick as he wheeled around and rammed his fist out, pointing his finger, "because of her! Her! Her! No one can talk without her going batty with her damn nerve pills!" Naomi was huge-eyed with shock. He'd almost poked her in the face. [p. 159]

. . . When Rick approached Naomi she jumped, she was that afraid of him. [p. 205]

Rogers had been smoking a cigar but when the cameramen began taking the jurors' pictures as they got off the bus Rogers hid his cigar and looked like a bad little boy. Victor had noticed it and asked what the trouble was and Rogers had said, "I don't want my wife to see me smoking on the TV. Oh, she'd be mad." After that it had become a joke at break time when Rogers lit up a cigar to say, "Watch out! There's your wife!" And he'd fall for it every time, hiding his cigar. [p. 179]

"I thought, my, what if we let Corona go and he not only returns to killing more old men but he harms his own children?" [Villaseñor, 1977, p. 112]

To the stimulus-response theorist, questions are directed at the learning process. What events preceded the development of certain habits? In the case of Rogers, for example, negative comments from his wife led to his habit of hiding his cigar. Similarly, during the course of deliberations, some jurors learned to respond to other jurors in particular ways, depending on whether they had been praised or criticized in earlier interactions.

again. For example, sociologist George Homans has written "If a man takes an action that is followed by a reward, the probability that he will repeat the action increases" (1970, p. 321). In contrast, those actions that are not rewarded tend to be discarded, and actions that are punished may be actively avoided. In more technical language, an S-R association gains strength if its consequences are reinforcing (Shaw & Costanzo, 1970).

S-R theorists see complex behaviors as chains of simpler S-R associations. Complex behaviors may get more complicated but are not any different "in kind" (Jenkins, 1974, p. 786). For example, the verbal behavior used in giving a complicated answer to a highway patrol officer's question "Why were you speeding?" may be analyzed as a chain of specific responses, or verbal associations. Similarly, a student's pursuit of a college degree may be represented as a chain of specific S-R connections.

Within the stimulus-response framework, several different models have been proposed, each emphasizing different constructs. Yet the importance of reinforcement

is reflected in each: in Miller and Dollard's emphasis on imitation, in the social-learning theories developed by Bandura and by Rotter, and in the various social-exchange theories.

1. *Miller and Dollard on Imitation.* Stimulus-response theory originated in the field of learning, but its applications to social behavior have been rich and varied. Several decades ago, Neal Miller and John Dollard (1941) proposed that imitation could be explained by extending the concepts of stimulus-response relationships and reinforcement. Their basic assumptions were (1) that imitation, like most human behavior, is learned and (2) that social behavior and social learning can be understood through the use of general learning principles. Miller and Dollard gave imitation a central place in explaining how the child learns to behave socially and, specifically, in how the child learns to talk—which is, after all, a social act. Furthermore, they proposed that imitation was important in maintaining discipline and conformity to the norms of a society. Suppose, for example, that both a young boy and his older brother wait for their father to arrive home from work. It is the father's custom to bring each son a piece of candy. The older brother starts running toward the garage because he hears a car pull up in the driveway. The younger child imitates his brother's response and discovers that he is rewarded for it. In other situations, the younger son continues to emulate his brother's behavior: he reacts to frustration by screaming; he combs his hair the same way; he begins using the same four-letter words.[2] Imitation has become rewarding, and the imitative response is generalized to many situations.

2. *Social-Learning Theory.* An extension of the basic stimulus-response approach, social-learning theory (Bandura, 1965, 1977; Bandura & Walters, 1963) is concerned with any learned behavior that occurs as a result of social aspects of the environment—specifically, other people, groups, cultural norms, or institutions (McDavid & Harari, 1974). Bandura and his colleagues have emphasized the role of *observation* in the learning of responses to social stimuli (Bandura, 1965, 1969; Bandura, Ross, & Ross, 1961, 1963a). They have shown that, if a child witnesses an adult (or *model*) being rewarded for making a certain response to frustration, the child is more likely to imitate the adult's response when placed in a similarly frustrating situation. The reinforcement that occurs in such instances can be *vicarious* (Berger, 1962). That is the case when the child as an observer makes no response—and so cannot be reinforced—yet still learns to make the response, even without a practice trial. Such learning can have embarrassing outcomes; as Kaufmann (1973) notes, a 5-year-old boy may hear certain obscenities but give no evidence of having retained them until he bursts out with them in front of his first-grade teacher and class. The principles of social learning and of modeling and imitation are certainly not limited to children, however. Each of us may acquire new re-

[2]This story is adapted from Miller and Dollard (1941).

sponses on the basis of observation of other models, and the social-learning theory can be applied widely, as we shall discover in later chapters.

3. *Social-Exchange Theories.* A third type of S-R theory, emphasizing *social exchange,* also reflects a strong reliance on the principle of reinforcement. For instance, Homans (1958) views social behavior as an exchange of both material and nonmaterial "goods" (such as approval and prestige). He believes that those who give to others create pressure in others to reciprocate, in order to create an equitable relationship and perhaps a profit.

Although John Thibaut and Harold Kelley (1959) would not classify themselves as S-R theorists, like Homans they have developed a social-exchange theory of social interaction that may be readily translated into S-R principles. Thibaut and Kelley maintain that each participant in an interpersonal interaction is dependent on every other participant. If each participant finds that the rewards are greater than the costs, then interaction will continue; if the costs become greater than the rewards, interaction is terminated. An exchange analysis may be applied to a variety of social situations, from the selection of a bridge partner to the maintenance of a marriage.

B. *Contributions to Social Psychology*

Although it originated in experimental psychology, stimulus-response theory deals effectively with many more complex activities than the maze learning of rats or humans' muscle twitches (Berger & Lambert, 1968; Kaufmann, 1973). The contributions of S-R theory to the understanding of social behavior are extensive; many people, in fact, would argue that it has been the dominant theoretical theme in most of social psychology (for example, Rychlak, 1975). In succeeding chapters we will see how various forms of stimulus-response theory have been applied to interpersonal attraction (Chapter 6), moral development (Chapter 8), aggression (Chapter 10), attitude formation and change (Chapters 12 and 13), and a number of other aspects of social behavior. In each instance, a stimulus-response-reinforcement model underlies many of the research questions.

Still another use of the reinforcement principle is reflected in the work of B. F. Skinner (1953, 1971) on operant conditioning. Although Skinner rejects the label of S-R theorist and, indeed, has explicitly rejected the notion of any theory, he has been most influential in applying the notion of reinforcement to a number of tasks, including the establishment of a hypothetical utopian community (Skinner, 1948). The frequency of behavior is a major focus of his work, and he has tended to disregard any internal mechanisms that could be offered as "causes."

C. *Applications to the Jury*

Approaching the jury setting, an S-R theorist would look for patterns of stimulus-response-reinforcement and phrase questions in those terms. As evidenced in the quotations in Box 1-4, such associations are often easy to detect. Naomi, for example, learned to fear Rick because of his frequent attacks on her thinking. Similarly, Rogers had learned to hide his cigar, on the basis of previous associations between the act of smoking and negative reinforcement. The jury member who is speculating on the future behavior of Juan Corona is also implying that S-R principles are operating. In this case, **stimulus generalization** is hypothesized: whereas killing had previously been a response to old winos, the juror suggests that it may generalize to Corona's own children.

Because there are so many varieties of S-R theory, there are many questions that the investigator could pose. One approach, of course, would be to look at the immediate situations. What reinforcements are present in the situation that might influence the behavior of a particular juror? Social-learning theory could direct us toward the importance of models—how might the behavior of one particular juror serve as a model for new responses to be learned by other jurors? We could proceed to the more com-

plex notions of social-exchange theory and ask: What rewards and costs are involved for each juror? How are interactions among jurors influenced by the principles of exchange? Indeed, the whole concept of procedural justice has been examined by Thibaut and Walker (1975), who, in a series of experiments, considered the ways in which various procedures will lead to a belief in justice and a feeling of satisfaction.

S-R theory can also deal with the past causes of behavior, and the investigator might choose to focus on particular sequences of stimulus, response, and reinforcement that lead people to their present behavior patterns. Tapp (1976), for example, has discussed *legal socialization*, a concept that refers to the ways in which legal attitudes and behaviors are learned and used. Specific past experiences are analyzed in order to determine how they affect an individual's present legal attitudes.

V. Gestalt Theory and Cognitive Theory

A. *Basic Assumptions and Concepts*

Gestalt is a German word that is not easily translated into English; generally speaking, it means "pattern" or "total whole nature" (Koffka, 1935). A basic assumption of the Gestalt approach is that *the whole is greater than the sum of the parts.* In other words, if we choose to break behavior down into specific stimulus-response associations, we lose its essence and ignore the totality of human experience. Mozart's Piano Concerto No. 23 is more than a sequence of keyboard sounds, and *Gone with the Wind* is more than a sequence of light frames on a movie screen. In this respect, Gestalt theory is diametrically opposed to the stimulus-response theories we've just reviewed.

To the Gestaltists, human behavior is integrated, purposeful, and goal oriented; hence Gestalt psychology contrasts with the stimulus-response approach in regard to what is emphasized in the study of social behavior. To the Gestaltists, focusing on habits and chains of stimulus-response bonds and reducing human behavior to a series of passive reactions is insufficient to explain the human condition. Gestalt theorists criticize the S-R approach for failing to recognize that human responses are always interrelated, moving people toward goals they are striving to achieve.

Gestalt theory also assumes that the brain actively fits sensations and perceptions into a larger cognitive structure; for example, when we hear a strange sound in the middle of the night, we not only hear it but interpret it and put it into context (see Box 1-5). The nervous system and brain are considered *organizers* and *interpreters*. In contrast, stimulus-response theory focuses on peripheral processes—that is, the action of sensory receptors and muscle responses.

Some Gestalt theorists use the **phenomenological approach,** which is oriented toward "as naive and full a description of direct experience as possible" (Koffka, 1935, p. 73). Thus the phenomenological approach states that knowing how a person *perceives* the world is most useful in understanding that person's behavior. In the words of sociologist W. I. Thomas, "situations defined as real are real in their consequences" (quoted in Hollander, 1971). In other words, we may act on the basis of what we believe to be true—and those beliefs may, in turn, affect the behavior of those around us.

In the past couple of decades, social psychology has seen the growth of general cognitive theories, many of them derived at least loosely from the Gestalt approach.

Like Gestalt theory, cognitive theories focus on organized conscious experience; but, unlike Gestalt theory, the emphasis is not exclusively on the perceptual process. Terms such as *cognition, cognitive structure, scripts,* and *schemata* have become common. Although the cognitive theorist may use terms like *stimulus* and *response,* their meaning is much more complex than the meaning assigned to them by S-R theorists. For cognitive theorists, a stimulus involves a complex pattern of organization rather than a simple external object, an idea that reflects the origin of this thinking in Gestalt theory. Cognitive theorists are also much more likely than S-R theorists to use concepts such as *meaning* that rely on learning and central cognitive processing (Shaw & Costanzo, 1970).

Box 1-5. Gestalt Theory.

"Okay, George, what do you remember about Mr. Whitacre, victim number one?" [p. 23]

They were just talking, going over the evidence, and trying to remember what they'd heard and seen during the five months of the trial, and surprisingly they were discovering that, as a group, as a collective memory, they were recalling much more than any one of them individually ever did. [pp. 32–33]

"That woman, Dr. Guy, who talked so much nobody could shut her up, was one of the people who saved our child . . . and she was eminently qualified and in *Who's Who* and in *Men and Women of Science.* . . . And I looked at Hawk and saw him belittling her . . . and I said to myself, hey, this Hawk isn't the good guy." [p. 71]

"So what are we going to do, let her argue for an acquittal with evidence that's nonexistent?" [p. 164]

"Ah, do you think you and I or anyone else has the right to tell a person on a jury that what they believe to be true isn't true but what we believe to be true is true?" [Villaseñor, 1977, p. 164]

How do people perceive events, and how do those perceptions affect behavior? Gestalt theorists are concerned primarily with these perceptual processes. As illustrated in the quotes above, perceptions— even of the same event—vary widely, and the reasons for these variations provide fertile ground for the Gestalt theorist.

Although current cognitive theories relate to the Gestalt model, they are not identical to it in their assumptions. Gestalt theory dealt more heavily with concepts such as psychophysiological isomorphism (a belief that the physiological experience and the psychological experience were one and the same) and other assumptions about the central role of perception in human behavior (Ausubel, 1965). More recent cognitive theorizing, while rejecting the strict mechanistic principles of the more rigid S-R theorists, is also open to a greater variety of mechanisms by which cognitive behavior may develop.

B. *Contributions to Social Psychology*

The interests and assumptions of many social psychologists reflect a basic Gestalt orientation to social behavior (Zajonc, 1968b). Early work by Solomon Asch (1946) on impression formation is one good example of such an orientation. To one group of students, Asch read a list of characteristics of a fictitious person that included the words *intelligent, skillful, industrious, warm, determined, practical,* and *cautious*. He read the same list of words to a second group, except that the word *cold* was substituted for the word *warm*. This single change had strong effects; the two groups formed quite different impressions about the imaginary person, thus supporting the Gestalt idea of perception as a whole rather than a simple sum of the parts. In Chapter 3 we will discuss the area of impression formation in greater detail.

The **halo effect,** or the tendency to use one's general impression of another person to shape an opinion about a specific characteristic of that person, is another very common tendency that supports this same idea. When someone asks us if our friend Diane is "sensible," we may respond "yes"—not because we have ever observed her in situations requiring good sense but because our overall impression of her is that "she's a good person." The phenomenological element in Gestalt psychology reminds us that our behavior is influenced if we assume that things are related, even if in reality they are not related.

A more recent development that derives from the Gestalt approach is **attribution theory** (Heider, 1958; Jones & Davis, 1965; Kelley, 1971). In essence, this theory is concerned with how we infer causes of action—other people's and our own (Kelley, 1967). For example, if Tony apparently sees you coming through the cafeteria line but fails to wave you over to his table, how do you interpret his behavior? Do you attribute it to poor vision ("Maybe he really didn't see me") or to his wanting to be alone so he can study for a test? Or do you take it as reflecting something negative about you personally? Attribution theory reflects the Gestalt assumption that we cannot process stimuli from the outside world apart from other information that we have acquired from being perceivers. To say, as communications theorist Marshall McLuhan (1964) does, that "the medium is the message" is an exaggeration of this viewpoint. But attribution theory does note that the *medium* (that is, the speaker, the source, or the communication mode) clearly influences the perception, interpretation, and acceptance of the message (see Figure 1-6). As we shall see in Chapter 3 and beyond, these perceptions and conclusions clearly affect our behavior as well.

We can see yet another influence of Gestalt theory and cognitive theories in social psychology in consistency models (Abelson, Aronson, McGuire, Newcomb, Rosenberg, & Tannenbaum, 1968; Zajonc, 1968b). Basic to all of these models, which will be discussed in more detail in Chapter 12, is the idea that people seek consistency in their beliefs and actions. For example, Festinger's (1957) theory of **cognitive dissonance** proposes that, when we hold two cognitions or beliefs that are in opposition to each other, we are motivated to relieve the discomfort, or dissonance, that is caused by the conflict between the beliefs. These basic ideas of consistency have been applied to a variety of areas, including impression management (Chapter 4), interpersonal attraction (Chapter 6), and attitudes (Chapter 12).

C. Applications to the Jury

Returning to the courtroom of the Juan Corona trial, we can see that each juror was forming impressions and drawing conclusions on the basis of information presented. Yet not every juror was forming the *same* impression or drawing the *same* conclusion. As shown in Box 1-1, some jurors thought they had heard evidence that others believed was nonexistent. How and why do such differences occur? For the social psychologist interested in the cognitive and judgmental aspects of decision making, the jury setting is a rich environment. Kaplan and his colleagues (Kaplan, 1977; Kaplan, Steindorf, & Iervolino, 1978), for example, have used a model called *information integration theory* to describe how jurors may combine various types of information in making their judgments. Both the individual juror's own values and the nature of the evidence presented can be combined in this model, allowing a prediction of juror decisions.

Figure 1-6. "I hold that a little rebellion, now and then, is a good thing, and as necessary in the political world as storms are in the physical."

Who said it, and what difference does it make? When students read this quotation and were told that Lenin, the leader of the Russian Bolshevik Revolution, had made the statement, they interpreted "rebellion" to mean "revolution" and talked about "purging the old order" or "letting loose of pent-up forces." When told that U.S. President Thomas Jefferson had made the statement, students emphasized "a *little* rebellion" and spoke of a need for "new ideas in government and politics." The effect of substituting one purported author for another was "to alter the cognitive content of the statement" (Asch, 1952, p. 422). Perceivers interpreted the content of the statement according to their assumptions about the author and the author's intent, demonstrating the Gestalt assumption that the whole is greater than the sum of its parts. The actual author of the statement was Jefferson. (The Bettmann Archive.)

Attribution theory, too, offers a rich source of hypotheses about jury decision making. For many cases, a basic task of the juror is to make judgments about the cause for a defendant's behavior. Decisions of guilt or innocence may be based on where that cause is assigned—whether, for example, a jury believes the individual was responsible or whether there were extenuating circumstances that shift the locus of responsibility to other individuals or environmental factors. Other aspects of the legal system lend themselves equally well to an attribution analysis. For example, Carroll (1978) found that, when parole officers believed an offender's criminal history was due to stable factors (such as basic personality problems), they were much less likely to recommend parole than when the cause of crime was unstable, such as loss of a job or provocation by the victim. Unstable causes are presumably changeable—hence the recommendation of parole—whereas stable causes are seen as permanent, and thus the criminal is less likely to be trustworthy in the future.

Another feature of the trial situation that lends itself to explanation by Gestalt theory and cognitive theory is the eyewitness report. When a person witnesses a crime, how accurate is the recall? Judging from the confusion that often surrounds the stories of different witnesses, we can be quite certain that the process is not a simple one of presenting a stimulus and obtaining a response (Clifford & Bull, 1978). Instead, people respond to various features in a situation and arrive at an overall judgment —that may or may not be accurate (Loftus, 1974). Furthermore, the witness' perceptions may be influenced by his or her physiological or psychological state; thus, observers who are anxious or preoccupied have been found to be less efficient in recalling details of an event (Siegel & Loftus, 1978). Eyewitness testimony is a fascinating application of cognitive principles to social problems (and will be discussed at greater length in Chapter 3).

In summary, the jury setting offers wide evidence of the importance of cognitive and perceptual processes in human behavior.

For the investigator operating out of this theoretical framework, the questions to be tested are unlimited.

VI. Field Theory

A. *Basic Assumptions and Concepts*

The last orientation we will consider is that of **field theory.** The Gestalt approach and field theory are similar, but the differences are great enough to warrant separate treatment. The fundamental contribution of field theory, as developed by **Kurt Lewin** (1951), is the proposition that human behavior is a function of both the person and the environment; expressed in symbolic terms, $B = f(P,E)$. The first implication of this proposition is that a person's behavior is related both to characteristics within the person (heredity, abilities, personality, state of health, and so on) *and* to the social situation in which the person presently exists (for example, the presence of others, the extent to which the person's goals may be blocked, and the like). This two-factor explanation (which will be discussed in more detail in Chapter 16) is different from some of the other theories that we have discussed. Whereas psychoanalytic theory tends to focus primarily on the individual and role theory concentrates on the situational demands, field theory proposes to take both factors into account simultaneously (see Box 1-6).

A second implication of a field theory of social behavior derives from the earlier use of field theory in physics. As used in physics, and as used by Lewin in psychology, field theory assumes that "the properties of any event are determined by its relations to the system of events of which it is a component" (Deutsch, 1968, p. 414). In other words, every action is influenced by the field in which it takes place—and the field includes both the person and the environment. The more current term, *general systems theory*, is founded on a similar assumption.

The most basic construct in field theory is the **life space,** the total subjective environment that each of us experiences

Box 1-6. Field Theory.

"And I would again emphasize that in your further deliberations no juror should change any vote or any opinion merely as an accommodation to any other jurors, but should do so only if convinced that his previous opinion or vote is erroneous." [p. 158]

"I got nothing to say. It's too late in the day and people will now vote according to how hungry or how tired they are, so I say why talk?" [p. 92]

"But," said Naomi, "my sister will leave if I don't tell her I'm coming home tomorrow. Look, I'm the holdout juror and I've changed my mind and tomorrow I'm going to give them my vote and it will then be a unanimous verdict, and so you can tell my sister I'm coming home." [p. 209]

"Before you sign these twenty-five cards I would like Naomi to tell us how she feels. Did she change her vote out of some sort of convenience or does she now believe Corona is really guilty?"

"Well," said Naomi, "I think I've changed my mind. Yesterday you gave me a day's rest and I relaxed and I saw things differently. Like when George spoke to me and, basically, I now think you people are right and I do think Corona is guilty." [Villaseñor, 1977, p. 213]

The field theorist, who looks at both individual and situational factors, would see in these quotations the influence of both factors. On the one hand, such a theorist would look to the personal characteristics of Naomi that led her to vote with the other jurors. On the other hand, this theorist would also explore the situational factors—her sister's expectations, the pressure from other jurors—as possible causes for Naomi's decision.

(Lewin, 1938). All psychological events—including thinking, acting, and dreaming—are a function of the life space, "which consists of the person and the environment viewed as one constellation of interdependent factors" (Deutsch, 1968, p. 417). Whereas the S-R theorists see behavior as a function of an external stimulus, Lewin claimed that it was meaningless to consider the determinants of behavior without reference to both the individual and the environment (Lewin, 1938). Thus the statement "He became leader of the group because of his aggressiveness" is an unacceptable explanation to field theorists (Deutsch, 1968). Equally simplified and unacceptable is a statement such as "a highly cohesive group will be more productive than a less cohesive group." Both the specific situation and the specific personalities must be considered.

Another major emphasis of field theory is *the here and now.* To Lewin, psychological events must be explained by the properties of the life space that exist in the present.

Thus the concept of historic causation, as employed in psychoanalytic theory and S-R theory, is rejected. According to field theorists, if a 29-year-old man is unmarried, shy, and self-deprecatory in his relationships with others, the fact that an auto accident permanently disfigured his face at age 12 is not sufficient explanation for his later behavior. The young man's present reluctance to date is only a function of contemporary properties of the field—properties that may, however, include his present feelings about his appearance or his present memories of humiliating comments about his face. The past can influence present behavior only indirectly, in the form of representations or alterations of past events carried into the present.

The concept of the *tension system* is also basic to field theory. Psychological needs that have been aroused but not yet satisfied create unresolved tension systems; these systems serve to engage people in actions that will move them toward the goal of satisfying those psychological needs. According to Lewin, unfinished tasks perpetuate unresolved tension systems; the tasks are better remembered until they are completed. When the task is completed, the associated tension is then dissipated and the task is less well remembered.

B. *Contributions to Social Psychology*

The influence of field theory on social psychology is very broad. Much of this influence has taken the form of general approaches to problem solving rather than a specific use of Lewin's constructs. A large part of its influence is due to the impact of Lewin himself. Rychlak (1973) observes that Lewin "probably did more for the establishment and development of social psychology than any other theorist in the history of psychology" (p. 409). Lewin originated the term *group dynamics* and founded the influential Research Center for Group Dynamics (now located at the University of Michigan). He and his associates also initiated the T-group movement (see Chapter 17) and were pioneers in the development of action research (see Chapter 20). Lewin's ideas have stimulated such diverse approaches to the study of social behavior as Roger Barker's **ecological psychology** (1963, 1965, 1968), described in Figure 1-7, and Morton Deutsch's work on the effects of cooperation and competition on small-group functioning (Deutsch, 1949a, 1949b).

The specific theoretical constructs that Lewin introduced are not used much in current social-psychological theorizing, but the general orientation that he espoused is very much in evidence. The belief that social-psychological phenomena can be studied experimentally, that psychological events must be studied in relation to one another, that both the individual and the group are important—these ideas are a part of the Lewinian legacy and continue to influence both theory and research (Deutsch, 1968).

C. *Applications to the Jury*

While the defense attorney for Juan Corona awaited the jury's verdict, he thought about the characteristics of juries.

"He'd never liked waiting for a jury's verdict. Juries were as fickle as women, in his estimation. You could never tell how a jury would interpret the proceedings in the courtroom" (p. 66). Such thoughts reflect the flavor of Lewinian field theory, an approach that stresses the dynamic interplay among various forces, involving both persons and environmental characteristics in the here and now. Similarly, Naomi's eventual decision to concur with the majority (see Box 1-6) illustrates the combination of individual and situational factors.

The investigator approaching the jury with a field-theory orientation would of necessity consider both individual and situational factors. Research on conformity, for example (see Chapter 14), reflects this dual approach. On the one hand, there are situational forces acting to increase the extent to which an individual conforms; on the other hand, there continue to be individual differences in the amount of conformity that different people display. Thus field theorists would formulate their questions in terms of both types of factors and would analyze the situation in terms of the pressures that existed in that particular situation. Field theorists would be more likely to study the deliberation process of the jury itself rather than static characteristics of the jurors, reflecting Lewin's concern with group dynamics as an active rather than passive process.

VII. A Comparison of Theories

Each of the five theories that we have discussed makes a set of specific assumptions about human behavior, defining certain variables as important and others as incidental. Each theory, in turn, points an investigator in certain directions, suggesting some questions to ask and ignoring others. Whether the setting is the jury, the classroom, or the laboratory, a theory provides a basic framework in which research is carried out. Having considered the central features of each theory separately, let's now compare them directly. First, we can make a comparison of the basic assumptions of each theory (Table 1-1 summarizes the results of such a comparison).

Figure 1-7. How much does setting influence behavior? **Ecological psychology** is the label given to the approach of social psychologists who use naturalistic observations to explore the relationship of behavior to the environment in which it takes place. Developed by Roger Barker and his associates (Barker, 1963, 1965, 1968; Barker & Schoggen, 1973; Gump, Schoggen, & Redl, 1957; Wicker, 1968, 1969b), the ecological approach analyzes real-life environments through the use of the construct **behavior settings**—the home, the office, a concert hall, and a wooded trail. The principal assumption of ecological psychology, that much important behavior is related to the setting in which it occurs, is an extension of Lewinian field theory. (© Cary Wolinsky/Stock, Boston.)

Historical versus Contemporary Emphasis. One general point of divergence among these theories is the extent to which they emphasize historical versus contemporary causes for behavior. Of the five approaches, field theory most strongly emphasizes that only present events can explain social behavior. Role theory and Gestalt theory also place importance on the present. In contrast, psychoanalytic theory assumes that present behavior is strongly influenced by past events—often by events that occurred when the child was six years or younger in age. Stimulus-response theory, while assuming that behavior can be changed through the modification of reinforcements, also recognizes that antecedents (or the person's reinforcement history) are important. Indeed, the compatibility between psychoanalytic and S-R theories of behavior in terms of the historical assumption has led to a number of attempts to translate the concepts of one model into the other (for example, Dollard & Miller, 1950).

TABLE 1-1 / *A Comparison of Theories in Social Psychology*

Theory	Causes of Behavior (Historical or Contemporary)	Internal versus Situational Factors	Units of Analysis	Assumptions about Human Nature
Psychoanalytic theory	Emphasis on historical but recognition of contemporary	Emphasis on internal factors (personality, motives)	Personality traits and general characteristics	The initially asocial infant learns to control his or her impulses and perhaps becomes an altruistic, loving adult.
Role theory	Contemporary ("You *are* what role you now hold.")	Emphasis on roles and situational influences; internal factors ignored.	Responses to various situations	People act in response to the expectations for roles they hold.
S-R theory	Contemporary, although concerned with antecedents of behavior also	Largely situational (emphasis on reward structure) but recognizes that internal factors may determine what is rewarding	Specific responses, habits— each treated as a unit	People can be molded into almost any behavior pattern through reinforcement.
Gestalt theory	Contemporary; emphasis on phenomenological approach	Both internal and situational factors recognized	More molar behaviors, although often unspecified	Human nature is active and purposive, seeking goals and self-improvement.
Field theory	Strongly contemporary	Emphasis on both types of factors	Great variation in units used, although "life space" is central	There are few substantive assumptions.

Internal versus Situational Factors. A second dimension on which theories differ is the extent to which they emphasize the role of the individual or the role of the situation in determining behavior. The field of personality has traditionally emphasized the importance of the individual (see Chapter 16), and thus psychoanalytic theory gives major emphasis to the personality and motives of the participants as determinants of interpersonal behavior. Role theory, in contrast, virtually ignores individual differences and looks instead at the common features of roles, role conflicts, and role expectations as the determinants of behavior. In the middle ground, we find field theory, with its conviction that every interpersonal action is a result of both the person and the environment.

Units of Analysis. How specific should the units of study be when we consider social behavior? Stimulus-response theory and Gestalt theory represent the extremities on this issue. S-R theory assumes that social behavior can be adequately described and explained only by looking at specific stimulus-response-reinforcement connections. Gestalt theory adamantly rejects this assumption, claiming that subdividing behavior into discrete elements destroys its essence. Similarly, most recent cognitive models assume a complex interdependence between processes of perception, memory, thought and action.

Assumptions about Human Nature. Both S-R theory and role theory assume that human nature lacks an essence; rather, people act in response to stimuli (S-R theory) or in response to the expectations of the role they are fulfilling (role theory). Gestalt theory and field theory, in contrast, emphasize that human nature is purposive and goal oriented. To varying degrees, they both assume that people develop long-term aspirations and act in accordance with these goals. Psychoanalytic theory, as explicated by Sigmund Freud, portrays instinc-

tual human nature as selfish and aggressive but held in abeyance by social restrictions.

A second way to compare these five theories is to look at how well they fit the criteria proposed by Shaw and Costanzo (1970) as requirements of a good theory (discussed earlier in this chapter). How well does each of these theories meet the standards of logical consistency, agreeability with data, and testability? Stimulus-response theory fares well; it is logically consistent, agrees with a considerable body of data within its domain, and shows easy testability. Psychoanalytic theory is often subject to criticism concerning its ability to be tested empirically but fulfills the first two criteria reasonably well. Although the other three theories—role theory, field theory, and the Gestalt and cognitive models—lack the well-integrated set of propositions that we should demand of a formal theory, they all have proved useful in generating a good deal of research.

There is little likelihood that any one broad theory will come to dominate social psychology in the future. In fact, there is a current trend toward the development of "theories of the middle level" (Merton, 1968) —that is, theories that seek to explain a narrower range of behavior or a more specific phenomenon. We will see many examples of such middle-level theories in the chapters that follow. These middle-level theories, although they do not aim for the scope of the broader theoretical frameworks that we have discussed, also make specific sets of assumptions that in turn shape research. "In simplest terms, a theory is a guide to tell you where to look for what you want to observe" (Runkel & McGrath, 1972, p. 23). And, as we have seen, each theory guides us toward some questions while ignoring others. Even when the theories are not made explicit, implicit theories and assumptions of the investigator will act as a guide (see Figure 1-8). Yet, as Bacon observed, "truth emerges more easily from error than from confusion," and the investigator who is aware of the basic assumptions that guide his or her research will probably fare better than the one who is not.

Figure 1-8. This researcher probably has certain theoretical assumptions, implicit or explicit, that lead her to investigate some questions and to ignore others. (© Cary Wolinsky/Stock, Boston.)

VIII. Summary

Social psychology is the field of study concerned with interpersonal behavior. It includes in its domain not only actual interpersonal behavior but also any behavior in which the presence of others is imagined or anticipated. Thus very little human behavior lies outside the realm of social psychology.

Psychoanalysis, basically a theory of personality structure and development, explains social behavior in terms of the level of personality development and the forces at work within the personality of each participant. Experiences during childhood are considered to be strong determinants of adult social behavior.

Role theory seeks to explain social behavior through an analysis of roles, role obligations, role expectations, and role conflicts. A role is a socially defined pattern of behavior that accompanies a particular position within a social context.

Stimulus-response theories study the associations between specific stimuli, responses, and reinforcements. These approaches assume that complex social behavior can be understood as a chain of simple responses and that the consequences of a social behavior are highly influential in determining whether similar behaviors will occur in the future.

Gestalt theory holds that social behavior cannot be properly understood if it is separated, analyzed, and reduced to specific responses. To the Gestalt psychologist, the essence of social behavior is complex, interrelated, and purposive. "The whole is greater than the sum of its parts" is the credo of Gestalt psychology. More recently developed cognitive theories share some of these same assumptions, although they do not necessarily accept all of the Gestalt principles. *Phenomenological* approaches assume that understanding a person's perceptions of the environment is more important in explaining that person's social behavior than is an objective description of the environment.

Field theory assumes that social behavior is always a function of both the person and the environment at a specific point in time. Although less specific than some of the other theories, the general concept of person/situation interaction is an important one.

As we saw using the case of Juan Corona and the jury, differences among theories will lead the student of human behavior to examine certain aspects of that behavior and to disregard others. The factors that help determine what kinds of questions a given theory will generate include: the belief in historical versus contemporary causation; the importance of internal versus situational factors; the unit of analysis that is studied; and the assumptions about human nature on which the theory is founded. In spite of the variation among theories on all of these dimensions, all theories serve as a guide to the investigator who is seeking explanations for human behavior.

Glossary Terms

anal stage	field theory	phallic stage
attribution theory	genital stage	phenomenological approach
behavior settings	Gestalt	reinforcement
cognitive dissonance	halo effect	response
construct	hypothesis	role
defense mechanisms	id	socialization
ecological psychology	libido	stimulus
ego	life space	stimulus generalization
	neo-Freudian	superego
	norms	
	oral stage	

Research is the invasion of the unknown.   DeWITT STETTON, Jr.

2

Methods
of Studying
Social
Behavior

A chapter on methods for the first and second editions of this book was prepared by Stuart Oskamp. Some of that material has been included in the present chapter.

Theories give us ways to look at the world. They provide a general framework for our understanding, and they also tell us what specific events to look for. As we saw in Chapter 1, a social-learning theorist may look for models that influence a person's behavior, whereas the investigator with a Freudian bent may turn to early childhood experiences to find the causes of adult behavior. Phrased in another way, it has been said that "we are prone to see what lies behind our eyes rather than what appears before them" (Beveridge, 1964, p. 99).

"Behind our eyes," however, encompasses a lot of territory, and it is from this territory that experimental hypotheses emerge. Social psychologists, like other scientists, begin their pursuit of knowledge with an idea and then proceed to test that idea to determine its validity. All of the research that will be discussed in this book began with an idea: sometimes a formally derived hypothesis, sometimes an intuitive leap, and sometimes a simple accident. How ideas develop will be the first topic of this chapter; how ideas are translated into scientific study will be our focus in the remainder of the chapter.

I. Formulating Hypotheses

Perhaps the best way to describe the development of an idea is to describe what is historically considered the first social-psychological experiment. Norman Triplett, who was a psychologist at Indiana University in the late 19th century, was also a bicycle enthusiast. In studying the records of the Racing Board of the League of American Wheelmen, Triplett observed that cyclists' times were faster when the cyclists were racing against each other rather than simply racing against a clock (see Figure 2-1). On the basis of this observation, Triplett proposed a theory of dynamogenesis (which is an origin of current theories of social facilitation, to be discussed in Chapter 17). Basically, his model suggested that the presence of other people acts as a stimulant to the performer. If such a

model were true, Triplett reasoned, it would hold for activities other than bicycle riding.

To test his hypothesis, Triplett returned to his psychology laboratory and engaged 40 children in a task of winding fishing reels, either alone or in competition with another child. His hypothesis was confirmed: children in competition performed faster than children alone (Triplett, 1897). Thus Triplett began with a simple observation, outside of his laboratory pursuits, and translated that thought into a psychological experiment that dealt with one of the core issues of social psychology: how the actions of others can influence the individual.

There are, of course, many ways to test any given idea: the diversity of these methods will be the concern of the majority of this chapter. First, however, it is important to give some additional consideration to where ideas come from. It has been said that "most of the knowledge and much of the genius of the research worker lie behind (the) selection of what is worth observing" (Beveridge, 1964, p. 103). But how are selections made?

Curiosity and observation must be the starting points (Silverman, 1977). For the social psychologist, this curiosity will concern human behavior; observation will focus on people and their interactions. Research ideas may develop from a general interest in some topic, such as persuasion or group processes or love. In other instances, a specific event may be perplexing, and, like Sherlock Holmes, the social psychologist will try to unravel the mystery and arrive at a solution. In still other cases, an investigator may be involved in one project and, like the fabled princes of Serendip, accidentally discover some other significant information about human behavior, quite removed from the original research focus. In each case, however, curiosity and observation are at the root of the investigation.

William McGuire (1973) has suggested some specific ways in which testable hypotheses about human behavior may be derived (see Table 2-1). Some of these approaches are based on a considerable body of past research; the investigator builds on past theory and data to develop

Figure 2-1. From bicycle racing to research: the inspiration for Norman Triplett. (The Bettmann Archive.)

increasingly complex hypotheses. Other approaches begin from more direct observation of people's behavior, as the investigator tries to define the basic psychological processes that may underlie the observed events. One example of the latter approach is to analyze the practitioner's rule of thumb (see No. 6 in Table 2-1).

Consider the style of the door-to-door encyclopedia representative. You yourself may have been on the receiving end of such house calls, in which the seller begins the pitch with a simple request. Having granted the sales representative five minutes of your time, you may have found yourself two hours later still listening to a talk on the virtue of the books. Such an experience, although annoying at the time, could nonetheless be the source of an experimental hypothesis if you were a social psychologist. In fact, research on this very issue has been conducted, and the results are referred to, not inappropriately, as the "foot-in-the-door" effect. Social psychologists have learned that a large request is more likely to be granted if it is preceded by the granting of a small request than if no request precedes it (Freedman & Fraser, 1966). This particular issue of compliance will be discussed at greater length in Chapter 14. For the present, however, it serves to illustrate how mundane the sources of some experimental ideas can be.

Other hypotheses may be developed from much more sophisticated theoretical networks or from a large body of previous research. Some of the sources that McGuire suggests deal with these more developed bases of hypothesis generation. The hypothetico-deductive method, for example, is perhaps best represented by Clark Hull's learning theory, in which numerous postulates were formulated that then allowed the prediction of specific relationships, such as the relationship between level of hunger and speed of learning a response.

TABLE 2-1 / *Some Approaches to Hypothesis Generation*

1. Intensive case study
   Example: Most psychoanalytic theory began with the extended analysis of individual patients. In treating a hysterical patient named Dora, for instance, Freud developed some of his theories about unconscious sexual impulses.

2. Accounting for a paradoxical incident
   Example: A cult of Illinois citizens in the mid-1950s fervently predicted the end of the world. Yet when the designated day arrived and the world did not end, the enthusiasm of the believers for their cause did not wane (Festinger, Riecken, & Schachter, 1956). This incident led to a hypothesis about the effects of commitment on subsequent behavior.

3. Use of analogy
   Example: Borrowing from the medical principles of immunization as a means of resisting disease, McGuire (1964) developed research showing how familiarity with attitudinal issues could increase later resistance to persuasion.

4. Hypothetico-deductive method
   Example: In this more formal method, the investigator combines a number of principles from previous research and, through logical deductive methods, arrives at a set of predictions. Hullian learning theory exemplifies this approach.

5. Functional or adaptive approach
   Example: The investigator considers a particular pattern of events and then generates the principles that must be operating in order for the event to occur. Kohlberg's theory of moral development (see Chapter 8) can illustrate this strategy.

6. Analyzing the practitioner's rule of thumb
   Example: Television commercials and magazine advertisements frequently show a celebrity praising a product, which suggests that advertisers believe that status sells products. This observation could lead to a series of hypotheses about the effects of communicator status on attitude and behavior change.

7. Trying to account for conflicting results
   Example: Many people believe, and research often shows, that our first impressions of a person have the most lasting effect. Yet other research indicates that the most recent information carries the greatest weight. Research hypotheses can be developed to predict when "primacy" will be important and when "recency" will be important (see Chapter 3).

8. Accounting for exceptions to general findings
   Example: Most research shows that a performance by a woman will be rated less favorably than an equivalent performance by a man. Yet on a few occasions, this devaluation will not occur (Taynor & Deaux, 1973). These exceptions to the rule provide an intriguing source of hypotheses.

9. Reducing observed complex relationships to simpler component relationships
   Example: The complex process of attitude change can be broken down into separate stages, as the investigator might form hypotheses about the initial reception of the message, the cognitive processing of the arguments, or the long-term retention of change (see Chapter 13).

Adapted from McGuire, 1973.

All of the approaches that McGuire suggests have been used on some occasion to develop the hypotheses that social psychologists have posed. Once a hypothesis is formulated, the investigator must then devise some means of testing that hypothesis. And although the hypothesis-generation phase of research is in many ways the most exciting aspect of the research process, the latter stages are no less critical. Nor are they simple or automatic, as **Box 2-1** illustrates.

II. Testing Hypotheses

Contrary to what some people believe, there is no one right way to test a hypothesis. Social psychologists have developed a warehouse of methods, many of which may be appropriate for any single question. In fact, every method has certain strengths and weaknesses, and the ultimate strategy of the scientist should be to test a single hypothesis through a diversity of methods, thereby increasing one's confidence in the validity of the hypothesis. Before delving into the characteristics of each method, however, let us consider how a single hypothesis might be tested in a variety of settings: the laboratory, the field, and across cultures.

A. *The Hypothesis*

The behavior of the individual in a group is one of the central issues of social psychology. Although the effects of a group are numerous, let us for the moment consider only one aspect: **deindividuation.** This descriptive term, suggested by Festinger, Pepitone, and Newcomb (1952), refers to a state of relative anonymity, in which the group member does not feel singled out or identifiable. In the late 19th century, LeBon (1896) observed crowd behavior and postulated a similar notion to explain why persons in a mob lose their sense of responsibility. From these general observations, then, it is possible to develop a specific hypothesis concerning the effects of anonymity on subsequent behavior. Let us focus on the following hypothesis: Greater degrees of anonymity will result in a greater frequency of antisocial behavior.

Formulating such a hypothesis represents the first stage of the research process. The next step is to develop a means to test

---

Box 2-1. If at First You Don't Succeed . . . .

Research reports in professional journals often make the research process sound easy. Apparently the investigators came up with a good hypothesis, tested it, obtained interesting results, and then quickly published their findings in the journal. In truth, the course of research is not so smooth.

Alan Gross and Anthony Doob (1976) provide an interesting account of their attempts to test the frustration-aggression hypothesis in a natural setting. Although inexperienced, they decided to move outside the laboratory to see if experiencing frustration leads people to become more aggressive. After considerable thought, they decided that traffic jams were a good source of frustration, and, although they did not think it reasonable to cause a series of major traffic jams, it seemed possible to arrange for a single driver to stall a car at a traffic light. The honking that occurs on such occasions could be used as a likely measure of aggression—but what factors might affect that aggression? Various bumper stickers on the stalled car were one possibility; the number of people in

the car was another. Finally Gross and Doob decided on the status of the car as the aggression factor, suggesting that people would be less likely to honk at a high-status car than at a low-status car. For graduate students, finding a low-status car was no problem; however, obtaining a high-status car posed more of a problem. A rented Chrysler proved to be the solution.

After a few more practical problems were encountered and solved, the field experiment was conducted. Data were collected and analyzed, and the statistical analyses showed that the data supported the initial hypothesis: people were less likely to honk at the driver of a stalled high-status car. So far, so good. But when the report was written up and submitted to a journal, the editor of that journal found the study uninteresting. The editor of a second journal concurred. Fortunately, however, this story has a happy ending. On their third try, Doob and Gross had a positive response, and the study of horn honking now occupies a place in the social-psychology literature (Doob & Gross, 1968).

the validity of that hypothesis. As noted before, there are many ways that a single hypothesis can be tested. To demonstrate the truth of this assertion, we will consider three different studies in three different settings, each of which was designed to test the relationship between anonymity and antisocial behavior.

B. *A Laboratory Investigation*

In a psychology laboratory at New York University, **Zimbardo** (1970) conducted a study in which four students were asked to share the responsibility for giving another student a set of electric shocks. The guise for giving those shocks was that the experimenter was interested in people's reactions to the pain of another person; in fact, however, the experimenter was interested in the level of aggressive behavior (as measured by the duration of electric shocks given) as a function of anonymity. (We will discuss the issue of deception in a later section of this chapter.) To vary the conditions of anonymity, Zimbardo had half of his subjects dressed in hoods. These students never gave their names, and they performed the experiment in the dark. (Several of the deindividuated students are pictured in **Figure 2-2**.) The other half of the subjects in this experiment had their individuality emphasized: they were greeted by name, given large name tags, and got to know each other on a first-name basis. Both groups of subjects were free to give as much or as little shock to the other student as they wished.

In this laboratory setting, the deindividuation hypothesis was confirmed: subjects in the anonymity condition gave more shock to the other students than did subjects in the individuated condition. Although the laboratory has been the setting most frequently used by social psychologists to test their hypotheses (the laboratory experiment will be discussed in more detail later in this

Figure 2-2. Subjects in the deindividuated condition in Zimbardo's laboratory experiment.

chapter), it is certainly not the only setting available. Let us consider two other settings that were used to test the same hypothesis.

C. A Field Investigation

The social psychologist who moves outside the laboratory to test a hypothesis is basically concerned with increasing the natural quality of the situation: naturalness of the behavior, the setting, and the treatment (Tunnell, 1977). Often the investigator's role in such a study is simply to observe what occurs, with little or no intervention. To test the hypothesis concerning deindividuation, one might therefore look for natural settings that would differ in the degree of anonymity they provided. For example, in a large urban center, we might expect anonymity to be much more pervasive than in a small university town where people are more likely to be acquainted. Thus greater antisocial behavior could be predicted, on the basis of our hypothesis, in the large as opposed to the small town.

To test the deindividuation hypothesis in these circumstances, Zimbardo and Fraser bought a used car and left it on a busy street adjoining the Bronx campus of New York University. At the same time, a similar car was left on a street near the Stanford University campus in Palo Alto, California. Within 26 hours the car in New York was stripped of battery, radiator, air cleaner, radio antenna, windshield wipers, side chrome, all four hubcaps, a set of jumper cables, a can of car wax, a gas can, and the one tire worth taking. Meanwhile, in Palo Alto, the second car remained unharmed. In fact, one day when it rained a passerby lowered the hood so the motor would not get waterlogged!

Although automobile-parts thieves and hooded students are obviously quite different, from the point of testing a hypothesis the conclusions remain the same: greater anonymity leads to a greater frequency of antisocial behavior.

D. A Cross-Cultural Investigation

What is true in industrialized countries may not be true in other parts of the world. Thus experimenters who want to determine the universality of their hypotheses may often look to other societies for a means to test their ideas. One source for such tests is the Human Relations Area File (HRAF), a collection of information assembled by ethnographers on more than 200 cultures throughout the world.

Watson (1973) used the material available in this file to test the anonymity-antisocial behavior hypothesis in yet another context. He assumed that the extensive use of masks and face and body paint by warriors serves as a guarantee of anonymity. Consequently, he hypothesized that those societies in which use of paint and disguise was extensive would have a tradition of more aggressive and ferocious warfare than would those societies in which disguise was less frequent. To test the hypothesis, Watson simply categorized societies described in the HRAF on two dimensions: intensity of warfare (as indicated by reports of such practices as torture, sacrifice of prisoners, headhunting, and fighting to the death in all battles) and the presence or absence of paints and disguise as a prelude to battle. Once again, the hypothesis concerning anonymity and aggression was supported: those societies that engaged in more aggressive forms of warfare were also more likely to don heavy disguises than were the more peaceful cultures (see Table 2-2).

TABLE 2-2 / *Relationship between Changes in Physical Appearance prior to Battle and Extremity of Aggression in Warfare among 23 Independent (Linguistically and Geographically) Cultures*

Item	Deindividuation Changed appearance	Unchanged appearance
Aggressive	12	1
Nonaggressive	3	7

Note: $N = 23$; $x^2 = 7.12$, $df = 1$, $p < .01$.

From "Investigation into Deindividuation Using a Cross-Cultural Survey Technique," by R. I. Watson, Jr., *Journal of Personality and Social Psychology*, 1973, *25*, 342–345. Copyright 1973 by the American Psychological Association. Reprinted by permission.

In this latter study, it is more difficult to determine the direction of cause and effect than it is, for example, in the laboratory study. Because the data are obtained through a **correlational method,** we cannot be certain which factor causes the other. Although the use of disguise may lead to more intensive warfare, it may also be true that a propensity for aggression encourages the use of disguise. In the laboratory, in contrast, anonymity was manipulated by the experimenter, so that we can be relatively sure that aggression did not cause the deindividuated state.

The above examples should serve to illustrate the point that there are multiple ways and places to test a single hypothesis. Furthermore, you may begin to suspect that no single method or setting is perfect. The high degree of control in the laboratory, for example, is often sacrificed to obtain a more natural setting in the field. Given such profusion of methods and settings, how does the investigator decide on a means of testing a hypothesis? The reasons for a particular choice are many and include such factors as convenience, a particular investigator's preference, and the history of past research in the area. In addition, the investigator must carefully consider the strengths and weaknesses of each method as they may affect the outcome. It is to this more detailed presentation of each method that we now turn.

III. Major Methods of Social-Psychological Research

Social psychologists have developed an extensive repertoire of methods to aid in the understanding of human behavior. We will discuss seven of these methods in the following pages: laboratory experiments, field experiments, quasi-experimental research, field studies, archival research, simulation and role playing, and surveys and interviews. In each case, we will consider both the advantages and disadvantages of the method as a means of learning about social behavior.

A. *The Laboratory Experiment*

Zimbardo's study of the effect of anonymity on students' willingness to shock another student is one example of a laboratory experiment. As another example, consider the following study by Deaux and Emswiller (1974). College students reported to a laboratory at Purdue University, where they were told that they would be asked to explain and evaluate the performance of another student. This other student was supposedly being asked to identify blurred pictures and to verbally name each item. The subjects, who were seated individually in booths, heard the student's answers over a set of headphones; in addition, they had a sheet with the correct answers in front of them. When the other student (either a male or a female) had successfully completed the test, each subject was asked to evaluate the performance on a questionnaire provided by the experimenters.

In this study, as in other laboratory experiments, the researcher's aim is to test the effects of one or more independent variables on one or more dependent variables. **Independent variables** in an experiment are those factors that are controlled or arranged by the experimenter and may often be considered the cause of a behavior. **Dependent variables** refer to those behaviors of the subject that are observed or recorded by the experimenter.

In the Deaux and Emswiller experiment, there were two independent variables: the sex of the student performing the visual discrimination task, and the sex-linkage of the task itself. In some cases, the objects of the task discrimination were female-linked objects, such as whisks, colanders, and pin cushions. In other cases, the list of objects included traditionally male-identified things, such as Phillips screwdrivers, lug wrenches, and tire rods. The dependent variable in the Deaux and Emswiller experiment consisted of a series of questions concerning the student's performance. Of particular interest was one question that asked how much luck versus skill was responsible for the observed student's performance.

The results of this study showed that when a male did well on a masculine task, subjects were apt to conclude that his performance was largely the result of skill. When a woman did well on the same task, subjects rated her as lucky. On the feminine task, there was no difference in the reasons given for the successful performance of males and females. Thus the investigators were able to conclude that evaluations of performance (the dependent variable) vary as a function of the sex of the performer and the type of task (the independent variables).

Characteristic of the laboratory experiment is the investigator's ability to control the independent and dependent variables. Indeed, this aspect of control is one of the most important features of the laboratory experiment. In the above example, the experimenters were able to manipulate systematically the performance that subjects observed: the sequence of responses that the student made, the number of correct and incorrect answers, and the specific items on the test were all determined by the experimenters. Through this control, numerous extraneous variables could be eliminated. For example, many judgments are influenced by the attractiveness of the person being judged. However, Deaux and Emswiller were not interested in this variable, and they were able to effectively eliminate it by allowing the subjects to hear only voices and not actually see the person they were judging. Similarly, in terms of the dependent variable, the experimenters were able to phrase the evaluation questions in exactly the manner they wished, enabling them to focus precisely on the issue of causal explanations.

In addition to control, the laboratory experiment also offers another important advantage: the ability to assign subjects randomly to conditions. In order for an investigator to draw conclusions regarding cause and effect, he or she must be sure that the pattern of results was not due to some systematic difference in the groups being compared. By randomly assigning subjects to listen to either a male or a female and to evaluate either a masculine or a feminine task, the experimenters can control for the possibility that some people may be more familiar with one or the other task and bias their judgments accordingly. On the average, **randomization** ensures an equality of subject characteristics across the various experimental conditions. Such a principle has been important in the development of other sciences and is important to the development of social-psychological knowledge as well.

One other characteristic of the laboratory experiment should be mentioned: the **manipulation check.** Although experimenters are able to control the independent variable, it is still important for them to be sure that the subjects in the experiment perceive the manipulation as it is intended. Thus, in the above example, it was critical for the experimenters to know that subjects did perceive the objects of the perception task to be masculine and feminine. To be sure of this, the experimenters included a question in their set of dependent measures that asked subjects how masculine or feminine they perceived the task to be. Significant differences on this question as a function of the task condition gave the experimenters confidence that their results were due to the variables that they manipulated.[1]

Advantages. The advantages of the laboratory experiment as a means of acquiring knowledge have been largely summarized above. Principal among these is the ability of the experimenter to control the independent variables and to randomly assign subjects to conditions. These two capabilities provide some basis for conclusions regarding cause and effect. Furthermore, the laboratory allows the investigator to "sort out" factors—to simplify the more complex events of the natural world by breaking them down into their component parts.

Other advantages of the laboratory experiment are somewhat more mundane, convenience being one of the major ones. Most psychological laboratories are located

---

[1] Experimenters must also consider the possible effects of their manipulation checks on other dependent variables. For further discussion of this issue, see Kidd (1976).

Figure 2-3. Experimental realism and mundane realism. *Experimental realism* refers to the amount of impact in the situation—that is, the extent to which the subject is involved and paying attention to the situation. Mundane realism refers to the similarity of the situation to "real-world" events. In the photograph on the left, mundane realism is low (people rarely encounter shock machines in the "real world"), but the experimental realism is high. In the photograph on the right, both mundane and experimental realism might be high. (© Stanley Milgram, left; © Jerry Berndt, Stock/Boston, right.)

on university campuses, where there is an abundant supply of students to serve as subjects and where the experimenter has easy access to facilities. Procedures at many universities make a "subject pool" readily available, and hence the investigator is spared the difficulty of contacting persons individually to engage their participation.

Disadvantages. Although the laboratory experiment has some considerable advantages in terms of its ability to isolate and control variables, it has some substantial disadvantages as well. In recent years, these disadvantages have become the topic of considerable debate. Three of the major issues of concern have been the possible irrelevance of the laboratory setting, the reactions of subjects to the laboratory setting, and the possible influence of experimenters on their results. (A fourth concern centered on deception and ethics, although primarily focused on certain laboratory experiments, is not exclusive to this method and will be discussed in more general terms in a later section of this chapter.)

The issue of irrelevance concerns the artificiality of the laboratory setting and the fact that many of the situations created in the laboratory bear little direct relationship to the situations a person encounters in real life. Aronson and Carlsmith (1968) have argued persuasively for the distinction between **experimental realism** and **mundane realism** (see Figure 2-3). They contend that, in the laboratory, one can devise situations that have impact and that evoke valid psychological processes (experimental realism), even if the situation itself does not look like the real world (mundane realism). Yet, despite the persuasiveness of Aronson's and Carlsmith's arguments, it remains true that many laboratory tasks seem suspiciously artificial and their **external validity** has not been demonstrated. *External validity* refers to the "generalizability" of research findings to other populations, treatment variables, and measurement variables (Campbell & Stanley, 1966). Although this criterion must be applied to all social-psychological studies, it is in the case of laboratory experiments that its applicability has been questioned most vigorously. Thus, although college students' evaluations of the performance of another student on an object-perception task *may* parallel the judgments of a supervisor rating male and female employees in an organization, it remains the responsibility of the experimenter to demonstrate this parallelism.

A second criticism of the laboratory experiment focuses on the reactions of subjects to the laboratory setting. These reactions may involve **demand characteristics** and **evaluation apprehension.** The first term refers to the fact that the experimental setting may evoke certain demands—that is, expectations on the part of subjects to act in the way that they think the experimenter would wish (Orne, 1969). Thus, for example, if you were in a psychology experiment in which somebody asked you to indicate your attitude toward zero population growth, then asked you to listen to a speech in which zero population growth was advocated, and then once again asked for your attitude, you might well suspect that the experiment was concerned with attitude change. A subject in this situation who was concerned with pleasing the experimenter or doing the "right thing" might well indicate a change of attitude on paper, without having experienced it in reality. Such a response would represent an influence of the demand characteristics of the situation but not necessarily the influence of the experimenter's intended variable.

Evaluation apprehension refers to the concerns that a subject has about being observed and judged while in the laboratory setting. Because subjects come to a laboratory experiment knowing that the investigator is interested in some aspect of their behavior, they may try to present themselves in a favorable light. (This specific problem concerning the laboratory setting is related to the more general issue of impression management, which will be discussed in Chapter 4.) Again, the issue is the veridicality of subjects' behavior; that is, are the subjects acting as they normally would in such a situation, or are they modifying their behavior *because of* the laboratory setting?

An interesting experiment by Sigall, Aronson, and Van Hoose (1970) examined the problem of evaluation apprehension. In this experiment, subjects were faced with the choice between cooperating with the experimenter, which meant conveying negative information about themselves, and negating the experimenter's demands and looking good. Looking good was the option chosen by most subjects, underlining the importance of self-presentation strategies to the individual and the possible limitations of the experimenter's power to influence behaviors that are not consistent with the subjects' own aspirations.

A final criticism of the laboratory experiment concerns **experimenter expectancies** (Rosenthal, 1966). It has been shown in a variety of situations that an experimenter, knowing the hypothesis of the study, can unknowingly influence the results of the study. For example, in tests involving rats running down an alley, Rosenthal and his colleagues found that experimenters who believed their rats were the fastest group obtained results that supported their belief —even though their rats were in fact no more predisposed to speed than other groups of rats. With human interaction, the influence of expectation is obviously even more likely. The experimenter can, through vocal inflection or subtle facial movements, clearly influence the behavior of the subject and thus bias the results. In this instance, we are questioning the **internal validity** of the experiment (Campbell & Stanley, 1966): are the results due to the independent variables that were manipulated or to some other uncontrolled element in the situation?

The influence of these experimenter expectancies can be controlled to a large extent. For example, many experiments involve instructions that have been tape recorded in advance, thus assuring constancy in experimenter approach to all subjects. Other techniques include the use of a "blind" experimenter, wherein the individual conducting the experiment is not informed of the experimental hypotheses and thus is less likely to exert a systematic bias on the results.

In summary, the laboratory experiment offers the most precise control of variables and the greatest ability to isolate those factors that are believed to be important, uncontaminated by extraneous variables and competing events. At the same time, however, the artificiality of the laboratory setting can create another set of problems that reduce the correspondence between laboratory-obtained findings and real-life behavior.

B. *The Field Experiment*

During 1968, more than 4000 passengers on the IND subway line in New York City saw another passenger fall down on the floor of the train. Although the passengers didn't know it, they were subjects in a field experiment designed to assess helping behavior (see **Figure 2-4**). The experimenters (Piliavin, Rodin, & Piliavin, 1969) arranged the situation so that the characteristics of the person needing help would vary. Four different "victims" were used at various times in the study: the victim was either Black or White, and was either apparently drunk (carrying a liquor bottle wrapped in a brown bag and reeking of alcohol) or slightly disabled (using a cane). After the victim fell, the experimenters, who were also present on the subway car, noted the number of people who offered help to the victim and the speed of the helping responses. The race of these helpers was also noted. The experimenters found that an apparently ill person is much more likely to receive aid than is the person who appears to be drunk: 95% of the "disabled" victims were offered some help by the other passengers, whereas only 50% of the "drunken" victims were helped. Race of the victim had little effect on helping behavior except when the victim was drunk, when help was offered more frequently to a member of the same race than to a member of another race. In addition, men in general were far more likely to offer help than were women.

This study is a classic example of the field experiment. Like the laboratory experiment, in the field experiment the experimenter has control of the independent variables and the random assignment of subjects to conditions. In the case of the subway study, the independent variables controlled by the experimenter were the race and the physical state of the victim. The subjects in the experiment (in this case the passengers on the subway) were essentially randomly assigned to their conditions, in that the experimenters had no idea who would be riding the train when they determined which victim would appear on which train. By such randomization procedures, we can assume that the passengers who saw a White victim fall were not systematically different from the passengers who saw a Black victim.

In contrast to the laboratory experiment, the setting of the field experiment is a natural one and the subjects are not generally aware that they are subjects in an experiment. Rather than contriving an artificial situation in a laboratory, the investigator who uses a field experiment to test a hypothesis is looking at behavior in its natural setting. The dependent variable in the field experiment is thus under somewhat less control. The investigator must select a behavior or set of behaviors that tend to occur naturally and observe them without intervening.

Advantages. The advantages of the field experiment are probably obvious. By focusing on behavior in a natural setting, the experimenter can be much more certain of the external validity of his or her findings. Furthermore, because subjects are generally unaware of their status as subjects, the problems of reactivity and the subjects' desire to be seen in a positive light are eliminated. In addition, because control over the independent variable and principles of randomization are maintained, the field experiment allows the same possibilities for conclusions about cause and effect as does the laboratory experiment.

Figure 2-4. Altruism on the IND. In subway cars such as the one shown below, social psychologists have observed whether people are willing to offer help to a stranger. What would you do if you were sitting on this car? (© Harry Wilks/Stock, Boston.)

Disadvantages. **Although the field experiment may seem to ideally combine the application of the strict rules of experimentation with the realism of natural behavior settings, it too has some disadvantages. These disadvantages relate to the nature of the independent variable, the nature of the dependent variable, the ethics of the experiment, and the practical difficulties involved.

Because the experimenter is working in a complex natural setting where many events may be occurring simultaneously, the independent variable in the study must be quite obvious to the potential subject. Subtle manipulations of a variable may simply go unnoticed. The experimental independent variable is, in effect, competing with all of the other stimuli present in the setting. Thus, in the subway study, it was arranged for the victim to fall down in the *middle* of the subway car at times when the train was not full to capacity. In contrast, if the investigators had conducted the experiment during rush hour, the victim would have had little room to fall, and, even if he had, few people would have seen him. Similarly, if the victim had merely tripped or dropped a package, his behavior might have gone unnoticed by the majority of passengers. Thus the investigator conducting a field experiment must be sure that the independent variable is sufficiently visible for potential subjects to have the opportunity to react. Otherwise, a failure to respond becomes difficult to interpret.

The dependent variable in a field experiment must also be selected carefully. The experimenters must be able to readily observe and reliably judge the dependent-variable behavior. In the subway experiment, for example, experimenters may not have noticed a number of passengers' responses to the victims. Facial expressions may have indicated sympathy or disgust. Passengers' comments to each other may have indicated their attitudes toward the victim. Yet without sophisticated recording equipment, such as videorecorders (which would clearly alter the situation by making passengers aware of their status as subjects), such subtle responses cannot be assessed by the field experimenter. Conse-**quently, the dependent variables that are selected tend to be rather large-scale behaviors, frequently scored in a present-or-absent fashion. (The limits of such measures for statistical purposes will be discussed later in this chapter.)

An additional problem in field experimentation concerns ethics. Is it reasonable for the investigator to involve individuals in an experiment without their knowledge or permission? This question has been discussed extensively by social psychologists (Carlsmith, Ellsworth, & Aronson, 1976; Kelman, 1968; McGuire, 1967b; Selltiz, Wrightsman, & Cook, 1976). The issue is invasion of privacy and the degree to which the experimenter is unreasonably infringing on the individual's activities. Although there is no single answer to this question, most social psychologists would agree that field experiments are reasonable if the independent variables concern normal occurrences in the subject's daily life and if the setting is a public one. The less that the experimenter's intervention inconveniences the subjects or involves them emotionally, the less serious the ethics question becomes. Thus, for example, an experiment in which someone drops packages on the street raises fewer questions on ethics than one in which persons are accosted by a stranger who is having an "epileptic fit." The latter situation would probably be viewed as ethically unacceptable by most investigators, whereas the former would be judged acceptable. On each occasion, however, the investigator must carefully consider the potential harm or inconvenience that his or her experimental intervention could cause.

Finally, the field experiment often poses practical problems. In contrast to the investigator in the laboratory, the investigator in the field has no control over the majority of events in the environment; unexpected events may reduce or destroy the effectiveness of the manipulation. Subways can stall, weather can affect plans, and unexpected events may divert subjects' attention from the experimenter's intended variable. These possibilities make it necessary for the field experimenter to study the setting carefully in advance of the experiment and to be aware of as many contingencies as possible. Often the experimenter must also get permission from shop owners, subway conductors, or from the local police force before an experiment is carried out, to ensure that the events being staged are not misinterpreted and do not violate local laws. Many shopping centers, for example, have ordinances prohibiting soliciting, and an experiment that is concerned with people's responses to requests for charitable contributions could be in conflict with such laws.

In summary, the field experiment has many advantages, combining many control and randomization principles with a setting more realistic than the laboratory. At the same time, because the investigator in the field cannot control the environment, the precision of the laboratory experiment cannot be attained. In addition, the field experiment raises serious practical and ethical issues.

C. *Quasi-Experimental Research*

A change in the British highway-traffic law provided the occasion for a "natural" experiment by Ross, Campbell, and Glass (1970). In an attempt to lower the highway death rate by getting drunk drivers off the road, the new law established criteria for

defining drunkenness and authorized police to give an on-the-scene breath test to drivers who were suspected of being drunk, committing moving-vehicle traffic offenses, or causing an accident. The Breathalyser test measured the percentage of alcohol in the driver's blood. Stiff punishment was established for driving under the influence of alcohol, and the starting date of the crackdown was widely publicized in advance.

The British Ministry of Transport reported that highway deaths dropped by 1152 in the first year of the Breathalyser crackdown. The dramatic drop in deaths and serious injuries is shown in Figure 2-5. Although the number of deaths occurring during the hours that pubs were closed did not change with the advent of the new law, deaths and injuries during those times when the pubs were most frequented decreased sharply.

This study is an example of quasi-experimental research. The defining characteristics of quasi-experimental research are that the investigator does not have full experimental control over the independent variables but does have extensive control over how, when, and for whom the dependent variable is measured (Campbell & Stanley, 1966, p. 34). Generally these experiments involve behavior in a natural setting

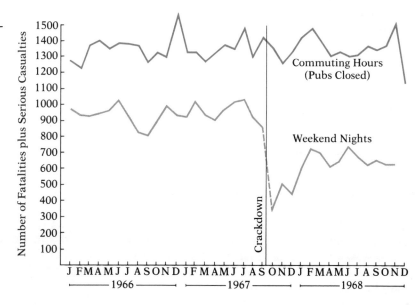

Figure 2-5. Results of the British Breathalyser crackdown. (Adapted from "Determining the Social Effects of a Legal Reform: The British 'Breathalyser' Crackdown of 1967," by H. L. Ross, D. T. Campbell, and G. V. Glass, *American Behavioral Scientist*, 1970, *13*(4), 493–509. Copyright 1970 by Sage Publications, Inc. Used by permission.)

and focus on the effect of intervention in a system of ongoing behavior. Often these interventions are the result of a policy decision—for example, by a governmental agency in the case of the Breathalyser study and by a legislative body in the case of the Mazur-Hart and Berman study (1977). In the latter study, investigators examined the change in divorce rates in Nebraska after the state legislature had passed a no-fault divorce law in 1972. By comparing the divorce rates in a three-year period preceding the law with the rate in a three-year period following the law, Mazur-Hart and Berman were able to conclude that the new law, which would appear to make divorce easier to obtain, had no reliable effect on the rate of divorce.

In other cases, the intervention may be a natural disaster, such as a flood, earthquake, or tornado. Power blackouts in New York City and other urban centers, for example, could serve as the independent variable in a study of reactions to stressful events. The experimenter would have no control over the independent variable, but he or she could carefully select a set of dependent variables to measure the effects of stress.

Advantages. One unique advantage of quasi-experimental research conducted in a natural setting is that it allows for the study of very strong variables that cannot be manipulated or controlled by the experimenter. In the case of a tornado, for example, the investigator has the opportunity to study responses to highly distressing and consequential events, the magnitude of which could never be simulated in the laboratory or purposefully manipulated in the field. Often, too, quasi-experimental research deals with policy decisions that have consequences for very large numbers of people: the entire population of England, for example, in the case of the Breathalyser policy, and the married population of Nebraska in the study of no-fault divorce laws. The broad impact of such decisions gives considerable weight to the external validity of the study, in a manner that can rarely be matched in the more limited laboratory or field experiment.

Disadvantages. Because the investigator has no control over the primary independent variable in quasi-experimental research, it is always possible that other uncontrolled variables are affecting the dependent-variable behavior. Random assignment of subjects to conditions can rarely be assumed in the quasi-experimental design, either. However, there are a number of statistical procedures by which investigators can increase their confidence in the validity of the proposed cause-and-effect relationship (cf. Campbell & Stanley, 1966).

When a natural disaster is the independent variable, the investigator faces the additional problem of preparation. Natural disasters usually arrive with little or no warning, thus giving the investigator little time to conceptualize his or her study and to prepare appropriate measuring instruments. Often such research must literally be done "on the run." Furthermore, the arbitrariness of events in the quasi-experimental world precludes the experimenter's ability to vary factors according to any theoretical model. Intensity of a stressful event, for example, might be an important variable in predicting the nature of response to stress. Nonetheless, it is clearly impossible for the experimenter to control such a variable, and hence the levels of intensity would need to be accepted as they naturally occurred.

In summary, quasi-experimental research offers some clear advantages to investigators in terms of the impact and complexity of situations that can be studied; in addition, it allows investigators to study some situations that cannot be studied in any other manner. At the same time, experimenters have less control in this situation than in the true experiment, and thus they must interpret results more cautiously.

D. *The Field Study*

A 12' × 57' steel cylinder, placed 205 feet below the surface of the Pacific Ocean, provided the site for an exotic field study by Radloff and Helmreich (1968). This cylinder, capable of sleeping 10 persons, was named SEALAB II and was designed by the U.S. Navy to study human capabilities for living and working under water (see Figure

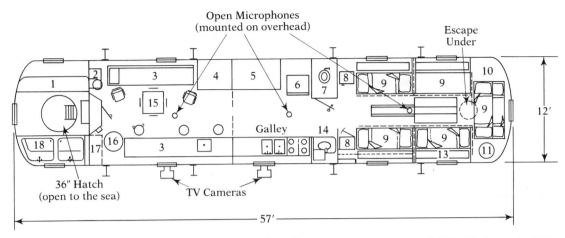

SEALAB II. Interior arrangement; Top removed—looking down. 1. Swim gear stow. 2. TV. 3 Lab bench. 4. Fan room. 5 Electric power and light. 6. Reefer. 7. Head. 8. Locker. 9. 2-Berths. 10. Stow. 11. CO_2 can. 12. Table. 13. Bench. 14. Lav. 15. Table and chairs. 16. Water heater. 17. Can stow'g. 18. Tub and shower.

Figure 2-6. Diagram of SEALAB II. (From Radloff, Roland and Robert Helmreich, *Groups Under Stress: Psychological Research in Sealab II.* © 1968 by Irvington Publishers, Inc. Reprinted by permission.)

2-6). Radloff and Helmreich were interested in the effects of psychological stress on human behavior, and they were able to obtain the permission of the Navy officials to study intensively the behavior of the aquanauts who participated in the Navy study.

The conditions in SEALAB II were undoubtedly stressful. In addition to the potential physical dangers from a ruptured wall or broken porthole, the living conditions themselves were unpleasant. The inside of the capsule was extremely confined and crowded, and there was little opportunity for privacy. To make matters worse, the habitat rested unevenly on the ocean floor at a 6° angle, causing drawers to slide open or shut and objects to slide off tables. In addition, the aquanauts were expected to make a series of diving expeditions outside the capsule, where they were subjected to the typical hazards of deep-sea diving at 200 feet.

In their intensive study of this small group of men, Radloff and Helmreich collected literally hundreds of different pieces of information. Some of this information consisted of objective behavioral measures: for example, number of excursions made outside the capsule, number of telephone calls made to the surface, and types of activ-

ities conducted within SEALAB. Other dependent measures were collected by questionnaire, measuring various personality characteristics and moods before and after dives. Still other information comprised demographic facts such as birth order, marital status, age, and years of diving experience.

From these measures, the investigators were able to gain a wealth of information about the behavior of groups of men in a stressful situation and the factors that may predict successful or unsuccessful adjustment. For example, they found that men who were born in small towns adjusted better to the SEALAB environment than men who were raised in urban areas. At a group level, the investigators observed an increase in camaraderie as the test period wore on.

Not all field studies are conducted in such exotic locales. Barker and Schoggen (1973), for example, focused their study on the residents of a small Midwestern town, population 830, and compared behaviors observed there to those seen in a similarly small English village. A major goal of this research was to make a complete classification of each town's behavior settings, defined as public places or occasions that evoke their own typical pattern of behavior. Newcomb (1961) conducted his year-long field study of students at Bennington College in Vermont, focusing on the change in values and attitudes of students from the beginning of the year to the end.

Most field studies are characterized by their indepth consideration of a limited group of people. The investigator in this setting plays a more reactive role than in the field experiment. Rather than manipulate some aspect of the environment and observe the changes that occur, the investigator in the field study records as much information as possible about the characteristics of that situation without altering the situation in any substantial way. Most often, people in the environment are aware of the investigator's presence and the general purpose of the investigation. Many times the investigator is a **participant observer**—that is, someone actively engaged in the activities of the group while at the same time maintaining records of the group members' behaviors.

√ Observation is the key element of the field-study method. However, because "people watching" is a fairly common activity for most of us, it is often hard to appreciate how difficult systematic scientific observation can be. Considerable time must be devoted in advance to familiarizing oneself with the environment and becoming aware of the kinds of behaviors that are most likely to occur. Next, one must decide which types of behavior are to be recorded. For example, should one focus on easily recorded behaviors, such as (in the case of the SEALAB study) telephone calls made from the underwater laboratory or excursions taken outside the laboratory? Or is one interested in charting the locations that are used and the number of people in each location? Or is the interest in smaller units of behavior, such as facial expressions and vocal pitch? The choice of one or more of these categories is in large part dependent on the questions that the investigator has posed. Although field-study investigators do not purposefully manipulate conditions, they are no less likely than any other experimenters to have a specific set of questions formulated in advance of the actual study. Without such questions, field observation becomes mired in a hopeless array of competing events.

Once categories of behavior are selected for observation, the investigator must devise specific methods of recording the desired information. Finally, the observer must conduct a series of preliminary investigations to determine the **reliability** of the measures. In other words, it must be demonstrated that a series of different observers watching the same event and using the methods chosen to record observations will code the behavior in the same way. Without such reliability, a coding system merely reflects one observer's biases and cannot be used as a basis for a scientific statement.

Advantages. The major advantage of the field study lies in its realism. The focus of the study is on events as they normally occur in a real-life setting. Furthermore, because most field studies take place over an extended period of time, they provide information about the sequence and development of behaviors that cannot be gained in the one-shot observation typical of field and laboratory experiments. Additionally, the duration of the field study generally allows for the collection of several different types of dependent measures. For example, in the study of aquanauts, the measures included observations, questionnaires, and demographic information. Such a variety of measures, when they are directed at the assessment of a limited number of concepts, may give one greater confidence in the conclusions than if any one of the measures were taken alone.

Disadvantages. Although well-conducted field studies furnish a wealth of data, the lack of control in such settings can be a problem. Because there is no controlled independent variable, it is difficult to form conclusions regarding cause and effect. Although there are some statistical techniques available to assist in making causal conclusions, the process is a more difficult one than in the controlled experimental design. A second potential problem in the field study is the subjects' awareness of the investigator's observations. When subjects are aware of being observed, their behavior may be **reactive**—that is, influenced by the process of observation. Most experienced observers believe, however, that in a long-term field study the subjects become indifferent to the observer's presence, though the problem remains a serious one in briefer studies.

In summary, the field study allows the investigator to study intensively a series of events in a real-life setting. Although field studies are not always the best means of testing specific experimental hypotheses, they may serve as a rich source of information that can provide the basis for more stringent experimental tests.

E. *Archival Research*

Lurid accounts of murder-suicides are often featured on television and in newspapers. Do these stories affect the behavior of people who read or see the reports? One testable hypothesis is that the reports of such events may trigger similar behavior in others. To test this hypothesis using an archival method, Phillips (1978) compiled a list of published reports in which an individual killed one or more persons and then committed suicide. In each case, the story was carried on the front pages of a major newspaper or reported on a major television network news program. A second set of data consisted of incidents of noncommercial airplane fatalities in which both the pilot and one or more passengers were killed. In selecting these data, Phillips assumed that such crashes might not always be accidental but could instead be intentional murder-suicides. The results in Figure 2-7 show that his chilling hypothesis was supported. The frequency of fatal noncommercial airplane crashes involving two or more persons went sharply up immediately following the published reports. In contrast, the frequency of crashes involving only one person showed no change; it was presumably not influenced by the stories of multiple deaths.

Archival research refers to the analysis of any existing records that have been produced or maintained by persons or organizations other than the experimenter. In other words, the original reason for collecting the records was not a social psychological experiment. Newspaper reports and government records of airplane fatalities are two forms of archival data. Other sources of

material include books and magazines, folk stories of preliterate societies, personal letters, and speeches by public figures. The study of the use of war paint and societal aggression discussed earlier in the chapter provides another example of archival research. In this case, the material in the Human Relations Area File was originally compiled by social scientists (generally anthropologists) but not for the reason of testing the hypothesis of deindividuation and aggression.

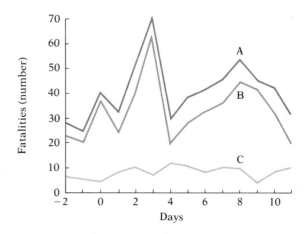

Figure 2-7. The relationship between noncommercial plane fatalities and reported murder-suicides. This graph shows the daily fluctuation of U.S. noncommercial plane fatalities for a 2-week period before, during (day 0), and after publicized murder-suicides. (Curve A) Fluctuation of fatalities for all noncommercial plane crashes: (curve B) fluctuation of fatalities for multifatality noncommercial plane crashes: and (curve C) fluctuation of fatalities for single-fatality noncommercial plane crashes. Noncommercial flying refers to "the use of an aircraft for purposes of pleasure, personal transportation, . . . private business, in corporate/executive operations, and in other operations, wherein there is no direct monetary fee charged"*(3)*. Planes owned in the United States but crashing outside the 50 states are excluded from this analysis. (From "Airplane Accident Fatalities Increase Just After Newspaper Stories About Murder and Suicide," by D. P. Phillips, *Science,* 1978, *201,* 748–750. Copyright 1978 by the American Association for the Advancement of Science. Reprinted by permission of the author and publisher.)

Advantages. Archival research has a number of advantages. First of all, it allows the investigator to test hypotheses over a wider range of time and societies than would otherwise be possible. Many records date back for centuries, a period of time that cannot be examined today using the other methods we have discussed. Demonstrating the validity of a hypothesis in a number of different cultures and historical periods, instead of being restricted to a specific group in the present time and place, gives us considerable confidence in the validity of that hypothesis as a test of human behavior in general.

A second advantage of the archival method is that it uses **unobtrusive measures:** measures that did not cause reactivity in the participants at the time they were collected (Webb, Campbell, Schwartz, & Sechrest, 1966). Because the information used in archival research was originally collected for some other purpose, there is little or no chance that demand characteristics or evaluation apprehension will be problems for the present investigator. (Airplane crashes, for example, lie far outside the realm of experimenter influence.)

Disadvantages. Although experimenters doing archival research did not collect the data personally and thus are spared some problems in terms of reactivity, they may encounter some difficulties in terms of data availability. Frequently an investigator will not be able to locate the kind of data needed to test a hypothesis. Not being able to design the dependent measures, the investigator is left at the mercy of those who collected the data. Sometimes, of course, creativity and ingenuity will help the investigator to locate the kinds of data needed; in other cases, however, missing or inaccurate records will prevent an adequate experimental test. Even if the material is available, it is sometimes difficult to categorize it in the way necessary to answer the research question. Careful methods of content analysis must be developed for material that is nonquantitative in nature, much as categories are developed for observational research described earlier (see p. 50).

Such procedures are time consuming, although the development of computer programs has provided a welcome assist in some instances.

In summary, archival research offers the investigator tremendous opportunities for examining data from a wide range of times and places. Although relying on data that were collected for another purpose may cause problems for the investigator, the appeal of archival research, particularly when used in conjunction with other research methods, is strong.

F. *Simulation and Role Playing*

One of the most dramatic studies in social psychology is the prison-**simulation** experiment (see Figure 2-8) conducted at Stanford University by Phillip Zimbardo and his colleagues (Haney, Banks, & Zimbardo, 1973). The simulation began with wailing police sirens as nine young men were picked up at their homes, spread-eagled and frisked, handcuffed, taken to the police station and booked, and finally driven blindfolded to a "prison" in the basement of the Stanford psychology building. There, three other young men dressed as guards supervised the "prisoners'" activities in a small area of the building that had been outfitted with typical prison cells, a small "yard," and even a solitary-confinement "hole."

The subjects in this research project were college students who had answered a newspaper ad for volunteers to take part in a psychological study of prison life. Prior to acceptance, all applicants were screened, and those selected were judged to be the most stable, most mature, and least antisocial students. All the students agreed to serve in either the guard or prisoner role and were randomly assigned to one of the two roles by the experimenter.

At the Stanford University "prison," conditions were made as realistic as possible. Prisoners were referred to only by number; their meals were bland and their toilet visits were supervised; they were assigned to work shifts and were lined up three times a day for a count. The guards were allowed to set up most of their own rules for running the prison; however, the use of punishment or physical aggression was prohibited. The project was scheduled to run for two weeks.

During this time, the experimenters maintained constant observation of the situation, using both audio and videotape equipment, and they administered a series of questionnaire measures as well. However, the intended two-week simulation study had to be abruptly terminated at the end of six days.

Within that six-day period, the behavior of the college men had degenerated rapidly. Guards increasingly enjoyed their power; for example, they issued arbitrary commands to do pushups and refused requests to go to the toilet. Prisoners lapsed into depression and helplessness and began to develop both physical and emotional distress symptoms. It was clear to the experimenters that, although the reality of a prison had undoubtedly been created, the situation was too dangerous. After terminating the experiment, the researchers held several sessions with the participants to deal with their emotional reactions to the experience, and they maintained contact with each student for a year after the study to ensure that the negative effects of the prison simulation did not persist.

Not all simulation studies are so dramatic. In some instances, subjects are simply brought to a bare room, given the description of an experimental setting, and asked to act as if they were in the real situation (Mixon, 1972). In this case, the participant in the simulation is being asked to play the role of a subject, rather than a more dramatic role, such as a prisoner or a guard. Somewhere between these two extremes are studies that simulate international decision making, in which subjects are given a large playing board and asked to make political and economic decisions for imaginary countries (Streufert, Castore, & Kliger, 1967).

Although the range of simulation studies is considerable, the aim of each is to imitate some aspect of a real-world situation in order to gain more understanding of people's psychological processes. Subjects in these studies are typically asked to *role*

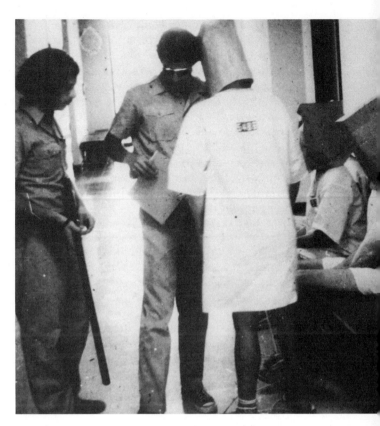

Figure 2-8. "Prisoners" and "guards" in the Stanford prison experiment. (Courtesy of Stanford University.)

play: to adopt a part and act as if they were in the real situation. In advance of their participation, the subjects are fully informed about the situation and are asked to develop their part to the best of their ability.

Advantages. The success of a simulation or role-play study depends heavily on the degree of involvement that the experimental setting can engender (Geller, 1978). If the subjects get deeply involved in the setting, then the simulation may well approximate the real-life conditions that it intends to match. Furthermore, because participants are fully informed of the purposes of the study in advance, they basically take on the role of co-investigators, a role that is both ethically and humanistically more satisfying in many respects than the more typical experimental subject role in which the subject is unaware of many of the experimenter's intentions (Kelman, 1968). An additional advantage of the simulation is that it may allow the investigator to study in the laboratory phenomena and situations that are difficult to study in the real world. For example, it is difficult for social scientists to gain access to prisons and international political conferences; however, the investigator can simulate them in the laboratory with the additional advantages of experimental control of variables and random assignment of subjects.

Disadvantages. In spite of their advantages, simulation and role playing are two of the most controversial methods in the social psychological repertoire (Cooper, 1976; Forward, Canter, & Kirsch, 1976; Hendrick, 1977; Miller, 1972). Critics of the method claim that when one asks subjects to act as if they were in a certain role, the subjects will do only what they think they *might* do and not necessarily what they *would* do in the real situation (Aronson & Carlsmith, 1968; Carlsmith, Ellsworth, & Aronson, 1976).

In addition, the problems of experimental demands and evaluation apprehension, discussed earlier in relation to laboratory experiments, are even more serious when the subject is fully informed of purposes of the study. On the other hand, proponents of role playing argue that, to some degree, the participant in an experiment is always playing a role, whether it is the general role of subject or a more specific role defined by the investigator.

This controversy is difficult to resolve and will probably continue for several years. Some of the issues in the controversy can be resolved empirically, by social psychologists conducting experiments directed at the methodological practices themselves. Other aspects of the argument may be more philosophical and, as in the case of the theories of Chapter 1, may reflect overriding views of human nature.

G. *Surveys and Interviews*

An assessment of the quality of life in the United States was the objective of a large-scale interview study conducted by Campbell, Converse, and Rogers (1976). Using a carefully selected sample of 2164 persons, 18 years or older and representing all segments of the population and all regions of the country, these investigators conducted lengthy interviews to determine how satisfied people were with their life in general and with particular areas such as job, marriage, and health. The initial results of the study showed that most people were reasonably happy with their lives. However, a closer analysis showed that subjective feelings of satisfaction are very clearly related to objective characteristics of the life situation. For example, degree of marital satisfaction is related to educational level, as illustrated in Figure 2-9. Those people with less education are more likely to report that they are completely satisfied with their marriage than are those with more education. It is also worth noting that the differences between men and women in reported marital satisfaction are greatest at the two extremes of educational level.

This study of the perceived quality of life is an example of an **interview** study, in which a researcher questions people according to a predetermined schedule and records their answers (see Figure 2-10). Similar to this is the **questionnaire survey,** in which respondents read the questions themselves and provide written answers (Jacoby, 1980). Although many other methods in social psychology make use of questionnaires as part of their procedures, survey and interview methods rely *solely* on this type of information. In both cases, the investigator defines an area for research and designs a set of questions that will elicit the beliefs, attitudes, and self-reported experiences of the respondent in relation to the research topic.

Designing a good questionnaire is not as easy as it might appear. Some considerations that enter into the design include the wording of questions, the provision of sufficient responses, and the format of the questionnaire itself (Jacoby, 1980). For example, the wording of a question may systematically bias the answers. Politicians often use this tactic to their advantage. Thus a question that begins "I agree that Candidate X . . ." is more likely to receive a positive re-

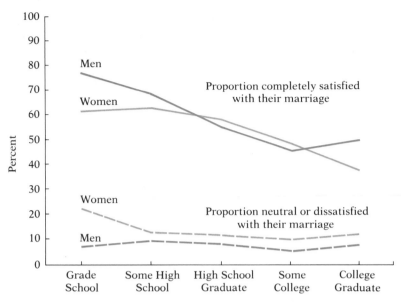

Figure 2-9. Relationship of marital satisfaction to educational level. (From *The Quality of American Life: Perceptions, Evaluations, and Satisfactions,* by A. Campbell, P. E. Converse, and W. L. Rogers. Copyright 1976 by the Russell Sage Foundation. Reprinted by permission.)

sponse than a question begun with "Does Candidate X." Considerable pretesting is necessary to assure that the questions are objective, unbiased, understandable to the average respondent, and specific enough to elicit the desired information.

When the questionnaire is being presented by an interviewer, additional precautions against biasing the responses are necessary. The issue of experimenter bias, discussed earlier in relation to laboratory experiments, can be a problem in the interview method if the interviewer consciously or unconsciously encourages some responses and discourages or seems uninterested in others. Thus, interviewers must be carefully trained to standardize the delivery of questions to respondents. In addition, the interview method requires some skills on the part of the interviewer in developing rapport, so that the respondent will be willing to answer questions in a straightforward and honest manner.

In both questionnaire surveys and interviews, the investigator must be concerned with *sampling procedures*. If the researcher wants to generalize to a larger population, say for example the entire population of the United States and Canada, it is not necessary to contact every member of that population. A sample or a subset of perhaps 2000 people can be chosen that will, if selected properly, prove to be an accurate reflection of the total population. Improper sample

selection, however, is almost certain to produce inaccurate results. For example, many televised news programs feature a roving reporter who asks passing pedestrians their opinion on some topical issue. Such samplings are undoubtedly not systematic and probably tell us very little about the general population.

Figure 2-10. Interviews may take place on the street, in the home, or in a variety of other situations. (© Charles Gatewood/Magnum Photos, Inc.)

Advantages. A major advantage of both survey questionnaires and interviews is that they allow the investigator to formulate the issues of concern very specifically. Rather than devising a situation to elicit desired behavior or finding a natural situation in which to observe that behavior, constructors of questionnaires directly question people about the behavior or area under investigation. In some cases, this is the only approach to desired information. For example, if you were interested in the events of a person's childhood, directly asking the person about those events might be the only way to obtain that information.

Interview and survey-questionnaire research methods also have their own particular advantages and disadvantages, which tend to balance out. For instance, survey questionnaires are easier and more economical to use than interview procedures. In addition, they provide greater anonymity for the respondent, which is important in the case of sensitive or personal issues. Face-to-face interviews, on the other hand, allow the interviewer to gather additional information from observation. Furthermore, the interviewer can clarify questions that may be confusing to the respondent and assure that the person intended to answer the questions is indeed the person responding.

Disadvantages. Perhaps the major difficulty with self-report data, whether from interviews or surveys, is the issue of accuracy. In the case of questions about childhood events, for example, a respondent may or may not recall what actually happened. Even in the case of more recent events, unintentional or deliberate bias may occur. Surveys of sexual behavior are frequently questioned on these grounds, with critics suggesting that people may be less than honest in describing their own sexual practices. Other topics may lead to embellishments by the respondent, who attempts to appear favorably. (This process represents another form of evaluation apprehension, discussed earlier in relation to the experimental method.)

As suggested earlier, survey questionnaires and interviews also have opposite sets of weaknesses. The survey questionnaire gives the investigator less control over the situation and cannot assure the conditions under which the questionnaire is being administered, who is answering it, and whether the respondent fully understands the questions. For its part, the interview is more costly, more time consuming, and is more susceptible to examiner bias.

In summary, questionnaire and interview methods allow the investigator to ask directly about the issues of concern. Particularly in the case of questionnaires, very large-scale studies are possible, thus allowing greater generalizability of the results. Both methods, however, rely on the accuracy and honesty of the respondent and depend on self-reports of behavior rather than observations of the behavior itself.

IV. Some Issues in Research

The variety of research methods that social psychologists have at their disposal is numerous indeed. From this wealth of possibilities, how does the investigator decide on one particular method? Further, having formulated a question or hypothesis and selected a research method, what other issues must be considered? In this section, we will deal with some of the major concerns that face the experimenter as an idea becomes translated into a research project.

A. *Selection of Method and Setting*

As we have seen, each of the methods available to the investigator has its own set of advantages and disadvantages. It is clear, therefore, that the choice of a method cannot simply be based on which one is best. In the abstract, there is no best method. In a specific case, however, there may be a method that is most appropriate to use, and this decision returns us to a consideration of hypothesis formulation.

As the investigator begins to think about research, the questions may be only vaguely defined. In some instances, the interest may be in something concrete, such as communes, the jury system, or a particular religious group. Such topics would probably guide the investigator to the natural setting—that is, to a field study—or to the use of a survey or interview method. In other cases, the investigator's questions may involve something more abstract in nature: for example, why people like each other, what causes aggression, or how we attribute intentionality to others' behavior. In the latter instance, the possibilities for study are much more numerous. To illustrate this distinction, reconsider the case of Triplett, who did the first study in social psychology. Had he been interested in the behavior of cyclists, his likely choices would have been to observe or to ask questions of the cyclists themselves, or perhaps to dig into the archival records of past races. His concern was not, however, the concrete topic of cyclists but rather the more abstract concept of competition and the effect of the presence of others on performance. With this concept in mind, he was free to retreat to his laboratory, use children instead of cyclists, and fishing reels instead of racing bikes.

Ellsworth (1977), in discussing the selection of a research method, notes that there are some basic concerns that the investigator always has. "In brief, one wants an instance that is capable of disconfirming the hypothesis, that allows for fairly precise specification of both independent and dependent variables, that is free of serious confounds, and that is informative, allowing the investigator to collect supplementary data that will be helpful in understanding the results" (Ellsworth, 1977, p. 606).

The possibility of disconfirming the hypothesis is an important one. Although scientists, like most other people, enjoy finding out that they are right, it is crucial that their experiments be not simply a demonstration of what was known all along but rather a true questioning process. As the eminent biologist Albert Szent-Györgyi once stated, "research means going out into the unknown with the hope of finding something new to bring home. If you know in advance what you are going to do or even

find there, then it is not research at all: then it is only a kind of honorable occupation" (Szent-Györgyi, 1971).

For these reasons, it is important for the investigator to consider very carefully the setting in which a hypothesis is to be tested. Sometimes an investigator begins in the laboratory, testing a theory under highly controlled conditions, and then moves out to the field to see if the same principles hold. On other occasions, a reverse strategy is used, as when relationships observed in a field study are then taken back to the laboratory for testing with the hope of more precisely defining cause-and-effect relationships. Such a back-and-forth strategy was, in fact, one of the dictums of Kurt Lewin, often considered the forefather of modern group dynamics.

The advantages of such a strategy should be evident after our discussion of the various research methods. Because each method has its own particular set of weaknesses, it is impossible for reliance on any single one to yield a full understanding of a phenomenon. Thus the question is not which method is best, but which set of methods will be best. As Webb and his colleagues note, "If a proposition can survive the onslaught of a series of imperfect measures, with all their irrelevant error, confidence should be placed in it" (Webb et al., 1966, p. 3). This principle of *triangulation*—of focusing on a single concept from a variety of vantage points—represents a key strategy in the conduct of social psychological research.

B. *Units of Analysis*

The investigator's decisions do not end with the definition of a question and the choice of a research method. The next decisions to be made concern the types of data that will be collected and the procedures to be used for analyzing those data. Depending on the way a hypothesis is framed, an investigator may be interested in the *frequency*, the *rate*, or the *level* of a particular behavior. For example, we might ask how often married couples engage in physical aggression, or what percentage of people are willing to help a person who has fallen down in a subway. These are questions whose answers concern frequency of occurrence. On other occasions, the concern may be with the rate of a behavior, as measured in units of behavior per person or per segment of time. Thus a question might concern the number of contacts a teacher has with his or her kindergarten pupils per day. Still other questions might focus on the specific level of a behavior, as when one measures the degree of attraction between two people or the level of shock administered in an aggression experiment.

A second and related issue concerns how we analyze the data that we collect. Although this is not the place for an elaborate discussion of statistics, a few basics should be mentioned that will aid in understanding the research to be discussed in later chapters. In general, we can talk about four types of questions that may be asked when analyzing data: they involve central tendency, variability, association, and measures of difference.

In the case of *central tendency*, we are asking what is the average response for a group of people. For example, what is the average income of a college graduate, or what is the average attitude of Canadians on the issue of independence for Quebec?

Variability refers to the dispersion of responses (Thorngate, 1974). For example, rather than knowing the average opinion of Canadians about independence for Quebec, it might be more informative to know the degree to which these opinions varied. Are most Canadians generally favorable toward the separatist movement, or do the opinions vary widely from strong opposition to strong support?

A third question that the investigator may ask involves the *association* between two variables. In the Phillips (1978) study, for example, the analysis dealt with the correlation between two types of data—reported murder-suicides and fatal airplane crashes.

Finally, the investigator may be concerned with the *differences* among two or more groups. "Are men more satisfied with marriage than women?" is an example of this type of question. Another example

would be a study concerned with the difference between high-status and low-status speakers in their effectiveness in changing listeners' attitudes.

In each of the last two examples, we are concerned only with one factor: sex in the first example and prestige of the communicator in the second example. Often, however, social psychologists are interested in looking at the effects of two or more independent variables simultaneously. For example, earlier in the chapter we discussed an experiment by Deaux and Emswiller (1974) in which subjects were asked to evaluate the performance of either a male or a female who successfully completed either a masculine or a feminine task. This study is an example of a 2 × 2 factorial experiment: one factor was the sex of the stimulus person (either male or female) and the other factor was the sex-linkage of the task (also with two levels, masculine and feminine).[2] The advantage of combining factors in a single experiment is that it presumably more closely approximates the real world, where many factors may operate simultaneously. Often the results of such experiments give us more information than we would have if we only studied one variable at a time. These results are frequently found in the form of **interaction**, as shown in Figure 2-11. *Interaction* is a statistical term referring to the fact that the effect of one variable depends on the level or state of the other variable. Thus, in the example in Figure 2-11, the evaluations that subjects made about the male and the female students' performances depended on the type of task. In the case of the masculine task, judgments about the male and female students were very different, whereas on the feminine task, the judgments were almost identical. In such a case, information about the **main effects**—the effect that either one of the variables has by itself, not considering the other factor—is much less informative than the combined information represented by the interaction.

---

[2] Actually, the Deaux and Emswiller experiment had a third factor, the sex of the subject, thus making it a 2 × 2 × 2 factorial design. This factor did not affect the results, however; male and female subjects made the same judgments.

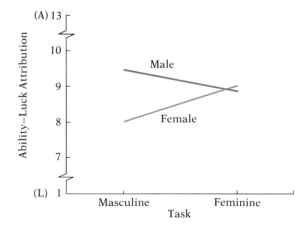

Figure 2-11. Ability-luck attributions as a function of sex of task and performer. (From "Explanations of Successful Performance on Sex-Linked Tasks: What Is Skill for the Male Is Luck for the Female," by K. Deaux and T. Emswiller, *Journal of Personality and Social Psychology*, 1974, *29*, 80–85. Copyright 1974 by the American Psychological Association. Reprinted by permission.)

C. *Ethics of Research*

Beyond the technical issues already discussed, there is another set of concerns that an investigator must consider before conducting an experiment. In addition to determining the potential scientific value of the study, an investigator must give careful thought to the ethical issues involved. In recent years, social psychologists have become increasingly aware of the ethical questions involved in research. In part, pressures for such consideration have originated in the federal and state governments. The U.S. Department of Health, Education, and Welfare has issued a set of guidelines, for example, that all recipients of grants and contracts must follow. Within the profession, there has been considerable concern as well, evidenced in numerous books and articles (for example, Carlsmith, Ellsworth, & Aronson, 1976; Cook, 1976; Kelman, 1968; Schlenker & Forsyth, 1977) and by a set of guidelines developed by the American Psychological Association (APA, 1973). In fact, some research has shown that social psychologists are far more stringent in their ethical evaluation of research practices than

other academicians, law professors, and the students who frequently participate in such research (Rugg, 1975).

The issues involved in the ethical conduct of research are both numerous and complex, and they cannot be fully resolved in this chapter. There are, however, a number of important points we should consider briefly.

One concern is the level of pain or stress to which a subject may be exposed. Although this question is more prominent in the medical and biological sciences, where experimentation with new drugs and experimental cures for disease can have irreversible effects, the general issue is one that social psychologists must also consider in some cases. Most often, the concern of the social psychologist is framed in terms of psychological rather than physical harm. For example, an investigator interested in the effects of negative personal evaluation on subsequent interaction may purposefully expose the subject to uncomplimentary information. Such information has the potential of causing considerable stress for the subject. Other experimental situations may provide the subject with the opportunity to shock another individual, sometimes with coercion from the experimenter to increase the levels of shock (Milgram, 1963). In such instances, even if no shock is actually being delivered, subjects may experience considerable stress as they attempt to comply with the experimenter's demands.

The experimenter's concern should always be to minimize the amount of stress that a subject experiences, both in terms of intensity and duration. At the same time, however, it is difficult to argue that stressful experiences should never be studied (West & Gunn, 1978). Although it is certainly more pleasant to focus one's research attention on positive forms of human behavior, it is undoubtedly true that humans display a reasonable amount of undesirable behaviors as well. The social psychologist, in seeking to understand the full range of human behavior, is obligated to consider both positive and negative aspects of human interaction.

One means of dealing with the problem of exposing subjects to pain or stress is through the use of *informed consent*. Insofar as possible, the experimenter should inform subjects in advance about the requirements of the experiment and obtain their consent to participate. Thus, if a subject is to be exposed to electric shock, it is the experimenter's obligation to inform the subject of that fact in advance. Although informed consent is an important principle for any area of study, it is clearly more important in those studies where the potential for stress or pain is high.

Informed-consent procedures are relatively easy to institute in the laboratory experiment, where the investigator has a great deal of control over the total situation. But what of the field experiment? As we discussed earlier, field experiments are generally carried out without the knowledge of the participants. For that reason, the investigator must plan field experiments carefully. Issues of *invasion of privacy* become paramount. To the extent that a subject has been fully informed of procedures and has given consent, the experimenter in most cases will not be intruding unfairly. In a situation such as the field experiment, however, where informed consent is not the rule, the investigator must be particularly concerned about unreasonable intrusion. Although it is difficult to formulate specific criteria for an acceptable field experiment, we saw in our earlier discussion of these experiments that their similarity to a normal situation is a working rule of thumb. The use of an independent variable that could normally be expected to occur in a public setting reduces the ethical concerns in a field experiment. Exposing unaware citizens to stressful events or invading private domains are far more questionable practices.

In the field study, in which the experimenter does not tamper with the environment, some of the ethical concerns are resolved. Even in this setting, however, investigators must consider carefully the potential for invading the privacy of individuals, especially when they are not identified to the participants.

Another ethical concern of experimenters relates to the practice of deceiving subjects, either by withholding certain information or by purposefully misleading them. Such procedures were unfortunately very common in the laboratory experiments of social psychologists in past years. Scientifically, there is some justification for such procedures. As we discussed earlier, the problems of demand characteristics and evaluation apprehension lead many investigators to develop elaborate scenarios so that the subject will be unaware of the true purpose of the experiment. However, although deception can occasionally be justified, it is undoubtedly true that the technique has been abused. To counter this practice, many social psychologists have argued strongly for role playing as an alternative approach to research, although, as we have seen, that method is not without its own set of problems.

To the extent that informed consent is required, deceptive experiments are less likely to occur. When they are conducted, however, it is critical that the experimenter undertake a thorough debriefing with all participants as soon as the experiment is completed. **Debriefing,** a term borrowed from the space program and the military, refers to the process whereby an experimenter reveals the complete procedure to the subject. In cases where stress or deception has been part of the experimental process, it is the investigator's obligation to be sure that subjects are not permanently harmed by the experience and that they leave the laboratory feeling no worse than they did on entering.

A final ethical concern of the social psychologist concerns the confidentiality of the data that are obtained. It is important that once the data are collected, they cannot be identified with any particular individual and that anonymity of the participants be maintained. Such precautions to protect subjects' confidentiality should be taken routinely by investigators, and the subjects should be informed that confidentiality is preserved.

Few of the ethics questions we have discussed are easily resolved, and often the investigator must carefully weigh the question of scientific value against the rights of the subject. Ultimately, investigators must make their own decisions whether or not to conduct an experiment, although numerous checks exist in the form of colleague and review-committee sanctions. Each time a study is begun, the investigator must consider all of the available options and determine the best way to answer the research question, keeping a multitude of complex factors in balance.

In conclusion, the process of "invading the unknown" is a complex but exciting one. The investigator must make numerous decisions along the way, and each one will contribute to the ultimate success or failure of the project. Not all questions are easily answered; their solutions may take dozens of studies and years of effort by many different investigators. The results of many such efforts will be the topic of the remainder of this book.

V. Summary

Research is an exacting and exciting endeavor. The process of research is a lengthy one, beginning with an idea and moving through decisions on how to test the idea, the completion of the actual research, and, finally, the analysis and interpretation of the data. Each of these stages is important to the final product, which is the answer to a question about human behavior.

Sources for experimental hypotheses are numerous, ranging from casual observation to complex hypothetico-deductive systems. Once a question is formulated, there are many different ways to attempt to answer it. Any question can be answered using several different methods.

At least seven specific methods are available to the social psychology researcher. These methods are: laboratory experiments, field experiments, quasi-experimental research, field studies, archival research, simulations and role playing, and surveys and interviews. Each of these methods has certain advantages over the other methods, and each has certain disadvantages as well.

The selection of any one research method depends in part on the question that is being asked. In the long run, however, it is important for the investigator to test each question with a variety of different methods, thereby canceling out the disadvantages of each single method and gaining more confidence in the validity of the research results. Also, different types of statistical analysis techniques are required to test different hypotheses.

Finally, throughout their research, investigators must give careful thought to the ethical issues that are involved. Social psychology research involves people, and the rights of these participants in the research process must be recognized and protected at all times.

Glossary Terms

archival research
correlational method
debriefing
deindividuation
demand characteristics
dependent variable
evaluation apprehension
experimental realism

experimenter expectancies
external validity
independent variable
interaction
internal validity
interview
main effect
manipulation check

mundane realism
participant observation
questionnaire survey
randomization
reactive measure
reliability
simulation
unobtrusive measure

*Yond Cassius has a lean and hungry look; . . . such men
are dangerous.* WILLIAM SHAKESPEARE

JOHN WILDE. *WEDDING PORTRAIT.* (1943.) PENCIL. 27¾ x 17¾ INCHES.
COLLECTION OF THE WHITNEY MUSEUM OF AMERICAN ART. GIFTS OF THE ARTIST IN MEMORY OF HELEN WILDE.

JOHN WILDE. *WEDDING PORTRAIT.* (1943.) PENCIL. 27¾ x 17¼ INCHES.

*To know one's self is wisdom, but to know one's neighbor
is genius.* MINNA ANTRIM

3

Social Perception: Impressions and Explanations of People

Curiosity about people certainly is not limited to social psychologists. Although the social psychologist may have more extensively developed theories and more exacting means of testing those theories, all of us during the course of our lives develop ideas and beliefs about what people are all about. These impressions of people form the basis for many of our interactions and experiences. In some sense, they precede most of the other aspects of social behavior that will be discussed in later sections of this book.

Consider the following example. It is 6 P.M. and you are at home alone. A short, redheaded man in his late 30s comes to the door carrying a suitcase and asks to use your phone. Somewhat nervously, you think, he claims that his car has broken down and that he wants to phone for help. What impressions do you form of him? How do you respond? Your reaction probably will depend on a series of quick judgments that you make about his personality, his intentions, and the reasons for his request. Such judgments fall within an area called *social perception*, a general term for the process of forming judgments about the qualities of other people.

If you did encounter this particular stranger, you might consider a number of issues. First, you may have some general beliefs about people that you apply in all situations. You might believe that people generally are trustworthy and thus quickly open your door to the stranger. Or, you might believe that people generally are not to be trusted and thus hurriedly turn the stranger away. Beyond this very general level, however, specific stereotypes can come into play. A belief that redheads are friendly, for example, might lead you to welcome this particular redheaded stranger.

Yet, each person acts as a specific stimulus, and our reactions involve far more than general beliefs. In this case, your impression of the stranger probably would be formed partly by studying his facial expressions, observing his clothes, and listening to his voice. Each of these pieces of information—and others as well—would influence your impression of the man and, in turn, your reaction to his request for help.

Beyond the question of what a person is like, we also ask why: what are the causes or reasons for a person's behavior? **Attribution theory** is concerned with the way people assign characteristics or intentions to other persons or to objects. This theory suggests that we do not form static impressions but, instead, actively attempt to explain behavior. In the case of the stranger at the door, for example, you might notice that he constantly looks over his shoulder, and you might conclude that he is concerned about onlookers. This may be because he is embarrassed to be asking for help, or it may be that he is worried that there will be witnesses to his approach.

Each of the questions you would ask yourself about the redheaded stranger represents a different level of the social-perception process. Using an analogy of an onion, we can consider how we continually peel down our reactions, beginning with the outer, surface layer and then considering the less obvious, hidden layers. Before we begin this peeling process, however, we should ask why the process is important.

I. The Need to Predict and Understand Others

In science fiction movies, when Earth people venture onto other planets, they typically encounter strange terrains, exotic machinery, and uncertain climates. Even more strange in most instances are the beings (human and otherwise) that they meet, and a central theme of the plot is often the Earthlings' attempts to predict the behavior of these strangers. The difficulty of these predictions results from a lack of knowledge about the strangers' behavior and the absence of experience with what beings of this sort will do.

Such confusion emphasizes the importance of our ability to know and understand the behavior of others. Other people significantly influence our successes and failures in life. The way professors grade a student's course work may affect whether that student can continue school and the kind of career that will be open to the student. When we approach other people to seek friendship, we may find love or rejection. We make important assumptions about other drivers, whose actions, if erratic, can have dire consequences.

Other people play such an influential part in our lives that, for most of us, the desire to understand and predict their behavior is of crucial importance. At a specific level, our direct experience with an individual will provide a basis for anticipating his or her future behavior and thus will affect how we relate to that person in the future (see Figure 3-1). At a more general level, we combine our experiences and our general understanding into broader **philosophies of human nature,**

which are expectancies that people will possess certain qualities and will behave in certain ways (Wrightsman, 1974). These general attitudes provide a base whereby we can predict the behaviors of people whom we haven't met and thus reduce the uncertainty involved in strange encounters with new people. Of course, our predictions may or may not be correct; philosophies of human nature refer to our *expectancies* concerning the behavior of others and not necessarily to what people really *are*.

A. *Philosophies of Human Nature*

An analysis of writings by philosophers, theologians, and social scientists has generated the proposition that our beliefs about human nature have six basic dimensions (Wrightsman, 1964). These dimensions,

Figure 3-1. Charlie Brown's assumptions about human nature. (© 1968 by United Feature Syndicate, Inc. Reprinted by permission.)

which are summarized in Table 3-1, are believed to represent a basic framework, or template, by which we judge the actions and characteristics of others.

To find evidence of differences in the first dimension of belief, *trustworthiness versus untrustworthiness*, we don't need to look any further than the influential viewpoints in psychotherapy. Carl Rogers, the originator of client-centered therapy, has written (1957): "In my experience I have discovered [people] to have characteristics which seem inherent in [the] species . . . terms such as positive, forward-moving, constructive, realistic, trustworthy" (p. 200). In contrast, Sigmund Freud, the father of psychoanalysis, wrote in a letter to a colleague that "with a few exceptions, human nature is basically worthless" (E. L. Freud, 1960, p. 79). Of course, many people's beliefs lie somewhere between these two extremes. Furthermore, beliefs may gradually shift with time. Research has shown, for example, that, while college students in the 1960s were quite optimistic, later generations of students have become more pessimistic in their beliefs about the basic trustworthiness of people (Baker & Wrightsman, 1974; Hochreich & Rotter, 1970).

The second dimension of philosophies of human nature is *strength of will and rationality versus lack of will power and irrationality*. U.S. culture, and perhaps to a lesser extent Canadian culture, traditionally has been characterized by a belief in the effectiveness of will power and motivation. The self-help movement, from Mary Baker Eddy to Dale Carnegie to Werner Erhard, has long been a strong force in amateur North American philosophy. Yet the opposite view has had its adherents as well. St. Paul believed that will power was not enough: "I can will what is right, but I cannot do it."

T A B L E 3 - 1 / *The Dimensions and Subscales of the Philosophies of Human Nature Scale*

The Philosophies of Human Nature (PHN) scale measures one's beliefs about human nature. It is a Likert-type scale, with each subscale being composed of 14 statements (items). Subjects indicate their agreement or disagreement with each item by circling a number from +3 to −3. The range for each subscale is +42 to −42. The six subscales are:

1. Trustworthiness versus untrustworthiness
   + = belief that people are trustworthy, moral, and responsible
   − = belief that people are untrustworthy, immoral, and irresponsible

2. Strength of will and rationality versus lack of will power and irrationality
   + = belief that people can control their outcomes and that they understand themselves
   − = belief that people lack self-determination and are irrational

3. Altruism versus selfishness
   + = belief that people are altruistic, unselfish, and sincerely interested in others
   − = belief that people are selfish and self-centered

4. Independence versus conformity to group pressures
   + = belief that people are able to maintain their beliefs in the face of group pressures to the contrary
   − = belief that people give in to pressures of group and society

5. Variability versus similarity
   + = belief that people are different from each other in personality and interests and that a person can change over time
   − = belief that people are similar in interests and are not changeable over time

6. Complexity versus simplicity
   + = belief that people are complex and hard to understand
   − = belief that people are simple and easy to understand

The first four subscales (T, S, A, and I) can be summed to give a *positive-negative* score (range +168 to −168), indicating general positive or negative beliefs about substantive characteristics of human nature. The last two subscales (V and C) can be summed to give a *multiplexity* score (range +84 to −84), indicating beliefs about the extent of individual differences in human nature.

This second dimension of philosophies of human nature also includes beliefs about human rationality and irrationality. *Rationality* here means that one's ego is in control and that cognitions dominate emotions. As an example of a belief in the irrational end of this dimension, we can consider Freud's views of U.S. President Woodrow Wilson (Freud & Bullitt, 1967). In this posthumously published book, President Wilson's virtues are portrayed as weaknesses and his visions as the fruits of compulsion; his idealization of the League of Nations is interpreted by Freud as evidence of a passive, dependent relationship between Wilson and his father. According to Freud, subconscious emotional factors are the major influence on decisions even at the highest levels of international affairs.

The third dimension of philosophies of human nature is *altruism versus selfishness.* An optimistic view of this aspect of human nature is that people are generally interested in others. However, a number of well-publicized events in which persons seeking help were ignored by passersby have caused many people to reevaluate their beliefs about the extent of altruism in human nature. For example, a number of years ago in Queens, New York, a woman was murdered while 38 witnesses failed to help or call for help. This incident received much publicity, generated considerable commentary on the apathy of modern life, and provided the impetus for an extensive research program by Latané and Darley (1970) on the factors affecting altruistic behavior (see Chapter 9).

The fourth dimension of philosophies of human nature is *independence versus conformity to group pressures,* or the extent to which one believes that people can maintain their convictions in the face of pressures to conform from a group, a society, or some individual authority figure (see Figure 3-2).

Figure 3-2. As is true of the other dimensions of philosophies of human nature, independence-versus-conformity may not be an either/or proposition. As we observe behavior, we may see evidence of both. In the photograph below, conformity in dress coexists with independence of behavior. (© Abigail Heyman/Magnum Photos, Inc.)

Stanley Milgram's work on obedience (to be discussed at greater length in Chapter 14) provides the basis for a fairly pessimistic view concerning people's ability to maintain independence (Milgram, 1963). In this project, men from the local community were hired to participate in what appeared to be a learning experiment. In the course of the study, the men were told by the experimenter (appropriately uniformed in a white lab coat) to give ever-increasing levels of shock to another person, who responded by screaming in pain and pounding on the wall. Milgram's basic research question was "What percentage of the people would continue to obey the experimenter, despite the apparent pain that their 'student' was suffering?" Prior to the experiment, Milgram had asked psychologists and Yale undergraduates to estimate what percentage of subjects would continue to administer shocks; in effect, Milgram asked for a measure of their beliefs about human nature. The most pessimistic respondents predicted that 3% of the subjects would continue to the highest level of shock. In actuality, 65% of Milgram's subjects administered the maximum shock. Such results are provocative and disturbing evidence of the willingness of people to obey the demands of an authority figure, and they provide a dramatic laboratory analog to the events of the Holocaust during World War II (Milgram, 1974).

Two additional dimensions of the philosophies of human nature proposed by Wrightsman (1964) concern beliefs in the variation that exists among human beings. These two dimensions are *similarity versus variability* and *complexity versus simplicity*. For the former dimension, we can compare people who believe that most individuals are the same with those who believe that there is extensive variety among people. Two people, for example, might both believe strongly in the basic trustworthiness of human nature, but, whereas one might think that everyone was equally trustworthy, the other might see considerable variability in people's trustworthiness. In personality theory, the *idiographic* approach, as represented most strongly by Gordon All-

port (1961, 1962), represents a belief in the uniqueness of each individual; in contrast, the *nomothetic* approach tends to classify people in large groups or categories when attempting to explain behavior.

Complexity versus simplicity refers to the extent to which one believes that people are complicated and hard to understand as opposed to simple and easy to understand. Muhammad Ali's theory of people, as shown in Box 3-1, seems to represent a relatively simple conception of people. In contrast, many psychologists would argue that human behavior is much more complex and requires more than a hardness–softness dimension for explanation.

In extensive research with the Philosophies of Human Nature scale with people of different ages, sexes, races, and occupations, Wrightsman and his colleagues have found that the average person believes human nature to be (1) neither extremely trustworthy nor extremely untrustworthy; (2) somewhat rational and possessing a moderate degree of will power; (3) neither extremely altruistic nor extremely selfish; (4) somewhat more likely to conform to group pressures than to remain independent; (5) moderately variable and unique; and (6) moderately complex and hard to understand (Wrightsman, 1974; Wrightsman & Satterfield, 1967).

Although this pattern of beliefs is a fair description of people in general, there are substantial differences between various groups of people. Students in schools in the Southern part of the United States, for example, generally have more trusting beliefs than do students from Eastern U.S. colleges (Wrightsman, 1974). Furthermore, dramatic events may change, at least temporarily, people's beliefs about human nature. After the assassination of U.S. President John F. Kennedy, many people became much more negative in their beliefs about human nature. Several months later, however, these people's beliefs had returned to their previous level, suggesting that philosophies of human nature may be fairly pervasive ways of looking at the world and the people in that world.

Box 3-1. Muhammad Ali's Views of People.

Invited by the graduating seniors to speak at Harvard University's commencement ceremonies, former heavyweight boxing champion Muhammad Ali expressed his theory about people, which is built around four personality types. These are the walnut, "hard on the outside, but soft on the inside"; the prune, "soft on the outside but hard on the inside"; the pomegranate, "hard on the inside and the outside"; and the grape, "soft on the inside and the outside." He also stated that of all the fruits in the bowl the grape is the most attractive. He said that he usually lets the public see only his "walnut" personality, but confessed to being more of a "grape." (© Vicki Lawrence/ Stock, Boston.)

B. *Implicit Personality Theory*

The general dimensions proposed by Wrightsman describe some basic factors that many people use in interpreting the behavior of others. However, we also know that people have much more individualized conceptions of human behavior. Through development and experience, each of us develops our own **implicit personality theory,** or unstated assumptions about what traits are associated with each other. Such theories are considered implicit because they are rarely stated in formal terms; nonetheless, they are often a dominant factor in our judgments of other people (Bruner & Tagiuri, 1954; Cronbach, 1955; Schneider, 1973; Schneider, Hastorf, & Ellsworth, 1979; Wegner & Vallacher, 1977).

For example, Rosenberg and Sedlak (1972) have found that college students, in describing the people they know, use the terms *intelligent, friendly, self-centered, ambitious,* and *lazy* with the greatest frequency. The usage of these terms is not random, however. People described as intelligent are also likely to be described as friendly. In contrast, people described as intelligent are rarely described as self-centered. Thus for many people there is apparently an implicit personality theory that says intelligence and friendliness are related, whereas intelligence and self-centeredness are not. Implicit personality theories are assumptions people make that two or more traits are related so that, if a person has one of the traits, he or she will have another specific trait as well. Such theories may be true or may be false when compared to the actual occurrence of such characteristics in real life. In fact, one of the features that distinguishes implicit personality theories from more formal psychological theories is their lesser likelihood of being tested and found incorrect. Because we may not even be aware that we make an association between, for example, intelligence and friendliness, we may be much less likely to notice exceptions to the rule. Thus we will continue to form impressions with our implicit theories intact.

The use of such implicit theories reflects our need to simplify and integrate information, enabling us to deal more easily with the complexities of human interaction. Given a limited amount of information, we can fill in the details and make a person more understandable in terms of our own experience.

Each of us probably has our own implicit personality theory, which could be assessed through our conversations and letters or from free descriptions elicited by experimenters. In an interesting use of the archival method, Rosenberg and Jones (1972) showed that it is possible also to assess the implicit personality theories of historical figures, in this case the writer Theodore Dreiser. Analyzing *A Gallery of Women* (1929), a collection of sketches about 15 women, these investigators tabulated all of the traits used by Dreiser in describing women (a summary of the 99 most frequently occurring traits is shown in Table 3-2). With further statistical analysis, Rosenberg and Jones were able to reduce these traits to three basic dimensions: hard–soft, male–female, and conforms–does not conform. Hardness was closely related to maleness in Dreiser's implicit theory but not identical

TABLE 3-2 / *The 99 Most Frequently Occurring Trait Categories in* A Gallery of Women, *by Theodore Dreiser*

Trait Category	Frequency	Trait Category	Frequency
Young	100	Fool, good-looking, literary, pagan	14
Beautiful	67		
Attractive	44	Aspirant, determined, good, had means, sad, society person, not strong, tasteful	13
Charming, dreamer	41		
Poetic	39		
Interesting, worker	32	Ambitious, careful, defiant, different, erratic, genial, happy, lonely, man, varietistic	12
Artistic	29		
Gay	26		
Practical, romantic, writer	25	Clever, genius, indifferent, Irish, manager, nice, old, pale, quiet, restless, serious, shrewd, sincere, successful, suffering, sympathetic, thin, understanding	11
Conventional, girl	24		
Free, strong	23		
Woman	22		
Unhappy	20	American, communist, crazy, critical, emotional, enthusiastic, fearful, fighter, forceful, great, handsome, hard, lovely, had money, painter, physically alluring, playful, repressed, reserved, skilled, sophisticated	10
Intellectual, radical, sensitive, sensual	19		
Kind, cold	18		
Vigorous	17		
Able, drinker, generous, troubled	16		
Colorful, graceful, intelligent, poor, reads, religious, studies, tall	15		

From "A Method for Investigating and Representing a Person's Implicit Theory of Personality," by S. Rosenberg and R. Jones. In *Journal of Personality and Social Psychology*, 1972, *22*, 372–386. Copyright 1972 by the American Psychological Association. Reprinted by permission of author and publisher.

with it; in contrast, sex and conformity were believed to be quite independent characteristics. It is interesting to consider this pattern of Dreiser's in conjunction with current stereotypes about men and women (to be discussed in more detail in Chapter 11). On the one hand, he was clearly concerned with the outward physical characteristics of women, as evidenced by the relative frequencies of traits listed in Table 3-2. Although such descriptions might suggest a rather superficial view of women, it is also true that he did not associate women with conformity, thus deviating from at least one aspect of the commonly held stereotype.

Another approach to understanding people's implicit personality theories is represented in the work of psychologist George Kelly. Kelly, in developing a cognitive theory of human behavior, was concerned with the links between our perceptions and our behavior. A crucial mediating link in this chain is our interpretation of the events and stimuli in our world. As Kelly asserts:

[People] look at [their] world through transparent patterns or templets which [they] create and then attempt to fit over the realities of which the world is composed. . . . Let us give the name constructs to these patterns that are tried on for size. They are ways of construing the world [1955, pp. 8–9].

Construct is a key term for Kelly. It is a way of interpreting the world and a guide to behavior. Kelly's fundamental assumption is that we are all scientists. Just as a scientist tries to understand and predict events, each human being tries in the same way to choose constructs that will make the world understandable and predictable. According to Kelly's theory, people do not strive for reinforcement or seek to avoid anxiety; instead, they try to *validate their own construct systems.* Furthermore, Kelly has discarded the notion of an objective, absolute truth in favor of a phenomenological approach— that is, conditions have meaning only as they are construed by the individual.

According to Kelly, every construct we use (such as "cheap" or "likable") gives us a basis for classifying the similarities and differences between people, objects, and events. Each person has developed only a

limited number of constructs, often arranged in order from more to less important. One person's constructs are never completely identical with another person's, although they may be similar. To the extent that their construct systems are similar, Kelly believed that people's behavior would be similar as well.

The method George Kelly developed to measure personal constructs is called the Role Construct Repertory Test, or "Rep Test." On the test form, a number of roles are listed (self, spouse, boss, friend, person you dislike, and so on). The subject is asked to name ways in which two of the individuals in these roles are like each other and at the same time different from a third individual. For example, a subject might say that her spouse and best friend are smart, while her boss is dumb. This process is repeated many times for different combinations of roles, and the traits named most frequently by subjects represent their major personal constructs. A test form appropriate for use with children also has been developed (Vacc & Vacc, 1973). Additional work with this approach has allowed the measurement of the more general characteristics of complexity and simplicity in the construing of social behavior. In these instances the interest is not in the particular constructs that one uses but, rather, in the general cognitive complexity of a respondent (Bieri, Atkins, Briar, Leaman, Miller, & Tripodi, 1966).

II. Forming Impressions

Our philosophies of human nature and our implicit personality theories form a basis for judging the people we encounter. Yet, our reactions to people are much more complex than this. Not only do we bring our own general theories to the situation, but we also react to what we see before us. Some of our impressions are based on surface characteristics; like the analogous onion skin, we may look first at skin color, gender, or other physical characteristics. Then we may look further for less apparent indicators in our attempt to understand the essence of the other person.

A. *The Use of Group Stereotypes*

Archie Bunker provides a vivid example of the use of group stereotyping. In his weekly monologues, Archie routinely ascribes traits to Italians, Blacks, liberals, feminists, and virtually any other group that he can label. Although Archie's ascriptions may be more vivid than some, most of us probably possess some stereotyped images. **Stereotypes** are relatively rigid and oversimplified conceptions of groups of people in which all individuals in a given group are labeled with the so-called group characteristics. Such stereotypes about members of a certain group, in turn, may affect the impressions we form of a single individual who can be identified as a member of that particular group.

As an example of how this stereotyping process can affect our judgments, consider a study conducted by Goldberg, Gottesdiener, and Abramson (1975). These investigators asked a group of subjects to look at photographs of 30 different women and to try to identify which women were feminists. With no information other than these pictures, subjects tended to select the least attractive women as probable feminists, while guessing that the more attractive women were not feminists. Such results clearly suggest a stereotyped link between attractiveness and feminism. To test the validity of this stereotyped link, these investigators also asked the women whose photographs were used to indicate their beliefs concerning feminism. The results indicated that there is no basis for the stereotype. The physical attractiveness of a woman (as judged by an independent set of raters) was in no way related to her feminist beliefs. In a similar study of stereotypes, Jacobson and Koch (1978) found that many people believe that unattractive women endorse feminism because they lack other goals, whereas attractive women presumably have more positive reasons for joining the movement.

Such stereotyped judgments concerning the relationship between attractiveness and feminism are an example of an **illusory correlation,** which is an overestimation of the strength of a relationship between two variables (Chapman & Chapman, 1969). In an illusory correlation, the variables may not be related at all, or the relationship may be much weaker than believed. One explanation for this kind of bias relates to the frequency of the events that we try to explain. Hamilton and Gifford (1976), for example, have shown that, if two different types of information both occur infrequently, we will tend to make an association between them even if no real association exists. To demonstrate this bias, these investigators presented subjects with a set of descriptive statements about a variety of people. Two-thirds of these people were identified as being members of Group A, while the remaining third were identified as members of Group B. In addition to their group identification, each person was also described by a single behavior, either a desirable behavior (for example, "John visited a sick friend in the hospital") or an undesirable behavior (for example, "John always talks about himself and his problems"). Among both Group A and Group B members, approximately two-thirds of the individuals were described by positive behaviors and approximately one-third were described by negative behaviors. Thus, in this experiment there were two factors: group membership and type of behavioral information presented. When asked to make judgments about the typical member of each group, subjects showed evidence of the illusory correlation. They judged members of Group B to be less likable than members of Group A, suggesting a perceived link between frequencies. The smaller number of Group B members was associated with the smaller number of undesirable behaviors, even though the proportions of undesirable behaviors were identical for the two groups.

Categorizing information on the basis of group membership may be more economical—it is easier to talk about 1 group than about 20 individuals—but it obviously has its problems. As another example, Rothbart and his colleagues have shown that the presence of a few deviant individuals in a group may color our perception of the group as a whole (Rothbart, Fulero, Jensen, Howard, & Birrell, 1978). Similarly, if we are asked to recall the details of a group discussion, we tend to remember what members of certain groups said (for example, what some woman said) but often forget which particular individual was responsible for the remark (Taylor, Fiske, Etcoff, & Ruderman, 1978).

Thus, many of our stereotypes are based on cognitive "errors." These "errors" are most likely to occur when we do not have extensive contact with the group in question and when we do not have any additional information about the individual members of the group. Because undesirable behaviors are also believed to be less common than desirable behaviors (Kanouse & Hanson, 1972; Lay, Burron, & Jackson, 1973), these two sets of infrequent and unfamiliar events (contact with a group we infrequently encounter and an undesirable behavior) may be linked in our mind, creating stereotypes that we use in the future (Hamilton, 1976, 1979). When we first meet someone, the surface layer of characteristics may elicit our past stereotypes, and our impressions will be affected by that information.

B. *Central Traits*

We may be able to avoid stereotypes by a conscious decision to "peel off" that first layer. But can we avoid emphasizing certain characteristics as the building blocks in forming our impressions of others? The Gestalt psychologists say no. **Solomon Asch** (1946), for example, suggested that, when we form an impression of another person, some pieces of information carry greater weight and thus modify the whole picture. Asch called such influential characteristics **central traits.** Asch showed that the *warm– cold* dimension was a central one that strongly affected the organization of people's impressions. For instance, when the adjective *cold* was included in a list of seven stimulus words purportedly describing a person, only about 10% of the subjects believed the person in question also would be generous or humorous, which were traits included on the response list. However, when the adjective *warm* was used as a stimulus instead of *cold*, about 90% of the subjects described the person as generous, and more

than 75% described the person as humorous. Responses to many other traits also were markedly affected by the presence of the words *warm* and *cold* in the brief stimulus lists.

By contrast, when the words *polite* and *blunt* were substituted for *warm* and *cold*, the resulting impressions were not much different from each other. Because of their lack of effect, the terms *polite* and *blunt* were not considered central traits by Asch. The results of Asch's study and those of several other researchers seemed to support for a time the aspects of Gestalt theory that Asch advocated.

However, further studies by Wishner (1960), by Warr and Knapper (1968, Experiments 10–13), and by Rosenberg, Nelson, and Vivekananthan (1968) provided a more refined analysis that cast a somewhat different theoretical light on the topic of central traits. Wishner began by having more than 200 undergraduates rate their course instructors on 53 pairs of traits that were used by Asch. From these ratings, Wishner then computed the correlation coefficients between each trait and every other trait; that is, he found out to what degree ratings of generosity, for example, went hand in hand with ratings of punctuality, bluntness, and so on.

Wishner's results showed that the centrality of a trait depends not only on the stimulus information but also, and perhaps more importantly, on the information provided in the response list. For example, he found that on Asch's original list, warm– cold did not correlate strongly with the other traits on the stimulus list but did relate highly to traits on the response list. Furthermore, the other stimulus traits showed no strong relationship to the response traits. In other words, in the particular case that Asch chose, warm–cold was providing considerable new information in the stimulus description and was highly predictive of the particular response traits that were selected. How central the trait is depends as much on the response choices you are given as it does on the stimulus information you are given.

As a final demonstration of the power of

his analysis, **Wishner** showed that he could create a situation that would produce exactly the sort of personality impression he predicted. On the basis of his trait-correlation matrix, Wishner selected a new stimulus list and a new response checklist so that the two lists were relatively uncorrelated. Then he chose *humane–ruthless* as a central trait that was not correlated with the other traits on the stimulus list. Finally, Wishner correctly predicted that this central trait would have great weight in leading a subject to endorse a response with which the central trait was highly correlated and little weight in leading the subject to endorse a response with which the central trait was not correlated.

These studies have made an important theoretical contribution to our understanding of impression formation. Asch considered the stimulus traits as a Gestalt, which led him to conclude that whether a trait was central or peripheral would depend on its relationship to its context—that is, to the other stimulus traits. However, **Wishner's** analysis has shown that stimulus traits are less important in determining centrality than the central trait's relationship with the response traits. In this situation, then, stimulus-response theory seems more successful than a Gestalt analysis.

More recently, however, the line between these two theoretical stances has become more clouded. Borrowing from the work of cognitive psychologists with their models of information processing, social psychologists have begun to explore the ways in which people code information about other people. Cantor and Mischel (1977, 1979) have suggested that we all have basic categories, or prototypes, that we use to organize information. A **prototype** is an abstract representation of the attributes associated with personality types that is stored in the memory and used to organize information about an individual. Cantor and Mischel have shown that various kinds of trait information are organized around these basic prototypes to form a coherent impression of another person. For example, you may have a prototype of *extroverted* and organize a considerable amount of informa-

tion around this characteristic. Later information that you acquire about an extroverted person will either be fitted into this prototype or ignored if it does not fit your particular prototype.

This conception of prototypes is much more dynamic than any of the earlier formulations. Whereas certain traits still may be considered central, they are central always in terms of the active perceiver and not apart from that person. Thus this approach combines the individual emphasis of implicit personality theory with the earlier literature on static trait descriptions. From this perspective, both Gestalt and stimulus-response theories have some value for understanding how we form our impressions of others.

C. *Adding versus Averaging in Impression Formation*

Often, when we ask what someone is like, we are given a list of personality traits that presumably describe the person. For example, you might be told by a friend that your blind date for Friday night is "open-minded, clever, and modest, but kind of quiet." How do you integrate these pieces of information? Social psychologists have developed two basic models to explain how this kind of information is combined: the *additive model* and the *averaging model* (Brewer, 1968; Hendrick, 1968; Rosnow & Arms, 1968). To illustrate how these models work, let us consider your hypothetical blind date. Would your impression of the person differ if you had been told only that the date was open-minded and clever?

Both the additive and the averaging models begin by assuming that traits can be scaled in their likability, with some traits conveying very favorable information about an individual while others indicate negative information. (An example of the rank ordering of some common traits, derived from a longer list developed by **Anderson**, 1968b, is shown in Table 3-3.)

The *averaging model* claims that we use the mean value of the traits provided to form our impression of a person (Anderson, 1965, 1974; Anderson & Alexander, 1971). In

T A B L E 3 - 3 / *The Likableness of Personality-Trait Words*

What is the "best" thing you can say about someone's personality? What is the "worst"? Norman H. Anderson and his associates have obtained likableness ratings for 555 different words that are used as personality-trait descriptions; that is, subjects rated each word on a seven-point scale ranging from "least favorable or desirable" to "most favorable or desirable." The average ratings given each word by the 100 college students form the value for that word. In the list below, only the relative rankings are given; in using these words in research, numerical values are assigned to each trait. Such a listing is tremendously useful in research on impression formation, for it gives us an empirical indication of the value of different traits. Of course, these likableness ratings are colored by the particular group of raters; some other group might rate "polite" as more or less favorable than this group (which made it 53rd in a list of 555 terms). Also, the likableness of traits can change over time; "logical" may not be as highly valued as it once was (in this group it is 94th).

Such a listing is interesting in what it reveals about our preferences. "Sincere" is rated most favorably of all 555 terms, while "liar" and "phony" are the very least desirable. These say something about our values. Interestingly, the very middle term in the list (278th in ranking) is "ordinary." The entire list cannot be reprinted here, but some extremes and highlights are included.

Rank	Term	Rank	Term	Rank	Term
1.	sincere	80.	ethical	531.	loud-mouthed
2.	honest	100.	tolerant	540.	greedy
3.	understanding	150.	modest	546.	deceitful
4.	loyal	200.	soft-spoken	547.	dishonorable
5.	truthful	251.	quiet	548.	malicious
6.	trustworthy	278.	ordinary	549.	obnoxious
7.	intelligent	305.	critical	550.	untruthful
8.	dependable	355.	unhappy	551.	dishonest
9.	open-minded	405.	unintelligent	552.	cruel
10.	thoughtful	465.	disobedient	553.	mean
20.	kind-hearted	500.	prejudiced	554.	phony
30.	trustful	520.	ill-mannered	555.	liar
40.	clever				

Adapted from "Ratings of Likableness, Meaningfulness, and Likableness Variances for 555 Common Personality Traits Arranged in Order of Decreasing Likableness," by N. H. Anderson, *Journal of Personality and Social Psychology*, 1968, 9, 272–279. Copyright 1968 by the American Psychological Association. Used by permission.

the case of the blind date, the averaging model predicts that you would have a more favorable impression of your blind date if you were given only the description "open-minded and clever," because both of these traits are very desirable and thus have high values, or scores near the top of the ranked list in Table 3-3. The inclusion of the traits "modest" and "quiet" would reduce the average, as they are less attractive traits and have low values, or scores near the bottom of the ranked list.

The *additive* (or *summation*) model, in contrast, predicts that one's judgment is based on the sum of the trait values, rather than on the average (Anderson, 1962). According to this model of information integration, adding the values of the traits

"modest" and "quiet" to the values for "clever" and "open-minded" would increase the favorability of the overall evaluation. Table 3-4 shows more precisely how these two models work.

Which model is correct? There is some evidence in support of each. The additive model received support from a study by Fishbein and Hunter (1964), who showed that people who knew five strongly positive characteristics about a target person had somewhat more positive feelings about the person than did people who knew only two strongly positive characteristics of the person. However, the majority of the evidence appears to be more strongly supportive of the averaging model. (Anderson, 1965; Anderson, Lindner, & Lopes, 1973). To

TABLE 3-4 / *Adding versus Averaging in the Integration of Impressions*

When given a list of traits that describe another person, how do we integrate the information given by these traits? The adding model and the averaging model agree that we, in effect, assign a value to each trait. But the models differ in regard to how these values are integrated.

Consider the data below, bearing in mind that we have assigned relative likableness values to each trait.

Let us say that we are given the following traits for two men:

Gary		Steve	
Understanding	$(+3)$	Understanding	$(+3)$
Poised	$(+2)$	Sharp-witted	$(+2)$
Confident	$(+1)$	Congenial	$(+2)$
		Resourceful	$(+2)$
		Loud-mouthed	(-3)

The additive model would sum the values for each person, giving each a score of $+6$. Thus the additive model would predict that our overall impressions of both men would be equally favorable. On the other hand, the averaging model would get a mean value for the traits for each, giving Gary a $+2$ and Steve a $+1\frac{1}{5}$. The averaging model would predict that our overall evaluation of Gary would be better than that of Steve.

further complicate the issue, however, it appears that a simple average is not the best solution. Some traits are more important than others in influencing our impressions. To account for these variations, Anderson (1968a) has proposed a weighted-averaging model, which predicts impressions on the basis of an average of scores that have each been weighted according to their importance. This more complicated version of the averaging model appears to best account for our integration of information about people.

D. *Primacy and Recency Effects*

Most of us probably exert extra effort to look nice and be charming when meeting someone for the first time, such as on a job interview or on our first meeting with new in-laws. In doing this, we are assuming that another person's first impression of us may be an influential one. What evidence is there for the power of first impressions? Put another way, is the first information in another person's perception of us (**primacy effect**), or is the latest information, more influential (**recency effect**)?

To study the effects of first impressions, Luchins (1957a, 1957b) wrote two short paragraphs describing some of the day's activities of a boy named Jim. In one paragraph, Jim walked to school with friends, basked in the sun on the way, talked with acquaintances in a store, and greeted a girl whom he had recently met. In the other paragraph, Jim's activities were similar but his style was different: he walked home from school alone, stayed on the shady side of the street, waited quietly for service in a store, and did not greet the girl whom he had recently met. The first paragraph (E) made subjects think of Jim as an extrovert; the second paragraph (I) made him seem an introvert.

Luchins then combined the two paragraphs in either the E–I order or the I–E order. After reading the two paragraphs, subjects were asked to rate Jim on a personality-trait checklist. The results of this and several other studies showed evidence of a primacy effect. In other words, subjects rated Jim as more extroverted when the E paragraph came first and more introverted when the I paragraph was first, despite the fact that each narrative contained identical information. Thus, first impressions are apparently very important in determining our final impressions of other people.

Under certain conditions, however, these results can be altered and a recency effect occurs instead. For example, if some additional activity intervenes between the two parts of the description, then the most recent information will have a larger effect (Luchins, 1957b, 1958; Mayo & Crockett, 1964; Rosenkrantz & Crockett, 1965). Thus, if you met Joan at a party last month and formed a slightly negative impression but then encountered her again this week and reacted positively, your impression is more likely to be positive than negative. However, if one is specifically instructed to combine all known information about a person, the recency effect may be eliminated (Leach, 1974).

E. *Memory and Distortion*

Up to this point, we have assumed that our impressions of people are the result of rationally integrating our information about them. Some traits may be more important than others and the order of information may affect the judgment, but we have nonetheless assumed that each new piece of information is taken at face value. Is this assumption true?

Twenty-five years ago, the study of social perception focused primarily on the issue of accuracy of impressions. Despite a great deal of research activity, the overall result was one of frustration. In part, this frustration resulted from methodological dead ends. Traits, after all, are not concrete entities that can be weighed and measured; rather, they are psychological constructs. Thus, to determine whether a judgment is accurate, we must first have a reliable way of assessing the presence or absence of a given trait in the person being judged. The obstacles to such assessment, however, have proved insurmountable so far.

Even when an observer is asked to make judgments about objective events, it is evident that accuracy is an elusive characteristic. Reported eyewitness accounts of sudden and unpredictable events provide ample evidence that a consensus of impressions is difficult to obtain. The variability of eyewitness accounts is illustrated in reports of the murder of U.S. Senator Robert F. Kennedy by Sirhan Sirhan, discussed in Box 3-2.

Such inconsistencies are not unusual. For example, Buckhout, Alper, Chern, Silverberg, and Slomovits (1974) staged a series of crimes to test witnesses' immediate recall and their ability to recognize the lawbreaker in a police lineup. Many witnesses were incorrect in describing what happened immediately afterward, and only 14% of the witnesses were able to pick the culprit out of the lineup.

In another study, Buckhout and his colleagues (Buckhout, Figueroa, & Hoff, 1974) staged an assault on a professor in a classroom in front of 141 students. Seven weeks later the students were asked to select the assailant from a set of six photographs. More than 60% of the witnesses—including the professor—picked an innocent man. Yet, despite numerous demonstrations of this kind of error (Loftus & Palmer, 1974; Loftus, 1974; Wall, 1971), eyewitness testimony continues to be a major factor in getting convictions of accused lawbreakers (Levine & Tapp, 1973).

Accuracy is indeed an elusive quality, but social psychologists' interest in the accuracy of social perception waned for other reasons as well. Social psychologists came to realize that the *processes* involved in how we perceive others are more important than the question of how well we do it. The impression that we form of another person is real to us, whether it is true in some more abstract sense or not. Acknowledging this psychological reality has opened the door to many interesting questions about the ways in which we process information about other people.

Many of these questions deal with the specific ways in which we distort information presented to us. For example, if you believe that your best friend is an honest person, you may be less likely to interpret a questionable deduction on her income tax return as dishonest, and thus you will be able to maintain your impression of her as an honest person. Also, recollection of past events can be distorted by new information

Box 3-2. The Variability of Eyewitness Accounts.

In June, 1968, U.S. Senator and presidential candidate Robert F. Kennedy was assassinated as he walked through a kitchen of the Ambassador Hotel in Los Angeles. Nearly 100 people were in the kitchen when the shots were fired, and many reported seeing Sirhan Sirhan spring forward, raise his gun, and fire. Yet the reports of the event differed widely.

Langman and Cockburn (1975), who spent three years investigating the assassination, report:

The eyewitnesses, many of them standing next to each other, saw—or remembered they saw—very different things. Against the recollections of the assistant maitre d'hotel, who says that he was holding Kennedy's hand and leading him along—toward Sirhan—one can place the recollections of at least four other people who testified that Kennedy was turning to his left at the time Sirhan fired in order to shake hands with one of the waiters. Frank J. Burns, a friend of Kennedy's, was standing off Kennedy's right shoulder when the shots were fired, and he testified at Sirhan's trial that Kennedy had turned "almost ninety degrees" at the time and therefore was not facing Sirhan's gun muzzle but indeed presenting his right and hinder side to it. It is difficult to find witnesses—apart from the assistant maitre d'hotel—who directly contradict his recollections and those of many others, such as Edward Minasian, Martin Petrusky, Jesus Perez, and Vincent Di Perro, all employed in the Ambassador's kitchen.

It is, however, impossible to find witnesses who directly corroborate the autopsy evidence that the gun was practically touching Kennedy's head. Their estimates vary widely. Pete Hamill, the columnist, put Sirhan seven feet from Kennedy. Juan Romero, a busboy who had just shaken hands with Kennedy, estimated "approximately one yard." Valerie Schulte, a college student, said at the trial that "Sirhan's arm and gun" were "approximately five yards from me, approximately three yards, something like that, from the Senator." Edward Minasian, who was walking about a yard in front of Kennedy, thought the barrel of Sirhan's gun was "approximately three feet" from Kennedy. The closest to Kennedy that one can place the gun muzzle, going on these recollections, is about two feet—a distance calculated from one recollection that Sirhan was "three or four" feet away from Kennedy [1975, pp. 18–20].

From "Sirhan's Gun," by B. Langman and A. Cockburn. Copyright 1974 by *Harper's Magazine*. Reprinted from the January 1975 issue by special permission.

about a person. To demonstrate this particular form of distortion, Snyder and Uranowitz (1978) asked people to read an extensive narrative about the life of Betty K., covering her childhood, education, and choice of profession. After reading this narrative, subjects (a) were told that Betty was a lesbian, (b) were told that Betty was a heterosexual, or (c) received no further information about Betty. One week later, when investigators asked the subjects to recall information about Betty's early life, they found that the people in groups (a) and (b) above had distorted their recall of the events in the narrative to match the later information about Betty's sexual preference. Those people who had been told that Betty was a lesbian "remembered" more incidents that suggested homosexuality than did either the group that was given a heterosexual label or the group that was given no specific sexual label for Betty.

These and other forms of distortion are pervasive in impression formation and underline how often we, like the theorists discussed in Chapter 1, may see not what lies in front of our eyes but what lies behind them.

III. The Attribution of Cause

In most cases we are not content simply to form static impressions of other people's personalities. Rather, we seek more actively to understand *why* people behave as they do

Figure 3-3. Attributions of causality. (© 1978 by King Features Syndicate, Inc. Reprinted by permission.)

—that is, to explain the causes for the events that we observe. Why did Susan run away from Joe at the restaurant? Why did Howard suddenly start a fight with Tom? Why did Alice get passed over for promotion? The answers to questions such as these fall in the domain of attribution theory, a rapidly developing area of research within social psychology (Harvey, Ickes, & Kidd, 1976, 1978, 1980; Manis, 1977; Shaver, 1973).

Fritz Heider, whose work (1944, 1958) serves as the mainspring for much of the current work on attribution theory, suggested that we all act as "naive psychologists," attempting to discover cause-and-effect relationships in the events that occur around us. These attempts to make sense of our world are the central focus of attribution theory.

More specifically, we can state three basic assumptions that underlie most of the current work in this area (Jones, Kanouse, Kelley, Nisbett, Valins, & Weiner, 1972). First, in accordance with Heider, it is assumed that people attempt to assign causes for events. As was assumed also by George Kelly, it is not necessary that these explanations be accurate. We may be wrong in our interpretation of an event, but the explanation can still satisfy our need to understand. Second, the assignment of causes for events is systematic. In other words, social psychologists believe that there are definite patterns in the explanations we use. The attribution of cause is not random, then, and is influenced by some very specific fac-

tors. Finally, and perhaps most importantly, the explanations we derive have consequences for our feelings and behaviors. Depending on how we interpret an event, we may like or dislike, admire or detest, approach or avoid the persons involved.

Any event can have a variety of possible causes (see Figure 3-3 for an example of this multiplicity). To create some order in this abundance, Heider suggested that causes can be classified into two basic types: *dispositional* (or personal) and *situational* (or environmental). In the case of Figure 3-3, for example, Lois has come up with a variety of situational causes for her first grey hair. In each case, the claimed cause is external to her, relying on some person or event in the environment. Alternatively, it would be possible for Lois to assign a dispositional cause to the event (for example, the fact that she is growing older).

This distinction between dispositional and situational causes, first proposed by Heider, is basic to much of the work in attribution theory. Later theorists, however, have carried this basic idea further, exploring the more complicated ways in which our attributions of causality are formed. Let us now look closely at some of the more recent developments: principles of covariation and causal schemata, the process of correspondent inference, and the attribution of causes for success and failure. Each of these developments can be identified closely with a particular social psychologist, although many investigators have contributed research to each model.

A. *Covariation and Causal Schemata: The Work of Harold Kelley*

Harold Kelley assumes that we try to explain events in much the same way as a scientist would: armed with a series of observations of people's behavior, we try to figure out what possible cause is responsible for a particular action. According to the principle of *covariation*, "an effect is attributed to the one of its possible causes with which, over time, it varies" (Kelley, 1967, p. 108). In other words, Kelley believes that we look for a systematic pattern of relationships and infer cause and effect from those patterns. This model obviously assumes that we have more than one opportunity to observe a particular person, and it assumes that we have observed other people in similar situations as well.

Building on Heider's general distinction between dispositional and situational causes, Kelley has pointed to three general types of explanation that may be used when trying to interpret someone's behavior: an attribution to the *actor*, or the person who is engaging in the behavior in question; an attribution to the *entity*, or the target person with whom the actor is behaving; and an attribution to the *circumstances*, or the particular setting in which the behavior occurs (Kelley, 1967). Thus, when Susan runs away from Joe at the restaurant, we might attribute the event to something about Susan ("she is a basically hysterical person"), to something about Joe ("he just told Susan that he was going to marry someone else"), or to the particular circumstances ("the restaurant's vichyssoise had mold in it, and it made Susan sick").

Each of these explanations is reasonable; the trick is to decide on one as *the* explanation. Kelley suggests that, to do this, we use three basic kinds of information: consensus, consistency, and distinctiveness. *Consensus* information refers to the knowledge we have about the behavior of other actors in the same situation. For example, if everyone in the restaurant jumped up and ran out, we would say the behavior had high consensus. In contrast, if Susan ran out alone, her behavior would have low consen-

sus. The second source of information, *consistency*, refers to the knowledge we have about the actor's behavior on other occasions. Does Susan habitually run out of restaurants and out of movies and concerts as well, or is this the only time that she has created such a scene? Finally, one can use distinctiveness as a source of information. *Distinctiveness* is concerned with the variation in behavior among different entities, or targets. Does Susan run away only from Joe, or has she also run away from Rita, Peter, and Lila on other occasions?

Kelley suggests that, if we have information about each of these three factors, our causal explanations will be quite predictable. These predictable explanations, which have been confirmed by subsequent research (McArthur, 1972; Major, 1978; Orvis, Cunningham, & Kelley, 1975), are outlined in Table 3-5. Depending on the particular combination of information we have about the people involved, we will explain the event by attributing it to the actor, to the entity, or to the circumstances. When the pattern of information is less clear than that outlined in Table 3-5, we may use some combination of these three factors to explain the event (Major, 1978; McArthur, 1972).

Although the covariation model has a kind of precise elegance, it is clearly an idealized model. Often we do not have available the kinds of information the model requires: we may not have observed a person on previous occasions or we may not know how other people have behaved in the same situation. What do we do in such cases if we want to explain behavior? Kelley (1972) suggests that we rely on causal schemata. According to Kelley, a **causal schema** is "a conception of the manner in which two or more causal factors interact in relation to a particular kind of effect" (1972, p. 152). From our observations of people, we develop certain beliefs about causes and effects. These beliefs, or schemata, are then used to explain a particular person's behavior. In other words, Kelley is suggesting that we rely on some general beliefs, rather than needing all possible information about one person in one situation, when we attempt to explain a particular behavior.

TABLE 3-5 / *Kelley's Model of Attribution: Why Did Professor Martinez Criticize Paul?*

Attributions are made to the actor when:
  Consensus is low
  Consistency is high
  Distinctiveness is low
Example: No other professors criticize Paul (low consensus); Professor Martinez criticized Paul last year, last month, and twice last week (high consistency); and Professor Martinez criticized every other student in the class as well (low distinctiveness). Conclusion: The behavior is attributed to Professor Martinez—for example, "Professor Martinez is a mean professor."

Attributions are made to the entity when:
  Consensus is high
  Consistency is high
  Distinctiveness is high
Example: Every other professor criticizes Paul (high consensus); Professor Martinez criticized Paul last year, last month, and twice last week (high consistency); and Professor Martinez was friendly to all the other members of the class (high distinctiveness). Conclusion: The behavior is attributed to Paul—for example, "Paul is stupid and lazy."

Attributions are made to the circumstances when:
  Consistency is low
Example: Professor Martinez has never criticized Paul before (low consistency). Conclusion: The behavior is attributed to a particular set of circumstances and not to either Paul or Professor Martinez—for example, "Paul said something today that Professor Martinez misinterpreted."

There are, of course, many possible kinds of causal schemata, but let us consider just two of the more general ones. For some events, we may use a *multiple sufficient-cause model*. In this case, we decide that any number of factors may be responsible for a particular event. For example, if we see a father give his son an affectionate hug, we could decide either that the father was generally a warm person or that the son had just done something special. Either of these explanations is possible; the one we select will depend on the information we have available. If we knew that the son had done nothing special, we would decide that the father was an affectionate person; if we knew that the father was generally inhibited about showing affection, we would conclude that the son had done something unusual to deserve the hug. The point here is that either attribution would be sufficient to explain the event.

In other cases, we use a *multiple necessary-cause model*. In this model at least two causes are necessary to explain the event. Often we use the multiple necessary-cause model to explain fairly extreme events. For example, Howard suddenly starts fighting with Tom. Did Tom do something to provoke Howard, or is Howard the kind of person who is likely to start a fight? In such a case, most people would conclude that both statements were true: Tom provoked Howard and Howard is the kind of guy who starts fights. It takes two people to start an argument, so the saying goes; or, in other terms, it takes two causes to explain an effect.

In summary, causal schemata are a kind of shorthand. If we have unlimited information, the covariation model may represent our inference processes accurately. But in many situations we try to explain events without having all of the information, and in such cases we will rely on causal schemata to make sense of the behavior we observe.

B. *Correspondent Inference: The Work of Edward Jones*

In our attempts to explain the events that occur around us, we do, as suggested by the covariation and causal schemata models, make a general distinction between dispositional and situational causes. Beyond this general process, however, we also make some very specific attributions about the personal characteristics of the actor. Edward Jones and his colleagues (Jones & Davis, 1965; Jones & McGillis, 1976) have focused primarily on the ways in which we make these dispositional attributions; that is, on the way we observe an event and infer the intentions and characteristics of the actor.

If you are watching someone act in a certain situation, you're probably aware not only of the behavior itself but also of some of the consequences of that behavior. For example, if you see John give Maria a bouquet of flowers at the office, you may also observe that Maria is very pleased by the gift. Perhaps, you may infer, John's intention was simply to make Maria happy. However, if you happen to know that Maria is the vice-president's personal secretary and that John is trying to get a promotion, you may begin to suspect that the intended consequences of John's actions were not simply to please Maria. This illustrates one of the factors that Jones and his colleagues believe is most important in our inference process: the consequences of an action. Jones suggests that, in observing a person's behavior, we consider not only the effects of that behavior itself but also the possible effects of alternative behaviors that the person might have engaged in. For example, if you knew that John had two tickets for a hit play but did not ask Maria to go with him, you might suspect that making Maria happy was less important to John than being seen as a friendly person around the office. In this analysis, the impression John makes in the office would be a *noncommon effect*— that is, a consequence that could be achieved only by giving the flowers to Maria at work—whereas the effect of making Maria happy could have been achieved in at least two ways. Jones and his colleagues believe that the fewer the number of noncommon effects, the more likely the consequences are to be influential in our attribution of characteristics to the actor. Research has supported this prediction (Newtson, 1974).

Jones also suggests that our tendency to infer dispositional causes for another person's behavior is influenced by what we initially expect the actor to do (Jones & McGillis, 1976). If the actor does something quite divergent from what we expect, we are much more likely to wonder why the event happened and to seek an explanation in the personality of the actor. Two kinds of expectancies have been defined. The first, *category-based expectancies*, refers to assumptions we make based on the individual's membership in a particular group or category. Stereotypes, which we discussed earlier, represent one form of such category-based expectancies. For example, if we assume that most men are not gentle, then we would probably take particular note of a man who was playing gently with children and tend to attribute his behavior to something special about his personality. A second form of expectancies is *target based*. These expectancies are based on information we have about the particular individual in other situations. For example, having seen Lionel behave gently with many children on many occasions, we would probably expect Lionel to be gentle, no matter what our general expectations of men were.

You may notice that these two kinds of expectancies are very similar to the concepts of consensus and consistency that were discussed earlier. Both category-based expectancies and consensus refer to information that we have about a group of people, which we may use in inferring the causes for a particular individual's behavior. Similarly, target-based expectancies and consistency both rely on our information about the particular actor.

Although the attribution models of Kelley and Jones are similar in some respects, Jones pays much more attention to the specific dispositional attributions that are made. To use his terms, the concern is with the **correspondence** between a behavior and a dispositional attribution. If John performs a friendly act, do we infer that John is a friendly person? As we have seen, in making this inference we look to the consequences of the action; that is, to the number of noncommon effects and to the expectedness of the effects. When both of these factors are low, we are likely to infer that the person intended the behavior, and in turn we will infer that the intention was a result of a particular personality disposition—in this case, friendliness. Under other conditions, such as when the behavior is expected and the noncommon effects are numerous, there may be low correspondence; we will not infer a particular personality disposition in order to explain the behavior. Thus the Jones model takes us one step further in explaining behavior, from pointing generally to something about the person to labeling the specific traits that are believed to be responsible.

C. *Causes for Success and Failure: The Work of Bernard Weiner*

Bernard Weiner has developed a model of attribution that refers to a much more specific area of behavior than do the models of Kelley and Jones. Weiner's model deals with the explanations we arrive at for the success and failure of people on particular tasks (Frieze, 1976; Weiner, 1974; Weiner, Frieze, Kukla, Reed, Rest, & Rosenbaum, 1972). Why did Linda get promoted so quickly? Why did David flunk the calculus exam? These are the kinds of questions that Weiner's model attempts to answer.

As was true of the Kelley and Jones models, Weiner's basic model rests on the foundations established by Fritz Heider. Like Kelley, Weiner believes that one of the dimensions of our judgments is a comparison between dispositional and situational causes, which he refers to as the *internal–external* dimension. In addition, he posits a second dimension that is called *temporary–stable.* Weiner suggests that these two dimensions are independent of each other, and thus we can describe causal explanations by means of a two-by-two table (see Figure 3-4).[1]

Internal–external dimension	Temporary–Stable Dimension: Temporary	Temporary–Stable Dimension: Stable
Internal	Effort, mood, fatigue	Ability, intelligence, physical characteristics
External	Luck, chance, opportunity	Task difficulty, environmental barriers

Figure 3-4. Weiner's model of causal attribution. (Adapted from B. Weiner, I. Frieze, A. Kukla, L. Reed, S. Rest, and R. M. Rosenbaum, "Perceiving the Causes of Success and Failure." In *Attribution: Perceiving the Causes of Behavior,* by E. E. Jones, D. E. Karouse, H. H. Kelley, R. E. Nisbett, S. Valins, and B. Weiner. Copyright 1971 by General Learning Corporation. Used with permission of Silver Burdett Company.)

In each of the categories, there is a variety of possible causes that we can use to explain someone's performance (or to explain our own performance). The two dimensions are important to keep in mind, however, because they have different consequences. The temporary–stable dimension is assumed to be most important to us in forming expectancies, or predictions of how someone will do in the future (Valle & Frieze, 1976). For example, if we believe that Linda's excellent job performance was due to her ability or to the fact that the assignment was an easy one, we would expect her to do well again if she were given the same assignment. If we decide that the reason for her success was a temporary situation, such as a fleeting good mood or pure chance, we would be unlikely to be confident of her future success. In trying to explain failure, the same principles hold true. Failure that is attributed to stable factors is likely to yield predictions of future failure, whereas failure that is attributed to more temporary causes allows the possibility of future improvement. (Lucy's explanation of outcome, described in Figure 3-5, illustrates the latter type of explanation.)

The second dimension of causal attribution in Weiner's model—internal versus external explanation—is believed to relate primarily to the rewards or punishments

[1] More recently, Weiner has suggested that there is a third important dimension—intentionality—that cross-cuts the other two dimensions. However, because less work has dealt with this dimension, we shall limit our discussion to the locus of control and stability factors.

Figure 3-5. Causal attributions for failure. (© 1978 by United Feature Syndicate, Inc. Reprinted with permission.)

that follow a performance. We are more likely to reward people if we believe that their success was of their own making—due, for example, to their ability or their hard work—than if we think that chance or some other external factor was responsible. At the same time, punishment is also more likely when failure is attributed internally, rather than externally. If David failed his exam because he didn't try hard enough, we are likely to be much more critical of him than we would be if we thought his failure was the consequence of an unreasonably hard test.

The important point here is that attributions are not "the end of the line"; instead, the explanations that we form may influence other kinds of behavior. Heilman and Guzzo (1978) have provided a vivid demonstration of some of these consequences. In a simulated organizational setting, business students were asked to assume the role of an employer and to make raise and promotion decisions for a set of hypothetical employees. The information provided about the employees stressed one of four causes for their recent successful job performance: high ability, considerable effort, a relatively easy assignment, or pure chance. The behavior of the role-playing supervisors strongly supported the validity of Weiner's two dimensions. Supervisors recommended raises only to those employees whose performance had been explained by either ability or effort; in other words, rewards were given for internally caused success but were not given when external factors were be-

lieved to be responsible. Promotion was reserved for those employees who were said to be high in ability. Presumably, subjects believed that future performance could be ensured only if high ability (an internal *and* stable characteristic) was present but not necessarily if exceptional effort (a more temporary characteristic) had been shown.

Weiner's model of attribution is more limited than the others we have considered, focusing strictly on explanations for successful and unsuccessful performances in an achievement context. Nevertheless, it is an important approach because, more so than the others, it points to some of the consequences that attribution patterns may have for other behaviors.

IV. Biases in the Attribution Process

In the models discussed so far, we have considered people as fairly rational creatures, observing behavior, weighing the evidence, and assigning plausible causes for events. However, the attribution process is not always that rational. Perhaps the most interesting work in attribution theory concerns the biases that systematically affect our judgment. Some of these biases have a motivational base; in other words, we may actively seek explanations that put our own behavior, or that of friends, in a favorable light. In other cases the biases have a cognitive basis, reflecting how we process information, even when trying to be fair.

A. *Overestimating Dispositional Causes*

One of the most basic tendencies of the observer is to overemphasize the actor as a cause of events (Ross, 1977). Like a personality theorist, we tend to see something in the actor as the cause of an event, neglecting situational factors as possible influences.

As an example of this bias, imagine yourself watching a quiz show in which a woman is asked to make up questions and a man is asked to answer them. The questioner, drawing on her own area of expertise, poses a difficult set of questions, and the respondent is only moderately successful in providing answers. When asked to judge the general intellectual ability of each contestant, whom would you rate more favorably? If you are like the subjects in an experiment conducted by Ross, Amabile, and Steinmetz (1977), you would probably rate the questioner as more intelligent than the respondent. Yet, in this judgment, you would be neglecting an important situational factor—specifically, the control and choice assigned to the questioner, which allowed her to select particular areas and avoid others. Had the roles in the situation been reversed so that the woman became the respondent and the man became the questioner, the man probably would have displayed similar finesse and your judgments of intelligence would have been reversed.

You may have experienced this same phenomenon in playing a game of trivia with a friend. In tapping your own area of expertise, you feel quite intelligent as your friend fails to answer several questions in a row. Yet, when your friend takes over the questioning, he or she appears to be the intelligent one. Ross and his colleagues point out how this particular error can be pervasive in our judgments of the powerful and the powerless: we may overestimate the capability of those in power, forgetting to consider the role requirements that give the powerful an advantage over the powerless.

In general, the actor in a situation is often simply more prominent than the other aspects of the environment. We tend to focus directly on the actor in many situations, and then we place undue reliance on that which we have observed most closely. Investigators who have manipulated the prominence of a person—for example, by having one individual wear a bright red shirt while others in the setting wear more neutral clothing—have shown that the prominence of the red-shirted actor does lead to a greater number of dispositional attributions by observers (McArthur & Post, 1977; Pryor & Kriss, 1977; Taylor & Fiske, 1975).

B. *Actors and Observers*

This general tendency to overestimate dispositional factors often stops short of our own behavior. Jones and Nisbett (1972) have suggested that, although we are likely to attribute the behavior of other people to their personality traits, we are prone to believe that our own behavior is situationally determined. Thus, if asked why your friend Ira likes Denise, you're likely to respond by listing Ira's personality characteristics. Yet, if asked why *you* like Denise, you will probably describe more of Denise's traits than your own (Nisbett, Caputo, Legant, & Maracek, 1973).

This particular attributional bias has been the focus of considerable research activity (Gurwitz & Panciera, 1975; Harvey, Harris, & Barnes, 1975; Miller, 1977; Miller & Norman, 1975; Taylor & Koivumaki, 1976; West, Gunn, & Chernicky, 1975), and it is clear that a number of factors can alter the pattern. For example, if you are asked to empathize with the person you're observing (Brehm & Aderman, 1977), you will be less likely to use dispositional explanations and more likely to find situational ones. Also, switching from the role of actor to the role of observer of oneself leads to a decrease in situational attributions (Storms, 1973).

More generally, Monson and Snyder (1977) have suggested that differences in the information available to the participants are important to the prediction of differences in the attributions made by the actor and the observer. Often, the observer has little information about the historical determinants—what has happened before—and thus will focus totally on the here and now.

In watching an actor give in to a social-influence attempt, for example, the observer may conclude that the person is weak willed and easily persuaded. In contrast, the actor has a great deal of information about his own past behavior. Knowing that past social-influence attempts generally have been unsuccessful, the actor may attribute his present behavior to the persuasiveness of the speaker. Such differences between actors and observers are often particularly apparent in laboratory experiments, where situational forces generally are quite strong.

In summary, actors may give more causes for a behavior than observers do, and, because their base of information is broader, they may be more nearly correct. At other times, actors may give more dispositional attributions for a behavior than an observer does, again because they have more information on which to base their explanation. Obviously, these patterns of attribution are complex. The main point to remember, however, is that our ways of making causal attributions are not always the same: different perspectives and different kinds of information will bias our explanations in one direction or another.

C. *Underusing Consensus Information*

Many attribution models assume that we explain an individual's behavior by using information about what other people have done. Yet, this consensus information often seems to be far less important than information about the individual (Major, 1978; McArthur, 1972). At times we may completely ignore consensus information. For example, Nisbett and Borgida (1975) gave subjects information about how people in general had behaved in previous studies of altruism and obedience. The information that virtually no one had been willing in the past to help in a particular experiment had no effect on the subjects' predictions of a target person's behavior when asked to participate in the same experiment. The subjects confidently predicted that the target person would help in the experiment. In other words, consensus information was ignored, which is a behavior pattern consis-

tent with the general disregard of base-rate information described by Kahneman and Tversky (1973). As noted earlier, we like to focus on the salient individual and may neglect other relevant information in making our judgments.

On some occasions, however, consensus information may be important, and a number of investigators are trying to identify those occasions (Wells & Harvey, 1977; Kassin, 1979; Hansen & Stonner, 1978; Ruble & Feldman, 1976; Zuckerman, 1978a, 1978b). Yet, in general it appears that we often look first to the actor in making our attributions and disregard the more abstract information about other people in the same situation on other occasions.

D. *Relationship to the Actor*

Another source of attributional bias occurs when we are asked to make judgments about people who have some relationship to us. Jones and Davis (1965) have pointed to two factors that increase our tendencies to make dispositional attributions: hedonic relevance and personalism. **Hedonic relevance** refers to the extent to which a person's actions are rewarding or costly to the observer. To the extent that Anna's behavior has a direct effect on you, you are more likely to attribute causality to Anna than you would be if her actions did not affect you. **Personalism** is a closely related concept that refers to the perceived intentionality of a person's actions, or the degree to which a perceiver believes that another's behavior is directed at him or her. If you believe that Anna intended to affect you by her behavior, your attributions about Anna will be made more strongly (Potter, 1973). Not only the kind of attributions made then, but the act of making attributions at all is affected by our perceived relationship with the actor (Leone, Graziano, & Case, 1978).

Even when we are not directly involved in a situation, our feelings toward the actor can affect our causal explanations. For example, if Pete is a friend of yours and does something unpleasant, you are far more likely to look for situational causes for his behavior than you would be if Pete were your enemy. Similarly, positive behaviors by a friend are more likely to be attributed to dispositional causes than are positive behaviors by someone you don't like (Regan, Strauss, & Fazio, 1974). In part, such attributions may have a motivational basis. We don't like to believe that our friends do bad things, and we do like to believe that they do good things. Making the appropriate attributions thus protects our beliefs. But such attributions may be rational as well. In knowing a friend for many years, you learn a great deal about your friend's good qualities and very little about his or her bad qualities. That's why the person is a good friend. Thus, historical information can make a dispositional attribution quite a rational one, rather than merely an enhancement of your established beliefs.

V. The Consequences of Attributions

The process of making causal attributions is no idle exercise. Although critics may claim that attribution theory leaves the person "lost in thought," many of the important decisions we make and actions we take are contingent on the causal explanations we form. The legal system, for example, relies on judicial decisions about why events happened. Decisions concerning the intentionality of an action (for example, first-degree murder versus involuntary manslaughter) affect the punishment that is handed out to the defendant. The Patricia Hearst trial (see Figure 3-6) was a vivid illustration of this process of attribution. The jury was asked to make causal attributions for the behavior of the defendant: on the basis of the reported events, did Patricia Hearst willingly commit the crimes of which she was accused, or was there an external explanation, such as force by her captors, that could satisfactorily explain her behavior? In this case, the judge and jury essentially made a dispositional attribution, explaining Ms. Hearst's behavior by factors related more to Hearst than to her captors. Consequently, Patricia Hearst was sentenced to a 7-year jail term.

Figure 3-6. Should President Carter have pardoned Patricia Hearst? Decisions such as these, like those of the original judge and jury, are influenced by attributions of responsibility. (© United Press International.)

Decisions in rape cases are a vivid example of the way in which causal attributions can affect subsequent behavior. To the extent that a judge or jury believes that the woman was responsible for the rape (a pervasive attitude documented by Brownmiller, 1975), the defendant is likely to receive very lenient treatment, in many cases being excused with no penalty whatsoever. In this regard, it is striking to note that Feild (1978) found that police officers and rapists were highly similar in their beliefs about the causes of rape and both groups' beliefs differed significantly from those of rape counselors. These patterns suggest important differences in the way that rape victims may be treated by courts, police, and rape counselors. Social psychologists have been very active in recent years in studying the process of judicial decision making. Much of this research has focused on the process of causal attribution and on the consequences that such attributions may have on judgments of guilt and innocence.

In other arenas as well, causal attribution has important effects. For example, the study by Heilman and Guzzo (1978) that was mentioned in Section III. C. of this chapter showed that explanations for events can affect employers' decisions on raises and promotions. Although the external validity of this finding remains to be demonstrated in an actual job setting, the implications of the role-playing study are strong.

In later sections of this book, we will consider a variety of social behaviors—topics such as attraction and love, aggression and conflict, and cooperation and helping. We will see that often these behaviors depend on our assumptions about causality. Your willingness to reciprocate a favor, for example, can depend on the degree to which you believe that the other person was genuinely altruistic (a dispositional cause), rather than compelled to be helpful by some other pressure (a situational cause). Similarly, if another person's actions were frustrating to you, you might excuse the person's actions if you believed that there were extenuating circumstances. However, the same frustrating actions might lead you to what you would consider justifiable aggression if you believed that dispositional causes were involved (Burnstein & Worchel, 1962; Cohen, 1955; Carpenter & Darley, 1978; Pastore, 1952). Thus our assignment of causes, although not the only factor influencing our behavior, is nevertheless one very important determinant of social interaction.

VI. Summary

Everyone makes assumptions about the nature of people in general in order to predict and understand behavior. One way of conceptualizing these assumptions is to use philosophies of human nature, which are expectancies that people in general possess certain qualities and will behave in certain ways. Six dimensions of philosophies of human nature have been identified; four of these are substantive dimensions and the other two deal with beliefs about individual differences in human nature.

More individualized conceptions of human behavior are termed *implicit personality theories*. These theories, formulated by each of us, describe certain traits as occurring together and affect the way that we perceive people in our environment. George Kelly's personal-construct theory is one important conceptualization of this kind of personal theorizing.

Many specific factors affect the kinds of impressions we form. Stereotypes about the characteristics of groups of people can affect our judgment of an individual member of that group. Often such judgments are inaccurate and reflect illusory correlations between unrelated characteristics.

Some descriptive traits carry more information than others; these central traits are more important than others, however, only when they are highly correlated with the traits we wish to predict. Trait information can be organized around certain prototypes, which in turn affect our processing of future information. When combining a number of traits to make an overall judgment, we apparently compute a mental average of these traits, rather than simply summarizing the elements.

The impressions that we form of people are not necessarily accurate, although accuracy of impressions is difficult to assess. Distortions in our impressions and in our memory of the events upon which those impressions are based are prevalent, despite the fact that impressions are often of great practical importance, as in the case of eyewitness reports.

Attribution theory deals with the causes we assign to events. In general, actions may be given either a dispositional attribution (the person is seen as the cause) or a situational attribution (the environment is seen as a cause). Harold Kelley, Edward Jones, and Bernard Weiner each have developed models of the attribution process, deriving from the early work of Fritz Heider. Each of these models deals with the relationship between the available information and the inferences that we draw in trying to explain the cause of an event.

As in the case of the simpler impression-formation process, biases in causal attributions are frequent. For example, we tend to overestimate the influence of dispositional factors. Actors and observers often emphasize different causes for events, in part because of differences in the information available to them. Consensus information may be ignored in favor of the immediate behavior of the actor. Events that have personal relevance for the observer or involve friends of the observer often are judged differently from events that have no personal relevance or involve the observer's enemies.

The consequences of these cognitive processes are extensive, affecting areas ranging from judicial decision making to job evaluation. Many forms of social behavior are mediated, in part, by our beliefs about their causes.

Glossary Terms

attribution theory
causal schemata
central trait
correspondence
hedonic relevance
illusory correlation

implicit personality theories
personalism
philosophies of human nature

primacy effect
prototypes
recency effect
stereotype

The image of myself which I try to create in my own mind in order that I may love myself is very different from the image which I try to create in the minds of others in order that they may love me   W. H. AUDEN

GEORGE TOOKER. *MIRROR II*, 1963. ADDISON GALLERY OF AMERICAN ART, PHILLIPS ACADEMY, ANDOVER, MASSACHUSETTS.

This world is governed more by appearances than by realities, so that it is fully as necessary to seem to know something as to know it.   DANIEL WEBSTER

Impression Management: The Self in Social Interaction

This chapter was written by **Mark Snyder.**

The quest for knowledge of ourselves, the desire for a meaningful identity, and the search for answers to the questions "Who am I?" and "How can I be me?" are experiences familiar to all who share the cultural heritage of the Western world. Parents and teachers draw upon the wisdom of poets and philosophers as they exhort each of us to "Know thyself" and "Unto thine own self be true." Authors of self-help books offer techniques for discovering ourselves, for liking ourselves, for respecting ourselves, and for asserting ourselves.

The concept of **self** is one of the oldest and most enduring in psychological considerations of human nature. For centuries, students of human nature have struggled to define the nature of those attributes of behavior and experience that individuals regard as "me." In so doing, they have sought to discover the nature of the self and the influence of the self on social interaction and interpersonal relations. Their discoveries have challenged some of our most cherished assumptions about human nature. We typically assume that each individual has one and only one true self; not so: each individual has not one, but many selves. Moreover, much as we might like to believe that the self is an integral feature of personal identity, the self is to a great extent the product of the individual's social relationships with other people. Furthermore, conventional wisdom to the contrary, there frequently exist striking gaps and contradictions between the public appearances of the self that an individual presents to other people in social interaction and the private realities of that individual's actual beliefs and attitudes about his or her self. This chapter is concerned with the nature of the self in social interaction.

I. Who Am I?—The Nature of the Self

Contemporary treatments of the self echo the classical viewpoints, in particular those laid down by the influential and articulate writings of the philosopher and psychologist William James (1890). For James, the sense of self—or that which a person regards as "me"—was to be defined in the broadest possible terms:

In its widest possible sense, however, a man's Self is the sum total of all that he can call his, not only his body and psychic powers, but his clothes and his house, his wife and children, his ancestors and friends, his reputation and works, his land and horses, and yacht and bank account. All these things give him the same emotions. If they wax and prosper, he feels triumphant; if they dwindle and die away, he feels cast down—not necessarily in the same degree for each thing, but in much the same way for all [1890, Vol. 1, pp. 291–292].

James believed that the experience of selfhood is very much a social experience—that is, our personal identities are critically dependent on our relationships with other people. In fact, it was James who first sensitized us to the identity-threatening consequences that would befall us if all our relationships with people were eliminated:

If no one turned around when we entered, answered when we spoke, or minded what we did, but if every person we met "cut us dead," and acted as if we were non-existing things, a kind of rage and impotent despair would ere long well up in us, from which the cruelest bodily tortures would be a relief; for these would make us feel that, however bad might be our plight, we had not sunk to such a depth as to be unworthy of attention at all [1890, Vol. 1, pp. 293–294].

Although James's views are expressed in 19th century prose that may seem archaic to us today, his writings contain the seeds of virtually every feature of modern theory and research on the self.

A. *The Constituents of the Self*

James divided the elements of the "me" into three categories: the material me, the social me, and the spiritual me. Included in the material me are the body, clothing, family, house, and all other material possessions. The central component of the social me is the recognition received from friends and acquaintances—in particular, the favorable regard experienced in relationships with other people. Characteristic of the spiritual me are the inner experiences, abilities, sensibilities, values, and ideals, which are the most enduring and intimate parts of the sense of selfhood.

Of course, certain constituents of the "me" may be more meaningful to some people than to others. One person may focus on the material me; another person, on the social me. To chart the features of a person's identity, psychologists have developed the **"Who am I" technique** of asking people to write answers (usually 15 or 20) to the simple question Who am I? (For details of this technique, see Bugental & Zelen, 1950; Gordon, 1968; Kuhn & McPartland, 1954.) Answers to the question Who am I? frequently reveal a great deal about an individual's self-concept. For an example of a particularly revealing set of answers to the "Who am I" technique, see Figure 4-1. When the "Who am I" question is put to college students, the most common answer categories are gender, age, student status, interpersonal style (shy, friendly), personality characteristics (moody, optimistic), and body image (Gordon, 1968).

B. *The Organization of the Self*

One's awareness of and one's concern with the features of "me" may vary from time to time. In fact, there are times when individuals are particularly likely to focus their attention inward and contemplate aspects of their self-concept. In such states of **objective self-awareness,** individuals are particularly sensitive to shortcomings in themselves and to discrepancies between their "real" self and their "ideal" self (Duval & Wicklund, 1972; Wicklund, 1975).

In addition, one's sense of "Who am I?" may shift dramatically from situation to situation. Thus, for example, a Black woman may be particularly aware of her identity as a Black when she is with an all-White group; this same Black woman, however, may be more aware of her identity as a woman when she is with an all-male group. William McGuire has coined the term **spontaneous self-concept** to refer to the extent to which particular "selves" and "identities" are brought to mind by social surroundings (McGuire, McGuire, Child, &

Figure 4-1. President Lyndon B. Johnson had these answers to the question Who am I? "I am a free man, an American, a liberal, a conservative, a Texan, a taxpayer, a rancher, a business man, a consumer, a parent, a voter, and not as young as I used to be nor as old as I expect to be—and I am all those things in no fixed order" (quoted by Gordon, 1968, p. 123). (Wayne Ingram, *Portrait of President Lyndon B. Johnson*, 1968. The Lyndon Baines Johnson Library and Museum, Austin, Texas.)

Fujioka, 1978; McGuire, McGuire, & Winton, 1979; McGuire & Padawer-Singer, 1976). In their research, McGuire and his colleagues have found, time and again, that it is those features of identity that make people *distinct* from those around them that are most prominent in their spontaneous self-concepts. Thus, in one investigation, McGuire, McGuire, and Winton (1979) instructed fourth-grade children to "Tell us about yourself." As the results displayed in Figure 4-2 clearly indicate, children were much more likely to spontaneously mention their gender when they came from households in which their gender was in the

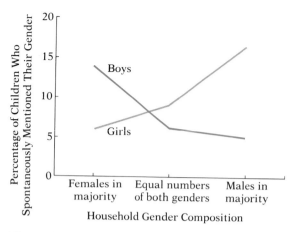

Figure 4-2. Prominence of gender and the spontaneous self-concept. (Adapted from "Effects of Household Sex Composition on the Salience of One's Gender in the Spontaneous Self-Concept," by W. J. McGuire, C. V. McGuire, and W. Winton, *Journal of Experimental Social Psychology,* 1979, *15,* 77–90. Used by permission of the author and Academic Press, Inc.)

minority. Thus, for example, being male was a particularly important feature of the spontaneous self-concepts of boys who came from families with females in the majority. These boys were more than three times as likely to mention their gender when defining their identities as were boys from homes with males in the majority.

Not only are some features of identity more prominent than others in an individual's self-concept, but also some features of identity are more clearly defined than others. For example, individuals with clearly defined conceptions of themselves as honest persons find it very easy to bring to mind the many and diverse honest deeds that they have performed, the many situations in which they have performed these honest deeds, and the many future opportunities that they anticipate having for acting upon their self-conception of honesty. When individuals have organized their knowledge of themselves in a particular domain of behavior and experience (in this case, honesty) in such clearly defined fashion, they are said to possess a **self-schema** in that domain (Markus, 1977). Presumably, individuals are particularly likely to organize their knowledge of their behavior and experience into

well-defined self-schemata in those domains of identity that are most relevant and important to them. Thus, individuals for whom independence and autonomy are central features of identity would develop well-defined self-schemata in those domains. By contrast, individuals for whom sensitivity and nurturance are central features of identity would acquire clearly defined self-schemata in those domains.

C. *Not One, but Many, Selves*

Central to James's ideas about the self was the proposition that each person has not one, but *many,* selves. Again, in his words:

A man has as many social selves as there are individuals who recognize him and carry an image of him in their mind. . . . But as the individuals who carry the images form naturally into classes, we may practically say that he has as many different social selves as there are distinct *groups* of persons about whose opinions he cares. He generally shows a different side of himself to each of these different groups. Many a youth who is demure enough before his parents and teachers swears and swaggers like a pirate among his "tough" young friends. We do not show ourselves to our children as to our club companions, to our masters and employers as to our intimate friends. From this there results what practically is a division of the man into several selves; and this may be a discordant splitting, as where one is afraid to let one set of his acquaintances know him as he is elsewhere; or it may be a perfectly harmonious division of labor, as where one tender to his children is stern to the soldiers or prisoners under his command [1890, Vol. 1, p. 294].

That each person may possess many selves challenges one of our basic assumptions about human nature: the assumption that each person has one and only one true self. We generally assume that people are fairly consistent and stable beings. We assume that the social individual is sociable in all—or at least most—social contexts, that a person who is generous in one situation is also generous in other situations, and so on. Yet, James's ideas about multiple selves suggest that some people may be strikingly inconsistent in the selves they present under different circumstances. In the fashion of the chameleon, they project whatever self suits the here and now. In different situations and with different people, they may act in very different ways.

II. Who Should I Be?—The Presentation of Self

William James's notions that individuals in social interactions present different selves to different people has been echoed by successive generations of theorists and researchers concerned with the self. In particular, theorists within the impression management tradition have proposed that the quest to be (or, at least, to appear to be) the right person in the right place at the right time is a basic fact of social life.

Impression management refers to all the strategies and techniques that individuals use to control the images and impressions of their "self" that they project to other people. Consider an everyday example of impression management in action. Imagine, if you will, that you are being interviewed for a job. Wouldn't you "put your best foot forward," "show your best profile," be careful to make the most favorable impression so that you'll get the job you want? You probably would choose your clothes carefully in order to project just the right job-winning image and try to determine the kind of candidate the interviewer prefers so that you could tailor your own image to meet those preferences. Even if you, personally, would not practice the art of impression management in this situation, no doubt you can readily appreciate that many other people would do so.

A. *The Necessity of Impression Management*

Many students of social behavior have suggested that impression management is necessary for effective functioning in interpersonal relations. Thus, theorists of the tradition known as *symbolic interactionism,* notably C. H. Cooley (1902) and G. H. Mead (1934), have stressed that participants in social interactions attempt to "take the role of the other" and see themselves as others see them. This process both allows them to know how they are coming across to others and

allows them to guide their social behavior so that it has the desired effect. Thus, by taking the role of the other, a politician can choose the right clothes and speech patterns to please rural constituents and then effectively change each of these to court the favor of party bosses. Similarly, by considering the perspective and background of each audience, a college professor can tailor her presentation of the latest developments in relativity theory so that it is meaningful to college sophomores on one occasion and to distinguished researchers at a scientific convention on another occasion. (See also **Figure 4-3** for a more fanciful example.)

Figure 4-3. One-upsmanship. The late **Stephen Potter**, author of *Gamesmanship, One-Upsmanship,* and other books, devoted his life to the development and analysis of successful impression management. Potter's books are full of tricks, rejoinders, and actions that will give one an advantage over others. The young man below would appear to be a disciple of Potter. (© Robert Burroughs/Jeroboam, Inc.)

Impression management is at the core of Erving Goffman's (1955, 1959, 1963, 1967) theory of the *presentation of self in everyday life*. Goffman has described social interaction as a theatrical performance in which each individual acts out a "line." A *line* is a set of carefully chosen verbal and nonverbal acts that express one's self. Of course, the line can shift from situation to situation as, for example, the roles of obedient employee, sensitive friend, and aggressive handball player change in degree of importance to the individual. People have many motives for trying to control the impressions that others receive of them and of the nature of their interaction. In particular, the desire for social approval and the motive to control the outcomes of social interaction will result in impression management. Each person in the interaction attempts to maintain an image appropriate to the current social situation and to secure an evaluation from the others that is both pleasant and self-assuring. A participant whose image successfully elicits social approval is said to be "in face"; one whose image fails is said to be "out of face." For Goffman, one of the fundamental rules of social interaction is mutual commitment. By this he means that each participant will work to keep all members of the interaction in face through impression management. To do so, each person has a repertoire of face-saving devices, an awareness of the interpretation that others place on his or her acts, a desire to sustain each member's face, and the willingness to use his or her repertoire of impression-management tactics.

Maintaining face is not the goal of social interaction. Rather, maintaining face is a necessary background for social interaction to continue. Incidents that threaten the face of a participant also threaten the survival of the relationship. Thus, when events challenge the face of a participant, corrective processes called face-work are initiated to avoid any embarrassment that might interfere with the conduct of the relationship. Thus, we conspicuously overlook or help others apologize for the social blunders and potentially embarrassing *faux pas* that they commit. (For examples of research on face-

saving behavior, see Brown, 1968; Brown, 1970; Brown & Garland, 1971; Modigliani, 1968.) In short, for Goffman, social interaction requires its participants to be able to regulate their self-presentation so that it will be perceived and evaluated appropriately by others.

In a related approach, C. N. Alexander also has suggested that impression management is a fundamental facet of social interaction (Alexander & Knight, 1971; Alexander & Lauderdale, 1977; Alexander & Sagatun, 1973). According to the **theory of situated identities,** there is for each social setting or interpersonal context a pattern of social behavior that conveys an identity particularly appropriate to that setting. This behavioral pattern is called a *situated identity.* Alexander claims that people strive to create the most favorable situated identities for themselves in their social encounters. Thus a college instructor might aim for a somewhat professorial and academic situated identity during lectures but shift to a more casual and informal situated identity at a social gathering of friends and acquaintances. Clearly, the concept of a situated identity is similar to that of a *role* (see Chapter 1). But a situated identity is tied much more to a specific situational context than a role is. Moreover, roles focus on behaviors that are expected or appropriate; situated identities deal more with the image one chooses to project in a particular social interaction

From the perspective of impression-management theorists, social interaction requires (a) an awareness of the interpretations that others place upon our acts, (b) a desire to maintain "face" or the appropriate situated identity, (c) a wide range of self-presentational skills, and (d) the willingness to use this repertoire of impression-management strategies. In short, social interaction requires the ability to manage or control our verbal and nonverbal self-presentation in order to foster desired images in the eyes of our beholders.

This ability, incidentally, is what produces successful stage actors (Metcalf, 1931). In William Shakespeare's *As You Like It,* the character Jacques expresses a view of human behavior that is strikingly similar to the theatrical image of human nature proposed by impression-management theorists:

All the world's a stage,
And all the men and women merely players;
They have their exits and their entrances;
And one man in his time plays many parts.[1]

Perhaps for this reason, the theoretical framework of impression management is sometimes referred to as the "dramaturgical" perspective (see Brisset & Edgley, 1975).

All theories of impression management (including the three viewpoints discussed in this section—symbolic interactionism, presentation of self, and situated identities) have something in common despite the apparent differences in language and emphasis that characterize the individual theories. Their common factor is this: other people are always forming impressions of us and using these impressions to guide their interactions with us (Chapter 3 explores this point in detail). Accordingly, it is to our benefit to understand other people's perceptions of us and to create images that we find acceptable. This makes us better able to predict, understand, and influence the flow of social interaction. From this perspective, any attempt to influence the image that others form of us is a direct consequence of the fact that others do form impressions of us and do act on them. Impression management is, quite simply, the inevitable consequence of social perception. What, then, determines the particular image or self-presentation that an individual will project to another person in a social interaction? Two of the most powerful influences on self-presentation are the *characteristics of the other person* and the *motivational context of the interaction*.

B. *Choosing an Image*

Would you act the same way with a boastful, conceited person as you would with a modest, self-effacing individual? An experi-

[1] From William Shakespeare's *As You Like It*, II, viii, 139.

ment by Gergen and Wishnov (1965) simulated precisely this situation, and the participants in that experiment presented themselves very differently in the two contexts. Those who had been paired with the boastful egotist afterward described their personalities much more positively than they had a month before the experiment. However, those who had been paired with the humble and modest partner played down their own virtues and emphasized their shortcomings. Clearly, the subjects in this experiment chose to project self-images similar to those of their partners. Perhaps, in a situation as novel and unfamiliar as a psychological experiment, these individuals were somewhat unsure of how to behave. Thus, they turned to their partners as guides in choosing a self-presentation appropriate to the situation.

Our beliefs about others influence also the way we express our attitudes about social issues. Imagine that you are a college student during the days of intense U.S. involvement in the Vietnam War. You have agreed to communicate your opinions on the war to an extremely pro-war audience and then to an extremely anti-war audience. You are a moderate on the Vietnam War issue. Might you present your position differently to the two audiences? The undergraduates studied by Newtson and Czerlinsky (1974) certainly did. These students expressed more hawkish views when communicating with a pro-war audience and more dovish attitudes when addressing an anti-war audience. In a similar experiment political "middle-of-the-roaders" became more liberal for an audience of liberals and more conservative for an audience of conservatives. Even though the students in both studies had been instructed to present their opinions as accurately as possible, they still presented themselves as more similar to the audience than they actually were. Why? Perhaps they were trying to win the social approval of the audience by exaggerating their similarities to the audience members. Opinion conformity certainly is one powerful tactic of ingratiation (see Section IV of this chapter) that can be used by those who want to win the positive regard of others. In fact, there is some evidence that the opinion shifts displayed by the participants in these and similar investigations (Cialdini, Levy, Herman, & Evenbeck, 1973; Hass & Mann, 1976; Manis, Cornell, & Moore, 1974; Tesser & Rosen, 1972) may represent attempts by communicators to ingratiate themselves with their audiences (Moore, 1975).

Will people always choose those self-presentations that maximize similarity with their interaction partners? What if you were interacting with an obnoxious and unlikable person who nevertheless persisted in expressing attitudes and opinions strikingly similar to yours? Might you not take care to express your attitudes in such a way as to maximize any differences between you and the obnoxious person? This was precisely the outcome of an experimental investigation by Cooper and Jones (1969). Participants altered their stated attitudes whenever an obnoxious interaction partner expressed viewpoints similar to theirs. Thus, the goals of self-presentation are not always to maximize similarity between self and other. When similarity is not particularly desirable, people may use impression management to establish social distance.

The nature of the interaction environment also helps determine the image that a person strives to create. Gergen and Taylor (1969) arranged for Navy cadets to work together on a problem-solving task. For half of the groups, social compatibility and solidarity were stressed. For the remaining groups, productivity and output were the primary goals. After the problem had been described to each person and the compatibility or productivity orientation had been explained, each person was asked to describe himself to his partner. These descriptions were used as the measure of self-presentation. Those cadets with the productivity orientation became considerably more positive in their self-descriptions; those anticipating a compatibility orientation were quite modest and even self-critical in their self-presentations. Apparently, the Navy cadets in this study believed that the best guarantee of productivity was to let their partners know about their competence and qualifications and that the best guarantee of compatibility was modesty.

C. *Maintaining an Image*

People not only seek by their self-presentation to create an image but also seek to maintain an existing one. Consider the case of an individual with a favorable image—one that he or she would wish to maintain—who did something that cast doubt on that image. Mr. Boss, for example, believes that he has a good record of supporting equal-opportunity hiring programs. He turns down a female applicant because there are no openings in his department. As she leaves Mr. Boss's office, the woman's expression clearly suggests that she feels that she has been a victim of sex discrimination. Mr. Boss feels that his nonsexist, equal-opportunity image is threatened. Will he bend over backward to fill the next vacancy in his department with a female worker? Several studies demonstrate that just such a "bending-over-backward" effect exists in impression management.

Dutton and Lake (1973) made the following request of White undergraduates at the University of British Columbia who valued equality and considered themselves relatively unprejudiced: Would you take a "lie detector" test that would be capable of registering signs of racial prejudice? After administering the "lie detector" test, Dutton and Lake led some students to believe that they had shown physiological signs of racial prejudice. No doubt this experience challenged both their private self-concepts and their public images as relatively unprejudiced persons. Other subjects in the study were told that their responses were typical of the unprejudiced person. Afterward, the experimenters arranged for each student to be approached either by a White panhandler or by a Black panhandler. Dutton and Lake wanted to find out whether those students whose self-concepts had been threatened would take advantage of the opportunity offered by the panhandlers to restore their feeling that they were not prejudiced. Indeed, they did! In fact, the results were an impressive example of *reverse discrimination* in action. The Black panhandler received considerably more money from students who feared that they might be prejudiced (average donation = 47¼¢) than from those who had not had their self-images threatened by the physiological feedback (average donation = 16¾¢). The White panhandler received approximately equal amounts of money from both groups of students (average donation = approximately 28¢).

Clearly, the students who had been threatened with the possibility of prejudice over-reacted and bent over backward to prove to themselves and to other people that they were not prejudiced about Blacks. Reverse discrimination thus may be seen as an attempt by those people who consider prejudice undesirable—but are uncertain about their own level of prejudice—to prove that they are free of prejudice. But, in their efforts not to discriminate against one group, they may discriminate against another group. Such attempts to appear unprejudiced, however, may produce only token acts that later serve as rationalizations for avoiding more significant commitments to the eradication of prejudice.

In a follow-up to the experiment described in Section II.C., Dutton and Lennox (1974) once again used the "lie detector" technique to convince students that they were prejudiced. Again, some individuals were approached by a White panhandler, others by a Black one. The next day a person apparently not connected with the original study asked each subject to donate time to an interracial-brotherhood effort. Those who previously had been panhandled by the Black were much more stingy with their time than either those who had been approached by the White panhandler or members of a comparison group who had not been panhandled.

D. *When Saying Is Believing*

The message from research on impression management is a clear one. Some people are quite flexible in their self-presentation;

with skill and grace, they can put on one face for one person and another face for another person. But what effects do these shifts in public appearance have on the more private realities of self-concept? In some circumstances, we are persuaded by our own appearances: we become the person we are trying to appear to be. This phenomenon is particularly likely to occur when the image we present wins the approval and favor of the people around us. In an experiment by Jones, Gergen, and Davis (1962), participants who had been instructed to win the approval of an interviewer presented very flattering images of themselves. Half of these participants (chosen at random) then received favorable reactions from their interviewers; the rest did not. All participants later estimated how accurately and honestly their self-descriptions had mirrored their true personalities. Those persons who had won the favor of their interviewers considered their self-presentations to have been the most honest of all. One interpretation of this finding is that those who won the favor of their interviewers were operating with rather pragmatic definitions of their self-concept: the self-description that produced the most positive results was considered an accurate reflection of the true inner self (Gergen, 1968).

The outcome of this experiment suggests that impression management can blur the distinction between public appearance and private reality; in other words, *we come to believe our own performances*. Furthermore, the reactions of other people to our performance can make it all the more likely that we will become what we claim to be. If other people accept our self-presentations at face value, they then may treat us as if we really were who we pretend to be. For example, if I act as if I like Jennifer, chances are good that Jennifer will like me in return. She probably will treat me in a variety of friendly ways. As a result of Jennifer's friendliness, I may come to like her, even though I did not like her in the beginning. Once again, appearances have created reality.

III. The Skilled Impression Manager

The message of theory and research on impression management is a clear one: individuals strive to influence the images that others form of them during social interaction. Researchers have meticulously and exhaustively cataloged the strategies and techniques used, and sometimes exploited, by those who practice impression management. To a greater or lesser extent, individuals know which behaviors on their part will create what impression in the mind of the beholder. At times, individuals are able convincingly and naturally to perform precisely those verbal and nonverbal acts that will create the desired image in the mind of the beholder.

There are, however, striking and important differences in the extent to which people can and do control their self-presentations: some people engage in impression management more often and with greater skill than do other people. The skilled impression manager has long been a mainstay of the world of fiction. The successful con artist, the artful seducer and charmer, the man or woman of many faces are forever popular. Masters of the arts of deception, hypocrisy, and pretense never fail to intrigue us. Molière's 17th-century stage comedy *Tartuffe*, for example, is virtually guaranteed to charm theatergoers. The title character is a pious-faced hypocrite who, behind a mask of religious propriety, proceeds to dupe the gullible Orgon of his property and steal his wife. Tartuffe, who in reality is a small-time criminal, puts on a show of deep religious piety. He hopes that others will accept this image and not stifle his attempts to live off their wealth. Tartuffe shifts among his various faces with the ease of a chameleon switching colors to match its surroundings. Moviegoers, too, have applauded the exploits of confidence artists in such screen classics as *The Great Imposter, The Sting*, and *Paper Moon*.

Skilled impression managers are found outside the world of fiction as well. Clearly, professional actors can manipulate the images they project far better than most of us can. Successful politicians, too, long have practiced the art of wearing the right face for the right constituency. Onetime mayor of New York, Fiorello La Guardia, was particularly skilled at adopting the expressive mannerisms characteristic of a variety of ethnic groups. In fact, he was so good at this that, in watching silent films of his campaign speeches, it's very easy to guess which group's vote he was soliciting. In recent years, presidential candidates have turned to advertising and media experts to help them cultivate presidential and statesmanlike images (McGinniss, 1970; Shrum, 1977; Witcover, 1970). With highly skilled performers, it is hard indeed to tell whether the self-presentation is genuine or one contrived to create a particular image (see Box 4-1).

A. *The Concept of Self-Monitoring*

Of course, actors and politicians are the exception, rather than the rule. Nonetheless, people do differ in the extent to which they can and do exercise control over their verbal and nonverbal self-presentation. These differences are captured by the psychological construct of **self-monitoring** (Snyder, 1979). High self-monitoring individuals are particularly sensitive to the expressions and the self-presentations of others in social situations, and they use these as cues in monitoring their own self-presentation for purposes of impression management. They regard themselves as rather flexible and adaptive individuals who shrewdly and pragmatically tailor their self-presentations to the circumstances that confront them. High self-monitoring individuals are identified by their high scores on the Self-Monitoring Scale (Snyder, 1974). For example, the high self-monitoring individual endorses such statements as:

1. When I am uncertain of how to act in a social situation, I look to the behavior of others for cues.
2. In different situations and with different people, I often act like very different persons.
3. I am not always the person I appear to be.
4. I may deceive people by being friendly when I really dislike them.

According to their peers, high self-monitoring individuals are good at learning

Box 4-1. Deception in Presidential Press Conferences.

An ancient Greek philosopher once said "Those who cannot lie cannot govern." Alker (1976) examined the presidential press conferences of Presidents Eisenhower, Johnson, Kennedy, Nixon, and Ford for signs of deception. His analysis revealed substantial differences among the Presidents in their first formal press conferences: Nixon ranked first in the overall number of indicators of deceptive communication, followed by Kennedy, Ford, Johnson, and Eisenhower, in that order. Of particular interest to Alker were three press conferences (Kennedy on the Bay of Pigs invasion, Johnson on the Gulf of Tonkin incident, and Nixon on Watergate) in each of which, history tells us, the President employed more than routine amounts of deception. In each case, the President actually showed very few signs of deception; apparently, in these instances, the Presidents very carefully controlled their speech and successfully managed to give every appearance of telling the truth.

James Gill, *In His Image*, 1965.

what is socially appropriate in new situations, have good control of their emotional expressions, and can effectively use these abilities to create the impressions they want. They also are particularly skilled at intentionally expressing and accurately communicating (nonverbally) a wide variety of emotions by facial and vocal means. In fact, high self-monitoring individuals are such polished actors that they can effectively adopt the mannerisms of a reserved, withdrawn, and introverted individual and then do an abrupt about-face and equally convincingly portray themselves as friendly, outgoing, and extroverted (Lippa, 1976; 1978). High self-monitoring individuals also can exploit their self-presentational skills to practice deception in face-to-face interviews (Krauss, Geller, & Olson, 1976).

In self-presentational situations, high self-monitoring individuals are quite likely to seek out and consult social-comparison information about appropriate patterns of self-presentation. They invest considerable effort in attempting to "read" and understand others (Berscheid, Graziano, Monson, & Dermer, 1976; Jones & Baumeister, 1976). At times, they even will go so far as to acquire, at some cost to themselves, information that may aid them in choosing their self-presentation in a forthcoming interaction with another person (Elliott, 1979).

B. *Self-Monitoring and Impression Management*

It would seem that high self-monitoring individuals are well-suited to practice the arts of impression management. And, indeed, they are skilled impression managers. In one experiment (Snyder & Monson, 1975), group-discussion conditions sensitized individuals to different peer reference groups that could provide cues to the social appropriateness of one's self-presentation. High self-monitoring individuals were keenly attentive to these differences. They were conforming when conformity was the most appropriate interpersonal orientation and nonconforming when reference-group norms favored autonomy in the face of social pressure (see Figure 4-4). Low self-monitoring individuals were virtually unaffected by the differences in social setting. Presumably, their self-presentations were very accurate reflections of their own personal attitudes and dispositions. What these

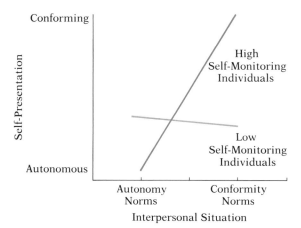

Figure 4-4. High self-monitoring individuals are ready and willing to practice the arts of impression management. They present themselves as conformists in situations that call for conformity and as autonomous individuals in situations that call for autonomy. Low self-monitoring individuals are unlikely to tailor their self-presentations to their situations. (From "Persons, Situations, and the Control of Social Behavior," by M. Snyder and T. C. Monson, *Journal of Personality and Social Psychology*, 1975, *32*, 637–644. Copyright 1975 by the American Psychological Association. Reprinted by permission.)

results mean is that those persons who are most skilled at impression management (high self-monitoring individuals) are also those most likely to practice the arts of impression management.

The well-developed impression-management skills of high self-monitoring individuals give them the flexibility and adaptiveness to cope quickly and effectively with a diversity of social roles. They can choose with skill and grace the self-presentation and social behavior appropriate to each of a wide variety of social situations. Yet, there can be costs to the interpersonal orientation of high self-monitoring individuals. For example, the high self-monitoring orientation may be purchased at the cost of having one's actions reflect and communicate very little about one's private attitudes, feelings, and dispositions. In fact, correspondence between private attitudes and public behavior is often minimal for high self-monitoring individuals (Snyder & Swann, 1976; Snyder & Tanke, 1976). Evidently, the words and deeds of high self-monitoring individuals often reveal very little information about their true inner feelings and attitudes.

High self-monitoring individuals are highly skilled not only at practicing impression management but also at detecting the impression-management attempts of other people. To demonstrate the finely tuned ability of high self-monitoring individuals to "read" others, Geizer, Rarick, and Soldow (1977) used videotaped excerpts from the old television program "To Tell the Truth." On this program, one of the three contestants (all male in the excerpts chosen for the study) is the "real" Mr. X, but all three contestants claim to be him. Of course, two of them are lying. Participants in this study watched each excerpt and then tried to identify the real Mr. X. High self-monitoring individuals were much more accurate than low self-monitoring individuals in correctly identifying the truthful contestant and reading through the attempted deceptions of the other two contestants. No doubt, contestants on "To Tell the Truth" were selected in part for their skill in deceiving others. In addition, the excerpts chosen for this investigation were particularly difficult ones; in each case, at least one of the celebrity panelists on the program had failed to identify the real Mr. X. Viewed from this perspective, the ability of high self-monitoring individuals to accurately detect the deceptive impression management by the contestants is all the more remarkable.

C. *Self-Monitoring and Social Relationships*

What would happen if two previously unacquainted individuals found themselves together in a room in which they were free to interact, or not, as they pleased? Any social interaction that occurred under these circumstances would be unstructured and spontaneous. It would therefore provide an ideal "laboratory" for observing the impact of self-monitoring on acquaintance processes and social relationships. Ickes and Barnes (1977) created just such a situation. They arranged for pairs of strangers to spend time together in a waiting room, ostensibly to wait for a psychological experiment to begin. They then audio- and video-recorded the verbal and nonverbal behaviors of both individuals over a 5-minute observation period. These conversational dyads represented all possible pairings of same-sex undergraduates at high, moderate, and low levels of self-monitoring. Ickes and Barnes then scrutinized their tapes for evidence of the impact of self-monitoring on the interactional dynamics of these spontaneous encounters between strangers.

The influences of self-monitoring on the dynamics of these social relationships were impressive. In these encounters—as, apparently, in so many other areas of their lives—high self-monitoring individuals suffered little or no shyness (Pilkonis, 1977). Early in the interaction, individuals high in self-monitoring took an active and a controlling role in the conversation: the higher self-monitoring members of the dyads were inclined to talk first and to initiate subsequent conversational sequences. They also experienced, and were seen by their partners as having, a greater need to talk. Their

partners viewed them as having been the more directive member of the dyad. It was as if the high self-monitoring individuals were particularly concerned about managing their social behavior in such a way as to create, facilitate, and maintain a smooth flow of conversation throughout the course of the interaction. In the service of these goals, high self-monitoring individuals took an active role in initiating and maintaining the conversation. It is perhaps this regulatory orientation to interpersonal relationships that accounts for the frequent emergence of high self-monitoring individuals as leaders of groups (see Garland & Beard, 1978).

D. *Detecting Self-Monitoring in Others*

Often in social relationships, we want to know which of a person's behaviors truly reflect underlying attitudes and feelings and which are impression-management techniques being used to create an image. Thus, when the life insurance agent compliments me on my taste in home furnishings, is she sincerely complimenting me or is she softening me up for the big sell? When an admirer tells me what beautiful brown eyes I have, is this admiration or seduction? When a job applicant recites a litany of impressive credentials, should I regard this as accurate self-presentation or as self-serving impression management? In order to react appropriately to another person's messages and overtures, we need to be able to tell accurate self-presentation from strategic (and possibly self-serving) impression management.

But how are we to read through the masks of impression management? If the actions of high self-monitoring individuals are typically the products of strategic impression management, then we ought to search out and be responsive to information about the self-monitoring levels of the people we meet. As it happens, people usually do know something about the self-monitoring propensities of those with whom they are well-acquainted, even if the term *self-monitoring* is not a part of everyday vocabulary (Snyder, 1974). Presumably, we can use this knowledge to appropriately interpret and react to the messages and overtures of the high self-monitoring individuals in our lives. Knowing which individuals characteristically use impression management in their social relationships can help us to see beyond the facades of their impression-management efforts.

Of course, we don't always know others well enough to shrewdly assess their self-monitoring tendencies. How, then, are we to know when strangers and casual acquaintances are engaged in self-monitoring? Are there some channels of expression and communication that are more revealing than others about a person's true inner "self," even when he or she is practicing the arts of impression management? Both scientific and everyday observers of human behavior have suggested that nonverbal behaviors such as facial expression, tone of voice, and body movement can reveal meaningful information about a person's attitudes, feelings, and motives (for a detailed treatment of nonverbal communication, see Chapter 5).

At least one experiment points to the usefulness of nonverbal behaviors as cues to the true attitudes held by those attempting impression management. Weitz (1972) reasoned that, on college campuses with strong normative pressures supporting a tolerant and liberal value system, all students would avoid saying anything that would indicate racial prejudice—whether their private attitudes supported such behavior or not. In fact, Weitz found that among "liberal" White males at Harvard University, the most racially prejudiced students (as determined by behavioral measures of actual attempts to avoid interaction with Blacks) bent over backward to *verbally* express liking and friendship for a Black in a simulated interracial encounter. However, their *nonverbal* behaviors betrayed them: their true racial attitudes showed through in the tone of voice they used. Thus, although the prejudiced individuals made every effort to say kind and favorable things, they did so in a cool and distant tone of voice. It is as if they knew the words but not the music; that is, they knew what to say, but not how to say it. (For another ex-

ample of the nonverbal betrayal of prejudice, see **Figure 4-5.**)

IV. Self-Disclosure: The Private "I" Goes Public

At times, the goal of impression management is to effectively present a true and honest image to other people—one that will not be misinterpreted by them. Consider the case of a woman on trial for a crime that she did not commit. Her task on the witness stand is to carefully present herself so that everything she does and says clearly communicates to the jurors her innocence so that they will vote for her acquittal. Chances are good, however, that the members of the jury will be somewhat skeptical about the defendant's claims of innocence. "After all," they might reason to themselves, "the district attorney would not have brought this case to trial were the state's case against her not a convincing one." The defendant must carefully manage her verbal and nonverbal behaviors so as to ensure that even a skeptical juror will form a true impression of her innocence. In particular, she must avoid the pitfalls of an image that suggests that "she protests her innocence too much and therefore must be guilty." To the extent that our defendant skillfully practices the art of impression management in the courtroom, she will succeed in presenting herself to the jurors as the honest person that she truly is.

Of course, few of us will ever have to engage in impression management in a courtroom in order to convince jurors of our innocence. There are times in all our lives, however, when we seek to make ourselves transparent to others and when we strive to present unvarnished images of our true selves. Such self-presentation is called self-revelation, or **self-disclosure.**

A. *Self-Disclosure and Self-Discovery*

Many psychologists believe that the ability to allow one's true self to be known to at least one significant other is necessary for a "healthy," or self-actualized, personality. In fact, Sidney Jourard, who was long a leading theorist in the domain of self-disclosure, believed that it was only through self-disclosure that we could achieve self-discovery and self-knowledge:

Through my self-disclosure, I let others know my soul. They can know it, really know it, only as I make it known. In fact, I am beginning to suspect that I can't even know *my own soul* except as I disclose it. I suspect that I will know myself "for real" at the exact moment that I have succeeded in making it known through my disclosure to another person [Jourard, 1964, p. 10].

Although Jourard believed that self-disclosure was necessary for effective psychological functioning, he also claimed

Figure 4-5. Gay is beautiful—at a distance. One way in which individuals nonconsciously reveal prejudices is in the distance they keep from the targets of their prejudice. To demonstrate this phenomenon, Morin (1975) arranged for college students to be interviewed about their attitudes toward homosexuality. Half of the interviewers wore "GAY AND PROUD" buttons and mentioned their membership in the Association of Gay Psychologists. The other half of the interviewers wore no buttons and simply mentioned that they were graduate students doing thesis research. The researchers then measured, without the subjects' knowledge, the distance that they placed their chairs from the interviewer. This measure of social distance proved to be a highly revealing sign of attitudes toward gay people. When the subject and the interviewer were of the same sex, subjects tended to establish distance between themselves and the gay interviewer. In fact, they placed their chairs an average of 32 inches away from the identifiably gay interviewers but only 22 inches away from the apparently "straight" interviewers. This is a difference of almost one foot, on the average. Interestingly, most of the subjects had already expressed tolerant—at times, favorable—attitudes toward gay people in general. However, the distances they chose to put between themselves and the gay interviewers betrayed their underlying negative attitudes. (© Leonard Freed/Magnum Photos, Inc.)

that either too little or too much self-disclosure could cause problems of adjustment (Jourard, 1959, 1964). The person who never discloses might be unable to establish any close and meaningful relationships with others. But those people who habitually pour out their souls to anyone who will listen could be maladjusted and morbidly preoccupied with themselves. Jourard believed that it would be ideal to disclose a lot to a few close friends and a moderate amount to others. Although Jourard's viewpoint is intuitively appealing, research has yet to fully chart the relationship between self-disclosure and psychological adjustment. Much is known, however, about the patterns of self-disclosure in interpersonal relationships.

B. *Self-Disclosure: By Whom? About What? To Whom?*

Just how prevalent is self-disclosure in interpersonal relationships? How frequently, if ever, do people disclose things that they have never before revealed to others? To what extent is self-disclosure a routine feature of interpersonal relationships? (See **Figure 4-6** for a lighthearted look at self-disclosure.)

To measure the frequency of self-disclosure, Jourard (1964) developed a questionnaire measure that covered ten global domains of the self within which a person could engage in self-disclosure. For example, within the domain of personality, a person might or might not be willing to disclose "the aspect of my personality that I dislike, worry about, that I regard as a handicap to me." Similarly, within the domain of the body, a person might or might not be willing to disclose "my feelings about my adequacy in sexual behavior—whether or not I feel able to perform adequately in sex relationships." For a full listing of the 60 items of Jourard's Self-Disclosure Questionnaire, see pages 161–163 of Jourard's book *The Transparent Self: Self-Disclosure and Well-Being* (1964).

In his research, Jourard (1971) asked people whether they had disclosed any aspects of themselves that were covered in the Self-Disclosure Questionnaire; and, if so, to whom they had made the disclosures. He found that people were much more willing to disclose some information than other information. For example, people reported much more self-disclosure about their attitudes and opinions than they did about their personalities and their bodies. Moreover, some people were more willing to disclose themselves than others. Thus, women reported more self-disclosure than men did. Similarly, Whites indicated more self-disclosure than Blacks. Finally, it appeared that some people were more desirable targets for self-disclosure than others were. In general, the subjects in Jourard's re-

Figure 4-6. Self-disclosure in social interaction. (© 1971, '72, G. B. Trudeau. Used by permission of Universal Press Syndicate. All rights reserved.)

search preferred to disclose themselves to people with whom they had relatively intimate relationships (for example, immediate family members and close friends).

C. *Liking, Intimacy, and Self-Disclosure*

Liking and self-disclosure often go hand in hand, but apparently this is true only of women. Jourard and Landsman (1960) found no relationship at all for males between those whom they liked and those to whom they disclosed themselves. Similarly, Ehrlich and Graeven (1971) could find no influence whatsoever of self-disclosure on liking in research involving males. And, Rubin and Shenker (1978) have reported that friendship and intimate disclosure were more highly related among women than among men. These sex differences may very well reflect the more general differences in sex-role socialization of the expression of liking and intimacy.

When asked whom they like, females usually indicate those individuals to whom they disclose themselves (Jourard, 1959; Jourard & Lasakow, 1958). In addition, self-disclosure and satisfaction in marriage seem to go together (Levinger & Senn, 1967). Moreover, self-disclosure frequently is tied to the social approval received for being intimate and self-revealing. Taylor, Altman, and Sorrentino (1969) trained confederates to provide subjects with (a) continuous positive reward, (b) continuous negative feedback, or (c) mixed reactions during conversation. As expected, those subjects who received either continuous positive approval or increases in social approval over the course of the conversation became increasingly willing to talk about themselves in an intimate and revealing fashion.

Do we like those who are self-revealing? At times, we do (Worthy, Gary, & Kahn, 1969); but, at other times, overly intimate disclosures can arouse anxiety in the listener (Cozby, 1972). Two factors that help determine our reactions to those who disclose themselves to us are the timing and the nature of the self-disclosure (Jones & Gordon, 1972). For example, when individuals let us know of their virtuous accomplishments (for example, "I want you to know that I was student body president of my junior high school"), we respond to them most favorably if they have modestly delayed these revelations until we already know the person well and are actively soliciting these positive self-disclosures. However, when individuals confess their more shameful deeds (for example, "I think you should know that I was once caught shoplifting"), we are most sympathetic to these disclosures when they occur spontaneously early in the course of the relationship.

V. The Quest for Social Approval

Why do people engage in impression management? What personal benefits do they receive as a consequence of managing the impressions of themselves that they present to the people with whom they interact? One likely consequence is social approval: by choosing one self-presentation rather than another, the impression manager hopes to win the approval and acceptance of others. In fact, there is clear evidence that people use impression management when they are seeking a socially appropriate image and the social approval that it brings. Jones, Gergen, and Davis (1962) studied college women who were about to be interviewed by a trainee in clinical psychology. Half of these women were told to say whatever they felt was necessary in order to secure the favorable approval of the interviewer. The remainder of the women were instructed to be candid, honest, and accurate in their self-presentations. Not surprisingly, the women who were seeking approval described themselves much more favorably than those oriented toward candor. Either those women searching for approval exaggerated their good qualities, or those women striving for accuracy in presenting themselves played down their assets. But, despite these differences, the two groups did *not* differ in how honest they felt they had been with the interviewer.

Reassuring social approval is more necessary when one has experienced a failure than when one has been successful. One social psychologist (D. J. Schneider, 1969) built upon this principle to study the effects of the experience of failure on impression management. He arranged for some individuals to fail at a task and for others to succeed at the same task. He then had the subjects describe themselves to another person. Those who had just failed—and presumably were in need of social approval—described themselves more positively than those who had just succeeded. However, this outcome occurred only when the person to whom they were describing themselves actually was capable of providing the social approval they so eagerly sought. When the target could not offer social approval, the failed individuals described themselves more negatively than the successful individuals.

A. *Self-Handicapping Strategies*

Clearly, there are times when we do our best to soothe the pain of failure by seeking reassuring social approval from sympathetic others. However, at other times, we seek to prevent ourselves from experiencing the pain of failure by arranging circumstances so that we and others need not interpret our poor performance as a failure. Thus, students who just before taking examinations complain to their peers about how few hours of sleep they had the night before are setting up in advance ready-made excuses that they conveniently can exploit should they happen to get low grades: "Oh, well, what could you expect from someone who only slept two hours before the test?" The job candidate who makes it known to his friends that he had quite a few drinks the night before an important job interview is manufacturing an alibi to use should the interview go badly: "It wasn't that I was unqualified for the job, it was just that I had this unbelievable hangover that day." Of course, should these individuals manage to succeed in the face of the roadblocks they have put in their own paths, they will be quick to give themselves added credit for their successes: "Two hours of sleep and a B; think what I could have done with six hours of sleep!"; "I got the job even with a hangover; no hangover, and they might have hired me as manager of the company!"

The strategies by which individuals manufacture protective excuses for any possible future failures are called **self-handicapping strategies** (Berglas & Jones, 1978; Jones & Berglas, 1978).

In an empirical demonstration of self-handicapping strategies in action, Berglas and Jones (1978) observed that male college students who had reason to anticipate that they might not perform well on a problem-solving task chose to take drugs that would interfere (or so they were led to believe) with their subsequent problem-solving performance. Should they then have performed poorly, they would have provided themselves with readily available explanations for their failure that in no way would have threatened their image of self-competence. In the language of attribution theory (see Chapter 3), they used *situational attributions* for their failure (for example, "I failed because of the drug"). However, should they have performed well, they might have prided themselves for being sufficiently intelligent and competent to overcome the handicap of the performance-inhibiting drug. In the language of attribution theory, they would have been making *dispositional attributions* for their success (for example, "I succeeded because I'm smart").

More generally, Jones and Berglas (1978) have proposed that, to the extent that individuals are concerned with maintaining an image of self-competence, they will try to choose settings and circumstances that maximize their chances for enhancing that image and minimize their chances for threatening that image. To the extent that individuals can use their self-handicapping strategies to meet these criteria, they will manage to live their lives in worlds that both protect and enhance their images of being competent and intelligent people.

B. *Basking in Reflected Glory*

It is understandable that we often feel the need to publicly crow about our successes and explain away our failures. There is little doubt that such impression management can help to maintain or increase other people's regard for our abilities. In fact, so strong is the desire to have others view us favorably that often we publicly advertise our connections with other people who are successes. Who among us is not quick to point out all the famous people who were born in the same city as we, or who went to the same schools, or who belong to the same ethnic group, and so on? These attempts at **basking in reflected glory** are particularly evident on college campuses where there are winning athletic teams. On the Monday morning after a victory, students proudly wear clothing that clearly identifies them as student body members and talk excitedly about how "we" won the big game. But, on those Monday mornings after defeats, the school jackets and sweatshirts stay hidden in closets and students talk glumly about how "the team" lost the game. In a series of investigations of the phenomenon of basking in reflected glory, Cialdini, Borden, Thorne, Walker, and Freeman (1976) not only have documented the tendency to publicly advertise one's association with winners but also have provided evidence that basking in reflected glory is an impression-management strategy designed to enhance the esteem in which one is held by others.

C. *Seeking an Appropriate Sex-Role Image*

The approval motive can powerfully influence impression management in the domain of sex-role behaviors. In one study by Zanna and Pack (1975), for example, female Princeton undergraduates were asked to describe themselves for the benefit of a male partner who was described to them as either (a) an attractive, 6'1", 21-year-old Princeton senior with no woman friend and a strong interest in meeting female college students or (b) an unattractive, 5'5", 18-year-old non-Princeton freshman with a girlfriend and no interest in meeting other women. (These women did not meet the men in question. They simply were asked to provide a self-description, which supposedly would be given to the man.) The researchers also told the women either that the man's idea of the ideal woman conformed to the traditional female stereotype (emotional,

deferent to her husband, home oriented, passive, and so on), or that it was the opposite of the traditional stereotype (analytical, independent, career-oriented, competitive, and so on).

What effect did this information about the partner and his beliefs have on the women's self-presentations? When the partner was the unattached senior, the women presented themselves as extremely conventional if his ideology was conventional and as much more liberal if his ideology was unconventional. When the partner was the unattractive freshman, his ideas about women did not have much impact on the images of themselves conveyed by the women in this experiment.

Clearly, expectations shaped the women's self-presentations. In anticipation of meeting an attractive but traditional man, some women described themselves in very conventional terms. In anticipation of meeting an attractive but nontraditional man, other women described themselves in relatively unconventional terms. Of course, the women in this experiment never had the opportunity to meet and interact with these men, so the question remains: if these women had interacted with the men described to them, would they actually have acted out the conventional or unconventional sex roles that would have fulfilled the expectations of the man?

Perhaps so. In a follow-up experiment, von Baeyer, Sherk, and Zanna (1979) scheduled female job applicants to be interviewed by male interviewers. Once again, the women learned that the male interviewer's idea of the ideal woman conformed either to the traditional stereotype or to its opposite. Of major concern to the researchers was the appearance (clothing, accessories, makeup, and so on) of the women when they arrived for their interviews. Indeed, the women in this experiment strategically dressed to meet the stereotyped expectations of the interviewer. Women who anticipated a traditional interviewer looked decidedly feminine, not only in terms of their overall appearance and demeanor but also in terms of their use of makeup and choice of accessories. During the actual interviews, these women offered traditionally feminine answers to questions such as "Do you have plans to include children and marriage with your career plans?"

We do not know what would happen if men were asked to present themselves to attractive women or to prospective employers. It seems quite likely that some similar shifts in presentation would occur. More generally, this research suggests that many supposed sex differences may merely reflect different images that people project in their attempts to act out sex roles that may be expected in particular situations (see Box 4-2). As stereotyped expectations about sex roles change, so too may the sex-role behaviors themselves. In fact, autobiographical statements by individuals who have undergone surgical sex reassignments have pointed to the power of such processes in facilitating adjustment to the new life as a member of the other sex. Thus, writer Jan Morris in her autobiographical chronicle of her transition from James to Jan observed, "The more I was treated as a woman, the more woman I became" (Morris, 1974, p. 165).

D. *Forcing the Stigmatized to Play Their Role*

A **stigma** is a characteristic that is considered undesirable by most people. In the United States, Canada, and other Western nations, being physically or mentally handicapped, having non-White skin color, being poor, being old, and being gay all can sometimes be stigmatizing experiences. The eminent social observer Goffman (1963) has written insightfully of such experiences. Essentially, he argues that other people intentionally or unintentionally "force" the stigmatized to play the role laid down for them. For example, he claims that people want to feel sorry for and charitable to the handicapped. Therefore, such individuals can anticipate sizable gains from behaving in ways that evoke pity. Thus the original stereotype that the handicapped are pitiful is confirmed because they purposely have conformed to those expectations. For the handicapped to behave in an independent manner would provoke only perceptions of

ingratitude. The net result is that the handicapped often accept their fate and act out the role that society has defined for them. Weinberg and Williams (1974) have suggested a similar effect. Based upon results of extensive cross-cultural survey research on gay males, they have speculated on the ways in which widely held but essentially untrue social stereotypes can shape the behavior of some gay men to fulfill those stereotypes. The impression-management process underlying these stereotypes is the same: "I am an X. Everyone believes that all X's act in way Y. Therefore I will act in way Y too." The stereotype is made to come true.

The evidence supports this viewpoint; people who are made to feel stigmatized come to behave as if they were in fact branded with shame and disgrace. For example, Farina, Gliha, Boudreau, Allen, and Sherman (1971) measured the impact on mental patients of their belief that others were aware of their psychiatric history. Mental patients interacted with another individual (actually a confederate) in a cooperative task. Half of the patients were told that their partner knew that they were mental patients. The remainder believed that their partners did not know that they were mental patients. In fact, the confederates never knew whether their partners were patients or nonpatients. The effects of these conditions were impressive. Believing that others were aware of their status caused the identified patients to feel less appreciated, to find the task more difficult, and to perform poorly. Moreover, objective observers perceived them to be more tense, more anxious, and more poorly adjusted than the patients who believed that their partners did not know of their status. Apparently, the belief that others might perceive them as stigmatized individuals caused them to act in ways consistent with such a deviant status. Evidently, these individuals were willing and able to "play the role" of stigmatized psychiatric patients. In fact, a considerable amount of research now suggests that many schizophrenics in psychiatric institutions actually play out complex impression-management processes (Braginsky, Braginsky, & Ring, 1969). It seems that

Box 4-2. The Self-Fulfilling Nature of Stereotypes about Women and Men.

Can one individual's stereotyped beliefs about the nature of the sexes influence the dynamics of social relationships in ways that actually cause another person to behave in a manner that confirms these stereotypes? To answer this question, Skrypnek and Snyder (1979) arranged for pairs of unacquainted individuals to interact in a situation that permitted them to control the information each one received about the sex of the other. The two people, located in separate rooms so that they could neither see nor hear each other, communicated by means of a signaling system. They were required to negotiate a division of labor for a series of worklike tasks that differed in their sex-role connotations. The tasks were simple activities that varied along the dimensions of masculinity and femininity (for example, sharpening a hunting knife = masculine; polishing a pair of shoes = neutral; ironing a shirt = feminine). One member of the dyad was led to believe, in one condition of the experiment, that the other member ("the target") was *male*, and, in the second condition of the experiment, that the target was *female*. These dyads then negotiated (communicating by means of the signaling system) their division of labor for the tasks. During the course of the negotiations, the first member's belief about the sex of the partner influenced the outcome of the negotiations. Thus, female targets whose partners believed that they were males chose relatively many stereotypically masculine tasks; female targets whose partners believed that they were females chose relatively many stereotypically feminine tasks. In this experiment, it was possible

to separate the target's "real" sex from her "apparent" sex and to demonstrate that the target would display behaviors traditionally associated with her "apparent" sex, even if those behaviors were stereotypically inappropriate to her "real" sex. Of course, in everyday life, "real" and "apparent" sexes are (with rare exceptions) the same. Nonetheless, this experiment suggests that many sex-role behaviors may be the product of other people's stereotyped beliefs about our "apparent" sex.

Drawing by Wm. Hamilton; © 1978 The New Yorker Magazine, Inc.

"I guess I'll just play out my stereotype."

some schizophrenics deliberately project carefully crafted images of incompetence so that they may remain in psychiatric institutions that shelter them from the stressful demands of everyday life.

In another study, Farina, Allen, and Saul (1968) led college students to believe that they had revealed to another person that they were stigmatized (for example, that they had a history of mental illness). In fact, the other person always received the same neutral information. However, merely believing that another person viewed them as stigmatized influenced the students' behaviors and caused them to be rejected by the other person. Possibly, then, stigmatized individuals expect to be viewed negatively by others and rejected by them; therefore, they accept and play the role that leads to this rejection. Ironically, they may be conforming to these expectations in the vain hope that they will be accepted if only they do what others expect of them. In their quest for approval, they actually cause the rejection they seek to forestall.

E. *Need for Approval: Some People More Than Others*

It appears that some people have a greater **need for approval** than others. Such individuals can be identified by their high scores on the Marlowe-Crowne Social Desirability Scale, a measure of the tendency to describe oneself in favorable, socially desirable terms (Crowne & Marlowe, 1964). Individuals with a great need for approval are likely to make claims like the following: "I never hesitate to go out of my way to help someone in trouble," "I have never intensely disliked anyone," "I always try to practice what I preach," "I'm always courteous to people who are disagreeable," and other socially approved claims. Presumably, people who make such claims do so because they crave the social approval that they believe is accorded to such individuals.

There is in fact considerable evidence that, in a wide variety of situations, those individuals with a high need for approval do give socially desirable responses. They conform more than do the low-need-for-approval individuals, they do not show overt hostility toward those who insult and double-cross them, and they are less likely to use "dirty" words. Strangely enough, these same people who desire social approval so intensely are frequently social isolates. Their peers describe them as individuals who spend most of their time alone, who don't go out of their way to make friends,

who don't talk much, and who don't act friendly toward others (Crowne & Marlowe, 1964, pp. 162–163).

VI. The Strategic Self: Winning Friends and Influencing People

Impression management often plays a strategic role in social relationships, because some people use impression management to win friends and influence people. The front cover of a recent printing of Dale Carnegie's *How to Win Friends and Influence People* (originally published in 1936) claims that more than 8,400,000 copies of that book have been sold. This number grows at the rate of over 250,000 copies each year. Dale Carnegie human-relations courses are offered in more than 1000 cities in the United States and Canada (an advertisement for the course is reproduced in Figure 4-7). The heart of the Dale Carnegie approach is a set of basic rules, each with a tactical purpose. For example, Carnegie offers six ways to make others like you:

Rule 1: Become genuinely interested in other people.
Rule 2: Smile.
Rule 3: Remember that a man's name is to him the sweetest and most important sound in any language.
Rule 4: Be a good listener. Encourage others to talk about themselves.
Rule 5: Talk in terms of the other man's interest.
Rule 6: Make the other person feel important—and do it sincerely.

It is all too easy to make light of the Carnegie method because he makes it seem so simple. Occasionally Carnegie's message seems a trifle simplistic, if not trite; for example, "Actions speak louder than words, and a smile says 'I like you. You make me happy. I am glad to see you.' " Yet the advice is eminently reasonable and practical. It also fits well with social-psychological theory and research. Thus, there is some truth to the Carnegie prescription that one's own "name is . . . the sweetest and most important sound in any language." For example, interviewers who call their interviewees

"The Dale Carnegie Course gets you to recognize and use your capabilities."

Terri Sopp Rae, Downey, California

Roland Schultz, Professor of Chemistry,
Oklahoma Christian College, Oklahoma City, Oklahoma

■ "I know now that I had a tendency to under-rate my own abilities," recalls Roland Schultz, "but after taking the Dale Carnegie Course, I have the self-assurance to be comfortable and at the same time more effective in putting across ideas to my students.

"This also shows up in my life-style. I have become active in organizations I wouldn't have considered before I took the Course. It's one of the best investments I ever made."

■ Terri Sopp Rae believed she needed to improve her self-image. "In college classes, I was afraid to volunteer even when I knew the answers. I thought I'd make a mistake and everyone would laugh at me.

"After my brother Randy enrolled in the Dale Carnegie Course and I saw what it did for him, I was convinced I could improve with Carnegie training.

In the Course, I developed a much stronger feeling of assurance. Now I can express myself and feel good about it. I find people listen to me, too, even when I'm talking to a group.

"My parents have noticed I'm a lot easier to get along with. I even found that my Dad and I have a lot in common. It's great discussing things with him. I'm really glad I took the Course while I'm young."

The Dale Carnegie Course leads men and women to new confidence, better relationships and greater recognition of their abilities—these and many other benefits can be yours. Dale Carnegie training is offered in more than 1,000 U.S. communities, including all major cities and in 51 other countries. For more information write us today.

DC DALE CARNEGIE COURSE

SUITE 115T • 1475 FRANKLIN AVENUE • GARDEN CITY, NEW YORK 11530

Figure 4-7. An advertisement for the Dale Carnegie Course in Effective Speaking and Public Relations. (Courtesy of Dale Carnegie & Associates, Inc., Garden City, New York.)

by name frequently during the course of their interviews are often better liked than interviewers who avoid calling their interviewees by name (Kleinke, Staneski, & Weaver, 1972).

A. *The Tactics of Ingratiation*

The term **ingratiation** refers to those tactics of impression management that a person consciously uses to increase a specific target person's liking for him or her. Edward E. Jones (1964) has made an in-depth social-psychological analysis of strategic approaches to interpersonal relationships, including ingratiation. He suggests that there are four sets of tactics that the ingratiator can use to gain the liking of a target person.

1. *Compliments or Other-Enhancement.* This technique is outright flattery. It assumes that people find it hard to resist liking people who think highly of them. However, the ingratiator must be careful to present these compliments with sufficient credibility and spontaneity so that they will be believed and accepted as sincere. Jones believes that flattery is most effective when the target needs the reassurance that a compliment can provide: "It is a person's doubts about an attribute in which he wishes to excel which render him open to flattery" (1964, p. 29). The ingratiator should also strive to appear discriminating in the use of praise and flattery. In fact, there are times when we react more positively to those who carefully temper their praise with a little criticism than we do to those who have nothing but kind words for us (see Aronson & Linder, 1965; Mettee, 1971). However, Jones would advise an ingratiator who practices this strategy to restrict the criticism to relatively minor and inconsequential faults and to offer any criticisms only after having offered lavish praise in some area of greater importance to the target (Jones & Wortman, 1973).

2. *Conformity in Opinion and Behavior.* In Molière's *The Miser*, the character Valère attests to the success of conformity as a tactic of ingratiation: "I find that the best way to win people's favour is to pretend to agree with them, to fall in with their precepts, encourage their foibles, and applaud whatever they do." Valère's tactic correctly assumes that we like people whose beliefs, attitudes, and behaviors are similar to our own. Once again, however, the ingratiator must maintain credibility. One strategy for doing so is that of discriminating conformity: the successful ingratiator mixes disagreement on unimportant points with agreement on crucial issues for which the target will reward social support with liking. Another approach is to limit the use of obvious conformity when the target suspects ingratiation (Kauffman & Steiner, 1968). However, if we can believe Molière's Valère, it may be only the rarest of targets who ever will suspect ingratiation: "One need have no fear of overdoing (it). . . . When it comes to flattery, the most cunning of men are the most easily deceived."

3. *Self-Presentation.* An ingratiator can court favor by presenting a favorable self-image. Or, as Sir Francis Bacon is reputed to have said, "Praise yourself daringly; something always sticks." This is exactly what participants did in the Jones, Gergen, and Davis (1962) study: they described themselves in very flattering, self-congratulatory terms when instructed to win the approval of interviewers. However, ingratiators tend to be discriminating in their use of self-enhancement. When they realize that someone has an unfavorable impression of one of their personal characteristics, they often conspicuously avoid making claims about that characteristic. Instead, they attempt to compensate for the negative impression by bending over backward to portray all the more favorably their other virtues and redeeming features (Baumeister & Jones, 1978). However, as Stires and Jones (1969) have pointed out, there are times when modesty is the best policy. Although self-enhancement was the preferred mode of ingratiation in the Stires and Jones research, dependent ingratiators inhibited this tendency in favor of more modest self-presentations when they knew that the target was aware of his or her power over the ingratiator. Modesty also can be particularly potent in the service of ingratiation when an overly positive self-presentation might threaten the target. Here, modesty plays to the target's vanity. Samuel Taylor Coleridge, English poet and philosopher, urged this rule for deciding between modesty and self-enhancement: "If you would stand well with a great mind, leave him with a favorable impression of yourself; if with a little mind, leave him with a favorable impression of himself" (quoted by Edwards, 1972, p. 297).

4. *Rendering Favors.* This tactic is a straightforward application of the everyday principle that people are attracted to those who give them gifts or do other pleasant and rewarding things for them. It is important, however, to distinguish between feelings of social indebtedness and feelings of liking provoked by gifts. Only the latter is correctly called ingratiation. In fact, we tend to react more favorably to those whose gifts we regard as appropriate than to those who make inappropriate offerings to us (S. B. Kiesler, 1966).

B. *The Goals of Ingratiation*

What psychological and social goals are met by ingratiation? In other words, why do people ingratiate themselves? Jones (1964) claims that there are three major motives for ingratiation: acquisition, protection, and signification.

1. *Acquisition.* The ultimate aim of acquisitive ingratiation is self-gain. The ingratiator hopes that liking will lead to favorable treatment from the target person. The employee who ingratiates herself with the boss in order to get a raise practices acquisitive ingratiation.

2. *Protection.* The goal of protective ingratiation is to keep the target from inflicting either psychological or physical harm on the ingratiator. Jones suggests that those in dependent positions use protective ingratiation to acknowledge the power held by those in control of their fate. The prisoner who curries favor with a sadistic guard engages in protective ingratiation.

3. *Signification.* We try to make others like us because of what their liking says about our personal worth; to be genuinely liked by others means that we are worthy of their liking. Perhaps, too, we wish others to like us so that we may like ourselves. But there is potential irony here. The harder we work to win another's liking, the less we may value it because we feel that the other person would not have liked us if we had not expended all that effort. However, if the ingratiation attempt succeeds in taking in the target, the chances are that the ingratiator will not even be aware of how deceitfully that liking was gained (Jones, Gergen, & Davis, 1962). Thus, self-deception and ingratiation may work hand in hand to guarantee that both the ingratiator and the target have favorable regard for the ingratiator.

Underlying Jones's analysis of ingratiation is a social-exchange view of human interaction: ingratiators use tactics designed to increase their reward value to targets, and the targets, in turn, increase their liking for the ingratiators. This "give to get" perspective on social interaction reflects the social-exchange theory (Homans, 1961) briefly described in Chapter 1 as a type of stimulus-response analysis of social behavior.

C. *Research on Ingratiation: Means and Ends*

Jones not only has insightfully analyzed the ingratiation process but also has extensively researched the phenomenon in both laboratory and field settings. In one study, Jones, Gergen, and Jones (1963) investigated the effects of one's position in a status hierarchy on one's choice of ingratiation tactics. To do this, they paired undergraduate Naval Reserve Officer Training Corps (NROTC) cadets for discussions of opinion issues under controlled conditions designed to maximize (condition one) or minimize (condition two) ingratiation motives. One member of each pair was of high status (an upperclassman); the other was of low status (a freshman). In the ingratiation interaction, the researchers told the cadets to be as compatible as possible so that the researchers could study the effects of compatibility on leadership effectiveness. In the noningratiation interaction, the researchers stressed the importance of honesty and sincerity of self-presentation. In both groups, the partners exchanged opinions and self-presentations by passing written messages.

The researchers then coded these messages for signs of opinion conformity, self-presentation, and other-enhancement—three of the major tactics of ingratiation emphasized in Jones's theory. Status clearly made a difference in the form of ingratiation preferred by the partners.

1. *Opinion Conformity.* Cadets of low status conformed more than those of high status on opinions relevant to the Navy and to NROTC (such as whether graduates of the naval academy at Annapolis should be favored over NROTC graduates for positions of authority in the Navy). There was some tendency for cadets with high status to conform more than those with low status on items that were peripheral to NROTC (such as opinions about college courses and extracurricular activities).

2. *Self-Presentation.* Partners of high status in the ingratiation interaction described themselves more modestly, on both important and unimportant items, than did those in the noningratiation interaction. Cadets with low status made quite different use of this tactic of ingratiation: when these cadets were courting the favor of their superiors in the ingratiation interaction, they were more modest on important items—but more assertive on unimportant items—than were those in the noningratiation interaction (see **Figure 4-8**). Perhaps, as these researchers have suggested, the low-status freshmen avoided describing themselves too favorably on important attributes so that they would not be viewed as presumptive upstarts.

3. *Other-Enhancement.* The freshmen cadets were more than willing to flatter their upperclass counterparts to butter them up. Apparently, they were willing to risk the obviousness of such a blatant ploy.

What this experiment shows is that people of all status levels are quite willing to play the ingratiation game; they just play their cards differently. Other research suggests the ends to which ingratiation can be the means. Jones, Gergen, Gumpert, and Thibaut (1965) examined the use of ingratiation by a worker to tease and coax from a

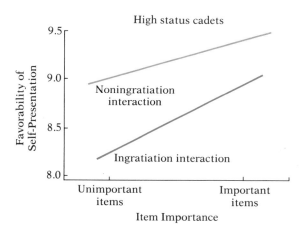

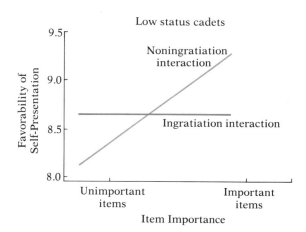

Figure 4-8. Although all naval cadets studied by Jones, Gergen, & Jones (1963) used self-presentation to ingratiate themselves with their discussion partners, high-status cadets and low-status cadets made quite different use of this tactic of ingratiation. (Adapted from "Tactics of Ingratiation among Leaders and Subordinates in a Status Hierarchy," by E. E. Jones, K. J. Gergen, and R. G. Jones, *Psychological Monographs*, 1963, 77 [Whole No. 566]. Copyright 1963 by the American Psychological Association. Used by permission.)

supervisor the judgment that the worker had performed his task well. To do this, the researchers created the following situation. A worker is involved in an ambiguous problem-solving task. He quickly becomes aware that he is not doing well. He then engages in an interaction with his supervisor. They exchange opinions and self-presentations in the usual message-passing format.

However, a few new twists are added to the ingratiation situation. The worker learns either (a) that the supervisor is free to subjectively decide after each trial whether a solution is correct or (b) that the supervisor is bound and committed to a set of solutions worked out in advance. Presumably, the worker-ingratiator would be more likely to make ingratiating moves when the supervisor had the freedom to define standards of good performance than when there was little to be gained by ingratiation. Moreover, the supervisor is characterized either as one who valued togetherness and solidarity or as one who cared only for good performance. Presumably, the worker would tailor the ingratiating strategy to the personal orientation of the supervisor.

The results supported both expectations. The workers were most ingratiating when they believed that they could influence the supervisor's judgment. Otherwise, they avoided ingratiation. This strategy is a reasonable one: few students would waste time ingratiating themselves with a supervisor at the College Board exams in an effort to gain admission to college, but many would put on a good show for an admissions interviewer who had the power to select the new admissions.

The workers in the Jones et al. study tailored their strategies to their beliefs about the supervisor. When the supervisor was togetherness oriented, they sought his approval through conformity with his opinions and attitudes. When he was productivity oriented, many workers chose a self-presentational strategy: they claimed to be efficient, diligent, reliable; in short, they stressed those qualities that define a good worker. This strategy, too, is a quite reasonable one. A candidate for public office would hardly court favor with financial backers and with voters in the same fashion —at least, not if that politician wanted both substantial donations and a decisive vote.

D. *Does Ingratiation Work If It Is Obvious?*

Essentially, an ingratiator is out to gain the liking of a target. To be maximally effective, the ingratiator must hide this manipulative intent and any deceit or pretense that may be involved. Yet, even if the target does notice the devious intent of the ingratiator, there may be strong motivation not to challenge the ingratiator. In Emerson's words: "We love flattery even though we are not deceived by it, because it shows we are of importance to be courted" (Emerson, quoted by Jones, 1964, p. 164). Thus, even unabashed ingratiation attempts often succeed. Such is the nature of human vanity.

VII. The Manipulative Self: Machiavelli and Company

Just as some people use impression management to be liked and to influence those in positions of power, other people put impression management to even more devious use, with goals that include the manipulation and control of others for their own personal gain. The silver-tongued confidence artist is a specialist in the not-always-honest manipulation of other people, and Yellow Kid Weil is sometimes considered *the* American con artist of the 20th century. His escapades rivaled those of the great confidence men of fiction—Herman Melville's *The Confidence Man* (1857/1964) and Thomas Mann's *Confessions of Felix Krull, Confidence Man* (1954/1955). The Yellow Kid was an equal-opportunity swindler: he dealt indiscriminately in all manner of fraud, including non-existent properties, paper securities, false letters of credit, and get-rich-quick schemes hatched in the twilight zones of legality. The legendary King of Flimflam, who netted millions during his heyday in the 1920s and went on to lose his fortune on high living and travel, died penniless in a convalescent home in 1976 at the age of 100. When asked by novelist Saul Bellow to describe his personal philosophy, the Yellow Kid had this to say: "I have never cheated any honest man, only rascals. They may have been respectable, but they were never any good. They wanted something for nothing. I gave them nothing for something" (1956, p. 42). For the Yellow Kid, victims got only what they deserved.

The confidence artist's view of the world is not all that different from the one portrayed by Niccolò Machiavelli, the 16th-century advocate of the use of manipulation and deceit for personal and political benefit (Christie & Geis, 1970; Jensen, 1960). In *The Prince* (1940), Machiavelli advised the Prince of Florence, among other things, that "It is safer to be feared than to be loved"; "Most men mourn the loss of their patrimony more than the death of their fathers"; and "Humility not only is of no service but is actually harmful." He described people as objects to be manipulated with cool calculation and emotional detachment and had little regard for conventional morality; he endorsed lying, cheating, and deceit when the ends justified the means. And, for Machiavelli, the ends of increased personal and political power almost always justified the means. The inborn baseness and manipulativeness of other people were, for Machiavelli, further justification for a manipulative interpersonal orientation.

A. *The Machiavellians among Us*

Whether or not Machiavelli was right about human nature, there are those people among us who accept and act upon the same kind of personal philosophy he employed. In fact, manipulative people often are called *Machiavellians*, after Machiavelli himself. Christie and Geis (1970) have constructed a simple paper-and-pencil scale to measure each person's level of **Machiavellianism.** Those with high scores on this "Mach Scale" agree with statements such as: "The best way to handle people is to tell them what they want to hear"; "Anyone who completely trusts anyone else is asking for trouble"; and "It's safest to assume that all people have a vicious streak that will come out when it is given a chance."

By contrast, those with low scores on the Mach Scale express very different views about human nature and morality. They prefer a different approach to social interaction: "When you ask someone to do something for you, it is best to give the real reasons, rather than giving reasons that might carry more weight"; "One should take action only when sure it is morally right"; and "There is no excuse for lying to someone."

To some extent, scores on the Mach Scale reflect socialization backgrounds. Higher scorers are frequently males, often come from urban backgrounds, are relatively young, and tend to be in people-oriented professions such as psychiatry, clinical psychology, and business administration. However, scores on the Mach Scale are unrelated to scores on the Self-Monitoring Scale discussed in Section III of this chapter.

B. *What Machiavellians Do*

Those individuals who endorse Machiavelli's world view are both willing and able to use Machiavellian tactics to outmaneuver, manipulate, and exploit the non-Machiavellians of the world. A fascinating way to witness the Machiavellian in operation is the "$10 bargaining game" (Christie & Geis, 1970). Three people, one with a high score on the Mach scale, one with a medium score, and one with a low score, together face the task of dividing $10 among themselves. Easy, you say? Not so, for there is a catch. The money must be divided between only *two* of the players. One unfortunate person gets squeezed out.

Not surprisingly, highly Machiavellian people rush in to exploit this situation and arrange coalitions for their own profit at the expense of those persons who are less Machiavellian. The latter individuals refrain from using manipulative tactics that might violate their ethical concerns about fighting over money. On the average, High Machs engineered deals that netted them $5.57, Middle Machs walked away with $3.14, and Low Machs contented themselves with $1.29 and the knowledge that they had practiced the morality they preached. (Had Machiavellianism been unrelated to success in this game, the average winnings for each player would, of course, have been $3.33.) The bargaining game clearly demonstrates the manipulative skill of the Machiavellian.

No doubt some of the Machiavellian's success at "con games" derives from a keen ability to accurately perceive and size up the manipulativeness of others. In fact, non-Machiavellians are noticeably inaccurate in their perceptions of others and tend to consistently (and trustingly) underestimate the amount of Machiavellianism that characterizes others (Geis & Levy, 1970).

Machiavellians not only are skilled in the control of others but also are able to successfully resist the attempts of others to influence their attitudes and change their behavior (Christie & Geis, 1970). These steely-eyed people can be counted on to violate conventional moral standards and cheat on tests, particularly when there is little risk of getting caught and the potential rewards from cheating seem substantial (Bogart, Geis, Levy, & Zimbardo, 1970; Exline, Thi-baut, Hickey, & Gumpert, 1970). Furthermore, when put in worklike situations in laboratory experiments, Machiavellians may go so far as to steal money from their supervisors, particularly if their supervisors happen to be trusting individuals who regard their workers as honest and do not make frequent inspections of their workers' performance on the job (Harrell & Hart-nagel, 1976). And, as if to add insult to injury, when accused of dishonesty, cheating Machiavellians will stare their accusers straight in the eye as they coolly deny their guilt (Christie & Geis, 1970). As you might expect, Machiavellians also derive considerable personal satisfaction from their manipulative escapades (see **Box 4-3** for an example of the Machiavellian at work).

C. *The Young Machiavellians*

Machiavellian orientations appear even in our junior citizens. In one study, **Bragin-sky** (1970) offered 10-year-olds 5¢ for each

---

Box 4-3. Beware the Machiavellian!

Given license to distract a subject taking a test, one highly Machiavellian tester went through the following gestures.

[The tester] rubs hands together in the stereotyped gesture of anticipation, bends over double, unties shoe, shakes foot, reties shoe; jingles contents of pocket noisily, pulls out Chapstick and applies it while staring absentmindedly at ceiling; whistles, slaps leg and straightens up noisily and abruptly in chair; taps pencil rhythmically on table; hums, reaches around divider and carefully knocks it over (this produces a loud crash and sends paper on table flying in all directions); after 10-second dead silence, apologizes profusely to [test-taker] for distracting him; erases vigorously on blank margin of [test-taker's] score sheet (divider board prevents [test-taker] from seeing that "examiner" is not erasing actual marks); comments with serious frown at one-way vision mirror, "I feel like I'm on TV, don't you?" (followed by grin at mirror as soon as [test-taker] returns his attention to test booklet); holds matchbook in both hands above divider board in full view of [test-taker] (pretending to ignore stopwatch), tears out matches one by one, dropping each into ashtray; dismantles a ballpoint pen behind divider board, uses spring to shoot it, parts flying, across the room; jumps from chair, dashes across room to retrieve pen parts saying, "Sorry, I'm a little nervous."

All this occurred in the 15 minutes or so necessary to administer ten embedded-figures problems! The innocent subject should indeed beware of the Machiavellian!

bitter-tasting cracker they could induce another child to eat. Children with high scores on a version of the Mach Scale that is modified for use with youngsters (called the "Kiddie Mach") accepted their mission with zeal. They readily lied about the taste of the crackers, offered bribes, and, with straight faces, falsely claimed that the experimenter wanted the child to eat the crackers. Their tactics paid off: the budding Machiavellians coaxed, bribed, or coerced their targets into eating an average of 6.46 bitter-tasting crackers. Low Mach children, by comparison, persuaded their targets to eat only 2.79 crackers. These young Machiavellians may have learned the tricks of their trade at home, because children who are skilled manipulators tend to have been raised by rather Machiavellian parents (Kraut & Price, 1976).

D. *Machiavellianism and Modern Society*

Fortunately for the trusting members of our society, Machiavellians are not always able to put their abilities to work. Their dispositions serve them best in those social situations that provide face-to-face interaction with their targets, some latitude for improvisation and the tailoring of their tactics to their targets and goals, and opportunities to use emotional arousal to distract their targets and make them more susceptible to control. One implication of these constraints on Machiavellians is that they should not be able to con their way to success on standardized, objective tests of ability and achievement (Singer, 1964). In fact, there is no relationship between Machiavellianism and intelligence-test scores. Moreover, Machiavellians probably would not rise to power in tightly structured bureaucratic organizations. However, they probably would succeed in loosely structured organizations.

Do Machiavellians collect more of society's rewards than non-Machiavellians? When Turner and Martinez (1977) examined a national sample of people in the work force, they found the following intriguing pattern of links between Machiavellianism

and social achievement. For men with college educations, Machiavellians had reached higher levels of occupational prestige and earned larger incomes than their non-Machiavellian counterparts; however, for men without college educations, it was the non-Machiavellians who had experienced the greatest occupational success. In general, the social attainments of Machiavellian women exceeded those of non-Machiavellian women, regardless of level of education.

In reflecting on years of research on Machiavellianism, Christie and Geis (1970) have suggested that modern society is becoming increasingly Machiavellian. One possible reason is "defensive Machiavellianism." It is easy to understand and appreciate why, in the face of frequent manipulative attempts, some non-Machiavellians might protectively adopt manipulative countermeasures to preserve their own independence and autonomy. It simply may be a case of the "best defense is often an offense." Indeed, the popularity in recent years of books such as Michael Korda's *Power: How to Get It, How to Use It* (1975) and Robert Ringer's *Looking Out for Number One* (1978) and *Winning through Intimidation* (1978) attests to the increasing concern with manipulativeness experienced by so many members of our society.

VIII. A Time to Reflect: Impression Management and Human Nature

Impression management appears to be a basic fact of social life. There are a variety of ways that people can and do influence the images of their "selves" that they project to other people. At times, these strategies and tactics are used in the quest for social approval, in the service of ingratiation, and even in attempts to manipulate and control other people. Yet, at other times, impression management is used to aid the processes of self-disclosure and self-revelation. Therefore, one cannot help but ask: Is impression management a good thing—something to be valued and prized? Or, is it a part of the seamier side of human nature?

A skilled wordsmith could give impression management either a bad image or a good one. First, the bad image: Impression management makes humans into social chameleons, forever putting on new faces to accommodate themselves to their current settings, forever being molded and shaped like Silly Putty creatures into the "right" person in the "right" place at the "right" time. Clearly, this image of impression management provides an unflattering view of human nature, because, from this perspective, impression management legitimizes deception, pretense, and hypocrisy. Now, the good image: Impression management gives us the flexibility and adaptiveness to quickly and consistently cope with the diversity of roles required of the individual in modern society. It allows us to choose with skill and grace the self-presentation and social behaviors appropriate to a wide variety of situations. This viewpoint certainly conveys a more comfortable image of human nature. According to this viewpoint, impression management "greases the wheels" of social interaction and interpersonal relations. (For a related discussion of the "goodness" and "badness" of impression management, see Box 4-4.)

Is one perspective more "correct" than the other? Of course not, for they both describe impression management. By carefully choosing shades of meaning, the skilled wordsmith can portray impression management either as a virtue or as a vice. It's the same concept—only the words have been changed to make it seem good or bad. Impression management in and of itself is neither good nor bad. The same practices can be applied to creating an honest image or a deceptive one, to influencing others for altruistic purposes or for exploitative ones. We may or may not approve of a specific goal that impression management serves, but certainly impression management is an integral part of everyday social interaction.

IX. Summary

Theories of the self are concerned with the nature of the self and the influence of the self on social interaction. Most theories of the self embody the views of William James. For him, the sense of self was defined broadly and included the material me, the social me, and the spiritual me. For James, the experience of selfhood was a fundamentally social experience that depended

---

Box 4-4. How Much Impression Management?

One approach to evaluating the "goodness" or "badness" of impression management is to consider the personal consequences of engaging in impression management. The question thus becomes "What are the effects of too little or too much impression management?" The writings of sociologist Erving Goffman provide some answers:

Too little perceptiveness, too little *savoir faire* [that is, too little impression management], too little pride and considerateness, and the person ceases to be someone who can be trusted to take a hint about himself or give a hint that will save others embarrassment. Such a person comes to be a real threat to society; there is nothing much that can be done with him. . . . Too much *savoir faire* [im-

pression management] or too much considerateness, and he becomes someone who is too socialized, who leaves the others with the feeling that they do not know how they really stand with him, nor what they should do to make an effective long term adjustment [Goffman, 1955, p. 227].

Thus, Goffman warns of the potential dangers both of too little and of too much impression management. For Goffman, deficits and excesses of impression management threaten the social order. Presumably, he would advise that one choose a middle-ground and engage in moderate amounts of impression management—just enough to ensure a smooth and pleasing flow of social interaction.

on interactions with other people. Modern researchers have expanded on James's viewpoint. The "Who am I?" technique identifies aspects of the self that are most meaningful to individuals. Individuals are most likely to attend to and to evaluate critically their selves when they are in a state of objective self-awareness. Moreover, those attributes that make people distinctive are most prominent in their spontaneous self-concepts. Finally, for some aspects of the self, knowledge of behavior and experience are organized into self-schemata.

Central to James's theory was the proposition that each person has not one but *many* selves and that these multiple selves are manifested in social interaction. That individuals might present different sides of themselves to different people in different situations has become the basic tenet of theories of impression management. *Impression management* refers to those strategies and techniques that individuals use to control the images and impressions that others form of them during social interaction. To successfully practice impression management, individuals must know which behaviors will create what impression in the minds of beholders. They must be skilled at taking the role of the other and be able to convincingly and naturally perform the verbal and nonverbal acts that will create the desired image. The images created by impression management may or may not be accurate reflections of a person's true nature.

Several factors determine the particular self-presentation that a person will choose to project in a social interaction. In general, people tailor their self-presentations to stress their similarities with what is expected of them, except when it would be personally uncomfortable to feel similar to an undesirable other. One important motivational determinant of self-presentation is the desire for compatibility and solidarity. Often people will bend over backward to maintain a public image that is personally and socially desirable. Although people are quite flexible in their self-presentations, they tend to feel that their various images are each accurate reflections of their true selves.

Some people are more skilled than others in the arts of impression management. These individuals, identified by their high scores on the Self-Monitoring Scale, are particularly likely to use their well-developed self-presentational skills for purposes of impression management in social relationships. High self-monitoring individuals also are highly skilled at detecting impression-management attempts by other people.

In some social contexts, people will reveal or disclose personal and intimate aspects of their behavior and feelings. Many psychologists believe that this self-disclosure is necessary for effective psychological adjustment. The frequency with which individuals disclose themselves, as well as the topics about which and the targets to whom they disclose themselves, are measured with the Self-Disclosure Questionnaire. Among the factors linked to self-disclosure are liking, intimacy, and social approval.

One important motivational determinant of impression management is social approval. When in need of social approval after failure, people will present favorable images to those who can offer such approval. People also often manufacture excuses, known as *self-handicapping strategies*, for any possible failures and "bask in the reflected glory" of successful others in attempts to maintain and enhance the esteem in which they are held. The quest for social approval can be seen in the domain of sex-role images and in the self-presentation of stigmatized individuals. Some people (identified by the Social Desirability Scale) are more dependent on approval than others.

Ingratiation refers to those activities designed to increase the attractiveness of an individual to another person. One analysis of ingratiation suggests that there are four tactics of ingratiation (other-enhancement, conformity, self-presentation, and rendering favors) and three goals of ingratiation (acquisition, protection, and signification). Research suggests that one's choice of ingratiation tactics depends on one's place within a status hierarchy and on the characteristics of the target of the ingratiation attempt.

Impression management can be used for purposes of social influence. Manipulativeness, or Machiavellianism, as a personal orientation is measured by the Mach Scale. Machiavellians outmaneuver non-Machiavellians in bargaining situations, are keen perceivers of the manipulative personality in others, and are able to resist the influence attempts of other people. Machiavellianism can be observed in children, too; Machiavellian children tend to have been raised by Machiavellian parents. Machiavellians are best able to put their abilities to work in situations that provide face-to-face interaction, latitude for improvisation, and opportunities to use distracting emotional arousal.

Glossary Terms

basking in
  reflected glory
impression
  management
ingratiation
Machiavellianism
need for approval

objective
  self-awareness
self
self-disclosure
self-handicapping
  strategies
self-monitoring

self-schema
theory of situated
  identities
spontaneous
  self-concept
stigma
"Who am I"
  technique

Language exists only when it is listened to as well as spoken. The hearer is an indispensable partner. JOHN DEWEY

DAVID FREDENTHAL. *THE PEOPLE.* THE UNIVERSITY OF ARIZONA MUSEUM OF ART, GIFT OF C. LEONARD PFEIFFER.

Those of us who keep our eyes open can read volumes into what we see going on around us. E. T. HALL

5

Interpersonal Communication

Interpreting the behavior of other people and defining our own self-concepts are fascinating processes. But do these activities really constitute social psychology? Isn't social psychology the study of actual *interaction* between people, rather than just an examination of the judgments and perceptions of individuals? Indeed, interaction is at the core of social psychology; many definitions of the field explicitly state that interaction between people is the substance of the field. In this chapter we will look at how people get together and interact—that is, how they communicate with one another.

Communication processes are basic to the study of most of the material in the remainder of this book. Expressions of friendship, affection, and love depend on the ability of people to communicate their feelings; so do expressions of anger, mistrust, and hatred. Relationships may begin to falter as people claim they can't communicate any more; international negotiations are beset with "communication breakdowns." Communication often seems like the most important concept in the understanding of human behavior. Yet just what does the word mean, and how is the communication process conceptualized?

I.   The Meaning of Communication

It has often been said that one can't *not* communicate. In other words, although a particular interaction may be filled with tension and stress, and verbal communication may actually cease, the communication process continues. Signs and messages continue to be transmitted between one person and the other, even if the goals of the interaction may have changed. This chapter focuses on the ways messages can be communicated; but first let's consider some basic definitions of the communication process itself.

The term *communication* is widely used and has been applied to situations ranging from intrapersonal information processing

on the one hand, to large-scale sociocultural systems, mass communication and influence, and communication networks on the other hand. We will focus primarily on a situation somewhere between these extremes: interpersonal communication—that is, the interactions that take place between two people. Such interactions are characterized by the close proximity of the interactants, the maximal number of communication channels that are available, and the immediacy of the feedback (Miller, 1978).

Communication theorists have developed a large number of models in an attempt to represent the communication process. For example, an early and influential model by Shannon and Weaver (1949) conceptualized the communication process as shown in Figure 5-1. According to this model, there are five necessary components of the communication process: source, transmitter, channel, receiver, and destination. In addition, Shannon and Weaver introduced the concept of *noise*, defined as any disturbance that interferes with transmission. Later this model was revised to include a concept of *feedback*, which attempted to deal with the fact that the receiver may not always receive the same message that the transmitter has sent.

Shannon and Weaver's model has had a tremendous influence on the study of communication, particularly in the field of computer sciences. Yet more recent communication theorists have had some problems with the model. Perhaps the most basic difficulty lies in the one-way assumptions of the model, as illustrated by the arrows in Figure 5-1. Can communication be accurately described as a one-way street? Recent theorists don't think so. For example, if Joan is talking with Elena, Joan is indeed transmitting a message verbally and may be sending a variety of nonverbal messages as well. Yet at the same time that Elena is interpreting those messages, attempting to understand what Joan is saying and meaning, Elena herself will probably be communicating as well. By her posture, her facial expression, and her general attentiveness, she will be sending messages to Joan at the same time as she is receiving them.

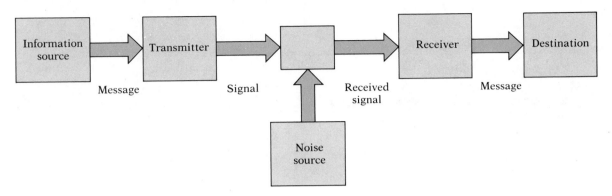

Recent work in communication theory, developing beyond the Shannon and Weaver model, has stressed at least four aspects of the communication process. First, communication is assumed to be a *shared social system*—a system in which two or more people are involved, both with their own expectations and intentions (Scott, 1977). Second, communication is an *ongoing dynamic system*. From this viewpoint, studying sequences of behavior is more important than studying isolated stimulus-and-response connections. Each action can, in fact, be seen simultaneously as a cause and as an effect (Fisher, 1978). Third, most recent communication theorists believe that verbal and nonverbal communications are part of the same system. Although it is sometimes useful to isolate specific communication channels for analysis (for example, speech, eye behavior, or physical distancing), it is important to remember that they naturally occur together and may parallel or contradict each other in important ways (Miller, 1978). Finally, many recent investigators have pointed out the importance of the *relational* component of communication. Rather than focusing exclusively on the content of communication, these investigators also examine how the exchange of messages may define a relationship, particularly in terms of the balance of power that exists between the two participants (Miller & Rogers, 1976; Parks, 1977; Rogers & Farace, 1975). In other words, the focus is not only on *what* is being said, but *how* it is being said.

Although recent models of the communication process seem more realistic than the earlier models, they have made the study of communication much more complicated. Instead of looking at isolated segments in an interchange or taking simple summary measures of the frequency of various behaviors, recent investigators have begun to conduct painstaking analyses of ongoing patterns of interaction, frequently breaking the analyses down into very fine-grained segments (Duncan & Fiske, 1977). An example of the relational analysis of conversation is shown in Box 5-1. By approaching the coding of communication in this manner, investigators are able to look more closely at the *meaning* of an interchange—at how the people are complementing or contradicting each other and how they may be establishing stable patterns or fighting for control. This analytical approach to communication is surely more complicated than just examining *what* is being said.

Because communication involves so many different elements, it is no wonder that so-called communication breakdowns and communication gaps occur so often. It is also not surprising that the study of communication is important to our understanding of human behavior and fundamental to social psychology. Having considered some of the basic issues in the conceptualization of communication, let us now turn to a consideration of the channels through which communication takes place—remembering,

Box 5-1. Relational Analysis.

Relational analysts believe that each individual message can be described by one of three control dimensions (Rogers & Farace, 1975). A "one-up" message represents an attempt to gain control in an exchange; a "one-down" message indicates that one is yielding control by either seeking or accepting the control of the other person; and a "one-across" message represents a movement toward neutralizing the control in the interaction. To see how these dimensions work, consider the following conversation between a husband and wife. The arrow after each statement indicates whether the statement is coded as one-up (↑), one-down (↓), or one-across (→).

Wife: We don't do anything together any more. ↑

Husband: What do you mean? ↓
Wife: Well, as a family we don't do very much. ↑
Husband: Oh, I don't know. →
Wife: Don't you feel I do the major portion of the disciplining of the children? ↓
Husband: The time we're together you don't. ↑
Wife: Well, just for the record, I have to disagree. ↑
Husband: Well, just for the record, you're wrong. ↑
Wife: Well, then, we completely disagree. ↑

From "Analysis of Relational Communication in Dyads: New Measurement Procedures," by L. E. Rogers and R. V. Farace, *Human Communication Research*, 1975, *1*(3), 222–239. Copyright © 1975 by the International Communication Association. Reprinted by permission of Transaction, Inc.

however, that none of the channels is ever used alone.

II. Channels of Communication

When the word *communication* is mentioned, many people think automatically of language. Speech has, after all, often been designated as a unique human ability, which distinguishes humans from other primates. Yet many other channels of communication serve us in exchanging messages with others and can be just as important: among these are facial expressions, eye contact, physical touch, body gestures, and even the distance that we put between ourselves and others. However, because speech is perhaps the most obvious of the communication channels, we shall begin there.

A. *Language and Paralanguage*

"When I use a word, it means just what I choose it to mean, neither more nor less," said Humpty-Dumpty in Lewis Carroll's classic *Through the Looking Glass.* Such confidence in the encoding of one's message is admirable but perhaps not realistic. Although the choice of words and the combination of these words into sentences represents our most controlled form of communication, the levels of meaning involved in such choices are numerous.

Linguists have developed a number of models to represent the language process. The elements in these models are numerous, and we can only deal briefly with their components. At the most basic level are *phonemes*—that is, sequences of elementary sounds in any language, such as a "p" sound or a "th" sound. At a slightly higher level are *morphemes*, which refer to the minimal meaningful forms in the language (Brown, 1965); in somewhat oversimplified terms, they are the basic word forms in a language. Dog, chase, and cat are examples of morphemes. At a higher level, the linguist deals with grammar, which combines a set of rules for the construction of words (morphological rules) and a set of rules for the construction of sentences (syntactic rules).

Although these concepts are basic to linguistic analysis, our own concern really lies at the level of *semantic analysis*—what is the meaning transmitted through our verbal language? To begin with, meaning depends in part on the cultural context. In other words, when speaking with people, we tend to assume we share a set of meanings—that is, we believe that the meaning we invest in words or sentences will be perceived in the same way by the listener. Such assumptions do not always hold true, however. For example, people from different cultures are more likely to misunderstand one another than people from the same culture, even though they all speak the same language.

Even within a single culture, however, a variety of meanings may be implied in very similar sentence structures. One recent approach to analyzing the various meanings is *grammatical case analysis:* the examination of the underlying features of various grammatical forms. Such analysis has shown, for example, that men and women tend to use different language structures in their speech. College men are more apt to use sentence cases that are neutral, objective, and describe the initiator of an action, whereas college women more frequently use cases referring to the experience and style of an action (Barron, 1971; Cashell, 1978). For instance, men might be more likely to talk about actions, such as "he hit the ball" or "she kicked the stone." Women, in contrast, are more likely to describe feelings, such as "he hates the professor" or "she feels sad."

At a simpler level, it is evident that we can convey an entire range of moods and emotions through our choice of words. The parent who tells a child "You make me furious" is obviously conveying a different message from one who says "You make me very happy." Thus a one- or two-word change in a sentence can entirely change its meaning. Another example of the importance of our choice of words is the recent development of *assertiveness training*, which stresses the choice of language that people use to achieve their goals. Assertiveness training differentiates between assertive, aggressive, and submissive forms of com-

munication, all of which may be aimed at accomplishing the same goal (see Box 5-2). Although nonverbal forms of communication may also differ, assertiveness training's primary emphasis has been on the verbal language chosen to express one's point.

Not all verbal communication is expressed in words and sentences; communication can also be made through vocal sounds and modifications that are not considered language but that nonetheless convey meaning. These sounds are called **paralanguage.** The study of paralanguage deals with *how* something is said and not *what* is said (Knapp, 1978). Examples of paralanguage include speech modifiers such as pitch, rhythm, intensity, and pauses, as well as vocalizations such as laughing, crying, yawning, groaning, sneezing, and snoring (Trager, 1958). Each of these paralanguage forms can convey meaning in a communication. For example, the person who yawns while you are talking obviously sends a very clear message of boredom; less obviously perhaps, the person who speeds up his or her speech while talking to you may be conveying either anxiety or excitement.

Recently, glowing claims have been made that objective analysis of voice patterns can detect if someone is telling the truth. Proponents of the spectrographic analysis of vocal stress patterns have argued for this method as a reliable lie detector. Although such claims appear to be overstated, it is true that we can transmit a considerable amount of information through paralinguistic cues. For example, a low voice pitch tends to convey pleasantness, boredom, or sadness, whereas a high pitch conveys anger, fear, surprise, or general activity. Moderate variations in pitch may communicate anger, boredom, or disgust, whereas more extreme voice variations indicate pleasantness, happiness, and surprise (Knapp, 1978; LaFrance & Mayo, 1978).

Paralinguistic cues also play an important role in managing communication. The rules of turn taking in a conversation, for example, are highly dependent on vocal cues, in many instances even more than on the actual content of the communication (Duncan & Fiske, 1977; Wiemann & Knapp,

Box 5-2. The Assertive Response.

In many interactions, we disagree with the statements or actions of another person. How do we respond? Recently, many advocates of assertiveness training have suggested that there are three possible responses to most situations: a passive response, an aggressive response, or an assertive response. The passive response is to do nothing—to inhibit one's own feelings for fear of offending the other person. An aggressive response, in contrast, directly attacks the other person. With the third possibility, the assertive response, a person can make his or her feelings known without attacking the other person.

As an example, pretend that you have spent several hours preparing an elaborate birthday dinner for a friend, and then the friend shows up an hour late, at which point the roast is burnt and the salad is soggy. What would you say? The passive response might be to say nothing—perhaps pouting as you ate or not engaging in conversation but refusing to deal with the problem directly. An aggressive response is easy to picture: pots and pans could go sailing across the room, and angry verbal attacks on your onetime friend could accompany them. A third strategy of response would be assertive: to state that you are annoyed but without verbally attacking your friend. These three different strategies would probably produce quite different results, and they illustrate the importance of both language and paralanguage in interaction.

Courtesy of Impact Publishers, Inc., San Luis Obispo, CA. Reprinted by permission of the publisher.

1975). For instance, if you want to keep talking even though you sense that the other person wants to take a turn, you may increase the volume and rate of your speech and decrease the frequency and duration of pauses (Knapp, 1978; Rochester, 1973). At the same time, the other person may persist in an attempt to gain entrance by using vocal "buffers" (like "Ah . . ." or "Er . . .") or by increasing the rapidity of responses, as if to say "Hurry up so I can talk."

Even though we know that words sometimes fail (see **Figure 5-2**), it may seem as if the tremendous variety of linguistic and paralinguistic forms of communication is sufficient to communicate virtually any thought or feeling. Yet beyond these verbal forms of communication, there is a wealth

PEANUTS

Dearest darling,

How I love you.

Words cannot tell how much I love you.

So forget it.

Figure 5-2. (© 1975 by United Feature Syndicate, Inc. Reprinted by permission.)

of nonverbal communication modes that sometimes support, sometimes contradict, and sometimes go beyond the verbal message.

B. *Eye Contact*

"Drink to Me Only with Thine Eyes," "the eyes of a woman in love," "seeing eye to eye" are all examples of expressions and song titles in our culture that testify to the importance of eyes as communicators. The pervasiveness of optic symbols in myth and religion also exemplifies the importance we assign to this mode of communication. Indeed, we perhaps depend more on the eye behavior of other people than any other nonverbal communication form, although, as we shall see later, this dependence sometimes can cause problems.

Investigators of the phenomena of *gaze* (looking directly at the face of another person) and *mutual gaze* (two people looking directly at each other)[1] show that they serve four major communication functions: regulating the flow of conversation, monitoring feedback, expressing emotions, and communicating the nature of the interpersonal relationship (Argyle, Ingham, Alkema, & McCallin, 1973; Kendon, 1967; Knapp, 1978).

[1] Gaze and mutual gaze are often used interchangeably with the term *eye contact* in general usage. However, many investigators prefer to use the former terms because actual eye contact is difficult to measure in the laboratory. Looking in the general direction of someone's face cannot be distinguished from direct eye-to-eye contact (von Cranach & Ellgring, 1973).

Regulating Conversation. Gaze serves an important role in initiating communication and in maintaining it once a conversation has begun. For example, if your professor is looking around the classroom for someone to supply the correct answer, you are likely to avoid eye contact if you failed to read the material the night before; however, you will probably return the professor's gaze if you know the correct answer and can discuss it. Similarly, you will probably ignore a gaze from a stranger at a bar if you don't want to be bothered, but you might return the look if you were interested in establishing a new relationship.

Observing unacquainted college students meet in a laboratory setting, Cary (1978) found that mutual gaze predicted the beginning of conversations. If students looked at one another upon meeting, they were more likely to engage in conversation. If the students looked at each other again, as the student who entered the room where the other student was sitting moved away from the door, conversation was even more likely.

Once a conversation has begun, gaze continues to play an important role. Consider these figures from a study by Argyle and Ingham (1972). During a typical two-person conversation, gaze occurs approximately 61% of the time, and mutual gaze accounts for 31% of the total interaction time. The average length of an individual gaze is about three seconds, whereas the average duration of mutual gaze is slightly more than one second. White adult speakers tend to gaze at the other person more often when they are listening (75% of the time) and less often when they are speaking (41%). Among Blacks, however, this pattern reverses, although the overall amount of gaze remains the same (LaFrance & Mayo, 1976; see Table 5-1).

T A B L E 5 - 1 / *Mean Other-Directed Gaze in Film Frames per 50 Frame Units*

	Conversational Role	
Subculture Group	Speaking	Listening
Black-Black Dyad		
First Black	31.05	19.57
Second Black	27.83	23.83
Black-White Dyad		
First Black	31.02	19.07
White	21.47	41.92

This table shows the results of a study by Marianne LaFrance and Clara Mayo (1976). When two Blacks were talking to each other, they both looked at each other more while they were talking rather than while they were listening. In contrast, when a Black and White were paired with each other, the White person gazed at the other person much more while listening (about 80% of the time), whereas the Black person looked at his or her partner primarily while talking. As a result, while the White was talking and the Black was listening, little eye contact occurred.

From "Racial Differences in Gaze Behavior during Conversations: Two Systematic Observational Studies," by M. LaFrance and C. Mayo, *Journal of Personality and Social Psychology*, 1976, *33*, 547–552. Copyright 1976 by the American Psychological Association. Reprinted by permission.

Ethnic differences in typical patterns of gaze can create substantial problems in communication. For example, LaFrance and Mayo observed that when Blacks and Whites converse, they often misinterpret the signals for taking turns in the conversation. "When the White listener . . . encountered a pause with sustained gaze from a Black speaker, the White was cued to speak, and both found themselves talking at once. In the obverse situation, by directing his gaze at the Black listener, the White speaker often did not succeed in yielding the floor and had to resort to direct verbal questioning" (LaFrance & Mayo, 1976, p. 551). Such differences can certainly create discomfort

in a conversation, and they may cause errors in judgment about the other person's intentions and motives as well.

Monitoring Feedback. Gaze also serves the function of conveying feedback to the speaker; it is interpreted as a sign of attention, interest, or attraction. In fact, people trying to convey a feeling of interest often deliberately gaze directly at the speaker. Also, persons with strong needs for approval engage in a higher proportion of direct gazing than do those less inclined to seek approval (Lefebvre, 1975). However, observers apparently are not oblivious to such behavior (Lefebvre, 1975); although they rated the high-gazer as warmer and friendlier, they also believed that the person was ingratiating in an attempt to be better liked (see Chapter 4).

Although the motives for gaze may sometimes be suspect, it is clear that we do tend to respond positively to eye contact. In fact, even the belief that the other person has gazed at us often seems to engender liking. In a demonstration of this effect, Kleinke and his colleagues (Kleinke, Bustos, Meeker, & Staneski, 1973) asked male and female subjects to engage in a ten-minute conversation. At the end of the period, the subjects were told either that their partner had gazed at them far more or far less than the average number of times, independent of the actual direct gaze frequency. When told that the gaze frequency was less than normal, subjects rated their partners as less attentive. Interestingly, the report of supposedly above-average rates of gazing produced different effects on men and women. When women thought their male partner had looked at them more than might be expected, their attraction to him did not increase. For males, the effect was the opposite: they were more attracted to the woman when they believed she had gazed at them more than the average number of times.

Expressing Emotions. The eyes also convey emotion. Although we will discuss this in greater detail later when we consider facial expressions, it is worth noting at this point that the eyes are one of three major areas of the face that convey emotion (the other two being the brows and forehead, and the lower face and mouth). People are often described as smiling with their eyes, as having an icy stare, or as having a glint in their eyes that indicates an emotional state. Paul Ekman and his colleagues have done extensive work in charting exactly what movements of the eyes and face indicate which emotions (Ekman, 1972; Ekman & Friesen, 1975). As just one example, the emotion of anger is generally conveyed by drawing the brows together, tensing the lower and upper eyelids, and staring hard with the eyes. Our dependence on the eyes as a sign of emotion is easily illustrated by the discomfort we feel when conversing with a person in opaque sunglasses, when "I can't tell what they're thinking" is a frequent complaint.

Defining Relationships. The fourth function of gaze, and perhaps the most relevant for social psychology, is the communication of the nature of interpersonal relationships. Like and dislike are clearly conveyed by the use of direct gaze; so are status relationships of dominance and submission.

We tend to look more at people we like than at people we dislike (Efran & Broughton, 1966; Exline & Winters, 1965). This gaze pattern has been observed in the laboratory with people who have interacted only briefly. It has also been observed with dating couples, whose interactions are obviously much more extensive. Couples who score higher on a measure of romantic love (see Chapter 6) spend more time looking at each other than those who report being less involved in a relationship (Rubin, 1970).

In addition to conveying positive feelings, extended gaze may also indicate the intensity of a relationship. Kimble and Forte (1978) found in an experiment that women who were asked to communicate a message to a male assistant looked at him more when they were asked to act as if they were strongly involved in the message and gazed at him less when they were instructed to be ambivalent about the message. This effect of intensity was true for both positive and negative messages and was in fact slightly stronger for the negative messages.

Another example of how gaze conveys intensity in a negative as well as a positive sense is supplied by Ellsworth and Carlsmith (1968). They arranged for an interviewer to evaluate college students either positively or negatively in the context of a laboratory experiment. If the interviewer engaged in a lot of eye contact with the student while making complimentary remarks, then the student rated the interviewer quite positively. In contrast, if the interviewer gazed at the student frequently while giving him or her a negative evaluation, then the student rated the interviewer lower than in a similar situation without eye contact. An even more dramatic demonstration of how prolonged direct gazing can convey intensity was shown by an experiment at traffic intersections. When drivers were stopped at an intersection, a stare from a person standing on the corner caused the drivers to depart much more rapidly than when no one was staring at them (Ellsworth, Carlsmith, & Henson, 1972).

Gaze is also an important indicator of status differences in a relationship. In a series of experiments, Ralph Exline and his colleagues found that when two people are of different status, the low-status person will spend more time looking at the high-status person than vice versa (Exline, 1971; Exline, Ellyson, & Long, 1975). In some of their studies status differences were manipulated by the experimenter; in other studies, the investigators looked at real-life status relationships, such as that between an ROTC officer and a lower-status ROTC cadet.

Although the higher-status person gazes directly at other people generally less than a lower-status person, Exline and his colleagues have observed a specific pattern in the gaze behavior of the high-status person. *Visual dominance behavior,* characteristic of people in high-status positions, involves a greater tendency to look at the other person when speaking than when listening. The effectiveness of this visual dominance pattern was demonstrated convincingly in a field study of ROTC officers at their training camp. Those leaders who showed a visual dominance pattern were given the highest leadership ratings, whereas those officers who engaged in a lower ratio of direct gaze while speaking to direct gaze while listening were rated less favorably on leadership abilities. From this study it is of course difficult to know whether individuals who engage in visual dominance behavior are more likely to be selected as leaders or whether occupying a leadership position encourages the development of visual dominance behavior. Nevertheless, the effectiveness of such behavior in communicating power and status is clear.

Henley (1977) has suggested that the status differences described above may help to explain the pervasive sex differences in eye behavior. In general, women engage in much more eye contact than do men (Duncan, 1969), consistent with the finding that the lower-status person looks directly at others more often than a higher-status person (in this case, the male). Women are also less likely to engage in staring and are more apt to avert the gaze of the other (Henley, 1977).

Overall, it is evident that eye contact or gaze provides substantial amounts of information in the communication process. The eyes are not the only channel, however; other nonverbal channels also convey important information.

C. *Facial Expressions*

The study of facial expressions has a long scientific history, dating from the classic work of Charles Darwin on *The Expression of Emotions in Man and Animals* (Darwin, 1872). Darwin's position was that there are evolutionary connections between animal and human facial expression and that certain facial expressions may serve to communicate the same message across species.

Investigators since Darwin have continued to be interested in the ways that facial expressions convey emotions. Most investigators have focused their attention on six primary emotions: surprise, fear, anger, disgust, happiness, and sadness (see Figure 5-3). An extensive research program by Paul Ekman and his colleagues has provided an exact description of the facial expressions involved in each of these emotional states

Figure 5-3. a. Edvard Munch, *The Shriek*, 1896. Lithograph, printed in black. $20^5/_8'' \times 15^{13}/_{16}''$. Collection, The Museum of Modern Art, New York, Matthew T. Mellon Fund. b. Pablo Picasso, *Weeping Head with Handkerchief.* Guernica Studies and "Postscripts," June 22, 1937. Oil on canvas, $21^5/_8'' \times 18^1/_8''$. On extended loan to The Museum of Modern Art, New York, from the estate of the artist. c. Henri Matisse, *Girl in a Ruffled Blouse* (The White Jabot), 1936, The Baltimore Museum of Art, The Cone Collection. d. Robert Henri, *Laughing Child*, 1907. Oil on canvas, $24'' \times 20''$. Collection of Whitney Museum of American Art, New York. Lawrence H. Bloedel bequest.

(Ekman, 1972; Ekman & Friesen, 1975; Ekman, Friesen, & Ellsworth, 1972). For example, in depicting surprise, an individual will typically raise the eyebrows and drop the jaw; there will be horizontal wrinkles across the forehead; the upper eyelid will be raised while the lower lid is drawn down, and the white of the eye will show above the iris and often below as well. Ekman terms this the **facial affect program:** the connection between an emotional experience and a particular pattern of facial-muscle activity. Other investigators also have shown, using a technique called *facial electromyography*, that subtle muscular activity in the face differentiates among various emotional states (Schwartz, Fair, Salt, Mandel, & Klerman, 1976).

Interestingly, both sides of the face may not show the same degree of emotional expression. Using the six emotional expressions that Ekman identified, Sackeim and his colleagues (1978) made composite pictures, either combining two left sides of a face or two right sides (see Figure 5-4). As shown in Figure 5-4, two different pictures resulted. With the exception of happiness, the left-side composites were always judged as more intense expressions than were the right-side composites. One interpretation of these results relates to the different functions of the right and left hemispheres of the brain. In this case, it is suggested that the right hemisphere (which controls the left side of the body and which also tends to be less involved in verbal skills) plays a greater role in emotional expression.

a.

b.

c.

d.

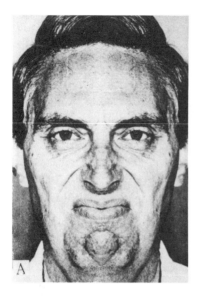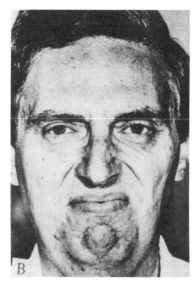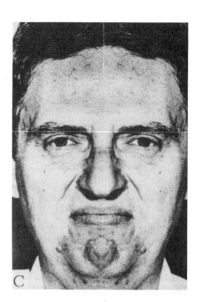

Figure 5-4. The center photograph above is the original picture of a man expressing disgust. The picture on the left was formed by taking only the right side of the original picture and reversing it to make a complete facial composite. Similarly, the picture on the right was formed by using only the left side of the original photograph. What differences can you detect between the two composite pictures? (From "Emotions are Expressed More Intensely on the Left Side of the Face," by H. A. Sackheim, R. C. Gur, and M. C. Saucy. In *Science*, 1978, *202*, 434–436. Copyright 1978 by the American Association for the Advancement of Science. Reprinted by permission.)

In support of the universality of emotional expression postulated by Darwin, Ekman and others have also shown that members of very different cultural groups show a consistency in labeling emotional expressions. Thus samples of people from Europe, South America, and preliterate societies in New Guinea all were able to correctly identify most of the primary emotions (Ekman, Friesen, & Ellsworth, 1972; Izard, 1969).

However, the fact that an emotion can be recognized by respondents from different cultures does not mean that the same emotion will always be displayed in similar circumstances. In some societies, for example, it is not considered appropriate to display emotional reactions in actual communication, even though such emotions might be experienced. Similarly, even within our own society, certain situations may call for restraint in the expression of an emotion. As an example, consider what your reaction would be to the sight and smell of the overflowing and odorous garbage can in a neighbor's kitchen. Although you might experience disgust, it is also quite likely that you would mask your emotional expression when talking with your neighbor. These qualifications of emotional expression are described by Ekman as **display rules** and can result from either personal habits, situational pressures, or cultural norms.

The recognition of display rules brings us closer to the central issue of this chapter, namely communication. Although the abstract expression of emotions is of interest in its own right, it is the ways in which we transmit these emotions to the other person that affect the communication process. This distinction between the expression of emotion and the communication of emotion is an important one. As an example of this distinction, consider a recent study by Kraut and Johnston (1979) on smiling behavior. Exploring a wide range of natural settings, including bowling alleys, hockey games, and public walkways, these investigators observed the frequency of smiling and attempted to relate these occasions to simultaneously occurring events. Their results showed that people were most likely to smile when talking to other people; in contrast, when people experienced positive emotional events alone, they were far less likely to smile. Figure 5-5 shows the results of two of these studies, which dealt with reactions to scores at a bowling alley and discussions of weather conditions in a public walkway.

The results of the study by Kraut and Johnston suggest that a major function of the smile is to *communicate* happiness to other persons. In other words, facial expressions such as a smile may be less an automatic response to a particular stimulus than a conscious choice to affect the communicated message. This idea of course allows for the possibility that a smile may be used to mask some other emotion that is being experienced, and, as we shall see later, such masking attempts are common.

D. *Body Movements and Gestures*

Other parts of the body get involved in the communication process as well. Movements of the head, the hands, the legs, and feet and torso can all serve to communicate messages. To impose some order on the multitude of possible body movements, Ray Birdwhistell proposed a model called **kinesics**, which is intended to parallel the previously mentioned model for verbal communication called linguistics (Birdwhistell, 1970). Continuing the linguistics-kinesics analogy, Birdwhistell proposed the terms *kinemes* and *kinemorphs* to represent basic units of body movement (these terms are similar in meaning to the phonemes and morphemes that we discussed earlier). On the basis of extensive observations conducted primarily in the United States, Birdwhistell proposed that there are approximately 50 to 60 basic kinemes—that is, classes of body movements that form the core of nonverbal body language. For example, he suggests there are four basic kinemes of the nose area: a wrinkled nose, compressed nostrils, both nostrils flared, and a single nostril flared. Continuing the parallel to linguistics, Birdwhistell suggests that kinemes, like phonemes, rarely occur in isolation. Instead, several basic units may occur simultaneously, constituting a kinemorph. Although Birdwhistell's approach to classifying body movements is ambitious, it is not without criticism. In particular, the usefulness of the kinesics-linguistics analogy has been questioned (Dittman, 1971). A major point of argument is whether kinesics is a separate language in itself or whether kinemes depend in large part on their verbal context. Nonetheless, whether the analogy holds or not, Birdwhistell's work has

		Score: Good	Score: Not Good	
Social Interaction	Yes	42%	28%	31%
	No	4%	3%	3%
		46%	31%	
	N	(26)	(90)	(116)

(a)

		Weather: Good	Weather: Bad	Total
Social Interaction	Yes	61% (61)	57% (60)	59% (121)
	No	12% (264)	5% (288)	8% (552)
	Total	21% (325)	14% (348)	

(b)

Figure 5-5. (a) Percentage of bowlers smiling after a good or other score, when the bowlers were facing the pins or facing their teammates; (b) social interaction, the weather, and percentage of pedestrians smiling.

been important in categorizing the wide variety of body movements that are displayed.

Nonverbal behaviors that are directly linked with spoken language have been termed **illustrators** (Ekman & Friesen, 1972). For example, if you are asked to direct someone to the library, it is likely that you will gesture as well as use verbal explanations. Other research has shown how speech and movement behavior are tightly bound together; if a person is unable to use one channel (gestures, for example, when talking on the telephone), the other channel may be used more extensively (Graham & Heywood, 1975; Condon & Ogston, 1966).

Not all body gestures accompany verbal language, however. On some occasions, a gesture may substitute for a spoken phrase. Such gestures, termed **emblems,** are nonverbal acts that are clearly understood by the majority of the members of a culture (Johnson, Ekman, & Friesen, 1975). For example, the wave of a hand in greeting is widely recognized in our society. Other emblems may be shared by smaller groups, such as the two-fingered horns sign of Texas football fans or the occasionally obscene finger gestures of American teenagers. As you might suspect, the meaning conveyed by the same emblem across cultures can differ dramatically. A similar gesture may convey two quite different meanings, whereas the same meaning may be translated into different gestures. Because emblems typically replace rather than accompany other forms of communication, these disparities in meaning can cause much confusion among members of different cultures.

So far we have discussed body language as an accompaniment or as a substitute for specific verbal phrases. In addition to this function, body movements and gestures can also indicate the nature of the relationship between two people in a conversation. For example, status differences in a relationship are often communicated by body position (see Figure 5-6). The higher-status person in a relationship will generally look more relaxed: arms and legs in asymmetrical positions and a backward lean to the body. In

contrast, the lower-status person is more likely to maintain a fairly rigid position, with body upright, feet together and flat on the floor, and arms close to the body (Mehrabian, 1969b, 1972; Scheflen, 1972). Once again, these status differences in nonverbal behavior frequently parallel observed sex differences in body language (Henley, 1977): men are far more apt to adopt an open stance, whereas women more frequently show the closed positions typical of a lower-status person.

Attraction can also be conveyed through body movements and gestures. People who like each other are more likely to lean forward with their bodies, to have a direct body orientation to the other person, and to show a more relaxed body position (Mehrabian, 1969a, 1972). These signs are clearly interpreted, and in turn may create feelings of liking or disliking for the other person (Clore, Wiggins, & Itkin, 1975).

E. *Touch*

Perhaps one of the most basic means of communication is touch. Long before language develops and before body illustrators and emblems have been learned, people communicate through tactile contact. The parent and child, for example, depend on touch for much of their early communication. As children grow older, however, the frequency of touch decreases (Willis & Hoffman, 1975), and among adults in many Western societies, touching is regarded with considerable ambivalence (Montagu, 1971).

Early investigators of touch behavior stressed the positive aspects of physical contact, either as an indication of affiliation and warmth (Mehrabian, 1972) or as an index of sexual intent (Jourard & Rubin, 1968; Morris, 1971). Yet one type of physical contact is not always interpreted the same way. Nguyen, Heslin, and Nguyen (1975), for example, have found that men and women perceive some kinds of touching quite differently. Women make a distinction between forms of touching that indicate warmth and friendship and those that indicate sexual desire; for men, in contrast, these two forms of touching are interchangeable in meaning.

Sex differences in response to touch have been observed frequently, even when the touch itself is of very brief duration. For example, in an experimental study in the Purdue University library, students who checked out books were briefly touched or not touched on the hand by the library clerk (Fisher, Rytting, & Heslin, 1976). The female students who were touched briefly responded positively: they liked the clerk and even the library more than those who had not been touched. Among males, however, similar increases in liking did not occur. An even more striking demonstration of sex differences in reaction to touch is provided by Whitcher and Fisher (1979). Male and female patients in an Eastern U.S. university hospital were either touched or not touched during a preoperative teaching interaction with the nurse. The touches themselves were relatively brief and professional,

consisting of a short touch on the patient's hand and an approximately one-minute contact on the patient's arm. The dependent measures in this study included both questionnaire responses and actual physiological measures taken immediately after surgery. The results showed striking evidence for the positive effects of touch on women. Female patients who had been touched reported less fear and anxiety on the questionnaire measures and showed lower blood pressure readings after surgery. For the male patients, in contrast, the brief touch by the nurse produced negative effects; these men showed less positive reactions than a no-touch control group and had increased blood pressure readings.

The striking sex differences in reactions to touching as a form of communication suggest that more than one message may be conveyed by touch. Indeed, recent work on

Figure 5-6. Body position and status. Can you make an estimate of the relative status of these two men by looking at their body positions?

What other cues would you use to judge status differences? (© Charles Harbutt/Magnum Photos, Inc.)

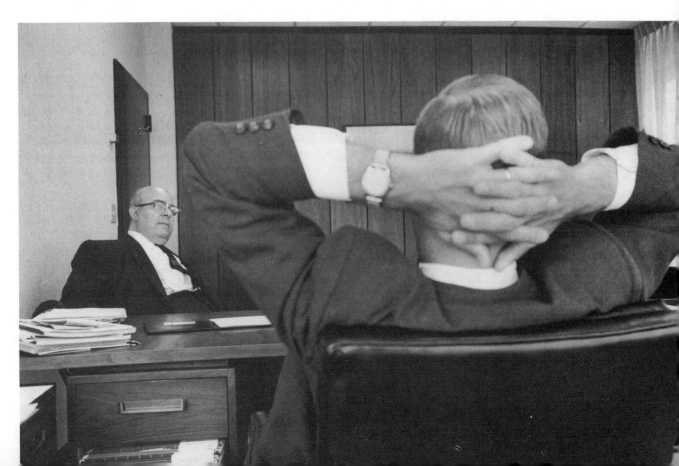

touch has shifted in focus from the positive and affiliative message of touch to the status concerns that may be conveyed. Recalling our earlier discussion of gaze and body movements, we should not be surprised to learn that touch can also serve to define status. Observational studies have found that the higher-status person is more likely to initiate touch, whereas the lower-status person is more apt to be touched (Henley, 1977). Similarly, as observers, we are more apt to attribute characteristics of dominance and high status to the person who initiates a touch and qualities of submissiveness and low status to the person who receives the touch (Major & Heslin, 1978).

Once again, we also find that male–female differences in touching parallel the high–low status differences in touch behavior (Henley, 1977). Such sex differences in reactions to touching as they relate to perceived status may help to account for the divergent findings of Whitcher and Fisher (1979), which we discussed earlier. In the case of the men in the hospital, the touch may have communicated to them that their status was low, and it may have increased the feelings of dependency that the hospital context engenders. Thus their typical previous high-status position may have been threatened, whereas for women the offered touch may have been a nonthreatening and possibly supportive gesture.

The divergent reactions of males and females to physical touch underline the difficulty inherent in the communication process. Whereas the original transmitter (to use Shannon and Weaver's terminology) may intend one kind of message, the decoding process of the receiver may result in a quite different communication. Communication between people is filled with the possibilities of misunderstanding and confusion.

F. *Interpersonal Distance*

The forms of communication that we have discussed so far have all involved some part of the body as a way of transmitting messages. At this point we shall turn to something more abstract—the distance between bodies as a mode of communication

(see **Figure 5-7**). Anthropologist Edward Hall (1959, 1963, 1966) is probably the individual most responsible for pointing out how the *interpersonal distance* that is established between two or more people can communicate a variety of messages. Based on extensive observations, primarily within the United States, Hall has proposed a categorization of *distance zones* to describe the patterns typically found in different types of interactions. The four major zones are termed *intimate, personal, social,* and *public. Intimate zones* range in distance from actual physical contact to about 18 inches (approximately .5 meter). In the intimate zone

The presence of the other person is unmistakable . . . because of the greatly stepped-up sensory inputs. Sight (often distorted), olfaction, heat from the other person's body, sound, smell, and the feel of the breath all combine to signal unmistakable involvement with another body [Hall, 1966, p. 116].

This zone generally indicates a high level of intimacy between the participants, although there are exceptions, such as when strangers are crowded together on an elevator. In the latter instance, the distance is uncomfortable because it conflicts with the feelings that the occupants may have for the total strangers against whom they are crushed.

The *personal distance zone* extends from 1½ to 4 feet (about .5 to 1.25 meters) and typifies the distance that we usually maintain between ourselves and friends (at the closer end) and ourselves and acquaintances in everyday conversations, for example (at the further end).

Greater distances, ranging from 4 to 12 feet (1.25 to 3.5 meters), represent the *social distance zone* and are typically used for business interactions or very casual social interactions. For example, your interactions with a clerk at the grocery store probably fall into this category, as well as the typical professor/student interaction.

Finally Hall describes a *public distance zone* where interpersonal distance ranges from 12 to 25 feet (about 3.5 to 7.5 meters). Interactions at these distances are typically quite formal, such as a public address or an interaction with a judge or celebrity.

Figure 5-7. Interpersonal distance. What distance zone is shown in the scene above? What inferences could you draw about this interaction? (© Abigail Heyman/Magnum Photos, Inc.)

As indicated by Hall's categorization, decreasing interpersonal distance generally indicates increasing immediacy of the relationship (Mehrabian, 1972). In other words, greater liking is usually communicated by smaller interpersonal distance. Considerable empirical support has been collected to support this relationship. For example, the optimal distance between friends is less than the distance between two interacting strangers (Sundstrom & Altman, 1976). Also, both college students and junior high school students have been observed to sit closer to people that they like (Byrne, Ervin, & Lamberth, 1970; Aiello & Cooper, 1972). On the reverse side of the coin, people will report being uncomfortable when the distance between them and others is greater than usual during a conversation (DeRisi & Aiello, 1978).

The high degree of correlation between the degree of intimacy in our interactions and the interpersonal distances we keep during them is the basis for the communicative information of interpersonal distance. Thus if you want to communicate liking for another person, you will probably decrease the distance between yourself and the other person. In a demonstration of this behavior, Rosenfeld (1965) asked female students to talk with another student (actually a confederate of the experimenter) with the goal of either appearing friendly or of avoiding the appearance of friendliness. Approval-seeking women placed their chairs an average of 4.75 feet from the confederate, whereas those students seeking to avoid affiliation placed their chairs an average of 7.34 feet away.

As is true for many of the nonverbal forms of communication, interpersonal distance can convey status messages as well as affiliative messages. In general, peers stand closer together than do people who are of unequal status (Mehrabian, 1969b). For example, Lott and Sommer (1967) observed seating patterns of students of different academic rank and found that seniors sat closer to other seniors than to either first-year students or to professors. In a field study, Dean, Willis, and Hewitt (1975) observed conversations between military personnel. Navy men maintained a greater distance when they initiated a conversation with a superior than when they began a conversation with a peer, and this difference grew larger as the difference in ranks increased. For the superiors, however, such differences did not exist, indicating the freedom of the higher-status person to define the boundaries of the conversation.

Once again, we find that a nonverbal form of communication can convey a variety of messages. Because of the many possibilities involved in all forms of communication, it is necessary to maintain a broad perspective when interpreting communicative behavior. In addition to considering the mode of communication, we must also examine the setting and the overall pattern of communicated messages.

III. Combining the Channels

As this chapter has shown, communication is a multichanneled phenomenon. In only the most unusual cases do we rely on just one form of communication; most often messages are transmitted back and forth through a variety of verbal and nonverbal modes. But just how do these channels combine? And are the various channels always used synchronously? Let's see how the various pieces of the communication puzzle fit together.

A. *Basic Dimensions of Communication*

Although the ways in which we communicate with other people may seem to have endless variety, investigators have discovered that there are three major dimensions of communicative behavior. Osgood, Suci, and Tannenbaum (1957), dealing mainly with verbal material, defined these three dimensions as general *evaluation, so-*

cial control, and *activity.* Earlier investigators of facial movements and the expression of emotion defined three similar dimensions: pleasantness–unpleasantness, sleep–tension, and attention–rejection (Schlosberg, 1954). More recently, Mehrabian (1969a) analyzed a variety of nonverbal behaviors and, through a statistical technique known as factor analysis, described three similar factors. As shown in Table 5-2, Mehrabian relates evaluation or liking to a series of intimacy cues, social control or status to relaxation cues, and responsiveness to activity cues.

Thus, according to Mehrabian, when you are attracted to someone, you are most likely to communicate this feeling through a variety of intimacy cues—by touching, by decreasing the distance between yourself and the other person, by leaning forward and by maintaining eye contact. Dislike would be communicated in just the opposite way—by refraining from physical contact, increasing the interpersonal distance, leaning away and avoiding eye contact. In a similar manner, status relationships can be communicated by a combination of relaxation cues. In general, Mehrabian proposes that the greater the communicator's status relative to the addressee, the more the communicator will be relaxed (Mehrabian, 1969a). Finally, Mehrabian suggests that the responsiveness of one person to the other is primarily communicated by activity cues, including amount of facial activity and rate of speech.

Although intimacy, status, and responsiveness *all* seem to be important aspects of the communication process, many investigators have focused on the intimacy factor in interpersonal communication and have developed models to explain how people may combine different modes of communication at different levels of intimacy. Two of these are the equilibrium model and the arousal model.

B. *Equilibrium Model of Intimacy*

We have seen that there are a variety of cues that indicate the level of intimacy in a relationship, such as amount of eye contact and distance between the participants.

These cues may serve as an index of the intimacy level; they may also be used to regulate intimacy. To explain how these various cues combine to produce the desired level of intimacy in a social encounter, Argyle and Dean (1965) have proposed an *equilibrium model.* According to these authors, every interpersonal encounter engenders both approach and avoidance pressures; a person may seek warmth, love, or security, but, at the same time, he or she may also fear rejection and seek to avoid certain contacts with the other person. Depending on the situation, an appropriate balance, or state of equilibrium, will be established through regulation of the nonverbal channels of communication. If this equilibrium is disturbed, as, for example, by one person's press for more intimacy than the other person wants, Argyle and Dean suggest that the latter individual will alter some of the nonverbal channels to restore the equilibrium. For instance, during a casual conversation with an acquaintance, the other person sits much closer to you than seems appropriate. Such an imbalance would probably lead you to alter your own nonverbal communication—either by increasing the distance between the two of you or perhaps by avoiding eye contact,

---

T A B L E 5 - 2 / *Nonverbal Cues of Liking, Status, and Activity*

Immediacy cues (indicate like or dislike for the other person)
    Touching (as in holding hands or touching shoulders)
    Distance (physical distance separating the two people)
    Forward lean
    Eye contact
    Orientation (facing directly or angled away from the other person)

Relaxation cues (indicate status differences between two persons)
    Arm position asymmetry (for example, hands clasped or arms folded symmetrically)
    Sideways lean
    Leg position asymmetry (both feet flat on the floor or legs crossed)
    Hand relaxation
    Neck relaxation
    Reclining angle

Activity cues (indicate responsiveness to the other person)
    Movements
        Trunk-swivel movements
        Rocking movements
        Head-nodding movements
        Gesticulation
        Self-manipulation
        Leg movements
        Foot movement
    Facial expressions
        Facial pleasantness
        Facial activity
    Verbalization
        Communication length
        Speech rate
        Halting quality of speech
        Speech-error rate
        Speech volume
        Intonation

Derived from "Some Referents and Measures of Nonverbal Behavior," by A. Mehrabian, *Behavioral Research Methods and Instrumentation*, 1969, *1*, 203–207. Used by permission.

orienting your body away from the person, or making facial signs that indicate discomfort. Thus the basic assumption of the model is that loss of equilibrium in one channel of communication can be compensated for by alterations in other channels—in other words, the model proposes a set of compensatory functions.

To test this model, investigators have manipulated one of the communication channels and looked at the effects of these manipulations on another channel. For example, investigators may vary the distance between persons and then assess the amount of eye contact or gaze between participants. Considerable support for the equilibrium model has been found using this method (Patterson, 1973). For example, it was found that, as people interact at closer distances, the amount of eye contact tends to decrease (Argyle & Dean, 1965; Goldberg, Kiesler, & Collins, 1969; Russo, 1975). In similar fashion, body orientation becomes less direct as interpersonal distance decreases (Aiello & Jones, 1971; Patterson, Mullens, & Romano, 1971; Pellegrini & Empey, 1970). Still other research has shown that, as an interviewer's questions become increasingly personal, the inter-

viewee will initiate less eye contact with the interviewer (Carr & Dabbs, 1974; Schulz & Barefoot, 1974).

Not all research supports the equilibrium model, however. For example, males and females may react differently to disturbances of equilibrium in a relationship (Aiello, 1972, 1977a, b). Although the model generally holds true for men—in that they increase their gaze behavior as the distance between them and another person increases—women show a different pattern. When the distance between participants is greater than 6 to 8 feet, women no longer increase their gaze behavior, as shown in Figure 5-8. This figure also shows that women engage in more eye contact at short distances than do men, suggesting that the sexes have different equilibrium points for intimacy in relationships.

Thus, although the Argyle and Dean equilibrium model is helpful in explaining how nonverbal communication cues establish intimacy levels in a relationship, it must be modified to allow for individual differences in the point of equilibrium. Cultural differences may also affect the way in which equilibrium is established, as described in Box 5-3.

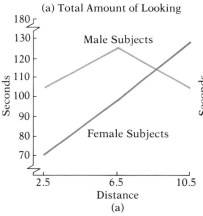
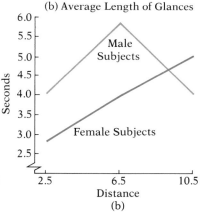

Figure 5-8. Sex differences in gaze and distance. Measured either by total amount of looking (a) or by the average length of glances (b), men and women show different gaze patterns as a function of distance. (From "A Further Look at Equilibrium Theory: Visual Interaction As a Function of Interpersonal Distance," by J. R. Aiello, *Environmental Psychology and Nonverbal Behavior*, 1977, *1*, 122–140. Copyright 1977 by Human Sciences Press: Reprinted by permission.)

Box 5-3. Bilingualism and Nonverbal Behavior.

Many people have observed that people from different cultures show different nonverbal behaviors. But what of the person who is bilingual? In a fascinating demonstration of the close connection between verbal and nonverbal channels of communication, Grujic and Libby (1978) studied French Canadian bilinguals who were equally proficient in both French and English. In their study, Grujic and Libby varied both the spoken language in a 30-minute conversation and the ethnic identification of the partner. Thus, in some cases, the subject would speak French to a person identified as English; in other cases, the subject would speak English to a person identified as English, and so on. The results showed that the ethnic identification of the partner didn't matter, but the language of the conversation did. When French was spoken, sub-jects sat closer to their partner at the beginning of the conversation, moved closer during the course of the conversation, gestured more (primarily with the left hand, again suggesting right-hemisphere dominance), and interacted for a longer period of time.

In terms of the compensation principle, this study suggests that different ways of establishing intimacy are used in English versus French. When speaking English, subjects maintained intimacy by looking at the partner more but smiling less. When speaking French, just the reverse occurred: there was more smiling but less gaze. Thus, in both cases, some intimacy was established—but the language of the conversation had strong effects on the nonverbal channels that were used.

The equilibrium model confronts an additional problem when one considers that compensation may not be the only response to a change in equilibrium (Breed, 1972). Surely there are occasions when an increase by one person in the level of intimacy is reciprocated rather than avoided. For example, when you are with someone you like in a romantic setting, wouldn't you be more apt to respond positively to increases in intimacy rather than to try to reduce the intimacy level? The following model takes this possibility into account.

C. *Arousal Model of Intimacy*

Miles Patterson (1976) has proposed a model of intimacy behavior that allows for either reciprocal or compensatory reactions to a change in the equilibrium level (see Figure 5-9). Basically, his model relies on the concept of *arousal*. Patterson suggests that small changes in the intimacy level will probably not be noticed and hence no behavior changes will occur. At some thresh-old point, however, a sufficient change in the intimacy level of the interaction will be noticed and some behavioral adjustment will be necessary.

What adjustment will be made, however, depends on how the person labels the state of arousal. Following a model developed by Schachter (1964), Patterson assumes that a given state of arousal can be labeled either positive or negative depending on the circumstances. Thus, if we return to the romantic setting suggested earlier, physical contact or intensified gazes initiated by your lover would probably be a positive experience and would lead you to reciprocate the behavior. In contrast, the same behavioral display by a stranger on a park bench would most likely be labeled negatively and would in turn lead to compensatory adjustments on your part—turning your body away, avoiding the gaze, or getting up and leaving. Thus the arousal model of intimacy incorporates the equilibrium principles proposed by Argyle and Dean (1965) but adds another dimension as

B's Reaction

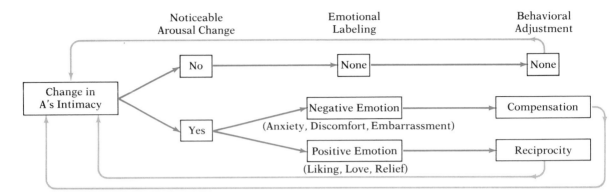

Figure 5-9. Diagram of the arousal model of interpersonal intimacy. (From "An Arousal Model of Interpersonal Intimacy," by M. L. Patterson, *Psychological Review*, 1976, 83[3], 235–245. Copyright 1976 by the American Psychological Association. Reprinted by permission of the author and publisher.)

well. By this model, we can predict that the same type of change in the behavior of one person may lead to two quite different reactions in the other person, depending on a variety of situational factors. To increase our power to predict reactions, however, we will need to develop a more specific means of defining situations in terms of their positive or negative properties. Without such specification, the arousal model will be limited to after-the-fact explanations rather than predictions.

D. *The Relative Importance of Channels*

Thus far we have assumed, to paraphrase Gertrude Stein, that a channel is a channel is a channel. In other words, we have acted as if all of the channels of communication are equally important. But is that assumption true? What if communication cues are not consistent with one another? Which ones do we tend to rely on the most?

Mehrabian and his colleagues (Mehrabian & Weiner, 1967; Mehrabian & Ferris, 1967) conducted a set of experiments in which vocal, facial, and verbal cues were combined in inconsistent fashion. Thus positive words might be spoken in negative tones, or positive facial expressions might accompany a negative message. On the basis of these experiments, the investigators derived the following formula:

Perceived attitude =
.07 (verbal) + .38 (vocal) + .55 (facial)

This formula suggests that people use facial cues the most to interpret communications and verbal cues the least.

Although the numbers in the above formula may apply only in the specific situation used by Mehrabian and his colleagues, other investigators have also found that visual cues have far more influence than auditory cues on the interpretation of communication. In a series of experiments, Rosenthal and his colleagues paired various combinations of auditory and visual messages and examined their effects in the communication of dominance and liking (DePaulo, Rosenthal, Eisenstat, Rogers, & Finkelstein, 1978). Once again, visual cues proved to be more influential than vocal cues. In this study, subjects' preference for visual information was most noticeable when facial expressions were paired with auditory cues; body gestures did not exert as strong an effect as did the facial cues. These investigators also found that visual cues are more significant when people are interpreting liking messages and less so when the messages concern status or dominance. Finally, women showed a greater reliance on visual messages than did men.

There are instances, however, when the visual message may be discarded in favor of the spoken message. Consider a series of studies by Daphne Bugental and her colleagues (Bugental, Kaswan, & Love, 1970; Bugental, Love, & Gianetto, 1971). These investigators asked children to interpret situations in which either a woman or a man was conveying one message with the face while expressing a contradictory verbal message. In judging women, the children tended to believe a negative verbal message and ignore an accompanying smile. With men, in contrast, the children relied more on the facial expression than on the verbal message. Why would the children's reactions to men and women be different? To explore this question, Bugental and her colleagues observed the behavior of fathers and mothers with their children. They found that mothers tended to be less consistent in combining channels of communication—they were just as likely to smile when vocalizing negative statements as when saying positive things. Fathers, on the other hand, were more consistent, smiling when they said positive things and not smiling when they said negative things. As a result, children may learn to disregard the facial channels of their mothers' communication, because it is a less reliable indicator of meaning, and pay more attention to their fathers' facial messages.

Work on the relative significance of various communication channels has only begun. The implications of this work are fascinating, however, and testify to the considerable complexity of human communication.

IV. Some Special Cases of Communication

We obviously spend a great deal of our time communicating with other people. Although it is clearly impossible to consider all of the situations in which interpersonal communication takes place, let's look at a few specific cases of the communication process.

A. *Initial Encounters*

When we meet someone for the first time, the initial encounter is often accompanied by some uncertainty. Not knowing the other person, we can't predict how he or she will behave; we are also unfamiliar with the style of speech, the nonverbal behaviors, and the beliefs, attitudes, and values of that stranger. Communication theorists have suggested that one of the functions of communication in initial encounters is to reduce this level of uncertainty (Berger & Calabrese, 1975). As an interaction develops, this uncertainty may decrease and our communication patterns may change as well. For example, Lalljee and Cook (1973) studied in detail the first nine minutes of conversation between previously unacquainted college students and found that speech patterns shifted considerably in the course of that short interchange. In the earliest stages of the interaction, speech rate was considerably less than in later stages of the interaction. Also, in the initial stages of the interaction, students were more likely to fill pauses in the conversation with "ers," "ahs," and "ums," reflecting the uncertainty of the encounter. It has also been suggested that nonverbal behaviors increase in frequency as communication progresses (Berger & Calabrese, 1975).

Other investigators have focused directly on the structure of conversation in an attempt to discover how communication develops. Questions appear to be an important device whereby we begin to structure an interchange and develop a process of turn-taking. And such turn-taking in itself is important in the development of communication, contributing to the ease or discomfort with which two people interact (Knapp, 1978; La France & Mayo, 1978). When participants in a conversation are not allowed to use questions, considerable disruption can occur (Kent, Davis, & Shapiro, 1978). The length of each participant's turn tends to increase, because the main mechanism for turning over the floor is absent. Interestingly, a ban on questions disrupts nonverbal behavior as well, as interactants in this situation gaze less at each other than do people who are conversing in more normal circumstances. Finally, conversations in which questions are not allowed are much less structured, and when people are asked to reconstruct the dialogues from these conversations, given only a list of the individual sentences out of order, they find it difficult.

The sex of the participants in initial encounters has considerable influence on the nature of the developing communication. Two women, for example, will show much more immediacy in their initial encounters than will two men: they orient their bodies more directly toward the other person, they talk more, gesture more, and gaze more at the other person (Ickes, 1978). When men and women interact, the situation becomes somewhat more complex. Nonverbal expressions of stereotypical masculinity and femininity (Lippa, 1978b) become an additional component of the situation. Somewhat surprisingly, it appears that the male and female who are most traditionally sex-typed (a male who is highly masculine in his personality characteristics and a female who is highly feminine) have the most difficulty in initial encounters (Ickes & Barnes, 1978). Compared to male–female dyads who are less traditionally sex-typed, these couples talk less, gesture less, and look at each other less frequently. They also smile less often and laugh less frequently than do less sex-typed couples during the course of an informal five-minute encounter. Not surprisingly, these couples report being less attracted to each other at the end of the brief encounter. These dramatic differences in communication patterns in a short five-minute interchange certainly illustrate the variety that exists in initial encounters.

We do not always approach initial encounters in total ignorance, however. On some occasions, we may have advance information about the person with whom we are going to interact. Does such advance information affect the communication pattern? Research suggests that it does indeed (Snyder, Tanke, & Berscheid, 1977; Snyder & Swann, 1978). In one study, male students engaged in a ten-minute telephone conversation with a female student whom they believed to be either physically attractive or unattractive. Analysis of these conversations showed that males who believed they were interacting with an attractive female were friendlier, more outgoing, and sociable, and they took the initiative in the conversation more often than did men who believed that they were talking to a less attractive woman. Perhaps even more interesting, however, were the differences in the women's communication. In actuality, these women did not differ in physical attractiveness, and they did not know what impression the men had been given. Nonetheless, women who conversed with men who believed they were highly attractive were rated as more sociable, poised, and humorous by objective observers. Thus the expectations that we have about an encounter can dramatically affect the communication patterns that develop, not only for the individual who has formed the prior expectations but for the other person as well. Such interdependency well illustrates the weakness of any model that considers only one direction of a communicated exchange.

B. *Self-Disclosure*

The process of self-disclosure refers to the revealing of personal information about one's self. As discussed in Chapter 4, there are a number of factors that affect our tendency to self-disclose. In this section, we are concerned with the characteristics of the interpersonal exchange that may affect the level of self-disclosure. As we might expect, given the decrease in uncertainty that accompanies the development of a relationship, the intimacy of self-disclosures increases as the interchange progresses (Davis, 1976). Reciprocity is often observed in such interchanges: in other words, if one person increases the intimacy of the disclosures, the other person is likely to respond with a similar increase in intimacy (Cozby, 1973; Davis & Skinner, 1974; Jourard & Jaffe, 1970; Worthy, Gary, & Kahn, 1969). However, two people do not generally reciprocate equally. Instead, one member of the dyad generally assumes the role of leader, initiating more intimate topics, whereas the other person tends to follow the lead (Davis,

1976, 1978). In a male–female dyad, the male often is the architect of the encounter, determining the rate at which intimacy of the exchange increases (Davis, 1978).

In longer-term relationships, however, strict reciprocity is no longer the rule in communication (Altman, 1973; Derlega, Wilson, & Chaikin, 1976; Morton, 1978). Although the overall intimacy level of such exchanges tends to be higher than in new relationships, there does not seem to be a one-for-one exchange of intimate information in any single conversation. Over the course of many conversations, however, these more intimate relationships probably also evidence a balance in level of self-disclosure. In other words, the specific rules of communication may change considerably as we move from the initial encounter to more stable relationships (which are discussed in more detail in Chapter 6).

The intimacy of an individual's self-disclosing statements may be related to nonverbal communication channels as well. For example, in a study by Ellsworth and Ross (1975), male and female subjects were asked to present a self-revealing monologue to a silent listener. Although the listener did not speak, the amount of gaze directed at the speaker was varied. Women subjects who received direct gaze from another woman were more personal and self-revealing in their monologues than women whose listener tended to avoid their gaze (see Figure 5-10). That the level of intimacy was higher in the former situation was agreed on not only by both the speaker and the listener, but by a neutral observer as well. For male subjects, however, the results were more complex. Males who received direct gaze from a male listener believed that they revealed more personal information; however, both the listener and the neutral observer agreed that men in this situation were less revealing than were men whose gaze was avoided. Why the difference between women and men? Certainly it is not the first instance of sex differences in communication behavior. One possible explanation concerns the different functions that eye contact or other communication channels can serve. In the case of women,

Figure 5-10. Gaze in conversation. (Isabel Bishop, *Two Girls*, 1935. The Metropolitan Museum of Art.)

eye contact may have served as a reinforcer for the more intimate disclosure and led to continued disclosure at relatively high levels. For men, however, the disagreement between observer and listener, on the one hand, and the speaker himself, on the other hand, suggests that different messages might have been communicated by the gaze. The male speaker may have considered the continuing gaze of the male listener to indicate that his disclosure must be reaching fairly intimate levels. Neutral observers of this same interaction, however, could judge the disclosure level of the speaker's monologue on its own merit, which did not indicate greater intimacy.

C. *Deceptive Communication*

In discussing self-disclosure, we often assume that people convey honest information about themselves. Yet there is no doubt that people sometimes lie. Political scandals, criminal proceedings, and extra-marital affairs are often the occasion for determined attempts to tell another person something other than the truth.

It is often believed that such deceptive communications are easily detected. In 1905, for example, Sigmund Freud suggested that "He that has eyes to see and ears to hear may convince himself that no mortal can keep a secret. If his lips are silent, he chatters with his fingertips; betrayal oozes out of him at every pore" (Freud, 1905/1959). More recently, trial lawyer Louis Nizer has pointed to cues that are associated with witnesses' attempts to deceive the jurors (Nizer, 1973). Included among these cues are a tendency to look at the ceiling, a self-conscious covering of the mouth before answering questions, and a crossing of the legs. Are these beliefs in the detectability of deception justified? Do liars regularly expose themselves through the various communication channels? To answer these questions first we must determine whether there are reliable verbal and nonverbal messages that are sent when a person is lying, and, second, we must find out whether an observer can reliably interpret those cues.

Research directed at the first part of our answer has revealed a wide variety of communicative cues that accompany deception. In other words, although the liar may be controlling the content of the message, many of the other communication channels appear to "leak" information. For example, people who are being deceptive use speech differently: they make factual statements less often, they are prone to make vague sweeping statements, and they frequently leave gaps in their conversation, apparently in an attempt to avoid saying something that would give them away (Knapp, Hart, & Dennis, 1974). The voice alters as well, in that liars are apt to have a higher pitch than truth tellers (Ekman, Friesen, & Scherer, 1976; Krauss, Geller, & Olson, 1976). An increase in manipulative gestures also accompanies lying in many instances: the deceiver is more apt to touch the face with the hand, for example, echoing the observations of Louis Nizer (Ekman & Friesen, 1974), or to play with glasses or some other external object (Knapp, Hart, & Dennis, 1974). Facial expression, in contrast, seems to be a less reliable indicator of deception. Some people smile while they are lying, whereas others maintain a placid expression (McClintock & Hunt, 1975; Mehrabian, 1971). Perhaps the latter situation is due to the fact that we have much more control over our facial expressions: we are aware of what emotion is being expressed in our face, but we are less aware of what the other parts of our body are saying.

With the abundance of cues, it might seem that deception can be easily detected. Indeed, many people claim such powers for themselves—"I can tell if she's lying by whether she looks me in the eye." Research suggests, however, that such powers may be more imagined than real. In most studies that have been conducted, people are able to distinguish between a truthteller and a liar at little better than chance frequencies (Bauchner, Brandt, & Miller, 1978; Littlepage & Pineault, 1978). Thus if you were to observe a group of 12 people, half of whom were telling the truth and half of whom were lying, the evidence suggests that you would correctly identify who was and who was not telling the truth only 50% of the time (Knapp, 1978). It is important to remember, however, that most of the studies of deception have been done in the laboratory, using people who are unrelated to each other and who have not seen each other in any other context. Thus it is quite possible that our ability to detect deception is markedly improved when we are communicating with close friends. In support of this suggestion, Ekman and Friesen (1974) found that people could detect deception in another person by body cues alone—if they had also had the opportunity to observe that person's behavior under other conditions where honest messages were being transmitted.

Furthermore, although the overall ability to detect deception is not impressively high, there are conditions that will increase our accuracy. Body cues, for example, seem to be a more reliable cue than facial cues from the observer's point of view, reflecting the earlier observation that these channels are more likely to "leak" nonverbal messages (Ekman & Friesen, 1969, 1974; Littlepage & Pineault, 1979).

Results of deception studies underline the complexity of communication. We send messages through many channels and we receive messages through many channels, and there is no guarantee that the various messages are consistent with one another. Thus interpretation is subject to error, and so-called "communication breakdowns" are not surprising. Of course, we do not analyze communications in a vacuum. Often we have previously formulated ideas about the other person's intentions, as suggested in Chapter 3, and these prior conceptions may substantially alter our predisposition to read falsehood in the messages of others.

D. *Telecommunication*

Although we tend to think of most communication occurring in face-to-face settings, there are many occasions when communication is mediated through some artificial means. Telephone conversations, for example, allow only the speech and vocal cues to come through. The communication industry has also begun to develop telephone systems in which video contact will be possible as well as the more standard audio contact, and the television industry has begun to experiment with cable television systems in which the viewer will be able to "talk back" to the program through a push-button system. How do these mediated forms of communication compare to the more direct face-to-face situation? Is communication different depending on the medium through which it occurs?

Some years ago Marshall McLuhan (1964) gained instant fame by proposing that "the medium is the message." For example, he suggested that television and radio could be contrasted as "cold" and "hot" media and that different personalities would be effective in the two different forms. In his analysis of the 1960 U.S. Presidential elections, he hypothesized that the television debates worked in John F. Kennedy's favor and Richard Nixon's disfavor because one personality was more suited to to the "coolness" of the television media. From what we know of the many channels through which communication can occur, we too might suspect that the media could

make a difference. In live interaction all of the channels are available, whereas video and audio forms eliminate some of those channels.

As you might expect, the differences between audio-only communication and face-to-face communication are great. In audio-only conversations, there are fewer interruptions and fewer pauses than when people interact in person (Cook & Lalljee, 1972; Williams, 1978). Audio-only conversations are also more narrow in focus, as well as more depersonalized and more argumentative (Stephenson, Ayling, & Rutter, 1976; Williams, 1977). Consequently, friendship formation seems to be hampered by this form of communication, and bargaining and negotiation become harder and more self-centered. Although adding the possibility of visual contact through videotape would be expected to improve the situation dramatically, the research to date suggests that this is not the case: communication through audio-visual media is much more similar to audio-alone situations than to face-to-face interaction (Williams, 1977). On the one hand, this research suggests that nonverbal communication channels, such as eye gaze, facial expression, and gestures, are less important than we have been led to believe. More likely, however, such evidence indicates the importance of the interactive nature of communication; the constant and direct interchange that face-to-face interaction allows may not be replicated in totality by artificial communication media.

V. Summary

The communication process underlies most aspects of human social behavior. Although the forms of communication are varied, it has been truthfully said that we can't *not* communicate. Early models of the communication process described a one-way flow from a transmitter to a receiver. More recent models stress the fact that communication (1) is a shared social system, (2) is an ongoing and dynamic process, (3) combines both verbal and nonverbal channels, and (4) contains relational as well as content messages.

There are many channels through which we can communicate. Among these are language and paralanguage, eye contact and gaze, facial expressions, body movements and gestures, touch, and interpersonal distance. Through each of these channels we can communicate emotions, liking and disliking, and indications of dominant or submissive status.

Language is the most obvious form of communication. *Paralanguage*, which refers to other types of meaningful vocalization, can also convey meaning ranging from excitement to boredom.

Eye contact or gaze serves at least four functions in a communicative interaction: (1) regulating the flow of conversation, (2) monitoring feedback, (3) expressing emotions, (4) and communicating the nature of the relationship. Both sex and ethnic differences have been observed in the use of gaze as a means of communication.

Facial expressions can convey a variety of emotions, and these basic emotional expressions can be identified by people in very different cultures throughout the world. However, although the *facial affect program* (the connection between an emotional experience and a particular pattern of facial-muscle activity) may be constant across cultures, there are tremendous variations in the *display rules* that regulate whether an emotion will be expressed. Many facial expressions, such as the smile, may be less the automatic expression of an emotion than a chosen way to communicate an emotion.

Body movements and gestures have been classified in a system called *kinesics* that attempts to parallel linguistic models. Some body movements (called *illustrators*) are directly linked with spoken language; others (called *emblems*) substitute for a spoken phrase.

Touch is one of the earliest forms of communication, although its use decreases as people grow from childhood to adulthood. Like many other forms of nonverbal communication, touch is used and reacted to quite differently by women and men.

The distance between two people also communicates a variety of messages. Four zones have been identified that are typical of different types of interactions: (1) intimate zones, (2) personal distance zones, (3) social distance zones, and (4) public distance zones.

In most communication situations, the various channels of communication are combined. Three major dimensions of communication have been identified (liking, status, and responsiveness), each of which is indicated by a variety of nonverbal cues. With particular regard to the liking dimension, two models of intimacy have been proposed. The *equilibrium model* proposes a balance between approach and avoidance pressures in an interaction and suggests that pressures for intimacy in one channel will result in compensatory moves away from intimacy in other channels. The *arousal model* suggests that responses to changes in the intimacy level of an interaction will depend on how that situation is defined: sometimes increases in intimacy will be reciprocated and other times they will be avoided.

All communication channels do not carry the same weight. Some evidence suggests that facial expressions, for example, are much more important than verbal messages in interpreting an interaction.

In initial encounters, particular patterns of speech and nonverbal behaviors have been observed. Also, the characteristics of an initial encounter vary greatly depending on the sex and personality of the participants, as well as on the expectations they have about each other. Self-disclosure between people in an interaction often tends to show reciprocity.

When people are being deceptive, a variety of verbal and nonverbal cues are displayed that differ from the normal state. However, our ability to detect lying in another person is not very good, particularly when we have no previous knowledge about the other person.

Finally, studies of telecommunication suggest that communication via media is not as effective as face-to-face interaction.

Glossary Terms   display rules   illustrators   paralanguage
                      emblems   kinesics
                      facial affect
                        program

CONSTANTIN BRANCUSI. *THE KISS.* PHILADELPHIA MUSEUM OF ART, THE LOUISE AND WALTER ARENSBERG COLLECTION.

6

Affiliation,
Attraction,
and Love

Those of us who need people "are the luckiest people in the world," a popular song tells us. But don't we all need people? For many of us, at least, friends and lovers are among the most important aspects of life, and the process of developing relationships is one of our most challenging goals. When we look at other people, when we look at ourselves, and when we develop channels of communication, we are beginning to move toward relationships with other people. The kinds of relationships we form are numerous. Some people are only casual acquaintances; others become spouses or lovers. Some relationships last; others end in boredom or distress. And sometimes we may prefer isolation to any relationship at all. These many forms of interpersonal involvement are the concern of this chapter.

I. Alone or Together?

A. *Reactions to Isolation*

Suppose you were offered $20 a day to remain in a room by yourself. You are free to leave whenever you want. The room has no windows but is equipped with a lamp, a bed, a chair, a table, and bathroom facilities. Food is brought at mealtime and left outside your door, but you see no one. You are allowed no companions, no telephone, no books, magazines, or newspapers, and no radio or television. If you were to volunteer for such a project, how long could you remain?

In an effort to understand people's needs to affiliate with other people, Schachter (1959) placed five male students in settings like the one described. All of the participants were volunteers. One of them was able to remain in the room for only 20 minutes before he had an uncontrollable desire to leave. Three volunteers remained in their rooms for two days. Afterward, one of these students said that he had become quite uneasy and would not want to do it again, but the other two seemed rather unaffected by their isolation. The fifth volunteer remained in isola-

tion for eight days. Upon his release the student admitted that he was growing uneasy and nervous, but no serious effects from the isolation were observed.

No one—including Schachter himself—would regard this study as a definitive one. It was simply an exploratory investigation of the reactions of normal people to voluntary social isolation. Yet the substantial differences in the reactions of the five volunteers to identical situations is a fascinating finding. Some people apparently have vastly greater needs than do others for the presence of people or for social surrogates such as radio, television, and telephones.

Social-psychological studies that single out the effects of isolation are quite limited (Suedfeld, 1974). Often such studies consider not only isolation but also the effects of restricted environment, as in Schachter's study. The element of choice is probably a very important factor as well. Suedfeld (1974) notes that Admiral Byrd survived an Antarctic winter completely alone, with his physical and mental faculties intact (Byrd, 1938). People have sailed around the world without experiencing any psychological harm. But these experiences may be quite different from that of the prisoner placed in solitary confinement, who has no choice in the situation (see Figure 6-1).

Prolonged isolation results initially in severe anxiety, but this stage passes. Periods of calm adaptation and then boredom develop in individuals isolated for long periods of time. For example, Burney (1961), who spent 526 days in solitary confinement in a Nazi prison in Germany, adapted to isolation so thoroughly that, when he was finally able to have contact with other prisoners, he "found conversation an embarrassment" (1961, p. 146, quoted in Suedfeld, 1974). Perhaps the best summary of the effects of isolation comes from Suedfeld (1974):

. . . there appears to be trustworthy evidence that isolation disrupts the ordinary everyday coping procedures, and leads to special kinds of psychological events. These frequently include hallucinations and vivid dreams, and a great openness to experience. These unusual states last for varying, but sometimes quite prolonged, periods.

If the individual does not return to the normal social environment, he begins to adapt and to develop habitual methods of behaving in isolation. These may appear bizarre by "normal" standards, but in fact represent a best fit response to a bizarre environment [p. 10].

Such descriptions refer to extreme cases of isolation, in which the lack of social contact extends for months or even years. Few people would voluntarily choose such a situation. Yet, in less extreme circumstances, many people choose to remain alone for varying periods of time. As Schachter's demonstration showed, people may vary widely in their need for other people. In more normal circumstances, for example, some people may prefer to live by themselves, whereas others prefer the company of a roommate, spouse, or lover.

Our tendency to believe in the basic need of people to affiliate is nicely illustrated by the stereotypes we hold of people who choose to live alone. Parmelee and Werner (1978a, 1978b) asked subjects to evaluate people who differed only in their living preferences and found that those people who voluntarily choose to live by themselves are judged as less socially desirable and less active (but also more organized and more efficient) than people who choose a joint living situation.

These stereotypes may or may not be true. What is clear is that people differ in the extent to which they need other people. Another way of phrasing this is to say that individuals differ in the optimal level of social stimulation they prefer. Hebb (1955) has presented a general arousal model in which the optimal level of stimulation may vary from person to person. Some people may need very little social contact; others may need a great deal.

In a more social context, Altman (1975, 1977) has conceptualized the need for privacy as a dynamic process in which people shift back and forth from seeking interaction to avoiding it. The need for privacy thus leads to a voluntary choice of isolation. At times, each of us may experience a state of "interaction overload." Perhaps we have gone from a crowded bus to a football game and then to a rock concert. Our social needs are not only met but oversupplied, and we have to be alone for a while.

At other times, a long day of isolation may lead us to brave the rain or cold in the hope of finding someone to interact with. At these times, we may be feeling *lonely*—experiencing less interaction than we desire (Peplau, Russell, & Heim, 1978). Such shifts from seeking affiliation to avoiding it are probably a continual dynamic of our lives. But what are the reasons for affiliation? What do we gain from social interaction that we cannot experience alone?

B. *Reasons for Affiliation*

There are several reasons why we may wish to affiliate with people or become a member of a group of people. For example, **social-exchange theory** would suggest that

Figure 6-1. Involuntary isolation. (© Jeff Albertson/Stock, Boston.)

people affiliate as a means to an end (for more on this theory, see Section II. B.). In this case, the individual has goals that can be met only by affiliating with others. Thus Irv, a tennis buff, needs to have at least one other companion who plays tennis; he may even join a tennis club in order to achieve his goals.

Reinforcement theory suggests that other people represent rewards in and of themselves. According to this viewpoint, needs such as those for approval and for development of an identity can be met only by other people (see, for example, Burk, Zdep, & Kushner, 1973). Although it is sometimes difficult to distinguish these two theories, the basic distinction has to do with means versus ends. Of course, the same person or group of persons may serve both goals: companionship in and of itself may be important, along with the achievement of some goal such as a tennis match.

Another implicit value of affiliation is that the process offers a means of self-evaluation. By comparing ourselves with other people, we can evaluate our own skills and beliefs. It is true that some characteristics can be evaluated with little or no reference to other people. The bachelor who has just cooked his first cheese soufflé can evaluate his cooking ability by looking at the soufflé and by tasting it. A 15-year-old who cannot do a single chin-up may easily conclude that he or she is not very strong. However, the evaluation of many skills, aptitudes, attitudes, and values can be done only by comparing oneself with other people. Festinger (1954) developed **social-comparison theory** to explain this process. The theory states that, in the absence of a physical or objective standard of correctness, we will seek other people as a means of evaluating ourselves. Whether it is our attitudes toward Eskimos or a new hairstyle or the latest rock group, we are motivated to evaluate our own beliefs and abilities by comparing them with social reality (Latané, 1966; Radloff, 1961; Singer & Shockley, 1965; Suls & Miller, 1977).

Self-evaluation through social comparison is more fruitful when we choose to make our comparisons with people who are generally similar to us (Bleda & Castore, 1973;

Castore & DeNinno, 1977; Goethals & Darley, 1977). Thus, if Ann is trying to evaluate her golf game, she does not choose tournament champion Nancy Lopez to compare herself to; nor would she be likely to choose a 6-year-old who just picked up a club. Rather, she would compare to other friends of somewhat equal ability. The sex of the comparison person appears to be one of the more important dimensions of similarity that we rely on. Thus, when subjects in an experiment are allowed to choose one person with whom they would like to compare their performance, both males and females generally show the greatest preference for someone of the same sex (Suls, Gaes, & Gastorf, 1979; Suls, Gastorf, & Lawhon, 1978; Zanna, Goethals, & Hill, 1975).

Still another purpose that affiliation serves is as a way of reducing anxiety (see Figure 6-2). Considerable research has been conducted on this particular topic. Let us consider it in somewhat greater detail.

C. *Affiliation as a Response to Anxiety*

We saw earlier that the initial reaction to isolation can be a state of extreme anxiety. If this is true, Stanley Schachter reasoned, perhaps the reverse is true as well: that anxiety may lead to a desire for affiliation.

In his initial study, Schachter (1959) led female introductory-psychology students at the University of Minnesota to believe that they would receive a series of electric shocks. Those subjects in the "high anxiety" conditions were told that the shocks would be painful but that there would be no permanent damage. In contrast, subjects in the "low anxiety" condition were led to expect virtually painless shocks that would feel, at worst, like a tickle. The basic purpose of the study was to determine whether anxious subjects would seek the presence of others more than less anxious subjects would. After receiving this description, the students were told that there would be a 10-minute delay while the equipment was set up. Each subject was allowed to choose whether she wanted to wait by herself or wait with some of the other subjects in the same experiment. After they had made this choice, the

Figure 6-2. Does misery love miserable company? (Isabel Bishop, *Idle Conversation*, 1932. Etching, 5″ × 5^{15}/$_{16}$″. Collection of The Whitney Museum of American Art. Purchase.)

experiment was terminated. Schachter's concern was only with the choices that subjects would make, and no shocks were actually administered.

As expected, the level of induced anxiety influenced the waiting preferences. Of the 32 subjects in the high-anxiety condition, 20 wanted to wait with other subjects; only 10 of the 30 subjects in the low-anxiety conditions chose to wait with others. The adage that "misery loves company" was confirmed.

What is it about being with others that makes affiliation so desirable for highly anxious subjects? There are at least two possible explanations. First, the presence of others may serve as a distraction. Alternatively, people in this situation may be unsure of their reactions and seek out other people as a means of social comparison. If the first explanation is true, then any other person would be desirable. On the other hand, if social comparison is critical, then it would be important to seek out people who were in a similar situation.

To test out these two explanations, Schachter (1959) conducted a second experiment. This time all subjects were told that they would receive painful electric shocks; hence all subjects were in a high-anxiety condition. Each subject was given the choice of waiting alone or with others, but the characteristics of the others were varied. Subjects in the *same-state condition* were given the choice of waiting alone or waiting with other female students who were taking part in the same experiment. Subjects in the *different-state condition* could wait either alone or with female students who were not participating in the experiment but instead were waiting to see their faculty advisors.

The results of the study were clear. Subjects who had the opportunity to wait with others in the same experiment showed a clear preference to do so. In contrast, those subjects who could wait with students not involved in the experiment showed a unanimous preference to wait alone. These findings suggest that distraction is apparently *not* an explanation of the link between anxiety and affiliation. Further, instead of concluding that misery loves company, it would be more appropriate to say that "misery loves miserable company." However, it may be that the company should not be too miserable. Rabbie (1963) found that subjects did not want to wait with others who were extremely fearful, perhaps because they might cause the subject's own fears to increase.

Other factors may affect the relationship between anxiety and the desire for affiliation. For example, as suggested earlier, similarity of the other person in terms of personality appears to be important—equally or more important than the similarity of experience (Miller & Zimbardo, 1966).

Someone who is very different from us may simply not be very relevant as we try to interpret our own reactions. Also, in a situation that is highly embarrassing, a person may prefer to wait alone rather than be exposed to the scrutiny of others (Firestone, Kaplan, & Russell, 1973; Sarnoff & Zimbardo, 1961; Teichman, 1973). Individual differences among people, as in their birth order, may also affect the choice to affiliate.

The data in Table 6-1 indicate that the heightened desire to affiliate under conditions of high anxiety occurs primarily among individuals who are the firstborn in their family. Evidence for this relationship has been found outside the laboratory as well. Schachter (1959) has reported an unpublished study by Weiner and Stieper of military veterans who were outpatients at a Veterans Administration Center. Over 75% of the veterans who were firstborn applied for psychotherapy, presumably to reduce their anxiety, whereas only 59% of the later-born veterans applied.

In another example, when Los Angeles experienced a major earthquake in 1971, two social psychologists at UCLA used the natural event to assess birth-order differences in people's responses to anxiety (Hoyt & Raven, 1973). Firstborn persons reported talking to significantly more people within the first 15 minutes after the quake than did later-born persons, suggesting a greater need for affiliation under stress.

Although the evidence quite clearly supports the relationship between anxiety and the desire for affiliation, it is much less cer-

T A B L E 6 - 1 / *Birth-Order Differences in the Tendency to Affiliate When Anxious*

Birth Order	High-Anxiety Condition Waiting Preference		Low-Anxiety Condition Waiting Preference	
	Together	Alone or Don't Care	Together	Alone or Don't Care
First and only child	32	16	14	31
Later born	21	39	23	33
	$X^2 = 10.70$ $p < .01$		$X^2 = 1.19$ $p = $ N.S.	

Adapted from *The Psychology of Affiliation*, by Stanley Schachter, with the permission of the publishers, Stanford University Press. © 1959 by the Board of Trustees of the Leland Stanford Junior University.

tain whether such affiliation actually does *reduce* anxiety. Evidence has been presented on both sides of the argument (Buck & Parke, 1972; Epley, 1974; MacDonald, 1970; Ring, Lipinski, & Braginsky, 1965; Wrightsman, 1960; Wrightsman, 1975). Yet, whether or not affiliation is an effective anxiety reducer, the fact that people choose to affiliate when they are anxious remains important for our understanding of affiliative behavior.

D. *Affiliation Patterns in Everyday Life*

In laboratory experiments such as those described above, it is possible to determine some of the reasons why people might choose to affiliate with other people. Yet, although such laboratory experiments are a very good way to verify cause-and-effect relationships, they tell us little about people's natural patterns of affiliation in everyday life. How often do people choose to spend time with other people as opposed to being by themselves? What kinds of people are selected for affiliation and interaction?

Social psychologists have paid very little attention to these questions in the past. Recently, however, a few investigators have conducted some observational studies that begin to answer these questions. For the most part, these investigators have begun in their own backyards—on the college campuses where they themselves are located. Latané and Bidwell (1977), for example, simply observed people in a variety of locations on the Ohio State and University of North Carolina campuses, recording whether each person they observed was alone or in the presence of other people. Overall, approximately 60% of the people they saw were with at least one other person. Interestingly, women were much more likely to be with other people than were men, suggesting that, at least in public places, women may affiliate more than men.

Pursuing this general strategy, Deaux (1978b) asked college students at Purdue University to keep records of their interactions over a three-day period, recording at each 15-minute interval of their waking hours whether they were alone or with

other people. The advantage of this strategy, as compared to the simple observation method, is that data could be collected for a single individual over a longer period of time, and private as well as public affiliation patterns could be tapped. However, the possible disadvantage of this method is that the investigator had to rely on self-report data, the shortcomings of which were discussed in Chapter 2.

College students in this study reported spending approximately 25% of their waking time alone, underlining the fact that affiliation is not a constant state. The remaining time was spent with other people; 12% (of total waking time) was reported spent with a person of the opposite sex, 15% with a person of the same sex, 17% with a group of people of the same sex, and 30% with a mixed-sex group. In general, men and women did not differ in their overall patterns of affiliation. The only exception was in the case of same-sex groups: men reported 20% of their time in such groups, whereas women reported only 14%. This particular difference is intriguing in that it supports the arguments of anthropologist Lionel Tiger (1969), who has suggested that males are more likely to bond together as a result of hereditary links to earlier animal behavior. The greater participation of men in team sports may also help to explain the difference.

One other interesting sex difference emerged when a closer look was given to the kinds of activities in which the students were engaged. Focusing on those periods when students reported talking, which we might consider to be most indicative of affiliation, Deaux (1978b) found that women spent more time engaged in conversation than did men; furthermore, women were more likely to talk with a person of the same sex than were men.

Looking more closely at social-interaction patterns, Wheeler and Nezlek (1977) asked first-year college students to keep track of all interactions that they had during a two-week period in both the fall and the spring semesters. By limiting the interactions to those that lasted for ten minutes or more, the investigators hoped to focus on those situations in which affiliation was actually occurring, as opposed to more casual exchanges such as getting a homework assignment or checking a book out of the library. By these criteria, there is evidence of a much higher same-sex affiliation. Fifty-six percent of the first-year students' interactions were with a person of the same sex. During the first semester, the women students spent significantly more time engaged in some kind of interaction than did the men; but, by the second semester, these differences had disappeared. To explain this difference, Wheeler and Nezlek suggest that the adjustment to college life may represent a much sharper transition for women than for men. With a relatively greater increase of freedom, women may be more likely to explore new relationships for the first few months and then to draw back somewhat as the novelty of the situation wears off.

Outside of the boundaries of the college campus, much less research has been done. In one of the few studies to consider a broader range of people, Booth (1972) interviewed 800 adults in Nebraska. He found that, although men and women reported having a similar number of close friends, women seemed to have closer and more frequent contact with their friends and relatives than did men. It is risky, of course, to conclude anything about basic sex differences because the occupational status of the men and women in this sample were very different. Most of the men were employed in jobs outside the home, whereas the majority of the women were homemakers and may therefore have had more time to develop and maintain friendships of a close and personal nature.

These studies begin to provide us with a picture of human social interaction. It is clear, for example, that, even on the high-density college campus, people do spend a substantial proportion of their time alone. When we do spend time with other people, it is interesting to note how often we choose to be with someone of the same sex. Although opposite-sex interactions frequently draw more attention, affiliation with someone of the same sex is an obviously important aspect of many people's social life.

II. Attraction

So far we have considered why people choose to affiliate, and we have looked at some of the general patterns of social interaction. Yet, given these general needs for affiliation, how do we choose which people we want to be with? Why are we friendly with or attracted to some people, while we reject or dislike others? In this section we move from the general nature of affiliation to the specific reaction of attraction. We shall review some of the characteristics of other people that make them attractive; then several theoretical explanations for the findings will be discussed.

A. *The Antecedents of Interpersonal Attraction*

Considerable research has been conducted on interpersonal attraction, perhaps reflecting the importance that many of us place on being liked. On the basis of this research, we can say that the odds are in favor of our liking a person if that person:

1. has similar beliefs, values, and personality characteristics;
2. satisfies our needs;
3. is physically attractive;
4. is competent;
5. is pleasant or agreeable;
6. reciprocates our liking; and
7. is in geographical proximity to us.

Let's consider each of these factors in turn.

1. *Similarity of Beliefs, Values, and Personality.* We like people whose attitudes and values appear to agree with ours, and we dislike those who seem to disagree with us (Byrne, 1971; Griffitt, 1974; M. F. Kaplan 1972). If their personalities are like ours, the attraction is even stronger. Most of the early studies that demonstrated this relationship were done in the laboratory, using verbal descriptions of hypothetical persons, and the findings were consistent and sometimes even surprising. For example, researchers found that Whites preferred associating with Blacks who had attitudes like their own, rather than with Whites who had opposing attitudes (Byrne & Wong, 1962;

Moss & Andrasik, 1973; Rokeach, 1968; Stein, Hardyck, & Smith, 1965). However, the value of these findings was challenged because of their artificial nature; that is, the other person is described only on paper, and the subject is explicitly made aware of the degree of similarity or dissimilarity in attitudes, thus creating the possibility of strong demand characteristics (Levinger, 1972; Wright & Crawford, 1971).

Field studies should help clarify the relationship. In an early field study, Newcomb (1961) gave college students free housing if they agreed to fill out seemingly endless questionnaires about their attitudes and their liking for their housemates. The results of this massive study showed generally that students whose attitudes were similar at the beginning of the semester came to like one another more by the end of the testing period. Although this interpretation is not beyond question, subsequent tests of the hypothesis in more controlled settings have reconfirmed the conclusion (Griffitt & Veitch, 1974). More recently, Kandel (1978) conducted an extensive questionnaire study with over 1800 adolescents, varying in age from 13 to 18. By comparing the attitudes and values of each student with those of his or her best friend, she was able to show strong support for the similarity relationship. Some areas of similarity were more important than others, however. Best friends were most apt to be similar with respect to certain demographic variables such as grade, sex, race, and age. Friends also tended to have similar attitudes toward drug use; in contrast, attitudes toward parents and teachers were not always shared by friends.

People who are dissimilar are not always disliked, however. In fact, on some occasions we may even *prefer* the dissimilar person. For example, if a person is stigmatized (Novak & Lerner, 1968) or is of lower status (Karuza & Brickman, 1978), we may prefer that person to be dissimilar to us in attitudes, perhaps because too much similarity to a less desirable person is threatening to our own self-image. Furthermore, even our initial tendency to dislike those who are dissimilar to us can be modified,

and often quite easily. Simply having the opportunity to predict a person's attitudes (Aderman, Bryant, & Donelsmith, 1978) or being allowed to discuss areas of disagreement (Brink, 1977) will substantially increase our liking for the initially dissimilar person.

2. *Complementarity of Need Systems.* In contrast to the preceding condition, there may be cases where seeming opposites attract. According to the theory of need **complementarity,** people choose relationships in which their basic needs can be mutually gratified (Winch, 1952; Winch, Ktsanes, & Ktsanes, 1954). Sometimes the result of this choice is a pairing of apparent opposites, as when a very dominant person is attracted to a very submissive partner. Other times the opposition may be more apparent than real, as when women with traditional views of their own roles prefer men with traditionally masculine attributes (Seyfried & Hendrick, 1973). In this case, both partners may believe in traditional sex roles, but the specific characteristics they favor in themselves and their partners may be opposite. In general, this idea seems reasonable, and there is some support for the complementarity principle in long-term relationships (Kerckhoff & Davis, 1962). Other investigators (Levinger, Senn, & Jorgensen, 1970) have been less encouraging, however, and we must conclude that the complementarity principle probably only operates on a few limited dimensions in a limited number of situations.

Perhaps one reason for the ambiguous findings in this area is that investigators have failed to consider the total picture of needs in a relationship. Needs may exist in various domains, and the resources that one person brings to the relationship may be exchanged for some virtue in another area (Foa, 1971). In an intriguing demonstration of this more complex pattern of needs, Harrison and Saeed (1977) examined 800 advertisements that had been placed in the lonely-hearts column of a widely circulated weekly tabloid. By analyzing both what people offered (such as "good-looking woman of high moral standards who will offer good company") and what they sought ("seeks wealthy older man with good intentions"), these investigators discovered some interesting aspects of the exchange relationship in male/female pairs. For example, women were more likely to offer physical attractiveness, and men were more likely to seek it. In similar fashion, men were more likely to offer financial security and women to request it. Supporting the similarity principle, good-looking advertisers of both sexes sought a good-looking partner. Further, some evidence of the more complex exchanges that may occur was shown by the self-described attractive women who sought financially well-to-do men.

Thus both similarity and complementarity may play some role in attraction. To date, however, the evidence for similarity is much stronger and much more broadly based as well, applying to both same-sex and opposite-sex friendships in both laboratory and field settings. Complementarity, on the other hand, has been found primarily in opposite-sex pairings of a romantic nature and is of uncertain status in either same-sex friendship relationships or even in homosexual romantic pairs.

3. *Physical Attractiveness.* Aristotle wrote that "Beauty is a greater recommendation than any letter of introduction," and things have not changed much in the last 2300 years. A beautiful or handsome physical appearance remains a critical determinant of success in our society (Berscheid & Walster, 1974), and the vast amounts of money spent on cosmetics, plastic surgery, diet foods, and contemporary fashions attest to the degree of concern that we invest in our appearance.

Such investments seem to pay off, because there is an implicit assumption in our society that "what is beautiful is good" (Dion, Berscheid, & Walster, 1972). As one example, Dion (1972) showed college women some photographs of children who had allegedly misbehaved. Some of the children were physically attractive, and others were not. Particularly when the misbehavior was a severe one, the beautiful children were given the benefit of the doubt. Respondents tended to disregard the misbehavior of the attractive children, whereas less beautiful children who committed the same acts were called maladjusted and deviant. Even children themselves are aware of these differences. Dion (1977) has found that children as young as three years will prefer pretty children to less attractive peers. (Such an awareness of the virtues of attractiveness is humorously illustrated in Figure 6-3.)

In fact, it is difficult to overestimate the effect that another person's physical appearance has on our initial impressions. Studies have shown that the highly attractive person is more likely to be recommended for hiring on a job interview (Dipboye, Arvey, & Terpstra, 1977; Dipboye, Fromkin, & Wiback, 1975), to have his or her written work evaluated favorably (Landy & Sigall, 1974), and to be seen as effective psychological counselors (Cash, Begley, McCown, &

Figure 6-3. (© 1978 by United Feature Syndicate, Inc. Reprinted by permission.)

Weise, 1975) and is less likely to be judged maladjusted or disturbed (Cash, Kehr, Polyson, & Freeman, 1977). Such studies powerfully demonstrate the extent to which we rely on physical appearance in making our judgments of others. Even a characteristic such as height, over which the person has no control, may be the basis for greater or less liking, as shown in Figure 6-4.

One reason why we are beckoned by the physically attractive lies in our hope that their attractiveness will "rub off" on us. Many years ago sociologist W. W. Waller (1937) observed that we gain a great deal of prestige by being seen with an attractive person of the other sex. This "rating and dating" complex has been verified in some recent research. For example, Sigall and Landy (1973) found that a male gets the most favorable impression from outside observers when he is accompanied by a good-looking female companion. He is viewed most negatively when his female companion is physically unattractive. Such "rub-off" effects may be slightly one-sided, however. Although men gain in likability when their female partner is highly attractive, women do not necessarily receive equal benefits. Bar-Tal and Saxe (1976a) showed subjects slides of presumably married couples, in which both the husband and the wife varied in their physical attractiveness. The unattractive male who was paired with an attractive wife was judged to have the highest income, the greatest professional success, and the highest intelligence. In contrast, the unattractive woman paired with an attractive husband gained no advantage by the pairing—she was judged solely on her own level of attractiveness. This and other evidence suggests that physical attractiveness is a much more potent cue in our judgments of women than of men (Bar-Tal & Saxe, 1976b). As the values of the culture change, such inequality in the importance of physical characteristics may change as well.

Yet, although physical attractiveness is apparently less important for men than for women, it is not totally incidental. In fact, there is considerable evidence for the importance of similarity of attractiveness between men and women. Often termed the **matching hypothesis,** research has shown that people tend to relate to people who approximately equal them in evaluated beauty (Murstein, 1972; Murstein & Christy, 1976; Price & Vandenberg, 1979; Silverman, 1971). Such is the case not only for opposite-sex relationships but for same-sex friends as well (Cash & Derlega, 1978). Thus in the abstract we may prefer the most attractive person (Walster, Aronson, Abrahams, & Rottman, 1966), but in more reality-based settings we choose someone who is close to our own level of attractiveness. Apparently, in making such choices, we combine information about the person's attractiveness with our own probability judgment of being accepted (Shanteau & Nagy, 1979)—and, with such a strategy, matching often results.

4. *Competence.* We like people who are intelligent, able, and competent more than we do those who are not. Although physical attractiveness is a more readily apparent piece of information, intelligence may be ultimately more important. Thus, when Solomon and Saxe (1977) provided people clear information about a woman's physical appearance and her intelligence, intelligence was a much more important determinant of attraction toward that person. In addition, the perception that someone is intelligent can generalize to other characteristics as well. Reversing the "beautiful is good" pattern, Gross and Crofton (1977) demonstrated that what is good is beautiful: people described by a positive set of characteristics, including intelligence, were judged as more physically attractive than those described in less glowing terms.

Although the generality of our attraction to intelligent and competent people has been well established (Aronson, Willerman, & Floyd, 1966; Helmreich, Aronson, & LeFan, 1970; Spence & Helmreich, 1972), there are some important exceptions. For example, men judging women at a distance readily report preferring a competent woman to an incompetent woman (Deaux, 1972; Spence & Helmreich, 1972). However, if faced with a situation in which they will actually interact with that woman, men no

Figure 6-4. The higher the better? It is widely believed that taller people are viewed more positively than shorter people. For example, Michael Korda, in his popular book, *Power: How to Get It, How to Use It!*, states that "Height means something to people, and it's wise not to forget it" (1975, p. 51). In support of this contention, Feldman (1971) has reported that short men receive lower starting salaries and are less likely to be hired than are tall men, and that in U.S. Presidential elections, the taller candidate nearly always wins (Jimmy Carter was an exception in 1976). Laboratory data are much less consistent on this point, however. Although we do tend to estimate men as taller the higher their status (Wilson, 1968), there may be a curvilinear relationship between height and attraction (Graziano, Brothen, & Berscheid, 1978). In other words, moderately tall men (5'9" to 5'11") may be preferred to short men (5'5" to 5'7"), but the taller man (for example, a 6'4" man) becomes less liked than his more average peer. Whether these findings are also true of women is not known. (William H. Johnson, *Lincoln at Gettysburg III*, ca. 1939–42. National Collection of Fine Arts, Smithsonian Institution. Gift of the Harmon Foundation.)

longer show a preference for competence (Hagen & Kahn, 1975). Males also show some interesting exceptions when judging a highly competent person who has committed a blunder. Reminiscent of the increased popularity of Muhammad Ali after he lost the world championship boxing match or of U.S. President John F. Kennedy's increased popularity ratings after the disastrous Bay of Pigs invasion plan, research has shown that men will prefer a highly competent person who makes a small blunder (such as spilling a cup of coffee) to one who does not (Aronson, Willerman & Floyd, 1966). Such research seems to suggest that "to err is humanizing." The less competent person who has the same accident, however, does not gain in attractiveness; he or she is rated even less favorably than an equally incompetent but less clumsy peer. For some reason, however, this pattern is not found when women are involved. Women themselves do not show favoritism to the blunderer, nor do either men or women judge a clumsy female favorably (Deaux, 1972). Such findings suggest that many characteristics may not be certain guarantees of attraction; rather, they depend on the sex of the person and perhaps other characteristics as well.

5. *Pleasant or Agreeable Characteristics.* Not surprisingly, we like people who are nice or who do nice things. As discussed in Chapter 3, personality characteristics vary in their likability, and we will be more attracted to someone who possesses various positive traits than to someone who demonstrates more negative habits (Kaplan & Anderson, 1973). Beyond evaluating the characteristics of another person in and of themselves, however, we are also concerned with the interpersonal implications of these traits (Clore & Kerber, 1978). In other words, when evaluating another person's characteristics, we give some consideration to what those traits or behaviors mean for us. For example, "considerate" not only is a favorable description of another person but also implies that we ourselves will receive some positive outcomes from interacting with that person. At the more negative pole, we tend to be least attracted to those individuals who can be described in terms that not only suggest negative aspects of their personality but that imply negative consequences for us as well (such as "unappreciative" or "dishonest").

6. *Reciprocal Liking.* We are attracted to people who like us. Heider's balance theory, to be considered in Chapter 12, predicts that if, for example, Susan likes herself and Bonnie likes Susan, a cognitively balanced state will result in which Susan likes Bonnie in return. In other words, liking and disliking are often reciprocal. Backman and Secord (1959) found that, if members of a discussion group were told that other group members liked them very much, they were most likely to choose those same members when asked to form smaller groups later in the experimental session. The opposite is also true: we tend to dislike those people who have indicated negative feelings toward us. Finally, our tendency toward balance can be taken even one step further. Aronson and Cope (1968) have demonstrated the truth of the maxim "My enemy's enemy is my friend." Two people who share in their dislike for a third person will tend to be more attracted to each other than those who do not share this common bond.

7. *Propinquity.* All else being equal, we tend to like people who live close to us better than those who are at some distance. This factor of **propinquity** has even been put to music, as in the song from *Finian's Rainbow* that says "When I'm not near the one I love, I love the one I'm near." More recently, Stephen Stills has advised us to love the one we're with. At a more scientific level, Festinger, Schachter, and Back (1956) found that residents of an apartment complex were more apt to like and interact with those who lived on the same floor of the building than with people who lived on other floors or in other buildings. Members of Air Force bomber crews develop closer relationships with coworkers who are stationed near them than with coworkers stationed a few yards away (Kipnis, 1957). And students in a classroom where alphabetical seating is required are more likely to report friendships with people whose names begin with the same letter than those whose names are at some distance away in the class roll (Byrne, 1961).

Why is propinquity a factor in attraction? In part, the effect may be due to simple familiarity (see Figure 6-5). There is a mass of evidence for the **mere exposure effect**; that is, repeated exposure to the same stimulus leads to greater attraction toward that object (Harrison, 1969; Matlin, 1970; Saegert, Swap, & Zajonc, 1973; Zajonc, 1968a). Thus we are more likely to see people who live close to us than those who live far away, and just that frequency of contact may increase our liking for the person.

In addition, it has been found that simple social interaction will increase our liking for people (Werner & Latané, 1976; Insko & Wilson, 1977). In fact, even the anticipation of interaction seems to increase our liking for another person (Darley & Berscheid, 1967), particularly when those people are either initially disliked or are ambivalently valued (Tyler & Sears, 1977). As Tyler and Sears (1977) suggest, we may even come to like obnoxious people when we know that we must live with them.

B. *Theoretical Explanations of Interpersonal Attraction*

We have seen how a variety of antecedent conditions contribute to interpersonal attraction. Now let's explore some of the possible explanations for these relationships, using theories as a way of helping to understand and organize the multiple findings. The basic models that we will consider are the *reinforcement-affect model*, *social-exchange theory*, and *equity theory*, and, specifically, we'll apply them to the specific phenomenon of interpersonal attraction.

Reinforcement-Affect Theory. **Perhaps** the most basic explanation of interpersonal attraction relies on the concept of reinforcement—that we like people who reward us and dislike people who punish us. As formulated by Byrne and Clore (1970), interpersonal attraction can be conceptualized as a basic learning process. This model assumes that most stimuli can be classified as rewards or punishment, and it assumes that rewarding stimuli elicit positive feelings or affect, whereas punishing stimuli elicit negative feelings or affect. Our evaluations

Figure 6-5. The effects of "mere exposure." Can you see any difference between these two photographs? In a clever test of the mere-exposure hypothesis, Mita, Dermer, and Knight (1977) asked subjects to indicate their preference for one of two pictures of themselves. In fact, the two photographs were identical, but in one case the image was simply reversed in printing. Friends of the subjects were also asked to indicate their preferences. The subjects themselves showed a strong preference for the mirror image—in other words, for the picture that looked like the image they saw of themselves daily in the mirror. Friends of the subjects, in contrast, preferred the true image—the face as they saw it in their interactions with the subject. (© Gail Kefauver.)

of people or objects are in turn based on the degree of positive or negative affect we experience, and neutral stimuli that are associated with the affect will gain the capacity to produce similar feelings. Lott and Lott (1974) have proposed a similar model.

To look at this theory in more concrete terms, let's consider some of the factors we discussed previously. Somebody doing nice things for us, for example, would undoubtedly be a positive or a rewarding experience. Byrne and Clore (1970) would suggest that the reward value of this experience would create positive affect and in turn would lead us to positively evaluate (or like) the person associated with that reward. To take it one step further, they would also predict that other people and objects associated with that situation (for example, the place where the interaction occurred or other people present at the time) would also tend to be liked more because of the conditioning process. Byrne and his colleagues (Byrne, 1971) have marshaled an impressive array of support for this apparently simple principle.

Social-Exchange Theory. The general assumption that reinforcement is an important basis of interpersonal attraction is not challenged by social-exchange theory. However, unlike the simple reinforcement theory just discussed, social-exchange theory is much more explicit about considering *both* people involved in the relationship. Attraction does, after all, involve two people, and it seems reasonable to assume that we should consider how the two people interact, rather than focus only on the characteristics of the other person while ignoring the perceiver. From the field of sociology, symbolic-interaction theory places a similar stress on the interaction between the people involved in a relationship, although it is less tied to reinforcement as the basic factor.

In social-exchange theory, the positive and negative reinforcements are conceptualized as costs and gains. Thus a person in a relationship presumably weighs the rewards or gains against the costs; to the extent that the gains outweigh the costs, the

attraction and positive feelings for the other person will be stronger. In addition, Thibaut and Kelley (1959) have suggested that people may compare the gains in a relationship to some baseline that they have come to expect. This *comparison level* is based on past experiences, and any present relationship will be judged as satisfactory or positive only if it exceeds the comparison level. Furthermore, these authors suggest that we may compare alternatives when we commit ourselves to one particular relationship; commitment thus depends on the degree to which the rewards of one relationship exceed the possible rewards of another relationship.

Equity Theory. **Equity theory** takes us one step further in considering both parties in a relationship. According to equity theory, we consider not only the costs and rewards that we experience in a relationship but the costs and rewards for the other person as well (Berscheid & Walster, 1978; Walster, Walster, & Berscheid, 1978). Ideally, there will be a balance between these two ratios. Basically, then, this theory suggests that we have some notion of what we deserve from a relationship, and this notion is based in part on what the other partner in the relationship is getting. The individual who feels that the relationship is out of balance will become distressed and will attempt to restore the balance, either by actually altering the inputs and outcomes or by psychologically altering the perception of the gains and costs that both people are experiencing.

Each of these three theories points to important aspects of the attraction process. At the most basic level, reinforcement theory tells us a great deal about the factors that will influence our attraction for another person. Most of the antecedents to attraction that we discussed earlier can in fact be handled by a simple reinforcement model. Yet, when we consider a more active interaction between two people, additional factors are needed to explain interpersonal attraction. Equity theory begins to take us in that direction, considering both people as necessary components of the explanation.

With this in mind, let's move beyond the simple cataloging of factors that affect attraction and consider some of the deeper relationships that people have.

III. Romance and Love

Perhaps the ultimate in affiliation and attraction is love. Philosophers and songwriters, novelists and poets have for centuries debated the meaning of love; yet until quite recently social psychologists have avoided the subject. Berscheid and Walster (1978) suggest three reasons for this neglect. First, "Love and marriage were regarded as belonging to the field of romance, not of science" (Burgess & Wallin, 1953, p. 11). Thus, although simpler forms of attraction might be studied by the social scientist, it was believed that real love is too mysterious and too intangible for scientific study. Even when the possibility of the study of love was acknowledged, however, the subject was often considered taboo. Like sexual behavior, love was considered to be a topic off limits to researchers, representing an unreasonable intrusion into personal and intimate matters. Thus, in the 1920s, a professor was fired from the University of Minnesota because he approved a questionnaire on attitudes toward sex (which included such "unreasonable" questions as "Have you ever blown into the ear of a person of the opposite sex in order to arouse their passion?") A third and perhaps more practical reason for the lack of study of love is simply that it is difficult. Without claiming it impossible, many investigators nonetheless have found it hard to approach this complex topic. Certainly, the laboratory tradition of social psychology in which subjects participate in brief, one-time sessions does not lend itself easily to the study of love. Love can't really be manipulated in the laboratory, and the causes and consequences of love are not easily isolated in a single brief session. Despite these barriers, social psychologists have recently begun to study love in earnest.

A. *Conceptions of Love*

Whereas attraction can be defined simply as "a tendency or predisposition to evaluate a person or symbol of that person in a positive or negative way" (Berscheid & Walster, 1978), definitions of love have generally been more complex. Walster and Walster (1978) suggest that there are two kinds of love: *passionate* (or romantic) *love* and *companionate love*. They offer the following description of passionate love:

A state of intense absorption in another. Sometimes "lovers" are those who long for their partners and for complete fulfillment. Sometimes "lovers" are those who are ecstatic at finally having attained their partners' love, and, momentarily, complete fulfillment. A state of intense physiological arousal [p. 9].

In contrast to this more intense state of feeling, Walster and Walster suggest that there is a second, and perhaps more familiar, form of love. *Companionate love* is defined as the affection we feel for those with whom our lives are deeply intertwined. In contrast to the sometimes momentary state of romantic love, companionate love reflects longer-term relationships and may be a later stage in a romantic relationship.

It should be noted that the gender of the lovers is not an implicit part of these definitions. Although social psychologists have tended to focus on the heterosexual relationship, it is probable that love relationships between persons of the same sex may also be considered in the same framework.

B. *The Measurement of Romantic Love*

The description of love is far easier than its measurement. One could, of course, simply ask people whether they were in love. However, to know what this feeling means to the people involved, more specific questions need to be asked. Social psychologist Zick Rubin (1970, 1973) has taken some of the initial steps in this measurement process, by devising a Love Scale to measure degrees of romantic involvement. Some of the statements from this scale are shown in **Figure 6-6**, along with a few items from a Liking Scale that he developed at the same time. In constructing this scale, Rubin included three components of romantic love: (1) attachment, (2) caring, and (3) intimacy. The concept of liking as reflected in the Liking Scale items includes two components: (1) a perception that the target person is similar to oneself and (2) a favorable evaluation of and respect for the target person.

Love-Scale Items
1. If I could never be with _____, I would feel miserable.
2. I would forgive _____ for practically anything.
3. I feel that I can confide in _____ about virtually everything.

Liking-Scale Items
1. I think that _____ is unusually well adjusted.
2. Most people would react very favorably to _____ after a brief acquaintance.
3. _____ is the sort of person who I myself would like to be.

Figure 6-6. Examples of Rubin's liking and love scales. Scores on individual items can range from 1 to 9, with 9 always indicating the positive end of the continuum. There are nine items on each scale. (From "Measurement of Romantic Love," by Z. Rubin, *Journal of Personality and Social Psychology*, 1970, *16*, 267. Copyright 1970 by the American Psychological Association. Reprinted by permission of the author and publisher.)

These scales were presented to 158 couples at the University of Michigan who were dating but not engaged. They were asked to complete both the Love Scale and the Liking Scale with respect to their dating partner and then with respect to a close friend of the same sex. The average scores for the men and women in Rubin's study are shown in Table 6-2, which shows that the love scores of men and women for their respective dating partners were almost identical. However, women *liked* their dating partners significantly more than they were liked in return. This difference is due to the fact that women rated their partners higher on task-oriented dimensions such as intelligence and leadership potential, perhaps consistent with certain stereotypes about men and women. Men and women reported liking their same-sex friends equally, but women indicated greater love toward their same-sex friends than did males. This deeper involvement in same-sex associations for women is consistent with some research about affiliation patterns we discussed earlier, such as Booth's (1972) report that women had affectively deeper relationships with their same-sex friends.

The results of Rubin's work show that there is a conceptual distinction between liking and romantic love. Other findings that suggest that these two measures are different include the finding that the two partners' love scores were more closely

TABLE 6-2 / *Love and Liking for Opposite-Sex Partners and Same-Sex Friends*

Index	Women		Men	
	$\overline{X}$	SD	$\overline{X}$	SD
Love for partner	89.46	15.54	89.37	15.16
Liking for partner	88.48	13.40	84.65	13.81
Love for same-sex friend	65.27	17.84	55.07	16.08
Liking for same-sex friend	80.47	16.47	79.10	18.07

Note: Based on responses of 158 couples.

From "Measurement of Romantic Love," by Z. Rubin, *Journal of Personality and Social Psychology*, 1970, *16*, 267–268. Copyright 1970 by the American Psychological Association. Reprinted by permission of the author and publisher.

related to each other than were their liking scores (in the former case, the correlation between the partners' scores was + .42; in the latter case, it was only + .28). In addition, Rubin found that the higher the partners' love scores, the more likely they were to expect that they would marry in the future; liking scores, in contrast, were less strongly related to this future estimate.

C. *Stimulants to Romantic Love*

The romantic ideal suggests that we meet someone, immediately become smitten, and fall deeply in love with the person, who then completely fulfills our ideal (Averill & Boothroyd, 1977). However, this image of two people in love and unaffected by circumstances may be oversimplified. A number of studies have suggested that situational factors may strongly affect the degree to which we report being in love.

Parental interference is one such factor. If two people are in love, what effect will the attitude of their parents have on the development of their relationship? It was widely reported, for example, that Prince Rainier and Princess Grace of Monaco were less than enthusiastic about their daughter Caroline dating a French commoner and playboy. What effect might this resistance have had on the relationship? Some research would suggest that parental disapproval will only strengthen the romantic ties of a young couple. Driscoll, Davis, and Lipetz (1972) conducted a test of this so-called *Romeo and Juliet effect*. They asked 91 married couples (married on the average for four years) and 49 dating couples (who had dated for an average of eight months) to respond to a variety of questionnaire measures. Included were measures of assessed parental interference, romantic love, and conjugal love (the latter similar to our earlier definition of companionate love). Not too surprisingly, parental interference and romantic love were not strongly related for those couples who were already married. However, for the unmarried couples, greater parental interference was associated with stronger romantic love (the correlation was +.50). Conjugal love was less strongly re-

lated to parental interference. From these data, it cannot be said with certainty that heightened parental interference intensified the relationship; but Driscoll and his colleagues repeated the measures six to ten months later to determine changes in both interference and reported love. Here they found even stronger evidence for the Romeo and Juliet effect. Reports of increasing parental interference were accompanied by greater feelings of romantic love, and less parental interference appeared to diminish the reports of love. Thus the Montagues and the Capulets, in Shakespeare's play of young romance, may have set a pattern for future generations of parents; and, as was true for Romeo and Juliet, the interference of the parents produced the opposite effect from what was intended.

Other situations involving frustration and challenge may also accelerate the development of romantic love. For example, it has been suggested that the challenge of the "hard-to-get woman" makes her especially attractive to men. Although etiquette books may prescribe this strategy for young women, research has shown that the strategy is not so certain (see **Box 6-1**).

Some writers have suggested that even negative emotional experiences may be associated with feelings of passion. In what is probably the first study conducted on a wobbly suspension bridge over a canyon, Dutton and Aron (1974) had a female interviewer ask males who were crossing the bridge to fill out a brief questionnaire and to compose a story based on one of the pictures from the Thematic Apperception Test (TAT). After the men had completed this task, while standing 230 feet above the rocks, the female experimenter gave each man her telephone number, saying that if he were interested she could explain the experiment to him at a later time. As a comparison group, Dutton and Aron arranged for other young men to have a similar encounter but this time on a much more solid bridge only ten feet above a shallow stream. Fear did appear to increase attraction: men on the high bridge were more likely to call the interviewer later and showed more sexual imagery in their TAT stories. Nine of the

Box 6-1. Playing Hard to Get.

According to folklore, men are attracted to women who are "hard to get." For example, Bertrand Russell has stated that "the belief in the immense value of the lady is a psychological effect of the difficulty of obtaining her" (quoted in Berscheid & Walster, 1978, p. 171). Dear Abby and Ann Landers would probably agree. But research suggests that such a conclusion must be qualified (Walster, Piliavin, & Walster, 1973; Walster, Walster, Piliavin, & Schmidt, 1973). Uniformly "hard to get" women were often rated by men as being undesirable, because they were "too picky" or "snotty." The most desired woman was the one who liked the man doing the rating but did not like other men. Generally hard to get and generally easy to get women were both liked less. Walster and her colleagues conclude that "a woman will be most successful in attracting any given man if she appears to be highly selective in her expressions of affection" (Walster, Piliavin, & Walster, 1973, p. 83).

But why is the highly selective woman liked? One reason, suggested by Walster and her colleagues, is that she is seen as having more desirable characteristics. Another possibility, however, is that, in being selective, she makes the man whom she does select feel particularly good. In other words, she causes an increase in his self-esteem, and he in turn likes the person who is responsible for the experience (Matthews, Rosenfield, & Stephan, 1979).

Charles Dana Gibson, illustration from *The Social Ladder.* © 1901 by Life Publishing Co.

18 subjects in the high-fear condition called the experimenter later, whereas only 2 of the 16 in the low-bridge condition did. Thus, an unrelated frightening event does seem to be related to increased sexual attraction.

Such evidence of unrelated arousal being linked to attraction has led Walster and her colleagues (Berscheid & Walster, 1978; Walster & Berscheid, 1974; Walster & Walster, 1978) to propose a two-component theory of passionate love. They derive their theory from the work of Stanley Schachter (1964), who proposed that emotional experiences are dependent on both cognitive and physiological factors. Briefly, Schachter suggested that a state of physiological arousal is necessary before we will experience an emotion such as fear, anger, or joy. In addition to the physiological state, however, we need an appropriate set of cognitive labels to explain the situation. Thus, if we have "butterflies in our stomach," we will seek some explanation of that feeling. Often the situation will provide such explanations for us when we are uncertain of the reasons. An uneasy stomach experienced in the presence of an unpleasant roommate may be interpreted as anger; the same stomach condition at the Super Bowl may be viewed as excitement.

Transferring this model to the area of passionate love, Walster and her colleagues suggest that love may be a combination of physiological arousal and the appropriate cognitive labels. They suggest that, if the situation is right and if certain cognitions about another person are present, then almost any situation that increases our physiological arousal may be interpreted as romantic love. This theory has some important implications. For example, being caught in a tornado with an attractive blind date would be more likely to elicit romantic feelings than a less arousing encounter. Similarly, some of the exercises of **sensitivity training** may also engender arousal. For example, a male and a female may be blindfolded and asked to become familiar with each other's faces through touching. The arousal in this situation, resulting from a new and unfamiliar experience, may well

lead the participants to a search for labels. Love, or at least infatuation, is one possible explanation.

Alternatively, however, the person may simply ascribe his or her arousal to the general characteristics of the situation. Particularly when the reasons for the arousal are fairly clear, situational attributions may be preferred. For example, in laboratory studies testing the fear and attraction link suggested by Dutton and Aron, little evidence has been found for misattribution (Kenrick, Cialdini, & Linder, 1979). Instead, male subjects in these experiments correctly attributed their excitement to the shock apparatus and did not transfer any arousal to the female confederate.

In summary, the two-component theory of passionate love points to certain irrational aspects of romance. Under the right conditions, arousal caused by external events may be interpreted as a sign of love. If other explanations are apparent, however, love may not be the answer.

D. *Stages in the Development of Love*

Earlier we discussed the distinction between romantic and companionate love, suggesting that the latter state represents more long-term relationships and focuses on more than the momentary stage of passion. Let's now consider this aspect of love more thoroughly, by looking at the development of relationships over time.

Social psychologist George Levinger (1974, 1978) has defined a sequence of stages of relationships, which can serve to illustrate the development of companionate love (see Figure 6-7). He begins this sequence with a *zero contact* point—those cases, representing thousands of instances in our life, in which we have absolutely no contact with the other person. Obviously, if we paired all of the possible people in the world, the majority of relationships could be classified in this zero-contact category. At the next level, Levinger suggests an *awareness stage*. Many of our relationships with other people probably fall into this category: we are aware of another person, perhaps even form an impression, but still

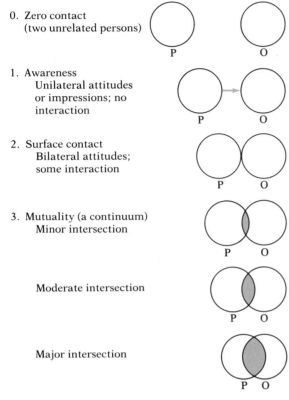

0. Zero contact
   (two unrelated persons)

   P   O

1. Awareness
   Unilateral attitudes
   or impressions; no
   interaction

   P   O

2. Surface contact
   Bilateral attitudes;
   some interaction

   P   O

3. Mutuality (a continuum)
   Minor intersection

   P   O

   Moderate intersection

   P   O

   Major intersection

   P   O

Figure 6-7. Levinger's stages of relationships. (From "Attraction in Relationship: A New Look at Interpersonal Attraction," by G. Levinger and J. D. Snoek. Copyright transferred to authors in 1978. [Morristown, N.J.: General Learning Press, 1972.] Reprinted by permission of the authors.)

have no actual interaction. Much of the material discussed in Chapter 3 concerning impression formation and attribution patterns is illustrative of this stage of a relationship. In addition, many of the variables affecting attraction that we discussed earlier in this chapter fall into the same category. Studies in which a subject is simply provided with a verbal or visual description of another person, who may be attractive or unattractive, similar or dissimilar in attitudes, are examples of this one-sided form of a relationship.

The remaining levels of Levinger's model refer to relationships between people in which there is actually some form of interaction. *Surface contact* (Level 2) is the beginning stage of these real interactions. Level 2, however, represents only the initial

contacts—exchanges that we have with casual acquaintances in which we may exchange names and pleasantries but little else. Many of our relationships probably are limited to this basis and progress no further. The dental assistant who cleans our teeth, the bus driver on our regular route, or the person we meet occasionally at a cocktail party in the neighborhood are all examples of this level of contact.

Beyond these initial stages, Levinger posits *mutuality*, represented as a continuum of increasing contact and interchange. In the early stages of mutual relationships, we may share only a small portion of ourselves with the other person. Gradually, however, we are willing to open up and share more experiences and feelings with the other person. Ultimately, in companionate love, for example, we may consider the relationship to represent the major intersection that Levinger suggests. Altman and Taylor (1973), in discussing the development of interpersonal relationships, also point to a sequence of development as a person begins to interact with another in a mutual fashion. According to their model, there are four stages in this development: *orientation, exploratory affective exchange, affective exchange,* and *stable exchange.* The progression through these stages can be likened to the peeling of an onion; at each level, the person is willing to reveal more personal and intimate aspects of the self. Many relationships do not go through the entire sequence, of course. Probably only a very few of our interactions with people can be represented by the final stage of major intersection or stable exchange. Those few relationships could be considered examples of companionate love.

Both of these theoretical models underline the importance of a sequence of development. Whereas social psychology has often concerned itself with a single point in time, it is now generally recognized that long-term relationships can be studied only by considering their development over time. Different factors may be important, depending on the stage that a relationship is in.

Yet the models themselves are fairly general. Just what specific behaviors might be different at different stages in a relationship? Rands and Levinger (1979) approached this question by simply asking people to rate the likelihood of a set of behaviors for four different degrees of closeness: casual acquaintances, good friends, very close relationships, and marriage. In general, the closer the described relationship, the more likely subjects were to believe that the couple would be *behaviorally interdependent*—in other words, would do things with or for one another. Examples of such behaviors include planning a joint project, offering to do an errand, and even showing irritation at the other person's behavior. Not surprisingly, greater amounts of physical contact were also expected with closer relationships, but this factor seemed less important than the behavioral interdependence.

In summary, as relationships develop, they change not only in intensity but also in the range of behaviors that are allowed and encouraged. Much more remains to be learned, however, about the sequence of these changes in the development of successful relationships.

IV. Falling Out of Love

In the movies of the 1930s, the story always ended with boy and girl together. Although the Hollywood version of romance has changed even in Hollywood itself, it has surely never been true of all real-life relationships. People do meet and fall in love and live together or marry. Yet some of these same people fall out of love, break off engagements, and separate or get divorced. Why do some relationships work out and others fail? Are there certain factors that influence the course of relationship, and might we be able to predict the positive and negative outcomes? It is to this side of the attraction coin that we now turn.

A. *Breaking Up Is Hard to Do*

Many relationships that begin with the glow of romantic or passionate love do not go on to fulfill their initial promise; others endure and lead to marriage, children, and golden anniversaries. Are there any patterns that can be detected in those relationships that break up versus those that last? In an attempt to answer this question, Hill, Rubin, and Peplau (1976) conducted an extensive two-year study, following the course of 231 couples in the Boston area. At the end of the two-year period, 103 couples (45% of the original sample) had broken up; 65 others were still dating, 9 were engaged, 43 were married, and 11 could not be contacted.

To understand the process of breaking up, Hill and his colleagues first looked at the initial questionnaire results that each couple had completed at the beginning of the two-year period. Were there any clues at that stage that could predict the course of the relationship? Not surprisingly, those couples who reported feeling closer in 1972 were more likely to be together in 1974. Yet those reported feelings were not a perfect predictor; many couples who reported feeling close at the initial testing still did break up in the subsequent two-year period. Consistent with our earlier discussion, scores on a love scale were more predictive than scores on a liking scale. In addition, women's love scores were a better indicator of whether the relationship would last than were the men's love scores. Thus, for some reason, the feelings of the woman in the relationship seem to be a more sensitive index of the health of the relationship. Unrelated to the future success of the relationship were whether the couple had had sexual intercourse and whether they had lived together. A couple was equally likely to maintain a relationship whether or not they had engaged in these more intimate forms of interchange.

Similarity of the two partners, discussed earlier as an important factor in attraction, also was important among these Boston couples. As shown in Table 6-3, similarity with respect to age, education, intelligence, and attractiveness were all more important for the couples that stayed together than for those who broke up. On the other hand, similarity of religion, sex-role attitudes, and desired family size did not appear to be important in predicting the

TABLE 6-3 / *The Relationship between Similarity and Breaking Up: Couple Similarity by Status Two Years Later*

Correlation of Partners'	All Couples (N = 231)	Together Couples (N = 117)	Breakup Couples (N = 103)
Characteristics			
Age	.19**	.38**	.13
Highest degree planned	.28**	.31**	.17
SAT, math	.22**	.31**	.11
SAT, verbal	.24**	.33**	.15
Physical attractiveness	.24**	.32**	.16
Father's educational level	.11	.12	.12
Height	.21**	.22*	.22*
Religion (% same)	51%**	51%**	52%**
Attitudes			
Sex-role traditionalism (10-item scale)	.47**	.50**	.41**
Favorability toward women's liberation	.38**	.36**	.43**
Approval of sex among "acquaintances"	.25**	.27**	.21*
Romanticism (6-item scale)	.20*	.21*	.15
Self-report of religiosity	.37**	.39**	.37**
Number of children wanted	.51**	.43**	.57**

Note. Total N for SAT scores = 187, for physical attractiveness = 174. Physical attractiveness based on ratings of color photographs by 4 judges. Religion categorized as Catholic, Protestant, or Jewish; random pairing would have yielded 41% same religion.

Probability of difference between Together and Breakup correlations (one-tailed) for age is $p < .05$, for SAT math and SAT verbal is $.05 < p < .10$, for highest degree planned and for physical attractiveness is $.10 < p < .15$.

Significance levels indicated in the table are for chance probabilities.

*$p < .05$.

**$p < .01$.

From "Breakups Before Marriage: The End of 103 Affairs," by C. T. Hill, L. Rubin, and L. A. Peplau, *Journal of Social Issues,* 1976, *32,* 147–168. Reprinted by permission.

long-term success of relationships. However, on each of these variables, couples were fairly well matched at the beginning of the study, suggesting they may be important in initial partner selection.

Another factor that proved to be an important predictor of the success of the relationship was the man's need for power (Stewart & Rubin, 1976). As measured by stories told in response to TAT cards, need for power is conceptualized as a stable tendency to seek impact on others, either through direct action or through more subtle influence attempts. Men who scored high in need for power in the Boston couples study were more likely to anticipate problems in the relationship and were more like-

ly to express dissatisfaction with the relationship at the initial stage of testing. True to the expectations of these men, a couple in which the man had a high need for power was much less likely to be together two years later. In fact, 50% of these relationships had broken up, compared to only 15% of those in which the man was low in the need for power. Although need for power was measured for the women partners as well, their scores showed absolutely no association to the success or failure of the relationship. This disparity might suggest that men and women express their power needs differently: perhaps men fulfill the "Don Juan" role by seeking many conquests, whereas women are more likely to find satisfaction in a single long-term relationship. Such an explanation is only speculative, of course, and even if true may be altered as the double standard for men and women becomes less pervasive.

To gain more understanding of the breakup process, Hill and his colleagues used a second method of data collection: intensive interviews with some of the couples who had broken up. These interviews provided many new insights into the process of breaking up, even including such facts as when the breakup occurred. Considering that the majority of the couples in this study were college students, it may not be surprising to learn that these relationships were most likely to break up at critical points in the school year—at the beginning of the fall semester and at the end of the fall and spring semesters. Apparently these natural break points in the calendar year allowed couples to break up their relationships more easily. However, it was also true that the less involved partner in a relationship was more likely to precipitate a breakup at one of these natural break points. In contrast, when the partner who had reported being more involved chose to end the affair, the timing was more likely to be in the middle of the school year rather than at the end. For the less involved partner, the separation of a summer vacation may provide a good excuse for ending the relationship, testifying to the truth of the maxim "Absence extinguishes small passions and increases great ones" (La Rochefoucauld, quoted in Hill et al., 1976, p. 158).

Most of the breakups that occurred were perceived to be somewhat one-sided, with over 85% of both men and women reporting that one person wanted to end the relationship somewhat more than the other. These perceptions were not totally accurate, however. Although there was considerable agreement in many cases, there was also a systematic bias in the reports. People were more likely to say that they were the one who wanted to break off the relationship than to say that their partner wished it. Such a strategy is, of course, self-protective: those partners who did the breaking up

were considerably happier, less lonely, and less depressed (but more guilty) than those partners who were the "broken-up-with" ones (see Figure 6-8).

Figure 6-8. The end of a relationship. (Edvard Munch, *Man and Woman*, 1899. Oslo Kommunes Kunstamlinger, Munch-Museet.)

Just who does the breaking up in the traditional male/female couple? Although some cases are clearly mutual decisions, in those cases where one person initiates the split it is more likely to be the woman. Rubin and his colleagues (Rubin, Peplau, & Hill, 1978) have suggested that in our society men tend to fall in love more readily than women, and women fall out of love more readily than men. Although such an assertion may contradict many of the stereotypes of the romantic woman and the "strong, silent" man, the data do support the argument. An interesting by-product of men's greater unwillingness to end the relationship is found in the relationship that the partners reported having after the breakup. If the man broke up the relationship, the couple was very likely to remain casual friends; however, if the woman was the one to end the relationship, staying friends was apparently much more difficult and happened less than half the time (see Figure 6-9 for a humorous version of ending an affair).

"I'm sorry, but it just isn't working out between us, Jeffrey. You're an orange, and I want an apple."

Figure 6-9. (Drawing by Koren; © 1975 The New Yorker Magazine, Inc.)

The end of an affair is probably less traumatic than the end of a marriage. Nevertheless, the factors that contribute to breakups in shorter relationships may also have something to do with those that occur in more long-term bonds. Even in itself, however, the breakup of an affair provides important continuity in our understanding of the development of love between two people.

B. *Inequity and Impermanence*

Earlier in the chapter we discussed the application of equity theory to interpersonal relationships. Whereas we desire equity from our interactions, the perception of in-

equity may be a factor in ending those relationships. For example, you might feel that you put a lot into a relationship, giving your partner emotional support and comfort but receiving little in return. If at the same time you feel that your partner is giving little to the relationship in exchange for your kindness, what would you do? Equity theory would predict that if the imbalance was too great, you would probably choose to end the relationship. In a test of this prediction, 511 men and women at the University of Wisconsin were interviewed about their relationships with their dating partner (Berscheid & Walster, 1978, pp. 189–191). At the initial testing each person was asked to evaluate his or her dating relationship in terms of the contributions and the benefits that each partner was receiving. For example, the person was asked to consider all of the things that might contribute to a relationship (such as personality, emotional support, help in making decisions) and to rate his or her own contribution on a scale from $+4$ to -4. They were then asked to make a similar rating for their partners' contributions. Each person was also asked to make a rating of the benefits received from the relationship, such as love, excitement, security, or a good time, again made for both the self and the partner. From these four estimates, the investigators were able to determine how equitable the relationship was perceived to be.

Three months later, the people were interviewed again and asked whether they were still going out with the same partner and how long they expected the relationship to last in the future. People who had reported equitable relationships at the earlier session were more likely to still be dating at the second testing period. They were also more likely to predict that the relationship would last than were those persons who reported a less equitable relationship. Thus, although it may be difficult to accurately measure all of the factors that contribute to a relationship, it seems clear that our perceptions of the costs and benefits of a relationship are directly related to our willingness to stay in that relationship.

C. *Marriage and Divorce*

The affair that breaks up probably prevents a marriage that would not have worked. Yet marriage itself is obviously not a guarantee of life-long attraction—in the United States, for example, the rate of divorce has been increasing rapidly in recent years (Levinger & Moles, 1979). What happens in these more extended relationships to cause a split? Are the factors similar to those identified in shorter-term dating relationships?

Once two people are married, the development of a relationship does not stop. Although our earlier discussion of stages of development suggested a stopping point when mutual interaction and stable ex-

change were achieved, a closer look at the dynamics of relationships may show a constant flux in attraction and exchange. Swenson (1978), for example, has studied couples ranging from newlyweds to those married for 60 years and has found a steady shift in the patterns of relationship. Over time, a couple's expression of love for each other drops steadily: expressions of love and affection, moral support, and interest and concern for the other person all seem to decrease as the marriage lengthens. At the same time, however, the problems in the relationship also seem to diminish, suggesting that the earlier intensity of romantic love has shifted to a less intense companionate relationship.

Yet in some couples this balance between rewards and costs does not stabilize, and in these cases divorce may be the solution. Levinger (1976) has offered a descriptive analysis of marital relationships, based on the combination of attractions and barriers that are present. Some of the attractions that he identifies are material rewards, such as family income; others are either symbolic, such as status, or affectional, such as companionship and sexual enjoyment. Barriers are conceived of as the potential costs of divorcing the relationship, such as financial expenses, feelings toward children, and religious constraints. Finally, Levinger suggests that people will also weigh the alternative attractions, a concept similar to Thibaut and Kelley's comparison level. Possible alternative attractions that a husband or wife might consider are the values of independence or a preferred companion or sexual partner. This framework is helpful in identifying some of the factors that may come into play when individuals decide whether to continue or to end a relationship. In general, we can predict that, when the attractions of the present relationship decrease, the barriers to getting out of the relationship diminish, and the strength of alternative attractions increases, then at that point an individual would choose to get out of the relationship. Unfortunately, however, this framework is only descriptive. Although there is evidence that many of the attractions and barriers are indeed related to marital stability, we are still a long way from being able to predict precisely when and how a marital relationship will be ended. Often a single event will precipitate a crisis, providing the final straw for a relationship that was already on shaky ground (Jaffe & Kanter, 1976; R. S. Weiss, 1976).

These unresolved questions demonstrate the extensive territory into which future research may go. In 1958, psychologist Harry Harlow wrote "So far as love or affection is concerned, psychologists have failed in their mission. The little we know about love does not transcend simple observations, and the little we write about it has been written better by poets and novelists" (1958, p. 673). Although some people may conclude that Harlow's statement is still essentially accurate, there are reasons for optimism. Many more investigators have become interested in the topic of love, and the issue is no longer taboo. Furthermore, the wider variety of methodologies that are now being used by social psychologists make it possible to investigate more fully complex and long-term relationships.

V. Summary

The need to affiliate, or to be with others, is an exceedingly strong one in many individuals. Some of the reasons for affiliation include the value that other people have in helping us attain goals, the intrinsic value of companionship, and the usefulness of other people in providing a standard for social comparison and self-evaluation. Under conditions of increased situational anxiety, there is also a greater desire to be with others, particularly those who are in the same situation.

Studies of real-life affiliation patterns have provided descriptive data on the extent to which people choose to be alone or with others and suggest that same-sex af-filiation is important, particularly among women.

The following factors make another person more attractive to us: similarity of beliefs, values, and personality; complementarity of needs; physical attractiveness; competence; pleasant or agreeable characteristics; reciprocal liking; and propinquity. Theories that have been proposed to explain interpersonal attraction include reinforcement-affect theory, social-exchange theory, and equity theory.

Two kinds of love have been defined, both of which are different from simple liking. Romantic (or passionate) love is believed to be more momentary; companionate love represents a longer-term relationship. Measurement of love and liking supports the distinction between these two feelings.

Often situational determinants affect the expression of romantic love. Parental interference is one such factor. Unrelated states of arousal may also be interpreted as signs of love, supporting a two-component theory that proposes that both cognitions and physiological arousal are important factors.

Romantic love is not a static phenomenon. Levinger has proposed a series of stages (zero contact, awareness, surface contact, mutuality) to describe the development of a relationship and has suggested that different factors will be important at different points in time.

People fall in love and people fall out of love. Initial feelings of intimacy and similarity of interests are related to breakups; perceptions of inequality in the relationship are also a factor. Even after couples marry, relationships continue to change. The choice to divorce has been represented as the result of an imbalance between attractions, barriers, and alternative attractions.

Glossary Terms

complementarity
equity theory
matching
  hypothesis

mere exposure
  effect
propinquity
sensitivity
  training

social-comparison
  theory
social-exchange
  theory

Sexual relationship is an interpersonal relationship, and as such is subject to the same principles of interaction as are other relationships.

LESTER A. KIRKENDALL   R. W. LIBBY

EDNA MANLEY. THE TREES ARE JOYFUL. NATIONAL GALLERY OF JAMAICA.

Custom controls the sexual impulse as it controls no other.   MARGARET SANGER

7

The Social Psychology of Sexual Behavior

Sexuality is a very obvious part of our lives and of our culture. As romantic love develops and relationships are formed, sexuality generally becomes an issue to be dealt with. Most of us remember our first sexual experience; many of us fantasize about future sexual encounters. People joke about sex, worry about sex, and enjoy sex. Sexual experiences are a part of human social interaction.

At a broader societal level, popular treatments of sexuality become best-sellers, and sex-therapy clinics develop in abundance. In newspapers, magazines, and television commercials, much of the advertising capitalizes on our sexual desires, and in any major city, large numbers of movie theaters offer exclusively X-rated films. Societies develop rules and standards for the expression of sexuality, and groups within the society may accept or challenge those rules.

It is not surprising, then, that the topic of sexual behavior finds a place in a social psychology text. It is an important part of human interaction, and it relates to our attitudes, to societal norms, and to basic learning processes as well. In this chapter, we will consider a number of facets of sexual behavior: the frequency of various forms of sexual behavior, theoretical models concerning the development of sexual behavior, the role of sexuality in interpersonal relationships, the influence of erotic material, and the related issues of contraception and family planning.

I. A Background for the Study of Sexual Behavior

In the Victorian era, when Freud proposed that sexuality was central to human nature, shock waves resounded through the literate world. His ideas were considered not only revolutionary but immoral and evil as well. Although some people still believe in the immorality of much sexual behavior, many others today—while not necessarily adopting Freudian theory—would nonethe-

less argue for the centrality of sexuality to human social behavior. Certainly it is difficult to avoid the topic of sex in newspapers, magazines, or the streets (see **Figure 7-1**). Yet, despite our irrepressible sexual habits and their pervasive effects, science has been quite timid in its investigation of sexual attitudes, behavior, and physiology.

For many years, sexual behavior was a taboo topic for the social scientist. Even the teaching of college-level courses on human sexuality has been a development of the last two decades. Other than a course on sex that was taught at Indiana University many years ago by the famous sex researcher **Alfred Kinsey**, the first university course with a title like "human sexuality" apparently was initiated in **1964** by **James L. McCary** at the University of Houston. The community hostility toward the public discussion of such topics at that time is reflected pungently in one of the many letters that Dr. McCary received. It read:

Dear Sir:

I want you to know that as a Christian I resent what you are teaching them boys and girls at that university. Furthermore, I am going to write the school trustees and let them know what you are doing. I hope you burn and suffer on doomsday, you son-of-a-bitch.

Sincerely yours,

Mr. _____

[Reprinted in McCary, 1975, p. 17.]

As we saw in the last chapter, even the topic of love was considered taboo for many years. Small wonder, then, that the study of sex aroused considerable antagonism and created innumerable difficulties for those scientists who pursued the topic. Even today, investigators who are concerned with the area of sexual behavior often encounter forms of hostility and antagonism not experienced by those conducting research on less controversial topics.

Yet, at the same time, many people are fascinated by the results of sex research, and findings are often quickly publicized and circulated in the mass media. Works by Kinsey and by Masters and Johnson, for example, became best-sellers even though they were written in a technical style and in-

Figure 7-1. The salience of sexuality in contemporary society. (© Peter Menzel/Stock, Boston.)

tended primarily for the professional audience. Such popularity poses an additional problem for the sex researcher, in that findings may be taken for absolute truth when they reflect only a preliminary stage of understanding. Popular "experts" are all too common in the area of human sexuality.

An example of this popularization is David Reuben's famous book *Everything You Always Wanted to Know about Sex but Were Afraid to Ask*. The book became an immediate best-seller when it was published in 1969, and it continues to be referred to quite frequently. Although much of the information contained in the book is correct, the author often generalizes from his personal experience as a psychiatric practitioner. His discussions of homosexuality, prostitution, and impotence, for example, reflect more of his own personal values than of the latest research. Table 7-1 lists some of his statements and compares them with what the scientific evidence actually indicates. By mixing facts with his own personal opinion

disguised as facts, Reuben has undoubtedly caused considerable confusion and, in some cases, distress on the part of his readers.

Not all case history investigations are subject to such popularization or to such error. The earliest scientific reports of sex, for example, were based primarily on the case history records of practicing psychiatrists. In addition to the obvious example of Sigmund Freud, the work of Havelock Ellis (1899/1936) at the turn of the century was based on clinical practice. Yet, in both cases, much of the focus was on abnormal sexual functioning, rather than general descriptions of sexual behavior as a social phenomenon. More recently, some investigators have turned again to the case study method —but with normal populations—and have shown how rich a source of data that can be (Abramson, in press).

Apart from the clinical case history approach, how do investigators study human sexual behavior? Because sex is primarily a private behavior, some of the

T A B L E 7 - 1 / *David Reuben versus the Research Findings*

As a popular guide, the book *Everything You Always Wanted to Know about Sex but Were Afraid to Ask* has been highly successful. Unfortunately, it makes many statements that contradict the empirical evidence (Rollin, 1972). Some of these are listed below.

Dr. Reuben says:	*The evidence indicates:*
1. About 70% to 80% of Americans engage in simultaneous cunnilingus and fellatio.	1. Actual rates of *simultaneous* actions are not available. Recent reports of either activity performed separately indicate rates of 45% to 65%.
2. The best douche available for women is Coca-Cola.	2. Such a procedure could lead to peritonitis, or even to gas embolism, causing death.
3. After the penis is within the vagina, the woman can, by muscle movements, stroke the penis from tip to base.	3. Masters and Johnson's research indicates that this action is impossible for most women.
4. Gentle stroking of the pubic area of a female initiates erection of the clitoris.	4. Masters and Johnson state: "The clitoris does not erect under direct or indirect forms of stimulation." Clitoral erection is a well-established fable usually used in pornography.
5. There is always bleeding when the hymen breaks.	5. Innumerable women have lost their hymens without overt evidence of bleeding.
6. Since the precise moment of orgasm usually brings on the lapse of consciousness, neither partner is able to enjoy the orgasm of the other.	6. Most men and women do *not* lose consciousness during orgasm.

methods discussed in Chapter 2 are not appropriate for this topic. The most common approach has been the survey, using questionnaires and interviews to investigate the range and frequency of people's sexual activities. Kinsey's studies, for example, were based exclusively on this method. He conducted detailed interviews with a large sample of U.S. citizens (Kinsey, Pomeroy, & Martin, 1948; Kinsey, Pomeroy, Martin, & Gebhard, 1953). Similar procedures, often using mailed questionnaires, have continued to be used in recent years (Hite, 1976; Hunt, 1974). The primary advantage of this method, particularly when the questionnaires are anonymous, is that it allows respondents a considerable degree of privacy in discussing intimate aspects of their sexual lives. Potentially embarrassing topics can be dealt with more easily when no face-to-face encounter is involved.

There are some problems with the survey method, however (Byrne & Byrne, 1977). One difficulty concerns the representativeness of the sample of subjects. Subjects in any survey are to some degree self-selected; in other words, after the investigator determines an initial sample, the selected subjects must agree to participate. Particularly in the area of sex research, it is probable that those people who agree to participate are not a random sample. Some people may be quite willing to discuss or to describe their sexual experiences, while others are aghast at the very thought. Generalizing the results of surveys to the total population is thus a very risky venture. A second related problem concerns the accuracy of the answers themselves. As in any self-report measure, the investigator must be concerned with the accuracy of the subject's information. In the area of sex, where norms and values are so strong, the difficulties of accepting self-report data as completely accurate are particularly acute. On the one hand, people may be reluctant to report behavior that is viewed as non-normative; on the other hand, some people may exaggerate their reported activities in order to appear exciting, progressive, or even normal in our age of high sexual pressures. Despite these limitations, however, the survey method will continue to be used when the concern is with describing normative patterns of sexual behavior.

A more recently adopted alternative to the survey method is the laboratory experiment. For example, investigators have conducted numerous studies in which subjects are exposed to a variety of pornographic films and asked to indicate their reactions to the material or to engage in other forms of behavior, such as aggression toward a confederate. In some instances, most notably the work by Masters and Johnson (1966), subjects engage in actual intercourse in the laboratory setting. Such approaches gain the advantages of the experimental method but still have some problems. Self-selection of subjects remains as a weakness, because all of these procedures require fully informed consent before the subject participates in the experiment. People who do not wish to watch pornographic films can choose not to participate, and those that do choose to participate are probably not a random sample. The laboratory also is a highly artificial setting for behaviors that typically occur in very private situations. Although this criticism has been applied to many areas of research, it is probably more severe in the case of sexual behavior.

Despite the problems and difficulties inherent in the study of sexual behavior, progress has been made in recent years. We are finally beginning to learn a good deal about sexual behavior—its frequency, its role in intimate relationships, factors that affect its occurrence, and, perhaps most importantly, the consequences of sexual behavior for social problems such as contraception and overpopulation. In this chapter we will consider each of these points as it relates to the social psychology of sexual behavior.

II. Forms and Frequency of Sexual Behavior

Who engages in which types of sexual behavior under what circumstances? In seeking the answer to this question, we can look to the results of a number of survey studies completed during the past 30 to 40 years. The original, of course, was the work of Kinsey (Kinsey, Pomeroy, & Martin, 1948; Kinsey, Pomeroy, Martin, & Gebhard, 1953). More recently, a large-scale survey by Hunt (1974) has provided an update on the earlier Kinsey data. Other recent surveys have concentrated exclusively on female sexuality (Hite, 1976; Levin & Levin, 1975). In addition, we have detailed information about the sexual attitudes and behavior of college students—a state that reflects the greater ease of access to this population.

A. Kinsey's Studies of Male and Female Sexual Behavior

Because Kinsey's original investigations are benchmark studies in our society and because they were pioneering efforts in the study of sex in any modern society, their major findings are worth reviewing. A few preliminary comments are in order, however. We must always remember that the Kinsey subjects were volunteers selected from diverse sections of the society; they were not selected in a fashion designed to ensure the representativeness of the sample. Also, the data were collected in face-to-face interviews, where inhibition is a real possibility. Yet, while there are many possible methodological artifacts in the original Kinsey procedures (sampling bias, interviewer bias, self-report distortions by the subjects), comparisons between the Kinsey findings and those of other investigators have produced generally consistent outcomes.

Some of the more general findings of Kinsey and his associates are shown in Figure 7-2. As can be seen, during the late 1940s and early 1950s when these data were collected, men more frequently than women reported a variety of sexual activities. It is also important to note that, while a substantial number of people of both sexes

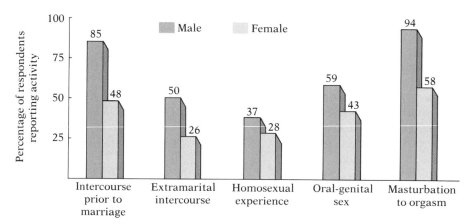

Figure 7-2. Frequencies of various forms of sexual behavior among males and females in the Kinsey surveys.

(37% of the males, 28% of the females) reported having had at least one homosexual experience, relatively few people of either sex (4% of the males, 3% of the females) reported themselves as being exclusively homosexual.

For both sexes, socioeconomic status was one of the most significant variables in predicting the incidence of most sexual behaviors. College-educated people, even though as children they had begun most sexual practices later than noncollege men and women, reported less inhibition in most sexual behaviors and were more likely to engage in masturbation, oral-genital sex, homosexuality, and a variety of coital positions. Although differences among religious denominations were not as striking, those persons who described themselves as nonreligious were more likely to masturbate, to pet to orgasm, and to have premarital coitus and extramarital affairs.

B. *Hunt's More Recent Survey*

In the early 1970s, **Morton Hunt (1974)** conducted a survey of 2026 people in the United States, generally matching the U.S. adult population in regard to most demographic characteristics. Interestingly, this study was financed by the Playboy Foundation in an effort to develop an accurate current picture of U.S. sexual attitudes and practices. Although this survey still is subject to some of the methodological problems discussed earlier, particularly in terms of subject self-selection, the results nonetheless give us some indication of current attitudes and behavior concerning sexuality.

In considering people's expressed attitudes toward various forms of sexuality, Hunt did not have much basis for comparison, as Kinsey had considered only people's reported behavior and not their reported attitudes. Even without this comparison, however, Hunt's findings suggest a considerable degree of permissiveness in attitudes toward sexuality. For example, more than 75% of his sample believed that schools should teach sex education. The vast majority of the people surveyed believed that the man should not always be the one to initiate sexual intercourse, and nearly as many people reported that nonmarital sex was acceptable. Positive attitudes toward specific sexual practices, such as cunnilingus and fellatio, also showed wide acceptance.

What about the actual behavior reported by people in this survey? In comparison with the earlier Kinsey data, Hunt's data indicate a number of changes, although not so many as some people might think. For example, extramarital intercourse appears to have decreased slightly for males (from 50% down to 41%), while the incidence of extramarital intercourse remained fairly constant for females. However, those who did engage in extramarital affairs did so earlier in the marriage than did the people in Kinsey's sample. As a possibly related factor, we can consider the results for divorced persons (the frequency of which is twice as high as it was at the time of the Kinsey survey). Divorced males and females both report considerably more sexual activity than did the divorced persons in the Kinsey sample. In the Hunt sample, divorced males reported a median of 8 sexual partners a year, and divorced women reported an average of 3.5.

Nonmarital sex was found to be much more common among the women in Hunt's sample (75% as compared to 48% in the Kinsey study), but there was little change in the incidence of nonmarital sex for the men. At the same time, men reported substantially less use of prostitutes in the 1970s than they did in the 1940s and 1950s. Between marriage partners, the frequency of intercourse appears to have increased somewhat; for couples in the 26 to 35 age range, the average was 2.6 times per week in comparison to the earlier figure of 2.0 times per week. One of the most striking differences was in the frequency of oral-genital contact. Paralleling the permissive attitudes that were expressed, figures showed that more than two-thirds of the people had tried this form of sexual activity.

The incidence of homosexuality does not appear to have changed much since Kinsey's study, despite the considerable publicity that the Gay Liberation Movement has garnered in recent years. Hunt's findings were similar to the Kinsey findings: 6% of the men and 3% of the women reported having had a homosexual experience within the preceding year. The percentage of people in Hunt's study who reported having had at some time at least one homosexual experience was nearer to 25%.

In summary, the results of Hunt's survey suggest that there has been some relaxation (a) of the pressures operating against sexual activity (particularly in the forms of sexuality), (b) in the sexual activities of women, and (c) in the sexual activity of divorced persons. At the same time, many areas have shown relatively little change between the 1940s and the 1970s, suggesting that the apparent increase in sexuality in our society may be only a change in expressed attitudes, rather than any drastic shift in behavior.

C. *Changes in Sexual Attitudes and Behavior among College Students*

We have reviewed findings for the incidence of sexual behavior in the general population with a focus on changes in the last three decades. What can we say about the sexual behavior of college students in particular? Here, of course, the majority of sexual activity is nonmarital, because the majority of college students are single.

Early work (reviewed by Smigel & Seiden, 1968) found that approximately 45% of college men and 12% of college women did not endorse sexual abstinence for single people. Later work by Reiss (1960, 1967), using a U.S. sample that included both Black and White high school and college students in both Northern and Southern schools, found that sexual standards had been noticeably liberalized. In 1959, when the first study by Reiss was done, nearly 70% of the males and 27% of the females accepted nonmarital intercourse as appropriate for themselves. It should be noted that, when these figures were compared to a typical adult population, the college students' beliefs were considerably more liberal than those of the adults.

The attitudes of college students toward nonmarital intercourse are related to a number of factors (McCary, 1978; Athanasiou, 1973). Among the men, acceptance of greater intimacy is related to race, age, semester in college, strength of religious feelings, and region of the country. Older men who are indifferent or hostile to religion and who attend Eastern, Western, or Southern schools are more permissive in their attitudes than younger, religious Midwestern males. Among college women, the crucial factor apparently is being in love. In a series of studies at the University of Colorado (Kaats & Davis, 1970) and in broad surveys (Freeman & Freeman, 1966; Nutt & Sedlacek, 1974), up to 70% of the women endorsed sexual intercourse for themselves when they are in love, but 40% or less found it acceptable when only strong affection exists. Among college women, acceptance of greater intimacy is very strongly related to having been in love two or more times or to being in a significant dating relationship.

As recently as 1970, attitudes expressed by college students indicated a continued acceptance of the double standard—that sexual behavior for singles is more acceptable for men than for women (Kaats & Davis, 1970). As shown in Table 7-2, both men and women reported acceptance of this double standard, wherein the expectations for women's behavior are more restricted than those for men. Whether this same double standard persists in the 1980s is uncertain, although there is some evidence to suggest erosion of the standard (King, Balswick, & Robinson, 1977).

People's attitudes may not always be expressed in their behavior, however. Athanasiou and Sarkin (1974) report that a substantial number of the respondents in their U.S. national sample believed that nonmarital sex was wrong but still did not wait until marriage to experience sexual intercourse. What are the findings regarding the actual sexual behavior of college students?

Curran (1977) asked 164 U.S. college students at a large, relatively conservative, Midwestern university to complete a questionnaire about their sexual experience. The results of his study, which looked at a large variety of sexual behaviors, are shown in Table 7-3. As indicated in the table, the majority of behaviors show no strong differences between males and females. There is, however, some suggestion from the percentage figures that college men and women may experience some sexual behaviors in different orders. For example, more women

T A B L E   7 - 2 / *Mean Scores for College Male and Female Respondents on Items Measuring Male/Female Sexual Equalitarianism*

Item[a]	Males (N = 110)	Females (N = 162)
1. It is important to me to be a virgin at the time of my marriage.	1.80	3.15
2. Virginity in a prospective mate is important to me.	2.92	1.98
3. If he asked my advice about having sexual intercourse, I would encourage a brother of mine *not* to engage in it before marriage.	2.48	2.63
4. If she asked my advice about having sexual intercourse, I would encourage a sister of mine *not* to engage in it before marriage.	3.47	3.65
5. I would lose respect for a male who engaged in premarital intercourse with a girl he did not love.	2.19	2.87
6. I would lose respect for a girl who engaged in premarital intercourse with a boy she did not love.	3.11	3.80
7. I think having sexual intercourse is more injurious to a girl's reputation than to a boy's reputation.	4.26	4.47
8. I have higher standards of sexual morality for females than for males.	3.52	3.79

[a] Subjects indicated their degree of agreement or disagreement with each statement. The choices were keyed as follows: 1 = strongly disagree, 2 = moderately disagree, 3 = neutral, 4 = moderately agree, 5 = strongly agree. Thus, a mean of 1.80 means an average score close to moderate disagreement (2.00) but a little stronger.

Adapted from "The Dynamics of Sexual Behavior of College Students," by G. R. Kaats and K. E. Davis, *Journal of Marriage and the Family*, 1970, 32(3), 390–399. Copyright 1970 by the National Council on Family Relations. Reprinted by permission of the authors and publisher.

TABLE 7-3 / *Sexual Behavior among College Students*

Have you ever engaged in the following behavior with a member of the opposite sex?	Percentage of Males Saying "Yes"	Percentage of Females Saying "Yes"
1. One minute of continuous kissing on the lips?	86.4	89.2
2. Manual manipulation of clothed female breasts?	82.7	71.1
3. Manual manipulation of bare female breasts?	75.5	66.3
4. Manual manipulation of clothed female genitals?	76.4	67.5
5. Kissing nipples of female breast?	65.5	59.0
6. Manual manipulation of bare female genitals?	64.4	60.2
7. Manual manipulation of clothed male genitals?	57.3	51.8
8. Mutual manipulation of genitals?	55.5	50.6
9. Manual manipulation of bare male genitals?	50.0	51.8
10. Manual manipulation of female genitals until there were massive secretions?	49.1	50.6
11. Sexual intercourse, face to face?	43.6	37.3
12. Manual manipulation of male genitals to ejaculation?	37.3	41.0
13. Oral contact with female genitals?	31.8	42.2
14. Oral contact with male genitals?	30.9	42.2
15. Mutual manual manipulation of genitals to mutual orgasm?	30.9	26.5
16. Oral manipulation of male genitals?	30.0	38.6
17. Oral manipulation of female genitals?	30.0	41.0
18. Mutual oral-genital manipulation?	20.9	28.9
19. Sexual intercourse, entry from the rear?	14.5	22.9
20. Oral manipulation of male genitals to ejaculation?	22.7	26.5
21. Mutual oral manipulation of genitals to mutual orgasm?	13.6	12.0

From "Convergence Toward a Single Sexual Standard," by J. P. Curran, *Social Behavior and Personality*, 1977, *3*, 189–195. Reprinted by permission.

have experienced cunnilingus and fellatio than have experienced intercourse, while for males that pattern is reversed. These findings suggest that, in some instances, women are enjoying various forms of sexual satisfaction while still remaining technically virgins. Similar patterns of results have been found by other investigators as well (Bentler, 1968a, 1968b; Curran, Neff, & Lippold, 1973). Thus, the sequence of behaviors may be somewhat different for males and females, but the overall frequency of sexual behavior in the late 1970s is not terribly different for men and women, suggesting that a double standard of behavior may not be pervasive in the college population.

The overall rates of intercourse for males and females in this sample (coming from a Midwestern U.S. population) appear to be slightly lower than figures reported from other locales. Over all locations, however, the percentage of college students who have engaged in sexual intercourse varies between 55% and 65% for women and between 70% and 75% for men (King, Balswick, & Robinson, 1977; Maxwell, Sack, Frary, & Keller, 1977). Similar studies in Canada, done a few years earlier, have shown rates of about 40% for women and 55% for men (Perlman, 1973).

The prevalence of sexual behavior, among the single as well as the married, surely testifies to the importance of sex as one aspect of social interaction. Yet, the frequency data, although interesting, tell us only what is being done and not why. What are the reasons for sexual behavior? What theoretical frameworks have been offered to explain sexuality? We will explore these questions further.

III. Theoretical Issues in Sexual Behavior

The variation in standards for sexual behavior is tremendous. If we look across various cultures, we find an incredible diversity of attitudes toward sexual behavior. In some cases, sex is seen as pleasurable, in others as innocuous, and in still others as a potentially dangerous event. Members of one society may say that sex is "the best thing in life," while other groups view sex as "a little like work" (Broude, 1975). How are these variations in sexual behavior explained?

A. *Freudian Theory of Sexuality*

Sigmund Freud was perhaps the first person to insist that sexuality is a basic part of the human personality. In his theorizing at the turn of the century, Freud proposed that sexual energy is the basic motivator of human behavior, and he described a sequence of stages paralleling supposed changes in the locus of sexual tension (Freud, 1938). Infantile sexuality centered on *oral* and *anal* areas of the body, but at the age of 5 or so, the *genital* area became central to the expression of sexuality. At this stage, too, Freud postulated critical differences between male and female development—differences that he believed contributed to significant variations in the sexual behavior of adult males and females. More specifically, Freud suggested that women could experience true sexuality only through vaginal orgasms as a result of penetration by the penis. Other modes of achieving orgasm, such as masturbation, were considered by Freud to reflect inadequate femininity, which he believed derived from the young girl's early penis envy. Although Freud believed that there is a physical as well as a psychological distinction between clitoral and vaginal orgasms, later research has demonstrated that the physiological experience of the two forms is identical (Masters & Johnson, 1966).

Freud also believed that his proposed sequence of the development of sexuality, including the famous Oedipal period, was universal. In other words, members of every culture and society were believed to go through the same sequence of events in the development of their sexuality. Although the socialization practices of various cultures might modify the expression of sexual energy, Freud for the most part believed that similar sexual motivations and conflicts would be found in every society.

B. *Cognitive Aspects of Sexual Behavior*

Many people disagree with Freud's theory of sexuality, but few deny that sexual behavior is basic to humans and animals alike. As a necessity for reproduction of the species, sexual intercourse is performed fairly instinctively, although the forms and cycles of sex vary among species (Ford & Beach, 1951; Daly & Wilson, 1978). In human beings, in particular, the variation in forms of sexual behavior is considerable, and it is difficult to account for these differences on the basis of instinct alone. Consequently, many recent theorists in the area of sexual behavior have begun to focus on cognitive factors that surround the choice and experience of sexuality.

As Paul Abramson (in press) states in explaining his model of the sexual system, "The underlying assumption in the present schema is that all decisions regarding sexual expression are controlled by a mechanism which has been represented as a cognitive structure." A careful examination of Figure 7-3 will show how this assumption works. Abramson assumes that a variety of factors influence the cognitive structure: parental standards, social norms, maturation, and previous sexual experience. For example, parents may instruct us as to what is proper sexual behavior. Other norms and values may be learned from our church or from our peers. The process of maturation itself, especially the onset of puberty, can influence our beliefs about sexuality. And finally, actual sexual experience—whether fantasy, masturbation, or intercourse—will play an important role in our beliefs. From the sum of these experiences, we develop a set of principles about sexual behavior. (This idea is, of course, very similar to the

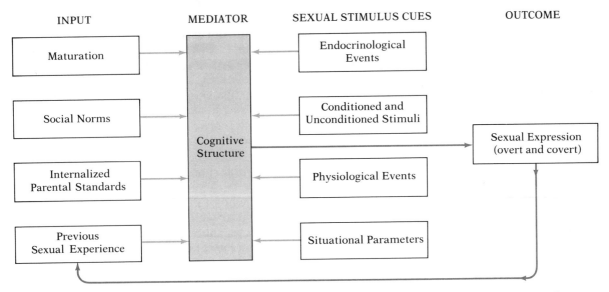

INPUT | MEDIATOR | SEXUAL STIMULUS CUES | OUTCOME

Figure 7-3. The sexual system. In this model proposed by Paul Abramson, cognitive structures are a major influence on sexual expression. The structures are formed on the basis of various inputs, and they, in turn, monitor various sexual stimulus cues to determine eventual sexual expression. (From *The Sexual System: A Theory of Human Sexual Behavior*, by P. R. Abramson. Copyright 1979 by Academic Press. Reprinted by permission of the author and publisher.)

concepts of schemata and prototypes that we discussed in Chapter 3.)

But past experience isn't the only thing that determines our sexual expression. A variety of sexual stimulus cues, both internal and external, can be influential, and these cues also are processed by the mediating cognitive structure. Internally, there are the influence of hormones and the nervous system. Externally, there are a variety of stimuli that may be associated with sexuality, such as erotic movies, racy novels, and particular people. Certain situations also may encourage sexual expression: environments in which sexual permissiveness is fostered or in which alcohol or other drugs are being used. On the basis of the principles that people have established, they will then weigh the acceptability of certain forms of sexual behavior and eventually make a choice.

Abramson's model is admittedly complex. Yet, it rests on a couple of very simple assumptions. First, it assumes that we learn from past experience and that principles of learning can be applied as easily to sexual behavior as they can to other forms of behavior. Second, it assumes that our cogni-

tions about sexuality are important—in other words, that sexual expression is not instinctual, but rather is the outcome of rational thought. Freud probably would disagree with both assumptions, but especially with the latter. Most current investigators of sexual behavior, however, have adopted some combination of learning and cognitive principles to explain sexual behavior (Byrne, 1977; Rook & Hammen, 1977) and the early results appear to justify their assumptions.

C. *Heterosexual and Homosexual Choices*

Evidence that learning plays an important part in our definition of and response to sexual stimuli also is related to the issue of heterosexual versus homosexual behavior. Why do some people prefer sexual partners of the same sex rather than partners of the other sex? Before discussing this, we must understand the distinction between gender identity and sexual preference. **Gender identity** refers to one's self-awareness of being male or female

(Money & Ehrhardt, 1972). Early theories of homosexuality often assumed that, for the homosexual, gender identity was opposite to the biological sex. In other words, some argued that the male homosexual in fact identified himself as a female and hence preferred a male sexual partner. This *sex-role inversion* theory suggested that homosexuals dress, act, and behave as much like the other sex as possible. More recently, it has been recognized that gender identity and *sexual preference* are quite distinct— that homosexuals have no confusion about their gender identity but simply prefer sexual partners of the same sex.[1]

Although there is no society in which homosexual expression is the dominant form (Ford & Beach, 1951), homosexual behavior has been common throughout history. In early Greek times, Sappho was born on the island of Lesbos (from which the word *lesbian* is derived) and wrote passionate love poems describing both homosexual and heterosexual love. Romans were fairly relaxed about all forms of sexual behavior, but, with the advent of Christianity, the norms regarding homosexual behavior became more restrictive. In the 19th century, Oscar Wilde was jailed and ruined, despite his creative output, when a court found him guilty of homosexual practices (Money & Tucker, 1975). Even in recent years, the majority of people in a national U.S. sample stated that homosexuality is sick, disgusting, and should be outlawed (Levitt & Klassen, 1974). In the United States, numerous referenda have been proposed (and frequently passed) to limit the civil rights of homosexuals.

The strong feelings aroused by indications of homosexuality and the disagreement about the causes of homosexual behavior obviously have a long history. Freud, for example, although he did not consider homosexuality an illness, was ambivalent about the normality of such behavior (see **Box 7-1**). In 1973, however, the **American Psychiatric Association** officially removed homosexuality from its list of mental disorders, thus endorsing the view that the choice of a sexual partner of the same gender is no more an indication of mental illness than is choice of a partner of the other gender. Even more recently, an extensive investigation sponsored by the **Kinsey Institute** (Bell & Weinberg, 1978) indicates that people who prefer a same-sex partner are every bit as well adjusted, on the average, as a comparable sample of heterosexuals. The majority of the homosexuals studied were or had been involved in steady relationships (though often of shorter duration than those of heterosexuals), derived satisfaction from their jobs, had a wide circle of friends, and described themselves as "pretty happy."

Yet, the question that still remains for research and theory is why some people prefer homosexuality while others prefer heterosexuality. Some investigators have sought genetic and physiological explanations for homosexuality (for example, Kallmann, 1952), but the evidence to date does not support an argument for biological differences between homosexuals and heterosexuals (Katchadourian & Lunde, 1975). A more common approach has been to look to early experiences in the socialization process as possible causes of homosexual behavior. From a Freudian viewpoint, such early experiences are considered critical blocks in the normal sequence of development. Freud believed that people are inherently bisexual (Freud, 1930), but he also believed that in the normal course of development the object choice becomes limited to members of the other sex. As a further illustration of the basic Freudian position, **Deutsch** described female homosexuality as a neurosis, deriving from penis envy and a psychological attachment to the mother (O'Leary, 1977). This position has received little empirical support, however (Mannion, 1976).

Investigators less wedded to a psychodynamic explanation of sexuality have looked simply at specific socialization ex-

[1] **Transsexualism,** in contrast, refers to the case in which one's gender identity is in opposition to one's bodily appearance and sexual organs. The writer James Morris, who became Jan Morris after a sex-change operation, described the feelings of a transsexual as follows: "I was born with the wrong body, being feminine by gender but male by sex, and I could achieve completeness only when the one was adjusted to the other" (Morris, 1974).

Box 7-1. A Letter from Freud.

April 9, 19_____

Dear Mrs. _____ ,

I gather from your letter that your son is a homosexual. I am most impressed by the fact that you do not mention this term yourself in your information about him. May I question you, why do you avoid it? Homosexuality is assuredly no advantage, but it is nothing to be ashamed of, no vice, no degradation, it cannot be classified as an illness; we consider it to be a variation of the sexual function produced by a certain arrest of sexual development. Many highly respectable individuals of ancient and modern times have been homosexuals, several of the greatest men among them (Plato, Michelangelo, Leonardo da Vinci, etc.). It is a great injustice to persecute homosexuality as a crime, and cruelty too. If you do not believe me, read the books of Havelock Ellis.

By asking me if I can help, you mean, I suppose, if I can abolish homosexuality and make normal heterosexuality take its place. The answer is, in a general way, we cannot promise to achieve it. In a certain number of cases we succeed in developing the blighted germs of heterosexual tendencies which are present in every homosexual; in the majority of cases it is no more possible. It is a question of the quality and the age of the individual. The result of the treatment cannot be predicted.

What analysis can do for your son runs in a different line. If he is unhappy, neurotic, torn by conflicts, inhibited in his social life, analysis may bring him harmony, peace of mind, full efficiency, whether he remains a homosexual or gets changed. If you make up your mind he should have analysis with me (I don't expect you will!!) he has to come over to Vienna. I have no intention of leaving here. However, don't neglect to give me your answers.

Sincerely yours with kind wishes,

Dr. Sigmund Freud

periences, assuming that learning plays a major role in one's choice of sexual partners. Investigations of this type have reported that often the homosexual male has had a poor relationship with his father, was closer to his mother than to his father, and began relatively early to avoid typical masculine pursuits (Bieber, Dain, Dince, Drellich, Girand, Gundlach, Kremer, Rifkin, Wilbur, & Bieber, 1962; Evans, 1969). There are indications that, for these men, normative masculine role behavior was not encouraged by either parent and that, although many homosexual males reported engaging in heterosexual experiences during adolescence, they found the experience unsatisfactory or a source of rejection (Stephan, 1973).

Female homosexuality has been investigated less extensively than male homosexuality, although a few studies are available (Gundlach & Riess, 1968; Wolff, 1971). In these studies, there is some indication that homosexual women had mothers who were somewhat indifferent toward their daughters, and there is a suggestion of greater family instability among homosexual women as compared to heterosexual women. Often these women displayed some forms of "tomboy" behavior as children, although the frequency of such behavior in heterosexual women certainly rules against its being causal in the development of homosexual preferences.

To summarize these findings, there is some evidence that certain social-psychological factors may be influential in the development of homosexual versus heterosexual preferences. Three factors that seem to be important are (1) relationship with parents, (2) source and rewardingness of early sexual behavior, and (3) peer relationships in adolescence and adulthood. Yet, it is important to note that many of the same conditions may be present in the early experience of the heterosexual as well, and thus in themselves they are not sufficient to determine sexual choice.

Perhaps the most instructive approach to understanding sexual-behavior choices is not to think in terms of the two categories "homosexual" and "heterosexual," but rather to consider sexual choice as a continuum. Kinsey and his colleagues (Kinsey et al., 1953), based on their extensive study of sexual behavior in the United States, advocated this position. Although a fairly limited proportion of the population is exclusively homosexual, a considerably larger proportion has had at least one homosexual experience. Furthermore, another sector of the population is essentially **bisexual**—that is, engages in sexual behavior with both the same and the other sex during similar periods of time. Such varieties in sexual preference point to the danger in oversimplifying the categories in which we place people. At the same time, occasional homosexual activity on the part of people who are predominantly heterosexual points to the importance of situational influences in one's choice of sexual experience. In discussing bisexuality, for example, Blumstein and Schwartz (1977) identify three kinds of circumstances that are common influences: (1) experimentation in a friendship context (particularly common among women), (2) liberal hedonistic environments where group sex and other activities are explored, and (3) erotically based ideological positions wherein sex represents one aspect of a more general philosophy of life. Other situations that may encourage or permit homosexual behavior by persons who generally consider themselves heterosexual include prisons, military camps, and prep schools, in all of which heterosexual outlets are absent or severely limited. The influence of such situational factors on sexual behavior surely points to sexuality as a social phenomenon, influenced by circumstances and not totally dependent on internal psychological or biological factors.

IV. Sexual Behavior in Relationships

Thus far we have considered sexual behavior from the perspective of the individual, looking at the frequency with which people report experiencing sexual activities and the theoretical issues involved in an individual's decisions about when and how to have sex. Yet, it is clear that sexual behavior is for the most part a shared experience—in other words, it is an important social and interpersonal event. Let's look, then, at the role of sexuality in interpersonal relationships.

A. *Sexuality in Nonmarital Relationships*

In Chapter 6 we discussed an extensive study of more than 200 dating couples in the Boston area, focusing on the ways in which partners fall in and out of love. This same study included an in-depth investigation of the sexual behavior of these couples and provides us with one of the most thorough reports on the nonmarital sexual behavior of college students in the 1970s (Peplau, Rubin, & Hill, 1977).

The majority of these couples were very positive about sexuality in a relationship. Not only did 80% of the couples believe that it was completely acceptable for couples who love each other to have intercourse, but also their behavior was consistent with these expressed beliefs: 82% of the couples had had intercourse in their current relationship. This figure does not imply that the number of college students who have intercourse is this high; our earlier discussion of the frequency of sexual behavior among college students showed the percentage was somewhat lower. Among couples who are "going with" someone, however, the incidence of sexual intercourse is quite high.

Although the majority of the couples in the Peplau et al. study had experienced intercourse with their current partner, 18% of the couples reported abstention. In these couples, it appeared that the woman was the primary source of restraint. Of the men, 64% reported that it was their partner's desire to abstain that kept them from engaging in sexual activity. Another reason for abstention in these couples, endorsed by nearly half of the men and the women, was a fear of pregnancy. In addition, women also said that sex would violate their ethical standards and that it was too early in the relationship to consider sexual activity. The religious background of the woman also was related to the sexual behavior of the couple. Approximately 27% of the Catholic women in the sample refrained from intercourse, compared to 16% of Jewish women and only 2% of Protestant women. Interestingly, the man's religious background had no effect on the presence or absence of sexual intercourse in the relationship.

Among the couples who had engaged in intercourse during their relationship, approximately half of the couples had done so within one month after the first date. Comparing these couples to the ones who began sexual activity at a later stage in the relationship, Peplau and her colleagues found that characteristics of the woman again were more related to the couple's activities than were characteristics of the man. As shown in Table 7-4, the women in those couples where sexual intercourse had occurred early reported themselves as less religious, more oriented toward a career, less oriented toward the homemaker role, and higher in self-esteem as assessed by a number of self-ratings.

The three types of couples observed in this study (those who abstain, those who have sex fairly early in the relationship, and those who first engage in sex at a later point in the relationship) viewed the relationship between sex and emotional intimacy in rather different ways. For the abstaining couples, sexuality was viewed in quite traditional ways, and a permanent commitment of marriage was a necessary prerequisite for sexual behavior. The women in these relationships were typically virgins, although the men may have had limited sexual experience in other relationships. Those couples who experienced sexual activity very early in the relationship, in contrast, indicated their approval of casual sex. They said that, although love is desirable in a sexual relationship, sex without love also is accept-

TABLE 7-4 / *Characteristics of Women in "Early Coitus" and "Later Coitus" Couples*

	Early Coitus (N = 90)	Later Coitus (N = 92)
Self-rating on religiosity (9-point scale)	3.4	4.2
Preference for being full-time housewife in 15 years (mean rank among 4)	2.8	2.3
Preference for being single career woman in 15 years (mean rank among 4)	3.0	3.5
Authoritarian submission (10 items)	1.8	2.3
Adherence to alternative lifestyle (9-point scale)	6.2	5.3
Self-ratings (all 9-point scales)		
Creative	6.4	5.9
Intelligent	7.0	6.6
Self-Confident	5.8	5.0
Desirable as a date	6.8	6.2

Note. All early-late differences significant at $p < .05$ or better. Similar analyses for men failed to reach statistical significance. (Early = within one month of first date.)

From "Sexual Intimacy in Dating Relationships," by L. A. Peplau, Z. Rubin, and C. T. Hill, *Journal of Social Issues*, 1977, *33*(2), 86–109. Reprinted by permission.

able. Often sexual intercourse for these couples served as a means of developing emotional intimacy, rather than being the result of such feelings. In between these two extremes were the couples that Peplau and her colleagues termed *sexual moderates*. For these couples, sex occurred later in the relationship, after love and emotional intimacy had been established. Ethical reasons did not appear to delay the onset of sexual activity, but romantic concerns were a necessary element. Despite the diversity in the views toward sexuality among these three kinds of couples, the long-term success of the relationship was equally likely for all three patterns. Two years after the initial interviews, an equal percentage of each type of couple had married (20%), had continued to date (34%), or had broken up (46%).

One final area of interest in this study concerns the differences between men and women in their attitudes toward sexuality. Men were somewhat more positive in their attitudes toward sex in a casual relationship (which is consistent with the attitude surveys we discussed earlier), but both men and women agreed that sex was acceptable in a love relationship. Contrary to some assumptions, the relationship between love and sexual satisfaction in the relationship was no different for men than for women. For both sexes, reported love was moderately correlated with reported sexual satisfaction.

Perhaps the most striking difference between the sexes in this study concerned the issue of loss of virginity. Commentators often have suggested that the loss of virginity is a more important step for a woman than for a man (Bernard, 1975), and the results of this study of Boston couples support that suggestion. The issue of whether the man was a virgin prior to the existing relationship had no noticeable effect on the couple's feelings of commitment, but the woman's sexual status prior to the relationship did affect the couple's commitment. Couples in which the woman had been a virgin prior to the existing relationship reported more love for each other and a higher probability of marriage. In addition, these women reported more closeness and greater satisfaction in the relationship than did women who had experienced intercourse prior to the existing relationship. It is interesting, however, that the previous virginity of the woman had no long-term effect on the relationship: couples in which the woman had been a virgin prior to their relationship were no more likely to stay together than were those couples in which the woman had had prior sexual experience.

In summary, the nonmarital sexual behavior of college students covers a wide range of styles. Although sexual activity of any kind (such as petting or genital manipulation) is most likely to occur when there is a sense of equity in the relationship (Walster, Walster, & Traupmann, 1978), the actual experience of intercourse may happen early, late, or not at all. Its occurrence seems to have little to do with predicting the long-term success of the relationship.

B. *Sexuality in Marital Relationships*

Although nonmarital sex appears to have little effect on the stability of dating relationships, we might ask whether it has any long-term effects at all. Specifically, for the couple who does get married, does their premarital sexual experience have any effect on their subsequent marital satisfaction? Ard (1974) asked this question of a sample of 161 couples who each had been married for approximately 20 years. Of these couples, who married in the 1930s, nearly half reported having had premarital intercourse with their future spouse. (This figure very closely approximates the Kinsey data but may prove surprising to some students. College students, when asked to estimate the extent of their parents' sexual activities, tend to grossly underestimate the levels of such activity, whether it is premarital, marital, or extramarital, as studies by Pocs and Godow, 1978, have shown.) When persons in this sample of married couples were asked whether their premarital sexual experience—either intercourse or the lack of it—had any effect on their marriage, the majority of couples in both groups reported that there was little effect. More people reported a favorable effect than an unfavorable effect, regardless of the level of activity, although wives who had not experienced premarital intercourse with their spouse were inclined to be most favorable about the effects of premarital abstention on subsequent marital happiness.

Within the marital relationship itself, sex often is believed to be a critical determinant of marital happiness. For example, Golden (1971) has concluded: "There are couples for whom the only good thing in marriage is sex. And there are sexless marriages which are satisfactory to husband and wife. But both these situations are rare. Usually in a discordant marriage the sex life is unsatisfactory, too" (p. 185). Research has tended to support this relationship between sexual satisfaction and marital satisfaction. For example, Thornton (1977) asked married people to monitor the frequency of their sexual intercourse for 35 days and at the end of that period to rate their marital happiness. The two indices were highly related ($r = +.70$), suggesting that sex and marital happiness do go together. In this same study, Thornton found that marital happiness was negatively related to the frequency of reported arguments, as might be expected, and that the frequency of sex was negatively related to the frequency of arguments as well. Although these latter relationships are not surprising, they are important because they remind us that correlational data cannot demonstrate causality. The frequency of sex and the frequency of arguments both may affect marital happiness; in turn, both of these factors may be affected by some third variable, such as job difficulties, health worries, or the presence of interfering relatives in the home.

The fact that sexual activity and marital happiness are related to a large number of other variables is clearly demonstrated by the results of a large-scale survey conducted by *Redbook* magazine (Levin & Levin, 1975). In this survey, nearly 100,000 women responded to a series of questions about the sexual satisfactions of their marriage. Nearly 70% of these women, regardless of how long they had been married, reported that their marital sex life was either good or very good. Interestingly, women who said that they were strongly religious were more likely to report a satisfying sexual life than were women who reported not being religious. At the same time, those women who said that they were nonreligious were less positive about other aspects of their marriage, and about themselves as well, when compared to the more religious women. The sexual satisfaction of these married women appeared to vary directly with the reported frequency of intercourse, which is consistent with earlier findings. For example, only 9% of those women who reported no sex in their marriage were willing to say that that was a satisfactory state of affairs. In a similar vein, sexual satisfac-

tion was reported to be greater when the women had frequent orgasms and when they felt that they could discuss their sexual feelings with their husband on most occasions.

From these studies, we can conclude that sexual behavior is indeed an important aspect of most marriages. Although it surely is not the sole determinant of marital happiness and may be affected by many other kinds of behaviors and events, sexual behavior is nonetheless central in most people's marital relationships.

V. Erotic Material and Sexual Arousal

In all of the kinds of social behavior that we've discussed, we have found that external stimuli and events can affect our behavior and our feelings. The area of sexuality is no different. What is sexually arousing? Is the state of arousal influenced by the setting in which it occurs? What are the effects of sexual arousal on other forms of behavior? In this section we will consider the specific influences of erotic stimuli on a variety of responses and the relationship between sexual arousal and other forms of behavior.

A. *Definitions of Erotic Stimuli*

Defining erotic stimuli is probably one of the most difficult tasks in this area of study. The terms *erotica*, *obscenity*, and *pornography* have all been used interchangeably but they each have somewhat different meanings. The word **obscenity** originally meant that which was considered publicly offensive and therefore proscribed— primarily derogatory statements about the church and government (W. C. Wilson, 1973). The incorporation of sexual terms and activities within the realm of obscenity developed around the middle of the 19th century; more recent developments in the United States have completed the process by limiting legal obscenity to the sexual realm (Bender, 1971). At one point the U.S.

Supreme Court set three criteria by which material could be judged obscene: (1) material appeals to prurient interest in the average person, (2) material goes substantially beyond community standards with regard to the depiction of sex, and (3) material is without redeeming social value (Money & Athanasiou, 1973). Yet, in subsequent court cases, it has been discovered that these criteria are very difficult to define. The question of what is obscene remains unresolved.

Pornography has been the term most used in recent years to refer to any written, visual, or verbal material that is considered sexually arousing. Although this term has been distinguished from obscenity in legal usage, it too has its problems. *Pornography* may refer to a wide range of materials, from sexually explicit films that portray genuine love and affection to books that depict hostility, aggression, and sadomasochistic relationships. Some recent investigators have preferred to use the term **erotica** (Byrne, Fisher, Lamberth, & Mitchell, 1974), presumably with the intent of removing negative connotations from the concept. However, very little investigation has been devoted to specifying the content of erotic stimuli (Diamond, in press). Although it is true that what is sexually arousing to one person can be boring to another, it is nonetheless essential that we classify types of erotic stimuli according to their content. Purely sexual stimuli are different from those materials that (all too frequently) combine both sexual and aggressive elements. To understand the effects of erotic stimuli on subsequent behavior, we must have a better way of describing the independent variable (that is, the erotic stimuli). Although this issue cannot be resolved at the present time, we should keep in mind as we consider the effects of erotic stimuli on other forms of behavior that there is no clear and universally accepted definition of erotic stimuli. First, we will consider the effects of sexual arousal on physiological responses and on psychological responses (fantasy); then we will turn to a consideration of the effect of sexual arousal on a variety of behaviors, including both sexual activity and aggression (see Figure 7-4).

B. *Physiological Responses to Erotic Stimuli*

There are several methods used to determine physiological reactions to erotic stimuli. For example, actual measurement of the reactions by sexual organs can be made. A device called the penile plethysmograph can be attached to the penis to measure its volume and size (Freund, Sedlacek, & Knob, 1965; Zuckerman, 1971), and the female's responses can be measured by vaginal contractions and by the temperature of the clitoris (Jovanovic, 1971) or by blood volume and pulse pressure in the genital area (Heiman, 1975). Other methods of measuring physiological responses include analysis of the content of urine to determine changes in its chemical composition (Barclay, 1970) and simple self-reports by subjects about how physiologically aroused they feel (Schmidt, Sigusch, & Meyberg, 1969; Mosher, 1973).

Most studies of physiological responses to erotic stimuli find that subjects do report sexual arousal. For example, in a study by Schmidt, Sigusch, and Meyberg (1969), male college students in Germany were the subjects studied. Approximately 80% of the men who observed sexually explicit photos reported that they had had an erection, and almost one-fifth reported the emission of some pre-ejaculatory fluid. In a later study that included female college students, most of the women reported some bodily reactions in the genital area (Schmidt & Sigusch, 1970). Similar results were found in a study conducted with U.S. college students (Mosher, 1973).

Although the physiological responses to erotic material are consistent, there is some evidence that the effect diminishes over time, at least for the typical college student. For example, in a study done for the U.S. Commission on Obscenity and Pornography, Howard and his colleagues (Howard, Liptzin, & Reifler, 1973; Howard, Reifler, & Liptzin, 1971) found that exposure to erotic material could be satiating. Each male subject, approximately 22 years of age, spent 90 minutes a day for three weeks alone in a room that contained a large and diverse col-

"The sex isn't so much, but the violence is marvellous!"

Figure 7-4. Problems in the definition of pornography. (Drawing by Koren; © 1971 The New Yorker Magazine, Inc.)

lection of erotic materials, including books, photographs, and movies, as well as some nonerotic material. All measures—including the amount of urinary acid phosphates, penile erections, and self-rating of arousal—decreased over time. Subjects spent less and less time with the erotic material and even resorted to reading *Reader's Digest*. However, the introduction of new erotic stimuli heightened the response once more, suggesting that the satiation may be specific, rather than general.

Sexual arousal also can occur without the presence of such erotic materials in the environment. Self-generated fantasies and other cognitive processes can lead to arousal, and their effects on physiological re-

sponses can be demonstrated in a laboratory setting (Geer, 1974). In such studies, subjects are asked to sit in a comfortable chair, to imagine a sexual scene, and to "turn themselves on" by doing so. Within two or three minutes, changes in physiological responses have been observed.

C. *Psychological Responses to Erotic Stimuli*

Responses to erotic material occur at a psychological level as well as a physiological one. People often respond to erotic stimuli by engaging in sexual fantasies, for example, imagining future encounters or recalling past events. These cognitive reactions to erotic stimuli clearly are a part of what is generally called sexual arousal.

In the original Kinsey studies (Kinsey et al., 1953), it was reported that women were less likely to be sexually aroused by erotic stimuli than were men. Although this sex difference was accepted without question for many years, recent investigations suggest that it is no longer accurate. Both men and women report sexual arousal in response to erotic stimuli, although certain qualitative aspects of the reported fantasies may differ. Fisher and Byrne (1978) asked undergraduate students, who had previously agreed to be involved in an experiment dealing with sexual material, to watch a 10 minute film in which a couple undressed and engaged in heavy petting. Both sexes reported considerable arousal in response to the sexual presentation, and the investigators found no sex differences in the responses to the film. Interestingly, when the investigators varied the background description for the film—describing the couple as married, in a prostitute-customer relationship, or as casual acquaintances—both men and women reported being most aroused by the casual-sex theme.

Other investigators (for example, Carlson & Coleman, 1977) have simply asked subjects to completely relax for a short period and to fantasize about an erotic situation. Reported fantasies during this period again show no quantitative differences between males and females, but there is some evidence that women have more complex and emotionally richer fantasies than do men (Carlson & Coleman, 1977). Similarly, when men and women are asked to describe the thoughts and ideas they've had during sexual activity, women tend to report more imaginary fantasies, while men are more apt to think of past experiences and current behavior (McCauley & Swann, 1978). Again, however, the overall level of fantasy is no different for males than for females, suggesting that the Kinsey conclusions are no longer warranted.

Not all responses to erotic stimuli are positive, however. For many people, guilt can be a primary reaction. For such people, viewing erotic stimuli is more of an aversive situation; in fact, people who score high on a measure of sex guilt are less likely to view erotic material (Schill & Chapin, 1972) and show less physiological arousal when they are exposed to such material (Pagano & Kirschner, 1978).

Erotic stimuli also can be classified as basically positive or negative. The degree to which erotic stimuli are viewed in a negative way has been shown to be related to judgments of the material as pornographic and to recommendations for greater restrictions on such material. Positive affect, in turn, relates to more liberal responses to such questions (Byrne, Fisher, Lamberth, & Mitchell, 1974). Similarly, people who find erotic stimuli positive are more likely to make choices that lead them to exposure to erotic stimuli, whereas people who find erotic stimuli negative are likely to avoid such outcomes (Griffitt & Kaiser, 1978).

Sexual arousal also can affect the ways in which we evaluate other people, particularly people with whom some sexual interactions can be imagined. For example, Stephan, Berscheid, and Walster (1971) found that sexually aroused males rated photographs of women as more attractive than did nonaroused males. This perception of the woman's increased attractiveness was particularly strong when the men believed that they would actually have a date with the woman. As might be expected in looking at a primarily heterosexual, college student population, increases in the attractiveness evaluation occurred only with regard to other-sex persons and not with regard to same-sex persons (Griffitt, May, & Veitch, 1974). Presumably, if a similar study were conducted with a homosexual population, stronger effects would be found for same-sex than for other-sex targets.

D. Behavioral Responses to Erotic Stimuli

Exposure to explicit sexual materials leads to a state of physiological arousal, to fantasy, and to more positive evaluation of sexual targets. But does it lead to increased sexual activity? This question has been one of the core issues in the debates concerning the availability of pornographic material in our society. A related issue concerns the effect of sexual arousal on nonsexual forms of behavior—specifically, the frequently suggested link between sex and aggression.

A number of groups in our society are concerned with the effect of explicit sexual material on subsequent sexual behavior (see Figure 7-5). The assumption generally made is that exposure to erotic material will cause an increase in the sexual activity of the observer. Investigators have attempted to test this assumption in the following way. First, the typical sexual activity of subjects (who volunteer for the study) is assessed through a self-report that describes their sexual activities for the previous week or month. Then, the subjects are shown erotic materials (usually films), and at a later time —perhaps a day later, perhaps a week— they are asked to report again on their sexual activities. The procedural problems in this methodology are probably apparent. The use of volunteers may mean that the sample contains too high a proportion of sensation-seeking subjects. There may be

demand characteristics that influence the subjects to engage in or to report more sexual activity after watching the films (Amoroso & Brown, 1971). Nevertheless, results from these studies are still preferable to uninformed speculation.

The results of such studies show a relatively limited effect of erotic material on subsequent behavior. By way of summary, we can report the following conclusions: (1) heightened sexual activity occurs for only a brief period of time, such as on the night the subjects view the film (Cattell, Kawash, & DeYoung, 1972); (2) there are no reports of increased sexual activity over a prolonged period—say, 12 weeks—even in response to four viewings of sexually explicit films (Mann, Sidman, & Starr, 1971, 1973); and (3) there is apparently no change in types of sexual activity (Amoroso, Brown, Pruesse, Ware, & Pilkey, 1971). Mosher (1973), in reviewing studies by himself and others, offers the generalization that "erotic films lead to increased sexual activity immediately following the films only if there is a well-established sexual pattern" (p. 109). And

Figure 7-5. Does exposure to sexual material affect a person's behavior? (By permission of Jules Feiffer, © 1980. Distributed by Field Newspaper Syndicate.)

even those mild increases are not found in younger and less experienced viewers. Thus the exposure to specifically erotic stimuli appears to have a relatively weak effect on subsequent sexual activity, at least under the conditions studied to date.

Yet, the effects of erotic material cannot be discussed fully without considering another possible link—that between sexual stimuli and aggressive behavior. As we discussed earlier, pornographic material may differ in a number of ways. Some films and book passages describe gentle, love-oriented sexual activity; other sources depict violent and exploitative sex, where aggressive elements are as prominent as sexual ones. Much of the concern over the effects of pornography is, in fact, related not to the possibility of increased sexual behavior but to the possible link between sex and aggression and to the possible link between pornography and the incidence of sex crimes such as rape.

Freud was one of the first to suggest that sexual behavior and aggression are closely linked. He stated that "the sexuality of most men shows an admixture of aggression, of a desire to subdue" (Freud, 1938, p. 659). Recent psychoanalytic theory has continued to argue for this connection, as evidenced in the following statement: "Hostility, overt or hidden, is what generates and enhances sexual excitement, and its absence leads to sexual indifference and boredom" (Stoller, 1976, p. 903). Is there evidence for such a link between sex and aggression? Some research suggests that there is, although the relationship may be considerably more complex than was first believed.

Some investigators have found clear evidence that exposure to erotic stimuli leads to increased aggression (Jaffe, 1975; Jaffe, Malamuth, Feingold, & Feshbach, 1974). In these studies, subjects either viewed erotic films or read erotic passages and were then given the opportunity to electrically shock another person. Compared to control groups, subjects who had been exposed to erotic material delivered more intense shocks. Other investigators, however, have suggested that sexual stimuli actually can inhibit subsequent aggression. For ex-

ample, Baron and Bell (1977) exposed college males to pictures of women in bathing suits, pictures of nude women, pictures of acts of lovemaking, or to erotic passages from literature. A control group was shown pictures of scenery. As shown in **Figure 7-6**, exposure to most of the erotic materials was followed by a decrease in aggressive responses, as compared to the control condition in which neutral scenery was viewed. Similar results were found for college women in a later study (Baron, unpublished manuscript). On the basis of these results, Baron has suggested that mild erotic stimuli may inhibit aggressive responses, insofar as they may serve as a distraction or as a source of incompatible responses. More intensive stimuli can result in increased aggression. It should be noted, however,

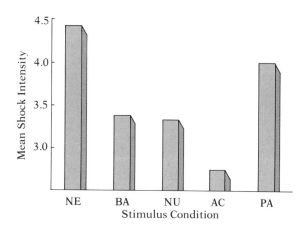

Figure 7-6. Mean intensity of shocks directed against the confederate by subjects exposed to nonerotic stimuli (NE), women in bathing suits (BA), nudes (NU), sexual acts (AC), or erotic passages (PA). After observing women in bathing suits, nude women, or acts of lovemaking, college males were significantly less aggressive toward another male than they were if they had looked at nonerotic pictures of scenery. Exposure to erotic passages from literature, however, did not decrease aggression. (Adapted from "Sexual Arousal and Aggression by Males: Effects of Type of Erotic Stimuli and Prior Provocation," by R. A. Baron and P. A. Bell, *Journal of Personality and Social Psychology*, 1977, 35, 79–87. Copyright 1977 by the American Psychological Association. Reprinted by permission of the author and publisher.)

that in this study the exposure to the most arousing stimuli was relatively brief and the stimuli did not include elements of hostility.

Feshbach, in discussing the evidence concerning links between sex and aggression, suggests that because both are viewed as taboo in this society, the link is a fairly strong one (Feshbach, 1978; Malamuth, Feshbach, & Jaffe, 1977). He has shown that not only may sexual arousal lead to aggression but also aggressive arousal may lead to sexual arousal. While some investigators cite this as evidence of the generalizability of any state of arousal (Berkowitz, 1971; Meyer, 1972), Feshbach believes that the specific connection between sex and aggression is one that is learned through the examples of the culture. As a correction, he recommends that aggression and sex be discriminated much more sharply during the course of socialization.

Certainly many pornographic films contain heavy mixtures of both sex and violence, and it is this combination that is perhaps the most serious aspect of the pornography issue. It is this combination, too, that has confused some of the research that has been conducted. In the laboratory, for example, most of the erotic material that has been used contains little or no aggressive or violent elements. In contrast, erotic material available in the society—in films, books, and magazines—frequently combines these elements. Investigations of the effect of this kind of mixed erotic material on subsequent behavior have been relatively infrequent, and the results of the investigations that have been done have been decidedly mixed. For example, a widely publicized study in Denmark considered the frequency of sex offenses following the removal of all restrictions on the sale of pornographic materials (Kutchinsky, 1973). The initial results of this "natural experiment" suggested that sex crimes declined markedly, and the study gave rise to a "safety-valve" theory (Kronhausen & Kronhausen, 1964). Thus it was argued that potential sex offenders may have obtained sufficient sexual satisfaction through the reading and viewing of pornographic materials, most probably combined with masturbation

(Kutchinsky, 1973). However, more recent figures from Denmark show an increase, rather than a decrease, in rape statistics (Court, 1976; Bachy, 1976): "a rise to a new level higher than anything experienced in the previous decade" (Court, 1976, p. 143). Admittedly, these data are correlational, and thus we cannot be certain that lifting restrictions on pornography caused the increase in sex crimes in Denmark. The recent findings do, however, present serious questions for the safety-valve theory and for those who would argue that pornography is harmless to a society.

Because pornography often contains such a mixture of elements, the question of whether purely erotic stimuli can lead to an increase in aggressive behavior must remain somewhat unsettled. For the scientist, it is important to devote more attention than before to classifying erotic material according to the presence or absence of hostile and aggressive material. For the citizen, too, it is important to realize that all erotic material is not the same.

VI. Sexual Behavior and Contraception

As everyone knows, sexual behavior may be more than an end in itself. It can also have future consequences—specifically, pregnancy and the birth of children. Or *does* everyone know? Many of the current debates and concerns about overpopulation and about the dramatic increase in teenage pregnancies in the United States point to the fact that the connection between sexual intercourse and future pregnancy is not always recognized, at least at the time the action occurs.

Based on figures from the U.S. Census Bureau, it has been estimated that 1 out of every 11 children is born out of wedlock, and that 40% of these births occur among teenage mothers (Fugita, Wagner, & Pion, 1971). In one study of marriage and birth records, 73% of the 16-year-olds who got married gave birth less than 8 months following the marriage (Tillack, Tyler, Paquette, & Jones, 1972). Such statistics are startling and certainly provide evidence that contraception, although readily available, is often not used during sexual activity (see Figure 7-7).

A number of reasons have been suggested for the failure of people, and particularly adolescents, to use effective contraceptive devices. One reason is the appearance of "premeditation" that the use of contraceptives suggests (Sorenson, 1973). Particularly among young females, the use of contraceptives is believed to indicate negative characteristics about the user. Another reason for the nonuse of contraceptives has been termed the "personal fable" (Cvetkovich, Grote, Bjorseth, & Sarkissian, 1975). Many adolescent women seem to believe that they cannot become pregnant, that their own chances of becoming pregnant are somehow different from the general laws of probability that apply to other people. "It won't happen to me," unfortunately, is all too often a myth.

Byrne and his colleagues (Byrne, Jazwinski, De Ninno, & Fisher, 1977) have suggested four steps that occur in the decision to use contraception. These four steps are (1) planning to engage in intercourse, (2)

acknowledging one's sexual intentions, (3) communicating with the partner about sex and contraception, and (4) practicing contraception. For the individual who wishes to believe that sexual intercourse is an impulsive, romantic occurrence, such a sequence of steps would be unthinkable.

The use of contraceptives also relates to a person's general attitudes toward sexuality. Even retaining information about contraception can depend on the person's general feelings about sex. For example, S. Schwartz (1973) presented a lecture on the biological and medical aspects of abortion to a group of college students who had previously been assessed on a measure of sex guilt. Those students who were high in guilt about sexual activities retained less information about the lecture than students who were low in guilt, presumably because anxiety about sexual matters interfered with retention of the material. Byrne (1977) has suggested that generally negative feelings about sexuality may also relate to the actual practice of birth control. People who feel generally negative about sex are less likely to practice contraceptive techniques and more likely to have large families. Similarly, people who have negative feelings toward sexual matters are more likely to rate those people who use contraceptives as immoral than are people who do not have negative feelings (Miller & Byrne, 1978). Our general attitudes toward sexuality, then, may have important consequences, and understanding these links can help us in dealing with problems such as overpopulation in the world.

VII. Summary

Sexual behavior is an important aspect of social interaction, although, until fairly recently, scientific study of the topic was considered taboo. Initial work in this area relied on case studies of clinical patients. More recently, methods have also included survey research and laboratory experimentation.

Kinsey's landmark work provided information on the frequency with which U.S. adults engaged in various forms of sexual

Figure 7-7. The reality of teenage pregnancy. (© Arthur Grace/Stock, Boston.)

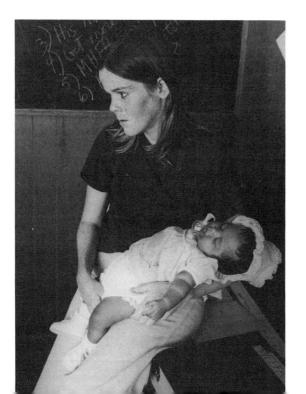

behavior. More recently, Hunt has updated the Kinsey information and found a gradual increase in the sexual behavior of U.S. adults, particularly among women.

Similar studies conducted with college students show that nonmarital sexual activity is fairly frequent. Variations in reported sexual activity among college students are related to age, religion, and geographic location.

Freud was among the first to insist that sexuality is a basic part of the human personality. His theories on infantile sexuality and the differences between male and female sexuality were influential for many years. Other theoretical discussions of sexuality point to the importance of cognitive factors. These theories stress the importance of socialization experiences and the role of learning in determining what situations and stimuli will be perceived as sexually arousing.

Gender identity refers to one's self awareness of being male or female and is independent of one's sexual preference. Thus, homosexuals may be quite certain of and satisfied with their maleness or femaleness but still prefer same-sex, rather than other-sex, partners for romantic and sexual activity. Societal attitudes toward homosexuality have often been quite negative, although in recent years the American Psychiatric Association has removed homosexuality from its list of mental disorders.

Explanations for the development of homosexual versus heterosexual preferences are uncertain. Some evidence suggests that, as children, homosexuals are encouraged less in traditional role behaviors by either parent and tend to be ignored by the parent of the same sex. Yet, many heterosexuals have had similar childhood experiences, so such factors cannot be isolated as a primary cause of homosexuality.

Bisexuals are people who engage in sexual behavior with both the same and the other sex. The relative frequency of some degree of bisexuality is consistent with Kinsey's arguments that sexual behavior is perhaps best considered on a continuum, rather than as just two categories— homosexual and heterosexual.

Studies of sexual activity in nonmarital relationships show little connection between the presence or absence of such activity and the future success of the relationship. Characteristics of those couples who abstain, those who have sex in the early stage of a relationship, and those who engage in sex at later stages of a relationship do differ, however, in terms of values and beliefs.

In marital relationships, reports of marital happiness are related to frequency of sexual activity. It is possible, however, that both of these variables may be related to some other factors in the marital relationship.

Studies of the influence of erotic stimuli on sexual behavior must begin with a consideration of the distinctions between the terms *obscenity*, *pornography*, and *erotica*. Considerable work remains to be done in specifying the characteristics of erotic material.

Responses to erotic material include physiological activity, fantasy, guilt, and changes in the attractiveness evaluations of other people. Actual sexual behavior may be affected by exposure to erotic stimuli, although the effects are fairly short term. Some evidence shows that exposure to erotic stimuli leads to an increase in aggressive behavior; under other conditions, however, aggression may actually decrease following such exposure. Part of the confusion in this area relates to the nature of the erotic material itself, some of which contains considerable aggression and violence in addition to erotic themes.

An obvious consequence of sexual activity is pregnancy. Attitudes and behaviors toward birth control are related to more general attitudes toward sexuality.

Glossary Terms

bisexual	gender identity	transsexualism
erotica	obscenity	

One has not only a legal but a moral responsibility to obey just laws. Conversely, one has a moral responsibility to disobey unjust laws. MARTIN LUTHER KING, JR.

BEN SHAHN, *NO MAN CAN COMMAND MY CONSCIENCE!* 1968. NEW JERSEY STATE MUSEUM COLLECTION, TRENTON. GIFT OF BERNARDA BRYSON SHAHN.

The history of the world, my sweet / Is who gets eaten and who gets to eat.
STEPHEN SONDHEIM (from *Sweeney Todd*)

Moral Judgments and Behavior

A chapter on moral judgments for the first and second editions of this book was prepared by John O'Connor. Some material from those chapters has been included in the present chapter.

Sex is immoral and evil, some say, whereas others extol the possibilities of free expression. Even early research on love, as we discovered in Chapter 6, encountered resistance from persons who felt that the subject was and should remain taboo. Other judgments of morality focus on behaviors such as cheating, lying, and inflicting pain on others. At a societal level, we find numerous examples of people making choices between what they feel is right and what the laws or their superiors encourage them to do. Throughout the Watergate incident in the United States, for example, associates of former President Nixon ignored questions of right and wrong in favor of expediency—that is, they believed in whatever would win the election. In wartime, conscientious objectors adhere to their own judgments of right or wrong, while commanders order troops into battle. And in Nazi Germany, the moral crime of genocide was justified under the guise of a great Aryan mission.

How do standards of morality develop? And why, in the face of many clear religious doctrines, are there so many variations and individual differences in standards of morality? How is **socialization** important—that is, how do we acquire the behaviors, norms, and values of our society? In this chapter, we will consider the socialization process. We shall also look at the consequences of immoral actions and the theories that attempt to explain how we relate to other people in just and unjust ways.

I. Conceptions of Morality in Western Culture

Throughout the recorded history of Western civilization, human beings have been preoccupied with the nature of their own morality in their search for justice and liberty. Ancient Greek philosophers considered reason the highest attribute of the virtuous person. Training and education were seen as the pathways to goodness, even though the skeptical Socrates admitted that

he didn't know what virtue really was or how it could be taught (Sizer & Sizer, 1970). With the rise of an organized Christian dogma we were given a new definition of moral judgment and conduct. According to doctrines advanced by St. Augustine, every human is born in sin, is basically evil, and can never hope to achieve virtue by the power of reason alone. Therefore, people must be educated to faith. During early Christian times, the good person was seen as one who glorified God; later the Catholic church taught that moral thought and conduct were the means to ensure a person's eternal salvation. In the era of the reformation, many people returned to reason and science in their search for an answer to the perplexing question of morality.

With the writings of Sigmund Freud in the early 1900s, our ability to reach moral decisions through reason alone again came into serious question. Civilization was ripe for a more complex, sophisticated analysis of the nature of morality (although a more pessimistic one). Had Freud not advanced his theories, someone else doubtless would have. Although Freud's concern was with the transformation of the child into a socialized adult, he was one of the first to point systematically at irrational psychosexual urges as a primary determinant of behavior and to the apparent necessity for all of us to place constraints on our feelings and behavior.

The early part of the 20th century saw the beginning of a scientific study of morality that derived its impetus not just from the clinical insights of Freud, but from academic social psychology as well. William McDougall (1908) conceptualized the problem in the following way in one of the first textbooks on social psychology:

The fundamental problem of social psychology is the moralization of the individual into the society into which he is born as an amoral and egoistic infant. There are successive stages, each of which must be traversed by every individual before he can attain the next higher: (1) the stage in which the operation of the instinctive impulses is modified by the influence of rewards and punishments, (2) the stage in which conduct is controlled in the main by anticipation of social praise or blame, (3) the highest stage in which conduct is regulated by an ideal that enables a man to act in the way that seems to him right regardless of the praise or blame of his immediate social environment [p. 6].

Although Freud and McDougall agree on some points (for example, the amoral nature of infants and a fixed sequence of child development), they disagree on many others. A major difference concerns the emotional versus the cognitive base of moral development. Do we learn about morality through dynamic motivational (emotional) processes, or does moral judgment reflect a more cognitive process of learning rules and principles? These two approaches to moral development result in quite different research strategies.

Another central issue in the study of morality is the ways in which situational factors may enhance or detract from moral conduct. Is our sense of a moral standard maintained in all situations? Or can particular circumstances influence our beliefs in what is right and wrong? Philosophical discussions of the concept of "situational ethics" represent a shift in emphasis from immutable standards of morality to a more momentary decision-making process. As we shall see, this issue of internal versus external influences on moral conduct represents a second theme that pervades much of the theoretical and empirical research on transgression.

II. Theoretical Explanations of Moral Development

Three major theoretical approaches have been proposed in the area of moral judgment. Freud's **psychoanalytic theory** uses emotional and motivational constructs to explain the development of personality and character, and it stresses internal constructs, such as the superego, to explain moral behavior. In contrast, **cognitive theories** focus on the development of rules and the acquisition of universal principles; they stress cognitive rather than motivational processes, but they also maintain a focus on internal factors. A third approach to the study of moral development, exemplified by **reinforcement theories** and **social-**learning theories,** is most concerned with the influence of situational factors on the acquisition and performance of moral or immoral behaviors. Although both cognitive and motivational factors are considered in the acquisition process, the emphasis in this case is clearly on external rather than internal factors. Each of these theories, as you might suspect, has generated a different understanding of morality.

A. *Psychoanalytic Explanations of Moral Development*

Freud's psychoanalytic explanation merits first coverage for more than historical reasons. Although this theory is often criticized, its influence on the choice of problems in morality research (the concept of conscience, for example) is pervasive, even if not always acknowledged.

In developing his emotional-motivational approach to personality and morality, Freud (1917/1963) postulated that three systems of energies operate within every individual. Each system—the **id,** the **ego,** and the **superego**—has its own province of the mind, and each functions as a relatively independent system, although continually interacting with the other two systems.

In psychoanalytic theory, the *id* can roughly be equated with the quantity of biologically determined energy in the organism. The id is below the level of awareness (in other words, it is part of the **unconscious**) and is the source of irrational impulses that persistently strive for selfish gratification. Although the id is said to be inborn, according to Freudian theory the *ego* is developed through learning and through encounters with one's environment. The basic purpose of the ego is to maintain the organism on its path toward realistic goals; in doing so, the ego mediates among the "three harsh masters"—the id, the superego, and external reality. The ego begins to develop at birth, and its development continues throughout life. According to psychoanalytic theory, the ego emerges as a result of the child's failures to gratify his or her needs.

In some of his formulations, Freud seemed to conclude that the ego possesses no energies of its own but rather borrows energy from the id and the superego. Many psychologists regard this as a rather curious conclusion, because it suggests that the major integrative and organizing aspect of the personality—the ego—is only a derivative of more basic impulses. Neo-Freudians— Freud's more recent followers—have elevated the status of the ego, proposing that it is innate and has a source of energy all its own. In effect, they reject Freud's assumption that humans are passive slaves to primitive instinctual urges (Shaffer, 1977). Many current researchers have focused on the concept of ego and ego development (for example, Block, 1973; Loevinger, 1966; Loevinger & Wessler, 1970), and these findings will be discussed in Section III.

The *superego* in Freud's system is the central point for moral judgments. According to Freud, the superego consists of the conscience (the censorship function of the personality) and the ego ideal (a perception of the kind of person one would like to be). Parents, teachers, siblings, and others in the environment contribute to the formation of the superego. What the child absorbs from these agents is principally prohibitions. Since Freud saw the young child as amoral, preoccupied with the satisfaction of instincts, he considered these prohibitions necessary. At the onset, the child conforms to parental dictates only because he or she fears punishment. Later, around the age of 6, if development has been optimal, the child comes to identify with the parents— their image and standards become internalized as the child's own (see Figure 8-1). According to Freud, this act of identification occurs in relation to sexuality and is dependent on a resolution of the **Oedipus conflict**. The parents play a critical role at this stage. Freud suggested that, in the absence of adequate parental figures to emulate, the super ego—and hence a sense of morality— may fail to develop. In extreme cases, the adult behavior of children raised in such circumstances may become what is called psychopathic—that is, without any apparent concern about wrongdoing.

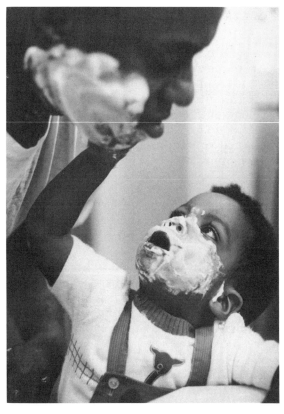

Figure 8-1. Identification with the parent. (© Burke Uzzle/Magnum Photos, Inc.)

With this formulation in mind, we can see why psychoanalytic theory proposes that by the age of 6 the nature of an individual's major drives and interpersonal relationships has been established and that this organization remains basic throughout the person's life. Later periods of development (for example, the latency period between 6 and 14, or the genital stage at 14 and beyond) are believed to have little effect on basic character traits.

Neo-Freudians, notably Erik Erikson (1963a, 1963b, 1964) and Harry Stack Sullivan (1953), have disagreed with this position, arguing that developments of considerable importance do occur after the age of 6 and that these developments play a major role in the moral judgments and conduct of the individual.

Erikson, who had been a high school dropout and a wandering artist in his youth, was never a conventional psychoanalyst.

For example, his work with the Oglala Sioux Indians (the tribe that killed Custer and in turn had their hoped-for freedom finally crushed at the Battle of Wounded Knee) and the Yurok Indians of Northern California convinced him that traditional psychoanalytic theory was not adequate for explaining the emotional problems of native North Americans. The Indians' dilemma was that they could neither live as their ancestors had nor identify with White people's values. Their difficulty appeared to have more to do with ego and cultural values than with sexual drives.

Erikson emphasizes three major concepts in the study of the ego that differ dramatically from Freud's. He suggests that:

1. Along with Freudian psychosexual developmental stages, there are also psychosocial developmental stages. Later stages of development concentrate on the creative, adaptive, and reality-oriented aspects of personality rather than on sexual drives.

2. Personality development continues throughout life and centers on nuclear conflicts particular to each period of development.

3. Each psychosocial stage has a positive as well as a negative component.

Erikson's eight stages of development, together with the construct that is achieved through the successful resolution of each stage, are described in Table 8-1. According to Erikson, the sequence of these stages is invariant—in other words, one must face the problems of one stage before beginning to deal with the next conflict.[1] Although Erikson accepts the validity of Freud's stages, he adds to them in two ways: (1) he suggests an additional sequence of stages beyond puberty, and (2) he believes that social-psychological events are as important as biological events at each stage. For example, according to Erikson, in the first stage of development the child not only experiences oral tension but he or she also de-

velops a sense of basic trust or mistrust in the world. In essence, Erikson suggests that the child at this stage learns to "trust others when it is appropriate and distrust them when that is justified." This ratio of trust to mistrust is then maintained throughout adult life. At each of the other seven stages of development, another basic construct is developed, as shown in Table 8-1.

Problems at any stage of development (or *nuclear conflicts,* as Erikson has termed them) can result in permanent impairment. Thus Erikson believes that, if, for example, a child does not develop a sense of purpose during the third (or phallic) stage, then that child will have a weak sense of purpose throughout life. In addition, this same child would have difficulties in later stages of development because each stage builds on the previous one. In effect, developmental stages have a snowballing effect; each stage adds something specific to all later stages and creates a new ensemble. This constant transformation of morality is called *epigenesis.* Optimum moral development at each stage must be supported by strong cultural institutions—first by the parents and later by all the various aspects of society.

Erikson's theory of moral development is more "social" than Freud's, and it stresses the positive qualities as well as the dangers of growing up (Elkind, 1974). However, both theories are alike in their assumption of specific stages of development and in their emphasis on motivational determinants. Both theories also assume a basic consistency of the personality.

How valid are these assumptions? For a consideration of the general issues of stages, motivation, and consistency, we will wait until we have discussed the other theories of moral development. At this point, however, we can conclude that some of the particulars of Freudian theory are questionable. Peck and Havighurst (1960), for example, found that the child's moral growth does continue beyond the age of 6, and other evidence has questioned the Freudian assumption that conscience develops only in the phallic stage via Oedipal conflict (Sears, Maccoby, & Levin, 1957). Thus, although the general concept of stages may still be

---

[1] It is interesting to note, however, that Erikson's theory, like many others, tends to assume a male model. Thus, although proposing an invariant sequence for men, Erikson has suggested that women must acquire intimacy and a relationship (stage 6) before they truly attain identity (stage 5).

TABLE 8-1 / *Erikson's Stages and Conflicts*

Stage of Life (or Nuclear Conflict)	Construct Ideally Realized or Achieved	Age or Equivalent Freudian Stage
1. Acquiring a basic sense of trust versus a sense of mistrust	Hope	Oral-sensory stage
2. Acquiring a sense of autonomy versus a sense of doubt and shame	Will	Anal-muscular
3. Acquiring a sense of initiative versus a sense of guilt	Purpose	Phallic
4. Acquiring a sense of industry versus a sense of inferiority	Competence	Latency period
5. Acquiring a sense of identity versus a sense of identity diffusion	Fidelity	Puberty and adolescence
6. Acquiring a sense of intimacy and solidarity versus a sense of isolation	Love	Young adult-hood
7. Acquiring a sense of generativity versus a sense of self-absorption or stagnation	Care	Adulthood
8. Acquiring a sense of integrity versus a sense of despair and disgust	Wisdom	Maturity

Adapted from "Stage and Sequence: The Cognitive-Developmental Approach to Socialization," by L. Kohlberg. In D. A. Goslin (Ed.), *Handbook of Socialization Theory and Research*. Copyright © 1969 by Rand McNally & Company, Chicago. Reprinted by permission.

posited, specific suggestions about the timing of superego development are not well grounded.

B. *Cognitive Theories of Moral Development*

Unhappy with the exclusive emphasis on motivational issues, both Jean Piaget, in Switzerland, and Lawrence Kohlberg, in the United States, turned their attention to the cognitive basis of moral development. These theorists and their followers believe that our moral judgments and conduct are learned through cognitive rather than purely emotional processes. We learn rules, laws, and higher principles, and reason be-

comes paramount, much as it was for many of the early Greek philosophers.

1. *Piaget—Two Stages of Moral Development.* Like Freud, **Piaget** developed his theory from extensive interviews coupled with observations of people. But, whereas Freud spent much of his time seated behind a patient's couch, listening to the dream descriptions of neurotic Viennese, Piaget squatted on the sidewalks of Geneva playing marbles with children. From these interactions he formulated his theory of cognitive development.

In his general theory of mental development, Piaget (1926, 1965) proposed that all children move through four stages of increasingly abstract reasoning. As used by Piaget, the term *cognitive stages* implies the following characteristics:

a. Children of different ages possess qualitatively different ways of thinking and solving the same problems.

b. These different ways of thinking are ordered in an invariant sequence; that is, there is a consistent series of steps in the sequence, along which each child must progress as he or she gets older [Piaget, 1960].

c. Each way of thinking forms a structured whole. This means that, at each stage, the individual beliefs are all organized around that particular way of thinking. Piaget believes that these ways of thinking, or structures, are "really there" controlling thought, much as the moon is really there controlling tides [Brainerd, 1974].

d. Each successive cognitive stage is an integration of what has gone before. Higher stages do not replace lower stages but instead reintegrate them.

Piaget proposes only two stages of moral development, and these rest on the prior development of basic cognitive skills. First, in the **heteronomous stage**, or the stage of moral realism, the child accepts rules as given from authority. In the second stage, the stage of **autonomous morality**, or moral independence, the individual believes in modifying rules to fit the needs of the situation.

These descriptions of moral-development stages, however, sound fairly abstract. What, after all, do rules mean to a child? And how can the investigator observe what rules the child may have in his or her head? Cleverly, Piaget decided to observe children at play. He played marbles and other street games with them and, as the games progressed, he asked them about the rules that they used. For your own investigation of this behavior, you might ask young children questions like "Who makes the rules?" or "Can you change the rules in this game?" and see how explanations differ from children of different ages.

Piaget found that when children of about 3 years play marbles together, they have no rules and no cooperative play. Children that young really do not play together, even though they may share the same space at the same time. From ages 3 to 5, a trend toward playing together starts to emerge, but each child is egocentric and considers his or her own view as the only possible one. At this age, children lack **empathy** (Shantz, 1974); they are unable to put themselves in someone else's place because they are unaware that the other person has a point of view. Around the age of 7 or 8, *incipient cooperation* emerges—the first incidence of concern about mutual benefits and the unification of rules. Even then, however, the ideas about rules are still rather vague. It is not until around the age of 11 or 12, the period of *codification of rules,* that every detail of the game is fixed and agreed on.

While children progress in the practice of rules, their attitudes toward rules, or their consciousness of rules, are also changing. To the 3-year-old, rules are received almost without thought. During the next few years, rules are believed to be sacred and untouchable; 4- and 5-year-olds see rules as coming from adults and lasting forever, even though children at this age often break rules indiscriminately. At the ages of 10 and 11, children view rules as laws formed by mutual consent, and this represents a shift from the heteronomous stage to the autonomous stage of moral development. At this age, rules are seen as modifiable, but the ones actually agreed on are adhered to scrupulously. For example, in response to the question "Are you allowed to change the rules at all?" a 13-year-old responds with "Oh, yes, some want to, and some don't. If the boys play that way (changing something), you have to play like that" (Piaget, 1965, p. 68).

The child's conception of rules is not the only thing that changes between the stage of moral realism and the stage of moral independence. Conceptions of the seriousness of crimes also change. In seeking to understand these changes, Piaget chose to deal with occurrences common to many children—clumsiness and lying. The young of any species are incredibly clumsy—puppies are forever stumbling and crashing into things, and children are constantly dropping and breaking things or otherwise disturbing the tranquility of the adult

A. A little boy who is called John is in his room. He is called to dinner. He goes into the dining room. But behind the door there was a chair, and on the chair there was a tray with fifteen cups on it. John couldn't have known that there was all this behind the door. He goes in; the door knocks against the tray; bang go the fifteen cups, and they all get broken!

B. Once there was a little boy whose name was Henry. One day when his mother was out he tried to get some jam out of the cupboard. He climbed onto a chair and stretched out his arm. But the jam was too high up, and he couldn't reach it and have any. While he was trying to get it, he knocked over a cup. The cup fell down and broke.

Figure 8-2. Piaget's moral-decision stories. (From J. Piaget, *The Moral Judgment of the Child.* Copyright 1935 by Routledge & Kegan Paul, Ltd. Copyright 1965 by The Macmillan Company. Reprinted by permission of the publishers. Photo © Jim Pinckney.)

world. The loss of tranquility does not often go unnoticed; an angry reaction often follows, and the child in turn inevitably attaches some meaning to the adult's reactions to the transgression.

Piaget asked children to compare the seriousness of two kinds of clumsiness—one that did considerable damage but was well intentioned, and one that had negligible consequences but was the result of disobedience. Stories such as the ones presented in Figure 8-2 were used. Piaget found that younger children judged actions according to their *material consequences;* to them, the boy who broke the most cups was the naughtiest. Older children took *intentions* into account and judged the second boy in Figure 8-2 (Henry) as committing the more serious offense. As we discussed in Chapter 3, this concept of intentionality also pervades adult judgments—for example, judgments of guilt in homicide trials.

Piaget found that the nature and consequences of lying also change between the stage of moral realism and the stage of moral independence. In response to the question "Do you know what a lie is?" younger children told Piaget that it was a "naughty word" or something bad "like words no one is supposed to say." Intent to deceive did not enter into the younger child's definition of a lie. For example, Piaget (1965) compared younger and older children's reactions to a story told innocently about a dog as big as a horse with their reactions to a less-farfetched story told with the deliberate intent to deceive. Younger children judged the first tale to be worse, whereas older children thought the second story was worse because it was a deliberate lie.

Piaget and his associates also studied the types of punishment that children advocate when rules are broken. He defined two types of punishment: expiatory and reciprocity. **Expiatory punishment** demands in a rather authoritarian manner that the transgressor must suffer (Sherwood, 1966); the severity of the punishment is directly related to the severity of the offense and may not educate the transgressor about the implications of his or her misdeed. Examples of expiatory punishment are plentiful:

spanking, revoking a child's allowance, or placing a child's toys (or the family car) off limits for a time. In contrast, **reciprocity** attempts to relate the punishment to the crime, so that the rule-breaker will be able to understand the implications of his or her misconduct. One type of reciprocity involves *restitutive* punishment, such as having a child pay for and replace the window that he or she broke. Such tactics have occasionally been used by judges as well; for example, they may demand that the offenders repay the victims for property damage and vandalism. *Exclusion* is another type of reciprocity, exemplified by statements such as "I'm not going to play with you any more because you play too rough."

Punishment by reciprocity corresponds with the more advanced stage of moral independence. For example, when Piaget interviewed 100 children between the ages of 6 and 12, he found that reciprocity was preferred by only 30% of the 6- and 7-year-olds, compared to 50% of the 8- and 10-year-olds and 80% of the 11- and 12-year-olds.

Along with moral realism and the advocacy of expiatory punishment, the younger child also believes in **immanent justice**— the concept that justice dwells within the things involved and that misdeeds will be punished by natural acts or occurrences. Thus if a girl is running across a bridge when she should be walking, and *if* the bridge collapses and tosses her into icy water, younger children will conclude that the girl was punished for being bad. Piaget finds that, although nearly all younger children believe in immanent justice, less than one-fourth of the 11- and 12-year-old children believe in it.

2. *Kohlberg—An Extension of the Cognitive-Stage Approach.* Just as Erikson was a revisionist of Freud, so Lawrence Kohlberg has extended Piaget's basic theory. Like Piaget, Kohlberg used the method of presenting hypothetical stories and measuring responses to study moral development, although Kohlberg's stories are considerably more complex and are more often used with adults (Box 8-1 gives an example of a Kohlberg story). Because these stories often

involve opposition between a law (or norm) and a human need, they encourage respondents to judge the stories on the basis of their general theory of morality (Brown, 1965). On the basis of responses to these stories, Kohlberg (1958, 1963, 1968) proposed that there are three different levels of moral maturity; each of these levels comprises two separate stages, thus there are six different stages of development experienced by children. These different stages of development are shown in Table 8-2.

At the initial, or preconventional, level of morality, a child is responsible to cultural rules and labels such as "good" and "bad," or "right" and "wrong"; however, the child interprets these labels in light of the consequences of actions or with a view to the physical power of those who define the rules. Here, might means right. In the earliest stage of the preconventional level, consequences alone determine morality. Getting caught means to the child that something is bad; not getting caught means it must be all right. At the second stage of the preconventional level, the hedonistic stage, the child begins to think in terms of his or her own needs. Unselfish acts, for example, are considered right only if they benefit the actor as well. As Kohlberg (1968) said, "You scratch my back and I'll scratch yours" is a characteristic view at this stage of moral development.

At the conventional level of moral development, maintaining the expectations of one's family, group, or nation is perceived as valuable in its own right, regardless of the consequences. Loyalty becomes a primary value. As an example of this form of moral reasoning, consider the view of some of the participants in the Watergate episode during the Nixon presidency. They said that they felt a deep sense of loyalty to the President and that they were concerned with being team players. These loyalties then presumably justified the morality of their actions, which history later showed to be less than moral in many people's eyes.

The two stages of the conventional level are interpersonal concordance (the good boy/good girl orientation) and the law-and-order orientation. In the first of these (Stage

Box 8-1. Kohlberg's Decision Story.

Kohlberg's moral-judgment stories tend to set up an opposition between a legal rule or social norm and a human need (R. Brown, 1965). Here is a typical example (from Kohlberg, 1963):

In Europe, a woman was near death from a special kind of cancer. There was one drug that the doctors thought might save her. It was a form of radium that a druggist in the same town had recently discovered. The drug was expensive to make, but the druggist was charging ten times what the drug cost him to make. He paid $200 for the radium and charged $2,000 for a small dose of the drug. The sick woman's husband, Heinz, went to everyone he knew to borrow money, but he could only get together about $1,000, which is half of what it cost. He told the druggist that his wife was dying, and asked him to sell it cheaper or let him pay later. But the druggist said, "No, I discovered the drug and I'm going to make money from it." So Heinz got desperate and broke into the man's store to steal the drug for his wife.

Should Heinz have done that? Was it actually wrong or right? Why?

Is it a husband's duty to steal the drug for his wife, if he can get it no other way? Would a good husband do it?

Did the druggist have the right to charge that much when there was no law actually setting a limit to the price? Why?

If the husband does not feel very close or affectionate to his wife, should he still steal the drug?

Suppose it wasn't Heinz's wife who was dying of cancer, but it was Heinz's best friend. His friend didn't have any money, and there was no one in his family willing to steal the drug. Should Heinz steal the drug for his friend in that case? Why?

Suppose it was a person whom he knew that was dying but who was not a good friend. There was no one else who could get him the drug. Would it be right to steal it for him? Why?

What is there to be said on the side of the law in this case?

Would you steal the drug to save your wife's life? Why?

If you were dying of cancer but were strong enough, would you steal the drug to save your own life?

Heinz broke in the store and stole the drug and gave it to his wife. He was caught and brought before the judge. Should the judge send Heinz to jail for stealing, or should he let him go free? Why?

Adapted from "Stage and Sequence: The Cognitive-Developmental Approach to Socialization," by L. Kohlberg. In D. A. Goslin (Ed.), *Handbook of Socialization Theory and Research.* Copyright © 1969 by Rand McNally & Company, Chicago. Reprinted by permission.

3), loyalty is directed toward other persons, whereas in the latter stage (Stage 4), loyalty is shown to the social order simply because it is the existing social order (Kohlberg, 1968).

At the third and highest level of moral development, which Kohlberg calls the postconventional or principled level, the person tries to define moral values and principles whose validity does not depend on the authority of the groups or persons who advocate these principles or the person's identification with these groups. At the first stage of the postconventional level, moral action is defined by how well it reflects general individual rights. Yet the person at Stage 5 realizes that there are individual differences in personal values and opinions; as a result, importance is placed on procedural rules for reaching a consensus among views and establishing a social contract. Although the legal point of view is accepted at Stage 5, as it is in Stage 4, a person at Stage 5 will recognize the possibility of changing the law in order to best accommodate the members of a society (Kohlberg, 1968). Democratic governments, as exemplified by the U.S. Constitution, illustrate a belief in this fifth-stage view of morality.

T A B L E 8 - 2 / *Kohlberg's Stages of Moral Development*

Preconventional level
  Stage 1: Punishment and obedience orientation
    No differentiation is seen between the moral value of life and its physical or social-status value.
  Stage 2: Hedonistic orientation (instrumental-relativist)
    The value of human life is seen as instrumental to the satisfaction of the needs of its possessor or of other persons.
Conventional level
  Stage 3: Interpersonal concordance (good boy/good girl orientation)
    The value of a human life is based on the empathy and affection of family members and others toward its possessor.
  Stage 4: Law-and-order orientation
    Life is conceived as sacred in terms of its place in a categorical moral or religious order of rights and duties.
Postconventional or principled level
  Stage 5: Social contract, legalistic orientation
    Life is valued both in terms of its relation to community welfare and in terms of being a universal human right.
  Stage 6: Universal ethical principles
    Belief in the sacredness of human life as representing a human value of respect for the individual.

Adapted from "Stage and Sequence: The Cognitive-Developmental Approach to Socialization," by L. Kohlberg. In D. A. Goslin (Ed.), *Handbook of Socialization Theory and Research.* Copyright © 1969 by Rand McNally & Company, Chicago. Reprinted by permission.

At Kohlberg's highest stage of development, what is morally right is defined by one's own conscience in accordance with self-determined ethical principles that are broad and abstract. These principles might include respect for the dignity of human beings, equality of human rights, or universal principles of justice. Martin Luther King, Jr.'s statement at the opening of this chapter reflects this level of moral development. On occasion, of course, we might have our own ethical principles that we know are not shared by others. For example, a pacifist might say "My conscience makes me do this, but yours may not." Such individualistic ethics are considered by Kohlberg to represent a transition stage between 5 and 6, termed the *individual conscience orientation.* Even at Stage 6, however, people can disagree on the ultimate right or wrong of a course of action. For example, beliefs regarding the acceptability of abortion may reflect one's principles about the sanctity of human life or about the rights of individuals to control their own bodies. A belief in the

universality of certain principles does not mean that everyone will accept the belief or the implications of that value.

Like Piaget, Kohlberg proposes that, in order to achieve Stage 6 of moral development (which Kohlberg clearly believes is the best level), one must pass through the other five stages in an invariant manner. The assumption that a principle-oriented morality is higher than a law-oriented morality is obviously loaded with value judgments, and for this reason Kohlberg has received his share of criticism. But before considering these specific criticisms, as well as the more general issues of stages and cognition involved in the Piaget and Kohlberg models, let us turn to the third general theory of moral development.

C. *Social-Learning Explanations of Moral Development*

Social-learning theory, as we learned in earlier chapters, relies on an analysis of the specific events that a person experiences to explain the kinds of behavior that develop. Unlike either psychoanalytic or cognitive theorists, social-learning theorists do not believe that there is an invariant sequence of development in moral judgment or conduct, but rather that these evaluations and behaviors are specifically learned in the course of socialization. Learning occurs either through direct reward and punishment or, more often, through observational learning, whereby the child (or adult) imitates behavior that he or she previously observed.

Although in the early development of social-learning theory it was assumed that the observer would model the exact behavior that was witnessed, later developments in the theory propose **abstract modeling** (Bandura, 1977). This is an important extension of the theory, particularly in terms of our understanding of moral behavior. Essentially, this extension allows for the development of rules and principles that may initiate behavior more general than any specific behaviors observed. As explained by Bandura, "In abstract modeling, observers extract the common attributes exemplified in diverse modeled responses and formulate rules for generating behavior with similar structural characteristics" (Bandura, 1977, p. 41). In other words, on the basis of a series of observations, the child or adult may begin to see patterns and will develop his or her own set of moral guidelines that fit these observations. Such a process can be applied not only to the acquisition of moral judgments, but to language acquisition as well. Clearly this view is not the mechanistic view of earlier learning theorists, such as John B. Watson (1930), who argued that environmental determinants were all powerful. Rather, modern learning theorists have taken into account the human capabilities for reason, thought, and active self-regulation and self-reinforcement and have proposed a model that combines external events with individual decision-making.

Yet social-learning theorists still rely heavily on environmental factors in determining just what will be learned or what moral principles will be extracted. They

direct particular attention to the characteristics of the behavior models and the circumstances in which these models appear. For example, a social-learning theorist in analyzing moral judgments would want to consider the characteristics of the model, the nature of the act itself, the immediate and long-term consequences of the act, and a variety of other features of the setting in which a particular moral or immoral act occurred (Bandura, 1977).

However, we know that, in addition to direct observation, children learn about morality from direct instruction, as when parents or teachers lecture on good and evil. Children also learn from experiencing the consequences of their acts: some behaviors may result in praise, whereas others are followed by harsh punishment. Yet these experiences are surely not always consistent. How does the child extract general rules from what must be a very diverse set of experiences? The answer to this question is twofold. First, social-learning theorists do not assume that moral judgments are as unified as do the other types of theorists that we have discussed. Individuals, they believe, will make a complex mixture of moral judgments that depend on particular experiences and may be applied in particular situations. Secondly, however, they believe that the human, as an active information processor, will weigh the experiences individually, considering some more important than others. Thus a person whom you respect may be a much more important model than someone you do not respect. Certain dimensions may be given more weight than others; for example, when Bryan and Walbek (1970a, b) contrasted the effect on children of what a model practiced and what a model preached, they found that the behavior was more influential than the verbal message in affecting the children's subsequent actions.

Assuming that an individual has developed a set of moral rules or standards from various kinds of experiences, what does that tell us about that person's actual moral behavior or conduct? More than either of the other theoretical approaches that we have discussed, social-learning theory has been concerned with moral *be-havior* as well as moral rules. In early research on this topic, a primary concern was the influence of either direct punishment or modeling on an individual's subsequent response, with little attention to any internal norms or standards. Thus investigators would administer punishment for a particular behavior, for example, and then look to its effect on subsequent resistance to temptation (Cheyne & Walters, 1970; LaVoie, 1973; Parke, 1969). In addition, implicating the importance of cognitive processes, Aronfreed (1968) found that children who were given a reason for their punishment were more resistant to subsequent temptation than children who were given no clue as to why they were being punished. Other experiments considered the effectiveness of various models in influencing an observer's subsequent behavior (Bandura & McDonald, 1963; Berger, 1971; Rosenkoetter, 1973). Using such a strategy, experimenters learned that the time interval between misdeed and delivery of punishment and the severity of the punishment were both important factors in the learning process, regardless of whether animals or children were the subjects (Cheyne & Walters, 1970).

These studies showed that, in the laboratory at least, children could learn to model virtually any behavior, including moral judgments and moral conduct (Keasey, 1973; Prentice, 1972; Turiel & Rothman, 1972). Termed by Hetherington and McIntyre (1975) the *whoopee! studies* (as in "Whoopee! We can condition _____ !"), these experiments certainly showed that moral behaviors can be learned through observation and modeling. More recently, however, social-learning theorists have become more cognitive in their emphasis, seeking to explain those situations in which the internal rules or standards of moral behavior will or will not be expressed in moral conduct.

In this search for explanation, the social-learning theorists have relied on concepts of **self-censure** and **exonerative moral reasoning.** Let's consider these concepts in more detail. Generally, social-learning theorists would claim, people will avoid engaging in behavior that violates their moral

principles because they anticipate *self-censure* (Bandura, 1977). In other words, if we anticipate that we could not excuse a particular behavior to ourselves in terms of the moral principles that we have developed, we will probably avoid doing that behavior. On other occasions, *exonerative moral reasoning* may weaken this internal restraint. We may be able to find reasons, perhaps even highly moral ones, for engaging in a particular behavior and thus justify that behavior to ourselves and perhaps to others as well (Bandura, 1973; Kurtines & Greif, 1974). There are many historical examples of this strategy. For instance, executioners in Nazi Germany did not believe that they were doing anything morally wrong; instead, they justified their crimes by claiming service to a higher moral good, in this case the Aryan culture. Parents who severely beat their children often use a similar exonerative strategy—they were not trying to hurt the child, but it was for the child's own good. In one case in Indianapolis in 1978, the worthy goal was allegedly to teach the child to spell *butterfly*, but the child's death cut the lesson short.

Deindividuation provides another example of a strategy whereby people disassociate their actions from the consequences and thus avoid moral self-censure. Similarly, diffusion of responsibility, whereby one person feels less responsible for the effects of an action when others are present, may also allow a person to behave immorally when he or she otherwise would not (Bandura, Underwood, & Fromson, 1975). Thus for the social-learning theorist, both acquired moral standards and specific situational factors must be considered when attempting to understand moral behavior.

D. *Comparison of the Three Viewpoints*

We have now covered the three major orientations to moral development—the psychoanalytic, the cognitive, and the social-learning viewpoints. Although, as we have seen, there are variations of each of these viewpoints, there are still some major differences among them. In the psychoanalytic model, especially as developed by

Freud, there is an overriding moral consistency in one's personality development, and the superego, which develops in early childhood, is believed to determine all later moral conduct. In this model, situational factors are thought to be of little importance once the basic structure of the personality is set. For the cognitive theorists, and for Erikson as well, moral development is conceptualized as an invariant sequence of stages. Not only do these stages always occur in the same order, but they are also generally assumed to occur at particular times in development. Thus, by knowing only the age of a child, cognitive-stage theorists would feel that they could make a good approximation of a child's level of moral judgment. Situational factors are also relatively unimportant for these theorists. They would agree that the moral judgment level of the individual alone would determine behavior in any situation. In marked contrast to both of these positions, social-learning theorists see a much less unified internal standard, although they do not deny the importance of internal rules of conduct. In further distinction, they place great importance on the role of situations and circumstances in moral development, not only as sources of original acquisition of moral standards, but also as influences in the subsequent adherence to or deviance from moral rules of conduct.

Not all theories of moral development can be so clearly delineated, however. For example, Hogan (1973) has proposed a theoretical framework that integrates ideas from each of the models that we have discussed. Hogan explains the development of moral character in terms of five separate dimensions: moral knowledge, socialization, empathy, autonomy, and a dimension of moral judgment. Together with both the cognitive theorists and the social-learning theorists, he considers the human to be a rule-formulating species. Socialization experiences are important in Hogan's system, but he also argues that there are some biological bases for morality, in the sense of internal templates that can compare and evaluate conduct according to a predetermined standard. Hogan's model also incorporates sequences of development, but, unlike the

stage theorists, he does not believe that these stages are invariant.

It is difficult, of course, to evaluate these various theoretical positions in the abstract. Although one or another theory may sound reasonable, we are obliged, as curious scientists, to look at the evidence for the various assumptions.

III. Research on Morality

Many issues that have been raised by the various theories of moral development have been topics of considerable empirical research. For example, investigators have considered whether morality is a unitary trait, whether there is an invariant sequence in moral development, and whether situational factors can influence moral behavior. In addition, research has dealt with the consequences of immoral action—what happens when someone behaves counter to moral standards? Let's look at the results of these studies.

A. *Generality of Moral Judgments and Moral Conduct*

Both the psychoanalytic and the cognitive approaches, although different in many of their assumptions, see morality as a general trait; that is, it is the same for each person across different situations. Although not wedded to either of these theoretical viewpoints, Hartshorne and May (1928–1930) conducted the most massive investigation of this assumption in a project grandly titled "The Character Education Inquiry." Testing thousands of children between the ages of 8 and 16 in a variety of settings and on a variety of tasks, these investigators sought to show the consistency of various forms of moral judgment, moral opinions, and moral conduct such as cheating and lying. Their results did not show such consistency, however. A child who cheated in scoring an exam was not necessarily more prone to express less moral opinions than other children nor even to steal money from the teacher's desk. As a result of generally low correlations between their various measures, Hartshorne and May proposed the "doctrine of specificity" and suggested that the commonality among various aspects of *situations* has more to do with the generality of moral behavior than does any internal character trait; that is, moral behavior may be influenced more by the characteristics of the situation than by those of the person.

In fact, there was somewhat greater consistency among behaviors than Hartshorne and May originally believed. More sophisticated analysis of the original data by Burton (1963) found some support for a general morality factor and a tendency for moral consistency to increase with age. Later the team of Nelson, Grinder, and Mutterer (1969), using six measures of resistance to temptation with sixth-grade children, found some evidence for a general morality factor, but again the evidence was much weaker than some of the theoretical viewpoints would assume. Other investigations, attempting to find correlations not only among behaviors, but between behavior and guilt, for example, have been even less successful in establishing the generality of morality (Hoffman, 1977). Thus we must conclude that, although there is some consistency of moral judgment and behavior across situations, we need more than a knowledge of the individual's level of morality to predict moral behavior.

B. *Invariant Sequences of Moral Development*

Erikson, Piaget, and Kohlberg all claim that morality develops in a predetermined sequence of stages, with each stage a prerequisite to the next stage. Relatively little research has been done to test Erikson's assumptions, although some investigators have reported that genuine intimacy occurs only when a reasonable sense of identity is established (Orlofsky, Marcia, & Lesser, 1973) and that conformity is greater when identity is less firmly established (Toder & Marcia, 1973) (see Table 8-1). Although both of these findings are consistent with the sequence suggested by Erikson, they obviously cover only a small section of the range that he suggests.

Piaget's idea of moral development progressing from specific to general and from the more concrete to the more abstract

has generally been supported (Gesell, Ilg, & Ames, 1956), and there is fairly consistent evidence that older children place more emphasis on intentions in evaluating the severity of a mistake (Baer & Wright, 1974). Yet the time periods Piaget proposed for his stages have not been universally accepted; it has been suggested by Bronfenbrenner (1970) that Piaget's specifications become less applicable the further one moves from Geneva, Switzerland. Despite disagreement on the age levels at which Piaget's stages occur, however, the general notion of a lower and higher stage of morality has been supported (Hetherington & McIntire, 1975). At the same time, many critics claim that the simple two-stage theory offered by Piaget is just that—too simple—and believe that it must be elaborated to adequately represent moral development (Isaacs, 1966; E. Lerner, 1937).

Kohlberg's theory obviously provides greater complexity, with its six distinct stages of moral development. Has the complexity of his theory been justified? Kohlberg, as you might suspect, believes that it has. In one test of this sequential theory, sixth graders who had been assessed on moral-judgment level were given the opportunity to cheat on four different tests (Krebs, 1967). As shown in Figure 8-3, higher stages of moral development were associated with less cheating behavior.

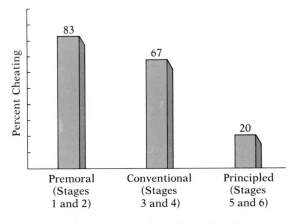

Figure 8-3. Percentage of students cheating. (From "Some Relations between Moral Judgment, Attention, and Resistance to Temptation," by R. Krebs. Unpublished doctoral dissertation, University of Chicago, 1967.)

In a much more extensive and more relevant test of Kohlberg's stage theory, Haan, Smith, and Block (1968) attempted to relate the moral-judgment levels of university students to their political behavior, their participation in student protests, and a number of other background variables. Students from the University of California at Berkeley, from San Francisco State, and Peace Corps volunteers served as subjects. Although 957 respondents were originally tested, only 54% of the sample was used in the final analysis, because the moral-judgment responses of the other persons did not clearly fall into a single level of moral judgment. (Such occurrences indicate either that the measuring instrument is not precise enough to classify every subject, or that some subjects are not clearly in a single stage at a given point of time. Probably both possibilities are true, suggesting a certain weakness in the Kohlberg model.)

As shown in Figure 8-4, few of the students were at the preconventional stage; about two-thirds of the men and 80% of the women were at the level of conventional moral judgment (Stages 3 and 4), and 28% of the males and 18% of the females had

reached the stage of principled morality. The difference between the sexes is explained by Kohlberg as a result of women's greater allegiance to children and stronger socialization pressures. Some people have argued, however, that the nearly exclusive use of male figures in Kohlberg's stories (see Figure 8-2) is an influencing factor (Poppen, 1974), whereas others have questioned the assumption that the sequence necessarily reflects increasingly higher levels of morality.

When Haan and her colleagues looked specifically at the moral-judgment levels of those students who had been arrested in sit-ins connected with the Berkeley Free Speech Movement, a number of interesting patterns were observed (see Figure 8-5). As Kohlberg would predict, a majority of both men and women at the principled level of moral judgment were involved in student activism. Yet somewhat surprisingly, a considerable proportion of students at the preconventional stages of moral development were involved as well. The authors suggest that different moral principles caused the activism of the two groups: "Principled arrestees (Stage 6) were more concerned with the basic issues of civil liberties and rights and the relationship of students as citizens within a university community. The IR's (Stage 2) reasons were more often concerned with their individual rights in a conflict of power" (Haan, Smith, & Block, 1968, p. 98). Findings such as these underline the difficulty in connecting moral judgments to moral conduct. Two people may engage in exactly the same action, but their reasons for doing so and their assessed level of morality may be quite different. Thus the predictive validity of Kohlberg's stage theory—its ability to predict behaviors of people at different levels of moral development—remains somewhat questionable.

Another critical assumption of Kohlberg's stage model is that the sequence of stages is invariant; everyone, Kohlberg assumes, begins at Stage 1 and moves toward Stage 6 (though not everyone will reach Stage 6). However, this assumption has also been questioned (Hoffman, 1977; Kurtines & Greif, 1974; Simpson, 1974). Although the evidence suggests that there

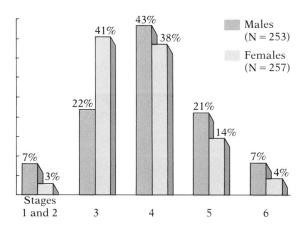

Figure 8-4. Percentages of subjects at each of Kohlberg's stages in the study of university students and Peace Corps volunteers. (From "Moral Reasoning of Young Adults: Political-Social Behavior, Family Background, and Personality Correlates," by N. Haan, M. B. Smith, and J. Block, *Journal of Personality and Social Psychology*, 1968, *10*, 183–201. Copyright 1968 by the American Psychological Association. Reprinted by permission.)

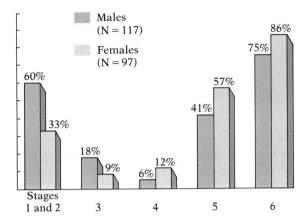

Figure 8-5. Percentages of pure moral types arrested in the Berkeley Free Speech Movement sit-in. (From "Moral Reasoning of Young Adults: Political-Social Behavior, Family Background, and Personality Correlates," by N. Haan, M. B. Smith, and J. Block, *Journal of Personality and Social Psychology*, 1968, *10*, 183–201. Copyright 1968 by the American Psychological Association. Reprinted by permission.)

may be a general movement from Stage 1 through Stage 3, there is considerably less evidence that this systematic progression continues through later stages. In fact, the entire ordering of the later sequences, and Kohlberg's assumptions that they represent a higher moral state, have been subject to considerable scrutiny. For example, Simpson (1974) emphasizes the importance of a person's sex and culture in determining moral development. She claims that in the United States the concept of equality has different meanings to persons of different social classes. The working class may view equality in economic terms, whereas the upper middle class defines equality socially. Simpson also attacks the strong emphasis that Kohlberg places on language ability. Can you be a Stage 5 or a Stage 6 only if you are verbally skilled? Criticisms like these must be taken seriously. We must conclude, then, that the assumption of invariance of stages has not been strongly supported.

C. *Situational Factors in Moral Behavior*

The question of how important situational factors are in determining moral conduct relates back to the issue of generality.

For those who believe that there is a general moral standard—that is, a moral standard that is valid for a person *all* the time—situational variations are thought to be relatively unimportant. For others, most notably the social-learning theorists, situations are considered to be equally or more important than internal standards in predicting the whens and whys of moral conduct. Mischel and Mischel (1976), for example, suggest that moral behavior is dependent on the person's ability to anticipate different outcomes in different situations, rather than on some general moral tendency. As we have seen, other studies in the social-learning tradition have pointed to the impact of immediate situational factors in encouraging moral or immoral behavior. Often the presence of models is an important influence, not only in the acquisition of a behavior, but in its subsequent display. For example, Kimbrell and Blake (1958) watched subjects who had just been in a dry-cracker-testing experiment walk past a drinking fountain that was labeled "Do not use." In some cases, a model (an accomplice of the experimenter) was drinking from the fountain as the subject walked by. In those cases, subjects themselves were much more likely to ignore the sign and take a drink, as compared to a situation in which no model was present.

The Milgram studies (discussed in Chapter 3), in which a person is encouraged to administer painful shocks to another human being, also point to the importance of external influences in moral development. In a similar fashion, the lifting of moral restraints may cause an increase in immoral or illegal behavior. As an example, Ross and DiTecco (1975) cite the wholesale looting that occurred in Montreal in 1969 when the police went on a 16-hour strike. Similar events in other cities since that time also point to the significant influence of situational factors on moral conduct.

The fact that external pressures and extreme temptations can sharply affect our behavior does not, of course, mean that individuals have no moral standards (Hoffman, 1977). Our earlier discussion certainly points to the existence of moral standards at the internal level. However, under certain conditions, large numbers of normally moral people may be guilty of immoral conduct, pointing once again to the importance of understanding situational factors in our search to understand social behavior.

D. *Morality: Abstract or Interpersonal?*

To a large extent, the research and theorizing on moral judgment has assumed that people develop a set of abstract rules and then apply these rules in specific situations. Particularly for the models of Kohlberg and Piaget, this process is largely cognitive and very general, and it tends to be unconcerned with interpersonal aspects of the situation. Recently, in diverging from these assumptions, Haan (1978) proposed an **interpersonal morality.** Here we have a very social conception of moral judgment. People, she suggests, engage in dialogues with each other with the intent of achieving new or maintaining old moral balances (Haan, 1978). In a study of adolescent friendship groups, Haan involved both Black and White teenagers in a series of games that required negotiation among the participants and some form of action as the result. In support of her contention, more of the adolescents used some form of interpersonal reasoning (based on compromise and induction) than formal reasoning (more individual and deductive) in the action situations. Also, echoing criticisms that Kohlberg's levels may apply only to people from certain social classes and certain ethnic backgrounds, Haan found that Blacks scored higher on interpersonal levels of morality than formal levels, whereas Whites showed the reverse pattern. Although Haan's approach to moral reasoning is still new, it represents an important reconceptualization. As social animals, we may indeed be dependent on interaction to be able to form moral judgments; indeed, interaction may be equally or more important than the more abstract cognitive development.

E. *The Consequences of Immoral Actions*

What are the "wages of sin?" So far we have concentrated on the ways in which moral judgment and moral behavior de-velop. We have assumed that most people learn some kind of morality and that they act according to these moral standards. Yet, as we have also discovered, on many occasions people will act counter to their moral standards. What happens in these situations? What are the effects on the person of immoral action?

Not surprisingly, guilt is one immediate reaction (see Figure 8-6) (Klass, 1978). Other negative feelings may develop as well, but these, in contrast to guilt, tend to be limited to the immediate situation. For example, there is no evidence that people who transgress generally feel any less self-esteem than other people, nor do they feel particularly negative about the context of their immoral act. They do, however, report feeling uncomfortable about the actual act (Noel, 1973; Shaffer, 1975a), and these feelings of discomfort have been shown to persist (Ring, Wallston, & Corey, 1970).

Making amends is also a common response to immoral conduct (Klass, 1978). For example, Carlsmith and Gross (1969) found that subjects who had done harm to another person were much more apt to comply with anyone's request for help, even when that help in no way would reduce the previous harm. The more guilty someone is, the more likely he or she is to agree to help another person.

Although Freud suggested that repression comes into play when we commit an immoral action—that is, that we tend to forget what we've done wrong—the research evidence suggests that this is not the case. People do remember their actions, even though these memories may cause some subjective distress. In at least one experiment, for example, it was found that people tended to remember their lies better than they remembered the truth (Maslach, 1971). Perhaps, because for most of us, lying is less common than truth-telling, we may be more aware of or pay more attention to those instances and so remember them better later on. Consider, for example, the case of the teenager who lies to his or her parents about a dented fender in the family car; while he or she may be claiming that the damage was caused by a hit-and-run driver, a picture of the wall that he or she backed

Figure 8-6. The "wages of sin." (© Mitchell Payne/Jeroboam, Inc.)

into will be clear in his or her mind. We could guess that that incident would be remembered long afterward (and perhaps this has happened to you).

Our minds have other ways to reduce the stress of guilt. On many occasions, we may begin to believe the lies that we have told. The theory of cognitive dissonance, which we will discuss in Chapter 12, suggests that we try to make our beliefs fit in line with our behaviors. Thus the person who tells a lie may come to believe that lie

(Carlsmith, Collins, & Helmreich, 1966; Cooper & Goethals, 1974) and so reduce the discomfort resulting from the awareness of saying one thing and doing another. In the case of the bent fender, for example, the teenager may begin to believe in the hit-and-run theory, gradually forgetting that his or her own carelessness caused the wall and the car to meet.

The specific responses to immoral acts that we have discussed make it clear that studies of moral behavior cannot stop simply with an understanding of the development of moral judgment. Beyond the specific factors that may influence moral judgment, there exists the reality of human behavior.

IV. Theories of Justice

In our less-than-perfect world, moral beliefs are not always reflected in moral behavior. Injustices may occur despite our belief that they shouldn't. How do we cope with these events? Are there any general principles of morality and justice that we can apply, not only to explain immorality but also to provide a basis for action when circumstances seem unjust? There are two general models of moral systems that may help us answer these questions: equity theory and the justice motive.

A. *Equity Theory*

In earlier chapters (see Chapter 6) we discussed the general notion of equity as it applies to interpersonal relationships: it meant that people seek a balance in their relationships and that they desire to have their contributions or inputs be equal to their rewards or outcomes. Equity theory, however, has been applied much more broadly, referring not only to two-person interchanges, but to general societal laws as well.

Such a concern with the laws of society is of course neither recent nor unique to social psychologists. Aristotle was perhaps the first to propose a concept of justice, when he suggested that there are two basic forms: equal justice, when rewards are divided equally among individuals, and distributive justice, when rewards are distributed according to merit. The contrast between these two forms of justice is still a basic philosophical issue in societies today, where governments must decide whether to reward people according to merit and contribution, or whether to assure equality in the distribution of resources. In many countries, such as the United States and Canada, the government's position lies between these two points.

Equity theory, as developed by social psychologists, deals with interpersonal exchanges rather than government policies. The basic propositions of equity theory are quite simple (Walster, Berscheid, & Walster, 1973). First, the theory assumes that individuals will try to maximize their outcomes (where outcomes equal the rewards minus the costs). Secondly, the theory assumes that groups can maximize their collective outcome by developing accepted systems for distributing rewards and costs fairly among members. To make such a system acceptable, the society must in turn find ways to reward those members who adhere to the equity norm. Why is all this necessary? In part, the answer is that equity is not objective. In order to avoid conflicts between individuals who weigh inputs and outcomes differently, the society must develop a common standard. A final assumption of equity theory is that the experience of inequity is unpleasant and that people will try to restore equity to an inequitable relationship.

In applying equity theory to the legal system, investigators have considered primarily the role of an impartial observer—such as a judge or a juror—in determining equity between harmdoers and victims (Austin, Walster, & Utne, 1976). A major question in such deliberations is how much the harmdoer should suffer, or how much punishment should be prescribed. The question of legal punishment is one that has never been thoroughly resolved by legal scholars. Various goals have been discussed, such as rehabilitation, the protection of society, or, as Durkheim suggested, simple retaliation.

And in truth, punishment has remained, at least in part, a work of vengeance. It is said that we do not make the culpable suffer in order to make him suffer; it is nonetheless true that we find it just that he suffer [Durkheim, 1933, p. 88].

Because the standards for punishment are not fully agreed on in principle, the allotment of justice will ultimately depend on the judgments of jurors and judges. In these decisions, principles of equity theory have been found to have relevance.

One prediction that equity theory would make is that, in determining the punishment that a harmdoer should receive, a judge will take into account the suffering that the harmdoer has undergone as a result of the crime. This circumstance is commonly used by attorneys in defense of their clients, as is perhaps most vividly illustrated by Elliot Richardson (then U.S. Attorney General) in his plea for leniency in the sentencing of former vice-president Agnew for charges of bribery and tax fraud. Richardson stated (as quoted in Austin, Walster, & Utne, 1976, p. 184):

I am firmly convinced that in all the circumstances leniency is justified. I am keenly aware, first, of the historic magnitude of the penalties inherent in the vice president's resignation from his high office and his acceptance of a judgment of conviction for a felony. To propose that a man who has suffered these penalties should, in addition, be incarcerated in a penal institution, however briefly, is more than I as head of the government's prosecuting arm, can recommend or wish.

A similar rationale was offered by President Ford in justifying his pardon of former U.S. President Richard Nixon.

This balancing of suffering and punishment against the crime has shown up in research studies as well. For example, Austin, Walster, and Utne (1976) report a study in which students were asked to play the role of a judge in determining the sentence of a defendant who was guilty of purse snatching and who, in the getaway, had either suffered moderate or severe wounds, or who had not suffered at all. The students' decisions were dramatically influenced by the amount of suffering that the defendant had undergone (see Table 8-3). The more the defendant suffered in the getaway, the more lenient was the punishment assigned. However, studies in which the suffering is less physical—for example, time spent in jail prior to a trial—do not seem to produce the same compensation strategy (Legant, 1973). It may be that the suffering has to be quite real and personal in order for a reduction in sentence to be warranted and for a perception of equity to be established.

In many ways, equity theory presents a very optimistic viewpoint. Like early wild-west films with heroes in white hats and villains in black hats, equity theory assumes

TABLE 8-3 / *Number of Months Assigned to Prison as a Function of a Criminal's Suffering and Sex of the Observer for Low Crime Severity (Purse Snatching)*[a]

| | Amount of criminal suffering | | | |
	None	Moderate	Excessive	$\overline{M}$
Male observer	15.83	10.83	3.44	10.04
Female observer	22.72	14.39	7.89	15.00
$\overline{M}$	19.28	12.61	5.67	

[a] The range of the prison sentence set by the law was 0 (suspended sentence) to 60 months in prison.

From "Equity and the Law: The Effect of a Harmdoer's 'Suffering in the Act' on Liking and Assigned Punishment," by W. Austin, E. Walster, and M. K. Utne. In L. Berkowitz and E. Walster (Eds.), *Advances in Experimental Social Psychology*, Vol. 9. Copyright 1976 by Academic Press, Inc. Reprinted by permission.

that a fair and ultimate balance eventually results. Yet it has been observed that people do not live by equity alone (Weick, 1966). On some occasions, perceptions of equity and justice may not prevail, victims may not be compensated for their losses, and harmdoers may go unpunished. Is there any way to account for these exceptions?

B. *The Justice Motive*

In a formulation that is in some respects similar to equity theory, social psychologist Melvin Lerner has proposed the existence of a justice motive. Basically, this construct assumes the *belief in a just world*—a belief that "there is an appropriate fit between what people do and what happens to them" (Lerner, 1966, p. 3). Lerner suggests that people develop such a personal "contract" in order to operate effectively in the environment—that we develop a sense of our own deservingness and that, in turn, we realize that a belief in our own deservingness is contingent on a belief that others also get what they deserve in the world.

But what happens if events appear to be unjust? Lerner suggests that these events threaten our belief in a just world and that, accordingly, we will try to correct the situation in some way (Lerner, 1975, 1977; Lerner, Miller, & Holmes, 1976). On some occasions we may rectify the situation by compensating the victim—by giving aid to refugees, for example. Other times we may try to punish the harmdoer (if we can find one). Yet in other instances where we do not seem to be able to reestablish justice, we may convince ourselves that no injustice has occurred.

By blaming the victim, we can maintain our belief that people get what they deserve (Ryan, 1971). A psychiatrist named Martin Symonds (1975) has interviewed hundreds of victims of rapes, assaults, and kidnappings and finds that many of these victims receive, instead of sympathy, inquisitions and censure from their friends and family. When a person has been mugged, for example, a frequent response of friends, family, and the police is to interrogate the person relentlessly about *why* he or she got into such an unfortunate situation. "Why were you walking in that neighborhood alone?" "Why didn't you scream?" "Why were you carrying so much money?" Such reactions reflect our pervasive need to find rational causes for apparently senseless events. Recently, social psychologists have found considerable evidence for the high frequency of such reactions, particularly in the case of rape (for example, Clark, Hren, & Sanchez, 1978; Feild, 1978; Jones & Aronson, 1973; Krulewitz, 1977). In general, these studies show a consistent tendency for observers to attribute responsibility to the woman who is the victim of rape. Such a tendency is most pronounced when other explanations for the event are not apparent. For example, a victim who is described as unacquainted with her assailant is seen as more responsible for a rape than when she is acquainted with him (Smith, Keating, Hester, & Mitchell, 1976). Consistent with the speculations of Susan Brownmiller (1975), men in general are more likely to attribute responsibility to the female victim than are women (Feild, 1978; Selby, Calhoun, & Brock, 1977).

Our tendency to attribute responsibility for events to the people they happen to ex-

tends to less traumatic situations as well. For example, Lerner (1965) observed that, when one member of a work group received an arbitrarily assigned large bonus, observers were persuaded that the worker had earned the bonus by an outstanding performance. At a broader level, the same rationale has been used by some people to account for the assassination of public figures (see Figure 8-7).

Even when responsibility for an outcome cannot reasonably be assigned to the victim, belief in a just world leads people to personally derogate the victim. Lichtman (cited in Lerner, 1966), for example, asked ninth-grade children to evaluate a boy named Bill Johnson who had suffered a bad automobile accident as the result of a blown-out tire. When these students believed that Bill had acted responsibly to avoid such an accident (by buying new tires when he was told the old ones were likely to blow), they rated him as *less* attractive than when they were told he had not bought the tires. One might tend to explain such irrationality as simply the product of ninth-grade minds; but Lerner and his colleagues have found similar results with college undergraduates (Lerner, 1965, 1970, 1974; Lerner & Becker, 1962; Lerner & Matthews, 1967; Lerner & Simmons, 1966).

Derogation of the victim does not always occur, however. Indeed, it is particularly unlikely when someone else's suffering threatens our own feelings of deservingness and justice. For example, Sorrentino and Boutilier (1974) found that observers who are told to expect a similar fate to that of the victim are less likely to malign the victim. Subjects in their experiment observed a female undergraduate receive a series of electric shocks as a "learner" in a teaching-effectiveness project. Some of the subjects were told that they would also serve as "learners" later; others were told that they would not. Anticipation of a similar fate led to a significant reduction in the assignment of negative characteristics to the learner. Such a pattern is, of course, consistent with the sex differences in attribution of responsibility for rape, where we can assume that women are more likely to anticipate a similar fate than are men.

"I DON'T KNOW WHAT WILL HAPPEN NOW. WE HAVE GOT DIF-
FICULT DAYS AHEAD, BUT IT DOESN'T MATTER WITH ME BE-
CAUSE I'VE BEEN TO THE MOUNTAIN TOP. LIKE ANYBODY ELSE
I WOULD LIKE TO LIVE A LONG LIFE. BUT IM NOT CONCERNED
WITH THAT. I JUST WANT TO DO GOD'S WILL AND HE HAS AL-
LOWED ME TO GO UP THE MOUNTAIN. I SEE THE PROM-
ISED LAND. I MAY NOT GET THERE WITH YOU, BUT I WANT YOU
TO KNOW TONIGHT THAT WE AS A PEOPLE WILL GET TO THE
PROMISED LAND. I AM HAPPY TONIGHT THAT I AM NOT WOR-
RIED ABOUT ANYTHING. I'M NOT FEARING ANY MAN. MINE
EYES HAVE SEEN THE GLORY OF THE COMING OF THE LORD."

Figure 8-7. Martin Luther King, victim of assassination. In April 1968, right after Dr. King's murder, a representative sample of 1337 American adults were asked: "When you heard the news [of the assassination], which of these things was your strongest reaction: (1) anger, (2) sadness, (3) shame, (4) fear, (5) he brought it on himself?" About one-third (426) of the respondents chose the response "brought it on himself" (Rokeach, 1970). For these respondents, Lerner's "just world" hypothesis applies: since Dr. King was killed, he must have deserved to be killed. (Ben Shahn, *Martin Luther King*, 1968. Collection of the New Jersey State Museum. Gift of Mr. and Mrs. Martin Bressler.)

At a more general level, Lerner (1977) has suggested that the individual's first concern is his or her own deservingness and the ability to believe in a world where justice prevails. Often this belief leads a person to simply ignore evidence of injustice. Thus we may skip those articles in the newspaper that deal with suffering in other countries, and we may avoid neighborhoods in our own town where evidence of poverty is prominent. Yet many of those same occasions may lead to direct help and assistance —perhaps because they represent only a minimal threat to our own state of justice and deservingness. Not being personally threatened, we may feel free to offer assistance and to correct the unjust consequences of others (Miller, 1977). In contrast, when the threat to our own state of deservingness is apparent, we seem to be much more likely to choose other strategies, such as blaming the victims and seeing them as a direct cause of their own misfortunes, thereby sparing ourselves the fear that a similar fate may befall us. Justice and morality thus become very personal matters, and, again, this poses a problem for those who assume that there are universal moral standards that prevail in all situations.

V. Summary

In seeking to understand the development of morality, some theorists, such as Freud and Erikson, have emphasized motivational and emotional determinants, whereas others, including Piaget and Kohlberg, have stressed cognitive factors. Learning theories, in contrast, have focused on situational factors rather than internal characteristics of the person.

Freud proposed three systems of energy—the id, the ego, and the superego. The superego, which develops out of the Oedipal conflict, represents the central base for moral judgments. Neo-Freudians, such as Erik Erikson, postulate psychosocial developmental stages as well as psychosexual ones.

Piaget's theory is an example of a cognitive approach to moral development, emphasizing the acquisition of rules, laws, and principles. He suggests that children pass from an initial stage of moral realism (accepting rules as given by authority) to a stage of moral independence (rules may be altered by consensus to fit the needs of the situation). According to Piaget, as the child moves from one stage to the other, he or she comes to emphasize the intentions rather than the consequences of an act; he or she also begins to favor reciprocal rather than expiatory types of punishment and discards a belief in immanent justice.

Kohlberg has extended Piaget's theory to include three levels of moral development: preconventional, conventional, and postconventional (also called the autonomous or principled level). Within these levels, there are six stages of moral development, through which, according to Kohlberg, a child must pass in an invariant order.

Social-learning theory emphasizes specific reinforcements and observational learning experiences in the development of morality. Through abstract modeling, a person may formulate general rules that then apply to a variety of situations. Social-learning theorists have been particularly concerned with moral *behavior* and the factors that may influence such behavior.

Research has cast doubt on the assumption that morality is a general trait. Situational factors also play an important role in influencing the morality or immorality of behavior. Evidence for an invariant sequence of stages, as proposed by Kohlberg, has been mixed: although the early stages appear to be supported, there is considerable question concerning the invariance and the values that may be inherent in the latter stages. Research also shows that there are many ways people will try to deal with guilt —one of the primary consequences of immoral action. For example, they will attempt to make amends or to believe their own lies to escape the stress of guilt.

Equity theory is a general model of a moral system that proposes that people desire to have inputs equal outcomes, on a societal level as well as the individual level. Applying this theory to the legal system, we can find evidence for a balance between the severity of a crime and the amount of suffering people feel a harmdoer should experience. Although equity theory suggests that a balance will nearly always be achieved, Lerner, in discussing the *justice motive,* suggests that on many occasions we will engage in a variety of distortions in order to maintain our belief in a just world. Blaming the victim, for example, justifies the otherwise senseless wrong that he or she may have suffered. However, if we expect to experience a similar fate, we will tend not to blame the victim. For Lerner, maintaining our belief in our own deservingness is our initial concern, and the attempt to believe in a just world is a pervasive strategy for maintaining that belief.

Glossary Terms

abstract modeling
autonomous stage
    of morality
cognitive theory
ego
empathy
equity theory
exonerative moral
    reasoning

expiatory punish-
    ment
heteronomous
    stage of morality
id
immanent justice
interpersonal mor-
    ality
Oedipus conflict
psychoanalytic
    theory

reciprocity
reinforcement
    theory
self-censure
socialization
social-learning
    theory
superego
unconscious

It is more blessed to give than to receive. THE NEW TESTAMENT, ACTS 20:35

HENRY MOORE. *FAMILY GROUP.* BRONZE, 1950. COLLECTION, THE MUSEUM OF MODERN ART, NEW YORK. A. CONGER GOODYEAR FUND.

If it is more blessed to give than to receive, then most of us are content to let the other fellow have the greater blessing. SHAILER MATHEWS

Prosocial Behavior: Cooperation and Helping

This chapter was written by Carol Sigelman.

Often it seems that all we read about in the newspapers are violence, war, and corruption. Yet people do behave in more likeable ways. They join forces to accomplish their goals; they do favors for one another; occasionally they even risk their lives to save others. Are such behaviors unusual, or are they a basic part of human nature? What do we know about positive forms of social behavior?

Following the lead of Wispé (1972), we define **prosocial behavior** as behavior that has positive social consequences—that contributes to the physical or psychological well-being of another person. A host of behaviors fall into this category; among them are altruism, aiding, attraction, bystander intervention, charity, cooperation, friendship, helping, rescue, sacrifice, sharing, sympathy, and trust. Although all of these behaviors certainly contrast with antisocial forms of behavior, the present chapter will focus on only a few of them.

Cooperation (that is, working together for mutual benefit) is a prosocial behavior that has received a great deal of attention, particularly as it contrasts with **competition** (striving to excel in order to obtain an exclusive goal). When two people cooperate, the action of each brings both closer to a goal; when two people compete, the behavior of one actually makes it less likely that the other will attain the goal.

Helping behavior, defined generally, is behavior that benefits another person rather than oneself. It may take several forms. A *favor,* such as holding a door open for someone, is a helping act that requires little self-sacrifice in time or effort but that benefits another person. *Donation* is the provision of goods or services to a person or organization in need. It requires material sacrifice, although the degree of sacrifice may be large or small. *Intervention in an emergency* is a potentially costly form of helping behavior, performed under stressful conditions, with little possibility of reward. Such helping behavior may cause you to think of the term **altruism**. Although some researchers use the word *altruism* to refer to helping behavior in general, most use it more narrowly to refer to unselfish behavior on behalf of others that involves a sacrifice.

We have no hesitancy about applying the term *altruism* to the actions of the Good Samaritan (Luke 10:30–35), who aided a man wounded by thieves. Unlike the priest and the Levite who "passed by on the other side," the Samaritan went to the wounded man, carried him to an inn, cared for him, paid the innkeeper, and offered money for any further expenses. Walster and Piliavin (1972) pinpointed why this parable serves as a model of altruism. First, the Samaritan was not responding to pressures or obligations. His act was voluntary and, in fact, nonconforming, since other community leaders had failed to help. He was not of the same ethnic group as the victim and had no special responsibility for him. Moreover, his behavior was costly, involving sacrifices on his part of time, effort, and money. Finally, he sought no reward, nor did he receive one.

When we take both the behavior and the motives behind the behavior into account, then, we see that altruism is a very special form of helping behavior that is voluntary, costly, and motivated by something other than the anticipation of reward.[1]

The study of prosocial behavior has become one of the liveliest areas of research in social psychology (for example, see Staub, 1978, 1979; Wispé, 1978). One reason for

---

[1] We encounter some problems when we try to define prosocial behavior. Here we have described it in terms of its consequences.

But who decides whether the consequences are positive or negative? Suppose you break up a fight, but the fighters call you a meddler. Alternatively, we can insist, as many researchers do, that a desire to benefit another person must be the motive for an act if it is to be called prosocial. But is someone really behaving prosocially by giving gifts to a politician when he or she also hopes to receive some favor in return? And are you behaving prosocially if you drown a person during a well-intentioned but clumsy rescue attempt? Can we always determine whether the motives for an act are selfish or unselfish? There is a great deal of controversy about what prosocial behavior is and whether it is always something to be encouraged.

this interest is that prosocial behavior is difficult to explain with existing theories of human behavior. A second reason is more practical than theoretical: when people fail to act prosocially, not only are we concerned but our assumptions about human nature are challenged.

I. Prosocial Behavior and Human Nature

The motivations for prosocial behaviors, especially altruistic ones, pose a challenge to social psychologists. Recall two of the major theories presented in Chapter 1. Stimulus-response theory states that those behaviors that are followed by rewarding consequences tend to be repeated or strengthened. How, then, would altruism increase in strength, or even exist, if it is associated with negative consequences such as loss of resources, injury, or even death? How can psychoanalytic theory, which rests on the assumption that human nature is instinctively selfish and aggressive, explain behavior that is apparently unselfish and beneficial to others? The theorist's challenge is to explain why people do something that is apparently not reinforcing or that goes against what is considered to be basic human nature.

Some psychoanalytic theorists have dealt with the challenge of explaining altruism by viewing it as a sign of psychological disorder or as a disguised attempt to manipulate people; others have attempted to understand how positive forces in personality development could reduce the strength of selfish motives (Ekstein, 1978). Various stimulus-response and social-learning theorists have also responded to the challenge. Some have rejected the concept of altruism; others have argued that there *are* rewards to seemingly altruistic acts but that the rewards are subtle (for example, Rosenhan, 1978). An increased feeling of self-esteem or even an expectation of reward in an afterlife may motivate helpers. But such arguments often seem circular—they seem to assume that, because the helping behavior occurred, its consequences must have been reinforcing. Still other researchers acting within an S-R framework have tried to demonstrate that helping is in fact reinforcing (for example, Aronfreed & Paskal, 1965; R. F. Weiss, Buchanan, Altstatt, & Lombardo, 1971). However, such researchers have not been able to explain why people sometimes help others at a huge cost to themselves.

Another debate centers around whether altruism is part of our basic biological nature. The traditional Darwinian theory of evolution emphasizes that it is the genes contributing to survival that are passed on to future generations and that become more prevalent in a species. But how could genes for altruism be passed on when altruists endanger their very survival for others? Some fascinating attempts to answer this question have come from the emerging discipline of **sociobiology** (for example, Barash, 1977; Dawkins, 1976; E. O. Wilson, 1975, 1978). In his landmark textbook on the subject, Harvard zoologist Edward O. Wilson (1975) defined sociobiology as ". . . the systematic study of the biological basis of all social behavior" (p. 4).

Consider the evolution of a species of social insects. Why would female worker bees be sterile themselves but devote their lives to caring for the queen bee's offspring and even commit suicide defending the hive? The explanation is a genetic one (W. D. Hamilton, 1964; Trivers & Hare, 1976). The female workers, as offspring of a single queen, share ¾ of their genes in common. By contrast, if a worker were able to reproduce, she would pass on only half of her genes to her own offspring. The key concept that sociobiologists introduce at this point is the concept of *kin selection,* as opposed to individual selection. They argue that it is the survival of genetic material (which is shared with relatives), rather than the survival of individuals, that matters in evolution. The worker bees can actually pass more of their genetic material to future generations by helping the queen to produce and care for more and more sisters than they could by reproducing themselves. Similarly, when an animal dies to save its offspring or relatives, it may optimize the amount of its family's genetic material that survives, even though its own genes die. In this view, altruism is a matter of selfishness —though not in any conscious sense—in the interest of passing on as much of one's genetic formula as possible.

But what about altruism on behalf of strangers? Here the concept of *reciprocal altruism* has been introduced (Trivers, 1971). I may well risk myself to help you, the argument goes, if I can anticipate help in return—help that will pay me back for my original sacrifice and that will mean both of us gain in the final analysis. (Notice, again, that what appears to be altruism is interpreted as an act of genetic self-interest.)

By applying these principles of genetic self-interest, sociobiologists have painted an unsettling picture of human nature. Taken to its extreme, this view suggests that "we are survival machines—robot vehicles blindly programmed to preserve the selfish molecules known as genes" (Dawkins, 1976, p. ix). However, critics point out that no genes for altruism have been identified, that there are important differences between social insects and humans, and that there is plenty of reason to believe that cultural influences and learning play a major role in the evolution of prosocial behavior (Boehm, 1979; D. T. Campbell, 1978, 1979; R. Cohen, 1978; Sahlins, 1976).

Such controversies over the nature (and even the possibility) of altruism are debates about the very nature of human beings. Psychoanalytic theory, stimulus-response theory, and sociobiology all assume that humans are basically selfish and interpret altruistic behavior as basically selfish, too. Altruism continues to defy major conceptions of human nature; for this very reason, it will continue to fascinate social psychologists.

There are also practical reasons for being interested in the study of prosocial behavior. Not only do we deplore violence, but we are alarmed when people fail to help when help is needed. An incident that symbolizes this failure occurred in New York City in 1964. The stabbing of Kitty Genovese might have passed for "just

another murder" except for some peculiar circumstances.

For more than half an hour thirty-eight respectable, law-abiding citizens in Queens watched a killer stalk and stab a woman in three separate attacks in Kew Gardens.

Twice the sound of their voices and the sudden glow of their bedroom lights interrupted him and frightened him off. Each time he returned, sought her out and stabbed her again. Not one person telephoned the police during the assault; one witness called after the woman was dead [*New York Times*, March 27, 1964].

Police and community experts could offer no explanation—particularly since witnesses needed only to make a call from the safety of their apartments. Social psychologists immediately attempted to find explanations; if we understand what happened perhaps we can prevent it from happening in the future. We also have a stake in determining why many people do not support charitable causes; why individuals and groups, including nations, do not cooperate with one another; and why even the simple courtesies or favors of life are not always forthcoming. And, on the positive side, we have a stake in determining what motivates people to behave prosocially. Social psychologists have responded by conducting a variety of studies of prosocial behavior in the laboratory as well as in subways, streets, and shopping malls.

What can we learn from this research? The first topic of this chapter is cooperation —a form of prosocial behavior that has "something in it" for the actor. We will explore the conditions that make people more or less likely to cooperate or to compete, and we will see how these behaviors are learned. Then we will turn to a variety of helping behaviors. In explaining these behaviors, we will focus on situational factors, the effects of other people, momentary psychological states, personality characteristics and other background variables, and the characteristics of the recipient of help. Three explanatory models—one emphasizing emotional reactions to the needs of others, another pointing to the operation of

norms or standards of behavior, and a third focusing on the costs and rewards of helping or failing to help—will tie together the loose ends of research findings. Finally, we will apply what we have learned to the task of building a more prosocial society.

II. Cooperation: Working for Mutual Benefit

As noted above, *cooperation* is a prosocial behavior in which persons act for mutual benefit. When people cooperate, they coordinate their efforts so that each individual's actions bring everyone closer to achieving a goal. In fact, people who cooperate can often achieve a goal that none could obtain alone, as when it takes four people pushing together to roll a car out of a muddy rut.

We cannot fully understand cooperation without comparing and contrasting it with *competition*. When people compete, they strive individually to obtain the same goal, one that not all of them attain (Deutsch, 1949a). One person's progress toward the goal decreases the probability that other competitors will attain it. We are not suggesting that competition is necessarily antisocial rather than prosocial. People often have rewarding and positive interactions while they compete. However, competitors cannot make a high priority of benefiting their rivals or they will lose the contest.

Analysis of cooperation and competition is often clouded because the two terms not only describe behavior but also refer both to the *reward structures* inherent in a situation and to the individual's *motives* as he or she enters a situation. Consider one very familiar situation—the classroom. A professor may grade on a curve, so that only 15% of the students will receive A's in the course. Students then find themselves in a **competitive reward structure,** in which the successes of their peers actually decrease their own chances of success (assuming that "success" is defined as receiving an A grade). College students often have to operate in such situations, competing with others for

honors, athletic awards, and job openings that not all of them can attain.

Another professor might introduce a **cooperative reward structure** into the classroom by saying "Each team that I have formed in this classroom must work as a team to complete a series of projects. If the team does excellent work, everyone on the team will receive an A in the course." As in the competitive reward structure, students' outcomes are interdependent; the actions of one have implications for the outcomes of others. The critical difference is that in a competitive reward structure, one person's gain is another person's loss, while in a cooperative reward structure, one person's contribution increases not only his or her own rewards but also those of other group members (Deutsch, 1949a).

Consider still another commonly employed grading system. The professor says "I reward competent work. If you complete your assignments successfully, you will receive an A. The grade you receive has no bearing on the grades others receive; in fact, I would be happy to see all of you produce high-quality work and receive A's." Here students' outcomes are not interdependent, since goal attainment by one has no effect on the probability of goal attainment by another. In this **individualistic reward structure**, individuals are freer to cooperate or compete with others as they choose—or simply to go about their own business.

In analyzing cooperation and competition, we also need to consider the cognitions and motives of individuals. Some people always seem to want to share resources and cooperate, whereas others seem to become cutthroat in even the friendliest of games. In a class with an individualistic reward structure, for example, if an individual primarily seeks the outcomes most beneficial to all students, he or she is governed by a cooperative motive. A person with a competitive motive seeks not only to achieve personal success but also to cause others in the situation to fail. Finally, the person with an individualistic motive seeks to optimize personal rewards, without regard to how others fare.

Naturally, reward structures influence the motives of individuals. A competitive reward structure tends to draw out the competitive motives in students. For example, premed students competing for scarce openings in medical schools sometimes find themselves in a "sort of academic guerrilla war" (*Time*, May 20, 1974, p. 62). To further their career chances, students reportedly give up their social lives, emphasize grades over learning, refuse to help other students, deliberately give misleading information to others, tear pages from important library readings, and ruin other students' laboratory experiments. No wonder people sometimes perceive competitive situations as aversive and attempt to escape them (Steigleder, Weiss, Cramer, & Feinberg, 1978). On the other hand, competitively motivated individuals can sometimes pursue their ends even in a cooperative reward structure.

In real life we rarely encounter purely cooperative or purely competitive reward structures. Rather, we enter many *mixed-motive* situations, in which we must choose between cooperating and competing. Consider the predicament called the **Prisoner's Dilemma**:

Two subjects are taken into custody and separated. The district attorney is certain they are guilty of a specific crime, but he does not have adequate evidence to convict them at a trial. He points out to each prisoner that each has two alternatives: to confess to the crime the police are sure they have done or not to confess. If they both do not confess then the district attorney will book them on some very minor trumped-up charge . . . ; if they both confess, they will be prosecuted, [and] he will recommend [a rather severe] sentence; but if one confesses and the other does not, then the confessor will receive rather lenient treatment for turning state's evidence whereas the latter will get the "book" slapped at him [Luce & Raiffa, 1957, p. 95].

Put yourself in the place of one of the prisoners. It seems easy enough to keep your mouth shut and receive a light sentence for a minor crime. Yet, if your partner confesses, you will pay dearly. On the other hand,

you can confess to gain a lenient sentence and worsen your partner's position relative to yours, but again you run the risk that he or she will confess also, ensuring that you will both suffer. The Prisoner's Dilemma is a mixed-motive situation precisely because the action that is the best choice for each individual separately will, if chosen by both individuals, result in a losing outcome (Dawes, 1974).

In the Prisoner's Dilemma, concealing the crime is considered to be a cooperative choice, whereas confessing is a competitive choice. Hundreds of college students have played laboratory games involving these two choices, although they play for money or points rather than for prison sentences (see Box 9-1). Prisoner's Dilemma research tells us a great deal about the determinants of cooperation and competition in game situations (the interested reader is referred to Davis, Laughlin, & Komorita, 1976; Pruitt & Kimmel, 1977; Rapoport & Chammah, 1965; Swingle, 1970; and Wrightsman, O'Connor, & Baker, 1972). For example, the strategy of the other player influences one's own tendency to cooperate. Generally people do not act more cooperatively if the other player is cooperative on every trial, but they quickly learn to make more cooperative choices if the other player matches their own choices "tit-for-tat," cooperating in response to a cooperative choice and competing in response to a competitive choice (Oskamp, 1971). Another strategy for increasing the cooperation of the other player is the "reformed sinner" approach, in which a player shifts from being noncooperative at first to being very cooperative. Cooperation is also facilitated if players can communicate with one another—provided they do not use the opportunity for communication to make threats—and come to an understanding of the benefits of cooperation (Swingle & Santi, 1972).

Personal characteristics also affect rates of cooperation. Whereas some people are generally cooperatively motivated, others are more competitively motivated, even when the task is not specifically introduced as calling for either cooperative or competi-

Box 9-1. The Prisoner's Dilemma Game.

		Second person chooses between:	
		C	D
First person chooses between:	C	$10, $10	−$10, $15
	D	$15, −$10	−$5, −$5

Imagine yourself playing this game in a psychology experiment. The first figure in each box indicates the amount to be won or lost by the first player; the second figure indicates the amount to be won or lost by the second player. Suppose that your opponent, moving first, chooses C. By choosing C yourself, you can get $10 for each of you. By choosing D, you can exploit your opponent, making him or her lose $10 while you win $15. If the first player chooses D, you can let yourself be exploited by choosing C, or you can choose D and make the outcome a loss of $5 for each of you. Clearly the most desirable strategy over the long run is for both of you to choose C and engage in mutual cooperation. However, college students in the laboratory often attempt to exploit the other and earn more for themselves. If both players do this, however, they often end up with the undesirable outcome in the lower righthand box—a loss of $5 for each.

There are many variations of this Prisoner's Dilemma game (and many other types of games as well). The game may involve just one choice by each player or it may be played over a long series of trials. Players may choose simultaneously or take turns. They may play against other subjects, against a confederate executing a prearranged strategy, or against a computer. These variations, as well as others, often influence the strategies used.

tive behavior. Perceptions of the situation and of the other player's intentions often prove to be very important (Braver & Barnett, 1974; see also Chapter 3). A variety of attitudes, personality characteristics, and motives have been shown to influence behavior in Prisoner's Dilemma games (see R. J. Harris, 1971). These include Machiavellianism, trusting attitudes, risk taking, and self-concept. Such personal variables interact with characteristics of the situation, such as strategy of the other player and opportunity to communicate. However, personal influences on behavior are generally weak in comparison to situational influences (Terhune, 1970).

According to some critics, Prisoner's Dilemma studies place subjects in an unrealistic situation and do not clearly separate cooperative and competitive motives from a host of other motives (Gergen, 1969; Nemeth, 1972; Pruitt & Kimmel, 1977). Some researchers (for example, Rapoport, Guyer, & Gordon, 1976), concerned with developing mathematical theories of rational play in game situations, admit that such research may have no implications for real life. Critics (for example, Pruitt & Kimmel, 1977) lament this and feel that the thousand studies done to date have yielded surprisingly little knowledge and understanding of real-world behavior.

We will highlight some of the more realistic studies in order to compare cooperation with helping behavior, typically studied under the most naturalistic conditions possible. We'll look at the effects of reward structures on group cohesiveness and productivity and the development of cooperative and competitive motives in children.

A. *Group Cohesiveness and Productivity*

If a competitive reward structure can produce antisocial behavior among premed students, does a cooperative reward structure lead people to behave more prosocially? The answer is yes, at least for well-developed groups in field situations. Cooperative reward structures are associated with increased communication among participants, greater group cohesiveness, and higher satisfaction (Raven & Eachus, 1963). Even before beginning to work together, group members who expect a cooperative orientation report more attraction to the group (Rabbie, 1974; Rabbie & Wilkens, 1971). Haines and McKeachie (1967) compared methods of running discussion sections in an introductory psychology course by grading individual performance in some groups and group projects in others. Not only was tension higher in the groups with the competitive reward structure, but students in the cooperative sections enjoyed their classes more.

Similar differences in atmosphere were found in an employment agency (Blau, 1954). In one section of the agency, an employment interviewer's job security depended on his or her filling more job openings and serving more clients than did other interviewers in the section. In a second section, the supervisor encouraged interviewers to develop a common purpose and make as many placements as possible without regard to relative standings among interviewers. As expected, interviewers in the first section became competitively motivated. They rarely communicated with one another, and they actually concealed information about job openings. Interviewers in the second section enjoyed each other's company and actually helped one another place clients.

However, there is more to job efficiency than group satisfaction and cohesiveness. Productivity is usually a more important criterion. In Blau's study, the cooperative section actually placed more job applicants than did the competitive section. In a study of four types of discussion groups in an in-troductory psychology course, cooperative groups produced a high percentage of mature, goal-oriented comments (Dunn & Goldman, 1966). In fact, members of the most productive groups had been instructed to cooperate with one another to best other groups. The only problem with students in this intergroup-competition/intragroup-cooperation condition was that they were not as accepting of fellow group members as were students in the purely cooperative reward structure. By comparison, competitive groups and individualistic groups were both very unproductive and uncohesive.

On the whole, competitive reward structures within groups tend to breed distrust, to disrupt cohesiveness, and even to lower productivity. Cooperative reward structures have positive effects on group cohesiveness (see Figure 9-1) and often increase productivity (assuming group members don't conspire to produce as little as possible). These effects are most noticeable when the tasks are such that two heads (or pairs of hands) are better than one (Raven & Eachus, 1963). When sheer quantity of work is required and individuals can work best without assistance, a competitive reward structure may enhance productivity (L. K. Miller & Hamblin, 1963).

Recently some researchers, convinced of the advantages of cooperation, have attempted to alter reward structures in the public schools. Consider the *jigsaw method* of learning developed by Elliot Aronson and his colleagues (Aronson, Blaney, Sikes, Stephan, & Snapp, 1975; Aronson, Blaney, Stephan, Sikes, & Snapp, 1978; Blaney, Stephan, Rosenfield, Aronson, & Sikes, 1977). These researchers took the view that traditional classrooms, with their competitive reward structures, inevitably produce winners and losers—and hard feelings among students as a result. Their alternative, the jigsaw method, forces students to cooperate in order to learn. It was introduced to facilitate racial integration of schools in Austin, Texas.

In one demonstration, fifth graders were to study the biography of Joseph Pulitzer. In the jigsaw classroom, students were

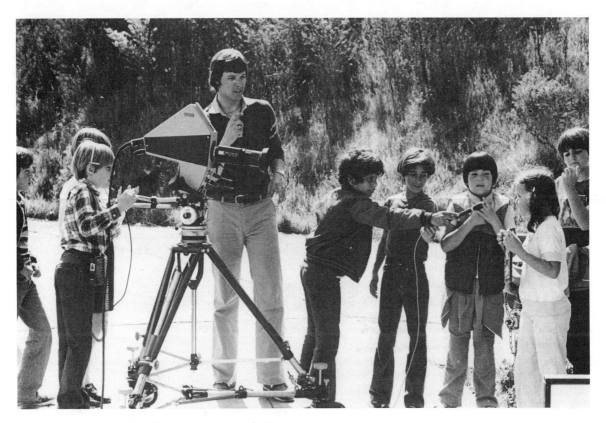

Figure 9-1. Cooperation for a common goal. (©
George T. Kruse/Icon.)

divided into heterogeneous, multi-ethnic
teams. Each child in the team was given a
section of the material on Pulitzer and, after
mastering it, had to teach it to the others in
the group. Thus each child depended on
others in the group for parts of the "jigsaw."

In studies conducted over six-week
periods, the jigsaw method was compared
to traditional classrooms run by teachers
identified as good teachers by their colleagues. The experiments were preceded by
workshops to train teachers and by "team-
building" exercises to help students put
aside their competitive motives. The teams
met for about 40–45 minutes a day, at least
three times a week. Overall, the comparisons of jigsaw and control classes indicated
the following about the jigsaw approach: (1)
jigsaw students grew to like their group-
mates; (2) Anglo and Black children,

although not Mexican-Americans, developed
more favorable attitudes toward school; (3)
students' self-esteem increased; (4) Black
and Mexican-American students tended to
master more material, while Anglo students
did no worse in the jigsaw classes than in
traditional ones; and (5) jigsaw children
were more likely to express cooperative attitudes and see their classmates as learning
resources. Others have tested similar team-
learning systems and found them to be successful in improving group relations without interfering with learning (for example,
DeVries, Edwards, & Slavin, 1978; Johnson
& Johnson, 1975; Weigel, Wiser, & Cook,
1975). One of the best things about these
systems is that they often motivate better
students to help slower students.

Would children exposed to such cooper-
ative-learning experiences throughout their

schooling be more cooperative as adults? To answer that question, let's consider how we learn to cooperate and compete.

B. *Learning to Cooperate and Compete*

Children 2 or 3 or even 4 years old are not capable of cooperation or competition, because both behaviors require coordinating one's actions with the actions of others (McClintock, Moskowitz, & McClintock, 1977). Young children, egocentric in their thinking, tend to play alone or to play beside others without really playing with them. (See Chapter 8 for a discussion of how children develop understandings of competitive games.) By the age of about 5 or 6, however, the child has learned the necessity of cooperation and, somewhat earlier, has begun to enjoy demonstrating mastery of skills through competition (H. Cook & Stingle, 1974; McClintock & Moskowitz, 1976).

An important task is learning when to cooperate and when to compete. Children's choices have been studied through the use of games. When playing the game pictured in Figure 9-2, Israeli children from a communal kibbutz were more cooperative than urban Israeli children brought up in a more achievement-oriented subculture (Shapira & Madsen, 1969), and Blackfoot Indian children were more cooperative than non-Indian Canadian children (A. G. Miller & Thomas, 1972). In many of these studies, the more cooperative children appeared to slow down, as though they were avoiding competition. In fact, among some Indian tribes that attach great value to group cooperation, children may hesitate to start a race, knowing that the winner will be ridiculed by other children (Erikson, 1963a). Middle-class children in the United States, by contrast, have learned competition so well and value it so highly that they compete in such games even when cooperation is the more "rational" strategy—a trend that becomes stronger with age (Knight & Kagan, 1977; Madsen, 1967, 1971; Madsen & Shapira, 1970). This increase in competitive behavior occurs in a variety of cultures, but levels of competitiveness in any given age group

vary from culture to culture (Avellar & Kagan, 1976; Toda, Shinotsuka, McClintock, & Stech, 1978).

In part, then, cooperative and competitive motives develop as the child's intellectual and social skills develop. However, the

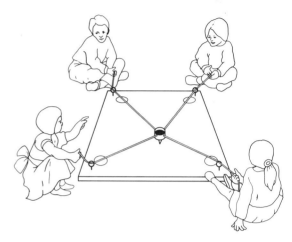

Figure 9-2. Deciding whether to cooperate or compete. Each child holds a string that can be pulled to move the marking pen in the center. As Madsen (1967) and his colleagues have structured the game, the children are first placed in a cooperative reward structure. They must move the pen through the four target circles in sequence to be rewarded. On the next series of trials, each child receives a reward only when the pen moves through his or her own designated target circle. Even when the instructions are changed in this way, cooperation is still the best strategy because, if the children pull against one another at cross-purposes, chances are that no one will receive many prizes. What do you think children actually do?

Three groups of Mexican children—middle-class urban, poor rural, and poor urban children—played the game in one study (Madsen, 1967). Although all groups cooperated on the first task, middle-class urban children became highly competitive when the instructions were altered and, as a result, did not reap as many benefits as did the rural and urban poor children who continued to use a cooperative strategy. Madsen attributed these differences to subcultural background, noting that the rural and urban poor children had learned to work together for family survival and to avoid greedy, competitive behavior, whereas the middle-class urban children were exposed to parental models who competed in business.

acquisition of a preference for one behavior over the other in a given situation may depend on the culture or subculture in which a child grows up—or, more precisely, on the values transmitted by parents and other adults. In some societies, such as the Sioux tribes, cooperation is so highly valued within the group that competitive motives are rarely expressed. On the other hand, we must wonder whether mainstream society in North America emphasizes competitive motives so heavily that cooperative behaviors receive too little exercise. Perhaps today's attempts to expand the use of cooperative reward structures in the classroom will help to correct this imbalance, but we cannot yet be sure.

III. Helping Behavior: From Handouts to Heroism

If it is often difficult to induce people to cooperate for mutual benefit, we might guess that it is even harder to make them work for another person's benefit—to engage in helping behavior. But people do help one another. What factors influence whether they do or do not?

A. Sizing Up the Situation

Any of us may find ourselves in a situation that calls for giving the time of day, returning a lost wallet, donating to charity, or jumping into a lake to rescue a drowning swimmer. How does the potential helper size up each situation and decide whether to help? Latané and Darley (1970) developed a five-stage model for analyzing behavior in emergencies, a model that appears to be applicable in a variety of nonemergency situations as well (see Figure 9-3).

This model may sound too "cold and calculating" if it is taken literally as a sequential decision-making process. Nonetheless, its elements—noticing the event, interpreting it, determining personal responsibility, choosing a form of assistance, and implementing that assistance—must be present in some form for helping to occur.

Muggings, car accidents, and tornadoes are all examples of emergencies. Latané and Darley (1970) claimed that emergencies can be characterized as dangerous, unusual, unique, unforeseen, and pressing. As a result, they produce arousal or stress that is not present in nonemergencies and that may interfere with efficient decision making and action (Bar-Tal, 1976; Piliavin & Piliavin, 1973). Now consider a nonemergency: you are walking down a street and a man approaching you on crutches drops a book, apparently unaware that he has done so. The event is easily noticed and easily interpreted as one requiring help, particularly since crutches signal dependency. You readily assume personal responsibility because you are the only other person on the street; if you do not help, no one else will. Moreover, the costs of helping are minimal, since picking up a book is a well-learned and painless form of assistance. At each step, the decision to help is relatively easy to make—easier, in fact, than walking by and feeling guilty for the rest of the day. Given the characteristics of this situation, it is not surprising that 100% of the subjects in one study rendered aid (F. W. Schneider, 1973).

Now suppose strangers approach you on the street and ask for each of the following: the time, directions to a well-known place, change for a quarter, your name, or a dime. Here again, the process of noticing a need for help is easy. But which requests would you be most likely to honor? Latané and Darley (1970) asked people in New York City to comply with these requests and obtained the results shown in Table 9-1.

People were fairly willing to provide these types of help, but they were significantly less likely to give their names or hand over dimes than they were to honor the other requests. Why? Perhaps because of slightly higher costs. Giving one's name to a stranger posed a threat; many of the subjects were surprised, asked why the experimenter wanted to know, and usually gave only their first names. Giving away a dime involved a small financial cost to the actor. However, it must be noted that the requester gave no reason for the request. Elaborating their requests for help, strangers collected even more dimes (1) when they stated you interpret them. If movie cameras surrounded the men, for example, you might perceive the event as a staged incident. In contrast, without cameras and with blood or cries for help, you are more likely to think that the victim needs help and go on to Step 3. (3) *Assume personal responsibility.* One man above appears to have offered his help, while the other onlookers seem to be avoiding any responsibility. What might account for the difference? In assessing the costs and rewards of intervening, people consider a variety of factors—for example, the severity of the situation, the availability of other potential help-givers and their own knowledge and ability to help. If this analysis prompts you to assume personal responsibility for intervening, you are ready for the next step. (4) *Choose a form of assistance.* Here again, costs and rewards must be calculated—this time, the costs and rewards of alternative helping responses. Should you try to give medical assistance? Maybe your treatment would only make the situation worse. Should you call the police or a hospital? That may take too much time. The intervention process may break down at this point if you are so distressed that you cannot settle on a course of action. (5) *Implement the assistance.* Having decided what to do, you must execute the behavior—if you can. Actual help will depend on your ability to do what you have decided to. Can you yell loudly enough to attract a police officer's attention? Or are you strong enough to lift the man to a safer place? Even here, at the fifth stage, help may not be given. (© Ellis Herwig/Stock, Boston.)

Figure 9-3. Deciding to intervene in an emergency. What would you do if you witnessed this? According to Latané and Darley (1970), there are five critical steps in the intervention process: (1) *Notice that something is happening.* Have all the people in this scene noticed the fallen man? If you are hurrying to a job interview or are distracted by a bus screeching to a halt across the street, you may not notice. But if you do see the man, you are ready for the next step. (2) *Interpret the situation as one in which help is needed.* Your interpretation of the scene depends on how many and what types of cues are available, and how

their names first and then made the request (49% response), (2) when they requested the dime and added that they needed it to make a phone call (64%), and (3) when they explained that their wallets had been stolen (72%). Altogether, these findings suggest that people are very responsive to requests for low-cost help, particularly if they are given a plausible explanation that aids them in interpreting the need for help as legitimate (Harrell, 1977).

Even when the need is clearly stated in a series of requests, however, the potential helper considers the costs of complying with each request. In a study by Suedfeld, Bochner, and Wnek (1972), male participants in a peace demonstration were approached by a

TABLE 9-1 / *Frequency of Response to Different Requests*

	Number Asked	Percentage Helping
"Excuse me, I wonder if you could . . .		
a. tell me what time it is?"	92	85
b. tell me how to get to Times Square?"	90	84
c. give me change for a quarter?"	90	73
d. tell me what your name is?"	277	39
e. give me a dime?"	284	34

From *The Unresponsive Bystander: Why Doesn't He Help?* by B. Latané and J. M. Darley. Copyright 1970. Reprinted by permission of Prentice-Hall, Inc., Englewood Cliffs, New Jersey.

young woman who stated that her male friend was feeling ill. All 80 subjects followed the woman to her sick friend and 79 agreed to help move him out of the way. Whereas a large majority (66%) agreed to help carry him to a first-aid station, only 19% agreed to help when they learned that he preferred to go to his apartment 7 miles away, and only 11% offered money when the woman finally asked for bus fare to get there. As the cost of helping, in terms of time or money, increased, helping behavior decreased.

Although we have by no means said all that can be said about situational factors that influence helping behavior, we have introduced a five-stage model of the intervention process that will permit us to analyze a variety of personal and situational factors influencing decisions by a potential helper. The ambiguity of a situation—as it is affected by the nature of the need, the legitimacy of the need, and the manner in which it is transmitted to the helper—is an important consideration. And the perceived costs and rewards of helping or failing to help will be a recurring theme in the analysis of helping behavior.

B. *The Influence of Other People*

At the heart of social psychology is the truth that people influence one another. If you witness a car accident along with others, the other witnesses become part of the situation from your perspective. They can serve as a source of reinforcement or punishment, perhaps approving of you if you act, perhaps scorning you for doing so. They can demonstrate, or model, helping behavior. Or they can display behavior that is unresponsive, influencing you in still another way. The first two types of influence—reinforcement and **modeling**—account for much human behavior and learning. The last type of influence—termed the "bystander effect"—has special implications for helping behavior and suggests why 38 witnesses did not act while Kitty Genovese was slain.

Reinforcement. A simple way to increase the strength of almost any behavior is to follow it by positive consequences. As we have already seen, helping may be rewarding in itself. But helping behavior can be given an extra boost if it is followed by external rewards, or it can be made less likely in the future if it is punished (M. K. Moss & Page, 1972; Rushton & Teachman, 1978). One important qualification is that *promising* rewards for helping in advance may have a boomerang effect (Batson, Coke, Jasnoski, & Hanson, 1978; Garbarino, 1975). In such situations, people come to perceive themselves as motivated by the reward rather than by altruistic motives. They are then less likely to behave altruistically in subsequent situations where reward is not present.

Reinforcement principles aid in understanding how children learn to help. Helping is made profitable for children if they receive material or social rewards after sharing or helping. They also can develop the ability to experience the emotions of others vicariously and to act to increase the joy and reduce the distress of others (Aronfreed, 1968).

Modeling. A second proven method of teaching or eliciting a behavior is to model it, allowing the learner to see the behavior and, better yet, to see positive consequences following it (White, 1972). When the collector for the United Fund calls, you may be more likely to contribute if you have already seen your friends do so and know that they have the stickers on their doors and the virtuous feelings to prove it. Even watching television programs in which prosocial behavior is modeled may affect your behavior (see Figure 9-4). Modeling effects have been demonstrated in many studies of helping behavior (Rushton, 1976). For example, Bryan and Test (1967) demonstrated that simply watching someone else change a flat tire or donate to the Salvation Army makes one more likely to help in these situations. However, how modeling works—that is, the nature of the mediating processes—is not always clear (Aderman & Berkowitz, 1970). A model can remind the observer of what is proper or appropriate in a situation (see Chapter 8), show the observer how to perform a helpful act, reduce the inhibitions against acting, and/or cue the observer to the consequences of a helpful act.

What do these modeling effects suggest to parents who are attempting to make their children more helpful? Must a parent set a glowing example, or is it enough to instruct children to be helpful? What if there is a discrepancy between words and deeds, between preaching and practice?

Grusec and Skubiski (1970) of the University of Toronto had elementary school children play a game to see if they would donate part of their winnings to charity. Some children saw an adult model donate half of his or her winnings to charity, others heard the model advocate donating to charity, and still others were not exposed to a model. Actions spoke louder than words— the modeling of donating behavior produced larger contributions than did the

preaching. Only when the child was a girl and the model had established a warm relationship with her beforehand was preaching more effective than nothing at all.

To determine the effects of hypocrisy— a contradiction between word and deed— Bryan and Walbek (1970a, 1970b) conducted a series of experiments in which children observed models who either donated or refused to do so, while either delivering a statement unrelated to charity, preaching charity, or preaching greed. The most powerful influence on children's donations was what the model did. If the model preached one thing and practiced another, *it was the behavior that was imitated.*

However, words were not entirely lost on the children. Verbal modeling influenced the children's evaluations of the model as well as their own verbalizations when they were asked to tape a message for the next player. Any statement about charity by a model—whether it expressed charitable or greedy sentiments—tended to elicit charitable statements from the children. By contrast, the model's behavior had little influence on children's preachings. Some research does suggest that preaching charity can increase children's donations if it is strongly stated or mentions reasons for giving (Grusec, Saas-Korlsaak, & Simutis, 1978; Midlarsky & Bryan, 1972; Rushton, 1975). However, it is still most effective to practice what you preach.

The Bystander Effect. Doesn't it seem logical to expect that the more people who witness an emergency, the more likely it is that at least one witness will provide aid? This is one reason that New Yorkers were so shocked by the complete failure of 38 witnesses to help Kitty Genovese. Were these people callous, or was there something about the situation that made the onlookers fail to help?

Bibb Latané and John Darley sought an answer. They actually hypothesized that the presence of other bystanders decreases the probability of helping behavior by any individual witness. In one of their first studies, male college students who were completing questionnaires were exposed to pungent

Figure 9-4. Television and prosocial behavior. Much evidence has accumulated to indicate that watching aggression on television and in movies fosters aggression in children (for example, see Liebert & Schwartzberg, 1977; Parke, Berkowitz, Leyens, West, & Sebastian, 1977; and Chapter 10 of this book). Is it true, then, that exposure to prosocial programs increases the prosocial behavior of children? In one key study, nursery-school children saw either prosocial programming in episodes of "Mister Rogers' Neighborhood," aggressive cartoons, or neutral programs for four weeks (Friedrich & Stein, 1973). Aggressive programs produced more aggressive behavior at school among children who were already above average in aggression. Prosocial programs led to more prosocial behavior, but only among lower-income children. Thus, the television programs had effects, but not all children were affected to the same degree. In another study, exposure to an episode of "Lassie," in which a boy helped a dog, increased the willingness of children to help puppies in distress in a test situation (Sprafkin, Liebert, & Poulos, 1975). Effects of the media have been demonstrated, then, although often the learning of prosocial behavior through modeling does not appear to generalize to different situations. For example, Paulson (1974) found that the modeling of cooperative behavior on "Sesame Street" produced cooperation in young children but did not have more general effects on prosocial behavior. (Photo by Robert Fuhring. © Children's Television Network.)

smoke puffing through a vent into the testing room (Latané & Darley, 1968). Subjects were either alone, with two other "naive" subjects, or with two passive confederates of the experimenter, who noticed the smoke but shrugged and continued writing. Being with two deliberately nonreactive confederates considerably reduced the subject's likelihood of reporting the smoke. But even three naive witnesses together were less likely to act than was a single subject. This study provided initial evidence that individuals are less likely to help when they are in the presence of others than when they are alone—the phenomenon called the **bystander effect.** However, as Latané and Darley noted, the puffing smoke—at least at first—was not clearly an emergency, and subjects who remained seated, coughing and rubbing their eyes, may have misguidedly wanted to appear brave. In the presence of others, they may have thought "Well, if you can take it, so can I."

Consequently, a study was devised in which the emergency was less ambiguous and did not threaten the subjects themselves. Latané and Rodin (1969) staged an incident in which subjects working on questionnaires heard a crash, a scream, and words of anguish ("Oh, my God, my foot") from an adjoining room where the woman who had given them their instructions had just gone. Subjects were alone, with a passive confederate, with another naive subject unfamiliar to them, or with a close friend. Again, there was little safety in numbers: 70% of those who were alone helped the woman, but only 40% of the pairs of strangers and 7% of the subjects coupled with a passive confederate did so. Help was provided by 70% of the pairs of friends. Clearly the victim was not safe in the hands of pairs of strangers or subjects paired with a deliberately passive witness. In the smoke study and in this one, the presence of others, particularly passive others, may have made subjects less likely to interpret an event as an emergency requiring action.

Latané, Darley, and others have provided a great deal of evidence for the so-called bystander effect in emergencies. Of course, these findings pertain to an individual's likelihood of acting. There is still some safety in numbers in the sense that the larger a group of witnesses, the more likely it is that at least one hero will be present; and if one person intervenes, others may join in due to modeling effects (Masor, Hornstein, & Tobin, 1973). But a person in a group who notices an event is still often less likely than a person who is alone to interpret it as a situation calling for helping behavior. This *social influence* may exist because people look to others to decide how they should interpret a situation. The ap-

parent indifference or coolness of group members while they are trying to read cues in the situation may foster the conclusion by each that nothing is seriously wrong. Moreover, even if people conclude that something is wrong, they may fail to act because of a **diffusion of responsibility**; that is, when other potential helpers are available, an individual may be less likely to accept personal responsibility for helping (Latané & Darley, 1970).

However, the bystander effect has not been observed in all studies. This suggests that it occurs only under some conditions and that there are ways to prevent it. Taking the Kitty Genovese incident as an example of the bystander effect, we can try to identify elements in that situation that produced a dramatic failure to help and to imagine a different outcome given different circumstances.

A study by Bickman (1972) offers some guidance in this regard. Female students heard via an intercom "another subject" declare that something had fallen from a bookcase in her testing room, get up from her chair, and then cry out "It's falling on me." This was followed by a scream and a loud crash. A confederate then interpreted the event over the intercom as either a certain emergency, a possible emergency, or no emergency at all. This other "bystander" was either able to help (was in the same building as the victim and subject) or unable to help (was located in a distant building). The more the interpretation by another witness indicated that an emergency was taking place, the more often subjects stated afterwards that they thought the victim needed help and the faster they actually provided help. Furthermore, subjects responded faster when they thought the other bystander was in a distant building and could not easily assume responsibility for acting.

The reactions of other bystanders are simply a subset of the situational cues that a person must process and interpret. As already noted, the bystander effect is diminished if friends rather than strangers witness an event, perhaps because friends are more likely to see behind each other's initial hesitancy and coolness (Latané & Rodin, 1969). It also appears to be important for witnesses to actually observe each other's reactions if alarm is likely to be registered. J. M. Darley, Teger, and Lewis (1973) found that naive subjects who were facing each other were as likely to respond to an emergency in an adjoining room as were subjects alone when the emergency occurred, but pairs of subjects seated so that they could not read each other's faces for cues were much less helpful.

Judging from this information, might anything that makes a situation less ambiguous dampen the "unresponsive-bystander effect"? It seems so. R. D. Clark and Word (1972) obtained 100% rates of helping from groups of bystanders when a maintenance man fell and cried out in pain in the next room. The presence of others inhibited helping only when the emergency was more ambiguous (when the fall but not the cry was heard). These researchers argued that in the Latané and Rodin (1969) experiment helping rates were low because the situation was tape-recorded and ambiguous. They also pointed to lack of ambiguity to account for high helping rates in a study by I. M. Piliavin, Rodin, and Piliavin (1969). Here larger groups actually responded faster than smaller groups when a man collapsed in a subway car. In this situation, the subjects could directly see the emergency (rather than overhearing it from another room), could see for themselves what other witnesses were doing or not doing, and had no way to escape the situation. Subsequent research (R. D. Clark & Word, 1974; Solomon, Solomon, & Stone, 1978) also suggests that the bystander effect is much more likely to occur when the situation is ambiguous than when there is a clearcut need for help.

Assuming that bystanders interpret an event as an emergency, acceptance of personal responsibility is more likely if witnesses have a special bond or commitment to the victim (Geer & Jarmecky, 1973; Moriarty, 1975; Tilker, 1970) or think that the other person is especially dependent on them personally (Berkowitz, 1978). Further-

more, if a bystander feels more competent to deal with the emergency than other witnesses, he or she is more likely to accept personal responsibility (Korte, 1971). For example, A. S. Ross (1971) found that subjects helped more when the other bystander was a young child than they did when the other was an equally competent adult. On the other hand, if you know that another witness is a medical student who works in an emergency room, you may be less likely to assume responsibility, deferring to the medical student's expertise (S. H. Schwartz & Clausen, 1970). All of this suggests that people who do not feel particularly competent are concerned about appearing foolish if they act. Anything that might make people less concerned about how other bystanders will evaluate them should facilitate helping behavior (Becker-Haven & Lindskold, 1978).

To summarize, the social-influence process by which other bystanders inhibit helping behavior can be lessened if (1) someone in the group voices the opinion that an emergency is occurring; (2) the bystanders can detect signals of alarm in one another's reactions, and (3) the incident is difficult to interpret as anything other than an emergency. Diffusion of responsibility is less likely if bystanders have some special bond of responsibility to the victim or feel more competent to act (or less worried about acting) than other bystanders.

How does this information help us understand the Kitty Genovese slaying? First, the 38 witnesses were subject to the kind of social influence that Latané and Darley described; that is, it was not just a case of "bystander apathy." Since the street was dark, there was room, at least initially, for alternate interpretations of the situation (for example, as a lover's quarrel). More importantly, witnesses could not see each other and, with no cues to the contrary, they may have assumed that others were not interpreting the event as an emergency. In addition, responsibility was diffused. Although some bystanders may have known one another and even known Ms. Genovese, no witness felt singled out for responsibility.

Each may have assumed that someone else had already phoned the police or that someone else would rush into the street.

Thus there are limits to the bystander effect and ways to reduce its power. Many studies underscore people's willingness to get involved and provide help. However, the Kitty Genovese incident can play itself out time and again if the conditions are right.

C. *Psychological States and Helping*

With so many situational factors influencing helping behavior, we begin to wonder if the characteristics of potential helpers matter much. Do some people possess personality characteristics that make them more likely to aid others? Before searching for such personality traits, we will consider the effects of more fleeting moods and feelings—psychological states.

Suppose you have had a very good day, with money, grades, and love all coming your way at once. Do you want to spread happiness throughout the world, or do you jealously guard your good feelings, refusing to let anyone spoil your good mood? A variety of moods and feelings affect helping behavior. We will consider the effects of: (1) prior success and good moods caused by something other than success; and (2) negative psychological states.

Success and Good Moods. **Isen (1970)** administered a battery of tests to teachers and college students, telling some that they scored very well, others that they had performed poorly, and still others nothing at all. A fourth group was spared from taking the tests. The successful subjects became more helpful than the other groups, donating more to a school fund and more often helping a woman struggling with an armful of books. Subjects who thought they had failed were no less helpful than those who received no feedback. Isen therefore spoke of a "warm glow of success," which makes people more likely to provide help. Berg (1978) saw the same phenomenon in observations of professional football games. Players were more likely to help other players to their feet when their own teams were ahead than

when they were behind! By contrast, failure may actually decrease concern for others (Crandall, 1978). Succeeding on a task increases helping behavior, then, but why? Possibly success creates a feeling of happiness, in which case happiness rather than success may be essential to the formula.

Isen and Levin (1972) set out to produce good moods that had nothing to do with success. In their first attempt, a confederate passed out free cookies to students in certain rows of library carrels. A second confederate later asked both students who had received cookies and students who had not to volunteer for an experiment that required either aiding or distracting subjects whose creativity under pressure would be tested. Interestingly, beneficiaries of cookies were more willing than control subjects to help future subjects but less willing to distract them. This suggested that the good moods induced by cookies did not lead to compliance with just any request.

But was this just another demonstration of the modeling effect, with the cookie distributor modeling helping behavior? In their second study, Isen and Levin controlled for this possibility. They arranged for some subjects to find a dime in the coin return of a pay phone. As predicted, people made happy by the seemingly small good fortune of a free dime were more likely to help a woman who dropped a pile of papers than were those who found no dimes. Here the subjects were exposed to no model of helping behavior; being in a good mood was enough to increase rates of helping. Other studies have supported these findings (Isen, Clark, & Schwartz, 1976; P. F. Levin & Isen, 1975).

Could we still argue that subjects got something for nothing and were prompted to restore balance in the world by giving of themselves? Probably not. Even experiences such as reading aloud statements expressing elation or recalling pleasant events from one's childhood can increase the rate of helping (Aderman, 1972; B. S. Moore, Underwood, & Rosenhan, 1973). Good moods consistently produce helpful behavior in a variety of circumstances.

Alice Isen and her colleagues propose

that a "loop" of positive cognitions is set up after a person is made happy and that helping others adds to this chain of positive thoughts (Isen, Shalker, Clark, & Karp, 1978). If, in order to be helpful, subjects must do something unpleasant, they are not as likely to help because helping would interfere with their good moods (Isen & Simmonds, 1978).

Negative Psychological States. If good moods make helping behavior more likely, do negative moods make it less likely? The answer is not a simple one. First consider self-concern, or preoccupation with one's own circumstances and outcomes. In several studies reported by Leonard Berkowitz (1972), self-concern lowered the rate and amount of helping behavior among college students waiting to learn how they had done on an important test. Simply being in a hurry for an appointment may make one less likely to provide help. Darley and Batson (1973) led seminary students who were leaving for a speaking engagement to think that they were already quite late, that they would arrive just in time, or that they would have time to spare. The percentages of subjects in these three groups who stopped to help a man slumped in an alley on the way were 10%, 45%, and 63%, respectively. In fact, even subjects scheduled to speak about the parable of the Good Samaritan were less likely to help when they were in a hurry! But were those in a hurry too self-concerned to be concerned about others? In a subsequent study, subjects were told either that their presence in a research lab was vital to a project or that their presence was unimportant (Batson, Cochran, Biederman, Blosser, Ryan, & Vogt, 1978). Only those who thought their presence was vital were less helpful when they were in a hurry. Those who believed they were late for an unimportant appointment were just as helpful as subjects who had plenty of time. This suggested to the researchers that being in a hurry for an important engagement simply puts people in a dilemma about whether to stop and help. However, in some studies self-concerned people have actually been more helpful than control

subjects (Hildebrand & Berkowitz, reported by Berkowitz, 1972; Isen, Horn, & Rosenhan, 1973).

Other researchers have attempted to create bad moods that have nothing to do with failure or anxiety about performance on a task. Here, too, the evidence is mixed. Robert Cialdini and Douglas Kenrick (1976) attempted to reconcile the findings. They noticed that studies in which bad moods increased helping (for example, Donnerstein, Donnerstein, & Munger, 1975) were often done with adult subjects, whereas studies in which bad moods decreased helping (for example, Underwood, Froming, & Moore, 1977) were often done with children. In their **negative-state-relief model**, Cialdini and Kenrick proposed that we come to learn that helping can alleviate negative moods. They then demonstrated that, although young children are less helpful when they are in bad moods, by high school age, children become more helpful when in bad moods.

But even this model may not be enough to explain all of the inconsistencies. For example, in one recent study adults in bad moods were very likely to volunteer to help if helping was easy and potentially very beneficial (Weyant, 1978). However, they were unlikely to help if helping was costly or was for an unimportant cause. In this study, people in good moods were not so greatly affected by the costs and benefits of helping; they were generally more helpful than control subjects. Researchers have also found that people in bad moods are sometimes less likely to notice a need for help and may be more helpful only if the need is clearly pointed out to them (McMillen, Sanders, & Solomon, 1977). All of this suggests that bad moods do not lead to helping in the same direct way that good moods do. Apparently people in bad moods have to perceive the need for help and perceive helping as likely to improve their mood in order for the effect to work.

The same logic can be applied to another common finding in the research literature: people who injure someone are likely to make amends by helping the victim (Carlsmith & Gross, 1969; Konečni, 1972).

In fact, simply witnessing harm being inflicted can motivate helping behavior (Kenrick, Reich, & Cialdini, 1976; Konečni, 1972; Rawlings, 1970). The concept of negative-state relief again appears to be useful. If people who have inflicted or have witnessed harm receive an unexpected monetary reward or social approval immediately afterward, they are less helpful than subjects who are left in a bad mood (Cialdini, Darby, & Vincent, 1973; McMillen, 1971). In other words, if negative feelings such as guilt or sympathy created by inflicting or witnessing harm can be erased in some other manner, helping behavior may not occur. Moreover, harm-doers or witnesses of harm can sometimes bend reality to escape the feeling that compensation of the victim is in order (Walster, Berscheid, & Walster, 1970). They sometimes derogate the victim ("That fool deserved it"), deny responsibility ("It wasn't really my fault"), or minimize the extent of suffering ("It really didn't hurt all that much"). On the basis of several studies, Walster, Berscheid, and Walster (1970) suggested that compensation is most likely to be made when such rationalizations cannot easily be justified and when it is possible to compensate just the right amount (as opposed to too little or too much). This line of thinking follows from **equity theory** (Adams, 1965), which is described in Chapter 8.

As we have seen, the effects of psychological states on helping behavior are complex. Success and good moods generally make people more likely to help than they normally would be. Self-concern and bad moods (including those brought about by inflicting or witnessing harm) may or may not increase rates of helping behavior. Such negative psychological states are most likely to increase the rate of helping when helping is perceived as a way of improving one's mood or of restoring equity in a relationship.

D. *Finding the Good Samaritan: Background and Personality*

We have identified factors that make most people more or less helpful than usual. But aren't some people consistently more

helpful than others? For instance, **Mahatma Gandhi** renounced his titles and lived in poverty to train young Indian freedom fighters in passive resistance. He suffered imprisonment, long fasts, and finally assassination in the long struggle for Indian independence and unity. Surely he would have been the first to return a lost wallet, pick up a book, or lend a stranger a dime. On the other hand, most of us have met people who almost literally will not give us the time of day unless there is "some percentage in it."

Several studies (see Huston & Korte, 1976) have attempted to identify background and personality variables that would predict helping behavior. The findings have been mixed. According to **Latané and Darley** (1970), none of several standard paper-and-pencil tests—measuring authoritarianism, alienation, trustworthiness, Machiavellianism, need for approval, or social responsibility—predicted helping behavior. Of the background variables considered by Latané and Darley (1970)—for example, father's occupation, church attendance, and number of siblings—only size of hometown predicted helping behavior. Subjects who grew up in small towns were somewhat more likely to help than those who grew up in larger cities or towns. This finding has been replicated (Gelfand, Hartmann, Walder, & Page, 1973; House & Wolf, 1978; Korte & Kerr, 1975), although a few studies have failed to demonstrate lower rates of helping among city dwellers or city-raised persons (for example, Hansson, Slade, & Slade, 1978; Korte, Ypma, & Toppen, 1975; see also Figure 9-5).

A person's background—particularly his or her family life—has been found to influence helpfulness in another way. **London** (1970) reported on interviews with people who had rescued Jews from the Nazis. Most of the rescuers were people who had a love of adventure; many of them lacked close personal relationships (and therefore perhaps had less to lose by their nonconformity to Nazi authority). Most interestingly, almost all identified strongly with at least one parent who had high moral standards and perhaps served as a model of altruism. This theme of identification with a moral

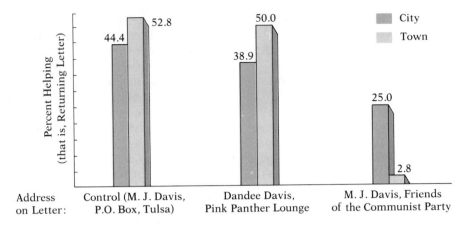

Figure 9-5. Helping in cities and towns. Are small-town folks really more helpful than city folks? Well, some of the time, but not all of the time. Hansson and Slade (1977), using the "lost letter technique," scattered letters with the three types of addresses shown above around Tulsa, Oklahoma, and 51 small towns in Oklahoma. They predicted that intolerance for deviants in small towns would make town dwellers less likely to help a communist. City dwellers were predicted to be less concerned with differentiating among people in deciding whom to help. Small-town residents were more helpful (that is, returned more lost letters) than city dwellers except when the letter was addressed to a communist. Here they were less helpful than city dwellers. In this study, the overall return rate from towns (49.4%) was lower than the return rate from the city (50.6%). Thus, the finding that town people are more helpful than city dwellers does not generalize to all types of situations calling for help. Judging from this study, town dwellers are choosy about whom they are willing to help.

parent was echoed by Rosenhan (1970), who conducted interviews with civil-rights workers in the early 1960s. Finally, M. L. Hoffman (1975a) found that altruistic children had parents with altruistic values who disciplined by pointing out the consequences of behavior for other people. We can conclude, then, that experiences during socialization may account for some differences among adults in their willingness to help (Rushton, 1976).

Personality variables, such as the belief that one's fate lies within one's own control, mature moral judgment, need for social approval or self-esteem, and the tendency to ascribe responsibility for others' welfare to oneself, have predicted helping behavior in one or more studies (Eisenberg-Berg, 1979; Rushton, 1975; Satow, 1973; Schwartz & Clausen, 1970; Staub, 1974). However, the evidence is not strong enough for us to use these characteristics to separate the Good Samaritans from the bulk of humanity. Even the factors we have identified here—a small-town upbringing, exposure to an altruistic parental model, and certain personality traits—are relatively weak predictors of helping behavior. In short, while some researchers would disagree (Huston & Korte, 1976; Severy & Ashton, 1973), the search for the stable personality traits and background characteristics of helpful people seems to have fallen short of clearly profiling the Good Samaritan (Bar-Tal, 1976; Mussen & Eisenberg-Berg, 1977; Schwartz, 1977).

Some of the snags in this search were pointed out by Gergen, Gergen, and Meter (1972), who gave a battery of personality tests to 72 college students and then noted their responses to five different requests for help from the psychology department. Although several relationships between personality scores and volunteering were significant, a trait often predicted one type of helping but failed to predict, or was even negatively associated with, another. To make matters more confusing, relationships that held for male students rarely held for female students, and vice versa. The researchers were forced to conclude that different types of students were looking for different types of payoffs by volunteering as they did.

The point Gergen's study makes so forcefully is that the characteristics of the situation and of the request for help *interact* in complex ways with personal characteristics (see Chapter 16 for a broader discussion). The same point was made in Figure 9-5, where town dwellers were more helpful than city dwellers in two situations but less helpful in a third (where a communist sympathizer was the person in need).

An individual's background and personality characteristics are bound to influence how he or she interprets a situation and responds to it. Some theorists (for example, Huston & Korte, 1976; D. Krebs, 1978) ✓ would argue that researchers have put so much emphasis on situational factors that personal factors have been neglected. However, it may be futile to search for personal characteristics that will predict behavior in *all* situations calling for help.

E. *People Who Need People: The Recipients of Help*

We have devoted much attention to helpers; now it seems only fair to give the recipients of help equal time. Who receives help? As you might expect, we are unlikely to identify characteristics that elicit help in all situations. Characteristics of the potential helper and characteristics of the potential recipient of help must be considered together, because the characteristics of the recipient are situational cues that a potential helper reads and interprets. Thus our attention to the recipient of help will shed still more light on the determinants of helping behavior.

Dependency. By its very nature, helping is a response to a person in need, but the nature of the recipient's dependency influences the rate of helping behavior. Dependency can be a stable characteristic of a person (for example, a mentally retarded child)

that elicits helpful behavior from almost everyone; it can be a function of a relationship between two people (for example, between parent and child or between bus driver and passenger); or it can result from a temporary plight (for example, a sprained ankle). Dependency can seem to be caused by forces outside one's control, as when one is struck by a falling beam, or may be attributable to one's own actions, as when a person is debilitated by an overdose of heroin. Dependency can also be more or less legitimate (for example, wanting someone to drive you to the race track versus to the hospital).

In a variety of studies, Leonard Berkowitz and his colleagues demonstrated that if dependency is introduced into the relationship between two people, helping behavior will follow. Typically, the subject was assigned the role of "worker," and his or her supervisor's rewards depended either heavily or very little on the worker's productivity. Subjects worked harder when the supervisor depended on their performance (Berkowitz, 1978; Berkowitz & Daniels, 1963).

Potential helpers also weigh the legitimacy of a recipient's dependency. Imagine how you would react if a woman approached you in the supermarket and asked for ten cents to buy milk. Then imagine the same woman asking for a dime for frozen cookie dough. When Bickman and Kamzan (1973) arranged these two situations, 58% of the shoppers contributed for milk but only 36% contributed for cookie dough. The more legitimate the need, the more help will be received.

Potential helpers also react to what they perceive as the source or cause of dependency (Ickes & Kidd, 1976). Suppose that a man collapses on the subway, either carrying a cane and appearing ill, or carrying a bottle and smelling of liquor. I. M. Piliavin, Rodin, and Piliavin (1969) found that groups of bystanders were less likely and slower to help the "drunk" than to help the "sick man"—possibly because a drunk can be blamed for his dependency. Contributors to charitable causes are more likely to help innocent victims than to help people whose dependency is attributable to personal weakness or immorality (Benson & Catt, 1978; Bryan & Davenport, 1968). Generally people who can be blamed are helped less than those who are dependent through no fault of their own.

However, even if a person's dependency is legitimate and even if it appears to be no fault of the victim, potential helpers consider the costs of helping. In a realistic study conducted in shoe stores, dependency and cost were both manipulated (Schaps, 1972). Salespersons had to serve either a dependent customer who limped in with a broken heel or a "normal" customer. The cost of devoting a great deal of time to these customers was either low, because the store was almost empty, or high, because the store was busy and the salesperson risked losing valuable business with other customers. When the costs of helping were low, the dependent customer received more service, but when the costs were high, the dependent woman actually received somewhat less service than the normal one. Similarly, on subway platforms in Canada, a person with an eyepatch was actually helped significantly less than a person with normal vision when the cost of helping was relatively high (Ungar, 1979). Thus, when the costs of helping escalate, even the most dependent persons may not elicit the helping behavior to which they seem entitled.

Friends, Relatives, and Attractive or Similar People. Relationships between friends or relatives imply mutual dependency and an obligation to help. Naturalistic studies of such disasters as tornadoes indicate that people tend to help members of their families first, then friends and neighbors, and finally strangers in the stricken area (Form & Nosow, 1958). Even a brief acquaintance with someone increases the rate of helping in experiments (Latané & Darley, 1970; Liebhart, 1972).

Similarly, the attractiveness of a recipient of help may increase the rate of helping (L. R. Daniels & Berkowitz, 1963; Gross, Wallston, & Piliavin, 1975). This suggests that people may be especially helpful to those who are similar to themselves in dress, ideology, race, and nationality. For example, Emswiller, Deaux, and Willits

(1971) reported that "hippie" and "straight" subjects were more likely to give dimes to those who resembled them in appearance than to dissimilar solicitors. People also tend to help those who share their opinions or beliefs (Sole, Marton, & Hornstein, 1975). When Nixon workers and McGovern workers dropped their campaign literature near the voting polls in 1972, they were helped 71% of the time if their preference was congruent with that of the voter (as determined by an interview after the incident) and 46% of the time if the beliefs were incongruent (Karabenick, Lerner, & Beecher, 1973).

People are often, but not always, most helpful to members of their own ethnic group (Gaertner & Bickman, 1971; Wispé & Freshley, 1971). Similarly, people tend to be more helpful to compatriots than to foreigners. The major study done by R. E. Feldman (1968) in Boston, Athens, and Paris examined such behaviors as giving directions, mailing unstamped letters, and returning overpayments for goods in stores. Citizens were generally more helpful to compatriots, although not in all situations studied.

Who, then, elicits helping behavior? First, the people who receive help almost always signal to potential helpers that they are dependent. When the potential helper perceives that the need is legitimate and is no fault of the victim, he or she is more likely to help, unless the costs of helping a highly dependent person are prohibitive. When the helper and recipient are bound by kinship or friendship, or by any special relationship that makes one person dependent on another, help is usually more likely. Furthermore, the attractiveness of the recipient, which is sometimes a function of his or her similarity to the potential helper in dress, ideology, race, or nationality, often elicits helping behavior.

F. *Explanations of Helping Behavior*

We have seen that helping behavior is influenced by a host of situational and personal variables, but we still have not approached a full understanding of helping. Some theorists have claimed that **empathy**

—the vicarious experience of another person's perceptions and emotions—plays a central role in motivating prosocial behavior. Other theorists have argued that we can understand helping behavior by referring to *norms*—socially defined expectations about what is appropriate behavior. However, others have argued that normative explanations are unsatisfactory and that we can understand helping behavior best by analyzing the costs and rewards of helping. We will look briefly at these three ways of integrating research findings.

Empathy. Several researchers have suggested that the ability and tendency to empathize with other people is a key motivator of helping behavior. Martin Hoffman (1975b, 1976) has offered a theory of the development of empathy and views it as the basis for a variety of moral and prosocial behaviors. He believes that children initially help others in order to relieve their own distress. Then, during their development, they shift to helping behavior that is motivated by a learned ability to empathize and a desire to relieve the distress of others (Aronfreed, 1968, 1976; Hoffman, 1975b; Mussen & Eisenberg-Berg, 1977). In one study of secondary-school students, students scoring high on a measure of empathy were more advanced in their moral reasoning about prosocial behavior than were students low in empathy (Eisenberg-Berg & Mussen, 1978). Empathy was related to actual helping behavior, but only among males, and there was also evidence that the discipline practices used by the parents of males were associated with their degree of empathy. Although not all research with children supports the idea of a causal link between empathy and helping in children (Iannotti, 1978), there appears to be some association between the two.

Empathy has also been proposed as a motivator of helping among adults. When empathy can be produced, helping behavior is more likely to follow. For example, D. Krebs (1975) attempted to create empathy by convincing some subjects that they were similar to a person whom they watched re-

ceiving rewards and punishments in a roulette game. Their own reports and a variety of physiological measures indicated that they were indeed more emotionally aroused than subjects who thought the roulette player was different from themselves, and they were more likely to help the other person at a cost to themselves. Similarly, Coke, Batson, and McDavis (1978) found that by raising subjects' empathic arousal they could increase the likelihood that they would help. These researchers suggest that people must first take the perspective of a person in need. This in itself is not enough, but, if empathic emotion is thereby aroused, this emotion will in turn motivate helping behavior. In a somewhat similar formulation, Harvey Hornstein (1976, 1978) emphasizes the motivational role of tension produced when someone we define as part of our "we-group" rather than as an outsider is in trouble. Whether people help to reduce their own emotional discomfort or to reduce the discomfort of another person is not known. What this line of theorizing *does* suggest is that there is an emotional basis for some kinds of helping behavior.

Norms and Helping. Normative explanations of helping behavior suggest that we help because we have internalized certain societal standards for behavior. For example, the **social-responsibility norm** states that we should help those who need help. We have seen that people are indeed likely to help those who appear dependent on them. However, we have also noticed that helpers consider the legitimacy and origin of dependency as well as the risks involved in helping a dependent person. More importantly, agreement with the norm of social responsibility does not automatically produce helpful behavior. Bryan (1972) noted that most elementary-school children believe that it is good to help the needy. But reminding children of the norm is not sufficient to elicit helping behavior, for children, like adults, are able to live with contradictions between their verbal endorsements of the norm and their actual behavior (Bryan & London, 1970).

The **reciprocity norm** holds somewhat more promise as a consistent motivator of behavior. As conceptualized by Gouldner (1960), it states that people should help those who have helped them and that people should not injure those who have helped them. It is closely related to concepts in equity theory emphasizing the imbalance produced in a relationship when one person helps (or harms) another (Walster, Berscheid, & Walster, 1976; Walster, Walster, & Berscheid, 1978). Gouldner argued that the norm of reciprocity is universal and essential in maintaining stable relationships among people in society. The only people exempt from the requirement to reciprocate help are the dependent—young children, the aged, or the sick—the very people whom the norm of social responsibility tells us to help.

Perhaps the greatest testimony to the strength of the reciprocity norm is the fact that gifts and other forms of help can be used to control and dominate others. To cite just one example, prison inmates may attempt to "buy" newcomers.

Aggressive inmates will go to extraordinary lengths to place gifts in the cells of inmates they have selected for personal domination. These intended victims, in order to escape the threatened bondage, must find the owner and insist that the gifts be taken back [McCorkle & Korn, 1954, p. 90].

No wonder people sometimes bite the hands that feed them! When someone does a favor, the obligation to reciprocate may make us uncomfortable. As Jack Brehm (1966) explains it, we experience **psychological reactance,** a motivation to reestablish freedom of behavior when our options are reduced (see Chapter 14). In fact, by determining when the norm of reciprocity fails to operate, we get a better understanding of when help is not appreciated. For example, people reciprocate less when a favor appears to have been accidental rather than intentional (Goranson & Berkowitz, 1966). A favor that seems motivated by selfishness is less appreciated than one motivated by altruism (Tesser, Gatewood, & Driver,

1968). Several researchers have taken up the study of how recipients of help react to the help given and to its source (for example, Gergen, 1974; Fisher, Nadler, & Whitcher, 1978).

Thus there are exceptions both to the norm of social responsibility and to the norm of reciprocity. The two normative explanations taken together still leave something to be desired, as noted by critics (Krebs, 1970; Latané & Darley, 1970; S. H. Schwartz, 1973). First, norms are so general that they may not tell us what to do in specific situations that differ drastically from one another. Second, if most people in society subscribe to such norms, how can norms explain individual differences in helping behavior? Third, two conflicting norms may seem equally applicable in a situation. For example, the norm of social responsibility is contradicted by a norm that says "Don't meddle in other people's affairs." Fourth, unless the conditions that activate a norm are specified in advance, we are left in the position of arguing circularly that the norm must have been operating because helping behavior occurred.

This is not to say that we should drop the word "norm" from our vocabularies, however. For example, Shalom Schwartz (1973, 1977) has developed a normative theory of helping that overcomes many of the problems in other normative theories. Instead of focusing on broad social norms, he and his colleagues have measured **personal norms,** or the individual's feelings of moral obligation to act in a given way in a particular situation. For example, Schwartz (1973) included this question designed to measure a personal norm in a medical survey of clerical workers: "If a stranger to you needed a bone marrow transplant and you were a suitable donor, would you feel a moral obligation to donate bone marrow?" Three months later, respondents received a mail request to actually donate bone marrow. Those with strong personal norms were more likely to volunteer, but even more importantly, the relationship between norms and behavior depended on another factor. Personal norms strongly predicted volunteering among people who, as indicated by questions in the first survey, had a strong tendency to assume responsibility for their actions but did not predict volunteering among those who tended to deny responsibility for the consequences of their action. These latter respondents may have felt an obligation to help, but when it came down to deciding, they may have talked themselves out of feeling personally obligated. In another study, housewives with strong personal norms about aiding welfare recipients acted according to their norms (Schwartz & Fleishman, 1978). However, those with no strong feelings of obligation one way or another were swayed by a situational factor included in the study's design: the legitimacy of the need for help.

In a variety of studies, the strength of personal norms has proved useful in predicting behavior, whereas endorsement of social norms has not (Schwartz, 1977). More interesting still, personal norms interact with other personal and situational factors in predictable ways. People appear to differ in their personal norms and in the likelihood that any feelings of obligation they have will be acted upon. In this view, some, but not all, people do act in ways consistent with their beliefs, and others, lacking strong beliefs, are more swayed by situational factors (see Chapter 11 for more discussion of this issue). By measuring strength of belief in personal norms in advance and by looking carefully at factors that determine whether they are activated and then acted upon in given situations, Schwartz and his colleagues have brought new life to the notion that our attitudes about helping do influence our behavior.

The Costs and Rewards of Helping. Whatever their normative beliefs, people are generally motivated to increase the rewards and decrease the costs of their actions. We have already seen that external rewards—such as money or praise—increase the likelihood of future helping behavior. Furthermore, as children learn to associate their own pain and pleasure with that of other people, their empathic feelings can serve as sources of reward and punishment. Acting

in accordance with a well-accepted norm may be rewarding because it leads to social approval and is consistent with our belief that we are helpful people.

On the other hand, increasing the costs of helping reduces the likelihood that help will be forthcoming. For example, we have seen that requests for dimes are less well received than requests for the time of day, that bloody victims are helped less frequently than "clean" victims, and that customers are helped less when the store is busy than when it is almost empty.

Since the potential helper is faced with two alternative actions—helping or not helping—it is essential to consider not only the rewards and costs of helping but also the rewards and costs of *not* helping. J. A. Piliavin and Piliavin (1973) have set forth a cost-reward analysis of helping, the general characteristics of which are illustrated in Box 9-2. Lynch and Cohen (1978) have developed a more complex model that takes into account both the probability that various consequences will occur and perceptions of how positive or negative each consequence would be. Obviously, the human being is not always the rational animal portrayed in Box 9-2. A potential helper is unlikely to coldly calculate all costs and rewards, particularly in an emergency calling for a quick decision under stress. However, researchers can use such analyses to predict the probability of helping behavior when potential costs and rewards are varied. Perhaps the greatest strength of a cost-reward analysis is that it allows us to enter both situational and personal variables into our equations.

As was the case with normative explanations, the researcher must specify in advance those factors associated with high and low cost and *then* determine whether helping rates fall as costs of helping escalate or costs of not helping decrease. Several researchers have done so and have confirmed cost-benefit predictions (for example, R. D. Clark, 1976; Cowan & Inskeep, 1978; Gross, Wallston, & Piliavin, 1975; Lynch & Cohen, 1978; Salter, Dickey, & Gulas, 1978). However, occasionally it proves difficult to predict in advance which of the many possi-

Box 9-2. The Mind of the Rational Helper: Cost-Reward Analysis.

Old man, I see you slumped in the gutter, looking half dead. I realize that you need help. Will I be the one?

What will it cost me if I help? Maybe you're drunk and will slobber all over me. Maybe you'll get surly. What if I make things worse and am held liable? Call that 10 cost points.

Besides, if I just pass by, I'll be on time for my job interview and will probably get the position. Rewarding indeed —at least 5 reward points, which I'll lose if I help.

Then again, maybe there's something in it for me if I help. I feel for you, old man, and I can imagine your joy if I help. I like to think of myself as a helpful person. Maybe the job interviewer will be

snowed when I explain why I was late. I know my friends will think well of me if I help. That adds up to 6 reward points.

It's going to hurt me some if I don't help, too. Maybe somebody I know will see me callously walk by and tell everyone. I'll feel guilty, I know; I'll wonder if I killed you, old man. Those costs are worth 3 points.

Time for the final tally. It will cost me 10 points to help, and I'll also lose 5 points I could have if I walk by. The total cost is 15 points. Helping is worth 6 reward points to me, and I'll avoid the 3-point cost of failing to help. The total reward value is 9 points.

Goodbye, old man. Perhaps when I'm in a better mood.

ble cost and reward factors will be influential (Bloom & Clark, 1976). And finally, despite its overall power to predict, cost-reward analysis has not successfully explained the motivation of heroic altruism, in which the costs are immense and the rewards few. Unless the cost-reward analyst can uncover hidden rewards for altruism, the altruist will continue to baffle us.

IV. Toward a Prosocial Society

Can knowledge of prosocial behavior be used to strengthen prosocial tendencies? We have already seen that the use of cooperative reward structures in classrooms can promote cooperation and helping as well as learning. There is even evidence that being taught the information about the bystander effect presented in this chapter makes students less likely to fall prey to it themselves (Beaman, Barnes, Klentz, & McQuirk, 1978; Rayko, 1977). In this final section, we will consider briefly the goals of raising funds for charitable causes, increasing the responsiveness of the helping professions, counter-

ing the dampening effects of urban life on prosocial behavior, and legislating a prosocial society.

A. *Enlisting Support for Charities*

Charity is big business, as evidenced by efforts of advertising agencies to sell diseases as if they were laundry soaps (see H. Katz, 1975; Liston, 1977; Rosenbaum, 1974). Competing charitable organizations bombard us with posters, literature, commercials, and telethons, appealing to our sympathy, guilt, and desire for a just world (see Figure 9-6).

However, as we have seen, appeals to norms of social responsibility are not notably effective. A better strategy is to reduce the costs of donating and increase the rewards. Hence, fund raisers make it easy for us to give at the office, allow us to pay on time installments, and highlight the fact that donations are tax-deductible. Door-to-door fund raisers make use of sound social-psychological principles. For example, a recent drive for multiple sclerosis sent only 12-year-olds to collect money—presumably

WHAT HURTS A LITTLE BUT FEELS GREAT?

Giving blood.

Figure 9-6. Soliciting help for charitable causes.
(Courtesy of Irwin Memorial Blood Bank of the
San Francisco Medical Society.)

because they are young enough to look dependent on us but old enough to handle our money. It is no accident that volunteers are recruited to solicit money from their immediate neighbors. The potential donor, susceptible to modeling, may think "The Joneses are behind this cause, and look how rewarding it has been for them," or may fear rejection if he or she appears unchari-table. The fund raiser may also help the cause by putting the potential donor in a good mood. Or in mail campaigns we may receive a small gift—perhaps as small as a penny as in one campaign by the Epilepsy Foundation of America (Liston, 1977)—intended to make us feel obligated to reciprocate. Straightforward appeals to a sense of social responsibility are likely to become less effective in societies that are increasingly pressed by so many needs and worthy causes. Fund raisers will need to become even more ingenious in the future to motivate charitable behavior.

B. *Helping in the Helping Professions*

As the population increases, the life span lengthens, and resources grow scarcer, social services will continue to expand in the United States and Canada; hence, more and more of us will find ourselves in salaried helping roles (Danish & Hauer, 1973; Pollak, 1976). However, serving as a helper within a large bureaucracy is far more complicated than helping friends and neighbors in need, which was the mode of social service in earlier times (see Lenrow, 1978, for a comparison). There are immense problems in informing people of services to which they are entitled, linking them with the appropriate agencies, inducing them to use such agencies, and seeing that their needs are actually met.

One of the most important tasks is to alter the nature of the relationship between helper and client so that recipients of bureaucratic help are not made to feel uncomfortably dependent and, as a result, resentful of the aid giver. We might restructure the ways in which aid is given to reduce the likelihood that the recipient will experience a threat to self-esteem (Fisher & Nadler, 1974; Fisher, Harrison, & Nadler, 1978). Since human-service workers without advanced education have generally been found no less effective helpers than degreed professionals (Durlak, 1979), they are sometimes employed to bridge the gap between client and helper (Sahlein, 1973).

Still another challenge is to alter the ways in which helping professionals are rewarded for their efforts. A client may receive better service from a professional paid on a fee-for-service basis than from the same professional paid a flat salary, perhaps because salaried helpers are not always motivated to go beyond the call of duty (Deniels, 1969). Ideally, professionals should be rewarded for providing effective help, but too often perhaps they are actually rewarded for other things such as cutting costs, not making waves, and so on. Perhaps in the future, salary and promotion will be used more directly as rewards for competent, creative, and well-received help.

C. *Urban Life and Prosocial Behavior*

Knowing that people who live in large cities are often less prosocial than their country cousins is cause for some alarm, since urban centers are here to stay. Stanley Milgram (1970) has offered an explanation for the lower rate of prosocial behavior in cities by suggesting that urbanites experience a kind of sensory and cognitive "overload." As a result, they must be selective. They shut off some sources of stimulation entirely (for example, by getting an unlisted phone number), they give less attention to each input (for example, by serving customers in a brusque manner), and they set priorities (for example, by helping friends but not strangers). These adaptations are necessary, Milgram argued, if the urbanite is to avoid being psychologically crushed by the demands of city life. What may appear to be callous disregard for others is, for the urbanite, a strategy for coping with city life.

Is there any support for this view? Milgram's **stimulus-overload theory** was partially supported in a study where a measure of the amount of environmental stimulation in a neighborhood (noise, traffic, and so on) was somewhat related to helpfulness (Korte, Ypma, & Toppen, 1975). However, this study was not clearly supportive of Milgram, for although towns were lower in environmental input than cities, town dwellers did not prove to be more helpful. Better support for Milgram's hypothesis came from a laboratory study in which college students had to listen for numbers read orally and proofread a text in the presence of distracting background noise (Sherrod & Downs, 1974). Subjects who experienced stimulus overload were less helpful when a confederate later asked them to work math problems than were those who had not experienced the distracting noise while completing the tasks. Mathews and Canon (1975) also found that loud noise reduced rates of helping. However, in the Sherrod and Downs study, if subjects were told that they could control the irritating noise, even if they did not actually turn it off, the effects of stimulus overload were lessened.

Perhaps there are ways to increase our sense of control over our environment. In some cities, citizens develop a sense of community control by localizing schools, human-service agencies, and governmental structures in small geographical areas or neighborhoods. Not only can neighborhood organizations convert strangers to acquaintances and friends, but they can foster a sense of common purpose and cooperation.

D. *Legislating a Prosocial Society*

At present, laws in North America are quick to define and punish antisocial behavior but are less concerned with punishing failures to help other people (J. A. Kaplan, 1978). We do punish failure to help in apprehending a criminal. And we may hold bystanders accountable if they have a special relationship to the victim (for example, father to son or doctor to patient), if they are responsible, even accidentally, for the plight of the victim, or if they actually worsen a victim's plight by intervening. By contrast, other countries such as France and the Netherlands also punish the failures of bystanders to help strangers in emergencies (J. A. Kaplan, 1978).

A more popular solution is to reduce the costs of helping. For instance, "Secret Witness" programs permit a person to call anonymously to report information about a crime, thus avoiding the fear of retaliation by the criminal and the time and effort involved in bouts with red tape. "Good Samaritan" laws have been passed to protect doctors from liability for all but the grossest negligence when they stop on the road to help injured motorists (Ratcliffe, 1966).

It is also simple to provide rewards for prosocial behavior. We still see offers of rewards on posters in the post office; Secret Witnesses are offered rewards for useful information; and organizations such as the Carnegie Foundation award medals for heroic altruism. Perhaps we can make it easier and more rewarding to help, but our society's emphasis on individualism stands in the way of mandating prosocial behavior in the future (J. A. Kaplan, 1978).

We will probably always struggle to increase prosocial tendencies and reduce antisocial ones. As Harvey Hornstein (1976) put it, . . . "human beings are potentially the cruelest and kindest animals on earth" (p. 66).

V. Summary

Prosocial behavior—behavior that has positive social consequences—occurs when two or more people cooperate for mutual benefit or when one person helps another by doing a favor, donating resources, or intervening in an emergency. Altruism is a special form of helping that is voluntary, costly, and motivated by something other than the anticipation of reward. Altruism poses challenges to assumptions about human nature reflected in psychoanalytic theory, learning theory, and sociobiology.

Cooperation is typically contrasted with competition. We refer to cooperative, competitive, or individualistic reward structures and distinguish the structure of a situation from an individual's motives—cooperative, competitive, or individualistic. Research using laboratory games tells us that we are more likely to cooperate with another person if the other person matches our choices tit-for-tat, if we can communicate, and if we come to the situation with attitudes and motives conducive to cooperation. In field situations, including classrooms, cooperative reward structures within groups often produce higher group cohesiveness, greater satisfaction, and more productivity than do competitive reward structures. Young children acquire the cognitive ability to cooperate and compete; then the values of their culture or subculture influence whether they prefer to cooperate or compete in given situations.

Helping behavior is also influenced by both situational and personal factors. In order to help, one must notice an event, interpret it as one requiring help, assume personal responsibility for acting, choose a form of assistance, and implement that assistance. Some situations, especially those that are unambiguous and do not pose a costly threat to the potential helper, elicit higher rates of helping behavior than do others.

Another important aspect of the situation is the presence and behavior of other people. Being reinforced by others for helping, or seeing someone else help, increases rates of helping. However, as the bystander effect indicates, people are often less likely to help when they are with others than when they are alone. This is so because of a social-influence process that makes witnesses less likely to interpret an event as an emergency and because of a diffusion of responsibility that makes witnesses less likely to accept personal responsibility for acting.

The psychological state of the potential helper is also important. Success and good moods generally increase the rate of helping, whereas self-concern and bad moods often inhibit helping but sometimes motivate it. Negative feelings aroused after one inflicts or witnesses harm may also motivate helping behavior, although sometimes people justify the harm rather than try to help. Researchers have had difficulty identifying more enduring personality traits and background characteristics of helpful people, although people from small towns and people who have been exposed to altruistic parents and have acquired certain values seem more helpful. Whatever their personal characteristics, people most often help those who are dependent, especially when the need is legitimate and is no fault of the victim. They also tend to be more helpful to friends, relatives, and people who are attractive or similar to themselves.

One theory of prosocial behavior emphasizes the motivational role of empathy. Helping behavior has also been explained by reference to norms or standards of behavior. The norm of social responsibility, which says that we should help those who need help, is more an ideal than an accurate description of typical behavior. The norm of reciprocity, which states that people help, or at least do not injure, those who have helped them, is a more powerful norm. In fact, it explains why people often feel that their behavioral freedom is threatened when they feel obligated to return a favor. Personal norms are better predictors of behavior than is endorsement of societal norms.

Finally, it appears fruitful to consider the costs and rewards of helping or not helping. People are generally more helpful if helping behavior is rewarded and less helpful if they must sacrifice a great deal by helping.

Knowledge of the dynamics of prosocial behavior can help us to build a more prosocial world, particularly if we change situations—for example, by altering reward structures to encourage cooperation among school children, by using social-psychological techniques to elicit donations, by changing aspects of the urban environment that inhibit prosocial behavior, and by drafting legislation to reduce the costs and increase the rewards of prosocial behavior.

Glossary Terms

altruism
bystander effect
competition
competitive reward structure
cooperation
cooperative reward structure
diffusion of responsibility
empathy

equity theory
helping behavior
individualistic reward structure
modeling
negative-state-relief model
norms
personal norms
Prisoner's Dilemma

prosocial behavior
psychological reactance
reciprocity norm
social-responsibility norm
sociobiology
stimulus-overload theory

Violence is as American as cherry pie.   RAP BROWN

GEORGE BELLOWS. *DEMPSEY-FIRPO FIGHT*. ADDISON GALLERY OF AMERICAN ART, PHILLIPS ACADEMY, ANDOVER, MASSACHUSETTS.

One of television's great contributions is that it brought murder back into the home where it belongs.   ALFRED HITCHCOCK

10

Aggression and Violence

During the approximately 5600 years that humans have recorded their history, more than 14,600 wars have occurred, averaging out to nearly 3 wars per year throughout our history (Montagu, 1976). Since the beginning of the 20th century, more than 900,000 civilians in the United States have died as a result of criminal acts. In fact, among stable industrialized societies, the United States has the highest rates of homicide, assault, rape, and robbery.

One could easily conclude from these facts that violence and aggression are integral facets of human society. Indeed, some behavioral scientists assume that aggression is the natural result of a "killer instinct" in human nature. Robert Ardrey (1961) has ✓ placed this **instinct** in an evolutionary context, stating that "Man is a predator whose natural instinct is to kill with a weapon." Other scientists, however, believe that aggression can be explained completely as a learned social behavior that is predictable and controllable.

The latter approach rests on somewhat different evidence than that presented in the first paragraph in this chapter. For example, societies exist in which instances of violence are minimal or totally absent. Moreover, there are wide variations among people in the extent to which they display aggressive behavior. Such variations among people and cultures pose serious questions for those who assume that aggression is a universal instinct.

Definitions and interpretations of aggressive behavior are determined by theoretical viewpoints; and when we consider the nature of aggression, we find more than enough theories to go around. These theoretical perspectives differ in a variety of ways: in the extent to which they consider aggression innate or learned, in the extent to which the person, versus situational factors, is considered influential, and in the proposed ways in which aggression might be controlled in the future. This chapter describes and evaluates three dominant, yet conflicting, assumptions about the nature of aggression. In addition, a number of related issues are considered. We ask, for example, how alcohol and drugs affect aggressive behavior, how the presentation of violence on television and in films affect the observer, how aggression is expressed in the home, and how violence might be controlled in the future.

Before we look at these more complex issues, however, some of the basic questions in the area of aggression need to be addressed. A definition of aggression is first in order of importance.

I. Definitions of Aggression

Different theories of aggression offer different definitions of aggression and different assumptions about its causes. According to the psychoanalytic approach, aggression is an inevitable expression of our psychic energy. According to the approach of ethology, or the study of species in their natural settings, aggression serves protective and life-saving functions. A third viewpoint, most commonly expressed by experimental social psychologists, treats aggression as a learned behavior.

A. *Aggression: The Psychoanalytic Definition*

The orthodox Freudian or psychoanalytic framework assumes that aggressive energy is constantly generated by our bodily processes. For example, the intake of food leads to the generation of energy. Aggressive urges, like sexual urges, must be "released" —that is, expressed directly or indirectly. These urges can be discharged in either socially acceptable ways (such as a vigorous debate or an athletic activity) or in less socially acceptable ways (such as insults or fights). The destructive release of aggressive urges does not necessarily have to be directed against other people; it can be aimed toward the self, as in suicide.

Some Freudians maintain that aggression plays a beneficial role in the ego's rational activities, but the typical psychoanalytic view defines aggression as an underlying urge that must seek expression. Therefore, aggression can become destructive to the self or to other people whenever it cannot be expressed in socially acceptable ways. Freud believed that one function of society is to keep natural aggression in check—to restrain its expression.

B. *Aggression: The Ethological Definition*

The noted ethologist Konrad Lorenz ✓ (1966) describes aggression as "the fighting instinct in beast and man which is directed *against* members of the same species" (p. ix). According to Lorenz's hypothesis, aggression is not a bad thing in itself; rather, it functions to preserve the species as well as the individual. Fights serve to reduce the number of members within a species or disperse the members over an area so that *the species as an entity* can survive. Through his investigations, Lorenz states, he has found the following:

The danger of too dense a population of an animal species settling in one part of the available biotope and exhausting all its sources of nutrition and so starving can be obviated by a mutual repulsion acting on the animals of the same species, effecting their regular spacing out, in much the same manner as electrical charges are regularly distributed all over the surface of a spherical conductor. This, in plain terms, is the most important survival value of intraspecific aggression [1966, p. 31].

The dangers of the human population explosion have always been apparent to Lorenz, who supports the notion that increased crowding will lead to increased aggression.

Lorenz concludes that an organism is far more aggressive toward members of its own species than toward members of other species. The basic purpose of such aggression is to keep members of the species separated—to give each member enough area to survive. Intraspecies aggression also affects sexual selection and mating; the stronger are more likely to mate. Thus, it assures that the best and strongest animals will carry on the species.

In Lorenz's view, aggression becomes undesirable only when the species—the human species, for example—fails to develop the usual instinctual inhibitions against it. Intraspecies fights do not usually end in death, but rather in acts of appeasement by the loser (see **Figure 10-1**). According to Lorenz, all humans' troubles arise from their "being a basically harmless, omnivorous creature, lacking in natural weapons with which to kill (their) big prey, and, therefore, also devoid of the built-in safety devices which prevent 'professional' carnivores from abusing their killing power to destroy fellow members of their own species" (1966, p. 241). Lacking the innate ability to kill without weapons, the human species also has failed to evolve inhibitory mechanisms to prevent aggression. If humans had no weapons at their disposal, they wouldn't be equipped to kill members of their species. What if all killing of other people had to be done with our hands and teeth? Wouldn't that not only reduce the murder rate but also restrain our desire to kill?

C. *Aggression: The Experimental Social Psychologist's Definitions*

In contrast to the psychoanalysts and the ethologists, most social psychologists do not consider aggression to be an innate instinct; however, even among social psychologists, there is not complete agreement on the nature of aggression. Some theorists consider aggression to be based on a motive or a drive. Such a drive, which is satisfied through aggressive behavior, is assumed to be elicited by various external circumstances. Although the concept of arousal is basic to these formulations, the definition of aggression itself is often limited to the behavioral reaction. For example, Berkowitz ✓ distinguishes between aggression—the behavior—and the emotional state "which may facilitate and perhaps even 'energize' the aggressive response" (Berkowitz, 1969, p. 3). This intervening emotional state is arousal, or anger.

Other social psychologists have found the concept of arousal unnecessary in the

Figure 10-1. The agony of defeat. In the photo above, the wolf on the left has accepted defeat, although the signs of her submission are quite subtle. The position of the ears and the tail are two signs of submission. (Photo by T. M. Huffman. Printed with permission of Wolf Park, Battle Ground, Indiana.)

explanation of aggression. Instead, they focus on the behavior itself, considering aggression to be a learned response much like other social behaviors. From this perspective, there is nothing automatic about aggressive behavior: it is not innate, nor is it the inevitable response to a particular state of arousal. It is acquired through specific learning processes and maintained as a result of consistent situational cues.

D. *Differences among the Definitions*

Each of the definitions of aggression described here implies a different phenomenon. The psychoanalyst focuses on an unconscious urge; the ethologist stresses a purposeful belligerence, particularly toward members of the same species; and the ex-perimental social psychologist emphasizes a specific behavior and the specific circumstances that elicit that behavior. These varying emphases must be kept in mind as we explore the issue of whether aggression is innate or learned.

To simplify our task we will adopt the following working definition of aggression: *Aggression is any form of behavior directed toward the goal of harming or injuring another living being who is motivated to avoid such treatment* (Baron, 1977). This definition, which is acceptable to most social psychologists, clearly focuses on a behavior and avoids the issue of the source of the behavior. A few other implications of this definition should be noted. First of all, the definition limits aggression to those forms of behavior in which an individual *intends* to harm a victim. If you accidentally knock someone over while riding your bicycle, for example, that act would not be considered an act of aggression. Similarly, when a nurse gives a patient a routine injection, her intention is not to do harm, although pain might well be the result. But what if the patient has just insulted the nurse, who then jams the needle in with unnecessary force? Certainly there is a component of aggression in this behavior. Although it is often difficult to establish intention with complete certainty, as the proceedings of criminal trials well indicate, the concept of intentionality is important in separating aggressive behavior from other forms of behavior that might lead to some harm.

Our working definition doesn't limit aggression to physical harm. Verbal insults are considered forms of aggression, and even the refusal to give a person something that he or she needs can be considered a form of aggression. Our definition does, however, limit aggression to those behaviors that involve other living beings, either human or animal. Although a person clearly expresses anger by kicking a wall, this behavior is not considered to be aggressive according to this definition. Finally, instances of aggression are limited to those cases in which the other person would prefer to avoid the pain. Behaviors most clearly ruled out by this clause are those of a sadomasochistic nature.

II. Theoretical Positions on Aggression

Definitions represent only the beginning of our understanding of aggression. Theorists in this area have developed a number of broad models of aggression, emphasizing different aspects of the cause, the consequences, and the related factors that may affect aggressive behavior. In this section, we consider three major viewpoints regarding aggression: the instinctual position, the drive (or motivation) position, and the position that emphasizes aggression as a learned behavior.

A. *Instinctual and Biological Explanations of Aggression*

Sigmund Freud once wrote "The tendency to aggression is an innate, independent, instinctual disposition in man" (1930, p. 102). Freud was a physician, and the psychoanalytic position that he developed was closely tied to his study of bodily functions and human physiology. Accordingly, Freud believed that an instinct is a mental entity in the id that represents an inner somatic source of stimulation (Hall & Lindzey, 1968); in other words, instincts result from tensions created by biological needs. Therefore, aggressive energy generated within the body is energy that must be dissipated; it can either be neutralized or discharged (Freud, 1963).

Freud frequently revised his theory, and his followers have introduced further revisions. **Neo-Freudians** have conceptualized aggressive behavior as a part of the ego (or the reality-oriented part of the personality) rather than placing aggression among the irrational processes of the id (Hartmann, Kris, & Loewenstein, 1949). According to the neo-Freudians, aggressive drives are healthy; they represent adaptations to the realities of the environment of every human being. For the most part, however, these revisionist theorists maintain the belief that aggression develops from innate and instinctive forces.

Psychoanalytic interpretations of aggression were derived originally from medicine and physiology. The ethological position on aggression is based on animal behavior. As we indicated earlier, **ethology** is the subfield of biology concerned with the instincts and action patterns common to all members of a species operating in their natural habitat (Eibl-Eibesfeldt, 1970). Ethologists observe the normal behavior of fish, birds, and other animals in the field and attempt to determine similarities and causes in their action patterns. As Crook (1973) has stated, in many cases, one may justifiably assume that these patterns are under innate or instinctual control. Lorenz (1952, 1966, 1970) has painstakingly observed needlefish, greylag geese, hedge-hogs, and Alsatian dogs, noting the characteristic behavior patterns of each species (see Figure 10-2). Lorenz has applied his conclusions to the behavior of human beings. More recently, sociobiologists also have proposed an innate basis for aggression, relying on Darwinian notions of evolution through natural selection and the concept of "genetic fitness" (Wilson, 1978). However, other ethologists, such as Tinbergen (1968), have emphasized that differences among species may reduce generality and the ability to apply one's conclusions to the more advanced species, such as humans.

In some ways, Lorenz's approach resembles that of the psychoanalyst. As an ethologist, he assumes that the expression of any fixed action pattern depends on the accumulation of energy. But according to ethologists, the release of energy—or the instigation of aggression—occurs *when triggered by an external stimulus* (E. H. Hess, 1962). The concept of *releasers* is used by ethologists to explain the relationship between internal factors and external stimuli. Specifically, a releaser is a cue in the environment that allows an organism to express aggressive or other drive-related behaviors. Essentially, this is a two-factor theory of the expression of aggression: it has an advantage over orthodox psychoanalytic theory and the neo-Freudian approaches in recognizing that environmental changes contribute to the aggressive response.

Although the psychoanalytic viewpoint and the view of ethologists and sociobiologists differ in some important respects, such as the role of the environment in contributing to aggressive behavior, they share some basic assumptions. Most importantly, both positions consider aggression to be an

Figure 10-2. Nobel prize-winning ethologist Konrad Lorenz. (© Yves De Braine/Black Star.)

innate and an instinctual behavior, and, therefore, a basic part of the human condition. When and where aggression might be displayed can be argued, but proponents of these positions allow no doubt as to *whether* it will be displayed. They believe that aggression always has existed and always will.

B. *Motivational Explanations of Aggression*

Although most social psychologists have been unwilling to accept aggression as an inevitable and instinctual behavior, the concept of aggression as a general motive, or drive, that can be either learned or innate has been widely accepted. In 1939, a group of psychologists at Yale University (Dollard, Doob, Miller, Mowrer, & Sears, 1939) introduced a hypothesis that has influenced thought and generated more empirical research than any other theory of aggression (until very recently). These psychologists hypothesized that frustration causes aggression. More specifically, this frustration-aggression hypothesis postulated that "the occurrence of aggression always presupposes frustration" (N. E. Miller, 1941, pp. 337–338). A second part of the hypothesis was usually interpreted to mean that any frustrating event would inevitably lead to aggression; however, this part of the hypothesis was later clarified by one of the authors, Neal Miller (1941), who argued that there were no implications that frustration would always cause aggression. "Frustration produces instigations to a number of different types of responses, one of which is an instigation to some form of aggression" (Miller, 1941, p. 338). In summary, although the link between frustration and aggression is considered to be a common one, frustration does not necessarily explain all aggressive behavior. Does this theory account for the incidence of aggression in society? To answer this question, we must look more carefully at the components of the frustration-aggression theory.

1. *What is Frustration?* To say the least, *frustration* is a vague term that is subject to many different interpretations (see Berkowitz, 1969). In common usage, frustration can refer to the external event that causes a reaction, or it can refer to the reaction itself. Suppose a young man is ready to drive his car to the airport to meet a female friend when he discovers that his car battery is dead. What is the frustration? Is it the dead battery or the fact that the car won't start (the external instigating conditions)? Or is frustration the young man's feelings of increased tension and the pounding of his heart—or does it refer to his pounding on the car? In the original frustration-aggression formulation, the Yale theorists defined frustration as the state that emerges when circumstances interfere with a goal response: "an interference with the occurrence of an instigated goal-response at its proper time in the behavior sequence" (Dollard et al., 1939, p. 7). This emphasis on observables suited the behavioristic orientation of the Yale group at that time, but psychologists who have tested the frustration-aggression hypothesis have not always defined the term *frustration* so clearly. This lack of a definition of the term has led Berkowitz (1969) to conclude that many of the failures to verify the frustration-aggression hypothesis reflect the ambiguity and inconsistency in definitions rather than any essential lack of validity in the formulation.

2. *Is the Relationship between Frustration and Aggression Innate?* There is a tendency to regard the frustration-aggression relationship as inevitable, or instinctual. Dollard and his colleagues fostered this belief when they stated that "the frustration-aggression hypothesis assumes a universal causal relation between frustration and aggression" (Dollard et al., 1939, p. 10). Although Miller (1941) later qualified this statement, leaving open the question of whether the basis of the relationship was learned or innate, many critics recently have challenged the universality of the proposed relationship. These critics suggest that, because people can learn to inhibit their aggressive reactions or learn different responses to frustration, the possibility of innate behavior is excluded (Bandura, 1973; Bandura & Walters, 1963; Berkowitz, 1969).

For example, if your boss severely criticizes your performance, you might quickly learn to inhibit tendencies to strike back. Does that mean that the frustration/aggression link is not innate? Not necessarily. Evidence of learning does not rule out the possibility of innate causes. Learning can alter or modify built-in patterns. Although frustration might instinctively heighten the likelihood that a certain type of response (such as aggression) will be instigated, learning can alter or disguise the manifestation of this response. The original formulators of the theory appeared to fall back to this position. In 1964, Miller wrote "It seems highly probable that . . . innate patterns exist, that they play an important role in the development of human social behavior, and that these instinctual patterns are modifiable enough so that they tend to be disguised by learning, although they may play crucial roles in motivating, facilitating, and shaping socially learned behavior" (p. 160).

3. *Does Research Support the Frustration-Aggression Hypothesis?* Evidence derived from studies using both human and nonhuman subjects seems to support the notion that aggression *may* be caused by frustration (see Azrin, Hutchinson, & Hake, 1966; Rule & Percival, 1971). For example, Buss (1963) subjected college students to three types of frustration: failing a task, losing an opportunity to win money, and missing a chance to earn a better grade. Each type of frustration led to approximately the same level of aggression, and in each case the level of aggression was greater than in a control condition where no frustration was experienced. Yet the level of aggression exhibited was not very great in any case. Perhaps the aggression was minimal because it could not serve to overcome the cause of the frustration. Buss (1961, 1966) suggests that frustration and aggression may be linked only when the aggression has *instrumental value*—that is, when aggressive behavior will help to override the frustration. Other studies also have reported no increase in aggression as a result of the degrees of frustration produced in human subjects in the laboratory (Gentry, 1970; Taylor & Pisano, 1971).

We know less about the possible links between frustration and aggression outside the laboratory. On the one hand, an extensive observational study of children's everyday behavior found little evidence to suggest that frustrating behavior leads to aggression (Fawl, 1963). In contrast, some investigators have suggested that most homicides can be interpreted as aggressive acts that result from frustration (Berkowitz, 1974). Although it is true that most homicides are not planned, but instead are fairly quick reactions to a situation (Mulvihill & Tumin, 1969), the somewhat automatic nature of the aggressive response does not necessarily prove the existence of frustration. Other precipitating causes, such as direct attack, have been found to be potent causes of aggression in the laboratory (Gaebelein & Taylor, 1971; Rule & Hewitt, 1971) and may be assumed to precipitate aggression outside the laboratory as well.

Most researchers believe that factors other than frustration are necessary to elicit aggressive behavior, and a number of revisions of the frustration/aggression formulation have been proposed. The most influential of these revisions has been proposed by Berkowitz (1965b, 1969, 1971), who emphasizes *the interaction between environmental cues and internal emotional states.*

Berkowitz suggests that the reaction to frustration creates "only a *readiness* for aggressive acts. Previously acquired aggressiveness habits can also establish this readiness" (Berkowitz, 1965b, p. 308). In other words, Berkowitz maintains that the occurrence of aggressive behavior is not solely dependent on frustration (a point that Neal Miller also is willing to grant) and that an intervening variable—a readiness—must be added to the chain.

According to Berkowitz, a second factor in the occurrence of aggressive behavior is the presence of aggressive cues in the environment that serve as triggers for the expression of aggression. Frustration creates the readiness of anger; stimulus cues can actually elicit aggression. Furthermore, the cues themselves can increase the strength of the aggressive response, particularly when the aggressive response is impulsive in nature (Zillman, Katcher, & Milavsky, 1972).

Although stimulus cues aren't always necessary for aggression to occur, Berkowitz would argue that they generally increase the probability of aggressive behavior.

Do aggressive cues really elicit aggressive behavior? In a systematic research program conducted by Berkowitz and his colleagues at the University of Wisconsin, considerable support for this position has been established. In a typical experiment, a male college student is introduced to another subject, who, in reality, is a confederate of the experimenter. The confederate either angers the subject deliberately or treats him in a neutral manner. Immediately after this phase of the experiment, both people watch a brief film clip—either a violent prize-fight scene from the film *Champion* or a neutral film showing English canal boats or a track race. After watching the film clip, the subject is given an opportunity to administer electric shocks to the accomplice. Using this basic paradigm, Berkowitz and his colleagues have developed a variety of tactics to create aggressive cues in the environment. In one experiment, for example, the accomplice was introduced either as a nonbelligerent speech major or as a physical education major who was interested in boxing. When the confederate was introduced as a boxer, the subjects administered more severe shocks (Berkowitz, 1965a). In another experiment, the confederate was introduced either as Kirk Anderson (presumably providing an association with Kirk Douglas, who was the actor in the film) or as Bob Anderson. Once again, the aggressive-cue value of the confederate affected

the level of aggression displayed by the subject (see Table 10-1).

Other experiments in this series have focused on the aggressive cue value of weapons (Berkowitz & LePage, 1967). For example, in one such experiment, male university students received either one or seven electric shocks from a student (confederate) and then were given an opportunity to administer shocks in return. While some subjects participated in the study, a rifle and a revolver were placed on a nearby table; for other subjects, no objects were present. As one might expect, the subjects who had been shocked more by the confederate were apt to administer shocks in return. More importantly, the presence of the guns increased the average number of shocks administered from 4.67 to 6.07. The results of this experiment have important theoretical and practical implications. At a theoretical level, they clearly support Berkowitz's hypotheses concerning the role of aggressive cues in eliciting aggression. At a more practical level, the results suggest the dangers in a society that allows the free display of dangerous weapons. As Berkowitz has phrased it, "Guns not only permit violence, they can stimulate it as well. The finger pulls the trigger, but the trigger may also be pulling the finger" (Berkowitz, 1968, p. 22). Examination of the difference between Canada and the United States seems to support these findings. In Canada, where firearms such as revolvers and submachine guns must be registered and may not be owned for the purposes of "protection," the homicide rate is considerably lower than in

T A B L E 10 - 1 / *Mean Number of Shocks Given to Accomplice*

Accomplice's Name	Aggressive Film		Track Film	
	Angered	Nonangered	Angered	Nonangered
Kirk	6.09$_a$	1.73$_c$	4.18$_b$	1.54$_c$
Bob	4.55$_b$	1.45$_c$	4.00$_b$	1.64$_c$

Cells having a subscript in common are not significantly different (at the .05 level) by Duncan multiple range test.

From "Film Violence and Cue Properties of Available Targets," by L. Berkowitz and R. G. Geen, *Journal of Personality and Social Psychology*, 1966, *3*, 525–530. Copyright 1966 by the American Psychological Association. Reprinted by permission.

the United States. Similarly, in England, where even the police do not carry guns, reported incidents of violence are markedly lower than in the United States.

Although the archival sources of homicide rates appear to be consistent with the findings of Berkowitz and LePage, their experiments have not gone unquestioned. Some experiments have demonstrated a similar "weapons effect" (Frodi, 1975; Leyens & Parke, 1975), but others have failed to do so (Buss, Booker, & Buss, 1972; Page & Scheidt, 1971). Some people have suggested that the effect might be due to demand characteristics (recall our discussion in Chapter 2), although Berkowitz and LePage (1967) do not believe that this is a sufficient explanation. Others have suggested that the presence of weapons is not sufficient if the person fails to interpret the weapons appropriately (Fraczek & Macaulay, 1971; Turner & Simons, 1974). At this point, then, it is best to conclude that, although weapons sometimes increase the probability of aggressive behavior, we aren't yet certain of the exact conditions under which such effects occur.

To summarize the frustration-aggression theory, we can say with considerable certainty that frustration and aggression often are related; however, although frustration sometimes leads to aggression, it can lead to other actions as well. Similarly, aggression can sometimes be the direct result of frustration, but aggressive behavior has a number of other possible causes. Furthermore, Berkowitz has demonstrated that aggressive cues in the environment can increase the probability of aggressive behavior, although whether they are essential and whether they always increase aggression remain questions for future research.

C. Social-Learning Explanations of Aggression

Our third theoretical explanation of aggression views aggression as a totally learned behavior. Rather than focusing on the concept of instinct or an innate drive to be aggressive, social-learning theorists look to the conditions in the environment that

lead someone to acquire and maintain aggressive responses.

Many psychologists believe that, although the aggressive behavior of lower animals can be explained by instinctual processes, the behavior of humans is not regulated by internal drives—rather, it is learned. Psychologist J. P. Scott has concluded that "all research findings point to the fact that there is no physiological evidence of any internal need or spontaneous driving force for fighting; that all stimulation for aggression comes eventually from forces present in the physical environment" (Scott, 1958, p. 98). If aggressive behavior is indeed learned, how does such learning take place? Proponents of this viewpoint have suggested two methods: instrumental learning and observational learning (Bandura, 1973).

The principle of **instrumental learning** suggests that, if a particular behavior is reinforced, or rewarded, that behavior will be more likely to occur in the future. Therefore, if a person acts aggressively and receives a reward for doing so, he or she is more likely to act aggressively on other occasions. Although instrumental-learning studies in animals generally limit the reinforcement to food, the possible range of reinforcements for humans is broad (Baron, 1977). For example, social approval or increased status can act as reinforcements of aggressive behavior (Geen & Stonner, 1971; Gentry, 1970). Money can act as a reinforcement for adults (Buss, 1971; Gaebelein, 1973), and candy has proved to be an effective reward for children (Walters & Brown, 1963). For the person who is extremely provoked, evidence of a victim's suffering can serve as a form of reinforcement (Baron, 1974; Feshbach, Stiles, & Bitter, 1967), suggesting a mechanism whereby mass executioners are able to perform their activities.

Although many aggressive responses can be learned through direct reinforcement, most investigators believe that **observational learning**, or social **modeling**, is a more frequent method of acquiring aggressive behaviors. Specifically, it has been demonstrated on many occasions that we learn new behaviors through observing the actions of other people (called *models*). Consider the following situation. A child in a nursery school is brought to a room and asked by an experimenter to join in a game. The experimenter then takes the child to one corner of the room and shows him or her how to make pictures by using potato prints and colorful stickers. Soon thereafter, the experimenter brings an adult into the room and takes that person to another corner, where a mallet, a set of Tinker Toys, and an inflated Bobo doll are placed.

After the experimenter leaves the room, the adult begins to play with the "adult toys." In a nonaggressive condition, the adult plays quietly with the Tinker Toys for ten minutes. In an aggressive condition, the adult spends most of the time attacking the Bobo doll, hitting it, kicking it, pounding its nose, and yelling aggressive comments such

as "Sock him in the nose!" The experimenter returns and takes the child to another room with another set of toys. After frustrating the child briefly by telling him or her that play with a favorite toy is not allowed, the experimenter gives the child an opportunity to play with any of the other toys in the room. These include aggressive toys (such as a Bobo doll, a mallet, and several dart guns) and nonaggressive toys (such as crayons, toy bears, a tea set, and plastic farm animals).

In this and similar experiments by Bandura, Ross, and Ross (1961, 1963a) experimenters were interested in the ways in which the observation of an adult's aggressive behavior would affect a child's play choices. The adult's behavior did have an effect (see **Figure 10-3**). The children who had watched an aggressive adult model were consistently more aggressive than the

Figure 10-3. Children playing with Bobo doll after observing an aggressive model. (From "Imitation of Film-Mediated Aggressive Models," by A. Bandura, D. Ross, and S. A. Ross, *Journal of*

Abnormal and Social Psychology, 1963, 66, 3–11. Copyright 1963 by the American Psychological Association. Reprinted by permission.)

children who had watched a nonaggressive model. (They also were more aggressive than members of control groups, who had watched no model at all.) Although these experiments demonstrate that children can model behaviors that they observe, some critics have suggested that they do not really focus on aggression (Klapper, 1968). Recall that, in our definition, we suggested that aggression should be limited to those instances in which behavior is directed against another living being. A Bobo doll doesn't seem to qualify; however, recent investigations have shown that aggressive behavior directed toward a Bobo doll does relate to other forms of aggression. Nursery school children who behaved most aggressively toward the inanimate doll also were rated as being most aggressive in general by their teachers and their peers (Johnston, DeLuca, Murtaugh, & Diener, 1977).

Even if an attack on a Bobo doll cannot be considered a true case of aggression, Bandura (1973) has argued for the importance of the experiments in demonstrating the ways in which aggressive behaviors can be acquired. He makes the important distinction between *learning* and *performance* of a response. Presumably, the modeling of the attacks allows the child to learn, or acquire, a response; subsequently, behaviors involving human beings might allow the *performance* of the acquired response. Many studies with adults attest to the importance of modeling (Bandura, 1973). Although most adults have acquired the knowledge of aggressive behavior, their willingness to perform such behavior is often based on the presence of an aggressive model. The model might not serve as an instructional source, but he or she could act as a *disinhibiting* factor—an example that says "it's all right to be aggressive in this situation."

In summary, social-learning theorists focus their attention not only on the ways in which aggressive behavior is learned but also on the conditions under which it is instigated and maintained (Bandura, 1973; Baron, 1977). They focus on the external conditions that lead to aggressive behavior and, on the opposite side of the coin, control aggression. We will return to the issue of control later. At this point, however, it is important to note that, to the extent that aggression is externally rather than internally determined, the possibilities of controlling aggression may be more promising.

III. Conditions That Influence Aggression

We've examined three theoretical perspectives that differ in the degree to which they believe aggression is caused by innate, or intrapersonal, factors. Although they also differ in the degree to which they consider environmental, or external, factors to be causal, each perspective gives some recognition to the importance of environmental factors: as a releasing mechanism for the ethologists, as a stimulus cue in the revised frustration-aggression hypothesis, and as a direct source of learning and performance for the social-learning theorists. Let us now turn to a consideration of some of the factors and situations that influence the occurrence and the extent of aggressive behavior.

A. *Frustration*

As we said earlier, some evidence suggests that an experience of frustration—the blocking of a goal-directed response—leads to aggressive behavior on some occasions. For example, Geen (1968) asked subjects to work on a jigsaw puzzle. In one condition (task frustration), the puzzle was insoluble; in another condition (personal frustration), the task was soluble, but the experimenter's confederate continually interfered with students as they worked, preventing them from completing the puzzle. In both conditions, subsequent aggression toward the confederate was greater than in a control condition. Yet other studies have failed to find a relationship between frustration and aggression, suggesting, as we've discussed earlier, that the relationship between the two factors is not an automatic one. Two conditions are important in predicting whether frustration will lead to aggression: (1) the magnitude of the frustration experienced by the potential aggressor, and (2) the extent to which the thwarting they experience is arbitrary or unexpected (Baron, 1977).

Apparently, frustrations of a fairly mild nature are unlikely to result in aggression; in contrast, intense frustration often leads to aggressive behavior. Although studies that systematically vary the level of frustration across a number of levels have not been conducted, a field study by Harris (1974) suggests the importance of the level of frustration. Harris and her confederates purposefully cut in ahead of people standing at different points in lines for movies, theaters, and grocery stores. If the confederate cut in ahead of the person who was second in line, that person tended to become quite aggressive (verbally), whereas a person who was twelfth in line exhibited many fewer aggressive reactions. Presumably, when you are close to the checkout counter or the ticket window, an interference is much more frustrating than when you still have a considerable way to go.

The second suggestion—that aggressive responses depend on how arbitrary the frustration is—has also received support. In one demonstration of this relationship, Burstein and Worchel (1962) found that group members whose progress was impeded by a member who had a hearing problem were much less aggressive than those group members who had equal difficulty because of one member who appeared to be deliberately blocking the group's progress. Other studies have shown that frustration does not lead to aggression when difficulty is anticipated, but it does lead to aggression when the goal blocking is not expected (Worchel, 1974).

B. *Verbal and Physical Attack*

Although frustration occupied early investigators seeking the causes of aggression, recently the focus has turned to an even more obvious determinant of aggressive behavior—direct verbal and physical attacks. When someone yells at you for no apparent reason, are you likely to scream back? Or if someone walked up to you in the street and began to shove you, what would your reac-

tions be? In all probability, you would be tempted (and might well act) to retaliate with some form of verbal or physical aggression.

Research has shown that attacks are a much more reliable provocation to aggressive behavior than frustration. For example, in the experiment in which Geen (1968) manipulated two types of frustration while students were working on a jigsaw puzzle, a third experimental condition was included in which the subjects were allowed to complete the puzzle (thus eliminating the possibility of frustration). At the completion of the task, however, the confederate proceeded to insult the subject, attacking both his intelligence and his motivation. In this condition, subsequent aggression toward the confederate was stronger than in either of the frustration conditions. In line with these findings, many laboratory investigations of aggressive behavior have included verbal attack prior to the assessment of aggression (Berkowitz, 1965a; Rule & Hewitt, 1971; Buss, 1966).

Other investigations of the importance of direct attack on subsequent aggression have been conducted by Taylor and his colleagues (Taylor, 1967; Taylor & Epstein, 1967). In these experiments, the subjects weren't asked to administer shocks to a passive learner; instead, they engaged in a two-person interaction in which both persons were allowed to administer shocks. (In actuality, the subject's opponent was a confederate of the experimenter or was fictitious—the subject is told that another person is returning the shocks, but, in fact, the schedule of shocks is arranged by the experimenter). In general, these experiments provide clear evidence of reciprocity—subjects tended to match the level of shock that their opponent delivered. If the opponent continued to increase the level of shock, the subject also increased the intensity. Although the absolute level of shock can vary with certain factors—for example, both males and females are more reluctant to administer shock to a female than to a male (Taylor & Epstein, 1967)—the general pattern of increases and decreases in response to the partner's pattern holds true.

We do not always retaliate immediately when we are attacked by another person. Remembering our discussion of attribution in Chapter 3, we might suspect that our judgments of another person's intention to cause us harm would affect our reactions (Rule & Ferguson, 1978). That is indeed the case. In experiments conducted by Dyck and Rule (1978), college men received bursts of aversive noise from a male opponent. The noises were described as either typical of most people (high consensus) or atypical of most people (low consensus). A second variable that the experimenters manipulated was whether or not the opponent had any knowledge of the consequences of his action —whether or not he knew the type and level of noise that he was giving to the subject. Both factors affected the extent to which the subjects exhibited aggressive behavior in return. Less retaliation was shown when the behavior was believed to be typical (thus leading the attribution away from the specific individual), and when the subject believed that the opponent was not aware of the consequences of his actions. An even stronger demonstration of the important role of intent is provided by Greenwell and Dengerink (1973), who found that the intentions of the opponent could be more important than the amount of harm he caused.

Even the perception of our own state of anger can affect the aggression we exhibit. Following the model of Schachter and Singer (1962), Younger and Doob (1978) considered subjects' responses to a provoking opponent after they had been given a placebo that was supposed to either relax or arouse them. When the subjects had an explanation for their arousal—that the pill caused it—they were less likely to shock their opponent than they were when there was no explanation for the stress caused by the opponent's attack (see Table 10-2).

C. *Third-Party Instigation*

Aggression doesn't always occur when two people are in isolation. Often there are witnesses and bystanders who become involved in the interaction. At a prize fight, for example, members of the audience can

TABLE 10-2 / *Mean Number of Shocks Delivered by Condition*

Condition	Pill conditions	
	Arousal	Relaxation
Provocation	8.00_a	12.62_b
No provocation	8.75_{ab}	9.62_{ab}

$N = 8$. Means having no subscript in common are significantly different at better than the .025 level by t test (two tailed).

From "Attribution and Aggression: The Misattribution of Anger," by J. C. Younger and A. N. Doob, *Journal of Research in Personality*, 1978, *12*, 164–171. Reprinted by permission.

enthusiastically urge their favorite to pulverize his opponent. Newspapers frequently report incidents in which pedestrians urge a potential suicide victim to jump. What are the effects of such third-party instigations on the frequency and intensity of aggressive behavior?

In a famous series of experiments, Milgram (1963, 1964, 1965, 1974) explored the effect of an experimenter's commands on the willingness of subjects (in this case, male citizens in New Haven and Bridgeport) to administer shock to another person under the guise of a learning experiment. Many of the subjects agreed to administer the maximum shock level, and Milgram described his findings as analogous to the situations surrounding the Holocaust in Nazi Germany. In subsequent studies, Milgram removed the experimenter pressure but substituted peers who were instructed to urge the subject on. Once again, the effect of external pressure was clear: subjects who were exposed to pro-aggression influences delivered much greater shocks than did those subjects who acted alone.

Not all bystanders are so intrusive, however (see, for example, **Figure 10-4**). What happens when a witness simply observes the aggressive behavior but neither urges nor condemns it? Borden (1975) has demonstrated that the effect of the observer depends in large part on the implicit values he or she conveys. For example, in one case,

Figure 10-4. Aggressive behavior in the presence of a disinterested observer. (Ben Shahn, *Laissez-Faire*, ca. 1947. Collection of the New Jersey State Museum. Gift of Mr. and Mrs. Michael Lewis.)

male subjects participating in the standard shock experiment were observed by either a male or a female student. Subjects who were observed by a male showed a significantly higher level of aggression than did subjects who were observed by a female. After the male observer left, the subjects reduced their level of aggression, whereas subjects' behavior was relatively unaffected by the departure of the female. Why did the sex of the observer have an effect? Borden hypothesized that the norms of our society implicitly suggest that males approve of violence, whereas females are opposed to it. In order to test this hypothesis of implicit values, Borden conducted a second experiment in which the observer belonged either to a karate club (aggressive observer) or to a peace organization (pacifistic observer). In this case, the sex of the observer also was varied, so that both males and females assumed the aggressive and pacifistic roles. With a control over the explicit values of the observer, the sex of the observer had no effect; however, the explicit values were influential. Subjects who were observed by a member of the karate club showed significantly more aggression than did subjects who were observed by a member of a peace organization. Once again, the departure of the aggressive instigator led to a decrease in shock levels, but the departure of the pacifist resulted in no increase in shocks.

Let's look at one more aspect of third-party instigation. Turning the tables slightly, let's consider the ways in which the behavior of the aggressor affects the behavior of the instigator. In other words, what conditions will encourage or discourage the instigator in his or her behavior? Gaebelein has conducted a series of studies that examine the behavior of an instigator of aggression (Gaebelein, 1973, 1977a,b, 1978; Gaebelein & Hay, 1974; Mander & Gaebelein, 1977). These studies indicate that an instigator will become more aggressive in his or her urging if the person actually performing the aggressive behavior is cooperative. Noncooperative partners who refuse to set intense shocks, for example, reduce the recommendations of the instigator. Therefore, when observers are effective in their recommendations of aggressive behavior, they are likely to continue and to increase the pace; when they are unsuccessful, they are less likely to persist. An instigator's urge to increase aggression is minimized when he or she becomes more directly involved in the situation. Gaebelein and Hay (1974) found that instigators tend to "cool it" when they themselves are vulnerable to shock.

In summary, direct urging by an observer or audience member will increase the amount of aggression a person displays. Furthermore, a passive observer who reflects aggressive values can cause increases in aggressive behavior. The instigator is not totally removed—his or her behavior is affected by the cooperation or noncooperation of the aggressor, and the instigations might wane when the recommended aggression is not forthcoming.

D. *Deindividuation*

When people can't be identified, they are more likely to perform antisocial acts. As we saw in Chapter 2, students who participated in a laboratory experiment that involved administering electric shocks were more likely to be aggressive when they were completely disguised by hoods and sheets than when they were identified by name tags (Zimbardo, 1970). Other experiments have used similar manipulations of anonymity and have found that people express more verbal hostility when their own identity is not stressed (Festinger, Pepitone, & Newcomb, 1952; Cannavale, Scarr, & Pepitone, 1970). In discussing the process of **deindividuation,** Zimbardo (1970) has suggested that conditions that increase anonymity serve to minimize concerns with evaluation and in turn weaken the normal

controls that are based on guilt, shame and fear. As a result, the threshold for behaviors that are normally inhibited is lowered, and the individual is more likely to engage in aggressive and other non-normative acts.

The concept of deindividuation can be applied to the victim as well as to the aggressor. For example, Milgram (1965) found that people were more willing to administer electric shocks when they couldn't see the victim and when the victim couldn't see them. In some ways, aggression under these conditions is dehumanized— because people cannot see the consequences of their actions, these actions may be easier to perform. It is probably significant that the genocide of World War II involved gas chambers that could be controlled from a distance and that hoods are often placed over the heads of execution victims. Even when aggression is not severe (for example, honking your horn at a stalled driver in front of you), the inability to see the victim (manipulated by drawing a curtain across the back of the rear window) has been found to increase the tendency of drivers to honk at a stalled motorist (Turner, Layton, & Simons, 1975).

E. *Drugs and Alcohol*

The use of drugs and alcohol is widespread in our society, and the effects of this usage are assumed to be numerous. Popular wisdom, for example, suggests that alcohol facilitates aggression, and cartoons of the hostile drunk are common. Similarly, many people believe that marijuana has the opposite effect—that it tends to "mellow" people out and minimize any tendencies toward aggression. In this instance, the popular wisdom appears to be close to the mark, although research on the topic is still in an infant stage. Taylor and his colleagues have begun a series of studies in which various dosages of either alcohol or THC (the major active ingredient of marijuana) are administered to subjects before they participate in an aggression experiment (Shuntich & Taylor, 1972; Taylor & Gammon, 1975, 1976; Taylor, Vardaris, Rawtich, Gammon, Cranston, & Lubetkin, 1976; Taylor,

Schmutte, & Leonard, 1977). In the aggression situation, subjects compete against a partner in a reaction-time experiment; each player has an opportunity to shock the player who loses on a trial. These specific conditions are important to remember, because it appears that effects are found only when a person is provoked or attacked (Taylor, Gammon, & Capasso, 1976). What happens when alcohol or THC is present in the bloodstream of a potential attacker? As shown in Figure 10-5, the two substances have quite different effects. Although low doses of alcohol (.5 ounces of alcohol per 40 pounds of body weight, or the equivalent of one cocktail) actually reduce the level of aggression (compared to a group that has had no alcohol), larger doses of alcohol (1.5 ounces per 40 pounds of body weight) have quite the opposite effect. (Substantially higher shock was administered by subjects who had consumed large doses of alcohol.)

Marijuana has a different effect. Small amounts of THC (1.82 milligrams per 40 pounds of body weight) have virtually no effect on aggressive behavior, whereas larger doses (5.44 milligrams per 40 pounds of body weight) decrease the tendency toward

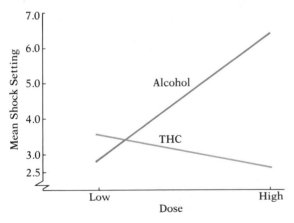

Figure 10-5. Mean shock settings as a function of high and low doses of alcohol and THC. (From "The Effects of Alcohol and Delta-9-Tetrahydrocan-Nabinol on Human Physical Aggression," by S. P. Taylor, R. M. Vardaris, A. Rawtich, C. B. Gammon, J. W. Cranston, and A. Lubetkin, *Aggressive Behavior*, 1976, *2*(2), 153–161. Copyright 1979 by Alan R. Liss, Inc. Reprinted by permission.)

aggressive behavior. Although too little research has been done to regard these results as conclusive, they certainly suggest that reasonably large amounts of alcohol can cause an increase in aggressive behavior— at least in response to provocation— whereas marijuana acts as an inhibitor or a depressant of aggressive reactions.

F. *Environmental Factors*

Psychologists have only recently become interested in the effects of the environment on our behavior, a topic that will be discussed at greater length in Chapter 19. Popular wisdom, however, has suggested links between the physical environment and behavior. For example, you might complain that you feel grouchy because the air conditioning in your room doesn't work on a hot day, or because the noise of construction outside your office makes you irritable. Do these conditions—specifically, noise and heat—have any demonstrated effect on aggressive behavior?

Research suggests that, under some conditions, unpleasant levels of noise cause an increase in aggressive behavior. For example, Donnerstein and Wilson (1976) found that, when subjects were exposed to loud bursts of noise while given the opportunity to administer shocks to a partner, the intensity of the delivered shocks was significantly higher than when either low-level noise or no noise was present. Other investigators have had similar results (Geen & O'Neal, 1969; Konečni, 1975a). In each case, however, increases in aggression were found only when the subjects had been provoked or angered. As in the case of alcohol, the external stimulus in and of itself is insufficient to produce aggression, but it does lower the threshold so that, when an instigation to aggression is present, the aggression will be displayed more readily.

The supposed effects of heat on aggressive behavior have been more widely proclaimed than the effects of noise. During the 1960s, when the outbreak of civil disturbances in the United States was extensive, the mass media frequently emphasized the "long hot summer" effect (see Box 10-1).

Heat was cited as a cause of riots. Indeed, the majority of disturbances did occur during the summer months (U.S. Riot Commission, 1968).

Laboratory experiments do not support a simple relationship between temperature and aggressive behavior. In a series of experiments, Baron and his colleagues (Baron, 1972; Baron & Bell, 1975; Baron & Bell, 1976; Bell & Baron, 1976) found that, under some conditions, heat increases the tendency toward aggression, even in subjects who haven't been angered; however, in other cases, higher temperatures seem to decrease the tendency toward aggression. Although the initial set of findings was somewhat confusing, Baron (1977) has provided an intriguing explanation that appears to incorporate all of the findings. Specifically, he suggests that aggression is mediated by the level of negative affect or discomfort that a person experiences, and that the relationship between this discomfort and aggression is a curvilinear one. In other words, at very low levels of discomfort or at very high levels of discomfort, aggression is minimized. Aggression is most likely to occur at intermediate levels of discomfort.

This complex explanation has been supported by other laboratory findings. For example, Palamarek and Rule (1979) either insulted or did not insult college males in a room that was either fairly comfortable (about 73° F) or unreasonably warm (about 96° F). When they were given a choice of tasks to perform, the men who had been insulted were more likely to choose a task that allowed them to aggress against their partners when the temperature was comfortable, but they were less likely to choose the aggressive task when the room was excessively warm. Again, these results support the curvilinear interpretation: moderate arousal, caused by *either* insult or heat, leads to greater aggression, but when both factors are present *or* when both are absent, less aggression occurs.

G. *Cross-Cultural Comparisons*

Those who explain aggression as a learned response claim that, if there are societies in which no aggressive behavior is manifested, one can conclude that learning, rather than instinct, plays a dominant role in aggression. Such societies *do* exist. For example, in the United States and Canada, members of isolated communities such as the Amish, the Mennonites, and the Hutterites strive to achieve peaceful coexistence. The Hutterites advocate a life of pacifism; aggressive acts in their society go unrewarded (Eaton & Weil, 1955, cited in Bandura & Walters, 1963). Gorer (1968) has reviewed anthropological evidence of societies whose goal is peaceful isolation; these societies include the Arapesh of New Guinea, the Lepchas of Sikkim, and the Pygmies of central Africa.

The societies described by Gorer have several characteristics in common that facilitate the development and maintenance of nonaggressive behavior. First, they tend to exist in rather inaccessible places that other groups do not covet as a living area. Whenever other groups have invaded their territory, the response of the members of these societies has been to retreat into even more inaccessible areas. Second, members of these societies are oriented toward the concrete pleasures of life—such as eating, drinking and sex—and an adequate supply of these pleasures apparently satisfies their needs. Achievement or power needs are not encouraged in children: "the model for the growing child is of concrete performance and frank enjoyment, not of metaphysical symbolic achievements or of ordeals to be surmounted" (Gorer, 1968, p. 34). Third, these societies make few distinctions between males and females. Although differences between male and female roles exist in each of these societies, no attempt is made to project (for instance) an image of brave aggressive masculinity.

Although the majority of societies in the world exhibit some forms of aggression (Rohner, 1976), the existence of nonaggressive societies reminds us of the malleability of human nature and the great diversity in "normal" behaviors from one society to another (Eisenberg, 1972). Both within and between societies, there appears to be a variety of conditions that encourage or discourage the display of aggression. Any instinctual readiness to aggress, if it exists,

Box 10-1. Violence as a Function of Temperature.

Is there a "long hot summer" effect? If so, what is its function? Do riots increase only up to a certain point as the temperature rises? Temperature and aggression are almost certainly related, but the exact form of that relationship is still subject to dispute.

Using archival data, Baron and Ransberger (1978) attempted to test the relationship between temperature and instances of collective violence. First, they identified the instances of collective violence in the United States between 1967 and 1971. Then they obtained records of the average temperature on the days on which the violence occurred. Plotting these two pieces of information on the same graph, they found the results shown in this graph. (Because a number of the riots surrounded the death of Martin Luther King, Jr., two separate graphs were calculated, although the two do not appear to differ very much.) In general, the results seem to support Baron's contention that temperature and aggression are related in a curvilinear manner: riots are more likely to occur as the days get hotter—but only up to a point.

This conclusion has not gone unchallenged, however. Underlining some of the problems of archival studies, Carlsmith and Anderson (1979) have suggested that Baron and Ransberger did not take account of the number of days in different temperature ranges. In other words, if 80-degree days are more common than 90-degree days, simple probability would lead us to expect more riots in the former periods than in the latter. To demonstrate their point, Carlsmith and Anderson showed that the frequency of baseball games played by the New York Mets in 1977 also could be represented as a curvilinear relationship, very similar to the one presented by Baron and Ransberger.

Is there any way to determine the true relationship in the nonexperimental field setting? By using simple probability theory, Carlsmith and Anderson calculated the likelihood of a riot for each temperature interval. Their corrected results suggest a simple linear relationship—the higher the temperature, the more likely a riot.

This controversy illustrates some of the problems involved in moving from the controlled laboratory to the uncontrolled field. The move certainly should be made, but the initial outcomes are not always clear-cut.

From "Ambient Temperature and the Occurrence of Collective Violence: The 'Long Hot Summer' Revisited," by R. A. Baron and V. M. Ransberger, *Journal of Personality and Social Psychology*, 1978, 36, 351–360. Copyright 1978 by the American Psychological Association. Reprinted by permission.

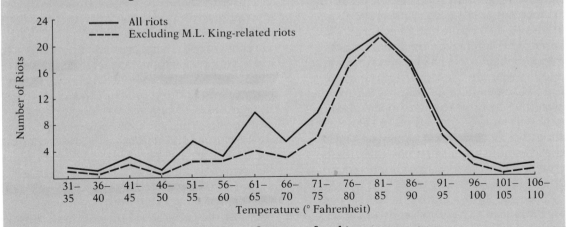

Frequency of collective violence (riots) as a function of ambient temperature.

can surely be modified by the learning experiences that occur.

IV. Violence and the Mass Media

A woman was driving through the Roxbury section of Boston when her car ran out of gas. As she returned to the car with a 2-gallon can of gasoline, she was forced into a back yard by six young men, who beat her and ordered her to douse herself with the fuel. Then one of the men tossed a burning match on her—the woman burned to death. Just two nights prior to this incident, the film *Fuzz*, in which a similar crime is depicted, had been shown on national television.

In San Francisco, a 9-year-old girl was raped with a discarded beer bottle by four teenagers, enacting a scene similar to one shown four days earlier in the made-for-TV movie *Born Innocent*. The mother of the girl sued the network that broadcast the film for $11 million in damages, claiming that the television drama had inspired the attack.

In Florida, a 15-year-old boy killed his 82-year-old neighbor for no apparent reason. The lawyer for the defendant claimed that the boy was legally insane at the time of the murder as a result of watching too much television (see Figure 10-6).

Do presentations of violence in the media—on television and in films—encourage the observer to act aggressively? Is aggression in our society greater than it would be if such presentations were not available? These questions are of great importance not only to social psychologists but also to the population in general. The existence of violence on television is not subject to dispute. It has been estimated, for example, that, by the age of 16, the average child (who spends more time watching television than he or she spends in the classroom) will have witnessed more than 13,000 killings on TV (Waters & Malamud, 1975). Yet the establishment of a possible link between observation and subsequent aggression has been a difficult task.

The first claims that witnessed aggression could lead to aggression by observers emanated from Bandura's studies of chil-

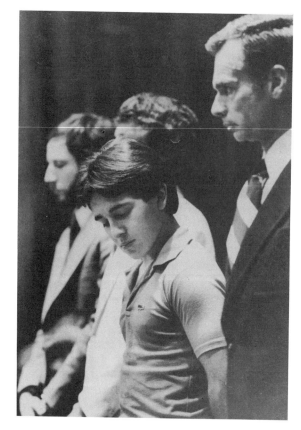

Figure 10-6. Ronney Zamora in court. The defense attorneys in the Zamora case attempted to prove that their defendant was innocent by virtue of television-induced insanity. Their attempts were unsuccessful, and young Zamora was convicted of murder. (© United Press International.)

dren's behavior with a Bobo doll, which we discussed earlier. In some of these studies, the aggressive model was a live actor who was in the room with the child; in other cases, the model was presented on film or in the form of a cartoon character (Bandura, Ross, & Ross, 1961, 1963a). Although Bandura (1965) pointed out that the acquisition of aggressive responses does not automatically ensure that such responses will be used on subsequent occasions, other investigators have suggested a relationship between play behavior and aggressive behavior in other situations (Johnston, DeLuca, Murtaugh, & Diener, 1977). Yet there were many criticisms of the generalizability of these initial findings (see Klapper, 1968). Critics pointed out that the laboratory situation was a highly artificial one: Bobo dolls are not people, films of adults hitting Bobo dolls are not the typical TV fare, and the opportunity to commit identical acts in a laboratory does not prove that people will learn from a TV show and then act more aggressively (Baron, 1977).

Responding to these criticisms, investigators attempted to study situations that were similar to the actual television-viewing experience. In laboratories, they began to use material from actual television shows and to consider their effects on various forms of aggression. For example, Liebert and Baron (1972) showed children excerpts from either *The Untouchables,* a television crime show that was popular during the 1960s, or from a televised sports event. After watching one of the two films, children had an opportunity to either help or hurt another child (actually nonexistent) by pushing a signal button. The children who had watched the excerpts from crime shows were more likely to push the "hurt" button than were the children who watched the sports event. Children who watch violent films also are more likely to believe that other people behave aggressively (Thomas & Drabman, 1977) and to tolerate aggression in others (Drabman & Thomas, 1974; Thomas & Drabman, 1975). Moreover, studies have found similar patterns of results with adults (Berkowitz & Geen, 1966, 1967; Walters, Llewellyn-Thomas, & Acker, 1962). Although these studies are consistent with the original Bandura findings, other evidence suggests that the relationship between observed violence and subsequent aggression is not an automatic one. For example, Berkowitz and Alioto (1973), have proposed that the observed violence must be justified in the film presentation in order for aggression to result. Other investigators suggest that the effects of observed aggression might be very short-lived and that they could have little consequence beyond a brief period of time (Doob & Climie, 1972; Buvinic & Berkowitz, 1976). Still other studies have found no increase in aggression following exposure to a violent film (Manning & Taylor, 1975), although, in the Manning and

Taylor study, the film clip presented was little more than a minute in length.

Since laboratory studies do not clearly establish a relationship between observed violence and aggression, many investigators have turned to field experiments and field studies in an attempt to assess the relationship under more realistic circumstances. In the case of field studies, many investigators have examined the relationship between the amount of violence watched on TV and the amount of aggressiveness exhibited in everyday behavior, as assessed, for example, by the ratings of peers (Eron, 1963). Such a relationship has been found. In fact, there is a modest correlation (approximately + .30) between the amount of TV watched at age 8 and the amount of aggressiveness exhibited ten years later (Eron, Huesman, Lefkowitz, & Walder, 1972). Such correlational studies, of course, allow for a variety of possibly causal explanations. For example, perhaps children who are aggressive choose to watch violence on TV and continue to exhibit aggressive behavior throughout their lives. Although the connection is an interesting one, it doesn't prove that television viewing causes aggression.

In an attempt to isolate cause-and-effect relationships more clearly, a number of investigators have conducted more controlled field experiments. For example, Feshbach and Singer (1971) attempted to regulate the television programs that boys in selected boarding schools and residential schools watched during a 6-week period. Some boys were allowed to watch only programs that were high in aggressive content, whereas other boys were told they could watch only nonviolent programs. (In fact, this manipulation was not completely effective; members of the nonaggressive group protested the restriction, and some allowances in their programming were made.) The results of this experiment showed that boys who watched aggressive programs engaged in less aggressive behavior than did the boys in the other group—they engaged in fewer fist fights and less verbal aggression. However, the methodological difficulties involved with this experiment have led many people to question the value of its results.

A more controlled experiment, conducted in Belgium, produced quite different results (Leyens, Camino, Parke, & Berkowitz, 1975). The manipulation of violent content was achieved through the use of a special "Movie Week," during which teenage boys were surveyed regarding their reactions to films that were shown nightly. During Movie Week, the TV sets in the dormitories in which the boys lived were disconnected. The boys lived in four small dormitories, and previous observation had shown that aggressive behavior was relatively high in two of the dormitories and low in the other two. During the week of film watching, the residents of one aggressive dormitory and one nonaggressive dormitory saw only films that were saturated with violent content (the films included *Bonnie and Clyde*, *The Dirty Dozen*, and *Iwo Jima*). The residents of the other two dormitories saw nonviolent films, including *Lili* and *La Belle Americaine*. As did Feshbach and Singer, Leyens and his associates trained observers to rate the amount of aggressive behavior exhibited by each boy during Movie Week and the week thereafter.

The boys who saw the violent films showed increases in physical aggression. The authors concluded that "the films evoked among the spectators the kind of aggression they had been exposed to" (Leyens et al., 1975, p. 353). Verbal aggression, on the other hand, increased only among the residents of the aggressive dormitory who were shown violent films. Residents of the nonaggressive dormitory who saw the violent films actually exhibited a decrease in verbal aggression. As might be expected, the effects of the content of the films were much more extreme immediately after viewing than they were during later observation periods. Other studies conducted recently in the United States have found similar results (Parke, Berkowitz, Leyens, West, & Sebastian, 1977).

The question of the relationship between observed violence and subsequent aggressive behavior is not totally resolved. Some critics still maintain that there is no evidence to support the suggested link (Kaplan & Singer, 1976). Others, although not so negative, still prescribe caution in drawing conclusions (Stein, 1974; Baron, 1977). Perhaps the safest conclusion to draw, based on available evidence, is that witnessed aggression does make a contribution to future tendencies toward aggression, although the impact might be considerably smaller and perhaps of a shorter duration than the most vocal partisans would suggest. Furthermore, it is important to recognize that many other factors can influence this relationship. For example, the social context in which aggression is witnessed might either exaggerate or minimize subsequent aggressive behavior. For instance, if a child watches violence on television in the presence of an adult who condemns the violence, that child is less likely to behave aggressively in subsequent situations. On the other side of the coin, condoning or encouraging comments made by an adult can result in a greater display of aggressive behavior on the part of a child (Hicks, 1968; Horton & Santogrossi, 1978). These and other contextual factors could prove to be important mediators in the relationship between observed violence and aggression, and they may serve as important keys to the control of aggressive behavior.

V. Violence in Society

Research concerning the effects of violence in the media has taken investigators out of the laboratory and shifted their focus from aggression as measured by shock intensities on laboratory apparatus to aggression in the forms of fights and interactions among people. Let's look more closely at some real-life aggression—behavior that is, unfortunately, very common in U.S. society and in many others as well.

A. *Violence in the Home*

Apparently, when it comes to aggressive behavior, "there's no place like home." Commuter students, asked to describe episodes of anger that had occurred to them, reported that episodes of verbal or physical aggression were most likely to occur in the home, and that relatives (such as parents, offspring, and spouses) were the most frequent targets of aggression (Fitz & Gerstenzang, 1978). Indeed, terms such as *wife beating*, *husband beating*, and *battered children* have become common in recent years. Some social scientists have described the family as the "cradle of violence" (Steinmetz & Straus, 1973).

Straus and his colleagues have conducted an extensive series of studies in an attempt to describe and explain the incidence of family violence (Steinmetz & Straus, 1974; Straus, 1973). Their research shows that aggressive behavior in the family is terribly frequent, if not commonplace. For example, in a study of more than 2000 married couples in the United States, these investigators found that more than 25% of the couples had engaged in some form of physical violence during their married life (Straus, 1977). Both husbands and wives engaged in acts of violence, but the rates for husbands were higher for the more harmful forms of violence, such as beating or using a knife or a gun (see Table 10-3). Comparisons of social-class differences tended to challenge some popular stereotypes. Although white-collar workers indicated less approval of marital violence than did blue-collar workers, the reported frequency of actual aggressive behavior did not differ very much between the two groups. The fact that aggression between spouses is so common (and that such incidents are far more frequent than physical attacks between strangers or mere acquaintances) provides support for Straus' somber description of "the marriage license as a hitting license" (Straus, 1975).

Family violence is not restricted to parents. Children, too, become statistics of domestic violence. For example, a survey of university students revealed that more than half of the students had experienced either actual or threatened physical punishment during their final year of high school (Straus, 1971). Reports of child beating have become increasingly prominent in recent years. Although parent/child aggression is an obvious problem in and of itself, there also are suggestions that the consequences of such aggression extend far beyond the

TABLE 10-3 / *Percent of Couples Engaging in Each Type of Violent Act* (N = 2143)		
	Percent in:	
CRT Violence Item	*1975*	*Ever*
Threw something at spouse	6.7	16.7
Pushed, grabbed, shoved spouse	13.0	23.5
Slapped spouse	7.4	17.9
Kicked, bit, or hit with fist	5.2	9.2
Hit or tried to hit with something	4.0	9.5
Beat up spouse	1.5	5.3
Threatened with a knife or gun	1.0	4.4
Used a knife or gun	0.5	3.7
Any of the above	16.0	27.8

Source: Data from *Behind Closed Doors: Violence in the American Family*, by M. A. Straus, R. J. Gelles, and S. K. Steinmetz. (New York: Doubleday, 1980)

immediate incident. For example, Owens and Straus (1975) report that individuals who experience violence as a child are more likely to favor violence as a means of achieving personal and political ends as adults. In other words, through learning and role modeling, individuals can perpetuate the aggressive behaviors they learned as children.

B. *Violence in the Streets*

Although the home is the most common site of violence, aggressive behavior in our society is by no means limited to the family. Reports of homicides, rapes, and other forms of aggression can be found daily in the newspapers, often as feature articles in some of the more sensational tabloids. According to the Federal Bureau of Investigation and the Royal Canadian Mounted Police, crime rates in the United States and Canada have been increasing yearly. Many behavioral scientists, however, are unconvinced of the accuracy of crime-rate comparisons across years. A portion of the increase in reported crime rates could be due to more extensive disclosure of crimes or to more accurate recording by officials. Even within a single year, it is difficult to state the exact frequency of violent crimes. In the case of rape, for example, it is estimated that a substantial percentage of incidents go unreported, because the victims are embarrassed or are unwilling to face the ensuing legal process, which often focuses questions on the defendant rather than the accused (see Brownmiller, 1975; Russell, 1975).

Although the exact figures on incidents of aggression are difficult to obtain, there is little doubt that violence is extensive in many societies. (Reported statistics show that the United States has the dubious distinction of leading most of the industrialized nations of the world in this regard.) Such evidence certainly testifies to the importance of understanding the causes of aggression and seeing the problem of aggression as more than an academic issue.

C. *Collective Violence*

Collective violence—violence between nations or between identifiable groups within a nation—has always been a part of Western civilization (see Figure 10-7). In surveying the field, Tilly concludes that "historically, collective violence has flowed regularly out of the central political processes of Western countries. Men seeking to seize, hold, or realign the levers of power have continually engaged in collective violence as part of their struggles. The oppressed have struck in the name of justice, the privileged in the name of order, those in between in the name of fear" (Tilly, 1969, pp. 4–5).

Figure 10-7. Violence between Catholics and Protestants has become a way of life in Northern Ireland. (© Gilles Peress/Magnum Photos, Inc.)

An analysis of comparative levels of political violence in the United States has indicated no general chronological trend in the direction of either increased or decreased violence (Levy, 1969). The most violent incidents occurred in the decade between 1879 and 1889, but the subsequent decade had only a moderate rate of such incidents. The 1940s and 1950s had low rates, but the 1960s had one of the highest rates of violent incidents. Canada, too, has had its share of collective violence. Since confederation in 1867, Canadians have fought in four major wars and have rioted over unemployment in the 1930s, conscription in the 1940s, and confederation itself in the 1960s and 1970s.

Some people believe that prolonged, severe hardship is all that is necessary to trigger the collective violence of a revolution. Davies (1962, 1969), however, concludes that the precipitating factor in a revolution is a sudden sharp decline in the status of the underprivileged that comes about immediately after a steady increase in their status. The earlier increase in their socioeconomic or political satisfaction leads people to expect the continuation of such improvements (the curve of rising expectations). As we have seen, predictability is important in making our assumptions about human nature. When expectations are frustrated for many people by an abrupt shift in status, a discrepancy termed a *revolutionary gap* results (Tanter & Midlarsky, 1967) and collective violence is more likely to occur (see Figure 10-8). Under these circumstances people perceive a state of **relative deprivation**; they compare their conditions to earlier conditions or to the conditions of others who serve as a reference group. Among the preconditions of a state of relative deprivation is the belief that one is not responsible for the failure to possess a desired outcome (Crosby, 1976). General support for this analysis is found in a variety of cases, ranging from the French and Russian revolutions to the Civil War in the United States. The possibilities of incidents of collective violence in our society should not go unrecognized. The National Commission on the Causes and Prevention of Violence (1969)

suggests that the rate of violence is a social bellwether: "dramatic rises in its level or modifications in its form tell us something important is happening in our political and social systems" (1969, p. 2).

VI. The Future: How Can Aggression Be Controlled?

Although some form of violence has always existed in our society, we can question whether aggression is inevitable. Can aggressive behavior be controlled or eliminated? The answer to this question is not a simple one.

A. *The Instinctual and Biological Views*

Those theorists who believe that aggression is an innate characteristic of human beings are predictably the most pessimistic about the possibilities of controlling aggressive behavior. As Freud grew older and witnessed the devastation of World War I, he became increasingly resigned to the inevitability of aggression. His theoretical postulation of a death instinct—or a compulsion in all human beings "to return to the inorganic state out of which all living matter is formed" (Hall & Lindzey, 1968, p. 263)—represented the culmination of his pessimism. He saw aggression as a natural derivation of the death instinct.

Psychoanalysts who adopt this position see little chance of restraining our violent behaviors. Freud himself wrote that there is "no likelihood of our being able to suppress humanity's aggressive tendencies" (quoted in Bramson & Goethals, 1968, p. 76). However, two procedures might provide some hope. One, at an international level, is a combining of forces to restrain the aggressive actions of powerful nations. At an individual level, the development of the superego can serve as a way of restraining innate aggressive impulses. Additionally, neo-Freudians advocate participation in socially acceptable aggressive activities (sporting events, debates, and the like) as a way of releasing aggressive energy.

According to ethologists and sociobiologists, who believe that aggression

Figure 10-8. Collective violence in U.S. history: protesting steel workers versus the South Chicago police on Memorial Day, 1937. (Philip Evergood, *The American Tragedy*, 1937. Oil on canvas, 29½″ × 39½″. The Whitney Museum of American Art, New York. Photo by Geoffrey Clements.)

is innate, the possibility of eliminating aggression is unlikely. Our task, then, becomes one of channeling aggression into socially acceptable behaviors. Lorenz (1966), for example, believes that Olympic games, space races to Mars, and similar international competitions provide opportunities for the direction of aggressive behaviors into relatively harmless pursuits (see Figure 10-9). The ethologists encourage us to try to identify, and thereby control, the cues that trigger the expression of aggression.

B. *The Motivational View*

According to motivational theorists, frustration is a major cause of aggression, creating a drive or arousal state that will be expressed in the presence of appropriate cues. Consequently, we might look to ways of reducing frustration as a means of controlling aggression. Ransford (1968) interviewed Blacks living in the Watts area of Los Angeles and found that those with intense feelings of dissatisfaction and frustration were more prone to violent action. The attendant violence of Quebec's separatism movement has been attributed to social and economic frustrations. There are numerous actions that community leaders can take to reduce such frustrations: by providing better services, introducing human-relations training for police, and dealing directly with the causes of frustration, they could reduce aggression and violence.

Motivational theorists have suggested **catharsis** as a means of controlling aggressive behavior. Originally introduced by Freud, catharsis refers to the discharge of energy through the expression of aggressive emotions or through alternative forms of behavior. The role of catharsis in reducing aggressive behavior is stated clearly by Dollard and his colleagues: "The expression of any act of aggression is a catharsis that reduces the instigation to all other acts of aggression" (1939, p. 33). Proponents of the catharsis hypothesis have suggested that fantasy is one way in which aggression can

Figure 10-9. Olympic basketball competition between Canada and Mexico: a release of aggressive energy? (© United Press International.)

be reduced. Although investigators have found that aggressive behavior can result in a decrease in aggressive fantasies (Murray & Feshbach, 1978), the more important relationship (if one is interested in controlling aggressive behavior)—that fantasies can serve to reduce aggressive behavior—has not received much support (Hartmann, 1969; Walters & Thomas, 1963). There is somewhat more support for the notion of behavioral catharsis—that the opportunity to express aggression at the time of frustration reduces subsequent aggressive behavior (Konečni, 1975b). Behavioral catharsis, however, does not reduce the overall incidence of aggressive behavior—it simply controls the future expression at the cost of present violence.

More optimistic grounds for control of aggressive behavior concern the role of appropriate environmental cues. Because such cues are important in the elicitation of aggression, and might even increase the strength of the aggressive impulse, the removal of such cues should serve to reduce aggressive behavior. Therefore, limits on the availability of guns and other aggression-eliciting stimuli could serve as a means of controlling aggressive behavior.

c. *The Social-Learning View*

The social-learning view is far more optimistic concerning the possibilities of controlling aggression. Because social-learning theorists believe that environmental factors control the acquisition and maintenance of aggressive behaviors, they maintain that appropriate changes in environmental conditions can cause a decrease in aggression and violence. For example, social-learning theorists suggest that observation of nonaggressive models leads to the acquisition of nonaggressive behavior. In an experiment that demonstrated this effect, students observed a subject administer electric shocks to a "victim" before the students were given their turn (Baron & Kepner, 1970). As shown in Figure 10-10, the students who observed an aggressive model administered more shocks to the "learner" than did subjects who had not

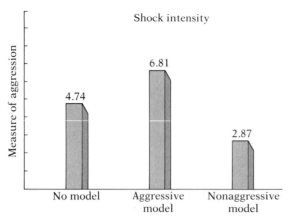

Figure 10-10. The impact of models on overt aggression. (From "Model's Behavior and Attraction Toward the Model as Determinants of Adult Aggressive Behavior," by R. A. Baron and C. R. Kepner, *Journal of Personality and Social Psychology*, 1970, *14*, 335–344. Copyright 1970 by the American Psychological Association. Reprinted by permission.)

observed a model. In contrast, students who witnessed a restrained, nonaggressive model decreased their own aggressive behavior. Other investigators have found similar results (see Donnerstein & Donnerstein, 1977), although the success of the model in reducing an opponent's aggression might be an important qualification (Lando & Donnerstein, 1978). Even more importantly, research has shown that, if both types of models are present, the nonaggressive model can effectively negate the influence of the aggressive model (Baron, 1971). Therefore, even if we cannot eliminate the presence of all aggressive models in society, we might be able to reduce aggression by adding more nonaggressive models to the environment.

Learning theorists advocate nonreinforcement of aggressive responses (Brown & Elliott, 1965). If a person is not rewarded for displays of aggression, aggressive behaviors are less likely to be acquired or maintained. Some people also have suggested that actual punishment or the threat of punishment might serve as a deterrent to aggressive behavior; however, the evidence for

these assumptions is not conclusive. Actual punishment might be an effective deterrent under certain conditions. Baron (1977) suggests four necessary conditions: (1) the punishment must be predictable, (2) it must immediately follow the aggressive behavior, (3) it must be legitimized by existing social norms, and (4) the persons administering the punishment should not be seen as aggressive models (see Figure 10-11). If these conditions are not met, punishment could encourage aggression. The conditions under which the threat of punishment can reduce aggression are perhaps even more limited. A threat appears to be effective only when the person making the threat is not terribly angry, when the anticipated punishment is very great and the probability of its delivery is high, and when the potential aggressor has relatively little to gain by being aggressive (Baron, 1977). These apparent limitations suggest that, in general, threatened punishment is not a very effective means of reducing aggressive behavior.

Investigators have pointed to incompatible responses as a third means of controlling violence. Basically, they suggest that it's difficult to do two things at once; therefore, when conditions induce responses that are incompatible with the expression of aggression, the performance of violent acts should be reduced. Demonstrations of the effectiveness of this strategy have included the use of humorous cartoons (Baron & Ball, 1974), mild sexual arousal (Baron, 1976), and conditions that foster empathy (Rule & Leger, 1976). In each case, subjects were less aggressive when an alternative response was available than they were when aggression was their only choice.

Finally, social-learning theorists have pointed to cognitive factors that might inhibit aggressive behavior. Specifically, they suggest that information concerning mitigating circumstances can lead to reduced aggression. Basically, this theory suggests that explaining a person's aggressive behavior—providing reasons that suggest that the provocation was beyond the person's control—reduces the tendency to counterattack (Zillman & Cantor, 1976; Zillman, Bryant, Cantor, & Day, 1975). Of course, such mitigating explanations are not always available; however, to the extent that they can be introduced and accepted as reasonable, they allow individuals to consciously choose to reduce their aggressive tendencies.

In summary, the social-learning view of aggressive behavior provides a basis for

optimism as we look to the future. A belief in innate aggressive tendencies might lead us to throw up our hands and say "there's nothing to be done; war is inevitable and people are naturally violent," but social-learning theorists point to specific environmental factors that can be controlled and changed. Even if such factors do not

Figure 10-11. There is evidence that punishment may actually serve to encourage aggressive behavior if certain conditions are not met (Baron, 1977). One of these conditions is that the punishment immediately follow the aggressive act. (© Julie O'Neil/Stock, Boston.)

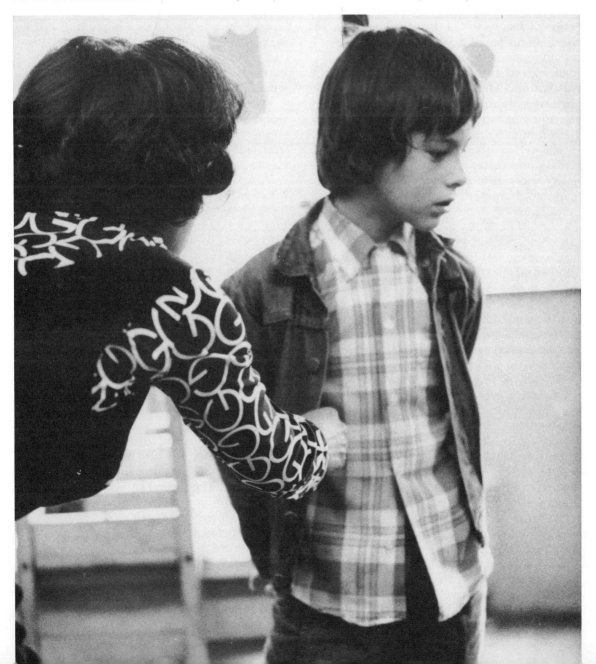

account for all aggressive behavior, they clearly account for a portion of it. These facts should not be overlooked as we seek a more peaceful human existence.

VII. Summary

According to Freud and orthodox psychoanalysts, aggression is an urge that is generated by the body: it must eventually find release. Ethologists believe that intra-species aggression has survival value, be-cause it facilitates selective mating and dis-persion of a species. On the other hand, most experimental social psychologists believe that aggressive behavior can be learned (much like other social behaviors). Many investigators define aggression as any form of behavior that is directed toward the goal of harming or injuring another living being who is motivated to avoid such treatment.

The various theoretical explanations of aggression focus on different causes and consequences. Biological explanations stress the innate character of aggression and con-sider aggression to be part of the basic hu-man condition. Motivational explanations focus on aggression as a drive (either learned or innate) that can be elicited by en-vironmental cues. The frustration-aggression hypothesis is a major statement of this position. Experimental research sup-ports the contention that frustration can lead to aggressive behavior, but frustration is not a necessary condition for aggression to occur.

Social-learning explanations of aggres-sion stress the ways in which aggressive be-havior is acquired and maintained as a function of forces that are present in the physical environment. Both instrumental learning and observational learning are be-lieved to be important processes in the ac-quisition of aggressive behavior. By observ-ing aggressive behavior in other people, an observer can learn how to be aggressive; however, other conditions may be necessary in order for the learned behavior to be per-formed.

Many conditions can influence the occurrence of aggressive behavior. Frustra-tion and direct physical or verbal attack can cause aggression; similarly, instigation by a third party can cause an increase in a per-son's aggressive behavior. Factors such as the level of frustration, the intentions of the person who attacks, and the availability of alternative reasons for anger can affect the amount of aggression exhibited. Aggressive behavior is more likely to occur when the potential aggressor is not readily identifi-able—when he or she is in a deindividuated state.

Preliminary research suggests that moderate amounts of alcohol increase levels of aggressive behavior; marijuana, in con-trast, appears to act as a deterrent. Environ-mental factors such as noise and heat also can affect the amount of aggression exhib-ited, but the relationship is not always a simple linear one.

Cross-cultural comparisons suggest con-siderable variety in the levels of aggression, supporting the argument for learning as an important determinant of aggressive be-havior.

Depiction of violence in the mass media may lead to increases in aggressive behav-ior, although the evidence is not conclusive. Laboratory studies provide fairly strong evidence to support this theory, but field ex-periments suggest that the link between observed violence and aggressive behavior is weak and of fairly short duration.

A large proportion of the violence in our society occurs in the home, between spouses and between parents and children. Other forms of violence in our society include homicide and rape, as well as incidents of collective violence—violence between na-tions or between identifiable groups within a nation. One explanation for the origin of revolutions and other forms of collective violence involves the concept of relative de-privation. When a group experiences an abrupt shift away from past increases in economic and political satisfaction, its members are more likely to revolt or ex-press collective violence.

Prospects for the control of aggression in the future depend in large part on one's theoretical assumptions. A belief that aggression has an innate and instinctual basis leads to relatively pessimistic out-looks. Although aggression might be diverted into socially acceptable forms, its expression is inevitable. Motivational theorists, who believe that catharsis is a means of diverting aggression, point to the added importance of environmental cues. Social-learning theorists rely totally on environmental factors and, as a result, present the most optimistic picture of the control of aggression in the future. Suggested strategies to be employed in reducing aggression include the use of nonaggressive models, nonreinforcement and punishment, incompatible responses, and information regarding mitigating circumstances.

Glossary Terms

catharsis	instrumental learning	observational learning
deindividuation	modeling	relative deprivation
ethology	neo-Freudians	
instinct		

The concept of attitudes is probably the most distinctive and indispensable concept in contemporary American social psychology. GORDON ALLPORT

People are disturbed not by things, but by the views which they take of them. EPICTETUS

You're going to find racism everyplace. In fact, I have never lived a day in my life that in some way—some small way, somewhere—someone didn't remind me that I'm Black. HENRY AARON

11

Attitudes, Prejudice, and Discrimination

With this chapter, we begin the exploration of a different aspect of social psychology—the study of attitudes and attitude change. The concept of attitude has been a central one in psychology. Nearly 50 years ago **Gordon Allport (1935)** grandly described it as "the keystone in the edifice of American social psychology" (p. 798). The concept of attitude is central in most of our daily lives as well. Public opinion pollsters report the results of their latest surveys to eager political candidates. A bachelor cook nervously asks for his guests' opinion on the cheese soufflé. And television network executives impatiently await the report on audience response to their new fall programming.

Attitudes also are important in their own right, serving as an index of how we think and feel about people, objects, and issues in our environment. In addition, they can serve as a clue to future behavior, predicting the ways that we will act when encountering the objects of our beliefs. At an even more general level, the concept of attitude relates to some of the broadest and most serious social issues in our society: the problems of prejudice and discrimination, racism, and sexism. Consider the following examples:

Aloysius Maloney has grown up in Grates Cove, C.B., Newfoundland, one of the many poor fishing villages of the province. His father, a fisherman, was lost at sea. His mother receives only a small welfare check in addition to the family allowance for the family's livelihood. Aloysius is very intelligent and desperately wants to go to a university on the mainland. But a university admissions officer tells him that he can't be admitted to the university because the academic quality of his school is so low. "Everyone knows that Newfoundland's schools are so inferior that no one from that province could survive in college," he is told.

Patricia Wilson has just completed a Ph.D. in history and is seeking a college teaching position somewhere in the Chicago area. Her husband works for a nationwide company there, but it is possible that he will be transferred to another city in the future. Despite her strong credentials and the fact that there are several openings in the area, Patricia gets no job offers. She learns that many heads of departments believe that hiring married females is risky because of their childbearing propensities, their domestic responsibilities, and the likelihood that they will follow their husbands elsewhere.

In these examples, behaviors toward a specific individual are being influenced by general attitudes that are held about groups of people. Prejudice and discrimination are very vivid illustrations of the ways that attitudes and behaviors are related, and we will begin our consideration of attitudes with an exploration of these issues of prejudice and discrimination. Then we can consider the concept of attitude in finer detail, and finally we will return to the general issue of the relationship between attitudes and behaviors.

I. Prejudice and Discrimination: Some Case Studies

Prejudice and discrimination, although the terms are often used interchangeably, are actually two distinct concepts. **Prejudice** refers to an intolerant, unfair, or unfavorable *attitude* toward another group of people (Harding, Proshansky, Kutner, & Chein, 1969); **discrimination** refers to specific *behaviors* toward members of that group which are unfair in comparison with behavior toward members of other groups. To illustrate the ways in which prejudice and discrimination operate, we will consider three "isms": racism, sexism, and the issues surrounding separatism in French-speaking Canada.

A. *Racism*

The term *racism* is somewhat difficult to define, although most people would agree that it includes both prejudice and discrimination as components. **Marx (1970)** has suggested that it includes "hostility, discrimination, segregation and other negative action expressed toward an ethnic group" (p. 101). The **U.S. Commission on Civil Rights (1969)**, in a booklet entitled *Racism in Amer-*

ica and How to Combat It, defines racism as "any attitude, action, or institutional structure which subordinates a person because of his or her color" (p. 1). Thus, racism may exist on an individual level or on an institutional one. In the latter case, we are talking about formal laws and regulations that discriminate against certain ethnic groups as well as about informal social norms that limit the opportunities available to certain ethnic groups (Weissbach, 1977).

Examples of racism are unfortunately all too numerous in our world. In both Great Britain and Canada, for example, attitudes and behaviors toward settlers from India and Pakistan frequently reflect extreme prejudice and discrimination. In South Africa, 3.5 million Europeans live in domination over 12.7 million Africans, and segregation of the races is virtually total. Although some policies are at last changing, Africans have been punished for staying overnight in White areas, are jailed for holding meetings and forming political parties, and must produce pass permits on demand to members of the ruling police force. Few newspapers are allowed to print articles critical of the ruling Nationalist party, and it was not until 1975 that the government permitted any television in South Africa.

During World War II, shortly after the Japanese attack on Pearl Harbor, pressure built in the United States to evacuate Japanese-Americans from the West Coast of the United States and restrict them to internment camps in the interior. Both the mass media and government officials insisted that these Japanese-Americans, two-thirds of whom were U.S. citizens, were a threat to the country's security. Early in 1942, more than 110,000 Japanese-Americans were moved to hastily constructed camps where they were detained for three years (see Figure 11-1). During this same period, other Japanese-Americans, although not moved to camps, were nonetheless subjected to severe prejudice and discrimination. Similarly, thousands of Japanese-Canadians in British Columbia were uprooted and resettled in the interior, most of them losing their homes, farms, and businesses in the process.

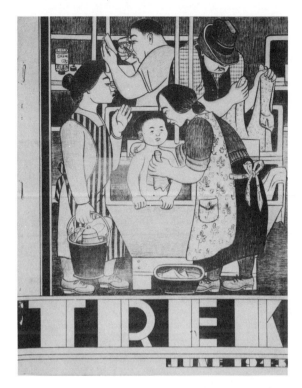

Figure 11-1. Japanese-American relocation often meant crowded conditions and little privacy, as shown in the drawing above made by a Japanese-American artist. (Japanese/American internment camp art, in *Trek* journal, 1942–1943. Oakland Museum.)

Although examples of racism at both the individual and the institutional level are numerous, we will focus our discussion on the role of Black people in U.S. society, in part because this example of racism has been studied most extensively.

At the heart of racism are often stereotypical conceptions of what the target group is like. As we discussed in Chapter 3, **stereotypes** are simplified conceptions about groups of people. Originally the word *stereotype* referred to a metal printer's mold, which could exactly reproduce a printed page. Walter Lippman (1922) borrowed this concept to refer to "pictures in our heads," whereby we tend to see all members of a particular group as being alike in their traits and characteristics (Weissbach, 1977). In the case of Blacks, the stereotypic traits have included characteristics such as laziness, superstitiousness, musical ability, and a pleasure-loving nature (D. Katz & Braly, 1933; Brigham, 1971; Karlins, Coffman, & Walters, 1969).

To some extent, these particular stereotypes have been breaking down in recent years. For example, recent studies show that class distinctions may be more important than racial classification in the stereotypes held by college students (Smedley & Bayton, 1978).

The elimination of stereotypes does not mean the automatic elimination of racism, however. Racism is based on a complex set of attitudes and behaviors at the individual level, on social norms, and on sets of rules and regulations at the institutional level, all of which may remain even after the stereotypes seem to have faded. Brigham and his colleagues, for example, have defined a set of 11 attitude dimensions that interrelate quite highly and that can be used to describe the attitudes of Whites toward Blacks (Brigham, Woodmansee, & Cook, 1976; Woodmansee & Cook, 1967). Included among these dimensions are attitudes toward integration, views on interracial marriage, approaches to racial equality, and attitudes toward Black militance. Each of these dimensions goes beyond the more limited notion of stereotypes about the personality characteristics of particular group members. At the institutional level, many habitual patterns of behavior may contribute to the perpetuation of racism. For example, the real estate agent who resists showing houses in all-White neighborhoods to prospective Black buyers may be following norms, rather than acting on the basis of any individual stereotypes about Blacks.

Social distance is another aspect of prejudice and discrimination and of racism in particular. The term **social distance** is used to refer to a person's acceptable degree of relationship with members of a given group (Westie, 1953). Social distance is usually measured by asking whether the person would accept members of group X as close friends, whether the person would invite them to a party, whether the person would live in the same neighborhood with them, and so on.

In recent years, some controversy has developed among social psychologists about the meaning of social distance. If a White rejects a Black, for example, does the rejection occur because the White assumes that Blacks hold different values or because of more blatant racial reasons? In *The Open and Closed Mind*, social psychologist Milton Rokeach (1960) argued that prejudice or rejection can be largely a result of perceived dissimilarity in values. Rokeach argues that if a White person rejects Blacks, he or she does not do so on the basis of their being Black per se but because the person sees Blacks as possessing different values, habits, and life-styles than Whites. Rokeach, Smith, and Evans (1960) designed two studies in which subjects indicated how friendly they would feel toward a variety of persons who differed in racial and religious backgrounds and in beliefs on important issues. They found that predictions of friendship were based much more on congruence of beliefs between the subject and the stimulus person than on racial or religious similarity.

In contrast, Harry Triandis, another social psychologist, has argued that people *do* reject other individuals because of their race per se: "People do not exclude other people from their neighborhood, for instance, because the other people have different (values), but they do exclude them because they are Negroes" (Triandis, 1961, p. 186). Subsequent research has shown that both positions have some truth (Stein, Hardyck, & Smith, 1965). The degree to which race is a factor in social distance depends on the particular situation. As shown by Triandis and Davis (1965), prejudice can be conceptualized as being made up of several different factors (these factors are described in Table 11-1). The relative impact of characteristics such as race and values may differ considerably from one factor to another. For example, similarity of values is more important than race in determining formal social rejection, but race is a more important factor in friendship rejection. In specific items referring to social distance (Factor IV), race appears to be the most important factor. Triandis and Davis conclude that, in the

T A B L E 11 - 1 / *Five Prejudice Factors Derived by Triandis and Davis*

Factor I. Formal Social Acceptance with Superordination versus Formal Social Rejection, defined by high loadings on items such as "I would admire the idea of," "I would admire the character of," "I would obey," "I would cooperate in a political campaign with."

Factor II. Marital Acceptance versus Marital Rejection, defined by high loadings on "I would marry," "I would date," "I would fall in love with."

Factor III. Friendship Acceptance versus Friendship Rejection, defined by high loadings on "I would accept as an intimate friend," "I would eat with," "I would gossip with."

Factor IV. Social Distance, defined by high loadings on items such as "I would exclude from the neighborhood," "I would prohibit admission to my club," "I would not accept as a close kin by marriage."

Factor V. Subordination, defined by high loadings on items such as "I would obey," "I would not treat as a subordinate," "I would be commanded by."

From "Race and Belief as Determinants of Behavioral Intention," by H. C. Triandis and E. Davis, *Journal of Personality and Social Psychology*, 1965, *2*, 715–725. Copyright 1965 by the American Psychological Association. Reprinted by permission.

case of intimate behaviors, the race of the other person is a determinant for most subjects: Blacks are rejected by Whites even if they are known to be similar in values.

These studies, however, rely on pencil-and-paper measures of abstract situations, and they have been criticized for creating a situation far removed from actual interaction. More realistic studies conducted by Rokeach and his colleagues (Rokeach, 1968; Rokeach & Mezei, 1966) have dealt with students' choices of group members in a discussion task or with employment practices in an actual job setting. These studies showed that values were more important than racial identity in the choices that were made. Although these experimental situations certainly do not represent terribly intimate behavior, the results of these studies do give cause for optimism because of their suggestion that values may outweigh superficial characteristics such as skin color at least in some circumstances.

Although these results are encouraging, they do not ensure that bringing together Whites and Blacks with similar values will bring about social acceptance. As Triandis (1961) and Stein et al. (1965) point out, in the majority of instances of racial discrimi-

nation, the White person does not inquire into the beliefs and values of the Black person to determine whether they are congruent or incongruent with his or her own. Rather, the typical White, with no further information, makes the assumption that the Black's values are different (Stein et al., 1965; Byrne & Wong, 1962). In fact, a highly racist White may *want* to believe that Blacks have values different from his or her own; such beliefs serve as a justification for the White person's prejudice and discrimination. Indeed, Byrne and Wong (1962) found that strongly anti-Black persons assumed more dissimilarity than did less prejudiced persons.

Racism is not just a matter of individual prejudices and attitudes, however. Carmichael and Hamilton (1967), for example, define racism as "the predication of decisions and policies on considerations of race for the purpose of subordinating a racial group and maintaining control over that group" (1967, p. 3). At this level, we must consider how the laws and practices of a society can enforce and perpetuate discrimination against one group by another. In South Africa, as we noted earlier, there is a wide-ranging body of laws and restrictions that keep the Black South Africans separate from the ruling White minority. Until fairly recently, the Untouchable class in India was controlled by a similar set of policies and long-standing norms; members of that class were not allowed to participate freely in the society. Similarly, in the United States, numerous policies have existed that kept Blacks "separate but equal" and perpetuated institutional racism. Many of these policies have changed in recent years. In 1954 the famous *Brown* vs. *The Board of Education* case was evaluated by the Supreme Court, and the decision was made that schools could not be separate—that equality could not be gained through separation of Black and White because such separation would always psychologically imply inequality. Yet, despite considerable gains, it is clear that racism still exists in the United States and that the larger social structure must be considered as important a factor in racism as individual attitudes of prejudice (Wellman, 1977; Willie, 1977).

B. *Sexism*

Sexism operates in much the same way as racism. In the case of sexism, however, the prejudice and discrimination are directed against people by virtue of their *gender* (their physical identity as male or female), rather than according to ethnic or racial group. Sexism incorporates a host of beliefs and behaviors that result in the unfair treatment of women in society (see Figure 11-2). In many respects, racism and sexism are similar forms of prejudice. Kirkpat-

Figure 11-2. Many people, such as those pictured below, believe that passage of the Equal Rights Amendment is necessary to reduce discrimination against women in the United States. The amendment, which states that "Equality of rights under the law shall not be denied or abridged by the United States or by any state on account of sex," has been a focus of considerable debate. (© United Press International.)

rick (1963) has discussed these similarities, pointing to more than 30 ways in which parallels can be drawn, including assumptions of biological inferiority, discriminatory practices in education, and stereotypes of typical characteristics.

As in the case of racism, pervasive stereotypes about the differences between two groups—in the case of sexism, women and men—lie at the heart of the prejudice. Many researchers have asked groups of people to describe what the average man and the average woman are like, and they have found that there is a surprisingly high degree of consensus as to which traits are typical of each sex (Ellis & Bentler, 1973; Rosenkrantz, Vogel, Bee, Broverman, & Broverman, 1968). Frequently the ascribed characteristics fall into two general groups: one collection of traits representing competence and independence and a second group focusing on warmth and expressiveness (I. K. Broverman, Vogel, Broverman, Clarkson, & Rosenkrantz, 1972). Males are generally seen as embodying the competence cluster, whereas women are seen as characterized by the expressive cluster. Table 11-2 lists

some of the traits most frequently associated with males and with females.

Although it might be argued that these two patterns—competency and expressiveness—are different but do not represent more favorable or less favorable impressions, other evidence suggests that the picture is not so optimistic. For example, studies of stereotyping generally find that many more of the characteristics that our Western societies *value* are associated with men than with women. Perhaps even more indicative of the rather negative stereotype associated with women is a study by I. K. Broverman and her colleagues (I. K. Broverman, Broverman, Clarkson, Rosenkrantz, & Vogel, 1970). These authors asked 79 practicing mental-health clinicians (clinical psychologists, psychiatrists, and social workers) to describe the characteristics of one of three types of persons: a normal adult male, a normal adult female, and a normal adult person with sex unspecified. The clinicians were asked to characterize the healthy, mature, socially competent person in each category. The results, not particularly encouraging if sexual equality is our

---

T A B L E 11 - 2 / *Stereotypic Items Typically Used to Describe Males and Females*

Competency Cluster

Feminine	Masculine
Not at all aggressive	Very aggressive
Not at all independent	Very independent
Very submissive	Very dominant
Not at all competitive	Very competitive
Very passive	Very active
Has difficulty making decisions	Can make decisions easily
Not at all ambitious	Very ambitious

Warmth-Expressive Cluster

Feminine	Masculine
Very tactful	Very blunt
Very quiet	Very loud
Very aware of feelings of others	Not at all aware of feelings of others
Very strong need for security	Very little need for security
Easily expresses tender feelings	Does not express tender feelings at all easily

Adapted from "Sex-Role Stereotypes: A Current Appraisal," by I. K. Broverman, S. R. Vogel, D. M. Broverman, F. E. Clarkson, and P. S. Rosenkrantz, *Journal of Social Issues*, 1972, *28*(2), 59–78. Copyright 1972 by the Society for the Psychological Study of Social Issues. Used by permission.

goal, were quite clear-cut. Both male and female clinicians saw the healthy adult male and the healthy adult person as nearly synonymous; the healthy adult female, in contrast, was significantly different from the healthy adult person. For example, both the healthy adult person and the healthy adult male were described by adjectives from the competency cluster (independent, active, competitive), whereas the healthy adult female was seen as possessing far less of each of these characteristics. The healthy adult female was viewed as more submissive, more concerned about her appearance, and more excitable in minor crises—a set of characteristics not attached to either the healthy adult or the healthy male.

Although the existence of less favorable stereotypes of women has an impact in its own right, it also is important in the effect that it can have on other judgments. Beliefs about what men and women are like can have the effect of a **self-fulfilling prophecy**. If women are assumed to be less competent, for example, their performance may be judged as less successful than it actually is. Or, if women are assumed to be less competent, they may be given less opportunity to assert themselves and prove their competence (with the result that they may be viewed as less assertive!). As in the case of racism, sexism does not stop simply with the stereotypes; discriminatory behaviors are practiced as well.

In employment categories, females are under-represented in nearly all professional and prestige occupations. In part, such under-representation may stem from the kinds of behaviors that women encounter as they attempt to prepare themselves for these occupations (see **Figure 11-3**). For example, **Ann Harris (1970)** reports the following responses given by male faculty members to female applicants for doctoral work: "You're so cute, I can't see you as a professor of anything"; "Any woman who has got this far has got to be a kook. There are already too many women in this department"; "I know you're competent, and your thesis advisor knows you're competent. The question in our minds is are you really serious about what you're doing?" and "Why don't you find a rich husband and give this all up?" (A. S. Harris, 1970, p. 285).

Such comments may seem frivolous, but the evidence that women are under-represented in professions and that the full-time working woman has a salary equal to approximately 60% of the salary of the full-time working man are much more serious matters. In fact, it has been estimated that the woman college graduate earns approximately the same salary as the White male with less than a high school education.

Figure 11-3. (Copyright 1974, G. B. Trudeau. Used by permission of Universal Press Syndicate. All rights reserved.)

Numerous studies have documented the existence of bias in hiring women. For example, Fidell (1970) sent a number of academic résumés to department heads of psychology departments at major universities in the United States and asked each head to evaluate the applicant as a potential professor in that department. Two forms—identical except for the sex of the applicant—were used, each going to half of the selected chairmen. The results of the study showed that men were generally offered a higher position than women (that is, associate professor rather than assistant professor), despite the equality of the backgrounds. Lest we infer that only psychologists are biased, it should be noted that A. Y. Lewin and Duchan (1971) found similar results in physics departments.

Dipboye, Fromkin, and Wiback (1975) asked college recruiters from major organizations to rate the desirability of hiring a number of candidates who varied in both sex and competence. Although the academic qualifications of the candidate were clearly the most important factor in the recruiters' decisions, sex again had an effect. Recruiters showed a significant preference for the male candidate over the equally qualified female candidate. In another simulated hiring study, Terborg and Ilgen (1975) found that women were hired as often as men but were offered lower starting salaries. Once hired, these women were more likely to be assigned to routine tasks, thus further limiting their performance on the job.

Whereas the studies just discussed held the job constant and attempted to compare the judgments about males and females, occupations in real life vary tremendously and men and women are distributed unevenly across various occupations. The majority of doctors, carpenters, and steelworkers, for example, are male, and the majority of elementary school teachers, nurses, and secretaries are female. Perhaps not surprisingly, the average salaries in these occupations vary as well, with male-dominated occupations generally receiving higher salaries than the predominantly female occupations.

Part of the explanation for the salary differences for men and women is that occupations with higher prestige ratings generally have a higher percentage of men in the field (Bose, 1973). From one vantage point, this doesn't seem unreasonable. Men pursue advanced education more often than do women and then enter professions requiring this advanced education. Occupations requiring less training will more often be held by women. Do these differences in occupations suggest evidence of discrimination? Probably not. But evidence from Touhey (1974a, 1974b) suggests that occupational prestige is influenced not only by the qualifications required but by the sex of the typical occupant as well. To demonstrate this bias, Touhey presented subjects with descriptions of several traditionally masculine occupations (for example, lawyer, college professor, architect) and asked subjects to rate the prestige of each occupation. In half the cases, the job description pointed out that *an increasing number of women* were expected to enter the field within the next 25 years, while in the other half of the cases the percentage of men was expected to *remain stable*. Without exception, occupations were given lower prestige ratings when the percentage of women in them was expected to increase. Touhey then reversed the situation; he conducted a similar experiment using traditional female occupations (for example, kindergarten teacher, registered nurse, librarian) and described the percentage of men in the job as either stable or increasing. Jobs that more men were expected to enter showed an increase in prestige. Touhey's results are illustrated in Figure 11-4.

These findings show that there are indeed many parallels between racism and sexism. In both instances, negative stereotypes are accompanied by discriminatory behavior in a wide range of areas, including education and employment. There are some important differences between the two "isms," however. For example, the social-distance concept that we discussed in reference to racism does not really apply in the case of sexism. Women's lives have always been intimately intertwined with members of the dominant male group, and

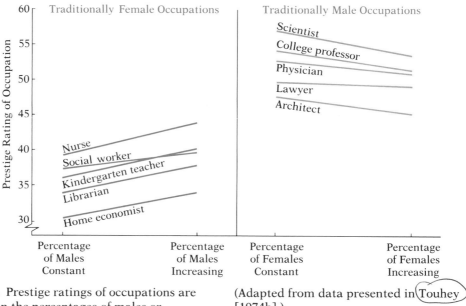

Figure 11-4. Prestige ratings of occupations are dependent on the percentages of males or females who engage in those occupations.

(Adapted from data presented in Touhey [1974b].)

women have experienced far greater informal power through these liaisons than have Blacks (Cameron, 1977). Historically, too, although both Blacks and women have been denied the vote and treated as property by the dominant male, the record of Black slavery is probably a more blatant example of discrimination than the marriage contracts and dowries of women.

C. *Separatism*

In his 1979 New Year's message, Canadian Prime Minister Trudeau warned of the potential for violence in his country. Among other sources of violence, he cited "the prejudices that French-speaking and English-speaking Canadians harbor against one another" (see Figure 11-5). As the third of our "isms," separatism is somewhat different from racism and sexism. The term itself refers to a political movement in Canada, centered in Quebec province and advocating the secession of that province from the rest of Canada. Many of the issues that underlie this movement, however, relate very closely to our discussion of racism and sexism, because a major reason for the movement is the perception by French-

speaking Canadians that there is prejudice and discrimination toward them on the part of English-speaking Canadians. In this case, it is not a physical characteristic, such as skin color or gender, that differentiates the groups; it is language and ethnic origin. Nevertheless, many of the problems are similar.

Stereotypes exist about French Canadians. For example, Canadian students describe French Canadians as excitable, talkative, impulsive, emotional, haughty, religious, and tenacious (Gardner, Wonnacott, & Taylor, 1968). Some of the students had more negative images, viewing French Canadians as unreliable and uncultured; these students were in turn much less favorable about French Canadians as a group. Evidence of discriminatory practices also exists. Studies of the career advancement of

Figure 11-5. Street signs are one indication of the bilingual nature of Canadian society. In the scene opposite, photographed in the province of Quebec, French predominates, and tensions between French-speaking and English-speaking citizens are most prominent here as well. (© Owen Franken/Stock, Boston.)

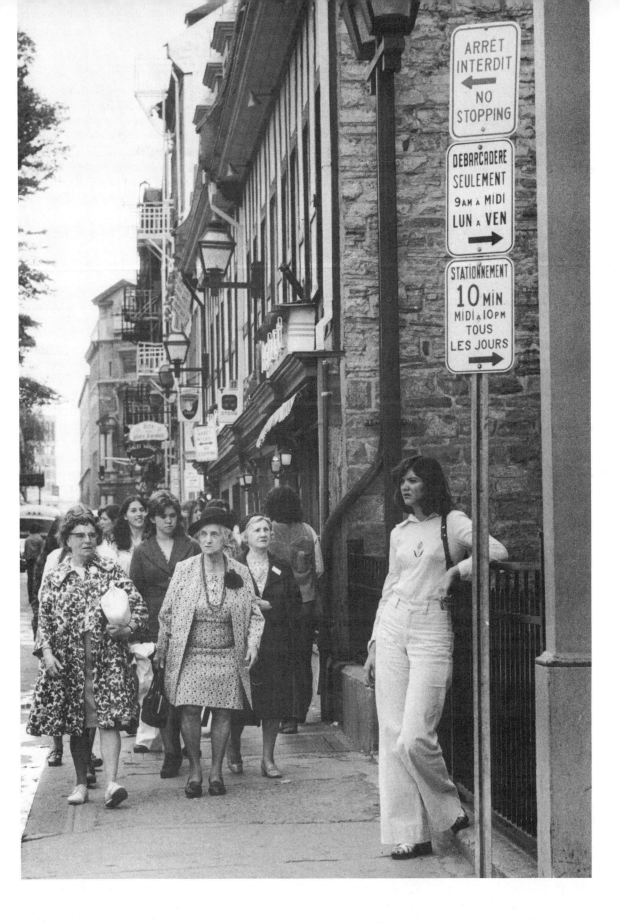

civil servants have shown that French-speaking Canadians make less money on the average than do English-speaking Canadians when factors of age, education, and seniority are equivalent (Beattie & Spencer, 1971). As in the case of racism and sexism, some attempts to explain these disparities between the two groups have focused on characteristics of the more powerful group; other explanations have looked to traits of the group that is discriminated against (Richer & Laporte, 1973). The nature of the explanation that is chosen has important consequences for the actions that are taken to reduce prejudice and discrimination.

II. The Causes of Prejudice and Discrimination

Many theories have been advanced in an attempt to explain why prejudice and discrimination occur. In general, these theories represent two different levels of analysis—the societal and the individual (Ashmore, 1970). Societal explanations are concerned with situational effects on prejudice in given societies, social systems, and

groups and with institutional factors that may encourage and perpetuate discrimination. The individual level of analysis asks why one person is more prejudiced than another. Gordon Allport's classic and readable book *The Nature of Prejudice* (1958) has outlined these various levels (represented in Figure 11-6), and we will discuss each type of theory in turn.

A. *Historical and Economic Emphasis*

The historian reminds us that the causes of prejudice cannot be fully understood without studying the historical background of the relevant conflicts. At the societal level of analysis, it is a sad fact that most prejudices have a long history. Allport points out that anti-Black prejudice in the United States, for example, has its roots in slavery and the slaveowner's treatment of Black families, in the exploitation of Blacks by carpetbaggers, and in the failure of Reconstruction in the U.S. South after the Civil War.

Certain historically oriented theories of prejudice emphasize economic factors. For example, advocates of the theories of Karl

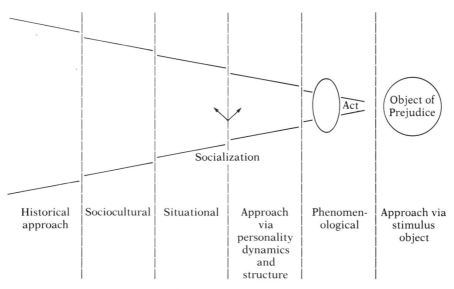

Figure 11-6. Theoretical and methodological approaches to the study of the causes of prejudice. (Adapted from "Prejudice: A Problem in Psychological and Social Causation," by G. W. Allport, *Journal of Social Issues*, Supplement Series No. 4, 1950. Copyright 1950 by the Society for the Psychological Study of Social Issues. Reprinted by permission.)

Marx see prejudice as a way of letting the rulers exploit the laboring class. As O. C. Cox has stated, "Race prejudice is a social attitude propagated among the public by an exploiting class for the purpose of stigmatizing some group as inferior so that the exploitation of either the group itself or its resources may both be justified" (1948, p. 393). Treatment of Black slaves before the U.S. Civil War, of Oriental immigrants in California at the turn of the century, and of Chinese laborers brought in to build the Canadian Pacific Railroad are all examples of the haves vilifying the have-nots. We saw in Chapter 8 how blaming the victim is a strong response when people attempt to solidify their beliefs in a just world; the act of oppression leads to reactions which, in effect, "prove" that such oppressive acts were warranted.

Economic exploitation, however, is of more than historical interest. Women today are denied education and career opportunities, thus permitting their "employment" as homemakers. Similarly, we have seen that occupations in which women are typically employed, though often essential for the society's functioning, are nonetheless paid lower wages than male-dominated occupations. Kenneth B. Clark (1965) has shown how the political, economic, and social structure of Harlem in New York City is in many ways that of a colony, and Eugene McCarthy referred to Black Americans as a colonized people during his 1972 U.S. presidential campaign (see Figure 11-7).

Despite its usefulness in the understanding of prejudice against some minority groups, the historical approach does not provide an all-inclusive answer to the question of the causes of prejudice. It does not explain why some people in power are more prejudiced than others or why some groups are the object of more prejudice than others. The economic-exploitation theory does not explain why certain immigrant groups that came to North America were exploited without suffering the degree of prejudice that Blacks and Jews have received. In the U.S. South, White sharecroppers are exploited by the ownership class to the same degree as Black sharecroppers, yet they

Figure 11-7. A colonized people? An artist's depiction of Harlem. (Romare Berden, *Fortune* cover, 1967, Special Urban Crisis Issue. Offset lithography.)

have not been harassed by lynch mobs or arsonists. Despite these weaknesses, however, consideration of historical and economic factors is important in understanding prejudice and discrimination, particularly in terms of seeing how discrimination may be fostered by institutional factors.

B. *Sociocultural Emphasis*

Sociologists and anthropologists emphasize sociocultural factors as determinants of prejudice and discrimination. Among these sociocultural factors are (1) the phenomena of increased urbanization, mechanization, and complexity; (2) the upward mobility of certain groups; (3) the increased emphasis on competence and training, the scarcity of jobs, and the competition to get them; (4) the increased population in the face of a limited amount of usable land and a lack of adequate housing; (5) the inability of many people to develop internal standards, leading to reliance on others (individuals, organizations, the mass media, or advertising) and a conforming type of behavior; and (6) changes in the role and function of the family, with concomitant changes in standards of morality.

The overt racism demonstrated in the 1970s by members of the British working class may reflect the threat to full employment posed by the influx of large numbers of Pakistanis, Indians, and West Indians (Esman, 1970). The covert racism of a former Canadian government's "Green Paper" on immigration and a more recent report of the Ontario Royal Commission on Education undoubtedly reflects the concern of many White Canadians over the perceived threat to the "stability" of Canadian society posed by the increased numbers of "nontraditional" immigrants, such as Blacks from the United States and the Caribbean and Orientals from Vietnam.

Increased urbanization also can be considered a cause of prejudice against ethnic groups. G. Watson (1947) found that many of the people he studied became more anti-Semitic after they had moved to the New York City area. In big cities, depersonalization is the rule; the New York subway rider, for example, rarely sees the same commuters from one day to the next. Also, the masses in the city follow the conventions of the times. Material values are often emphasized, and the poor are shunned because they have not reached the level of material existence prescribed by the sociocultural conventions (E. Herzog, 1970; J. H. Peterson, 1967). But even as people submit to the pressure of materialistic values, they despise the city that promotes them. Supposed urban traits—dishonesty, deceit, ambitiousness, vulgarity, loudness—were, several decades ago, reflected in the stereotype of the Jew. The late sociologist Arnold Rose believed that "the Jews are hated . . . primarily because they serve as a symbol of city life" (1948, p. 374). More recently, Blacks and Puerto Ricans have been the recipients of the blame for urban "crime in the streets."

This sociocultural emphasis is a logical explanation of prejudices toward urbanized minority groups as well as toward groups that have not accepted White middle-class values. But it does not explain the hostility toward hard-working Japanese-American and Japanese-Canadian farmers during World War II, or the fact that farm dwellers—isolated from the depersonalized city—may be as prejudiced as city dwellers.

C. *Situational Emphasis*

Let us now turn to explanations that operate at a more individual level: those that begin to deal with the question of why some people are prejudiced while others are not. The situational emphasis is perhaps the most purely social psychological in nature in that it is oriented toward the present. It states that prejudice is caused by current forces in the environment. As we saw in Chapter 8 in discussing some of the determinants of moral behavior, situational pressures can influence a person to act in moral or immoral ways. Similarly, pressures in the immediate situation can lead us to act in prejudiced and discriminating ways. Conformity to others is a strong influence on prejudice, according to theories that look to the situation for the causes of prejudice. As Schellenberg (1974) indicates, we gain social approval by conforming to the opinions that are held by our friends and associates. During the 1960s in the U.S. South, for example, many restaurant owners claimed that they themselves were not prejudiced but that other customers would object if the owners allowed Blacks to be served.

Changes over time in specific stereotypes of racial or national groups often reflect this situational emphasis. During World War II, U.S. citizens were exposed to government propaganda that led to an adoption of negative stereotypes of the Japanese and the Germans and to favorable stereotypes of allies, including the Russians. Early in the war most U.S. citizens described the Russians as hardworking and brave. In 1948, as postwar conflicts between the two great powers emerged, the stereotypes were quite different, as Figure 11-8 indicates. Although "hardworking" was still considered an appropriate description of the Russians, more people in the United States in 1948 believed that Russians were cruel. In a world where the Soviet Union was no longer an ally but a competitor, assumptions about the nature of Russians had changed. In recent years a different change has begun to take place in regard to the assumptions held by many U.S. citizens about mainland Chinese: negative attitudes about these people may be moderating with the advent of rapprochement and such things as Coca-Cola franchises in China.

D. *Psychodynamic Emphasis*

In contrast to the situational emphasis is the view that sees prejudice as a result of the prejudiced person's own conflicts and maladjustments. Here we find theories that are essentially psychological, in contrast to the historical, economic, and sociological emphases of previous approaches. According to these theories, if you want to alter prejudice and discrimination, you must focus directly on the prejudiced person.

Two types of psychodynamic theories of prejudice are used. One of these assumes that prejudice is rooted in the human condition, because **frustration** is inevitable in human life. Frustration and deprivation lead to hostile impulses, "which if not controlled are likely to discharge against ethnic minorities" (Allport, 1958, p. 209). In this interpretation, we can of course see the frustration-aggression hypothesis (discussed in Chapter 10) finding its place in the explanation of discrimination. **Scapegoating**—the displacement of hostility upon less powerful groups—is hypothesized to result from frustration when the original source of the frustration is not available for attack or is not attackable for other reasons. Lynching of Blacks, burning of synagogues, and other assaults on representatives of minority groups are instances of such behavior (see Figure 11-9).

Ashmore (1970) has reviewed the evidence for a frustration theory of prejudice and found that some studies demonstrate scapegoating but that others do not. For example, Allport and Kramer (1946) report that, among Catholic students, those who complained of being discriminated against because they were Catholic were more anti-Black and more anti-Semitic than were other Catholic students. However, children with highly punitive parents (as measured by the children's own ratings) are not more prejudiced toward minority groups than are children with less punitive parents (R. Epstein & Komorita, 1965a, 1965b, 1966). In evaluating frustration theories, Feshbach and Singer (1957) make a very useful distinction between shared threats and personal threats. A shared threat, such as the possibility that one's community might be hit by a hurricane, has the effect of bringing people together; such a threat has been found to reduce anti-Black prejudice. But a personal threat, as frustration theory would predict, has an escalating effect on prejudice.

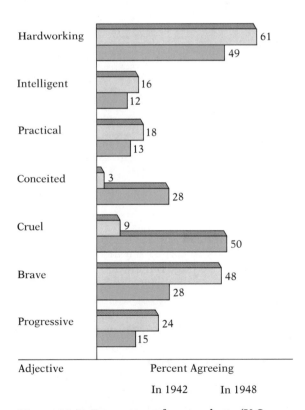

Adjective	Percent Agreeing

Hardworking — 61 / 49
Intelligent — 16 / 12
Practical — 18 / 13
Conceited — 3 / 28
Cruel — 9 / 50
Brave — 48 / 28
Progressive — 24 / 15

In 1942   In 1948

Figure 11-8. Percentage of respondents (U.S. citizens) who agreed that the adjectives listed above described the Russians. (From *How Nations See Each Other,* by W. Buchanan and H. Cantril. Copyright 1953 by the University of Illinois Press. Reprinted by permission.)

Figure 11-9. Members of the Ku Klux Klan and the American Nazi party both advocate White supremacy, expressing hostility toward Blacks and Jewish people. The displacement explanation would suggest that members of these groups are frustrated—by economic conditions, for example—and displace their aggression on easily identifiable, nonpowerful groups. (© United Press International.)

Within the psychodynamic emphasis, a second approach focuses on the hypothesis that prejudice develops only in people who have a personality defect or a weak character structure. This approach does not accept prejudice as normal; it postulates that prejudice is the result of the strong anxieties and insecurities of neurotic persons. A similar approach derives from research on authoritarianism, which conceptualizes prejudice as a function of the antidemocratic orientation of certain people.

A book called *The Authoritarian Personality* (1950) was a landmark in the history of social psychology. Written by the German social scientists T. W. Adorno and Else Frenkel-Brunswik and their colleagues at the University of California at Berkeley, this huge book (990 pages) included clinical hunches, extensions of psychoanalytic theory, multiple item-analyses of various attitude scales, in depth interviews, and post hoc theory. Although written 30 years ago, this work is still of contemporary interest (Cherry & Byrne, 1977).

The initial focus of the Adorno et al. research program was an understanding of prejudice and discrimination as they are evidenced in *anti-Semitism,* or negative attitudes and behaviors toward Jewish people. Gradually, however, the focus of the program shifted toward prejudice, or what the

California group chose to call *ethnocentrism*. They preferred the latter term to prejudice, because ethnocentrism refers to a relatively consistent frame of mind—a rejection of all outgroups and aliens. The ethnocentric person has a dislike for anything and everything different. For example, it has been found that highly ethnocentric subjects are less likely to have foreign-made automobiles (Day & White, 1973). This emphasis on ethnocentrism reflected the California group's assumption that prejudice results from some characteristic of the ethnocentric person, rather than from the characteristics of a specific minority group.

We will discuss the concept of authoritarianism more extensively in Chapter 16, but for the present we should note that research on authoritarianism has viewed prejudice in very individual terms. In particular, it has interpreted prejudice from a psychoanalytic viewpoint. Thus to researchers on authoritarianism, the authoritarian personality results from a strict and rigid superego, a primitive id, and a weak ego structure (N. Sanford, 1956), which lead to predictable patterns of behavior (prejudice) toward minority groups.

As Pettigrew (1961) has shown, each of these explanations of prejudice within the psychodynamic approach represents an externalization process in which people apply their ways of dealing with personal problems to the structuring of outside events. Yet, there exist prejudiced persons to whom the psychodynamic emphasis does not apply. The psychodynamic approach is particularly inadequate to explain cases in which prejudice and discrimination pervade the entire social structure.

E. *Phenomenological Emphasis*

The phenomenological emphasis advances the notion that what should be studied is not the objective world but the individual's perception of the world. Unlike the psychodynamic view, which stresses more durable personality characteristics, the phenomenological emphasis stresses the immediate perceptions of a person. As we saw in Chapter 3, there are often many possible interpretations of a single event. Our interpretation can be influenced by a variety of factors: our past experience with the person, the behavior of other people in the same situation, our selective attendance to certain aspects of the situation. The combination of these factors will in turn affect our behavior. For example, the assertive behavior of a woman, seen in the context of more passive women, may be interpreted as "too aggressive" and "pushy," even though the behavior may be comparable to that of a man in the same situation. Discriminatory behavior may follow. In contrast, previous experience with that same woman, or comparison of her behavior with others in a similar situation, might result in quite different behavior on our part. In other words, the phenomenological interpretation of prejudice and discrimination emphasizes immediate influences and pays little attention to broad and historical causes.

With the phenomenological emphasis, we have reached the immediate level of causation as represented in Figure 11-6. But our survey of approaches is not complete until we consider the stimulus object of prejudice.

F. *Emphasis on Earned Reputation*

All the previous approaches have localized the source of prejudice in the observer. They have failed to consider that minority groups, by their behavior or characteristics, may precipitate the negative feelings that are directed toward them. The *earned-reputation* theory postulates that minority groups possess characteristics that provoke dislike and hostility. There is some evidence to support the earned-reputation theory. For example, Triandis and Vassiliou, in a study of people from Greece and the United States, conclude: "The present data suggest that there is a 'kernel of truth' in most stereotypes *when they are elicited from people who have firsthand knowledge of the group being stereotyped*" (1967, p. 324, italics in original). A careful review by Brigham (1971) concludes that ethnic stereotypes can have a "kernel of truth" in the sense that different groups of respondents agree on which traits identify a particular object group. Furthermore, in at least some cases, these beliefs about the characteristics of members of another group may be relatively accurate (McCauley & Stitt, 1978).

None of these theories of the causes of prejudice is sufficient to explain every case; a phenomenon as pervasive as prejudice has many sources. Thus we must acknowledge the multiple causes of prejudice, while realizing that attempts to identify specific causes for individual cases of prejudice are helpful.

III. The Nature of Attitudes

Prejudice and discrimination are "big" concepts: they involve stereotypes and beliefs about groups of people and about individuals who represent those groups, they involve actions and behaviors toward these people, and they may involve norms and institutional policies that influence beliefs and behaviors. Are all of these aspects included in the concept of attitude? In a general sense, yes. Yet, because these phenomena are so complex, social psychologists have attempted to break down their analysis of such events into smaller components. By defining the components more precisely, it then becomes possible to put the pieces back together and look at the broader phenomena of prejudice and discrimination. Let us look, then, at how the basic concept of attitude is conceptualized in social psychology. Then, with the component pieces in hand, we can return to the broader issues of prejudice, discrimination, and the general relationship between attitudes and behavior.

A. *Definitions of Attitude*

Because "attitude" can mean so many things to so many people, it is not surprising that social psychologists have entertained many different definitions of the concept of attitude. In one of the earliest uses of the concept, attitude related primarily to a physical posture or a body position. Thus in the early experiments on reaction time, experimenters would talk about a subject's attitude when referring to a readiness to respond to the onset of a stimulus (Himmelfarb & Eagly, 1974). For most of recent history, however, the use of the term *attitude* has been limited to mental rather than physical states, although the notion of a readiness to respond to objects has often been maintained in the definition (Allport, 1935).

Many theorists have proposed that attitudes have three basic components: the cognitive, the affective, or emotional, and the behavioral (D. Katz & Stotland, 1959). As McGuire (1969) has noted, the proposition that people take three existential stances in regard to the human condition—knowledge, feeling, and acting—has been advanced by philosophers throughout history. As far back as Plato, the terms *cognition, affect* and *conation* were used to refer to the three components of what we may call attitude (Oskamp, 1977). In this analysis of attitudes, the cognitive component refers to the beliefs and ideas a person has about some attitude object (Harding et al., 1969). For example, the beliefs that women are more intuitive than men, that all welfare recipients are lazy, and that politicians are dishonest all represent the cognitive aspect of attitudes toward objects. The affective component of an attitude refers to the emotional feelings one has about the attitude object or one's like or dislike for the object. Positive feelings might include respect, liking, and sympathy; negative feelings might be contempt, fear, and revulsion. The behavioral, or conative, component of an attitude refers to one's action tendencies toward the object. For example, does a legislator vote for or against the Equal Rights Amendment? Does an individual donate money to the Cancer Society?

Obviously, it causes some confusion to imply three separate things when talking about the single word *attitude*. In some cases, however, these three components relate very highly to each other, thus reducing possible confusion. For example, D. T. Campbell (1947) constructed scales that attempted to tap a variety of components of attitudes toward various ethnic groups. His results showed reasonably high correlations within each group; in other words, the various components of attitudes toward Japanese were more similar than was any single component toward a number of ethnic groups. Later research, however—including discussion by Campbell himself (D. T. Campbell & Fiske, 1959)—has pointed to the problems involved in this original study, due in part to the fact that the method of measurement was the same from scale to scale. Thus the correlations may have been high due to commonalities in the measuring instruments, rather than in the conceptual components themselves. Furthermore, as we will discuss at greater length in subsequent sections, many investigators have found considerable discrepancy between, for example, a person's *expression* of liking for an object and his or her *behavior* toward that object.

Because of this potential confusion, whereby a single concept refers to three separate kinds of response, many recent investigators have become much more precise in their use of the term *attitude*. Fishbein and Ajzen (1972), for example, suggest that the term *attitude* be used only in reference to the evaluative dimension, to indicate like or dislike toward the object. Their argument is certainly a justifiable one. Most of the measurements of attitudes, which we will discuss in the next section, in fact are simple measures of like and dislike. This approach to the definition of attitudes has considerable merit, and in our remaining discussion we will accept attitude as an indicant of liking and disliking.

If we do accept this definition of attitude, however, how then do we refer to the other components of what has been called an attitude in the past? *Beliefs* is a term that has been used to refer to the cognitive component. In Fishbein and Ajzen's terms (1972), beliefs are probabilistic judgments about whether a particular object has a particular characteristic. For example, if I say that professors are smart people, I am indicating my belief that smartness and professors are related. Other beliefs about the properties of professors might include arrogance, absentmindedness, and liberalism. Such beliefs may be held with varying degrees of certainty. For example, the person

who says that the planet Venus might be inhabitable is indicating a lower probability, or a weaker belief, than the person who swears that life exists on Venus. In and of themselves, such statements do not indicate overall liking or disliking; in other words, they are conceptually distinct from attitudes as an evaluative statement. Together, they may be able to predict some kinds of behavior that relate to a particular attitude object.

To refer to the conative (or behavioral) component, Fishbein and Ajzen (1972) offer the concept of *behavioral intention*. This refers to a person's stated intention to perform a particular behavior with respect to the object of consideration. In summary, attitudes, beliefs, and behavioral intentions can be used to represent the affective, cognitive, and conative components of attitudes.

There are a couple of other terms that we should mention before we go further into the nature of attitudes, because these terms are sometimes confused with attitudes and beliefs. *Values* are broader and more abstract goals that an individual may have, and they lack a specific object or reference point. Bravery, beauty, and freedom are values. They serve as criteria for judgments or as abstract standards for decision making, through which the individual may develop specific attitudes and beliefs (Rokeach, 1973). Thus, if beauty is a primary value for you, many of your beliefs may revolve around the issue of whether a particular object is beautiful. In turn, your attitude toward that object may be influenced by the degree to which you think it is aesthetically pleasing. For other people, the value of practicality or efficiency may be more important, and thus their attitudes and beliefs toward the same object might differ sharply from yours.

Opinion is a term that is less easily defined, and has often been used interchangeably with both attitudes and beliefs. In fact, McGuire (1969) has suggested that these are "names in search of a distinction, rather than a distinction in search of a terminology" (p. 152). Yet, the term *opinion* continues to be used widely, particularly in reference to public opinion polling, where the focus is on the shared attitudes and beliefs of large groups of people (Oskamp, 1977). Generally these public opinions combine aspects of attitudes, beliefs, and behavioral intentions. For example, a television poll may ask respondents "Do you like Candidate X?" "Do you think Candidate X is interested in the problems of minorities?" and "If the election were held today, would you vote for Candidate X?" In our discussion, we will avoid the use of the term *opinion* and maintain the distinctions between attitudes, beliefs, and intentions. When you next see the results of a public opinion survey, however, you might want to analyze the questions according to this three-way distinction.

B. *Measurement of Attitudes*

Attitudes, like many variables of central interest to social psychology, are not observable entities. You can't smell, feel, or touch an attitude. It is an underlying construct that must be inferred. To make this inference, psychologists have developed many methods of measurement, all designed to tap the underlying attitudes of people toward various objects and issues in their environment. Most of the methods of attitude measurement are concerned with the evaluative dimension; in other words, they attempt to determine how much an individual likes or dislikes a particular object. (It is for this reason, among others, that we are comfortable in limiting the term *attitude* to the affective dimension and reserving the term *beliefs* for cognitive aspects.)

There are literally hundreds of methods that have been devised to measure attitudes. In the simplest form, a method might consist of open-ended questions—for example, What do you think about space exploration? Such questions have the advantage of eliciting a broad range of respondent viewpoints and sometimes more detail than some of the other forms. However, open-ended questions also have the disadvantage of having low reliability (often, a person will answer quite differently on two different occasions), and it is difficult to compare the answers of different respondents because their answers may vary so widely.

Although open-ended questions can be quite useful in the initial stage of an investigation—when you are not sure of all the issues that may be involved—later stages of attitude research generally use more closed-ended questions that allow more precision.

It is impossible to detail all of the methods of attitude measurement that have been developed. We will, however, briefly discuss three of the most common methods in use in order to provide a sense of the strategies that investigators use in this complex area.

1. The Thurstone Method of Equal-Appearing Intervals. In this method of attitude measurement, developed early in the history of attitude research (Thurstone, 1928), the goal of the investigator is to construct a scale marked off in equal units. Although such a goal might seem relatively easy to attain, the procedure for developing this kind of scale is in fact quite complex. Initially, the investigator develops a large number of statements about the attitude object of interest—abortion, nuclear energy, violence on television, and so on. These statements are then rated by a large group of people who indicate their favorable or unfavorable attitude toward the topic. The rating is accomplished by asking each person to place each statement in one of 11 piles, with the first pile indicating an extremely unfavorable statement and the last pile indicating an extremely favorable statement. For example, if you were a judge in this procedure and the topic was attitudes toward North American Indians, you might place a statement such as "I would rather see the White people lose their position in this country than keep it at the expense of the Indians" in one of the piles at the favorable end of the continuum. A statement such as "I consider that the Indian is only fit to do the dirty work of the White community" might be placed in one of the piles at the unfavorable end.

Once this initial group of statements has been judged, the investigator then selects a smaller number of statements (about 20 is typical) for the final attitude scale. Statements that show considerable disagreement in ratings among judges will be discarded, and the statements chosen will represent a spread of scale values (based on the median of the judges' ratings) along the entire dimension of favorable to unfavorable, with approximately equal intervals between each scale value.

All of this work is preliminary to using the scale to measure a person's attitude. Once the items have been selected, they are presented in random order (with no mention of the scale values) to a sample of the population of interest. People are then asked to check those items that they agree with, and the investigator determines that person's attitude by calculating the mean or median of the scale values of those items checked. Thus in the final analysis, a person's attitude will be represented by some number between 1 and 11.

2. *The Likert Method of Summated Ratings.* Responding in part to the difficulty of using the Thurstone method, Likert (1932) proposed an alternative procedure for measuring attitudes that is considerably simpler and, as a result, has been more widely used in recent years than the Thurstone method. In the Likert method, there is no effort to find statements that are distributed evenly along a continuum; rather, only statements that are definitely favorable or unfavorable to the object are used. The investigator compiles a series of these statements and then asks subjects to indicate their degree of agreement or disagreement with each statement. An example of this format is shown in Figure 11-10.

A Likert scale will contain a series of such items, and a person's final attitude score will be the sum of the responses to all of the items. Thus, if there are 20 items on the scale, a person's score can range from 0 to 100. In refining a Likert scale, an investigator will generally do an item analysis to determine which questions are the best measures of the attitude in question. Specifically, the investigator will determine the correlation of each item with the total score and will keep only those items that show a substantial correlation with the total score.

3. *The Semantic-Differential Technique of Osgood, Suci, and Tannenbaum.* Both the Thurstone and Likert methods, to varying degrees, require the investigator to do considerable initial development before a scale can be used to assess a person's attitude on the topic of interest. In contrast, the semantic-differential method uses a scale that is general enough to be applied to any topic and asks the person to evaluate the attitude object directly (Osgood, Suci, & Tannenbaum, 1957). In this method, which was originally developed to measure the meaning of an object (thus the term *semantic*), the person is asked to rate a given concept on a series of seven-point, bipolar rating scales as shown in Figure 11-11. Any concept—a person, a political issue, a work of art, or anything else—can be rated using this same format.

In addition to the Thurstone, Likert, and semantic-differential methods, there are many other measures of attitude that have been developed. These three, however,

Figure 11-10. A sample item from the Likert scale of attitude measurement.

"The policy of encouraging Indians to remain on reservations should be terminated immediately."

Strongly disapprove	Disapprove	Undecided	Approve	Strongly Approve
(1)	(2)	(3)	(4)	(5)

Figure 11-11. A sample item from the semantic differential scale of attitude measurement.

The subject is asked to rate a given concept (such as "North American Indian") on a series of seven-point, bipolar rating scales. Any concept—a person, a political issue, a work of art, a group, or anything else—can be rated. The usual format is as follows, with the person placing an X to indicate his or her rating on each bipolar dimension:

North American Indian

Fair	_ _ _ _ _ _ _	Unfair
Large	_ _ _ _ _ _ _	Small
Clean	_ _ _ _ _ _ _	Dirty
Bad	_ _ _ _ _ _ _	Good
Valuable	_ _ _ _ _ _ _	Worthless
Light	_ _ _ _ _ _ _	Heavy
Active	_ _ _ _ _ _ _	Passive
Cold	_ _ _ _ _ _ _	Hot
Fast	_ _ _ _ _ _ _	Slow

are probably the most widely used measures in attitude research today. Furthermore, while the assumptions and characteristics of each of these methods differ, the responses to all three scales generally have been found to be highly related (Fishbein & Ajzen, 1974). In other words, a person whose responses to a Thurstone scale indicate a highly favorable attitude toward North American Indians probably would also show a positive attitude on the Likert and semantic-differential scales.

With this variety of measurement techniques in hand, social scientists have investigated a tremendous range of attitudes. Attitudes on virtually every topic—religion, politics, the environment, drugs, sex, and many others—have been investigated with nearly every segment of the population. Often the investigator's concern is with a comparison between different segments of the population. For example, R. W. Griffeth and Cafferty (1977) have compared the attitudes and values of police officers to those of both Black and White citizens. They found many similarities but a number of striking differences as well. Police valued

equality less than the citizen groups did and valued an exciting life more highly than the citizen groups did. Other investigators have considered how men and women differ, as in a study by Powell and Borden (1978), which found that women are more concerned than men about environmental problems but that men are more knowledgeable than women about environmental problems. Public opinion pollsters often are concerned with the differences in attitudes among people living in different parts of a country, as for example in assessing the popularity of the Canadian Prime Minister in the western provinces as compared to the eastern provinces.

Such investigations are of interest in their own right, because they indicate the ways that people think and their feelings toward a variety of objects and issues in the environment. Yet, attitudes have been of central importance to social psychologists not only as an interesting phenomenon in and of themselves but because it was widely believed that attitudes, measured in the ways that we have discussed, would serve as predictors of subsequent behavior.

IV. Attitudes as Predictors of Behavior

A. *Are Attitudes Predispositions to Action?*

The implicit assumption among those who have studied attitudes has always been that attitudes are related to behaviors. In other words, if we measure a person's attitude toward Spanish-speaking Americans and find that it is negative, then we should be able to predict that this person would engage in a number of discriminatory behaviors toward any individual Spanish-speaking American. But can we make this prediction? Fairly early on in the history of attitude research, investigators learned that relationships between attitudes and behavior and relationships among various behaviors were not nearly so neat as early theoretical work would have predicted. As a result of several studies showing inconsistency in such relationships, many social scientists in the early 1970s began to regard the concept of attitude as nearly useless (Eagly & Himmelfarb, 1978).

The classic study used by critics as evidence for inconsistency was done by Richard LaPiere, back in 1934. At that time there were strong feelings against Orientals in the United States, particularly along the West Coast. LaPiere, a highly mobile sociologist, took a Chinese couple on a three-month automobile trip, twice across the United States and up and down the West Coast. The trio stopped at 250 hotels and restaurants during their trip, and only once were they refused service. Later LaPiere wrote to each of these establishments, asking whether they would accept Chinese patrons. Only about one-half of the proprietors bothered to answer, but, of these, 90% said that they would not serve Chinese!

In a similar study, Kutner, Wilkins, and Yarrow (1952) arranged for a Black woman to join two White women seated at a restaurant, repeating this procedure in 11 different restaurants. In no case was the Black woman refused service. However, later telephone calls requesting reservations for an interracial party produced six refusals and only five grudging acceptances of the reservation. Although both of these studies suggest some discrepancy in behavior, they are not without their problems. For example, in neither case was attitude actually assessed. Instead, an indication of intended behavior (or a *behavioral intention*) was compared to an actual behavior. Dillehay (1973) has argued that these studies actually are comparing types of role behavior, and he notes that "the unit sampled is suprapersonal, the establishment rather than the individual" (p. 888). Similarly, Triandis (1971) has pointed out that there is no way of knowing whether the person who refused the reservation by letter or by phone was actually the same person who admitted the Chinese and Black persons when they were at the establishment.

Although the variety of problems in these early studies of discriminatory behavior still might not lead us to discard any notion of attitude-behavior consistency, more recent studies that have eliminated some of the problems have often been no more successful in establishing a relationship between attitudes and behavior. Wicker (1969a), in a review of many of these studies, concluded that attitudes were a very poor predictor of subsequent behavior.

B. *Why Don't Attitudes Predict Behavior More Consistently?*

In the face of numerous failures to find expected relationships between measured attitudes and observed behavior, many social psychologists began to believe that the concept of attitude was not a useful concept in their attempt to understand human behavior. Other investigators, however, rather than throwing the baby and the bath water out together, have pointed to a number of reasons why the expected relationship may not always be strong and, at the same time, have charted new directions for the investigator of attitudes. Let us consider some of these reasons for the weak relationship.

First, consider the *level of specificity* at which attitudes and behaviors are defined. Often, investigators have used a very general measure of attitudes (for example, attitudes toward psychology) and then looked at a very specific measure of behavior (for example, willingness to enroll in a social psychology course taught at Classic University by Professor Knowlittle). In many ways, it is not surprising that such a general measure of attitudes would not fare well in predicting such a specific behavior. In contrast, experiments in which the measure of attitude is more specific have had much more success in predicting specific behavior. For example, Weigel, Vernon, and Tognacci (1974) measured people's attitudes toward general issues, such as the environment, and toward more specific objects, such as the Sierra Club (see Figure 11-12). Later they gave subjects the opportunity to volunteer for activities of the Sierra Club. While a relationship between general environmental attitudes and Sierra Club activities was not found (correlations were .06), there was a strong relationship ($r = +.68$ between the more specific attitudinal measures and the actual behavior.

Figure 11-12. These volunteers are cleaning up after an oil spill on the California coast. Such behavior has been shown to correlate more highly with people's attitudes about a *specific* object (for instance, the Sierra Club) than with their attitudes about more general concepts (such as the environment). (© Ilka Hartmann/Jeroboam, Inc.)

A related issue in considering the attitude-behavior relationship concerns the question of single acts versus multiple acts. Generally, when investigators have studied this problem, they have selected a single behavior to test their predictions. Yet, if we are interested in a general issue, such as attitudes toward women, then it probably makes more sense to look at a series of possible behaviors. In other words, although a person's general attitude toward women may not be an accurate predictor of his or her response to a particular woman in an employment interview, that attitude may be a much more accurate predictor when a whole series of behaviors related to women is taken into account. For any single act, there may be a variety of factors that influence the behavior; over a wide range, however, the general attitude may exert a more powerful influence.

One of the reasons for seeking this broader range of indices is that behavior is complex and multidetermined. Our attitude toward an object may affect some of our behavior, but there may be other influencing factors as well. For example, suppose an elderly man tells his friend that "the less contact he has with Blacks the better" and then boards a bus. Noting that all the seats but one are occupied, the man takes the available one—next to a Black. We cannot conclude that his verbal statement is false just because his choice of seats has repudiated it. Even the apparently simple action of taking a seat may be multidetermined. Although it may be upsetting for the old man to sit next to a Black, his feet may be hurting him so much that sitting, under any conditions, is more tolerable than standing. On the other hand, observation of future behavior might prove more enlightening. Perhaps the man would refuse to take that bus any more or would change his schedule to avoid crowded bus hours. Even more broadly, other situations involving the man's interactions with Blacks might show a consistency between expressed attitude and actual behavior. In short, one-shot measures of behavior may not give us much information about the strength of the attitude-behavior relationship.

Situational factors also may influence behavior, as we have seen repeatedly in earlier chapters. In the case where situational pressures are strong, people of widely differing attitudes may act in a similar manner. For example, if a young White child were about to be hit by a car, most people, no matter what their attitude toward Whites, probably would attempt to save the child. Yet, in other cases where the situation was not one of life or death, varying attitudes toward Whites might influence one's reaction to a White child. In general, we can say that the stronger the situational pressures toward some behavior, the less likely the individual differences in attitudes are to affect the behavior. (We shall have reason to return to this general point in Chapter 16.)

A related issue in considering the attitude-behavior relationship is that a given behavior may be related to more than one attitude. For example, in the case of the White child about to be struck by a car, a person might have one set of attitudes toward Whites and another set of attitudes toward children. Which attitude would best predict the person's behavior? Thus, the relationship between behavior and a single attitude may appear inconsistent because other attitudes have greater influence (Wicker, 1969a; S. W. Cook & Selltiz, 1964). In one study, Insko and Schopler (1967) used a person whose attitudes were favorable to the civil rights movement but who refused to contribute money to the movement. Perhaps this person had stronger attitudes about caring for the needs of his or her family, maintaining a good credit rating, and the like.

Understanding the competing role of different attitude domains may facilitate future prediction of behavior.

Other personal characteristics also may influence behavior. For example, some people are simply more consistent in their attitudes and behaviors. S. H. Schwartz (1978), for example, found that those people whose general set of attitudes regarding altruism was highly stable were more likely to show consistency between attitudes and behavior than people whose attitudes were less stable.

C. *Resolving the Attitude/Behavior Issue*

All of the reasons already mentioned tend to diminish the observed relationship between attitudes and behavior. Yet, they do not mean that we should throw up our hands in despair and accept the claim that there is no relationship. Instead, these problems in showing the relationship indicate some directions whereby we can take these complexities into account and become far more successful in predicting behavior on the basis of attitude measures.

Izek Ajzen and Martin Fishbein (1969, 1970, 1972, 1977; Fishbein & Ajzen, 1975) have done exactly that. In analyzing the field of research on attitudes and behaviors, these investigators have shown that there are indeed some grounds for confidence. On the basis of their review (Ajzen & Fishbein, 1977), they conclude that "a person's attitude has a consistently strong relation with his or her behavior when it is directed at the same target and when it involves the same action" (p. 912). Thus, if we carefully construct our attitude measure and carefully select the behavior to be observed, we can indeed predict behavior from attitudes. In general, these investigators suggest that attitudes toward specific behaviors (for example, a person's attitude toward recycling wastes) will provide the best predictor of single-act criteria (for example, the specific act of taking bottles to the local recycling center), while more general attitudes toward objects (such as attitudes to ecology) are more suitable for multiple-act criteria (such as a combination of behavioral measures, including taking bottles to a recycling center, reducing the thermostat, and using recycled paper for correspondence). Clearly this a more complex approach to attitude-behavior assessment than early investigators used, but it appears to be a much more profitable one as well.

Fishbein and Ajzen have also proposed a model for predicting people's behavioral intentions and actual behavior. This model includes both a measure of the person's attitude toward the action as well as his or her normative beliefs about the desirability of the action (Fishbein, 1967; Fishbein & Ajzen, 1975). With the inclusion of this latter factor, these investigators are able to consider how other people may influence a person's behavior in ways that are or are not consistent with the person's actual attitude toward the specific object. Triandis (1977a) has proposed a similar model that also includes a habit factor, reflecting the number of times that a particular action has been performed by the person in the past. Both of these models have received considerable support and testify to the usefulness of taking a more complex view of the attitude-behavior relationship.

While Fishbein, Ajzen, and Triandis have focused on defining the components of attitudes and their relationship to behavior, other investigators have begun to consider the factors that may directly influence the consistency between attitudes and behavior. For example, Regan and Fazio (1977) have shown that attitudes formed through direct experience with the object show more consistent relationships to behavior than do attitudes formed less directly. For example, when a student has participated in several psychology experiments, a measure of that student's attitude toward psychology experiments is much more likely to predict his or her future participation than is the attitude of a student who has only read about experiments (Fazio & Zanna, 1978). At a more esoteric level, your attitude toward Martians is far less likely to predict your actual behavior, should you ever encounter a Martian, than your attitude toward professors is likely to predict your classroom behavior.

These developments in attitude research are important ones. As noted before, however, these developments do make life more complicated. Recalling our earlier discussion of racism, for example, we can be much less certain that there is a racist personality, whose attitude can be assessed and whose every behavior toward Blacks can be predicted. Although there certainly may be some generality, many of the behaviors that fall into the category of racial discrimination may be predicted only by quite specific attitudes and may occur only in particular circumstances. Knowledge of this complexity does not make us any less concerned about issues of racism, sexism, prejudice, and discrimination, but it should make us realize that these problems are highly complex ones and that any strategies for solution and change will necessarily be complex as well.

V. Summary

Attitude is and always has been a central concept in social psychology, and it is related to a variety of important phenomena. *Prejudice* refers to an intolerant attitude toward a group of people; *discrimination* refers to specific unfair behaviors toward members of that group.

Racism is a specific form of prejudice and discrimination, directed toward an ethnic group. It may exist at either the individual or the institutional level. Sexism is a similar form of prejudice, but in this case the behavior is directed against a person by virtue of gender, rather than race. *Separatism,* a Canadian political movement, is propelled by evidence of prejudice and discrimination toward French-speaking Canadians. In each of these cases, negative stereotypes are accompanied by discriminatory behavior in a wide range of areas.

Theories about the causes of prejudice make a distinction between prejudice existing in the society at large and the degree of prejudice held by different individuals. The historical emphasis hypothesizes that prejudice is often the result of traditions and relationships that have existed for generations. Economic exploitation of less powerful groups is advanced as one cause of prejudice.

Sociologists and anthropologists emphasize sociocultural factors as causes of prejudice. Among these are increased urbanization, competition for scarce jobs, and changes in the functions of the family. The situational emphasis states that prejudice is caused by current forces in the environment.

Psychodynamic theories of the causes of prejudice posit that prejudice results from personal conflicts and maladjustments within the prejudiced person. Among specific factors are low frustration tolerance, authoritarianism, and personality deficit. The phenomenological emphasis argues that a person's perception of his or her environment is of crucial importance in understanding that person's behavior.

Throughout the years, many definitions of attitude have been offered. Although beliefs, behaviors, and evaluations have all been considered a part of the attitude concept at one time, more recent usage limits the term *attitude* to only the evaluative (like or dislike) dimension. *Beliefs* refer to cogni-

tions or ideas that one has about an object, apart from any liking or disliking. *Behavioral intentions* describe tendencies toward action. *Values* refer to broader and more abstract goals and lack a specific reference point.

Three major methods for measuring attitudes are the Thurstone method of equal-appearing intervals, the Likert method of summated ratings, and the semantic-differential technique.

A major question has always been the relationship between assessed attitudes and observed behaviors. Many early investigations found little relationship between the two. Some of the factors that may affect the relationship are the level of specificity of the attitude measured, the question of single-versus multiple-act criteria for behavior, the influence of situational factors, and the fact that several attitudes may be relevant to one specific behavior.

Recent investigations have shown considerable correspondence between attitudes and behaviors when these various factors are taken into account and when both the attitude and the behavior are assessed carefully.

Glossary Terms	discrimination	scapegoating	social distance
	frustration	self-fulfilling	stereotypes
	prejudice	prophecy	

We are incredibly heedless in the formation of our beliefs, but find ourselves filled with an illicit passion for them when anyone proposes to rob us of their companionship. JAMES HARVEY ROBINSON

PHOTO © JANE SCHERR, ICON.

Some praise at morning what they blame at night, but always think the last opinion right. ALEXANDER POPE

12

Theories of Attitude Change

The attitudes we have and the ways in which these attitudes are related to behavior are a topic of interest in their own right. Yet perhaps even more interesting are the ways in which we alter our attitudes, our beliefs, and our actual behavior. Virtually every day, some of our attitudes are challenged by pressure from others or by questions from ourselves.

Consider, for example, a few moments in the life of a young woman named Joan O'Malley. It is a dreary Monday morning. Joan drags herself out of bed and flips on the television. She hopes the early morning program will provide some provocative piece of news that she can share with people at the office. Instead, a commercial praises a new hair rinse that promises to transform her into the essence of charm, popularity, and sexuality. That's the last thing she needs, Joan thinks—to heighten her sexuality. The phone rings—it's Ernie, still trying to convince her to go away with him for the weekend. But Joan is resistant; she's never *done* that before. She finally terminates the conversation by telling Ernie that she'll see him at lunch and discuss it further then. She sighs for a moment, then quickly prepares her breakfast, swallows her sugar-coated corn flakes, and scans the front page of the newspaper. The headlines are about efforts to persuade Congress to pass a new nuclear arms agreement. Joan wonders how persuaded her own Congressional representative has been. As she leaves for work, the mail arrives, but it contains nothing but some throwaway ads.

If Joan O'Malley had nothing else to do all day, she might to be able to keep track of the number of efforts made to change her attitudes or behavior. On this particular morning, she has already been inundated by advertisements emanating from several media—including even the cereal box! It may seem to her that every story in the newspaper is concerned with changing attitudes or behavior—whether it's pressures on a President or Prime Minister, a local petition campaign to build a new park, or a terrorist's threats to destroy a hijacked plane unless certain demands are met. And then there's always Ernie and his constant persuasion campaign.

When we consider these events as typical of the ever-present assault on our sensibilities (see **Figure 12-1**), it's no wonder that social psychologists have taken an immense interest in attitude change. Especially during the 1960s, theories of attitude change proliferated, and several long and detailed books appeared. One such book, dealing only with consistency theories, was 901 pages long (Abelson, Aronson, McGuire, Newcomb, Rosenberg, & Tannenbaum, 1968)!

Despite the information overkill brought about by these books and hundreds of additional research articles, we are still some way from understanding all the dynamics of attitude change. There are a number of theories of how attitude change takes place, but each theory has a different focus and thus may explain only certain cases of attitude change. It may well be, as Zimbardo and Ebbesen (1969) claim, that theorists and researchers studying attitude change are not primarily concerned with changing attitudes. Rather, their major interest may be in "using the attitude change paradigm to study basic psychological processes and the operation of theoretically relevant variables" (p. v). On the other hand, many of the theories have been important in at least suggesting the kinds of variables that should be of interest when attitude change is desired.

At the same time, it's also true that much of our knowledge of attitude change stems from studies done outside the framework of any theory or involves a combination of elements from several theories. For example, if a company hires a new employee who holds strongly anti-Black attitudes, we can specify a number of specific aspects of the working conditions that are likely to bring about favorable attitude change in this employee—but many of these conditions are not tied directly to any single theory. Thus the area of attitude change has a rather split character. On the one side,

Figure 12-1. Attempts to change attitudes and to influence behavior. (© J. R. Holland/Stock, Boston.)

there are the theories and laboratory research; on the other side are programs of field research on real-world topics, such as the effects of advertising propaganda. Because of this apparent division and because of the vast importance of the issue, we shall devote two chapters to attitude change. In this chapter we shall compare theories, describing the basic concepts and typical research of each theory and then examining its application to a real-world situation. In Chapter 13, we will look at some more specific examples of attitude change—programs that often borrow concepts from several different theories.

The theories to be described can be related to the basic orientations presented in Chapter 1. The first, *learning and reinforcement theories*, reflect the stimulus-response orientation that has been derived from basic

experimental psychology. The second and third, *social-judgment theory* and the *consistency theories*, are outgrowths of Gestalt theory and field theory. The fourth theory of attitude change, *functional theory*, is an eclectic one, although it draws mainly on psychoanalytic theory and other orientations that emphasize personal needs.

Attitude-change theories reflect assumptions about human nature. In specifying how the process of change occurs, they are forced to make certain decisions about the human condition. Do people have a strong need to make their separate attitudes consistent with one another? Does a person's attitude change only if the new attitude is more profitable in some personal sense? In the face of new evidence, is change more or less likely than a refusal to change? By looking at the assumptions held by each theory, we can compare each with our own conceptions of human nature and the information we have about human behavior. Bearing these considerations in mind, let's examine the first type of attitude-change theory.

I. Learning and Reinforcement Theories

As indicated in Chapter 1, stimulus-response theory focuses on the relationship between specific stimuli and responses. Behavior is analyzed by being broken down into units of habits and other separable responses. A response is more likely to be made again if it is reinforced (rewarded). It follows from this analysis that a stimulus-response theory of attitude change will place great emphasis on the characteristics of the communication (message, appeals, and so on) that try to make us change our attitudes and on the rewards that we may derive from doing so.

There are two general types of learning theory that have been developed to explain attitude change. In the first, concepts of classical and instrumental conditioning developed in the animal laboratories have been applied rather faithfully to the attitude-change situation. In the second, the adoption of classical-learning terms has been somewhat looser, although the general philosophical assumptions remain similar. Let's look at each of these approaches.

A. *Conditioning Theories of Attitude Change*

The work of **Arthur Staats** exemplifies the use of basic conditioning principles in developing a model of attitude formation and change (Staats, 1967; Staats & Staats, 1958). Building on earlier work by Doob (1947), Staats has used a classical-conditioning model, like that developed by Pavlov with his dogs, to explain the acquisition of attitudes. In the now familiar experiments by **Pavlov**, an unconditioned stimulus (UCS) is paired with a new stimulus, called the conditioned stimulus (CS), and through

the process of association the animal learns to make the same response to the CS as it previously did to the UCS (see **Figure 12-2**). This new response, called a conditioned response (CR), is what Staats defines as an *attitude*—a conditioned evaluative response to some object in the environment. Further work by **Staats (1968)** has amplified this model, adding other concepts from both animal and human learning, in an attempt to more fully represent the complexity of human behavior. In this more recent model (Staats calls it *the A-R-D system*), attitudes are treated as classically conditioned responses, as reinforcements for other behaviors, and as stimuli that may serve as goals or motivators. In each case, concepts of attitude and attitude change are related to more basic learning principles.

In another example of the use of learning theory in the explanation of attitude change, R. F. Weiss (1962, 1968) directly borrowed from Hull-Spence learning theory, incorporating terms such as *drive*, *incentive motivation*, and *habit* into his mod-

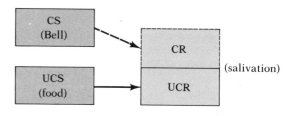

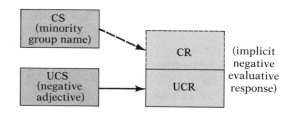

Figure 12-2. Classical-conditioning model. (Adapted from "Orientations to the Study of Attitudes and Their Change," by S. Himmelfarb and A. H. Eagly. In S. Himmelfarb and A. H. Eagly (Eds.), *Readings in Attitude Change.* Copyright 1974 by John Wiley & Sons, Inc. Used by permission.)

el of attitude change. In this approach to attitude change, a major effort is made to find appropriate equivalents to the concepts developed in the animal laboratory. For example, habit strength in the Hull-Spence theory is believed to be a function of the number of trials that a rat has in an alley. The parallel in Weiss's theory of attitude change is the number of persuasion attempts that a person receives (R. F. Weiss, 1968). Similarly, in the original Hull-Spence model, the magnitude of reinforcement that a rat receives (for example, how many pellets or how much wet mash) is considered to affect incentive motivation. For Weiss, the corresponding variable in human attitude change is the strength of the persuasive argument. Drawing these kinds of parallels, Weiss then proceeds to conduct numerous experiments in a controlled laboratory setting, in which he shows that similar relationships can be found between independent and dependent variables, thus providing weight for his analogous model.

Both of these approaches to attitude change rely very heavily on basic learning principles. Many critics suggest that the reliance is too heavy. In order to refine their measures in such a way that learning concepts can be applied precisely, both of these investigators have had to sacrifice a good deal of reality in their study of attitudes. For example, Weiss's dependent variable is usually the speed with which a person agrees with the persuasive statement, a form of response that is not directly applicable to the real-world setting (Himmelfarb & Eagly, 1974). Such criticisms are not true of all learning approaches to attitude change, however, as the Hovland research program demonstrates.

B. *Hovland's Communication Research Program*

During the late 1940s and 1950s, a highly energetic and productive group of social psychologists gathered at Yale University under the direction of Carl Hovland. Together they developed a model of attitude change that remains influential even today. Unlike Staats and Weiss, these investigators

did not attempt to develop a systematic theory of attitude change but, rather, used learning principles only as guiding assumptions in developing principles and specifying critical factors in the attitude-change process. Their approach did, however, reflect some basic assumptions of learning theory, and they believed that the principles applicable to acquiring verbal and motor skills could also be used to understand attitude formation and change (Hovland, Janis, & Kelley, 1953).

In the learning of new attitudes, three variables were believed to be important: attention, comprehension, and acceptance. The relationship of these processes is illustrated in Figure 12-3. The first of these factors, *attention*, recognizes the fact that not

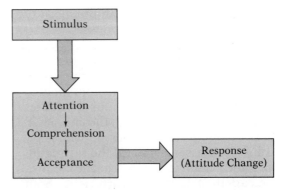

Figure 12-3. Steps in the attitude-change process, according to the Hovland-Janis-Kelley model.

all message stimuli that we may encounter are noticed. Driving down a highway littered with billboards, for example, you may notice only a fraction of the persuasive messages that you pass by. Lacking your attention, the attempted persuasion will very likely not be successful. But even when an appeal is noticed, it may not be effective. The second factor posited by Hovland and his colleagues, *comprehension*, recognizes the fact that some messages may be too complex or too ambiguous for their intended audience to understand. Thus a highly complex treatise on the balance-of-payments deficit, for example, may be totally ineffective in persuading the economic novice to vote for or against a particular bill. Finally, in the third step, a person must decide to accept the communication before any real attitude change takes place. The degree of *acceptance* is largely related to the incentives that are offered: the message may provide arguments or reasons for accepting the advocated point of view, or it may engender expectations of rewards or other pleasant experiences (Insko, 1967). For example, the billboard on the highway may tell you that a nationally known restaurant is only minutes off the highway, thus promising you something better than you had planned to get at the next truck stop. More than any other approach, the stimulus-response and reinforcement theories regard this assumption as basic—that attitudes are changed only if the incentives for making a new response are greater than the incentives for making the old response.

A major contribution of learning-based theories is the specification of factors that may influence the acceptance of the persuasive communication. These factors include (1) the communication stimulus (its content, arguments, and appeals); (2) the characteristics of the source or the person who is presenting the message; and (3) the setting in which the person is exposed to the communication, including characteristics both of the audience and of the recipients themselves.

This analysis has led to the following types of research questions:

1. If a salesperson is trying to convince you to adopt a certain point of view, should he or she review both sides of the argument or present only his or her own side? If he or she chooses to present both sides of the argument, which side should be presented first? (This latter question is known as *the primacy-recency issue.*)

2. How does the source of the persuasive communication affect attitude change? For example, if the source is highly believable or authoritative, is there more attitude change than if the source is untrustworthy?

3. Does it matter what the audience is required to do when the message is being presented? For example, what happens if the audi-ence is required to repeat the arguments after they are presented, as opposed to sitting and listening passively?

The Yale Communication Research Program has generated a great deal of research on these aspects of persuasive communication; we shall describe many of the findings in Chapter 13, when we deal with the outcomes of attempts to change attitudes.

C. *Assumptions about Human Nature*

It has become fashionable to state that stimulus-response and reinforcement theories assume that humans respond to stimuli in a rather passive, robot-like fashion. A careful reading would indicate, however, that such a notion does not reflect S-R theory fairly. For example, the Yale Communication Research Program recognized that the recipient must attend to and comprehend a stimulus before his or her attitude can be changed by it. Although it is true that researchers using the S-R approach have been interested primarily in aspects of the stimulus and the communicator, they also recognize that the recipient's characteristics can influence the extent of attitude change. Contemporary S-R theories are more accurately called S-O-R theories, in that they recognize the place of the organism that intervenes between stimulus and response.

Basic to S-R and reinforcement approaches is the notion that incentives for change must be stronger than incentives for maintaining the status quo. Behind this notion may be a recognition of each person's individuality, in the sense that, to predict the person's response, his or her past history of reinforcements must be understood and accounted for. Underlying this recognition, however, there is an assumption that, if the past history of reinforcements is known by the communicator, it can be used to manipulate the recipient's attitudes. Reinforcement theorists will claim that, if they had enough information about the recipients and if they had sufficient resources at hand, they could bring about attitude change in every recipient through the same general techniques.

D. *Representative Research*

Research using learning-theory approaches to attitude change has been varied, reflecting the diversity of theoretical approaches that learning-based theorists have used. Investigators in the classical-conditioning tradition, for example, have focused on issues such as the effect of verbal reinforcement on attitude change. Other investigators, building on the Yale Communication Program, have been more concerned with the sequence of the attitude-change process. We will briefly consider examples of each of these approaches.

In ordinary conversation, expressions of some of our most fervently held attitudes can fall on deaf ears. When we express other attitudes, our listener may respond enthusiastically with comments such as "You're so right!" or "I wish I'd said that!" Are those statements that are verbally reinforced more likely to be made in the future? Does a positive reaction from others tend to establish a belief more firmly in our repertory?

Insko (1965) attempted to answer these questions by conducting a verbal-reinforcement study via the telephone. Students at the University of Hawaii were phoned by an interviewer who sought their opinions about "Aloha Week" (festivities held every fall in Honolulu). For half the students, the investigator responded with "Good" when the student indicated a favorable opinion about Aloha Week; for the other half of the students, a "Good" response followed statements of negative attitudes toward Aloha Week. By this means, verbal conditioning was instituted—for some of the students positive attitudes were reinforced, and for others negative attitudes were reinforced.

Approximately one week after the telephone calls, the same students completed an apparently unrelated "Local Issues Questionnaire" in their regular class meeting, and one of the items in this questionnaire asked for their attitudes on Aloha Week.

Students who had been verbally reinforced by the telephone interviewer for positive attitudes expressed more favorable views than did those subjects who had been verbally reinforced for negative attitudes. The effect of verbal reinforcement thus appeared in another setting one full week later.

Verbal reinforcement has been used to modify such phenomena as wearing clothes of certain colors (Calvin, 1962); expressing prejudiced attitudes (Mitnick & McGinnies, 1958); adhering to certain philosophies of education (Hildum & Brown, 1956); and holding particular attitudes toward capital punishment (Ekman, 1958). In each case, the reinforcement of a specific attitude enhances the future expression of that attitude. There are, however, limitations to these conclusions. First of all, the verbal-reinforcement procedure can cause the respondent to accentuate his or her previously held attitudes, but it does not apply to a reversal in the direction of attitudes. In other words, this procedure requires that a person already hold an attitude and express it; then the experimenter is limited to reinforcing and perhaps thereby strengthening the original attitude. A second criticism of this approach to attitude change is that most of the attitudes studied have been rather unimportant or irrelevant ones. Most University of Hawaii students, for example, are probably indifferent as to whether Aloha Week is held once a year, once a month, or once a century. Even changes in attitude about a more important question such as capital punishment may occur without much investment on the part of the changer.

A third concern in this area is the exact nature of the reinforcement. Why does a verbal response such as "Good" lead to changes in expressed attitudes? One possibility is that the person believes that conformity to his or her present opinion will result in a variety of future reinforcements; however, this explanation is not totally convincing (Insko, 1967). Other people have questioned whether the reinforcement itself is really the cause of changes in attitudes, suggesting that *demand characteristics* may be a more reasonable explanation. Thus, in the Insko study, it is possible that students may have expressed either more favorable or more unfavorable attitudes toward Aloha Week on the Local Issues Questionnaire because they felt that they were supposed to, rather than because any true shift in attitude had occurred (M. M. Page, 1969, 1971, 1974).

This issue is not totally resolved. Investigators seem to agree that **contingency awareness** is necessary—in other words, a person must realize that statements such as "Good" are being used in reaction to particular attitude statements (thus refuting the popular idea of "hidden persuasion")—but they do not agree on whether a person must also realize that a specific persuasive attempt is being made (Insko & Oakes, 1966; Page, 1969).

Research developing from the Yale Communication Program has been concerned with a substantially larger number of variables than have the classical-conditioning theories. For example, one line of research developing from this program has focused on the relationship between personality variables and various stages of the communication process. As we noted earlier, this model of research considers three separate stages in the attitude-change process—attention, comprehension, and acceptance of the message. McGuire (1968) has developed a model of attitude change that predicts the relationship between various personality factors and these separate stages—often with opposite effects for a particular personality characteristic on the separate stages. For example, he suggests that intelligence will be positively related to the comprehension stage but negatively related to the acceptance stage. Thus, a bright person will be more apt to understand complex arguments than will an unintelligent person, and therefore one might predict greater attitude change for the intelligent person. In contrast, the less bright person might be more apt to accept a message than would the more intelligent person, thus causing a greater likelihood of change at this stage of the process. Although these relationships can be very complex, the important point to note is that the likelihood of

attitude change may vary with the different stages in the attitude-change process.

E. *Applications of Learning Theories to Attitude-Change Procedures*

To see how these theories might apply to a real-life attitude-change situation, let's take as an example a White female college student who finds a summer job at a local research company. Now let's add two conditions: first, the White student is strongly prejudiced against Blacks, and, second, she will be required to work on a team throughout the summer with a Black female student from another nearby university. What procedures would reinforcement theory advocate to reduce the White student's prejudice?

First, reinforcement theory would suggest that any expression of acceptance by the White toward the Black should be positively reinforced. If the White student should happen to compliment the Black on her clothes or task skills, then other staff members should verbally reinforce the prejudiced White for giving such compliments. Negative gestures by the White toward the Black should, in turn, be given no positive reinforcement. As the conditioning research has shown, even subtle nonverbal responses —a smile or intense concentration on what the speaker is saying—can be reinforcing, and our hypothetical change procedures should make use of these reinforcements when the response is appropriate.

Drawing from the learning model of the Yale Communication Program, we would want to consider each stage of the attitude-change process. For example, if the company has an active program designed to eliminate racial prejudice, it would be important to know that each stage of the attempted attitude-change process was being realized. Thus it would be necessary first to ensure that the prejudiced White college student (and others sharing her beliefs) paid attention to the company's program. Second, it would be important to ensure that the prejudiced White understood the message that was being conveyed. Individual sessions might increase the probability of such acceptance, as would relating the ideas to concepts that the student already had learned in previous schooling. Finally, it would be important to facilitate acceptance of the message. The concept of incentives is important here. The prejudiced person must become motivated to make a new response; the appropriate incentives to bring about this change must be identified and used. The incentive for one person may be social acceptance; for another it may be money.

Once the prejudiced White has accepted the Black, the stimulus-response theorist would seek **stimulus generalization**—or the acceptance by the prejudiced White of Blacks in general. If conditioning has been effective in establishing a new response (attitude) toward the Black participant, the laws of learning predict that stimulus generalization will take place. The more similar the other Blacks to the target, the more likely such generalization is to occur.

II. The Social-Judgment Theory of Attitude Change

Social-judgment theory represents a much more cognitive approach to the study of attitude change. Whereas learning theories deal with the objective nature of the stimulus and assume that this is constant across a wide variety of people, social-judgment theory emphasizes the individual's perception and judgment of the persuasive communication and views these judgments as mediators of attitude change. Thus, for the social-judgment theorist, the cognitive (judgment) and affective (evaluation) components are closely interrelated, and both must be taken into account in predicting attitude change. The major developer of this approach to attitude change has been **Muzafer Sherif** (Sherif & Hovland, 1961; Sherif, Sherif, & Nebergall, 1965).

A. *Basic Concepts of Social-Judgment Theory*

To understand the principles of social-judgment theory as developed by Sherif, we need to look briefly at some issues in

psychophysics, from which the theory was developed. In their early work, Sherif and his colleagues were interested in the basic question of how simple judgments are affected by the context. First they asked subjects to judge the heaviness of a series of weights (ranging from 55 to 141 grams) on a 6-point scale, where 1 was to be used for the lightest weight and 6 for the heaviest weight. Sherif and his colleagues (Sherif, Taub, & Hovland, 1958) found that, with only this set of weights on which to base their judgments, subjects tended to distribute their judgments equally across the 6-point scale (see the top panel of Figure 12-4).

In the next stage of the experiment, Sherif and his colleagues altered the judgment context by introducing an **anchor**—a reference point that is used in making judgments. They did this in two ways. First, they gave subjects a weight of 141 grams and told them that this weight should be rated a 6. With this weight as an anchor, subjects showed **assimilation effects**: judgments tended to pile up toward the anchored end of the scale, rather than be equally distributed as they had before (see the middle panel of Figure 12-4). In a second demonstration of judgment effects, the investigators gave subjects an anchor weighing 347 grams and told them that this weight should be rated a 6. In this case, when judging the original series of weights, subjects showed a **contrast effect**—their judgments tended to pile up at the "lightest" end of the distribution, as they rated the weights to be much lighter in contrast to the anchor stimulus (illustrated in the bottom panel of Figure 12-4).

Although weights may seem a bit abstract, we all make these kinds of judgment shifts fairly regularly. Consider, for example, the resident of snowbound Minneapolis or Ottawa in the winter, who would probably rate a winter day when the thermometer went above 32 degrees Fahrenheit as warm and balmy, showing a contrast effect in judgment compared to the below-zero anchor points that are typically experienced. On the other hand, that same temperature in the summer (or in a Florida winter) might be judged as cold, comparing it

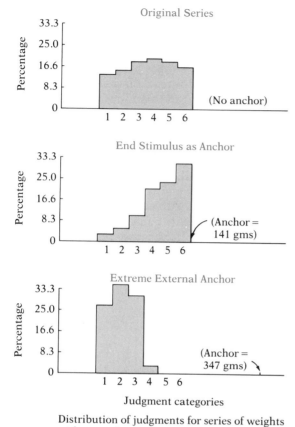

Original Series

End Stimulus as Anchor

(Anchor = 141 gms)

Extreme External Anchor

(Anchor = 347 gms)

Judgment categories

Distribution of judgments for series of weights without anchor (top) and with anchors at two distances above original series.

Figure 12-4. Distribution of judgments of weights without anchor (top) and with anchors (middle and bottom). In the **Sherif** et al. study, there were an equal number of stimuli at each of the six weight levels. In the absence of an anchor, subjects made an equal percentage of judgments to each of the six categories. When an anchor was introduced, judgment patterns changed. In the middle panel, we see that nearly 30% of the weights were judged to be heaviest, showing assimilation toward the 141-gram anchor. A contrast effect is evident in the lower panel. None of the weights were judged as heaviest when the anchor was much heavier, and a high percentage of judgments were made to the lighter categories. (Adapted from "Assimilation and Contrast Effects of Anchoring Stimuli on Judgments," by M. Sherif, D. Taub, and C. I. Hovland, *Journal of Experimental Psychology*, 1958, *55*, 150–155, Copyright 1958 by the American Psychological Association. Used by permission.)

to the anchor-point days with temperatures in the 60s and 70s.

Sherif used these basic principles of psychophysics to develop his social-judgment theory of attitude change. Persuasive communications that are similar to our own view (an internal anchor) will be judged as more similar than they really are, whereas communications at some distance from our own position will be contrasted, or judged as further away than they actually are. To explain how these judgments of assimilation and contrast are related to actual attitude change, Sherif introduced three new concepts: *latitude of acceptance, latitude of rejection,* and *latitude of noncommitment* (Sherif & Hovland, 1961; Sherif, Sherif, & Nebergall, 1965). The principle of latitudes reflects Sherif's belief that a person's attitude cannot be represented by a single point on a scale; rather, an attitude consists of a range of acceptable positions. Thus, if you are presented a set of statements on a particular issue (using, for example, a Thurstone scale), you would be asked to indicate all of those statements that you felt were consistent with your attitude on the issue. These statements would constitute your latitude of acceptance (see **Figure 12-5**). The range of statements that a person finds unacceptable or objectionable is defined as the latitude of rejection, and statements that are neither acceptable nor unacceptable constitute the latitude of noncommitment.

When a person encounters a persuasive communication, his or her first reaction is to make a judgment as to where this communication falls on the dimensions in question and, specifically, whether it falls inside or outside of the latitude of acceptance. Once this judgment is made, then attitude change may or may not occur. Social-judgment theory states that attitude change is most likely to occur when a communication falls inside of a person's latitude of acceptance (Atkins, Deaux, & Bieri, 1967). Attitude change has also been shown to occur when the message falls within an individual's latitude of noncommitment, approaching but not within the latitude of rejection (Peterson & Koulack, 1969).

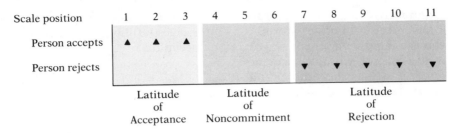

Figure 12-5. Latitudes of acceptance, rejection, and noncommitment. Each number represents a particular statement that the person is asked to accept or reject. For example, if the issue were birth control, a statement at 1 might be "Birth control devices should be available to everyone, and the government and public-welfare agencies should encourage the use of such devices." At the other extreme, a statement might be "All birth control devices should be illegal, and the government should prevent them from being manufactured." (From "Width of the Latitude of Acceptance as a Determinant of Attitude Change," by A. Eagly and K. Telaak, *Journal of Personality and Social Psychology*, 1972, *23*, 388–397. Copyright 1972 by the American Psychological Association. Reprinted by permission.)

B. *Assumptions about Human Nature*

Compared to some of the other theories, the social-judgment model appears to assume that people hold more precise attitudes; that is, the theory says that each person localizes his or her attitude at some point along a scale that includes areas of acceptance and rejection. Social-judgment theory sees the human as a cognitive being, in the sense that people know what their attitudes are, where they stand along a continuum, which other attitudes they would accept, and which they would reject. These cognitive judgments are assumed to precede any actual changes that are made.

As we shall see in the next section, however, social-judgment theory also assumes that other factors can affect the judgment process. For example, the extent of a person's ego involvement in an issue will have predictable effects on the size of the various latitudes and hence will relate to subsequent attitude change. Thus cognitive and affective components are intertwined in this theory, and each may affect the other.

C. *Representative Research*

Research done within the framework of social-judgment theory has concentrated on two issues: (1) What are the effects of ego involvement in an issue on the latitudes of acceptance and rejection and hence on attitude change? (2) How much is attitude change influenced by the discrepancy between the communication and the recipient's position?

Ego Involvement and the Latitudes. A question of major concern to Sherif and his colleagues has been how the size of a person's latitude of acceptance, rejection, and noncommitment may differ as a function of that person's involvement in the issue at hand. In other words, if you are extremely committed to an issue (see, for example, Figure 12-6), will you be apt to find a smaller range of positions acceptable than if your concerns are less intense? Surprisingly, Sherif and his colleagues found no difference in the size of the latitude of acceptance as a function of a person's involvement in an issue. As shown in Figure 12-7, people who were strongly committed to either a Republican or a Democratic position did not differ from uncommitted or neutral people in the size of their acceptable range of positions (although obviously the content of statements within those ranges did differ considerably). Differences did occur in the width of latitudes of noncommitment and rejection. People at either extreme of the scale found considerably more positions unacceptable and were neutral or noncommitted on far fewer items. In other words, the person who is a fanatic about some issue, such as gun control, will not necessarily find any fewer positions acceptable than will a less ego-involved advocate—but that person will reject more anticontrol positions and be neutral about very few positions. Not all research is consistent with Sherif's findings, however, and the exact relationship between ego involvement and size of latitudes is still uncertain (Eagly & Telaak, 1972; N. Miller, 1965).

The question of the size of the latitude of acceptance is important in Sherif's theory because it serves as the basis for predictions of attitude change. A person with a narrow latitude of acceptance would not be expected to change his or her position easily, whereas the person with a wider range of

acceptance should find more persuasive messages falling in or near the boundaries of acceptability.

Effects of the Discrepancy between the Communication and the Position of the Recipient. Based on the principles of the latitudes, social-judgment theory predicts a curvilinear relationship between discrepancy and attitude change. If you consider the implications of the various latitudes, the reasons for this prediction become clear. Messages that fall very close to the person's own position should be assimilated, and no real change would be necessary. On the other end, messages that are highly discrepant with one's own position would probably fall within the latitude of rejection and would not be acceptable or effect any change. Between these two extremes, when

Figure 12-6. Commitment to an issue: The case of people opposed to the use of nuclear energy. (© Christopher Brown/Stock, Boston.)

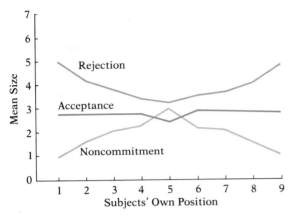

Figure 12-7. Average size (number of positions) of latitudes of acceptance, rejection, and noncommitment for persons endorsing different positions as most acceptable in the 1960 presidential election. Positions along base line range from 1 (most extreme Republican) through 5 (nonpartisan) to 9 (most extreme Democrat). (From *Attitudes and Opinions,* by S. Oskamp. Copyright © 1977 by Prentice-Hall, Inc. Originally adapted from *Attitude and Attitude Change: The Social Judgment Approach,* by C. W. Sherif, M. Sherif, and R. E. Nebergall. Copyright 1965 by W. B. Saunders Company. Used by permission of Prentice-Hall, Inc., and W. B. Saunders Company.)

messages fall somewhere in the latitude of noncommitment, their persuasive impact should be the greatest. Research results generally support this prediction (Hovland, Harvey, & Sherif, 1957; Peterson & Koulack, 1969).

Social judgment has also attempted to incorporate other variables such as the credibility of a persuasive source into its models. For example, social-judgment theorists have suggested that, if the persuasive agent is a highly respectable and highly credible one, attitude change will be more likely to occur. Although other theorists, such as the Yale Communication Program, have predicted similar effects, the rationale for the social-judgment prediction is slightly different. They argue that source credibility affects the perception of the message and thus effectively broadens the latitudes of acceptance and noncommitment, which in turn makes attitude change more likely.

Research has supported the effect of source credibility. Bochner and Insko (1966), for example, found that more discrepant messages were effective in changing a person's attitude toward sleep requirements when the source was a Nobel-prizewinning physiologist than when the source was a YMCA director.

D. *Applications of Social-Judgment Theory to Attitude-Change Procedures*

In applying social-judgment theory to our real-life situation, we must realize that the theory has some intriguing possibilities but some limitations as well. On the positive side of the ledger, there is evidence that it can be successfully applied in real settings, such as Sherif's own work with voter attitudes and referenda toward prohibition (Sherif, Sherif, & Nebergall, 1965) and other projects designed to make salespeople more successful with resistant customers (Varela, 1971). On the other side, it remains true that the theory itself is somewhat limited, dealing only with the variables of message discrepancy and a person's ego involvement in the issue. Nevertheless, let's consider how these two factors might be applied to the situation in which a prejudiced White is working with a Black.

To change the attitude of the prejudiced White student, we would first recognize that attitudes are more likely to change in the desired direction if the persuasive messages fall within—or close to—the subject's latitude of acceptance. Therefore, the limits of acceptance would first have to be determined. If, in contrast, the persuasive message directed toward the subject fell solidly within her latitude of rejection, the message would be very unlikely to have the desired effect. In fact, it would be more apt to reinforce her initial stand or even produce boomerang effects—that is, make her more prejudiced than she originally was.

The greater the discrepancy between the persuasive communication and the position of the subject—as long as the communication is within the acceptance limits —the more we can expect a shift in the person's position. (However, social-judgment theory has only rarely considered individual differences in breadth of acceptance.) What if our target's latitude of acceptance is so narrow that she can only tolerate positions very close to her own? The results of the Eagly and Telaak (1972) study, among others, would suggest that in such a situation very little change would be possible. In these situations, then, social-judgment theory provides very little ground for optimism about achieving significant changes.

Finally, the general concept of anchors might be applied by considering a list of behaviors or alternatives that could be presented to the subject. For example, if other options were presented to the prejudiced student, such as working as the only White in an all-Black group or conducting the project on a predominantly Black university campus, these might serve as external anchors. With such possibilities to serve as anchors, the person's reaction to her present situation might be a more tolerant one than it would be in the absence of such anchors.

Clearly such applications must be developed in greater detail to be of any real use—and even then they may prove cumbersome. The main attraction of social-judgment theory is its recognition of an optimum distance between the subject's attitude position and the position of the persuasive communication. As we shall see in the next section, however, other theories with a broader range of coverage also make this same prediction from a different theoretical stance.

III. Consistency Theories of Attitude Change

The third type of theory, the consistency theories of attitude change, shares with social-judgment theory an emphasis on cognitive processes. They assume that we are aware of our attitudes and behaviors and, more importantly, that we want these various aspects of ourselves to be consistent with each other. From this perspective, attitude change occurs when we perceive some inconsistency among our beliefs or between our attitudes and our behavior. Although

consistency theory assumes that we are thoughtful, it does not necessarily posit that we are rational. Indeed, Abelson and Rosenberg (1958) have coined the term *psycho-logic* to refer to the process whereby we may alter our beliefs so that they are psychologically consistent without necessarily following the strict rules of formal logic. For example, if you know that cigarettes can cause cancer and yet continue to smoke, the belief and the behavior are inconsistent. To resolve this uncomfortable state of inconsistency, you may deny the fact that cigarettes have anything to do with disease. Such a choice is not a totally rational one, yet the denial allows your continued smoking behavior to be consistent with your beliefs.

There are a variety of cognitive-consistency theories, most of them developed in some form from Heider's original balance model (Heider, 1946, 1958). These theories include Osgood and Tannenbaum's *congruity theory* and Festinger's *cognitive-dissonance theory*. Although each theory has some unique characteristics, they also share some common assumptions. Each assumes that people are motivated to be and to appear consistent; each assumes that a person's awareness of his or her own inconsistency is tension producing and cannot easily be tolerated; and, finally, each assumes that attitude change is a principal tool for resolving inconsistencies.

A. *Heider's Balance Theory*

Fritz Heider (1946, 1958) was the first to develop a theory about the ways people view their relationships with other people and with their environment, based on a principle of consistency. For simplicity, Heider limited his analysis to two persons (P and O) and to one other entity (X). The person P is the focus of analysis, and O represents some other person; X can be an idea, a person, a thing, or an attitude object. Heider's goal was to discover how the relationships among P, O, and X are organized in P's cognitive structure. Heider proposed that there were two possible relationships that could exist between these three elements—a *unit relationship*, which refers to the extent to which two elements belong together, as in ownership or similar-group membership, and a *liking relationship*. We will concentrate on the liking relationship, which includes all forms of positive or negative sentiments or affect between two or more elements.

Heider proposed that the relationships among P, O, and X may be either balanced or unbalanced, depending on the pattern of like and dislike links among elements. Consider the following example. P, who has spent all summer as a volunteer worker for the Republican presidential candidate, enters the state university as a freshman in the fall. He is assigned to Professor O as a faculty advisor. When P meets O to plan a first-semester schedule, P observes that O is wearing a campaign button for the Democratic candidate. Will P like O? Will P think much of O's recommendations about which courses to take? Probably not—because P does not feel comfortable in unbalanced relationships. If X in this example stands for the Democratic party candidate, a balanced state exists when P likes O, P likes X, and O likes X. The only way a balanced state can exist within P's cognitive structure—as long as P dislikes X and O likes X—is for P to dislike O. P can say, in effect, "Professor O is

no good, which fits because she's a big supporter of Candidate X."

Heider proposed that balanced states exist either when all three relations are positive (as in liking) or when two relations are negative (disliking) and one is positive (see Figure 12-8). The preceding example fits the latter possibility. Of course, if P had found that his advisor was a Republican supporter and if P had come to like O, then balance theory would describe the relationship as P likes O, P likes X, and O likes X. As can be seen in Figure 12-8, unbalanced states do occur; people do like other people who differ in their attitudes toward important issues or objects. The reverse situation is also possible: you may discover that someone you hate intensely likes the same rather obscure art works that you do. What do you do about such a state? Heider proposes that such unbalanced states produce tension and generate forces to achieve or restore balance.

Heider's approach is a highly simplified one. Indeed, its greatest limitation may be that it's too simplified, for the approach fails to consider degrees of liking, relationships that consist of more than three elements, or more than one direction of liking —for example, it does not consider whether

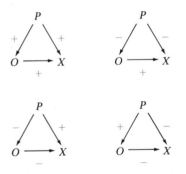

Balanced States

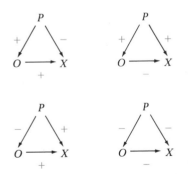

Unbalanced States

Figure 12-8. Heider's balance theory. Examples of balanced and unbalanced states according to Heider's definition of balance. In each case, P is the person whose attitudes are of concern. P can either like or dislike O and both P and O can have either positive or negative attitudes toward X. Can you find any pattern in the def-

inition of balanced and unbalanced states? (Adapted from "The Concepts of Balance, Congruity, and Dissonance," by R. B. Zajonc, *Public Opinion Quarterly*, 1960, 24, 280–296. Copyright 1960 by Columbia University Press. Used by permission.)

O likes P but only whether P likes O (Oskamp, 1977). At the same time, the theory is capable of accounting for a wide variety of phenomena, including interpersonal attraction, verbal reinforcement of attitudes, and liking for political candidates (Insko, Songer, & McGarvey, 1974; Kinder, 1978).

B. Osgood and Tannenbaum's Congruity Theory

The congruity theory of Osgood and Tannenbaum (1955) is an extension of the balance notion and one that has been particularly concerned with the direction and amount of attitude change. Somewhat more limited than Heider's balance theory, congruity theory deals exclusively with attitude change that occurs when some source makes a statement about some object (see Figure 12-9). This statement can represent an *associative bond* (an indication of liking, favor, or approval) or a *dissociative bond* (an indication of disliking, disfavor, or disapproval). For example, if Robert Redford (a source) says that he is in favor of the ecology movement (an object), that statement would represent an associative bond. A dissociative bond would be exemplified by Jane Fonda stating that she is against capital punishment.

According to this theory, a state of congruity or balance exists when a source and concept that are linked by an associative bond have exactly the same evaluation or when a source and an object that are linked by a dissociative bond have exactly the opposite evaluations. Let's take an example to see how this theory works. Consider Professor Jones, who has supported Senator Smith in past elections (+) and who also believes that the National Science Foundation is a valuable institution (+). If Senator Smith were to praise the National Science Foundation, congruity would exist in Professor Jones's cognitive system (a + is linked by an associative bond with a +). But when Senator Smith castigates the NSF for its support of social-science research, calling it trivial and worthless, an inconsistency arises for Professor Jones. The dissociative bond between a positive source and a positive object creates a state of incongruity, which can be resolved only by changing one's attitudes. Because this is a dissociative bond, congruity would occur only if the evaluations of the two concepts were opposite, as, for example, if Senator Smith were now evaluated negatively and the NSF continued to be evaluated positively.

Congruity theorists have taken this approach a step further, by specifying the degrees of evaluation of each source and object. In congruity theory, every source and every object is scaled using a semantic-differential method, on a scale ranging from $+3$ to -3. By using such a graduated scale, the theory allows us to make more finely tuned predictions about attitude change. For example, if Professor Jones is strongly favorable toward the National Science Foundation ($+3$) and only mildly favorable toward Senator Smith ($+1$), even a positive statement by Senator Smith toward the National Science Foundation would result in some shift in attitudes, because the two elements do not have an identical evaluation as the theory requires when an associative bond exists. Unique to congruity theory is the notion that attitude change will occur toward both elements. In this case, we could predict that Professor Jones would become slightly less favorable toward the National Science Foundation but, at the same time, become more favorable toward Senator Smith (the exact prediction would be that both the Senator and the Foundation would end up being rated as a $+2\frac{1}{2}$). Notice that the more extremely held attitude—in this case the National Science Foundation—is more resistant to change than the less strongly held attitude.

C. Festinger's Cognitive-Dissonance Theory

Cognitive-dissonance theory, as first proposed by Leon Festinger (1957), has certainly been the most influential of the consistency theories, not only in the area of attitude change but in a wide variety of other areas of social psychology as well. The basic assumptions of the theory are quite

Photo by Grant Edwards

"THESE FILES ARE FULL OF CHILDREN CRYING OUT FOR YOUR HELP."
Sally Struthers

"In a room at Christian Children's Fund headquarters, there are file cabinets that look like any other file cabinets. Until you look inside. These files are full of children. Children with no one to care for them.

"Unless someone, like you, will help.

"There are children like little Angela. Her health is poor, but her family can't afford a doctor. And Rapson. He suffers from severe malnutrition. And Sri, who rarely eats anything but rice and corn.

"These poor children have known more suffering and want in their short lifetimes than you or I will ever know. But you can help change that. You can become a sponsor through Christian Children's Fund."

For $15 a month—just 50¢ a day— you can help give one of these children warm, nourishing meals, medical attention, the chance to go to school, or whatever the child needs most to live a healthy, productive life.

You needn't send any money now. First learn more about the child who needs you. Just send in the coupon. Christian Children's Fund will send you a child's photograph and tell you about the child's way of life. The child's age, interests and family background. We'll also tell you how this child can be helped, and give you details on how you can write to him and share a very special part of his life.

After you find out more about the child and Christian Children's Fund, then you can decide if you want to become a sponsor. Simply send in your first monthly check or money order for $15 within 10 days.

Please take this opportunity to open your heart to a child who needs you. And receive something very special in return.

Love.

FOR THE LOVE OF A HUNGRY CHILD.

Dr. Verent J. Mills
CHRISTIAN CHILDREN'S FUND, Inc., Box 26511, Richmond, Va. 23261
I wish to sponsor a ☐ boy ☐ girl. ☐ Choose any child who needs help. NNWK61
Please send my information package today.
☐ I want to learn more about the child assigned to me. If I accept the child, I'll send my first sponsorship payment of $15 within 10 days. Or I'll return the photograph and other material so you can ask someone else to help.
☐ I prefer to send my first payment now, and I enclose my first monthly payment of $15.
☐ I cannot sponsor a child now but would like to contribute $_____

Name_____
Address_____
City_____ State_____ Zip_____
Member of American Council of Voluntary Agencies for Foreign Service, Inc.
Gifts are tax deductible. Canadians: Write 1407 Yonge St., Toronto, Ontario M4T 1Y8.
Statement of income and expenses available on request.

CHRISTIAN CHILDREN'S FUND, INC.

Figure 12-9. For those people who have a positive attitude toward Sally Struthers, the appeal pictured here would probably lead to favorable attitudes toward children of poverty.

simple. Cognitive dissonance is said to exist when a person possesses two cognitions that contradict each other. **Cognitions** are thoughts, attitudes, beliefs, and also behaviors of which the person is cognitively aware. For example, the following statements could be considered cognitions: "It's a nice day today," "I am a thoughtful person," "I believe that schools are repressive institutions," and "I forgot my father's birthday." According to Festinger, such cognitions can either be relevant or irrelevant to one another. For example, "It's a nice day today" and "Schools are repressive institutions" would probably be considered irrelevant, in that the one cognition does not imply anything about the other. In contrast, "I am a thoughtful person" is relevant to "I forgot my father's birthday" because the one cognition relates to the other in a psychological sense. Two relevant cognitions may exist either in a state of *consonance* or in a state of *dissonance*. In the case of dissonance, exemplified by "thoughtful person" and "forgetting father's birthday," the two elements do not fit with each other—or, to use a term of Festinger's, the one element implies the obverse of the other.

A basic assumption of dissonance theory is that a state of dissonance motivates the person to reduce or eliminate the dissonance. Dissonance, the theory says, is uncomfortable and produces a state of psychological tension. Just how uncomfortable this state is or how great the magnitude of the dissonance depends on two factors: (1) the ratio of dissonant to consonant cognitions and (2) the importance of each cognition to the person (Sherwood, Barron, & Fitch, 1969). In other words, two cognitions may exist in a state of dissonance, but, if neither is terribly important or central to your beliefs, then the tension experienced will be only minimal. When important beliefs or behaviors are at stake, however, dissonance theory would predict considerable tension and considerable effort to reduce that tension.

How is dissonance reduced? One method is to decrease the number or importance of the dissonant elements. If a man has forgotten his father's birthday, he may convince himself that celebrating birthdays

is meaningless or that his father would just as soon not be reminded that he's getting older. Or the man may increase the number or importance of the consonant cognitions. To reaffirm that he is a thoughtful person, for example, he may buy his father tickets for the Super Bowl, ask him out for dinner, or engage in other behaviors that are consistent with being a thoughtful person.

A third way of reducing dissonance is, of course, to change one of the dissonant elements so that it is no longer inconsistent with the other cognitions. Often this reduction involves changing one's attitude, so that it is consistent with a behavior already performed. In our example, the man might change his self-perception and no longer consider himself a terribly thoughtful person. This latter example underlines one of the unique aspects of dissonance theory. Because the theory proposes that any of the elements in the relationship may change when dissonance is experienced, it allows one to treat the attitude/behavior relationship from both directions. A change in one's cognitions about the self, for example, may lead to future changes in behavior. On the other hand, it is equally possible that a change in one's behavior may lead to a change in one's attitudes—thus attitude change may result from behavior as well as causing behaviors.

The flexibility of this theory has made it extremely popular, and it has been applied to a wide variety of situations, ranging from controlled laboratory experiments on attitude change to participant observation of religious cults. At the same time, the openness of the theory has presented certain problems as well: for example, it is often difficult to specify with any precision just what elements are relevant to a particular situation and how important those elements may be to a specific person. Nonetheless, the theory has generated a huge body of research and, as any good theory should, has suggested many new and significant questions.

D. *Assumptions about Human Nature*

Each of the consistency theories—balance theory, congruity theory, and dissonance theory—assumes that holding conflicting attitudes is intolerable or at least uncomfortable and that people will be motivated to change their attitudes or their behavior in order to feel and appear consistent. Each of the theories also assumes a very cognitive orientation to the world, in that they view people thinking about their attitudes, weighing beliefs, and making conscious choices to change certain attitudes or behaviors. Yet, although the models assume cognition, they do not necessarily assume rationality. Indeed, many of the changes predicted from these models might be appropriately considered rationalizations rather than logical deductions. In other words, they predict a search for a *psychologically* balanced state but do not require that this balance accurately reflect the state of the world. For example, the three-pack-a-

day smoker who denies any evidence of a link between smoking and disease may not be acting realistically—but he or she will nonetheless resolve the dissonance by believing that smoking causes no harm.

There are some limits to consistency theory. The wholesale assumption that people always abhor inconsistency has more recently been rejected in favor of the notion that at least some people sometimes act in such a way as to minimize inconsistencies. But on other occasions people can live with their inconsistencies quite well, and seeking consistency may be less important than seeking novelty, complexity, approval, achievement, or power (Shaw & Skolnick, 1973). See Figure 12-10 for an intriguing example. In addition, recent formulations of dissonance theory have often stressed the

Figure 12-10. President Anwar Sadat of Egypt, President Jimmy Carter of the United States, and Prime Minister Menachem Begin of Israel sign agreements for negotiation of a Middle East peace treaty. Is this behavior consistent with the attitudes of these men? Is it consistent with some attitudes and inconsistent with others? Or are other motives more important than consistency? (© United Press International.)

importance of the self. Thus cognitions may be dissonant but may not necessarily create tension unless some element of personal responsibility is involved (Aronson, 1968; Greenwald & Ronis, 1978).

Although the three theories of cognitive consistency are alike in their major assumptions, each one also has some unique characteristics. Balance theory, for example, assumes a rather simple model of thought and a restricted number of elements; it also assumes that judgments are made on a dichotomous like/dislike basis. Congruity theory, in contrast, assumes that we make finer gradations in our judgments of like and dislike. It also assumes that, in the case of incongruity, we will generally reevaluate both components rather than change only one attitude to resolve the balance. More than either of the other two theories, cognitive-dissonance theory specifically assumes that inconsistency is motivating and that we will experience tension or discomfort when cognitions do not fit with one another. Dissonance theory is also a more "active" theory in the sense that it deals with behavior as well as with attitudes and predicts that changes in actions as well as attitudes will be carried out in order to resolve inconsistency.

E. *Representative Research*

Each of the consistency theories has been subjected to empirical tests. Studies of the relationship between attitude similarity and attraction, for example (as discussed earlier in Chapter 6), are basically derived from Heider's model. If you like pizza with pepperoni and mushrooms and your new roommate has the same preference in pizza, then you are more apt to like your roommate than if the person is an anchovy freak. Similarly, a rave movie review from a friend will make you more inclined to rate that movie positively than you would if your friend had pronounced the movie a dud. In the realm of political opinion, balance theory has also shown its relevance. Kinder (1978) studied voters' perceptions of 1968 U.S. presidential candidates Nixon,

Humphrey, and Wallace, together with the respondents' views on a number of current political and social issues and their perception of the candidates' stands on these same issues. In line with balance theory, respondents who thought that the solution to urban unrest was the use of more force, for example, also tended to see their preferred candidate as sharing similar views on the issue. In other words, people were attempting to achieve a balanced relationship among the triad consisting of: (1) their attitude toward an issue; (2) their attitude toward a candidate; and (3) the candidate's attitude toward that issue.

Research testing the congruity model has also achieved some success, although, as we noted earlier, the model is a limited one and thus has not been used extensively. In contrast, cognitive-dissonance theory has found applications over a wide range of areas—more than 500 studies have been completed using this single theoretical framework. Let's take a look at a few of the major issues on which that research has focused.

1. *The Consequences of Decision Making.* More than most other theories of attitude change, dissonance theory has been concerned with the consequences of making a decision on subsequent attitudes and behavior. According to the theory, any time one is forced to choose between two attractive options, postdecision dissonance exists (Festinger, 1957). The more difficult or important the decision, the more likely a person is to find reasons that support the choice that was made and to minimize the attractive qualities of the foregone choice. For example, if you are undecided about which of two persons to invite to the Super Bowl game, dissonance theory predicts that, once you have made your choice, you will find many ways of "spreading apart" the alternatives—your chosen date will seem more attractive than he or she did before and the rejected date will seem less attractive than before. This same strategy has been evidenced in a variety of settings, including election polling areas and race tracks (see Box 12-1).

Box 12-1. Postdecision Dissonance Reduction at Post Time.

"Put your money where your mouth is" was an admonition followed by Robert Knox and James Inkster (1968), who were not content to test cognitive-dissonance theory only under artificial laboratory conditions. These researchers went to a local racetrack in Vancouver and interviewed bettors at the $2 window about the chances of their horse's winning. Subjects who were interviewed as they stood in line waiting to place their bets thought their horse had a little better than a fair chance to win. In contrast, subjects interviewed right after they had placed their bet were significantly more confident, rating their chances as good. These results suggest that the act of committing oneself by placing the bet creates dissonance and leads to the dissonance-reducing rating of greater confidence in one's choice. A similar process was observed by Frenkel and Doob (1976) at polling areas in a Toronto election. Voters polled after they had cast their ballot were more likely to believe that their candidate was best and that he or she would win than those voters polled before they entered the polling area. (© United Press International.)

2. *Selective Exposure to Information.* Another way to confirm that we have made a correct decision is to seek out information that is consistent with our choice and to avoid information that is discrepant. For ex- ample, after purchasing a new car, you might be more prone to read magazine re- ports on the virtues of the car that you bought and to avoid advertisements for the competing car that you did not buy. This selective-exposure hypothesis seems intuitively reasonable and can be used to explain the failure of many media campaigns, for example, if we assume that people who are against the persuasive message simply don't pay attention to it. Yet, despite the intuitive appeal, a number of laboratory experiments designed to demonstrate selective exposure had little success (Feather, 1963; Freedman & Sears, 1965; Rosen, 1961). More recently, however, several investigators have demonstrated that selective exposure is a real phenomenon (Cotton & Heiser, 1978; Frey & Wicklund, 1978). The critical variable, it appears, is a person's choice in the matter: if a person has a high degree of choice in making the initial decision, then he or she will selectively seek information that is consistent with that choice and avoid information that is discrepant. In contrast, the person who had little choice in the matter apparently feels little need to shore up support for the decision.

3. *Counterattitudinal Advocacy.* When a person is forced to take a public position contrary to his or her private attitude, dissonance theory proposes that the conflict will lead to attitude change (usually in the private attitude). The theory also makes the somewhat surprising prediction that, the less a person is induced to advocate a public position that violates the private attitude, the more likely the person is to shift the privately held attitude. The now classic study that first tested this prediction (Festinger & Carlsmith, 1959) paid male students either $1 or $20 to lie to other students. After participating for an hour in a series of dull, meaningless tasks (for example, putting 12 spools in a tray, emptying the tray, and then refilling it, time and time again), the student was paid to tell a prospective subject that the experiment was interesting, educational, and highly worthwhile. Later, under the guise of a survey unrelated to the experiment, each subject who lied for either $1 or $20 answered a questionnaire about his private attitudes toward the experiment. Festinger and Carlsmith found that students who had been paid only $1 rated the experimental task as more enjoyable than did those students who were paid $20. Presum-

ably, the students who were paid $20 for the lie could easily justify the reasons for their behavior—money did talk, in this instance. The other students, however, who received only $1 in payment, had to find some other reason for their behavior—hence the attitude change, whereby they said that the experiment was enjoyable because they believed it was.

Not everyone has accepted this conclusion. The methodology of cognitive-dissonance studies, particularly those that involve deception, has been severely criticized, and questions have been raised about the validity of some of the results (Chapanis & Chapanis, 1964). Critics have also questioned the plausibility of some of the manipulations and suggested suspicion on the part of the subjects. Rosenberg, for example, has argued that paying large monetary rewards in cognitive-dissonance experiments has led to an increase in the subject's **evaluation apprehension**, defined as "an active, anxiety-toned concern that he win a positive evaluation from the experimenter, or at least that he provide no grounds for a negative one" (M. J. Rosenberg, 1965, p. 29). This apprehension, presumably greater when more money is involved, might cause the subject with the $20 payment to resist admitting any change in private opinion.

Controversy surrounding the effects of counterattitudinal advocacy continued for more than a decade after the original Festinger and Carlsmith experiment, resulting in dozens of studies and numerous lively debates. In the aftermath of this debate, it seems clear that the basic hypothesis of Festinger does indeed hold true, when certain conditions are met. In brief, these conditions are: (a) there is low incentive (for example, money) to perform the behavior; (b) the person has a high degree of perceived choice to perform the behavior; (c) the action has unpleasant consequences for someone; and (d) the person believes that he or she has a high degree of personal responsibility for the action and its consequences (Kiesler & Munson, 1975; Oskamp, 1977). Furthermore, some degree of arousal related to the inconsistency is necessary as well. Subjects who are administered a tranquilizer in the forced-compliance situation, for example, show little attitude change (Cooper, Zanna, & Taves, 1978). Although the behavior of these subjects is still counter to their attitudes, the tranquilizer presumably reduces any tension that might arise from the dissonance between attitude and behavior—and, without tension, there is no pressure to change the attitude. Thus, as is true of the consistency notion in general, some behaviors that are discrepant with previously held attitudes will not cause any subsequent attitude change; however, those that are more important, more personal, and less readily justified may indeed lead us to modify our attitudes.

F. *Self-Perception Theory: A Different View of Dissonance*

In the wake of the enthusiasm for dissonance theory's explanations of forced compliant behavior, Daryl Bem proposed a radically different interpretation of the results based on his own self-perception theory. According to Bem, people come to "know" their attitudes and other internal states partially by inferring them from observations of their own behavior (D. J. Bem, 1965, 1967, 1972). Bem's theory, which is in large part based on the reinforcement principles of B. F. Skinner, essentially views the person forming attitudes in the same way that an observer would infer the person's attitudes. Both use the available external cues in order to infer the internal state of mind.

To illustrate the self-perception theory, let's look at how Bem would reinterpret the Festinger and Carlsmith findings. In this case, Bem makes the same predictions as would dissonance theorists—that subjects paid $1 will report a more favorable attitude toward the experiment than will subjects paid $20—but he does so for different reasons. According to Bem, the person who was paid $1 will look to the environment to find reasons for this behavior. Not finding sufficient reasons ($1 is hardly enough), the person will then infer that his or her attitude toward the experiment must have been favorable and will report it accordingly when asked by the experimenter. To demonstrate this thought process, Bem performed

an "interpersonal replication" of the Festinger and Carlsmith experiment. He presented a group of subjects with the basic information about the situation and then asked these subjects to infer the actor's attitude on the basis of the described behavior. Bem describes the process as follows:

The hypothetical observer is then asked to state the actual attitude of the individual he has heard. If the observer had seen an individual making such statements for little compensation ($1), he can rule out financial incentive as a motivating factor and infer something about the individual's attitudes. He can use an implicit self-selection rule and ask: "What must this man's attitude be if he is willing to behave in this fashion in this situation?" Accordingly, he can conclude that the individual holds an attitude consistent with the view that is expressed in the behavior: He must have actually enjoyed the tasks. On the other hand, if an observer sees an individual making such statements for a large compensation (e.g., $20), he can infer little or nothing about the actual attitude of that individual, because such an incentive appears sufficient to evoke the behavior regardless of the individual's private views. The subject paid $20 is not credible in the sense that his behavior cannot be used as a guide for inferring his private views [1972, p. 7].[1]

Self-perception theory proposes that participants in Festinger and Carlsmith's experiment behaved just like this hypothetical observer. They considered their own behavior and implicitly asked themselves: "What must my attitude be if I am willing to behave in this fashion in this situation?" Their final attitudes are self-attributions based on their behavior and the apparent compensation for it.

As you might expect, Bem's reinterpretation of dissonance findings has not gone without criticism. The fact that passive observers can replicate the findings obtained from involved actors does not necessarily mean that both are engaging in

[1] From "Self-Perception Theory," by D. J. Bem. In L. Berkowitz (Ed.), *Advances in Experimental Social Psychology*, Vol. 6. Copyright 1972 by Academic Press, Inc. Reprinted by permission of the author and publisher.

the same process, nor does it mean that dissonance is not experienced by the actor. As Zajonc has observed, "Most subjects are also able to guess the trajectory of an apple falling from a tree, without doing serious damage to the laws of classical mechanics" (1968, p. 375). Although a rash of so-called "critical" experiments attempted to prove one theory superior (for example, D. Green, 1974; Shaffer, 1975; Snyder & Ebbesen, 1972; Ross & Shulman, 1973), most of them failed to show that one theory was demonstrably superior to the other (Greenwald, 1975). Because the same observable behaviors are being predicted in most cases, it may in fact be impossible to do so.

More recently, however, some investigators have suggested that it may be more appropriate to look for areas where the two theories do not compete, rather than areas where they do. Fazio, Zanna, and Cooper (1977) have suggested that self-perception theory may be most appropriate in those situations in which behavior is congruent with an attitude, whereas dissonance theory may have the edge in those cases where behavior is discrepant with one's attitude. For example, if you are reasonably in favor of conserving energy, active involvement in an energy-saving campaign would probably lead you to become more pronounced in your attitude toward energy conservation. Such a change would not reflect dissonance reduction—the original attitude and the behavior were not inconsistent—but some reevaluation of your attitude would occur, based on observations of your behavior, as self-perception theory would predict. Of critical importance here is the concept of *tension*. When attitudes and behavior are not contradictory, no tension should be expected. In contrast, when an attitude and a behavior are in contradiction, tension is experienced and dissonance theory becomes the more powerful explanation.

G. *Applications of Consistency Theories to Attitude-Change Procedures*

Each of the consistency theories offers some general strategies that could be applied toward changing the attitude of a prej-

udiced White person toward a Black co-worker. Balance theory, for example, would predict that, if both the Black and the White person had similar attitudes toward some important issue or object (for example, toward their immediate supervisor), then the White person would be more apt to like the Black, thus creating a balanced state. Congruity theory, from its basis of communicated messages, would formulate a situation in which the Black (presumably evaluated -2 or -3 on the White person's internal scale) would be positively associated with some positively valued concept or person. Thus, if the president of the company were considered a $+3$, then positive statements by the president about Black/White relationships might lead to an increase in the Black's perceived placement in the prejudiced White person's mind. The danger of this particular strategy, however, is that the president would also be devalued at the same time, a consequence that might not be desirable. Alternatively, it would be possible for the Black worker to show dislike of some person or issue that the White dislikes as well. Such a strategy, from congruity-theory predictions, would lead to a more favorable attitude toward the Black person.

Brehm and Cohen (1962) have applied cognitive-dissonance theory specifically to the task of desegregation and integration. They propose that most prejudiced White persons who interact closely with a Black will experience dissonance arousal as their attitudes will seem discrepant with their behavior. Dissonance will be particularly increased if this behavioral commitment is irrevocable. As dissonance is unpleasant, efforts will be made by the prejudiced Whites to bring their attitudes closer to their behavior. As Brehm and Cohen have stated:

In effect, we expect that, among other things, the dissonance-reduction process should result in a more favorable perception of the social climate shared with the Negroes and a change toward more favorable attitudes toward Negroes. Thus, everything else being equal, commitment to an irrevocable interracial policy should result in at least some change in attitudes toward the Negroes: Forcing a person to behave in a fashion discrepant from what he believes can result in a change in private opinion [1962, p. 272].

Some of the factors controlling the magnitude of dissonance experienced and the consequent amount of attitude change include the extent of contact with a Black, the extent of freedom of choice, and the initial attitude position. The greater the contact (in terms of proximity, intimacy, frequency, or duration), the greater the dissonance and the greater the efforts to reduce dissonance. With regard to the variable of choice, Brehm and Cohen have proposed that, the more a person is compelled to make a commitment, the less dissonance is created and hence the less attitude change. To facilitate attitude change, the person must be given some choice in interacting with Blacks. Once he or she does behave in a positive way, the person should then not be given a chance to disclaim his or her action, for such a disclaimer reduces dissonance and creates less need to change the original attitude (Harvey & Mills, 1971; Helmreich & Collins, 1968). Finally, the more unfavorable the initial attitude position of the anti-Black White, the more the White's attitude should change in a favorable direction—assuming that the White has, through the exercise of choice, become committed to some interaction with Blacks. However, those who wish to apply a cognitive-dissonance model to such a situation must be careful in trying to force compliance. If persons refuse to act in ways inconsistent with their prejudiced attitudes, their attitudes may become even more negative than before (Darley & Cooper, 1972; Kiesler, 1971).

The consistency theorist would try to marshal an attractive situation that the White person would enter of his or her own free will. Once the White finds himself or herself in the situation and committed to making the job a success, he or she should be oriented toward the discrepancy between attitudes and behavior. The attitude will then shift, being more amenable to change than the behavior.

IV. Functional Theories of Attitude Change

We now turn to the fourth and final type of attitude-change theory, the functional theory. You will find it to be quite different from the previous ones.

A. *Basic Position*

The basic proposition of a functional theory of attitude change is a simple one: people hold attitudes that fit their needs, and, in order to change those attitudes, we must determine what their needs are. The functional approach is a phenomenological one; it maintains that a stimulus (for example, a television commercial, a new piece of information, or an interracial contact) can be understood only within the context of the perceiver's needs and personality. Different people may have quite different needs, and consequently the same persuasive message may not be equally effective for all people.

Two rather similar functional theories have been developed, one by Katz (1960, 1968; Katz & Stotland, 1959) and one by Smith, Bruner, and White (1956). Each theory proposes a list of functions that attitudes serve. The two theories have some differences, but Kiesler, Collins, and Miller (1969) have helpfully synthesized the functions of each, as shown in Table 12-1. We

TABLE 12-1 / *The Functions of Attitudes*

Katz	Smith, Bruner, and White
Types:	
1. Instrumental, adjustive, utilitarian	Social adjustment
2. Ego defense	Externalization
3. Knowledge	Object appraisal
4. Value expressive	Quality of expressiveness

From *Attitude Change: A Critical Analysis of Theoretical Approaches*, by C. A. Kiesler, B. E. Collins, and N. Miller. Copyright 1969 by John Wiley & Sons, Inc. Reprinted by permission.

will describe each general function, drawing heavily on the analysis of Kiesler and his associates.

First, attitudes may serve an *instrumental, adjustive,* or *utilitarian* function. According to Katz, a person develops a positive attitude toward those objects that are useful in meeting his or her needs or that are effective in preventing negative events. If an object, or another person, thwarts the person's needs, he or she develops a negative attitude toward that object or person. As we can see, this particular basis of attitudes draws heavily on learning principles, suggesting that a person's past history of reinforcement or punishment with a particular attitude object will serve as the basis for attitude formation and change.

Second, attitudes may serve an *ego-defensive* or *externalizing* function. Here, Katz's functional theory is influenced by psychoanalytic thought. An attitude may develop or change in order to protect a person "from acknowledging the basic truths about himself or the harsh realities in his external world" (D. Katz, 1960, p. 170). For example, derogatory attitudes toward out-groups and minority groups may serve as a means of convincing oneself of one's own importance. Without utilizing psychoanalytic supports, Smith, Bruner, and White see attitudes as functioning in a similar way, permitting the externalization of internal reactions.

The *knowledge* function, or *object appraisal,* is a third function of attitudes. Attitudes may develop or change in order "to give meaning to what would otherwise be an unorganized chaotic universe" (Katz, 1960, p. 175). This will happen particularly when a problem cannot be solved without the information associated with the attitude. Smith, Bruner, and White see attitudes as a "ready aid in 'sizing up' objects and events in the environment from the point of view of one's major interests and going concerns" (1956, p. 41). Some of the consistency notions are relevant here, as we may view new situations in terms of the previous beliefs that we have about the situation. Object appraisal "stresses the role that gathering information plays in the day-to-day adaptive activities of the individual" (Kiesler et al., 1969, p. 315).

Value expression is a fourth function of attitudes. According to Katz, people gain satisfaction from expressing themselves through their attitudes. For example, one's attitude toward the latest Mazda may be a reflection of a general self-image, one which in this case is centered on fast cars and new trends. Beyond this, the expression of attitudes may help people form their own self-concepts. Smith, Bruner, and White diverge most widely from Katz at this point. To them, the expressive nature of attitudes does not mean that any need for expression exists but rather that a person's attitudes "reflect the deeper-lying pattern of his or her life" (Smith et al., 1956, p. 38). In other words, they do not see this fourth type of attitude as serving any real function or satisfying any real need but rather as being simply a reflection of some general aspects of the personality.

If we consider that attitudes may be serving any one of these four different functions, then the process of attitude change can become considerably more difficult. First of all, different conditions may arouse different attitudes. For example, posed threats or a rise in frustration may activate ego-defensive needs. In contrast, new information presented in an intellectual way may arouse attitudes based on the knowledge function. In turn, different types of influences are predicted to be effective in changing each type of attitude. The promise of social approval from an important peer group, for example, might be effective in changing an instrumentally based attitude. Attitudes based on ego-defensive needs would probably be unaffected by such a strategy but might be more influenced by some form of self-insight therapy.

B. *Applications of Functional Theory to Attitude-Change Procedures*

Consider our example of the prejudiced White student who is working on a summer project with a Black. This person may have expressed anti-Black attitudes because she was exposed to such attitudes in her environment and learned them from her friends. On the other hand, her prejudice may reflect a deep-seated personality problem. That is, her internal feelings of personal worthlessness may be so threatening to her that she defends against them by disparaging Blacks, Chicanos, Catholics, or any other identifiable group. A functional theory proposes that the effective attitude-change techniques in these two situations would vary. Thus, functional theory would first seek to determine what needs were being met by the White person's anti-Black attitudes. A series of projective tests or clinical interviews would probably be used to make this determination, although the exact procedures are not specified by the theory.

If the person was anti-Black because such attitudes gained her approval from friends and family, then the best strategy might be to institute a different set of rewards in the job situation. Positive attitudes toward Black workers could win approval from her employer and camaraderie from other workers. Anti-Black attitudes, in contrast, would be negatively reinforced.

If the person's anti-Black attitudes were based simply on misinformation, then the approach to change might be even easier. Simply providing new information, perhaps through a general orientation course, could

in itself be effective (see Figure 12-11). In contrast, if the person's anti-Black attitudes were ego defensive in nature, based on some internal conflicts, then a deluge of information will have little effect. In this case, therapeutic procedures such as catharsis and developing insight into the ego-defensive function served should be more beneficial. Obviously, however, such a procedure would hardly be practical in the average summer-job setting.

C. *Assumptions about Human Nature*

The functional theories emphasize individual differences in human nature. To change another person's attitude, we must first recognize his or her specific needs and then choose specific change strategies consistent with the need base. The functional theory reflects assumptions about the complexity and variability of human nature.

D. *Representative Research*

As Kiesler and his colleagues (1969) point out, a straightforward test of functional theory would be to select two subjects whose attitudes toward an object are similar but are based on different needs and

Figure 12-11. More information — presented in a newspaper editorial or gained in conversation with another person, for example — may sometimes be sufficient to change attitudes. (Joseph Hirsch, *Two Men*, 1937. Oil on canvas, 18⅛" x 48¼". Collection, The Museum of Modern Art, New York, Abby Aldrich Rockefeller Fund.)

then to determine the effectiveness of various kinds of attitude-change techniques. Unfortunately, however, this straightforward approach has not really been used, largely because of the difficulty in determining just what function a particular attitude serves for a particular individual.

A more general approach is demonstrated in a study by McClintock (1958), in which groups of subjects were assessed on two general personality measures (need for conformity and ego defensiveness) and then presented with one of several different messages concerning prejudice. In one case, for example, the message was informational, stressing the cultural-relativism arguments against prejudice; in the other case, the message was interpretational, focusing on the internal dynamics that can lead to prejudice. McClintock predicted that those subjects high in conformity would be more susceptible to the informational appeal, whereas subjects high in ego defensiveness would be more persuaded by the interpretational appeal. (Notice that the investigator is assuming that, for a person high in ego defensiveness, any attitude is presumed to have that basis. Such an assumption is very risky and does not really test the individual approach of functional theory.)

Despite a number of methodological problems in this study, one of the hypotheses was confirmed. Among subjects who read the informational message, more high-conformity subjects than low-conformity subjects changed their attitudes. In contrast, high-ego-defensive persons were less likely to show attitude change than were low-ego-defensive persons. Results for the interpretational message were much less consistent. Conformity showed no relationship to change, and, for the ego-defensiveness measure, greatest change was shown by those in the middle range of the scale. Although Katz would argue that those high in ego defensiveness are simply too rigid to make any changes, at least in such an impersonal setting, we must conclude that the results are not wholehearted support for functional theory. Furthermore, later attempts to demonstrate the utility of functional theory have also not been very successful (Katz, Sarnoff, & McClintock,

1956; Smith & Brigham, 1972; Stotland, Katz, & Patchen, 1959).

A functional theory of attitudes is appealing to anyone who recognizes that attitude change is a function of both the message and the recipient of that message. More than any other approach, this one recognizes individual differences in persuasion, and for that reason it should not be dismissed lightly. But the development of the theory is hampered by a lack of adequate measurement of needs. Until such measures are better developed, we must conclude that the theory has little practical use. Nevertheless, it does serve as a suggestive model, highlighting contributions of consistency, learning, psychoanalytic, and self theories in the formation of attitudes and in programs for change. As a general heuristic model, it may be more widely accepted than as a specific and testable theory.

V. Summary

The number of theories and models of attitude change that have been developed reflects the importance that we place on understanding how a person's attitude may be altered through a variety of persuasive tactics. Four of the major theoretical approaches are learning and reinforcement theories, social-judgment theory, the consistency theories, and functional theory. Each theory has different assumptions about human nature.

Conditioning theories of attitude change rely on basic principles developed in the experimental laboratory. Concepts such as conditioned and unconditioned stimuli, reinforcement, and habit strength are used to explain the effect of persuasive communications on the recipient.

The Yale Communication Research Program relied more loosely on learning principles and stressed a three-stage process of attitude change—attention, comprehension, and acceptance. This program of research also identified three general factors that may influence attitude change: the communication stimuli, source characteristics, and the setting. More than any other approach, learning theories make the assumption that attitudes are changed only if the incentives for making a new response are greater than the incentives for maintaining the old response.

Social-judgment theory represents a more cognitive approach to attitude change and emphasizes the individual's perception and judgment of a communication as prerequisites to predicting attitude change. Borrowing from the principles of psychophysics, social-judgment theorists have demonstrated the importance of anchors, or reference points, in our judgments of the position of a communication. Concepts of assimilation and contrast are used to describe these shifts in our judgments. In Sherif's theory, an attitude is described by a range of positions along a scale, called the latitude of acceptance. Other opinion points on the scale may fall either in the latitude of rejection or the latitude of noncommitment. Attitude change is believed most likely to occur when a persuasive communication falls in or near a person's latitude of acceptance. Research within the social-judgment framework has focused on two major variables: (1) the effects of a person's ego-involvement in an issue and (2) the amount of discrepancy between a persuasive communication and the person's own position.

The consistency theories of attitude change include Heider's balance theory, Osgood and Tannenbaum's congruity theory, and Festinger's cognitive-dissonance theory. Common to these is an assumption that people change their attitudes in order to reduce or remove inconsistency between conflicting attitudes and behaviors. Although these theories assume that we are thoughtful, they do not require that we be rational either in our perception of inconsistency or in its resolution.

Heider's balance theory deals with the relationship between a person P, another person O, and some object X, and his general theory has been used in many areas such as interpersonal attraction in addition to attitude change. The congruity model is limited to the case in which some source makes a statement about some object and the changes in a person's attitudes toward both the source and the object. Of all the consistency theories, Festinger's cognitive-dissonance model has generated the most research and also the most controversy. Dissonance is said to exist when a person possesses two cognitions, one of which is contradictory to the other. Such dissonance is believed to be uncomfortable and to motivate the person to eliminate the dissonance by changing either the behavior or the attitude. Research within the cognitive-dissonance framework has focused on the consequences of decision making, selective exposure to information, and the effects of counterattitudinal advocacy.

Bem's self-perception theory offers a critique of the dissonance model and suggests that people infer their attitudes from their behavior and from external cues in the same way that an uninvolved observer would.

The basic proposition of the functional theories of attitude change is that people hold attitudes that fit their needs and that, to change these attitudes, we must determine what the particular needs are. Among the functions that attitudes may serve are: (1) the instrumental, adjustive, or utilitarian function; (2) the ego-defensive or externalization function; (3) the knowledge or object-appraisal function; and (4) the value-expressing function. These theories have not generated much research, but they serve as general models, incorporating many of the assumptions of more specific attitude-change theories.

Glossary Terms

anchor	contingency	stimulus generalization
assimilation effects	awareness	
cognitions	contrast effect	
	evaluation apprehension	

We have too many high sounding words, and too few actions that correspond with them. ABIGAIL ADAMS

13

Attitude and Behavior Change: Outcomes

As we saw in Chapter 12, there is no shortage of theories concerning the nature of attitude change; however, when we turn to an actual situation in which attitude change is desired, we often find that no one of these theories is totally successful in prescribing a strategy. In part, this limitation results from the fact that each theory has defined a limited set of concepts or variables on which to build its structure. Actual attitude-change settings aren't so neatly partitioned, and they often call for a dip into many theoretical pots with their particular variables of concern. Stuart W. Cook (1970) refers to this approach as one that uses *event* theories, rather than the *process* theories that we described in Chapter 12. Event theories include hypotheses that seek to explain recurring patterns of events. For example, are we more likely to change our attitudes if an expert or authority, rather than a friend, tries to persuade us to change? Are rational, fact-filled communications more persuasive than communications based on emotion? You can see from these questions that event theories attempt to isolate factors that may influence changes in attitude and behavior. They deal more with specific factors than with the larger theoretical network.

In this chapter, we consider the specific variables that have been identified as important in attitude change and the factors that account for resistance to persuasion. Then we turn to some specific examples of attitude-change practices and programs, looking at areas such as politics, health, and interracial contact.

I. Major Components of Persuasion

Journalism students are often told that a good news article should identify "who said what to whom under what circumstances." In similar fashion, students of attitude and behavior change (most notably, the members of the Yale Communication Program) have traditionally identified four elements that are involved in most persuasion situations: the source of the persuasive communication, the characteristics of the message, the context in which the message is delivered, and the personality of the recipient of the message. Within each of these elements, there are a variety of factors that affect the success of persuasion.

A. *The Source*

Often, the person who says something to you influences your reactions to what is said. Recommendations from a close friend are generally treated more seriously than advice from a total stranger or an enemy. Commercial business enterprises invest thousands of dollars on the assumption that we are more likely to buy their products when they are endorsed by celebrities rather than anonymous individuals (see Figure 13-1).

One major concern of investigators has been the credibility of a source, which includes the components *expertise, trustworthiness,* and *impact* (Schweitzer & Ginsburg, 1966; R. G. Smith, 1973). Not surprisingly, the majority of studies have found that we are more apt to be persuaded by a credible source than by a noncredible source (Hovland & Weiss, 1951; Karlins & Abelson, 1970). The study that was conducted by Bochner and Insko is an example of this phenomenon, because the advocacy speech was presented by either a Nobel prize-winning scientist or a YMCA director. In this paired comparison, the scientist won (see Chapter 12). Of course, just how credible a source is may depend on the point of view of the recipient (Rosnow & Robinson, 1967); for example, judges are among those used as highly credible sources, but some people may have reason to distrust any statement that is made by a judge.

Although sources may be credible in an abstract sense, their effectiveness in a particular situation also can be influenced by their apparent motives. For example, when we believe that a person is arguing against his or her own best interests, we may be more persuaded by the message than we are when we suspect that a person stands to gain some personal rewards through our acceptance of a message (Walster, Aronson, & Abrahams, 1966). Eagly, Wood, and Chaiken (1978) have discussed this process in terms of attribution theory and our perceptions and expectations of other people. If, for example, a local business vice-president is scheduled to address the Junior Chamber of Commerce on the topic of ecology, we might anticipate that the vice-president will adopt an anti-environmental stance that is appropriate to both his company's interests and the audience's disposition. If, however, that vice-president delivers a pro-environmental speech, we would be much more apt to be persuaded by the speech than by a similar talk given by a Sierra Club officer to a local ecology club. In other words, we may implicitly make assumptions regarding the stance a source is likely to take—assumptions that are based on other things that we know about the source. Messages that contradict those assumptions and seem unlikely to reflect self-interest are much more credible and, therefore, more apt to result in attitude change.

There are other obvious limits to the credibility effect. For example, if an audience is not motivated to receive a communication and pays no attention to the attempt, the credibility of the source will make little difference (Brock & Becker, 1965). Thus, an anti-abortion group would be unlikely to change their attitude, whether the spokesperson for reproductive rights was a highly prestigious physician or an unknown person. Such findings, while certainly not surprising, remind us of the importance of considering different stages of the attitude-change process, as learning theorists propose.

Figure 13-1. Assumptions of source effectiveness. (Photo © Gail Kefauver.)

Characteristics of the source also may be influential. Physically attractive communicators, for example, have been shown to be more effective than less attractive sources, even though they may not be judged as more credible (Horai, Naccari, & Fatoullah, 1974; Mills & Aronson, 1965; Snyder & Rothbart, 1971). Therefore, the use of movie stars and beautiful people in TV commercials seems to have empirical support, perhaps vindicating sponsors' lavish investments. A source's clothing, grooming, and general physical appearance also can influence the extent of attitude change (Cooper, Darley, & Henderson, 1974). Race may be an additional influence, especially for those who are prejudiced against a particular ethnic group (Aronson & Golden, 1962). Perceived similarities between a source and a recipient that are relevant to the issue at hand also are effective in producing attitude change (Berscheid, 1966).

B. *The Message*

Imagine that you were asked to persuade an audience concerning the virtues of yearly medical checkups. Assume that you know everything there is to know about the topic and that you have been designated as the source. How would you organize your arguments? What medium would you use? What particular appeals would you stress? These questions deal with the communicated message itself. Considerable research has been conducted in an effort to isolate those factors of communication that are most effective. In general, we can place these factors in three categories: the content, the organization or format, and the medium used.

One of the major concerns in considering the content of persuasive messages has been the effectiveness of fear-arousing appeals. In our example of yearly medical examinations, for example, would it be wise to describe serious diseases? Or would it be better to stress the positive effects of having a medical exam, in terms of improved health, greater self-assurance, and the like?

In an early experiment, Janis and Feshbach (1953) presented subjects with a message that was designed to encourage proper

dental care. The level of fear-arousing content in the message ranged from low (some small cavities might occur) to high (pictures of advanced gum disease were included). These investigators found the greatest reported change among those subjects who had been exposed to low levels of fear-arousing material. More recent evidence contradicts this conclusion, however, often finding greater attitude change following high fear appeals (Higbee, 1969; Leventhal, 1970; McGuire, 1969). In many cases, advertising agencies appear to have been affected by the results of these later studies (see Figure 13-2). One resolution of these contradictory results has been proposed by McGuire in the form of a curvilinear relationship, or a U-shaped curve, relating the amount of fear to the degree of attitude change. According to this formulation, very low levels of fear and very high levels of fear-arousing material are both ineffective. Low levels of fear might be insufficient for even gaining an audience's attention, and very high levels of fear may cause defensiveness and avoidance. On the other hand, at intermediate levels of fear, it is predicted that both attention and reception may be high; therefore, communication may be most effective at this level.

A message that arouses fear will probably be ineffective unless it clearly recommends actions by which the feared consequences can be avoided. In other words, it does no good to exhibit lurid pictures of gum decay unless you also provide your audience with the means of avoiding that consequence. In discussing this area of research, Rogers (1975) has proposed that three factors are important in any fear appeal: the magnitude of unpleasantness of the described event, the probability that the event will really occur if the recommended action is not taken, and the perceived effectiveness of the recommended action. For example, most people probably see the chances of developing severe gum disease as unlikely, even though they may forget to brush their teeth for days. Other people may disregard anti-smoking campaigns that warn of lung cancer and heart attacks, assuming that they are not going to die in the near future whether or not they quit

IS THIS WHAT YOUR KISSES TASTE LIKE?

If you smoke cigarettes, you taste like one.

Your clothes and hair can smell stale and unpleasant, too.

You don't notice it, but people close to you do. Especially if they don't smoke.

And non-smokers are the best people to love. They live longer.

AMERICAN CANCER SOCIETY®

This space contributed by the publisher as a public service.

Figure 13-2. The use of fear appeals. (Courtesy of the American Cancer Society, California division.)

smoking. In summary, a message that arouses fear may not be effective unless the source focuses on the specific behavior that is desired and considers the beliefs that relate to that specific behavior (Fishbein & Ajzen, 1975).

Another issue that relates to the content of persuasive messages is the question of one-sided communications versus two-sided communications. For example, if you are arguing in favor of reduced television time for children, should you present only arguments that are favorable to your position, or should you acknowledge and attempt to refute an opposing viewpoint? In answering this question, we again see that few answers are "all or none"; instead, specific conditions must be considered in each case. As Karlins and Abelson put it:

> When the audience is generally friendly, or when your position is the only one that will be presented, or when you want immediate, though temporary, opinion change, present one side of the argument. [But when] the audience initially disagrees with you, or when it is probable that the audience will hear the other side from someone else, present both sides of the argument [1970, p. 22].

If there are occasions in which it is most effective to present both sides of an argument, which side should be presented first for maximum impact? Here we face the issue of primacy versus recency effects, also discussed in regard to impression formation in Chapter 3. As in the case of forming first impressions, there can be no absolute rule in favor of either primacy or recency. More than 50 years ago, Lund (1925) formulated a "law of primacy in persuasion," because he found that the side of an argument that was presented last changed attitudes somewhat, but not as much as an initial message did. Other researchers question the generality of Lund's law (Hovland & Mandell, 1952; Insko, 1964; Lana, 1963a, 1963b, 1964a, 1964b; Rosnow, 1966). This research has shown that a number of variables determine whether the side presented first or the side presented last will be the more persuasive. One of the most thorough summaries is offered by Rosnow and Robinson:

> Instead of a general "law" of primacy, or recency, we have today an assortment of miscellaneous variables, some of which tend to produce primacy, . . . others of which, to produce recency. . . . Still others produce either order effect, depending on their utilization or temporal placement in a two-sided communication. . . . Nonsalient, controversial topics, interesting subject matter and highly familiar issues tend toward primacy. Salient topics, uninteresting subject matter, and moderately unfamiliar issues tend to yield recency [1967, p. 89].

A third question, in addition to the content and organization of the persuasive message, concerns the medium by which the message is delivered. In Chapter 5, we considered the ways in which communication can be either encouraged or hampered by various modalities. In the present instance, we are concerned with a one-way aspect— how persuasive a communication can be, depending on the modality of transmission. Again, the answer is not a simple "one is better, one is worse." Although some early investigators reported that live or video-taped messages were more effective than audiotaped messages, which were more effective than written messages, recent evidence isn't so clear-cut (Eagly & Himmelfarb, 1978). One resolution of the confusion (Chaiken & Eagly, 1976) has proposed that we consider the separate stages of comprehending and yielding to a message. A written communication may be more effective in conveying information, particularly information that is complex and difficult to grasp. In contrast, more direct communications, such as videotaped or live presentations, may be more effective when the focus is on yielding rather than comprehension. Therefore, if you want to present a complex proposal to your supervisor at work, written communication might be preferable in the initial presentation stage. Later, however, when the options have been reduced to "yes" or "no," a face-to-face presentation should be more effective.

C. *The Context*

Up to this point, we have discussed persuasive communications as though they take place in a vacuum. Although some laboratory experiments have structured situations in just that way, it is evident that, in the real-life persuasion context, many factors may be operating at the same time. For instance, a television commercial suggesting that you buy a particular brand of aspirin may have to compete with a family argument, the stereo in the next room, and a knock at the door. What effect do distractions have on the effectiveness of a persuasive message?

Although you might think that any distraction would automatically reduce the effectiveness of a persuasive message, that's not necessarily true. Apparently, distraction inhibits the thoughts that we have and men-

tally rehearse while we listen to a communication (Petty, Wells, & Brock, 1976). If a message is one with which we are in sympathy, distraction prevents us from rehearsing supportive arguments; therefore, the communication proves less effective than it would under more neutral circumstances. However, if a message contradicts our beliefs, distraction reduces our ability to generate arguments.

Distractions in laboratory experiments generally involve asking a subject to do two tasks simultaneously. A more natural version of distraction can be seen in the political heckler, who makes comments from the audience while a speaker tries to present an argument. Studies of heckling have found, in contrast to the laboratory situation, that this form of distraction generally reduces the persuasiveness of a message (Silverthorne & Mazmanian, 1975; Sloan, Love, & Ostrom, 1974) among listeners who are initially neutral, although it may serve to moderate positions of listeners who were originally extreme. Why do these results differ from the results of laboratory-based studies of distraction? One reason may be that a heckler not only serves as a distractor (as a competing laboratory task does) but also provides information and an opposing viewpoint. When uninvolved members of an audience are presented with another side of an argument, the speaker's position may seem much less convincing than it otherwise would. Consistent with the research on two-sided communications, however, a speaker who responds to hecklers in a calm and relevant manner apparently can overcome their effects (Petty & Brock, 1976).

D. *The Recipient*

Are some people, by the nature of their personalities, more responsive than others to an attempt to change their attitudes, regardless of the source, the content, or the context of a message? Conversely, are some people able to resist efforts—even the best designed and most appropriate ones—to change their attitudes? The answer is yes, to a slight degree (McGuire, 1968a, 1968b). However, in the majority of cases, the personality of the recipient interacts with other factors to determine whether or not a change in attitude will take place.

Early attempts to relate personality to persuadability focused on single variables, such as intelligence, self-esteem, the need for social approval, and gender. Generally, these simple approaches met with little success. For example, despite the frequently held belief that women are more apt to be persuaded than men, recent reviews find that, in the standard attitude-change setting, men and women have nearly equal tendencies to change their attitudes (Cooper, 1979; Eagly, 1978). Although early research suggested that people low in self-esteem would automatically be more prone to change their attitudes (Janis & Field, 1959), this assumption proved to be inaccurate when subjected to a wider range of tests (Barach, 1969; Bauer, 1970; Cox & Bauer, 1964).

One alternative to this simple but unsuccessful approach has been proposed by McGuire (1968b) (see Chapter 12). If we consider the attitude-change process as a series of separate stages, we can look at the effects of personality variables at different stages of the process. For example, people of high intelligence might be able to comprehend a complex message more easily than persons less intellectually endowed; or, more intelligent persons might be less prone to yield to persuasion, because they have greater confidence in their own critical abilities (see Figure 13-3). In testing this hypothesis, Eagly and Warren (1976) found that high intelligence is related to attitude change when a message is complex—people higher in intelligence changed their attitudes more than less intelligent people. When a message is weak and unsupported by arguments, only people of lower intelligence are likely to change their attitudes.

In considering the murky field of personality and persuadability, some researchers distinguish among attitudes, intentions to perform a behavior, and actual behavior. For example, Rozelle and his colleagues (Rozelle, Evans, Lasater, Dembroski, & Allen, 1973) focused on the relationships between a person's need for social approval

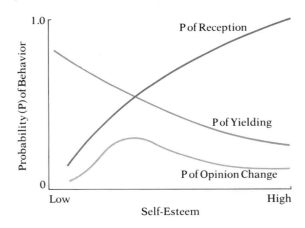

Figure 13-3. The relationship between self-esteem and reception and yielding stages. (Adapted from "Personality and Susceptibility to Social Influence," by W. J. McGuire In E. F. Borgatta and W. W. Lambert (Eds.), *Handbook of Personality Theory and Research.* Copyright 1968 by Edgar F. Borgatta. [Chicago, Illinois: Rand McNally, 1968.] Used by permission.)

and his or her response to a persuasive message advocating better dental care. People who were high in need for social approval reported stronger intentions to improve their dental care; yet, in actual behavior, there were no differences between people who were high and those who were low in need for social approval. Once again, we see that attitude change is no simple matter, and the need for a more complex analysis becomes apparent.

Up to this point, we've dealt with attitude change in a static way that is reminiscent of the Shannon and Weaver model discussed in Chapter 5. We've viewed the source as having a set of stable characteristics and the recipient as having a set of stable characteristics, and we have looked at the possible matches, or persuasive tendencies, between these units. In fact, attitude change, like communication in general, is an active and dynamic process; the source and the recipient can greatly affect each other. For example, if the position of an audience is known, communicators have been shown to shift their message toward the position of the audience (Crawford, 1974; Newtson & Czerlinsky, 1974). Observers of political campaigns are well aware of this tendency. Speakers often shift the content and organization of their message when they perceive an unfriendly or unfavorably disposed audience, stressing problems and issues (a two-sided approach) rather than simple solutions (Hazen & Kiesler, 1975). Therefore, recipients of a persuasive communication not only receive—they can actively shape the content and the organization of the persuasive message as it is being delivered.

II. When Attitudes Don't Change

Discussions of research in attitude change often convey the impression that all people change their attitudes almost all the time. That is not the case. In many cases, shifts in attitude are quite temporary, and in other cases, strong resistance to change is exhibited.

Some people maintain that most of the attitude change exhibited in laboratory settings is merely artifact, reflecting the subjects' responses to the demand characteristics of the settings. This position is undoubtedly too extreme; however, many of the shifts that have been observed in the laboratory may indeed be quite transitory; a decay in persuasion can occur within a single experimental session (Ronis, Baumgardner, Leippe, Cacioppo, & Greenwald, 1977).

A. *Anticipatory Attitude Change*

Investigators have found evidence to suggest that attitudes may shift even before a person is exposed to a persuasive message. In the initial demonstration of this effect, McGuire and his colleagues (McGuire & Millman, 1965; McGuire & Papageorgis, 1962) observed that people who anticipated a persuasive message shifted their attitudes in the direction of the forthcoming message. Are such changes in attitude real? If so, why do they occur in the absence of any actual persuasion? Early explanations of this phenomenon stressed self-esteem, suggesting that people change their attitudes in ad-

vance of a communication in order to avoid appearing gullible later (Deaux, 1968; McGuire & Millman, 1965). More recently, investigators have stressed two factors in attitude change. First, as Cialdini and his colleagues have described it, there is "elasticity" in a person's attitudes (Cialdini, Levy, Herman, & Evenbeck, 1973; Cialdini, Levy, Herman, Kozlowski, & Petty, 1976). In response to various pressures, people may moderate their position within a limited range (perhaps comparable to the latitude of acceptance); however, when the outside pressures disappear (for example, when the promise of a persuasive speech is withdrawn), their attitudes "snap back" to their original positions. Cialdini and his colleagues raise the possibility that most of the attitude change observed in the laboratory reflects this principle of elasticity rather than any real change.

At a more general level, we can think of these anticipatory changes as a form of impression management (Hass, 1975; Hass & Mann, 1976). In other words, when people anticipate a persuasive message, they may try to manage the impression that others are forming, and, in an attempt to appear broad-minded, they may moderate their original position. Such strategies are no doubt common in real life as well as in the laboratory. Consider the way in which you would state your opinion regarding a longer school year if you were discussing that issue with a friend who is in favor of the extension. Such concerns with appearing moderate and reasonable may only occur, however, when people are not personally invested in an issue. Indeed, Cialdini and his colleagues (Cialdini et al., 1976) found that, when an issue is of great importance to a subject, anticipatory shifts are in the direction of greater polarization rather than greater moderation. Again, such a shift may represent a careful tactic on the part of a subject —by taking an extreme position, a subject can allow for the possibility of later compromise, moving to a position similar to the one initially held. Attitudes may indeed be elastic; and the expression of attitudes may serve a variety of motives in addition to the accurate expression of values.

B. *Resistance to Persuasion*

Although a forewarning of persuasion may lead to some initial shifts in the direction of the forthcoming communication, some evidence suggests that, in the long run, forewarning may encourage resistance to the persuasive attempt—or, in the words of Petty and Cacioppo (1977), "forewarned is forearmed."

In an experiment that was conducted during the months preceding President Truman's announcement that Russia had produced an atom bomb, Lumsdaine and Janis (1953), members of the Yale Communication Program, considered the effects of one-sided messages versus two-sided messages. Their special focus was on which of these two types of messages would be most likely to encourage resistance to subsequent counterpropaganda. Their results showed that two-sided communication was more effective in inducing resistance to propaganda, and they suggested that the presentation of counterarguments initially serves to "inoculate" subjects against later persuasive attempts.

McGuire (1964) pursued this explanation in a more elaborately designed set of studies. Prior to hearing a persuasive message, his subjects were presented with arguments that supported their initial beliefs, arguments that refuted the counterarguments that would be used in the subsequent persuasion, or arguments that refuted counterarguments that would not be used in the actual communication. The subjects who had heard only the arguments that supported their initial position showed the least resistance to subsequent persuasion. In contrast, those subjects who had already been exposed to a weakened form of the counterarguments showed resistance when the actual message was presented (see Figure 13-4). Using a medical analogy, McGuire suggests that exposure to weakened forms of a message can be effective in producing defenses. In other words, the exposure inoculates a person against the subsequent attack. Presumably, this strategy is most effective when a person's initial position is relatively "germ free"—when it hasn't been questioned.

Even when counterarguments are not supplied, forewarning can be effective in allowing individuals to provide their own counterarguments and become more resistant to later attacks. For example, Petty and

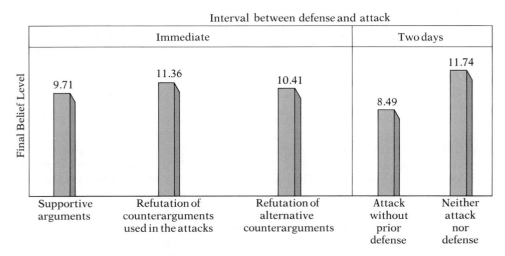

Interval between defense and attack

Figure 13-4. Persistence of the resistance to persuasion conferred by three types of prior belief defense. (Adapted from "Inducing Resistance to Persuasion," by W. J. McGuire. In L. Berkowitz (Ed.), *Advances in Experimental Social Psychology*, Vol. 1. Copyright 1964 by Academic Press, Inc. Used by permission of the author and publisher.)

Cacioppo (1977) have shown that, when people are warned of a forthcoming message and are given time to think about the issue, they consider their own positions and alternative positions, and they generate cognitive defenses against the impending assault. Therefore, one of the most effective ways of encouraging resistance to persuasion is to warn a person that a persuasive attempt is about to be made, identifying the specific content of a message (so that counterarguments can be rehearsed), or simply indicating that persuasion will be attempted, in which case a more general resistance or a more cautious reaction to the message may result (Kiesler & Kiesler, 1964). Given these findings, it isn't surprising that commercials are often introduced with little warning, or that government leaders often call "surprise" press conferences to announce new policy initiatives.

III. Attitude Change in Society

As we've suggested, studies of attitude change in the laboratory have resulted in numerous theories, and they point to dozens of specific variables that appear to be influential in the change process. In controlled studies, each of these factors can be isolated and its unique influence readily determined; however, in a complex societal setting, all these factors may exist concurrently. How does a person who wants to make changes decide which variables are most important, or most relevant, to a particular situation? Often, this choice process is fairly haphazard and subject more to intuitive hunches than laboratory findings. An advertising agency may operate on the assumption that celebrities are influential or that a commercial inserted in the middle of World Series coverage is indeed worth hundreds of thousands of dollars. A more systematic approach involves careful assessment of a situation to determine the most important factors and consideration of theoretical and conceptual variables that may be brought to bear. To get a flavor of the ways in which our knowledge of attitude change has been applied in real-life settings, we will consider

a number of important topics: voting behavior, health-related behaviors, and interracial contact. In each case, we will examine the ways in which the principles of attitude change operate in the complex environment of the real world.

A. *Political Attitudes and Voting Behavior*

Politicians must be able to convince their electorates to vote for them on election day. Phrased in other terms, this project amounts to a program of persuasion that is intended to convince supporters to remain committed and convince other voters to change their attitudes.

Students of political opinion have used a number of strategies in attempting to assess the general opinion of the electorate. At one level, investigators have tried to find out where voters stand on a general liberal/conservative dimension; however, the utility of this approach is questionable. For example, Free and Cantril (1967) sampled over 3000 respondents in the United States, asking them general questions concerning issues such as federal interference, government regulation, and individual initiative. On the basis of these results, they reported that 50% of the citizens in the United States considered themselves completely conservative, 34% considered themselves middle of the road, and only a small percentage could be identified as completely or predominantly liberal. A second set of questions, which focused on *operational* liberalism and conservatism, produced quite different results. (The questions dealt with specific issues, such as Medicare, urban renewal, and federal aid to education.) In this case, the majority of people were found to be liberal in their political ideology (see Figure 13-5). As a result of such discrepancy, many investigators question whether general ideology is related to specific voting patterns.

A much more promising approach involves an assessment of voters' beliefs regarding specific issues and their perceptions of the candidates' beliefs. Using this strategy, we can ignore the general categories of liberal and conservative, which may

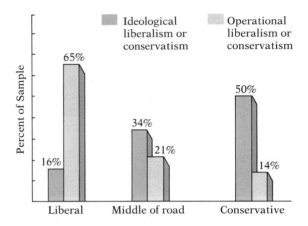

Figure 13-5. Ideology versus operationalism in political beliefs. (From *The Political Beliefs of Americans: A Study of Public Opinion*, by Lloyd A. Free and Hadley Cantril. Copyright © 1967 by Rutgers, the State University. Reprinted by permission of Rutgers University Press.)

have little significance, and focus on the specific issues that voters feel are important. It is, of course, true that voters may not have an accurate perception of their chosen candidate's stand on an issue. As we saw in Chapter 12, voters tend to distort their perceptions of a candidate's stand in order to achieve consistency in their beliefs. Nevertheless, these beliefs may determine subsequent voting behavior. By assessing voters' beliefs regarding specific issues in the 1976 U.S. presidential elections, Jaccard, Knox, and Brinberg (1979) were able to predict (with considerable accuracy) individuals' actual voting behavior. Studies of British elections, using the same techniques, proved equally successful (Fishbein, Bowman, Thomas, Jaccard, & Ajzen, 1979).

For politicians, simply knowing the voters' attitudes and intentions is not enough; their goal, after all, is to change attitudes so that they may be elected. What strategies do politicians use to create attitude change in the electorate?

In recent years, media campaigns have been used to inform the electorate of a candidate's opinions on relevant issues. Commercials, televised debates, and general media coverage have been used to convey information regarding candidates. As a means of conveying specific information, however, these campaigns are not always successful. As we noted in Chapter 12, there are a number of stages in the attitude-change process. At the first level, the potential audience must attend to the persuasive message. Such attention is not always gained by politicians: flyers are thrown into the wastebasket, commercials are aired while the television viewer goes to the kitchen for a snack, and even billboards are ignored. Having gained *some* attention, however, candidates must attempt to present messages that will be understood by a potentially wide audience. Moreover, candidates must convince people to vote for them despite pressures from friends and family members, party identification, and job-related issues. With such a range of possible pressures, it may not be surprising to learn that attitude change is most likely to be found among individuals who have an initially weak party identification (Sears, 1969).

Because of the increased use of television in recent political campaigns, many investigators have begun to focus on the effects that exposure alone can have on voting behavior. Laboratory research by Zajonc (1968) has shown that mere exposure to a stimulus can increase our positive feelings regarding that stimulus (see Chapter 6). In other words, the more we see something, the more we are apt to like it. Apparently, this simple principle applies to political elections. Grush, McKeough, and Ahlering (1978) predicted 83% of the winners in the 1972 U.S. congressional primaries by calculating the amount of media coverage devoted to each candidate. In light of this finding, it isn't surprising that Grush and his colleagues have found that wealthy candidates are very likely to win elections (Grush & Schersching, 1978). With money, a candidate can buy extensive television coverage. The frequency of exposure in the media apparently provides a strong force for attitude change—specifically, a vote for the candidate on election day.

Whose attitudes are changed? Most studies show that attitude change is most likely to occur among those voters who have the least interest in the campaign (Oskamp,

1977). Many of the complex methods of attitude change, such as focusing on the content of particular messages or the order of presentation, have little effect on these voters. Simple variables, such as the frequency of exposure, have much more impact on individuals whose attention is at a relatively low level. Such a finding makes good social psychological sense; nonetheless, it appears slightly discomforting to those who believe in a literate and thinking electorate.

B. *Health-Related Attitudes and Behaviors*

Many individuals and agencies are concerned with changing people's attitudes toward health-related behaviors (see Figure 13-6). Dentists are interested in improving people's teeth-care practices. The U.S. Surgeon General's office has waged an extensive campaign to reduce cigarette smoking, publicizing the health dangers posed by extensive smoking. Governments throughout the world have attempted to convince their citizens that a reduced birth rate is in their best interests. Each of these examples represents an attempt to change attitudes and behaviors. What tactics have been used?

As we saw earlier, appeals that induce fear are often used in attempts to change a number of health-related behaviors. Leventhal and his colleagues (Leventhal, 1970) have conducted numerous investigations into the effects of fear-arousing communications on attitudes and behaviors regarding dental practices and chest X-rays. The results of these studies have been mixed. Although a number of studies have shown that fear appeals change expressed attitudes toward a targeted behavior and increase

Figure 13-6. "Let me show you what you should do." Attitude campaigns about dental practices are often directed at young children. (© Bob Clay/Jeroboam, Inc.)

anxiety, they have been less successful in altering actual behavior (Evans, Rozelle, Lasater, Dembroski, & Allen, 1970; Leventhal, 1970). One conclusion drawn from this collection of studies is that attempts to change behavior should be directed at a specific action, such as going to the dentist, rather than more general classes of behaviors, such as taking better care of one's teeth (Fishbein & Ajzen, 1975).

Another important factor in changing health-related behaviors is the similarity of the source to the target audience. In another study of the effect of fear appeals on subsequent behavior, Dembroski, Lasater, and Ramirez (1978) found that the content of a communication had no effect on subsequent tooth-brushing behavior. (In this study, the investigators did not rely on self-reports of brushing behavior; instead, a chemical dye that measures actual bacteria concentration was applied to the subjects' teeth.) Among the Black high school students in the study, however, a Black communicator was much more effective than a White communicator, suggesting that similarity of the source may be an important variable in eliciting changes in health-related behaviors.

Other efforts to change health-related behaviors have focused on cigarette smoking, particularly among young children. Let's consider one such program conducted by Richard Evans and his colleagues at the University of Houston (Evans, 1976; Evans, Rozelle, Mittelmark, Hansen, Bane, & Havis, 1978). In initial interviews with a group of fifth-grade, sixth-grade, and seventh-grade students, the investigators learned that, although most of the children believed that smoking was dangerous to their long-range health, more immediate pressures in the environment often encouraged them to smoke. Three pressures that were particularly strong were: peer influence, parents who smoked, and media presentations of smokers.

To counteract these specific pressures, Evans and his colleagues designed a program to help children deal with the situation. Through a structured videotaped presentation, children were presented with information regarding the dangers of smoking, as well as a discussion of the pressures that peers, parents, and the media can exert on behavior. Identification of the pressures was coupled with a detailed set of techniques that the children could use to cope with the pressures. Reflecting the findings that we discussed earlier, the investigators used children of similar ages as the communicators in the film, thus increasing the similarity between source and audience. In addition, the immediate physiological consequences of smoking (as opposed to the long-range effects) were described. To determine the effectiveness of their program, the investigators used not only self-reports of smoking behavior but also a saliva test that detects the presence of nicotine in the body.

The results of this multifaceted appeal are encouraging. Ten weeks after the treatment, only 10% of the students had begun to smoke, compared with 18% of the students in a control group. Therefore, although the treatment did not eliminate smoking behavior, it affected that behavior considerably.

This program illustrates the combination of factors that must be considered by those who attempt to change attitudes and behaviors in the field. Any single factor in itself may have little effect; therefore, a campaign needs to consider numerous elements simultaneously, if any substantial change is to be effected.

A similar point has been made by Fishbein and his colleagues in discussing programs aimed at reducing population growth (Fishbein, Jaccard, Davidson, Ajzen, & Loken, 1979). Programs that stress the dangers of overpopulation have been notoriously ineffective in changing a specific family's child-bearing behavior. On the other hand, programs that stress the effectiveness of contraceptives may change people's beliefs regarding the usefulness of contraceptives but have little effect on other salient beliefs that determine usage. Therefore, a woman who feels that contraceptives are immoral will exhibit little change in behavior, even though she may agree that contraceptives are effective. Again, a multifaceted approach is called for: all the relevant beliefs of the people involved must be identified, and a program must be designed to deal with each of the issues of concern.

C. *Attitudes regarding Race*

Prejudice is often deeply ingrained and, therefore, extremely resistant to change. At the same time, the existence of prejudice poses a real dilemma for a society that values equality. As a result, many projects have been conducted to explore the ways in which negative racial attitudes and behaviors might be changed. In Chapter 12, we discussed a number of possible tactics that might be used in this endeavor, deriving predictions from theories of attitude change. In this section, we discuss other factors that have been found to be important in changing racial attitudes, and we describe one project that attempted to control these factors.

Many people have made the optimistic assumption that, if two racial or religious groups could be brought together, the hostility, antagonism, and prejudice often expressed by each group toward the other would erode, and positive attitudes would develop. This, in essence, is the **intergroup contact hypothesis**. Quite obviously, this hypothesis must be qualified before it can be considered valid. French Canadians enrolling in "English" schools, Catholics and Protestants fighting in the streets of Northern Ireland, and parolees and police officers playing together in softball games are events that show that intergroup contact can have either beneficial or deleterious outcomes. Mere frequency is not very important; the nature of the contact is the determinant.

S. W. Cook (1970) has described five characteristics of the contact situation that are critical to predicting whether attitude change will occur: (1) the potential for acquaintance, (2) the relative status of the participants in a contact situation, (3) the nature of the social norm concerning contact of one group with another, (4) the presence of a cooperative reward structure rather

than a competitive one, and (5) the characteristics of the individuals who are in contact.

1. *The Potential for Acquaintance.* A person can experience daily contact with another person over a number of years and not get to know that person as an individual. Our experiences with janitors, letter carriers, and cashiers are examples of this type of contact. In big cities, apartment dwellers may know little about the family in the next apartment, despite numerous passing contacts. When we come to know people as individuals, learning their aspirations, fears, likes, and dislikes, attitude change can result. For example, when Black and White homemakers living in the same apartment building are brought together and given a chance to get to know one another, attitude change in the direction of greater acceptance is the typical result (Deutsch & Collins, 1965; Wilner, Walkley, & Cook, 1955).

2. *The Relative Status of the Participants in a Contact Situation.* Beneficial attitude change is more likely to occur when the minority-group member and the prejudiced person occupy the same social status. When the minority-group member occupies either a lower status or a higher status, the interaction is likely to be role oriented, with less opportunity for authentic relationships to develop between the participants. In other words, equal status implies equal power among the people who interact (Ramirez, 1977).

3. *The Nature of the Social Norm concerning Contact of One Group with Another.* In some situations, people feel that a friendly association is appropriate; beneficial attitude change is more likely to occur in such situations. Attitude change isn't as likely to occur when the people involved have no expectation of a social relationship, as in some business contacts.

Social norms are often reflected in pronouncements made by public officials. The White school principal who tells irate parents "I don't like school desegregation either, but I have to enforce it" creates a social norm that discourages changes in the attitudes of the White students and their parents toward Blacks, Puerto Ricans, and Chicanos. If the principal complies with the law and reflects positive attitudes, there is a greater chance that the students and their parents will comply with the new policies and perhaps come to accept their merit.

4. *The Presence of a Cooperative Reward Structure Rather than a Competitive One.* A great deal of recent evidence suggests that a cooperative orientation can reduce interracial tension (DeVries & Slavin, 1975; Weigel, Wiser, & Cook, 1975). Cooperation leads to mutual interdependence—that is, the task goals of one group can be attained only when the other group achieves its goals. One impressive example of this situation is found in the project of Elliot Aronson and his colleagues (Aronson, Blaney, Sikes, Stephan, & Snapp, 1975; Aronson, Blaney, & Stephan, 1975), which was discussed in Chapter 9. These social psychologists responded to a "crisis call" from the Austin public-school system, where increased hostility among racially mixed groups of elementary-school children was presenting severe problems.

Aronson and his colleagues believe that most classrooms are arenas for competition rather than cooperation; this competition exacerbates tensions among children who come from various backgrounds, "look different," and "talk different." In Aronson's project, teachers were trained in the development of cooperative work groups for their students. Each child was assigned a small portion of a lesson. Then the children communicated their information in a process that resembled the assembling of a jigsaw puzzle. The procedure led to some dramatic changes in behavior:

The children quickly learned that the only way they could learn the whole lesson (and do well on an upcoming exam) was to cooperate with the students in the group by listening attentively and helping each of them teach (by asking good questions, etc.). This required about one week for students to realize that the usual kinds of put-downs and insults were no longer functional [Aronson, Blaney, & Stephan, 1975, p. 2].

By emphasizing common goals and requiring mutual interdependence among group members, such general procedures have the effect of increasing attraction toward members of other racial groups and reducing interracial conflict in the classroom.

5. *The Characteristics of the Individuals Who Are in Contact.* Attitude change is more likely to occur when the participating members do not conform to commonly held, unflattering stereotypes of their group. Interaction with a Black who is hardworking, bright, restrained, and not particularly musical or religious may stimulate attitude change on the part of a White. Similarly, a White who is not condescending, arrogant, and "uptight" may encourage attitude change in a Black. Similarity of interests also may help to dispel stereotypes (Blanchard, Weigel, & Cook, 1974).

In addition, of course, one must consider the intensity and the basis of each individual's attitude. As we indicated in Chapter 12, the causes of a person's prejudice may determine the degree to which that person will change. The intensity of the attitude held by the prejudiced person also can influence the degree of attitude change. Moreover, interaction effects may occur; that is, after contact, the overall group may appear to be just as prejudiced as it was before contact, when, in reality, some of its members have become less prejudiced and others have become more so. Cook (1957) has cited a study by Taylor concerning the ways in which Whites reacted to Blacks living on the same block. The Whites who had been in favor of residential desegregation before the first Black family moved in became even more positive in their attitude after Blacks had been living nearby for several weeks. The Whites who had initially been against the idea of desegregation became even more negative after desegregation occurred. In some cases, contact can intensify whatever initial attitude a person possesses.

Stuart Cook (1964, 1970, 1971) conducted an elaborate 10-year project to test the validity of the contact hypothesis. He tried to include each of the factors that we have discussed as being critical to the positive outcome of interracial contact. Recognizing that involuntary interracial contact is common in the United States, Cook designed an experiment in which White subjects were involuntarily placed in contact with a Black individual. The project was conducted in a large city in the Southern part of the United States. The subjects for the project came from four of the city's predominantly White colleges.

The project was conducted in three separate stages. In the first stage, female students were recruited through advertisements in the student newspaper for a test-development study sponsored by the bogus "Institute for Test Development." Students who volunteered were asked to complete a series of questionnaires and told that they would be retested several months later on these same tests (again, for pay). One questionnaire, of course, dealt with interracial attitudes and provided the basis for selection of participants in the second stage of the project.

Cook and his colleagues were interested in studying students whose attitudes could clearly be considered anti-Black. From the total number of students who volunteered for the first session, the researchers selected those who were most strongly prejudiced in their attitudes. (On a sentence-completion task, for example, these students wrote the responses shown in Table 13-1.) The students who were selected for the project on this basis were then contacted by a faculty member at "St. George's College" (not the true name of the college) and asked to apply for part-time work on a group project (apparently unrelated to the first testing session). This project, which would require two hours per day for a 1-month period, was described as a management task being used as part of a government project to train groups of strangers to work together, presumably with the aim of understanding how crew members at isolated bases might be able to work with one another.

If the student agreed to participate, an appointment was made, some perfunctory interviews were conducted, and a contract

TABLE 13-1 / Responses of Prejudiced Whites to Sentence-Completion Test

1. If they began admitting Negroes to the club to which I belong, I would . . .
   "drop out."
   "find another club."
   "stop it."

2. If my boss began hiring many Negroes, I would . . .
   "quit right away."
   "tell him to hire Whites or I'd leave."
   "not like it at all."

3. If someone at my church suggested inviting the Young People's group at a Negro church to a joint supper meeting, I would . . .
   "vote against it."
   "feel uncomfortable."
   "throw up."

was signed. The student agreed to work for the specified time period, with the understanding that she would be paid only if she completed the work. The purpose of this device was to discourage the prejudiced subject from withdrawing from the project when she discovered that interracial contact was involved. Although such withdrawal might seem unlikely to us now, it should be recalled that this project was conducted in 1961, when it was still very unusual for Southern Blacks and Whites to work together or eat together under conditions even approaching equal status.

The task that was chosen for the project is called the Railroad Game (Jensen & Terebinski, 1963), in which a group is required to operate a railroad system composed of ten stations, six lines, and 500 freight cars of six types. The group itself consisted of five people, as illustrated in Figure 13-7: a White female supervisor, a Black female helper, three crew members (two of whom were confederates—one Black and one White—and one of whom was the White subject). The three-member crew could communicate directly with one another, but they could talk to the supervisor and her helper only by telephone. In addition, two members of the experimental team acted as observers and were not visible to the participants. During the course of the game, the crew had to make numerous decisions concerning routes and equipment and then telephone their decisions to the supervisor and her helper.

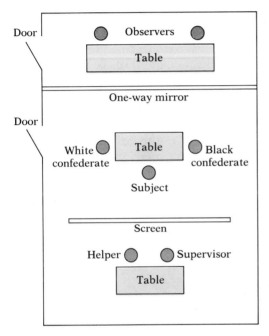

Figure 13-7. The railroad game.

In the middle of each day's 2-hour session, there was a 30-minute lunch break, which gave the subjects an opportunity to get to know one another and gave the experimenters an opportunity to create some of the situational characteristics that increase the benefits of interracial contact. For example, *acquaintance potential* was facilitated by the conversation of the confederates. During each lunch break, the Black confederate talked about herself, her family, her plans, and her likes and dislikes. Some of these comments were volunteered; others were evoked by preplanned questions that were posed by the White confederate.

With regard to the second situational characteristic, *relative status of the participants,* the Black confederate and the other

crew members were of equal status. Built into the procedure was a rotation of crew assignments, which reinforced the equality of status for the three participants.

Social norms regarding contact of one group with another were established by making it clear to all participants that the situation favored acceptance of Blacks. Beyond the implied norms of the situation itself, other devices were used. For example, the White confederate expressed sympathy with the Black confederate and disapproval of segregation.

The *presence of a cooperative reward structure* was established through the structure of the Railroad Game. For instance, when the group did well, a bonus was paid to each member. In addition, the Game's procedure led to close interaction and mutual assistance between the prejudiced White person and the Black confederate, especially when they were paired as the dispatcher and the status keeper. Moreover, the rotation of crew assignments put the prejudiced White person in a position of both teaching the Black and being taught by her.

Finally, the *characteristics of the individuals in contact* also were considered. The Black confederate was presented throughout as being personable, able, ambitious, and self-respecting. Care was taken to see that the Black performed her game tasks well. The Black participant was quite different from the stereotype that the prejudiced White might have expected.

Throughout the four weeks that the crew was together, the Black confederate presented information concerning the injustices and indignities she had suffered as a result of racial discrimination. For example, one topic of conversation was shopping for clothing. (In the early 1960s, department stores in the South wouldn't permit a Black to try on clothes at the store. Instead, the store delivered clothes to the Black's home, where they could be tried on without the knowledge of Whites.) As the project continued, the White confederate became openly upset about the ways in which Blacks were being treated in U.S. society. However, the confederate didn't ask the subject to agree with this opinion, under the assumption that such a direct question would cause defensiveness and rigidity of attitudes.

The third stage of this elaborate project consisted of a follow-up call from the "Institute for Test Development." The student was asked to retake the tests that she had taken several months earlier. Again, it is important to remember that the "Institute" had no apparent connection with "St. George's College" and the Railroad Game. Responses to attitude questionnaires administered at a follow-up session were used as indicators of the effectiveness of the intervention procedures.

The Cook study was a far more intensive attempt to change attitudes than most experiments conducted by social psychologists. What was the outcome? At the anecdotal level, a number of incidents suggested that some real changes had taken place among White students in their attitudes toward their Black coworkers (see Box 13-1). A number of subjects were visibly influenced by the content of lunch-time conversations and were particularly touched when the Black confederate recounted the indignities she had suffered. The conversations provided opportunities for relearning. Many of the Whites had never realized, for example, that Blacks traveling in the South during the early 1960s could never be sure whether they could use the rest rooms at gasoline stations. The subjects had not known that the textbooks used in Black high schools were outdated hand-me-downs from White schools, and that many Blacks who had struggled to complete college found that only menial jobs were available to them. The communications that took place during the lunch breaks served to focus the attention of the subjects—a necessary factor in the attitude-change model advanced by the Yale Communication Research Program.

Many objective measures of change were observed in the course of Cook's project. For example, observers stationed behind a one-way mirror recorded the number of comments that subjects directed to the confederates. At the beginning of the month, the subject directed her questions and comments almost entirely to the White confed-

erate and rarely turned her head toward the Black confederate. Toward the end of the project, approximately 60% of the subject's comments were directed to the White confederate, and 40% of her comments were directed to the Black confederate.

Behaviors such as these suggest changes in many of the White subjects' attitudes toward a specific Black person. A larger question is whether these changes were generalized to include all Blacks. Using several different standardized measures of attitudes toward Blacks, Cook and his colleagues found that approximately 35%–40% of the subjects in the project exhibited a significant shift in their favorability toward Blacks, whereas 40% exhibited essentially the same attitudes. Approximately 20% of the subjects became even more prejudiced in their attitudes toward Blacks. (As a comparison, those women who had turned down the opportunity to participate in Cook's project exhibited very little change in either direction).

What are we to make of these results? In one sense, the findings provide some hope that attitudes can indeed be changed. More than one-third of the subjects who were initially prejudiced exhibited positive attitude change after only 40 hours of actual contact. In other ways, however, the results are less satisfactory. For example, in Cook's study, we do not know whether the observed changes continued to be evidenced over a period of time. Although the changes were observed one month after the contact, we cannot know whether a subject who returns to a typical environment will continue to show a positive attitude toward Blacks when the pressures against such attitudes may be pervasive.

Another source of dissatisfaction with Cook's findings is the limited percentage of people who changed in a positive direction. And why did 20% of the subjects exhibit an increase in negative attitudes toward Blacks? Answers to these questions lie in a more thorough understanding of individual differences in change potential. In an attempt to understand more about such individual differences, Wrightsman and Cook (1965) compared a small group of subjects

Box 13-1. One Outcome of the Cook Study.

At the beginning of Cook's project, the idea of eating with a Black was probably unpleasant to every one of the prejudiced Whites. In light of this base, the following incident is particularly remarkable. One high point of the daily lunch was dessert. On one particular day, the subject decided that she didn't want a piece of pie, but the Black confederate ordered one. When the lunches arrived, the crew discovered that blackberry pie was being served—the subject's favorite.

As the Black confederate ate her pie, the subject kept turning her eyes to the pie, as if hypnotized. Finally, after the Black confederate pushed aside her half-eaten pie, the subject turned to her and said "Betty Jean, would you mind if I ate the rest of your pie?" Surely, if the prejudiced White had been told one month earlier that she would soon be eating a Black person's leftovers, the suggestion would have been met with ridicule. (© Bruce Davidson/Magnum Photos, Inc.)

who had shown positive change with a group that had shown no change. The researchers used a variety of personality tests as the basis of comparison. Few differences were found with regard to characteristics such as rigidity, hostility, and initial level of anti-Black attitudes. In three areas, however, there were notable differences. The sub-

jects who had exhibited positive change were more likely to have positive attitudes toward people in general and a need for social approval; they were more apt to feel negative about themselves.

We have examined the Cook study in detail, because it represents a far more extensive attempt to change attitudes than many other projects that could be described here. At the same time, the results of the project clearly show that attitude change in real settings with highly involving issues is not as easily managed as some advocates of change might suggest.

IV. Summary

Programs of attitude change often draw their hypotheses from several theories. In most attitude-change settings, four general characteristics are considered important: the source, the message, the context, and the recipient.

Generally, messages that are delivered by a source who is highly credible (expert, trustworthy, and impactful) are more likely to change attitudes than messages that emanate from a source who has little credibility. Perceptions of the source's intentions also are important; when people appear to argue against their own self-interest, their message is more effective. Other characteristics of the source that are important include physical appearance and similarity to the recipient.

Studies of fear-arousing communications have shown that moderate levels of arousal may be more effective than either high or low levels. A fear-arousing message should contain specific recommendations by which the depicted consequences can be avoided. Other studies of message content have shown that the effectiveness of one-sided communication versus two-sided communication depends on the beliefs of the audience and the desire for temporary change versus long-term change. The order of presentation (the primacy/recency issue) has complex effects. The relative effects of various media presentations depend on whether comprehension or yielding is more critical in a particular case.

Distraction may either facilitate attitude change (when the initial position of the audience is counter to the message being delivered) or encourage attitude change (when the message is consistent with the audience's position), by reducing the ability to rehearse arguments. The presence of a heckler may reduce attitude change through distraction and the presentation of an alternative viewpoint.

Specific personality variables may be related to different stages in the attitude-change process and to different measures of attitude change, such as attitudes, intentions, and behavior. It is important to recognize that characteristics of the audience may affect the position of the source, thus underlining the interactive nature of persuasion.

Although emphasis has been placed on the factors that bring about change, we also should consider the factors that increase resistance to change. Studies of anticipatory attitude change suggest that some changes may simply reflect an "elasticity," with people consciously presenting their opinions as moderate in order to appear flexible. When a person is forewarned of a persuasive communication, he or she may be inoculated against subsequent change as a result of that warning.

Research regarding political attitudes has shown that general concepts, such as liberal and conservative, are not very useful in predicting voting behavior, whereas more operational definitions that consider specific beliefs and issues can be quite accurate. Media exposure also influences voting behavior.

Health-related behaviors are more apt to be changed when a persuasive message focuses on a specific behavior rather than a general attitude toward health practices. Other factors that contribute to change in health-related behaviors include the similarity of the source to the audience, direct instruction concerning the potential pressures of peers, and feedback. In every case, it is important to consider the variety of beliefs that may determine a particular behavior.

Intergroup contact is more likely to result in a change in racial attitudes when: (1) there is a potential for acquaintance, (2) the relative status of the participants is equal, (3) the social norms favor acceptance, (4) the reward structure of the task is cooperative rather than competitive, and (5) the characteristics of the individuals involved do not conform to stereotypes.

Even when these conditions are present, however, not all interracial contacts lead to a reduction in prejudice. In Stuart Cook's elaborate intergroup-contact project, approximately 40% of the subjects shifted their attitudes in a positive direction; others remained the same or, in a few cases, showed increased negative attitudes. The intrapersonal characteristics that facilitated reduction of prejudice in Cook's project included a positive attitude toward people in general and a negative self-concept.

Glossary Term   intergroup
                          contact
                          hypothesis

As for conforming outwardly, and living your own life inwardly, I do not think much of that.   HENRY DAVID THOREAU

PHOTO © BOB ADELMAN, MAGNUM.

There is no subjugation so perfect as that which keeps the appearance of freedom, for in that way one captures volition itself.   JEAN-JACQUES ROUSSEAU

14

Social Influence and Personal Control

Attitude change is one example of social influence, one that relies on verbal comprehension and generally assumes that human behavior has a cognitive basis. Yet there are many other ways in which we can be influenced and even controlled by others — through the use of power strategies, direct orders, specific requests, and even simple example. In many cases, succumbing to social influence is adaptive: driving on the right side of the road in the United States and Canada, for example, is a simple matter of safety, just as doing the opposite in Great Britain is more socially functional. In other cases, conformity behavior may be questionable, as when members of a junior high school clique determine what clothes are acceptable to wear and reject people who choose a different dress style. How we respond to the requests or orders of others will vary across a wide range of situations; we do not respond the same way to a friend who asks us for a favor, a door-to-door salesperson who's pressuring us to buy a gadget we don't need, and a dictator in a repressive society.

Each time we encounter an attempt by a person or persons to influence our behavior or attitudes, we must decide whether to comply or resist. At the heart of this process is the issue of control—the degree to which we feel we have control over our own lives versus the degree to which others have the power to affect our behavior.

This very basic issue of influence and control is the focus of this chapter. First we will consider the various forms of control—conformity, compliance, and obedience. Then we will look more carefully at why control is an important issue and how people respond to a loss of control in their lives.

I. Conformity

A. *The Asch Situation*

A male college student has volunteered to participate in a research project. He is to be a subject in a visual-perception experiment. Along with six other "subjects" (who are, in fact, confederates of the researcher), he is seated at a circular table. The group is shown a board with a vertical line drawn on it. With this line still in view, all the group members look at another board, which has three vertical lines of different lengths. One of these lines is identical in length to the line on the first board; the other two lines are different enough so that in controlled tests (done individually, not in groups) more than 95% of subjects make correct judgments about the length of the lines. In the group experiment, the subjects are asked to state their choices out loud and one at a time. The real subject is seated so that he is always the next-to-last person to respond. On the first and second trials, everyone gives the same response, and this response is the one that the real subject has judged to be correct. (The volunteer begins to think that this task is easy.) The same outcome occurs on several more trials. Then, on a subsequent trial—where the choice appears as clear-cut as those before—the first confederate gives a response that the subject perceives to be obviously incorrect. All the other confederates follow suit, giving the wrong response. When it comes time for the subject to respond, all the preceding respondents at the table have given an answer that he believes is wrong. What does he do? Does he stick to his convictions, remain independent, and give the correct response? Or does he conform to the group, giving an answer that he knows is wrong? Or does he convince himself that he must be wrong and that the group's answer is correct?

This was the procedure used in an early set of studies on conformity by social psychologist Solomon Asch (1951, 1956, 1958), and it illustrates some of the basic characteristics of the process of influence and control. In its most basic sense, **conformity** refers to a yielding to group pressures when no direct request to comply with the group is made. Thus, in the Asch situation, the confederates did not directly ask the subject to go along with their judgment. Nevertheless, the subject undoubtedly perceived some real pressures to have his judgment be consistent with those of the other group members.

How does the volunteer in the Asch conformity situation respond? In the standard Asch procedure, there were 12 critical trials on which confederates gave the wrong response, interspersed with a large number of trials on which all confederates gave the correct answer. The conformity behavior of 50 subjects is shown in Figure 14-1. When we consider the responses of all true subjects on all of the critical trials, we find that 32% of the responses were conforming or that subjects on the average conformed on 3.84 out of 12 possible trials. But the averages are deceiving; in the Asch study the distribution of conforming responses is important because of the great range of individual differences. Notice in Figure 14-1 that 13 of the 50 subjects never yielded to the majority on any of the critical trials, whereas 4 subjects yielded on 10 or more of those trials. Thus, although some conformity was certainly shown in the Asch procedure, it is certainly not true that every subject conformed every possible time.

Asch's work on conformity was influenced by the even earlier studies of Muzafer Sherif (1935) on the autokinetic effect. If you look at a stationary light in an otherwise completely dark room, the light will appear to move, because your eyes have no other reference point (J. Levy, 1972). Sherif capitalized on this autokinetic phenomenon to study the effects of another person's response and found that a subject's reports of movement were highly influenced by other people's estimates. In this case, it is not totally surprising that some conformity occurred; the stimulus was ambiguous, and there was no other source of information. In contrast, the results of the later Asch studies are more surprising because the stimulus was almost devoid of ambiguity.

B. Situational Influences on Conformity

Since these early pioneering investigations, many additional studies of conformity behavior have been conducted (Allen, 1965; Kiesler, 1969; Nord, 1969; Montmollin, 1977). One major conclusion that we can draw from these later studies is that a great many situational factors influence the degree to which an individual will conform to group pressure. For example, what is the effect of group size? One might expect that the larger the number of subjects who form a unanimous majority, the more often the true subject will conform. This is true, but only to a degree. Asch (1956, 1958) and others (S. C. Goldberg, 1954; L. A. Rosenberg, 1961) have studied the extent to which people yield to unanimous majorities (varying from only 1 to 15 persons). More conformity occurs when two confederates

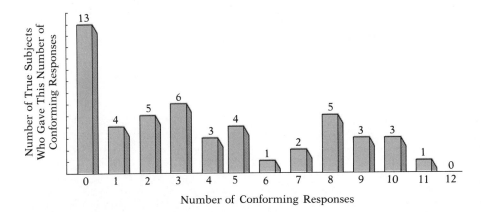

Figure 14-1. Distribution of conformity responses in the original Asch study. (Modified from Asch, 1958, p. 177.)

give false answers than when only one does (see Table 14-1). Groups of three or four confederates have the greatest influence in inducing conformity responses; groups of eight or more persons are somewhat less effective, indicating the possible limits of increasing numbers (Stang, 1976). In the real world, however, further increases in group size may continue to increase conformity; Krech, Crutchfield, and Ballachey (1962) see the greater possibility of threats of reprisal as one reason why conformity may increase with increases in the size of real-life groups.

Another important factor in considering the effect of the group is the extent to which members of the group are regarded as a single unit (Wilder, 1975). Consider the difference between a situation in which four individuals all give the wrong answer and one in which those four persons are viewed as a single group or club. In the latter case, conformity pressures are apparently less effective and may more closely approximate the pressure exerted by only a single individual. In other words, the four opinions are actually considered to represent only one voice, and hence the size of the majority becomes less important.

In the studies described thus far, all of the confederates were instructed to respond falsely on predesignated trials. However, it is unclear whether conformity is influenced by the sheer number of others or by the unanimity of their response (Allen & Levine, 1968; Moscovici, 1974). What if one of the eight confederates (for example, the one seated fourth in the row) were to give the correct response on every trial? This tactic results in much less conformity. In such experiments, only 5.5% of the true subjects' responses are conforming, compared with 32% in the original experiment.

Being in a relatively large group (eight to ten persons) with one other kindred soul is less likely to result in conformity than being in a smaller group (four persons) where everyone else disagrees with you. When a kindred soul is not present but the subject knows that someone else in the past has responded as the subject wants to, less conformity behavior occurs (Wilder & Allen, 1973). Thus the principle of "divide and conquer" has validity in the sense that, when a person is removed from all others who give support, he or she is much more likely to succumb to the pressures of the majority, even if the unanimous majority is not a large group (D. Graham, 1962; Moscovici & Faucheux, 1972).

The status and the competence of the group members will also affect the extent of conformity shown by the subject (Endler & Hartley, 1973). High school students, for example, may conform more to the majority's judgments when the other participants are introduced as college seniors than when they are depicted as other high school students (Crutchfield, 1955). The subject's own feelings at the time can also influence conformity. In a demonstration of the effects of stress, Davis, Brown, and White (1978) looked at the extent to which fraternity pledges would conform to the opinions of the active members across the course of "Hell Week." As the physical and mental stress of the week increased, pledges showed an increasing tendency to adopt the views of the senior members.

T A B L E   14 - 1 / *Extent of Conformity with Unanimous Majorities of Different Sizes*

	1	2	3	4	8	10–15
Size of majority						
N of true subjects	10	15	10	10	50	12
Mean no. of conforming responses	0.33	1.53	4.0	4.20	3.84	3.75
Range in no. of conforming responses per subject	0–1	0–5	1–12	0–11	0–11	0–10

From Asch (1958, p. 181).

C. *Issues in the Study of Conformity*

Conformity in behavior does not always reflect a private acceptance of the position that a behavior reflects. Thus, as Allen (1965) has pointed out, a person's outward behavior may or may not conform to the group, and, at the same time, the internal belief in that position may also be in agreement or disagreement with the group. For example, a tourist at Disneyland (see Figure 14-2) might comply with the dress code without agreeing to the philosophy supporting those dress codes, because he or she wishes to enjoy what Disneyland has to offer. In such a case, public agreement or conformity would not necessarily reflect any private acceptance of the position. Alternatively, many of the people at Disneyland who are conforming to the code may also privately agree with the Disney philosophy. Therefore, since apparent conformity of behavior may not be terribly informative about an individual's true beliefs, some psychologists would argue that we should consider only behavior and give up on attempts to define internal beliefs.

If conformity is yielding to group pressure, what is the opposite of conformity? We may think of two different types of opposing, nonconformity responses. One is *independence*, defined as the maintenance of expression of behavior without regard to the group norms. Thus the person who wears blue jeans when they are popular and continues to wear them when the styles change might be considered to demonstrate independence—the person who "does his or her own thing." In contrast to this type of behavior that is independent of group pressure, the term **anticonformity** or counterconformity is used to label the response that is opposed to the majority response on all occasions. The anticonformist might choose to wear blue jeans when more formal clothes are in style, but switch to more formal wear when blue jeans become popular. Thus the actions of two persons may appear similar in some situations but may, in fact, reflect quite different motives if we consider the total context. For example, in studying the reasons why some U.S. soldiers who

Figure 14-2. Conformity pressures at Disneyland. (Photo courtesy of Disneyland.)

were prisoners of war did not collaborate with their Communist Chinese captors during the Korean war, psychologists identified two types of resisters. Some soldiers resisted because they knew that admitting guilt for the war and broadcasting peace appeals were wrong actions; these men were labeled as independent resisters. Another group of men had a long history of unwillingness to accept any kind of authority; they did not conform to commands from officers in the U.S. Army *or* to orders from the Chinese (Kinkead, 1959; Schein, 1957). These men displayed anticonformity or counterconformity.

Use of terms such as *conformist, anticonformist,* and *independent* seems to suggest that we may classify people into one of these categories, implying that someone who conforms in one situation will conform in every other. The wide variation in responses to the Asch task led many investigators to explore the various personality types that might accompany conformity. A number of differences were reported. Crutchfield (1955), for example, in studying a group of businessmen and military officers, reported that independent subjects showed "more intellectual effectiveness, ego strength, leadership ability, and maturity of social relations, together with a conspicuous absence of inferiority feelings, rigid and excessive self-control, and authoritarian attitudes" (p. 194). Other studies using the same basic paradigm have found conforming subjects to have a stronger need for affiliation (McGhee & Teevan, 1967), stronger tendencies to blame themselves (Costanzo, 1970), and lower levels of self-esteem (Stang, 1972). Yet despite these seemingly strong patterns, a conforming personality is not so easily pinned down. Evidence for the consistency of conformity behavior across a variety of situations has been much less impressive, and the search for a single conforming type of person has proved somewhat futile (McGuire, 1968b).

At a more general level, popular social critics such as David Riesman (1950) and William H. Whyte, Jr. (1956), considering the society as a whole, have argued that conformity has increased. In *The Organization Man*, Whyte argued that the complexities of modern society have increased the need to rely on others. A social ethic that emphasized "getting along with others" as a norm or standard was replacing the Protestant ethic that had valued hard work. Riesman's discussion of the prevalence of the "other-directed" person in our society reflects a similar viewpoint. As Riesman sees it, U.S. citizens several generations ago were more "inner directed," meaning that they determined their own values and goals. "Other directed" individuals, in contrast, look to peers to determine their behavior, and Riesman believed this orientation was increasing in the society.

However, such global depictions of conformity are inevitably oversimplified. If the laboratory research on conformity has demonstrated anything, it is that situational factors are of great importance in eliciting conformity behavior. Furthermore, it is undoubtedly a mistake to consider conformity as a reflexive reaction to some group pressure. Rather it is important to consider the reasons for individual choices. Some have argued that a person in the typical conformity situation is simply seeking to resolve his or her own uncertainty. For example, if a person is unfamiliar with the topic being discussed or if the required judgments are ambiguous, that person will be more likely to go along with the opinions of other people than when the topic is a familiar one and the required decision is clear (Montmollin, 1977). With this perspective, we may view conformity as simply one outcome of an attempt to solve problems and reach conclusions about one's surroundings. Such a perspective is an important one and should be considered before one too quickly adopts a value stance that conformity is always and forever bad. As Collins has stated:

> It would be a mistake to oversimplify the question and ask whether conformity is good or bad. A person who refused to accept anyone's word of advice on any topic whatsoever . . . would probably make just as big a botch of his life . . . as a person who always conformed and never formed a judgment on the basis of his own individual sources of information [1970, p. 21].

II. Compliance

The term **compliance** has often been used interchangeably with conformity (Kiesler & Kiesler, 1969). Here, however, we will use the term more specifically, limiting its use to those situations in which a direct request is made and the person agrees to behave in accord with that request. Unlike conformity, where the pressure to comply is indirect, in the compliance situation there is some direct pressure to comply. Such demands are made of us daily. For example, a professor may ask you to stop by after class, a door-to-door salesperson may suggest that you buy a new vacuum cleaner, or a panhandler may stop you on the street and ask for a quarter for a cup of coffee. Many experimental studies of compliance have in fact taken their lead from these common events.

A. *The "Foot-in-the-Door" Effect*

The **foot-in-the-door effect** has been developed from the sales lore that suggests that, once the seller has his or her foot in the door, a subsequent sale will be no problem (see Figure 14-3). Phrased in other terms, a person who complies with one small request is much more likely to comply later with a larger and more substantial demand.

In an initial test of this hypothesis, Freedman and Fraser (1966) arranged for two undergraduate experimenters to contact suburban housewives in their homes—first with a small request and later with a larger request. The housewives were first asked either to place a small sign in their window or to sign a petition about driving safely or keeping California beautiful. Two weeks later, a different experimenter returned to each home and asked each housewife to place a large and unattractive billboard promoting auto safety on her lawn for the next couple of weeks—a rather substantial request. A second group of housewives (the control group) was contacted only about the second, large-billboard request. The results showed a very strong "foot-in-the-door" effect—subjects who had complied with the earlier trivial request were much more likely to comply with the larger request several weeks later. More

Figure 14-3. (Drawing by Koren; © 1973, The New Yorker Magazine, Inc.)

"Good morning. I'm your Fuller Brush person."

intriguing yet was the apparent generality of the effect; signing a petition to "keep California beautiful" led to greater compliance with a different experimenter on a different issue.

Why does the "foot-in-the-door" effect occur? One explanation offered by social psychologists stresses people's perceptions of themselves. Having once agreed to help, a person may decide that he or she is basically a helpful person. A second request—even a burdensome one—may then be granted because the person wishes to maintain that image of helpfulness. Considerable evidence supports this interpretation (DeJong, 1979). However, at least two conditions are apparently necessary for the effect to occur. First, the initial request must be large enough to cause people to think about the implications of their behavior. Offhandedly telling someone the correct time, for example, might not be enough to cause you to think about yourself, whereas giving a set of complicated directions to someone who was lost might lead to self-perceptions. A second necessary condition is a perception of free choice. If a person feels forced to comply, then there is no reason to make attributions to internal dispositions. In fact, any external justification for the compliance will weaken or eliminate the foot-in-the-door effect. Thus homemakers who were offered money for agreeing to a 5-minute telephone interview were no more likely to comply with a later request for a 25-minute interview than were women who did not receive the initial request. Demonstrating the foot-in-the-door effect, women not offered the monetary justification were more likely to agree to the later request (Zuckerman, Lazzaro, & Waldgeir, 1979).

What about people who refuse the initial request? The self-perception explanation would suggest that these people would be *less* likely to comply with subsequent requests. In contrast to people who agree to help, these noncompliers should view themselves as nonhelpful people and act accordingly on future occasions. A clear demonstration of the importance of this labeling process is provided by Kraut (1973). In his experiment, subjects who gave to charity were either labeled as charitable or not labeled. For example, following their donation, subjects in the labeling condition might be told "You are really a generous person. I wish more people were as charitable as you are." Similarly, subjects who refused to give to charity were either labeled as uncharitable or not labeled. All subjects were later asked by another canvasser to contribute to a second charity. Subjects who had been labeled as charitable gave more and subjects labeled as uncharitable gave less than their respective unlabeled peers.

Thus, consistent with sales lore, there is considerable evidence for the foot-in-the-door effect. A "foot in" makes future compliance more likely, but "no foot in" should reduce future compliance. But does the latter reduction in compliance always occur?

B. The "Door-in-the-Face" Effect

Coining the term *"door-in-the-face" effect*, Cialdini and his coworkers (Cialdini, Vincent, Lewis, Catalan, Wheeler, & Darby, 1975) suggested that on some occasions people who refuse an initial request may be *more* likely to agree to a subsequent request. These researchers approached college students with a socially desirable but highly demanding request: Would they serve as voluntary counselors at a County Juvenile Detention Center for two years? Virtually everyone politely refused, thus in effect slamming the door in the face of a demanding request for compliance. However, when a second and smaller request was made, specifically to chaperone juveniles on a trip to the zoo, many subjects readily agreed to the request.

Why wasn't there less compliance in this case, as the self-perception explanation would predict? Apparently, investigators have concluded, the door-in-the-face effect depends on a particular set of circumstances (DeJong, 1979). First, the initial request must be very large—so large that the person who refuses does not make any negative inference about the self. Thus the person who declined two years of voluntary service would probably conclude that hardly anyone would agree to such a large request and would not have to form a self-perception of unhelpfulness. Second, for the door-in-the-face effect to occur, the second request must be made by the same person who makes the first request. According to Cialdini and his colleagues (Cialdini et al., 1975), subjects view the toned-down request as a concession on the part of the experimenter, and they then feel pressure to reciprocate that concession. If a different person makes the second request, however, such conciliatory behavior is not necessary.

The fact that the refusal of an initial request may occasionally facilitate the chances of compliance with a later smaller request need not always apply to socially desirable activities. For example, the sequence of events in the Watergate incident may be analyzed in terms of the "door-in-the-face" effect. Gordon Liddy was able to persuade leaders of the Committee to Re-Elect the President to finance his attempt to "bug" the offices of the Democratic Party, despite the clear knowledge of John Mitchell and Jeb Magruder that such actions were illegal. The refusal of an initial request of much larger scope may have facilitated the approval of the Watergate plan that was later actually attempted.

C. *The "Low-Ball" Procedure*

Yet another investigation of compliance that was inspired by a practitioner's rule of thumb is the "low-ball" procedure (Cialdini, Cacioppo, Bassett, & Miller, 1978). Presumably widespread (and especially among new-car dealers), the technique of "throwing a low ball" consists of inducing the customer to purchase a car by offering an extremely good price (for example, $500 below what other competitors are offering). Once the customer has agreed to buy the car, the conditions of the deal are then changed, resulting in a higher purchase price than the customer originally agreed to. Reported techniques include a refusal to approve the deal by the salesperson's boss, a reduction in the trade-in figure given by the used-car manager, or the exclusion of various options from the purchase price offered.

As Cialdini and his colleagues demonstrated, this technique of inducing compliance works beyond the new-car showroom. University students, for example, were more likely to show up for an experiment at 7 A.M. if they had first agreed to participate in a general way than if they were initially told of the early hour. Although this technique of compliance is in many ways similar to the foot-in-the-door procedure, there is at least one important difference. In "low balling," the initial commitment is to the behavior to be performed; in the "foot" procedure, the commitment is first to a less demanding behavior.

D. *The Generality of Compliance*

In a normal day, probably dozens of requests are made of each of us. Research such as that just described has concentrated on showing different conditions under which compliance to a request is more or less likely. In some instances, a decision to comply with a request may be a rational choice, in which we consider the pros and cons of agreeing with the request. Often, however, our willingness to comply with a request may be much less considered. Langer, in fact, has argued that many such behaviors are essentially "mindless"—in other words, we go along with the request without much thought. To demonstrate that people may comply without giving much thought to their actions, Langer and her colleagues (Langer, Blank, & Chanowitz, 1978) conducted a series of studies in which people were asked to comply with requests with little or no justification. For example, people about to use a copying machine were interrupted by an experimenter who asked to go first, either for no reason, for a noninformative reason ("I have to make copies"), or for a real reason ("I'm in a rush"). As long as the request was a small one, people were equally likely to comply with the latter two requests—even though "I have to make copies" provided no real reason for letting the other person go first. (Less compliance occurred when no reason at all was offered.)

Although such "mindless" compliance may be common, studies of power strategies suggest that we may at times be quite sensitive to the form in which compliance is requested. French and Raven (1959) identified six bases of power or ways in which one person could induce compliance on the part of another. These six different strategies are shown in Table 14-2. As a variety of studies have shown (Raven, 1965, 1974), the likelihood of compliance will vary depending on which form of power is used. Furthermore, people will attribute the reasons for compliance differently depending on the power strategy chosen. For example, when either referent, informational, or reward power is used, attributions for compliance generally focus on the person who performs the compliant behavior. In contrast, when either coercive or legitimate power is used, explanations for compliance generally focus on the person making the request (Litman-Adizes, Raven, & Fontaine, 1978). Such findings suggest not only that there are differences in the immediate response to a

request for compliance but also that the attributional patterns may influence the extent of future compliance once the agent making the request is no longer present.

We have seen that willingness to comply with the request of another person may occur for many different reasons: at one extreme, there may be the "mindless" response, in which we comply in an almost automatic fashion, giving little thought to the reasons why we should or should not agree to carry out the behavior. This form of compliance is most likely to occur when the response is essentially overlearned, not requiring much conscious monitoring on our part. At the other end of the spectrum, there may be situations in which we carefully weigh the reasons for compliance and act accordingly. Yet, although rationality may contribute on many occasions, the sheer force of the request often determines our response. As we shall see in the case of obedience, once legitimate power has been established, a person may refuse to question the reasons for the agent's request and simply carry out orders because they are made.

III. Obedience

A special form of compliance, in which the request is made in the form of an order, is **obedience**. All of us feel some degree of pressure to obey certain symbols of authority, such as parents, police officers, and traffic lights. We can question, however, whether obedience can assume so powerful a position within a person's domain of behavior that it causes the person to perform socially unacceptable acts (Figure 14-4 illustrates one tragic outcome of obedience). Can destructive obedience occur? The cases of Lieutenant Calley and Adolf Eichmann are relevant. When he was tried for killing 100 Vietnamese villagers, U.S. Army Lieutenant Calley stated that he was simply following orders. Adolf Eichmann, in charge of exterminating 6 million Jews in Nazi Germany, also did what he was told. At his trial for war crimes, Eichmann denied any moral responsibility. He was, he said, simply doing his job.

TABLE 14-2 / *Forms of Power or Potential Influence*

Types of Power	Bases of Power
Coercion	Ability of agent to mediate punishment
Reward	Ability of agent to mediate rewards
Expertise	Attribution of superior knowledge or ability to influence agent
Reference	Agent is used as frame of reference for self-evaluation
Legitimacy	Acceptance of relationship in power structure such that agent is allowed to prescribe behaviors
Information	Content of communication establishes new cognitions

From "The Bases of Social Power," by J. R. P. French, Jr., and B. H. Raven. In D. Cartwright (Ed.), *Studies in Social Power.* Copyright 1959 by the University of Michigan. Published by the Institute for Social Research. Reprinted by permission.

A. *Milgram's Laboratory Studies of Destructive Obedience*

Although the Eichmann and Calley examples are real, they may be unusual cases. Stanley Milgram, a social psychologist, attempted to demonstrate that, under much more normal conditions, people will indeed obey an authority, even when the person believes that he or she is endangering the life of another person.

Through advertisements and direct-mail solicitations in New Haven, Connecticut, Milgram (1963) gathered 40 males of various ages and occupations for paid participation in a research project at Yale University. When each subject arrived for the experiment, he was introduced to the experimenter and another subject (actually an accomplice of the experimenter). The subjects were told that the purpose of the experiment was to determine the effects of punishment on learning. Subjects drew lots to determine who would be the teacher and who would be the learner, but the drawing was rigged so that the true subject was always the teacher and the accomplice was always the learner. At that point, the learner was strapped to a chair, electrodes were attached to his wrist, and the subject-teacher was then instructed in his task.

The lesson to be administered by the subject was a paired-associate learning task, in which the subject was to read a series of word pairs to the learner and then read the first word of the pair along with four other words. The learner's job was to indicate which of the four terms was the correct associate by pressing a switch that lit a light in the teacher's room. The teacher was told to administer a shock to the learner each time he gave a wrong response, using a shock generator with 30 separate switches. These switches increased by 15-volt increments from 15 to 450 volts and were labeled from "Slight Shock" at the low end to "Danger: Severe Shock" and finally an omnious "XXX" at the highest end. In fact, this equipment was a dummy generator and the confederate never received an actual shock, but its appearance was quite convincing.

After each wrong answer (of which the

Figure 14-4. Obedience to a destructive authority: the aftermath of Jonestown. (© United Press International.)

accomplice intentionally made many), the experimenter instructed the subject to move one level higher on the shock generator. When the subject reached 300 volts, the accomplice began to pound on the wall between the two rooms, and then, from that point on, he no longer made any answer to the questions posed by the subject. At this point, subjects usually turned to the experimenter for guidance. In a stoic and rather stern way, the experimenter replied that no answer was to be treated as a wrong answer and the subject was to be shocked according to the usual schedule.

Milgram's basic question was simply how many subjects would continue to administer shocks to the end of the series, following the orders of the experimenter. Table 14-3 presents the results. Of the 40 subjects, 26 (65%) continued to the end of the shock series. Not a single subject stopped prior to administering 300 volts—the point at which the learner began pounding on the wall. Five refused to obey at that point; at some point 14 of the 40 subjects defied the experimenter. Milgram concludes that obedience to commands is a strong force in our society, since nearly two-thirds of his subjects obeyed the experimenter's instructions even though they were led to believe that they were hurting another human being.

Milgram (1964a, 1965, 1974) then extended his program of research to study some of the situational factors that may lead a subject to obey or to refuse to obey when the experimenter (the authority figure) tells the subject to hurt another person. He found, for example, that, the closer the victim was to the subject, the more likely subjects were to refuse the command of the experimenter. Thus when the victim was in the same room as the subject and only 1½ feet away, only one-third of the subjects were willing to go to the maximum shock level. In another set of studies, Milgram showed that, if the experimenter was not physically present but, rather, presented his commands either by telephone or by tape recording, obedience was much less frequent. In fact, when the experimenter was absent, several subjects administered shocks of a lower voltage than was required, thus defying the authority of the experimenter. As Rada and Rogers (1973) note, the situation in which the authority figure is absent is probably more typical of everyday living, and thus defiance of authority may be more common than the Milgram results suggest. Yet Rada and Rogers also found that, when the authority figure had previously issued a strong command to obey, the subjects tended to obey whether the authority figure was present or not.

T A B L E 14 - 3 / *Distribution of Breakoff Points in Milgram's Study of Obedience*

Verbal Designation and Voltage Indication	Number of Subjects for Whom This Was Maximum Shock
Slight Shock	
15	0
30	0
45	0
60	0
Moderate Shock	
75	0
90	0
105	0
120	0
Strong Shock	
135	0
150	0
165	0
180	0
Very Strong Shock	
195	0
210	0
225	0
240	0
Intense Shock	
255	0
270	0
285	0
300	5
Extreme-Intensity Shock	
315	4
330	2
345	1
360	1
Danger—Severe Shock	
375	1
390	0
405	0
420	0
XXX	
435	0
450	26

From "Behavioral Study of Obedience," by S. Milgram, *Journal of Abnormal and Social Psychology*, 1963, 67, 371–378. Copyright 1963 by the American Psychological Association. Reprinted by permission.

B. *Criticisms of Milgram's Obedience Studies*

As provocative as these findings are, Milgram's program of research has not gone without criticism. Perhaps the strongest of the critics is Baumrind (1964), who believes the studies were not only unethical but also lacking in generalizability to real-world obedience situations. These two lines of criticism will be examined in turn.

Criticisms of the Ethics of the Experiment. Milgram's studies have been called unethical on several grounds. One claim is that the subjects' rights were not protected. No health examinations were given to the subjects prior to the experiment to determine whether some psychological maladjustment or physical problem should exclude certain subjects. No prior permission was obtained from the subjects allowing the experimenters to place them in distressful conflict situations. In fact, it is unlikely that the exact procedures of the Milgram study could be replicated today. In most cases, experimenters are required to give subjects more information before they consent to participate than Milgram provided his subjects.

A second claim is that there could have been long-term effects on the subjects from having participated in the study. Among these effects could be the subjects' loss of trust in future experimenters, the university, or science in general. Another type of long-term effect might have been on the subjects' self-concepts. Prior to the experiment, most subjects probably saw themselves as persons who would not deliberately inflict pain on another person unless the circumstances were extreme. As a result of the experiment, they would have to believe otherwise. One can certainly argue that such self-education might be beneficial, but it is probably not within the province of the experimental social psychologist to force such education on a subject.

A third criticism regarding the ethicality of the experiment centers on Milgram's reactions to the anguish and tension shown by some subjects as they methodically increased the shock levels trial by trial. Milgram reports with some awe, if not relish, the extreme degrees of tension that his subjects experienced—that subjects were observed to "sweat, stutter, tremble, groan, bite their lips, and dig their fingernails into their flesh. Full-blown uncontrollable seizures were observed for three subjects" (1963, p. 375). Critics have asked why the whole experiment was not terminated in the face of such incidents. Milgram has argued that debriefing at the end of the experiment was sufficient to eradicate these tensions. In describing the debriefing procedure, Milgram stated: "After the interview, procedures were undertaken to assure that the subject would leave the laboratory in a state of well-being. A friendly reconciliation was arranged between the subject and the victim, and an effort was made to reduce any tensions that arose as a result of the experiment" (1963, p. 374). Yet it is hard to believe that such extreme examples of tension could be erased by a short debriefing procedure. Milgram's critics remain unconvinced by his reports (1964b, 1968, 1974) that interviews by psychiatrists and follow-up questionnaires completed by the subjects indicated no long-term deleterious effects.

Criticisms of the Lack of Generality. Baumrind and others have also questioned whether the extreme degrees of obedience found in Milgram's subjects may be generalized to the real world. For example, trust in and obedience to the authority figure may be demand characteristics that are especially salient for subjects in experiments (Orne & Holland, 1968). In other words, subjects who will do as they are told in an experiment might disobey another authority figure, such as the physician who tells them to exercise daily or the employer who tells them to fire a popular coworker. Along with this criticism is the claim that the prestige of Yale University contributed to the high obedience rate; subjects may have assumed that anything carried out at Yale must be scientifically and socially acceptable—hence, they were more inclined to obey. Yet the available evidence contradicts this last claim. Milgram repeated the experiment in a rundown office building in a deteriorating area of Bridgeport, Connecticut, and found that almost 50% of the men obeyed the experimenter to the end of the shock series. Although the prestige of Yale apparently accounted for some obedience, the phenomenon still occurred in a blatantly nonuniversity setting.

The use of "prods" by the experimenter in the Milgram task may have contributed significantly to the high rate of obedience. If a subject was unwilling to continue, the experimenter used four verbal prods to urge him to continue, beginning with "Please continue" and advancing in strength to "You have no other choice—You *must* go on." We do not know what the rejection rate would have been if the prods had not been used, but it is probable that more subjects would have terminated their participation earlier.

Certainly there are problems in making a blanket generalization of Milgram's findings to real-world cases of destructive obedience. Several replications (Kilham & Mann, 1974; Rada & Rogers, 1973) have reported lower rates of obedience. But in real-world situations where prods or similar devices are used to keep people at tasks that are personally abhorrent, Milgram's findings may well be applicable, prompting Etzioni (1968) to conclude that humans are latently Eichmannistic. Whether that extreme conclusion is warranted or not, it is clear that Milgram's work has demonstrated that obedience is a much more pervasive phenomenon than had been thought. Neither a group of undergraduates nor a group of psychologists and psychiatrists, when told of the procedures, predicted that subjects would continue to obey when the high voltage levels were reached. Assumptions about human nature were more favorable than the actual outcomes.

IV. The Sense of Control

Theories of human behavior differ in their assumptions about human nature and hence are divided on the issue of personal control. As we saw in Chapter 1, phenome-

nological approaches to social behavior often rest on the assumption that as humans we have almost complete control over our behavior. In contrast, Skinner and his followers take the position that stimuli in the environment determine our behavior—that we are controlled by external rewards and punishments and that free will is merely a figment of our imagination (Skinner, 1971). Between these two positions lie a number of variations, although it is certainly fair to say that experimental social psychology has emphasized external influences more than individual choice.

The issue of control is particularly relevant when we talk about social influence. As we have seen, people will, under a variety of circumstances, conform to group pressure, comply with requests, and obey orders. In each of these cases, external forces appear to regulate the behavior and the issue of individual control seems peculiarly absent. Yet many people fervently believe that we do have nearly complete control over our behavior, and even those, like Skinner, who would disagree nevertheless admit that most people believe in a sense of personal control.

In the remainder of this chapter, we will consider the general issue of control—how we develop illusions of control, how a belief in control affects our behavior, and how we react to a loss of control in our lives.

A. *The Illusion of Control*

Magicians entertain by appearing to control events that we cannot explain. Although most of us cannot make rabbits appear out of hats or people float in air, we do believe in our ability to control more mundane events. Even for events that objectively are determined purely by chance, we often develop an "illusion of control" over the outcome. Ellen Langer and her colleagues have presented the most persuasive evidence for these beliefs (Langer, 1975, 1978a; Langer & Roth, 1975).

The lottery is clearly a situation in which the likelihood of winning is determined solely by chance—the "luck of the draw" allows little room for an individual to influence the outcome. To illustrate the illusion of control, Langer (1975) gave people the opportunity to buy $1 lottery tickets with the chance of a $50 prize. Two identical sets of tickets were used; each ticket had the name of a football player and his team written on it. When one of the tickets was purchased by the subject, its identical mate was deposited in the lottery box. To vary the illusion of control, the experimenters allowed one group of people to select the ticket they wanted; that is, they named the football player and team of their choice. Other participants received randomly selected lottery tickets from the experimenter (identical to those chosen by the first group). Prior to the random drawing of the prize ticket, all subjects were approached by the experimenter and asked if they would be willing to sell their ticket to someone who would pay more than the going price for the ticket. Subjects who had not been given a choice in the ticket they held were willing to sell their card for an average of $1.96. In contrast, those subjects who believed that they had some choice demanded an average of $8.67 for their ticket, presumably because they believed that they had a better chance of winning the random draw than did those subjects who had not exercised a choice.

There are many factors that can increase our belief in control. In general, the more similar a purely chance situation is in appearance to a real skill situation, the more likely we are to believe in our own ability to control the outcome. For example, competition increases our belief in control. Paired with a seemingly incompetent competitor, we will be much more confident of our success than when the competitor appears competent, even though the task itself is purely chance determined (Langer, 1975). Thus playing a Las Vegas slot machine with a 5-year-old at the next stand would probably lead us to believe that we had greater control over our outcome—despite the fact that the machines themselves are obstinately beyond our control. Similarly, involvement in the task, knowledge about the procedures that are in-

volved, and practice in performing the task all lead us to believe that we have more control than we in fact possess. Success at a task may also create the illusion of control. In another study, Langer and Roth (1975) asked subjects to predict coin tosses and structured the outcome so that people either experienced early success and later failure, early failure and later success, or a purely random order of outcome. In each case, however, the number of correct predictions was the same and did not differ from what could be expected by chance. Those people who experienced early success were much more confident of their ability on the task, predicting more future successes for themselves and viewing themselves as more skilled. Early experience with success apparently created a belief in the ability to control the outcome, a finding that is probably quite similar to the case of the novice gambler who hits the jackpot the first time around—and then proceeds to lose far more than was initially won!

Findings such as these do not mean that we never have real control over situations and outcomes. However, it is apparent that our belief in control may range far wider than the actual boundaries of our control.

B. *Consequences of a Belief in Control*

Why do we believe so strongly in our ability to influence events, often in the face of evidence that suggests we in fact have little or no control? One reason is that a belief in such control makes the world more predictable. If we are expecting to interact with someone in a competitive situation, for example, we would like to be able to predict that person's behavior and in turn our own outcomes, and experiments have shown that we may, in fact, exaggerate our ability to make such predictions. In one study, subjects who expected to compete with another subject were more certain that they would be able to infer the personality of their competitor than were subjects who expected only to observe the interaction (Miller, Norman, & Wright, 1978). Yet the belief in control is not something that exists only in our fantasies. Behavior, too, is altered when we believe that we have control over our circumstances.

Performance on routine tasks is better when we believe that we had control over loud noise that was present prior to the performance, even when that control was not actually exercised (Glass & Singer, 1972). People who have control over their environment perceive conditions as less crowded than do those who feel that they have no control; further, they judge their surroundings as more pleasant and their own mood as more positive (Rodin, Solomon, & Metcalf, 1978). In general, over a wide range of circumstances, we react more positively when we believe we have some control than when we do not. One of the reasons for severe depressions following major illnesses such as heart attacks, for example, is assumed to be the feelings that one has lost control over one's life (Glass, 1977).

Perhaps one of the most dramatic demonstrations of power of a belief in control is a study of aged people in institutions done by Ellen Langer and Judith Rodin (Langer & Rodin, 1976; Rodin & Langer, 1977). These investigators suggested that one of the reasons for the debilitated condition of many elderly residents of institutions was their perception of having no control. In contrast to their lives in their own homes, where dozens of decisions are required daily, these residents of institutions were placed in a decision-free environment where all of the control resided in others. Such psychological factors might be equally or more important than physical factors in determining the people's well-being (see also Figure 14-5).

To test this hypothesis, Langer and Rodin (1976) gained the cooperation of the staff of a Connecticut nursing home, divided the residents into two groups, and administered one of two communications. Residents of one floor received a message that stressed the staff's responsibility for them and for their activities. Residents were given a plant but were told that the nurses would care for the plant; they were informed they would be allowed to see a movie but that the staff would determine what day the

movie would be shown. In contrast to this message that minimized the resident's sense of control (and that probably paralleled the situation in most nursing homes), members of the other group were given a communication that emphasized their own responsibility. The message stressed the number of things that residents could do for themselves, from arranging the furniture in their room to deciding how to spend their time, and encouraged the people to make their complaints known if they were not satisfied with the current arrangements. Members of this group were also given a plant, but they were allowed to pick which plant they wanted and were told that it would be their responsibility to take care of it. Finally, these residents were also told that a movie would be shown and that they could decide when and if they would view it.

In many respects, the communication provided to the experimental group seems quite weak. The defined areas of responsibility are, after all, ones that most of us take for granted. It may be difficult to believe that a specific reminder would have much effect. But it did. Persons in the group in which personal control had been stressed reported significant increases in happiness when questioned three weeks later. Nurses judged these same residents to be improved in their mental outlook and reported substantially increased activity on the part of the residents—talking with other patients, visiting people from outside the nursing home, and talking to the staff. Even attendance at the promised movie was greater for those residents who had control over the time that they would see the film.

More dramatic evidence of the effects of control was found when Rodin and Langer (1977) returned to the nursing home 18 months later. Nurses continued to rate the responsibility-induced group of residents as more active, more sociable, and more vigorous; physicians rated these same patients as being in better health. Most striking of all was the difference in mortality rates. Whereas 30% of the patients in the control group had died in the months intervening, only 15% of the residents in the responsibility group had died. These results provide graphic and powerful evidence for the importance of control in a person's life.

C. *Individual Differences in Perceptions of Control*

Although situational factors can forcefully affect the extent to which we believe that we have power over events, it is also true that people differ widely in their general beliefs about control. The general question of individual differences in behavior will be discussed much more extensively in Chapter 16. Here, however, we should give some notice to the idea of **locus of control,** as originally proposed by Rotter (1966). Rotter suggested that people have a general tendency to believe that control of the events in their lives is either internal or ex-

ternal. Internal people, for example, tend to believe in their own ability to control events; external people believe that other people or events were the primary influences on their own circumstances. Some items from the scale that Rotter developed to measure these general orientations are shown in Table 14-4. More recent research has suggested that Rotter's ideas, though accurate in a general sense, may be too simplified. A belief in external control, for example, can imply a number of different dimensions: belief in fate, belief in powerful others, belief in a difficult world, and belief in a politically unresponsive world (Collins, 1974; Gurin, Gurin, Lao, & Beattie, 1969; Mirels, 1970).

In addition to the multidimensional nature of beliefs in control, other investigators have suggested that we have different be-

Figure 14-5. Early investigations of the causes of death in elderly people tended to stress physical causes. More recently, however, many investigators have become aware of the importance of psychological factors and environmental events in predicting the death of elderly people. Rowland (1977) reviewed much of this research and found two factors of considerable importance. The death of a significant other person, most often a spouse, increases the probability of a person's own death. Relocation, such as a move to a nursing home, also seems to increase the probability of death. In this case, the issue of control and the voluntary or involuntary nature of the move are important. Contrary to many beliefs, Rowland (1977) found no strong evidence suggesting that retirement precipitates an early death. (© United Press International.)

TABLE 14-4 / *Internal Versus External Locus of Control*

The concept of *internal versus external locus of control* (also called "internal versus external control of reinforcement") developed from Julian Rotter's social-learning theory (Rotter, 1954, 1975; Rotter, Chance, & Phares, 1972).

Although the *concept* deals with an intrapersonal orientation, Rotter's (1966) Internal-External (I-E) scale contains statements about both oneself and people in general. For example, the following two pairs of items reflect beliefs about people in general:

1. People's misfortunes result from the mistakes they make.
   versus
   Many of the unhappy things in people's lives are partly due to bad luck.
18. With enough effort we can wipe out political corruption.
    versus
    It is difficult for people to have much control over the things politicians do in office.

The above items contrast with the *personal* orientation of the following internal-external pairs:

19. There is a direct connection between how hard I study and the grades I get.
    versus
    Sometimes I can't understand how teachers arrive at the grades they give.
22. What happens to me is my own doing.
    versus
    Sometimes I feel that I don't have enough control over the direction my life is taking.

liefs when positive versus negative outcomes are considered (Crandall, Katkovsky, & Crandall, 1965; DuCette, Wolk, & Soucar, 1972). A person may, for example, believe that he or she has considerable control over positive outcomes while feeling that negative events are beyond personal control. Other people might believe just the opposite. At least one study suggests that the major difference between people who are internal or external in the general sense proposed by Rotter lies in their reaction to negative outcomes. Subjects in this experiment were asked to perform a difficult task that was described as dependent on skill (Gregory, 1978). When a reward was promised for a successful performance, internal and external persons behaved similarly. When the instructions were changed, stressing the avoidance of punishment if performance was successful, only internal subjects performed well. Externals, in contrast, seemed to default their responsibility and accept the inevitability of punishment from an outside agent.

Although the concept of a person's locus of control is not without ambiguity, considerable research has shown that people do differ, often dramatically, in their approach to the world and in their feelings of effectiveness over their environment (Phares, 1976; Strickland, 1977). Individual differences in such beliefs must ultimately be considered in conjunction with those situational factors that make us feel more or less in control of our world.

V. Reactions to a Loss of Control

Although most of us would like to believe that we have control over events, such control is not always possible. Often we are faced with situations in which someone else or something else appears to be in control of our fate, and our own freedom of choice is severely limited. In some cases, this sense of another's control may simply be exasperating or frustrating. Social observer L. Rust Hills (1973), for example, discussed the roles of social life in the contemporary United States and concluded that there are three "social cruel rules." One of these is the following: "(a) Whenever you really feel like going out you don't have an invitation; and in converse: (b) whenever you are invited to go out, you feel like staying at home" (p. 15). In this case, although the belief in control by others may not be overpowering, it is nonetheless influential on your activities. In other cases, a perception that others have control over our lives may be much more pervasive. Citizens living under a repressive dictatorship, for example, may feel that they have little control over their daily activities, their conversations, and even their thoughts. How do people cope with these perceptions of a loss of control?

A. A Theory of Reactance

Social psychologist Jack Brehm (1966, 1972) has proposed the concept of psychological reactance to explain some of the reactions that we have to a loss of control or freedom of choice. According to Brehm, reactance is a motivational state that is aroused whenever a person feels that his or her freedom has been abridged or threatened. Consider the following fairly commonplace example offered by Brehm:

Picture Mr. John Smith, who normally plays golf on Sunday afternoons, although occasionally he spends Sunday afternoon watching television or puttering around his workshop. The important point is that Smith always spends Sunday afternoon doing whichever of these three things he prefers; he is free to choose which he will do. Now consider a specific Sunday morning on which Smith's wife announces that Smith will have to play golf that afternoon since she has invited several of her lady friends to the house for a party. Mr. Smith's freedom is threatened with reduction in several ways: (1) he cannot watch television, (2) he cannot putter in the workshop, and (3) he must (Mrs. Smith says) play golf [1966, p.2].

Given this threat to his freedom, reactance theory would predict that Mr. Smith would attempt to restore his personal freedom. He might choose to stay in his workshop, for example, perhaps creating a clamor of protest in the process. Threats to freedom, according to this theory, create a psychological state of reactance, and this motivational state leads the person to take actions that will help to regain control and personal freedom (Wicklund, 1974; Worchel & Brehm, 1971).

The exact actions that the person chooses will, of course, depend on the na-ture of the threat and the freedom being threatened. For example, in the face of a threatening communication, a person might change an attitude in a direction opposite to that advocated, thus confirming a sense of independence and control (Brehm, 1966; Snyder & Wicklund, 1976). Another example of reactance is a situation in which certain alternatives are eliminated, so that our ability to choose freely is threatened. In one experiment, for example, subjects were initially given a choice of record albums and then later told that certain albums would not be available. Reacting to this threat to their freedom, these subjects showed increased positive feelings toward the threatened options (Brehm, Stires, Sensenig, & Shaban, 1966). Perhaps an even more relevant example of the effects of restrictions on people's feelings is the case of limitations on the availability of pornography. According to reactance theory, material that is restricted or censored would take on a greater appeal (Fromkin & Brock, 1973); in fact, Worchel, Arnold, and Baker (1975) found that censorship of a message caused a potential audience to change their attitudes in the direction of the position advocated by the communication, as well as to develop a greater desire to hear the communication. One interpretation (Ashmore, Ramchandra, & Jones, 1971) is that the potential audience felt that the censor was threatening their freedom to hold the attitude advocated by the censored message.

Many other examples of reactance can be imagined, in which a threat to freedom or a perception of external control may lead to actions geared at restoring a sense of personal control. Children who are told not to touch certain furniture, for example, often make a game of touching the forbidden objects. In such games, getting caught often seems to be part of the fun and may be viewed as a means for the child to demonstrate some control, however temporary it may be. Teenagers show similar behavior when they break a parent's imposed curfew, not because they lost track of time or were involved in anything of interest but simply as a means of demonstrating that they, and not their parents, control their activities.

Thinking back on your own behavior, you can probably easily think of cases when reactance may have been operating and when the sheer act of exerting a sense of control was more important than the particular action that you took.

Of course, it is not always to our advantage to be perceived as in control of a situation. For example, if a man points a gun in your face and demands your money, would you attempt to show that you were in control by wrestling with him? In such cases, in which an attempt to reestablish control could lead to personal injury, people are often content to acknowledge the other person's control (Grabitz-Gneich, 1971). In still other cases, personal harm may not be likely, but the responsibility of harm to someone else may be equally discomforting. "Passing the buck" is a case in point. Here people may voluntarily relinquish control in order to avoid the responsibility for some unpleasant outcome (Feldman-Summers, 1977). Thus in situations in which negative outcomes and personal responsibility for those outcomes are involved, we are willing to abrogate a sense of control; in many other cases, however, where outcomes are positive or simply neutral, we actively attempt to reassert control and preserve our sense of personal freedom.

B. *The Case of Learned Helplessness*

One aspect of our belief in personal control rests on the fact that outcomes are predictable—the issues of predictability and control are very closely related. Many routines in our life are based on a sense of predictability. For example, if you live in a city that has a subway system, you have probably learned to expect that, every time you put a token in the subway stile, it will click, turn, and allow you to board the next train. A failure of the stile to turn when the coin is dropped almost inevitably results in frustration. Such a break in the normal routine may involve threats to both predictability and control. On the one hand, the subway stile did not react as you predicted it would, and, on the other, its recalcitrance casts doubt on your ability to control your own outcomes.

Consider the adventures of Alice in Wonderland. Finding herself in a strange environment, Alice quickly discovers that all is not as she has learned it to be. On one occasion she drinks the contents of a bottle and quickly shrinks to a mere ten inches in height. Trying another bottle similarly labeled "Drink me," Alice grows to gigantic proportions. Such adventures, although fictional, nonetheless illustrate the principle of *noncontingency*—similar actions do not lead to similar outcomes. And there are many situations in life in which people may experience a similar fate—their actions appear to have little relationship to the outcomes that they experience.

The result of such experiences is a state that psychologist Martin Seligman (1975) has termed **learned helplessness**. As Seligman has stated simply, "When a person is faced with an outcome that is independent of his responses, he learns that the outcome is independent of his responses" (1975, p. 46). Although this statement probably seems obvious, it has some important implications. Three elements characterize the individual who is in a state of learned helplessness. First, it is necessary to have been exposed to situations in which outcomes are noncontingent on one's behavior. From that experience, the individual then develops a belief or an expectancy that his or her own responses have no effect, or are not instrumental, in influencing outcomes. Finally, a variety of cognitive and behavioral deficits result from that belief—performance will suffer and a sense of debilitation and lack of control will be experienced.

Early work in this area was done with animals. Seligman and his colleagues observed dogs placed in an apparatus and administered shock, from which there was no way they could escape. Nothing they did would terminate the shock. These same animals, when placed in a different apparatus in which a simple jumping response would terminate the shock, were unable to learn the new response. Unlike dogs that had not been exposed to the noncontingent experience, these dogs simply lay down and whined, unable to learn the fairly simple contingency.

It was quickly found that these effects are not limited to animals; learned helplessness is a human phenomenon as well. College students who are faced with a series of unsolvable puzzles, for example, will show striking deficits in a subsequent task where loud noise can be avoided (Seligman, 1975) or where simple responses are to be performed (DeVellis, DeVellis, & McCauley, 1978).

Noncontingency does not have to be experienced directly in order to produce a state of learned helplessness. As social-learning theory would predict, simply observing a model experience noncontingency of outcomes can be sufficient to induce a state of learned helplessness in the observer and affect that observer's own performance in a similar situation (Brown & Inouye, 1978; DeVellis et al., 1978). As we might further expect, the more similar the model is to the observer, the more likely the model's experience is to affect the observer's own performance (Brown & Inouye, 1978).

Learned-helplessness effects are not limited to artificial tasks performed in a laboratory setting. Like Alice's Wonderland, our natural environment may contribute strongly to feelings of learned helplessness. Crowded environments, for example, may affect a person's ability to regulate social control and thus contribute to a feeling of learned helplessness. Rodin (1976), for example, found that children living in a high-density residence were less likely to assume control of outcomes than children living in less dense settings. Similarly, children from more densely populated environments performed more poorly on puzzles than did children from lower-density homes.

But why do people fall, with such apparent ease, into a state of learned helplessness? Why don't they react against the situation, as reactance theory suggests they would? Sometimes they do. In a situation in which the person had no initial beliefs in control, learned helplessness may be the immediate response. In contrast, Wortman and Brehm (1975) predict that "reactance will precede helplessness for individuals who originally expect control" (p. 308). In a field study of this hypothesis, Baum, Aiello, and Calesnick (1978) selected residents of college dormitories who lived either in large or in moderate-sized groups and for whom the architecture of the building (long- or short-corridor design) either facilitated a sense of control and predictability in their interactions or diminished this sense of control. Taking these subjects into the laboratory to perform a standard social task that allows either cooperation or competition (the Prisoner's Dilemma, as described in Chapter 9), the experimenters considered the performance of subjects as a function of how long they had lived in the residence halls—either one, three, or seven weeks. Those students who had lived in the long-corridor dormitories for shorter periods of time (either one or three weeks) reported negative feelings about their living conditions, but at the same time they showed highly competitive behavior in the Prisoner's Dilemma game, which suggested an attempt to assert control. However, after living in the low-control situation for several more weeks, the students seemed to relinquish some of their attempted control. They became less negative and more accepting of the conditions, and their play in the game became less competitive, less involved and motivated, and more withdrawn. Thus, in the initial weeks, the students appeared to show reactance—attempting to restore their belief in freedom and feeling of control. Yet, because their attempts were presumably for the most part unsuccessful, regulated by the facts of the dormitory design, attempts to gain control were replaced with feelings of resignation and helplessness. In contrast, residents of short-corridor dormitories did not perceive any problems of control, and their behavior was more adaptive than the other residents' and did not change over the course of the study.

C. *Self-Induced Dependence*

Although learned helplessness is initially generated by an experience with uncontrollable outcomes, a feeling of loss of control may be caused by other factors as well. Langer (1978b, 1979) has suggested that there are a number of situations that may create an illusion of incompetence. Other people, for example, may imply or suggest directly that a person is incompetent, and that belief may be incorporated by the person himself or herself. With respect to the elderly, Langer has suggested that part of their apparent dysfunction may result directly from others labeling them as incompetent. As a society, we tend to disparage the elderly, assuming that they are past their prime, incapable of any significant physical or mental activity, and generally dependent on the aid of friends, relatives, and institutional personnel. Although such assumptions may not be totally unfounded, it is certain that they are vastly overdrawn. Such assumptions are not only inaccurate, Langer argues, but may also create the conditions that they presuppose. The elderly themselves, labeled as dependent, may come to believe the label.

The reality of such self-induced dependence is made clear in a study by Langer and Benevento (1978). In this study, male high school students were given the opportunity to perform a set of word-hunt problems and experienced success on the task. In a second phase, each boy worked in a team with another male (actually a confederate of the experimenter). By a predetermined draw, the student was assigned the role of assistant, and the confederate was assigned the role of boss. After working on a second task in this role of assistant, the subjects then took part in the third phase of the experiment, in which they were once again allowed to work individually on the word-hunt task they had performed during the first phase of the experiment. As Figure 14-6 shows, the performance of these boys dropped by 50%—they located only half as many words—after they had experienced a dependent role. In contrast, boys who did not participate in the assistant role showed little change in their performance level.

Perhaps the most surprising aspect of this experiment is how strong the performance effects were after only a brief experience in the role of assistant. If we imagine the elderly, or other groups who are frequently put in the role of dependents, we can easily see how pervasive and powerful self-induced dependence effects can be.

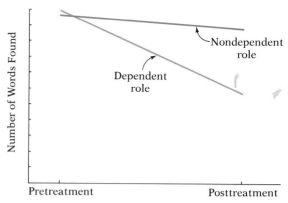

Figure 14-6. The effect of dependency on later performance. (From "Self-Induced Dependence," by E. J. Langer and A. Benevento, *Journal of Personality and Social Psychology*, 1978, *36*, 886–893. Copyright 1978 by the American Psychological Association. Reprinted by permission.)

VI. Summary

The issues of social influence and personal control are central to human behavior and are evident in everyday interactions as well as in more global issues of government and politics.

Conformity refers to a yielding to group pressure when no direct request to comply with the group is made. Asch conducted some of the earliest studies demonstrating the effect of a group's judgments on the behavior of the individual. Later investigators have shown that a variety of situational factors—such as the size of the group, the number of people who agree with the individual, the status of the group members, and the type of task—can affect the degree of conformity behavior that individuals will display.

Nonconformity behavior can be of two types. Independent behavior is that which occurs with no reference to the group position. In anticonformity behavior, in contrast, an individual does exactly the opposite of what the group does, thus showing that the group is still serving as a reference point for the individual's behavior. Conformity itself, although sometimes regarded as a purely negative type of behavior, also can serve a positive function by reducing a person's uncertainty in an unfamiliar situation.

Compliance refers to behavior that occurs in response to a direct request by some other person. In the "foot-in-the-door" technique, a small request is followed by a substantially larger request. Agreement with the first stage will increase the probability of compliance to the second request. The "door-in-the-face" effect works in the opposite way. In this case, the individual who initially refuses a fairly large request will be more likely to agree to a subsequent smaller request. A third technique for inducing compliance is the "low-ball" procedure, in which initial commitment to a behavior correlates with increased probability of compliance when the costs are increased.

Although compliance with some requests appears to be relatively "mindless," occurring without conscious thought, other acts of compliance evidence considerable thought, as when we evaluate the kind and amount of power that the agent has over our own situation.

Obedience studies show that people readily follow orders even when their compliance may cause harm to another person. Less obedience occurs when the victim is nearer to the subject (who is administering the shocks), and more obedience occurs if the experimenter is nearer.

Criticisms of Milgram's obedience studies focus on ethical questions and on their generalizability. In terms of ethics, critics cite the possible long-term effects on the subjects, the rights of consent of the subjects, and the wisdom of continuing the study despite high levels of distress shown by subjects. Generalizability questions focus on: (1) the nonrepresentative nature of the subjects; (2) the use of prods; and (3) the essential trust in experiments that most people feel.

In the face of these and other pressures, people maintain a pervasive belief in their own control. Even in situations that are obviously determined by chance, people have an illusion of control. Some of the factors that strengthen this illusion are competition, involvement in the task, knowledge and practice, and the similarity of the situation to a skill task.

Belief in personal control results in better performance and more positive affect than the lack of such belief. Studies have shown that even the death rate of persons in a nursing home is related to a feeling of personal control. Individual differences in perceptions of control exist; some people are inclined to believe in external control and others believe strongly in internal control.

Because beliefs in personal control are so pervasive, people often react strongly to a perceived or real loss of control. Psychological reactance refers to a motivational state that is aroused whenever a person feels that his or her freedom has been abridged. According to reactance theory, people will attempt to restore their sense of freedom when such threats are perceived. In some cases, however, as when harm to oneself or to others is involved, people show a willingness to relax their control and accept control as being in the hands of others.

Learned helplessness can be induced by exposing a person to a situation in which outcomes occur in a manner that is noncontingent (apparently random) on one's own behavior. People who experience such outcomes may develop beliefs that their own responses have no effect on subsequent outcomes and will show behavioral deficits even when the new situation does allow them the possibility of control.

Self-induced dependence may develop even without such outcomes. Labeling people as dependent can cause decrements in subsequent behavior, apparently because the labeled person begins to believe that his or her own behavior is dependent primarily on the actions of others.

| **Glossary Terms** | anticonformity
autokinetic effect
compliance
conformity | "foot-in-the-door"
  effect
learned helpless-
  ness | locus of control
obedience
reactance |

I deny that any one knows, or can know, the nature of the two sexes, as long as they have only been seen in their present relation to one another.
JOHN STUART MILL

RAINBOW PEOPLE. (DETAIL) 1972. PHOTO © ROBERT SOMMER.

The less intelligent the White man is, the more stupid he thinks the Black.
ANDRÉ GIDE

15

Variations in Social Behavior: Sex, Race, and Social Class

In *Gulliver's Travels*, the wandering Captain Gulliver visits a series of imaginary societies, encountering the Lilliputians, the Blefuscudeans, the Houyhnhnms, and a variety of other people and nations (Swift, 1960). In each case, he finds a group of people whose appearance, values, and behaviors are radically different from his own. In similar scenarios, science fiction writers describe human beings whose behaviors and thoughts are often quite different from those of the people we all know. Do these kinds of differences among groups represent mere fictional license, or do groups of people really differ in their behavior?

Many social psychologists assume that people are basically alike and that the primary causes of behavior are external to the person. This argument suggests that different situations produce different behaviors and that, given the same conditions, all people would generally have the ability to behave in the same way. In contrast, other observers of human behavior assume that various groups of people behave differently. For example, in the year 1909, newly inaugurated President William Howard Taft told a group of Black college students in Charlotte, North Carolina "Your race is adapted to be a race of farmers, first, last and for all times" (quoted in Logan, 1957, p. 66). Taft was not alone in making this kind of assumption. As we saw in earlier chapters, there are stereotypes of many groups. People maintain beliefs concerning men and women, Blacks and Whites, old people and young people, and the citizens of various countries. But to what extent do these beliefs reflect the truth? Are there any predictable differences in behavior that are a function of the categories of sex, race, and social class?

Such questions are deceptively simple. For example, on the surface, it shouldn't be difficult to determine whether men (on the average) are more aggressive than women, whether Blacks and Whites differ on a standard measure of self-esteem, or whether the values of upper-class people differ from those of lower-class individuals. Yet the answers to such questions are both scientifically complex and politically charged, particularly when we move from asking "What is the difference?" (if any) to "Why does such a difference exist?"

In this chapter, we deal with these questions. We examine distinctions such as sex, race, and social class to see whether they make a difference. Furthermore, when differences are found to exist, we ask why they exist.

I. Similarities and Differences among Groups

Since the beginning of recorded history, people have made comparisons between their own racial or geographical group and other groups (Gossett, 1963). For example, Aristotle believed that Greece's benign climate enabled the Greeks to develop physical and mental characteristics that were superior to those of other Europeans. This *chauvinistic* stance (a belief that one's own group is better than other groups) is certainly not unique to Aristotle. Often, when people make comparisons between their own country and other countries, between their own sex and the other sex, or between their own class and other classes, they tend to imply that their country, sex, and so on are superior. Such value-laden comparisons, unfortunately all too common, represent only one of the difficulties that arise when we attempt to make comparisons among groups.

In looking for differences, investigators can become blind to similarities between members of different groups. In anthropology, the term exotic bias has been coined to refer to the tendency of investigators to focus only on those aspects of a group or society that differ from their own society. North American social scientists visiting a South Seas island may first notice differences in style of dress and diet. If the society is a matrilinear one, in which status descends through women's lineage, this feature also may command the attention of investigators who are accustomed to a pat-rilinear system. On the other hand, aspects of the culture that correspond to the culture of the investigators may go unnoticed—since they aren't exotic or different, they may be taken for granted.

The effects of biases are not restricted to the anthropological field study. When-ever we set out to explore the ways in which two groups may differ (Blacks and Whites, or women and men, for example), we run the risk of ignoring the similari-ties between those groups, which may far outweigh the differences between them. Terms such as *race differences* or *sex differ-ences* can be misleading. Often, they convey the assumption that there *are* differences to be found—and that is a question we should ask, rather than a conclusion we can assume.

Even when we do observe differences between two identifiable groups, precau-tions are in order. For example, if you found a statistically significant sex difference in aggression, you wouldn't be able to assume that all men are more aggressive than all women. If you were to study aggressive be-havior in young children, you would find many little girls who are potential sluggers and many young boys who tend to shy away from physical confrontation. This concept of *overlapping distributions* is illustrated in Fig-ure 15-1. Most studies that find differences between races, social classes, or sexes ex-hibit this type of distribution. Although one group may differ from another, there are many people within each group who do not fit the pattern. We can't predict individuals' scores on a test simply by knowing their race, social class, and sex.

Perhaps the most difficult problem of all in the study of possible differences be-tween various demographic groups is in de-termining why differences occur. Recalling our discussion of methods in Chapter 2, we can speak of the independent variable in an experiment as one that is manipulated by the experimenter and randomly assigned across conditions. In such experiments, the assumption is rather safely made that the independent variable (for example, the number of bystanders present in an emergency) does not systematically vary with any other characteristics of the sub-jects. When our quasi-independent variable is race or sex, however, we can't make such assumptions. The experimenter has not ran-domly assigned sex or race, and many other factors could be associated with either one of those characteristics. In seeking to deter-mine what these other factors are, psychol-ogists have encountered innumerable ob-stacles and have often become embroiled in controversy.

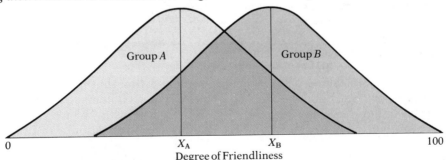

Figure 15-1. The concept of overlapping distri-butions.

In the above diagram, the curve on the left represents the distribution of "friendliness" scores for members of Group *A*, and the curve on the right represents the scores for members of Group *B*. Assume, for arbitrary purposes, that the highest score is 100 and the lowest score is 0. If we look at the group averages, indicated by an *X*, we see that members of Group *B* are, on the average, friendlier than members of Group *A*; however, many members of Group *A* have higher scores than some members of Group *B*, and some members of Group *B* are quite unfriendly. (Many members of *A* and *B* are alike on friendliness.) Most psychological traits and social behaviors exhibit this kind of overlap when two groups are compared.

Traditionally, investigators have focused on hereditary factors and environmental factors. Hereditary explanations stress the importance of genetic factors and often assume the inevitability of observed group differences. For example, as an explanation of racial differences, heredity has had a long history. In 1900, the dominant viewpoint held that the development of mental ability in Blacks stopped at an earlier age than in Whites. Similarly, in seeking explanations for observed differences between women and men, some investigators have posited genetic and hormonal variations between the sexes as causes of many differences in intellectual and social behaviors (see Broverman, Klaiber, Kobayashi, and Vogel, 1968). Even behavioral differences among social classes have sometimes been attributed to hereditary causes (Herrnstein, 1973).

Other investigators have looked for causes of observed differences in the socialization experiences of various groups. These explanations cover a broad range, including economic and environmental conditions, specific socialization practices of parents, and more general issues of racism and sexism (as discussed in Chapter 11).

Rather than focusing exclusively on either heredity or environment, however, most investigators prefer to consider the possible influence of both factors—although they may still differ considerably in the weight they attach to each factor.

In the following section, we discuss the evidence for differences between sexes, races, and social classes. In each case, we consider the possible causes of observed differences and try to weigh the hereditary and environmental arguments.

II. Women and Men

One of the major social and political developments of the 1970s was the reemergence of the movement for equality of the sexes—a movement encompassing women's liberation, men's liberation, and a host of related concerns. New legal requirements, spawned by the U.S. Civil Rights Act of 1964, Title IX of the U.S. Education Act Amendments of 1972, and the Canadian Bill of Rights, have forced changes in many customary social practices in the United States and Canada (see Figure 15-2). Similar developments have taken place in other countries. In Europe, Sweden set the pace with governmental support of equality between the sexes in both occupation and education. Even some of the most traditional societies have heard demands for a more active role for women, as evidenced by the protests that took place in Iran following the reinstatement of traditional dress codes (the chador) for women in 1979.

As in the case of any social change, the movement for equality of the sexes has met resistance. Little League baseball coaches argued that girls shouldn't play on their teams. The courts, however, ruled in favor of equality. On another level, opponents of the Equal Rights Amendment to the U.S. Constitution claim that women have the right to be financially supported by their husbands and that changes in legal requirements will ruin the family, the institution of marriage, and the future of children.

Underlying these arguments is a basic question: What is the nature of men and women? Let us look first at the evidence for differences between the sexes and then consider the possible causes of any observed differences.

A. Sex Differences in Intelligence and Aptitude

A question that has frequently been posed by psychologists, philosophers, and even comedians is "Who's smarter, men or women?" The question was, in fact, of major concern in the early research on brain localization, in which investigators attempted to find those areas of the brain that are responsible for intelligence. As Shields (1975) has vividly shown, these investigations were not without their problems. Shifts in thought regarding which area of the brain controlled intelligence were often followed by dramatic reversals in findings concerning which sex possessed the larger area of the supposed "seat of intelligence." According to

Figure 15-2. The recruitment of women into the U.S. Armed Forces is one example of changing roles for women. (© United Press International.)

these turn-of-the-century investigators, male dominance in social life was paralleled by male superiority in intelligence.

With the development of standard measures of intelligence, such as the Stanford-Binet Tests, you might think that it would be a simple matter to compare the scores of men and women. The very method that was used to construct this test, however, prohibits simple comparison. The designers of the Stanford-Binet Tests, Terman and Merrill (1937), discovered that females and males *did* differ in the correctness of their answers to some of the possible test items. To resolve this problem, the designers made the assumption that men and women do not differ in innate intelligence and that sex differences in scores on particular items simply reflect differences in experience (McNemar, 1942). Consequently, items that tended

to produce large differences between the sexes were eliminated from the final version of the test. As a result of this procedure, males and females average identical scores on the Stanford-Binet measure of intelligence. The construction of most other intelligence tests has been based on similar procedures.

Since general measures of intelligence have been structured so that they cannot reveal differences between men and women, investigators have turned their consideration to more specific measures of ability: in several cases, sex differences have been found. Females are generally better than males at academic achievement; they obtain better grades throughout grade school, high school, and college (Sherman, 1971). Females tend to outscore males on tests of verbal ability, whereas males are the higher scorers on tests of mechanical aptitude (Garai & Scheinfeld, 1968; Maccoby & Jacklin, 1974; Tyler, 1965). Males do better than females on tests of spatial ability, such as the Witkin Embedded Figures Tests (Witkin, Dyk, Faterson, Goodenough, & Karp, 1962). These tests call for both visual and analytic skills (Maccoby & Jacklin, 1974). It is important to note, however, that many of these sex differences do not appear until adolescence. For example, among grade school students, there are relatively few sex differences in mechanical, verbal, or spatial abilities.

B. *Sex Differences in Social Behavior*

For many years, experimental social psychologists were not particularly interested in any possible differences that might exist between men and women—or, for that matter, between the old and the young, the rich and the poor, or Blacks and Whites. In fact, there was a pronounced tendency for investigators to use primarily male subjects (Holmes & Jorgensen, 1971) and to generalize the findings from these studies to the general population (Dan & Beekman, 1972), apparently assuming that White males were representative of humanity as a whole. More recently, however, attention has been directed to possible differences (as well as similarities) between men and women. Although the areas in which comparisons could be made are as numerous as the chapters of this book, we focus on only a few areas in order to under-

stand the patterns that are found. Specifically, we consider sex-related patterns in aggression, conformity and social influence, achievement, and nonverbal behaviors.

1. *Aggression.* Are men more aggressive than women? In the frequently lively debates concerning possible differences between women and men, it is often conceded that men tend to be more aggressive than women. Some people argue that, although men are more aggressive physically, women excel in verbal aggressiveness. In a lengthy review, Maccoby and Jacklin (1974) concluded that men are indeed the more aggressive sex, and they suggested that there may be a biological base to this behavior that creates a greater readiness toward aggression in men than in women.

Subsequent analysis shows that this simple conclusion may be too simple. From a social psychological standpoint, we need to consider the various situational factors that may affect aggressive behavior, and in doing so, we find that the differences between men and women are somewhat complex. For example, although men are more likely than women to describe themselves as aggressive, actual behavioral measures show few differences between the sexes (Frodi, Macaulay, & Thome, 1977). When aggression has been provoked directly, through insult or previous attack, there is no evidence to suggest that women are less likely to react aggressively than men are (see **Figure 15-3**). On the other hand, women are less likely than men to instigate aggres-

Figure 15-3. Aggression in response to provocation. (© 1978 by United Feature Syndicate, Inc. Reprinted by permission.)

sive behavior or to act as third-party insti-gators of aggression (Frodi et al., 1977; Gaebelein, 1977b). Further, as we noted in Chapter 10, the forms of aggression chosen by men may be considerably more violent than those chosen by women. It has been suggested that women may consider aggres-sion to be inappropriate in many situations and may associate anxiety and guilt with aggression when direct provocation is not present (Frodi et al., 1977). Finally, contrary to many popular beliefs, there is no evi-dence to suggest that women are more aggressive than men verbally.

2. *Conformity and Social Influence.* Another area in which sex differences are often assumed is that of conformity and per-suadability. Although several generations of textbooks have supported this assumption, sex differences are much less striking than was previously thought (Eagly, 1978). In a scholarly review of dozens of studies, Eagly found that there are no general differences between men and women with regard to susceptibility to persuasive communica-tions; nor are there any sex differences in conformity when direct group pressure is not applied. When group pressure is pres-ent, there is evidence that women are more likely to conform than men (Cooper, 1979; Eagly, 1978). One possible explanation for this difference is that women are more con-cerned with group harmony—when group pressure is exerted, they may be more will-ing to go along with the group rather than exert their own judgment and risk dishar-mony.

If sex differences in social influence appear to be limited to certain situations, we might wonder why earlier investigators were convinced that women are more easily persuaded than men, or that they conform more readily. One explanation lies in the nature of the tasks that the investigators used. Sistrunk and McDavid (1971) have suggested that women are more likely to conform only in situations that are unfamil-iar to them and that earlier studies may have been biased in the types of issues and tasks they used. For example, a majority of conformity situations have involved stimu-lus material that requires spatial/perceptual

judgments, and, as we pointed out earlier, men tend to do better on these types of tasks. To test their hypothesis regarding task effects, Sistrunk and McDavid de-veloped a large number of items that could be sorted into three groups: one set with which men were more familiar, a second set with which women were more familiar, and a third set with which men and women were equally familiar. They then presented statements, indicating the percentage of people who agreed with each statement, and asked the subjects to indicate their own opinions. The degree to which subjects' opinions reflected the fictitious consensus indicated the degree of conformity. The re-sults of this experiment (shown in **Figure 15-4**) suggest that, when men and women are equally familiar with a topic, they don't differ in the degree of conformity they exhibit—at least in the absence of direct group pressure. When either sex is unfa-miliar with a subject, there is likely to be some conformity. One implication of this study is that we should consider the signifi-cance of situations in our attempts to deter-mine whether men differ from women. As we will see in our examination of other re-search studies, situational factors can be very important.

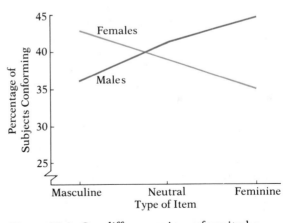

Figure 15-4. Sex differences in conformity be-havior. (Adapted from "Sex Variables in Con-forming Behavior," by F. Sistrunk and J. W. McDavid, *Journal of Personality and Social Psy-chology*, 1971, *17*, 200–207. Copyright 1971 by the American Psychological Association. Used by permission.)

3. *Achievement.* A basic definition of the term *achievement motivation* is: a striving for success in competition with a standard of excellence. Achievement behavior is pervasive in Western societies. Social psychologists have conducted extensive research in an attempt to understand the nature of *man's* strivings for excellence. *Man's* is quite appropriate in this context, because very little of the early research dealt with women. The reason for this disregard is quite simple: predictions derived from the theory did not apply to women. The problem was not that women exhibited no evidence of achievement motivation. In fact, when the task instructions were neutral, the stories that women told in response to Thematic-Apperception-Test (TAT) picture cards indicated the same degree of concern with achievement as did the stories told by men. When the instructions stressed the importance of the test in predicting intelligence and future success, women's scores did not increase. As the theory of achievement motivation predicted, men's scores did increase (McClelland et al., 1953). As a consequence, women were eliminated from much of the subsequent research on achievement motivation.

After a period of neglect, a number of investigators began to consider achievement in women. Some researchers suggested that women are motivated to affiliate rather than achieve (L. W. Hoffman, 1972). Women are described as seeking social approval rather than exhibiting an internally-based striving for standards of excellence. An alternative point of view, offered by Stein and Bailey (1973), contends that, although women and men are equally concerned with achievement, the areas in which women choose to excel differ from the areas chosen by men. Women in general may find it important to achieve in the areas of homemaking, cooking, and traditional female occupations, such as nursing and elementary education, but their concerns for doing well are motivated by achievement rather than affiliation. The specific areas of these strivings are undoubtedly influenced by social norms rather than an inherent preference for cooking versus carpentry, for example (see **Figure 15-5**).

Figure 15-5. In recent years more and more women — such as the corporate executive shown here — have been achieving in traditionally masculine fields. (© United Press International.)

Two other approaches to the study of sex differences in achievement behavior have stressed anxiety as a possible explanation (Frieze, Parsons, Johnson, Ruble, & Zellman, 1978). The first of these approaches focuses on anxiety that is associated with failure or the possibility of failure. In general, girls and women score higher on measures of anxiety than do boys and men; this provides some support for theories that focus on anxiety as a possible detriment to female achievement (Maccoby & Jacklin, 1974).

A somewhat less obvious, and considerably more popularized, explanation of sex differences in achievement behavior stresses anxiety that is associated with success. As originally proposed by Matina Horner (1970, 1972), **fear of success** is defined as: "a latent, stable personality disposition acquired early in life in conjunction with standards of sex-role identity" (Horner, 1972, p.

159). Horner suggested that most women have this "disposition to become anxious about achieving success because they expect negative consequences" (p. 159). Her original evidence suggested that few men evidenced a fear of success (as measured by responses to brief sentences); therefore, she proposed that differences in the strength of this motivation could account for sex differences in achievement.

Although the concept of a fear of success was quickly seized upon by both scientists and the popular press, more careful assessment has revealed a number of problems (Zuckerman & Wheeler, 1975). First of all, the higher scores of women on the measure proved to be unstable, and sex differences were found to disappear or even reverse, depending on age, race, geographical location, and type of university. Second, a number of people have suggested that the stories people tell may reflect the stereotypes they've incorporated, rather than their own motives and anxieties (Feather, 1975; Monahan, Kuhn, & Shaver, 1974). Therefore, when completing a story about Anne being at the top of her class in medical school (the traditional stem used by Horner and others), you might write a story reflecting what you think an "average Anne" would do. Furthermore, negative, or anxiety-laden, stories are not limited to descriptions of women in nontraditional positions; similar results occur when the stimulus deals with men in nontraditional positions. Therefore, a "John" at the top of his class in nursing school elicits the same form of "fear of success" stories (Cherry & Deaux, 1978).

In summary, most investigators have rejected the motivational explanation proposed by Horner. As Condry and Dyer (1976) point out, people do have a set of expectations, based on past experience, regarding the negative consequences that may occur if they deviate from accepted sex-role norms; but it is the consequences of success, and not success as such, that both men and women may fear. When negative consequences are not anticipated, fear of success disappears.

4. *Perceiving Nonverbal Cues.* As we saw in our discussion of communication patterns in Chapter 5, men and women often differ in their nonverbal behaviors. In the amount and patterning of eye contact, in body positions and gestures, in touching behavior, and in interpersonal distance, men and women exhibit reliable and often substantial differences (Henley, 1977; La-France & Mayo, 1978). In interpersonal interactions, women are more able to elicit warmth, whereas men elicit anxiety (Weitz, 1976).

Beyond these differences in actual behavior, women have been found to be more able to judge the affective, or emotional, state of other people (Hall, 1978). In other words, in situations that require an interpretation of another person's mood or intentions that is based on nonverbal cues, women prove to be superior to men. However, there are limits to this superiority. If a message is very brief, women seem to lose their advantage, suggesting that a certain minimal amount of information is necessary in order for the sex difference to appear (Rosenthal & DePaulo, 1979).

Sex differences also appear in the reception of deceptive messages. Women are more likely than men are to believe a deceptive message rather than interpreting the true state of affairs that underlies a cover-up. On the other side of the coin, women are more revealing senders of emotional cues. Men may be less expressive than women, who convey their moods and sentiments more clearly than men do (Rosenthal & De-Paulo, 1979).

Several hypotheses have been offered to explain these differences between men and women. One hypothesis suggests that women have been better trained to read cues and have been socialized to respond in a more emotionally expressive way. Another suggestion is that, because women have less power than men in many social situations (Henley, 1977), they learn by necessity the importance of interpreting the behaviors of others, going beyond the obvious verbal messages and seeking nonverbal cues of intentions. Finally, a third hypothesis suggests that such sex differences are innate. Hall (1978), in fact, has postulated that the early experiences of mothers with their infants may require them to be extremely sensitive to external threats to their young; therefore, women develop the ability to perceive the outside world more accurately than men do. Although each of these suggestions remains a possibility, there is no one hypothesis that has amassed the amount of evidence necessary for us to discard the others. In fact, it is quite possible that each of the hypotheses offers some insight into the causes of observed sex differences.

C. *Explaining the Differences*

We have covered only a small fraction of the areas in which sex differences have been found. In turn, there are a great many areas in which no evidence of differences between males and females appears. As a general rule of thumb, we might say that the majority of differences occur in those situations that involve social interaction; in more cognitive activities, such as individual problem solving, and issues of cognitive balance, sex differences are generally slight or nonexistent (Deaux, 1977). Moreover, we need to remember the issue of overlap discussed earlier in this chapter. Even when we find significant differences between men and women on the average, we cannot assume that all men and all women will exhibit those differences.

The causes of average sex differences *are* matters of concern. When men and women do differ, how can we explain the origins of those differences? Some differences may have biological causes; for example, it has been suggested that differences in spatial ability are of biological origin (Maccoby & Jacklin, 1974). Similarly, heredity has been pointed to as one cause of some of the observed differences in aggression. The following facts support a biological interpretation of sex differences in aggression: (1) males are more aggressive than females in most societies that have been studied, (2) male hormones usually increase aggressive behavior, and (3) animal studies have found greater male aggression than female aggression in many cases. However, even when biology can be invoked to explain male-female differences, it is important to remember that socialization factors may

increase or diminish such differences. Learning and experience have been shown to reduce or eliminate the sex differences in aggression (Bandura, 1965) and in spatial aptitude as well (Connor, Serbin, & Schackman, 1978).

Few people would argue with the contention that boys and girls are raised quite differently, and that early experiences play an important role in the development of adult differences. Social structures, opportunities, the specific reinforcements provided by parents, teachers, and peers, and models all provide possible sources for learning patterns of behavior. Not only do past learning experiences of males differ from those of females, but the continued pervasiveness of sex-role norms—beliefs regarding appropriate behavior for women and men—adds another element to the situation (Spence, Helmreich, & Deaux, 1981). As the John Stuart Mill citation at the beginning of this chapter indicates, it is difficult to determine the true nature of the sexes, because biology and socialization are so inextricably bound together (see Figure 15-6).

A final point that we should consider when attempting to explain sex differences concerns the nature of sex itself. Sex is a biological variable, and, although it denotes a specific set of physical and hormonal differences, it does not automatically denote a specific set of psychological differences. Indeed, many recent investigators prefer to use the word *gender* when they discuss the social behaviors of men and women. They use this term to refer to the psychological aspects of being male or female (or being masculine or feminine) as opposed to the strictly biological aspects. The interpretation of gender as a set of psychological characteristics associated with men and women requires us to focus on the ways in which particular patterns of behavior come to be associated with men or with women.

As we shall see in the next chapter, many investigators have begun to identify masculinity and femininity as sets of personality characteristics that both men and women may possess in various combinations. This shift from the division of the

THE WIZARD OF ID

by Brant parker and Johnny hart

Figure 15-6. (By permission of Johnny Hart and Field Enterprises, Inc.)

world into two mutually exclusive types of people to an approach that considers a broad range of psychological variations is probably a more realistic approach. Rather than assuming that some obvious physical characteristics determine all behavior, we can look to the specific situations and experiences that lead some people to behave in one way and other people to behave in another way. From this vantage point, men and women are not two totally different species; instead, they exhibit a broad range of human behavior and share many experiences.

III. Racial Groups

In many respects, popular assumptions regarding differences between members of various racial groups have been even more pervasive than beliefs concerning the differences between the sexes. Psychologists have tended to focus on Whites in their research, much in the same way that their studies have focused on males. In an illustration of this trend, Guthrie's (1976) summary of the history of psychological research is entitled *Even the Rat Was White.* In this volume, Guthrie deals not only with the assumptions that are made regarding the differences between Blacks and Whites but also with the often unrecognized contributions of Black psychologists to our body of scientific knowledge.

To understand the possible differences between Blacks and Whites, or the differences between members of other groups, such as Native Americans and Native Canadians, we must first understand exactly what the term *race* means.

A. *The Definition of the Term* Race

The task of defining the term *race* is not a simple one; there are many meanings associated with the term. We will simplify this task by dividing the definitions of *race* into two types: technical definitions and popular definitions. Technical definitions are those used by geneticists and anthropologists who study races; popular definitions reflect the ways in which people in general label someone's race.

1. *The Technical Definitions of Race.* What do scientists mean by *race?* In its simplest form, they define race as a population of people who live in the same geographical area and intermarry. However, throughout the history of the study of races, the means of identifying populations have changed. For instance, 200 years ago, classifications of races were usually based solely on differences in skin color. In 1735, Carolus Linnaeus described all humans as members of one species—a controversial position at that time—and divided that species into four skin-color varieties. Linnaeus ascribed different mental characteristics to each variety. Not surprisingly, given his own background, he considered Europeans to be "lively" and "inventive."

A century later, scientists rejected Linnaeus' use of skin color as a *sole* determinant of race and began to utilize a number of observable physical characteristics—head shape, facial features, body physique, and hair color and texture—as well as skin color. Note that such a classification system avoids the use of nonbiological attributes in defining race. Groups differing in culture, customs, and languages—but not in biological or physical characteristics—are now called **ethnic groups**; they are not considered to be different races, even though Italians, Irish, Nordics, Slavs, and others have been referred to as *races* at one time or another. (We will return to the issue of differences among ethnic and cultural groups later in this chapter.)

Although the classification of race according to physical attributes is scientifically acceptable, it suffers the handicap of being based on **phenotypes** (surface characteristics) rather than **genotypes** (underlying characteristics). The more recent definition of race uses underlying characteristics as its building blocks. This *genetic* approach to race classification makes the following assumptions (summarized from Dunn & Dobzhansky, 1952): (1) groups of people differ not only in observable features but also in characteristics such as blood type and susceptibility to certain diseases, (2) each of these characteristics is determined by patterns of genes, (3) groups of people differ in their genetic makeup, and certain groups of people can be distinguished on the basis of their possession of certain genes. According to this genetic approach, races are defined as "populations which differ in the frequencies of some gene or genes" (Dunn & Dobzhansky, 1952, p. 118).

The genetic approach makes the problem of classification much more complex than was earlier recognized. Significant differences in genetic compositions of different racial populations indicate that the concept of race is a viable one. At the same time, however, we must recognize that the genetic constituencies of two races are highly similar, and the differences in many cases are only in the proportions of particular characteristics (C. Jorgensen, 1975). In other words, races defined genetically differ only in a relative way (B. Glass, 1968).

Some investigators have questioned whether it is desirable to retain the term *race* at all. Anthropologist M. F. Ashley Montagu (1957, 1964) wants to remove the term *race* from the English language, arguing that it has caused a divisive, prejudicial orientation toward people. Other anthropologists favor the continued use of the term, as long as it conveys a biological meaning (Kilham & Klopfer, 1968; Washburn, 1964). Adherents of both positions, however, would agree that the popular definition of race, considered next, is oversimplified and misleading.

2. *The Popular Definition of Race.* Most often, the definition of race given by people is based on skin color alone. In the United States, a person's racial classification is often self-determined, although it is influenced by family tradition, custom, and law. In certain states, laws assign one's racial classification on the basis of the race of one's ancestors. Therefore, if one or more of a person's great-grandparents were "Negro," those states would classify that person as Negro. For example, a Black named Plessy protested having to sit in a separate railroad car because of his presumed Negro race. (Seven of his eight great-grandparents had been White.) The original U.S. Supreme Court decision (Plessy versus Ferguson, 1896) denying his claim was overturned by the 1954 desegregation decision (Logan, 1957). In addition, the popular definition of race includes only six classifications: White (or Caucasian), Black, Native American (Indian), Oriental, Asian Indian, and Brown (or Melanesian). These classifications correspond to the geographic groupings that are now considered to be too simplified.

A vital aspect of the popular definition of race is its all-or-none character. According to its approach, a person is clearly a Black, a White, or a member of one of the other four groups. Yet it has been estimated that 70% of U.S. residents classified as Blacks have some Caucasian genetic background. Moreover, approximately 20% of U.S. Whites are believed to have some Black genetic background (Reed, 1969; Stuckert, 1964). These estimates further emphasize the fact that differing "races" possess considerable similarities, not only in their environment but also in their genetic make-up.

Research that focuses on social/psychological similarities and differences *should* be based on the technical definition of race, to the extent that investigators go on to implicate the hereditary causes of observed differences. However, almost every researcher has used the popular definition of race. Group comparisons are made after researchers assign individuals to one "race" or another simply by looking at them or by using a self-labeling procedure (Schoenfeld, 1974). This point is an important one to remember as we look further at the evidence for differences between Blacks and Whites.

B. *Racial Differences in Intelligence*

One of the early concerns of investigators was to determine whether there are intellectual differences between members of various racial groups. The research regarding possible racial differences has been much more extensive than the research regarding sex differences. As a consequence, we will look fairly closely at the evidence, particularly at the arguments offered for the possible determinants of observed differences.

Numerous studies indicate that Black children (on the average) score approximately 15 points (or 1 standard deviation) lower than White children score on standard IQ measures (Jensen, 1973; Loehlin, Lindzey, & Spuhler, 1975). Recalling the concept of overlap, we need to recognize that this doesn't mean that all Blacks score lower than all Whites score; indeed, many Black children score above the population average of 100, and many White children score below the Black average. Studies indicate that the differences between Blacks and Whites appear regardless of the type of test used—group versus individual, verbal versus performance, or traditional versus *culture-free* tests. (Culture-free tests attempt to use materials that are uninfluenced by the environment in which the individual

taking the test lives; we doubt, however, that it is possible to achieve such a goal.)

The fact that such differences in test scores occur is recognized by those who believe that there are innate racial differences (the hereditarians) and by those who believe that the best explanation is based on environmental factors (the environmentalists). The controversy focuses on the causes—and, therefore, the importance—of the test-score differences. And the controversy has been an intense one, marked not only by emotion but also by scandal (see Box 15-1).

The hereditarian position, represented most strongly in recent years by Arthur Jensen (1969, 1973) and Richard Herrnstein (1973), suggests that racial differences in intelligence are primarily the result of genetic factors. To support their contentions, hereditarians often cite studies of identical twins reared together or apart. Although Jensen and Herrnstein don't totally discount the role of environmental factors, they believe that approximately 80% of the variation in intelligence is genetically determined.

If we accept the evidence for the heritability of intelligence *within* racial populations—and many researchers, such as Kamin (1974), would not—we need to examine the implications of such evidence regarding the differences *between* racial populations (specifically, between Blacks and Whites). Group differences don't necessarily reflect genetic differences. In the case of sex differences, for example, evidence for a genetic influence on aggressive behavior can't be cited as the sole cause, or even the principal cause, of observed differences in aggression between women and men. Environmental influences cannot be excluded.

In the case of racial differences in intelligence, environmental explanations have often been called into play. The average Black in the United States lives in an economically poorer environment than the average White does. Pettigrew's *A Profile of the Negro American* (1964), which is an excellent source of information, indicates that, among Blacks in the United States, unemployment rates are higher than those of Whites, health is poorer, incomes are lower, educational

Box 15-1. The Case of Sir Cyril Burt.

Cyril Burt, British psychologist, devoted a lifetime to the measurement of human intelligence. His work, particularly with separated twins, provided strong evidence for the heritability of intelligence. In his view, intelligence was almost totally the product of genetic factors. For his work, Burt was knighted in his native England and received the Thorndike Award from the American Psychological Association.

Shortly after Burt's death in 1971, a number of people began to look more closely at his data, which were used to support the hereditarian position. Serious flaws and inaccuracies became apparent (Kamin, 1974); apparently, Burt's data were invented rather than collected on numerous occasions. Indeed, Burt even invented research assistants and co-authors (Hearnshaw, 1979). As a result, Cyril Burt will be remembered in history not as a distinguished scholar but as one of the greatest frauds in psychological research.

levels are lower, and housing is poorer—all of which combine to lead to shorter life expectancy among Blacks, higher susceptibility to certain diseases (such as tuberculosis), and greater incidence of psychosis. The Equality of Educational Opportunity Study, or "Coleman Report" (Coleman, Campbell, Hobson, McPartland, Mood, Weinfield, & York, 1966) documents the inferior education given to Black children in the United States.

Pointing to the range of possible influences on intelligence is only suggestive. More direct evidence for the effect of environmental factors on intelligence scores can be found in studies that have specifically varied the environment of Black children. In the Early Training Project (S. W. Gray & Klaus, 1965, 1970; Klaus & Gray, 1965, 1968), a group of 20 children participated in a 10-week summer session in what the researchers considered an enriched environment. Throughout the year, a home visitor provided each child with new educational materials and encouraged parents and children to participate in activities together. Although the primary purpose of this particular project was not to change IQ scores, subjects' results on the Stanford-Binet Intelligence Test indicated that the progressive retardation commonly found among lower-class Black children in the South was arrested, while the members of control groups, who didn't participate in the project, continued to deteriorate.

Much more convincing evidence for the importance of cultural and environmental advantages is provided by Scarr and Weinberg (1976) in a study of 130 adopted Black and interracial children. The White families who adopted these children were highly educated and above average in both occupational status and income. At the time of testing, all the children were 4 years in age or older, and the majority of the children had been placed in adoptive homes during the first year of life. Results of this study showed that these adopted children scored above the IQ average of a standard White population—approximately 15–20 points higher than the average Black child in the United States. The earlier a child had been adopted, the higher was his or her IQ score. These results provide strong support for the environmental malleability of intelligence scores.

It should be noted that Scarr and Weinberg assessed the intelligence of the natural biological children of the parents in their study and found that their scores were higher than those of the adopted Black and interracial children. Such a result is not surprising, if we assume that there is *some* genetic variation in intelligence. Nor does it support an argument for racial differences in intelligence, if we assume that the adoptive parents were, on the average, more intelligent than those of the adopted children. In summary, as Scarr and Weinberg point out, "the social environment plays a dominant role in determining the average IQ level of Black children and . . . both social and genetic variables contribute to individual variation among them" (1976, p. 739).

C. *Racial Differences in Characteristics Other than Intelligence*

Although intelligence has figured prominently in the comparisons made between Blacks and Whites, it is not the sole focus of concern. Many investigators have considered differences between the self-concept, or self-esteem, of Blacks and that of Whites, often predicting that Blacks would be lower than Whites in self-esteem. The rationale for this prediction was that Blacks in the United States have borne a "mark of oppression" (Karon, 1958; Kardiner & Ovesey, 1951) that "represents the emotional wound of living in a White world of prejudice and discrimination" (I. Katz, 1969, p. 15). In other words, if we assume that self-concept develops as a result of experience with society's norms and values, then the prejudice toward Blacks should be reflected in a negative self-concept among Black persons. Studies that support this rationale have shown that some Black children value the opinions of Whites more than those of other Blacks (Cantor, 1975). Blacks have been found to disparage their own race, learning negative stereotypes of themselves and blaming themselves, rather than society at large, for the inferior status of their group (Gurin, Gurin, Lao, & Beattie, 1969; Proshansky & Newton, 1968).

More recently, however, investigators have begun to question whether all or even most Blacks adopt White standards as a basis for self-esteem (Baughman, 1971). The emergence of "Black is beautiful" in the United States during the 1970s suggested an alteration of standards, as described by Cross (1973) in his account of the "Negro-to-Black conversion experience." Changes such as these suggest that earlier assumptions re-

garding self-esteem among Blacks may be unwarranted. In fact, measures of self-esteem among Blacks (as well as Whites) can be influenced by a number of factors. In reviewing a series of recent studies, Gray-Little and Appelbaum (1979) found that studies reporting higher self-esteem scores among White students than among Black students, as well as studies reporting no difference between Blacks' scores and Whites' scores, were most apt to have been conducted at integrated schools. In contrast, studies conducted at segregated schools and desegregated schools with Black majorities generally indicated more positive self-concept scores among Black students than among Whites. Even the particular measure used can inflate or eliminate racial differences (Gray-Little & Appelbaum, 1979).

Other investigators have considered possible racial differences in athletic performance (see Figure 15-7). As is true of most work in this area, confounding factors are present. In summary, relatively little solid evidence exists for personality differences between Blacks and Whites at this time; correlated factors, such as social class and environment, must be taken into account.

D. *Explaining the Differences*

Although many popular beliefs suggest that the differences between racial groups are extensive, we have seen that relatively few differences have been established. Two issues are of major importance in this regard. First, most investigations use the popular definition of the term *race* and rely on observation and self-report rather than scientific evidence. Second, race is almost inevitably confounded with a variety of other factors, such as economics, health, social class, and environmental conditions. These factors make any "pure" test of racial differences almost impossible.

Even if these issues could be resolved, however, considerable attention would have to be paid to the setting in which investigations of racial differences occur and the assumptions that are made. For example, the concept of intelligence, which has been

Figure 15-7. Are there racial differences in athletic performance? Why are there so few Black quarterbacks, baseball pitchers, and golfers in professional sports? We believe it is simply a matter of prejudice against Blacks plus lack of opportunity to develop. Pitchers and quarterbacks are prestige positions; to some extent they have been "reserved" for Whites. But Morgan Worthy, a psychologist at Georgia State University, believes there is a different reason. Worthy (1974) notes that, within a professional sport, Blacks are *over*represented at some positions and *under*represented at others. For example, many defensive backs in football are Blacks; many outfielders in professional baseball are Blacks. Worthy (Worthy & Markle, 1970) reports evidence that White athletes excel at self-paced sports activities, whereas Blacks excel in reactive activities. Golf is self-paced, in that the golfer initiates action when he or she chooses; pitching in baseball would also reflect a self-paced response. But hitting is reactive; the individual must respond to actions of others or changes in the stimulus situation. But the differences in task responses also are found among Whites with different eye colors. Worthy finds that White persons with dark eyes tend to perform better "in tasks that require sensitivity, speed, and reactive responses; light-eyed organisms tend to specialize in tasks that require hesitation, inhibition, and self-paced responses" (Worthy, 1974). Eye color, rather than race *per se*, appears to be the determining variable. Worthy's early work—which made racial comparisons—may have been another example of race's being invoked as an explanation when something else was actually operating. (© United Press International.)

the subject of so much controversy, is basically culturally defined. On one of the standard tests of intelligence, a child is asked to determine which of two girls is prettier. Within one particular culture, there is probably a consensus regarding the "right" answer to the question, but there is no reason to believe that standards of beauty are universal with regard to facial features. Another example of possible cultural biases is illustrated in Box 15-2. Although Jensen (1979) has argued that standard IQ tests are not "culture loaded," the argument is far from resolved.

The testing situation itself may be another source of influence. Too often, investigators assume that, once a particular measuring instrument is devised, it will produce the truth—that characteristics of the administrator of the test, the situation, or other environmental factors will have little or no effect. Such an assumption has been shown to be wrong; it is particularly invalid when the purpose of the test is to explore differences between various cultural and minority groups. Table 15-1 lists some of the possible influences that are external to the measuring instrument itself.

As we might expect, many of the investigators of cultural differences have been Whites; this reflects their dominance in the field of social science. Often, it has been found that the responses obtained by White investigators from Black respondents differ from the responses obtained by Black investigators.

Box 15-2. Try the Chitling Test.

Black sociologist Adrian Dove was well aware of the cultural biases of the usual IQ tests when he constructed the Dove Counterbalance General Intelligence Test (the Chitling Test). He described his test for ghetto Black children as "a half-serious idea to show that we're just not talking the same language." Here is a sampling of the 30 items. How "culturally deprived" is the White middle-class child when the tables are turned?

1. A "handkerchief head" is (a) a cool cat, (b) a porter, (c) an Uncle Tom, (d) a hoddi, (e) a preacher.
2. Which word is most out of place here? (a) splib, (b) blood, (c) gray, (d) spook, (e) Black.
3. A "gas head" is a person who has a: (a) fast-moving car, (b) stable of "lace," (c) "process," (d) habit of stealing cars, (e) long jail record for arson.
4. "Bo Diddley" is a: (a) game for children, (b) down-home cheap wine, (c) down-home singer, (d) new dance, (e) Moejoe call.
5. If a pimp is up tight with a woman who gets state aid, what does he mean when he talks about "Mother's Day"? (a) second Sunday in May, (b) third Sunday in June, (c) first of every month, (d) none of these, (e) first and fifteenth of every month.
6. If a man is called a "blood," then he is a: (a) fighter, (b) Mexican-American, (c) Negro, (d) hungry hemophile, (e) Redman or Indian.
7. What are the "Dixie Hummingbirds"? (a) part of the KKK, (b) a swamp disease, (c) a modern gospel group, (d) a Mississippi Negro paramilitary group, (e) deacons.
8. T-Bone Walker got famous for playing what? (a) trombone, (b) piano, (c) "T-flute," (d) guitar, (e) "hambone."

Those who are not "culturally deprived" will recognize that the correct answers are: (1) c, (2) c, (3) c, (4) c, (5) e, (6) c, (7) c, and (8) d.

From "Taking the Chitling Test," *Newsweek*, July 15, 1968, Vol. 72, pp. 51–52. Copyright Newsweek, Inc., 1968.

TABLE 15-1 / *Possible Influences on Test Performance*

I. Variables of background and environment
   A. Cultural background (racial or ethnic group)
   B. Family characteristics
   C. Formal school training
   D. Experience with similar tests
   E. General health and special handicaps (for example, impaired sight, hearing, or coordination, emotional disturbance, and the like)
   F. Age

II. Personality and motivational variables
   A. Persuasibility or responsiveness to examiner
   B. Interest in test problems
   C. Effort and persistence
   D. Anxiety level
   E. Achievement motivation

III. Characteristics of the testing situation
   A. Perceived importance of the test
   B. Expectations of success or failure
   C. Temporary physical conditions (fatigue, transient respiratory or digestive ailments, or other temporary indispositions)
   D. Interference from the testing environment
   E. Influence of the tester

IV. Test demands
   A. Specific abilities required
   B. Speed of response required

Adapted from "Mental Abilities of Children from Different Social-Class and Cultural Groups," by G. S. Lesser, G. Fifer, and D. H. Clark, *Monographs of the Society for Research in Child Development*, 1965, *30*(4), 1–115. Copyright 1965 by The Society for Research in Child Development, Inc. Used by permission.

In the case of scores on intelligence tests, results have been mixed. Some investigations have found that Black children score higher on IQ tests administered by Black examiners than they score on tests administered by White examiners (Forrester & Klaus, 1964); however, other studies indicate that the race of the examiner has little effect on test results (Tanner & Catron, 1971). Many factors could cause these mixed results, of course, including several of those listed in Table 15-1. Both the experience and the attitude of the examiner, for example, could affect test results.

When we attempt to determine the attitudes of various cultural and racial groups, the problems appear to be even more severe. For example, Shosteck (1977) found that there were extreme differences between the statements regarding problems of concern given by Black respondents to Black interviewers and those they gave to White interviewers. Interestingly, when the Black subjects were categorized according to their degree of militancy, the highly militant Blacks gave Whites virtually the same answers that Black respondents in general gave to Black interviewers. In other words, self-esteem and self-confidence minimized differences in the responses, but, for the less confident or less militant Blacks, the race of the interviewer drastically affected the test results.

The number of variables involved is disturbing, since we are trying to gain a real understanding of possible cultural and racial differences. Although this problem is far from being solved, Montero (1977) has offered a number of suggestions that may help to eliminate artificial findings. First, the researcher needs to gain the acceptance of the people under study by becoming involved in their communities and using field-research methods that include direct participation. These strategies appear to be far more productive than surveys mailed from a distance by an unknown investigator. Second, the investigator should be sensitive to the specific concerns of the population being studied—in a theoretical sense (in terms of identifying those issues that are meaningful to the population) and in an ethical sense (using the results in a way that will help, or at least not harm, the group whose cooperation is being sought). These issues are, of course, more general in nature than the issue of studying racial groups. In Chapter 2, and elsewhere in this text, we have had reason to question the goals and objectives of social science investigators, as well as the ways in which their data are used.

IV. Social Class

As we have seen, race and social class often covary in our society. Although some people claim that the United States and Canada are classless societies, it is evident that, within these societies, certain types of people are grouped together (and separated from others) on the basis of interests, education, income, values, and other socioeconomic variables. Although these groupings are not always clear-cut, they are real, and they are important enough to be studied in their own right. Many studies that have allegedly examined differences between Blacks and Whites, or among other groups, have not controlled for differences in social class; therefore, the interpretations of the findings may focus on the wrong variables as causal or influential.

A. *The Definition of the Term* Social Class

A review of various definitions of the term *social class* (Krech, Crutchfield, & Ballachey, 1962) indicates that three methods are most commonly used to define the term: the objective method, the subjective method, and the reputational method.

1. The objective method. This approach measures social class by "objective charac-teristics (that) are likely to discriminate most sharply among the different patterns of social behavior which (the social scientist) conceives as class behaviors" (p. 313). The objective characteristics most frequently used are: amount and source of income, level of education, type of occupation, and type and location of housing.

2. The subjective method. This approach defines social class "in terms of how the members of the community see themselves in the status hierarchy" (p. 313).

3. The reputational method. This approach defines social class "in terms of how the members of a community place each other in the status system of the community" (p. 313). As an example of this approach, a number of surveys have shown that respondents make a clear-cut and consistent ranking of the socioeconomic status of various occupations. Table 15-2 presents one ranking of occupational prestige, based on data collected in 1964. Although such ratings are subject to some fluctuation (for example, in 1964 the occupation of a U.S. Congressional Representative ranked considerably higher than it does in more recent surveys), the figures provide an indication, however temporary, of the ways in which the majority of people view various occupations.

TABLE 15-2 / *Occupational Prestige Rankings.*

	Rank	Occupation	Prestige Score		Rank	Occupation	Prestige Score
	1	U.S. Supreme Court Justice	94		14	Dentist	88
	2	Physician	93	Tied	14	Architect	88
Tied	3.5	Nuclear physicist	92		14	County judge	88
	3.5	Scientist	92	Tied	17.5	Psychologist	87
Tied	5.5	Government scientist	91		17.5	Minister	87
	5.5	State governor	91		17.5	Member of the board of directors of a large corporation	87
Tied	8	Cabinet member (U.S. federal government)	90		21.5	Priest	86
	8	College professor	90		21.5	Head of a department in a state government	86
	8	U.S. Representative in Congress	90	Tied	21.5	Civil engineer	86
Tied	11	Chemist	89		21.5	Airline pilot	86
	11	Lawyer	89	Tied	24.5	Banker	85
	11	Diplomat in U.S. Foreign Service	89		24.5	Biologist	85
					26	Sociologist	83

TABLE 15-2 / *Occupational prestige rankings in 1964 (continued)*

	Rank	Occupation	Prestige Score		Rank	Occupation	Prestige Score
Tied	27.5	Instructor in public schools	82	Tied	57	Mail carrier	66
	27.5	Captain in U.S. Army	82		57	Railroad conductor	66
Tied	29.5	Public-school teacher	81		57	Traveling salesman for a wholesale concern	66
	29.5	Accountant for a large business	81		59	Plumber	65
Tied	31.5	Owner of a factory that employs about 100 people	80		60	Automobile repairman	64
	31.5	Building contractor	80	Tied	62.5	Playground director	63
Tied	34.5	Artist who paints pictures that are exhibited in galleries	78		62.5	Barber	63
					62.5	Machine operator in a factory	63
	34.5	Musician in symphony orchestra	78		62.5	Owner-operator of a lunch stand	63
	34.5	Author of novels	78	Tied	65.5	Corporal in U.S. Army	62
	34.5	Economist	78		65.5	Garage mechanic	62
	37	Official of an international labor union	77		67	Truck driver	59
Tied	39	Railroad engineer	76		68	Fisherman who owns his own boat	58
	39	Electrician	76	Tied	70	Clerk in a store	56
	39	County agricultural agent	76		70	Milk route man	56
Tied	41.5	Owner-operator of a printing shop	75		70	Streetcar motorman	56
	41.5	Trained machinist	75	Tied	72.5	Lumberjack	55
Tied	44	Farm owner and operator	74		72.5	Restaurant cook	55
	44	Undertaker	74		74	Singer in a nightclub	54
	44	Welfare worker for city government	74		75	Filling-station attendant	51
	46	Newspaper columnist	73	Tied	77.5	Dockworker	50
	47	Policeman	72		77.5	Railroad section hand	50
	48	Reporter on a daily newspaper	71		77.5	Night watchman	50
Tied	49.5	Radio announcer	70		77.5	Coal miner	50
	49.5	Bookkeeper	70	Tied	80.5	Restaurant waiter	49
Tied	51.5	Tenant farmer (one who owns livestock and machinery and manages the farm)	69		80.5	Taxi driver	49
				Tied	83	Farmhand	48
	51.5	Insurance agent	69		83	Janitor	48
	53	Carpenter	68		83	Bartender	48
Tied	54.5	Manager of a small store in a city	67		85	Clothes presser in a laundry	45
					86	Soda-fountain clerk	44
	54.5	Local official of a labor union	67		87	Sharecropper (one who owns no livestock or equipment and does not manage farm)	42
					88	Garbage collector	39
					89	Streetsweeper	36
					90	Shoeshiner	34

From "Occupational Prestige in the United States, 1925–1963," by R. W. Hodge, P. M. Siegel, and P. H. Rossi, *American Journal of Sociology, 1964, 70,* 286–302, by permission of The University of Chicago. Copyright © 1964 by The University of Chicago.

B. *Social-Class Differences in Behavior*

Many investigations of social class have focused on differences in intelligence. Generally, these investigations have found that intelligence scores are related to social class —the higher the social class, the higher the intelligence score. For example, the massive

Coleman Study (Coleman et al., 1966) found that children of low socioeconomic status scored below the national averages on both verbal and nonverbal tests at all grades tested (grades 1, 3, 6, 9, and 12). Differences in social-class level also are related to the tested IQ scores of adults. In both world wars, data from military recruits have shown variance in test scores according to occupation (Fryer, 1922; T. W. Harrell & Harrell, 1945; N. Stewart, 1947; Yerkes, 1921). In World War I, the highest Army Alpha means for U.S. enlisted men were obtained by engineers and accountants; in World War II, accountants, lawyers, and engineers obtained the highest means. In World War I, the groups with the lowest average scores were miners, farm workers, and unskilled laborers; in World War II the same groups (along with the teamsters) scored lowest. Similar differences have been found among military recruits in Sweden (Carlsson, 1955), employed adults in New York City (Simon & Leavitt, 1950), and employees of a large company in Great Britain (Foulds & Raven, 1948).

Beyond the issue of intelligence, there are many differences between people in various social strata. One of the basic beliefs held by the core of the middle class is that education is the portal to success (Gruen, 1964). Members of the working class may adhere less adamantly to this belief. R. Bell (1964) described examples of the value stretch present in the working class. Some working-class parents maintain high educational aspirations for their children; at the same time, they may think their children should marry by age 19 or 20 and that four or five children is a nice-sized family.

Even among members of a single social class, there may be strong differences in beliefs and values. Stephan and Stephan (1971), for example, found that rates of neurosis were higher among migrants to cities than among members of the same class who had been born in the city (in this case, Santiago, Chile). Urban-born subjects placed themselves in more roles than the migrants did, and they were better able to respond empathetically to the situations of other people.

C. *Explaining the Differences*

As in the case of other observed group differences, attempts to explain social-class differences focus on both heredity and environment.

Since 1870, when Sir Francis Galton's *Hereditary Genius* (1952) was published, it has been shown that the offspring of more prominent families are more successful than other children. The hereditarian position claims that intelligent people have more natural ability and, therefore, have gravitated to positions of eminence. Anastasi (1958) has summarized this position: "The more intelligent individuals would gradually work their way up to the more demanding but more desirable positions, each person tending eventually to 'find his level.' Since intellectually superior parents tend to have intellectually superior offspring, the children in the higher social strata would be more intelligent, on the whole, than those from the lower social levels" (p. 521). Herrnstein (1973) similarly argues for the influence of genetics on social-class standing. This argument does not, however, recognize the obstacles that a society can pose in the forms of sexism, racism, and other biases; rather, it assumes that the cream will rise to the top, unencumbered by countering forces.

Environment is a multifaceted phenomenon. Consider the differences between the environments of two 8-year-old girls, both living in the same geographical area of the United States. One lives in a prosperous suburb; the other lives in an inner-city slum. Their environments have differed markedly almost from the moment at which each of them was conceived. Just how numerous are these differences? Let's consider only a few. First, the prenatal environments of the two girls probably differed. The mother of the child in the slum probably received less extensive medical care, was less healthy, and ate a less adequate diet during pregnancy than the mother living in the suburbs. We know that poor nutrition in a pregnant woman can affect the physical state of her offspring; for example, Naeye, Diener, and Dellinger (1969) report that the newborns of poor mothers were 15% smaller than normal. Likewise, inadequate nutrition during pregnancy or a child's infancy can result in the impairment of the child's mental development (Eichenwald & Fry, 1969; Kaplan, 1972). Premature births, complications during pregnancy and delivery, and injuries at birth are all more probable in the lower class than in the middle class (Pasamanick & Knobloch, 1960; Pettigrew, 1964; Rider, Taback, & Knobloch, 1955). The mental abilities of children who survive such traumas may very well be affected by them.

A second environmental factor of concern is the type of stimulation present during the early years of life. Although Freud considered the first 5 years of life to be important in terms of his psychosexual theory, more recent investigators have focused on the types of sensory stimulation present and their effects on subsequent cognitive development. It may be that children of various social-class levels differ in the amount or type of sensory stimulation they receive during the first few years of life. Gray (1962) believes that the difference in absolute amounts of stimulation received by children of differing social classes is not great but that there is a social-class difference in the range and variety of the stimuli and in the order of presentation of the material. (Middle-class parents, for example, are often more interested than lower-class parents in choosing toys that increase mental development—that is, toys that lead to higher scores on IQ tests.)

Several recent attempts to alter the environment of lower-class children exemplify another demonstration of the role of environment in determining social-class differences in IQ scores. The Early Training Project in Tennessee (S. W. Gray & Klaus, 1965; Klaus & Gray, 1965, 1968) placed lower-class children in a 10-week preschool designed to stimulate the development of perceptual skills, aptitudes, language, and interest in school-related activities. Attempts were made to involve the families of the children as well. Early results showed definite improvement of the children in the project compared with control children, who

had received no special training. Although follow-up testing indicated some shrinkage of the differences between the two groups, the superiority of the special-training group was evident.

Conceptions of social class and cultural disadvantage are becoming increasingly unsatisfactory to many workers in the field, because of the broad nature and implied value judgments of these concepts. More precise, less evaluative definitions of environment are being advocated. B. S. Bloom (1964) reviewed attempts to measure the quality of environments and concluded that the dearth of adequate measures had led to an underemphasis of the role of environments in research and prediction. Among the characteristics of the environment that may be influential are: communication and interaction with adults, motivation to understand one's environment or to achieve, types of incentives, and the availability of adult role models (Bloom, 1964, p. 188). Furthermore, we must continue to be concerned with the types of comparisons that are being made. Although measures of intelligence have dominated research, they don't represent the only value in our society, and we know relatively little about the ways in which social classes differ with regard to the characteristics cited here.

Finally, the nature of overlap is as important in understanding social-class differences as it is in understanding racial and gender differences. Although the difference between the average scores of two groups may be large, members of each group may well exceed or fall under the average for their group (or for the other group). Although group factors may produce average differences, the use of a person's class, race, or occupation as an indication of his or her ability is completely unwarranted.

V. Other Group Comparisons

Although we've focused this discussion on the variables of gender, race, and social class, it is probably apparent that there are many other distinctions that can be made among people, allowing the possibility of a wide variety of group differences. Let us consider two additional ways in which people can be classified and compared.

A. *Cross-Cultural Comparisons*

Much of the work reported in this book has been based on samples of U.S. citizens. In part, this focus represents an ethnocentric bias, and, in part, it reflects the fact that the majority of those scientists who call themselves social psychologists are located in the United States. In fact, we are only at a beginning stage in terms of learning whether those facts of human behavior generated in the United States have relevance or truth value for people in other societies. Often, linguists, anthropologists, and other social scientists distinguish between etic constructs and emic constructs. **Etic constructs** refer to universal factors—those that hold across all the cultures we know or have investigated. For example, the concept of the family can be considered an etic construct, although the various forms of family life certainly differ across cultures (Triandis, 1977b). In contrast, an **emic** construct is one that is culture specific—that exists or has meaning only within a particular cultural framework. "Generation gap," for example, might have meaning only in the United States and in societies that are similar to the United States. We might suspect that many of the variables that we have covered in this text are *pseudoetic*—constructs that we believe to be universal, but that may in fact characterize only our own society.

Often, cross-cultural comparisons are made without a great deal of thought. For example, it is frequently assumed that the United States and Canada are quite similar in attitudes, behaviors, and values. However, the governments of these two countries differ, as do their basic constitutional premises and many of their social customs. In recent years, Canadians have pointed out that such differences do exist, and that past generalizations are not warranted (Berry, 1974; Sadava, 1978).

When the reader in the United States looks farther afield, differences become even more apparent. Moscovici (1972), for example, has argued that the concept of equity

theory is particular to capitalistic systems and may play a small role in the interpersonal behavior of people in countries that maintain other forms of government. Other writers have attempted to describe more specifically the character of people in a particular country. For example, in her work with the Japanese character, Lebra (1976) stresses the importance of social relativism as a basis for most behavior choices. In another example of this approach, Diaz-Guerrero (1975) has analyzed the character of the Mexican. Moreover, by using a measuring instrument that assesses *sociocultural premises*, Diaz-Guerrero has compared citizens of Mexico with citizens of the United States on a number of dimensions. He found that citizens of the U.S. are likely to respond to stress in an active way, whereas Mexicans tend to respond passively. In even broader terms, Diaz-Guerrero found that, according to Mexicans, interpersonal relationships are the most important part of life. They stress affiliation and love. In contrast people in the United States tend to stress liberty, equality, and individualism.

Although studies of specific cultures are a rich source of data on the characteristics of certain people, the future of cross-cultural comparisons probably rests on a broader and more theoretical approach (Malpass, 1977). In other words, we need to use a general theory of etic constructs and then attempt to determine their emic equivalents in various cultures. As an example of this strategy, several investigators have used basic models of attitude and behavior relationships (discussed in Chapter 11) in their attempt to assess the similarities and differences between Mexicans and U.S. citizens in their family-planning behavior (Davidson et al., 1976; Jaccard & Davidson, 1972). This type of strategy offers us the advantage of understanding both the similarities *and* the differences between members of various cultural groups. As a result, we can begin to construct a more general understanding of human behavior than the single culture approach allows. To phrase it in another way, the latter approach tends to give us isolated pieces of a structure; the former approach begins to tie those pieces together into an integrated whole.

B. *Age Comparisons*

Age is a variable that has been of relatively little concern to social psychologists, who have preferred to leave the issue of age comparisons in the hands of developmental psychologists. Although we will not give much consideration to the factor of age, it is undoubtedly an important basis of categorization that may reveal many differences. In the past, of course, investigators in other disciplines have been concerned with changes in physical and intellectual abilities as a function of age. At what age do intellectual functions peak? At what age does physical degeneration begin, and at what rate does it progress? Investigators of sexual behavior (see Chapter 7) have considered the ages at which men and women seem to reach the peak of their sexual interest and activity, although many of the earlier conclusions regarding such peaks have been challenged by more recent data.

In terms of other social behaviors, considerably less interest in age has been exhibited until recent years. The popular success of **Gail Sheehy's** *Passages* (1976) and the more scholarly investigations of Levinson (1978) have alerted many to the distinct stages through which people pass. Although some of these stages are undoubtedly related to physical and social maturation, many "crises" appear to reflect an interaction between a person of a particular age and the typical events that occur at certain predictable periods of time (Wrightsman, 1980). This question of age differences is a potentially rich one in which social and developmental psychologists can combine their skills, once again attempting to learn about the diversity of human behavior, as well as its similarities across groups.

C. *A Final Note*

Whether we are considering group differences in race, gender, age, or culture, it is important to remember that we are using handy descriptive categories to classify peo-ple. As we mentioned throughout this chapter, the concept of overlap is an important one. On virtually no characteristic is one group completely different from another; rather, there may simply be degrees of difference on a variety of characteristics. Discoveries of such differences are important—they tell us more about the variety, as well as the similarity, of human behavior. However, in many ways they serve merely as a starting point. They lead us to ask why such differences might exist, whether heredity plays a role, whether particular socialization experiences are critical, or whether some combination of these is significant. Therefore, the discoveries of differences serve as important markers—they encourage us to look further for the psychological causes and significance of observed differences. As we'll see in the next chapter, many psychological constructs have been developed in an attempt to classify and understand people in ways that depend on psychological differences, not physical differences. These psychological characteristics may be shared by a wide variety of people—Black, White, male, female, old, and young. The understanding of demographic group differences is a beginning point—the understanding of psychological complexities is the next step.

VI. Summary

One approach to the study of human behavior is to divide people into specified groups, generally on the basis of some physical characteristic such as sex or race. Although such comparisons often reveal group differences, it is important to remember that many similarities generally exist as well. Furthermore, the concept of overlap is important—average group differences do not mean that all the members of one group have more or less of a specific characteristic than all the members of another group. Both hereditary and environmental explanations are considered when group differences are found.

Comparisons between women and men show no overall difference in intelligence but have found some differences in specific skills, such as spatial ability, verbal ability, and mechanical aptitude. Most of these differences do not appear until adolescence. Areas of social behavior in which sex differences have often been assumed are: aggression, conformity, achievement and nonverbal behavior.

Men are more aggressive than women are in the absence of direct provocation. There are few sex differences in response to attack, although men report themselves as being more aggressive. Sex differences in conformity are minimal, unless direct group pressure exists; in such cases, women conform more readily than men do. The nature of the task is also critical in predicting sex differences in conformity behavior.

Early work in achievement dealt primarily with male subjects. More recently, comparisons between men and women have focused on anxiety associated with failure and success. In the latter case, the specific consequences of performance appear to be more important than any sex-linked motive. Nonverbal behavior differences between men and women are numerous. Women are better able to judge the emotional state of others.

Comparisons between members of different racial groups, primarily between Blacks and Whites, requires an understanding of the concept of race. The construct of race is technically defined either in terms of frequency of one or more genes (the definition preferred by geneticists and physical anthropologists) or in terms of certain physical characteristics (the definition preferred by social anthropologists and sociologists). The popular definition of race—based on skin color, self-determination, tradition, custom, and law—is oversimplified.

Research regarding racial differences has often focused on intelligence; the existence of differences in IQ test scores of Blacks and Whites is documented. The controversy centers on the relative importance of heredity and environment as causal factors. Natural observation and intervention studies have shown that, by improving environmental conditions, we can improve IQ scores. In interpreting differences in intelligence, it is important to consider factors such as the cultural definition of intelligence that is being used and the characteristics of the testing situation.

Research studies of social class indicate that children from upper-class and middle-class families surpass children from lower-class families on measures of intelligence. Environmental factors, which become effective at the moment of conception, may determine how closely one's level of intelligence approaches the genetically predetermined limit of one's abilities.

Many comparisons of groups have been derived from the tradition of cross-cultural research. Here, an attempt is made to determine how general our knowledge of human behavior is: whether our constructs are etic (truly universal) or emic (specific to a particular culture). Eventually, these kinds of investigations should provide us with a much fuller understanding of human behavior. Although age comparisons aren't often considered by social psychologists, they offer the potential for expanding our knowledge.

In each case of group comparisons, we are placing people in categories according to their physical appearance alone. Such a strategy, though useful, should be the prelude to a consideration of individual psychological differences.

Glossary Terms

emic	fear of	phenotype
ethnic group	success	sex-role
etic	genotype	norms
exotic bias		

To have one's individuality completely ignored is like being pushed quite out of life. Like being blown out as one blows out a light.   EVELYN SCOTT

CONSTANTIN BRANCUSI. *MADEMOISELLE POGANY II.* BRONZE. 1920. ALBRIGHT-KNOX ART GALLERY, BUFFALO, NEW YORK. CHARLOTTE A. WATSON FUND, 1927.

Each individual ego is endowed from the beginning with its own peculiar dispositions and tendencies.   SIGMUND FREUD

16

Individual Differences in Social Behavior

We can form broad, general theories regarding the ways in which various groups differ; however, as we saw in Chapter 15, members of outwardly differing groups (such as Blacks and Whites, or men and women) may be similar in their attitudes, values, and behaviors. Although the categorization of people may begin at a highly visible level, most of us pursue a system of classifying people that goes beyond obvious physical characteristics. Implicit personality theories (discussed in Chapter 3) may guide us in categorizing the people we know. We may, for example, see John and Harriet as being very similar in their extroverted, friendly personalities, whereas Robin and Peter may appear to be quiet and introverted. In trying to select people for a community project, we may consider a dimension of efficiency, and favor Alice and Al over Joan and Jim. In doing so, we are identifying a particular personality characteristic (efficiency) and we are assuming that personality can affect behavior (in this case, work on a community project).

Although the average person may have only general descriptive notions of the ways in which people differ, some psychologists have attempted to make such distinctions more precise. In other words, they have attempted to systematically conceptualize and measure the ways in which individuals differ. Entire books have been devoted to the topic of personality, and many college courses focus on the study of human personality. Although some questions regarding this topic are important to social psychologists, for reasons that we will explore, they typically have ignored the individuality of people in favor of seeking constant situational conditions that influence behavior. In this chapter, we consider the background of this issue, look at some specific examples of personality measures and explore their relationship to social behavior, and consider some of the broad issues involved in relating personality constructs to situational variables.

I. A Consideration of Personality

The concept of personality differences has not been entirely absent from our earlier discussions. In Chapter 4, for example, the characteristics of self-monitoring and Machiavellianism were discussed. When we considered moral development in Chapter 8, we looked at theorists who posited individual differences in people according to stages of moral growth. Locus of control was considered in Chapter 14. And our extensive discussion of attitude change implies that there are individual differences in people's beliefs and values. Despite this infiltration of personality measures, social psychologists have often been reluctant to really deal with the *issue* of personality. Let's examine the reasons for this neglect.

A. *The Social-Psychological Tradition*

As we saw in Chapter 1, there are many approaches that one can take in viewing human behavior. Although the alternatives are numerous, social psychology has tended to be dominated by only two of these approaches (Blass, 1977). The first approach is derived from early behaviorism, that of the S-R theorists. Here, the focus is on determining how certain stimuli in the environment cause certain responses; the characteristics of the individual performing the response are of minimal concern. In fact, the strongest proponents of this approach, such as Skinner, find any mentalistic notions completely unnecessary.

More traditionally, social psychology dates its heritage to Kurt Lewin, who represents one form of Gestalt theory. Lewin stressed the present psychological life space (Lewin, 1935, 1936) as a source of behavior, and he disdained past determinants. Although Lewin clearly recognized that both the person and the environment are important, most of his followers have tended to stress the environment, rather than the person. (Lewin's original formulation that B (behavior) $= f(P,E)$, where P and E represent the person and the environment respectively, clearly shows that he himself regarded personality and individual differences as being important).

As Helmreich has pungently stated, "Classic, laboratory social psychology has generally ignored individual differences, choosing to consider subjects as equivalent black boxes or as two-legged (generally white) rats from the same strain" (1975, p. 55). This situation is changing, however. Controversy has replaced complacency, and, although complete agreement hasn't been reached, the argument promises to be healthy for the growth of our understanding of human behavior.

B. *The Nature of Individual Differences*

The study of personality is one that has been fraught with controversy during much of its existence. A major concern, for example, is the extent to which we can classify all individuals on a single dimension versus the extent to which each individual must be viewed as a unique combination of characteristics (Allport, 1937; Mischel, 1977; Murray, 1938). In taking the former approach, termed the **nomothetic** approach, investigators isolate a single dimension of concern and attempt to categorize people in terms of one variable. In other words, the focus is on one trait, and the assumption is that all people have some "amount" of that trait. For example, a researcher who is interested in the concept of achievement behavior may develop a scale to measure need for achievement. With this scale in hand, the researcher can assess people's achievement needs, eventually developing a rank ordering of people, from those who score very high on need achievement to those who score very low. Then the researcher will try to determine how individuals with different scores on the measure will perform in selected situations.

In contrast, the **idiographic** approach to personality focuses on the interrelationship of events and characteristics within an individual—it is a person-centered focus. Here, the focus is not on making comparisons among individuals, but rather on understanding the complexity of a single individual and the way in which the component

parts of a person fit together. Idiographic personologists also are interested in the concept of choice and the ways in which individuals determine the environments in which they are found (Tyler, 1978). In other words, there is more interest in how people shape their environments than there is in how environments mold people.

The implications of these differences are numerous—they involve basic assumptions, methodologies, and goals—and the development of these positions goes far beyond the bounds of a social psychology textbook. For the social psychologist, the trait-centered (or nomothetic) approach has clearly been dominant (to the extent that personality has been considered at all). We will focus our attention on certain selected traits that exemplify this approach. At the same time, we will be mindful of the pitfalls that are associated with this approach. We will return to some of the more general issues of personality and social behavior in a later section.

The number of personality traits and personality measures that have been developed is staggering; it would be impossible for us to cover them all here (and such complete coverage would undoubtedly be boring). As a consequence, we will select only a few: authoritarianism, achievement, uniqueness, masculinity, femininity, and the concept of androgyny. In each case, we will try to explain the rationale behind the development of the concept and describe several of the social behaviors to which the concept has been related. Then we will return to the more general issues of predicting behavior on the basis of personality characteristics.

II. Authoritarianism

As we discussed briefly in Chapter 11, the concept of authoritarianism was the product of a group of social scientists, led by T. W. Adorno and Else Frenkel-Brunswik, who attempted to assess degrees of anti-Semitism. Clearly instigated by events in Germany during the 1930s under the reign of Hitler, this concept initially was seen as a series of separate components, including

Figure 16-1. Authoritarianism in action. A rigid belief in traditional standards and the acceptance of authority to enforce those standards may lead to extreme action, such as the book burning in Santiago, Chile, pictured here. (© United Press International.)

anti-Semitism, ethnocentrism, and political and economic conservatism (Adorno, Frenkel-Brunswik, Levinson, & Sanford, 1950).

A. Development and Measurement of the Concept

Aiming to develop a general measure of individuals' susceptibility to antidemocratic ideology (without specific reference to any particular group), the research team headed by Adorno and Frenkel-Brunswik constructed a measure of **authoritarianism**, popularly referred to as the *F* scale (*F* denoting Fascism). The California group postulated nine components of authoritarianism: conventionalism, authoritarian submission, authoritarian aggression, power and tough-

ness, anti-intraception, superstition and stereotypy, destructiveness and cynicism, projectivity, and overconcern with sex (see Figure 16-1, which illustrates authoritarianism in action). Each of these components is defined, with sample items from the original *F* scale, in Table 16-1. Although some of the items have been altered as the scale has come through a set of revisions, the third and final version of the scale contains many of the items listed in Table 16-1 (Cherry & Byrne, 1977).

In developing their conceptualizations, the California group relied on the theory of psychoanalysis and Freud's concepts of the ego, the superego, and the id (discussed in Chapter 1). Considering individually the constructs that entered into the theory of authoritarianism, we can say that the first three—conventionalism, authoritarian submission, and authoritarian aggression— refer to the functioning of the superego. Emphasis is placed on strict demands that are made by the superego; these demands are backed up by external reinforcements and by punishment in the name of authority figures to whom the highly authoritarian person has submitted.

Manifestations of a weak ego are reflected in the constructs of anti-intraception, superstition and stereotypy, and projectivity. As indicated in Table 16-1, anti-intraception reflects an early stage in the development of defense mechanisms that involves repression and denial. Superstition and stereotypy involve the shifting of responsibility onto an external world, implying that the ego has forsaken attempts to control behavior. Projectivity reflects a relatively primitive, immature way of avoiding one's anxieties. The dimension of power and toughness appears to signal a weak ego and a very conventional orientation held by the superego. This is indicated by the authoritarian person's reliance on will power, often to an extreme.

Destructiveness and cynicism, as well as an exaggerated concern with sex, reflect a rather undisguised and forceful id, though, in matters of sex, the superego often appears to dominate basic id instincts. In addition, authoritarians were believed to

TABLE 16 - 1 / *Components of Authoritarianism*

1. *Conventionalism. Rigid* adherence to and *over*emphasis on middle-class values, and overresponsiveness to contemporary *external* social pressure.
   Sample item: "A person who has bad manners, habits, and breeding can hardly expect to get along with decent people."
   Sample item: "No sane, normal person could ever think of hurting a close friend or relative."

2. *Authoritarian submission.* An exaggerated, emotional need to submit to others; an uncritical acceptance of a strong leader who will make decisions.
   Sample item: "People should have a deep faith in a supernatural force higher than themselves to whom they give total allegiance and whose decisions they obey without question."
   Sample item: "Obedience and respect for authority are the most important virtues children should learn."

3. *Authoritarian aggression.* Favoring condemnation, total rejection, stern discipline, or severe punishment as ways of dealing with people and forms of behavior that deviate from conventional values.
   Sample item: "Sex crimes, such as rape and attacks on children, deserve more than mere imprisonment; such criminals ought to be publicly whipped, or worse."
   Sample item: "No insult to our honor should ever go unpunished."

4. *Anti-intraception.* Disapproval of a free emotional life, of the intellectual or theoretical, and of the impractical. Anti-intraceptive persons maintain a narrow range of consciousness; realization of their genuine feelings or self-awareness might threaten their adjustment. Hence, they reject feelings, fantasies, and other subjective or "tender-minded" phenomena.
   Sample item: "When a person has a problem or worry, it is best for him or her not to think about it, but to keep busy with more cheerful things."
   Sample item: "There are some things too intimate and personal to talk about even with one's closest friends."

5. *Superstition and stereotypy.* Superstition implies a tendency to shift responsibility from within the individual onto outside forces beyond one's control, particularly to mystical determinants. Stereotypy is the tendency to think in rigid, oversimplified categories, in unambiguous terms of black and white, particularly in the realm of psychological or social matters.
   Sample item: "It is entirely possible that this series of wars and conflicts will be ended once and for all by a world-destroying earthquake, flood, or other catastrophe."
   Sample item: "Although many people may scoff, it may yet be shown that astrology can explain a lot of things."

6. *Power and toughness.* The aligning of oneself with power figures, thus gratifying both one's need to have power and the need to submit to power. There is a denial of personal weakness.
   Sample item: "What this country needs is fewer laws and agencies, and more courageous, tireless, devoted leaders whom the people can put their faith in."
   Sample item: "Too many people today are living in an unnatural, soft way; we should return to the fundamentals, to a more red-blooded, active way of life."

7. *Destructiveness and cynicism.* Rationalized aggression; for example, cynicism permits the authoritarian person to be aggressive because "everybody is doing it." The generalized hostility and vilification of the human by highly authoritarian persons permits them to justify their own aggressiveness.
   Sample item: "Human nature being what it is, there will always be war and confict."

8. *Projectivity.* The disposition to believe that wild and dangerous things go on in the world. In the authoritarian personality, the undesirable impulses that cannot be admitted by the conscious ego tend to be projected onto minority groups and other vulnerable objects.
   Sample item: "The sexual orgies of the old Greeks and Romans are kid stuff compared to some of the goings-on in this country today, even in circles where people might least expect it."
   Sample item: "Nowadays when so many different kinds of people move around so much and mix together so freely, people have to be especially careful to protect themselves against infection and disease."

TABLE 16-1 / (cont.)

9. *Sex*. Exaggerated concern with sexual goings-on, and punitiveness toward violators of sex mores.
   Sample item: "Homosexuality is a particularly rotten form of delinquency and ought to be severely punished."
   Sample item: "No matter how they act on the surface, men are interested in women for only one reason."

have unresolved Oedipal conflicts that would continue to plague them and determine their behavior.

Although the ideological framework of the concept of authoritarianism is clear, there were a number of problems and criticisms surrounding the actual measurement of authoritarianism (Hyman & Sheatsley, 1954; Bass, 1955). Without going into the details of these criticisms, we can say that some of the problems they raise have been resolved in more recent versions of the scale. Taking a more direct approach, we will examine the research that has been done on the *F* scale: Does authoritarianism allow us to predict behavior, and does it relate to concepts that the theory would suggest should be related?

B. *Research on Authoritarianism*

Two general approaches have been taken in relating authoritarianism to other variables. In the first approach, scores on the authoritarianism scale are correlated with other variables in an attempt to see how a package of variables might fit together. In the second approach—a social psychological approach—an investigator manipulates specific situations and observes the ways in which the personality variable leads to different behaviors in various situations. We will consider the evidence related to authoritarianism in each of these approaches.

1. *The Relationship between Authoritarianism and Other Variables.* Investigators of the authoritarian personality were interested in determining (1) the conditions that might lead to the development of an authoritarian personality, and (2) the characteristics that could accompany authoritarianism. In seeking answers to the first question, investigators turned to a consideration of the parents of highly authoritarian people. They found, for example, that highly authoritarian persons tend to have a more traditional family ideology, which includes strong parental control over family decisions, clear-cut roles for each parent, and restrictions on the rights of children to dissent. Less authoritarian persons appeared to prefer a more democratic family structure (Levinson & Huffman, 1955). Byrne (1965) looked specifically at the relationship between the *F* scores of parents and the scores of their children. Interestingly, highly authoritarian sons appeared to have been influenced by their mothers and fathers (who scored high on the *F* scale themselves), whereas daughters appeared to have been influenced only by the authoritarianism of their mothers. Moreover, Byrne observed that one low-authoritarian parent of either sex appears to be sufficient to produce a low-authoritarian child. Although these findings seem to establish the influence of parents on their children, Baumrind (1972), in comparing Black and White families, has provided a note of caution. Black parents scored higher on the *F* scale than White parents did, but these same Black parents tended to produce children who were independent, emotionally expressive, and apt to display a number of other characteristics not typically associated with authoritarianism. In summary, although there is certainly some evidence for the relationship between parents' characteristics and the characteristics of their children, it is clear that a number of factors may moderate these relationships. The home environment in itself cannot fully account for the development of an authoritarian personality.

The search for other characteristics that describe the authoritarian personality has been a prolific area of research. Literally hundreds of studies have been conducted that point to a number of features that provide a broad picture of the authoritarian personality. Prejudice, for example, has been shown repeatedly to relate to authoritarianism, from the time of the early California studies that related F scores to a general measure of ethnocentrism to a host of later studies that consistently show the high-F person to be more prejudiced against minority groups. This holds true whether the focus is White prejudice against Blacks (Martin & Westie, 1959), Arab prejudice against Jews (Epstein, 1966), or Israeli prejudice against Arabs (Siegman, 1961). A thorough summary of these findings has been provided by Hanson (1975).

Additional correlates of authoritarianism have been identified (Cherry & Byrne, 1977; Christie & Cook, 1958; Kirscht & Dillehay, 1967). In a general sense, highly authoritarian persons are made uncomfortable by situations that involve ambiguity (Zacker, 1973); in such situations, they try to impose a simplified structure. Similarly, Steiner and Johnson (1963a) found that authoritarian persons were reluctant to believe that "good people" can possess both good and bad attributes.

Highly authoritarian people tend to avoid several kinds of situations. For example, they aren't likely to complete mail questionnaires sent by psychologists (Poor, 1967) or volunteer for psychological experiments (Rosen, 1951; Rosenthal & Rosnow, 1975). This avoidance of personal involvement by high authoritarians is not limited to their interaction with psychologists. By interviewing a representative sample of adults in Philadelphia, Sanford (1950) found that authoritarian interviewees reported less interest in political affairs, less participation in politics and community activities,

and more characteristic preferences for strong leaders (in other words, let someone else do it) than did low authoritarians. In contrast, highly authoritarian people are more likely than less authoritarian people to attend church (Jones, 1958).

The picture of the authoritarian personality as one with conservative attitudes is reflected in political preferences. In U.S. presidential elections, authoritarians were shown to favor General Douglas MacArthur over other Republican candidates in the 1952 primaries (O. Milton, 1952) and to prefer Senator Barry Goldwater to Lyndon Johnson in 1964 (Higgins, 1965; Wrightsman, 1965). In both cases, the candidate who was preferred by the high authoritarian persons was generally considered to be more conservative and more militaristic than the other candidates.

More specific military involvement is also preferred by the authoritarian personality. For example, when the United States was involved in the Vietnam War, students who actively protested the war scored lower in authoritarianism than those students who supported U.S. involvement in Vietnam (Izzett, 1971). In a related study, an attitude scale toward Lieutenant Calley and the My Lai massacre was constructed by Fink (1973), who administered the attitude scale, along with the F scale, to a group of college students. The subjects who believed that Calley's actions were excusable, and that he shouldn't have been court-martialed, were more authoritarian than were those who were critical of Calley's actions. Defenders of Calley during that period were more apt to believe that Calley had no choice but to obey orders and that, therefore, he was not personally responsible for the outcome of actions carried out under his instructions (Kelman, 1973). Such opinions are highly consistent with the general belief in authority that is held by the authoritarian personality.

In summary, the search for correlates of authoritarianism has given us a picture of a person who is generally conservative in political and social attitudes, deferent to authority, and prone to look askance at deviations from the conventional moral order. In most cases, these conclusions are based on the relationship found between two types of pencil-and-paper measures (Titus & Hollander, 1957). Therefore, although a clear pattern seems to exist, we can continue to examine the ways in which the behavior of high-authoritarian persons differs from the behavior of low authoritarians—and whether particular situational characteristics are important in predicting their behavior.

2. *Authoritarian Behavior and Situational Factors.* As Kirscht and Dillehay (1967) have noted, "authoritarian deeds have more social consequence than authoritarian thoughts" (p. 2). Therefore, it becomes important to look at specific behaviors and determine whether the authoritarian personality is as easily predictable as the neat pattern of correlates would suggest. First, we should consider situations that are likely to elicit differences in behavior between highly authoritarian and less authoritarian people. Logically, we should predict that behavioral differences would be most apparent in those areas that relate to the specific construct—for example, conformity to authority and judgments of right and wrong.

Overall, studies that have attempted to relate authoritarianism to conformity behavior have been inconsistent (Cherry & Byrne, 1977). Perhaps this set of findings is surprising, but we must consider the source of conformity pressure more carefully. If that source is a clearly recognized figure of authority, we might well expect highly authoritarian persons to conform more readily than less authoritarian persons. In contrast, if the source of conformity pressure has little authority, is there really any reason to expect the authoritarian to exhibit substantial conformity? When we look at the evidence from this more reasoned perspective, the results seem to fall into place. Highly authoritarian people are more conforming and less hostile than those who are low on authoritarianism to high-status sources (Roberts & Jessor, 1958; Steiner & Johnson, 1963b).

The importance of the authority source, and its effect on the subject's behavior, is seen even more clearly in a study conducted by Mitchell (1973). In this study, two different versions of a scenario describing a rock concert that got out of hand were presented to the subjects. In one version of the scenario, a concertgoer was killed by a police officer; in another version, in which the basic description of events was the same, the police officer was killed by the concertgoer. High and low authoritarians who were asked to recommend punishment for the murderer responded quite differently to these two versions, as shown in **Figure 16-2**. Highly authoritarian subjects recommended strong punishment when the victim was the policeman, but not when the victim was the concertgoer; less authoritarian subjects exhibited exactly the reverse pattern, being punitive toward the high-authority person (the policeman), but not toward the citizen. In each case, however, judgments were made only after some negative information concerning the defendant had been presented.

Behavioral differences between high-authoritarian and low-authoritarian personalities have been observed in their perception of information, but the particular kind of information and the particular situation make a difference. For example, Levy (1979) asked a sample of registered voters in Detroit to evaluate the evening news commentators (Cronkite on CBS, Chancellor on NBC, and Reasoner and Smith on ABC) and to indicate how often they believed what their preferred source of information told them about race relations and Vietnam. Highly authoritarian listeners were much more likely to believe in the source that they had designated as an authority than were less authoritarian listeners. There is also evidence for differences between high and low authoritarians in their ability to recall information. Using one of the most famous trials of the 1970s, Garcia and Griffitt (1978) compared high and low authoritarian persons in their recall of evidence in the Patricia Hearst case. The subjects did not differ in the number of prosecution arguments recalled; however, high author-

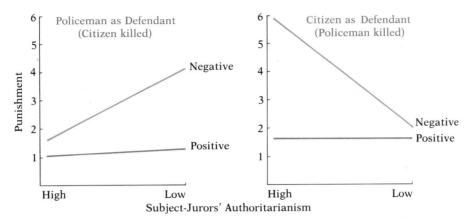

Figure 16-2. Punishment as a function of subject-jurors' authoritarianism, description of the defendant, and status of the defendant. (From "Affective and Informational Determinants of Juror Decision Making." Unpublished doctoral dissertation given at Purdue University by H. E. Mitchell, 1979. Reprinted by permission.

itarians recalled significantly fewer arguments presented by the defense attorneys than did low authoritarians. Moreover, high authoritarians were more likely than low authoritarians to infer guilt.

To summarize, high and low authoritarian persons do behave differently in some situations—but not in all situations. As we will discuss in more detail later in this chapter, it is important to consider the characteristics of the situation, as well as the characteristics of the person. Certain situations may trigger an authoritarian response; in such situations, the behavior of a high-F person will be predictably different from that of a low-F person. Other situations may simply be irrelevant to the authoritarian character; in those situations, personality characteristics may tell us nothing about the behaviors that might occur.

III. Achievement

In Chapter 15, we discussed the concept of a fear of success, which was developed in an attempt to explain differences in attainment and performance between men and women. This concept was preceded by decades of work on the more basic notion of achievement. Before we consider related research, let's look at the development and measurement of the concept of achievement.

A. *Development and Measurement of the Concept*

More than 25 years of research has been devoted to the concept of a need or motive to achieve. The basic research is centered at the University of Michigan, but it radiates throughout the United States and, as its objects of study, to societies as diverse as modern-day India, ancient Greece, and 15th-century England. Before following the pursuits of these investigations, however, we should define the basic concept of achievement motivation.

Achievement is believed to be an individual motive that includes concerns for meeting standards of excellence and excelling in performance against those standards. In our own society, with its emphasis on achievement and progress, it is no surprise that a substantial amount of time and energy has been devoted to understanding the development and operation of the achievement motive. Even beyond our own cultural boundaries, we know that, at various times and places, individuals and societies have been concerned with achieving, striving, getting ahead, and winning in competition.

The idea that there are basic sets of human motives, or drives, is not new; Freud, of course, posited such a set of drives, as did Murray (1938), Maslow (1954), and McClelland (1951). Early philosophers also posited such motives. The urge to measure these motives, however, is a more recent phenomenon—one that can be attributed primarily to psychologists. In fact, the beginnings of the research on achievement motivation did not begin with the concept of achievement, but rather with an attempt to measure hunger motivation. Using a group of naval recruits, Atkinson and McClelland (1948) attempted to devise a fantasy measure that could be used to measure degrees of hunger. The basic assessment tool was the Thematic Apperception Test, in which subjects are asked to write stories describing a set of pictures that are presented to them. Atkinson and McClelland found that there was a relationship between the content of the stories written by the subjects and the number of hours they had been deprived of food. The work on achievement motivation had begun.

Although the need, or motive, to achieve is less concrete than the number of hours that someone has been deprived of food, McClelland and his colleagues began to suspect that their research strategy could be used in the study of achievement motivation. A basic measure of achievement motivation was developed. The stories told in response to pictures were scored by means of an elaborate coding process and used to assess an individual's level of achievement. Figure 16-3 presents the description of a typical picture and some of the responses that would be scored either high or low in achievement imagery.

From these rather simple beginnings, a vast literature has been developed in an attempt to understand and explain the ways in which achievement motivation operates within an individual. This literature is exceedingly complex, and whole books have been devoted to its exposition (Atkinson, 1958; Heckhausen, 1967; McClelland, Atkinson, Clark, & Lowell, 1953). A complete examination of this literature is beyond the scope of this chapter; however, we will pre-

Figure 16-3. Achievement stories. (From *Motives in Fantasy, Action, and Society,* by J. W. Atkinson [Ed.]. Copyright 1958 by Van Nostrand Reinhold Company. Reprinted by permission.)

Description of the picture:
A boy about 18 years old is sitting at his desk in an occupied classroom. A book lies open before him, but he is not looking at it. The boy rests his forehead on one hand as he gazes pensively out toward the viewer.

High Story
1. This chap is doing some heavy meditating. He is a sophomore and has reached an intellectual crisis. He cannot make up his mind. He is troubled, worried.
2. He is trying to reconcile the philosophies of Descartes and Thomas Aquinas—and at his tender age. He has read several books on philosophy and feels the weight of the world on his shoulders.
3. He wants to present a clear-cut synthesis of these two conflicting philosophies, to satisfy his ego and to gain academic recognition from his professor.

4. He will screw himself up royally. Too inexperienced and uninformed, he has tackled too great a problem. He will give up in despair, go down to the G——, and drown his sorrows in a bucket of beer (p. 697).

Low Story
1. The boy in the checkered shirt whose name is Ed is in a classroom. He is supposed to be listening to the teacher.
2. Ed has been troubled by his father's drunkenness and his maltreatment of Ed's mother. He thinks of this often and worries about it.
3. Ed is thinking of leaving home for a while in the hope that this might shock his parents into getting along.
4. He will leave home but will only meet further disillusionment away from home (p. 697).

sent some of the basic concepts of the achievement motive.

The *motive to achieve success (M_s)* is measured by stories told in response to TAT pictures. A second (and related) concept is the *motive to avoid failure (M_f)*. Investigators recognized that, whenever there is a challenge to succeed, there is also a threat of failure, and that the balance between these two needs is crucial in predicting subsequent behavior. A measure was adopted to assess the motive to avoid failure, most commonly the Test Anxiety Questionnaire of Mandler and Sarason (1952). In general terms, we can say that a high-achievement-oriented person is one for whom the motive to achieve success is stronger than the motive to avoid failure; conversely, the low-achievement-oriented person is one for whom the motive to avoid failure is greater than the motive to achieve success.

Additional constructs have been introduced into the theory to increase the precision of predicting behavior. For any specific task, for example, one can consider the probability of being successful (P_s) and the importance (or incentive value) of success at that particular task (I_s). Similar concepts were adopted to accompany the measure of failure avoidance, the probability of failing to achieve a task (P_f), and the negative feelings associated with failing to achieve a particular task (I_f). Initially, these probabilities were considered to be standard across a group of people. More recent work, however, has shown that an individual assessment of these probabilities is more sensible and more reliable (Kuhl, 1978). Mathematically, these relationships can be shown in the following manner:

$$T_s = M_s \times P_s \times I_s$$
$$T_f = M_f \times P_f \times I_f.$$

Overall achievement motivation is then determined by subtracting the motive to avoid failure (T_f) from the motive to achieve success (T_s).

In addition, investigators have recognized the importance of other extrinsic factors that may affect task performance, such as social or financial rewards. Without going further into the theoretical elaboration of achievement motivation, we can summarize the characteristics that are believed to be typical of high-achievement-oriented persons and low-achievement-oriented persons. The former are generally attracted to activities that require skill, because they enjoy the challenge of doing something well. In contrast, the latter are threatened by failure; they avoid activities in which their performance might be evaluated either against a standard of excellence or against the performance of other people.

B. *Research on Achievement*

Investigators of achievement motivation have been concerned with actual behavior and the ways in which different situations interact with basic achievement needs. However, some early studies did explore the various correlates of achievement motivation.

1. *The Relationship between Achievement Motivation and Other Variables.* Some of the early investigations into achievement motivation were quite ingenious in their attempts to discover variations in the expressive styles of high achievers and low achievers (Brown, 1965). For example, Knapp (1958) found that high achievers preferred somber tartan plaid patterns in which shades of blue predominated. Low achievers, in contrast, preferred bright colors. Knapp suggested that the high achievers preferred a neutral background, against which they could impose their own hard-driving achievement needs, whereas low achievers presumably preferred to be absorbed by the background. These apparent differences in general expressive style led Knapp and Garbutt (1958) to explore preferences for literary metaphors. They found that high achievers preferred expressions such as "a dashing waterfall" and "a speeding train," whereas low achievers favored "a string of beads" and "a vast expanse of sky" (Brown, 1965). Even the doodles of high achievers and low achievers were shown to differ (Aronson, 1958). High scorers, for example, preferred s-shaped lines and discrete lines, whereas low scorers favored fuzzy overlaid lines and few diagonals. Some of these findings are amusing, and their replicability is, in some cases, uncertain. They do, however, suggest general expressive differences between high-achievement people and low-achievement people.

Investigators also were interested in the child-raising practices that might lead to the development of high (versus low) achievement needs (see **Figure 16-4**). Winterbottom (1953) interviewed the mothers of 29 boys (ranging in age from 8 to 10) and found that the mothers of high-achievement-oriented boys were concerned that their children learn to do new things independently (and at an early age). These mothers were more likely than mothers of low-achievement-oriented boys to reward their sons with physical signs of affection, such as hugging. Rosen and D'Andrade (1959) observed that parents of high-

achievement boys encouraged performance, whereas the fathers of low-achievement boys were directive, easily irritated, and generally authoritarian in their behavior.

More recent studies of the correlates of achievement have considered the patterns of causal attributions (see Chapter 3) that people use (Weiner, Frieze, Kukla, Reed, Rest, & Rosenbaum, 1972). There is evidence that highly achievement-oriented males are likely to use self-attributions (such as ability and personal effort) for their success, whereas low-achievement-oriented males turn to external factors, such as task ease and luck, to explain their success. It should be noted that these results did not hold true for females (thus extending the poor record of achievement research to account for *both* male and female behavior [see Chapter 15]). Additional research on achievement-related behaviors is presented in **Box 16-1**.

Figure 16-4. The development of achievement motivation in children may be influenced by parental attitudes and behavior, particularly by parents stressing independence on the part of their children. (Henri Matisse, *The Piano Lesson*, 1916. Oil in canvas, 96-½ × 83-¾ in. The Museum of Modern Art, New York, Mrs. Simon Guggenheim Fund.)

2. *Achievement Behavior and Situational Factors.* From its beginning, the investigation of achievement orientation emphasized the relationship between personality disposition and actual behavior and the ways in which various situations could affect the behavior of high-achievement and low-achievement scorers. On the basis of their theory, achievement investigators made a number of predictions regarding people of high and low achievement needs. For example, they predicted that highly achievement-oriented people would prefer tasks of intermediate difficulty, whereas less achievement-oriented individuals would prefer tasks that were either very easy or very difficult. In the latter case, the low achievers could be assured of success, though with very little payoff, or they could fail without any consequences. In contrast, highly achievement-oriented individuals initially select those tasks that involve a risk as well as a reasonable chance of success. These predictions have been supported (Atkinson & Feather, 1966). Moreover, individuals who have a strong need for achievement persist longer in the solution of a task than do less achievement-oriented individuals.

Box 16-1. Achievement of Scientists.

The Science Citation Index (SCI) is an index of the number of times a scientific paper is cited by scientists. Many people maintain that this index is a valid measure of scientific eminence. Unlike a simple count of a scientist's publications, the SCI focuses on the impact and (perhaps) the quality of the scientist's work.

Helmreich, Beane, Lucker, and Spence (1979) attempted to relate the SCI figures to individual achievement needs. To measure achievement orientation, they developed an instrument that separates components of work, mastery, and competition (Spence & Helmreich, 1978). Work refers to involvement and a task orientation; mastery deals with the chal-

lenge of accomplishing something; competition, as the word implies, is related to compared performance. Using this concept of achievement motivation, these authors found that the most frequently cited scientists scored *high* in work and mastery but *low* in competition.

Similar results appeared in a study of male graduates of the University of Texas Graduate School of Business. The men who ranked high in work and mastery and low in competitiveness were earning the highest salaries—$6000 more than their peers who were ranked high in competitive needs. Contrary to popular belief, competition may be detrimental to achievement!

Much of the early work on achievement motivation focused on simple tasks (in the laboratory) that had little consequence for future action. For example, young boys were asked to play a game of ringtoss, choosing the distance they would throw the ring. To the credit of investigators in this area, they have realized that real-life achievement is neither static nor unrelated to expected future consequences. For example, in proposing a dynamics of action, Atkinson and Birch (1970) have expanded the original theory of achievement motivation to account for sequential changes in behavior. In one test of their theoretical notions, Kuhl and Blankenship (1979) have shown that people shift to increasingly difficult tasks over time. Once again, we find a particular situation interacting with an individual-difference variable. (In this case, we have the additional variable of time.)

In an additional attempt to go beyond the one-shot situation, Raynor (1969, 1974) has developed a model that considers sequences of behavior, such as those that might be involved when you consider taking a particular course, majoring in a particular subject, and choosing a particular career as

steps in a sequence of events. Each of these events is contingent on the preceding one, and your initial approach to the first course should have some relationship to your later achievement aspirations. Although the general prediction assumes that people who have high achievement needs prefer tasks of immediate risk, Raynor suggests that "it is the future challenge which offers the moderate risk." Since these people "face the necessity of guaranteeing 'staying in the ballgame' long enough to achieve future career success" (Raynor, 1974, pp. 146–7), they may, in fact, be less risky than would be expected early in the sequence. Later on, however, as the earlier stages have been successfully completed, their behavior will tend to approach the predicted preference for tasks of intermediate difficulty. In contrast, people who are less strongly oriented toward achievement (or who have a more intense fear of failure) may initially tackle a more difficult task and, in the face of actual failure, move toward increasingly easy tasks.

The achievement literature is both extensive and complex; we have only been able to briefly review some of its high points. McClelland (1961) extended the concept of individual achievement to the societal level and found relationships between the achievement level of a society (as measured, for example, by the content of children's literature) and the subsequent growth or decline in capitalism and industrialization in that society. More recently, Atkinson and his colleagues (Atkinson, 1977; Atkinson & Birch, 1970) have attempted to make the theory of achievement motivation much more dynamic by accounting for changes in preferences over time rather than static tendencies. The significance of these developments is that they give us a more realistic view of human behavior as a constantly changing process.

IV. Uniqueness

On a variety of specific dimensions, such as achievement and authoritarianism, people display differences. At a more abstract level, we can consider the concept of "differentness" in and of itself. Is there a general trait that involves the perception of being the same as or different from other people? Sometimes, when a person is observed deviating from others, negative labels come into play: *weirdo, freak,* and *oddball* are terms that underscore the tendency of people to reject individuals who are "different." Conformity to norms (see Chapter 14) is often considered desirable behavior, whereas deviant behavior is ignored or punished. However, some people feel that being different is important. For these people, it may be more important to be different than it is to conform.

A. *Development and Measurement of the Concept*

Snyder and Fromkin (1980) have proposed that people differ in their need to be distinguished from other people. Rejecting the connotation of the term *deviance* as abnormal and maladjusted, these authors define *uniqueness* as "a positive striving for differences relative to other people" (Snyder & Fromkin, 1977, p. 518). They propose that people vary in their need to be unique: for

some, being different is very important, whereas, for others, it is more important to appear much like everyone else. In one case, people are stressing their similarities (much like the classic social psychological approach); in the other case, they are stressing their unique qualities (reflecting a more ideographic conception of human nature). To illustrate these differences, Snyder and Fromkin (1980) present statements made by Zeke and Dennis. Zeke says "I don't like being called an average guy. Sometimes, it seems like most of the people I know want to be like each other. . . . I usually say what I think, even when other people may think that I'm kind of weird. Maybe I am, but that's O.K. Actually, I do think I am different from other people, and I'm proud of it." In contrast to the high uniqueness needs of Zeke, consider Dennis: "Ever since I was a teenager, and probably before that, I have pretty much gone along with what other people say or do. . . . I guess you could say I am a pretty typical type of person. . . . Well, I'm probably just more comfortable when I'm one of the guys" (Snyder & Fromkin, 1980, p. 78).

Although people's statements and self-descriptions may reveal quite a bit about their need for uniqueness, a more reliable method of assessing differences in personality is the use of a standard personality questionnaire. Such a scale was developed to measure individual differences in the need for uniqueness (Fromkin & Lipshitz, 1976; Snyder & Fromkin, 1977). Some of the items on this scale are shown in Table 16-2. The scale consists of 32 items, and analysis has shown that three general factors constitute the concept of uniqueness: (1) a lack of concern regarding others' reactions, (2) a desire to break the rules occasionally, and (3) a willingness to publicly defend one's beliefs (Snyder & Fromkin, 1977).

Snyder and Fromkin conducted a number of studies to validate their scale—in other words, to show that people who score low in the need for uniqueness really differ from those who score high. For example, they asked friends of each of their subjects to rate the subjects in order to determine whether other people perceived their various levels of uniqueness needs. They did:

TABLE 16-2 / *Some Items from the Need for Uniqueness Scale*

I find it sometimes amusing to upset the dignity of teachers, judges, and "cultured" people.

Others' disagreement makes me uncomfortable.*

I always try to follow rules.*

If I must die, let it be an unusual death rather than an ordinary death in bed.

I would rather be known for always trying new ideas than for employing well-trusted methods.

As a rule, I strongly defend my own opinions.

Those items marked with an asterisk (*) are scored in the reverse direction.

From *Uniqueness: The Human Pursuit of Differences*, by C. R. Snyder and H. L. Fromkin. Copyright 1980 by Plenum Publishing Corporation. Reprinted by permission.

the people who scored high on the measure of uniqueness needs were rated more unique by their friends than were the people who scored low (Snyder & Fromkin, 1977). Members of specific groups, such as gay liberation, women's liberation, and Mensa (a group whose entrance criteria involve a test to demonstrate superior and unusual levels of intelligence), were tested on the Uniqueness Scale. The investigators assumed that the members of these groups would believe themselves to be more unique than a randomly selected group of control subjects. In each case, the predictions held true, further demonstrating the validity of the uniqueness scale.

B. *Research on Uniqueness*

Although uniqueness is a rather new variable in the annals of personality traits, a variety of studies have already shown its importance in explaining some human differences.

1. *The Relationship between Uniqueness and Other Variables.* Since people who have a strong need for uniqueness apparently enjoy being deviant, or at least somewhat different, we would expect that they would score low on measures that are designed to assess levels of social anxiety. Such an expectation appears to be justified: people who rank high in a need for uniqueness are found to score significantly lower on measures of social anxiety and audience anxiety than individuals who rank low in uniqueness needs. We should also expect that certain behavioral patterns of high-uniqueness individuals differ from those of low-uniqueness individuals. One's signature, for example, is a defining characteristic. Snyder and Fromkin (1977) have found that high-uniqueness individuals tend to have larger signatures than low-uniqueness individuals have. In a word-association task, in which people are asked to respond to one word by saying the first word that comes to mind (for example, saying *chair* after the experimenter reads the word *table*), high-uniqueness individuals offer more novel and unusual responses than low-uniqueness individuals do (Brandt, 1976).

Relatively little is known about the development of uniqueness. However, at least one study suggests that some of the pressures that push people toward uniqueness may occur quite early in life. By comparing people who had unusual first names (names that occurred only once in the entire college population) with people who had more common first names, Zweigenhaft (cited in Snyder & Fromkin, 1980) found that the former group had significantly higher scores on the Need for Uniqueness scale, suggesting that an individual's name may affect subsequent personality development. (Of course, there are other possible explanations. Parents who tend to assign unusual first names to their children may stress the importance of being unique in a variety of ways as their children grow up. Therefore, although the name itself may not be the most important single cause, it may reflect a general set of values.)

2. *Uniqueness and Situational Factors.* As in the case of other personality variables, we should expect that a situation would interact with a particular disposition. Although the research on uniqueness has not been extensive, the results suggest that this pattern of person/situation interaction exists.

Consider, for example, a situation in which you find out either that you are very similar to other people or that you are very different from them. How would this make you feel? If you have a strong need for uniqueness, the fact that you are similar to other people might be disturbing; it could lead to a decrease in your self-esteem. In contrast, if your need for uniqueness is low, being similar to other people might be a positive experience that could lead to an increase in your self-esteem. In an experimental test of this hypothesis, individuals were told that they were very similar to other college students (Snyder & Fromkin, 1980). The subjects reacted according to the degree of their need to be unique. For high-uniqueness people, the information resulted in a decline in self-esteem, whereas low-uniqueness people experienced a rise in self-esteem.

People who differ in the degree to which they need to be unique react differently to objects in their environment. Some objects in our environment are quite rare or are advertised as being exotic and distinct (see, for example, Figure 16-5). For the person who is strongly oriented toward uniqueness, such rarities should be desirable; however, for the person whose need for uniqueness is low, such distinctiveness may be unimportant. In a laboratory experiment in which subjects were asked to rate their preference for various pairs of boots, the experimenters varied the background information about the availability of the boots. In some conditions, the boots were described as being available to large numbers of persons; in other conditions, they were said to be available to only a few people. Those subjects who scored low in uniqueness were not affected by this information; high-uniqueness subjects, on the other hand, exhibited a marked preference for the boots when they were described as a scarce commodity.

It may be important to each of us to seem unique on some occasions, especially when the pressures for conformity seem very strong. However, for some people, this need is more pervasive and more important than for others. Therefore, the need for uniqueness serves as one more way in which we can separate "some of the people some of the time" from "all of the people all of the time."

V. Masculinity, Femininity, and Androgyny

In Chapter 15, we discussed differences and similarities between males and females —we treated sex as a demographic variable that can be used to divide the population roughly in half. For dozens of years, psychologists have been dissatisfied with such a gross dichotomy; they have sought to develop personality measures of masculinity and femininity that presumably could be found among males *and* females. In other words, they have assumed that, psycholog-

Figure 16-5. By stressing that no two women can share the perfume, this advertisement makes a direct appeal to people's need for uniqueness. (Courtesy of Prince Matchabelli.)

ically, some men and women may be more similar to one another than they are different from one another. They believe that a consideration of these psychological dimensions could be more fruitful than a reliance on the obvious physical characteristics of males and females.

A. *Development and Measurement of the Concept*

The early research in this area has been ably reviewed by Constantinople (1973). As she has pointed out, although the early investigators differed in some of the details of their measurement procedures, they made two common assumptions: (1) that masculinity and femininity represent two opposite points on a scale, and (2) that the dimension of masculinity to femininity is unidimensional (rather than a complex conglomerate of characteristics). More recently, investigators who examined male/female differences began to argue that masculinity and femininity are quite separable sets of characteristics, and that both men and women can possess varying degrees of each set (Bakan, 1966; Block, 1973; Carlson, 1971).

These theoretically based arguments were followed by a number of specific scale developments, in which investigators devised separate scales to measure masculinity and femininity (Bem, 1974; Berzins, Welling, & Wetter, 1975; Heilbrun, 1976; Spence, Helmreich, & Stapp, 1974). The assumption underlying each of these investigations is that there is a set of characteristics that may be considered masculine (or *agentic,* in Bakan's terms), and another set that may be considered feminine (or *communal*). Although these scales differ slightly, the masculinity scales contain items such as *independence, competitive,* and *self-confident,* whereas the femininity scales contain items such as *kind, gentle,* and *warm.* Although males, in general, score higher on the masculinity scale, and females, in general, score higher on the femininity scale, the two scales are unrelated (Bem, 1974; Spence & Helmreich, 1978). In other words, a person can score high on both scales, low on both scales, or high on one scale and low on the other. Statistically, this means that the correlation between the two scales approaches zero. In more descriptive terms, it means that both males and females can be either high or low in either masculinity or femininity; the presence of one set of characteristics does not imply the absence of the other, as earlier investigators had assumed.

To categorize people who have these varying combinations of characteristics, investigators have borrowed the term **androgyny** (originally used by the ancient Greeks to refer to individuals who combined the physical characteristics of both sexes). In its present use, the term refers to a combination of *psychological* characteristics. The classification of individuals according to their scores on masculinity and femininity scales is shown in Figure 16-6.

Although most investigators agree on the general method that is used to measure masculinity and femininity (and the subsequent classification of subjects into four categories), there is considerable disagreement concerning the categories' implications (Lenney, 1979). For Bem (1974), whose work was the first to be widely recognized in this area, the androgynous person is an ideal toward which we should strive. By combining positive masculine and feminine characteristics, the androgynous person, in Bem's view, can function effectively in a wide variety of situations that call for either masculine or feminine behavior. She believes that sex-typed persons, in contrast,

	Masculinity Score	
	Above Median	Below Median
Above Median	Androgynous	Feminine sex-typed
Below Median	Masculine sex-typed	Undifferentiated

Femininity Score

Figure 16-6. Categories of sex-type characteristics.

are more limited, because they are able to operate effectively in some situations, but not in others. Other investigators take a more cautious approach, arguing that the personality characteristics of masculinity and femininity may or may not relate to what we typically consider sex-role behaviors. For example, the personality characteristic of femininity may not be related to homemaking skills; rather, running a home may be related to both masculine and feminine (or agentic and communal) characteristics (Spence & Helmreich, 1978).

Still other critics have argued that the notion of androgyny is a phenomenon that is peculiar to the United States, where individuality is valued and interdependency is scorned (Sampson, 1977). According to this view, traditional sex roles and characteristics may be functional in most societies and at most times—or, at minimum, the advantages of the androgynous personality remain to be demonstrated. As we can see, the notion of androgyny has gathered its share of controversy since it was introduced into the psychological literature. However, the research on this topic is already abundant; we will review some of the findings in order to understand this new approach to masculinity and femininity.

B. *Research on Androgyny*

Before we consider the characteristics that are associated with masculine, feminine, androgynous, and undifferentiated persons, we might first consider the number of people who can be classified in each of these categories. Although the percentages can be considered only approximate, Spence and Helmreich (1978) have sampled a variety of subject populations and, by using the same point to split masculinity and femininity scores in each case, have provided a means by which we can examine the distribution of people into four categories. Some of the results of their work are shown in Table 16-3. As you can see, among an average college-student sample, approximately one-third of the males are masculine sex-typed, and one-third of the females are feminine sex-typed. One-fourth to one-third of the students score as androgynous; the remaining students are either undifferentiated or reverse sex-typed (masculine sex-typed females and feminine sex-typed males). Other groups deviate somewhat from these patterns, as shown by the data in Table 16-3. Now that we have some understanding of just who we're talking about, let's look at some of the research that has used these concepts.

TABLE 16-3 / *Percentage of Populations in the Four Sex-Type Categories*

	Masculine	Feminine	Androgynous	Undifferentiated
Female college students	14	32	27	28
Male college students	34	8	32	25
Female high school students	14	32	35	18
Male high school students	44	8	25	23
Female homosexuals	22	13	33	32
Male homosexuals	9	23	18	50
Female scientists	23	23	46	8
Male scientists	43	5	32	20

Data from Spence & Helmreich, 1978.

1. *The Relationship of Masculinity and Femininity to Other Variables.* If androgynous people are "better," as Bem has suggested, we might expect them to score higher on measures of self-esteem than persons in other categories do. In fact, it has been found that androgynous people have the highest scores in self-esteem, followed, in order, by masculine sex-typed persons, feminine sex-typed persons, and undifferentiated persons (Bem, 1977; O'Connor, Mann, & Bardwick, 1978; Spence, Helmreich, & Stapp, 1975; Wetter, 1975). One caution should be noted, however: since the existent measures of androgyny contain, for the most part, only positive characteristics, the relationship between these measures and a general measure of positive self-regard is more likely than it might be if the measures of masculinity and femininity contained negative characteristics as well. These findings hold true for both males and females, suggesting that the sex-type category may be more important than gender in explaining variations in behavior. In other cases, however, both gender and sex-type category seem to be important. For example, Wiggins and Holzmuller (1978) found that androgynous men were flexible in their interpersonal behavior, whereas androgynous women tended to adopt typically masculine modes of interacting.

Other investigators have attempted to relate the personality characteristics of masculinity and femininity to general political attitudes and, in particular, attitudes toward equal rights for women. Generally, these investigators have found no relationship between the measures (Bem, 1977; Spence & Helmreich, 1978), suggesting that these particular personality characteristics may not be closely related to political attitudes. In other words, a person may combine agentic and communal characteristics without having any predictable position on the issue of women's rights. Consider a traditional woman living on a Midwestern farm, for example. She may score high on warmth and expressiveness and on independence and assertiveness, but these characteristics are displayed in the context of her own home. She may be opposed to the Equal Rights Amendment to the U.S. Constitution, because she feels that sexual equality is contrary to basic morals, and so forth. Or she may support the amendment. The fact that there is no relationship between measures of masculinity and femininity and attitudes toward women's rights tells us that either of these situations is possible. We must be careful not to assume that a personality characteristic reflects a particular political stance.

In the area of achievement, which we discussed earlier, androgynous people tend to score higher on achievement concerns than their sex-typed counterparts do (Spence & Helmreich, 1978). Myers and Lips (1978) reported that androgynous women were more likely than traditionally sex-typed women to play competitive sports (badminton, squash, and racquetball). In this instance, masculine sex-typed persons of both sexes were frequent competitors as well.

The other avenue of investigation in seeking correlates of androgyny is, as you might suspect, the search for parental antecedents. What child-raising practices, and what types of parents, are most likely to produce androgynous offspring? There is some evidence to suggest that androgynous children are most likely to emerge from a home in which the parents also are androgynous (Orlofsky, 1978; Spence & Helmreich, 1978). High levels of warmth and involvement of parents with their children also were found to encourage the development of both masculine and feminine characteristics (Orlofsky, 1978). Androgynous characteristics are more apt to develop in females whose mothers are employed than in females whose mothers are not employed (Allgeier, 1975; Hannson, Chernovetz, & Jones, 1977). Maternal employment seems to have little effect on the development of these characteristics among males.

2. *Masculinity, Femininity, and Situational Factors.* In her initial work on the concept of androgyny, Sandra Bem was interested in showing that androgynous people could adapt more readily and more positively than their sex-typed counterparts to a variety of situations. Her first investigations attempted to demonstrate that androgynous people could display masculine independence and feminine playfulness and nurturance as readily as their sex-typed counterparts could (Bem, 1975; Bem, Martyna, & Watson, 1976). Furthermore, she attempted to show that traditionally sex-typed people would actively avoid those activities associated with the opposite sex (Bem & Lenney, 1976). Although the results of these studies are not clear-cut, they provide some support for the flexibility of androgynous people in a variety of situations and the limited ability of traditionally sex-typed people to function in situations that are considered out of range by traditional standards.

Androgynous and sex-typed persons appear to differ in their awareness of sex-role stereotypes and their responses to members of the opposite sex. Wolff and Taylor (1979) found that, although androgynous people are more aware of the stereotypes of both sexes, they are less evaluative in their stereotyping. Traditionally sex-typed people, in contrast, focus on the stereotypes of their own sex and are less cognizant of the stereotypes of the opposite sex. Androgynous people tend to react to both sexes in similar ways, whereas traditionally sex-typed persons (masculine males and feminine females) devote greater attention to males than they devote to females (Deaux & Major, 1977).

These differences in the perceptions of androgynous and sex-typed persons are reflected in their behavioral interactions. For example, androgynous people are likely to relate to an equal number of males and females and to disclose corresponding amounts of information to either sex. Sex-typed persons seem to prefer to disclose more to females; this is consistent with the notion that females are less threatening and more appropriate sources of emotional support (Deaux, 1977). In a group situation, both masculine sex-typed individuals and androgynous people are more positively regarded by their peers than are feminine sex-typed persons (Falbo, 1977).

The real social impact of personality types such as androgyny on actual behavior has been vividly demonstrated by Ickes and his colleagues (Ickes & Barnes, 1977, 1978). When male and female couples, representing various combinations of the sex-type categories, were allowed to interact freely in an initial meeting, the results were both fascinating and perhaps contrary to many of our expectations. The lowest levels of interaction and the lowest levels of reported enjoyment were found among couples in which the male was traditionally masculine sex-typed and the woman was feminine sex-typed. When both members of a couple were androgynous, the levels of interaction and mutual enjoyment were high, supporting the hypothesis that the possession of both masculine and feminine skills leads to rewarding encounters with a variety of people.

At this point, the critics of the androgyny construct are perhaps as numerous as its supporters; however, androgyny is bound to suffer its growing pains. On the more positive side, the concept has generated an amazing amount of research in a very brief period of time, and, unlike some faddish concepts, it has demonstrated an ability to predict behavior in a variety of situations. We must exercise caution when we assume that a single dimension of personality will allow us to predict behavior in each and every situation that can be imagined. Such assumptions have been the source of many disputes in social psychology that question whether personality dimensions are of any use at all in understanding social behavior. We have seen evidence that some personality constructs can predict some behaviors. Now let us consider, in greater depth, some of the underlying issues and controversies in this area.

VI. The Relationship between Personality and Social Behavior

As a result of our discussion to this point, you may wonder why there is any question regarding the ability of personality traits to predict social behavior, or the fact that individual differences can contribute to a broad understanding of human behavior. However, we have, admittedly, been selective in our coverage, choosing to focus on examples that have been successful in showing the relationship between personality measures and social behavior. Meanwhile, in the closets of personality psychology and social psychology, there are numerous examples of failure. How can we explain the successes and failures—why something that works on one occasion may not work on another occasion? To answer these questions, let us look at some of the basic issues that personality psychologists and social psychologists have been discussing in recent years.

A. *Some Questions about Measurement*

Suppose that, on several occasions, you were going to measure the dimensions of your bedroom with a rubber measuring device that continually fluctuated in length. Clearly, your measurements would vary, depending on the weather, the force with which you pulled the tape, and a variety of other factors. Although the construction of personality measures certainly aims to be solid, there is no doubt that many of the personality-trait measures that have been devised have low reliability. How can we expect them to accurately predict forms of behavior? A reliable measure, of course, is one that has been through a series of development procedures designed specifically to avoid such variation; however, even when such development procedures are employed, there is still margin for error.

Questions have been raised regarding the accuracy of people's reports of their own behaviors (Fiske, 1978). Instead of asking people to state how dominant, authoritarian, or unique they are, some investigators have argued strongly for straightforward observations of behavior. In other words, we would decide whether or not a person was friendly by observing the person's behavior in a variety of situations in which friendliness or unfriendliness might be displayed. As you might guess, the avoidance of this particular technique has not been based on rational grounds alone—it is obviously much more difficult to make a series of observations than it is to administer a sim-

ple paper-and-pencil questionnaire. Some investigators have found that, by combining a number of personality-assessment techniques—for example, biographical information, trait questionnaires, and behavioral sampling methods—they can predict actual behavior much more effectively than they can when they use only a single measure of personality (Alker & Owen, 1977).

One side of the coin of the argument regarding the relationship between personality and social behavior concerns the method of assessing personality traits; the other side, of course, concerns the kinds of social behavior that we are trying to understand. Often, an investigator will spend a great deal of time refining the personality instrument, and then he or she will choose the situation in which to predict social behavior with haste and little thought. Despite social psychologists' considerable involvement with the situational determinants of action, we do not have an adequate taxonomy of situations (Frederiksen, 1972); nevertheless, we do know enough about various situations to make some progress (Pervin, 1978).

The issue at stake here is similar to the one faced by investigators of attitudes, who have been attempting to predict behavior from measures of individual attitudes. As we saw in Chapter 11, there are a number of reasons to believe that such prediction can be achieved, if certain factors are taken into account and certain pitfalls are avoided. The same strategy can be applied here. For example, Jaccard (1974, 1977) has suggested that personality measures should be related to multiple-act criteria, but not to single-act criteria. In other words, if we measure a person's achievement motivation and set up a number of situations in which achievement traits might be exhibited, we should find that, overall, high-achievement individuals exhibit more achievement behavior than low-achievement individuals. At the same time, in any single situation, results may not be clear—some situations may result in little difference, whereas other situations may even show a reversal. A similar point has been made by Epstein (1979), who has pointed out that any single observation of behavior can involve considerable error and have limited generality. However, if we observe a person's behavior over a period of time, general personality measures become much more capable of predicting overall behavior.

Suppose that your friend Joe is someone you think of as an extroverted, outgoing, friendly individual. Yet, at a party on one particular Thursday evening, Joe (for any one of a number of reasons) stays pretty much to himself, talking to a few close friends and avoiding most of the people at the party. As a personality psychologist who believes that assessing personality should allow you to predict every single behavior, you might feel that your theory regarding Joe was wrong. It is more likely, however, that you would consider how Joe had acted in all of the other situations in which you had seen him—you would keep your assessment of his character intact.

B. *Some Questions about the Consistency of Personality*

The preceding arguments have made the assumption that personality traits are stable—that our only problem is in the measurement of either the trait or the behavior. Some critics, however, have questioned whether personality is, in fact, stable—whether such stability is only in the mind of the psychologist. The extreme position of pure *situationism* maintains that situational factors influence behavior, and that individual differences account for very little of the variance in behavior (Mischel, 1968). Social psychology has often been used to represent the pure-situational approach, although, as we have seen and will continue to see, the evidence is not clear-cut. There have been a number of critiques of this extreme position (see Bowers, 1973). Relatively few people today adopt the pure situational position.

A more moderate and more interesting argument concerning personality consistency has been proposed by Bem and Allen (1974). They argue, very simply, that some people will be consistent on some traits, but others will not. In other words, each person-

ality dimension devised by psychologists does not necessarily apply to every person. A particular dimension may be relevant to some individuals, but not to others. How can we find out whether people are consistent on a particular dimension? Again, Bem and Allen propose a simple answer—just ask them. For example, by asking people whether they are friendly in general, and how much they vary from situation to situation in their friendliness, researchers were able to show that people who perceive friendliness as one of their stable characteristics are consistent across a variety of situations. Those people who reported that they were less consistent in their display of friendliness were, in turn, less consistent across situations. The psychologist, in attempting to predict behavior, can at least predict some of the people some of the time.

Can psychologists do better than that? Is it possible to predict all of the people all of the time? Kenrick and Springfield (1980) suggest that it is possible, but only if we recognize that various traits have differing degrees of relevance from one individual to another. Extending Bem and Allen's reasoning, these investigators asked each individual subject to select a personality dimension on which his or her behavior was most consistent. Not surprisingly, the particular dimensions selected differed widely among the subjects. However, in analyzing the selections of subjects individually, the investigators found that there was a consistency of reported behavior—one that was reported by subjects themselves and seen by parents and friends.

Kenrick and Springfield take a more ideographic stance than that taken by most recent personality researchers: they begin with the person, rather than with norms (Mischel, 1977). Their approach is an intriguing one that helps to explain some of the inconsistency found in previous personality research. For example, when an experimenter provides a scale, and a subject scores somewhere in the middle of the scale, that could mean that the subject is moderate on that trait, that the trait is simply irrelevant, or that the subject is habitually inconsistent in that particular area. Either of the two latter cases would, of course, lower the experimenter's ability to predict behavior across a range of situations (Sorrentino & Short, 1977). In short, there is consistency in personality—and there is inconsistency. A Chinese philosopher would smile at the thought!

C. *The Interaction between Personality and Situations*

The consensus that has evolved—and that underlies most of this chapter—is that personalities *and* situations must be considered in order to completely understand human social behavior (see Figure 16-7). This *interactionist* position probably represents the views of most social psychologists today; however, there is controversy about the exact meaning of the term *interaction*. The interactionist position maintains that, in most instances, we can explain some behavior by considering only personalities and some behavior by considering only situations; but we can explain more behavior by considering the interface between personalities and situations. Many psychologists have come to adopt this position (Bem & Funder, 1978; Endler & Magnusson, 1976; Magnusson, 1976; Magnusson & Endler, 1977).

The interactionist position requires that we find effective methods of categorizing situations—perhaps methods that are similar to those that we have used to categorize personalities (Bem & Funder, 1978; Frederiksen, 1972; Pervin, 1978). If we adopt the interactionist position, we will probably begin to think of human behavior in active terms (Endler & Magnusson, 1976), considering the interaction between personalities and situations. As we saw in Chapter 5, communication is not a stable process, nor is the interaction of any single individual with his or her environment. Situations constantly change, often in very subtle ways, and a person's behavior may reflect subtle changes. Human behavior is more complex than we had originally thought it to be, and understanding that behavior is a far more exciting endeavor than we had imagined.

VII. Summary

Although social psychology traditionally has emphasized the importance of situational determinants of behavior, the study of personality has continued to emphasize the importance of individual differences. The *nomothetic* approach to the study of personality stresses general dimensions and norms that apply to all people; the *idiographic* approach focuses on the interrelationship of events and characteristics within an individual.

The concept of *authoritarianism* was developed by a group of social scientists who were interested in measuring anti-Semitism during World War II; the scale they developed is referred to as the *F* scale. Nine components of authoritarianism were described: conventionalism, authoritarian submission, authoritarian aggression, anti-intraception, superstition and stereotypy, power and toughness, destructiveness and cynicism, projectivity, and overconcern with sex. In conceptualizing the authoritarian personality, researchers relied on psychoanalytic theory, suggesting that a weak ego, a rigid and externalized superego, and a strong primitive id are characteristic of the authoritarian personality.

Highly authoritarian persons tend to come from authoritarian families with traditional family ideologies; however, family environment alone cannot explain the development of the authoritarian personality. Highly authoritarian persons tend to be prejudiced, intolerant of ambiguity, and politically conservative. Situational factors are important in predicting the behavior of authoritarians: in some cases, low-authoritarian people may be more punitive than high authoritarians.

The achievement motive focuses on meeting standards of excellence and on performing well. Research on the achievement motive has considered two components: a tendency to achieve success, and a tendency to avoid failure. Other components of the formula are: the probability of success or failure, the incentive value of success and failure, and extrinsic factors.

People who are high in achievement motivation tend to have a more expressive style than those who are low in achievement motivation. Parents of high achievers stress early independence. High achievers tend to select tasks of intermediate risk, whereas low achievers prefer either extremely simple or extremely difficult tasks. More recent work on achievement motivation has considered the sequences of behavior that are involved in a career choice and the relationship between achievement behavior and economic growth.

Uniqueness is a "positive striving for differences relative to other people." People who are high in uniqueness rank low in social anxiety, suffer decreases in self-esteem when they believe that they are similar to other people, and prefer rare commodities.

Although early research considered masculinity and femininity as opposite poles of a single dimension, recent investigators have shown that these concepts represent two unrelated dimensions. People who combine masculine and feminine psychological characteristics are *androgynous.* Although the concept of androgyny has been criticized on both methodological and theoretical grounds, it has generated a great deal of research in recent years.

People who are androgynous tend to be high in self-esteem and, in some cases, flexible in their interpersonal behavior. Moreover, androgynous people rank higher than traditionally sex-typed persons in achievement motivation. Androgynous people tend to behave in the same way toward members of both sexes, and interactions between two androgynous people are generally more active and more enjoyable than initial interactions between, for example, a masculine sex-typed male and a feminine sex-typed female.

The question of the relationship between personality variables and social behavior has a long history of controversy, although most people now accept the position that both contribute to our understanding of human behavior. Some of the issues that have been raised in the controversy focus on: (1) the procedures used in measuring personalities and situations, (2) the question of whether all people are consistent on all traits (or whether some dimensions of personality may be more stable and more relevant for some people than they are for others), and (3) the particular forms in which personality and situations interact.

Glossary Terms   androgyny   idiographic   nomothetic
                        authoritarianism

Figure 16-7. The interactionist view of human behavior maintains that, in order to understand human social behavior, we must look at both the personalities involved and the situation. (© Owen Franken/Stock, Boston.)

No man is an Iland, intire of itselfe. JOHN DONNE

We are all in the same boat in a stormy sea, and we owe each other a terrible loyalty. G. K. CHESTERTON

17

The Behavior of Groups

Watching Baryshnikov dance, an audience jumps to its feet in unison to shout "Bravo" as the performance comes to an end. When they realize that their plane is about to crash, the passengers of American Airlines Flight 191, leaving Chicago for Los Angeles in April 1979, suddenly grab one another and begin to share emotions and fears. A student in downtown San Francisco observes a demonstration and becomes involved in a riot that follows the demonstration. In each of these instances, individuals become involved with a group of persons, and their actions are influenced by the group.

In citing these examples, we are no longer focusing strictly on the individual, but rather on the behavior of a number of people: according to many people, this is the essence of social psychology. However, social psychologists often prefer to work at the level of the individual, stressing each person's perceptions, beliefs, and actions, and ignoring the interaction that takes place in groups. Some social psychologists have even suggested that groups are not real. The late Floyd Allport used to say "You can't stumble over a group," proposing that groups exist only in the minds of people. According to Allport, groups are no more than shared sets of values, ideas, thoughts, and habits that exist simultaneously in the minds of several persons. Others have argued just as impressively that groups are entities that should be treated as unitary objects in our environment (Durkheim, 1898; Warriner, 1956). Such advocates renounce the suggestion that all social behaviors can be explained adequately at the individual level; they stress the unique aspects of the group process in and of itself (Shaw, 1976).

Clearly, there are a number of perspectives that one can adopt regarding the influence of more than one person in a situation. Most people would probably agree that many of the activities of our lives involve other people. Football teams, families, facul-

ties, and fishing crews all involve the interaction of a group of people. But groups also may be composed of individuals who don't come into close proximity with one another or see one another often. The national sales manager for Frisbees, along with his or her field representatives, may constitute a group; likewise, all the members of an audience at the latest Woody Allen movie may constitute a group.

One basic question, of course, is "How can we define the term *group?*" Although many definitions have been offered (Cartwright & Zander, 1968), perhaps a simple working definition of a group is "Two or more persons who are interacting with one another in such a manner that each person influences and is influenced by each other person" (Shaw, 1976, p. 11). A more comprehensive definition of the term can include some of the following properties: "Interaction between individuals, perceptions of other members and the development of affective ties, and the development of interdependence or roles" (DeLamater, 1974, p. 39).

We can apply the term *aggregate* to collections of individuals who do not interact with one another. Persons standing on a street corner waiting for the light to change, passengers on an uneventful flight, and, in many cases, the members of a class—these people typically do not interact or share feelings to such a degree that they influence one another. However, as the case of the passengers on Flight 191 illustrates, an aggregate can become a group.

In this chapter, we consider the ways in which groups act—how they perform, how members of groups communicate with one another, and how they draw together or split apart. Our survey will look at both the carefully contrived laboratory group, which participants join on an involuntary basis, and real-life groups, such as juries, families, communes, and experiential groups. In addition, we consider relationships between groups and the conflicts that may result from their encounters. First, however, let us turn our attention to a simpler question—how does the presence of other people influence the behavior of the individual?

I. The Influence of Other People

Reaching back in the history of social psychology (and to our memories of the early chapters of this text), we can recall the experiment of Norman Triplett, who was interested in the effects of other people on individual performance. Creating an analogy to bicycle racing (see Chapter 2), Triplett (1897) asked children to wind fishing reels; their performance when they were alone was compared with their performance when another child was present. This experiment marks the earliest attempt to understand how the mere presence of other people—not necessarily acting as a group—can influence behavior. Considerable investigation has followed the initial Triplett venture.

A. *The Effects of an Audience*

On many occasions, we may act individually but, at the same time, be aware that others are watching us. For example, on entering a room full of strangers, we may be painfully (or gleefully) aware that many eyes are focused on us. A guest lecturer may present a talk and have no interaction with the members of the audience. How does awareness of an audience affect behavior?

Many people experience fear and anxiety in the presence of an audience. For example, a survey of people's fears showed that speaking in front of a group is feared more than height, darkness, loneliness, sickness, and even death (Borden, 1980). However, on some occasions, the presence of an audience can give us an extra "charge." For example, athletes report that they perform better before a crowd than they do in an empty stadium (Davis, 1969), and many actors comment on the difference between playing for a full house and playing for a theater that is nearly empty. What accounts for these differences?

First of all, let us define the basic characteristics of the audience situation. The individual is acting or performing a behavior in the presence of a group of people; however, there is no direct interaction between the individual and the audience—rather, the members of the audience are passive observers of the action that is taking place (Geen, 1980).

The influence of the audience depends on a number of factors. Latané and his colleagues (Latané, 1973; Latané & Nida, 1980) have suggested three factors: the number of people in the audience, the immediacy of the audience, and the strength (or status) of the members of the audience. In general, the larger the number of people in the audience, the greater the impact of that audience, although the increments in impact tend to decrease with the addition of each observer. Audiences that are physically present have more impact than those that are at some distance—for example, separated from the performer by a one-way mirror. Finally, the status of audience is important. Latané and Harkins (1976) observed that students who expected to sing before an audience of high-status people reported more tension than those who expected a low-status audience. In Chapter 10, we saw that the specific characteristics of an audience have an effect on performance, as shown by Borden's (1975) experiments with aggression. Observers who were believed to hold values favoring aggression caused an increase in the aggression of the performer; those observers who were believed to be more passive had less effect on the aggressive behavior of the subject.

As you might guess from our discussion in Chapter 16, there are individual differences in reactions to an audience (Paivio, 1965). Some individuals actively seek out an audience; they may be encouraged to improve their performance when an audience is present. The performance of individuals who are anxious about being observed may suffer as a result of the presence of others. Using a social-reinforcement model, Paivio has suggested that many of these differences are due to past experiences in similar situations.

B. *Social Facilitation*

It seems clear, and has been apparent since the early days of psychological research, that an audience can affect the performance of an individual. In some cases, the effects are positive, leading to an increase in the level of performance; in other cases, the effects are negative, causing decreases in the level of performance. Such a confusion of results in one area causes despair and begs for a theory—the history of research on social facilitation illustrates these reactions. **Social facilitation**, a term coined by Floyd Allport (1920), refers to the improvement of individual performance in the presence of other people. Remember, we are concerned with the effect of the mere presence of other people, not with interaction between a person and an audience.

Many years after Allport made his observations, Zajonc (1965) proposed a theoretical model to account for discrepant findings for the effects of an audience. Relying on a Hull-Spence model of learning, Zajonc (1965, 1968) suggested that the presence of others is a source of general arousal, or drive. In the case of responses that are well-learned (or *dominant,* in the Hull-Spence terminology), this drive results in increased levels of performance. In contrast, responses that are not well-learned suffer from increased arousal, since well-learned responses interfere with their performance (**Zajonc & Sales, 1966**). In other words, if you are asked to act in a community play, and it is your first experience with acting, the presence of an audience may be detrimental—you may drop lines, forget your entrance, or suffer a severe case of stage fright. In contrast, an experienced and well-rehearsed actor, appearing before a similar audience, should show improved performance, because arousal leads to an increase in well-learned behaviors. This explanation, which is based on rather simple assumptions, has been quite successful in accounting for most of the findings regarding the effects of an audience on performance (Cottrell, 1972; Geen & Gange, 1977).

Zajonc's formulation doesn't resolve all the issues concerning the effects of an audience. Although Zajonc seemed to assume that the arousal properties of an audience are innate (or wired into the organism), others, most notably Cottrell (1972), argue that the presence of others is a *learned* source of drive. According to Cottrell, it is not the mere presence of others that causes arousal, but rather the anticipation that an audience will make evaluations and judgments of performance. To demonstrate this distinction, subjects have been asked to perform alone, in front of a group of people who are either experts or who implicitly make evaluations, and in front of a group of people who are either nonexperts or who are unable to make evaluations (for example, observers who are blindfolded). These studies (Cottrell, Wack, Sekerak, & Rittle, 1968; Sasfy & Okun, 1974) have supported Cottrell's arguments. Subjects' performance in the first condition was equivalent to their performance in front of the nonexpert or nonevaluative groups, whereas subjects performing in front of judgmental experts showed the effects of greater arousal—increased levels of performance in the case of a well-learned response, and decreased levels of performance in the case of an unfamiliar and complex task.

Other investigators have argued that social-facilitation effects can be explained by a distraction hypothesis (Sanders & Baron, 1975; Baron, Moore, & Sanders, 1978; Sanders, Baron, & Moore, 1978). According to this hypothesis, the presence of an audience provides distraction, and this distraction serves as a source of drive.

As you can see, although there is little doubt that social facilitation occurs, the causes of this phenomenon are a source of lively debate.

C. *The Coacting Audience*

So far, we have concentrated on the effects of a passive audience that merely observes while the actor performs. However, if we go back to the origins of social-facilitation literature in the initial experiment of Triplett, we see that the audience was not passive; it performed a task. How does the situation involving the coacting audience differ from the situations we've described in this chapter?

How would you react in the Triplett situation, winding a fishing reel and being acutely aware of the person next to you engaged in the same task? Many people, particularly in Western societies, would see the situation as a challenge and attempt to do better than their companion. These competitive attitudes (discussed briefly in Chapter 9) were pointed out in early research by Dashiell (1930). He found that people in a coactive situation performed faster but less accurately than people who were working alone. Once again, as pointed out by Zajonc in his initial formulation, characteristics of the task are important. As a source of arousal, competition may improve performance of simple or well-learned tasks, but it may impair the performance of more complex or less familiar tasks. In fact, specific instructions encouraging cooperation in the completion of a complex task result in the improved performance of coactors (Laughlin & Jaccard, 1975), whereas the presence of competitive motives may impair their performance.

Performers in a coacting situation can use one another as sources of information. This modeling effect, discussed in earlier chapters, means that a performer can look to other people for information about the task. New responses can be learned simply by observing the other participants. These new responses are likely to be performed when the other participants are apparently successful in their actions (Bandura, 1965).

Finally, at a more cognitive level, a coacting audience provides a source of social comparison (Festinger, 1954). By observing the behavior of others, we can establish a basis for evaluating our own performance and gauging our reactions to a particular situation. (For another example of the coacting audience, see Box 17-1.)

II. Interaction in Groups

We have begun our consideration of people in interaction with an examination of a simple situation in which an individual is observed or accompanied by one or more persons. However, a group (as we defined the term at the beginning of this chapter) involves more than people performing an activity at a particular time and place. According to a comprehensive definition, groups involve interaction, the development of shared perceptions and affective ties, and interdependence of roles. Let us now turn from the individualistic emphasis and begin to look at the group, rather than the individual, as the unit of analysis.

A. Group Problem Solving and Performance

One question of major interest in the history of group research is whether individuals working together in a group perform more successfully or efficiently than individuals working alone. The reason for such interest is not hard to discover: any organization seeking to maximize its output needs to know how to structure its tasks.

Box 17-1. Coaction in the Movie Theatre.

You go to a funny film and find yourself alone in the theater. Would you laugh less than you would if the theater was filled? The results of a study by Sheldon Levy and William Fenley, Jr. (1979) suggest that you would. During the run of the film "M*A*S*H" in a Houston theater, these investigators instructed observers to sit through the film and record the reactions of the members of the audience during 25 representative scenes. The observers attended 15 showings of the film, and the number of people at the showings varied from 125 to 976. As social-facilitation theory would predict, the size of the audience *did* make a difference. The more people in the audience, the more likely any single member was to laugh heartily at the film. What are the possible explanations for this effect?

Although this question is straightforward, the answer is complex. To begin to formulate an answer, let us first consider two types of group performance: judgment and problem solving.

1. *Judgments and Observations.* If your car is rammed from behind, is it better to have one witness, or a group of onlookers, if you seek accurate testimony (see, for example, Figure 17-1)? If a decision is to be made as to which painting is the best entry in an art contest, is it better to have a single judge, or a team of judges? As a starting point, it is apparent that the particular individuals and the particular task are important considerations. We can assume that a group's performance will be better than that of the average individual acting alone when we are dealing with purely physical tasks, such as pulling a car out of the mud. However, with regard to judgments and

mental tasks, we can't assume that a group's performance will be better or more accurate than the performance of the most proficient group member acting alone; this would require a clear-cut contribution from the group, which is not readily predictable from simple observation or intuition.

In attempting to deal with the issue of group performance versus individual performance, researchers have developed two techniques (Shaw, 1976). The first is called the *statisticized group technique* (Lorge, Fox, Davitz, & Brenner, 1958). In using this technique, researchers average the individual responses of all group members and compare the resulting figure with the average of independent, noninteracting individuals. Although there is an indication that some "group" averages exhibit more accurate judgments of weights, temperatures, and other physical phenomena (Knight, 1921; K. Gordon, 1924), this method fails to consider

Figure 17-1. In a situation such as the one shown here, would a single witness or a group of onlookers be more likely to give an accurate account of what happened? (© Raimondo Borea/Editorial Photocolor Archives).

the social-psychological processes in group interaction (Preston, 1938).

The second technique compares the responses of separated individuals with the responses resulting from a group discussion. (The latter may consist of either a group consensus or individual judgments made after a group discussion.) A variety of judgments and observations have been obtained (Burtt, 1920; Marston, 1924; Jenness, 1932). The comparisons indicate some group superiority, but not as much as one might expect. Shaw's conclusion seems appropriately restrained:

In general, it appears that group judgments are seldom less accurate than the average individual judgment and are often superior. This can be accounted for by the number of judgments contributing to the estimate (Stroop, 1922), by the range of knowledge represented by the individual group members (Jenness, 1932), and by the effects of others on the less confident group members (Gurnee, 1937). It is also apparent that the kind of task may determine whether group judgment will be superior to individual judgments [1976, pp. 60–61].

In summary, when it comes to judgments, the group may or may not be better than the individual. For example, an individual Picasso might well make a more accurate artistic judgment than a group of high school students; in contrast, a group of college seniors might know more about the job market than any single one of those individuals.

2. *Problem Solving.* We can see how a dominant individual might cause a team or committee to make a subjective judgment that is less than optimal. However, are groups better able than individuals to perform problem-solving tasks for which there is one correct answer? Again, the answer is more complex than the question. The term *problem solving* has been used to refer to a wide variety of tasks, varying from counting dots to solving the problems faced by the managements of large business organizations (Hoffman, 1978). Furthermore, the requirements of these tasks frequently vary (Shiflett, 1979). Some tasks are easily divisible, so that the overall problem can be broken down into specialized subtasks, each of which may be performed by one person (Steiner, 1972). Other tasks cannot be broken down into subtasks. Even when subtasks can be defined, they may or may not be obvious to the participants; in the latter case, considerable judgment and negotiation may precede the actual problem-solving attempt (Steiner, 1972).

An example of a problem-solving task in which subtasks are not easily defined is described in Box 17-2. On the basis of a number of studies, we may conclude, along with

---

Box 17-2. Do Groups Solve Problems Better than Individuals?

You may recall the mental problem involving the missionaries and the cannibals. In the task, three cannibals and three missionaries must be transported across a river, in several trips, since the boat holds only two persons at a time. One of the cannibals and all three of the missionaries know how to operate the boat. The crossing must be carried out so that the cannibals on either shore never outnumber the missionaries. In a classic study, Marjorie E. Shaw (1932) used puzzles and problems like this one to compare group and individual problem solving. Subjects worked either in five groups of four persons each or as individuals. In solving such problems, 5 individuals out of 63 produced correct solutions (8%), compared with 8 out of 15 groups (53%). The groups took about 1½ times as long to solve the problems, however. The cost in person-hours was thus greater in the groups. Shaw concluded that the major advantage of the group was its ability to recognize and reject incorrect solutions and suggestions.

Shaw, that "groups produce more and better solutions to problems than do individuals, although the differences in overall time required for solution are not consistently better for either individuals or groups" (M. E. Shaw, 1976, p. 64). However, when the person-hours required for solution are considered, individuals have to be judged as superior.

Brainstorming is another example of a group problem-solving task in which subtasks may be developed but are not immediately apparent. About 25 years ago, an advertising executive named Osborn (1957) began to advocate brainstorming as a device by which groups could come up with new or creative solutions to difficult problems. The ground rules for brainstorming are shown in Table 17-1. Such a technique could be applied to a wide range of problems. For example, an advertising agency might use brainstorming to develop a new slogan, a government agency might use it to predict the effects of a policy change, or a school board might use it to discover ways of handling a teacher shortage.

TABLE 17-1 / *Rules for Brainstorming*

1. Given a problem to solve, all group members are encouraged to express whatever solutions and ideas come to mind, regardless of how preposterous or impractical they may seem.

2. All reactions are recorded.

3. No suggestion or solution can be evaluated until all ideas have been expressed. Ideally, participants should be led to believe that no suggestions will be evaluated at the brainstorming session.

4. The elaboration of one person's ideas by another is encouraged.

Osborn claimed great success with the brainstorming procedure. Empirical evaluations, however, have not consistently produced results to indicate that brainstorming is worth its time (Bouchard, Barsaloux, &

Drauden, 1974). For example, Taylor, Berry, and Block (1958) found that the number of suggestions made by groups did in fact exceed the number made by any given individual working alone. However, when the suggestions of four separate individuals operating under brainstorming instructions were combined, they produced almost twice as many ideas per unit of time as did the face-to-face brainstorming groups of four persons each. This also was the case when the subjects were research scientists who had worked together to solve problems (Dunnette, Campbell, & Jaastad, 1963). Lamm and Trommsdorf (1973) have summarized brainstorming research in the following way: "The empirical evidence clearly indicates that subjects brainstorming in small groups produce fewer ideas than the same number of subjects brainstorming individually. Less clear evidence is available on measures of quality, uniqueness, and variety" (p. 361).

Much of the research on brainstorming groups has been criticized, because it brings together individuals who do not know one another—individuals who are formed into "groups" (for the purpose of the experiment) and then disbanded (Bouchard, 1972). Members of such groups might be reluctant to express some of their wild flights of fancy in front of strangers, even under ground rules that prohibit criticism of any idea. Moreover, such transitory groups may not be highly motivated. It has been shown that training and practice can improve the performance of brainstorming groups (Parnes & Meadow, 1959; D. Cohen, Whitmyre, & Funk, 1960). One of the critical factors may be the degree to which separate subtasks can be defined. If members are selected who readily select subtasks, or areas of specialization, group brainstorming may not involve the mismanagement of time that it is often claimed to generate (R. D. Mann, 1959; Heslin, 1964; Bouchard, 1969; Graham & Dillon, 1974).

To summarize the work on group problem solving, we must consider both the task and the nature of the individuals engaged in the task. Under many circumstances, a group may be better able than an individual to solve a problem; for example, when a task can be divided into subtasks and individual skills can be matched with those particular subtasks (Steiner, 1972). However, when the division of tasks is unspecified, or when the members of a group lack the necessary skills, group performance may fall well below its potential (and even below the level of an individual performing the task alone).

B. *The Perils of Groupthink*

The group, as we have described it so far, appears to be a very rational creature: individuals come together, seek the best solution to a problem, and proceed to perform tasks to the best of their ability (see, for example, Figure 17-2). However, from experience, we know that such an ideal state is not always the case. Groups often make bad decisions, and then go on to defend those decisions with ardor. Social

psychologist Irving Janis, in analyzing a number of case studies in which government policy makers made serious errors, has coined the term **groupthink**, which he defines as "a mode of thinking that people engage in when they are deeply involved in a cohesive in-group, when the members' strivings for unanimity override their motivation to realistically appraise alternative courses of action" (Janis, 1972, p. 9).

Among the situations (or *fiascoes,* to use Janis's own term) analyzed were: the U.S. invasion of the Cuban Bay of Pigs, U.S. involvement in North Korea, the escalation of the Vietnam War, and the lack of preparedness on the part of the United States for the attack on Pearl Harbor during World War II. When is groupthink most likely to occur? Janis defines four conditions. First, a crisis situation is faced by a decision-making group. Second, the group itself must be cohesive—its members must have an esprit

Figure 17-2. A group in process. (© Abigail Heyman/Magnum Photos, Inc.)

de corps, and they need to work together on a continuing basis. Third, the decision-making group isolates itself from the judgments of qualified outsiders. Fourth, in most groupthink situations, the leader of the group presents a favored solution to a problem and actively promotes that solution. According to Janis's analysis, under these conditions, a number of typical symptoms are present. The group begins to perceive itself as invulnerable and unquestionably moral; outsiders are viewed as evil or stupid; and insiders who question the group's decision are pressured or censured so that a front of unanimity is maintained. Janis even suggests that, under these conditions, self-appointed "mindguards" emerge—members who protect the group from information that might shatter its complacency.

In a constructive vein, Janis goes on to suggest ways in which groupthink can be prevented. A leader should encourage dissidence, call on each member of the group to be critical, and reinforce those members who voice criticism of a favored plan. Furthermore, a leader should not present a favored plan at the outset; initially, he or she should describe a problem, not recommend a solution. Finally, Janis suggests that routine procedures should be established by which several independent groups could work on one problem. With such dispersion of energies, it is unlikely that a consensus will develop prematurely. Of course, in order to reach a final decision, the groups must merge.

Despite the fascinating nature of Janis's analysis, relatively few direct tests of his hypotheses have been conducted. One archival study used the public statements of leading decision makers involved in five U.S. foreign-policy crises, three of which were described by Janis as examples of groupthink (Tetlock, 1979). Consistent with Janis's hypothesis, groupthink decision makers made more positive references to the United States and to its allies than did the nongroupthink participants. Moreover, groupthink policy makers were more simplistic in their perceptions of the basic issues. However, in contrast to Janis's suggestion, groupthink members were no less negative than nongroupthink members toward Communist states and their allies.

One laboratory test of groupthink involved the experimental manipulation of group cohesiveness and leadership style (Flowers, 1977). Once again, Janis was partially supported; a closed-leadership style was found to lead to few suggested solutions and a limited use of available facts. Contrary to Janis's hypothesis, however, evidence of groupthink was apparent in both high-cohesive and low-cohesive groups, suggesting that the phenomenon may be more pervasive than Janis had thought. Although the precise symptoms of groupthink remain to be clarified, the fact that it is evidenced even among previously unacquainted college students in a psychology experiment may lead us to conclude that groupthink is a frequent outcome of the group process.

C. *The Polarizing Effects of Group Interaction*

Observations of group discussions reveal that pressures toward uniformity often occur during the decision-making process (Festinger, 1950). In a classic study of the group problem-solving process, Schachter (1951) arranged for one member of a group to maintain a position on a discussion topic that was quite at odds with the positions of the other group members. Initially, reactions to this person, who was called a *deviate* because of his position on the issue, involved a great deal of attention. Other members directed more of their communications toward him than toward each other. However, after it began to be clear that his position on the topic was not going to shift, the others terminated their communications to him and concentrated on resolving their own minor differences.

One very strong outcome of group discussions is a *polarization* of responses; that is, the consensus judgments and opinions resulting from group participation are more extreme than those of the individual participants beforehand (Myers & Lamm, 1976). Initial research in this area focused on the specific question of whether groups are more or less conservative in their decisions than are individuals. This question generated more than a decade of research on what was termed the *risky shift*. This research began with the initial finding by Stoner (1961) that group decisions were riskier than individual decisions, countering the common belief that groups tended to be more conservative than their individual members. (The view that groups are less productive and produce less satisfactory solutions than individuals still pervades popular wisdom; for example, consider the description of a camel as "a horse designed by a committee.")

Most of the research studies that followed Stoner's employed the choice-dilemma questionnaire developed by Kogan and Wallach (1964), one item of which is shown in Figure 17-3. Note that the definition of a risky choice is rather specific in this figure (Mackenzie & Bernhardt, 1968). Subjects are not asked whether they would recommend a risky or a conservative decision; instead, they are asked to estimate what the odds for success would have to be in order for them to choose a risky action. In the typical risky-shift experiment, members of a group respond to the questionnaire individually. Then they form a group to discuss each hypothetical choice and arrive at a unanimous group decision. Each subject is then asked to go back over each item on the questionnaire and, once again, indicate an individual decision. Most studies that used this method found that group decisions were indeed riskier, and a variety of theoretical formulations were offered to explain this initially unpredicted finding (Dion, Baron, & Miller, 1970; Cartwright, 1971; Clark, 1971; Pruitt, 1971a, 1971b; Vinokur, 1971). In a group, the shift toward risk is dependent on three conditions: group discussion, "a certain divergence between the individual positions, and a certain normative quality in the material on which the discussion is based" (Moscovici & Doise, 1974, pp. 271–272). In other words, the members of the group must show some disagreement at the beginning of the discussion, and the

Figure 17-3. A choice-dilemma questionnaire item. (From *Risk Taking: A Study in Cognition and Personality*, by Nathan Kogan and Michael A. Wallach. Copyright © 1964 by Holt, Rinehart and Winston. Reprinted by permission of Holt, Rinehart and Winston.)

Mr. A., an electrical engineer who is married and has one child, has been working for a large electronics corporation since graduating from college five years ago. He is assured of a life-time job with a modest, though adequate, salary and liberal pension benefits upon retirement. On the other hand, it is very unlikely that his salary will increase much before he retires. While attending a convention, Mr. A. is offered a job with a small, newly founded company which has a highly uncertain future. The new job would pay more to start and would offer the possibility of a share in the ownership if the company survived the competition of the larger firms.

Imagine that you are advising Mr. A. Listed below are several probabilities or odds of the new company proving financially sound. *Please check the lowest probability that you would consider acceptable to make it worthwhile for Mr. A. to take the new job.*

____ The chances are 1 in 10 that the company will prove financially sound.

____ The chances are 3 in 10 that the company will prove financially sound.

____ The chances are 5 in 10 that the company will prove financially sound.

____ The chances are 7 in 10 that the company will prove financially sound.

____ The chances are 9 in 10 that the company will prove financially sound.

____ Place a check here if you think Mr. A. should *not* take the new job no matter what the probabilities.

topic itself must have some implications for socially accepted values.

More recently, investigators have realized that, although group discussion often produces a shift in individual opinions, such a shift is not necessarily in the direction of greater risk. It has been shown that, if the initial opinions of the group tend toward conservatism, then the shift resulting from group discussion will be toward a more extreme conservative opinion (Myers & Bishop, 1970; Fraser, 1971). Therefore, the term **group polarization** has effectively replaced the term *risky shift* as a general description of this particular phenomenon.

Given the apparent pervasiveness of group polarization, we should ask *why* such polarization occurs. What causes the members of a group to shift their opinions toward an extreme position? Three general kinds of explanations have been offered. These explanations are based on group-decision rules, interpersonal comparisons, and informational influence (Myers & Lamm, 1976).

Explanations based on group-decision rules focus on the statistical prediction of the group product, using specific combinations of individual preferences. Although a variety of social-decision schemes exist (Davis, 1973), most investigators have examined the principle of majority rule; that is, a group will shift toward that pole favored by the majority of members, because initially deviant members fall in line with the majority. Some investigators have argued that group polarization effects are a statistical artifact rather than the outcome of a real, internalized change in opinions; others, however, have simply tried to predict specific changes without a concern for psychological underpinnings.

Although attempts to predict specific changes are laudable, we would like to have a better understanding of the psychological mechanisms involved in these changes. Explanations based on interpersonal comparison and informational influence provide this understanding. According to the *interpersonal-comparison* explanation, individuals in a group shift their opinions in order to conform to the opinion of the group

(see Chapter 14). Motives suggested for this behavior include the desire for a favorable evaluation by others and a concern for self-presentation. This explanation focuses on the characteristics of the group members, not on information that might develop in the course of group discussion. As stated by Myers and Lamm (1976), the interpersonal-comparison explanation suggests that "group polarization is a source effect, not a message effect" (p. 613). Andrews and Johnson (1971) have called one variation of this position the "climb on the bandwagon" effect, believed to be particularly evident when members of the group anticipate future interactions with one another in other settings.

Informational-influence explanations stress the cognitive learning that results from exposure to persuasive arguments during the course of group discussion. Here the emphasis is on the actual content (or the "message") of the group discussion, and the degree to which members are persuaded by the new information that is presented. This persuasion may involve mutual reinforcement. For example, Myers and Bishop (1971) found that 76% of the arguments in a group were in support of the position that was held by most of the members. Therefore, a shift toward extremity occurs because the tendency to accept dominant positions is reinforced by statements of attitudes that reflect one's own attitudes.

The adoption of a more extreme position is not caused solely by being exposed to arguments. In addition, when group members hear such arguments, they generally process the information, rehearse their arguments, and then actively commit themselves to the position of the group. Moscovici and Zavalloni (1969) believe that group discussion leads to an enhancement of participants' involvement with the issues and their confidence that their position is the correct one.

In summary, group polarization effects are indeed real; they may cause a group to become either more conservative or more risky, depending on the initial opinions of the majority of group members. When emphasis is placed on reaching a consensus, group members are more likely to shift their positions. Moreover, polarization is most likely to occur during active group discussions.

III. Qualities Affecting the Influence of Groups

Groups are as varied as individuals. Any discussion of the effects of groups must take into account some of their most variable and salient characteristics. In this section, we consider three of these characteristics: group size, communication opportunities, and cohesiveness.

A. *The Size of the Group*

Even within the limits of the definition of *group* that we introduced at the beginning of the chapter, it is possible to conceive of groups that range in size from a couple on their honeymoon to all the members of the U.S. Congress or the Canadian House of Commons. Most experimental research, however, has concentrated on small groups (that is, from 3 to 10 people). The most frequently studied topic has been the relationship between a group's size and its performance on mental tasks, although some investigators have considered physical tasks, as shown in Box 17-3.

There have been some efforts (probably unwise) to specify the "ideal size" of problem-solving groups. For example, P. E. Slater (1958) concluded that groups of 5 were the most effective for dealing with mental tasks in which group members collect and exchange information and make a decision based on the evaluation of that information. Osborn (1957), the developer of brainstorming, suggested that the optimum size of such groups ranges from 5 to 10 members.

Box 17-3. Many Hands Make Light the Work: The Case of Social Loafing.

Earlier, in discussing the relative merits of groups versus individuals, we suggested that, for some physical tasks, such as pulling a car out of the mud, a group would be clearly superior. But would each person work harder in such a situation than he or she would work alone? Two experiments by Latané, Williams, and Harkins (1979) suggest that "social loafing," rather than increased effort, takes place in group endeavors. In one situation, subjects were asked to clap as loudly as they could; in the second instance, they were asked to cheer as loudly as they could. In each case, subjects performed the task alone, in pairs, in groups of 4, and in groups of 6. As shown in the graph below, individual effort exhibited a precipitous drop as the size of the group increased. Part of this decrement was the result of faulty coordination: hearing other people creates problems in hearing one's own sounds and provides some distraction if the cheers and claps are not in synchrony. When these factors are controlled, however—when subjects cannot hear the other people—a decrease in individual performance is still found, suggesting that people "loaf" when other people share the load.

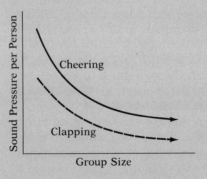

From "Many Hands Make Light the Work: The Causes and Consequences of Social Loafing," by B. Latané, K. Williams, and S. Harkins, *Journal of Personality and Social Psychology*, 1979, *37*, 822–832. Copyright 1979 by the American Psychological Association. Reprinted by permission.

Conclusions regarding the optimum size of problem-solving groups are probably oversimplifications. First, there are varying criteria for determining what is successful. Smaller groups may be more satisfying to participants, because they have a chance to express their opinions fully; however, the addition of a few more members may add essential skills and make for a better solution to the task, even if it hurts members' participation and morale. Second, tasks vary greatly in their demands. Some tasks may require only one person, whereas other tasks can be performed only by several individuals (Hackman & Vidmar, 1972; Steiner, 1972). Third, the amount of structure in the group interacts with its size (B. W. Jorgensen, 1973). Although it may be true that groups composed of more than 5 people are less satisfying than small groups, larger groups can be effective without any major loss of morale.

The effects of group size are important in everyday life. We know that the traditional jury in England, the United States, and Canada consists of 12 persons who must come to a unanimous decision. However, a number of U.S. states are experimenting—mostly in civil cases—with smaller juries and majority verdicts (Kalven & Zeisel, 1966). Several other countries already use trial juries of fewer than 12 people (Saks & Ostrom, 1975). What are the effects of these variations on group process and outcome? Do smaller juries spend less time in deliberation than 12-member juries? Are smaller juries more likely to reach guilty verdicts? Are their verdicts less likely to be correct?

A recent study used mock juries to examine some of these questions (J. H. Davis, Kerr, Atkin, Holt, & Meek, 1975). Juries composed of either 6 or 12 undergraduates listened to a 45-minute recording of a trial —an abbreviated version of the transcript of an actual rape trial. Some "juries" of subjects were instructed to come to a unanimous decision regarding the guilt or innocence of the accused rapist within 30 minutes. Others were told that their jury should reach a two-thirds-majority decision.

It was found that 89% of the 6-person juries and 83% of the 12-person juries judged the defendant to be innocent.

Moreover, the judgments of the groups forced to unanimity were similar to those of the two-thirds-majority groups (81% and 92%, respectively, returned a verdict of "innocent"). The major differences were found in the group *processes* rather than the verdicts. Table 17-2 indicates that unanimous juries needed a larger number of poll votes before reaching a verdict, as well as a longer deliberation time. On the basis of this study, it would first appear that Supreme Court decisions permitting majority decisions are safe enough. Unanimous juries and majority juries appear to produce about the same results. But this is not the whole story. Further analyses by Davis and his colleagues indicated that, of the 36 juries operating under the two-thirds rule, 26 had a two-thirds majority on their first poll (but did not have unanimity). Of these 26, a total of 9 juries (35%) decided *immediately* on the majority position, and several more deliberated only a short time after the first vote. The non-unanimous rule may lead to a "cursory consideration of dissenting views" (Davis et al., 1975, p. 12).

B. *Communication Opportunities*

Group size is meaningless when group members have difficulty in communicating with one another. Real-world groups sometimes establish restricted channels through which messages may go; for example, members of President Nixon's Cabinet complained that they were not allowed to speak with the president directly; they could speak only with his second-level staff members (Rather & Gates, 1974). Relationships between individuals may affect communication channels; there may be two members of the church's board of deacons who "haven't spoken to each other for years." Location of some group members in a different building may inhibit communication between them. (In Chapter 19, we consider some of the effects of the physical environment on group members' interactions.)

We refer to prescribed patterns of communication as **communication networks** (Shaw, 1964, 1978). A number of communication networks are represented schematically in Figure 17-4.

T A B L E 17 - 2 / *Mean Number of Polls and Mean Time (in Minutes) to Verdict in Each Experimental Condition in Davis et al. (1975) Study*

| Assigned Social-Decision Scheme | Jury Size | | Total |
	6 Persons	12 Persons	
Unanimity			
Polls	2.39	2.89	2.64
Time	13.28	19.22	16.25
Two-thirds majority			
Polls	1.94	1.78	1.86
Time	11.83	7.61	9.72
Total			
Polls	2.17	2.33	2.25
Time	12.56	13.42	12.99

From "The Decision Processes of 6- and 12-Person Mock Juries Assigned Unanimous and Two-Thirds Majority Rules," by J. H. Davis, N. L. Kerr, R. S. Atkin, R. Holt, and D. Meek, *Journal of Personality and Social Psychology*, 1975, *32*, 1–14. Copyright 1975 by the American Psychological Association. Reprinted by permission.

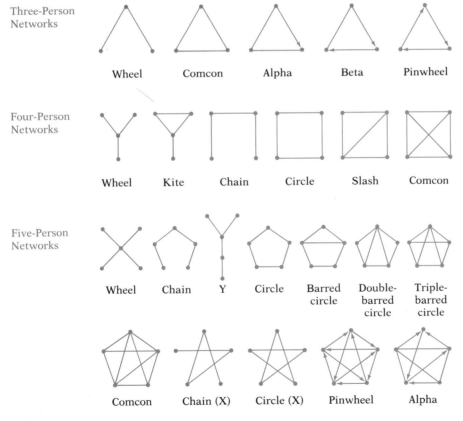

Figure 17-4. Communication networks used in experimental investigations. Dots represent positions, lines represent communication channels, and arrows indicate one-way channels. (From "Communication Networks," by M. E. Shaw. In L. Berkowitz (Ed.), *Advances in Experimental Social Psychology*, Vol. 1. Copyright 1964 by Academic Press, Inc. Reprinted by permission of the author and publisher.)

For example, among the five-person networks, consider the "wheel." This gives great control to the person in the middle; he or she can communicate with each of the other four members, but they (in *peripheral positions*) cannot communicate with each other. They can communicate only with the *central person.* If such a communication network were established as the ground rules at the formation of a new group, the central-position person would probably emerge as the leader (Hirota, 1953; M. E. Shaw, 1954; M. E. Shaw & Rothschild, 1956). In such cases, possession of information leads to power.

The "Y" and "chain" networks in Figure 17-4 lead to centralized organization, but the "circle" networks do not facilitate the emergence of a dominant leader (Leavitt, 1951). In real-life groups that have a "circle" communication network (a relatively unlikely one) or a "comcon" network, in which every member is able to communicate with everyone else, it is impossible to predict which position will lead to leadership and dominance. In the case of these networks, the individual personalities and skills of group members are the determining factors.

What effects do communication networks have on productivity? Which networks are most satisfying to group members? The second question can be answered simply. People prefer positions in which they have greater opportunities for communication and participation. "Silent" partners do not like to remain quiet. The central position in the "wheel," the "chain," and the "Y" is rated as a satisfying one, whereas the morale of persons in the peripheral positions in these same networks is poor (Leavitt, 1951). Networks that permit decentralized communication lead to higher morale for persons at each position.

The efficiency of various communication networks is dependent on the task faced by the group. Leavitt (1951) found that a centralized network—such as a "wheel" or a "Y"—was most efficient with respect to the time required for the solution of a problem, the number of errors made, and the number of messages communicated. However,

Leavitt used a simple symbol-identification task that required only the collection and straightforward assembling of information by one person, analogous to collecting the pieces of a simple jigsaw puzzle and putting them together.

M. E. Shaw (1954) used tasks that drew on the problem-solving abilities of group members and the active manipulation of information. Shaw found that, in dealing with complex problems, the "circle" was most efficient, whereas the "wheel" was least efficient, as measured in time required to reach a solution. The decentralized networks were able to detect and correct errors more rapidly than the "wheel" or the "Y." There is yet another aspect of the story. The "wheel" groups required fewer messages to find a solution. The difference in outcomes for simple and complex tasks is a consistent one, as Table 17-3 indicates. Once again, we see how important it is to consider the nature of the task when we ask questions about group composition.

C. *Cohesiveness*

The spirit of closeness—or lack of it—in a group can have an important effect on the behavior of its members. For example, sportswriters are fond of observing that certain athletic teams (see, for instance, Figure 17-5) have the "best material" or "personnel," but that "they just can't put it together." In such cases, it is likely that the absence of closeness—or even the presence of hostilities among team members—is influential in the team's less-than-expected performance. A number of terms have been used to describe the variable of closeness, including "we-feeling" and "emotional climate" (Vraa, 1974). The most frequently used term is group **cohesiveness**, defined as a "characteristic of the group in which forces acting on members to remain in the group are greater than the total forces acting on them to leave it" (J. H. Davis, 1969, p. 78). In other words, groups in which members like one another and want to remain in one another's presence are cohesive; groups in which members are un-

TABLE 17-3 / *Number of Comparisons Showing Differences between Centralized ("Wheel," "Chain," "Y") and Decentralized ("Circle," "Comcon") Networks as a Function of Task Complexity*

	Simple Problems[a]	Complex Problems[b]	Total
Time			
Centralized faster	14	0	14
Decentralized faster	4	18	22
Messages			
Centralized sent more	0	1	1
Decentralized sent more	18	17	35
Errors			
Centralized made more	0	6	6
Decentralized made more	9	1	10
No difference	1	3	4
Satisfaction			
Centralized higher	1	1	2
Decentralized higher	7	10	17

[a] Simple problems: identification tasks involving symbols, letters, numbers, and colors.

[b] Complex problems: arithmetic, word-arrangement, sentence construction, and discussion problems.

From "Communication Networks," by M. E. Shaw. In L. Berkowitz (Ed.), *Advances in Experimental Social Psychology*, Vol. 1. Copyright 1964 by Academic Press, Inc. Reprinted by permission of the author and publisher.

Figure 17-5. Successful performance by a team is partly the result of the cohesiveness, or spirit of closeness, among the team members. (© Paul Fusco/Magnum Photos, Inc.)

attracted to one another, and groups that are breaking up, are said to be low in cohesiveness. As **M. E. Shaw** (1976) notes, group members who are attracted to the group work harder to achieve its goals; therefore, cohesiveness leads to higher productivity. A close-knit fraternity, for example, is more likely to make elaborate house decorations for the homecoming weekend and engage successfully in intramural sports than a less cohesive fraternity. This example assumes that the goals or norms of the group favor productivity; in contrast, if the group norm is to *avoid* work, we could expect the highly cohesive group to be less productive.

Within any organization, there may be many groups that participate in overall activities. The goal of one particular group might not reflect the goal of the organization of which it is a part. However, highly cohesive groups are more likely than low cohesive groups to agree on a common goal (Schachter, Ellertson, McBride, & Gregory, 1951; L. Berkowitz, 1954; J. H. Davis, 1969). In our discussion of groupthink, we saw that highly cohesive groups present dangers, as well as the promise of better group performance, to their members.

Group cohesiveness is often related to the quality of task performance, because the members of cohesive groups enjoy one another and are not reluctant to involve one another in their search for solutions to tasks. However, there is a danger: as J. H. Davis (1969) notes, when the interaction of group members is extremely pleasurable in and of itself, little energy is devoted to the completion of the group's tasks.

Uniformity is stressed in cohesive groups. Back (1951) found that members of cohesive dyads changed their opinions in the direction of their partner's opinions more than members of less cohesive dyads. Similar findings with larger groups have been reported by Festinger, Gerard, Hymovitch, Kelley, and Raven (1952), and by Lott and Lott (1961). When you like the other members of a group, there may be a greater tendency to go along with their opinions, believing that harmony will enhance the good feelings that are present.

IV. Groups in Action

The history of social psychology's interest in group behavior presents a picture of waxing and waning concerns. During the 1940s and 1950s, with the impetus of Lewin's field theory, many investigators believed that groups should be studied extensively both within the confines of the laboratory and in natural settings. During the 1960s and early 1970s, however, many investigators retreated to their laboratories and, in many instances, abandoned the study of groups altogether. Some of the research conducted during that period was not very good. In fact, in reviewing literature on group processes during the 1960s, some observers suggested that research on groups had fallen victim to a psychological Gresham's law, by which "bad research drives out good" (Helmreich, Bakeman, & Scherwitz, 1973). Even those who maintained quality in their research changed their approach to the study of groups. As Steiner (1974) has observed, the study of groups became individualistic in its orientation. Group processes were studied from the perspective of individuals—their individual attitudes, satisfactions, and productivity.

During the 1960s, much of the laboratory research on groups seemed to violate the very definition of the term *group.* For example, in some studies, "groups" of students were formed on the spur of the moment and told that they would either like one another or dislike one another. Although it is true that the people in these groups did interact, the investigator specified roles and norms, and any affective ties that occurred were quite transitory and artificial (DeLamater, 1974).

Despite this history of abuse and neglect by social psychologists, groups have continued to flourish in the real world. The jury system continues to be a part of the judicial process; although their doom is occasionally forecast, families continue to form the basis of most societies; alternative forms of families, such as communes, appear repeatedly; and new forms of group therapy are discussed in the pages of psychiatric journals and the popular press. In this section we consider some of these groups.

A. *Juries*

Juries represent an important example of real-life groups in action; as we saw in Chapter 1, they are a rich area for social-psychological investigation. Unfortunately, legal restrictions preclude the study of actual juries in operation. Perhaps the closest approach to an actual jury situation is found in the work of Strodtbeck and his colleagues (Strodtbeck & Mann, 1956; Strodtbeck, James, & Hawkins, 1957; James, 1959), who drew their subjects from actual jury rosters, assembled them in a courtroom, and asked them to listen to a recording of a real trial in the presence of court officials. The subsequent jury-deliberation process was conducted in as realistic a manner as possible. Overall, Strodtbeck came as close as an investigator can come to observing jury behavior without intruding on the actual judicial process.

One focus of the Strodtbeck research was the roles that develop during the course of jury deliberations. High-status members participated more than low-status members, and they were perceived as being more influential. The foreman of the group was likely to be a high-status person. Sex differences appeared as well. Women expressed more positive reactions to other jurors during the deliberation phase, whereas men were more likely to attempt to give answers. Overall, the groups felt that the members who had offered the most answers were the most helpful, suggesting that the males were somewhat more valued in the group than the females.

James (1959) examined the specific content of jury deliberations and found that a surprising 50% of the discussion was devoted to personal experiences and opinions. Approximately 25% of the discussion was devoted to procedural issues, 15% to the actual testimony, and 8% to the judge's instructions to the jury. Highly educated jurors emphasized procedure and instruc-

tions, whereas those members with only a grade-school education were more likely to focus on opinion, testimony, and personal experiences (Gerbasi, Zuckerman, & Reis, 1977).

In contrast to these studies of jury process, studies of the outcome of jury deliberations have considered the ways in which various compositions of juries affect their ultimate decision regarding the accused. For example, in the study conducted by Davis and his colleagues that we discussed earlier, it was shown that the size of the jury (6 versus 12 persons) had little effect on their ultimate decision. Group-polarization effects have been found in simulated jury settings. When the evidence for guilt is weak, individuals tend to shift toward a more lenient decision after their deliberation; however, when the evidence for guilt is strong, deliberation leads to harsh judgments (Myers & Kaplan, 1976). The decision rules that are imposed on a jury also can have an effect (Davis, Bray, & Holt, 1976). For example, a hung jury is, not surprisingly, more likely to occur when unanimity is required than when only a majority decision is needed (Kerr, Atkin, Stasser, Meek, Holt, & Davis, 1976).

Jury behavior provides an exciting area of investigation for the social psychologist. Although many studies of the judicial process have focused on individual decision making (Davis, Bray, & Holt, 1976), reflecting the individualistic bias that Steiner (1974) noted in group research, there is a growing recognition that group behavior must be studied in context, and that the factors of duration and commitment present in a real jury may create a situation that is quite different from the simulated-jury situation in the laboratory experiment.

B. *Families*

In contrast to the jury, in which members initially are strangers, the family shows us a group in which members maintain extensive and long-term interaction. The dynamics of the family may be much more intensive, and much more complex, than those of the jury. This complexity has caused many investigators to shy away from the family as a focus of investigation, whereas others have attempted to create "simulated" families, in which specific factors can be controlled (Waxler & Mishler, 1978). Although certainly no one would argue that such an artificial family is the same as the real thing, such attempts have pointed to certain consistent factors that may operate in both simulated and real families. For example, Bodin (reported in Waxler & Mishler, 1978) found that artificial families and real families employed the same general modes of resolving problems; however, mothers in the real families were less compromising than the "mothers" in the ad hoc groups. After comparing real and artificial husband/wife dyads, Ryder (1968) concluded that "the differences between married and split dyads seem much better described by noting that subjects treat strangers more gently and generally more nicely than they do their spouses" (p. 237)!

Other investigators have preferred to study real families exclusively; for example, they investigate the ways in which demographic variables affect the pattern of family interaction. Strodtbeck (1951) studied husband/wife decision making among Protestant Texan, Navajo, and Mormon couples. He found that Mormon husbands were much more powerful than their wives; Navajo wives were more powerful than their husbands, reflecting the matriarchal nature of Navajo society; and the Protestant Texan couples exhibited equality in their decision-making process. Expanding the dyad to a triad (including a mother, a father, and an adolescent son), and considering two other cultures (Jewish and Italian), Strodtbeck (1958) again found evidence for cultural differences. Italian fathers were much more powerful than their wives and their sons; in Jewish families, parents shared power and had more power than their sons.

Although Strodtbeck's findings are intriguing, they tell us little about the causes of cultural differences. One way in which we could circumvent this problem would be to conduct extensive longitudinal studies of

families, observing a number of families over many years, noting changes in structure (for example, the birth of a child, or the death of a grandparent), and relating these structural changes to differences in the process of family interaction. Although attempts have been made to conduct this form of research (Scott, 1962; Borke, 1967), it is probably obvious that such an approach is incredibly time-consuming: the project could outlive the investigator! Furthermore, this approach doesn't permit us to make precise cause-and-effect statements, though very suggestive findings may emerge.

Recently, many investigators of family structure and process have introduced experimental interventions, attempting to show clearly how specific variables affect family interaction (Waxler & Mishler, 1978). For example, Bandura, Ross, and Ross (1963b) experimentally varied the status of parents' roles and their reward power, and then looked at the imitation behavior of children. Within this framework, they found that children are more likely to imitate the behaviors of the high-status parent, regardless of who is giving or receiving rewards.

Many people would, of course, question whether these experimental situations have much to do with real-life families, with their complex histories of interactions, joys, and sorrows. This question must be answered cautiously. On the one hand, it is quite likely that some of the characteristics of artificial groups and the results of laboratory group experiments are relevant to the family; they will help to point out some of the critical variables in family interaction. On the other hand, there may be no real substitute for more intensive, longitudinal studies of actual family interaction. The challenge of this kind of investigation is great, but its potential for expanding our understanding of group behavior is equally great.

C. Communes

The traditional nuclear family is generally a very small unit, although extended family structures can expand the group to include a large number of people. We can see communes as forms of the family, often developed as alternatives to traditional family units. Although religious and political communes have existed throughout history, the 1970s saw an acceleration of the development of communes. According to one estimate, more than 5000 communes were established in the United States alone during a five-year period around 1970 (Westhues, 1972).

The purposes of these communal developments varied (see Table 17-4). In one case, Twin Oaks in Virginia, a commune was formed in order to put scientific principles (in this case, Skinnerian behaviorism) to a real-life test. In other instances, such as the tragic example of the People's Temple group in Guyana, the alleged aim was religious freedom and an escape from perceived persecution. Although communes vary widely in size, purpose, and location, it is possible to form a general definition that encompasses most of the particular forms of communal living. We will define a *commune* as a group of people who share time, space, resources, and energy in an effort to create an alternative experiment in intimate group living. The inclusion of "alternative experiment" separates communes from fraternities, sororities, and traditional religious orders. Moreover, intimacy distin-

TABLE 17-4 / *Types of Contemporary Communes*

1. Hip-psychedelic and anarchistic communes (heavily into drugs; no consistent group goals)

2. Communes based on Skinnerian behaviorism (Twin Oaks, outside Louisa, Virginia, is the oldest example.)

3. Group-marriage communes (Harrad West, in California, is an example.)

4. Religious communes (includes both traditional ones such as Koinonia and "New Age" religious communes such as "Jesus People" groups)

5. Ideological communes (that possess a particular political or ideological viewpoint)

guishes communes from these other groups, though the inclusion of the term *intimate* in our definition should not be interpreted to mean that nontraditional sexual relationships are characteristic of all communal groups. Communes also can be defined in terms of their shared values, which usually include camaraderie, trust, openness, experimentation, and the unity of body and mind (see Figure 17-6).

Figure 17-6. Assumptions about human nature in communal groups. Most members of most communal groups share certain assumptions: that human nature is perfectible, that cooperation is natural, that individual needs and community needs can be integrated, and that there is a unity of body and mind. (Copyright 1973, G. B. Trudeau. Used by permission of Universal Press Syndicate. All rights reserved.)

Some communes do not last very long; others have been in existence for several generations (Zablocki, 1971). Can we distinguish successful communes on the basis of social/psychological qualities? In part, of course, such an effort depends on the way in which we define *success* for a commune. According to many observers, a commune is successful as an alternative experiment in group living if it lasts and achieves its specific goals. Group longevity, low turnover rates, and members' satisfaction are used as criteria for this assessment. Melville (1972) suggests that a commune's success is measured by the fate of the ideas it reflects. A more straightforward, if somewhat amusing, assessment was made by an advocate of communal groups: "Of course communes work—I'm in my fourth" (quoted by Kanter, 1972, p. 215).

Kanter sees the degree of members' commitment to the values of the communal group as central to the group's success. She suggests that a person commits to the group "to the extent that he sees it as expressing or fulfilling some fundamental part of himself; . . . to the degree that he perceives no conflict between its requirements and his own needs; . . . and to the degree that he can no longer meet his needs elsewhere. When a person is committed, what he wants to do . . . is the same as what he has to do" (1972, p. 66). Therefore, commitment ensures the stability of the group and its ability to overcome challenges from without and within.

Six social-psychological processes have been identified as crucial in building commitment to a group. Some of these processes involve "detaching" individuals from other allegiances; others involve "attaching" individuals to the group in order to increase their dependence. Two of the processes aim for a perception of the group as the provider of benefits in the form of energy and resources that members would lose if they left the group. For instance, the process of *sacrifice* requires the giving up of something (such as lucrative positions) in order to belong to the group. The process of *investment* mandates that all group members give a portion of their resources to the group. In the case of Jonestown, all money was turned over to the Reverend Jones, and in the grisly aftermath of the mass suicide, locked trunks containing hundreds of welfare checks, pension funds, and other financial resources were found in the private quarters of Jim Jones.

Two other processes—renunciation and communion—provide each group member with emotional gratification and secure the loyalty of each person to the group. *Renunciation* necessitates "giving up competing relationships outside the communal group and individualistic, exclusive attachments within" (Kanter, 1972, p. 73). *Communion* involves the development of a meaningful relatedness through the whole group.

A third set of commitment processes, which provides direction and purpose to the group members, involves a value orientation. *Mortification* is the term Kanter assigns to the rejection of certain elements of the person's former identity—those that might be at variance with the group's values. The other process, *transcendence*, involves finding a sense of meaning, "of rightness, certainty, and conviction" through the communal group.

Kanter suggests that, if these six processes are incorporated into the organization of a commune, the group will be able to develop the commitment necessary for its survival. Many of the specific strategies Kanter detected in her analysis of 19th-century utopian communities have been noted by observers of contemporary communes. (Many, for example, can be identified in the development of Jonestown, to again cite the most recent and most notorious example.) The fact that similar strategies have been observed by experts on organizational development and small-group dynamics contributes to the validity of generalizing from the experience of communes to other facets of society.

D. *Experiential Groups*

During the past 20 years, we have witnessed an increase in the number of experiential groups, in which individuals have sought to improve their own skills or lifestyles through participation in groups.

Through the group experience itself, individual changes are sought (Shaw, 1976). Such groups take many forms and have a variety of names: T-groups, sensitivity groups, encounter groups, EST, and consciousness-raising groups, to cite only a few.

T-group (which stands for "training group") is a technique originally developed by Kurt Lewin and his colleagues. They developed the technique while leading a workshop on the use of small groups as a vehicle for personal and social change (R. Lippitt, 1949). The methods they used in their workshop were rather traditional. During the evenings, the staff would meet to discuss the daily events. One evening, to the surprise of all, three trainees wanted to listen to the staff's discussion. In an interview obtained by Back (1972), Lippitt later described what happened:

And on this particular night, three of the trainees, three school teachers who hadn't gone home that evening, stuck their heads in the door and asked if they could come in, sit and observe and listen, and Kurt (Lewin) was rather embarrassed, and we all were expecting him to say no, but he didn't, he said, "Yes, sure, come on in and sit down." And we went right ahead as though they weren't there, and pretty soon one of them was mentioned and her behavior was described and discussed, and the trainer and the researcher had somewhat different observations, perceptions of what had happened, and she became very agitated and said that wasn't the way it happened at all, and she gave her perception. And Lewin got quite excited about this additional data and put it on the board to theorize it, and later on in the evening the same thing happened in relation to one of the other two. She had a different perception on what was being described as an event in that group she was in. So Lewin was quite excited about the additional data, and the three at the end of the evening asked if they could come back again the next night, and Lewin was quite positive that they could; *we* had more doubts about it. And the next night the whole fifty were there and were every night, and so it became the most significant training event of the day as this feedback and review of process of events that had gone on during the work sessions of the day. And as Ken Benne, Lee Bradford, and I discussed this, actually it was at a hamburger joint after one of these evenings, we felt the evi-

dence was so clear that the level of our observations of the phenomena about these sessions were a major basis for reorganizations of perceptions and attitude change and of linking up to some degree attitudes and values with intentions and behavior [Back, 1972, pp. 8–9].[1]

From this accidental beginning, a huge industry of group experiences has developed that uses the group as a basis for individual change. The original National Training Laboratory, developed by Lewin and his associates, generally does training with a specific purpose (Hare, 1976). Based in Washington, D.C. (with summer workshops in Bethel, Maine) NTL engages in work for personnel departments and government agencies, and it conducts sessions for individuals who are concerned with personal growth.

Encounter groups are a product of the freewheeling style of California; not surprisingly, a headquarters for encounter-group experiences is Esalen, located in the Big Sur area of northern California. Often, these groups stress experience for its own sake. As Wolfe (1968) has cynically noted, "Esalen was a place where educated middle-class adults came in the summer to try to get out of The Rut and wiggle their fannies a bit" (p. 119).

What are the effects of participation in experiential groups? Since such groups vary in composition, duration, purpose, and procedures, it's difficult to answer this question. Moreover, systematic research on the phenomenon of experiential groups is still in its infancy (Lieberman, 1976). The problems in establishing control groups are similar to those encountered in research on the effectiveness of psychotherapy. Changes in actual behavior are often difficult to detect, and they are difficult to measure after participants have returned to their homes. Much research falls back on the use of participants' self-reports regarding the benefits of experiential groups—a procedure that is rife with demand characteristics. (Someone

[1] From *Beyond Words: The Story of Sensitivity Training and the Encounter Movement*, by K. W. Back. Copyright 1972 by the Russell Sage Foundation. Reprinted by permission.

who has paid $250 for a weekend group encounter would be unlikely to admit that it was a flop.)

Despite the weak basis for drawing conclusions, Shaw (1976) has offered four tentative hypotheses concerning the effects of experiential groups:

1. The discrepancy between the perceived self and the ideal self decreases as a function of participation in experiential groups.

2. Participants in experiential groups perceive changes in their feelings and behavior as a consequence of the group experience.

3. Observers report perceived changes in members' behavior following participation in experiential groups.

4. Under some conditions, participation in experiential groups results in severe psychological disturbances.

In summary, it is difficult at this time to validate (in accepted scientific fashion) the exact effects of experiential groups. The structural elements present in the many varieties of these groups are only beginning to be identified (Lieberman, 1976). Nonetheless, experiential groups are popular and powerful, and they underline the pervasiveness of the group process.

V. Intergroup Conflict

Groups in our society are like a series of overlapping and interlocking boxes. On the one hand, small groups can be subsumed by large groups. For example, the family may be one part of a neighborhood, and the neighborhood may be one part of a city. Here the question is one of the level of analysis at which one wants to study groups —in small units, such as the family or a three-person laboratory group, or in large units, such as a commune or a large-scale multinational organization.

On the other hand, at either of these levels, we can consider the conflicts that may occur between groups. The legendary Hatfields and McCoys, for example, represent the history of two families in conflict. Modern politics often presents us with case studies of nations in conflict with one another. What happens when two groups are in conflict?

A. *Bargaining and Negotiation*

When two groups are in conflict, they must devise a means of resolving that conflict. For example, union and management negotiate contracts on a periodic basis, and nations often negotiate treaties. In these and many other situations, each group approaches the negotiation with its own particular set of goals, which might not reflect the goals of the other group. Union workers want higher wages, but management wants to hold down prices. Russia wants a strategic arms advantage, but the United States wants to ensure its military superiority. How are such conflicts resolved?

Social psychologists, as well as economists, political scientists, and mathematicians, have devoted considerable energy to the study of the bargaining process. (For summaries of this work, see Chertkoff & Esser, 1976; Davis, Laughlin, & Komorita, 1976; Pruitt & Kimmell, 1977; Murnighan, 1978; Miller & Crandall, 1980.) Often, however, such research has focused only on the two-person situation, which has little application to the broad group-against-group situation. Nonetheless, many of these efforts have aimed at establishing general principles that might be applied to the larger arena. Osgood (1959, 1962, 1966), for example, has developed a *GRIT model*— graduated and reciprocated initiatives in tension reduction. As shown in Table 17-5, this model proposes 10 basic principles that are hypothesized to lead to a reduction in tension between two groups or two nations. In large part, these principles aim for an increase in trust, thereby encouraging the reduction of conflict and the development of cooperation (Lindskold, 1978).

Other investigators have considered the ways in which perceptions of the outgroup can impede or facilitate cooperation. As we discussed in Chapters 3 and 11, prejudice often results from the categorization of people. In defining one group as "different," we favor our own ingroup and, to a lesser extent, act negatively toward the members of the outgroup (Tajfel, 1970; Brewer, 1979). However, Wilder (1978) has shown that, by individuating members of the outgroup, we

TABLE 17-5 / *Basic Principles of the GRIT Strategy*

1. A general statement is made that emphasizes intentions to reduce tension.
2. A clear announcement of each conciliatory initiative is made publicly.
3. Initiatives are carried out on schedule as announced.
4. The announcement of conciliatory initiative should invite reciprocity, but not demand it.
5. Initiatives are continued over time, even in the absence of reciprocation.
6. Initiatives are unambiguous and susceptible to verification.
7 & 8. Initiatives do not impair capacity to retaliate.
9. Initiatives are diversified.
10. Reciprocation is matched in future initiatives.

can diminish bias. In Wilder's study, members of one group (the ingroup) were told either that members of another group (the outgroup) were unanimous in their behavior, or that one member of the outgroup dissented from the majority. When the outgroup appeared to be completely homogeneous, considerable discrimination was exhibited by the ingroup. In contrast, when one member of the outgroup was deviant, discrimination toward all members of the group was reduced. In further work, Wilder showed that, when members of the outgroup responded as individuals, discrimination was much less than it was when a single group opinion was offered. The moral of this study seems clear: categorization of a group can increase conflict, whereas one-to-one interaction can reduce it. The preference for individual diplomacy shown by many government leaders would seem to be supported by these findings.

Other researchers have examined the role of the representative bargainer—the individual who is in a one-to-one bargaining situation to represent the interests of a large group (for example, the union president who represents the total union membership). In general, these studies show that representative bargainers are more competitive, make smaller concessions, and are less likely to reach agreements than individual bargainers (Davis, Laughlin, & Komorita, 1976). This is particularly true when the representatives are being observed or evaluated by their constituents. These findings obviously offer little promise of successful conflict resolution (note that third-party arbitrators are often called in to resolve conflicts). Laboratory experiments have shown that the role of an arbitrator is of considerable importance. Negotiators who anticipate binding arbitration are likely to concede and reach an agreement. Arbitrators prove to be more effective when they enter negotiations that have been deadlocked than when they enter a situation prior to a stalemate (Davis, Laughlin, & Komorita, 1976).

In the basic bargaining situation, we are talking about two groups who approach a situation with differing motives; they need to develop a means of resolving their conflict through concession and cooperation. However, in some cases, two groups may simply develop a working "peace" and continue to engage in their own group activities.

B. *Developing Superordinate Goals*

Conflicts between two groups can be resolved when the groups are merged in the pursuit of a single **superordinate goal**—an important goal that can be achieved only through cooperation. A classic example of this phenomenon is the Robber's Cave field study by Sherif and his associates (M. Sherif, Harvey, White, Hood, & Sherif, 1961; M. Sherif, 1966), which showed how two groups of people can be manipulated. In this study, hostilities between two groups were escalated, and then they were reduced to the point at which the two groups merged into one group.

The boys at Robber's Cave camp were well-adjusted 11-year-old and 12-year-old sons of stable, middle-class families. Although the boys did not know it, their summer camp was staffed by researchers who manipulated and observed their behavior. Two groups of boys were escorted to separate cabins on the first day, each group unaware that the other group existed. In order to develop cohesiveness within each group, the researchers planned activities that required the boys to cooperate for mutual benefit (for example, camping out, or cleaning up a beach). The boys soon came to recognize one another's strengths and weaknesses; leaders and lieutenants emerged on the basis of their contributions to the group. Each group developed a name for itself (the "Rattlers" and the "Eagles"), group jokes, standards for behavior, and sanctions for those who "got out of line."

Then the researchers introduced intergroup conflict; they simply placed the two groups in competition for rewards that only one group could attain. When the groups were brought together for a series of contests, fair play was replaced by an ethic akin to that of the former Green Bay Packer coach Vince Lombardi: "Winning isn't everything, it's the only thing." The groups began to call each other derogatory names, pick fights, and raid each other's camps. "Rattlers" downgraded all "Eagles," and vice versa, to the extent that neither group desired further contact with the other group. Muzafer Sherif (1966) remarked that a neutral observer who had no knowledge of what had happened would assume that the boys were "wicked, disturbed and vicious bunches of youngsters" (p. 58). However, the escalating hostility between groups appeared to produce a peak of solidarity within each group.

The researchers found that it was more difficult to reduce intergroup conflict than it was to produce it. Several strategies were tried and found wanting. The boys attended religious services that emphasized love and cooperation, but this appeal to moral values did not stop them from going right back to their war strategies after the services. Introduction of a third group, which served as "a common enemy," only widened the scope of conflict. Conferences between the leaders of the two groups were rejected, because concessions by the leaders could only be interpreted by their followers as traitorous sellouts of the group's interests. Intergroup contact under pleasant circumstances, such as going to the movies or shooting off fireworks on the Fourth of July, only provided more opportunities for the expression of hostility.

Enter the superordinate goal. First, the researchers arranged for a breakdown in the water-supply line. The boys joined forces in order to find the leak, but they resumed their conflict when the crisis had passed. The researchers then instigated a series of such joint efforts to achieve a superordinate goal: the groups pooled their money to rent a movie, and they used a rope to pull and start the food-supply truck. As a cumulative effect of these joint projects, the groups became friendlier with each other, began to see strengths in each other, and even developed friendships across group lines. In fact, the majority of the boys chose to return home on the same bus, and the group that had won $5 as a prize used the money to treat the other group. The introduction of superordinate goals apparently permitted conflict-reduction strategies (such as contact, increased knowledge of the other group, and communication) to become effective. Although superordinate goals cannot be fabricated, goals such as halting the arms race and solving the energy crisis may help to bring hostile nations into contact and open lines of fruitful communication.

VI. Summary

A *group* has the following properties: interaction between individuals, the development of shared perceptions, the presence of emotional ties, and the development of interdependence and roles. Collections of people that do not possess these characteristics are called *aggregates*.

Other people may influence our behavior, even when we are not part of a group. The presence of an audience, as well as the size of that audience and the status of its members, may affect our individual behavior. Zajonc's drive theory of *social facilitation* suggests that the presence of others is a source of general arousal and will result in increased performance of simple or well-learned responses; their presence causes a decrement in complex or unfamiliar tasks. Apparently, part of this effect is due to our anticipation of being evaluated by the audience.

Coacting audiences create a feeling of competition. In addition, they provide a source of modeling and of social comparison.

Group performance on skill tasks and problems may exceed that of the most skilled individual member, although the nature of the task is a critical variable. Brainstorming appears to be an inefficient use of time and resources. The evidence for the wisdom of subjective judgments made by a group is inconsistent; groups can be swayed, by a "groupthink" process, to ignore deviant positions that may be correct.

In general, group interaction tends to lead to a *polarization* of responses: opinions resulting from group discussions are more extreme than the opinions of the individuals prior to the group discussion. Explanations of group-polarization effects focus on statistical artifacts, interpersonal comparison, and informational influence.

Group productivity and morale are affected by the size of the group, its communication network, and its degree of cohesiveness. These variables often interact.

Real-life examples of groups in action include juries, families, communes, and experiential groups. Each of these types of groups has a set of unique properties; each, too, shows the applicability of social-psychological findings originally obtained in artificial laboratory settings.

Often, groups come into conflict with one another. Studies of bargaining and negotiation have established some of the ways in which conflicts can be resolved or escalated. Representative bargaining is likely to lead to more competitive interaction; third-party mediators often reduce the level of conflict.

Conflicts between two groups can be resolved when the groups are merged in the pursuit of a single superordinate goal—an important goal that can be achieved only through cooperation.

Glossary Terms	cohesiveness	group polari-	social facilita-
	communication	zation	tion
	networks	groupthink	superordinate
			goal

The question "Who ought to be boss?" is like asking "Who ought to be the tenor in the quartet?" Obviously, the man who can sing tenor.   HENRY FORD

PHOTO © ELIZABETH CREWS, ICON.

You can take people as far as they will go, not as far as you would like them to go.
JEANNETTE RANKIN

18

Leadership and Organizational Effectiveness

Groups, as we have described them, are collections of people interacting and working together toward a common goal. But are all members of a group equally influential in moving the group toward that goal? What role does leadership play in human interaction? Because the topic of leadership has always been a concern of social and organizational psychologists, we have chosen to devote an entire chapter to it.

The study of leadership has changed from a search for simplicity to a recognition of complexity. In early attempts to study leadership objectively, researchers attempted to find characteristics that all leaders, but no followers, possessed. Implicit in this approach was an assumption that certain traits—or a single trait—within a person lead that person to assume a leadership role on every occasion, whether it is the election of a captain of the church bowling team, the promotion of a company vice-president, or the selection of a jury foreman. But such a simplified approach was doomed to failure because it did not recognize the numerous functions of leaders, the variety of tasks performed by groups, the differing amounts of power held by different leaders, and the general nature of the system in which the leader and group operate.

As the studies progressed, researchers examined the complex interactions between leaders and groups in an effort to make an accurate statement about what makes a successful leader. The concept of leadership has thus been refined; its functions have been analyzed, and we now know a great deal more about leadership than we did earlier. Yet, as some observers comment, leadership often seems to more closely resemble a performing art than a science (Vaill, quoted by McCall & Lombardo, 1978), and many important questions remain to be answered.

I. The Search for Leadership Traits

What makes one person a successful leader, while another person fails in the same position? How have some revolutionary leaders—for example, Napoleon, Hitler, and Mao Zedong—been able to control the destiny of thousands of people, while other leaders come and go? Why does one person consistently become the class president, the director of the local city council, or occupy other positions of leadership? Patterns of this kind have led people to look for the limited set of traits or characteristics that can distinguish the leader from the follower.

A. *Do Leaders Possess Certain Traits?*

The earliest approach to studying leadership, and one that is still used to a small extent today, is to find a group of leaders and followers, give them a series of personality measures, and attempt to determine which characteristics distinguish the leaders from the followers. Although researchers were initially enthusiastic about this approach, it has become considerably less popular in recent years.

In part, the disillusionment with this approach resulted from the rather simplified assumptions that were made. Often, for example, investigators assumed that a single characteristic would be sufficient to separate leaders from followers. For example, Bird (1940) analyzed the results of 20 studies that had considered 79 different leadership traits. In these studies, leadership was usually defined in terms of school activities, but with great variation in the settings; for example, they included student councils, Girl Scout and Boy Scout troops, speech and drama groups, and athletic teams. Bird found little consistency in the results from one study to another. Of the 79 traits, 51 made a difference in only one study. Although the lack of consistency was partly the result of using different, but almost synonymous, terms in different studies (for instance, *more reliable* versus *more accurate in work*), the general result was a disappointment for those who assumed that leaders were somehow "special" in regard to many traits. High degrees of only four characteristics—intelligence, initiative, sense of humor, and extroversion—were identified often enough in leaders for Bird to consider them "general traits of leadership" (1940, p. 380).

Later reviews of studies of leadership characteristics (Jenkins, 1947; Stogdill, 1948) tended to arrive at the same conclusion: there is no consistent pattern of traits that characterizes leaders (Gibb, 1969, p. 227). Even high intelligence, which many academic investigators assumed should be a mark of the successful leader, did not turn out to be a general leadership trait. For example, Mann's (1959) review concludes "Considering independent studies as the unit of research, the positive association between intelligence and leadership is found to be highly significant. . . . However, the magnitude of the relationship is less impressive; no correlation reported exceeds .50 and the median r (correlation coefficient) is roughly .25" (p. 248). In some cases, the relationship between leadership and intelligence is negligible or even inverse (Lonetto & Williams, 1974).

Korman (1968), in his review of managerial performance, suggested that, although the intelligence levels of first-line supervisors could be related to their performance levels, there seemed to be little connection between the higher-level intelligence levels and success of management leaders. In part, of course, the lack of connection between intelligence level and performance of leaders at higher levels may be the result of a selection process: at these levels, perhaps all people in each group possess a relatively high level of intelligence, and thus other variables become more important in determining leadership. And, according to Gibb (1969), if there is too much discrepancy between a potential leader's level of intelligence and the intelligence level of other group members, his or her success in initiating and maintaining leadership is hampered. Leaders can be too bright for their followers. "The evidence suggests that every increment of intelligence means wiser government, but that the crowd prefers to be ill-governed by people it can understand" (Gibb, 1969, p. 218). In short, there is a lack of evidence to support the assumption that any *single* variable—be it a personality trait such as extroversion, a demographic variable such as height or age, or a cognitive characteristic such as intelligence—distinguishes leaders from followers.

Recent research has shown, however, that a certain *cluster* of traits does appear to reliably separate leaders from their followers, as well as distinguish effective leaders from ineffective leaders. As summarized by Stogdill (1974), this cluster of traits includes "a strong drive for responsibility and task completion, vigor and persistence in pursuit of goals, venturesomeness and originality in problem solving, drive to exercise initiative in social situations, self-confidence and sense of personal identity, willingness to accept consequences of decision and action, readiness to absorb interpersonal stress, willingness to tolerate frustration and delay, ability to influence other persons' behavior, and capacity to structure social interaction systems to the purpose at hand" (p. 81). This list represents a big change from the early single-trait approach and provides a much more complete and complex picture of the leader.

Recent research has also included situational characteristics along with personal traits in its examination of leadership determinants (this reflects the issues that we discussed in Chapter 16). Although the initial single-trait approach to the study of leadership has been found lacking, the abandonment of all trait concepts proved unsatisfactory as well.

B. *The "Great Man" Theory of Leadership*

The "great man" theory of leadership, in its boldest form, proposes that major events in national and international affairs are influenced by the people who hold positions of leadership "and that all factors in history, save great men, are inconsequential" (Hook, 1955, p. 14). Perhaps the greatest exponent of the "great man" theory was the historian Thomas Carlyle, who believed that genius would exert its influence wherever it was found.

A sudden act by a great leader could, according to this theory, change the fate of a nation. Thus, Germany became overtly nationalistic and belligerent in the 1930s solely because Adolf Hitler was in power; had there been no Hitler, says the theory, there would have been no World War II. The extreme form of the theory would go on to propose that, had a "great man" been in power in Great Britain or the United States at that time, World War II could have been averted in spite of Hitler's belligerence. Implicit in the "great man" theory is the assumption that leaders possess *charisma*, a set of personality characteristics that facilitate the accomplishment of their goals, even in the face of great obstacles.

A variant of the "great man" theory suggests that people who possess some of the qualities necessary for successful leadership will possess *all* such necessary qualities. This is an extremely naive idea, in that it assumes that all desirable qualities (sensitivity, intelligence, high energy level, and so on) are present in the same persons. Empirical studies show clearly that a single person does not usually possess all the characteristics of leadership (Bales, 1958; Collins, 1970). For example, the most valuable group member in terms of initiating ways to complete the group's task is seldom the best-liked group member (Bales, 1970; Borgatta & Bales, 1956; M. E. Shaw & Gilchrist, 1956; Stang, 1973).

An Opposing Viewpoint: The Zeitgeist and Social Determinism. A strong rebuttal to the "great man" theory is found in approaches that place emphasis on social forces, social movements, and changing social values as determinants of historic events. According to the *Zeitgeist* theory of history, leaders are like actors who play out the roles designed for them by broad social forces. *Zeitgeist* means "the spirit of the times" or "the temper of the times"; this theory sees the leader's temperament, motives, and ability as having little real influence in the face of social movements. As Victor Hugo wrote, "There is nothing in this world so powerful as an idea whose time has come"—a statement reflecting the perspective of the *Zeitgeist,* or social determinism. In seeking a determination of whether the "great man" or the *Zeitgeist* theory is more nearly correct, let's first discuss the historical evidence.

Study of the history of scientific discovery gives rather weak support to the "great

man" hypothesis. Although certain scientists rise notably above their peers, an analysis of scientific accomplishments by Simonton (1979) suggests that sheer chance plus the influence of the *Zeitgeist* (and of previous technological discoveries) are more important determinants of scientific eminence than personal qualities.

It is the relationship between the power and performance and the personal attributes of political leaders, however, that fostered the development of the "great man" theory. Can this theory of leadership be tested by relating the personal qualities of ruling monarchs to the extent of growth or decline in their countries during their reign? Frederick Adams Wood (1913), an early-20th century American historian, thought so. He made a detailed study of 386 rulers in 14 countries in Western Europe who lived between A.D. 1000 and the time of the French Revolution. All of the rulers that he studied had absolute power over their kingdoms. Each was classified as strong, weak, or mediocre on the basis of knowledge about his or her intellectual and personal characteristics (presumably independent of the strength or weakness of the nation at that time). The condition of each country was also classified as to whether it exhibited a state of prosperity, a state of decline, or no clear indication of either. (This classification was based on the country's economic and political status, not on its artistic, educational, or scientific development.)

Wood found a relationship between the monarchs' personalities and the state of their countries. He states his results as follows: "Strong, mediocre, and weak monarchs are associated with strong, mediocre, and weak periods respectively" (1913, p. 246). Although the correlation coefficient was reasonably strong (between $+.60$ and $+.70$), as with any correlation, we cannot infer a direct relationship between cause and effect. However, Wood clearly favors the interpretation that strong leaders cause their countries to flourish. On the other hand, it is equally possible that a state of prosperity in a country permits bright or brilliant rulers to emerge or to reign successfully with little strain. The interpretation that Wood favors can also be doubted because of the problems in establishing independent and objective measurements of the quality of a monarch and his or her country's development. King Charles I of England is a case in point. It is not enough that King Charles lost his crown and his head; the final indignity is that Wood called him two-faced and obstinate. Yet other observers, as Hook notes, might describe Charles as "shrewd and principled." Although we admire Wood's exhaustive approach to the study of "great men," we must conclude that his data do not permit an answer to his question.

How may the conflict between the "great man" theory and the *Zeitgeist* hypothesis be resolved? We have emphasized throughout this book that no one theory is always correct and that conflicting theories can each make a contribution to the understanding of complex social phenomena. Simonton (1979) concurs with this point in his analysis of scientific eminence, and Hook believes the "great man" plays a unique and decisive role "only where the historical situation permits major *alternative* paths of development" (1955, p. 109). Even if Christopher Columbus had not set sail in 1492, another explorer would have "discovered" the New World soon thereafter. The forces at work gave no alternative. Only when choices exist does the great man or woman influence history.

What may arise out of a clash between a particular leader and his times is a new set of values; for example, one effect of the nonviolent protest for Black rights led by Martin Luther King, Jr., was the consciousness among many Whites that certain citizens in the United States were being unfairly treated. This effect cannot be attributed to the man alone or to his times; it resulted from a creative interaction between the two (Elkind, 1971).

Furthermore, history changes as do people. In fact, Suedfeld and Rank (1976) have suggested that the most successful revolutionary leaders were those who could change their behavior with the demands of the situation (see Box 18-1).

The "Great Man" Theory in the Laboratory. A quite different approach to the "great man" theory of leadership involves using manipulations and experimental controls to determine how the behavior of the single person in the top position affects organizational performance. Borgatta, Couch, and Bales (1954) used this approach with three-man groups of military recruits. Each man participated in four sessions of 24 minutes each, with two new participants in each session. "Great men" were selected on the basis of their performance in the first session; the top 11 of 123 men were so classified. These 11 men were followed through the subsequent sessions so that their productivity could be assessed. (Productivity was measured by the number of acts initiated per time unit and the leadership and popularity ratings given each man by his coparticipants.) "Great men" selected on the basis of the first session continued to have an influence that led to relatively superior performance in their subsequent groups. Of the 11 top men, 8 were in the top 11 productivity ranks in the second and third sessions. Seven of the 11 were still in the top rank in the fourth session. Groups in the second, third, and fourth sessions with "great men" as participants demonstrated smoother functioning with fewer cases of anxiety or withdrawal from participation.

As supportive as these findings are, we are still a long way from verifying a "great man" theory of leadership in practice. The study by Borgatta et al. (1954) does indicate some consistency in group performance across groups with different leaders classified as "great"—over a 96-minute period. It does not, however, show the degree to which a charismatic leader can manipulate the content of eventful decisions over the course of months or years.

C. *Where Is the "Great Woman" Theory?*

Throughout history, there have been famous women leaders in addition to famous men (see Figure 18-1). The queens of France, Russia, and England can be matched with more recent counterparts such as Golda Meir, Indira Gandhi, and Margaret

Box 18-1. Long-Term Success of Revolutionary Leaders.

Social psychologists Peter Suedfeld and A. Dennis Rank (1976) hypothesized that during the phase of initial struggle, revolutionary leaders would need to be cognitively simple—categorical and single-minded in their approach to problems. After the revolution, however, the successful leader might need a broader, more complex view of the world. In an archival study, these investigators tested their hypothesis by analyzing the prerevolution and postrevolution writings of 19 leaders throughout history.

Their hypothesis was supported. Leaders who continued to be prominent after the revolution (such as Cromwell in England, Thomas Jefferson in the U.S., Lenin and Stalin in Russia, and Castro in Cuba) showed a shift toward greater complexity. In contrast, leaders who did not continue in power after the Revolution (such as Alexander Hamilton in the United States, Trotsky in Russia, and Guevara in Cuba) also showed little change in their initially simple patterns of cognitive functioning. (© Burt Glinn/Magnum Photos, Inc.)

Thatcher. Yet most of the research on leadership has focused primarily or entirely on men as leaders (Denmark, 1977). Indeed, a major bibliography of leadership research (Stogdill, 1977) does not even include sex in the index, although other variables such as race, age, and social class have numerous references. In the past, some researchers have justified this gap by pointing to the absence of women leaders in business, industry, politics, and academics, although the absence of women in these positions has never been as total as some commentators suggest. Accompanying this lack of atten-

Figure 18-1. Eleanor Roosevelt and Golda Meir, two women who have played leadership roles.

(© Inge Morath/Magnum Photos, Inc., left; © Marilyn Silverstone/Magnum Photos, Inc., right.)

tion is evidence that pervasive stereotypes exist to the effect that women do not make good leaders (Bass, Krusell, & Alexander, 1971; Shein, 1973, 1975). Thus in the trait approach to leadership, a common though rarely tested assumption is that being male is one of the characteristics essential to the good leader.

Recently, however, with the increasing appearance of women in leadership positions in many fields, it has become evident that the assumption of a sex difference in leadership ability can't remain untested. As the research begins to emerge, results are somewhat contradictory. Some studies have found little difference between male and female leaders (Schneier, 1978); others have found that groups of men perform somewhat better with a male than with a female leader (Rice, Bender, & Vitters, 1980); still

others have found that the evaluation of the leader depended on whether the group was successful or unsuccessful in its performance (Jacobson & Effertz, 1974). Although it is premature to draw any firm conclusions in this area, a couple of points can be made. First of all, it is unlikely that sex is one of the critical variables that distinguishes good leaders from poor leaders. Like other attempts to explain leadership on the basis of a single characteristic, this one too is doomed to failure. A second point is that the studies of male and female leadership need to look more closely at actual leadership behaviors and styles and at the interaction of the leader's personality with the situation. This point is similar to the one we made about early research on leader personality. Therefore, let's leave the question "who is a leader?" and consider "what do leaders do?"

II. Leadership Behavior

A. *Leadership versus the Designated Leader*

The relative futility of the quest for distinguishing traits of leaders had several ramifications. One was a rethinking of the difference between a designated leader and a person who exercised leadership (Stogdill, 1974). During the 1940s and 1950s, research focused on the *functions* of leaders; influential work was done by R. F. Bales at Harvard University and by John Hemphill, Ralph Stogdill, Carroll Shartle, and others at the Personnel Research Board of Ohio State University. The result of these efforts was a new focus on *influence* as the salient aspect of leadership (Hammer, 1974). For example, Stogdill defined leadership as "the process (act) of influencing the activities of an organized group in its efforts toward goal setting and goal achievement" (1950, p. 3).

According to such a definition, almost every member of every group has some leadership responsibility. Certainly all members of a football team have some such function—even the water carrier, if the provided refreshment really renews energy, effort, and efficiency. Of course, some group members exert much more influence toward goal attainment than do others, as Stogdill recognized. Members of a group, team, or organization can often be rank ordered according to the amount of influence they exert on each aspect of the group's task. In the case of a football team, the coaching staff and the quarterback may exert the most influence when it comes to selecting plays that are successful in moving the team toward the goal line. However, insofar as inspiration and motivation are concerned, some other player may be more important. Such a phenomenon demonstrates the place of *emergent leadership* (R. T. Stein, 1975; R. T. Stein, Geis, & Damarin, 1973), or the exercise of leadership functions by persons who are not designated leaders (see Figure 18-2, for example).

An emphasis on goal-oriented functions of leaders is a far cry from the earlier search for personality characteristics that were

Figure 18-2. The most obvious person in the group may not be the actual leader. Leadership functions may be exercised by people who at first glance seem to be in the background of a more visible spokesperson but later emerge as leaders in their own right. (William Gropper, *The Senate*, 1935. Oil on canvas, 25-⅛″ × 33-⅛″. The Museum of Modern Art, New York. Gift of A. Conger Goodyear.)

unique to leaders. In studying the functions of leadership, the initial research efforts examined what kinds of things leaders actually do. For example, the United States Army adopted 11 "principles of leadership" (Carter, 1952), which Gibb (1969, p. 228) has converted into seven possible behaviors: (1) performing professional and technical specialties, (2) knowing subordinates and showing consideration for them, (3) keeping channels of communication open, (4) accepting personal responsibility and setting an example, (5) initiating and directing action, (6) training people as a team, and (7) making decisions. Similarly, the survey by the Ohio State Leadership group (Hemphill & Coons, 1950) proposed nine basic dimensions of the leader's behavior; these are listed in Table 18-1.

B. *Actual Dimensions of the Leader's Behavior*

So much for analysis; what does a leader actually do? Halpin and Winer (1952) set

T A B L E 18 - 1 / *Nine Proposed Dimensions of Leader Behavior*

1. *Initiation.* Described by the frequency with which a leader originates, facilitates, or resists new ideas and new practices

2. *Membership.* Described by the frequency with which a leader mixes with the group, stresses informal interaction between him- or herself and members, or interchanges personal services with members

3. *Representation.* Described by the frequency with which the leader defends his or her group against attack, advances the interests of his or her group, and acts in behalf of his or her group

4. *Integration.* Described by the frequency with which a leader subordinates individual behavior, encourages pleasant group atmosphere, reduces conflict between members, or promotes individual adjustment to the group

5. *Organization.* Described by the frequency with which the leader defines or structures his or her own work, the work of other members, or the relationships among members in the performance of their work

6. *Domination.* Described by the frequency with which the leader restricts individuals or the group in action, decision making, or expression of opinion

7. *Communication.* Described by the frequency with which a leader provides information to members, seeks information from them, facilitates exchange of information, or shows awareness of affairs pertaining to the group

8. *Recognition.* Described by the frequency with which a leader engages in behavior that expresses approval or disapproval of group members

9. *Production.* Described by the frequency with which a leader sets levels of effort or achievement or prods members for greater effort or achievement

Adapted from *Leadership Behavior Description*, by J.K. Hemphill and A.E. Coons. Personnel Research Board, Ohio State University, 1950. Used by permission.

out to identify empirically the dimensions of a leader's behavior. After constructing questionnaire items and administering them to various sets of group members, the Ohio State researchers did a factor analysis of the responses (Stogdill, 1963). Four factors of leadership, or clusters of behaviors, emerged; of concern to us here are the two major ones, labeled **consideration** and **initiating structure.** (The other two factors were production emphasis, accounting for only about 10% of the variability, and sensitivity, or social awareness, accounting for only about 7% of the variability.)

Consideration. Halpin and Winer called the first dimension of leadership behavior *consideration.* This dimension reflects the extent to which the leader shows behavior that is "indicative of friendship, mutual trust, respect, and warmth" in relationships with the other group members (Halpin,

1966, p. 86). Genuine consideration by the leader reflects an awareness of the needs of each member of the group (Fleishman & Peters, 1962). Leaders high in this behavioral characteristic encourage their coworkers to communicate with them and to share their feelings (Korman, 1966). In Halpin and Winer's study, consideration accounted for almost half of the variability in behavior between different leaders.

Initiating Structure. A second dimension was called *initiating structure,* which was defined as "the leader's behavior in delineating the relationship between himself and members of the work group and in endeavoring to establish well-defined patterns of organization, channels of communication, and methods of procedure" (Halpin, 1966, p. 86). Thus initiating structure refers to the leader's task of getting the group moving toward its designated goal. (A part of initiating structure may be identifying and agreeing on the goal.) Initiating structure accounted for about one-third of the variability among leaders.

Other analyses of leadership have produced similar results. Bales (1953), for example, has concluded that leadership has two functions: *task orientation* (or thrust to achieve the group's goals) and *socioemotional orientation* (support of group members' morale and cohesiveness). Because there have been independent confirmations of the results of studies by Bales (1958) and others (Fleishman, Harris, & Burtt, 1955), we conclude that *initiating structure* and *consideration* (or similar factors) are two major dimensions of leadership behavior and not simply mutually exclusive leadership patterns (Gibb, 1969). In other words, the leadership process generally involves both of the leadership dimensions or orientations, and people may exhibit both in various degrees.

The most common method of assessing a leader in terms of leadership dimensions is to ask the group members to rate him or her on a set of descriptive statements, reprinted in Table 18-2. These form the Leader Behavior Description Questionnaire (LBDQ), devised by the Personnel Research Board at Ohio State University (Halpin, 1966; Schriesheim & Kerr, 1974; Stogdill, 1963, 1969).

In any organized group—whether it is a professional hockey team, the teaching staff at an elementary school, or a fire-fighting crew for an oil company—an evaluation can be made of the leader's behavior in terms of initiating structure and showing consideration. Some research indicates that the correlation between the levels of behavior shown on these two dimensions is quite low (Greenwood & McNamara, 1969). In other words, it may be difficult for the same person to fulfill both these functions successfully. The achievement-oriented leader must often be critical of the group members' ideas or actions; such a leader may constantly turn the members' attention back toward the goal when they digress. At the same time, another member of the organization may become the group-maintenance expert, concerned with arbitrating task-oriented disputes, relieving tensions, and giving every person a pat on the back or a chance to be heard. However, sometimes a given behavior may achieve both functions; a leader who helps a group solve a difficult problem may, by that action, develop solidarity and better morale (Cartwright & Zander, 1968).

In general, the challenges of successfully fulfilling both leadership functions are considerable. (You may wish to consider, for example, how many Presidents of the United States or Prime Ministers of Canada were successful in "getting the country moving again" at the same time that they were "bringing people together.") However, although the combination of behaviors may be difficult, leaders are rated as being most effective when they rank high on both dimensions (Stogdill, 1974).

Group performance level has also been shown to relate to leadership-skill ratings. For example, Canadian pupils scored higher on province-wide examinations when their teachers were rated highly on both consideration and initiating structure (Greenfield & Andrews, 1961). Even the rank of the school principals in terms of these two dimensions was related to the performance of the students (Keeler & Andrews, 1963). In another study, Hemphill (1955) asked faculty members at a liberal arts college to name the five departments in the college that had the reputation of being the best led or administered and the five departments that were least well administered. Faculty members in each department then rated their department head on the LBDQ, and the results are shown in Table 18-3. The department's administrative rating was consistent with the ratings that its staff gave the leader. In an entirely different setting, Korean War aircraft commanders were rated on overall effectiveness by their superiors (which included a performance assessment of each commander's group), while their crews completed the LBDQ (Halpin, 1953, 1954). Once again, the relationship between leadership effectiveness rating and group performance level held. Of the nine commanders who were rated in the upper 10%

TABLE 18-2 / *The Leader Behavior Description Questionnaire**

Initiating Structure	Consideration
1. He makes his attitudes clear to the staff.	1. He does personal favors for staff members.
2. He tries out his new ideas with the staff.	2. He does little things to make it pleasant to be a member of the staff.
3. He rules with an iron hand.[a]	3. He is easy to understand.
4. He criticizes poor work.	4. He finds time to listen to staff members.
5. He speaks in a manner not to be questioned.	5. He keeps to himself.[a]
6. He assigns staff members to particular tasks.	6. He looks out for the personal welfare of individual staff members.
7. He works without a plan.[a]	7. He refuses to explain his actions.[a]
8. He maintains definite standards of performance.	8. He acts without consulting the staff.[a]
9. He emphasizes the meeting of deadlines.	9. He is slow to accept new ideas.[a]
10. He encourages the use of uniform procedures.	10. He treats all staff members as his equals.
11. He makes sure that his part in the organization is understood by all members.	11. He is willing to make changes.
12. He asks that staff members follow standard rules and regulations.	12. He is friendly and approachable.
13. He lets staff members know what is expected of them.	13. He makes staff members feel at ease when talking with them.
14. He sees to it that staff members are working up to capacity.	14. He puts suggestions made by the staff into operation.
15. He sees to it that the work of staff members is coordinated.	15. He gets staff approval on important matters before going ahead.

Each item is answered by checking one of five adverbs: *always, often, occasionally, seldom,* or *never.*

* This questionnaire, developed 20 years ago, fails to recognize that leaders may be either male or female.

[a] Scored negatively.

From *Theory and Research in Administration*, by A. W. Halpin. Copyright © 1966 by Andrew W. Halpin. (New York: Macmillan, 1966.) Reprinted by permission.

of overall effectiveness by their superiors, eight were above the mean on both consideration and initiating structure, according to their crews. Of the ten commanders who were rated least effective, more fell below the mean than above the mean on both dimensions of leader behavior.

However, despite the results of the preceding studies, some questions remain. Stogdill, for example, summarizes the findings of these studies as follows: "the significance of consideration and structure is to be explained, not in terms of leadership, but in terms of followership. The two patterns of behavior emerge as important, not because they are exhibited by the leader, but because they produce differential effects on the behavior and expectations of followers" (1974, p. 141). Others have argued that the LBDQ does not provide ratings of actual leader behavior but instead reflects the *implicit leadership theories* of the person doing the rating (Lord, Binning, Rush, & Thomas, 1978; Rush, Thomas, & Lord, 1977). According to this explanation, most of us have an idea of what "appropriate" leadership

TABLE 18-3 / *The Relationship between the Reputation Achieved by College Departments and the Consideration and Initiating-Structure Scores of Department Chairmen Taken Conjunctively (N = 18)*

	Number of Chairmen	
Chairman's Leadership	With Dept. below Median in Reputation	With Dept. above Median in Reputation
Score of 41 or higher on consideration and a score of 36 or more on initiating structure	1	8
Score of less than 41 on consideration or less than 36 on initiating structure	8	1

From "Leadership Behavior Associated with the Administrative Reputation of College Departments," by J. K. Hemphill, *Journal of Educational Psychology*, 1955, *46*(7), 385–401. Copyright 1955. Reprinted by permission of Abrahams Magazine Service.

behavior is, and, even with minimal information about the leader, we will give high ratings when performance is good and low ratings when performance is poor. Such an explanation does not mean that real leader behaviors are not the source of *some* of the findings for the LBDQ ratings—but it does caution us against assuming that the questionnaire ratings are a completely accurate representation of behavior. One obvious solution to the problem of whether ratings reflect actual behavior or people's ideas about ideal leader behavior is to observe actual leadership behavior, rather than to rely solely on questionnaire ratings of the group members. Although this approach is difficult and time consuming, it is necessary if we are to fully understand the dynamics of leadership behavior.

III. A Contingency Theory of Leadership

The early research on basic personality traits of leaders was followed by a more functional approach to the topic, in which leadership *behaviors* became more important than the leaders' personality traits. But a functional analysis was not enough to fully understand leadership behavior. Not until the 1960s—beginning with the work of Fred E. Fiedler—was attention directed squarely at both the leader *and* the situation in which that leader must operate.

Fiedler (1967) defines the leader as the individual in the group who is given the task of directing and coordinating task-relevant activities or who—in the absence of a designated leader—carries the primary responsibility for performing these functions in a group. Fiedler's theory is called a *contingency theory of leadership* because it relates the effectiveness of the leader to aspects of the group's situation. Specifically, the theory predicts that the leader's contribution to group effectiveness is dependent on both the characteristics of the leader and the favorableness of the situation (Graen, Alvares, Orris, & Martella, 1970). To Fiedler, there is no one successful type of leader; task-oriented leaders may be effective under some circumstances but not under others. A permissive leader who is oriented toward human relations and who has been successful with one group may not be successful in a different group.

A. *Elements of the Fiedler Contingency Model*

There are four basic components in Fiedler's contingency model. One of these refers to the personality of the leader, whereas the other three describe characteristics of the situation in which the leader must lead. Let's consider the personality component first. To Fiedler, this means leadership style, which is defined as "the underlying need-structure of the individual that motivates his behavior in various leadership situations" (Graen et al., 1970, p. 286). Leadership style is assessed by the extent of the leader's esteem or liking for his or her "least-preferred coworker," or the LPC measure. Each leader is asked to think of all the people with whom he or she has ever worked and then to select the one with whom it has been most difficult to cooperate. This person represents the "least-preferred coworker," or LPC. The leader is then given a set of bipolar rating scales and is asked to rate this least-preferred coworker on each of the dimensions listed. Examples of these dimensions include pleasant/unpleasant, friendly/unfriendly, and rejecting/accepting (Fiedler, 1967).

The LPC score may be thought of as an indication of a leader's emotional reaction to people with whom he or she could not work well (Fiedler, 1969, 1972). Low-LPC leaders, who rate their least-preferred coworker quite negatively, are considered to be task-oriented administrators, who gain satisfaction and self-esteem from the group's completion of its tasks, even if the leader personally must suffer unpleasant interpersonal relationships for the tasks to be completed. For these leaders, a poorly performing coworker is a major threat to self-esteem. In contrast, High-LPC leaders (who rate their least preferred coworker more favorably) are more concerned about interpersonal relationships. To High-LPC leaders, satisfaction comes from happy group relationships; they are more relaxed, compliant, and nondirective. Low performance by a coworker is not terribly threatening and hence that worker is not rated as negatively. Thus High-LPC and Low-LPC leaders seek to satisfy different basic needs in a group. In a review of the LPC research, Rice (1978) describes the two types of leaders as differing in their basic value orientation. High-LPC leaders value interpersonal success relatively more than do Low-LPC leaders, and they tend to base a wide range of judgments about themselves, others, and the environment on interpersonal success.

Low-LPC leaders, in contrast, value task success relatively more than do High-LPC leaders, and their judgments are correspondingly based on task considerations.

As we noted before, the contingency model does not consider just the personality of the leader. Rather, contingency theory is important because it assumes an interaction between the situation and characteristics of the leader (Yukl, 1971); both of these factors, according to Fiedler, play a role in determining the nature of the leader's influence and the extent of the leader's effectiveness. The three situational components of the contingency model are leader-member relations, task structure, and leader position power.

1. *Leader-Member Relations.* The leader's personal relations with members of his or her organization can range from very good to very poor. Some leaders are liked and respected by their group, whereas others may be disliked, distrusted, or even completely rejected. Fiedler proposes that this general group atmosphere is the single most important factor determining the leader's influence in a small group (Fiedler, 1964).

2. *Task Structure.* The amount of structure in the task that the group has been assigned, often on an order "from above," can vary widely. Some tasks possess a great deal of *goal clarity;* that is, the requirements of the task are clearly known or programmed. For example, the factory team assembling a car or a refrigerator has little doubt about what it is supposed to do. Other tasks, such as those of ad hoc committees, policy-making groups, and creative groups, often lack goal clarity and structure—no one knows exactly what the group purposes are or how the group should proceed. A second element of task structure concerns *solution specificity* (M. E. Shaw, 1963)—that is, whether there is more than one way to complete the task. A third element is *decision verifiability:* once a decision has been made, how clearly does the group know that it is a correct one? All these aspects of task structure play a role in determining the effectiveness of different types of leaders.

3. *Position Power.* A third major component of the contingency model is the power and authority inherent in the leadership position. Does the leader have the authority to hire and fire? Can the leader reward persons by giving raises in pay or status, or is he or she limited in means of regulating the behavior of group members? Does the organization back up the leader's authority? For example, the person in charge of a group of volunteer workers in a political campaign would ordinarily have little position power over the volunteers. A football coach, an owner of a small business, and a police chief will often carry high degrees of position power.

B. *Putting the Elements Together*

Now that we have defined each of the four components of Fiedler's contingency model, how do we fit the parts together? For purposes of simplification and analysis,

Fiedler considers each of the last three components to be dichotomous. Leader-member relationships are either good or poor; task structure is either clear or unclear; and position power is either strong or weak. Because there are two categories in each of these situational components, we may conceive of a system of eight classifications (2 × 2 × 2), which would encompass all their possible combinations. Fiedler has then arranged these eight classifications on a dimension of favorability to the leader, as shown in **Figure 18-3**, based on his specific assumptions about the importance of each classification.

Favorable conditions emerge from situations that permit the leader to exert a great deal of influence on the group. For example, good leader-member relations, strong position power, and clear task structure are considered favorable for the leader in a general sense. In contrast, poor leader-

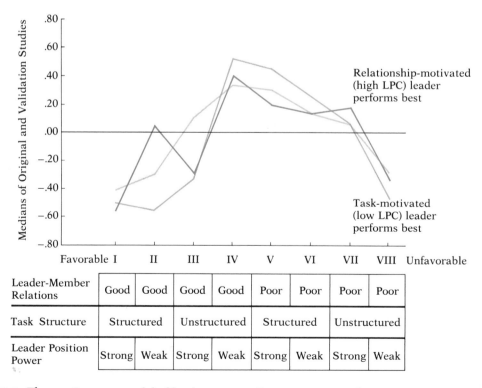

Figure 18-3. The contingency model of leadership and group performance. (From "Recent Developments in Research on the Contingency Model," by F. E. Fiedler. In L. Berkowitz (Ed.), *Group Processes.* Copyright 1978 by Academic Press, Inc. Reprinted by permission of the author and publisher.)

member relations, an unstructured task, and weak position power are considered to be unfavorable.

This is only the first part of the story, however. The second part concerns how the personality style of the leader relates to the different conditions of favorability. Fiedler hypothesizes that Low-LPC leaders (the task-oriented, controlling types) are most effective under group conditions that are either *very favorable* (classes I, II, and III) or *very unfavorable* (classes VII and VIII). In other words, the Low-LPC leader is most effective when he or she has either a great deal of influence and power or almost no influence or power. In contrast, High-LPC leaders (the relationship-oriented types) are most effective under conditions that are *moderately favorable or unfavorable* and in which the leader's influence and power are mixed or moderate (classes IV, V, VI). These predictions are also shown in Figure 18-3, where the predicted correlations between leader LPC score and group performance are graphed.

Many studies have supported Fiedler's contingency model of leadership (Fiedler, 1971; Fiedler & Chemers, 1974). In perhaps the strongest of these studies, Chemers and Skrzypek (1972), using West Point cadets as subjects, composed four-man groups that differed in leader position power, leader-member relations, and LPC scores. The investigators designated the leaders and asked each group to perform one structured and one unstructured task. These investigators found that the eight conditions of favorability and the LPC scores corresponded almost perfectly to the model. In a more limited test of the model, focusing only on class II, Schneier (1978) observed students enrolled in a personnel management course and allowed leaders to emerge naturally. As the Fiedler model would predict, those persons who emerged as leaders had lower LPC scores than the average group member—in fact, in 74% of the groups, the eventual leader had the lowest score among the four or five persons in the group. It is also of interest that this study found similar patterns for both male and female leaders, thus extending general validity of the model.

The most basic conclusion of Fiedler's massive program of research is that there is no such thing as a good leader for all situations. "A leader who is effective in one situation may or may not be in another" (Fiedler, 1969, p. 42). For example, consider a laboratory group in a chemistry class where the task structure is very clear (the instructor has made a definite assignment) but the position power of the group leader is weak (he or she has little authority to make decisions or assign grades). Who would be the best type of leader in this situation? It would depend on the leader-member relations, defining the group as either a class II or a class VI. If leader-member relations were good, then a task-oriented leader (with a low LPC score) would probably do the best job. In contrast, if the leader-member relations were poor, then a High-LPC leader should elicit a better performance from the group. Just these kinds of comparisons have been made in testing the model. For example, high school basketball teams (defined as having a structured task and weak position power) with good relationships between the captain and the other team members win more games if the captain is a task-oriented leader (Fiedler, 1964). You might want to analyze some of the groups that you belong to in terms of these dimensions and consider how the style of the leader leads to effective or ineffective performance of your group.

C. *Leadership and Change*

What if a leader is not effective? Are there ways to change the situation or the leader in order to improve group performance? Fiedler believes that it is more fruitful to try to change the leader's work environment than to try to change his or her personality or leadership style (Fiedler, 1969, p. 43; Fiedler, 1973). In fact, Fiedler and his colleagues (Fiedler, Chemers, & Mahar, 1976) have developed a leadership training program (called "LEADERMATCH") that helps leaders define and create situations in which they are most effective. For example, a leader can volunteer for structured or ambiguous task assignments and thus achieve the preferred level of task structure; power in a group can be shifted according to autocratic or participatory principles; and a leader can influence leader-member relationships either by socializing or remaining aloof (Fiedler, 1978). Fiedler reports that in a series of validation studies using Army cadets, middle managers, police sergeants, and leaders of Latin American volunteer public health organizations, leaders trained by the LEADERMATCH system are consistently more effective than untrained control group leaders (Fiedler, 1978). Although this approach probably represents a more direct attack on the problem of training effective leaders, other social scientists report that the application of positive reinforcement, dissonance, reactance, and other psychological principles can be successful in modifying the personality and behavior of the leader (Varela, 1969). In fact, the distinction between leadership style and specific leader behaviors may not be as clear as the Fiedler model suggests, and thus certain changes may alter the characteristics of both the leader's personality *and* the leader's group situation.

Although Fiedler's studies represent the most comprehensive research on leadership effectiveness to date, it will undoubtedly require refinement as more data are accumulated. Considerable variability in the performance of groups cannot be accounted for by the predictions of the contingency model. Furthermore, the correlations between LPC and group performance are often not significant. Fiedler chooses to verify his theory by showing that the majority of observed correlations are in the direction predicted by the theory. However, reliance on this relatively weak criterion leaves room for questions concerning the accuracy of the model (Graen et al., 1970; Butterfield, 1968).

Fiedler's contingency model is also static in nature; it appears to assume that leaders influence the group but that the group or organization has little or no effect on the leader. Recently, however, Fiedler (1978) has begun to deal with this issue and is formulating a more dynamic theory of the leadership process. One example of this new approach is provided by the study of ROTC

students at the University of Utah before and after training in a specific task (Chemers, Rice, Sundstrom, & Butler, 1975). At both times, the leader-member relationships were poor and the leader position had little power. However, as a result of training, the task structure shifted from weak to strong. Correspondingly, as shown in **Figure 18-4**, the effectiveness of the two types of leaders changed as well. Although relationship-oriented leaders performed better in the untrained condition, task-oriented leaders were superior after the task was learned. These results point out the importance of recognizing that groups and organizations are not static but instead may be constantly changing.

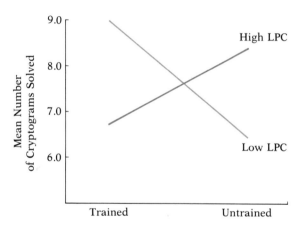

Figure 18-4. Comparison of task performance by High- and Low-LPC leaders with and without task training. (From "Recent Developments in Research on the Contingency Model," by F. E. Fiedler. In L. Berkowitz (Ed.), *Group Processes*. Copyright 1978 by Academic Press, Inc. Reprinted by permission of the author and publisher.)

IV. The Interaction of Leaders and Followers

Leadership is not a one-way street. As Fillmore Sanford noted more than 30 years ago, "Not only is it the follower who accepts or rejects leadership, but it is the follower who *perceives* both the leader and the situation and who reacts in terms of what he perceives" (1950, p. 4). Thus any complete understanding of leadership must include knowledge of followers as well as leaders—in terms of how the followers perceive the leader and how their behavior may alter the leader's behavior. This is a much more process-oriented approach than that of the contingency model. Like the critics who rejected the Shannon and Weaver model of communication (see Chapter 5), critics of the traditional models of leadership emphasize *process* and *transaction* in their attempt to define their topic of study.

A. *Perceptions of the Leader's Behavior*

Although the investigator of leadership may specify certain dimensions of leadership and manipulate those dimensions with some precision in the laboratory, it is not necessarily the case that followers will perceive leaders according to those dimensions. As we discussed in Chapter 3, people have a tendency to make attributions for events in their lives and to formulate their own theories about cause and effect. Recent research in leadership has pointed to the importance of these attributional processes as they relate to the follower's perceptions of and reactions to the leader (Mitchell, 1979). Pfeffer (1978), in fact, suggests that leadership may be an ephemeral phenomenon—that much of what we call *leadership* is based on the attributions of observers rather than on any real behavior of the designated leader. Pfeffer argues that, in any real organization, there are innumerable constraints on the leader's effectiveness. In analyzing the effects of individual mayors on city budgets, for example, Salancik and Pfeffer (1977) found that characteristics of the government structure and the particular year had more influence on budget allocations than the individuals who occupied the position of mayor.

Despite evidence to the contrary, however, we tend to think that the leader's personality is important. Why? Pfeffer suggests that we tend to attribute events to the leader because the leader is a more visible cause; the environment may be so complex that it is difficult to pinpoint environmental causes of events. As an example, Gamson and Scotch (1964) noted how the manager of a baseball team serves as a scapegoat when the team is performing poorly. It's unlikely that the owner would fire the whole team, or even a substantial portion of it, even if there were evidence that many players were performing poorly. In contrast, it's easy, if not always effective, to focus on the manager as the cause of the poor performance.

Hollander and his colleagues have conducted a series of studies exploring the factors that affect the follower's perceptions of the legitimacy of the leader and the leader's subsequent ability to influence the group members (Hollander, 1978; Hollander & Julian, 1970, 1978). Not surprisingly, they have found that leaders are rated more positively when they are successful than when they are unsuccessful and when they indicate an interest in the group activities or in the group members. Whether the leader is appointed or elected to his or her post also makes a difference in the expectations of the group members. Hollander and Julian (1970) suggest that when a leader is elected, the group has higher expectations for leadership performance. In such cases, the leader must be competent and the group must be successful in order for the group to endorse his or her performance. For the appointed leader, either individual competence *or* group success may be sufficient for group endorsement.

Our tendency to make attributions for events may also account for some of the leadership-study findings that focus on the sex of the leader. Fallon and Hollander (1976), for example, found that female leaders were perceived as less influential than male leaders, although the actual performance of the group was the same in both cases. Yet sometimes the different expectations that people tend to have for male and female leaders may work against the male. Jacobson and Effertz (1974) found that when a group failed, male leaders were judged more harshly than were female leaders, presumably because more was expected of the male leader. At the same time, however, female *followers* were evaluated more negatively than male followers. Again, if we can assume that people think women are better followers, then their failure in such a role is judged more stringently than is a similar failure by a male.

Perceptions of the leader may affect future actions by group members. For example, consider the case where the members of a group perceive the leader's behavior to be inequitable. Perhaps the leader takes more of the credit for a group performance than he or she deserves, or perhaps when salaries are determined the leader allocates an unfairly small proportion of the total resources to the group and a large proportion to him- or herself. Not surprisingly, followers in such a situation reduce their endorsement of the leader (Hollander & Julian, 1970; Michener & Lawler, 1975). They may also go further—acting on their perceptions of inequity by revolting against the leader and forming coalitions to counter the leader's behavior (Lawler & Thompson, 1978). Such revolts are much more likely to occur when the group members see the leader as responsible for the inequitable decision, as opposed to when the responsibility can be attributed to someone else—for example, when organizational policy is seen as constraining the leader's options (Lawler & Thompson, 1978). Group members may even choose to depose their leader. Although a crisis may temporarily increase the influence of the leader, particularly if that leader was elected by the group, continued failure will lead to dissatisfaction and an eventual ouster, if the group has the power to depose the leader (Hollander, Fallon, & Edwards, 1977).

B. *The Influence of Followers on the Leader's Behavior*

It is clear that a good leader must pay attention to reactions of the group members. In fact, Weick (1978) has suggested that a good leader should act as a medium, able to take in messages of various types from various sources and to reflect an understanding of those messages in subsequent behavior.

Yet even if the leader is not aware of all of the messages coming from subordinates

and the general system, there is considerable evidence that these messages can still significantly influence the leader's behavior. For example, Fodor (1978) found that supervisors adopted a more authoritarian style of control when they were faced with a stressful situation than when the situation involved less stress. Other studies have shown that situational demands will cause different effects, depending on the personality characteristics of the leader. When the situational demands of the situation increase, task-oriented leaders show less structure and instead begin to increase their consideration and concern for people. In the same situation, interaction-oriented leaders will show a decrease in social behaviors and an increased concern for task considerations (Stogdill, 1974).

Leadership is not a static process. There is a constant interchange between leaders and followers (Katz & Kahn, 1978), and each is influenced by the other in an ongoing process. Neither events nor leadership styles are static, and the shifting patterns that exist in an organizational setting provide a fascinating testing ground for the social scientist interested in dynamic, transactional processes.

V. Leadership, Organizational Effectiveness, and Assumptions about Human Nature

Organizations are composed of many different groups. Although these groups may differ dramatically in their style and function, the organization as a whole often illustrates the operation of some general assumptions about human nature. This section reviews the changing conceptions of human nature held by organizations and their leaders; we shall see an increasing sophistication and complexity arising from an accumulation of research and thought (Cyert & MacCrimmon, 1968).

Edgar Schein (1971), in a stimulating text called *Organizational Psychology*, introduces four different concepts about the nature of the worker. These four concepts, described in detail below, refer to the *rational-economic worker*, the *social worker*, the *self-actualizing worker*, and the *complex worker*. Whether we are looking at a basketball team, a homecoming committee, or a large steel plant, the operating principles of the organization will probably reflect one of these four concepts.

A. *The Rational-Economic Concept*

In the first quarter of this century the most influential voice in managerial psychology was that of Frederick Taylor (1911), who advocated what was called a *scientific-management approach*. In Taylor's view, the worker's only motivation was to make money, and hence Taylor's answer to the problem of motivating workers was a piecework system of pay (Tannenbaum, 1966).

If people are motivated by money—as assumed by the rational-economic model—then the leader's task is one of manipulating and motivating workers to perform their best within the limits of what they can be paid. The theory holds that workers' feelings are irrational and must be prevented from obstructing the expression of the worker's rational self-interest (Schein, 1971). This narrow concept resembles what Douglas McGregor (1960, 1966, 1967) called *Theory X*, or management's traditional concept of the worker. (McGregor included some additional assumptions under Theory X that are compatible with the rational-economic theory—namely, that humans are inherently passive, lazy, and gullible and that they are incapable of self-discipline and self-control.) In general, the rational-economic model says there is little to workers' motivations beyond their desire to obtain the largest possible paycheck at the end of the week.

The assembly line is an outgrowth of the rational-economic concept. The production of a light switch, a radio, or an automobile is broken down into thousands of specific tasks. A worker may have to make only one response—perhaps tightening one screw in every light switch that passes by on the never-ending assembly line (see Figure 18-5). Pay can be related to the number of switches processed. The goal of management is to produce as many finished prod-

ucts as possible; according to this concept, whether the worker is satisfied or bored is quite unimportant. "The fact that the employee's emotional needs were not fulfilled

Figure 18-5. Life on the assembly line. The single source of cohesiveness uniting auto workers on the assembly line is the never-ending monotony of it all. Partially assembled cars pass by at the rate of 50 to 65 an hour, and workers have less than a minute each to do their specific tasks—for example, to pound out a dent in a fender or re-weld an improperly joined seam. At the Dodge plant in Hamtramck, Michigan, the assembly line begins promptly at 6 A.M. There is a 30-minute lunch break at 10 A.M.—not enough time for some workers to get a hot lunch at the cafeteria. Some workers munch a sandwich from a bag, often while waiting in the long line to use the toilet. The only other breaks are an 11-minute one in the morning and a 12-minute one in the afternoon. This work shift ends at 2:30 P.M. To quote Henry Belcher, a welder, "Everything is regulated. No time to stop and think about what you are doing; your life is geared to the assembly line. I have lost my freedom." (© Burk Uzzle/Magnum Photos, Inc.)

on the job was of little consequence because he often did not expect them to be fulfilled" (Schein, 1971, p. 52).

There is no denying that better pay and merit bonuses are important motivators for workers. To that degree, the rational-economic model is valid. But the theory does not suffice; it fails to recognize other needs of workers that relate to satisfaction and productivity and to employee turnover and malingering.

B. *The Social Concept*

Between 1927 and 1932, employees of the Western Electric Company's Hawthorne works in Chicago were observed in a series of studies (Roethlisberger & Dickson, 1939; see also Carey, 1967; Landsberger, 1958; Parsons, 1974). A group of female workers assembling relay switches for telephones was moved to a special room; a number of innovations were introduced and their effects on the worker's productivity were studied. Some of these innovations were expected to lower productivity—the lighting was dimmed, the workday was shortened by an hour, and coffee breaks were added, thus reducing time on the job. In contrast, another alteration involved the institution of a longer workday without any rest periods or coffee breaks. To the surprise of the researchers, *every* change had the effect of *increasing* productivity. Output became higher than ever before. The researchers concluded that the workers' productivity had increased because they felt that the management was interested in them. Workers' previous feelings of alienation and loss of identity were replaced with a feeling that they were special. The *Hawthorne effect* subsequently became a term used to label this phenomenon of working harder and producing more because of a feeling of participating in something new and special.

One of the Hawthorne researchers, Elton Mayo (1945), developed a model that emphasizes the *social* concept of the worker. The assumptions of this model included the following:

1. Workers are basically motivated by interpersonal needs and determine their basic sense of identity through relationships with others.

2. As a result of the industrial revolution and the segmenting of tasks into specific activities, the meaning has gone out of work for many workers, who—now alienated—seek new meaning in the social relationships available on the job (Creedman & Creedman, 1972).

3. Working people are more responsive to the social forces of their peer group than to the incentives and controls of management. The working group can often determine and control what constitutes a normal rate of production, despite management's frenzied efforts to increase output. In another work group in the Hawthorne plant, one new worker was at first a "rate buster" —she turned out almost twice as many products a day as the others. But soon the other women had convinced her to slow down and to produce at an "appropriate" rate as the others were doing.

4. Workers are responsive to management to the extent that a supervisor can meet the subordinate's social needs and needs for acceptance (adapted from Schein, 1965, p. 51).

Thus, according to the assumptions of the social concept of the worker, the tasks of the leader—whether a shop manager or a department head—require that some attention be given to the needs of the subordinates. Even when they feel alienated, workers may perform tolerably or adequately, but their productivity (as well as morale and satisfaction) can be increased by a leader's or manager's recognition of their needs.

Although Mayo's model of the worker as a social being was an improvement over the rational-economic concept of workers, it was justifiably criticized by liberal sociologists such as C. Wright Mills (1948) as being pro-management and seeing the worker as only a means to ends defined by the company ownership. Yet a variety of studies in the 1940s and 1950s demonstrated the potency of the social concept of the worker. Many of these studies were stimulated by the thinking of Kurt Lewin, the father of group dynamics, who sensitized industry to the powerful effect of participatory decision making on job efficiency.

A prototype of a Lewinian study was conducted in a pajama plant in rural Virginia. One of the officers of the company, psychologist Alfred Marrow, invited Lewin to meet with the plant staff to discuss a basic problem: the inexperienced workers hired by the new company were not reaching the level of skill that was expected of them by the management. The company officials felt that they had tried everything. The workers were being paid more than they had been receiving on their previous jobs. The management had tried a multitude of reward systems, and all had failed.

Lewin made several suggestions. One was that the inability of the workers to meet management's standard might reflect a belief that the company's standard was impossibly high. Lewin advocated importing some experienced workers from other communities to work alongside the local workers. Although this was an unpopular suggestion, because the town officials strongly opposed giving jobs to outsiders, the frustrated plant officials were willing to give it a try. The skilled, experienced operators who were imported adapted to management's standards. When the local, unskilled workers saw the performance of the experienced outsiders, they vowed that they could also reach the desired level, and their production rate gradually began to increase.

Later studies at this same plant (French & Coch, 1948) dealt with resistance by production workers to changes in working methods. Signs of resistance included high rates of turnover, lowered levels of production, and verbal hostility toward the plant and coworkers. French, one of Lewin's associates, and Coch, the personnel manager, decided to try three methods of instituting changes in job duties, each involving a different amount of participation by the workers in planning the details of new job activities. The first group of workers was simply told about the planned changes in their jobs and what was expected of them; they did not participate in the decision. The second group appointed representatives from among themselves to meet with management to consider problems involved in changing working methods. The third group procedure involved every worker in the unit, not just representatives. All members of the third group met with management, participated actively in discussion, shared many suggestions, and helped plan the most efficient methods for mastering the new jobs.

Marrow reports the differences among these three groups in job adaptation. The findings offer support for the social concept of the worker.

The differences in outcome . . . were clearcut and dramatic. Average production in the nonparticipating group dropped 20% immediately and did not regain the prechange level. Nine percent of the group quit. Morale fell sharply, as evidenced by marked hostility toward the supervisor, by slowdowns, by complaints to the union, and by other instances of aggressive behavior.

The group which participated through representatives required two weeks to recover its prechange output. Their attitude was cooperative, and none of the members . . . quit their jobs.

The consequences in the total-participation group were in sharp contrast to those in the nonparticipating group. It regained the prechange output after only two days and then climbed steadily until it reached a level of about 14% above the earlier average. No one quit; all members of the group worked well with their supervisors, and there were no signs of aggression [1969, pp. 150–151].

A more recent study (Zander & Armstrong, 1972) found that, when work groups in a slipper factory were asked to set their own daily production goals, they tended to aim for high goals—even higher than the standard set by the manager.

Lewinian methods and social concepts of the worker may lead to better employee-leader relations, as well as to heightened productivity. Such efforts are not limited to the industrial plant. Lewin, Lippitt, and White's (1939) classic study of the social climate of boys' task groups has shown the wide applicability of the social concept of the worker. Small groups of 11-year-old boys met after school for several weeks to make masks and carry out similar activities. The adult leader of the groups acted in either an authoritarian, a democratic, or a laissez-faire manner. The authoritarian leader usually started by giving an order, frequently criticized the work, and often disrupted activity by suddenly making the children begin a new project. This type of leader gave the boys no indication of long-range goals and frequently remained aloof. In contrast, the democratic leader worked with the group to develop goals and the means for attaining them. All decisions were made by the entire group. In the third form of leadership, laissez-faire, the leader gave out information only on request and did not enter into the spirit of the task.

As in the pajama factory, these experimental variations produced changes in both performance and satisfaction. Authoritarian leadership resulted in more restlessness, discontent, aggression, fighting, damage to play materials, and apathy. Apathy dominated in groups with laissez-faire leaders as well. All but one of 20 boys in the groups preferred the democratic leadership. (Preferences were not a result of the specific person who served as leader, since three different men served as leaders in all three social climates.) Results regarding productivity were not as clear-cut. The largest number of masks was produced by the authoritarian groups, but democratic groups were better able to put forth a sustained effort when the leader was absent. Laissez-faire leadership led to low rates of productivity.

Subsequent studies have continued to explore the relationships among leadership style, group satisfaction, and productivity, often considering productivity for periods considerably longer than the boys' group measure of number of masks produced during short group sessions. In general, these later studies have found no consistent relationship between leadership style and productivity, although greater member satisfaction nearly always results from the democratic as opposed to the authoritarian style (Stogdill, 1974). More detailed consideration of groups suggests that leadership style interacts with the size and composition of the group. Democratic leaders are most satisfying when the group is small and interaction oriented (see Figure 18-6), whereas autocratic leadership may be more satisfying when the group is large and oriented toward a specific task (Stogdill, 1974).

If we can assume that democratic leadership instills in group members a greater desire to succeed, even without continuous supervision, we may conclude that democratic leadership has better long-term effects. This assumption is clearly behind the advocacy of a student-centered approach to learning, which stresses the active involvement of the student in preference to passive reaction to a professor's directives. To Carl Rogers (1969), a teacher-centered approach to the classroom has no long-range benefits in the development of the student as an authentic person. In order for education to be of real value to the learner, the quest for learning must come from inside; authoritarian demands that one learn are of short-term value only.

C. *The Self-Actualizing Concept*

The social view of the worker is more humane than the rational-economic view, but it is still not satisfactory to some social psychologists and social philosophers. To Abraham Maslow (1954), for example, people at their best are *self-actualizing* and make maximum use of all their resources. To Maslow, to Argyris (1964), and to McGregor (1960, 1966, 1967)—all social psychologists concerned with leadership in industry—most jobs in contemporary factories, offices, and shops do not permit workers to use their capacities fully. These jobs do not facilitate workers' understanding of the relationship between what they are doing and the total purpose of the employing organization (Schein, 1971).

The leader who adopts the view of people as self-actualizing feels concern about his or her employees but is more interested in making their work meaningful and satisfying than in fulfilling their social needs. Workers will be given as much responsibility as they can handle; as they achieve certain degrees of skill and responsibility, they are encouraged to move upward. In contrast to earlier theories that saw the worker as *extrinsically* motivated (reasons for working were artificially related to the job), the self-actualizing concept views people as *intrinsically* motivated. They have personal, internalized reasons for doing a good job, and they take pride in their work because it is

Figure 18-6. Leadership style appears to interact with the size and composition of a group. In a group that is relatively small, such as the one shown here, and that is oriented toward interac-tion among the members, a democratic leader-ship style may be the most satisfactory. (© Ellis Herwig/Stock, Boston.)

their work (D. A. Wood, 1974). If we ask peo-ple why they feel good about their jobs, as Herzberg, Mausner, and Snyderman (1959) have done, their reasons often center on their accomplishments and their feelings of increasing job competence. We interpret these interview responses as indications that self-actualization is a part of the nature of the worker. (Factors that made people feel bad about their job, such as poor pay, bad working conditions, and inadequate job security, are unrelated to self-actualization.)

It may be true that a self-actualization concept of human nature is more idealistic than realistic. Some workers may not care whether their job provides any challenge or autonomy (Meir & Barak, 1974; B. Schneid-er & Bartlett, 1970). Self-actualization may

not be applicable to many unskilled jobs or temporary activities (Larson & Spreitzer, 1973). Perhaps for these positions the goal should be to provide the worker with enough money so that he or she can find meaning and challenge off the job (Schein, 1971). But as Argyris (1964) and others have indicated, there is a great risk that rejecting self-actualization as a goal can lead to a se-rious waste of valuable human resources.

D. *The Concept of the Complex Worker*

Each of the previous sets of assump-tions about the nature of the worker reflects the problems of "simple and sovereign" theories. Although each has some accuracy and may be applicable to some individuals, each of these concepts is also oversimplified and overgeneralized. Schein postulates that the worker is not only "more complex within himself, but he is also likely to differ from his neighbor in the patterns of his own complexity" (1965, p. 60). Thus a model of the person as a complex being is necessary to complete our picture of the nature of the worker. Schein (1971) points to five aspects of potential complexity that must be recognized in any model of the worker.

1. Workers are not only complex, but also highly variable. Although their basic motives may be arranged in some hierarchy of importance, the hierarchy is subject to change from time to time and from situation to situation.

2. People can learn new motives through their organizational experience, and thus individual motives can interact with organizational experience in a complex fashion.

3. A person's motives may be different in different organizations or in different parts of the same organization. In complex jobs, such as that of a manager, various motives may operate in various aspects of the job.

4. Other factors also relate to productivity. "The nature of the task to be performed, the abilities and experience of the person on the job, and the nature of the other people in the organization all interact to produce a certain pattern of work and feelings. For example, a highly skilled but poorly motivated worker may be as effective *and satisfied* as a very unskilled but highly motivated worker" (Schein, 1971, p. 62).

5. No single managerial strategy will work for all people at all times.

There are many examples of the need for a complex concept of the worker in the study of leaders and organizations. In effect, the failure of any intervention to bring about identical results in every subject is an indication of the human complexity involved. When 19 out of 20 11-year-olds prefer democratic leadership, we must not overlook the single deviant and the interindividual variability that his or her response represents. (Very few interventions produce the almost unanimous response that was obtained in the original authoritarian-democratic leadership studies!) This represents one level of complexity resulting from individual differences. Another example of

complex individual differences comes from a study of a large trucking company (Vroom, 1960; Vroom & Mann, 1960). In this case, workers with different kinds of jobs and different personalities preferred different leadership styles. Men with relatively independent, solitary jobs (such as truck drivers and dispatchers) preferred a more task-oriented, authoritarian supervisor. But men whose work was interdependent preferred employee-oriented supervision.

Successful attempts to change the leadership preferences of workers further document the conclusion that it is desirable for every successful manager, chairperson, or group leader to possess a complex view of human nature (Hulin & Blood, 1968). None of the concepts of the worker as rational-economic, social, or self-actualizing applies to all workers at all times, and a static description of an organization will not apply to all situations within the organization.

VI. Summary

In the early search for characteristics that distinguished leaders from nonleaders, little consistency was found from one study to another. Although no single leadership trait has been consistently identified, there is a cluster of traits that are more typical of leaders than nonleaders: drive for responsibility, vigor and persistence, originality, initiative, self-confidence, willingness to accept consequences and to tolerate stress and frustration, ability to influence, and capacity to structure tasks.

Attempts to explain the emergence of great political leaders have considered both the charismatic qualities of the leader as well as the *Zeitgeist*, or the temper of the times.

Designated leaders of groups have two major functions: initiating structure and consideration. *Initiating structure* refers to the leader's behavior in identifying the group's goal and moving the group toward that goal. *Consideration* refers to the leader's concern with relationships between himself or herself and other group members. Leaders are rated as more effective when they are considered to fill both functions well.

Fiedler's contingency theory of leadership emphasizes that there is no one successful type of leader. The four basic components of Fiedler's model are the personality of the leader, leader-member relations, task structure, and position power. Depending on the favorability of the situation, either a task-oriented or an interaction-oriented leader may be more effective. Changes in the situation may allow a particular leader to become more effective.

Leaders and followers must be viewed as interacting in order to understand group behavior. The attributions that subordinates make about the leader's behavior will affect the group process and can alter the leader's behavior as well.

Leaders of organizations and groups operate according to assumptions about human nature. Four different types of models of human nature may be distinguished: rational-economic, social, self-actualizing, and complex.

The rational-economic model of the worker sees people as motivated by money and self-interest. Hence, the leader's task is seen as one of motivating workers to turn out the most they can within the limits of what they can be paid.

The social model of the worker sees people as basically motivated by social needs; relationships with others are primary. The task of the manager is to recognize these social needs and facilitate their fulfillment in order to increase production.

The self-actualizing model of the worker views people as striving to use their capacities fully. The leader using this model tries to make other employees' work meaningful and satisfying. Workers are given the most challenging jobs that they can handle and are encouraged to develop new skills and goals.

The complex model of the worker reflects the belief that different workers have different needs and capabilities. In addition, this model recognizes the different demands within any organization and the fact that both people and situations may change over time.

Glossary Terms   consideration
initiating struc-
    ture

Three little bugs in a basket, and hardly room for two.   ALICE CARY

We shape our buildings, and afterwards our buildings shape us.
WINSTON CHURCHILL

19

Physical Environment and Interpersonal Behavior

This chapter was written by Eric Sundstrom.

The Pruitt-Igoe housing project stood for fewer than 20 years before the city of St. Louis demolished the last of its 33 high-rise buildings. The project, which the city had finished before 1960, contained 2764 apartments for low-income families. As shown in Figure 19-1, the 11-story buildings occupied spacious, open grounds. At the time of its construction, the project represented a model for many architects and professional planners; however, despite optimistic publicity, the project soon became a miserable failure. After only three years, the buildings were physical wrecks, with broken windows, cluttered hallways, urine-stained stairwells, and other signs of neglect and decay. The buildings harbored criminals and juvenile delinquents; vacancy rates rose as high as 70%.

Research evidence suggests that the project failed, in part, because of the design of the buildings. In their former "slum" neighborhoods, the residents had spent much time chatting with one another on porches, in alleys, across back fences, and in other areas near their apartments. But the high-rise buildings of Pruitt-Igoe provided few places in which people could talk. The corridors were narrow and bare. The galleries, which were intended as informal gathering places, were rarely used (probably because they were far from the apartments and walkways). As a consequence, Pruitt-Igoe residents reported feelings of isolation (Yancey, 1971).

The buildings created problems for parents. When they lived in two-story or three-story "walk-up" apartments, they could watch their children playing in the streets. In contrast, they found it difficult to maintain supervision from the high-rise structures of Pruitt-Igoe, and the stairwells and corridors provided ideal hiding places for mischievous children. These same places gave cover to would-be muggers

Figure 19-1. The Pruitt-Igoe housing project in St. Louis provided modern apartments for low-income families—but the high-rise buildings were plagued with vacancy and vandalism. The apartments seemed to discourage residents from continuing their previous habits of interpersonal interaction. The few spaces designed for informal interactions, such as the galleries pictured on the left, were dissociated from the apartments. The open doors lead to what were laundry rooms. (From *Defensible Space*, by O. Newman. Copyright © 1972, 1973 by Oscar Newman. Reprinted by permission of Macmillan Publishing Co., Inc. and The Architectural Press Ltd.)

who preyed on the residents of the project. Crime was far more prevalent at Pruitt-Igoe than in neighboring areas (Newman, 1973).

The case of Pruitt-Igoe illustrates the effects of the physical environment on social behavior—effects that we often ignore. An anthropologist noted the general unawareness of physical setting in the title of his book on the subject—*The Hidden Dimension* (Hall, 1966). Perhaps this reflects our tendency to adapt to environments without thinking about them, as well as our habit of automatically coping with the difficulties our environments create. When something goes wrong, as at Pruitt-Igoe, routine means of adaptation and coping may not work, and the role of the environment—normally taken for granted—becomes obvious.

This chapter explores the role of physical settings in social behavior. The material is organized into five sections. The first section explores the ways in which we perceive our physical settings. The second section considers the physical environment as a means of obtaining privacy, of regulating social contact, and of organizing interactions; for example, through the establishment of "territories." In the third and fourth sections, we view physical settings as determiners of social behavior. We examine the consequences of environmental stress and the influences of built environments on contact between people, formation of friendships, and social overload. The last section looks at crowding, an environmentally determined failure of an individual's attempts to regulate social contact.

I. Perceiving Physical Environments

Consider a classroom at a local college or university, such as the one that houses your social psychology class. Perhaps it seems spacious, quiet, and friendly. Or maybe it seems crowded, noisy, and unfriendly. Your judgments reflect certain physical qualities of the room, in much the same ways that your perceptions of people reflect their visible characteristics and demeanor.

A. *Dimensions in the Perception of Places*

In the past, researchers tried to find psychological dimensions that reflect important qualities of physical environments. Such dimensions resembled the "central traits" in the perception of persons (see Chapter 3). For instance, a room may elicit differing responses when it is tidy and when it is messy. If so, tidiness would be a central dimension in the perception of the room. The search for universal dimensions has demonstrated the complexity of perceptions of environments (see Canter & Stringer, 1976). One aspect of this complexity concerns **scale**, or the size of the environment in relation to an individual. A room generally has a smaller scale than a building, a neighborhood, or a city. Because of differences in scale, the perceptual basis for judging a neighborhood might be quite different from the basis for judging a living room.

Physical settings differ in many ways. Of the qualities an environment can embody, we can distinguish two types. **Ambient conditions** refer to the physical qualities of the atmosphere surrounding an individual: sounds, light, air quality, temperature, and humidity (Parsons, 1976). *Architectural features* include more permanent aspects of a setting. In a room, these features might include the configuration of walls, floor, and ceiling, and the arrangement of furnishings and decorations. The architectural features of a building include the layout of each floor, the design and treatment of the exterior, and so on. The larger the scale, the more difficult it is to characterize a setting. In places as large as cities, the potential variety in physical features is almost endless.

Ambient conditions seem to go unnoticed, unless a setting becomes uncomfortable. For instance, as long as the temperature stays around 70° F, we pay little attention to it; however, if it drops to 55° F, or climbs to 95° F, we may take notice and try to restore our comfort. All of the ambient conditions have a range of comfort. As conditions depart from it, we experience the deviation in terms of its *intensity*. A temperature of 90° F is warm; 105° F is hot. Departures from the range of comfort motivate coping responses in proportion to the deviation. Other dimensions also may be important, such as complexity and variety (see Wohlwill, 1974).

Perceptions of architectural features of interiors are more complicated than perceptions of ambient conditions, because they can differ in so many ways: size and shape; type and arrangement of furniture; textures, colors, materials, objects, and so on. Studies of perceptions of interiors have recognized that people tend to select and simplify perceptions of places, as they do their perceptions of people (see Chapter 3). One finding from research on dimensions of interiors is a strong evaluative dimension. Features of interiors associated with favorable evaluations included: *interesting, friendly, soft,* and *bright* (Canter, 1969); and *stimulating, informal, harmonious, soft,* and *beautiful* (Acking, 1971).

Another study showed that people differentiated rooms in terms of "friendliness." Ratings of schematic pictures of rooms revealed that the friendliest rooms contained chairs arranged with no intervening barriers, along with other features shown in **Figure 19-2.** Researchers have identified other perceptual dimensions that might indirecty affect interpersonal behavior, such

as "flexibility"—the ease with which a room can be rearranged for a social encounter (High & Sundstrom, 1977).

Matters are more complex when it comes to large-scale settings, such as urban environments. A recent study uncovered 20 separate dimensions in preferences for urban areas, including aesthetics, feelings about living in the area, noise that disturbed outdoor activities, traffic safety, and noise that disturbed indoor activity (Carp, Zawadski, & Shokrkon, 1976). There was no strong evaluative dimension equivalent to the one that appeared in studies of perceptions of rooms. Another study identified five dimensions in ratings of urban areas: "cultural, contemporary, commercial, entertainment, and campus" (Herzog, Kaplan, & Kaplan, 1976). These dimensions have a functional character that may reflect the selection of only the most salient features of a complex environment.

B. *Adaptation: The Shifting of Perceptions*

After prolonged exposure to a physical setting, an individual may begin to view that setting differently. For instance, an individual who works in the downtown district of a large city is exposed to a constant

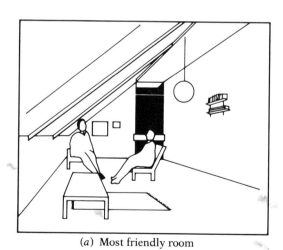

(a) Most friendly room

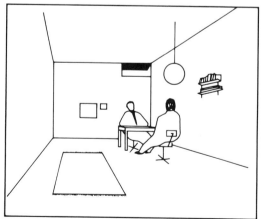

(b) Least friendly room

Figure 19-2. "Friendly" and "unfriendly" rooms. (This figure is from a paper by R. Wools and D. Canter entitled "The Effect of the Meaning of Buildings on Behavior" in Volume 1, No. 3, pp.

144–150 of *Applied Ergonomics*, 1970. Published by IPC Science and Technology Press Ltd., Guildford, Surrey, UK. Reprinted by permission.)

din of passing traffic. In time, the traffic noise may become background—no longer noticed by the individual; this is an example of **adaptation**. As one consequence of adaptation, people perceive new situations in terms that are familiar to them. For example, the urbanite who visits a suburb may find it quiet and peaceful—through implicit comparison with the downtown environment. An individual from a rural location (an individual who is accustomed to relative quiet) may find the same suburb noisy. Examples of adaptation include the inability of most people to smell subtle odors for more than a few seconds, and the automatic adjustment of the eye to bright light. These forms of adaptation reflect physiological mechanisms. Other examples of adaptation (such as the tendency for individuals to perceive a disco as intensely loud when they enter, but later not so loud) may reflect the allocation of attention to other things (see S. Cohen, 1978). One consequence of adaptation is that physical settings may have their greatest effects immediately after an individual's first exposure to them, which means that physical settings may have their greatest effect on the social behavior of newcomers.

As we adapt to environmental conditions, we change our internal standards for evaluation. Personal standards for perception are called **adaptation levels** (Helson, 1964; Wohlwill, 1974). An example of adaptation levels appears in a study involving people from small cities (24,000 or fewer), medium-sized cities (152,000–753,000), and large cities (more than 1 million). Participants viewed color slides of scenes from cities of various sizes and rated them in terms of crowding and congestion, noise, and other dimensions. As shown in Figure 19-3, the residents of small towns found the scenes to be crowded and noisy (Wohlwill & Kohn, 1973); apparently, they had low adaptation levels, and they judged the scenes by their experience.

C. The Big Picture: Cognitive Maps

Perceptions of a setting form large mental images of environments, called **cognitive maps**. This term refers to an individual's

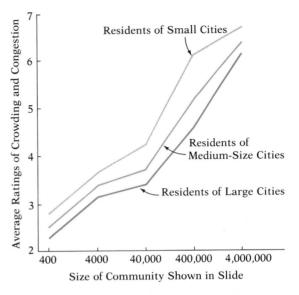

Figure 19-3. Adaptation levels. (Adapted from "The Environment as Experienced by the Migrant: An Adaptation-Level View," by J. Wohlwill and I. Kohn, *Representative Research in Social Psychology*, 1973, *4*, 135–164. Used by permission.)

mental image of a physical setting in the context of a larger environment (see Altman & Chemers, 1980; Downs & Stea, 1973). Cognitive maps differ in scale and amount of detail; people have images of the interiors of their homes or apartments, their neighborhoods, their cities, and their countries. Cognitive maps of large environments contain less detail than maps of small environments.

Figure 19-4 shows how a San Franciscan's cognitive map of San Francisco and the rest of the country might look. San Francisco occupies well over half the map, and Taylor Street seems to take up nearly as much mental space as the rest of the country. The drawing illustrates five characteristics of cognitive maps of cities identified in research (see, for example, Lynch, 1960): (1) *paths*, such as Geary Way and its walkways; (2) *nodes*, or places where paths cross, such as intersections of streets; (3) *edges*, or visible boundaries not generally used as paths; (4) *landmarks*, or physical features that serve as reference points, usually because they are visible from many parts of an environment; and (5) *districts*, such as the "Financial District" in San Francisco.

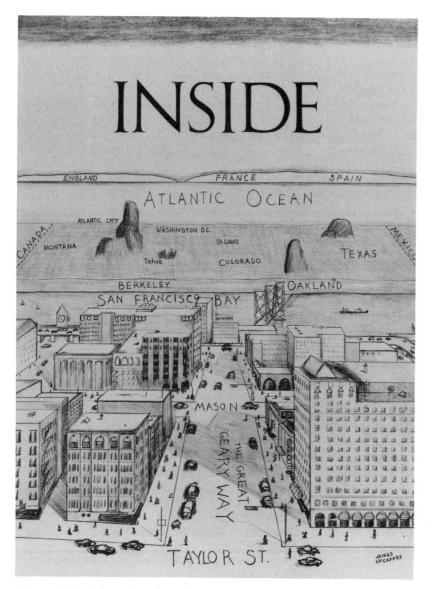

Figure 19-4. A San Franciscan's cognitive map. (James McCaffry, artist. Courtesy of Arts and Leisure Publications.)

Not surprisingly, cognitive maps tend to show greater accuracy and differentiation in areas in which a person lives or travels (see Altman & Chemers, 1980; Gould & White, 1974). For instance, one researcher asked college students and high school students from the U.S. and several other countries to draw maps of the world. Most of the students put their own countries at the centers of their maps, exaggerated the size of their home countries, and gave the greatest detail of areas near their homes (Saarinin, 1973). Similarly, in another study, researchers obtained cognitive maps of a college campus from students and recorded their use of various areas on campus through direct observation. The students were seen most frequently in areas that were emphasized in their cognitive maps (Holahan & Dobrowolny, 1978).

II. Using Physical Environments to Regulate and Organize Social Contact

Physical environments can limit the amount of social contact an individual experiences; for instance, by providing *privacy* when an individual wants to withdraw from social involvement. On the other hand, a setting can create accessibility when social contact is desired. For example, a student who lives in a dormitory room can lock the door and pull the curtains for privacy, or open the door and curtains to encourage interaction.

The theory that the physical environment helps in regulating interaction assumes that desires for interaction change from time to time, and that these shifting desires lead to active attempts to regulate involvement with others. Irwin Altman, who developed a theory of privacy, writes:

If a person desires a lot of interaction with another person and gets only a little then he feels lonely, isolated or cut off. And if he actually receives more interaction than he originally desired, then he feels intruded upon, crowded, or overloaded. However, what is too much, too little, or ideal shifts with time and circumstances, so what is optimum depends on where one is on the continuum of desired privacy. If I want to be alone, a colleague who comes into my office and talks for fifteen minutes is intruding and staying too long. If I want to interact with others, then the same fifteen minute conversation may be far too brief [1975, p. 25].

Altman claims that, whenever we desire more or less interaction than we experience, we use "privacy regulation mechanisms," including resources supplied by the physical setting, to achieve an optimal state of affairs. In other words, when we experience more or less social contact than we want—we cope.

A. *Privacy*

Privacy is generally defined as the ability to control access to oneself or to information about oneself (Altman, 1975; Margulis, 1977). Privacy implies the choice of

withdrawing from involvement with other people (Marshall, 1972). It involves control over both incoming stimulation and outgoing information. For example, two roommates talking in their dormitory room might experience a lack of privacy because of noise from neighboring rooms (lack of control over incoming stimulation), or because they think they might be overheard through the thin walls (lack of control over outgoing information).

In a widely cited book, Westin (1970) identified four varieties of privacy: solitude, intimacy, anonymity, and reserve. Solitude involves deliberate physical isolation when an individual wants to be alone. (Involuntary isolation is not a form of privacy, because it involves no choice.) Solitude allows reflection, self-evaluation, and emotional release. This form of privacy involves control of both incoming stimulation and outgoing information, as in a locked bedroom. Intimacy involves the isolation of a couple, family, or group from accessibility by others; it allows "protected communication" within a social unit. It also allows free expression of emotions that are not meant for other audiences. This form of privacy exists in most private residences, but it also can be found in certain public places, such as isolated campsites. The third type of privacy, anonymity, refers to the experience of being in a crowd and having no distinct identity. Anonymity depends little on the physical setting, nor does the fourth type of privacy, reserve, which means restraint in discussing details of one's personal life.

Some people view privacy as an ability to control interpersonal boundaries, including those around the individual and around social units, such as families. Seen in this way, privacy could represent a "cultural universal"—that is, it could appear in many cultures, or perhaps all cultures (Altman, 1977).

Privacy may be important in the maintenance of a sense of autonomy and self-identity (see Figure 19-5). By observing what happens when privacy is unavailable, we can understand its importance. In a correlational study, researchers circulated a questionnaire among first-year students in a

"HELLO, I'M TAKING A POLL ON HOW PEOPLE FEEL ABOUT INVASION OF THEIR PRIVACY..."

Figure 19-5. (*Dunagin's People*, by Ralph Dunagin, courtesy of Field Newspaper Syndicate.)

some country clubs; such boundaries are effective because of social norms. In our culture, for instance, access to restrooms is regulated by signs on doors and by social norms. The same sorts of norms dictate a knock before trying a closed door.

Several strategies are available for regulating social contact through the use of physical environments. First, a person can adjust the environment itself. This can involve temporary adjustments, such as opening or closing gates and doors, or long-term adjustments, such as moving a file cabinet into a double dormitory room to separate two beds. Second, an individual can negotiate the use of a place with other potential users. This includes inviting someone to visit, suggesting that someone leave, or working out a schedule of times for using a place. Third, a person can regulate social contact by changing locations; for example, by leaving the room to retreat to a more private place, or by going where people are likely to be found. A fourth strategy, regulating one's position in a setting, has received the most attention in research. This strategy depends on *immediacy behaviors* (discussed in Chapter 5), because a person's position in a setting establishes interpersonal distance, opportunities for eye contact, or the presence of intervening barriers. For instance, the face-to-face distance a person maintains from another individual may be seen as a sign of the desired degree of involvement and type of encounter. Findings on interpersonal distance (discussed in Chapter 5) suggest that people use their positions in a setting to regulate their involvement with one another.

college dormitory. Eighteen months later, they noted the students who had dropped out for nonacademic reasons. Responses made by the dropouts suggested that they had failed to develop the effective means of regulating interaction that the other students had found. For instance, dropouts were less likely than others to shut the doors of their rooms, find a quiet place, or arrange their rooms for privacy. At the same time, the dropouts weren't likely to use their environments in certain ways to seek company, such as using the bathroom at busy times or inviting people to their rooms (Brown, Vinsel, Foss, & Altman, 1978).

Some of the most obvious environmental resources for privacy appear in places that are commonly referred to as *private*, such as residences, rooms, offices, and clubs. Occupants of places such as these can literally regulate their boundaries by opening or closing gates to fences, doors, shades, drapes, and so on. Some boundaries are relatively flimsy, like the fences surrounding

B. *Territories and the Organization of Interaction*

Some theorists maintain that, like certain nonhuman animals, humans claim and defend territories. Altman's model of privacy regulation treats territoriality as one means of maintaining necessary interpersonal boundaries. Another theorist argues that territoriality is necessary for social organization (Edney, 1976).

Territories are specific places in which occupants exercise control over access by others; the term is derived from ethology, where it refers to a place that an animal marks with calls, scents, or other signs. An animal uses its territory for nesting, breeding, and as a base for hunting and foraging. If a member of the same species enters an animal's territory, a conflict usually ensues, along with posturing and threatening gestures. The intruder usually retreats (see Carpenter, 1958; Howard, 1920). However, not all species are territorial, and not all territorial species follow the same instinctive patterns of activity.

Apparently, territoriality serves many useful functions: it disperses animals evenly over a habitat (which ensures against overgrazing or overhunting), and it provides a place for caring for the young, feeding, propagation, and a means for social organization (Carpenter, 1958; Wynne-Edwards, 1962). One researcher observed domestic cats and discovered that, when two cats met outside their territories, the animal that was ranked lower in the dominance hierarchy usually retreated without a fight. In their own territory, however, animals nearly always drove away all intruders, even those with higher dominance ranks (Leyhausen, 1965). *Territorial dominance* allows even a low-ranked animal to keep its territory.

Are people territorial? Some writers claim that we are and argue that violence stems, in part, from instinctive responses to territorial encroachment (Ardrey, 1966; Lorenz, 1966; see Chapter 10). Humans *do* form attachments to places; however, human use of space is complex and varied, unlike the stereotypic behavior observed in some species (Sundstrom & Altman, 1972). If humans are territorial, we are unique in our habit of routinely entertaining guests (Edney, 1974). Although observations of nonhuman territoriality obviously do not generalize directly to humans, we still cannot rule out the idea that humans act territorial in some ways. People maintain homes and apartments, work at prescribed work stations, and temporarily claim tables in restaurants, spaces in parks, benches at bus stops, and other public places. Anybody who has strayed onto a farmer's field only to confront the owner's shotgun will think twice before completely dismissing the idea that humans have territories.

Types of Territories. Recognizing the complexities in the ways in which people use and control places, theorists have distinguished several types of territories (for example, see Goffman, 1971; Lyman & Scott, 1967; Taylor, 1978). Altman (1975) reviewed the theories and identified three common types of territories, which are described in Table 19-1. **Primary territories** are defined as places "owned and exclusively used by individuals or groups, . . . clearly identified as theirs by others, . . . controlled on a relatively permanent basis, and . . . central to the day to day lives of the occupants" (p. 112). Examples include homes and some private offices. Primary territories are used for relatively long periods of time, they are usually decorated and personalized by their occupants, and they may express personal or group identity. These places usually provide privacy; intrusion is a serious matter. **Secondary territories** are "less central, pervasive, and exclusive" (p. 114); they are used regularly by a specific group that attempts to control access. One example of a secondary territory is a neighborhood bar, where regular users sometimes glare at outsiders and make hostile remarks to them (Cavan, 1963). **Public territories** may be temporarily established in spaces that are available to practically anyone, such as telephone booths, tables in libraries, and picnic tables in parks. Occupants, however, are expected to conform to certain norms. For example, most restaurants forbid people to bring in brown-bag lunches. Some establishments refuse to serve men unless they wear a jacket and tie. Public territories allow very little control and incorporate few physical features to assure privacy.

A fourth kind of territory, sometimes not classified as such, is called an *interaction territory;* this refers to the area around two or more people as they talk (Lyman & Scott, 1967). Analogous to an individual's

TABLE 19-1 / *Types of Territories*

Type of Territory	Occupants	Use	Control and Privacy	Examples
Primary	Individual; Family; Primary group	Regular frequent use. Long-term occupancy. Personally important activities.	High degree of control over access; high degree of privacy.	Private room; residence; apartment; private office.
Secondary	Secondary group	Regular use for varying periods.	Moderate control over access by nonmembers.	Neighborhood bar, church, or park; classroom; apartment building; fraternity house.
Public	Individual or group	Temporary use for limited period.	Limited control, limited privacy.	Table in a restaurant; bench at a bus stop; seat in a theater.

Adapted from Altman, I., *The environment and social behavior.* Monterey, Calif.: Brooks/Cole, 1975. Pp. 111–120.

personal space (see Chapter 5), these areas are like invisible bubbles that last as long as the conversations within them last. Research suggests that people hesitate to invade a conversation space; intruders show signs of discomfort and submissiveness. The "permeability" of a conversation space depends on such things as the size of the group and the status of its members (Cheyne & Efran, 1972; Efran & Cheyne, 1972, 1973, 1974; Knowles, 1972, 1973).

Interactions in Primary Territories. As in nonhuman species, a form of **territorial dominance** has been reported among humans—in which people dominate encounters in their own territories. A physician noticed that patients appeared submissive in his office, but, when he called at their homes, they were confident and assertive (Coleman, 1968; Esser, 1970). This idea was tested directly in a college dormitory. Pairs of students debated about the appropriate jail sentence for a fictional criminal. One student argued for the prosecution; the other student argued for the defense. The debate took place in one student's room. The students who were in their own rooms argued more persuasively and spent more

time talking than their visitors (Martindale, 1971). In another study, pairs consisting of a dormitory resident and a visitor worked on a cooperative task in the resident's room. When attitudes were dissimilar, residents exerted more "dominant speech patterns." However, when attitudes were similar, residents deferred to the visitors in what was called a "hospitality effect" (Conroy & Sundstrom, 1977).

Territorial dominance applies to sports. A basketball team's home court may be seen as a primary territory, because of the frequency and exclusiveness of the team's practices and games there. Figure 19-6 shows the number of games won and lost by the University of Utah basketball and football teams during a 2-year period. The teams generally won more games at home than they did on the road (Altman, 1975). Familiarity with the home court or field may have helped, but perhaps being in their own territory gave the teams an added advantage in these competitive encounters.

One important feature of primary territories is personalization of a territory to reflect the individual's personality; this may be related to the individual's sense of control. A group of researchers counted the per-

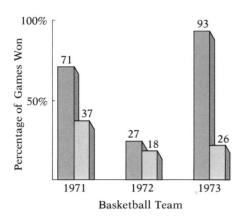
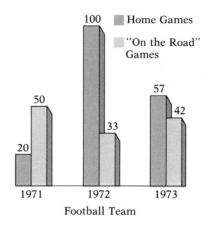

Figure 19-6. The home-court advantage in college sports.

sonal decorations, such as posters, rugs, and stereos, in a sample of college dormitories and later found out which students had dropped out of college. Drop outs had displayed fewer personal items than the other students (Hansen & Altman, 1976). Perhaps personalization had expressed the individual's commitment to the place. Another study on the same campus found more decorations in the rooms of those students who had dropped out 18 months later, but a closer analysis revealed that those decorations concerned other localities, such as former residences, whereas other students focused on their current locale (Brown et al., 1978). Moreover, the drop outs had failed to develop the strategies for privacy regulation that were used by other students; this suggests that drop outs had not realized the potential of their physical settings for privacy.

Another characteristic of primary territories is the maintenance of boundaries. A field study found that residents of houses with clearly marked boundaries, such as hedges and "no trespassing" signs, had lived in their houses longer and intended to stay longer than residents who didn't use such markers. Moreover, residents of marked houses answered their doors faster than other residents (Edney, 1972). In another study, it was found that elderly residents with marked boundaries or outdoor decorations felt protected from crime (Patterson,

1977), implying a link between physical boundaries and a sense of control.

Maintaining Group Territories. Areas controlled by groups who attempt to restrict access by nonmembers include apartment buildings and college dormitories. Urban planner Oscar Newman (1973) suggests that crime in such multiple dwelling units is related to their territorial boundaries. According to Newman, statistical data show that robberies become much more frequent as building height increases (see Figure 19-7). He claims that high-rise apartment buildings harbor crime, because people cannot easily distinguish intruders from residents in large buildings. High rises may lack boundaries that mark "zones of influence." Often, surveillance of those who enter high rises is extremely difficult.

For example, each building in the Pruitt-Igoe housing project contained more than 80 dwelling units, and the whole project could house over 2700 families; therefore, recognition of outsiders was difficult. The buildings stood on featureless grounds with neither physical nor symbolic boundaries. Each building had several entrances, which discouraged surveillance. The project provided none of the resources Newman sees as necessary for maintenance of territorial boundaries that inhibit crime.

One of the Pruitt-Igoe buildings turned out to be an exception. Workers had erected

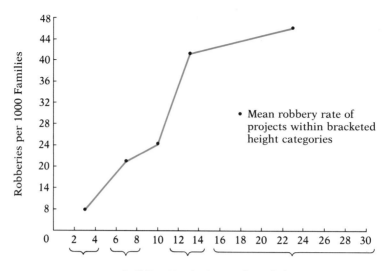

Building Height in Number of Floors

Figure 19-7. Mean rate of robberies per 1000 families in New York apartment buildings in 1969 as a function of building height (from Newman, 1973, p. 29). Note that many more robberies occur in buildings with 12 or more stories. One explanation is that high-rise dwellers cannot tell neighbors from intruders. Another possibility is that high-rise buildings allow less surveillance over space outside the apartments, such as lobbies and stairwells. According to Newman (1973), buildings with "defensible space" provide opportunities for residents to identify and monitor visitors. (From *Defensible Space*, by O. Newman. Copyright © 1972, 1973 by Oscar Newman. Reprinted by permission of Macmillan Publishing Co., Inc. and The Architectural Press Ltd.)

a chain-link fence around the building to protect construction material. When the workers left, residents of the building persuaded them to leave the fence. Two years later, the building enjoyed a vandalism rate 80% below that of the other buildings, and vacancies varied between 2% and 5%, compared with 70% in the other buildings. Residents of the building tended their "yard" and watched their gate (Newman, 1973). Of course, the fence itself may have done as much to deter criminals as the residents' territorial orientation. (Newman's ideas on territoriality are controversial and largely untested.)

Choosing Public Territory. For temporary claims on spaces in public places, people depend more on interpersonal distance than on boundaries. For example, observations in a library showed that most students who entered the library alone sat by themselves (64%); those who sat at tables with other students usually took chairs diagonally across the table. Only a few students sat directly across from or beside another student (Sommer, 1966). In studies conducted at other libraries, students maximized their distance from others or their belongings (Sommer, 1966) and stayed longest at tables where nobody else was seated (Becker, 1973).

One strategy for obtaining privacy in a public place is to occupy as much space as possible. In a study that explored this idea, students were shown diagrams of six-chair library tables and asked "If you wanted to be as far as possible from the distraction of other people, where would you sit at the table?" Or "If you wanted to have the table to yourself, where would you sit to discourage anyone else from occupying it?" These questions focused on two tactics: avoidance of other people (retreat), and attempts at keeping other people away (active defense). Most "retreat" subjects chose end chairs; the "active defenders" chose center chairs. Another study provided diagrams of an entire room with four tables and a door. "Retreat" subjects usually chose seats next to the wall, and both groups preferred seats facing away from the door at tables in the rear of the room (Sommer & Becker, 1969).

A sense of control over a public territory may depend on the length of time an occupant has been there. In an experiment conducted in a campus snack bar, a confederate approached people who had been seated for varying lengths of time and said "Excuse me, but you are sitting in my seat." Those who had been seated for only a few minutes tended to leave apologetically, but those who had been there longer tended to resist the attempted intrusion (Sommer, 1969). Another naturalistic study reported that, the longer a party of people had been on a beach, the larger the circular area they viewed as "theirs" (Edney & Jordan-Edney, 1974).

One way to establish a public territory is to mark it with personal belongings such as books or clothing. Occupants often use "markers" to reserve spaces in their absence. For instance, in an experiment conducted in a campus snack bar, either a newspaper, a paperback book, or a sweater was used to mark a seat. People sat in marked chairs in only 14% of the trials (Sommer, 1969). In an experiment conducted in a heavily used study hall, several combinations of markers were used, as shown in Figure 19-8. Each evening, an

observer recorded how long it took for a marked chair and a randomly chosen, unmarked chair to be occupied. A coat, a textbook, and a notebook consistently reserved a chair when an unmarked space was occupied after 20 minutes (Sommer & Becker, 1969). Moreover, the researchers noticed that, when an individual approached a marked chair, he or she usually asked someone whether the chair was taken. In subsequent experiments on "the good neighbor," a confederate sat at a table with another student, then left behind a stack of paperbacks. A second confederate approached. People generally did not defend the space, unless the confederate asked whether the seat was taken (Sommer & Becker, 1969). People sometimes place their own belongings in areas they had been asked to save (Hoppe, Greene, & Kenny, 1972). In another field study conducted in a library, it was found that even the "owner" of a marked space may choose another spot rather than confront an intruder (Becker & Mayo, 1971). This illustrates that claims on public spaces are tenuous. However, intrusions may be uncommon (except those made by social-psychology investigators); respondents in a survey unanimously claimed that they would not invade marked spaces (Becker, 1973). And one study found that, when a public territory is valuable enough, the occupant will defend it (Brooks & Taylor, 1979).

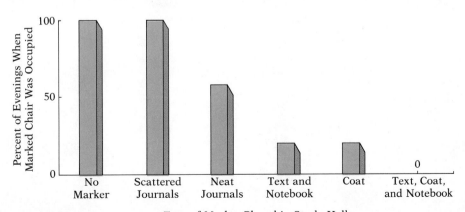

Figure 19-8. The effectiveness of different markers in establishing public territory.

Territorial Patterns within Groups. The use of physical settings indicates a person's position in a group and can help in organizing and expressing relations among members. In business organizations, for instance, an employee's status in a company is reflected by the workspace he or she occupies (see Figure 19-9, for example). Those employees who have higher ranks often enjoy private offices, whereas people of lower status work in areas with several coworkers. For executives in the CBS building in New York City, a promotion brings a larger office with more and nicer furniture—perhaps two chairs for visitors, instead of one—and a large wooden-topped desk, instead of a small metal one (see Sundstrom & Sundstrom, 1981).

A parallel between individual use of the environment and group organization appears in small groups, especially in insti-tutional settings. Sociologist **Erving Goffman** observed patients in a mental hospital and wrote:

Patients who had been on a given ward for several months tend to develop personal territories in the day room, at least to the degree that some inmates developed favorite sitting places and would make some effort to dislodge anybody who usurped them [1961, p. 244].

A systematic study found that the territorial habits exhibited by mental patients were related to their rank in the group **dominance hierarchy**—high-ranked patients tended to move throughout the entire ward, whereas those of lesser rank claimed a specific place in the ward (Esser, Chamberlain, Chapple, & Cline, 1964). Observations of a group of prison inmates showed that highly dominant group members were most mobile and had the most desirable bunks as "territo-

Figure 19-9. Physical aspects of the office environment provide clues to the status of the workers who use that office. (© Mark Godfrey/Magnum Photos, Inc.)

ries" (Austin & Bates, 1974). Apparently, these groups organized their use of the physical setting so that those with higher status enjoyed either more space or more desirable space (see Esser, 1973).

A longitudinal study of a group of boys in a reform school found that the dominant boys regularly used the most desirable spaces—but only until a change in group composition took place. After two highly dominant boys left and two new boys entered the group, the territorial behavior of the entire group decreased. The boys tended to rove about the cottage instead of using specific locations, and the tendency for dominant boys to use desirable places nearly disappeared. Cottage supervisors reported an increase of 50% in incidents of aggression. However, territorial behavior increased again during the last few weeks of observation, and aggression subsided (Sundstrom & Altman, 1974).

These findings suggest a link between territoriality and social organization in groups—a smoothly functioning group may have orderly territorial habits. Research on pairs of sailors in isolation showed that they formed habits with regard to the use of their settings; however, some of the pairs elected to quit before the study was finished. Comparisons revealed that the successful pairs established territorial habits early in their relationships, whereas the unsuccessful pairs did not (Altman, Taylor, & Wheeler, 1971). Research on families and couples suggests that territorial organization is important (Altman, Nelson, & Lett, 1972; Rosenblatt & Stevenson, 1973).

III. Influences of the Environment on Social Behavior: Ambient Conditions

So far, we have viewed the physical setting as a resource for regulating social involvements and organizing interactions. Now we view it as a determiner of the character of social encounters. For instance, a man preparing an apartment to entertain a woman he finds attractive may dim the lights, draw the drapes, play some mood

music, and put candles on the table. These efforts are intended to affect the "atmosphere" of the apartment and the encounter that is about to take place.

A. *Sociability and Pleasant Places*

The furnishings and decorations in a room can affect an individual's desire to remain and socialize. If a room makes you uncomfortable, you probably want to leave as soon as you can, and as a consequence you might rush through encounters with others. You can observe this effect in fast-food restaurants with hard plastic chairs. On the other hand, pleasant surroundings may make you feel sociable and encourage relaxed conversation.

Evidence for what could be called the "amiability effect" comes from a study in which students were ushered into one of three rooms of equal size to rate a series of photographs. The "average" room was a professor's office, well-kept but obviously a place of work. The "beautiful" room was carpeted, well-lit, pleasantly furnished, and tastefully decorated. At the other extreme, the "ugly" room looked like a janitor's storeroom. Its walls were gray, and its windows were half-covered by dirty shades; the room contained a single overhead light. The walls were lined with pails, mops, and brooms; the bare floor needed cleaning. A student interviewer asked each participant to evaluate 10 photographs of faces. Ratings were most positive in the "beautiful" room and most negative in the "ugly" room (Maslow & Mintz, 1956). The researchers unobtrusively observed the two interviewers in the study, and found that they finished their interviews more quickly in the "ugly" room. Asked to rate the photos themselves, the interviewers gave lower ratings in the "ugly" room (Mintz, 1956).

Participants in another research project viewed color slides of settings and rated them on "pleasurableness," along with their desire to be with other people in the settings. "Desire to affiliate" was greater for the slides rated as pleasurable (Russell & Mehrabian, 1978). Another study involving color slides of university professors' offices found that the addition of items such as a potted plant or an aquarium increased ratings of anticipated comfort in the setting, along with feelings of welcomeness (Campbell, 1978).

More evidence for the effect of environment on mood and associated interpersonal behavior comes from an experiment in which students listed either the positive or the negative features of their residences. Then they "ran into" another student—an accomplice in the experiment—who asked for help in a project that involved doing arithmetic problems. The students who had focused on the negative aspects of their residences were less likely to help than the students who focused on positive aspects. A second experiment revealed a similar effect on altruism after participants watched color slides of either attractive or unattractive settings (Sherrod, Armstrong, Hewitt, Madonia, Speno, & Teruya, 1977). The researchers concluded that the environment affected mood, but its influence depended to some extent on the aspects of the setting to which the individual directed his or her attention. The idea that rooms can produce a pleasant mood that affects interpersonal encounters has received only limited empirical support, but it is apparently not lost on business leaders, clinical psychologists, and other professional people who carefully decorate their offices to achieve comfortable settings.

B. *Interpersonal Effects of Environmental Stressors: Heat and Noise*

If a pleasant physical setting can encourage people to become amiable by creating a positive mood, perhaps aversive conditions have just the opposite effect. Two such conditions are heat and noise, which can produce stress. **Stress** is a physiological and psychological response to a demand or challenge that leads to arousal and mobilization of an individual's capacities for coping (see McGrath, 1970, 1976; Selye, 1971). Environmental stressors are most disturbing when they are intense and uncontrollable (see Averill, 1973; see Chapter 14 for a discussion of control). The intensity of the stress response seems to match the intensity of the stressor. For instance, soft "white" noise creates mild arousal and discomfort but apparently not enough to warrant action. Loud noise, like that produced by a police siren blaring nearby, can create intense discomfort. Most people cope with such noise by covering their ears or trying to interpose barriers.

Stress often brings about a "narrowing of attention"—when they are under stress, people ignore peripheral cues (Solly, 1969). This might reflect a reduction in individuals' capacities while they are under stress (Berkun, 1964) or a strategy for avoiding excessive input (Cohen, 1978). One potential effect of stress on social behavior is that, when they are under stress, people may ignore social cues that they would otherwise notice. To the extent that stress produces both arousal and a narrowing of attention, its effects on social behavior might involve both overresponsiveness to salient interpersonal cues and insensitivity to subtle cues.

Mild stress may produce enough discomfort to cause people to feel irritable and unsociable; as a result, heat may reduce interpersonal attraction. To examine this phenomenon, researchers placed groups of people in an environmental chamber. Half of the groups worked under "normal" temperature conditions; the other groups worked under "hot" conditions (100° F with 60% relative humidity). Participants performed simple tasks for 45 minutes. Then, after seeing an attitude scale that was supposedly completed by a stranger, they indicated how well they liked the stranger. Subjects in the "hot" condition gave the stranger lower ratings (Griffitt, 1970; Griffitt & Veitch, 1971). (For a more detailed discussion of this subject, see Chapter 10.)

Like heat, noise can produce stress; a widely cited experiment conducted by Glass and Singer (1972) illustrates this point. Participants worked for about 30 minutes on such tasks as addition of numbers and verbal reasoning problems; they were exposed to either quiet conditions or bursts of soft or loud noise. The loud noise was 108 decibels, about as loud as a power saw cutting wood. Noise was either predictable—in regular bursts—or unpredictable. The subjects who were in controllable noise conditions could press a button they were told would stop the noise if it became intolerable; the subjects who were in uncontrollable conditions had no such button. The researchers recorded errors during the tasks and measured physiological arousal. Results showed that noise had no effect on performance of simple tasks. In the beginning, participants exhibited elevated physiological response to noise, especially when it was unpredictable and uncontrollable; however, physiological reactions decreased with adaptation.

The experiment did not end with the completion of the first set of tasks. Participants continued to work in another room—a quiet one this time. They attempted to solve four puzzles, two of which were actually insoluble; the length of time they persisted indicated their "tolerance for frustration." They also proofread a manuscript. Those who had been exposed to unpredictable, uncontrollable noise showed the least tolerance for frustration and caught fewest errors in the manuscript. In other words, the unpredictable, uncontrollable noise produced *negative aftereffects* (see Gardner, 1978). Glass and Singer concluded that such noise ". . . should affect aggressiveness, exploitative behavior, liking for others, and general irritability in interpersonal relations" (1972, p. 159). These speculations have been borne out in research on aggression and altruism.

The fact that noise can produce temporary arousal suggests that it might increase the likelihood of aggression (see Chapter 10). In an experimental test of this idea, subjects were shown either aggressive or nonaggressive films. Then, in either a noisy or a quiet room, they had an ostensible opportunity to shock another person (an accomplice who did not receive the shock). As expected, participants gave more shocks under noisy conditions (Geen & O'Neal, 1969). In a similar study, students heard random bursts of either loud or soft noise; they then had an opportunity to give another person a "shock." Some subjects had been angered earlier by the research accomplice. Those subjects who were ex-

posed to loud noise and were angered gave more intense "shocks" (Donnerstein & Wilson, 1976). However, the researchers reported that, when the participants were given a button that was supposed to stop the noise, the noise no longer produced aggressiveness among those who had been angered, even when they did not exercise the control they believed they had (see Geen, 1978). These findings suggest that loud noise might increase the chances of aggression when the individual believes that the noise is uncontrollable.

If noise can make people more aggressive, it ought to make them less altruistic. One study showed lower rates of altruism among subjects even *after* exposure to noise. As they worked on a laboratory task, students heard background noise that was intended to be either distracting or soothing. When they finished and began to leave, another student (who was actually a confederate) asked for help in a project that involved arithmetic problems. The students who were exposed to distracting noise were less likely to help with the project (Sherrod & Downs, 1972). Glass and Singer predicted this sort of aftereffect as a consequence of stress. Noise also seems to decrease altruism *during* exposure. One researcher staged an accident in which a pedestrian dropped packages in a construction area. Fewer passersby stopped and helped in noisy conditions, especially when the noise was loud (Page, 1977). One explanation for this is that the noise created discomfort, which impelled people to keep moving rather than help. Another explanation is based on **overload.** This concept is derived from theories of information processing; it refers to situations in which an individual receives inputs at a faster rate or in greater numbers than he or she can process them (Miller, 1964). The environment can create overload through conditions that demand attention, such as noise, or exposure to many people. Whether excessive inputs come from the environment or from its occupants, the usual response is to try to reduce inputs, perhaps by ignoring some of them. For example, residents of New York City have been stereotyped as being insensitive to strangers;

this may be an accurate reflection of a tendency to pay little attention to the people they encounter—to avoid overload.

Noise may create overload and absorb so much of an individual's attention that none is left for someone who might need help (S. Cohen, 1978). If so, a lack of altruism may reflect a need to avoid any more inputs, or even an inability to process them. The results of a recent study support this overload interpretation. The study involved staged incidents in which an experimenter dropped a box of books. In half of the incidents, the experimenter's arm was in a cast. In some cases, a noisy power lawn mower was running nearby. When the mower was quiet, people gave more help when it was needed most—when the experimenter wore the cast. However, when the mower was running, passersby helped less frequently and were not affected by the cast (Mathews & Canon, 1975). Under noisy conditions, these people decreased their altruism and were apparently unaffected by an important social cue.

To test the idea that noise can divert attention from social cues, Cohen and Lezak (1977) showed color slides to students as they learned lists of nonsense syllables in either quiet or noisy conditions. The slides depicted people in either everyday activities or in dangerous situations. For example, one slide showed a man paying for oil at a gas station; another slide showed a man holding up a gas station. When the students were unexpectedly quizzed about the slides, those in the noisy conditions were unable to describe many of the dangerous situations. Apparently, noise decreased the amount of attention paid to social cues that might have been noticed under quiet conditions.

IV. Influences of the Environment on Social Behavior: Architecture

Architecture affects social behavior by creating opportunities for face-to-face contact or discouraging such contact through arrangements of buildings and rooms. Consider, for example, the isolation forced on the residents of the Pruitt-Igoe housing project by their buildings. The environment affects chances for conversation mainly through physical barriers that separate people. Similarly, the seating arrangement in a room can affect the character of an encounter through interpersonal distance and body orientation.

A. Interior Arrangements and Interaction

Anthropologist Edward Hall (1966) observed that, when two people work closer to each other than 10 feet, they may feel compelled to talk, because they are within conversational distance. When two people sit facing each other, the arrangement encourages eye contact and conversation.

An example of the effects of interior arrangements on social interaction can be seen in a new geriatrics ward for women at a Saskatchewan hospital. The ward room was cheerfully decorated and furnished; it was the showplace of the hospital. However, the patients seemed depressed; they sat in their new chairs staring into space. Sommer and Ross (1958) noticed that the chairs were lined up along the walls, side by side, all facing the same direction. Sommer persuaded the hospital staff to rearrange the chairs in circles around tables. The patients resisted the change, possibly because it disrupted their territorial habits; however, after a few weeks, the frequency of conversations had nearly doubled.

In a more formal experiment, students entered a well-furnished room in pairs to listen to music and give an opinion of it. They sat in chairs that were oriented directly toward each other or at angles of 90° or 180°; they were separated by various distances of up to 9 feet. As the participants waited for the music to begin, observers watched through a concealed two-way mirror and recorded affiliative behaviors, such as statements made and "positive verbal content." Distance had no effect within the range of 3 to 9 feet, but the more directly the subjects faced each other, the more affiliative they were (Mehrabian & Diamond, 1971a). In a similar experiment, groups of four strangers could choose their own seating in a room that allowed various distances and orientations. The more directly the participants faced each other, the more time they spent talking (Mehrabian & Diamond, 1971b).

The study in the geriatrics ward and those that followed illustrate what one psychiatrist dubbed *sociopetal space,* which brings people together, and *sociofugal space,* which keeps them apart (Osmond, 1957). An example of sociofugal space is the typical airport waiting area, in which chairs are bolted to the floor in rows facing the concourse. Other such spaces include some classrooms and reception rooms in hospitals. Designs that create sociofugal space may reflect deliberate attempts to provide arrangements in which people can go about their business without having to attend to one another. People go to certain places, such as lounges and bars, in order to talk. These places are usually partly sociopetal, with chairs grouped around tables to encourage conversation. Such architectural arrangements imply support of the idea that physical settings influence affiliative behaviors.

Furniture may not have much effect in a room that can easily be rearranged, provided the occupants think to rearrange it to suit their purposes—but they may not. An industrial consultant reports that, after the people in an office had moved to a new building, they found their desks in what appeared to be random disarray, but they went to work in their new places on the assumption that there was a reason for the way things were. It seems, however, that the workers had found the desks where the movers had left them (Steele, 1971). Such a tendency to overlook the physical setting or take it for granted is especially interesting in light of a recent experiment that found that people misconstrue the effects of their settings. The experiment called for conversations by pairs of people in uncomfortably distant chairs—11 feet apart—or in chairs placed at a comfortable distance. The subjects who conversed in the distant arrangement felt more ill at ease. Moreover, even though the environment allowed no choice in seating distance, participants in the distant condition held their partners responsi-

ble for their own negative feelings (Aiello & Thompson, 1978). In other words, they misattributed the effects of the setting to the people in the setting.

Seating Arrangement and Group Discussion. Just as orientation and proximity influence conversations in pairs of people, similar influences seem to operate in groups. In an experiment in which groups held discussions at circular tables, members addressed most remarks to those who were seated directly across the table (Steinzor, 1950). A related study simulated jury deliberations in groups of 12 people, who were told to elect their own foremen. The "juries" sat in rectangular tables with five chairs on the long sides and one chair at each end. Participants at the ends of the table were elected foremen more often than occupants of other positions. Moreover, people in end positions were seen as most influential, and they participated more than other members in group discussions (Strodtbeck & Hook, 1961). Perhaps dominant people chose end positions, or perhaps end positions facilitated leadership.

The idea that people address those whom they face may apply in classrooms. One study showed that, in rooms in which chairs were arranged in fixed rows, students in the front rows and in the middle sections of the classroom participated more than the students in the rear section (Sommer, 1967; see Figure 19-10). Another study showed that the grades of class members followed the same general pattern: the students who had the best grades sat in the front and middle sections of the room (Sommer, 1974). Perhaps students who face the instructor participate more, or perhaps students who do well choose "high participation" seats: a recent study confirms these hypotheses (Koneya, 1976).

Open-Plan Offices. One example of the effects of physical settings on interaction appears in an office design now popular throughout the U.S., called *office landscape,* or **open-plan office**. In this arrangement, people work in a large, open area; work spaces are separated only by moveable

| Instructor |

57%	61%	57%
37%	54%	37%
41%	51%	41%
31%	48%	31%

Figure 19-10. Classroom participation as a function of seating positions (from Sommer, 1967, p. 500). Note that students who tended to participate most were seated in the front row or in the center sections of the room. These students were relatively likely to make eye contact with the instructor. Students who sit in these seats also may obtain better grades (Sommer, 1974), but we do not know whether students who want to participate choose their seats in areas of high participation or whether the seating position influences participation. (Reproduced by special permission from "Classroom Ecology," by R. Sommer, *Journal of Applied Behavioral Science*, 1967, *3*(4), 489–503. Copyright 1967 by NTL Institute Publications.)

screens, furniture, bookcases, blackboards, and plants (see **Figure 19-11**). Compared with the undivided arrangement of open secretarial pools, office landscapes provide greater opportunities for privacy; however, they offer less privacy than individual offices (Pile, 1978). In an empirical study of an office landscape, two sections of a manufacturing firm simultaneously moved to new buildings; one of the sections moved to a landscaped arrangement. Six months later, the employees in both sections completed a questionnaire. The employees in the office landscape said they spent more time talking, cooperated less with coworkers, and accomplished less than they had prior to the move. They found the arrangement noisier and less private than their earlier quarters (Hundert & Greenfield, 1969). Another survey indicated that employees in

an open office who were satisfied with the arrangement reported having more opportunities for contact and greater solidarity (McCarrey, Peterson, Edwards, & Von Kulmiz, 1974). Employees who expressed dissatisfaction reported "too much noise, too many distractions, lack of ability to put sustained effort on a problem, lack of territory definition, overly great accessibility to others" (p. 402). Research on company moves to open-plan offices reveals that noise and communication usually increase and privacy usually decreases as a result of the open-plan arrangement (Sundstrom & Sundstrom, 1981).

Figure 19-11. In *office-landscape* arrangements, where desks are separated only by office furniture, workers have reported having less privacy and spending more time talking with others. Workers satisfied with the arrangement find opportunities for solidarity; dissatisfied workers report distractions and inability to control inputs. (Photos by Eric Sundstrom.)

B. *Residential Proximity, Interaction, and Friendship*

Just as physical proximity within a room can affect interpersonal relationships, so can the proximity of residences. A field study on this topic was conducted in a group of apartments for students. In one section of the project, called Westgate West, couples lived in two-story buildings; there were five similar apartments on each floor with front doors facing the same direction. Couples had been assigned to apartments as vacancies arose. Researchers asked each couple to name the three other couples with whom they socialized most often. Among residents of the same floor, the closer the residents' apartments were, the more often they mentioned one another. Of all next-door neighbors who could have been mentioned, 41% were chosen. Couples mentioned only 22% of the possible choices two doors away, and fewer still of the neighbors three and four doors away (Festinger, Schachter, & Back, 1950). Moreover, the results indicated that couples on the same floor mentioned one another as friends more often than those residing on differing floors, even though the physical distance between floors was small. Festinger and his colleagues introduced the concept of **functional proximity** to describe the extent to which the physical environment creates opportunities for conversation. For example, many second-floor couples were friends of first-floor couples who lived next to the stairs. Frequency of interaction, and consequent formation of friendships, may increase with functional proximity (see Chapter 6 for a discussion of other factors related to attraction).

Additional research associates friendship and functional proximity. A study of a Chicago suburb (Park Forest) reported that parties consisted mainly of neighbors from the same block (Whyte, 1956). However, this study, and the study we discussed in the preceding paragraph, were conducted among populations with high rates of turnover; most people had only recently moved into the area. If proximity helped to determine interaction and friendship, it apparently did so mainly during the initial phases of residents' relationships. Other research found that new residents in a dormitory formed initial friendships on the basis of proximity, but they later sought out people with attitudes similar to their own (Menne & Sinnett, 1971; Newcomb, 1961). Proximity doesn't influence long-term friendships unless additional conditions are present, such as similarity of attitudes and backgrounds (Gans, 1970), or necessity of continued mutual contact and assistance (Michelson, 1970).

Proximity also may contribute to animosity. In a field study conducted in a California apartment complex, researchers asked residents to name the couples they liked most and the couples they liked least. Friendships increased with proximity, but the people a resident disliked tended to live even closer than those he or she liked (Ebbesen, Kjos, & Konečni, 1976). Perhaps animosities arise in close proximity because neighbors are in a position to annoy one another by playing loud music, holding parties late at night, letting dogs run loose, and so on.

C. *Architecture and Social Overload*

If the arrangement of rooms or residences can bring people together, perhaps architecture can create too much social contact, or *social overload*. A series of studies on residential designs that encourage overload compared two types of college dormitories. In the traditional *corridor design*, students occupy rooms that are accessible from a long double-loaded corridor that is used by residents of 33 rooms; all residents share one bathroom. The *suite design* incorporates units of three double rooms clustered around a common lounge and bathroom, with rooms opening into the lounge, instead of into the corridor. When people in the suite arrangements leave their rooms, they might run into any of their five suitemates; those in the corridor arrangement might run into any of 67 other people who share a common bathroom. The corridor design creates conditions that lead to a great deal of unpredictable, uncontrollable social contact. The suite design creates conditions in which a group of suite residents can develop a "secondary territory" and control their interactions with outsiders (see Figure 19-12).

Research reveals that residents of corridor-design dormitories experience more unwanted interaction than suite-design residents, especially in rooms near the bathroom, and that they express a greater desire to avoid others. Residents of suites reported having more control over what happened on their floors. Observations in the dormitories showed that corridor residents spent more time in their rooms while they were in the dormitory, but they spent less time in the

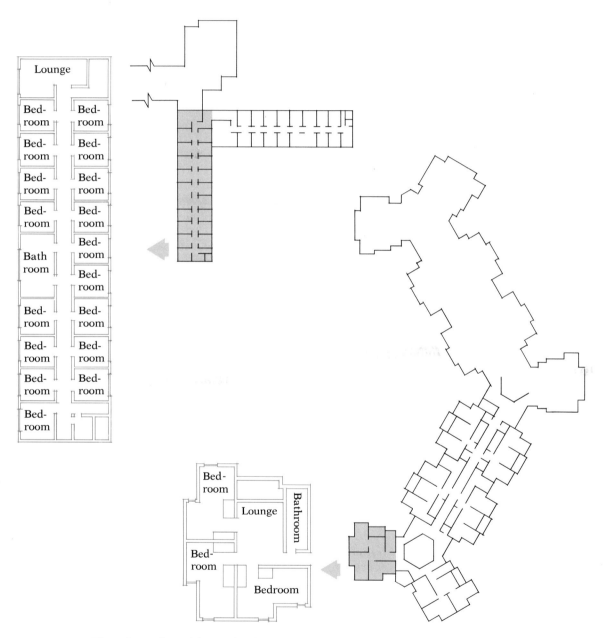

Figure 19-12. Floorplans of corridor-and-suite designs for dormitories. (From *Architecture and Social Behavior: Psychological Studies of Social Density*, by A. Baum and S. Valins. Copyright 1977 by Lawrence Erlbaum and Associates, Inc. Reprinted by permission.)

dormitory, perhaps to avoid excessive social contact (Baum & Valins, 1977).

A laboratory experiment illustrates the coping responses of corridor residents. First-year students who lived in the two types of dormitories went to a laboratory waiting room, where some waited with another student. Corridor residents maintained greater distance than suite residents, looked less frequently toward the student's face, and initiated fewer conversations. Corridor residents apparently did all they could to avoid social contact with a stranger. Such habits of social withdrawal extended to a group task in which corridor residents exhibited less desire than suite residents to rely on group consensus (Baum, Harpin, & Valins, 1975).

Residents involved in the laboratory experiment played a modified Prisoner's Dilemma game (see Chapter 9). This version of the game allowed three choices: a cooperative response, a competitive response, or a withdrawal response (in which neither party won). Reliance on withdrawal was thought to indicate helplessness. The corridor residents consistently gave more competitive and less cooperative responses than the suite residents, though both groups decreased in competitiveness over the three testing periods. By the end of the seventh week, the suite residents had become more cooperative; the corridor residents increasingly resorted to withdrawal. In postgame interviews, the corridor residents indicated that their competitive responses were designed to express dislike; they explained their choice with responses like "I don't really care what happens in the game." In order to cope with social overload created by their environment, corridor residents apparently withdrew, but they exhibited signs of learned helplessness (Baum, Aiello, & Calesnick, 1978).

In order to maintain the level of social contact they desire, corridor residents may prefer minimal interaction outside their dormitories. A recent experiment tested this idea. In the experiment, residents of both types of dormitories worked on a group task with two other people (actually confederates), who either included them in the group discussion or ignored them. Corridor residents were actually more comfortable when they were ignored, whereas suite residents were more comfortable in the "not ignored" condition (Reichner, 1979). People may not only avoid involvements with others in settings that encourage social overload but they also may carry their preference for minimal involvement into other settings.

D. *Urban Overload*

Like the corridor-design dormitories, some urban settings encourage overload, though on a larger scale. Cities bring many people into the same space; they also bring many environmental stressors—heat, noise, and air pollution, visual complexities (such as flashing neon signs and display windows), automobile traffic, and bustling crowds. One reaction you might expect from individuals is adaptation. Remember, for example, the study cited earlier in which city dwellers and residents of a small town had differing perceptual standards by which they judged various settings as "noisy" and "crowded." However, adaptation may not be enough—city dwellers probably develop other means of insulating themselves from overload, such as habitual withdrawal. This is exactly what the urban-overload hypothesis predicts (McCauley & Taylor, 1976).

Unfortunately, it is difficult to test the urban-overload hypothesis. Cities contain many sources of overload, both environmental and social; therefore, it is difficult to identify the important sources. Moreover, when city dwellers exhibit patterns of behavior that differ from those exhibited by residents of small towns, it is possible that differences in behavior reflect differences in norms or in personalities. For instance, Milgram (1970) found that urban residents are less likely than suburbanites to help strangers who ask for assistance. This finding supports the urban-overload hypothesis, but we do not know whether these findings reflect norms or personalities.

Recent research has begun to clarify some of the issues raised by the urban-overload hypothesis. For example, a study conducted in Holland involved the identification of "high-input" and "low-input" areas in certain neighborhoods of cities and rural towns. Input included noise, automobile traffic, and pedestrian traffic. In each area, researchers stationed a person who looked like a stranger in need of assistance. The person received more help in low-input areas of cities and small towns than in high-input areas (Korte, Ypma, & Toppen, 1975).

In an ingenious study of the avoidance of eye contact, researchers found that people in cities are less willing than people in suburbs or small towns to make eye contact with strangers (McCauley & Newman, 1977). In order to avoid rural/urban comparisons involving differing populations, McCauley, Coleman, and DeFusco (1978) observed commuters traveling from a quiet suburb to a busy area of Philadelphia. Male and female experimenters stood in commuter-train stations in Philadelphia in the mornings, and in the suburban stations in the evenings, and recorded the number of people leaving the trains who returned their gazes. Eye contact was consistently lower in the city, suggesting that the commuters were more likely to avoid social involvement with strangers in the city than in a setting with few sources of overload.

If the urban-overload hypothesis applies to involvement with strangers, perhaps it applies to relationships with acquaintances and friends as well. If so, urban patterns of social contacts would differ from patterns in suburbs and rural areas. Perhaps city dwellers have more acquaintances but maintain less involvement with each acquaintance. A study designed to test this hypothesis found that city dwellers reported fewer and longer conversations with friends and acquaintances, both by telephone and face to face, than suburban and rural residents (McCauley & Taylor, 1976). Apparently, the urban-overload hypothesis applies most clearly to involvement with strangers.

V. Crowding: Too Many People, Not Enough Space

As a consequence of living in a large city, people must sometimes carry out their activities in spaces that cannot accommo-date them comfortably. One possible result is **crowding**—a form of stress that can occur when people are concentrated into a relatively small space.

Popular conceptions equate crowding with high **population density**—a relatively large number of persons per unit of space. According to this oversimplified picture, a densely populated city necessarily produces crowding. Both high density and crowding are pictured as the causes of many social ills. At least 35 articles published between 1960 and 1970 in popular magazines linked high density with crime, war, alcoholism, drug addiction, poor education, family disorganization, and other social pathologies (Zlutnick & Altman, 1972). Few of these articles provided evidence to support what has become a widely accepted view. A few examples of concentration reveal flaws in the popular conception of crowding:

More than 1000 people reside in luxury apartments in a single city block of Chicago.

Eighty people attend a Manhattan cocktail party in a two-room hotel suite.

Football fans crowd into the rows of a stadium for a homecoming game.

A migrant farm-worker couple and their four children share a two-room shack for the winter.

Twelve people squeeze into an elevator in an office building.

Although these situations involve the concentration of many people into a limited space, important differences exist. First, high population density can create discomfort; however, at times, people actually seem to enjoy conditions of high density—for instance, in downtown apartments, at parties, and at football games. Second, the duration of exposure to high density is important. An elevator ride is brief compared with a winter in a crowded household. Third, the situations vary in the degree of control they give people over social contact. For instance, most cocktail parties involve a deliberate choice to seek social contact, and partygoers are free to leave. On the other hand, the farm workers and their children living in the shack may have serious problems in controlling their contact with one another.

These examples illustrate the necessity of distinguishing between the physical condition of high population density and the experience of it, and of recognizing the many different experiences that occur in high density. *Crowding* may be defined as a form of stress that *sometimes* accompanies high population density (see Stokols, 1972a). This definition assumes that high density produces stress only when it leads to the inability to maintain desired amounts of social contact (Altman, 1975; Stokols, 1972b; Sundstrom, 1975a). For example, an elevator containing 11 people might not produce crowding, unless the elevator stalls between floors, or the passengers talk too loudly, smoke, or stand in one another's way. Crowding occurs when control over interaction breaks down.

A. *The Social-Pathology Hypothesis*

The popular conception of crowding as a cause of various forms of social pathology not only inspired articles in the popular press but also encouraged research. The social-pathology hypothesis draws some of its support from studies of nonhuman animals.

Social Pathology among Nonhumans. One of the best known studies of crowding is Calhoun's (1962) experiment with rats. After building a colony of four connected pens that could comfortably house 48 rats, Calhoun supplied food and water, allowed the population to increase to 80 rats, and observed them. The crowded rats soon exhibited abnormalities in nest building, courting, mating, rearing of their young, and social organization. Some males became aggressive and disregarded the ritualized signals of submission that usually end a fight. Females often neglected their young, and as many as 75% of the infant rats died. Territories were ignored or maintained through force. Autopsies revealed signs of prolonged stress, including enlarged adrenal glands (see also Southwick, 1955).

Studies of social pathologies in crowded conditions have not been limited to laboratories. A naturalistic study of Sika deer on an island off the coast of Maryland revealed that the population had grown to an unusually high density of about one deer per acre—about 300 deer. During the winter two years later, more than 50% of the deer died, even though food was plentiful. Autopsies showed enlarged adrenal glands. More deer died the next winter, and the herd stabilized at approximately 80 animals (Christian, Flyger, & Davis, 1960). The social-pathology hypothesis is now fairly well established for many species (Freedman, 1972).

Social Pathology in the Cities. Early research revealed a correlation between the number of persons per acre and rates of mental illness and crime in cities (see Zlutnick & Altman, 1972). This evidence, though weak, supported the idea that the social-pathology hypothesis applies to human populations. However, early research overlooked the fact that crowded areas of cities usually are inhabited by poor people; social pathologies associated with high density could result from other aspects of ghetto life. A study designed to examine this issue involved Chicago census data, which showed positive correlations between the number of persons per acre and rates of death, tuberculosis, infant mortality, public assistance, and juvenile assistance. However, when factors such as occupation, income, education, ethnicity, and quality of housing were statistically controlled, the relationship between density and social pathology disappeared or became negative (Winsborough, 1965).

A second generation of correlational research distinguished between various types of density, such as *household density*—the number of persons within a residence—and *outside density*—the number of persons per acre (see Zlutnick & Altman, 1972). High household density is illustrated in the family of migrant farm workers living in a two-room house. High outside density involves contacts with people on sidewalks, in grocery stores, in parks, and other public places (see Figures 19-13 and 19-14).

The second generation of correlational research also takes account of socioeconomic status, ethnic background, and other possible confounding factors. An example of

Figure 19-13. High outside density, shown in this photo of New York City's Central Park. (© Bruce Davidson/Magnum Photos, Inc.)

Figure 19-14. High household density, illustrated here by artist Red Grooms. (Red Grooms, *Loft on 26th Street*, 1965–66. Joseph H.

Hirshhorn Museum and Sculpture Garden, Smithsonian Institution, Washington, D.C.)

this research distinguished four types of density: persons per room within a dwelling, rooms per dwelling, dwellings per structure, and structures per acre. Analysis of Chicago census data included statistical controls for differences in socioeconomic status and ethnicity. Results showed that the number-of-persons-per-room density was related to rates of mortality, public assistance, and juvenile delinquency. A similar study of New York data failed to reveal a relationship between household density and social pathology (Freedman, Heshka, & Levy, 1975). Other studies link household density to rates of violent crimes. One such study involved census tract data from 65 nations, including Canada, the United States, and Australia, and countries in Central and South America, Europe, Africa, and Asia. Even after researchers controlled statistically for socioeconomic factors, analysis of the data revealed a relationship between inside density and rates of homicide (Booth & Welch, 1973). A similar study conducted in the United States used data from 656 cities with populations of more than 25,000 people. Analyses controlled for race, education, and income and treated cities with populations of more than 100,000 separately. In larger cities, persons-per-room density accounted for significant increments in crimes against persons (such as murder, assault, and rape), especially among poor families. In smaller cities, where a crowded household is perhaps more easily escaped, the relationship between crime and household density was weaker (Booth & Welch, 1974). These studies suggest that the social-pathology hypothesis may apply to human populations, but in a limited form: high household density in large cities may be associated with high rates of violent crime, independent of socioeconomic factors (see also Kirmeyer, 1978; Verbrugge & Taylor, 1980).

B. *Theories of Crowding*

Theories regarding crowding have gone beyond the social-pathology hypothesis. For example, the identification of crowding as a form of stress inspired models that empha-size the sources of stress in high density, the processes of coping, and the settings in which crowding occurs. Other theories emphasize perceptions of situations and control over them.

Sources of Crowding. Crowding may stem from three types of antecedents that can occur in high density: overloading, thwarting, and overstaffing (Stokols, 1976, 1978). *Overloading* arises from large numbers of people or their proximity. *Thwarting* (Stokols, 1976), or *goal blocking* (Sundstrom, 1975a), occurs when many people occupy a limited space and interfere with one another's activities. For instance, in a crowded home, a teenager may be thwarted in his attempt to study in a bedroom that he shares with three brothers and sisters. Thwarting may create frustration, which could help to explain the connection between household density and violent crimes. The third source of crowding is called *overstaffing,* a term derived from Roger Barker's (1960, 1968) theory of *behavior settings* (see Chapter 1). Examples of behavior settings include classrooms, grocery stores, and banks. **Understaffed settings** contain fewer people than roles; as a result, individuals may take more responsibility and feel more involved than they do in conditions of optimal staffing. On the other hand, **overstaffed settings** contain more people than necessary to carry out requisite roles (Wicker, 1973, 1979). Here, people may feel not only crowded but also alienated. In an experiment on overstaffing in which participants worked on tasks in groups of three, the subjects felt less needed and less important when only two people could be accommodated than they did when the number of subjects matched the number of roles required to complete the task (Wicker & Kirmeyer, 1977).

Coping with Crowding. In order to cope with crowding, people may withdraw from a situation or from involvement with those present. For example, passengers on crowded elevators stand silently with their arms clenched to their sides, avoiding eye contact until they reach their floors. In an attempt to examine coping responses, researchers simulated a crowded situation. Groups of six male students worked on an impression-formation task in either a large room or a small room; researchers observed the subjects through one-way mirrors. The participants talked in pairs and rated one another's personalities. The groups contained three confederates, who, at times, introduced two types of interpersonal disturbance: intrusion and goal blocking. Intrusion involved inappropriate physical contact and excessive eye contact. Goal blocking involved inattention. The subjects who had intrusive partners rarely looked at their partner's face, especially in the small room; concurrent reports of discomfort decreased over time. Goal blocking led to more pervasive withdrawal: less gazing at the partner, less gesturing, and less willingness to discuss personal topics. Reports of irritation concurrently increased, implying that withdrawal was not effective in coping with goal blocking (Sundstrom, 1975b).

Other laboratory research shows withdrawal as a response to close proximity in crowded rooms (Greenberg & Firestone, 1977; Stokols, Rall, Pinner, & Schopler, 1973). Researchers also have observed people waiting with one or two persons in *anticipation* of being crowded, and report withdrawal among those "waiting for a crowd" (Baum & Greenberg, 1975; Baum & Koman, 1976; Greenberg & Baum, 1979). People can cope with interference by cooperating and by coordinating activities (Stokols, 1976). To deal with overstaffing, people can redistribute available tasks, creating new roles for those on the sidelines (see Wicker & Kirmeyer, 1977).

The Importance of Settings. **Daniel Stokols** (1976, 1978) maintains that crowding is most intense and difficult to resolve in **primary environments**, or places in which "an individual spends much time, relates to others on a personal basis, and engages in a wide range of personally important activities" (1976, p. 73). The best example of a primary environment is a residence. This concept resembles the "primary territory" in Altman's theory. Stokols suggests that,

in primary settings, sources of overload, thwarting, and overstaffing threaten a person's "psychological security." Moreover, crowding in such places may abridge an individual's ability to regulate social contact, since primary territories are major resources of such contact. In **secondary environments** "encounters with others are relatively transitory, anonymous, and inconsequential" (1976, p. 73). Shopping centers, sidewalks, corridors in schools, and elevators are examples of secondary settings. Crowding may be less threatening in secondary environments, because people can usually leave when they want to.

Stokols proposes that the setting determines the way in which people perceive the sources of crowding. Stokols claims that, in secondary environments, people see overload, thwarting, and overstaffing as neutral consequences of the environment; however, in primary settings, people may perceive similar sources of crowding as directed personally at themselves, which may intensify the effects of crowding. This suggests that high density in households may have more serious consequences than high density in public places—or in the laboratories of social psychologists.

The Importance of Perceptions. **Some** theorists contend that the situation affects the way in which people perceive conditions associated with crowding. For instance, Miles Patterson (1976) claims that crowding can occur when people experience arousal due to close proximity with other people, but only when they label their reaction as a negative response to the other people. (This idea follows the social-comparison theory, described in Chapter 6.) Other theorists argue that attribution of arousal to something other than the people in a room may diminish the experience of crowding. In a laboratory experiment designed to test this idea, students watched either an exciting fight film or a nonarousing film in either close or distant seating arrangements. Those who watched the fight film in close quarters apparently misattributed their arousal to the film and felt less crowded than the others (Worchel & Esterson, 1978).

C. *Effects of Crowding: Current Evidence*

Crowding in Neighborhoods and Public Places. A recent study involved the observation of residents' use of sidewalks and public places and a survey of their perceptions. Residents said they felt more crowded, encountered unfamiliar people more often, and had more unwanted social contact in business areas than they did in residential areas. People in crowded areas were less likely to use sidewalks or public places for interaction (Baum, Davis, & Aiello, 1978), revealing the difficulty of claiming space in crowded areas. Other studies have investigated crowding in neighborhoods as a source of social overload. Researchers dropped "lost letters" in the vicinity of high-density and low-density dormitories and reported that residents in low-density areas returned more letters (Bickman et al., 1973). Also in keeping with the overload model, people in a store noticed fewer details when the store was crowded than they did when it was not busy (Saegert, MacIntosh, & West, 1974).

Crowding in Residences and Institutions. Not surprisingly, research suggests that, as the number of people per room in a household increases, so does crowding. For instance, a survey among groups of students living in identical trailer houses reported increased crowding as the number of students living in each trailer increased, regardless of how many students shared a bedroom (Eoyang, 1974; see also Paulus, Cox, McCain, & Chandler, 1975). The stress associated with prolonged residential crowding may have serious consequences. For example, in a study in which students were randomly assigned to double rooms in groups of two or three, the "triples" maintained lower grades, despite their greater withdrawal (Glassman, Burkhart, Grant, & Vallery, 1978; see also Aiello, Epstein, & Karlin, 1975).

Short-Term Crowding in the Laboratory. Most laboratory experiments on crowding have asked groups of people to work for an hour or longer on a task in large or small rooms, in large or small groups, or in close or distant seating arrangements. *High density* typically means 4 to 8 square feet per person (think of an elevator containing six people seated in chairs). Participants have found such conditions to be uncomfortable (see Sundstrom, 1978). Crowded conditions also can produce physiological arousal. For instance, one experiment placed groups of 6 students in a very small room. Measurements of skin conductance indicated greater arousal in a small room than in a large room. Arousal in the small room continued throughout the experiment, indicating that the participants did not adapt to the setting (Aiello, Epstein, & Karlin, 1975; see also Evans, 1978). Laboratory research has focused on three major aspects of the effects of crowding: (1) performance of tasks, (2) adverse aftereffects, and (3) sex differences.

1. *Performance of tasks.* Early studies in the laboratory were based on the idea that, if crowding creates stress, it ought to lead people to perform poorly on tasks. However, some of the first studies failed to find a relationship between room density and the performance of students who worked on seven tasks in crowded conditions for several hours (Freedman, Klevansky, & Ehrlich, 1971). The tasks were relatively simple, involving such things as solving rudimentary arithmetic problems and crossing out certain letters in a printed text. Later research also failed to find any effects of room density on the performance of such tasks; a few studies found that subjects' performance of simple tasks was improved in crowded conditions (see Sundstrom, 1978). However, recent studies that have introduced more complicated tasks report poorer performance in crowded conditions. For instance, the performance of people who traced three-dimensional mazes suffered in crowded conditions (Paulus et al., 1976), as did the performance of people who did two things at once (Evans, 1979) or assembled things in cramped quarters where other people might get in the way (Heller, Groff, & Solomon, 1977; Saegert, 1974).

2. *Adverse aftereffects.* In an experiment modeled after Glass and Singer's studies on noise, groups of eight women worked on

tasks in either a small or a large room. Some women were told that they were free to leave at any time (to give them a sense of control). Results indicated that neither density nor control affected performance. However, when participants worked on another task in a more spacious room, those who had been crowded and had no control did worst on measures of tolerance for frustration (Sherrod, 1974; see also Cohen & Spacapan, 1978; Evans, 1979). The effects of short-term crowding may persist beyond the crowded situation, especially if crowding is uncontrollable.

3. *Sex differences.* In crowded rooms, females tend to react positively to one another, whereas males tend to react negatively to one another. For example, when groups of 8 men and 8 women worked on a task in either a large or a small room, the small room created crowding for everyone; however, women made more hostile comments under conditions of low density, whereas men made more hostile remarks under conditions of high density (Stokols et al., 1973). Parallel findings appear for cooperation versus competition (see Sundstrom, 1978).

VI. Summary

Perceptions of physical environments focus on ambient conditions (sound, temperature, air quality, lighting, and so on) and architectural features of interiors, buildings, and urban areas. Research on dimensions of perception reveals the selective and simplifying character of perception and the importance of the scale of the setting in relation to the individual. Experience with physical environments affects perceptions as a result of adaptation, or a shift in perception with continued exposure. People adapt to ambient conditions and develop perceptual standards called *adaptation levels.* Physical environments occupy places in cognitive maps, or mental images of an individual's wider environment.

We use our physical settings to attain the amount of social contact we desire at a given time, to isolate ourselves if we desire less interaction, or to increase the chances of seeing people when we want to visit. The ability to control access to the self by others is called *privacy*, which allows the choice of withdrawal from involvement with others. The environment can support two types of privacy: solitude of the individual, and intimacy in couples, families, or groups. Another way of using physical settings to regulate interaction concerns a person's position in a room, which determines interpersonal distance and opportunities for eye contact.

The use of physical environments to organize interaction can involve the establishment of territories, analogous to the claiming and defending of spaces by certain nonhuman animals. However, territorial patterns among humans are very complex; they involve numerous types of attachments to places. Primary territories, such as residences, are central to an individual's daily life, and they are subject to considerable control. Research on primary territories indicates that some people have an advantage in competitive encounters, analogous to the territorial dominance observed in other species. Secondary territories are used and controlled by the members of a group. Country clubs, neighborhood taverns, and apartment buildings are examples of secondary territories. Crime rates may be higher in apartment buildings that fail to provide the physical resources for residents to maintain territorial boundaries and monitor the activities of visitors. Individuals have little control over public territories; they are only temporarily established in places that are accessible to many people. Territorial patterns exist within groups who share an environment; when these patterns are not established, group functioning suffers.

The physical environment can influence interpersonal behavior through ambient conditions by affecting an individual's mood, or by creating stress—a complex response to a demand or challenge that brings about arousal and motivates coping responses. One environmental stressor, heat, may lead to decreased liking for other people. Another stressor, noise, can increase aggression and decrease altruism. Lowered altruism can occur when noise creates overload, which leads to inattention to certain social cues.

Architectural features can affect interpersonal behavior. Arrangements of interiors that encourage conversation, such as cocktail lounges in which chairs are grouped in circles around small tables, are called *sociopetal* spaces. Other settings discourage conversation, such as airport terminals in which chairs are bolted in rigid rows facing the concourses. In group discussions, people are most likely to talk if they face one another. This applies in classrooms, where high participation seats are in the front and in the center of the room. Current office design sometimes incorporates features that encourage interaction. In open-plan offices, conversation is made easier, but privacy is less available than it is in conventional offices.

The architecture of residences can encourage or discourage contact between people through proximity. Research evidence suggests that people choose friends from among close neighbors. However, some residences, such as dormitories of the corridor design, create too much social contact, which often produces social overload. One coping response to this type of situation is social withdrawal.

City dwellers often experience multiple sources of overload and stress. The urban-overload hypothesis suggests that urbanites decrease their involvement with other people. Evidence suggests that, in overloaded areas, people cope by engaging in less eye contact and performing fewer acts of altruism than people in suburban areas do. Such coping responses apply to strangers, but not to acquaintances and friends. City life also can involve a source of stress called *crowding*, which can occur when a physical environment cannot accommodate the people who occupy it. High population density, or a large number of persons per unit of space, has been equated with crowding; however, examples show that not all high density situations are uncomfortable, and people sometimes seek high density. *Crowding* is defined as a subjective response that sometimes occurs in high-density situations. The social-pathology hypothesis reflects the popular view of crowding and is based partly on evidence that links high density with behavioral aberrations among nonhuman species. Although early correlational research linked urban density with crime and mental illness, recent research suggests that social ills are most closely associated with household density.

Theories of crowding identify three sources of stress that might accompany high density: overloading, thwarting, and overstaffing. Overstaffed settings contain more people than jobs. All three sources of crowding elicit coping reactions, such as withdrawal in response to overload. Crowding may be more stressful in primary environments than in other settings, and it may depend on the attribution of arousal and discomfort to the other people in a setting.

Current evidence on crowding shows that crowding in residences may create health problems and lead to poor performance in school. Laboratory studies show that short-term crowding impairs performance of complex tasks and tasks that are subject to physical interference. In crowded rooms, females tend to react positively to one another, whereas males tend to react negatively to one another.

Glossary Terms

adaptation	open-plan office	scale
adaptation level	overload	secondary environment
ambient conditions	overstaffed settings	secondary territory
cognitive map	population density	stress
crowding	primary environment	territorial dominance
dominance hierarchy	primary territory	territory
functional proximity (distance)	privacy	understaffed settings
	public territory	

There is nothing so practical as a good theory. KURT LEWIN

One faces the future with one's past. PEARL S. BUCK

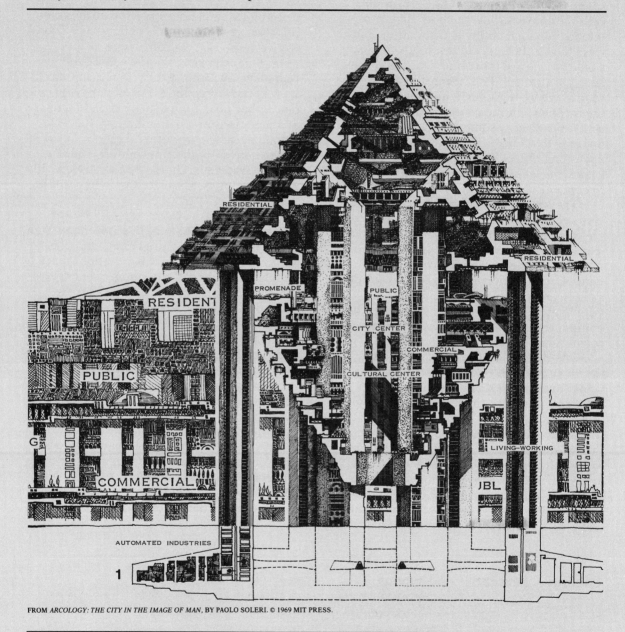

FROM *ARCOLOGY: THE CITY IN THE IMAGE OF MAN*, BY PAOLO SOLERI. © 1969 MIT PRESS.

A good society is a means to a good life for those who compose it; not something having a kind of excellence on its own account. BERTRAND RUSSELL

20

Social Psychology and Society

Social psychology has discovered a great deal about human behavior—how people love and hate, how they help and harm, how they perceive as individuals and how they relate in groups. Yet the more cynical reader might still ask "What good does this knowledge do?" After all, much of the research of social psychology has been conducted in laboratories, in a rarefied atmosphere removed from the currents of everyday life. Yet astronomy laboratories have put people on the moon, biological laboratories have developed cures for polio, and physics laboratories have produced nuclear energy, with both good and ill effects. Can social psychology match this record of contribution to society?

Some people argue that social psychology has done little. Virulent critics claim that social psychology *can't* do anything—that it has little to contribute to solving the problems of society. But there is evidence to the contrary. Although errors have been made and applications have not been as rapid as many people would like, there is substantial evidence of social-psychological contributions to understanding and solving social issues. And the potential for contribution is even greater.

Many have recognized the need for social-psychological contributions. Although technological developments in the past several decades have been tremendous, it often seems that humanity has made little headway over centuries. Yet we may be on the brink of changing that assessment—of using social psychology not to control people but to help them run their own lives in more profitable ways (see Figure 20-1). In his presidential address to the American Psychological Association, George A. Miller (1970) urged an extension of this viewpoint. He said "I can imagine nothing that we could do that would be more relevant to human welfare, and nothing that could pose a greater challenge to the next generation of psychologists, than to discover how best to give psychology away" (p. 21).

Miller, reflecting a theme of this book, notes that each of us makes assumptions about human nature. All people routinely "practice psychology" as they attempt to cope with the problems of their everyday lives. But, Miller states, they could practice it better if they knew which assumptions were scientifically verified—if the valid principles of psychology were "given away" to them. For some social psychologists Miller's words have served as a beacon. Throughout this textbook, we have tried to show how psychological knowledge can be applied to your own behavior—not only to interpersonal behaviors but also to the larger problems that our societies face now and in the future. The aim is an ambitious one, to be sure, but the potential consequences are substantial and possibly even critical to our future.

I. Pure Science or Applied Science—or Both?

The ideal of social scientists applying their knowledge to the solution of social problems sounds quite sensible. You may be surprised, however, to learn that many social psychologists have not tried to put their findings to any practical use. Moreover, considerable debate and controversy have raged about whether social psychologists *should* become involved in applied research, much less in social intervention. On the one hand, basic research scientists have felt that it is not part of their role as scientists to point out the practical value of their findings. In fact, some have held that "the pursuit of scientific knowledge is a good activity in its own right, and even better since scientific knowledge is an absolute good apart from its consequences" (Baumrin, 1970, p. 74). This position has been commonly referred to as *knowledge for knowledge's sake*. Other basic scientists, although they do not doubt that scientific findings will eventually prove useful, argue that application at this point in time is premature. Applied scientists, in contrast, advocate that science should study human problems now in order to work out solutions as well as to

Figure 20-1. People working together on neighborhood improvements where social interaction can be more important than technological advances. (© Bob Clay/Jeroboam, Inc.)

determine what the consequences of any action might be. Although arguments have flourished between these two polar positions, social psychology has, throughout its history, produced representatives of both camps, as well as individuals who conduct both basic and applied research, either simultaneously or in alternation. The brief look at social psychology's history in the next section will confirm this statement.

A. *The Waxing and Waning of Applied Interests*

The earliest work in social psychology, such as the experiments by Triplett described in Chapter 2, were primarily laboratory ventures. Although the problems were often inspired by real-world events (in Triplett's case, by bicycle racing), the objective was understanding basic principles rather than solving applied problems. Throughout the first forty years of this century, research encompassed both laboratory and field settings, although the laboratory took increasing precedence in the work of many social psychologists. Still, the problems were often very realistically defined, such as Floyd Allport's work on groups or the early stereotype work of Likert, Murphy, and Sherif (Deutsch, 1975).

During World War II, social psychology blossomed and was very often applied as well. Much of the early work on attitude change, as developed by the Yale Communication Research program (see Chapter 13) was aimed at very practical problem solving—how to maintain good morale and high performance in soldiers during the war. During this same period, Kurt Lewin was making major and highly influential contributions to the field of social psychology, and his program of **action research** (which we will discuss in more detail) was explicitly aimed at fusing basic and applied research into a single pursuit.

Despite Lewin's effort, however, many of his followers became more and more attracted to the laboratory. The research of the 1950s and 1960s focused increasingly on developing sophisticated theoretical models within a laboratory setting and disdaining any concern with real-life application (Ring, 1967, 1971). The reasons for this shift are numerous (Deutsch, 1975). In part it reflected an insecurity on the part of the fledgling field of social psychology and a belief that, by doing rigorously controlled laboratory experiments, more credibility would accrue to the discipline. In other words, the more controlled and "pure" the research was, the more scientific its practitioners could claim to be. Other external factors also played a part in this retreat to the ivory tower during the 1950s and early 1960s. Universities tend to reward the specialist—particularly the specialist who is highly productive in terms of papers and reports. Applied problems, in contrast, often require a more interdisciplinary emphasis and a much greater span of time for completion than does the more controlled laboratory experiment. During this period, applied psychologists more often worked in industry or for government organizations, whereas theoretically oriented psychologists remained in the university. Communication between the two camps was, unfortunately, often meager at best.

The past decade has witnessed a noticeable shift in the concerns of social psychologists. Although many continue to pursue primarily laboratory research, many others are actively engaging in problem-oriented research—choosing problems of high relevance, developing strategies to analyze those problems, and involving themselves in the implementation and evaluation of social programs. Lewin's legacy appears to be having a rebirth.

B. *Kurt Lewin and Action Research*

Kurt Lewin was probably the strongest early advocate of combining applied and theoretical social psychology within a single structure. In developing his **field theory** (discussed in Chapter 1), he argued that behavior must always be viewed in relation to the environment. And, although he was a passionate advocate of the importance of theory, he also argued that theory must deal with those variables in society that make a difference (Cartwright, 1978).

Lewin's statement that there is nothing so practical as a good theory has often served as the byword of the social-psychological enterprise. Yet, ironically, the context of this statement is often ignored, as investigators justify their exclusive laboratory experimentation and exclusion of applied problems. The full text of Lewin's statement gives a much more revealing picture of his beliefs:

[Close cooperation between theoretical and applied psychology] can be accomplished . . . if the theorist does not look toward applied problems with highbrow aversion or with a fear of social problems, and if the applied psychologist realizes that there is nothing so practical as a good theory [1951, p. 169].

Thus, although Kurt Lewin was interested in the development of theories, he was also interested in *doing* something with them. "Research that produces nothing but books will not suffice," he stated (1948, p. 203). Lewin tried to resolve social conflicts such as marital friction, management/worker disputes, and the psychosociological problems of minority groups. Describing his work in these areas as action research, Lewin noted that community organizations and agencies that are concerned with eliminating and preventing social problems are often unsuccessful, no matter how hard they seem to try. His goal was to transform such good will into organized, efficient action by helping community groups answer three questions: (1) What is the present situation? (2) What are the dangers? And, most important of all, (3) what shall be done? To Lewin, action research consists of "analysis, fact-finding or evaluation; and then a repetition of this whole circle of activities; indeed, a spiral of such circles" (N. Sanford, 1970, p. 4). In short, the action researcher obtains data about an organization, feeds these data into the organization, measures the change that occurs, and then repeats the process.

Lewin's goals were indeed lofty. They aimed at once at focusing on significant problems, developing solid social-psychological theory, and acting as change and intervention agents as well. Perhaps it is not surprising that such an ambitious program could not be realized in his lifetime. Yet, as we shall see, the roots were good ones, and, although the soil was inhospitable for some period and germination was slow, the products of Lewin's ideas are finally beginning to flourish.

II. Research on Significant Problems

Problem-oriented research requires a significant shift in thinking for most social psychologists. The traditional model of social psychology focuses primarily on theory and on the development of situations in which to test that theory (either laboratory or field). The problem-oriented investigator, by contrast, begins with a situation and then brings various theoretical notions to bear on that situation. At the outset, theory may be of little help; theoretical notions may come from a variety of sources, and "working speculations" may be used rather than well derived theories (Singer & Glass, 1975). As the work progresses, theories may evolve, and, through both laboratory and field research, a better understanding of the problem will emerge. With such understanding, specific interventions and programs can be developed. But let's return for a moment to the first step—the identification of the significant problems.

In recent years, social psychologists have begun to engage in many such research endeavors: health care, energy conservation, police protection, welfare policies, consumer protection, and the like. The list is a lengthy one, and we can deal with only a few of these issues. But these selections will, we hope, give increased validity to the contributions of social psychology to society. In effect, they answer the question "But what good is it?"

A. *Health Care and Medical Practice*

Health care is a major industry in many countries and a major concern in most countries throughout the world. In the United States, for example, more than 10% of personal income is devoted to health care, and the health industry is the largest service industry in the country (Taylor, 1978). In developing countries, health care often focuses on the young and on problems concerning birth and malnutrition. In more developed countries where zero population growth exists, more and more concern is being given to adult disease and the problems of the elderly. Despite the critical importance of these problems, the issues involved in health care have been primarily the province of medical personnel—of the doctors, nurses, and paramedics whose training is geared specifically toward health and illness. Yet, in recent years, social psychologists have become increasingly involved in this area and have often shown the value of social-psychological principles to the issues of health and disease.

Taylor (1978) has suggested that social psychology can contribute to five distinct areas of medicine and medical practice: etiology, prevention, management, treatment, and service delivery. Causes for ① etiology disease are often external to the person, centering on environmental factors or in particular situations. Glass (1977), for example, has conducted extensive work on the nature of the Type-A syndrome, a pattern of personality characteristics highly correlated with coronary disease, and on the ways in which situational factors affect this syndrome. Knowledge of etiology can in turn lead to recommendations for prevention. ② prevention Management, treatment, and delivery all in- ③-⑤ volve interactions between patients and the service-giving agents, and these interactions are distinctively social-psychological in nature. Although medical practice has traditionally moved forward through drugs, technology, and other external means, recent developments have shown the considerable importance of psychological factors (Friedman & DiMatteo, 1979). Social, cultural, and emotional factors are important in the treatment of illness, and "healing is seen as a process that is partially interpersonal" (Friedman & DiMatteo, 1979, p. 4). For this part of the process, social psychology is particularly well equipped. As Taylor has stated, a "special advantage of the social psychological perspective on medical issues is social psychology's orientation to situational variables which elicit, maintain, and control behavior" (1978, p. 516). Rather than relying on a clinical-psychiatric model that focuses strictly on the patient, the social-psychological perspective suggests a more interactionist view, looking at characteristics of the situation on one hand and of the patient on the other. Further, the specific communication that takes place between the provider and the recipient of services is a prototype of interpersonal communication.

There are many ways in which social-psychological principles can be applied to the specific problems of health-care services. Let's consider the application of some of these principles, first from the perspective of the physician or nurse who delivers services and then from the perspective of the patient who either accepts or rejects these services.

We often hear that doctors and nurses are "only human." If we pursue the implications of that statement, we see that many of the basic principles of perception and action that were discussed earlier in this book can be applied to the particular medical situation. For example, doctors and nurses may hold stereotypes about certain kinds of patients or certain kinds of illnesses. Alcoholics and alcoholism are good examples of this pattern of thought. Wallston and her colleagues (DeVellis, Wallston, & Wallston, 1978) found that nurses have generally negative perceptions of alcoholics. Furthermore, when asked to evaluate a particular alcoholic patient, these same nurses responded much more negatively than they did to patients with other illnesses of comparable severity. This same set of studies showed that sex discrimination also occurs in the hospital wards. Licensed practical nurses were asked to rate male and female patients who had identical illnesses. Consis-

tent with previous research discussed in Chapter 11, male and female patients were described in terms of stereotypic masculine and feminine traits. More importantly, the women patients were viewed more negatively and were considered to be less mentally healthy than the men—despite the fact that the illnesses were primarily physical rather than psychological in nature.

M. L. Snyder and Mentzer (1978) have suggested that physicians' diagnoses may be influenced by certain attributional biases. As one example, they cite Tversky and Kahneman's (1973) concept of availability, which postulates that people judge the probability of an event in terms of the psychological availability of that event. In other words, if a number of cases of a particular symptom are readily in mind (such as swine flu, perhaps), then a physician may be predisposed to make that diagnosis quite readily—even if the likelihood of that disease is quite low. There is little empirical evidence available either to support or to refute this suggestion. Yet, given the massive amount of information that physicians must store and recall—an amount that probably only a computer could do effectively—it seems quite likely that such judgment errors do occur both in the diagnosis of diseases and in the prescription of cures.

Diagnosis and evaluation are, of course, only the beginning points of the physician/patient interaction. Once having made the diagnosis, the doctor must then communicate information to the patient and attempt to elicit cooperation and compliance from the patient in the treatment of the illness. The communication process is often a difficult one, and in many cases a physician may resist giving patients complete information about their diseases. In the case of terminally ill cancer patients, for example, physicians are often reluctant to tell the patient of his or her prognosis, despite the fact that most surveys show that the majority of terminally ill people would prefer to be told that they are going to die (Snyder & Mentzer, 1978).

Hackett and Weisman (1962), in a discussion of the treatment of the dying, report a woman who had inquired about her headaches. When the doctor said it was probably nerves, she asked why she was nervous. He returned the question. She replied, "I am nervous because I have lost 60 pounds in a year, the Priest comes to see me twice a week, which he never did before, and my mother-in-law is nicer to me even though I am meaner to her. Wouldn't this make you nervous?" There was a pause. Then the doctor said, "You mean you think you are dying?" She said, "I do." He said, "You are." Then she smiled and said, "Well, I've finally broken the sound barrier; someone's finally told me the truth" (p. 122).

Susan Sontag (1978), in her insightful discussion of illness as metaphor, notes how the diagnosis of cancer is particularly secretive. Although heart attack patients may be equally likely to die as cancer patients, our society has little aversion to informing patients of heart disease, whereas cancer is often surrounded in secrecy.

The reluctance of the physician to transmit bad news appears to reflect a more general psychological principle, which Tesser and Rosen (1975) have labeled the "MUM effect." In a series of laboratory studies, these investigators have shown that people are generally much less likely to transmit bad news than good. Perceived emotional instability on the part of the recipient (a state that may well be attributed to the ill patient) increases the likelihood that bad news will be withheld. Yet, despite the difficulty that medical personnel may have in transmitting such information, most reports seem to suggest that both the patients and their families function better when information is fully disclosed (Glaser & Straus, 1965).

Particularly in the case of less serious illnesses, transmission of information is only a prelude to the recommendations for treatment. Here the role of the doctor, nurse, or other professional person is to persuade the patient to follow recommended procedures. Such a task is more difficult than one might think. One survey of patients, for example, found that an average of 42% of the patients did not comply with their physician's recommendations, and the range across a series of studies was from 4%

to 92% (Marston, 1970). Furthermore, physicians frequently underestimate this degree of noncompliance (Charney, 1972) and are often unable to judge which patients are in fact complying with their recommendations (Kasl, 1975).

Again, many social-psychological principles become relevant to this interaction. The literature of attitude change, discussed in Chapter 13, offers a number of suggestions. Stone (1979), in discussing the role of the doctor as expert, emphasizes the importance of communicating specific knowledge to the patients. Stone suggests that the physician explore the individual patient's situation fully, anticipate the patient's difficulties in following recommendations, and communicate information in a way that will maximize effectiveness. A number of skills may be involved in such a process. DiMatteo (1979) stresses the importance of the physician's nonverbal skills. As discussed in Chapter 5, a considerable amount of communication occurs through nonverbal channels, and it may be critical for the physician to be able to "decode" what the patient is saying—particularly those messages that convey fear and resistance on the part of the patient. In turn, physicians may be able to facilitate communication by being aware of nonverbal messages that they themselves are sending, because patients may rely more heavily on these—particularly when the verbal message is garbed in technical jargon not understood by the average patient.

Although the doctor's role vis-à-vis the patient is traditionally considered one of expert power, Rodin and Janis (1979) suggest that other sources of power may be more effective in the long run (see Chapter 14). *Expert* and *coercive power,* they suggest, may cause patients to react against recommendations or at least to feel that their fate is in the hands of someone else. In contrast, *referent power*, in which the physician is perceived as likeable, benevolent, and accepting, may allow patients to feel a greater sense of choice and control, as they *identify with* the source of power instead of feeling controlled by it. Rodin and Janis caution that not all situations may be suited for the use of referent power as opposed to the more traditional forms of expert and coercive power. However, their research shows that it is important to consider the specifics of the physician/patient interchange and that modifications in the traditional pattern of expert power may often lead to increased compliance and recovery.

This discussion of physician/patient relationships points up the importance of considering both parties in any health-care transaction. Not only must the physician diagnose illness and prescribe and deliver treatment, but the patient must first present the symptoms and then comply or not comply with the recommendations. Again, there are a variety of social-psychological principles that can be applied to the patient's situation.

Medical personnel rarely become involved in an individual's health care until that individual reports particular symptoms to them. Noticing such symptoms is, of course, the first step on the part of the patient, and Pennebaker and Skelton (1978) have suggested that a number of social-psychological factors may influence the reporting of such symptoms. Situations that focus attention on the body, for example, may lead to an increased awareness of physical problems. As just one example, national publicity given to public figures (such as Betty Ford) with breast cancer may make the individual woman more prone to perform self-examinations and/or to seek medical expertise. Even individual fluctuations in moods may increase or decrease the frequency with which symptoms are reported. Although it is quite likely true that the presence of actual symptoms can lead to negative mood states, the direction may go the other way as well—a negative mood may make someone more aware of perceived or actual physical disturbances. Indeed, these two factors may interact in what has been termed an *exacerbation cycle* (Storms & McCaul, 1976), with the result being an increase in the reporting of symptoms.

Awareness of one's symptoms does not always lead to an immediate search for medical attention. Often, the attributions that a person makes for the causes of his or her disability may hinder the quest (Rodin, 1978). A person may notice strange pigmentation of the skin, for example, but simply dismiss it as a bad case of sunburn rather than a potential skin cancer. Frequent stomach pains may be self-diagnosed as a minor case of nerves rather than a severe ulcer. Such inaccurate diagnosis can often result in serious delays in seeking medical help, often leading to far greater severity of the disease than would otherwise have been the case.

Even when medical problems are referred to qualified personnel, the patient may entertain a variety of causes for the illness, some of which may be unfavorable for rapid recovery. Taylor and Levin (1976), for example, found that many women blame their breast cancer on premarital sex and thus suffer guilt and remorse about their illness. Even victims of serious accidents often unreasonably attribute the misfortune to their own actions (Bulman & Wortman, 1977) and thus may engage in self-recrimination instead of self-help during the period of recovery.

The interaction between the patient and hospital personnel during the period of treatment and recovery can also be critical to the stress that a patient feels. As we discussed in Chapter 14, residents of an old-age home showed better health when they were given some control over their immediate environment. Similarly, Taylor (1979) has argued that, if patients are given a greater role in their own treatment, risks are reduced and health care is improved. Providing the patient with sufficient information about his or her illness and treatment seems to be one way to do this. As an example, abdominal-surgery patients who were given full information about the postoperative pain that they would experience required fewer narcotics and were able to leave the hospital sooner than were patients who did not receive that information (Egbert, Battit, Welch, & Bartlett, 1964). Langer, Janis, and Wolfer (1975) found that patients given both information and particular techniques for coping with the stress also showed more rapid recovery than patients who were not as involved with the process. Even in less severe or nonemergency situations, such as giving blood, it has been shown that having both information and choice (for example, choosing which arm to use for the blood sample) will lessen reactions to stress (Mills & Krantz, 1979).

In summary, the area of health care and medical practice is one to which social psychology has much to contribute. Until recently the concern of medicine was technological advancement, a trend that "created an array of tools with which to do things *to* people, thus resulting in less and less time to do things *with* people" (Wexler, 1976, p. 276), but a growing emphasis is now being placed on doing things with people. And, in this movement, social-psychological principles of situational factors and human interaction are becoming of major importance in the problem-solving venture.

B. *Energy Conservation*

Energy has clearly become a major societal problem in the past decade. As the OPEC nations continue to raise the price of oil, industrialized nations must find alternative ways to maintain their economic systems while relying less on foreign oil purchases. Some of the solutions to this problem are clearly outside the province of the social sciences; developing alternative sources of fuel, for example, is a problem for geologists, chemists, and engineers. Yet, as in the case of most such problems, the human element is as important as the technological element. As a result, problem-oriented social psychologists have turned their attention to the problems of energy conservation in recent years.

Energy conservation, on a national or international scale, clearly depends on more than a single individual's effort. This interrelationship between the individual's behavior and the consequences for society has become a focus of interest in recent years. Instigated by Garret Hardin's paper on the tragedy of the commons (see Box 20-1), social scientists have begun to discuss the concept of a **social trap**. As described by Platt (1973), social traps are situations that provide immediate individual incentives for

behaviors that in the long run may have unfortunate consequences for society if those behaviors are performed by large numbers of people. In the short run, each individual may benefit; in the long run, the society will suffer. Many of the problems of energy conservation can be related to this dilemma. Individuals may benefit from air-conditioned 65° temperatures in summer and from heated 75° temperatures in winter, but the ultimate outcome of hundreds and thousands of individuals adopting that same policy is a heavy use of energy and an eventual shortage for everyone.

What are the possible solutions to these problems? In recent years, hundreds of scientists and government officials throughout the world have labored over these questions. Some would argue that the political process is the only means of solution, with enforced controls by an external authority. *Mutually-agreed-upon coercion* is the term used by Hardin (1968). It is likely that some such forms of control will continue to be necessary. Other social scientists, however, have attempted to find ways in which individuals can be encouraged to voluntarily decrease their energy usage, and in doing so they have used a number of social-psychological principles. Among these principles are goal setting, feedback, commitment, and incentives. Each of these tactics requires some behavioral commitment on the part of the individual, reflecting the knowledge gained from early studies of race relations (see Chapter 11) that simple information is not enough—a lesson that has been relearned in some of the energy-conservation research (Geller, Ferguson, & Brasted, 1978).

One reason why a simple information campaign may not be effective in reducing people's energy consumption is that people hold a variety of beliefs about energy use—and, as we discussed in Chapter 13, unless the persuasive communication is directed at the beliefs in question, little attitude or behavioral change can be expected. To make matters more difficult, analyses of the components of people's beliefs about energy have shown that a major factor in energy use is a person's attitude about personal

Box 20-1. The Tragedy of the Commons.

The tragedy of the commons is an example of a problem with no technical solution (Hardin, 1968). Consider the example offered by Hardin. A number of people are raising cattle in a common pasture. For years, and perhaps centuries, the pasture has provided more than enough food for all of the cattle. Any number of events—for example, poaching, disease, or war—may allow each cattle herder to maintain his or her herd without infringing on the stock of others. Yet at some point this utopia may end, and the land may no longer support all of the cattle. How does this change occur?

Let us assume that each herder wants to maximize profit, raising as many cattle as possible for the meat or milk or hides that they can provide. A single herder may decide to add one additional animal to the stock. That herder will realize considerable profit from the addition. The common pasture, at the same time, will have to be divided more ways—yet our individual herder may notice less loss than gain. Eventually, however, as many herders increase their herds, the commons will be depleted. Or, as Hardin has stated, "Freedom in a commons brings ruin to all" (1968, p. 1244).

Such problems are essentially human problems, and hence they require human solutions. Social scientists have begun to study these problems. Early research suggests that neither information alone nor the knowledge of interdependence will be effective in reducing the exploitation of a resource (Linder, 1980). More promising results, using a laboratory analog, have been obtained when communication is encouraged and when subjects develop a sense of participating in the determination of how the resource is to be managed (Linder, 1980). Solutions such as these and others will have to be developed if we are to halt the depletion of common resources—the tragedy that Whitehead defines as a "remorseless working of things" (1925, p. 17).

comfort. In a survey administered by Seligman and his colleagues, including items related to belief in science, legitimacy of the energy crisis, efforts to conserve, and other relevant items, those questions that dealt most directly with a person's own comfort (see Table 20-1) were shown to be most predictive of energy consumption (Seligman, Kriss, Darley, Fazio, Becker, & Pryor, 1979). Although these results give clear support for the connection between attitudes and behavior, they make specific changes in this instance more difficult. It is far easier for an information campaign to change people's beliefs about more technical factors than about their own personal comfort.

In contrast, some behavioral techniques have been found to be reasonably effective in reducing individual energy consumption, often for extended periods of time. Pallak and Cummings (1979), for example, studied a group of homeowners who committed themselves to reducing energy consumption, both of natural-gas heating in the winter and electrical air-conditioning in the summer. Half of these homeowners were told that their efforts would be made public —their names would be listed in the paper —and the remaining participants were assured that they would not be personally identified. Public commitment proved to be a more effective deterrent, compared to either the private commitment of the other group of homeowners or no commitment at all (there was a control group that had no communication with the experimenters). In a further exploration, these same authors asked an additional group of subjects to keep an energy log, monitoring appliance usage, thermostat settings, and utility-meter readings. This procedure proved nearly as effective as the public-commit-

T A B L E 20 - 1 / *Energy-Related Questions Dealing with Personal Comfort and Family Health*

I find it very difficult to fall asleep without an air conditioner on at night.

It's essential to *my* health and well-being for the house to be air-conditioned in the summer.

How uncomfortable would you be if you turned your thermostat setting up 3 degrees from its usual setting?

While others might tolerate turning off the air-conditioner in the summer, my own need for being cool is high.

It's essential to my family's health and well-being for the house to be air-conditioned in the summer.

Reprinted by permission of V. H. Winston & Sons, 7961 Eastern Avenue, Silver Spring, MD 20910 from Seligman, Kriss, Darley, Fazio, Becker, and Pryor, "Predicting Summer Energy Consumption from Homeowners' Attitudes," *Journal of Applied Social Psychology*, 1979, Vol. 9, pp. 70 – 90.

ment condition, a result that suggests the value of self-controlled procedures.

These monitoring procedures provide direct feedback to the consumer and have frequently been shown to be effective in reducing energy consumption (Becker, 1978; Seligman & Darley, 1977). Having information readily available on just how well you're doing in your efforts can be much more effective than shutting off lights or turning down the air-conditioner without knowing whether your efforts are really making a difference. Specific goals have proved useful as well. Becker (1978) gave families a goal of 20% reduction in electricity during a several-week period in the summer, providing feedback as well, and, although those families did not quite meet the goal, their energy consumption did decrease by nearly 15%. In contrast, a group given a relatively easy goal of 2% reduction showed little change in energy use, not differing from a control group that had no goal.

Borrowing from learning and reinforcement models, other investigators have explored the use of financial incentives for reduced energy consumption. This straight-forward approach, suggested by Platt (1973) and based on an economic model of human behavior, assumes that rewarded behavior will be maintained whereas behavior that is punished or not rewarded will decrease. Using this approach, McClelland and Cook (1980) set up a contest among groups of apartment residents in a University of Colorado housing complex. In each of a series of two-week periods, the group that had conserved the most energy won $80 to use as it wished. The results of this competition were positive: over a 12-week period energy savings averaged over 6%. It was clear that "money talks." In designing a large-scale energy-saving plan, however, it would be important to consider whether the incentives awarded for energy savings exceeded the savings themselves! Furthermore, there are some serious questions as to whether energy-saving behavior will continue once the rewards are removed, and even the money itself (assuming the amounts are conservative) may lose its appeal after a short time (McClelland & Canter, 1979).

The energy question is going to continue to be a major one for decades to come. For the problem-oriented social psychologist, it is certainly an area of challenge and of potential benefit for the society.

III. From Problems to Solutions

Having looked at some specific problem areas in which social psychology has been active, let's turn our attention to the more general issue of the process of social change.

Social problems often lead to social programs and, by definition, to some form of social change. Much of the research in social psychology has been at a basic level, putting "its emphasis on the production of knowledge and (leaving) its use to the natural processes of dissemination and application" (Weiss, 1972, p. 6). However, with the recent growing emphasis on basic societal problems, the applications of social-psychological research principles have become much more extensive. Pizer and Travers (1975) have proposed that social-psychological research can contribute to the solution of social problems in at least three ways: (1) documenting problems that exist; (2) estimating the cost and benefits of alternative kinds of change; and (3) providing the means for change. Each of these areas of research has become increasingly active in the past decade.

A. *Documenting Problems*

A theme throughout much of the history of social psychology has been to document the problems that exist in society at large. Much of the early attitude research, for example, began with the goal of documenting various stereotypes and prejudices that exist in our society. An early and very famous example of research aimed at documenting existing problems is the work of Clark and Clark (1947), who administered projective tests to Blacks and Whites and demonstrated the effects of social prejudice. In the famous *Brown vs. The Board of Education* case of 1954, Kenneth Clark assumed an advocate role (Hornstein, 1975) and testified to the court as follows:

> I have reached the conclusion . . . that discrimination, prejudice, and segregation have definitely detrimental effects on the personality development of the Negro child. The essence of this detrimental effect is a confusion in the child's concept of his own self-esteem—basic feelings of inferiority, conflict, confusion in his self-image, resentment, hostility towards himself, and hostility towards Whites [Kluger, 1976, p. 353].

As those familiar with U.S. history know, the result of this case was the order to desegregate schools in the United States, under the assumption that separate educational facilities are inherently unequal. The Clarks and other investigators had defined a problem—racial prejudice. Yet it is important to note that, although they advocated a particular solution, their research had focused on the problem and not on the effectiveness of various solutions.

Later assessments have, in fact, suggested that the solution was far less beneficial than proponents would have hoped. Stephan (1979) has systematically reviewed the evidence for desegregation in terms of

the hypotheses implicitly or explicitly offered by social scientists in their testimony during the *Brown vs. The Board of Education* case. Disappointingly, he concludes that desegregation has not reduced the prejudices of Whites toward Blacks; that the self-esteem of Blacks has rarely increased in desegregated schools; and that desegregation generally has not reduced the prejudices of Blacks toward Whites. However, achievement levels of Blacks have increased in desegregated schools, providing support for the decisions if not for all of the hypothesized effects of desegregation. In this review, however, Stephan is careful to note that these conclusions are tentative. Much of the research had problems, and rarely were either the conditions of desegregation or the measures of effects constant across conditions. A clear moral of this case study is that defining problems is not enough for the concerned social scientist—solutions must be assessed as well as problems.

This is not to argue, however, that the stage of problem definition is unimportant. Indeed, it is quite impossible to devise a solution unless the problem itself is defined —a statement that, although obvious, is nevertheless ignored on occasion. Many tactics have been used to improve problem assessment. Surveys, for example, are often used to poll the opinions of various segments of the population (Andrews & Withey, 1976). Political polls often ask citizens to define the problems that are of most concern to them, and individual organizations may conduct internal surveys to assess their own particular needs. In addition, the last fifteen years have seen the development of **social indicators**—descriptive statistics about a society that facilitate concise, comprehensive, and balanced judgments about the quality of social existence (Bauer, 1966). Social indicators are most often direct measures of welfare: they may include, for example, statistics on longevity, access to medical care, crime frequency, educational enrollment, level of income, housing quality, and the use of leisure time (Executive Office of the President, 1973). Only measures that are employed repeatedly and at regular intervals can properly be considered indicators; in other words, social indicators are series of observations that allow comparisons over an extended period and that reflect long-term trends as well as unusually sharp fluctuations in rates (Sheldon & Freeman, 1970). Such numbers must of course be interpreted—in and of themselves they provide a reading, but interpretation is necessary to define the precise social problem that they may reflect.

B. *Evaluating Solutions to Social Problems*

Social scientists may or may not define a particular problem, but most often the solution to the problem is devised by politicians, bureaucrats, and other persons directly involved in the problem. In the past, social scientists were often content to maintain their role as citizens and observe the outcomes of such programs. But in 1969, Donald Campbell issued a challenge:

The United States and other modern nations should be ready for an experimental approach to social reform, an approach in which we try out new programs designed to cure specific social problems, in which we learn whether or not these programs are effective, and in which we retain, imitate, modify, or discard them on the basis of apparent effectiveness on the multiple imperfect criteria available [p. 409].

In effect, he argued for an experimenting society, and in the years since his challenge evaluation research has become one of the most active fields of social science (Guttentag & Struening, 1975; Rossi & Williams, 1972; Struening & Guttentag, 1975).

Although the term *evaluation research* has been used in many ways, a basic definition of the term is "research which is aimed at assessing or evaluating the effects of a given social action or program" (Hornstein, 1975, p. 214). This strategy can be and has been applied to a myriad of areas: college courses, mental health programs, compensatory education, income maintenance, and virtually any other social program, large or small, in which the effects of action or change can be measured. The evaluation

program can serve a few people or a few million people; it can focus on a single classroom, an entire nation, or several nations; it can last a few hours or go on indefinitely (Weiss, 1972).

Although the aim of evaluation research is quite simple, the process itself can be quite complex. Weiss (1972), in her definition of evaluation research, begins to hint at some of these complexities: "The purpose of evaluation research is to measure the effects of a program against the goals it set out to accomplish as a means of contributing to subsequent decision making about the program and improving future programming" (p. 4). Evaluation research must begin with specific questions, phrased in terms of the goals that an organization has set for itself. Again, this process might appear to be a simple matter, but in practice it often turns out to be more complex. "Program goals are often hazy, ambiguous, hard to pin down" (Weiss, 1972, p. 25). Officials of a program may have a general sense that they want their program to be better, but exactly how they want it to be better is often left vague and undefined. "Better" or "more modern" or "more effective" are general descriptions that must be translated into specific criteria before the evaluation research can proceed.

As one example, the announced goals of Operation Head Start, a program in compensatory education conducted in the United States during the late 1960s, were to compensate for the alleged educational disadvantages of poor children that caused them to have difficulties when they entered the first grades of school (Rossi & Williams, 1972). Yet the major evaluation showed that there was no noticeable improvement in cognitive skills as a result of the program. If the specific goal were a concrete improvement in cognitive skills, then the program evaluation for the most part showed the program to be a failure. However, in the swirl of controversy that surrounded this project (Hellmuth, 1970; Williams & Evans, 1972), many advocates argued that other goals were established by the project—for example, the physical health of the children may have been improved. Alternatively, cognitive skills may have improved in ways not tapped by the measures used. These kinds of controversy illustrate just a few of the problems that are involved in the specification of goals in a social program—and the care that the evaluation researcher must take to specify the exact objectives and to devise appropriate methods of measuring the outcomes of the program.

Once the exact objectives are specified, an evaluation-research program must devise methods to measure the desired effects. In such an effort, a vast arsenal of methods (as discussed in Chapter 2) may be used—interviews, questionnaires, existing records, observations, and any other available forms of data that appear to be relevant to the questions posed. Often, however, the true experiment, whether of a laboratory or field variety, is impossible to use. As a result, methodologists, most notably Donald Campbell and his colleagues, have been active in developing a number of **quasi-experimental research** designs that will approximate some of the experimental controls while allowing for the "messiness" of real live data (see Campbell & Stanley, 1966). As illustrated in Figure 20-2, considerable precautions must be taken in the interpretation of data in evaluation research. Because the investigator has little control over most of the independent variables, maintaining only some control over the data collection (the dependent variables), it is essential that very careful consideration be given to alternative explanations for the effects that are observed.

Still another feature of evaluation research is that it takes place in what Weiss (1972) has called a "turbulent setting." Social psychologists accustomed to the calm of their laboratory may find the activity of an on-site evaluation somewhat disquieting. Furthermore, the evaluation-research project itself is generally of secondary concern, at least to the members of the organization that is being evaluated. In most cases, these personnel are primarily concerned with giving service or producing a product. They are not concerned with the needs of the researchers, in many instances, and may in fact find their presence an annoyance or an inconvenience to the jobs that they are performing. Evaluation itself may affect the behavior of the personnel (see **Figure 20-3**). Personality conflicts may develop between the researcher and key personnel; the organization may suffer a crisis in some other aspect of its operation that will in turn affect the evaluation program; or the program itself may change during the course of its operation as a result of other pressures and needs. These are only some of the factors that make evaluation research a much more "turbulent" arena than the more traditional social-psychology setting.

Yet, despite the difficulties of evaluation research, its benefits can be substantial. Only through knowing how existing programs are actually working can we begin to develop the means for better solutions to the society's problems.

C. *Providing Means for Change*

Research need not be limited only to the evaluation of existing programs. In addition, social psychologists can contribute to the solution of society's problems by providing the means for change—by actually developing and testing procedures that can be used to change outcomes in a particular setting. Many of the research projects discussed in the sections on health and energy represent a beginning effort at this form of research. The studies by Langer and Rodin, discussed in Chapter 14, that attempted to increase the perceived control of residents of homes for the aged are another example of this strategy. Social psychologist Irvin Janis (1975) has conducted an extensive series of studies in the areas of smoking, weight control, and blood donation, and in each instance he has attempted to identify those conditions that will lead to success or failure. In each of these examples, social psychologists are using their experimental tools to compare various approaches to a specific problem—and, in the process of their interventions, they are creating the basis for a new social technology (Hornstein, 1975).

There is still another way in which research can contribute to the solutions of problems and provide the means for change

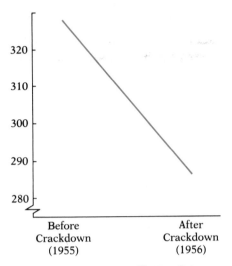

Connecticut Traffic Fatalities

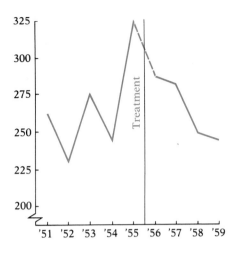

Connecticut Traffic Fatalities

Figure 20-2. **Reforms as experiments.** Donald T. Campbell, distinguished social scientist, makes a strong appeal for an experimental approach to social reform. He presents several research designs for evaluating specific programs of social amelioration. One of these is the interrupted time-series design. A convenient illustration comes from the 1955 Connecticut crackdown on speeding. After a record high of traffic fatalities in 1955, the governor instituted an unprecedentedly severe crackdown on speeding. At the end of one year of such enforcement, there had been 284 traffic deaths as compared with 324 the year before. These results are shown in the left-hand graph above, with a deliberate effort to make them look impressive. The right-hand graph includes the same data as the graph to the left, except that it is presented as part of an extended time series. Campbell acknowledges that the crackdown did have some beneficial effects, but he advocates the exploration of as many rival hypotheses as possible to explain the decline in traffic fatalities from 1955 to 1956. For example, 1956 might have been a particularly dry year, with fewer accidents due to rain or snow. There might have been a dramatic increase in use of seat belts. At least part of the 1956 drop is the product of the 1955 extremity. (It is probable that the unusually high rate in 1955 caused the crackdown, rather than, or in addition to, the crackdown's causing the 1956 drop.) Campbell asks for a public demand for hardheaded evaluation and for education about the problems and possibilities involved in the use of socially relevant data. (Adapted from "Reforms as Experiments," by D. T. Campbell, *American Psychologist*, 1969, *24*(4), 409–429. Copyright 1969 by the American Psychological Association. Used by permission.)

to occur. Consider the situation when one or more strategies have been shown to be effective in improving education, in reducing welfare rolls, or in reducing energy consumption. The translation of such knowledge into actual practice may be helped if we understand more about the policy-making process itself. Decisions are not made in a vacuum, and social conflict often results when a variety of opinions clash with one another. The practitioner of social change (see the next section) may have to deal with these issues as they arise; but the researcher may be able to contribute some information by studying the actual judgment process that occurs in a typical policy decision. Hammond (1965), for example, has suggested the use of a basic model of human judgment (the Brunswik "lens model") to explore the bases of judgmental conflict—how different policymakers may arrive at different positions on the same issue. Using this basic strategy, Summers and his colleagues (Summers, Ashworth, & Feldman-Summers, 1977) have explored people's solutions to the problem of overpopulation. They found

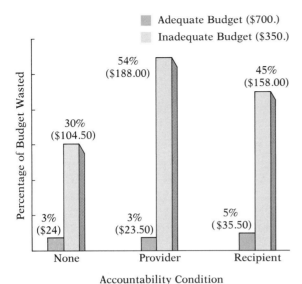

Figure 20-3. The consequences of accountability. Although many programs are currently being evaluated, the effects of such accountability on the participants in the program are not fully understood. However, social psychologists Sheldon Adelberg and C. Daniel Batson (1978) have found that when a help-giving agent is held accountable for his or her actions, the result may be fewer services to the client. The experimenters set up a fictitious service agency in which male students allocated financial resources among six applicants for financial aid. Students were given a budget that was either adequate or less than adequate to meet the demands; in addition, accountability was varied by telling subjects that they would report their decisions to the agency (provider accountability), to the applicants (recipient accountability), or to no one (no accountability). As shown in the table above, accountability made little difference when the budget was adequate. However, when the budget was inadequate, accountability resulted in a serious waste of resources. When subjects were accountable to the recipients, they tended to give some money to everyone, ignoring individual need and thus overpaying some subjects while underpaying others. When accountable to the agency, the subjects also wasted money. However, in this case, they gave either all or most of the money to only some of the applicants but still tended to ignore individual applicant needs and thus used the money in an inefficient manner. Here their goal appeared to be to spend as little money as possible, and, in the process of presumably satisfying their "agency," they neglected their clients.

(From "Accountability and Helping: When Needs Exceed Resources," by S. Adelberg and C. D. Batson, *Journal of Personality and Social Psychology*, 1978, *36*, 343–350. Copyright 1978 by the American Psychological Association. Reprinted by permission.)

that two dimensions were considered important to their respondents: (1) the voluntary or involuntary nature of a solution and (2) the economic or noneconomic nature of the proposed solution. In turn they showed that conflicts among their subjects, and presumably among real policymakers as well, could be understood more clearly in terms of these basic dimensions. Thus not only are the solutions of problems a target for social-psychological research, but the ways in which solutions can be developed and carried out can be a focus of research as well.

IV. The Nature of Social Change

Research can define the problem, evaluate alternative solutions, and provide the means for change. But the change process itself goes beyond research. As Hornstein (1975) has discussed this issue, the individual can confront a social problem and ask "Is more information needed?" If the answer is yes, then research such as we have discussed can be conducted. On the other hand, if the answer is "No, we have enough information" or even "Yes, more information is needed, but we don't have time to get it," then direct social change may be the chosen route.

A. *Strategies for Change*

The term **change agents** (R. Lippitt, Watson, & Westley, 1958; Bennis, Benne, & Chin, 1968) can be applied to those persons who are engaged in the planning and application of change methods in the society. Change can be brought about through the use of various strategies. Three major types of change strategies are (1) the empirical-rational strategy; (2) the normative-reeducative strategy; and (3) the power-coercive strategy. Since each strategy operates from a different set of assumptions about human nature, we will discuss each one separately.

The Empirical-Rational Strategy. This strategy assumes that people are rational and that they will act on the basis of the best information available. Therefore, in order to improve people's ability to make decisions, one need only present them with the facts. The **empirical-rational strategy** clearly is congenial with many Western values, such as will power and educability. Because of our belief in this strategy, we maintain public schools, write letters to our legislators, read newspapers regularly, and give money for cancer research. Of course, there are limits to how much we accept this strategy; that is, we also smoke, drive at excessive speeds, refuse to exercise, and often pick a new car by kicking its tires and slamming its doors instead of consulting *Consumer Reports* or *Canadian Consumer*. In short, we often act irrationally; hard facts have limited power to change behavior.

Another example of the limits of the empirical-rational strategy is reflected in the publication of the Pentagon Papers in the early 1970s. When Daniel Ellsberg removed these from the U.S. Department of Defense files and disseminated them, he thought his act would put an end to U.S. participation in the Vietnam War. Senator Mike Gravel, who later read the Pentagon Papers into his subcommittee records, shared this hope. In the introduction to a book in which they were reprinted, he wrote "Had the true facts been made known earlier, the war would long ago have ended." Both men were apparently convinced that an informed public was all that was necessary to compel the government to end an immoral war (Koning, 1972). Yet the publication of this information did not stop the war or even change the way the U.S. government presented information about the war to the public.

The professional role demanded by the empirical-rational strategy has been described as that of an analyst (Vollmer, 1970) —that is, one who tries objectively to diagnose a problem and to bring appropriate

data to bear on its solution. Etzioni (1978) advocates this strategy when he calls for "social scientists to make it their business to publicize data policymakers have repeatedly ignored" (p. 26). Expert testimony in front of government committees also represents a form of empirical-rational strategy. To take the argument a step further, one could easily argue that all governmental research is based on the empirical-rational strategy; that is, government agencies fund research that will produce facts, which can then be disseminated for the purpose of effecting change.

The empirical-rational strategy is limited in that no guarantee exists as to what kind of people will read the information or put it to use. As just one example of the limitations of the empirical-rational strategy, consider the outcomes of the work of the Federal Commission on Obscenity and Pornography, appointed by U.S. President Johnson in 1968. Even before the report was published in the fall of 1970, then-President Richard Nixon renounced many of the conclusions of the report. Moreover, several U.S. legislators denounced the report on national television, although these legislators admitted that neither they nor their staffs had read it! Obviously, the empirical-rational strategy is often insufficient, in and of itself, to promote extensive change.

The Normative-Reeducative Strategy. A second strategy for social change is based on different assumptions about human nature. The **normative-reeducative strategy** assumes that people are intelligent and rational, but it also assumes that they are bound up in their own particular culture. As a result, they have definite behavioral responses and patterns that are based on attitudes, values, traditions, and relationships with others. Before trying to change a person, group, or community, these cultural or normative determinants must be taken into account.

As we mentioned earlier, Kurt Lewin was one of the first to address the issue of using the normative-reeducative strategy in resolving social conflicts (Lewin, 1948), by reeducating groups through professional participation in the groups. Many police training programs that have developed since the 1970s reflect the normative-reeducative strategy. In response to riots and accusations of police brutality, analyses of activities by the police were conducted in many communities. Time-and-motion studies revealed that less than 20% of the working hours of police officers were spent in law-enforcement activities, whereas increasing portions of time were spent in a wide range of social-service activities. Bard (1970) has referred to the New York City police as a "human resource agency without parallel" and has pointed out that "maintaining order and providing interpersonal service—not law enforcement and crime suppression—are what modern police work is all about" (p. 129). Social scientists rediscovered what the police already knew—that crime in the streets is much less common than crime *off* the streets. One of the riskiest activities for police officers is handling family disputes (Driscoll, Meyer, & Schanie, 1973). In brief, the police were being trained in traditional law enforcement or property surveillance but were being called upon to serve a wide range of social-service functions (Flynn & Peterson, 1972).

To bring about change in this system, many social scientists adopted a normative-reeducative strategy for working police. They began riding in patrol cars, observing training programs, and generally acquainting themselves with the norms of law enforcement (Beilin, 1974; Peterson, 1974). Actual entry into the system was slow. Social psychologists first performed specific services for the police such as improving the ways of selecting new recruits. Next came lectures and sensitivity training that dealt with such matters as the emotionally disturbed, ways to deal with aggression, and the general area of interpersonal relations (Diamond & Lobitz, 1973; Fromkin, Brandt, King, Sherwood, & Fisher, 1974). Gradually, the social scientists became more involved in all aspects of police training—and more acceptable in the eyes of the police (Brodsky, 1974; Carlson, Thayer, & Germann, 1971).

The normative-reeducative process moves slowly; change depends upon a great deal of agreement and collaboration between the agents of change and the people in the selected system. But there have been payoffs. Bard (1970) has trained a special squad of patrol officers in the use of mediation and referral in handling domestic disturbances. This project has been highly successful in preventing homicides, reducing the number of assaults, reducing the number of arrests, and preventing injury to the police themselves. A central characteristic of this approach has been the predictability of change, which has been in the desired direction and has been approved by both the change agents and the police.

The Power-Coercive Strategy. This strategy differs from the first two in its use of power. The **power-coercive strategy** is based on political, economic, and social uses of power that have been both popular and effective in bringing about change. Federal legislation of civil rights has moved integration forward in the United States and has promoted bilingualism in Canada; labor strikes have affected economic policies; and boycotts have changed discriminatory hiring practices. Similarly, Martin Luther King, Jr., Cesar Chavez, and Saul Alinsky became famous for their power-coercive strategies in their quests for constructive change (Sharp, 1970, 1971).

In employing power-coercive methods, change agents have been concerned primarily with nonviolent strategies of change. Opposition to violent strategies is based on at least two principles. One is that the use of violence means denying human worth and that even the most favorable short-term outcome does not justify using violent methods. A second reason is that violent strategies introduce much more unpredictability into a social system than do nonviolent approaches (Fairweather, 1972). Predictability in this context refers to: (1) whether one accomplishes one's desired goals; (2) how long one's accomplishments last; and (3) whether any unanticipated, negative side effects result. When evaluated according to these three criteria, nonviolent strategies are found to be much more effective in establishing planned change throughout a broad social system. (For another point of view, see Figure 20-4.)

Nonviolent power-coercive methods have brought about much planned social change in the last two decades. Demonstrations have been accompanied by legal sanctions and class-action suits. One of the more interesting aspects of the power-coercive strategy is that it can take many forms. The case history described in Box 20-2 summarizes an unusually innovative approach to problem resolution by one of the masters of the power-coercive strategy. Despite their frequent effectiveness, power-coercive strategies are seldom sufficient change methods in and of themselves. Often they must be coupled with a normative-reeducative approach to maximize change. In fact, in most social-change endeavors, there will be occasion to use all three of these strategies in various ways at various times. Indeed, it is most difficult to use only one strategy. Yet, to be successful, the change agent must be aware of which strategy is being used, as well as how others perceive the strategy.

B. *The Role of the Social Scientist in Change*

Just as the form of social change can vary, so can the role of the social scientist vary in his or her relationship to the change process. Hornstein (1975) has discussed three different roles that the change agent may play: the expert, the collaborator, and the advocate.

The Expert Relationship. The suggested prototype of the expert relationship is the physician/patient interaction. In the analogous change situation, the social scientist plays the role of an outside expert, not directly collaborating with the change makers but, instead, offering advice from a distance. In such an endeavor, the role of the social scientist is most influential in the early stages of the change process, when plans are being formulated. Any single social scientist may, of course, be only one

Figure 20-4. The use of violent strategies. Some social scientists would argue that violent strategies may be successful as well. William Gamson (1974, 1975) analyzed the outcomes of a sample of 53 groups that sought change in the United States during the late 19th and early 20th centuries and concluded that violence was often a successful tactic when used by groups that possess a sense of confidence and a rising sense of power. Gamson's advocacy of violence as a successful tactic is qualified, however. He finds it used successfully when it is a secondary tactic, backing up primary nonviolent power-coercive strategies such as strikes, bargaining, and propaganda. "Violence, in short, is the spice of protest, not the meat and potatoes" (Gamson, 1974, p. 39). (William Gropper, *Strikebreaking, 1930s.* Courtesy of Mrs. Sophie Gropper.)

voice among many recommending directions or procedures for change. Congressional testimony is a clear example of many experts being called in, with the final decision representing some composite of the testimony of these various experts, with other political and idiosyncratic factors contributing to the final decision as well.

Box 20-2. The Employment of Power-Coercive Strategy.

The late Saul Alinsky was one of the foremost organizers of community-action groups; he trained such minority-group leaders as Cesar Chavez, who organized California's agricultural workers and then precipitated a national consumer boycott against California grapes. Alinsky was a proponent of the power-coercive strategy and used this strategy in quite different ways. One of the more novel uses of this approach was his Rochester, New York, battle with Eastman Kodak. Following a Rochester race riot that was partially due to a conflict over Kodak's inadequate training and job programs for Blacks, the local churches invited Alinsky to work in their Black ghetto. He accepted and soon founded a community-action group called FIGHT (Freedom, Integration, God, Honor, Today). Instead of depending on community-action tactics such as picketing and demonstrating, FIGHT began soliciting stock proxies from churches, individuals, and organizations as a direct power challenge to Kodak's policies. Enough proxies were turned over to FIGHT to enable the group to force Kodak to improve its policies concerning minority groups.

For the expert's advice to be taken most seriously, Hornstein (1975) suggests that three conditions are necessary: (1) policymakers must be experiencing a need for change; (2) proposed solutions must fall within the perceived capabilities and goals of the organization; and (3) policymakers must have the motivation to take action as required. If each of these conditions does not hold true, the expert's advice may fall on deaf ears. A number of factors can prevent one or more of these conditions from existing. The motivation to comply with suggestions, for example, can be hindered by an inability to translate the suggestions into action. Even when the translation process is feasible, organizations may be reluctant to take what they perceive as risks in following the recommendations. On some occasions, the organization may fear the results of the study or the publicity that might be given to those results. In the United States, for example, organizations are often reluctant to engage in studies of sex and ethnic discrimination, fearful that the results will reflect badly on the company and expose them to potential lawsuits.

The Collaborative Relationship. As Lewin recognized early on, many of the fears or motivational problems that may occur in the expert relationship are minimized when the social scientist takes a collaborative role. Indeed, it has been argued "that the adaptation of research findings is primarily determined by the motivational by-products of collaboration rather than by the technical expertise of a research effort" (Hornstein, 1975, p. 223). The work of Lewin and his colleagues, described in Chapter 18, is an example of the collaborative relationship in an industrial setting. Indeed, Lewin's whole strategy of action research exemplified the collaborative relationship between the social scientist and the target of change. Technical expertise is not sufficient in this kind of relationship; in addition, the social scientist must have skills in the interpersonal area to help facilitate group and individual functioning as the team moves toward its goal.

The Advocate Relationship. In both expert and collaborative relationships, the agent of change (the social scientist) and the object of change (the organization) tend to agree on the goals that are to be pursued. In contrast, in an advocate relationship, the social scientist may disavow collaboration and instead pursue a path of action aimed at changing the organization from outside. This role of the change agent is most evident in the use of the power-coercive strategy, although the extent of involvement and the forms of power used may vary widely. In some instances, for example, the social scientist may simply present the results of a study in a forceful and well-publicized manner: the Clarks' use of their data on self-concept among Blacks is an example of this strategy.

Kenneth Ring (1971), after criticizing much of earlier social-psychological activities, has argued for a new "psychology of the left," which would combine advocacy research and partisan social action. The work of social psychologist Hannah Levin (1970) exemplifies Ring's "new left" position. While working as a consultant to a community health center, Levin was dismayed by the fact that the people who lived near the health center had little or no say in its operation. The health authorities told the people that they could have an advisory board, but those who actually administered the health program would have to be physicians. However, the people wanted the operating policies to be determined by the local residents. In the confrontation that followed, Levin became a professional advocate for the people. Levin and the people's groups were informed that they could advise, or even participate, but not control. The health authorities were unable to see the difference between participation and control. According to Levin, the people's retort was "If you don't see any real difference between participation and control, then you can participate and the community will control!" (1970, p. 123). Through Levin's advocacy, the people were able to establish influence over the policies of the health center. One outcome of community control was a shift in priorities from programs that emphasized treatment of suicidal and acutely disturbed patients to programs that focused on young people. The people in the community declared that it was irresponsible of the health center to ignore the many health needs of school children for the sake of a "few suicides" and "psychotics."

C. *The Development of Social Technology*

Although most social psychologists believe that their research will eventually have practical applications, many resist applying current knowledge to current problems. Our knowledge is imperfect and our understanding inadequate, they claim. Yet, as we have seen, some other social psychologists are much more inclined to apply our findings now, believing that we already have a good deal of basic technology to use in the solution of social problems. Jacobo Varela (1971, 1975, 1977, 1978) has been perhaps the most passionate advocate of such a **social technology**. From his background in engineering, Varela moved to social sciences, attempting to use many of the same strategies but with a different set of tools. His arguments are persuasive:

The fact is that we already have most of the technology we need to solve an enormous range of social problems, from personal miseries to organizational conflict, from the marriage bed to the conference table. If we wait for pure research to come up with real-world answers, though, we will be waiting for Godot. . . . Engineers and physical scientists cannot wait for theoretical perfection. If the Romans had waited for the elegance of the Verrazano-Narrows Bridge instead of fooling around with stone arches, the course of civilization would have changed. The Roman arches had their faults, but they have lasted nineteen centuries [1978, p. 84].

Many would disagree with Varela's analysis. Yet, just as there are many methods for doing research, there are also many responses to the outcomes of research, and no single response or tactic has an exclusive claim on the truth. It is imperative that social psychologists continue to do basic theory-oriented research, both in the laboratory and in natural settings (McGuire, 1967b), for such research will add to our knowledge and form the basis for future social technologies. Yet at some point, we may be obligated to use the knowledge that we have in the solution of social problems. And many would argue that the time has come.

V. Futuristics and the Future

"If anything is important it is the future. The past is gone and the present exists only as a fleeting moment. Everything that we think and do from this moment on can affect only the future" (Cornish, 1977, p. vii). These words might be considered the creed of futuristics, a field devoted to looking forward to what will come and attempting to propose solutions to those future challenges. As defined by Cornish, **futuristics** is:

A field of activity that seeks to identify, analyze, and evaluate possible future changes in human life and the world. The word implies a rational rather than mystical approach to the future, but also accepts artistic, imaginative, and experiential approaches as offering contributions that can be useful and valid [1977, p. 258].

Within the past decade, there has been a proliferation of organizations devoted to the study of the future—although few social psychologists have been involved. Some of these future-oriented groups include the World Future Society and the Club of Rome. Organizations devoted to futuristics include the Institute for the Future in Menlo Park, California, the Hudson Institute, the Social Policy Research Institute at Stanford University, and a host of others. However, the study of the future is not a new endeavor. As long as people have thought and dreamed, there have been utopian thinkers, who shared their dreams about alternative futures. In works from Plato's *Republic* to Skinner's *Walden Two*, men and women have tried to define possible futures. The science fiction literature, from Jules Verne to the present, has consistently dealt with prediction of worlds to come. These predictions deal with both technical and human elements. As just one example of the latter, Isaac Asimov's *Foundation* trilogy depicts the struggle of social scientists applying "psycho-history" to the development of the society of the universe.

For many people, concern with the future was not made vivid until the 1970 publication of Alvin Toffler's book on future shock. **Future shock**, as defined by Toffler, refers to the shattering stress and disorientation that people experience when they are overwhelmed by an accelerating rate of change (see, for example, Figure 20-5). Toffler points to a variety of experiences in today's world that lead to the experience of future shock: increased transience of both people and products, novelty, greatly increased diversity in products and life-styles (often leading to a condition that could be called "over-choice"), a data deluge made possible by the advent of high-speed computers, and genetic innovation. There is considerable evidence that both the number and pace of these changes is greater than ever before. Yet, while such technology advances rapidly, Toffler suggests that the human may not be able to adapt so readily. Symptoms of future shock described by Toffler range from confusion, anxiety, and hostility, through physical illness, seemingly senseless violence, and self-destructive apathy. Victims of future shock feel continuously harassed and hence attempt to reduce the number of changes that they must come to terms with and the number of decisions they must make (Toffler, 1970).

A helpful way to grasp the implications of future shock is to look at a parallel term, *culture shock*. Novice world travelers experience culture shock when they find themselves in a totally new environment, cut off from the meaning of events around them and without familiar psychological cues. But such travelers have the comforting knowledge that they can go back to the culture they left behind—or, in many cases, can find islands of their own culture in the foreign country. Travelers from the United States, for example, may quickly seek out hamburger stands, English-language newspapers, and syndicated television shows to reduce their shock. Future shock may be viewed as a culture shock in one's own society, arising when a new culture is superimposed upon an old one. For the victim of future shock, however, there is little likelihood of returning to the familiarity that we left behind.

Because "we can't go home again," to borrow a phrase from Thomas Wolfe, futurists argue that it is imperative that we look to the future. Toffler (1970) says that every

Figure 20-5. The rapid growth of computers is both a cause and effect of change in society, creating future shock for some people and challenges for others. (© Leonard Freed/Magnum Photos, Inc.)

society faces not merely a succession of probable futures but an array of possible futures and a conflict over which future is preferable. "The management of change is the effort to convert certain possibles into probables, in pursuit of agreed-on preferables. Determining the probable calls for a *science* of futurism. Delineating the possible calls for an *art* of futurism. Defining the preferable calls for a *politics* of futurism" (Toffler, 1970, p. 409).

Technological changes are perhaps the most noticeable events and also the most predictable. In fact, futurists will state that "almost anything can be done in 20 years," (Cornish, 1977)—some might even say ten— and point to the development of atomic power in four years and putting people on the moon in eight years. Yet changes occur

not only on the technological level but on the human level as well. Values in the post-industrialized age have changed from those held in earlier periods (see Table 20-2), and technology is both a result and a cause of shifts in human behaviors and values (see, for example, Figure 20-6).

In looking to life in the year 2000, members of the World Future Society predict that people from different countries will be more unified in a world community; most people will have more leisure time and a higher standard of living; families will be less stable, and people will be more mobile and better educated. These are, of course, only possible futures or, as the early French futurist Bertrand de Jouvenal would say, *futuribles*—"events or situations that might logically develop from the present" (Cornish, 1977). Yet "since the future does not exist, it must be invented" (Cornish, 1977, p. 99). In other words, we must give some thought to the future in order to have any effect on it. Such prediction holds risk as well as challenge. Nevertheless, predictions of what lies ahead may help to clarify goals and provide alternative policies.

Where does social psychology fit into the study of the future? Some critics would suggest that the field has little to offer. A bold article by social psychologist Kenneth Gergen (1973) provides the most salient example of this criticism. Gergen proposed that social psychology is primarily a historical inquiry and that it will never be as successful as the natural sciences in building a cumulative structure of knowledge. In Gergen's view, social psychology deals mostly with "facts that are essentially nonrepeatable and which fluctuate markedly over time" (Gergen, 1973, p. 310). If this is the case, we would have to conclude that principles of social behavior, established today, would be of little use in predicting future social behavior.

Although many social psychologists have expressed disenchantment during the last decade over the seeming lack of progress in the field (Harré & Secord, 1972; Israel & Tajfel, 1972; McGuire, 1973; Shaver, 1974; Smith, 1972), few were prepared to accept the attack by Gergen on the fun-

Figure 20-6. The East Wing of the National Gallery in Washington, D.C., reflects a blend of artistic values and technological advances. (© Ann Chwatsky/Editorial Photocolor Archives, Inc.)

damental scientific orientation of the field. In a detailed critique, Schlenker (1974) has expressed faith in the traditional scientific approach and judges it to be the best approach to the orderly accumulation of knowledge about social behavior. In response to Gergen's claim that "facts" can be reversed over time, Schlenker notes that one of the necessary conditions for the formulation of generalizable theories is that they be phrased in sufficiently abstract form to allow for the effects of specific contingencies. Other respondents have noted that, although "facts" may change over time, the *processes* determining them remain constant. For example, Paige (1970) has shown that changes in attitude of Blacks toward Whites from the mid-1940s to the mid-1960s could be understood by considering the political context in which they operated. That is, whatever attitudes were expressed reflected a more general political orientation that specified how to deal with members of the White majority. To look at an even more basic example, the principles of reinforcement may continue to apply across generations; the specific characteristics of the reinforcer, however, may vary across both space and time.

Although Gergen's arguments seem to us unduly pessimistic, it is true that social psychology has not attained the exactitude of some of the physical sciences. Too rarely have we been concerned with making specific point predictions—that is, saying exactly how much of some behavior will occur or when it will occur (Deaux, 1978a)—and too often have we been content to simply make contrasts—for example, more aggression will occur under these conditions than those, more helping will occur when this variable is present than when it is not. Yet, throughout this book, we have seen some exceptions to this general statement: for ex-

TABLE 20-2 / *Changes in Emphasis in the Transition to Postindustrialism*

Type of Change	From	Toward
Cultural values	Achievement Self-control Independence Endurance of distress	Self-actualization Self-expression Interdependence Capacity for joy
Organizational philosophies	Mechanistic forms Competitive relations Separate objectives Own resources regarded as owned absolutely	Organic forms Collaborative relations Linked objectives Own resources regarded also as society's
Organizational practices	Responsive to crisis Specific measures Requiring consent Short planning horizon Damping conflict Detailed central control Small local units Standardized administration Separate services	Anticipative of crisis Comprehensive measures Requiring participation Long planning horizon Confronting conflict Generalized central control Enlarged local units Innovative administration Coordinated services

Adapted from "Between Cultures: The Current Crisis of Transition," by C. R. Price. In W. Schmidt (Ed.), *Organizational Frontiers and Human Values*. Reprinted by permission of the author.

ample, Zajonc and Markus have made some rather precise predictions of children's intelligence as a function of family size, and other investigators have begun to chart the exact relationship between temperature and aggression. In the coming years, we think that there will be more of this kind of research, as social psychologists attempt to take the principles that have been established and refine their predictions as to when the behaviors will or will not occur.

Furthermore, in studying the process of social change itself, we can be better prepared for the future. Understanding how people change may allow us to better cope with a future filled with change, and social psychologists may form a partnership with the futurists in leading toward the year 2001 and beyond.

VI. Summary

It is essential that social-psychological knowledge be applied so that we can remedy social problems and understand the social change that we encounter in everyday life. In fact, an important aspect of social psychology is its concern with problems that are relevant to our society and to each of us as social beings. The methodology of social psychology permits the study and understanding of complex social phenomena, but, despite this, many social researchers have not been interested in the real-world applicability of their research findings. However, this trend has shifted in recent years, representing a recognition of the early ideas of Kurt Lewin and his concept of action research.

Two significant problems that have received substantial research attention in recent years are health care and energy conservation. Within the health-care area, it has been recognized that healing is an interpersonal as well as a medical process. Principles of stereotyping and attribution have been applied to the perceptions that doctors and nurses have of their patients and to the diagnoses and treatments that may result from these perceptions. Principles of communication have also been used to understand the nature of physician/patient interactions. Similarly, concepts of persuasion and social influence have been applied to the problems of patient compliance with recommendations.

Attribution theory has also been used in understanding the ways in which patients view themselves, report symptoms, and request health care. Concepts of control have been applied to give patients a greater role in their own treatment.

Social traps are situations that provide immediate individual incentives for behaviors that in the long run may have unfortunate consequences for the society. Energy-conservation programs depend in large part upon an alteration of individual energy use for the good of the society as a whole. Various psychological principles have been applied to the problem of energy conservation; these include goal setting, feedback, commitment, and incentives.

Social psychology can contribute to the process of social change in three ways: by documenting problems that exist, by estimating the costs and benefits of alternative kinds of change, and by providing the means for change. Work on social indicators, programs of evaluation research, and the design of intervention strategies are just a few of the ways in which research can contribute to the solution of social problems.

Social scientists may also be involved in the process of change itself. Three strategies for planned change are the *empirical-rational strategy*, the *normative-reeducative strategy*, and the *power-coercive strategy*. The empirical-rational strategy assumes that people will act on the basis of the best available information and hence focuses on dissemination of information as a means to change. The normative-reeducative strategy assumes that our behavior is based on attitudes, values, and interpersonal relationships, and it takes these factors into account when planning change. The power-coercive strategy utilizes political, social, and economic pressures to bring about desired social change.

The social scientist can have three roles in the change process: as an expert, as a collaborator, or as an advocate. These roles vary in their level of involvement with the change process itself. *Social technology* is the application of social science principles to the solution of social problems.

The field of *futuristics* is concerned with the prediction of future changes in human life and the world. Although concern with the future and plans for utopian societies are not new, the concept of future shock is of more recent vintage. *Future shock* refers to the stress that people experience when they are overwhelmed by an accelerating rate of change, characteristic of much of the world today.

Some people have argued that social psychology has little to contribute to the understanding of the future; many others, however, believe that basic social processes remain unchanged and that an understanding of social behavior will allow us both to predict the future and to deal with that future more effectively.

Glossary Terms

action research
change agents
empirical-rational strategy
evaluation research
field theory

future shock
futuristics
normative-reeducative strategy
power-coercive strategy

quasi-experimental research
social indicators
social technology
social trap

Glossary

abstract modeling. From social-learning theory, the process of extracting common principles from a series of observations and formulating rules for behavior.

action research. Research that has as its goal the understanding or solution of social problems.

adaptation. Shift in perception of one's environment that occurs with continued exposure, often involving decreased sensitivity to aversive conditions, such as noise.

adaptation level. Personal, cognitive standard for evaluating new conditions, such as the noisiness of a city street.

altruism. A special form of helping behavior that is voluntary, costly, and motivated by something other than the anticipation of reward.

ambient conditions. Physical qualities of the atmosphere surrounding an individual: sounds, lighting, air quality, temperature, and humidity.

anal stage. The Freudian developmental stage that is characteristic of the 2- to 3-year-old child and centered on toilet training and elimination of waste.

anchor. A reference point that is used in making judgments.

androgyny. A term referring to a high degree of masculine (or agentic) traits and a high degree of feminine (or communal) traits; currently used by investigators to refer to psychological, rather than physical, characteristics.

anticonformity. Behavior that is directly antithetical to the normative group expectations. Also called counterconformity.

archival research. Analysis of existing documents or records, especially those contained in public archives.

assimilation effects. A term used in social-judgment theory that refers to shifts in judgments toward an anchor point.

attribution theory. A theory, stemming from the work of Fritz Heider and from Gestalt theory, concerning the way in which people assign characteristics or intentions to other persons or to objects.

authoritarianism. A basic personality dimension that includes a set of organized beliefs, values, and preferences, including submission to authority, identification with authority, denial of feelings, and cynicism.

autokinetic effect. The tendency for a stationary light, when viewed in an otherwise completely darkened room, to appear to be moving.

autonomous stage of morality. A later stage of moral development in which rules are seen as modifiable in order to fit the needs of a given situation.

basking in reflected glory. Publicizing one's association with successful others in order to maintain and enhance the esteem in which one is held.

behavior settings. A term used in Barker's ecological psychology to refer to every location-activity combination. Thus the term *behavior settings* refers not only to physical localities (a gymnasium, a street corner, a drugstore) but also to the activities that take place within them.

bisexual. One whose sexual behavior pattern includes both heterosexual and homosexual activity during similar periods of time. Popularly termed *AC-DC* (for alternating and direct current).

bystander effect. The finding that a person is less

likely to provide help when in the presence of other witnesses than when alone.

catharsis. The concept that engaging in "safe" or socially acceptable acts of aggression will discharge energy and reduce the tendency toward aggression.

causal schemata. A conception of the manner in which two or more causal factors interact in relation to a particular kind of effect; an assumed pattern of data in a complete analysis-of-variance framework.

central trait. A personal characteristic that strongly influences a perceiver's impressions of the person possessing the trait. Asch showed that the *warm–cold* personality dimension was such a central trait.

change agents. Persons who are engaged in the planning and application of change methods in the society.

cognition. A mental event in which perceptions, memories, beliefs, or thoughts are processed.

cognitive. Refers to thought or mental, rather than emotional, orientation.

cognitive dissonance. A state in which a person holds two beliefs or cognitions that are inconsistent with one another.

cognitive map. A mental image of a physical environment.

cognitive theory. A theory that emphasizes thinking and mental processes rather than emotional or motivational processes.

cohesiveness. The attractiveness that a group has for its members and that the members have for one another; the force that holds a group together.

communication networks. Representations of the acceptable paths of communication between persons in a group or organization.

competition. Striving to excel in order to obtain an exclusive goal.

competitive reward structure. A reward structure in which not all people striving for a reward can attain it and in which movement toward the goal by one person decreases the chances that others will attain it.

complementarity. Principle proposed by Winch to explain interpersonal attraction; refers to a pairing of different (and sometimes opposite) needs, such as dominance and submission.

compliance. Agreement to behave in accordance with a direct request.

conformity. Yielding to group pressures when no direct request to comply is made.

consideration. A dimension of leadership; the leader's concern with relationships between himself or herself and other group members and the maintenance of group morale and cohesiveness.

construct. A concept, defined in terms of observable events, used by a theory to account for regularities or relationships in data.

contingency awareness. Recognition of the connection or dependency between one event and a subsequent event.

contrast effects. A term used in social-judgment theory that refers to shifts in judgment away from an anchor point.

cooperation. Working together for mutual benefit. A prosocial behavior.

cooperative reward structure. A reward structure in which everyone in the group must achieve the reward in order for it to be attained by any one participant. Each person's efforts advance the group's chances.

correlational method. A study of the interrelation between two or more sets of events. Such a method does not allow conclusions about the causal relationship between the two events.

correspondence. As used in Jones's attribution model, the degree to which an observed behavior (for example, helping) is explained by inferring a similar personality disposition (for example, friendliness).

crowding. A psychological state of stress that sometimes accompanies high population density. (A similar term, *crowded*, refers to situations in which population density is relatively high.)

debriefing. Discussion conducted at end of experiment in which experimenter reveals complete procedures to subject and explains the reasons for any deception that may have occurred.

defense mechanisms. Devices used by the ego, operating at an unconscious level, that transform libidinal impulses into less threatening expression.

deindividuation. A state of relative anonymity, in which a group member does not feel singled out or identifiable.

demand characteristics. The perceptual cues, both explicit and implicit, that communicate what behavior is expected in a situation.

dependent variable. A variable whose changes are considered to be consequences or effects of changes in other (independent) variables.

diffusion of responsibility. A hypothesized cause of the *bystander effect*, whereby an individual is less likely to accept personal responsibility for helping when in the presence of other witnesses than when alone.

discrimination. Any behavior that reflects the acceptance of one person or rejection of another solely on the basis of that person's membership in a particular group.

display rules. Socially learned rules for controlling the expression of emotions.

dominance hierarchy. In a group, the ranking of the members in terms of influence or power. The most powerful or dominant member is highest in the hierarchy.

door-in-the-face technique. The effect in which refusal of a large request increases compliance with a subsequent smaller request.

ecological psychology. A viewpoint in social psychology that encourages us to study the behavior of the organism in the environment in which it occurs.

ego. According to Freud, that part of the personality that is oriented toward acting reasonably and realistically; the "executive" part of personality.

emblems. Body gestures that are substitutes for the spoken word.

emic. Referring to culture-specific constructs that have meaning only within a particular cultural framework.

empathy. The vicarious experience of another person's perceptions and feelings.

empirical-rational strategy. A strategy of planned change that holds that publishing the facts that support change is sufficient to initiate that change.

equity theory. A minitheory that specifies how people evaluate relative contributions to a relationship. Specifically, the theory suggests that ratios of inputs and outcomes should be equal for both participants.

erotica. Written, visual, or verbal material that is considered sexually stimulating.

ethnic group. A group sharing a common culture, customs, and language.

ethology. The study of the behavior of animals in their natural settings.

etic. Referring to universal factors; constructs that are not culture specific.

evaluation apprehension. A concern on the part of a subject in a study that he or she is performing correctly and will be positively evaluated by the researcher.

evaluation research. Research that assesses or evaluates the effects of a specific social action or program (Hornstein, 1975).

exonerative moral reasoning. Cognitive process of finding moral justification for an apparently immoral action.

exotic bias. A tendency, in observing another group or society, to focus on those aspects that are different from one's own group or society and to ignore similar features.

experimental realism. Arrangement of the events of an experiment so that they will seem convincing and have the maximum possible impact on the subjects. This is sometimes accomplished through the use of deception.

experimenter expectancies. Beliefs held by the experimenter and reflected in his or her behavior that may cause changes or distortions in the results of an experiment.

expiatory punishment. Punishment that is painful in proportion to the seriousness of the offense but not necessarily adapted to the nature of the offense. According to Piaget, younger children believe in this type of punishment (see *reciprocity*).

external validity. The "generalizability" of a research finding (for example, to other populations, settings, treatment arrangements, and/or measurement arrangements).

facial affect program. The connection between an emotional experience and a particular pattern of facial muscles.

fear of success. A personality disposition to become anxious about achieving success; originally hypothesized by Horner to explain a lack of achievement by women. Recent research does not support the motivational assumption.

field theory. A social-psychological perspective developed by Kurt Lewin that proposes that one's social behavior is a function not only of one's own attitudes, personality, and other intrapersonal factors but also of one's environment, or "field."

"foot-in-the-door" effect. A psychological effect whereby compliance with a small request makes it more likely that the person will comply with a larger (and less desirable) request.

frustration. The blocking of, or interference with, ongoing motivated behavior.

functional proximity. The extent to which the physical proximity of two persons' residences, along with the physical layout of the residences, affects their opportunities to interact.

future shock. Alvin Toffler's term for the disorientation that results from the superimposition of a new culture on an old one; a product of a greatly accelerated rate of change in society.

futuristics. A field of activity that seeks to identify, analyze, and evaluate possible changes in human life and the world (Cornish, 1977).

gender identity. One's self-awareness of

being male or female.

genital stage. The Freudian developmental stage from approximately age 14 up, centered on the development of mature sexuality and love for others.

genotype. An underlying characteristic; often a causal factor.

Gestalt. (German). Form or pattern. The basis of Gestalt theory, which emphasizes perception as a central process.

group polarization. A shift in opinions by members of a group toward a more extreme position.

groupthink. A mode of thinking, as defined by Janis, in which group members' strivings for unanimity override their motivation to realistically appraise alternative courses of action.

halo effect. A rating error in which the rater lets his or her general, overall impression of another influence the rating he or she gives the other person on some specific characteristic.

hedonic relevance. As used by Jones and Davis, the extent to which a person's actions are rewarding or costly to the observer.

helping behavior. Prosocial behavior that benefits another person rather than oneself.

heteronomous stage of morality. An early stage of moral development, in which the child accepts rules as given from authority.

hypothesis. A tentative explanation of a relationship between variables, or a supposition that a relationship may exist. A hypothesis generates some scientific method (such as an experiment) that seeks to confirm or disprove the hypothesis.

id. According to Freud, a set of drives that is the repository of our basic unsocialized impulses, including sex and aggression.

idiographic. Approach to the study of personality that focuses on the interrelationship of events and characteristics within a single individual.

illusory correlation. An overestimation of the strength of a relationship between two variables. Variables may not be related at all, or the relationship may be much weaker than believed.

illustrators. Nonverbal behaviors that are directly linked with spoken language.

immanent justice. According to Piaget, the belief held by younger children that misdeeds will lead naturally to negative consequences and that punishments emanate automatically from the objects of the misdeeds.

implicit personality theories. Assumptions people make that two or more traits are related so that, if a person has one of the traits, it is believed that he or she will have another

specific trait as well.

impression management. The process of attempting to control the images that others form of us.

independent variable. A variable that is manipulated in an experiment; a variable whose changes are considered to be the cause of changes in another (dependent) variable.

individualistic reward structure. A reward structure in which goal attainment by one participant has no effect on the probability of goal attainment by others.

ingratiation. A tactic used for impression management in which the person consciously tries to make others like him or her.

initiating structure. A dimension of leadership; the leader's behavior in identifying the group's goal and moving the group toward its goal.

instinct. An unlearned behavior pattern that appears in full form in all members of the species whenever there is an adequate stimulus.

instrumental learning. A type of learning in which a response is followed by a reward or reinforcement, resulting in an increase in the frequency of the response.

interaction. A joint effect of two or more variables such that the effect of one variable is different for various levels of the other variables.

intergroup contact hypothesis. The assumption that prejudice will be reduced and favorable attitudes will develop when members of two groups with negative attitudes toward each other are brought together.

internal validity. The conclusiveness with which the effects of the independent variables are established in a scientific investigation, as opposed to the possibility that some confounding variable(s) may have caused the observed results.

interpersonal morality. A system of moral reasoning proposed by Haan that develops within the context of social interaction; contrasted with formal morality of Kohlberg.

interview. A research method that involves asking another person a set of questions according to a predetermined schedule and recording the answers.

kinesics. A scheme developed by Birdwhistell for classifying body motions, intended to parallel linguistic categories.

learned helplessness. The belief that one's outcomes are independent of one's actions, learned through exposure to situations in which outcomes are noncontingent and resulting in behavior deficits and feelings of depression.

libido. In psychoanalytic theory, psychic energy

that is expended in the satisfying of different needs.

life space. In field theory, the person plus his or her environment, all of which is viewed as one set of interdependent factors.

locus of control. A construct developed by Julian Rotter, referring to a person's belief that events are within his or her own control (internal) or that outside forces are in control (external).

Machiavellianism. The belief that people can be manipulated through such means as flattery, threats, and deceit, and a zest for carrying out such manipulations.

main effect. The effect that levels of a single independent variable have on a dependent variable, not considering any other variables that may be affecting the results.

manipulation check. One or more questions posed to the subject(s) by the experimenter to assess the effectiveness of the experimental manipulation.

matching hypothesis. The proposition that people will be attracted to others who are approximately equal in physical beauty.

mere exposure effect. The finding that repeated exposure to an object results in greater attraction to that object.

modeling. The tendency for a person to reproduce the action, attitudes, and emotional responses exhibited by a real-life or symbolic model. Also called "observational learning."

mundane realism. Arrangement of the events in an experiment so that they seem as similar as possible to normal everyday occurrences.

need for approval. Differences in need of approval among individuals are measured by the Social Desirability Scale, a measure of the tendency to describe oneself in socially desirable terms.

negative-state-relief model. A hypothesis explaining the relationship between negative moods and helping behavior as a learned way of escaping negative psychological states.

neo-Freudians. Followers of Freud who depart in various ways from some of Freud's doctrines.

nomothetic. Approach to the study of personality that focuses on differences between people on a single norm or dimension selected by an investigator.

normative-reeducative strategy. A strategy of planned change that assumes that, before trying to change a person or group, one must take into account the cultural or normative factors (such as the past history of the person or group).

norms. Socially defined and enforced standards of behavior that concern the way an individual should interpret the world and/or behave in it.

obedience. A special form of compliance in which behavior is performed in response to a direct order.

objective self-awareness. A psychological state in which individuals focus their attention on and evaluate aspects of their self-concepts, particularly discrepancies between "real" self and "ideal" self.

obscenity. That which is considered offensive to the mass populace and therefore proscribed. Recent definitions have limited the meaning of *obscenity* to offensive sexual materials.

observational learning. A type of learning in which responses are acquired simply by observing the actions of others.

Oedipus conflict. The attraction of the child toward the parent of the other sex, accompanied by envy and hostility toward the parent of the same sex.

open-plan office. A popular arrangement of office environments in which employees work in a large, open area; work spaces are separated only by movable screens, furniture, bookcases, blackboards, and plants.

oral stage. The first stage in personality development, according to Freud. In this stage the child is concerned with satisfying the oral needs to suck and bite.

overload. Concept derived from information-processing that refers to a situation in which an individual receives inputs at a faster rate than they can be processed. Overload is often a source of stress.

overstaffed settings. Settings that contain more people than necessary to carry out requisite roles.

paralanguage. Vocalizations that are not language but that convey meaning; examples include pitch and rhythm, laughing and yawning.

participant observation. An observation method in which the observer becomes a member of a group being observed and participates in its activities but tries not to influence the activities.

personalism. As used by Jones and Davis, the perceived intentionality of a person's behavior; the degree to which a perceiver believes that another's behavior is directed at him or her.

personal norms. An individual's feelings of obligation to act in a given way in a certain situation; internalized norms.

phallic stage. A stage of personality development,

according to Freud; in this stage the child's concern is directed toward his or her sex organs.

phenomenological approach. A point of view in social psychology stating that the environment, as the person perceives it, is an important influence on behavior.

phenotype. A surface or observable characteristic; often a resultant rather than a causal factor.

philosophies of human nature. Expectations that people possess certain qualities and will behave in certain ways.

population density. The number of persons (or other animals) per unit of space; for example, the number of persons per acre.

power-coercive strategy. A strategy that uses either violent or nonviolent pressures (lobbying, petitions, strikes, riots, and so on) to bring about social change.

prejudice. An unjustified evaluative reaction to a member of a racial, ethnic, or other group, which results solely from the object's membership in that group; an intolerant, unfair, or unfavorable attitude toward another group of people.

primacy effect. The tendency for the first information received to have the predominant effect on one's judgments or opinions about persons, objects, or issues.

primary environment. A place in which a person spends much time, relates to others on a personal basis, and performs a wide range of personally important activities.

primary territory. An area that an individual or group owns and controls on a relatively permanent basis; such areas are central to the everyday lives of the occupants (Altman, 1975).

Prisoner's Dilemma. A mixed-motive situation in which people must choose between cooperating or competing; played as a matrix game in laboratory studies.

privacy. Ability to control access to the self or information about the self, especially when an individual wants less involvement with others.

propinquity. Proximity or geographical closeness; considered an important factor in interpersonal attraction.

prosocial behavior. Behavior that has positive social consequences and that improves the physical or psychological well-being of another person or persons.

prototypes. An abstract representation of the attributes associated with personality types that is stored in memory and used to organize information about an individual.

psychoanalytic theory. A theory of personality first developed by Sigmund Freud, which has implications for social behavior.

psychological reactance. (See *reactance.*)

public territory. A space in a public place that is temporarily used by an individual or group (for example, a bench, cafeteria table, or bus seat).

quasi-experimental research. Social research in which the investigator does not have full experimental control over the independent variable but does have extensive control over how, when, and for whom the dependent variable is measured.

questionnaire survey. A research method in which the experimenter supplies written questions to the subject, who provides written answers.

randomization. Assignment of conditions (for instance, assignment of subjects to treatment conditions) in a completely random manner—that is, a manner determined entirely by chance.

reactance. A theory stating that, if the opportunity to choose an object is severely limited, its desirability is increased.

reactive measure. A measurement of a variable whose characteristics may be changed by the very act of measuring it.

recency effect. The tendency for the most recent information received to have the predominant effect on one's judgment or opinion about persons, objects, or issues.

reciprocity. Punishment that is logically related to the offense so that the rule breaker will understand the implications of his or her misconduct. According to Piaget, older children usually believe in this kind of punishment (see *expiatory punishment*).

reciprocity norm. A norm or standard of behavior that says that people should help those who have helped them and refrain from injuring those who have helped them.

reinforcement. A consequence of a response that increases the probability that the response will be made again under the same stimulus conditions.

reinforcement theory. A theory that emphasizes that behavior is determined by the rewards or punishments given in response to it.

relative deprivation. One's perceived state in relation to the perceived state of others or in relation to unfulfilled expectations.

reliability. Consistency of measurement. Stability of scores over time, equivalence of scores on two forms of a test, and similarity of two raters' scoring of the same behavior are examples of three different kinds of reliability.

response. An alteration in a person's behavior that results from an external or internal stimulus.

role. The socially defined pattern of behaviors that is expected of an individual who is assigned a certain social function, such as spouse, clergyman, or baseball umpire.

scale. The size of a physical environment in relation to an individual.

scapegoating. The displacement of hostility on less powerful groups when the source of frustration is not available for attack or not attackable for other reasons.

secondary environment. A place in which a person spends little time, relates to others on an impersonal basis, and performs relatively unimportant activities (Stokols, 1976).

secondary territory. A physical area often claimed by a person or group, even though it is recognized that others may occupy that area at times.

self. Those attributes of behavior and experience that individuals regard as "me," including—in James's theory—the material me, the social me, and the spiritual me.

self-censure. Cognitive act of condemning or not excusing our own actions.

self-disclosure. Self-presentation that reveals personal and intimate aspects of behavior and feelings; self-revelation.

self-fulfilling prophecy. A belief that certain events are true, which leads them to become true in reality.

self-handicapping strategies. Strategies by which individuals manufacture protective excuses for anticipated failures in order to preserve and enhance their self-concept of competence.

self-monitoring. The use of cues from other people's self-presentations in controlling one's own self-presentation. High self-monitoring individuals, as identified by the Self-Monitoring Scale, use their well-developed self-presentational skills for purposes of impression management in social relationship.

self-schema. Organized knowledge of features of one's self within a particular domain of behavior and experience (for example, the domain of honesty).

sensitivity training. A group interaction process in which individuals deal with their beliefs and emotions and receive feedback about their interpersonal skills and their effectiveness in groups.

sex-role norms. Beliefs regarding appropriate behaviors for women and men.

simulation. A research method that attempts to imitate some crucial aspects of a real-world situation in order to gain more understanding of the underlying mechanisms that operate in that situation.

situated identities, theory of. A theory proposing that for each social situation, there is a certain pattern of behavior that conveys an identity appropriate to that setting.

social-comparison theory. A theory, developed by Festinger, that proposes that we use other people as sources for comparison, so that we can evaluate our own attitudes and abilities.

social distance. A person's acceptable degree of closeness (physically, socially, or psychologically) in regard to members of an ethnic, racial, or religious group.

social-exchange theory. A general theoretical model that conceptualizes relationships in terms of costs and gains to the participants.

social facilitation. The state in which the presence of others improves the quality of an individual's performance.

social indicators. Descriptive statistics about a society that are used to evaluate the quality of social existence.

socialization. A growing-up process in which children learn the norms of their society and acquire their own distinctive values, beliefs, and personality characteristics.

social-learning theory. A theory that proposes that social behavior develops as a result of observing others and of being rewarded for certain acts.

social-responsibility norm. A norm or standard of behavior that dictates that people should help persons who are dependent or in need of help.

social technology. The application of social-science principles to the solution of social problems.

social trap. A situation that provides immediate individual incentives for behaviors that in the long run may have negative consequences for society if large numbers of people perform the behaviors.

sociobiology. A new discipline concerned with identifying biological and genetic bases for social behavior in animals and humans.

spontaneous self-concept. The extent to which particular features of one's self-concept are brought to mind by one's social surroundings.

stereotype A relatively rigid and oversimplified conception of a group of people, in which all individuals in the given group are labeled with the so-called group characteristics.

stigma. A characteristic that is considered undesirable by most people (for example, a mental handicap).

stimulus. Any event, internal or external to the person, that brings about an alteration in that person's behavior.

stimulus generalization. A process whereby, after a person learns to make a certain response to a certain stimulus, other similar but previously ineffective stimuli will also elicit that response.

stimulus-overload theory. Stanley Milgram's concept of an abundance of sensory and cognitive inputs; used to account for the behavior of people who live in cities and are sometimes found to be less helpful than town dwellers.

stress. Complex physiological and psychological response to a demand or challenge, involving arousal and mobilization of capacities for coping.

superego. According to Freud, the part of personality oriented toward doing what is morally proper; the conscience. The superego includes one's ego ideal, or ideal self-image.

superordinate goal. An important goal that can be achieved only through cooperation.

territorial dominance. The phenomenon in which an individual dominates interactions with others when the interactions occur in the individual's own territory.

territory. For many nonhuman species, a specific geographic region that an animal marks with scents or calls, uses as a nesting place, and defends against intrusion by other animals of the same species. For humans, an area whose occupant(s) perceive it as under their own control.

transsexualism. A gender identity opposite to one's bodily appearance and sexual organs. A person with male sex organs whose gender identity is female, or vice versa, is a transsexual.

unconscious. According to Freud, that part of the human psyche that is below the level of awareness.

understaffed settings. Settings that contain fewer people than roles.

unobtrusive measures. A measurement that can be made without the knowledge of the person being studied. An unobtrusive measure is also nonreactive.

"Who am I?" technique. A method for measuring self-concept by examining an individual's answers to the question "Who am I?"

References

Abelson, R. P., Aronson, E., McGuire, W. J., Newcomb, T. M., Rosenberg, M. J., & Tannenbaum, P. H. (Eds.). *Theories of cognitive consistency: A sourcebook.* Chicago: Rand McNally, 1968.

Abelson, R. P., & Rosenberg, M. J. Symbolic psychologic: A model of attitudinal cognition. *Behavioral Science,* 1958, *3,* 1–13.

Abramson, P. R. *The sexual system: A theory of human sexual behavior.* New York: Academic Press, 1979

Abramson, P. R. *Sexual lives.* Unpublished manuscript, University of California, Los Angeles, 1980.

Acking, C. A. Factorial analysis of the perception of an interior. In B. Honikman (Ed.), *Proceedings of the Architectural Psychology Conference at Kingston Polytechnic.* London: R.I.B.A. Publications, Ltd., & Kingston Polytechnic, 1971.

Adams, J. Inequity in social exchange. In L. Berkowitz (Ed.), *Advances in experimental social psychology* (Vol. 2). New York: Academic Press, 1965. Pp. 267–299.

Adelberg, S., & Batson, C. D. Accountability and helping: When needs exceed resources. *Journal of Personality and Social Psychology,* 1978, *36,* 343–350.

Aderman, D. Elation, depression, and helping behavior. *Journal of Personality and Social Psychology,* 1972, *24,* 91–101.

Aderman, D., & Berkowitz, L. Observational set, empathy, and helping. *Journal of Personality and Social Psychology,* 1970, *14,* 141–148.

Aderman, D., Bryant, F. B., & Donelsmith, D. E. Prediction as a means of inducing tolerance. *Journal of Research in Personality,* 1978, *12,* 172–178.

Adorno, T. W., Frenkel-Brunswik, E., Levinson, D., & Sanford, N. *The authoritarian personality.* New York: Harper, 1950.

Aiello, J. R. A test of equilibrium theory: Visual interaction in relation to orientation, distance, and sex of interactants. *Psychonomic Science,* 1972, *27,* 335–336.

Aiello, J. R. A further look at equilibrium theory: Visual interaction as a function of interpersonal distance. *Environmental Psychology and Nonverbal Behavior,* 1977, *1,* 122–140. (a)

Aiello, J. R. Visual interaction at extended distances. *Personality and Social Psychology Bulletin,* 1977, *3,* 83–86. (b)

Aiello, J. R., & Cooper, R. E. Use of personal space as a function of social affect. *Proceedings, 80th Annual Convention, American Psychological Association,* 1972, *7,* 207–208.

Aiello, J. R., Epstein, Y. M., & Karlin, R. A. Effects of crowding on electrodermal activity. *Sociological Symposium,* 1975, *14,* 43–57.

Aiello, J. R., & Jones, S. E. A field study of the proxemic behavior of young school children in three subcultural groups. *Journal of Personality and Social Psychology,* 1971, *19,* 351–356.

Aiello, J. R., & Thompson, D. E. When compensation fails: Mediating effects of sex and locus of control at extended interaction distances. Paper presented at the annual convention of the American Psychological Association, Toronto, Canada, 1978.

Ajzen, I., & Fishbein, M. The prediction of behavioral intentions in a choice situation. *Journal of Experimental Social Psychology,* 1969, *5,* 400–416.

Ajzen, I., & Fishbein, M. The prediction of behavior from attitudinal and normative behaviors. *Journal of Experimental Social Psychology,* 1970, *6,* 466–487.

Ajzen, I., & Fishbein, M. Attitudes and normative beliefs as factors influencing behavioral intentions. *Journal of Personality and Social Psychology,* 1972, *21,* 1–9.

Ajzen, I., & Fishbein, M. Attitude-behavior relations: A theoretical analysis and review of empirical research. *Psychological Bulletin,* 1977, *84,* 888–918.

Alexander, C. N., & Knight, G. W. Situated identities and social psychological experimentation. *Sociometry,* 1971, *34,* 65–82.

Alexander, C. N., Jr., & Lauderdale, P. Situated identities and social influence. *Sociometry,* 1977, *40,* 225–233.

Alexander, C. N., Jr., & Sagatun, I. An attributional analysis of experimental norms. *Sociometry,* 1973, *36,* 127–142.

Alinsky, S. *Rules for radicals.* New York: Random House, 1971.

Alker, H. A. *Mystification and deception in presidential press conferences.* Washington, D.C.: American Psychological Association, 1976.

Alker, H. A., & Owen, D. W. Biographical, trait and behavioral-sampling predictions of performance in a stressful life setting. *Journal of Personality and Social Psychology,* 1977, *35,* 717–723.

Allen, V. L. Situational factors in conformity. In L. Berkowitz (Ed.), *Advances in experimental social psycholo-*

gy (Vol. 2). New York: Academic Press, 1965. Pp. 133–170.

Allen, V. L., & Levine, J. M. Social support, dissent, and conformity. *Sociometry*, 1968, *31*, 138–149.

Allgeier, E. R. Beyond sowing and growing: The relationship of sex-typing to socialization, family plans, and future orientation. *Journal of Applied Social Psychology*, 1975, *5*, 217–226.

Allport, F. H. The influence of the group upon association and thought. *Journal of Experimental Psychology*, 1920, *3*, 159–182.

Allport, G. W. Attitudes. In C. Murchison (Ed.), *Handbook of social psychology*. Worcester, Mass.: Clark University Press, 1935. Pp. 789–844.

Allport, G. W. *Personality: A psychological interpretation*. New York: Holt, 1937.

Allport, G. W. Prejudice, a problem in psychological and social causation. *Journal of Social Issues*, Supplement Series, No. 4, 1950.

Allport, G. W. *The nature of prejudice*. Garden City, N.Y.: Doubleday Anchor, 1958. (Originally published, 1954.)

Allport, G. W. *Pattern and growth in personality*. New York: Holt, Rinehart & Winston, 1961.

Allport, G. W. The general and the unique in psychological science. *Journal of Personality*, 1962, *30*, 405–422.

Allport, G. W. The historical background of modern social psychology. In G. Lindzey & E. Aronson (Eds.), *The handbook of social psychology* (Vol. 1) (2nd ed.). Reading, Mass.: Addison-Wesley, 1968. Pp. 1–80.

Allport, G. W., & Kramer, B. M. Some roots of prejudice. *Journal of Psychology*, 1946, *22*, 9–39.

Altman, I. Reciprocity of interpersonal exchange. *Journal of the Theory of Social Behaviour*, 1973, *3*, 249–261.

Altman, I. *The environment and social behavior: Privacy, personal space, territory, and crowding*. Monterey, Calif.: Brooks/Cole, 1975.

Altman, I. Privacy regulation: Culturally universal or culturally specific? *Journal of Social Issues*, 1977, *33*(3), 66–84.

Altman, I., & Chemers, M. *Culture and environment*. Monterey, Calif.: Brooks/Cole, 1980.

Altman, I., Nelson, P. A., & Lett, E. E. The ecology of home environments. *Catalog of Selected Documents in Psychology*. Washington, D.C.: American Psychological Association, Spring 1972.

Altman, I., & Taylor, D. A. *Social penetration: The development of interpersonal relationships*. New York: Holt, Rinehart & Winston, 1973.

Altman, I., Taylor, D., & Wheeler, L. Ecological aspects of group behavior in isolation. *Journal of Applied Social Psychology*, 1971, *1*, 76–100.

Altman, I., & Vinsel, A. M. Personal space: An analysis of E. T. Hall's proxemic framework. In I. Altman & J. Wohlwill (Eds.), *Human behavior and environment* (Vol. 2). New York: Plenum Press, 1978.

American Psychological Association. *Ethical principles in the conduct of research with human participants*. Washington, D.C.: American Psychological Association, 1973.

Amoroso, D. M., & Brown, M. *Some problems in studying the effects of erotic materials*. Research Report No. 28. Waterloo, Ontario, Canada: Department of Psychology, University of Waterloo, September 1971.

Amoroso, D. M., Brown, M., Pruesse, M., Ware, E. E., & Pilkey, D. W. An investigation of behavioral, psycho-logical, and physiological reactions to pornographic stimuli. *Technical Reports of the Commission on Obscenity and Pornography* (Vol. 8). Washington, D.C.: U.S. Government Printing Office, 1971.

Anastasi, A. *Differential psychology* (3rd ed.). New York: Macmillan, 1958.

Anderson, N. H. Application of an additive model to impression formation. *Science*, 1962, *138*, 817–818.

Anderson, N. H. Averaging versus adding as a stimulus-combination rule in impression formation. *Journal of Experimental Psychology*, 1965, *70*, 394–400.

Anderson, N. H. A simple model of information integration. In R. P. Abelson, E. Aronson, W. J. McGuire, T. M. Newcomb, M. J. Rosenberg, & P. H. Tannenbaum (Eds.), *Theories of cognitive consistency: A sourcebook*. Chicago: Rand McNally, 1968. Pp. 731–743. (a)

Anderson, N. H. Ratings of likableness, meaningfulness, and likableness variances of 555 common personality traits arranged in order of decreasing likableness. *Journal of Personality and Social Psychology*, 1968, *9*, 272–279. (b)

Anderson, N. H. Cognitive algebra: Integration theory applied to social attribution. In L. Berkowitz (Ed.), *Advances in experimental social psychology* (Vol. 7). New York: Academic Press, 1974. Pp. 1–101.

Anderson, N. H., & Alexander, G. R. Choice test of the averaging hypothesis for information integration. *Cognitive Psychology*, 1971, *2*, 313–324.

Anderson, N. H., Lindner, R., & Lopes, L. L. Integration theory applied to judgments of group attractiveness. *Journal of Personality and Social Psychology*, 1973, *26*, 400–408.

Andrews, F. M., & Withey, S. B. *Social indicators of well-being*. New York: Plenum Press, 1976.

Andrews, I. R., & Johnson, D. L. Small-group polarization of judgments. *Psychonomic Science*, 1971, *24*, 191–192.

Ard, B. N., Jr. Premarital sexual experience: A longitudinal study. *Journal of Sex Research*, 1974, *10*, 32–39.

Ardrey, R. *African genesis*. New York: Delta Books, 1961.

Ardrey, R. *The territorial imperative*. New York: Atheneum, 1966.

Argyle, M., & Dean, J. Eye contact, distance, and affiliation. *Sociometry*, 1965, *28*, 289–304.

Argyle, M., & Ingham, R. Gaze, mutual gaze, and proximity. *Semiotica*, 1972, *6*, 32–49.

Argyle, M., Ingham, R., Alkema, F., & McCallin, M. The different functions of gaze. *Semiotica*, 1973, *7*, 19–32.

Argyris, C. *Integrating the individual and the organization*. New York: Wiley, 1964.

Aronfreed, J. *Conduct and conscience: The socialization of internalized control over behavior*. New York: Academic Press, 1968.

Aronfreed, J. Moral development from the standpoint of a general psychological theory. In T. Lickona (Ed.), *Moral development and behavior: Theory, research, and social issues*. New York: Holt, Rinehart & Winston, 1976. Pp. 54–69.

Aronfreed, J., & Paskal, V. *Altruism, empathy, and the conditioning of positive affect*. Unpublished manuscript, University of Pennsylvania, 1965.

Aronson, E. The need for achievement as measured by graphic expression. In J. W. Atkinson (Ed.), *Motives in fantasy, action, and society*. Princeton, N.J.: Van Nostrand, 1958. Pp. 249–265.

Aronson, E. Dissonance theory: Progress and problems.

In R. P. Abelson, E. Aronson, W. J. McGuire, T. M. Newcomb, M. J. Rosenberg, & P. H. Tannenbaum (Eds.), *Theories of cognitive consistency: A sourcebook.* Chicago: Rand McNally, 1968. Pp. 5–27.

Aronson, E., Blaney, N., Sikes, J., Stephan, C., & Snapp, M. Busing and racial tension: The jigsaw route to learning and liking. *Psychology Today*, 1975, *8*(9), 43–50.

Aronson, E., Blaney, N., & Stephan, C. *Cooperation in the classroom: The jigsaw puzzle model.* Paper presented at the meeting of the American Psychological Association, Chicago, September 1975.

Aronson, E., Blaney, N., Stephan, C., Sikes, J., & Snapp, M. *The jigsaw classroom.* Beverly Hills, Calif.: Sage, 1978.

Aronson, E., & Carlsmith, J. M. Experimentation in social psychology. In G. Lindzey & E. Aronson (Eds.), *Handbook of social psychology* (Vol. 2) (2nd ed.). Reading, Mass.: Addison-Wesley, 1968.

Aronson, E., & Cope, V. My enemy's enemy is my friend. *Journal of Personality and Social Psychology*, 1968, *8*, 8–12.

Aronson, E., & Golden, B. W. The effect of relevant and irrelevant aspects of communicator credibility on attitude change. *Journal of Personality*, 1962, *30*, 135–146.

Aronson, E., & Linder, D. Gain and loss of esteem as determinants of interpersonal attractiveness. *Journal of Experimental Social Psychology*, 1965, *1*, 156–171.

Aronson, E., Willerman, B., & Floyd, J. The effect of a pratfall on increasing interpersonal attractiveness. *Psychonomic Science*, 1966, *4*, 157–158.

Asch, S. E. Forming impressions of personality. *Journal of Abnormal and Social Psychology*, 1946, *41*, 258–290.

Asch, S. E. Effects of group pressure upon the modification and distortion of judgments. In H. Guetzkow (Ed.), *Groups, leadership, and men.* Pittsburgh: Carnegie Press, 1951. Pp. 177–190.

Asch, S. E. *Social psychology.* Englewood Cliffs, N.J.: Prentice-Hall, 1952.

Asch, S. E. Studies of independence and conformity: A minority of one against a unanimous majority. *Psychological Monographs*, 1956, *70*(9, Whole No. 416).

Asch, S. E. Effects of group pressure upon the modification and distortion of judgments. In E. E. Maccoby, T. M. Newcomb, & E. L. Hartley (Eds.), *Readings in social psychology* (3rd ed.). New York: Holt, Rinehart & Winston, 1958.

Ashmore, R. D. Prejudice: Causes and cures. In B. E. Collins (Ed.), *Social psychology.* Reading, Mass.: Addison-Wesley, 1970. Pp. 243–339.

Ashmore, R. D., Ramchandra, V., & Jones, R. A. *Censorship as an attitude change induction.* Paper presented at the meeting of the Eastern Psychological Association, New York City, April 1971.

Athanasiou, R. A review of public attitudes on sexual issues. In J. Zubin & J. Money (Eds.), *Critical issues in contemporary sexual behavior.* Baltimore: Johns Hopkins University Press, 1973. Pp. 361–390.

Athanasiou, R., & Sarkin, R. Premarital sexual behavior and postmarital adjustment. *Archives of Sexual Behavior*, 1974, *3*(3), 207–225.

Athanasiou, R., & Yoshioka, G. A. The spatial character of friendship formation. *Environment and Behavior*, 1973, *5*, 43–65.

Atkins, A., Deaux, K., & Bieri, J. Latitude of acceptance and attitude change: Empirical evidence for a reformulation. *Journal of Personality and Social Psychology*, 1967, *6*, 47–54.

Atkinson, J. W. (Ed.). *Motives in fantasy, action, and society.* Princeton, N.J.: Van Nostrand, 1958.

Atkinson, J. W. Motivation for achievement. In T. Blass (Ed.), *Personality variables in social behavior.* Hillsdale, N.J.: Erlbaum, 1977. Pp. 25–108.

Atkinson, J. W., & Birch, D. *The dynamics of action.* New York: Wiley, 1970.

Atkinson, J. W., & Feather, N. T. (Eds.). *A theory of achievement motivation.* New York: Wiley, 1966.

Atkinson, J. W., & McClelland, D. C. The projective expression of needs. II. The effect of different intensities of the hunger drive on thematic apperception. *Journal of Experimental Psychology*, 1948, *38*, 643–658.

Austin, W. T., & Bates, F. L. Ethological indicators of dominance and territory in a human captive population. *Social Forces*, 1974, *52*, 447–455.

Austin, W., Walster, E., & Utne, M. K. Equity and the law: The effect of a harmdoer's "suffering in the act" on liking and assigned punishment. In L. Berkowitz & E. Walster (Eds.), *Advances in experimental social psychology* (Vol. 9). New York: Academic Press, 1976. Pp. 163–190.

Ausubel, D. P. Introduction. In R. C. Anderson & D. P. Ausubel (Eds.), *Readings in the psychology of cognition.* New York: Holt, Rinehart & Winston, 1965. Pp. 3–17.

Avellar, J., & Kagan, S. Development of competitive behaviors in Anglo-American and Mexican-American children. *Psychological Reports*, 1976, *39*, 191–198.

Averill, J. R. Personal control over aversive stimuli and its relation to stress. *Psychological Bulletin*, 1973, *80*(4), 286–303.

Averill, J. R., & Boothroyd, P. On falling in love in conformance with the romantic ideal. *Motivation and Emotion*, 1977, *1*, 235–247.

Azrin, N. H., Hutchinson, R. R., & Hake, D. F. Attack, avoidance, and escape reactions to aversive shock. *Journal of Experimental Analysis of Behavior*, 1966, *9*, 191–204.

Bachy, V. Danish "permissiveness" revisited. *The Journal of Communication*, 1976, *26*, 40–43.

Back, K. W. Influence through social communication. *Journal of Abnormal and Social Psychology*, 1951, *46*, 9–23.

Back, K. W. *Beyond words: The story of sensitivity training and the encounter movement.* New York: Russell Sage Foundation, 1972.

Backman, C. W., & Secord, P. F. The effect of perceived liking on interpersonal attraction. *Human Relations*, 1959, *12*, 379–384.

Baer, D. M., & Wright, J. C. Developmental psychology. In M. R. Rosenzweig & L. W. Porter (Eds.), *Annual review of psychology* (Vol. 25). Palo Alto, Calif.: Annual Reviews, 1974.

Bakan, D. *The duality of human existence.* Chicago: Rand McNally, 1966.

Baker, N. J., & Wrightsman, L. S. The *Zeitgeist* and philosophies of human nature, or where have all the idealistic imperturbable freshmen gone? In L. S. Wrightsman (Ed.), *Assumptions about human nature: A social-psychological approach.* Monterey, Calif.: Brooks/Cole, 1974. Pp. 166–180.

Bales, R. F. The equilibrium problem in small groups. In

T. Parsons, R. F. Bales, & E. A. Shils (Eds.), *Working papers in the theory of action.* Glencoe, Ill.: Free Press, 1953. Pp. 111–161.

Bales, R. F. Task roles and social roles in problem-solving groups. In E. E. Maccoby, T. M. Newcomb, & E. L. Hartley (Eds.), *Readings in social psychology* (3rd ed.). New York: Holt, Rinehart & Winston, 1958. Pp. 396–413.

Bales, R. F. *Personality and interpersonal behavior.* New York: Holt, Rinehart & Winston, 1970.

Bandura, A. Vicarious processes: A case of no-trial learning. In L. Berkowitz (Ed.), *Advances in experimental social psychology* (Vol. 2). New York: Academic Press, 1965. Pp. 1–55.

Bandura, A. Theoretical approaches to socialization. In D. A. Goslin (Ed.), *Handbook of socialization theory and research.* Chicago: Rand McNally, 1969. Pp. 213–262.

Bandura, A. *Aggression: A social-learning analysis.* Englewood Cliffs, N.J.: Prentice-Hall, 1973.

Bandura, A. *Social-learning theory.* Englewood Cliffs, N.J.: Prentice-Hall, 1977.

Bandura, A., & McDonald, F. J. The influence of social reinforcement and the behavior of models in shaping children's moral judgments. *Journal of Abnormal and Social Psychology,* 1963, *67,* 274–281.

Bandura, A., Ross, D., & Ross, S. Transmission of aggression through imitation of aggressive models. *Journal of Abnormal and Social Psychology,* 1961, *63,* 575–582.

Bandura, A., Ross, D., & Ross, S. Imitation of film-mediated aggressive models. *Journal of Abnormal and Social Psychology,* 1963, *66,* 3–11.   (a)

Bandura, A., Ross, D., & Ross, S. A comparative test of the status envy, social power and secondary reinforcement theories of identification learning. *Journal of Abnormal and Social Psychology,* 1963, *67,* 527–534.   (b)

Bandura, A., Underwood, B., & Fromson, M. E. Disinhibition of aggression through diffusion of responsibility and dehumanization of victims. *Journal of Research in Personality,* 1975, *9,* 253–269.

Bandura, A., & Walters, R. *Social learning and personality development.* New York: Holt, Rinehart & Winston, 1963.

Barach, J. A. Self-confidence, risk-handling, and mass communications. In P. R. McDonald (Ed.), *Marketing involvement in society and the economy.* Fall Conference Proceedings of the American Marketing Association, Series #30, 1969. Pp. 323–329.

Barash, D. P. *Sociobiology and behavior.* New York: Elsevier, 1977.

Barber, J. D. *The presidential character.* Englewood Cliffs, N.J.: Prentice-Hall, 1972.

Barclay, A. M. Urinary acid phosphate secretion in sexually aroused males. *Journal of Experimental Research in Personality,* 1970, *4,* 233–238.

Bard, M. Alternatives to traditional law enforcement. In F. F. Korten, S. W. Cook, & J. I. Lacey (Eds.), *Psychology and the problems of society.* Washington, D.C.: American Psychological Association, 1970. Pp. 128–132.

Barker, R. G. Ecology and motivation. In M. R. Jones (Ed.), *Nebraska Symposium on Motivation, 1960.* Lincoln: University of Nebraska Press, 1960. Pp. 1–49.

Barker, R. G. (Ed.). *The stream of behavior.* New York: Appleton-Century-Crofts, 1963.

Barker, R. G. Explorations in ecological psychology. *American Psychologist,* 1965, *20,* 1–14.

Barker, R. G. *Ecological psychology: Concepts and methods for studying the environment of human behavior.* Stanford, Calif.: Stanford University Press, 1968.

Barker, R. G., & Schoggen, P. *Qualities of community life.* San Francisco: Jossey-Bass, 1973.

Baron, R. A. Reducing the influence of an aggressive model: The restraining effects of discrepant modeling cues. *Journal of Personality and Social Psychology,* 1971, *20,* 240–245.

Baron, R. A. Aggression as a function of ambient temperature and prior anger arousal. *Journal of Personality and Social Psychology,* 1972, *21,* 183–189.

Baron, R. A. Aggression as a function of victim's pain cues, level of prior anger arousal, and exposure to an aggressive model. *Journal of Personality and Social Psychology,* 1974, *29,* 117–124.

Baron, R. A. The reduction of human aggression: A field study of the influence of incompatible reactions. *Journal of Applied Social Psychology,* 1976, *6,* 260–274.

Baron, R. A. *Human aggression.* New York: Plenum Press, 1977.

Baron, R. A. Heightened sexual arousal and physical aggression: An extension to females. Unpublished manuscript, Purdue University, 1978.

Baron, R. A., & Ball, R. L. The aggression-inhibiting influence of nonhostile humor. *Journal of Experimental Social Psychology,* 1974, *10,* 23–33.

Baron, R. A., & Bell, P. A. Aggression and heat: Mediating effects of prior provocation and exposure to an aggressive model. *Journal of Personality and Social Psychology,* 1975, *31,* 825–832.

Baron, R. A., & Bell, P. A. Aggression and heat: The influence of ambient temperature, negative affect, and a cooling drink on physical aggression. *Journal of Personality and Social Psychology,* 1976, *33,* 245–255.

Baron, R. A., & Bell, P. A. Sexual arousal and aggression by males: Effects of type of erotic stimuli and prior provocation. *Journal of Personality and Social Psychology,* 1977, *35,* 79–87.

Baron, R. A., & Kepner, C. R. Model's behavior and attraction toward the model as determinants of adult aggressive behavior. *Journal of Personality and Social Psychology,* 1970, *14,* 335–344.

Baron, R. A., & Ransberger, V. M. Ambient temperature and the occurrence of collective violence: The "long hot summer" revisited. *Journal of Personality and Social Psychology,* 1978, *36,* 351–360.

Baron, R. S., Moore, D., & Sanders, G. S. Distraction as a source of drive in social facilitation research. *Journal of Personality and Social Psychology,* 1978, *36,* 816–824.

Barron, N. Sex-typed language: The production of grammatical cases. *Acta Sociologica,* 1971, *14,* 24–42.

Bar-Tal, D. *Prosocial behavior. Theory and research.* Washington: Hemisphere (distributed by Halsted Press), 1976.

Bar-Tal, D., & Saxe, L. Perceptions of similarly and dissimilarly attractive couples and individuals. *Journal of Personality and Social Psychology,* 1976, *33,* 772–781. (a)

Bar-Tal, D., & Saxe, L. Physical attractiveness and its relationship to sex-role stereotyping. *Sex Roles,*

1976, *2*, 123–133. (b)

Bass, B. M. Authoritarianism or acquiescence? *Journal of Abnormal and Social Psychology*, 1955, *51*, 616–623.

Bass, B. M., Krusell, J., & Alexander, R. A. Male managers' attitudes toward working women. *American Behavioral Scientist*, 1971, *15*, 221–236.

Batson, C. D., Cochran, P. J., Biederman, M. F., Blosser, J. L., Ryan, M. J., & Vogt, B. Failure to help when in a hurry: Callousness or conflict? *Personality and Social Psychology Bulletin*, 1978, *4*, 97–101.

Batson, C. D., Coke, J. S., Jasnoski, M. L., & Hanson, M. Buying kindness: Effect of an extrinsic incentive for helping on perceived altruism. *Personality and Social Psychology Bulletin*, 1978, *4*, 86–91.

Bauchner, J. E., Brandt, D. R., & Miller, G. R. The truth/deception attribution: Effects of varying levels of information availability. In B. D. Ruben (Ed.), *Communication Yearbook I*. New Brunswick, N.J.: International Communication Association, 1977. Pp. 229–243.

Bauer, R. A. (Ed.) *Social indicators*. Cambridge, Mass.: M.I.T. Press, 1966.

Bauer, R. A. Self-confidence and persuasibility: One more time. *Journal of Marketing Research*, 1970, 7, 256–258.

Baughman, E. E. *Black Americans: A psychological analysis*. New York: Academic Press, 1971.

Baum, A., Aiello, J. R., & Calesnick, L. E. Crowding and personal control: Social density and the development of learned helplessness. *Journal of Personality and Social Psychology*, 1978, *36*(9), 1000–1011.

Baum, A., Davis, G. E., & Aiello, J. R. Crowding and neighborhood mediation of urban density. *Population Behavioral, Social, and Environmental Issues*, 1978, *1*, 266–279.

Baum, A., & Greenberg, C. I. Waiting for a crowd: The behavioral and perceptual effects of anticipated crowding. *Journal of Personality and Social Psychology*, 1975, *32*(4), 671–679.

Baum, A., Harpin, R. E., & Valins, S. The role of group phenomena in the experience of crowding. *Environment and Behavior*, 1975, 7(2), 185–198.

Baum, A., & Koman, S. Differential response to anticipated crowding: Psychological effects of social and spatial density. *Journal of Personality and Social Psychology*, 1976, *34*(3), 526–536.

Baum, A., & Valins, S. *Architecture and social behavior: Psychological studies of social density*. Hillsdale, N.J.: Erlbaum, 1977.

Baumeister, R. F., & Jones, E. E. When self-presentation is constrained by the target's knowledge: Consistency and compensation. *Journal of Personality and Social Psychology*, 1978, *36*, 608–618.

Baumrin, B. H. The immorality of irrelevance: The social role of science. In F. F. Korten, S. W. Cook, & J. I. Lacey (Eds.), *Psychology and the problems of society*. Washington, D.C.: American Psychological Association, 1970. Pp. 73–83.

Baumrind, D. Some thoughts on the ethics of reading Milgram's "Behavioral study of obedience." *American Psychologist*, 1964, *19*, 421–423.

Baumrind, D. An exploratory study of socialization effects on black children: Some black-white comparisons. *Child Development*, 1972, *43*, 261–267.

Beaman, A. L., Barnes, P. J., Klentz, B., & McQuirk, B. Increasing helping rates through information dis-

semination: Teaching pays. *Personality and Social Psychology Bulletin*, 1978, *4*, 406–411.

Beattie, C., & Spencer, B. G. Career attainment in Canadian bureaucracies: Unscrambling the effects of age, seniority, education, and ethnic linguistic factors in salary. *American Journal of Sociology*, 1971, 77, 472–490.

Becker, F. D. Study of spatial markers. *Journal of Personality and Social Psychology*, 1973, *26*, 439–445.

Becker, F. D., & Mayo, C. Delineating personal distance and territoriality. *Environment and Behavior*, 1971, *3*, 375–381.

Becker, L. J. Joint effect of feedback and goal setting on performance: A field study of residential energy conservation. *Journal of Applied Psychology*, 1978, *63*, 428–433.

Becker-Haven, J. F., & Lindskold, S. Deindividuation manipulations, self-consciousness, and bystander intervention. *Journal of Social Psychology*, 1978, *105*, 113–121.

Beilin, L. A. *Program design and curriculum development for police training*. Paper presented at the meeting of the American Psychological Association, New Orleans, September 1974.

Bell, A. P., & Weinberg, M. S. *Homosexualities: A study of diversity among men and women*. New York: Simon and Schuster, 1978.

Bell, P. A., & Baron, R. A. Aggression and heat: The mediating role of negative affect. *Journal of Applied Social Psychology*, 1976, *6*, 18–30.

Bell, R. *Self-concept and aspirations of working-class mothers*. Paper presented at the meeting of the American Psychological Association, New York, September 1964.

Bellow, S. A talk with the Yellow Kid. *The Reporter*, September 6, 1956, pp. 41–44.

Bem, D. J. An experimental analysis of self-persuasion. *Journal of Experimental Social Psychology*, 1965, *1*, 199–218.

Bem, D. J. Self-perception: An alternative interpretation of cognitive dissonance phenomena. *Psychological Review*, 1967, *74*, 183–200.

Bem, D. J. Self-perception theory. In L. Berkowitz (Ed.), *Advances in experimental social psychology* (Vol. 6). New York: Academic Press, 1972. Pp. 1–62.

Bem, D. J., & Allen, A. On predicting some of the people some of the time: The search for cross-situational consistencies in behavior. *Psychological Review*, 1974, *81*, 506–520.

Bem, D. J., & Funder, D. C. Predicting more of the people more of the time: Assessing the personality of situations. *Psychological Review*, 1978, *85*, 485–501.

Bem, S. L. The measurement of psychological androgyny. *Journal of Consulting and Clinical Psychology*, 1974, *42*, 155–162.

Bem, S. L. Sex role adaptability: One consequence of psychological androgyny. *Journal of Personality and Social Psychology*, 1975, *31*, 634–643.

Bem, S. L. On the utility of alternate procedures for assessing psychological androgyny. *Journal of Consulting and Clinical Psychology*, 1977, *45*, 196–205.

Bem, S. L., & Lenney, E. Sex-typing and the avoidance of cross-sex behavior. *Journal of Personality and Social Psychology*, 1976, *33*, 48–54.

Bem, S. L., Martyna, W., & Watson, C. Sex-typing and androgyny: Further explorations of the expressive domain. *Journal of Personality and Social Psychology,* 1976, *34,* 1016–1023.

Bender, P. Definition of "obscene" under existing law. *Technical Reports of the Commission on Obscenity and Pornography* (Vol. 2). Washington, D.C.: U.S. Government Printing Office, 1971.

Bennis, W. G., Benne, K. D., & Chin, R. *The planning of change.* New York: Holt, Rinehart & Winston, 1968.

Bennis, W. G., & Shepard, H. A. A theory of group development. *Human Relations,* 1956, *9,* 415–437.

Benson, P. L., & Catt, V. L. Soliciting charity contributions: The parlance of asking for money. *Journal of Applied Social Psychology,* 1978, *8,* 84–95.

Bentler, P. M. Heterosexual behavior assessment: I. Males. *Behavior Research and Therapy,* 1968, *6,* 21–25.(a)

Bentler, P. M. Heterosexual behavior assessment: II. Females. *Behavior Research and Therapy,* 1968, *6,* 27–30. (b)

Berg, B. Helping behavior on the gridiron: It helps if you're winning. *Psychological Reports,* 1978, *42,* 531–534.

Berger, C. R., & Calabrese, R. J. Some explorations in initial interaction and beyond: Toward a developmental theory of interpersonal communication. *Human Communication Research,* 1975, *1,* 99–112.

Berger, S. M. Conditioning through vicarious instigation. *Psychological Review,* 1962, *69,* 450–466.

Berger, S. M. Observer perseverance as related to a model's success. *Journal of Personality and Social Psychology,* 1971, *19,* 341–350.

Berger, S. M., & Lambert, W. W. Stimulus-response theory in contemporary social psychology. In G. Lindzey & E. Aronson (Eds.), *Handbook of social psychology* (Vol. 1) (2nd ed.). Reading, Mass.: Addison-Wesley, 1968. Pp. 81–178.

Berglas, S., & Jones, E. E. Drug choice as an externalization strategy in response to noncontingent success. *Journal of Personality and Social Psychology,* 1978, *36,* 405–417.

Berkowitz, L. Group standards, cohesiveness and productivity. *Human Relations,* 1954, *7,* 505–519.

Berkowitz, L. Some aspects of observed aggression. *Journal of Personality and Social Psychology,* 1965, *2,* 359–369. (a)

Berkowitz, L. The concept of aggressive drive: Some additional considerations. In L. Berkowitz (Ed.), *Advances in experimental social psychology* (Vol. 2). New York: Academic Press, 1965. Pp. 301–329. (b)

Berkowitz, L. Impulse, aggression, and the gun. *Psychology Today,* 1968, *2*(4), 18–22.

Berkowitz, L. The frustration-aggression hypothesis revisited. In L. Berkowitz (Ed.), *Roots of aggression: A re-examination of the frustration-aggression hypothesis.* New York: Atherton, 1969. Pp. 1–20.

Berkowitz, L. The contagion of violence: An S-R mediational analysis of some effects of observed aggression. In W. Arnold & M. Page (Eds.), *Nebraska Symposium on Motivation* (Vol. 18). Lincoln: University of Nebraska Press, 1971, Pp. 95–135.

Berkowitz, L. Social norms, feelings, and other factors affecting helping and altruism. In L. Berkowitz (Ed.), *Advances in experimental social psychology* (Vol. 6). New York: Academic Press, 1972. Pp. 63–108.

Berkowitz, L. Some determinants of impulsive aggression: Role of mediated associations with reinforce-

ments for aggression. *Psychological Review,* 1974, *81,* 165–176.

Berkowitz, L. Decreased helpfulness with increased group size through lessening the effects of the needy individual's dependency. *Journal of Personality,* 1978, *46,* 299–310.

Berkowitz, L., & Alioto, J. T. The meaning of an observed event as a determinant of its aggressive consequences. *Journal of Personality and Social Psychology,* 1973, *28,* 206–217.

Berkowitz, L., & Daniels, L. R. Responsibility and dependency. *Journal of Abnormal and Social Psychology,* 1963, *66,* 664–669.

Berkowitz, L., & Geen, R. G. Film violence and cue properties of available targets. *Journal of Personality and Social Psychology,* 1966, *3,* 525–530.

Berkowitz, L., & Geen, R. G. Stimulus qualities of the target of aggression: A further study. *Journal of Personality and Social Psychology,* 1967, *5,* 364–368.

Berkowitz, L., & LePage, A. Weapons as aggression-eliciting stimuli. *Journal of Personality and Social Psychology,* 1967, *7,* 202–207.

Berkun, M. M. Performance decrement under psychological stress. *Human Factors,* 1964, *6*(1), 21–30.

Bernard, J. *Women, wives, mothers.* Chicago: Aldine, 1975.

Berry, J. W. Canadian psychology: Some social and applied emphases. *The Canadian Psychologist,* 1974, *15,* 132–139.

Berscheid, E. Opinion change and communicator-communicatee similarity and dissimilarity. *Journal of Personality and Social Psychology,* 1966, *4,* 670–680.

Berscheid, E., Graziano, E., Monson, T., & Dermer, M. Outcome dependency: Attention, attribution and attraction. *Journal of Personality and Social Psychology,* 1976, *34,* 978–989.

Berscheid, E. & Walster, E. *Physical attractiveness.* In L. Berkowitz (Ed.), *Advances in experimental social psychology* (Vol. 7). New York: Academic Press, 1974. Pp. 158–216.

Berscheid, E. & Walster, E. *Interpersonal attraction* (2nd ed.). Reading, Mass.: Addison-Wesley, 1978.

Berzins, J. I., Welling, M. A., & Wetter, R. E. *The PRF ANDRO scale user's manual.* Unpublished manual, University of Kentucky, 1975.

Beveridge, W.I.B. *The art of scientific investigation.* London: Mercury, 1964.

Bickman, L. Social influence and diffusion of responsibility in an emergency. *Journal of Experimental Social Psychology,* 1972, *8,* 438–445.

Bickman, L., & Kamzan, M. The effect of race and need on helping behavior. *Journal of Social Psychology,* 1973, *89,* 73–77.

Bickman, L., Teger, A., Gabriele, T., McLaughlin, C., Berger, M., & Sunday, E. Dormitory density and helping behavior. *Environment and Behavior,* 1973, *5,* 465–490.

Biddle, B. J., & Thomas, E. J. (Eds.). *Role theory: Concepts and research.* New York: Wiley, 1966.

Bieber, I., Dain, H. J., Dince, P. R., Drellich, M. G., Girand, H. G., Gundlach, R. H., Kremer, M. W., Rifkin, A. H., Wilbur, C. B., & Bieber, T. B. *Homosexuality: A psychoanalytic study.* New York: Basic Books, 1962.

Bieri, J., Atkins, A., Briar, S., Leaman, R. L., Miller, H., & Tripodi, T. *Clinical and social judgment.*

New York: Wiley, 1966.

Bion, W. R. *Experiences in groups, and other papers.* New York: Basic Books, 1959.

Bird, C. *Social psychology.* New York: Appleton-Century-Crofts, 1940.

Birdwhistell, R. L. *Kinesics and context.* Philadelphia: University of Pennsylvania Press, 1970.

Blanchard, F. A., Weigel, R. H., & Cook, S. W. *The effect of relative competence of group members upon interpersonal attraction in cooperating interracial groups.* Unpublished manuscript, Institute of Behavioral Science, University of Colorado, 1974.

Blaney, N. T., Stephan, C., Rosenfield, D., Aronson, E., & Sikes, J. Interdependence in the classroom: A field study. *Journal of Educational Psychology,* 1977, *69*(2), 121–128.

Blass, T. On personality variables, situations, and social behavior. In T. Blass (Ed.), *Personality variables in social behavior.* Hillsdale, N.J.: Erlbaum, 1977. Pp. 1–24.

Blau, P. Cooperation and competition in a bureaucracy. *American Journal of Sociology,* 1954, *59,* 530–535.

Bleda, P. R., & Castore, C. H. Social comparison, attraction and choice of a comparison other. *Memory and Cognition,* 1973, *1,* 420–424.

Block, J. The assessment of communication role variations as a function of interactional context. *Journal of Personality,* 1952, *21,* 272–286.

Block, J. H. Conceptions of sex roles: Some cross-cultural and longitudinal perspectives. *American Psychologist,* 1973, *28,* 512–526.

Bloom, B. S. *Stability and change in human characteristics.* New York: Wiley, 1964.

Bloom, L. M., & Clark, R. D. The cost-reward model of helping behavior: A nonconfirmation. *Journal of Applied Social Psychology,* 1976, *6,* 76–84.

Blumstein, P. W., & Schwartz, P. Bisexuality: Some social psychological issues. *Journal of Social Issues,* 1977, *33*(2), 30–45.

Bochner, S., & Insko, C. Communicator discrepancy, source credibility, and influence. *Journal of Personality and Social Psychology,* 1966, *4,* 614–621.

Boehm, C. Some problems with altruism in the search for moral universals. *Behavioral Science,* 1979, *24,* 15–24.

Bogart, K., Geis, F., Levy, M., & Zimbardo, P. No dissonance for Machiavellians. In R. Christie & F. Geis (Eds.), *Studies in Machiavellianism.* New York: Academic Press, 1970. Pp. 236–259.

Booth, A. Sex and social participation. *American Sociological Review,* 1972, *37,* 183–192.

Booth, A., & Welch, S. *The effects of crowding: A cross-national study.* Unpublished manuscript, Ministry of State for Urban Affairs, Ottawa, Canada, 1973.

Booth, A., & Welch, S. *Crowding and urban crime rates.* Paper presented at the meeting of the Midwest Sociological Association, Omaha, Nebraska, 1974.

Borden, R. J. Witnessed aggression: Influence of an observer's sex and values on aggressive responding. *Journal of Personality and Social Psychology,* 1975, *31,* 567–573.

Borden, R. J. Audience influence. In P. B. Paulus (Ed.), *Psychology of group influence.* Hillsdale, N.J.: Erlbaum, 1980.

Borgatta, E. F., & Bales, R. F. Sociometric status patterns and characteristics of interaction. *Journal of*

Abnormal and Social Psychology, 1956, *43,* 289–297.

Borgatta, E. F., Couch, A. S., & Bales, R. F. Some findings relevant to the Great Man theory of leadership. *American Sociological Review,* 1954, *19,* 755–759.

Borke, H. The communication of intent: A systematic approach to the observation of family interaction. *Human Relations,* 1967, *20,* 1.

Bose, C. E. *Jobs and gender: Sex and occupational prestige.* Baltimore, Md.: Center for Metropolitan Planning and Research, Johns Hopkins University, August 1973.

Bouchard, T. J., Jr. Personality, problem-solving procedure, and performance in small groups. *Journal of Applied Psychology,* 1969, *53,* 1–29.

Bouchard, T. J., Jr. Training, motivation, and personality as determinants of the effectiveness of brainstorming groups and individuals. *Journal of Applied Psychology,* 1972, *56,* 324–331.

Bouchard, T. J., Jr., Barsaloux, J., & Drauden, G. Brainstorming procedure, group size, and sex as determinants of the problem-solving effectiveness of groups and individuals. *Journal of Applied Psychology,* 1974, *59,* 135–138.

Bowers, K. S. Situationism in psychology. An analysis and a critique. *Psychological Review,* 1973, *80,* 307–336.

Braginsky, B. M., Braginsky, D. D., and Ring, K. *Methods of madness: The mental hospital as a last resort.* New York: Holt, 1969.

Braginsky, D. Machiavellianism and manipulative interpersonal behavior in children. *Journal of Experimental Social Psychology,* 1970, *6,* 77–99.

Brainerd, C. J. Structures-of-the-whole: Is there any glue to hold the concrete-operational "stage" together? Paper presented at the meeting of the Canadian Psychological Association, Windsor, Ontario, June 1974.

Bramson, L., & Goethals, G. W. (Eds.). *War* (Rev. ed.). New York: Basic Books, 1968.

Brandt, J. M. *Behavioral validation of a scale measuring need for uniqueness.* Unpublished doctoral dissertation, Purdue University, 1976.

Braver, S., & Barnett, B. Perception of opponents' motives and cooperation in a mixed-motive game. *Journal of Conflict Resolution,* 1974, *18,* 686–699.

Bray, R. M., & Noble, A. M. Authoritarianism and decisions of mock juries: Evidence of jury bias and group polarization. *Journal of Personality and Social Psychology,* 1978, *36,* 1424–1430.

Breed, G. The effect of intimacy: Reciprocity or retreat? *British Journal of Social and Clinical Psychology,* 1972, *11,* 135–142.

Brehm, J. W. *A theory of psychological reactance.* New York: Academic Press, 1966.

Brehm, J. W. *Responses to loss of freedom: A theory of psychological reactance.* Morristown, N.J.: General Learning Press, 1972.

Brehm, J. W., & Cohen, A. R. *Explorations in cognitive dissonance.* New York: Wiley, 1962.

Brehm, J. W., & Cole, A. H. Effect of a favor which reduces freedom. *Journal of Personality and Social Psychology,* 1966, *3,* 420–426.

Brehm, J. W., Stires, L. K., Sensenig, J., & Shaban, J. The attractiveness of an eliminated choice alternative. *Journal of Experimental Social Psychology,* 1966, *2,* 301–313.

Brehm, S. S., & Aderman, D. On the relationship between empathy and the actor versus observer hypothesis. *Journal of Research in Personality*, 1977, *11*, 340–346.

Brewer, M. B. Averaging versus summation in composite ratings of complex social stimuli. *Journal of Personality and Social Psychology*, 1968, *8*, 20–26.

Brewer, M. B. In-group bias in the minimal intergroup situation: A cognitive-motivational analysis. *Psychological Bulletin*, 1979, *86*, 307–324.

Brigham, J. C. Ethnic stereotypes. *Psychological Bulletin*, 1971, *76*, 15–38.

Brigham, J. C., Woodmansee, J. J., & Cook, S. W. Dimensions of verbal racial attitudes: Interracial marriage and approaches to racial equality. *Journal of Social Issues*, 1976, *32*(2), 9–21.

Brink, J. H. Effect of interpersonal communication on attraction. *Journal of Personality and Social Psychology*, 1977, *35*, 783–790.

Brissett, D., & Edgley, C. *Life as theater: A dramaturgical sourcebook.* Chicago: Aldine, 1975.

Brock, T. C., & Becker, L. A. Ineffectiveness of "overheard" counterpropaganda. *Journal of Personality and Social Psychology*, 1965, *2*, 654–660.

Brodsky, S. L. *After the courtship: Psychologists and policemen work together.* Paper presented at the meeting of the American Psychological Association, New Orleans, September 1974.

Bronfenbrenner, U. *Two worlds of childhood: U.S. and U.S.S.R.* New York: Russell Sage Foundation, 1970.

Brooks, D. K., & Taylor, R. B. *Temporary territories: Spatial desirability and response to intrusions in a public setting.* Paper presented at the annual meeting of the Eastern Psychological Association, Philadelphia, 1979.

Broude, G. J. Norms of premarital sexual behavior: A cross-cultural study. *Ethos*, 1975, *3*, 381–402.

Broverman, D. M., Klaiber, E. L., Kobayashi, Y., & Vogel, W. Roles of activation and inhibition in sex differences in cognitive abilities. *Psychological Review*, 1968, *75*, 23–50.

Broverman, I. K., Broverman, D. M., Clarkson, F. E., Rosenkrantz, P. S., & Vogel, S. R. Sex-role stereotypes and clinical judgments of mental health. *Journal of Consulting and Clinical Psychology*, 1970, *34*, 1–7.

Broverman, I. K., Vogel, S. R., Broverman, D. M., Clarkson, F. E., & Rosenkrantz, P. S. Sex-role stereotypes: A current appraisal. *Journal of Social Issues*, 1972, *28*(2), 59–78.

Brown, B. B., Vinsel, A., Foss, C. L., & Altman, I. *Privacy management styles and prediction of college dropouts.* Paper presented at the annual convention of the American Psychological Association, Toronto, Canada, 1978.

Brown, B. R. The effects of need to maintain face on interpersonal bargaining. *Journal of Experimental Social Psychology*, 1968, *4*, 107–122.

Brown, B. R. Face-saving following experimentally induced embarrassment. *Journal of Experimental Social Psychology*, 1970, *6*, 255–271.

Brown, B. R., & Garland, H. The effects of incompetency, audience acquaintanceship, and anticipated evaluative feedback on face-saving behavior. *Journal of Experimental Social Psychology*, 1971, *7*, 490–502.

Brown, I., Jr., & Inouye, D. K. Learned helplessness through modeling: The role of perceived similarity in competence. *Journal of Personality and Social Psychology*, 1978, *36*, 900–908.

Brown, P., & Elliott, R. Control of aggression in a nursery school class. *Journal of Experimental Child Psychology*, 1965, *2*, 103–107.

Brown, R. *Social psychology.* New York: Free Press, 1965.

Brownmiller, S. *Against our will: Men, women and rape.* New York: Simon and Schuster, 1975.

Bruner, J. S., & Tagiuri, R. The perception of people. In G. Lindzey (Ed.), *Handbook of social psychology* (Vol. 2). Reading, Mass.: Addison-Wesley, 1954. Pp. 634–654.

Bryan, J. H. Why children help: A review. *Journal of Social Issues*, 1972, *28*(3), 87–104.

Bryan, J. H., & Davenport, M. *Donations to the needy: Correlates of financial contributions to the destitute.* (Research Bulletin No. 68-1). Princeton, N.J.: Educational Testing Service, 1968.

Bryan, J. H., & London, P. Altruistic behavior by children. *Psychological Bulletin*, 1970, *73*, 200–211.

Bryan, J. H., & Test, M. A. Models and helping: Naturalistic studies in aiding behavior. *Journal of Personality and Social Psychology*, 1967, *6*, 400–407.

Bryan, J. H., & Walbek, N. The impact of words and deeds concerning altruism upon children. *Child Development*, 1970, *41*, 747–757. (a)

Bryan, J. H., & Walbek, N. Preaching and practicing self-sacrifice: Children's actions and reactions. *Child Development*, 1970, *41*, 329–353. (b)

Buchanan, W., & Cantril, H. *How nations see each other.* Urbana: University of Illinois Press, 1953.

Buck, R. W., & Parke, R. D. Behavioral and physiological response to the presence of a friendly or neutral person in two types of stressful situations. *Journal of Personality and Social Psychology*, 1972, *24*, 143–153.

Buckhout, R., Alper, A., Chern, S., Silverberg, G., & Slomovits, M. Determinants of eyewitness performance on a lineup. *Bulletin of the Psychonomic Society*, 1974, *4*, 191–192.

Buckhout, R., Figueroa, D., & Hoff, E. *Eyewitness identification: Effects of suggestion and bias in identification from photographs* (Report No. CR-11). Center for Responsive Psychology, Brooklyn College, Brooklyn, N.Y., May 1, 1974.

Bugental, D. E., Kaswan, J. E., & Love, L. R. Perception of contradictory meanings conveyed by verbal and nonverbal channels. *Journal of Personality and Social Psychology*, 1970, *16*, 647–655.

Bugental, D. E., Love, L. R., & Gianetto, R. M. Perfidious feminine faces. *Journal of Personality and Social Psychology*, 1971, *17*, 314–318.

Bugental, J.F.T., & Zelen, S. L. Investigations into the self-concept. *Journal of Personality*, 1950, *18*, 483–498.

Bulman, R. J., & Wortman, C. G. Attribution of blame and coping in the "real world": Severe accident victims react to their lot. *Journal of Personality and Social Psychology*, 1977, *35*, 351–363.

Burgess, E. W., & Wallin, P. *Engagement and marriage.* Philadelphia: Lippincott, 1953.

Burk, B. A., Zdep, S. M., & Kushner, H. Affiliation patterns among American girls. *Adolescence*, 1973, *8*, 541–546.

Burney, C. *Solitary confinement* (2nd ed.). London: Colin MacMillan, 1961.

Burstein, E., & Worchel, P. Arbitrariness of frustration and its consequences for aggression in a social situation. *Journal of Personality*, 1962, *30*, 528–540.

Burton, R. V. Generality of honesty reconsidered. *Psychological Review*, 1963, *70*, 481–499.

Burtt, H. E. Sex differences in the effect of discussion. *Journal of Experimental Psychology*, 1920, *3*, 390–395.

Buss, A. *The psychology of aggression*. New York: Wiley, 1961.

Buss, A. Physical aggression in relation to different frustrations. *Journal of Abnormal and Social Psychology*, 1963, *67*, 1–7.

Buss, A. H. Instrumentality of aggression, feedback, and frustration as determinants of physical aggression. *Journal of Personality and Social Psychology*, 1966, *3*, 153–162.

Buss, A. H. Aggression pays. In J. L. Singer (Ed.), *The control of aggression and violence*. New York: Academic Press, 1971. Pp. 7–18.

Buss, A. H., Booker, A., & Buss, E. Firing a weapon and aggression. *Journal of Personality and Social Psychology*, 1972, *22*, 296–302.

Butterfield, D. A. *An integrative approach to the study of leadership effectiveness in organizations*. Unpublished doctoral dissertation, University of Michigan, 1968.

Buvinic, M. L., & Berkowitz, L. Delayed effects of practiced versus unpracticed responses after observation of movie violence. *Journal of Experimental Social Psychology*, 1976, *12*, 283–293.

Byrd, R. E. *Alone*. New York: Putnam, 1938.

Byrne, D. The influence of propinquity and opportunities for interaction on classroom relationships. *Human Relations*, 1961, *14*, 63–70.

Byrne, D. Parental antecedents of authoritarianism. *Journal of Personality and Social Psychology*, 1965, *1*, 369–373.

Byrne, D. *The attraction paradigm*. New York: Academic Press, 1971.

Byrne, D. Social psychology and the study of sexual behavior. *Personality and Social Psychology Bulletin*, 1977, *3*, 3–30.

Byrne, D., & Byrne, L. A. *Exploring human sexuality*. New York: Thomas Y. Crowell, 1977.

Byrne, D., & Clore, G. L. A reinforcement model of evaluative responses. *Personality: An International Journal*, 1970, *1*, 103–128.

Byrne, D., Ervin, C., & Lamberth, J. Continuity between the experimental study of attraction and real-life computer dating. *Journal of Personality and Social Psychology*, 1970, *16*, 157–165.

Byrne, D., Fisher, J. D., Lamberth, J., & Mitchell, H. E. Evaluations of erotica: Facts or feelings? *Journal of Personality and Social Psychology*, 1974, *29*, 111–116.

Byrne, D., Jazwinski, C., DeNinno, J. A., & Fisher, W. A. Negative sexual attitudes and contraception. In D. Byrne & L.A. Byrne (Eds.), *Exploring human sexuality*. New York: Thomas Y. Crowell, 1977. Pp. 331–342.

Byrne, D., & Wong, T. J. Racial prejudice, interpersonal attraction, and assumed dissimilarity of attitudes. *Journal of Abnormal and Social Psychology*, 1962, *65*, 246–253.

Calhoun, J. B. Population density and social pathology. *Scientific American*, 1962, *206* (2), 139–148.

Calvin, A. Social reinforcement. *Journal of Social Psychology*, 1962, *56*, 15–19.

Cameron, C. Sex-role attitudes. In S. Oskamp, *Attitudes and opinions*. Englewood Cliffs, N.J.: Prentice-Hall, 1977. Pp. 339–359.

Cameron, N. A. Role concepts in behavior pathology. *American Journal of Sociology*, 1950, *55*, 464–467.

Campbell, A., Converse, P. E., & Rogers, W. L. *The quality of American life: Perceptions, evaluations, and satisfactions*. New York: Russell Sage, 1976.

Campbell, D. E. *Interior office design and visitor response*. Paper presented at the annual convention of the American Psychological Association, Toronto, Canada, 1978.

Campbell, D. E., & Beets, J. L. Lunacy and the moon. *Psychological Bulletin*, 1978, *85*, 1123–1129.

Campbell, D. T. *The generality of a social attitude*. Unpublished doctoral dissertation, University of California, 1947.

Campbell, D. T. Reforms as experiments. *American Psychologist*, 1969, *24*(4), 409–429.

Campbell, D. T. On the genetics of altruism and the counter-hedonic components of human culture. In L. Wispé (Ed.), *Altruism, sympathy, and helping: Psychological and sociological principles*. New York: Academic Press, 1978. Pp. 39–57.

Campbell, D. T. Comments on the sociobiology of ethics and moralizing. *Behavioral Science*, 1979, *24*, 37–45.

Campbell, D. T., & Fiske, D. W. Convergent and discriminant validation by the multitrait multimethod matrix. *Psychological Bulletin*, 1959, *56*, 81–105.

Campbell, D. T., & Stanley, J. C. *Experimental and quasiexperimental designs for research*. Chicago: Rand McNally, 1966.

Cannavale, F. J., Scarr, H. A., & Pepitone, A. Deindividuation in the small group: Further evidence. *Journal of Personality and Social Psychology*, 1970, *16*, 141–147.

Canter, D. An intergroup comparison of connotative dimensions in architecture. *Environment and Behavior*, 1969, *1*, 37–48.

Canter, D., & Stringer, P. *Environmental interaction: Psychological approaches to our physical surroundings*. New York: International Universities Press, 1976.

Cantor, G. N. Sex and race effects in the conformity behavior of upper-elementary-school-aged children. *Iowa Testing Programs Occasional Papers*, No. 16, July 1975.

Cantor, N., & Mischel, W. Traits as prototypes: Effects on recognition memory. *Journal of Personality and Social Psychology*, 1977, *35*, 38–48.

Cantor, N., & Mischel, W. Prototypes in person perception. In L. Berkowitz (Ed.), *Advances in experimental social psychology*. New York: Academic Press, 1979. Pp. 4–52.

Carey, A. The Hawthorne studies: A radical criticism. *American Sociological Review*, 1967, *32*, 403–416.

Carlsmith, J. M., & Anderson, C. A. Ambient temperature and the occurrence of collective violence: A new analysis. *Journal of Personality and Social Psychology*, 1979, *37*, 337–344.

Carlsmith, J. M., Collins, B. E., & Helmreich, R. L. Studies in forced compliance: I. The effect of pressure for compliance on attitude change produced by face-to-face role playing and anonymous essay writing. *Journal of Personality and Social Psychology*, 1966, *4*, 1–13.

Carlsmith, J. M., Ellsworth, P. C., & Aronson, E. *Methods of research in social psychology*. Reading, Mass.: Addison-Wesley, 1976.

Carlsmith, J. M., & Gross, A. E. Some effects of guilt on compliance. *Journal of Personality and Social Psychology*, 1969, *11*, 232–239.

Carlson, E. R., & Coleman, C.E.H. Experiential and motivational determinants of the richness of an induced sexual fantasy. *Journal of Personality*, 1977, *45*, 528–542.

Carlson, H., Thayer, R. E., & Germann, A. C. Social attitudes and personality differences among members of two kinds of police departments (innovative vs. traditional) and students. *Journal of Criminal Law, Criminology and Police Science*, 1971, *62*, 564–567.

Carlson, R. Sex differences in ego functioning. *Journal of Consulting and Clinical Psychology*, 1971, *37*, 267–277.

Carlsson, G. Social class, intelligence, and the verbal factor. *Acta Psychologia*, 1955, *11*, 269–278.

Carmichael, S., & Hamilton, C. V. *Black power: The politics of liberation in America*. New York: Random House, 1967.

Carnegie, D. *How to win friends and influence people*. New York: Simon and Schuster, 1936.

Carp, F. M., Zawadski, R. T., & Shokrkon, H. Dimensions of urban environment quality. *Environment and Behavior*, 1976, *8*(2), 239–264.

Carpenter, B., & Darley, J. M. A naive psychological analysis of counteraggression. *Personality and Social Psychology Bulletin*, 1978, *4*, 68–72.

Carpenter, C. F. Territoriality: A review of concepts and problems. In A. Roe & G. Simpson (Eds.), *Behavior and evolution*. New Haven, Conn.: Yale University Press, 1958. Pp. 224–250.

Carr, S. J., & Dabbs, J. M., Jr. The effects of lighting, distance and intimacy of topic on verbal and visual behavior. *Sociometry*, 1974, *37*, 592–600.

Carroll, J. S. Causal attributions in expert parole decisions. *Journal of Personality and Social Psychology*, 1978, *36*, 1501–1511.

Carter, J. H. Military leadership. *Military Review*, 1952, *32*, 14–18.

Cartwright, D. Risk taking by individuals and groups: An assessment of research employing choice dilemmas. *Journal of Personality and Social Psychology*, 1971, *20*, 361–378.

Cartwright, D. Theory and practice. *Journal of Social Issues*, 1978, *34*(4), 168–180.

Cartwright, D., & Zander, A. (Eds.). *Group dynamics: Research and theory* (3rd ed.). New York: Harper & Row, 1968.

Cary, M. S. The role of gaze in the initiation of conversation. *Social Psychology*, 1978, *41*, 269–271.

Cash, T. F., Begley, P. J., McCown, D. A., & Weise, B. C. When counselors are seen but not heard: Initial impact of physical attractiveness. *Journal of Counseling Psychology*, 1975, *22*, 273–279.

Cash, T. F., & Derlega, V. J. The matching hypothesis: Physical attractiveness among same-sexed friends. *Personality and Social Psychology Bulletin*, 1978, *4*, 240–243.

Cash, T. F., Kehr, J. A., Polyson, J., & Freeman, V. Role of physical attractiveness in peer attribution of psychological disturbance. *Journal of Consulting and Clinical Psychology*, 1977, *45*, 987–993.

Cashell, D. J. *Sex differences in linguistic style*. Unpublished doctoral dissertation, Purdue University, 1978.

Castore, C. H., & DeNinno, J. A. Investigations in the social comparison of attitudes. In J. M. Suls & R. L. Miller (Eds.), *Social comparison processes: Theoretical and empirical perspectives*. Washington, D.C.: Halsted-Wiley, 1977. Pp. 125–148.

Cattell, R. B., Kawash, G. F., & DeYoung, G. E. Valida-tion of objective measures of ergic tension: Response of the sex erg to visual stimulation. *Journal of Experimental Research in Personality*, 1972, *6*, 76–83.

Cavan, S. Interaction in home territories. *Berkeley Journal of Sociology*, 1963, *8*, 17–32.

Chaikin, S., & Eagly, A. H. Communication modality as a determinant of message persuasiveness and message comprehensibility. *Journal of Personality and Social Psychology*, 1976, *34*, 605–614.

Chapanis, N. P., & Chapanis, A. C. Cognitive dissonance: Five years later. *Psychological Bulletin*, 1964, *61*, 1–22.

Chapman, L. J., & Chapman, J. P. Illusory correlations as an obstacle to the use of valid psychodiagnostic signs. *Journal of Abnormal Psychology*, 1969, *74*, 271–280.

Charney, E. Patient-doctor communication: Implications for the clinician. *Pediatric Clinics of North America*, 1972, *19*, 263–279.

Chemers, M. M., Rice, R. W., Sundstrom, E., & Butler, W. Leader esteem for the least preferred coworker score, training and effectiveness: An experimental examination. *Journal of Personality and Social Psychology*, 1975, *31*, 401–409.

Chemers, M. M., & Skrzypek, G. J. An experimental test of the Contingency Model of leadership effectiveness. *Journal of Personality and Social Psychology*, 1972, *24*, 172–177.

Cherry, F., & Byrne, D. Authoritarianism. In T. Blass (Ed.), *Personality variables in social behavior*. Hillsdale, N.J.: Erlbaum, 1977. Pp. 109–133.

Cherry, F., & Deaux, K. Fear of success vs. fear of gender-inappropriate behavior. *Sex Roles*, 1978, *4*, 97–101.

Chertkoff, J. M., & Esser, J. K. A review of experiments in explicit bargaining. *Journal of Experimental Social Psychology*, 1976, *12*, 464–486.

Cheyne, J. A., & Efran, M. G. The effect of spatial and interpersonal variables on the invasion of group controlled territories. *Sociometry*, 1972, *35*, 477–489.

Cheyne, J. A., & Walters, R. H. Punishment and prohibition: Some origins of self-control. In T. M. Newcomb (Ed.), *New directions in psychology* (Vol. 4). New York: Holt, Rinehart & Winston, 1970.

Christian, J. J., Flyger, V., & Davis, D. E. Factors in the mass mortality of a herd of sika deer, *cervus nippon*. *Chesapeake Science*, 1960, *1*, 79–95.

Christie, R., & Cook, P. A guide to the published literature relating to the authoritarian personality through 1956. *Journal of Psychology*, 1958, *45*, 171–199.

Christie, R., & Geis, F. L. (Eds.). *Studies in Machiavellianism*. New York: Academic Press, 1970.

Cialdini, R. B., Borden, R. J., Thorne, A., Walker, M. R., & Freeman, S. Basking in reflected glory: Three (football) field studies. *Journal of Personality and Social Psychology*, 1976, *34*, 366–375.

Cialdini, R. B., Cacioppo, J. T., Bassett, R., & Miller, J. A. Low-ball procedure for producing compliance: Commitment then cost. *Journal of Personality and Social Psychology*, 1978, *36*, 463–476.

Cialdini, R. B., Darby, B. L., & Vincent, J. E. Transgression and altruism: A case for hedonism. *Journal of Experimental Social Psychology*, 1973, *9*, 502–516.

Cialdini, R. B., & Kenrick, D. T. Altruism as hedonism: A social developmental perspective on the relationship of negative mood state and helping. *Journal of Personality and Social Psychology*, 1976, *34*, 907–914.

Cialdini, R. B., Levy, A., Herman, P., & Evenbeck, S.

Attitudinal politics: The strategy of moderation. *Journal of Personality and Social Psychology*, 1973, *25*, 100–108.

Cialdini, R. B., Levy, A., Herman, P., Kozlowski, L., & Petty, R. E. Elastic shifts of opinion: Determinants of direction and durability. *Journal of Personality and Social Psychology*, 1976, *34*, 663–672.

Cialdini, R. B., Vincent, J. E., Lewis, S. K., Catalan, J., Wheeler, D., & Darby, B. L. A reciprocal concessions procedure for inducing compliance. The door-in-the-face technique. *Journal of Personality and Social Psychology*, 1975, *21*, 206–215.

Clark, K. B. *Dark ghetto.* New York: Harper & Row, 1965.

Clark, K. B., & Clark, M. P. Racial identification and preference in Negro children. In T. M. Newcomb & E. L. Hartley (Eds.), *Readings in social psychology.* New York: Holt, 1947. Pp. 169–178.

Clark, N. T., Hren, R. F., & Sanchez, H. *Determinants of responsibility assignment to rape victims: Complicity, yes! Chauvinism, no!* Paper presented at the meeting of the Midwestern Psychological Association, Chicago, May 1978.

Clark, R. D., III. Group-induced shift toward risk: A critical appraisal. *Psychological Bulletin*, 1971, *76*, 251–270.

Clark, R. D. On the Piliavin and Piliavin model of helping behavior: Costs are in the eye of the beholder. *Journal of Applied Social Psychology*, 1976, *6*, 322–328.

Clark, R. D., III, & Word, L. E. Why don't bystanders help? Because of ambiguity? *Journal of Personality and Social Psychology*, 1972, *24*, 392–400.

Clark, R. D., III, & Word, L. E. Where is the apathetic bystander? Situational characteristics of the emergency. *Journal of Personality and Social Psychology*, 1974, *29*, 279–287.

Clifford, B. R., & Bull, R. *The psychology of person identification.* Boston: Routledge and Kegan Paul, 1978.

Clore, G. L., & Kerber, K. W. *Toward an affective theory of attraction and trait attribution.* Unpublished manuscript, University of Illinois, Champaign, 1978.

Clore, G. L., Wiggins, N. H., & Itkin, S. Gain and loss in attraction: Attributions from nonverbal behavior. *Journal of Personality and Social Psychology*, 1975, *31*, 706–712.

Cohen, A. R. Social norms, arbitrariness of frustration and status of the agent of frustration in the frustration-aggression hypothesis. *Journal of Abnormal and Social Psychology*, 1955, *51*, 222–226.

Cohen, D., Whitmyre, J. W., & Funk, W. H. Effect of group cohesiveness and training upon creative thinking. *Journal of Applied Psychology*, 1960, *44*, 319–322.

Cohen, R. Altruism: Human, cultural, or what? In L. Wispé (Ed.), *Altruism, sympathy, and helping: Psychological and sociological principles.* New York: Academic Press, 1978. Pp. 79–98.

Cohen, S. Environmental load and the allocation of attention. In A. Baum, J. E. Singer, & S. Valins (Eds.), *Advances in environmental psychology.* Hillsdale, N.J.: Erlbaum, 1978.

Cohen, S., & Lezak, A. Noise and attentiveness to social cues. *Environment and Behavior*, 1977, *9*, 559–572.

Cohen, S., & Spacapan, S. The aftereffects of stress: An attentional interpretation. *Environmental Psychology and Nonverbal Behavior*, 1978, *3*(1), 43–57.

Coke, J. S., Batson, C. D., & McDavis, K. Empathic mediation of helping: A two-stage model. *Journal of Personality and Social Psychology*, 1978, *36*, 752–766.

Coleman, A. D. Territoriality in man: A comparison of behavior in home and hospital. *American Journal of Orthopsychiatry*, 1968, *38*(3), 464–468.

Coleman, J., Campbell, E., Hobson, C., McPartland, J., Mood, A., Weinfield, F., & York, R. *Equality of educational opportunity.* Washington, D.C.: U.S. Government Printing Office, 1966.

Collins, B. E. *Social psychology.* Reading, Mass.: Addison-Wesley, 1970.

Collins, B. E. Four components of the Rotter Internal-External scale: Belief in a difficult world, a just world, a predictable world, and a politically responsive world. *Journal of Personality and Social Psychology*, 1974, *29*, 381–391.

Condon, W. S., & Ogston, W. D. Sound film analysis of normal and pathological behavior patterns. *Journal of Nervous and Mental Disease*, 1966, *143*, 338–346.

Condry, J., & Dyer, S. Fear of success: Attribution of cause to the victim. *Journal of Social Issues*, 1976, *32*(3), 63–83.

Connor, J. M., Serbin, L. A., & Schackman, M. Sex differences in children's response to training on a visual-spatial task. *Developmental Psychology*, 1977, *13*, 293–294.

Conroy, J., & Sundstrom, E. Territorial dominance in a dyadic conversation as a function of similarity of opinion. *Journal of Personality and Social Psychology*, 1977, *35*, 570–576.

Constantinople, A. Masculinity-femininity: An exception to a famous dictum? *Psychological Bulletin*, 1973, *80*, 389–407.

Cook, H., & Stingle, S. Cooperative behavior in children. *Psychological Bulletin*, 1974, *81*, 918–933.

Cook, M., & Lalljee, M. Verbal substitutes for visual signals in interaction. *Semiotica*, 1972, *6*, 212–221.

Cook, S. W. Desegregation: A psychological analysis. *American Psychologist*, 1957, *12*, 1–13.

Cook, S. W. *An experimental analysis of attitude change in a natural social setting.* Small grant proposal submitted to U.S. Commission of Education, July 1964.

Cook, S. W. Motives in a conceptual analysis of attitude-related behavior. In W. J. Arnold & D. Levine (Eds.), *Nebraska Symposium on Motivation, 1969.* Lincoln: University of Nebraska Press, 1970. Pp. 179–231.

Cook, S. W. *The effect of unintended racial contact upon racial interaction and attitude change* (Final report, Project No. 5-1320, Contract No. OEC-4-7-051320-0273). Washington, D.C.: U.S. Office of Education, Bureau of Research, August 1971.

Cook, S. W. Ethical issues in the conduct of research in social relations. In C. Selltiz, L. S. Wrightsman, & S. W. Cook (Eds.), *Research methods in social relations* (3rd ed.). New York: Holt, Rinehart & Winston, 1976.

Cook, S. W., & Selltiz, C. A. Multiple-indicator approach to attitude measurement. *Psychological Bulletin*, 1964, *62*, 36–55.

Cooley, C. H. *Human nature and the social order* (Rev. ed.). New York: Scribner's, 1922. (Originally published, 1902.)

Cooper, H. M. Statistically combining independent studies: A meta-analysis of sex differences in conformity research. *Journal of Personality and Social Psychology*, 1979, *37*, 131–146.

Cooper, J. Deception and role playing: In telling the good guys from the bad guys. *American Psychologist*, 1976, *31*, 605–610.

Cooper, J., Darley, J. M., & Henderson, J. E. On the effectiveness of deviant- and conventional-appearing communicators: A field experiment. *Journal of Personality and Social Psychology*, 1974, *29*, 752–757.

Cooper, J., & Goethals, G. R. Unforeseen events and the elimination of cognitive dissonance. *Journal of Personality and Social Psychology*, 1974, *29*, 441–445.

Cooper, J., & Jones, E. E. Opinion divergence as a strategy to avoid being miscast. *Journal of Personality and Social Psychology*, 1969, *13*, 23–40.

Cooper, J. C., Zanna, M. P., & Taves, P. A. Arousal as a necessary condition for attitude change following induced compliance. *Journal of Personality and Social Psychology*, 1978, *36*, 1101–1106.

Cornish, E. *The study of the future: An introduction to the art and science of understanding and shaping tomorrow's world.* Washington, D.C.: World Future Society, 1977.

Costanzo, P. R. Conformity development as a function of self-blame. *Journal of Personality and Social Psychology*, 1970, *14*, 366–374.

Cotton, J. L., & Heiser, R. A. *Cognitive dissonance and selective exposure to information.* Paper presented at the meeting of the Midwestern Psychological Association, Chicago, May 1978.

Cottrell, N. B. Social facilitation. In C. G. McClintock (Ed.), *Experimental social psychology.* New York: Holt, 1972. Pp. 185–236.

Cottrell, N. B., Wack, D. L., Sekerak, G. J., & Rittle, R. H. Social facilitation of dominant responses by the presence of an audience and the mere presence of others. *Journal of Personality and Social Psychology*, 1968, *9*, 245–250.

Court, J. H. Pornography and sex crimes: A reevaluation in the light of recent trends around the world. *International Journal of Criminology and Penology*, 1976, *5*, 129–157.

Cowan, G., & Inskeep, R. Commitments to help among the disabled-disadvantaged. *Personality and Social Psychology Bulletin*, 1978, *4*, 92–96.

Cox, D. F., & Bauer, R. A. Self-confidence and persuasibility in women. *Public Opinion Quarterly*, 1964, *28*, 453–466.

Cox, O. C. *Caste, class, and race.* New York: Doubleday, 1948.

Cozby, P. C. Self-disclosure, reciprocity, and liking. *Sociometry*, 1972, *35*, 151–160.

Cozby, P. C. Self-disclosure: A literature review. *Psychological Bulletin*, 1973, *79*, 73–91.

Crandall, J. E. Effects of threat and failure on concern for others. *Journal of Research in Personality*, 1978, *12*, 350–360.

Crandall, V. C., Katkovsky, W., & Crandall, V. J. Children's beliefs in their own control of reinforcement in intellectual-academic achievement situations. *Child Development*, 1965, *36*, 91–109.

Crawford, T. J. Sermons on racial tolerance and the parish neighborhood context. *Journal of Applied Social Psychology*, 1974, *4*, 1–23.

Creedman, N., & Creedman, M. Angst, the curse of the working class. *Human Behavior*, 1972, *1*(6), 8–14.

Cronbach, L. J. Processes affecting scores on "understanding others" and "assumed similarity." *Psychological Bulletin*, 1955, *52*, 177–193.

Crook, J. H. The nature and function of territorial aggression. In M.F.A. Montagu (Ed.), *Man and aggression* (2nd ed.). New York: Oxford University Press, 1973. Pp. 183–220.

Crosby, F. A model of egoistical relative deprivation. *Psychological Review*, 1976, *83*, 85–113.

Cross, W. E., Jr. The Negro-to-Black conversion experience. In J. A. Ladner (Ed.), *The death of white sociology.* New York: Vintage Books, 1973. Pp. 267–286.

Crowne, D. P., & Marlowe, D. *The approval motive.* New York: Wiley, 1964.

Crutchfield, R. S. Conformity and character. *American Psychologist*, 1955, *10*, 191–198.

Curran, J. P. Convergence toward a single sexual standard? *Social Behavior and Personality*, 1975, *3*, 189–195.

Curran, J. P., Neff, S., & Lippold, S. Correlates of sexual experience among university students. *Journal of Sex Research*, 1973, *9*, 124–131.

Cvetkovich, G., Grote, B., Bjorseth, A., & Sarkissian, J. On the psychology of adolescents' use of contraceptives. *Journal of Sex Research*, 1975, *11*, 256–270.

Cyert, R. M., & MacCrimmon, K. R. Organizations. In G. Lindzey & E. Aronson (Eds.), *Handbook of social psychology* (Vol. 1) (2nd ed.). Reading, Mass.: Addison-Wesley, 1968. Pp. 568–611.

Daly, M., & Wilson, M. *Sex, evolution and behavior.* North Scituate, Mass.: Duxbury Press, 1978.

Dan, A. J., & Beekman, S. Male versus female representation in psychological research. *American Psychologist*, 1972, *27*, 1078.

Daniels, J. *Ordeal of ambition: Jefferson, Hamilton, Burr.* Garden City, N.Y.: Doubleday, 1970.

Daniels, L. R., & Berkowitz, L. Liking and response to dependency relationships. *Human Relations*, 1963, *16*, 141–148.

Danish, S. J., & Hauer, A. L. *Helping skills: A basic training program.* New York: Behavioral Publications, 1973.

Darley, J. M., & Batson, C. D. "From Jerusalem to Jericho": A study of situational and dispositional variables in helping behavior. *Journal of Personality and Social Psychology*, 1973, *27*, 100–108.

Darley, J. M., & Berscheid, E. Increased liking as a result of the anticipation of personal contact. *Human Relations*, 1967, *20*, 29–39.

Darley, J. M., & Cooper, J. The "clean for Gene" phenomenon: The effect of students' appearance on political campaigning. *Journal of Applied Social Psychology*, 1972, *2*, 24–33.

Darley, J. M., Teger, A. I., & Lewis, L. D. Do groups always inhibit individuals' responses to potential emergencies? *Journal of Personality and Social Psychology*, 1973, *26*, 395–399.

Darwin, C. *The expression of the emotions in man and animals.* London: John Murray, 1872.

Dashiell, J. F. An experimental analysis of some group effects. *Journal of Abnormal and Social Psychology*, 1930, *25*, 190–199.

Davidson, A. R., Jaccard, J. J., Triandis, H. C., Morales, M. L., & Diaz-Guerrero, R. Cross-cultural model testing: Towards a solution of the etic-emic dilemma. *International Journal of Psychology*, 1976, *11*, 1–13.

Davies, J. C. Toward a theory of revolution. *American Sociological Review*, 1962, *27*, 5–19.

Davies, J. C. The J-curve of rising and declining satisfactions as a cause of great revolutions and a contained rebellion. In H. D. Graham & T. R. Gurr (Eds.), *Vio-*

lence in America. New York: New American Library, 1969. Pp. 671–709.

Davis, J. D. Self-disclosure in an acquaintance exercise: Responsibility for level of intimacy. *Journal of Personality and Social Psychology*, 1976, *33*, 787–792.

Davis, J. D. When boy meets girl: Sex roles and the negotiation of intimacy in an acquaintance exercise. *Journal of Personality and Social Psychology*, 1978, *36*, 684–692.

Davis, J. D., & Skinner, A.E.G. Reciprocity of self-disclosure in interviews: Modeling or social exchange? *Journal of Personality and Social Psychology*, 1974, *29*, 779–784.

Davis, J. H. *Group performance.* Reading, Mass.: Addison-Wesley, 1969.

Davis, J. H. Group decision and social interaction: A theory of social decision schemes. *Psychological Review*, 1973, *80*, 97–125.

Davis, J. H., Bray, R. M., & Holt, R. W. The empirical study of social decision processes in juries. In J. L. Tapp & F. J. Levine (Eds.), *Law, justice and the individual in society.* New York: Holt, Rinehart & Winston, 1976. Pp. 326–361.

Davis, J. H., Kerr, N. L., Atkin, R. S., Holt, R., & Meek, D. The decision processes of 6- and 12-person mock juries assigned unanimous and two-thirds majority rules. *Journal of Personality and Social Psychology*, 1975, *32*, 1–14.

Davis, J. H., Laughlin, P. R., & Komorita, S. S. The social psychology of small groups: Cooperative and mixed motive interaction. In M. R. Rosenzweig & L. W. Porter (Eds.), *Annual Review of Psychology*, 1976, *27*, 501–542.

Davis, M. J., Brown, D. H., & White, B. C. *Conformity within the fraternity system.* Paper presented at the meeting of the Midwestern Psychological Association, Chicago, May 1978.

Dawes, R. M. *Formal models of dilemmas in social decision-making.* Paper presented at the Human Judgment and Decision Processes Symposium, Northern Illinois University, October 1974.

Dawkins, R. *The selfish gene.* Oxford: Oxford University Press, 1976.

Day, H. R., & White, C. *International prejudice as a factor in domestic versus foreign car ownership and preferences.* Paper presented at the 20th International Congress of Psychology, Tokyo, Japan, August 1973.

Dean, L. M., Willis, F. N., & Hewitt, J. Initial interaction distance among individuals equal and unequal in military rank. *Journal of Personality and Social Psychology*, 1975, *32*, 294–299.

Deaux, K. Variations in warning, information preference, and anticipatory attitude change. *Journal of Personality and Social Psychology*, 1968, *9*, 157–161.

Deaux, K. To err is humanizing: But sex makes a difference. *Representative Research in Social Psychology*, 1972, *3*, 20–28.

Deaux, K. Sex differences. In T. Blass (Ed.), *Personality variables in social behavior.* Hillsdale, N.J.: Erlbaum, 1977. Pp. 357–377.

Deaux, K. Looking at behavior. *Personality and Social Psychology Bulletin*, 1978, *4*, 207–211. (a)

Deaux, K. *Sex-related patterns of social interaction.* Paper presented at the meeting of the Midwestern Psychological Association, Chicago, May 1978. (b)

Deaux, K., & Emswiller, T. Explanations of successful performance on sex-linked tasks: What is skill for the male is luck for the female. *Journal of Personality and Social Psychology*, 1974, *29*, 80–85.

Deaux, K., & Major, B. Sex-related patterns in the unit of perception. *Personality and Social Psychology Bulletin*, 1977, *3*, 297–300.

DeJong, W. An examination of self-perception mediation of the foot-in-the-door effect. *Journal of Personality and Social Psychology*, 1979, *37*, 2221–2239.

DeLamater, J. A definition of "group." *Small Group Behavior*, 1974, *5*(1), 30–44.

Dembroski, T. M., Lasater, T. M., & Ramirez, A. Communicator similarity, fear arousing communications, and compliance with health care recommendations. *Journal of Applied Social Psychology*, 1978, *8*, 254–269.

Deniels, A. K. The captive professional: Bureaucratic limitations in the practice of military psychiatry. *Journal of Health and Social Welfare*, 1969, *10*(4), 255–265.

Denmark, F. L. Styles of leadership. *Psychology of Women Quarterly*, 1977, *2*, 99–113.

DePaulo, B. M., Rosenthal, R., Eisenstat, R. A., Rogers, P. L., & Finkelstein, S. Decoding discrepant nonverbal cues. *Journal of Personality and Social Psychology*, 1978, *36*, 313–323.

DeRisi, D. T., & Aiello, J. R. *Physiological, social and emotional responses to extended interaction distance.* Paper presented at the meeting of the Eastern Psychological Association, Washington, D.C., April 1978.

Derlega, V. J., Wilson, M., & Chaikin, A. L. Friendship and disclosure reciprocity. *Journal of Personality and Social Psychology*, 1976, *34*, 578–582.

Deutsch, M. An experimental study of the effects of cooperation and competition upon group process. *Human Relations*, 1949, *2*, 196–231. (a)

Deutsch, M. A. theory of cooperation and competition. *Human Relations*, 1949, *2*, 129–152. (b)

Deutsch, M. Field theory in social psychology. In G. Lindzey & E. Aronson (Eds.), *Handbook of social psychology* (Vol. 1) (2nd ed.). Reading, Mass.: Addison-Wesley, 1968. Pp. 412–487.

Deutsch, M. Introduction. In M. Deutsch & H. A. Hornstein (Eds.), *Applying social psychology: Implications for research, practice, and training.* Hillsdale, N.J.: Erlbaum, 1975. Pp. 1–12.

Deutsch, M., & Collins, M. *Interracial housing: A psychological evaluation of a social experiment.* Minneapolis: University of Minnesota Press, 1951.

DeVellis, B. M., Wallston, B.S., & Wallston, K. A. Stereotyping: A threat to individualized patient care. In M. Miller & B. Flynn (Eds.), *Current issues in nursing*, 1978, Vol. 2. Pp. 252–264.

DeVellis, R. F., DeVellis, B. M., & McCauley, C. Vicarious acquisition of learned helplessness. *Journal of Personality and Social Psychology*, 1978, *36*, 894–899.

DeVries, D. L., Edwards, K. J., & Slavin, R. E. Biracial learning teams and race relations in the classroom: Four field experiments using Teams-Games-Tournament. *Journal of Educational Psychology*, 1978, *70*, 356–362.

DeVries, D. L., & Slavin, R. E. *Effects of team competition on race relations in the classroom: Further supportive evidence.* Paper presented at the meeting of the American Psychological Association, Chicago, September 1975.

Diamond, I. Pornography and repression: A reconsideration of "who" and "what." *Signs*, 1980.

Diamond, M. J., & Lobitz, W. C. When familiarity breeds respect: The effects of the experimental depolarization program on police and student attitudes toward each other. *Journal of Social Issues*, 1973, 29(4), 95–109.

Diaz-Guerrero, R. *Psychology of the Mexican: Culture and personality*. Austin: University of Texas Press, 1975.

Dillehay, R. C. On the irrelevance of the classical negative evidence concerning the effect of attitudes on behavior. *American Psychologist*, 1973, 28, 887–891.

DiMatteo, M. R. A social-psychological analysis of physician-patient rapport: Toward a science of the art of medicine. *Journal of Social Issues*, 1979, 35(1), 12–33.

Dion, K. Physical attractiveness and evaluation of children's transgressions. *Journal of Personality and Social Psychology*, 1972, 24, 207–213.

Dion, K. K. The incentive value of physical attractiveness for young children. *Personality and Social Psychology Bulletin*, 1977, 3, 67–70.

Dion, K. K., Berscheid, E., & Walster, E. What is beautiful is good. *Journal of Personality and Social Psychology*, 1972, 24, 285–290.

Dion, K. L., Baron, R. S., & Miller, N. Why do groups make riskier decisions than individuals? In L. Berkowitz (Ed.), *Advances in experimental social psychology* (Vol. 5). New York: Academic Press, 1970. Pp. 305–377.

Dipboye, R. L., Arvey, R. D., & Terpstra, D. E. Sex and physical attractiveness of raters and applicants as determinants of resumé evaluations. *Journal of Applied Psychology*, 1977, 62, 288–294.

Dipboye, R. L., Fromkin, H. L., & Wiback, K. Relative importance of applicant sex, attractiveness, and scholastic standing in evaluation of job applicant resumés. *Journal of Applied Psychology*, 1975, 60, 39–45.

Dittman, A. T. *Kinesics and context* by R. L. Birdwhistell. *Psychiatry*, 1971, 34, 334–342.

Dollard, J., Doob, L. W., Miller, N. E., Mowrer, O. H., & Sears, R. R. *Frustration and aggression*. New Haven, Conn.: Yale University Press, 1939.

Dollard, J. C., & Miller, N. E. *Personality and psychotherapy*. New York: McGraw-Hill, 1950.

Donnerstein, E., Donnerstein, M., & Munger, G. Helping behavior as a function of pictorially induced moods. *Journal of Social Psychology*, 1975, 97, 221–225.

Donnerstein, E., & Wilson, D. W. The effects of noise and perceived control upon ongoing and subsequent aggressive behavior. *Journal of Personality and Social Psychology*, 1976, 34, 774–781.

Donnerstein, M., & Donnerstein, E. Modeling in the control of interracial aggression: The problem of generality. *Journal of Personality*, 1977, 45, 100–116.

Doob, A. N., & Climie, R. J. Delay of measurement and the effects of film violence. *Journal of Experimental Social Psychology*, 1972, 8, 136–142.

Doob, A. N., & Gross, A. E. Status of frustrator as an inhibitor of horn-honking responses. *Journal of Social Psychology*, 1968, 76, 213–218.

Doob, L. W. The behavior of attitudes. *Psychological Review*, 1947, 54, 135–156.

Downs, R. M., & Stea, D. (Eds.). *Image and environment: Cognitive mapping and spatial behavior*. Chicago: Aldine, 1973.

Drabman, R. S., & Thomas, M. H. Does media violence increase children's tolerance of real-life aggression?

Developmental Psychology, 1974, 10, 418–421.

Dreger, R. M., & Miller, K. S. Comparative psychological studies of Negroes and Whites in the United States. *Psychological Bulletin*, 1960, 57, 361–402.

Dreger, R. M. & Miller, K. S. Comparative psychological studies of Negroes and Whites in the United States: 1959–1965. *Psychological Bulletin Monograph Supplement*, 1968, 70 (No. 3, Part 2).

Dreiser, T. *A gallery of women*. New York: Boni and Liveright, 1929.

Driscoll, J. M., Meyer, R. G., & Schanie, C. F. Training police in family crisis intervention. *Journal of Applied Behavioral Science*, 1973, 9, 62–81.

Driscoll, R., Davis, K. E., & Lipetz, M. E. Parental influence and romantic love: The Romeo and Juliet effect. *Journal of Personality and Social Psychology*, 1972, 24, 1–10.

DuBois, P. H. A test standardized on Pueblo Indian children. *Psychological Bulletin*, 1939, 36, 523.

Du Bois, W.E.B. *The world and Africa: An inquiry into the part which Africa has played in world history*. New York: Viking Press, 1947.

DuCette, J., Wolk, S., & Soucar, E. Atypical patterns in locus of control and nonadaptive behavior. *Journal of Personality*, 1972, 40, 287–297.

Duncan, S. Nonverbal communication. *Psychological Bulletin*, 1969, 72, 118–137.

Duncan, S., Jr., & Fiske, D. W. *Face-to-face interaction*. Hillsdale, N.J.: Erlbaum, 1977.

Dunn, L. C., & Dobzhansky, T. *Heredity, race and society* (Rev. ed.). New York: New American Library, 1952.

Dunn, R. E., & Goldman, M. Competition and noncompetition in relation to satisfaction and feelings toward group and nongroup members. *Journal of Social Psychology*, 1966, 68, 299–311.

Dunnette, M. D., Campbell, J., & Jaastad, K. The effect of group participation on brainstorming effectiveness for two industrial samples. *Journal of Applied Psychology*, 1963, 47, 30–37.

Durkheim, E. *The division of labor in society* (George Simpson, trans.). New York: Free Press, 1933.

Durkheim, E. Représentations individuelles et représentations collectives. *Revue de Métaphysique*, 1898, 6, 274–302. (In D. F. Pocock [trans.], *Sociology and philosophy*. New York: Free Press, 1953.)

Durlak, J. A. Comparative effectiveness of paraprofessional and professional helpers. *Psychological Bulletin*, 1979, 86, 80–92.

Dutton, D. G., & Aron, A. P. Some evidence for heightened sexual attraction under conditions of high anxiety. *Journal of Personality and Social Psychology*, 1974, 30, 510–517.

Dutton, D. G., & Lake, R. A. Threat of own prejudice and reverse discrimination in interracial situations. *Journal of Personality and Social Psychology*, 1973, 28, 94–100.

Dutton, D. G., & Lennox, V. L. Effect of prior "token" compliance on subsequent interracial behavior. *Journal of Personality and Social Psychology*, 1974, 29, 65–71.

Duval, S., & Wicklund, R. A. *A theory of objective self-awareness*. New York: Academic Press, 1972.

Dyck, R. J., & Rule, B. G. Effect of retaliation on causal attributions concerning attack. *Journal of Personality and Social Psychology*, 1978, 36, 521–529.

Eagly, A. H. Sex differences in influenceability. *Psycho-*

logical Bulletin, 1978, *85*, 86–116.

Eagly, A. H., & Himmelfarb, S. Attitudes and opinions. In M. R. Rosenzweig & L. W. Porter (Eds.), *Annual review of psychology*, 1978, *29*, 517–554.

Eagly, A., & Telaak, K. Width of the latitude of acceptance as a determinant of attitude change. *Journal of Personality and Social Psychology*, 1972, *23*, 388–397.

Eagly, A. H., & Warren, R. Intelligence, comprehension and opinion change. *Journal of Personality*, 1976, *44*, 226–242.

Eagly, A. H., Wood, W., & Chaiken, S. Causal inferences about communicators and their effect on opinion change. *Journal of Personality and Social Psychology*, 1978, *36*, 424–435.

Ebbesen, E., Kjos, G., & Konečni, V. Spatial ecology: Its effects on the choice of friends and enemies. *Journal of Experimental Social Psychology*, 1976, *12*, 505–528.

Edney, J. J. Property, possession, and performance: A field study in human territoriality. *Journal of Applied Social Psychology*, 1972, *2*, 275–282.

Edney, J. J. Human territoriality. *Psychological Bulletin*, 1974, *81*, 959–975.

Edney, J. J. Human territories: Comment on functional properties. *Environment and Behavior*, 1976, *8*(1), 31–47.

Edney, J. J., & Jordon-Edney, N. L. Territorial spacing on a beach. *Sociometry*, 1974, *37*, 92–104.

Edwards, T. *The new dictionary of thoughts*. Garden City, N.Y.: Doubleday, 1972.

Efran, J., & Broughton, A. Effect of expectancies for social approval on visual behavior. *Journal of Personality and Social Psychology*, 1966, *4*, 103–107.

Efran, M. G., & Cheyne, J. A. The study of movement and affect in territorial behavior. *Man-Environment Systems*, 1972, *3*, 348–350.

Efran, M. G., & Cheyne, J. A. Shared space: The cooperative control of spatial areas by two interacting individuals. *Canadian Journal of Behavioral Science*, 1973, *5*, 201–210.

Efran, M. G., & Cheyne, J. A. Affective concomitants of the invasion of shared space: Behavioral, physiological, and verbal indicators. *Journal of Personality and Social Psychology*, 1974, *29*, 219–226.

Egbert, L. D., Battit, G. E., Welch, C. E., & Bartlett, M. K. Reduction of postoperative pain by encouragement and instruction of patients. *New England Journal of Medicine*, 1964, *270*, 825–827.

Ehrlich, H. J., & Graeven, D. B. Reciprocal self-disclosure in a dyad. *Journal of Experimental Social Psychology*, 1971, *7*, 389–400.

Eibl-Eibesfeldt, I. *[Ethology: The biology of behavior]* (E. Klinghammer, trans.). New York: Holt, Rinehart & Winston, 1970.

Eichenwald, H. F., & Fry, P. C. Nutrition and learning. *Science*, 1969, *163*, 644–648.

Eisenberg, L. The *human* nature of human nature. *Science*, 1972, *176*, 123–128.

Eisenberg-Berg, N. Relationship of prosocial moral reasoning to altruism, political liberalism, and intelligence. *Developmental Psychology*, 1979, *15*, 87–89.

Eisenberg-Berg, N., & Mussen, P. Empathy and moral development in adolescence. *Developmental Psychology*, 1978, *14*, 185–186.

Ekman, P. *A comparison of verbal and nonverbal behavior as reinforcing stimuli of opinion responses.* Unpublished doctoral dissertation, Adelphi College, 1958.

Ekman, P. Universals and cultural differences in facial expressions of emotion. In J. K. Cole (Ed.), *Nebraska Symposium on Motivation* (Vol. 19). Lincoln: University of Nebraska Press, 1972.

Ekman, P., & Friesen, W. V. Nonverbal leakage and clues to deception. *Psychiatry*, 1969, *32*, 88–106.

Ekman, P., & Friesen, W. V. Hand movements. *Journal of Communication*, 1972, *22*, 353–374.

Ekman, P., & Friesen, W. V. Detecting deception from body or face. *Journal of Personality and Social Psychology*, 1974, *29*, 288–298.

Ekman, P., & Friesen, W. V. *Unmasking the face.* Englewood Cliffs, N.J.: Prentice-Hall, 1975.

Ekman, P., Friesen, W. V., & Ellsworth, P. C. *Emotion in the human face.* New York: Pergamon, 1972.

Ekman, P., Friesen, W. V., & Scherer, K. B. Body movement and voice pitch in deceptive interaction. *Semiotica*, 1976, *16*, 23–27.

Ekstein, R. Psychoanalysis, sympathy, and altruism. In L. Wispé (Ed.), *Altruism, sympathy, and helping: Psychological and sociological principles.* New York: Academic Press, 1978. Pp. 165–175.

Elkind, D. Praise and imitation. *Saturday Review*, January 16, 1971, 51ff.

Elkind, D. Erik Erikson's eight ages of man. *Command and Management Course 1 Phase 1 Management Fundamental Lesson #2: Individual Behavior*, 1974.

Elliott, G. C. Some effects of deception and level of self-monitoring on planning and reacting to a self-presentation. *Journal of Personality and Social Psychology*, 1979, *37*, 1282–1292.

Ellis, H. *Studies in the psychology of sex* (1899). New York: Random House, 1936.

Ellis, L. J., & Bentler, P. M. Traditional sex-determined role standards and sex stereotypes. *Journal of Personality and Social Psychology*, 1973, *25*, 28–34.

Ellsworth, P. C. From abstract ideas to concrete instances: Some guidelines for choosing natural research settings. *American Psychologist*, 1977, *32*, 604–615.

Ellsworth, P. C., & Carlsmith, J. M. Effect of eye contact and verbal consent on affective response to a dyadic interaction. *Journal of Personality and Social Psychology*, 1968, *10*, 15–20.

Ellsworth, P. C., Carlsmith, J. M., & Henson, A. The stare as a stimulus to flight in human subjects: A series of field experiments. *Journal of Personality and Social Psychology*, 1972, *21*, 302–311.

Ellsworth, P., & Ross, L. Intimacy in response to direct gaze. *Journal of Experimental Social Psychology*, 1975, *11*, 592–613.

Emswiller, T., Deaux, K., & Willits, J. E. Similarity, sex, and requests for small favors. *Journal of Applied Social Psychology*, 1971, *1*, 284–291.

Endler, N. S., & Hartley, S. Relative competence, reinforcement and conformity. *European Journal of Social Psychology*, 1973, *3*, 63–72.

Endler, N. S., & Magnusson, D. Toward an interactional psychology of personality. *Psychological Bulletin*, 1976, *83*, 956–974.

Eoyang, C. K. Effects of group size and privacy in residential crowding. *Journal of Personality and Social Psychology*, 1974, *30*, 389–392.

Epley, S. W. Reduction of the behavioral effects of aversive stimulation by the presence of companions. *Psychological Bulletin*, 1974, *81*, 271–283.

Epstein, R. Aggression toward outgroups as a function of authoritarianism and imitation of aggressive models. *Journal of Personality and Social Psychology*, 1966, *3*, 574–579.

Epstein, R., & Komorita, S. S. The development of a scale of parental punitiveness toward aggression. *Child Development*, 1965, *19*, 129–142. (a)

Epstein, R., & Komorita, S. S. Parental discipline, stimulus characteristics of outgroups, and social distance in children. *Journal of Personality and Social Psychology*, 1965, *2*, 416–420. (b)

Epstein, R., & Komorita, S. S. Prejudice among Negro children as related to parental ethnocentrism and punitiveness. *Journal of Personality and Social Psychology*, 1966, *4*, 643–647.

Epstein, S. The stability of behavior: I. On predicting most of the people much of the time. *Journal of Personality and Social Psychology*, 1979, *37*, 1097–1126.

Erikson, E. H. *Childhood and society* (2nd ed.). New York: Norton, 1963. (a)

Erikson, E. H. (Ed.). *Youth: Change and challenge.* New York: Basic Books, 1963. (b)

Erikson, E. H. *Insight and responsibility.* New York: Norton, 1964.

Eron, L. D. Relationship of TV viewing habits and aggressive behavior in children. *Journal of Abnormal and Social Psychology*, 1963, *67*, 193–196.

Eron, L. D., Huesman, L. R., Lefkowitz, M. M., & Walder, L. O. Does television violence cause aggression? *American Psychologist*, 1972, *27*, 253–263.

Esman, A. Toward an understanding of racism. *Psychiatry and Social Science Review*, 1970, *4*, 7–9.

Esser, A. H. Interactional hierarchy and power structure on a psychiatric ward. In S. J. Hutt & C. Hutt (Eds.), *Behavior studies in psychiatry.* Oxford, England: Pergamon Press, 1970. Pp. 25–59.

Esser, A. H. Cottage fourteen: Dominance and territoriality in a group of institutionalized boys. *Small Group Behavior*, 1973, *4*, 139–146.

Esser, A. H., Chamberlain, A. S., Chapple, E., & Kline, N. S. Territoriality of patients on a research ward. In J. Wortis (Ed.), *Recent advances in biological psychiatry.* New York: Plenum Press, 1964. Pp. 37–44.

Etzioni, A. A model of significant research. *International Journal of Psychiatry*, 1968, *6*, 279–280.

Etzioni, A. Social science vs. government: Standoff at policy gap. *Psychology Today*, November 1978, pp. 24–26.

Evans, G. Human spatial behavior: The arousal model. In A. Baum & Y. Epstein (Eds.), *Human response to crowding.* Hillsdale, N.J.: Erlbaum, 1978. Pp. 283–302.

Evans, G. W. Behavioral and physiological consequences of crowding in humans. *Journal of Applied Social Psychology*, 1979, *9*, 27–46.

Evans, R. B. Childhood parental relationships of homosexual men. *Journal of Consulting and Clinical Psychology*, 1969, *33*, 129–135.

Evans, R. I. Smoking in children: Developing a social psychological strategy of deterrence. *Journal of Preventive Medicine*, 1976, *5*, 122–127.

Evans, R. I., Rozelle, R. M., Lasater, T. M., Dembroski, T. M., & Allen, B. P. Fear arousal, persuasion and actual versus implied behavior change: New perspective utilizing a real-life dental hygiene program. *Journal of Personality and Social Psychology*, 1970, *16*, 220–227.

Evans, R. I., Rozelle, R. M., Mittelmark, M. B., Hansen, W. B., Bane, A. L., & Havis, J. Deterring the onset of smoking in children: Knowledge of immediate physiological effects and coping with peer pressure, media pressure, and parent modeling. *Journal of Applied Social Psychology*, 1978, *8*, 126–135.

Executive Office of the President: Office of Management and Budget. *Social Indicators, 1973.* Washington, D.C.: U.S. Government Printing Office, 1973.

Exline, R. V. Visual interaction: The glances of power and preference. In J. K. Cole (Ed.), *Nebraska Symposium on Motivation* (Vol. 19). Lincoln: University of Nebraska Press, 1971. Pp. 163–206.

Exline, R. V., Ellyson, S. L., & Long, B. Visual behavior as an aspect of power role relationships. In P. Pliner, L. Krames, & T. Alloway (Eds.), *Nonverbal communication of aggression* (Vol. 2). New York: Plenum Press, 1975.

Exline, R. V., Thibaut, J., Hickey, C. B., & Gumpert, P. Visual interaction in relation to Machiavellianism and an unethical act. In R. Christie & F. Geis (Eds.), *Studies in Machiavellianism.* New York: Academic Press, 1970. Pp. 53–76.

Exline, R., & Winters, L. Affective relations and mutual glances in dyads. In S. Tomkins & C. Izard (Eds.), *Affect, cognition, and personality.* New York: Springer, 1965.

Fairweather, G. W. *Social change: The challenge to survival.* Morristown, N.J.: General Learning Press, 1972.

Falbo, T. Relationships between sex, sex role, and social influence. *Psychology of Women Quarterly*, 1977, *2*, 62–72.

Fallon, B. J., & Hollander, E. P. *Sex-role stereotyping in leadership: A study of undergraduate discussion groups.* Paper presented at the meeting of the American Psychological Association, Washington, D.C., 1976.

Farina, A., Allen, J. G., & Saul, B.B.B. The role of the stigmatized in affecting social relationships. *Journal of Personality*, 1968, *36*, 169–182.

Farina, A., Gliha, D., Boudreau, L. A., Allen, J. G., & Sherman, M. Mental illness and the impact of believing others know about it. *Journal of Abnormal Psychology*, 1971, *77*, 1–5.

Fawl, C. L. Disturbances experienced by children in their natural habitats. In R. G. Barker (Ed.), *The stream of behavior.* New York: Appleton-Century-Crofts, 1963. Pp. 99–126.

Fazio, R. H., & Zanna, M. P. Attitudinal qualities relating to the strength of the attitude-behavior relationship. *Journal of Experimental Social Psychology*, 1978, *14*, 398–408.

Fazio, R. H., Zanna, M. P., & Cooper, J. Dissonance and self-perception: An integrative view of each theory's proper domain of application. *Journal of Experimental Social Psychology*, 1977, *13*, 464–479.

Feather, N. T. Cognitive dissonance, sensitivity, and evaluation. *Journal of Abnormal and Social Psychology*, 1963, *66*, 157–163.

Feather, N. T. Positive and negative reactions to male and female success and failure in relation to the perceived status and sex-typed appropriateness of occupations. *Journal of Personality and Social Psychology*, 1975, *31*, 536–549.

Feild, H. S. Attitudes toward rape: A comparative analysis of police, rapists, crisis counselors, and citizens.

Journal of Personality and Social Psychology, 1978, *36*, 156–179.

Feldman, R. E. Response to compatriot and foreigner who seek assistance. *Journal of Personality and Social Psychology*, 1968, *10*, 202–214.

Feldman, S. *The presentation of shortness in everyday life—Height and heightism in American society: Toward a sociology of stature*. Paper presented at the meeting of the American Sociological Association, Chicago, 1971.

Feldman-Summers, S. Implications of the buck-passing phenomenon for reactance theory. *Journal of Personality*, 1977, *45*, 543–553.

Feshbach, S. Sex, aggression and violence toward women. In L. Berkowitz (Chair), *Aggression and violence*. Symposium presented at the meeting of the American Psychological Association, Toronto, 1978.

Feshbach, S., & Singer, R. D. The effects of personal and shared threats upon social prejudice. *Journal of Abnormal and Social Psychology*, 1957, *54*, 411–416.

Feshbach, S., & Singer, R. D. *Television and aggression*. San Francisco: Jossey-Bass, 1971.

Feshbach, S., Stiles, W. B., & Bitter, E. The reinforcing effect of witnessing aggression. *Journal of Experimental Research in Personality*, 1967, *2*, 133–139.

Festinger, L. Informal social communication. *Psychological Review*, 1950, *57*, 271–282.

Festinger, L. A theory of social comparison processes. *Human Relations*, 1954, *7*, 117–140.

Festinger, L. *A theory of cognitive dissonance*. Stanford, Calif.: Stanford University Press, 1957.

Festinger, L., & Carlsmith, J. M. Cognitive consequences of forced compliance. *Journal of Abnormal and Social Psychology*, 1959, *58*, 203–210.

Festinger, L., Gerard, H., Hymovitch, B., Kelley, H. H., & Raven, B. The influence process in the presence of extreme deviates. *Human Relations*, 1952, *5*, 327–346.

Festinger, L., Pepitone, A., & Newcomb, T. Some consequences of deindividuation in a group. *Journal of Abnormal and Social Psychology*, 1952, *47*, 382–389.

Festinger, L., Riecken, H., & Schachter, S. *When prophecy fails*. Minneapolis: University of Minnesota Press, 1956.

Festinger, L., Schachter, S., & Back, K. *Social pressures in informal groups: A study of human factors in housing*. New York: Harper, 1950.

Fidell, L. S. Empirical verification of sex discrimination in hiring practices in psychology. *American Psychologist*, 1970, *25*, 1094–1098.

Fiedler, F. E. A contingency model of leadership effectiveness. In L. Berkowitz (Ed.), *Advances in experimental social psychology* (Vol. 1). New York: Academic Press, 1964. Pp. 149–190.

Fiedler, F. E. *A theory of leadership effectiveness*. New York: McGraw-Hill, 1967.

Fiedler, F. E. Style or circumstance: The leadership enigma. *Psychology Today*, 1969, *2*(10), 38–43.

Fiedler, F. E. Validation and extension of the contingency model of leadership effectiveness: A review of empirical findings. *Psychological Bulletin*, 1971, *76*, 128–148.

Fiedler, F. E. Personality, motivational systems, and behavior of High and Low LPC persons. *Human Relations*, 1972, *25*, 391–412.

Fiedler, F. E. The trouble with leadership training is that it doesn't train leaders. *Psychology Today*, 1973, *6*(9), 23–30ff.

Fiedler, F. E. Recent developments in research on the contingency model. In L. Berkowitz (Ed.), *Group processes*. New York: Academic Press, 1978. Pp. 209–225.

Fiedler, F. E., & Chemers, M. M. *Leadership and effective management*. Glenview, Ill.: Scott, Foresman, 1974.

Fiedler, F. E., Chemers, M. M., & Mahar, L. *Improving leadership effectiveness: The leader match concept*. New York: Wiley, 1976.

Fink, H. C. *Attitudes toward the Calley-My Lai case, authoritarianism and political beliefs*. Paper presented at the meeting of the Eastern Psychological Association, Washington, D.C., May 1973.

Firestone, I. J., Kaplan, K. J., & Russell, J. C. Anxiety, fear, and affiliation with similar-state versus dissimilar-state others: Misery sometimes loves nonmiserable company. *Journal of Personality and Social Psychology*, 1973, *26*, 409–414.

Fishbein, M. Attitude and the prediction of behavior. In M. Fishbein (Ed.), *Readings in attitude theory and measurement*. New York: Wiley, 1967. Pp. 477–491.

Fishbein, M., & Ajzen, I. Attitudes and opinions. *Annual Review of Psychology*, 1972, *23*, 487–544.

Fishbein, M., & Ajzen, I. Attitudes toward objects as predictors of single and multiple behavioral criteria. *Psychological Review*, 1974, *81*, 59–74.

Fishbein, M., & Ajzen, I. *Belief, attitude, intention, and behavior: An introduction to theory and research*. Reading, Mass.: Addison-Wesley, 1975.

Fishbein, M., Bowman, C. H., Thomas, K., Jaccard, J., & Ajzen, I. Predicting and understanding voting in British elections and American referenda: Illustration of the theory's generality. In I. Ajzen & M. Fishbein (Eds.), *Understanding attitudes and predicting social behavior*. Englewood Cliffs, N.J.: Prentice-Hall, 1979. Pp. 196–216.

Fishbein, M., & Hunter, R. Summation versus balance in attitude organization and change. *Journal of Abnormal and Social Psychology*, 1964, *69*, 505–510.

Fishbein, M., Jaccard, J., Davidson, A., Ajzen, I., & Loken, B. Predicting and understanding family planning behaviors: Beliefs, attitudes, and intentions. In I. Ajzen & M. Fishbein (Eds.), *Understanding attitudes and predicting social behavior*. Englewood Cliffs, N.J.: Prentice-Hall, 1980. Pp. 130–147.

Fisher, B. A. *Perspectives on human communication*. New York: Macmillan, 1978.

Fisher, J. D., Harrison, C. L., & Nadler, A. Exploring the generalizability of donor-recipient similarity effects. *Personality and Social Psychology Bulletin*, 1978, *4*, 627–630.

Fisher, J. D., & Nadler, A. The effect of similarity between donor and recipient on recipient's reactions to aid. *Journal of Applied Social Psychology*, 1974, *4*, 230–243.

Fisher, J. D., Nadler, A., & Whitcher, S. *Toward a model for conceptualizing recipient reactions to aid*. Paper presented at the annual meeting of the American Psychological Association, Toronto, Canada, August 1978.

Fisher, J. D., Rytting, M., & Heslin, R. Hands touching hands: Affective and evaluative effects of an interpersonal touch. *Sociometry*, 1976, *39*, 416–421.

Fisher, W. A., & Byrne, D. Sex differences in response to erotica: Love versus lust? *Journal of Personality and Social Psychology*, 1978, *36*, 117–125.

Fiske, D. W. *Strategies for personality research: The obser-*

vation versus interpretation of behaviors. San Francisco: Jossey-Bass, 1978.

Fitz, D., & Gerstenzang, S. Anger in everyday life: When, where, and with whom? Paper presented at the meeting of the Midwestern Psychological Association, Chicago, May 1978.

Fleishman, E. A., Harris, E. F., & Burtt, H. E. Leadership and supervision in industry. Columbus: Ohio State University Press, 1955.

Fleishman, E. A., & Peters, D. R. Interpersonal values, leadership attitudes and managerial success. Personnel Psychology, 1962, 15, 127–143.

Flowers, M. L. A laboratory test of some implications of Janis's groupthink hypothesis. Journal of Personality and Social Psychology, 1977, 35, 888–896.

Flynn, J. T., & Peterson, M. The use of regression analysis in police patrolman selection. Journal of Criminal Law, Criminology, and Police Science, 1972, 63, 564–569.

Foa, U. G. Interpersonal and economic resources. Science, 1971, 171, 345–351.

Fodor, E. M. Simulated work climate as an influence on choice of leadership style. Personality and Social Psychology Bulletin, 1978, 4, 111–114.

Ford, C., & Beach, F. A. Patterns of sexual behavior. New York: Paul Hoeber, 1951.

Form, W. H., & Nosow, S. Community in disaster. New York: Harper, 1958.

Forrester, B. J., & Klaus, R. A. The effect of race of the examiner on intelligence test scores of Negro kindergarten children. Peabody Papers in Human Development, 1964, 2(7), 1–7.

Forward, J., Canter, R., & Kirsch, N. Role-enactment and deception methodologies: Alternative paradigms? American Psychologist, 1976, 31, 595–604.

Foulds, G. A., & Raven, J. C. Intellectual ability and occupational grade. Occupational Psychology, London, 1948, 22, 197–203.

Fraczek, A., & Macaulay, J. R. Some personality factors in reaction to aggressive stimuli. Journal of Personality, 1971, 39, 163–177.

Fraser, C. Group risk-taking and group polarization. European Journal of Social Psychology, 1971, 1, 493–510.

Frederiksen, N. Toward a taxonomy of situations. American Psychologist, 1972, 27, 114–123.

Free, L. A., & Cantril, H. The political beliefs of Americans: A study of public opinion. New Brunswick, N.J.: Rutgers University Press, 1967.

Freedman, J. L. The effects of population density on humans. In J. T. Fawcett (Ed.), Psychological perspectives on population. New York: Basic Books, 1972. Pp. 209–238.

Freedman, J. L., & Fraser, S. C. Compliance without pressure: The foot-in-the-door technique. Journal of Personality and Social Psychology, 1966, 4, 195–202.

Freedman, J. L., Heshka, S., & Levy, A. Population density and pathology: Is there a relationship? Journal of Experimental Social Psychology, 1975, 11, 539–552.

Freedman, J. L., Klevansky, S., & Ehrlich, P. R. The effect of crowding on human task performance. Journal of Applied Social Psychology, 1971, 1, 7–25.

Freedman, J., & Sears, D. O. Selective exposure. In L. Berkowitz (Ed.), Advances in experimental social psychology (Vol. 2). New York: Academic Press, 1965. Pp. 57–97.

Freeman, H. A., & Freeman, R. S. Senior college women: Their sexual standards and activity. Journal of the National Association of Women Deans and Counselors, 1966, 29(3), 136–143.

French, J.R.P., Jr., & Coch, L. Overcoming resistance to change. Human Relations, 1948, 1, 512–532.

French, J.R.P., Jr., & Raven, B. H. The bases of social power. In D. Cartwright (Ed.), Studies in social power. Ann Arbor: University of Michigan Press, 1959. Pp. 150–167.

Frenkel, O. J., & Doob, A. N. Post-decision dissonance at the polling booth. Canadian Journal of Behavioural Science, 1976, 8, 347–350.

Freud, E. L. (Ed.). Letters to Sigmund Freud. New York: Basic Books, 1960.

Freud, S. Totem and taboo. London: Hogarth Press, 1913.

Freud, S. Civilization and its discontents. London: Hogarth Press, 1930.

Freud, S. Three contributions to the theory of sex. In A. A. Brill (Ed.), The basic writings of Sigmund Freud. New York: Random House, 1938.

Freud, S. Moses and monotheism. London: Hogarth Press, 1939.

Freud, S. Fragment of an analysis of a case of hysteria. In Collected papers (Vol. 3). New York: Basic Books, 1959. (Originally published, 1905.)

Freud, S. Introductory lectures on psychoanalysis. In J. Strachey (Ed.), The standard edition of the complete psychological works (Vols. 15 & 16). London: Hogarth Press, 1963. (First German edition, 1917.)

Freud, S., & Bullitt, W. C. Thomas Woodrow Wilson. Boston: Houghton-Mifflin, 1967.

Freund, K., Sedlacek, F., & Knob, K. A simple transducer for mechanical plethysmography of the male genital. Journal of the Experimental Analysis of Behavior, 1965, 8, 169–170.

Frey, D., & Wicklund, R. A. A clarification of selective exposure: The impact of choice. Journal of Experimental Social Psychology, 1978, 14, 132–139.

Friedman, H.S., & DiMatteo, M. R. Health care as an interpersonal process. Journal of Social Issues, 1979, 35(1), 1–11.

Friedrich, L. K., & Stein, A. H. Aggressive and prosocial television programs and the natural behavior of preschool children. Monographs of the Society for Research in Child Development, 1973, 38(4, Whole No. 151).

Frieze, I. H. Causal attributions and information seeking to explain success and failure. Journal of Research in Personality, 1976, 10, 293–305.

Frieze, I. H., Parsons, J. E., Johnson, P. B., Ruble, D. N., & Zellman, G. L. Women and sex roles: A social psychological perspective. New York: Norton, 1978.

Frodi, A. The effect of exposure to weapons on aggressive behavior from a cross-cultural perspective. International Journal of Psychology, 1975, 10, 283–292.

Frodi, A., Macaulay, J., & Thome, P. R. Are women always less aggressive than men? A review of the experimental literature. Psychological Bulletin, 1977, 84, 634–660.

Fromkin, H. L., Brandt, J., King, D. C., Sherwood, J. J., & Fisher, J. An evaluation of human relations training for police. Paper No. 469, Institute for Research in the Behavioral, Economic, and Management Sciences, Krannert Graduate School of Industrial Administration, Purdue University, August 1974.

Fromkin, H. L., & Brock, T. C. Erotic materials: A commodity theory analysis of the enhanced desirability that may accompany their unavailability. *Journal of Applied Social Psychology*, 1973, *3*, 219–231.

Fromkin, H. L., & Lipshitz, R. A. *A construct validity method of scale development: The Uniqueness Scale.* Institute for Research in the Behavioral, Economic and Management Sciences (Paper No. 591). West Lafayette, Indiana: Purdue University, 1976.

Fryer, D. Occupational intelligence standards. *School and Society*, 1922, *16*, 273–277.

Fugita, B., Wagner, N. N., & Pion, R. J. Contraceptive use among single college students. *American Journal of Obstetrics and Gynecology*, 1971, *109*, 787–793.

Gaebelein, J. W. Third party instigation of aggression: An experimental approach. *Journal of Personality and Social Psychology*, 1973, *27*, 389–395.

Gaebelein, J. W. The relationship between instigative aggression in females and sex of the target of instigation. *Personality and Social Psychology Bulletin*, 1977, *3*, 79–82. (a)

Gaebelein, J. W. Sex differences in instigative aggression. *Journal of Research in Personality*, 1977, *11*, 466–474. (b)

Gaebelein, J. W. Third party instigated aggression as a function of attack pattern and a nonaggressive response option. *Journal of Research in Personality*, 1978, *12*, 274–283.

Gaebelein, J. W., & Hay, W. M. Third party instigation of aggression as a function of attack and vulnerability. *Journal of Research in Personality*, 1974, *7*, 324–333.

Gaebelein, J. W., & Taylor, S. P. The effects of competition and attack on physical aggression. *Psychonomic Science*, 1971, *24*, 65–67.

Gaertner, S., & Bickman, L. Effects of race on the elicitation of helping behavior: The wrong number technique. *Journal of Personality and Social Psychology*, 1971, *20*, 218–222.

Galle, O. R., Gove, W. R., & McPherson, J. M. Population density and pathology: What are the relations for man? *Science*, 1972, *176*, 23–30.

Galton, F. *Hereditary genius: An inquiry into its laws.* New York: Horizon Press, 1952. (Originally published, 1870.)

Gamson, W. A. Violence and political power: The meek don't make it. *Psychology Today*, 1974, *8*(2), 35–41.

Gamson, W. A. *The strategy of social protest.* Homewood, Ill.: Dorsey, 1975.

Gamson, W. A., & Scotch, N. A. Scapegoating in baseball. *American Journal of Sociology*, 1964, *70*, 69–72.

Gans, H. J. Planning and social life: Friendship and neighbor relations in suburban communities. In H. Proshansky, W. Ittelson, & L. Rivlin (Eds.), *Environmental psychology.* New York: Holt, Rinehart & Winston, 1970. Pp. 501–509.

Garai, J. E., & Scheinfeld, A. Sex differences in mental and behavioral traits. *Genetic Psychology Monographs*, 1968, *77*, 169–299.

Garbarino, J. The impact of anticipated reward upon cross-age tutoring. *Journal of Personality and Social Psychology*, 1975, *32*, 421–428.

Garcia, L. T., & Griffitt, W. Evaluation and recall of evidence: Authoritarianism and the Patty Hearst case. *Journal of Research in Personality*, 1978, *12*, 57–67.

Gardner, G. T. Effects of federal human subjects regulations on data obtained in environmental stressor research. *Journal of Personality and Social Psychology*, 1978, *36*, 628–634.

Gardner, R. C., Wonnacott, E. J., & Taylor, D. M. Ethnic stereotypes: A factor analytic investigation. *Canadian Journal of Psychology*, 1968, *22*, 35–44.

Garland, H., & Beard, J. F. *The relationship between self-monitoring and leader emergence across two task situations.* Unpublished manuscript, University of Texas at Arlington, 1978.

Geen, R. G. Effects of frustration, attack and prior training in aggressiveness upon aggressive behavior. *Journal of Personality and Social Psychology*, 1968, *9*, 316–321.

Geen, R. G. Effects of attack and uncontrollable noise on aggression. *Journal of Research in Personality*, 1978, *12*, 15–29.

Geen, R. G. The effect of being observed on performance. In P. B. Paulus (Ed.), *Psychology of group influence.* Hillsdale, N.J.: Erlbaum, 1980.

Geen, R. G., & Gange, J. J. Drive theory of social facilitation: Twelve years of theory and research. *Psychological Bulletin*, 1977, *84*, 1267–1288.

Geen, R. G., & O'Neal, E. C. Activation of cue-elicited aggression by general arousal. *Journal of Personality and Social Psychology*, 1969, *11*, 289–292.

Geen, R. G., & Stonner, D. Effects of aggressiveness habit strength on behavior in the presence of aggression-related stimuli. *Journal of Personality and Social Psychology*, 1971, *17*, 149–153.

Geer, J. H. *Cognitive factors in sexual arousal—toward an amalgam of research strategies.* Paper presented at the meeting of the American Psychological Association, New Orleans, August 1974.

Geer, J. H., & Jarmecky, L. The effect of being responsible for reducing another's pain on subject's response and arousal. *Journal of Personality and Social Psychology*, 1973, *26*, 232–237.

Geis, F. L., & Levy, M. The eye of the beholder. In R. Christie & F. L. Geis (Eds.), *Studies in Machiavellianism.* New York: Academic Press, 1970. Pp. 210–235.

Geizer, R. S., Rarick, D. L., & Soldow, G. F. Deception and judgment accuracy: A study in person perception. *Personality and Social Psychology Bulletin*, 1977, *3*, 446–449.

Gelfand, D. M., Hartmann, D. P., Walder, P., & Page, B. Who reports shoplifters? A field-experimental study. *Journal of Personality and Social Psychology*, 1973, *25*, 276–285.

Geller, D. M. Involvement in role-playing simulations: A demonstration with studies on obedience. *Journal of Personality and Social Psychology*, 1978, *36*, 219–235.

Geller, E. S., Ferguson, J. F., & Brasted, W. S. *Attempts to promote residential energy conservation: Attitudinal versus behavioral outcomes.* Unpublished manuscript, Virginia Polytechnic Institute and State University, 1978.

Gentry, W. D. Effects of frustration, attack, and prior aggressive training on overt aggression and vascular processes. *Journal of Personality and Social Psychology*, 1970, *16*, 718–725.

Gerbasi, K. C., Zuckerman, M., & Reis, H. T. Justice needs a new blindfold: A review of mock jury research. *Psychological Bulletin*, 1977, *84*, 323–345.

Gergen, K. J. Personal consistency and the presentation of self. In C. Gordon & K. J. Gergen (Eds.), *The self in social interaction.* New York: Wiley, 1968,

Pp. 299–308.

Gergen, K. J. *The psychology of behavior exchange.* Reading, Mass.: Addison-Wesley, 1969.

Gergen, K. J. Social psychology as history. *Journal of Personality and Social Psychology,* 1973, *26,* 309–320.

Gergen, K. J. Toward a psychology of receiving help. *Journal of Applied Social Psychology,* 1974, *4,* 187–193.

Gergen, K. J., Gergen, M. M., & Meter, K. Individual orientations to prosocial behavior. *Journal of Social Issues,* 1972, *28*(3), 105–130.

Gergen, K. J., & Taylor, M. G. Social expectancy and self-presentation in a status hierarchy. *Journal of Experimental Social Psychology,* 1969, *5,* 79–92.

Gergen, K. J., & Wishnov, B. Others' self-evaluations and interaction anticipation as determinants of self-presentation. *Journal of Personality and Social Psychology,* 1965, *2,* 348–358.

Gesell, A., Ilg, F. L., & Ames, L. B. *Youth: The years from ten to sixteen.* New York: Harper & Row, 1956.

Gibb, C. A. Leadership. In G. Lindzey & E. Aronson (Eds.), *Handbook of social psychology* (Vol. 4) (2nd ed.). Reading, Mass.: Addison-Wesley, 1969. Pp. 205–282.

Ginsburg, B. E., & Laughlin, W. S. The distribution of genetic differences in behavioral potential in the human species. In M. Mead, T. Dobzhansky, E. Tobach, & R. E. Light (Eds.), *Science and the concept of race.* New York: Columbia University Press, 1968. Pp. 26–36.

Glaser, B. G., & Straus, A. L. *Awareness of dying.* Chicago: Aldine, 1965.

Glass, B. The genetic basis of human races. In M. Mead, T. Dobzhansky, E. Tobach, & R. E. Light (Eds.), *Science and the concept of race.* New York: Columbia University Press, 1968. Pp. 88–93.

Glass, D. *Behavior patterns, stress, and coronary disease.* Hillsdale, N.J.: Erlbaum, 1977.

Glass, D. C., & Singer, J. E. *Urban stress.* New York: Academic Press, 1972.

Glassman, J. B., Burkhart, B. R., Grant, R. D., & Vallery, G. C. Density, expectation and extended task performance: An experiment in the natural environment. *Environment and Behavior,* 1978, *10*(3), 299–315.

Goethals, G. R., & Darley, J. M. Social comparison theory: An attributional approach. In J. M. Suls & R. L. Miller (Eds.), *Social comparison processes: Theoretical and empirical perspectives.* Washington, D.C.: Halsted-Wiley, 1977. Pp. 259–278.

Goffman, E. On face-work: An analysis of ritual elements in social interaction. *Psychiatry,* 1955, *18,* 213–231.

Goffman, E. *The presentation of self in everyday life.* Garden City, N.Y.: Doubleday Anchor, 1959.

Goffman, E. *Asylums.* Garden City, N.Y.: Doubleday Anchor, 1961.

Goffman, E. *Stigma: Notes on the management of spoiled identity.* Englewood Cliffs, N.J.: Prentice-Hall, 1963.

Goffman, E. *Interaction ritual: Essays on face-to-face behavior.* Garden City, N.Y.: Doubleday, 1967.

Goffman, E. *Relations in public.* New York: Basic Books, 1971.

Goldberg, G. N., Kiesler, C. A., & Collins, B. E. Visual behavior and face-to-face distance during interaction. *Sociometry,* 1969, *32,* 43–53.

Goldberg, P. A., Gottesdiener, M., & Abramson, P. R. Another put-down of women? Perceived attractiveness as a function of support for the feminist movement. *Journal of Personality and Social Psychology,* 1975, *32,* 113–115.

Goldberg, S. C. Three situational determinants of conformity to social norms. *Journal of Abnormal and Social Psychology,* 1954, *49,* 325–329.

Golden, J. Roundtable: Marital discord and sex. *Medical Aspects of Human Sexuality,* 1971, *1,* 160–190.

Goranson, R. E., & Berkowitz, L. Reciprocity and responsibility reactions to prior help. *Journal of Personality and Social Psychology,* 1966, *3,* 227–232.

Gordon, C. Self-conceptions: Configurations of content. In C. Gordon & K. J. Gergen (Eds.), *The self in social interaction.* New York: Wiley, 1968.

Gordon, K. Group judgments in the field of lifted weights. *Journal of Experimental Psychology,* 1924, *7,* 389–400.

Gorer, G. Man has no "killer" instinct. In M.F.A. Montagu (Ed.), *Man and aggression.* New York: Oxford University Press, 1968. Pp. 27–36.

Gossett, T. F. *Race: The history of an idea in America.* Dallas: Southern Methodist University Press, 1963.

Gould, P., & White, R. *Mental maps.* New York: Penguin Books, 1974.

Gouldner, A. W. The norm of reciprocity: A preliminary statement. *American Sociological Review,* 1960, *25,* 161–178.

Grabitz-Gneich, G. Some restrictive conditions for the occurrence of psychological reactance. *Journal of Personality and Social Psychology,* 1971, *19,* 188–196.

Graen, G., Alvares, K., Orris, J. B., & Martella, J. A. Contingency model of leadership effectiveness: Antecedent and evidential results. *Psychological Bulletin,* 1970, *74,* 284–296.

Graham, D. Experimental studies of social influence in simple judgment situations. *Journal of Social Psychology,* 1962, *56,* 245–269.

Graham, J. A., & Heywood, S. The effects of elimination of hand gestures and of verbal codability on speech performance. *European Journal of Social Psychology,* 1975, *5,* 189–195.

Graham, W. K., & Dillon, P. C. Creative supergroups: Group performance as a function of individual performance on brainstorming tasks. *Journal of Social Psychology,* 1974, *93,* 101–105.

Gray, S. W. The performance of the culturally deprived child: Contributing variables. *Proceedings of Section II, Annual Professional Institute of the Division of School Psychologists, American Psychological Association,* 1962. Pp. 30–36. (Mimeographed)

Gray, S. W., & Klaus, R. A. An experimental preschool program for culturally deprived children. *Child Development,* 1965, *36,* 887–898.

Gray, S. W., & Klaus, R. A. The Early Training Project: A seventh year report. *Child Development,* 1970, *41,* 909–924.

Gray-Little, B., & Appelbaum, M. I. Instrumentality effects in the assessment of racial differences in self-esteem. *Journal of Personality and Social Psychology,* 1979, *37,* 1221–1229.

Graziano, W., Brothen, T., & Berscheid, E. Height and attraction: Do men and women see eye-to-eye? *Journal of Personality,* 1978, *46,* 128–145.

Green, D. Dissonance and self-perception analyses of "forced compliance": When two theories make competing predictions. *Journal of Personality and Social Psychology,* 1974, *29,* 819–828.

Green, R. F. *On the correlation between I.Q. and amount of "White" blood.* Paper presented at the meeting of the American Psychological Association, Honolulu, August 1972.

Greenberg, C., & Firestone, I. J. Compensatory responses to crowding: Effects of personal space intrusion and privacy reduction. *Journal of Personality and Social Psychology*, 1977, *35*, 637–644.

Greenberg, C. I., & Baum, A. Compensatory response to anticipated densities. *Journal of Applied Social Psychology*, 1979, *9*(1), 1–12.

Greenberg, M. S., & Frisch, D. M. Effect of intentionality on willingness to reciprocate a favor. *Journal of Experimental Social Psychology*, 1972, *8*, 99–111.

Greenfield, T. B., & Andrews, J.H.M. Teacher leader behavior. *Alberta Journal of Educational Research*, 1961, *7*, 92–102.

Greenwald, A. G. On the inconclusiveness of "crucial" cognitive tests of dissonance vs. self-perception theories. *Journal of Experimental Social Psychology*, 1975, *11*, 490–499.

Greenwald, A. G., & Ronis, D. L. Twenty years of cognitive dissonance: Case study of the evolution of a theory. *Psychological Review*, 1978, *85*, 53–57.

Greenwell, J., & Dengerink, H. A. The role of perceived versus actual attack in human physical aggression. *Journal of Personality and Social Psychology*, 1973, *26*, 66–71.

Greenwood, J. M., & McNamara, W. J. Leadership styles of structure and consideration and managerial effectiveness. *Personnel Psychology*, 1969, *22*, 141–152.

Gregory, W. L. Locus of control for positive and negative outcomes. *Journal of Personality and Social Psychology*, 1978, *36*, 840–849.

Griffeth, R. W., & Cafferty, T. P. Police and citizen value systems: Some cross-sectional comparisons. *Journal of Applied Social Psychology*, 1977, *7*, 191–204.

Griffitt, W. Environmental effects on interpersonal affective behavior: Ambient effective temperature and attraction. *Journal of Personality and Social Psychology*, 1970, *15*, 240–244.

Griffitt, W. Attitude similarity and attraction. In T. L. Huston (Ed.), *Foundations of interpersonal attraction.* New York: Academic Press, 1974. Pp. 285–308.

Griffitt, W., & Kaiser, D. L. Affect, sex guilt, gender and the rewarding-punishing effects of erotic stimuli. *Journal of Personality and Social Psychology*, 1978, *36*, 850–858.

Griffitt, W., May, J., & Veitch, R. Sexual stimulation and interpersonal behavior: Heterosexual evaluative responses, visual behavior, and physical proximity. *Journal of Personality and Social Psychology*, 1974, *30*, 367–377.

Griffitt, W., & Veitch, R. Influences of population density on interpersonal affective behavior. *Journal of Personality and Social Psychology*, 1971, *17*, 92–98.

Griffitt, W., & Veitch, R. Preacquaintance attitude similarity and attraction revisited: Ten days in a fall-out shelter. *Sociometry*, 1974, *37*, 163–173.

Gross, A. E., & Crofton, C. What is good is beautiful. *Sociometry*, 1977, *40*, 85–90.

Gross, A. E., & Doob, A. N. Status of frustrator as an inhibitor of horn-honking responses: How we did it. In M. P. Golden (Ed.), *The research experience.* Itasca, Ill.: F. E. Peacock, 1976.

Gross, A. E., Wallston, B. S., & Piliavin, I. M. Beneficiary attractiveness and cost as determinants of responses to routine requests for help. *Sociometry*, 1975, *38*, 131–140.

Gruen, W. *The composition and some correlates of the American core culture.* Canandaigua, N.Y.: Veterans Administration Hospital, 1964. (Mimeographed)

Grujic, L., & Libby, W. L., Jr. *Nonverbal aspects of verbal behavior in French Canadian French-English bilinguals.* Paper presented at the meeting of the American Psychological Association, Toronto, September 1978.

Grusec, J. E., Saas-Korlsaak, P., & Simutis, Z. M. The role of example and moral exhortation in the training of altruism. *Child Development*, 1978, *49*, 920–923.

Grusec, J. E., & Skubiski, S. L. Model nurturance, demand characteristics of the modeling experiment, and altruism. *Journal of Personality and Social Psychology*, 1970, *14*, 352–359.

Grush, J. E., McKeough, K. L., & Ahlering, R. F. Extrapolating laboratory exposure research to actual political elections. *Journal of Personality and Social Psychology*, 1978, *36*, 257–270.

Grush, J. E., & Schersching, C. *The impact of personal wealth on political elections: What has the Supreme Court wrought?* Paper presented at the meeting of the Midwestern Psychological Association, Chicago, May 1978.

Gump, P. V., Schoggen, P., & Redl, F. The camp milieu and its immediate effects. *Journal of Social Issues*, 1957, *13*(1), 40–46.

Gundlach, R., & Riess, B. F. Self and sexual identity in the female: A study of female homosexuals. In B. F. Riess (Ed.), *New directions in mental health.* New York: Grune & Stratton, 1968. Pp. 205–231.

Gurin, P., Gurin, G., Lao, R. C., & Beattie, M. Internal-external control in the motivational dynamics of Negro youth. *Journal of Social Issues*, 1969, *25*(3), 29–53.

Gurnee, H. A comparison of collective and individual judgments of facts. *Journal of Experimental Psychology*, 1937, *21*, 106–112.

Gurwitz, S. B., & Panciera, L. Attributions of freedom of actors and observers. *Journal of Personality and Social Psychology*, 1975, *32*, 531–539.

Guthrie, R. V. *Even the rat was white: A historical view of psychology.* New York: Harper & Row, 1976.

Guttentag, M., & Struening, E. L. (Eds.). *Handbook of evaluation research* (Vol. 2). Beverly Hills: Sage, 1975.

Haan, N. Two moralities in action contexts: Relationships to thought, ego regulation, and development. *Journal of Personality and Social Psychology*, 1978, *36*, 286–305.

Haan, N., Smith, M. B., & Block, J. Moral reasoning of young adults: Political-social behavior, family background, and personality correlates. *Journal of Personality and Social Psychology*, 1968, *10*, 183–201.

Hackett, T. P., & Weisman, A. D. The treatment of dying. *Current Psychiatric Therapies*, 1962, *2*, 121–216.

Hackman, J. R., & Vidmar, N. Effects of size and task type on group performance and member reactions. In L. Marlowe (Ed.), *Basic topics in social psychology.* Boston: Holbrook Press, 1972. Pp. 244–258.

Hagen, R., & Kahn, A. *Discrimination against competent women.* Paper presented at the meeting of the Midwestern Psychological Association, Chicago, 1975.

Haines, D. B., & McKeachie, W. J. Cooperative versus competitive discussion methods in teaching introductory psychology. *Journal of Educational*

Psychology, 1967, *58*, 386–390.

Hall, C. S., & Lindzey, G. The relevance of Freudian psychology and related viewpoints for the social sciences. In G. Lindzey & E. Aronson (Eds.), *Handbook of social psychology* (Vol. 1) (2nd ed.). Reading, Mass.: Addison-Wesley, 1968. Pp. 245–319.

Hall, C. S., & Lindzey, G. *Theories of personality* (3rd ed.). New York: Wiley, 1978.

Hall, E. T. *The silent language.* New York: Doubleday, 1959.

Hall, E. T. A system for the notation of proxemic behavior. *American Anthropologist*, 1963, *65*, 1003–1026.

Hall, E. T. *The hidden dimension.* Garden City, N.Y.: Doubleday, 1966.

Hall, J. A. Gender effects in decoding nonverbal cues. *Psychological Bulletin*, 1978, *85*, 845–857.

Halpin, A. W. Studies in aircrew composition: III. In *The combat leader behavior of B-29 aircraft commanders.* Washington, D.C.: Human Factors Operations Research Laboratory, Bolling Air Force Base, September 1953.

Halpin, A. W. The leadership behavior and combat performances of airplane commanders. *Journal of Abnormal and Social Psychology*, 1954, *49*, 19–22.

Halpin, A. W. *Theory and research in administration.* New York: Macmillan, 1966.

Halpin, A. W., & Winer, B. J. *The leadership behavior of the airplane commander.* Research Foundation, Columbus: Ohio State University, 1952. (Mimeographed)

Hamilton, D. L. Cognitive biases in the perception of social groups. In J. S. Carroll & J. W. Payne (Eds.), *Cognition and social behavior.* Hillsdale, N.J.: Erlbaum, 1976. Pp. 81–93.

Hamilton, D. L. A cognitive-attributional analysis of stereotyping. In L. Berkowitz (Ed.), *Advances in experimental social psychology* (Vol. 12). New York: Academic Press, 1979. Pp. 53–84.

Hamilton, D. L., & Gifford, R. K. Illusory correlation in interpersonal perception: A cognitive basis of stereotypic judgments. *Journal of Experimental Social Psychology*, 1976, *12*, 392–407.

Hamilton, W. D. The genetical evolution of social behavior, I & II. *Journal of Theoretical Biology*, 1964, *7*, 1–52.

Hammer, T. H. *Leadership as a multi-faceted concept: Integrating leadership, motivation and power.* Paper presented at the meeting of the American Psychological Association, New Orleans, August 1974.

Hammond, K. R. New directions in research on conflict resolution. *Journal of Social Issues*, 1965, *21*(3), 44–46.

Haney, C., Banks, C., & Zimbardo, P. Interpersonal dynamics in a simulated prison. *International Journal of Criminology and Penology*, 1973, *1*, 69–97.

Hansen, R. D., & Stonner, D. M. Attributes and attributions: Inferring stimulus properties, actors' dispositions, and causes. *Journal of Personality and Social Psychology*, 1978, *36*, 657–667.

Hansen, W. B., & Altman, I. Decorating personal places: A descriptive analysis. *Environment and Behavior*, 1976, *8*(4), 491–504.

Hanson, D. J. The influence of authoritarianism upon prejudice: A review. *Resources in Education*, 1975, *14*, 31.

Hansson, R. O., Chernovetz, M. E., & Jones, W. H. Maternal employment and androgyny. *Psychology of Women Quarterly*, 1977, *2*, 76–78.

Hansson, R. O., & Slade, K. M. Altruism toward a deviant in city and small town. *Journal of Applied Social Psychology*, 1977, *7*, 272–279.

Hansson, R. O., Slade, K. M., & Slade, P. S. Urban-rural differences in responsiveness to an altruistic model. *Journal of Social Psychology*, 1978, *105*, 99–105.

Hardin, G. The tragedy of the commons. *Science*, 1968, *162*, 1243–1248.

Harding, J., Proshansky, H., Kutner, B., & Chein, I. Prejudice and ethnic relations. In G. Lindzey & E. Aronson (Eds.), *Handbook of social psychoogy* (Vol. 5) (2nd ed.). Reading, Mass.: Addison-Wesley, 1969. Pp. 1–76.

Hare, A. P. *Handbook of small group research* (2nd ed.). New York: Free Press, 1976.

Harlow, H. F. The nature of love. *American Psychologist*, 1958, *13*, 673–685.

Harré, R., & Secord, P. F. *The explanation of social behavior.* Oxford, England: Blackwell, 1972.

Harrell, T. W., & Harrell, M. S. Army general classification test scores for civilian populations. *Educational and Psychological Measurement*, 1945, *5*, 229–239.

Harrell, W. A. Self-disclosure and reason for requested help as factors influencing helping behavior in a field setting. *Psychological Reports*, 1977, *41*, 1122.

Harrell, W. A., & Hartnagel, T. The impact of Machiavellianism and the trustfulness of the victim on laboratory theft. *Sociometry*, 1976, *39*, 157–165.

Harris, A. S. The second sex in academe. *American Association of University Professors Bulletin*, 1970, *56*, 283–295.

Harris, M. B. Mediators between frustration and aggression in a field experiment. *Journal of Experimental Social Psychology*, 1974, *10*, 561–571.

Harris, R. J. Experimental games as a tool for personality research. In P. McReynolds (Ed.), *Advances in psychological assessment.* Palo Alto: Science and Behavior Books, 1971.

Harrison, A. A. Exposure and popularity. *Journal of Personality*, 1969, *37*, 359–377.

Harrison, A. H., & Saeed, L. Let's make a deal: An analysis of revelations and stipulations in lonely hearts advertisements. *Journal of Personality and Social Psychology*, 1977, *35*, 257–264.

Hartmann, D. Influence of symbolically modeled instrumental aggression and pain cues on aggressive behavior. *Journal of Personality and Social Psychology*, 1969, *11*, 280–288.

Hartmann, H., Kris, E., & Loewenstein, R. M. Notes on a theory of aggression. *Psychoanalytic Study of the Child*, 1949, *3–4*, 9–36.

Hartshorne, H., & May, M. A. *Studies in the nature of character* (Vol. 1). *Studies in deceit.* New York: Macmillan, 1928.

Harvey, J. H., Harris, B., & Barnes, R. D. Actor-observer differences in perceptions of responsibility and freedom. *Journal of Personality and Social Psychology*, 1975, *32*, 22–28.

Harvey, J. H., Ickes, W. J., & Kidd, R. F. (Eds.). *New directions in attribution research* (Vol. 1). Hillsdale, N.J.: Erlbaum, 1976.

Harvey, J. H., Ickes, W. J., & Kidd, R. F. (Eds.). *New directions in attribution research* (Vol. 2). Hillsdale, N.J.: Erlbaum, 1978.

Harvey, J. H., Ickes, W. J., & Kidd, R. F. (Eds.). *New directions in attribution research* (Vol. 3). Hillsdale, N.J.: Erlbaum, 1980.

Harvey, J., & Mills, J. Effect of a difficult opportunity to revoke a counterattitudinal action upon attitude change. *Journal of Personality and Social Psychology*, 1971, *18*, 201–209.

Hass, R. G. Persuasion or moderation? Two experiments on anticipatory belief change. *Journal of Personality and Social Psychology*, 1975, *31*, 1155–1162.

Hass, R. G., & Mann, R. W. Anticipatory belief change: Persuasion or impression management? *Journal of Personality and Social Psychology*, 1976, *34*, 105–111.

Hazen, M. D., & Kiesler, S. B. Communication strategies affected by audience opposition, feedback, and persuasability. *Speech Monographs*, 1975, *42*, 56–68.

Hearnshaw, L. S. *Cyril Burt: Psychologist*. Ithaca, N.Y.: Cornell University Press, 1979.

Hebb, D. O. Drives and the C.N.S. (Conceptual Nervous System). *Psychological Review*, 1955, *62*, 243–254.

Heckhausen, H. *The anatomy of achievement motivation*. New York: Academic Press, 1967.

Heider, F. Social perception and phenomenal causality. *Psychological Review*, 1944, *51*, 358–374.

Heider, F. Attitudes and cognitive organization. *Journal of Psychology*, 1946, *21*, 107–112.

Heider, F. *The psychology of interpersonal relations*. New York: Wiley, 1958.

Heilbrun, A. B., Jr. Measurement of masculine and feminine sex role identities as independent dimensions. *Journal of Consulting and Clinical Psychology*, 1976, *44*, 183–190.

Heilman, M. E., & Guzzo, R. A. The perceived cause of work success as a mediator of sex discrimination in organizations. *Organizational Behavior and Human Performance*, 1978, *21*, 346–357.

Heiman, J. R. The physiology of erotica: Women's sexual arousal. *Psychology Today*, 1975, *8*(11), 90–94.

Heller, J., Groff, B. D., & Solomon, S. H. Toward an understanding of crowding: The role of physical interaction. *Journal of Personality and Social Psychology*, 1977, *35*, 183–190.

Hellmuth, J. (Ed.). *Disadvantaged child* (Vol. 3). *Compensatory education: A national debate*. New York: Brunner/Mazel, 1970.

Helmreich, R. Applied social psychology: The unfulfilled promise. *Personality and Social Psychology Bulletin*, 1975, *1*, 548–560.

Helmreich, R., Aronson, E., & LeFan, J. To err is humanizing—sometimes: Effects of self-esteem, competence, and a pratfall on interpersonal attraction. *Journal of Personality and Social Psychology*, 1970, *16*, 259–264.

Helmreich, R., Bakeman, R., & Scherwitz, L. The study of small groups. In P. H. Mussen & M. R. Rosenzweig (Eds.), *Annual review of psychology* (Vol. 24). Palo Alto, Calif.: Annual Reviews, Inc., 1973. Pp. 337–354.

Helmreich, R. L., Beane, W., Lucker, G. W., & Spence, J. T. Achievement motivation and scientific attainment. *Personality and Social Psychology Bulletin*, 1978, *4*, 222–226.

Helmreich, R. L., & Collins, B. E. Studies in forced compliance: Commitment and magnitude of inducement to comply as determinants of opinion change. *Journal of Personality and Social Psychology*, 1968, *10*, 75–81.

Helson, H. *Adaptation-level theory: An experimental and systematic approach to behavior*. New York: Harper & Row, 1964.

Hemphill, J. K. Leadership behavior associated with the administrative reputation of college departments. *Journal of Educational Psychology*, 1955, *46*, 385–401.

Hemphill, J. K., & Coons, A. E. *Leader behavior description*. Personnel Research Board, Ohio State University, 1950.

Hendrick, C. Averaging versus summation in impression formation. *Perceptual and Motor Skills*, 1968, *27*, 443–446.

Hendrick, C. Role-playing as a methodology for social research: A symposium. *Personality and Social Psychology Bulletin*, 1977, *3*, 454.

Hendrick, C., & Jones, R. A. *The nature of theory and research in social psychology*. New York: Academic Press, 1972.

Henley, N. M. *Body politics: Power, sex, and nonverbal communication*. Englewood Cliffs, N.J.: Prentice-Hall, 1977.

Herman, J. F., Kail, R. V., & Siegel, A. W. Cognitive maps of a college campus: A new look at freshman orientation. *Bulletin of the Psychonomic Society*, 1979, *13*(3), 183–186.

Herrnstein, R. *IQ in the meritocracy*. Boston: Atlantic Monthly Press and Little, Brown, 1973.

Herzberg, F., Mausner, B., & Snyderman, B. *The motivation to work*. New York: Wiley, 1959.

Herzog, E. Some assumptions about the poor. *Monthly Labor Review*, 1970, *93*(2), 42–49.

Herzog, T. R., Kaplan, S., & Kaplan, R. The prediction of preference for familiar urban places. *Environment and Behavior*, 1976, *8*(4), 627–645.

Heslin, R. Predicting group task effectiveness from member characteristics. *Psychological Bulletin*, 1964, *62*, 248–256.

Hess, E. H. Ethology. In R. Brown, E. Galanter, E. H. Hess, & G. Mandler, *New directions in psychology*. New York: Holt, 1962. Pp. 157–266.

Hetherington, M. E., & McIntyre, C. W. Developmental psychology. In M. R. Rosenzweig & L. W. Porter (Eds.), *Annual review of psychology* (Vol. 26). Palo Alto, Calif.: Annual Reviews, Inc., 1975. Pp. 97–136.

Hicks, D. Short- and long-term retention of affectively-varied modeled behavior. *Psychonomic Science*, 1968, *11*, 369–370.

Higbee, K. L. Fifteen years of fear arousal: Research on threat appeals: 1953–1968. *Psychological Bulletin*, 1969, *72*, 426–444.

Higgins, J. Authoritarianism and candidate preference. *Psychological Reports*, 1965, *16*, 603–604.

High, T., & Sundstrom, E. Room flexibility and space use in a dormitory. *Environment and Behavior*, 1977, *9*(1), 81–90.

Hildum, D., & Brown, R. Verbal reinforcement and interview bias. *Journal of Abnormal and Social Psychology*, 1956, *53*, 108–111.

Hill, C. T., Rubin, Z., & Peplau, L. A. Breakups before marriage: The end of 103 affairs. *Journal of Social Issues*, 1976, *32*(1), 147–168.

Hills, L. R. The cruel rules of social life. *Newsweek*, 1973, *81*(14), 15. (October 1, 1973 issue)

Himmelfarb, S., & Eagly, A. H. (Eds.) *Readings in attitude change*. New York: Wiley, 1974.(a)

Himmelfarb, S., & Eagly, A. H. Orientations to the study of attitudes and their change. In S. Himmelfarb & A. H. Eagly (Eds.), *Readings in attitude change*. New York: Wiley, 1974. Pp. 2–49.(b)

Hirota, K. Group problem solving and communication. *Japanese Journal of Psychology*, 1953, *24*, 176–177.

Hite, S. *The Hite report: A nationwide study of female sexuality.* New York: Macmillan, 1976.

Hochreich, D. J., & Rotter, J. B. Have college students become less trusting? *Journal of Personality and Social Psychology,* 1970, *15,* 211–214.

Hoffer, E. *The true believer.* New York: Harper, 1951.

Hoffer, E. *The ordeal of change.* New York: Harper Colophon, 1964.

Hoffman, L. R. Group problem solving. In L. Berkowitz (Ed.), *Group processes.* New York: Academic Press, 1978. Pp. 67–100.

Hoffman, L. W. Early childhood experiences and women's achievement motives. *Journal of Social Issues,* 1972, *28*(2), 129–155.

Hoffman, M. L. Altruistic behavior and the parent-child relationship. *Journal of Personality and Social Psychology,* 1975, *31,* 937–943. (a)

Hoffman, M. L. Developmental synthesis of affect and cognition and its implications for altruistic motivation. *Developmental Psychology,* 1975, *11,* 607–622. (b)

Hoffman, M. L. Empathy, role taking, guilt, and development of altruistic motives. In T. Lickona (Ed.), *Moral development and behavior: Theory, research, and social issues.* New York: Holt, Rinehart & Winston, 1976. Pp. 124–143.

Hoffman, M. Moral internalization: Current theory and research. In L. Berkowitz (Ed.), *Advances in experimental social psychology* (Vol. 10). New York: Academic Press, 1977. Pp. 85–133.

Hogan, R. Moral conduct and moral character: A psychological perspective. *Psychological Bulletin,* 1973, *79,* 217–232.

Holahan, C. J., & Dobrowolny, M. B. Cognitive and behavioral correlates of the spatial environment: An interactional analysis. *Environment and Behavior,* 1978, *10*(3), 317–333.

Hollander, E. P. *Principles and methods of social psychology* (2nd ed.). New York: Oxford University Press, 1971.

Hollander, E. P. *Leadership dynamics: A practical guide to effective relationships.* New York: Free Press/Macmillan, 1978.

Hollander, E. P., Fallon, B. J., & Edwards, M. T. Some aspects of influence and acceptability for appointed and elected group leaders. *Journal of Psychology,* 1977, *95,* 289–296.

Hollander, E. P., & Julian, J. W. Studies in leader legitimacy, influence, and innovation. In L. Berkowitz (Ed.), *Advances in experimental social psychology* (Vol. 5). New York: Academic Press, 1970. Pp. 33–69.

Hollander, E. P., & Julian, J. W. A further look at leader legitimacy, influence, and innovation. In L. Berkowitz (Ed.), *Group processes.* New York: Academic Press, 1978. Pp. 153–165.

Holmes, D. S., & Jorgensen, B. W. Do personality and social psychologists study men more than women? *Representative Research in Social Psychology,* 1971, *2,* 71–76.

Homans, G. C. Social behavior and exchange. *American Journal of Sociology,* 1958, *63,* 597–606.

Homans, G. C. *Social behavior: Its elementary forms.* New York: Harcourt, Brace & World, 1961.

Homans, G. C. The relevance of psychology to the explanation of social phenomena. In R. Borger & F. Cioffi (Eds.), *Explanation in the behavioral sciences.* Cambridge: Cambridge University Press, 1970.

Pp. 313–328.

Hook, S. *The hero in history.* Boston: Beacon Press, 1955.

Hoppe, R. A., Greene, M. S., & Kenny, J. W. Territorial markers: Additional findings. *Journal of Social Psychology,* 1972, *88,* 305–306.

Horai, J., Naccari, N., & Fatoullah, E. The effects of expertise and physical attractiveness upon opinion agreement and liking. *Sociometry,* 1974, *37,* 601–606.

Horner, M. S. Femininity and successful achievement: A basic inconsistency. In J. Bardwick, E. Douvan, M. S. Horner, & D. Gutmann, *Feminine personality and conflict.* Monterey, Calif.: Brooks/Cole, 1970. Pp. 45–74.

Horner, M. S. Toward an understanding of achievement-related conflicts in women. *Journal of Social Issues,* 1972, *28*(2), 157–176.

Horney, K. *The neurotic personality of our time.* New York: Norton, 1937.

Horney, K. *New ways in psychoanalysis.* New York: Norton, 1939.

Hornstein, H. A. Social psychology as social intervention. In M. Deutsch & H. A. Hornstein (Eds.), *Applying social psychology: Implications for research, practice, and training.* Hillsdale, N.J.: Erlbaum, 1975. Pp. 211–234.

Hornstein, H. A. *Cruelty and kindness. A new look at aggression and altruism.* Englewood Cliffs, N.J.: Prentice-Hall, 1976.

Hornstein, H. A. Promotive tension and prosocial behavior: A Lewinian analysis. In L. Wispé (Ed.), *Altruism, sympathy, and helping: Psychological and sociological principles.* New York: Academic Press, 1978. Pp. 177–207.

Horton, R. W., & Santogrossi, D. A. The effect of adult commentary on reducing the influence of televised violence. *Personality and Social Psychology Bulletin,* 1978, *4,* 337–340.

House, J. S., & Wolf, S. Effects of urban residence on interpersonal trust and helping behavior. *Journal of Personality and Social Psychology,* 1978, *36,* 1029–1043.

Hovland, C., Harvey, O. J., & Sherif, M. Assimilation and contrast effects in reactions to communication and attitude change. *Journal of Abnormal and Social Psychology,* 1957, *55,* 244–252.

Hovland, C., Janis, I., & Kelley, H. H. *Communication and persuasion.* New Haven, Conn.: Yale University Press, 1953.

Hovland, C., & Mandell, W. An experimental comparison of conclusion drawing by the communicator and by the audience. *Journal of Abnormal and Social Psychology,* 1952, *47,* 581–588.

Hovland, C. I., & Weiss, W. The influence of source credibility on communication effectiveness. *Public Opinion Quarterly,* 1951, *15,* 635–650.

Howard, D. *Territory and bird life.* London: John Murray, 1920.

Howard, J. L., Liptzin, M. B., & Reifler, C. B. Is pornography a problem? *Journal of Social Issues,* 1973, *29*(3), 133–145.

Howard, J. L., Reifler, C. B., & Liptzin, M. B. Effects of exposure to pornography. In *Technical report of the Commission on Obscenity and Pornography* (Vol. 8). Washington, D.C.: U.S. Government Printing Office, 1971. Pp. 97–132.

Hoyt, M. F., & Raven, B. H. Birth order and the 1971 Los Angeles earthquake. *Journal of Personality and Social*

Psychology, 1973, *28*, 123–128.

Hulin, C., & Blood, M. Job enlargement, individual differences, and worker responses. *Psychological Bulletin*, 1968, *69*, 41–55.

Hundert, A. J., & Greenfield, N. Physical space and organizational behavior: A study of an office landscape. *Proceedings, 77th annual convention, American Psychological Association*, 1969, pp. 601–602.

Hunt, M. *Sexual behavior in the 1970's*. Chicago: Playboy Press, 1974.

Huston, T. L., & Korte, C. The responsive bystander: Why he helps. In T. Lickona (Ed.), *Moral development and behavior: Theory, research, and social issues*. New York: Holt, Rinehart & Winston, 1976. Pp. 269–283.

Hutt, C., & Vaizey, M. J. Differential effects of group density on social behavior. *Nature*, 1966, *209*, 1371–1372.

Hyman, H. H., & Sheatsley, P. B. "The authoritarian personality"—A methodological critique. In R. Christie & M. Jahoda (Eds.), *Studies in the scope and method of "The Authoritarian Personality."* New York: Free Press, 1954. Pp. 50–122.

Iannotti, R. J. Effect of role-taking experiences on role-taking, empathy, altruism, and aggression. *Developmental Psychology*, 1978, *14*, 119–124.

Ickes, W. *The enactment of social roles in unstructured dyadic interaction*. Paper presented at the meeting of the Midwestern Psychological Association, Chicago, May 1978.

Ickes, W. J., & Barnes, R. D. The role of sex and self-monitoring in unstructured dyadic interactions. *Journal of Personality and Social Psychology*, 1977, *35*, 315–330.

Ickes, W., & Barnes, R. D. Boys and girls together—and alienated: On enacting stereotyped sex roles in mixed-sex dyads. *Journal of Personality and Social Psychology*, 1978, *36*, 669–683.

Ickes, W. J., & Kidd, R. F. An attributional analysis of helping behavior. In J. H. Harvey, W. J. Ickes, & R. F. Kidd (Eds.), *New directions in attribution research* (Vol. 1). Hillsdale, N.J.: Erlbaum, 1976. Pp. 311–334.

Insko, C. Primacy versus recency in persuasion as a function of timing of arguments and measures. *Journal of Abnormal and Social Psychology*, 1964, *69*, 381–391.

Insko, C. A. Verbal reinforcement of attitude. *Journal of Personality and Social Psychology*, 1965, *2*, 621–623.

Insko, C. A. *Theories of attitude change*. New York: Appleton-Century-Crofts, 1967.

Insko, C. A., & Oakes, W. F. Awareness and the "conditioning" of attitudes. *Journal of Personality and Social Psychology*, 1966, *4*, 487–496.

Insko, C. A., & Schopler, J. Triadic consistency: A statement of affective-cognitive-conative consistency. *Psychological Review*, 1967, *74*, 361–376.

Insko, C. A., Songer, E., & McGarvey, W. Balance, positivity, and agreement in the Jordan paradigm: A defense of balance theory. *Journal of Experimental Social Psychology*, 1974, *10*, 53–83.

Insko, C. A., & Wilson, M. Interpersonal attraction as a function of social interaction. *Journal of Personality and Social Psychology*, 1977, *35*, 903–911.

Isaacs, S. *Intellectual growth in young children*. New York: Schocken, 1966.

Isen, A. M. Success, failure, attention and reactions to others: The warm glow of success. *Journal of Personal-*

ity and Social Psychology, 1970, *15*, 294–301.

Isen, A. M., Clark, M., & Schwartz, M. F. Duration of the effect of good mood on helping: "Footprints on the sands of time." *Journal of Personality and Social Psychology*, 1976, *34*, 385–393.

Isen, A. M., Horn, N., & Rosenhan, D. L. Effects of success and failure on children's generosity. *Journal of Personality and Social Psychology*, 1973, *27*, 239–247.

Isen, A. M., & Levin, P. F. Effect of feeling good on helping: Cookies and kindness. *Journal of Personality and Social Psychology*, 1972, *21*, 384–388.

Isen, A. M., Shalker, T. E., Clark, M., & Karp, L. Affect, accessibility of material in memory, and behavior: A cognitive loop? *Journal of Personality and Social Psychology*, 1978, *36*, 1–12.

Isen, A. M., & Simmonds, S. F. The effect of feeling good on a helping task that is incompatible with good mood. *Social Psychology Quarterly*, 1978, *41*, 346–349.

Israel, J., & Tajfel, H. *The context of social psychology: A critical assessment*. New York: Academic Press, 1972.

Izard, C. E. The emotions and emotion constructs in personality and culture research. In R. B. Cattell (Ed.), *Handbook of modern personality theory*. Chicago: Aldine, 1969.

Izzett, R. Authoritarianism and attitudes toward the Vietnam War as reflected in behavioral and self-report measures. *Journal of Personality and Social Psychology*, 1971, *17*, 145–148.

Jaccard, J. J. Predicting social behavior from personality traits. *Journal of Research in Personality*, 1974, *7*, 358–367.

Jaccard, J. Personality and behavioral prediction: An analysis of behavioral criterion measures. In L. Kahle & D. Fiske (Eds.), *Methods for studying person-situation interactions*. San Francisco: Jossey-Bass, 1977. Pp. 73–91.

Jaccard, J. J., & Davidson, A. R. Toward an understanding of family planning behavior: An initial investigation. *Journal of Applied Social Psychology*, 1972, *2*, 228–235.

Jaccard, J., Knox, R., & Brinberg, D. Prediction of behavior from beliefs: An extension and test of a subjective probability model. *Journal of Personality and Social Psychology*, 1979, *37*, 1239–1248.

Jacobson, M. B., & Effertz, J. Sex roles and leadership: Perceptions of the leaders and the led. *Organizational Behavior and Human Performance*, 1974, *12*, 383–396.

Jacobson, M. G., & Koch, W. Attributed reasons for support of the feminist movement as a function of attractiveness. *Sex Roles*, 1978, *4*, 169–174.

Jacoby, J. *The handbook of questionnaire construction*. Boston: Ballinger, 1980.

Jaffe, D. T., & Kanter, R. M. Couple strains in communal households: A four-factor model of the separation process. *Journal of Social Issues*, 1976, *32*(1), 169–191.

Jaffe, Y. *Sex and aggression: An intimate relationship*. Unpublished doctoral dissertation, University of California, Los Angeles, 1975.

Jaffe, Y., Malamuth, N., Feingold, J., & Feshbach, S. Sexual arousal and behavioral aggression. *Journal of Personality and Social Psychology*, 1974, *30*, 759–764.

James, R. Status and competence of jurors. *American Journal of Sociology*, 1959, *64*, 563–570.

James, W. *The principles of psychology* (Vols. 1 and 2). New York: Henry Holt and Company, 1890.

Janis, I. L. *Victims of groupthink*. Boston: Houghton Mifflin, 1972.

Janis, I. L. Effectiveness of social support for stressful decisions. In M. Deutsch & H. A. Hornstein (Eds.), *Applying social psychology: Implications for research, practice, and training.* Hillsdale, N.J.: Erlbaum, 1975. Pp. 87–114.

Janis, I. L., & Feshbach, S. Effects of fear-arousing communications. *Journal of Abnormal and Social Psychology,* 1953, *48*, 78–92.

Janis, I. L., & Field, P. B. Sex differences and personality factors related to persuasibility. In I. L. Janis, C. I. Hovland, P. B. Field, H. Linton, E. Graham, A. R. Cohen, D. Rife, R. P. Abelson, G. S. Lesser, & B. T. King (Eds.), *Personality and persuasibility.* New Haven, Conn.: Yale University Press, 1959. Pp. 55–68.

Jellison, J. M., Jackson-White, R., & Bruder, R. A. *Fear of success? A situational approach.* Paper presented at the meeting of the Western Psychological Association, San Francisco, April 1974.

Jenkins, J. J. Remember that old theory of memory? Well, forget it! *American Psychologist,* 1974, *29*, 785–795.

Jenkins, W. O. A review of leadership studies with particular reference to military problems. *Psychological Bulletin,* 1947, *44*, 54–79.

Jenness, A. The role of discussion in changing opinion regarding a matter of fact. *Journal of Abnormal and Social Psychology,* 1932, *27*, 279–296.

Jensen, A. R. How much can we boost IQ and scholastic achievement? *Harvard Educational Review,* 1969, *39*, 1–123.

Jensen, A. R. *Educability and group differences.* New York: Basic Books, 1973.

Jensen, A. R. *Bias in mental testing.* New York: Free Press, 1979.

Jensen, B. T., & Terebinski, S. J. The railroad game: A tool for research in social sciences. *Journal of Social Psychology,* 1963, *60*, 85–87.

Jensen, D. L. (Ed.). *Machiavelli: Cynic, patriot, or political scientist?* Lexington, Mass.: Heath, 1960.

Johnson, D. W., & Johnson, R. T. *Learning together and alone.* Englewood Cliffs, N.J.: Prentice-Hall, 1975.

Johnson, H. G., Ekman, P., & Friesen, W. V. Communicative body movements: American emblems. *Semiotica,* 1975, *15*, 335–353.

Johnston, A., DeLuca, D., Murtaugh, K., & Diener, E. Validation of a laboratory play measure of child aggression. *Child Development,* 1977, *48*, 324–327.

Jones, C., & Aronson, E. Attribution of fault to a rape victim as a function of respectability of the victim. *Journal of Personality and Social Psychology,* 1973, *26*, 415–419.

Jones, E. E. *Ingratiation.* New York: Appleton-Century-Crofts, 1964.

Jones, E. E., & Baumeister, R. The self-monitor looks at the ingratiator. *Journal of Personality,* 1976, *44*, 654–674.

Jones, E. E., & Berglas, S. Control of attributions about the self through self-handicapping strategies: The appeal of alcohol and the role of underachievement. *Personality and Social Psychology Bulletin,* 1978, *4*, 200–206.

Jones, E. E., & Davis, K. E. From acts to dispositions: The attribution process in person perception. In L. Berkowitz (Ed.), *Advances in experimental social psychology* (Vol. 2). New York: Academic Press, 1965. Pp. 219–266.

Jones, E. E., Gergen, K. J., & Davis, K. Some reactions to being approved or disapproved as a person. *Psychological Monographs,* 1962, *76*(Whole No. 521).

Jones, E. E., Gergen, K. J., Gumpert, P., & Thibaut, J. Some conditions affecting the use of ingratiation to influence performance evaluation. *Journal of Personality and Social Psychology,* 1965, *1*, 613–625.

Jones, E. E., Gergen, K. J., & Jones, R. G. Tactics of ingratiation among leaders and subordinates in a status hierarchy. *Psychological Monographs,* 1963, *77*(Whole No. 566).

Jones, E. E., & Gordon, E. M. Timing of self-disclosure and its effects on personal attraction. *Journal of Personality and Social Psychology,* 1972, *24*, 358–365.

Jones, E. E., Kanouse, D. E., Kelley, H. H., Nisbett, R. E., Valins, S., & Weiner, B. *Attribution: Perceiving the causes of behavior.* Morristown, N.J.: General Learning Press, 1972.

Jones, E. E., & McGillis, D. Correspondent inferences and the attribution cube: A comparative reappraisal. In J. H. Harvey, W. J. Ickes, & R. F. Kidd (Eds.), *New directions in attribution research* (Vol. 1). Hillsdale, N.J.: Erlbaum, 1976. Pp. 389–420.

Jones, E. E., & Nisbett, R. E. The actor and the observer: Divergent perceptions of the causes of behavior. In E. E. Jones, D. Kanouse, H. H. Kelley, R. E. Nisbett, S. Valins, & B. Weiner (Eds.), *Attribution: Perceiving the causes of behavior.* Morristown, N.J.: General Learning Press, 1972. Pp. 79–94.

Jones, E. E., & Wortman, E. E. *Ingratiation: An attributional approach.* Morristown, N.J.: General Learning Press, 1973.

Jones, M. B. Religious values and authoritarian tendency. *Journal of Social Psychology,* 1958, *45*, 83–89.

Jorgensen, B. W. *Group size: Its effect on group performance and on individual acquisition of knowledge.* Paper presented at the meeting of the Eastern Psychological Association, Washington, D.C., May 1973.

Jorgensen, C. Personal communication on draft of Chapter 15, June 16, 1975.

Jourard, S. M. Healthy personality and self-disclosure. *Mental Hygiene,* 1959, *43*, 499–507. (a)

Jourard, S. M. Self-disclosure and other-cathexis. *Journal of Abnormal and Social Psychology,* 1959, *59*, 428–431.(b)

Jourard, S. M. *The transparent self: Self-disclosure and well-being.* Princeton, N.J.: Van Nostrand, 1964.

Jourard, S. M. *Self-disclosure.* New York: Wiley, 1971.

Jourard, S. M., & Jaffe, P. E. Influence of an interviewer's disclosure on the self-disclosing behavior of interviewees. *Journal of Counseling Psychology,* 1970, *17*, 252–297.

Jourard, S. M., & Landsman, M. J. Cognition, cathexis, and the "dyadic effect" in men's self-disclosing behavior. *Merrill-Palmer Quarterly,* 1960, *6*, 178–186.

Jourard, S. M., & Lasakow, P. Some factors in self-disclosure. *Journal of Abnormal and Social Psychology,* 1958, *56*, 91–98.

Jourard, S. M., & Rubin, J. E. Self-disclosure and touching: A study of two modes of interpersonal encounter and their inter-relation. *Journal of Humanistic Psychology,* 1968, *8*, 39–48.

Jovanovic, U. J. The recording of physiological evidence of genital arousal in human males and females. *Archives of Sexual Behavior,* 1971, *1*, 309–320.

Kaats, G. R., & Davis, K. E. The dynamics of sexual behavior of college students. *Journal of Marriage and the Family*, 1970, *32*(3), 390–399.

Kahneman, D., & Tversky, A. On the psychology of prediction. *Psychological Review*, 1973, *80*, 237–251.

Kallmann, F. Comparative twin study on the genetic aspects of male homosexuality. *Journal of Nervous and Mental Disease*, 1952, *115*, 283–298.

Kalven, H., Jr., & Zeisel, H. *The American jury*. Boston: Little, Brown, 1966.

Kamin, L. J. *The science and politics of I.Q.* Potomac, Md.: Erlbaum, 1974.

Kandel, D. B. Similarity in real-life adolescent friendship pairs. *Journal of Personality and Social Psychology*, 1978, *36*, 306–312.

Kanouse, D. E., & Hanson, L. R., Jr. Negativity in evaluations. In E. E. Jones, D. E. Kanouse, H. H. Kelley, R. E. Nisbett, S. Valins, & B. Weiner (Eds.), *Attribution: Perceiving the causes of behavior*. Morristown, N.J.: General Learning Press, 1972. Pp. 47–62.

Kanter, R. M. *Commitment and community: Communes and utopias in social perspective*. Cambridge, Mass.: Harvard University Press, 1972.

Kaplan, B. J. Malnutrition and mental deficiency. *Psychological Bulletin*, 1972, *78*, 321–334.

Kaplan, J. A. A legal look at prosocial behavior: What can happen if one tries to help or fails to help another. In L. Wispé (Ed.), *Altruism, sympathy, and helping: Psychological and sociological principles*. New York: Academic Press, 1978. Pp. 291–302.

Kaplan, M. F. Interpersonal attraction as a function of relatedness of similar and dissimilar attitudes. *Journal of Experimental Research in Personality*, 1972, *6*, 17–21.

Kaplan, M. F. Judgments by juries. In M. Kaplan & S. Schwartz (Eds.), *Judgment and decision processes in applied settings*. New York: Academic Press, 1977. Pp. 31–55.

Kaplan, M. F., & Anderson, N. H. Information integration theory and reinforcement theory as approaches to interpersonal attraction. *Journal of Personality and Social Psychology*, 1973, *28*, 301–312.

Kaplan, M. F., Steindorf, J., & Iervolino, A. Courtrooms, politics and morality: Toward a theoretical integration. *Personality and Social Psychology Bulletin*, 1978, *4*, 155–160.

Kaplan, R. M., & Singer, R. D. Television violence and viewer aggression: A reexamination of the evidence. *Journal of Social Issues*, 1976, *32*(4), 35–70.

Karabenick, S. A., Lerner, R. M., & Beecher, M. D. Relation of political affiliation to helping behavior on election day, November 7, 1972. *Journal of Social Psychology*, 1973, *91*, 223–227.

Kardiner, A., & Ovesey, L. *The mark of oppression*. New York: Norton, 1951.

Karlins, M., & Abelson, H. I. *How opinions and attitudes are changed* (2nd ed.). New York: Springer, 1970.

Karlins, M., Coffman, T. L., & Walters, G. On the fading of social stereotypes: Studies in three generations of college students. *Journal of Personality and Social Psychology*, 1969, *13*, 1–16.

Karon, B. P. *The Negro personality*. New York: Springer, 1958.

Karuza, J., Jr., & Brickman, P. *Preference for similar and dissimilar others as a function of status*. Paper presented at the meeting of the Midwestern Psychological Association, Chicago, May 1978.

Kasl, S. V. Issues in patient adherence to health care regimens. *Journal of Human Stress*, 1975, *1*, 5–18.

Kassin, S. M. Consensus information, prediction, and causal attribution: A review of the literature and issues. *Journal of Personality and Social Psychology*, 1979, *37*, 1966–1981.

Katchadourian, H. A., & Lunde, D. T. *Fundamentals of human sexuality* (2nd ed.). New York: Holt, Rinehart & Winston, 1975.

Katz, D. The functional approach to the study of attitudes. *Public Opinion Quarterly*, 1960, *24*, 163–204.

Katz, D. Consistency for what? The functional approach. In R. P. Abelson, E. Aronson, W. J. McGuire, T. M. Newcomb, M. J. Rosenberg, & P. H. Tannenbaum (Eds.), *Theories of cognitive consistency: A sourcebook*. Chicago: Rand McNally, 1968. Pp. 179–191.

Katz, D., & Braly, K. Racial stereotypes of one hundred college students. *Journal of Abnormal and Social Psychology*, 1933, *28*, 280–290.

Katz, D., & Kahn, R. L. *The social psychology of organizations* (2nd ed.). New York: Wiley, 1978.

Katz, D., Sarnoff, I., & McClintock, C. G. Ego-defense and attitude change. *Human Relations*, 1956, *9*, 27–45.

Katz, D., & Stotland, E. A preliminary statement to a theory of attitude structure and change. In S. Koch (Ed.), *Psychology: A study of a science* (Vol. 3). New York: McGraw-Hill, 1959. Pp. 423–475.

Katz, H. *Give! Who gets your charity dollar*. Garden City, N.Y.: Anchor/Doubleday, 1975.

Katz, I. A critique of personality approaches to Negro performance with research suggestions. *Journal of Social Issues*, 1969, *25*(3), 13–28.

Kauffman, D. R., & Steiner, I. D. Conformity as an ingratiation technique. *Journal of Experimental Social Psychology*, 1968, *4*, 400–414.

Kaufmann, H. *Social psychology: The study of human interaction*. New York: Holt, Rinehart & Winston, 1973.

Keasey, C. B. Experimentally induced changes in moral opinions and reasoning. *Journal of Personality and Social Psychology*, 1973, *26*, 30–38.

Keeler, B. T., & Andrews, J.M.H. Leader behavior of principals, staff morale, and productivity. *Alberta Journal of Educational Research*, 1963, *9*, 179–191.

Kelley, H. H. Attribution theory in social psychology. In D. Levine (Ed.), *Nebraska Symposium on Motivation, 1967* (Vol. 15). Lincoln: University of Nebraska Press, 1967. Pp. 192–238.

Kelley, H. H. *Attribution in social interaction*. Morristown, N.J.: General Learning Press, 1971.

Kelley, H. H. Causal schemata and the attribution process. In E. E. Jones, D. Kanouse, H. H. Kelley, R. E. Nisbett, S. Valins, & B. Weiner (Eds.), *Attribution: Perceiving the causes of behavior*. Morristown, N.J.: General Learning Press, 1972. Pp. 151–174.

Kelly, G. A. *A theory of personality: The psychology of personal constructs* (2 vols.). New York: Norton, 1955.

Kelman, H. C. *A time to speak: On human values and social research*. San Francisco: Jossey-Bass, 1968.

Kelman, H. C. Violence without moral restraint: Reflections on the dehumanization of victims and victimizers. *Journal of Social Issues*, 1973, *29*(4), 25–61.

Kendon, A. Some functions of gaze-direction in social interaction. *Acta Psychologica*, 1967, *26*, 22–63.

Kenrick, D. T., Cialdini, R. B., & Linder, D. E. Misattribution under fear-producing circumstances: Four failures to replicate. *Personality and Social Psychology Bulletin*, 1979, *5*, 329–334.

Kenrick, D. T., Reich, J. W., & Cialdini, R. B. Justification and compensation: Rosier skies for the devalued victim. *Journal of Personality and Social Psychology*, 1976, *34*, 654–657.

Kenrick, D. T., & Springfield, D. O. Personality traits and the eye of the beholder: Crossing some traditional philosophical boundaries in the search for consistency in all of the people. *Psychological Review*, 1980, *87*, 88–104.

Kent, G. G., Davis, J. D., & Shapiro, D. A. Resources required in the construction and reconstruction of conversation. *Journal of Personality and Social Psychology*, 1978, *36*, 13–22.

Kerckhoff, A. C., & Davis, K. E. Value consensus and need complementarity in mate selection. *American Sociological Review*, 1962, *27*, 295–303.

Kerr, N., Atkin, R., Stasser, G., Meek, D., Holt, R., & Davis, J. Guilt beyond a reasonable doubt: Effects of concept definition and assigned rule on the judgments of mock jurors. *Journal of Personality and Social Psychology*, 1976, *34*, 282–294.

Kidd, R. F. Manipulation checks: Advantage or disadvantage? *Representative Research in Social Psychology*, 1976, *2*, 160–165.

Kiesler, C. A. Group pressure and conformity. In J. Mills (Ed.), *Experimental social psychology*. New York: Macmillan, 1969. Pp. 233–306.

Kiesler, C. A. *The psychology of commitment: Experiments linking behavior to belief*. New York: Academic Press, 1971.

Kiesler, C. A., Collins, B. E., & Miller, N. *Attitude change: A critical analysis of theoretical approaches*. New York: Wiley, 1969.

Kiesler, C. A., & Kiesler, S. B. Role of forewarning in persuasive communications. *Journal of Abnormal and Social Psychology*, 1964, *68*, 547–549.

Kiesler, C. A., & Kiesler, S. B. *Conformity*. Reading, Mass.: Addison-Wesley, 1969.

Kiesler, C. A., & Munson, P. A. Attitudes and opinions. *Annual Review of Psychology*, 1975, *26*, 415–456.

Kiesler, S. B. The effect of perceived role requirements on reactions to favor doing. *Journal of Experimental Social Psychology*, 1966, *2*, 298–310.

Kilham, P., & Klopfer, P. H. The construct race and the innate differential. In M. Mead, T. Dobzhansky, E. Tobach, & R. E. Light (Eds.), *Science and the concept of race*. New York: Columbia University Press, 1968. Pp. 26–36.

Kilham, W., & Mann, L. Level of destructive obedience as a function of transmitter and executant roles in the Milgram obedience paradigm. *Journal of Personality and Social Psychology*, 1974, *29*, 696–702.

Kimble, C. E., & Forte, R. *Simulated and real eye contact as a function of emotional intensity and message positivity*. Paper presented at the meeting of the Midwestern Psychological Association, Chicago, May 1978.

Kimble, G. A. *Hilgard and Marquis's conditioning and learning*. New York: Appleton-Century-Crofts, 1961.

Kimbrell, D. L., & Blake, R. R. Motivational factors in a violation of prohibition. *Journal of Abnormal and Social Psychology*, 1958, *56*, 132–133.

Kinder, D. R. Political person perception: The asymmetrical influence of sentiment and choice on perceptions of political candidates. *Journal of Personality and Social Psychology*, 1978, *36*, 859–871.

King, K., Balswick, J. O., & Robinson, I. E. The continuing premarital sexual revolution among college females. *Journal of Marriage and the Family*, 1977, *39*, 455–459.

Kinkead, E. *In every war but one*. New York: Norton, 1959.

Kinsey, A. C., Pomeroy, W. B., & Martin, C. E. *Sexual behavior in the human male*. Philadelphia: Saunders, 1948.

Kinsey, A. C., Pomeroy, W. B., Martin, C. E., & Gebhard, P. H. *Sexual behavior in the human female*. Philadelphia: Saunders, 1953.

Kipnis, D. M. Interaction between members of bomber crews as a determinant of sociometric choice. *Human Relations*, 1957, *10*, 263–270.

Kirkpatrick, C. *The family as process and institution* (2nd ed.). New York: Ronald Press, 1963.

Kirmeyer, S. I. Urban density and pathology: A review of research. *Environment and Behavior*, 1978, *10*(2), 247–269.

Kirscht, J. P., & Dillehay, R. C. *Dimensions of authoritarianism: A review of research and theory*. Lexington: University of Kentucky Press, 1967.

Klapper, J. T. The impact of viewing "aggression": Studies and problems of extrapolation. In O. N. Larsen (Ed.), *Violence and the mass media*. New York: Harper & Row, 1968.

Klass, E. T. Psychological effects of immoral actions: The experimental evidence. *Psychological Bulletin*, 1978, *85*, 756–771.

Klaus, R. A., & Gray, S. W. Murfreesboro preschool program for culturally deprived children. *Childhood Education*, 1965, *42*, 92–95.

Klaus, R. A., & Gray, S. W. The early training project for disadvantaged children: A report after five years. *Monographs of the Society for Research in Child Development*, 1968, *33*(4, Whole No. 120).

Kleinke, C. L., Bustos, A. A., Meeker, F. B., & Staneski, R. A. Effects of self-attributed and other-attributed gaze on interpersonal evaluations between males and females. *Journal of Experimental Social Psychology*, 1973, *9*, 154–163.

Kleinke, C. L., Staneski, R. A., & Weaver, P. Evaluation of a person who uses another's name in ingratiating and noningratiating situations. *Journal of Experimental Social Psychology*, 1972, *8*, 457–466.

Kluger, R. *Simple justice*. New York: Knopf, 1976.

Knapp, M. L. *Nonverbal communication in human interaction* (2nd ed.). New York: Holt, Rinehart & Winston, 1978.

Knapp, M. L., Hart, R. P., & Dennis, H. S. An exploration of deception as a communication construct. *Human Communication Research*, 1974, *1*, 15–29.

Knapp, R. H. *n* Achievement and aesthetic preference. In J. W. Atkinson (Ed.), *Motives in fantasy, action and society*. Princeton, N.J.: Van Nostrand, 1958. Pp. 367–372.

Knapp, R. H., & Garbutt, J. T. Time imagery and the achievement motive. *Journal of Personality*, 1958, *26*, 426–434.

Knight, G. P., & Kagan, S. Development of prosocial and competitive behaviors in Anglo-American and Mexican-American children. *Child Development*,

1977, *48*, 1385–1394.

Knight, H. C. *A comparison of the reliability of group and individual judgments*. Unpublished master's thesis, Columbia University, 1921. (Cited in Shaw, 1971)

Knowles, E. S. Boundaries around social space: Dyadic responses to an invader. *Environment and Behavior*, 1972, *4*, 437–445.

Knowles, E. S. Boundaries around group interaction: The effect of group size and member status on boundary permeability. *Journal of Personality and Social Psychology*, 1973, *26*, 327–331.

Knox, R. E., & Inkster, J. A. Postdecision dissonance at post time. *Journal of Personality and Social Psychology*, 1968, *8*, 319–323.

Koffka, W. *Principles of Gestalt psychology*. New York: Harcourt Brace, 1935.

Kogan, N., & Wallach, M. A. *Risk-taking: A study in cognition and personality*. New York: Holt, 1964.

Kohlberg, L. *The development of modes of moral thinking and choice in the years ten to sixteen*. Unpublished doctoral dissertation, University of Chicago, 1958.

Kohlberg, L. Moral development and identification. In H. Stevenson (Ed.), *Child psychology* (62nd Yearbook of the National Society for the Study of Education). Chicago: University of Chicago Press, 1963.

Kohlberg, L. The child as a moral philosopher. *Psychology Today*, 1968, *2*(4), 24–30.

Komarovsky, M. Functional analysis of sex roles. *American Sociological Review*, 1959, *15*, 508–516.

Konečni, V. J. Some effects of guilt on compliance: A field replication. *Journal of Personality and Social Psychology*, 1972, *23*, 30–32.

Konečni, V. J. The mediation of aggressive behavior: Arousal level versus anger and cognitive labeling. *Journal of Personality and Social Psychology*, 1975, *32*, 706–712. (a)

Konečni, V. J. Annoyance, type and duration of postannoyance activity, and aggression: The "cathartic" effect. *Journal of Experimental Psychology: General*, 1975, *104*, 76–102. (b)

Koneya, M. Location and interaction in row-and-column seating arrangements. *Environment and Behavior*, 1976, *8*(2), 265–282.

Koning, H. Did the Pentagon Papers make any difference? *Saturday Review*, 1972, *55*(24), 13–15. (June 10, 1972, issue)

Korda, M. *Power: How to get it, how to use it!* New York: Random House, 1975.

Korman, A. K. "Consideration," "initiating structure," and organizational criteria—A review. *Personnel Psychology*, 1966, *19*, 349–361.

Korman, A. K. The prediction of managerial performance. A review. *Personnel Psychology*, 1968, *21*, 295–322.

Korte, C. Effects of individual responsibility and group communication on help-giving in an emergency. *Human Relations*, 1971, *24*, 149–159.

Korte, C., & Kerr, N. Response to altruistic opportunities in urban and nonurban settings. *Journal of Social Psychology*, 1975, *95*, 183–184.

Korte, C., Ypma, I., & Toppen, A. Helpfulness in Dutch society as a function of urbanization and environmental input level. *Journal of Personality and Social Psychology*, 1975, *32*, 996–1003.

Krauss, R. M., Geller, V., & Olson, C. *Modalities and cues in the detection of deception*. Paper presented at the meeting of the American Psychological Association, Washington, D.C., September 1976.

Kraut, R. E. Effects of social labeling on giving to charity. *Journal of Experimental Social Psychology*, 1973, *9*, 551–562.

Kraut, R. E., & Johnston, R. Social and emotional messages of smiling: An ethological approach. *Journal of Personality and Social Psychology*, 1979, *37*, 1539–1553.

Kraut, R. E., & Price, J. D. Machiavellianism in parents and their children. *Journal of Personality and Social Psychology*, 1976, *33*, 782–786.

Krebs, D. Altruism—an examination of the concept and a review of the literature. *Psychological Bulletin*, 1970, *73*, 258–302.

Krebs, D. Empathy and altruism. *Journal of Personality and Social Psychology*, 1975, *32*, 1134–1146.

Krebs, D. A cognitive-developmental approach to altruism. In L. Wispé (Ed.), *Altruism, sympathy, and helping: Psychological and sociological principles*. New York: Academic Press, 1978. Pp. 141–164.

Krebs, R. *Some relations between moral judgment, attention, and resistance to temptation*. Unpublished doctoral dissertation, University of Chicago, 1967.

Krech, D., Crutchfield, R., & Ballachey, E. *Individual in society*. New York: McGraw-Hill, 1962.

Kronhausen, E., & Kronhausen, P. *Pornography and the law* (Rev. ed.). New York: Ballantine, 1964.

Krulewitz, J. E. *Sex differences in rape attributions*. Paper presented at the meeting of the Midwestern Psychological Association, Chicago, May 1977.

Kuhl, J. Standard setting and risk preference: An elaboration of the theory of achievement motivation and an empirical test. *Psychological Review*, 1978, *85*, 239–248.

Kuhl, J., & Blankenship, V. Behavioral change in a constant environment: Shift to more difficult tasks with constant probability of success. *Journal of Personality and Social Psychology*, 1979, *37*, 551–563.

Kuhn, M. H., & McPartland, T. S. An empirical investigation of self-attitudes. *American Sociological Review*, 1954, *19*, 68–76.

Kuhn, T. S. *The structure of scientific revolutions* (2nd ed.) Chicago: University of Chicago Press, 1970.

Kurtines, W., & Greif, E. G. The development of moral thought: Review and evaluation of Kohlberg's approach. *Psychological Bulletin*, 1974, *81*, 453–470.

Kutchinsky, B. The effect of easy availability of pornography on the incidence of sex crimes: The Danish experience. *Journal of Social Issues*, 1973, *29*(3), 163–181.

Kutner, B., Wilkins, C., & Yarrow, P. R. Verbal attitudes and overt behavior involving racial prejudice. *Journal of Abnormal and Social Psychology*, 1952, *47*, 649–652.

La France, M., & Mayo, C. Racial differences in gaze behavior during conversations: Two systematic observational studies. *Journal of Personality and Social Psychology*, 1976, *33*, 547–552.

La France, M., & Mayo, C. *Moving bodies: Nonverbal communication in social relationships*. Monterey, Calif.: Brooks/Cole, 1978.

Lalljee, M., & Cook, M. Uncertainty in first encounters. *Journal of Personality and Social Psychology*, 1973, *26*, 137–141.

Lamm, H., & Trommsdorff, G. Group versus individual performance on tasks requiring ideational proficiency (brainstorming): A review. *European Journal of Social Psychology*, 1973, *3*, 361–388.

Lana, R. Controversy of the topic and order of presentation in persuasive communications. *Psychological Reports*, 1963, *12*, 163–170. (a)

Lana, R. Interest, media, and order effects in persuasive communications. *Journal of Psychology*, 1963, *56*, 9–13. (b)

Lana, R. The influence of the pretest on order effects in persuasive communications. *Journal of Abnormal and Social Psychology*, 1964, *69*, 337–341. (a)

Lana, R. Three theoretical interpretations of order effects in persuasive communications. *Psychological Bulletin*, 1964, *61*, 314–320. (b)

Lando, H. A., & Donnerstein, E. I. The effects of a model's success or failure on subsequent aggressive behavior. *Journal of Research in Personality*, 1978, *12*, 225–234.

Landsberger, H. A. *Hawthorne revisited.* Ithaca, N.Y.: Cornell University, 1958.

Landy, D., & Sigall, H. Beauty is talent: Task evaluation as a function of the performer's physical attractiveness. *Journal of Personality and Social Psychology*, 1974, *29*, 299–304.

Langer, E. J. The illusion of control. *Journal of Personality and Social Psychology*, 1975, *32*, 311–328.

Langer, E. J. The psychology of chance. *Journal for the Theory of Social Behaviour*, 1978, *7*, 185–207.(a)

Langer, E. J. The illusion of incompetence. In L. Perlmutter & R. Monty (Eds.), *Choice and perceived control.* Hillsdale, N.J.: Erlbaum, 1978. Pp. 301–312. (b)

Langer, E. J. Old age: An artifact? In *Biology, behavior and aging.* Washington, D.C.: National Research Council, 1979.

Langer, E. J., & Benevento, A. Self-induced dependence. *Journal of Personality and Social Psychology*, 1978, *36*, 886–893.

Langer, E., Blank, A., & Chanowitz, B. The mindlessness of ostensibly thoughtful action: The role of "placebic" information in interpersonal interaction. *Journal of Personality and Social Psychology*, 1978, *36*, 635–642.

Langer, E., Janis, I., & Wolfer, J. Reduction of psychological stress in surgical patients. *Journal of Experimental Social Psychology*, 1975, *11*, 155–165.

Langer, E. J., & Rodin, J. The effects of choice and enhanced personal responsibility for the aged: A field experiment in an institutional setting. *Journal of Personality and Social Psychology*, 1976, *34*, 191–198.

Langer, E. J., & Roth, J. Heads I win, tails it's chance: The illusion of control as a function of the sequence of outcomes in a purely chance task. *Journal of Personality and Social Psychology*, 1975, *32*, 951–955.

Langman, B., & Cockburn, A. Sirhan's gun. *Harper's*, January 1975, *250*(No. 1496), 16–27.

LaPiere, R. T. Attitudes and actions. *Social Forces*, 1934, *13*, 230–237.

Larson, D. L., & Spreitzer, E. A. Education, occupation and age as correlates of work orientation. *Psychological Reports*, 1973, *33*, 879–884.

Latané, B. (Ed.). Studies in social comparison. *Journal of Experimental Social Psychology, Supplement*, 1966, No. 1.

Latané, B. *A theory of social impact.* Paper presented at the meeting of the Psychonomic Society, St. Louis, 1973.

Latané, B., & Bidwell, L. D. Sex and affiliation in college cafeterias. *Personality and Social Psychology Bulletin*, 1977, *3*, 571–574.

Latané, B., & Darley, J. M Group inhibition of bystander intervention. *Journal of Personality and Social Psychology*, 1968, *10*, 215–221.

Latané, B., & Darley, J. *The unresponsive bystander: Why doesn't he help?* New York: Appleton-Century-Crofts, 1970.

Latané, B., & Harkins, S. Cross-modality matches suggest anticipated stage fright as multiplicative function of audience size and status. *Perception and Psychophysics*, 1976, *20*, 482–488.

Latané, B., & Nida, S. Social impact theory and group influence: A social engineering perspective. In P. B. Paulus (Ed.), *Psychology of group influence.* Hillsdale, N.J.: Erlbaum, 1980.

Latané, B., & Rodin, J. A lady in distress: Inhibiting effects of friends and strangers on bystander intervention. *Journal of Experimental Social Psychology*, 1969, *5*, 189–202.

Latané, B., Williams, K., & Harkins, S. Many hands make light the work: The causes and consequences of social loafing. *Journal of Personality and Social Psychology*, 1979, *37*, 822–832.

Laughlin, P. R., & Jaccard, J. J. Social facilitation and observational learning of individuals and cooperative pairs. *Journal of Personality and Social Psychology*, 1975, *32*, 873–879.

LaVoie, J. C. Punishment and adolescent self-control. *Developmental Psychology*, 1973, *8*, 16–24.

Lawler, E. J., & Thompson, M. E. Impact of leader responsibility for inequity on subordinate revolts. *Social Psychology*, 1978, *41*, 264–268.

Lay, C. H., Burron, B. F., & Jackson, D. N. Base rates and informational value in impression formation. *Journal of Personality and Social Psychology*, 1973, *28*, 390–395.

Leach, C. The importance of instructions in assessing sequential effects in impression formation. *British Journal of Social and Clinical Psychology*, 1974, *13*, 151–156.

Leavitt, H. J. Some effects of certain communication patterns on group performance. *Journal of Abnormal and Social Psychology*, 1951, *46*, 38–50.

LeBon, G. *The crowd.* London: Ernest Benn, 1896.

Lebra, T. S. *Japanese patterns of behavior.* Honolulu: University Press of Hawaii, 1976.

Lefebvre, L. Encoding and decoding of ingratiation in modes of smiling and gaze. *British Journal of Social and Clinical Psychology*, 1975, *14*, 33–42.

Legant, P. *The deserving victim: Effects of length of pretrial detention, crime severity, and juror attitudes on simulated jury decisions.* Unpublished dissertation, Yale University, 1973.

Lenney, E. Androgyny: Some audacious assertions toward its coming of age. *Sex Roles*, 1979, *5*, 703–719.

Lenrow, P. Dilemmas of professional helping: Continuities and discontinuities with folk helping roles. In L. Wispé (Ed.), *Altruism, sympathy, and helping: Psychological and sociological principles.* New York: Academic Press, 1978. Pp. 263–290.

Leone, C., Graziano, W., & Case, T. The effects of locus of control and utility on attributional processes. Paper presented at the meeting of the Midwestern Psychological Association, Chicago, May 1978.

Lerner, E. *Constraint areas and the moral judgment of children.* Menasha, Wisc.: Banta, 1937.

Lerner, M. J. Evaluation of performance as a function of performer's reward and attractiveness. *Journal of Personality and Social Psychology*, 1965, *3*, 355–360.

Lerner, M. J. *The unjust consequences of the need to believe in a just world.* Paper presented at the meeting of the American Psychological Association, New York, September 1966.

Lerner, M. J. The desire for justice and reactions to victims. In J. Macaulay & L. Berkowitz (Eds.), *Altruism and helping behavior: Social psychological studies of some antecedents and consequences.* New York: Academic Press, 1970. Pp. 205–229.

Lerner, M. J. Social psychology of justice and interpersonal attraction. In T. L. Huston (Ed.), *Foundations of interpersonal attraction.* New York: Academic Press, 1974. Pp. 331–351.

Lerner, M. J. The justice motive in social behavior. *Journal of Social Issues*, 1975, *31*(3), 1–19.

Lerner, M. J. The justice motive: Some hypotheses as to its origins and forms. *Journal of Personality*, 1977, *45*, 1–52.

Lerner, M. J., & Becker, S. W. Interpersonal choice as a function of ascribed similarity and definition of the situation. *Human Relations*, 1962, *15*, 27–34.

Lerner, M. J., & Matthews, G. Reactions to suffering of others under conditions of indirect responsibility. *Journal of Personality and Social Psychology*, 1967, *5*, 319–325.

Lerner, M. J., Miller, D. T., & Holmes, J. G. Deserving and the emergence of forms of justice. In L. Berkowitz & E. Walster (Eds.), *Advances in experimental social psychology* (Vol. 9). New York: Academic Press, 1976. Pp. 133–162.

Lerner, M. J., & Simmons, C. H. Observer's reactions to the "innocent victim": Compassion or rejection? *Journal of Personality and Social Psychology*, 1966, *4*, 203–210.

Lesser, G. S., Fifer, G., & Clark, D. H. Mental abilities of children from different social-class and cultural groups. *Monographs of the Society for Research in Child Development*, 1965, *30*(4), 1–115.

Leventhal, H. Findings and theory in the study of fear communications. In L. Berkowitz (Ed.), *Advances in experimental social psychology* (Vol. 5). New York: Academic Press, 1970. Pp. 119–186.

Levin, H. Psychologist to the powerless. In F. F. Korten, S. W. Cook, & J. I. Lacey (Eds.), *Psychology and the problems of society.* Washington, D.C.: American Psychological Association, 1970. Pp. 121–127.

Levin, P. F., & Isen, A. M. Further studies on the effect of feeling good on helping. *Sociometry*, 1975, *38*, 141–147.

Levin, R. J., & Levin, A. Sexual pleasure: The surprising preferences of 100,000 women. *Redbook*, September 1975, 51–58.

Levine, F. J., & Tapp, J. L. The psychology of criminal investigation. *University of Pennsylvania Law Review*, 1973, *121*(5), 1079–1131.

Levinger, G. Little sand box and big quarry: Comment on Byrne's paradigmatic spade for research on interpersonal attraction. *Representative Research in Social Psychology*, 1972, *3*, 3–19.

Levinger, G. A three-level approach to attraction: Toward an understanding of pair relatedness. In T. L. Huston (Ed.), *Foundations of interpersonal attraction.* New York: Academic Press, 1974. Pp. 100–120.

Levinger, G. A social psychological perspective on marriage dissolution. *Journal of Social Issues*, 1976, *32*(1), 21–47.

Levinger, G. *Models of close relationships: Some new directions.* Invited address presented at the meeting of the American Psychological Association, Toronto, August 1978.

Levinger, G., & Moles, O. C. *Divorce and separation: Context, causes and consequences.* New York: Basic Books, 1979.

Levinger, G., & Senn, D. J. Disclosure of feelings in marriage. *Merrill-Palmer Quarterly*, 1967, *13*, 237–249.

Levinger, G., Senn, D. J., & Jorgensen, B. W. Progress toward permanence in courtship: A test of the Kerckhoff-Davis hypotheses. *Sociometry*, 1970, *33*, 427–443.

Levinson, D. J. *The seasons of a man's life.* New York: Knopf, 1978.

Levinson, D. J., & Huffman, P. E. Traditional family ideology and its relation to personality. *Journal of Personality*, 1955, *23*, 251–273.

Levitt, E., & Klassen, A. Public attitudes toward homosexuality: Part of the 1970 national survey by the Institute for Sex Research. *Journal of Homosexuality*, 1974, *1*, 29–43.

Levy, J. Autokinetic illusion: A systematic review of theories, measures and independent variables. *Psychological Bulletin*, 1972, *78*, 457–474.

Levy, S. G. A 150-year study of political violence in the United States. In H. D. Graham & T. R. Gurr (Eds.), *Violence in America.* New York: New American Library, 1969. Pp. 81–92.

Levy, S. G. Authoritarianism and information processing. *Bulletin of the Psychonomic Society*, 1979, *13*, 240–242.

Levy, S. G., & Fenley, W. F., Jr. Audience size and likelihood and intensity of response during a humorous movie. *Bulletin of the Psychonomic Society*, 1979, *13*, 409–412.

Lewin, A. Y., & Duchan, L. Women in academia. *Science*, 1971, *173*, 892–895.

Lewin, K. *A dynamic theory of personality.* New York: McGraw-Hill, 1935.

Lewin, K. *Principles of topological psychology.* New York: McGraw-Hill, 1936.

Lewin, K. The conceptual representation and measurement of psychological forces. *Contributions to Psychological Theory*, Vol. I, No. 4. Durham, N.C.: Duke University Press, 1938.

Lewin, K. *Resolving social conflicts.* New York: Harper, 1948.

Lewin, K. *Field theory in social science.* New York: Harper, 1951.

Lewin, K., Lippitt, R., & White, R. K. Patterns of aggressive behavior in experimentally created "social climates." *Journal of Social Psychology*, 1939, *10*, 271–299.

Lewis, E. C. *Developing woman's potential.* Ames: Iowa State University Press, 1968.

Leyens, J. P., Camino, L., Parke, R. D., & Berkowitz, L. Effects of movie violence on aggression in a field setting as a function of group dominance and cohesion. *Journal of Personality and Social Psychology*, 1975, *32*, 346–360.

Leyens, J. P., & Parke, R. E. Aggressive slides can induce a weapons effect. *European Journal of Social Psychology*, 1975, *5*, 229–236.

Leyhausen, P. The communal organization of solitary mammals. *Symposium of the Zoological Society of London*, 1965, *14*, 249–253.

Lieberman, M. A. Change induction in small groups. In M. R. Rosenzweig & L. W. Porter (Eds.), *Annual Review of Psychology*, 1976, *27*, 217–250.

Lieberman, S. The effects of changes of roles on the attitudes of role occupants. In H. Proshansky & B. Seidenberg (Eds.), *Basic studies in social psychology*. New York: Holt, Rinehart & Winston, 1965. Pp. 485–494.

Liebert, R. M., & Baron, R. A. Some immediate effects of televised violence on children. *Developmental Psychology*, 1972, *6*, 469–475.

Liebert, R. M., & Schwartzberg, N. S. Effects of mass media. In M. R. Rosenzweig & L. W. Porter (Eds.), *Annual review of psychology* (Vol. 28). Palo Alto, Calif.: Annual Reviews, 1977. Pp. 141–173.

Liebhart, E. H. Empathy and emergency helping: The effects of personality, self-concern, and acquaintance. *Journal of Experimental Social Psychology*, 1972, *8*, 404–411.

Likert, R. A technique for the measurement of attitudes. *Archives of Psychology*, 1932, No. 140.

Lindskold, S. Trust development, the GRIT proposal, and the effects of conciliatory acts on conflict and cooperation. *Psychological Bulletin*, 1978, *85*, 772–793.

Lippa, R. Expressive control and the leakage of dispositional introversion-extraversion during role-played teaching. *Journal of Personality*, 1976, *44*, 541–559.

Lippa, R. The effect of expressive control on expressive consistency and on the relation between expressive behavior and personality. *Journal of Personality*, 1978, *46*, 438–461. (a)

Lippa, R. The naive perception of masculinity-femininity on the basis of expressive cues. *Journal of Research in Personality*, 1978, *12*, 1–14. (b)

Lippitt, R. *Training in community relations*. New York: Harper, 1949.

Lippitt, R., Watson, J., & Westley, B. *The dynamics of planned change*. New York: Harcourt Brace & World, 1958.

Lippman, W. *Public opinion*. New York: Harcourt, Brace and World, 1922.

Liston, R. A. *The charity racket*. Nashville, Tenn.: Thomas Nelson, 1977.

Litman-Adizes, T., Raven, B. H., & Fontaine, G. Consequences of social power and causal attribution for compliance as seen by powerholder and target. *Personality and Social Psychology Bulletin*, 1978, *4*, 260–264.

Littlepage, G., & Pineault, T. Verbal, facial, and paralinguistic cues to the detection of truth and lying. *Personality and Social Psychology Bulletin*, 1978, *4*, 461–464.

Littlepage, G. E., & Pineault, M. A. Detection of deceptive factual statements from the body and the face. *Personality and Social Psychology Bulletin*, 1979, *5*, 325–328.

Loehlin, J., Lindzey, G., & Spuhler, J. N. *Race differences in intelligence*. San Francisco: W. H. Freeman, 1975.

Loevinger, J. The meaning and measurement of ego development. *American Psychologist*, 1966, *21*, 195–206.

Loevinger, J., & Wessler, R. *Measuring ego development* (Vol. 1). San Francisco: Jossey-Bass, 1970.

Loftus, E. F. Reconstructing memory: The incredible eyewitness. *Psychology Today*, 1974, *8*(7), 116–119.

Loftus, E. F., & Palmer, J. C. Reconstruction of automobile destruction: An example of the interaction between language and memory. *Journal of Verbal Learning and Verbal Behavior*, 1974, *11*, 585–589.

Logan, R. W. *The Negro in the United States*. Princeton, N.J.: Van Nostrand, 1957.

London, P. The rescuers: Motivational hypotheses about Christians who saved Jews from the Nazis. In J. Macaulay & L. Berkowitz (Eds.), *Altruism and helping behavior: Social psychological studies of some antecedents and consequences*. New York: Academic Press, 1970. Pp. 241–250.

Lonetto, R., & Williams, D. Personality, behavioural, and output variables in a small group task situation: An examination of consensual leader and non-leader differences. *Canadian Journal of Behavioural Science*, 1974, *6*(1), 59–74.

Loo, C. M. The effects of spatial density on the social behavior of children. *Journal of Applied Social Psychology*, 1972, *4*, 372–381.

Lord, R. G., Binning, J. F., Rush, M. C., & Thomas, J. C. The effect of performance cues and leader behavior on questionnaire ratings of leadership behavior. *Organizational Behavior and Human Performance*, 1978, *21*, 27–39.

Lorenz, K. *King Solomon's ring*. New York: Crowell, 1952.

Lorenz, K. *On aggression*. New York: Harcourt, Brace and World, 1966.

Lorenz, K. *[Studies in animal and human behavior]* (Vol. 1) (R. Martin, trans.). Cambridge, Mass.: Harvard University Press, 1970.

Lorge, I., Fox, D., Davitz, J., & Brenner, M. A survey of studies contrasting the quality of group performance and individual performance, 1920–1957. *Psychological Bulletin*, 1958, *55*, 337–372.

Lott, A. J., & Lott, B. E. Group cohesiveness, communication level, and conformity. *Journal of Abnormal and Social Psychology*, 1961, *62*, 408–412.

Lott, A. J., & Lott, B. E. The role of reward in the formation of positive interpersonal attitudes. In T. L. Huston (Ed.), *Foundations of interpersonal attraction*. New York: Academic Press, 1974. Pp. 171–189.

Lott, D. F., & Sommer, R. Seating arrangements and status. *Journal of Personality and Social Psychology*, 1967, *7*, 90–94.

Luce, R. D., & Raiffa, H. *Games and decisions*. New York: Wiley, 1957.

Luchins, A. S. Experimental attempts to minimize the impact of first impressions. In C. I. Hovland (Ed.), *The order of presentation in persuasion*. New Haven: Yale University Press, 1957. Pp. 62–75. (a)

Luchins, A. S. Primacy-recency in impression formation. In C. I. Hovland (Ed.), *The order of presentation in persuasion*. New Haven: Yale University Press, 1957. Pp. 33–61. (b)

Luchins, A. S. Definitiveness of impression and primacy-recency in communications. *Journal of Social Psychology*, 1958, *48*, 275–290.

Lumsdaine, A., & Janis, I. Resistance to counterpropaganda produced by a one-sided versus a two-sided propaganda presentation. *Public Opinion Quarterly*, 1953, *17*, 311–318.

Lund, F. The psychology of belief. IV. The law of primacy in persuasion. *Journal of Abnormal and Social Psychology*, 1925, *20*, 183–191.

Lyman, S. M., & Scott, M. B. Territoriality: A neglected sociological dimension. *Social Problems*, 1967, *15*(2), 236–249.

Lynch, J. G., Jr., & Cohen, J. L. The use of subjective expected utility theory as an aid to understanding variables that influence helping behavior. *Journal of Personality and Social Psychology*, 1978, *36*, 1138–1151.

Lynch, K. *The image of the city*. Cambridge, Mass.: M.I.T. Press, 1960.

Maccoby, E. E., & Jacklin, C. N. *The psychology of sex differences*. Stanford, Calif.: Stanford University Press, 1974.

MacDonald, A. P., Jr. Anxiety, affiliation, and social isolation. *Developmental Psychology*, 1970, *3*, 242–254.

Machiavelli, N. *The prince*. New York: Modern Library, 1940.

Mackenzie, K. D., & Bernhardt, I. *The effect of status upon group risk taking*. Unpublished manuscript, Wharton School of Finance and Commerce, University of Pennsylvania, 1968.

Madsen, M. C. Cooperative and competitive motivation of children in three Mexican subcultures. *Psychological Reports*, 1967, *20*, 1307–1320.

Madsen, M. C. Developmental and cross-cultural differences in the cooperative and competitive behavior of young children. *Journal of Cross-Cultural Psychology*, 1971, *2*, 365–371.

Madsen, M. C., & Shapira, A. Cooperative and competitive behavior of urban Afro-American, Anglo-American, Mexican-American, and Mexican village children. *Developmental Psychology*, 1970, *3*, 16–20.

Magnusson, D. The person and the situation in an interactional model of behavior. *Scandinavian Journal of Psychology*, 1976, *17*, 253–271.

Magnusson, D., & Endler, N. S. (Eds.). *Personality at the crossroads: Current issues in interactional psychology*. Hillsdale, N.J.: Erlbaum, 1977.

Major, B. N. *Information acquisition and attribution processes*. Unpublished doctoral dissertation, Purdue University, 1978.

Major, B., & Heslin, R. *Perceptions of same-sex and cross-sex touching: It's better to give than to receive*. Paper presented at the meeting of the Midwestern Psychological Association, Chicago, May 1978.

Malamuth, N., Feshbach, S., & Jaffe, Y. Sexual arousal and aggression: Recent experiments and theoretical issues. *Journal of Social Issues*, 1977, *33*(2), 110–133.

Malpass, R. S. Theory and method in cross-cultural psychology. *American Psychologist*, 1977, *32*, 1069–1079.

Mander, A. M., & Gaebelein, J. W. Third party instigation of aggression as a function of noncooperation and veto power. *Journal of Research in Personality*, 1977, *11*, 475–486.

Mandler, G., & Sarason, S. B. A study of anxiety and learning. *Journal of Abnormal and Social Psychology*, 1952, *47*, 166–173.

Manis, M. Cognitive social psychology. *Personality and Social Psychology Bulletin*, 1977, *3*, 550–566.

Manis, M., Cornell, S. D., & Moore, J. C. Transmission of attitude-relevant information through a communication chain. *Journal of Personality and Social Psychology*, 1974, *30*, 81–94.

Mann, J., Sidman, J., & Starr, S. Effects of erotic films on sexual behavior of married couples. In *Technical report of the Commission on Obscenity and Pornography* (Vol. 8). Washington, D.C.: U.S. Government Printing Office, 1971. Pp. 170–254.

Mann, J., Sidman, J., & Starr, S. Evaluating social consequences of erotic films: An experimental approach. *Journal of Social Issues*, 1973, *29*(3), 113–131.

Mann, R. D. A review of the relationship between personality and performance in small groups. *Psychological Bulletin*, 1959, *56*, 241–270.

Mann, T. *Confessions of Felix Krull, confidence man*. New York: Modern Library, 1955. (Original German publication, 1954)

Manning, S. A., & Taylor, D. A. Effects of viewed violence and aggression: Stimulation and catharsis. *Journal of Personality and Social Psychology*, 1975, *31*, 180–188.

Mannion, K. Female homosexuality: A comprehensive review of theory and research. *JSAS Catalog of Selected Documents in Psychology*, 1976, *6*, 44.

Margulis, S. T. Conceptions of privacy: Current status and next steps. *Journal of Social Issues*, 1977, *33*(3), 5–21.

Markus, H. Self-schemata and processing information about the self. *Journal of Personality and Social Psychology*, 1977, *35*, 63–78.

Marriott, C. *Psycho-social patterns of dying*. Paper presented at the meeting of the American Psychological Association, New Orleans, August 1974.

Marriott, C., & Harshbarger, D. The hollow holiday: Christmas, a time of death in Appalachia. *Omega*, 1973, *4*, 259–266.

Marrow, A. J. *The practical theorist: The life and work of Kurt Lewin*. New York: Basic Books, 1969.

Marshall, J. J. Privacy and environment. *Human Ecology*, 1972, *1*(2), 93–110.

Marston, M. Compliance with medical regimens. *Nursing Research*, 1970, *19*, 312–323.

Marston, W. M. Studies in testimony. *Journal of Criminal Law and Criminology*, 1924, *15*, 5–31.

Martin, J., & Westie, F. The tolerant personality. *American Sociological Review*, 1959, *24*, 521–528.

Martindale, D. A. Territorial dominance behavior in dyadic verbal interactions. *Proceedings, 79th Annual Convention, American Psychological Association*, 1971, *6*, 305–306.

Marx, G. T. Civil disorder and agents of social control. *Journal of Social Issues*, 1970, *26*(1), 19–57.

Maslach, C. The "truth" about false confessions. *Journal of Personality and Social Psychology*, 1971, *20*, 141–146.

Maslow, A. H. *Motivation and personality*. New York: Harper & Row, 1954.

Maslow, A. H., & Mintz, N. L. Effects of three esthetic surroundings: I. Initial effects of three esthetic conditions upon perceiving "energy" and "well-being" in faces. *The Journal of Psychology*, 1956, *41*, 247–254.

Masor, H. N., Hornstein, H. A., & Tobin, T. A. Modeling, motivational interdependence, and helping. *Journal of Personality and Social Psychology*, 1973, *28*, 236–248.

Masters, W. H., & Johnson, V. E. *Human sexual response*. Boston: Little, Brown, 1966.

Mathews, K. E., Jr., & Canon, L. K. Environmental noise level as a determinant of helping behavior. *Journal of*

Psychology, 1975, *61*, 153–157.

Matlin, M. W. Response competition as a mediating factor in the frequency-affect relationship. *Journal of Personality and Social Psychology*, 1970, *16*, 536–552.

Matthews, K. A., Rosenfield, D., & Stephan, W. G. Playing hard-to-get: A two-determinant model. *Journal of Research in Personality*, 1979, *13*, 234–244.

Maxwell, J. W., Sack, A. R., Frary, R. B., & Keller, J. F. Factors influencing contraceptive behavior of single college students. *Journal of Sex and Marital Therapy*, 1977, *3*, 265–273.

Mayo, C. W., & Crockett, W. H. Cognitive complexity and primacy-recency effects in impression formation. *Journal of Abnormal and Social Psychology*, 1964, *68*, 335–338.

Mayo, E. *The social problems of an industrial civilization.* Boston: Harvard Graduate School of Business, 1945.

Mazur-Hart, S. F., & Berman, J. J. Changing from fault to no-fault divorce: An interrupted time series analysis. *Journal of Applied Social Psychology*, 1977, *7*, 300–312.

McArthur, L. A. The how and what of why: Some determinants of consequences of causal attribution. *Journal of Personality and Social Psychology*, 1972, *22*, 171–193.

McArthur, L. Z., & Post, D. L. Figural emphasis and person perception. *Journal of Experimental Social Psychology*, 1977, *13*, 520–536.

McCall, M. W., Jr., & Lombardo, M. M. Where else can we go? In M. W. McCall, Jr., & M. M. Lombardo (Eds.), *Leadership: Where else can we go?* Durham, N.C.: Duke University Press, 1978. Pp. 151–165.

McCarrey, M., Peterson, L., Edwards, S., & VonKulmiz, P. Landscape office attitudes: Reflections of perceived degree of control over transactions with the environment. *Journal of Applied Psychology*, 1974, *50*, 401–403.

McCary, J. L. Teaching the topic of human sexuality. *Teaching of Psychology*, 1975, *2*(1), 16–21.

McCary, J. L. *Human sexuality: Physiological, psychological, and sociological factors* (3rd ed.). New York: Van Nostrand, 1978.

McCauley, C., Coleman, G., & DeFusco, P. Commuters' eye contact with strangers in city and suburban train stations: Evidence of short term adaptation in interpersonal overload in the city. *Environmental Psychology and Nonverbal Behavior*, 1978, *2*(4), 215–225.

McCauley, C., & Newman, J. Eye contact with strangers in city, suburb, and small town. *Environment and Behavior*, 1977, *9*(4), 547.

McCauley, C., & Stitt, C. L. An individual and quantitative measure of stereotypes. *Journal of Personality and Social Psychology*, 1978, *36*, 929–940.

McCauley, C., & Swann, C. P. Male-female differences in sexual fantasy. *Journal of Research in Personality*, 1978, *12*, 76–86.

McCauley, C., & Taylor, J. Is there overload of acquaintances in the city? *Environmental Psychology and Nonverbal Behavior*, 1976, *1*(1), 41–55.

McClelland, D. C. *Personality.* New York: William Sloane, 1951.

McClelland, D. C. *The achieving society.* Princeton, N.J.: Van Nostrand, 1961.

McClelland, D. C., Atkinson, J. W., Clark, R. A., & Lowell, E. L. *The achievement motive.* New York: Appleton-Century-Crofts, 1953.

McClelland, L., & Canter, R. J. Psychological research on energy conservation: Context, approaches, methods. In J. Singer, S. Valins, & A. Baum (Eds.), *Advances in environmental psychology.* Hillsdale, N.J.: Erlbaum, 1978.

McClelland, L., & Cook, S. W. Promoting energy conservation in master-metered apartments through group financial incentives. *Journal of Applied Social Psychology*, 1980, *10*, 19–31.

McClintock, C. G. Personality syndromes and attitude change. *Journal of Personality*, 1958, *26*, 479–493.

McClintock, C. G., & Hunt, R. C. Nonverbal indicators of affect and deception in an interview setting. *Journal of Applied Social Psychology*, 1975, *5*, 54–67.

McClintock, C. G., & Moskowitz, J. M. Children's preferences for individualistic, cooperative, and competitive outcomes. *Journal of Personality and Social Psychology*, 1976, *34*, 543–555.

McClintock, C. G., Moskowitz, J. M., & McClintock, E. Variations in preferences for individualistic, competitive, and cooperative outcomes as a function of age, game class, and task in nursery school children. *Child Development*, 1977, *48*, 1080–1085.

McCorkle, L. W., & Korn, R. R. Resocialization within walls. *The Annals of the American Academy of Political and Social Science*, 1954, *293*, 88–98.

McDavid, J. W., & Harari, H. *Psychology and social behavior.* New York: Harper & Row, 1974.

McDougall, W. *An introduction to social psychology.* London: Methuen, 1908.

McGhee, P. E., & Teevan, R. C. Conformity behavior and need for affiliation. *Journal of Social Psychology*, 1967, *72*, 117–121.

McGinnis, J. *The selling of the President, 1968.* New York: Pocket Books, 1970.

McGrath, J. E. (Ed.). *Social and psychological factors in stress.* New York: Holt, Rinehart & Winston, 1970.

McGrath, J. E. Stress and behavior in organizations. In M. E. Dunnette (Ed.), *Handbook of industrial and organizational psychology.* Chicago: Rand McNally, 1976. Pp. 1351–1395.

McGregor, D. *The human side of enterprise.* New York: McGraw-Hill, 1960.

McGregor, D. *Leadership and motivation.* (W. G. Bennis & E. H. Schein, Eds.). Cambridge, Mass.: M.I.T. Press, 1966.

McGregor, D. *The professional manager* (C. McGregor & W. G. Bennis, Eds.). New York: McGraw-Hill, 1967.

McGuire, W. J. Inducing resistance to persuasion. In L. Berkowitz (Ed.), *Advances in experimental social psychology* (Vol. 1). New York: Academic Press, 1964.

McGuire, W. J. Some impeding reorientations in social psychology. *Journal of Experimental Social Psychology*, 1967, *3*, 124–139. (a)

McGuire, W. J. *Theory-oriented research in natural settings: The best of both worlds for social psychology.* Symposium paper presented at Pennsylvania State University, May 1967. (b)

McGuire, W. J. Personality and attitude change: A theoretical housing. In A. G. Greenwald, T. C. Brock, & T. M. Ostrom (Eds.), *Psychological foundations of attitudes.* New York: Academic Press, 1968. Pp. 171–196. (a)

McGuire, W. J. Personality and susceptibility to social influence. In E. F. Borgatta & W. W. Lambert (Eds.), *Handbook of personality theory and research.* Chicago:

Rand McNally, 1968. Pp. 1130–1187.(b)

McGuire, W. J. The nature of attitudes and attitude change. In G. Lindzey & E. Aronson (Eds.), *Handbook of social psychology* (Vol. 3) (2nd ed.). Reading, Mass.: Addison-Wesley, 1969. Pp. 136–314.

McGuire, W. J. The yin and yang of progress in social psychology: Seven koan. *Journal of Personality and Social Psychology*, 1973, *26*, 446–456.

McGuire, W. J., McGuire, C. V., Child, P., & Fujioka, T. Salience of ethnicity in the spontaneous self-concept as a function of one's ethnic distinctiveness in the social environment. *Journal of Personality and Social Psychology*, 1978, *36*, 511–520.

McGuire, W. J., McGuire, C. V., & Winton, W. Effects of household sex composition on the salience of one's gender in the spontaneous self-concept. *Journal of Experimental Social Psychology*, 1979, *15*, 77–90.

McGuire, W. J., & Millman, S. Anticipatory belief lowering following forewarning of a persuasive attack. *Journal of Personality and Social Psychology*, 1965, *2*, 471–479.

McGuire, W. J., & Padawer-Singer, A. Trait salience in the spontaneous self-concept. *Journal of Personality and Social Psychology*, 1976, *33*, 743–754.

McGuire, W. J., & Papageorgis, D. Effectiveness of forewarning in developing resistance to persuasion. *Public Opinion Quarterly*, 1962, *26*, 24–34.

McLuhan, M. *Understanding media: The extensions of man.* New York: McGraw-Hill, 1964.

McMillen, D. L. Transgression, self-image, and compliant behavior. *Journal of Personality and Social Psychology*, 1971, *20*, 176–179.

McMillen, D. L., Sanders, D. Y., & Solomon, G. S. Self-esteem, attentiveness, and helping behavior. *Personality and Social Psychology Bulletin*, 1977, *3*, 257–261.

McNemar, Q. *The revision of the Stanford-Binet scale: An analysis of the standardization data.* Boston: Houghton Mifflin, 1942.

Mead, G. H. *Mind, self and society.* (C. W. Morris, Ed.) Chicago: University of Chicago Press, 1934.

Megargee, E. I. The prediction of violence with psychological tests. In C. Spielberger (Ed.), *Current topics in clinical and community psychology.* New York: Academic Press, 1974. Pp. 98–156.

Mehrabian, A. Some referents and measures of nonverbal behavior. *Behavioral Research Methods and Instrumentation*, 1969, *1*, 203–207. (a)

Mehrabian, A. Significance of posture and position in the communication of attitude and status relationships. *Psychological Bulletin*, 1969, *71*, 359–372. (b)

Mehrabian, A. Nonverbal betrayal of feeling. *Journal of Experimental Research in Personality*, 1971, *5*, 64–73.

Mehrabian, A. *Nonverbal communication.* Chicago: Aldine-Atherton, 1972.

Mehrabian, A., & Diamond, S. Effects of furniture arrangement, props, and personality on social interaction. *Journal of Personality and Social Psychology*, 1971, *20*, 18–30. (a)

Mehrabian, A., & Diamond, S. Seating arrangement and conversation. *Sociometry*, 1971, *34*, 281–289. (b)

Mehrabian, A., & Ferris, S. R. Inference of attitudes from nonverbal communication in two channels. *Journal of Consulting Psychology*, 1967, *31*, 248–252.

Mehrabian, A., & Weiner, M. Decoding of inconsistent communications. *Journal of Personality and Social Psychology*, 1967, *6*, 109–114.

Meir, E. I., & Barak, A. Pervasiveness of the relationship between intrinsic-extrinsic needs and persistence at work. *Journal of Applied Psychology*, 1974, *59*, 103–104.

Melville, H. *The confidence man.* New York: Signet, 1964. (Originally published, 1857)

Melville, K. *Communes in the counterculture: Origins, theories, styles of life.* New York: Morrow, 1972.

Menne, J.M.C., & Sinnett, E. R. Proximity and social interaction in residence halls. *Journal of College Student Personnel*, 1971, *12*, 26–31.

Merton, R. D. *Social theory and social structure* (Rev. ed.). New York: Free Press, 1968.

Metcalf, J. T. Empathy and the actor's emotion. *Journal of Social Psychology*, 1931, *2*, 235–238.

Mettee, D. R. Changes in liking as a function of the magnitude and affect of sequential evaluations. *Journal of Experimental Social Psychology*, 1971, *7*, 157–172.

Meyer, T. P. The effects of sexually arousing and violent films on aggressive behavior. *Journal of Sex Research*, 1972, *8*, 324–331.

Michelson, W. *Man and his urban environment: A sociological approach.* Reading, Mass.: Addison-Wesley, 1970.

Michener, H. A., & Lawler, E. J. The endorsement of formal leaders: An integrative model. *Journal of Personality and Social Psychology*, 1975, *31*, 216–223.

Midlarsky, E., & Bryan, J. H. Affect expressions and children's imitative altruism. *Journal of Experimental Research in Personality*, 1972, *6*, 195–203.

Milgram, S. Behavioral study of obedience. *Journal of Abnormal and Social Psychology*, 1963, *67*, 371–378.

Milgram, S. Group pressure and action against a person. *Journal of Abnormal and Social Psychology*, 1964, *69*, 137–143. (a)

Milgram, S. Issues in the study of obedience: A reply to Baumrind. *American Psychologist*, 1964, *19*, 848–852. (b)

Milgram, S. Some conditions of obedience and disobedience to authority. *Human Relations*, 1965, *18*, 57–76.

Milgram, S. Reply to the critics. *International Journal of Psychiatry*, 1968, *6*, 294–295.

Milgram, S. The experience of living in cities. *Science*, 1970, *167*, 1461–1468.

Milgram, S. *Obedience to authority.* New York: Harper & Row, 1974.

Miller, A. G. Role playing: An alternative to deception? A review of the evidence. *American Psychologist*, 1972, *27*, 623–636.

Miller, A. G. Actor and observer perceptions of the learning of a task. *Journal of Experimental Social Psychology*, 1977, *11*, 95–111.

Miller, A. G., & Thomas, R. Cooperation and competition among Blackfoot Indian and urban Canadian children. *Child Development*, 1972, *43*, 1104–1110.

Miller, C. T., & Byrne, D. *Affective orientation to sexuality and attributions of contraceptors.* Paper presented at the meeting of the Midwestern Psychological Association, Chicago, 1978.

Miller, C., & Crandall, R. Bargaining and negotiation. In P. B. Paulus (Ed.), *Psychology of group influence.* Hillsdale, N.J.: Erlbaum, 1980.

Miller, D. T. Personal deserving versus justice for others: An exploration of the justice motive. *Journal of Experimental Social Psychology*, 1977, *13*, 1–13.

Miller, D. T., & Norman, S. A. Actor-observer differences

in perceptions of effective control. *Journal of Personality and Social Psychology*, 1975, *31*, 503–515.

Miller, D. T., Norman, S. A., & Wright, E. Distortion in person perception as a consequence of the need for effective control. *Journal of Personality and Social Psychology*, 1978, *36*, 598–607.

Miller, F. E., & Rogers, L. E. A relational approach to interpersonal communication. In G. R. Miller (Ed.), *Explorations in interpersonal communication*. Beverly Hills: Sage, 1976.

Miller, G. A. Psychology as a means of promoting human welfare. *American Psychologist*, 1969, *24*, 1063–1075. (Reprinted in F. F. Korten, S. W. Cook, & J. I. Lacey [Eds.], *Psychology and the problems of society*. Washington, D.C.: American Psychological Association, 1970. Pp. 5–21.)

Miller, G. R. The current status of theory and research in interpersonal communication. *Human Communication Research*, 1978, *4*, 164–178.

Miller, J. G. Adjusting to overloads of information. In R. Waggoner & D. Carek (Eds.), *Disorders of Communication*, 1964, *42*, 87–100.

Miller, L. K., & Hamblin, R. L. Interdependence, differential rewarding, and productivity. *American Sociological Review*, 1963, *28*, 768–778.

Miller, N. Involvement and dogmatism as inhibitors of attitude change. *Journal of Experimental Social Psychology*, 1965, *1*, 121–132.

Miller, N., & Zimbardo, P. G. Motives for fear-induced affiliation: Emotional comparison or interpersonal similarity? *Journal of Personality*, 1966, *34*, 481–503.

Miller, N. E. The frustration-aggression hypothesis. *Psychological Review*, 1941, *48*, 337–342.

Miller, N. E. Some implications of modern behavior theory for personality change and psychotherapy. In P. Worchel & D. Byrne (Eds.), *Personality change*. New York: Wiley, 1964. Pp. 149–175.

Miller, N. E., & Dollard, J. *Social learning and imitation*. New Haven: Yale University Press, 1941.

Mills, C. W. The contributions of sociology to studies of industrial relations. *Proceedings of the First Annual Meeting, Industrial Relations Research Association*, 1948, *1*, 199–222.

Mills, J. & Aronson, E. Opinion change as a function of communicator's attractiveness and desire to influence. *Journal of Personality and Social Psychology*, 1965, *1*, 173–177.

Mills, R. T., & Krantz, D. S. Information, choice, and reactions to stress: A field experiment in a blood bank with laboratory analogue. *Journal of Personality and Social Psychology*, 1979, *37*, 608–620.

Milton, G. A. *Five studies of the relation between sex role identification and achievement in problem-solving* (Technical Report No. 3). New Haven, Conn.: Yale University, 1958.

Milton, G. A. Sex differences in problem solving as a function of role appropriateness of the problem content. *Psychological Reports*, 1959, *5*, 705–708.

Milton, O. Presidential choice and performance on a scale of authoritarianism. *American Psychologist*, 1952, *7*, 597–598.

Mintz, N. L. Effects of esthetic surroundings: II. Prolonged and repeated experience in a "beautiful" and an "ugly" room. *The Journal of Psychology*, 1956, *41*, 459–466.

Mirels, H. L. Dimensions of internal versus external control. *Journal of Consulting and Clinical Psychology*, 1970, *34*, 226–228.

Mischel, W. *Personality and assessment*. New York: Wiley, 1968.

Mischel, W. On the future of personality measurement. *American Psychologist*, 1977, *32*, 246–254.

Mischel, W., & Mischel, H. N. A cognitive-social learning approach to morality and self-regulation. In T. Likona (Ed.), *Moral development and behavior*. New York: Holt, 1976.

Mita, T. H., Dermer, M., & Knight, J. Reversed facial images and the mere-exposure hypothesis. *Journal of Personality and Social Psychology*, 1977, *35*, 597–601.

Mitchell, H. E. *Authoritarian punitiveness in simulated juror decision-making: The good guys don't always wear white hats*. Paper presented at the meeting of the Midwestern Psychological Association, Chicago, May 1973.

Mitchell, T. R. Organizational behavior. In M. R. Rosenzweig & L. W. Porter (Eds.), *Annual Review of Psychology*, 1979, *21*, 243–272.

Mitnick, L., & McGinnies, E. Influencing ethnocentrism in small discussion groups through a film communication. *Journal of Abnormal and Social Psychology*, 1958, *56*, 82–90.

Mixon, D. Instead of deception. *Journal for the Theory of Social Behaviour*, 1972, *2*, 145–177.

Modigliani, A. Embarrassment and embarrassability. *Sociometry*, 1968, *31*, 313–326.

Molière, J.B.P. de. *Tartuffe*. New York: Harcourt Brace and World, Inc., 1963. (Original edition, 1669)

Monahan, J. (Ed.). *Community mental health and the criminal justice system*. New York: Pergamon, 1975.

Monahan, L., Kuhn, D., & Shaver, P. Intrapsychic versus cultural explanations of the "fear of success" motive. *Journal of Personality and Social Psychology*, 1974, *29*, 60–64.

Money, J., & Athanasiou, R. Pornography: Review and bibliographic annotations. *American Journal of Obstetrics and Gynecology*, 1973, *115*, 130–146.

Money, J., & Ehrhardt, A. A. *Man and woman; boy and girl*. Baltimore: Johns Hopkins Press, 1972.

Money, J., & Tucker, P. *Sexual signatures: On being a man or a woman*. Boston: Little, Brown, 1975.

Monson, T. C., & Snyder, M. Actors, observers, and the attribution process: Toward a reconceptualization. *Journal of Experimental Social Psychology*, 1977, *13*, 89–111.

Montagu, M.F.A. *Man: His first million years*. Cleveland: World, 1957.

Montagu, M.F.A. *Man's most dangerous myth: The fallacy of race* (4th ed.). Cleveland: World, 1964.

Montagu, M.F.A. *Touching: The human significance of the skin*. New York: Columbia University Press, 1971.

Montagu, A. *The nature of human aggression*. New York: Oxford University Press, 1976.

Montero, D. Research among racial and cultural minorities: An overview. *Journal of Social Issues*, 1977, *33*(4), 1–10.

Montmollin, G. de. *L'influence social: Phénomènes, facteurs et théories*. Paris: Presses Universitaires de France, 1977.

Moore, B. S., Underwood, B., & Rosenhan, D. Affect and self-gratification. *Developmental Psychology*, 1973, *8*, 209–214.

Moore, J. C. Audience effects in a communication chain:

An instance of ingratiation. *Personality and Social Psychology Bulletin*, 1975, *1*, 58–61.

Moriarty, T. Crime, commitment and the responsive bystander: Two field experiments. *Journal of Personality and Social Psychology*, 1975, *31*, 370–376.

Morin, S. *Attitudes toward homosexuality and social distance.* Paper presented at the annual meeting of the American Psychological Association, Chicago, 1975.

Morris, D. *Intimate behavior.* New York: Random House, 1971.

Morris, J. *Conundrum.* New York: Harcourt, Brace, Jovanovich, 1974.

Morton, T. L. Intimacy and reciprocity of exchange: A comparison of spouses and strangers. *Journal of Personality and Social Psychology*, 1978, *36*, 72–81.

Moscovici, S. Society and theory in social psychology. In J. Israel & H. Tajfel (Eds.), *The context of social psychology: A critical assessment.* New York: Academic Press, 1972.

Moscovici, S. Social influence I: Conformity and social control. In C. Nemeth (Ed.), *Social psychology: Classic and contemporary integrations.* Chicago: Aldine, 1974. Pp. 179–216.

Moscovici, S., & Doise, W. Decision making in groups. In C. Nemeth (Ed.), *Social psychology: Classic and contemporary integrations.* Chicago: Rand McNally, 1974. Pp. 250–287.

Moscovici, S., & Faucheux, C. Social influence, conformity bias, and the study of active minorities. In L. Berkowitz (Ed.), *Advances in experimental social psychology* (Vol. 6). New York: Academic Press, 1972. Pp. 149–202.

Moscovici, S., & Zavalloni, M. The group as a polarizer of attitudes. *Journal of Personality and Social Psychology*, 1969, *12*, 125–135.

Mosher, D. L. Sex differences, sex experience, sex guilt, and explicitly sexual films. *Journal of Social Issues*, 1973, *29*(3), 95–112.

Moss, M. K., & Andrasik, F. Belief similarity and interracial attraction. *Journal of Personality*, 1973, *41*, 192–205.

Moss, M. K., & Page, R. A. Reinforcement and helping behavior. *Journal of Applied Social Psychology*, 1972, *2*, 360–371.

Mulvihill, D. J., & Tumin, M. M. *Crimes of violence. Staff report to the National Commission on the Causes and Prevention of Violence* (Vol. 11). Washington, D.C.: U.S. Government Printing Office, 1969.

Murnighan, J. K. Models of coalition behavior: Game theoretic, social psychological, and political perspectives. *Psychological Bulletin*, 1978, *85*, 1130–1153.

Murray, H. A. *Explorations in personality.* New York: Oxford University Press, 1938.

Murray, J., & Feshbach, S. Let's not throw the baby out with the bathwater: The catharsis hypothesis revisited. *Journal of Personality*, 1978, *46*, 462–473.

Murstein, B. I. Physical attractiveness and marital choice. *Journal of Personality and Social Psychology*, 1972, *22*, 8–12.

Murstein, B. I., & Christy, P. Physical attractiveness and marriage adjustment in middle-aged couples. *Journal of Personality and Social Psychology*, 1976, *34*, 537–542.

Mussen, P., & Eisenberg-Berg, N. *Roots of caring, sharing, and helping.* San Francisco: W. H. Freeman, 1977.

Myers, A. M., & Lips, H. M. Participation in competitive amateur sports as a function of psychological androgyny. *Sex Roles*, 1978, *4*, 571–578.

Myers, D. G., & Bishop, G. D. Discussion effects on racial attitudes. *Science*, 1970, *169*, 778–789.

Myers, D. G., & Bishop, G. D. Enhancement of dominant attitudes in group discussion. *Journal of Personality and Social Psychology*, 1971, *20*, 386–391.

Myers, D. G., & Kaplan, M. F. Group-induced polarization in simulated juries. *Personality and Social Psychology Bulletin*, 1976, *2*, 63–66.

Myers, D. G., & Lamm, H. The group polarization phenomenon. *Psychological Bulletin*, 1976, *83*, 602–627.

Naeye, R. L., Diener, M. M., & Dellinger, W. S. Urban poverty: Effects on prenatal nutrition. *Science*, 1969, *166*, 1026.

National Commission on the Causes and Prevention of Violence. *To establish justice, to insure domestic tranquility.* New York: Award Books, 1969.

Neiman, L. J., & Hughes, J. W. The problem of the concept of role—a resurvey of the literature. *Social Forces*, 1951, *30*, 141–149.

Nelson, E. A., Grinder, R. E., & Mutterer, M. L. Sources of variance in behavioral measures of honesty in temptation situation: Methodological analyses. *Developmental Psychology*, 1969, *1*, 265–279.

Nemeth, C. A critical analysis of research utilizing the Prisoner's Dilemma paradigm for the study of bargaining. In L. Berkowitz (Ed.), *Advances in experimental social psychology* (Vol. 6). New York: Academic Press, 1972.

Newcomb, T. M. *The acquaintance process.* New York: Holt, Rinehart & Winston, 1961.

Newman, O. *Defensible space.* New York: Macmillan, 1973.

Newsweek. Taking the chitling test. 1968, *72*(3), 51–52. (July 15, 1968 issue)

Newtson, D. Dispositional inference from effects of actions: Effects chosen and effects foregone. *Journal of Experimental Social Psychology*, 1974, *10*, 489–496.

Newtson, D., & Czerlinsky, T. Adjustment of attitude communications for contrasts by extreme audiences. *Journal of Personality and Social Psychology*, 1974, *30*, 829–837.

Nguyen, T., Heslin, R., & Nguyen, M. L. The meanings of touch: Sex differences. *Journal of Communication*, 1975, *25*, 92–103.

Nisbett, R. E., & Borgida, E. Attribution and the psychology of prediction. *Journal of Personality and Social Psychology*, 1975, *32*, 932–943.

Nisbett, R. E., Caputo, C., Legant, P., & Marecek, J., Jr. Behavior as seen by the actor and as seen by the observer. *Journal of Personality and Social Psychology*, 1973, *27*, 154–165.

Nizer, L. *The implosion conspiracy.* New York: Doubleday, 1973.

Noel, R. C. Transgression—compliance: A failure to confirm. *Journal of Personality and Social Psychology*, 1973, *27*, 151–153.

Nord, W. R. Social exchange theory: An integrative approach to social conformity. *Psychological Bulletin*, 1969, *71*, 174–208.

Novak, D., & Lerner, M. J. Rejection as a consequence of perceived similarity. *Journal of Personality and Social Psychology*, 1968, *9*, 147–152.

Nutt, R. L., & Sedlacek, W. E. Freshman sexual attitudes and behavior. *Journal of College Student*

Personnel, 1974, *15*, 346–351.

O'Connor, K., Mann, D. W., & Bardwick, J. M. Androgyny and self-esteem in the upper-middle class: A replication of Spence. *Journal of Consulting and Clinical Psychology*, 1978, *46*, 1168–1169.

O'Leary, V. E. *Toward understanding women.* Monterey, Calif.: Brooks/Cole, 1977.

Orlofsky, J. L. Parental antecedents of sex-role orientation in college men and women. *Sex Roles*, 1979, *5*, 495–512.

Orlofsky, J. L., Marcia, J. E., & Lesser, I. M. Ego identity status and the intimacy versus isolation crisis of young adulthood. *Journal of Personality and Social Psychology*, 1973, *27*, 211–219.

Orne, M. T. Demand characteristics and the concept of quasi-controls. In R. Rosenthal & R. Rosnow (Eds.), *Artifact in behavior research.* New York: Academic Press, 1969.

Orne, M. T., & Holland, C. C. On the ecological validity of laboratory deceptions. *International Journal of Psychiatry*, 1968, *6*, 282–293.

Orvis, B. R., Cunningham, J. D., & Kelley, H. H. A closer examination of causal inference: The role of consensus, distinctiveness, and consistency information. *Journal of Personality and Social Psychology*, 1975, *29*, 426–434.

Osborn, A. F. *Applied imagination.* New York: Scribner, 1957.

Osborn, J. L. *Corporate employee information handling practices and employee perceptions.* Paper presented at the Organization for Economic Co-operation and Development's Symposium on Transborder Data Flows and the Protection of Privacy, Vienna, Austria, September 1977.

Osgood, C. E. Suggestions for winning the real war with communism. *Journal of Conflict Resolution*, 1959, *3*, 295–325.

Osgood, C. E. *An alternative to war or surrender.* Urbana: University of Illinois Press, 1962.

Osgood, C. E. *Perspective in foreign policy.* Palo Alto, Calif.: Pacific Books, 1966.

Osgood, C. E., Suci, G. J., & Tannenbaum, P. H. *The measurement of meaning.* Urbana: University of Illinois Press, 1957.

Osgood, C. E., & Tannenbaum, P. H. The principle of congruity in the prediction of attitude change. *Psychological Review*, 1955, *62*, 42–55.

Oskamp, S. Effects of programmed strategies in the prisoner's dilemma game. *Journal of Conflict Resolution*, 1971, *15*, 225–259.

Oskamp, S. *Attitudes and opinions.* Englewood Cliffs, N.J.: Prentice-Hall, 1977.

Osmond, H. Function as the basis of psychiatric ward design. *Mental Hospitals*, 1957, *8*, 23–30.

Owens, D. J., & Straus, M. A. The social structure of violence in childhood and approval of violence as an adult. *Aggressive Behavior*, 1975, *1*, 193–211.

Pagano, M., & Kirschner, N. M. Sex guilt, sexual arousal, and urinary acid phosphatase output. *Journal of Research in Personality*, 1978, *12*, 68–75.

Page, M. M. Social psychology of a classical conditioning of attitudes experiment. *Journal of Personality and Social Psychology*, 1969, *11*, 177–186.

Page, M. M. Postexperimental assessment of awareness in attitude conditioning. *Educational and Psychological Measurement*, 1971, *31*, 891–906.

Page, M. M. Demand characteristics and the classical conditioning of attitudes experiment. *Journal of Personality and Social Psychology*, 1974, *30*, 468–476.

Page, M., & Scheidt, R. The elusive weapons effect: Demand awareness, evaluation and slightly sophisticated subjects. *Journal of Personality and Social Psychology*, 1971, *20*, 304–318.

Page, R. Noise and helping behavior. *Environment and Behavior*, 1977, *9*, 311–334.

Paige, J. M. Changing patterns of anti-White attitudes among Blacks. *Journal of Social Issues*, 1970, *26*(4), 69–86.

Paivio, A. Personality and audience influence. In B. Maher (Ed.), *Progress in experimental personality research.* New York: Academic Press, 1965. Pp. 127–173.

Palamarek, D. L., & Rule, B. G. The effects of ambient temperature and insult on the motivation to retaliate or escape. *Motivation and Emotion*, 1979, *3*, 83–92.

Pallak, M. S., & Cummings, W. Commitment and voluntary energy conservation. *Personality and Social Psychology Bulletin*, 1976, *2*, 27–30.

Parke, R. D. Effectiveness of punishment as an interaction of intensity, timing, agent nurturance, and cognitive structuring. *Child Development*, 1969, *40*, 213–235.

Parke, R. D., Berkowitz, L., Leyens, J. P., West, S. G., & Sebastian, R. J. Some effects of violent and nonviolent movies on the behavior of juvenile delinquents. In L. Berkowitz (Ed.), *Advances in experimental social psychology* (Vol. 10). New York: Academic Press, 1977. Pp. 135–172.

Parks, M. R. Relational communication: Theory and research. *Human Communications Research*, 1977, *3*, 372–381.

Parmelee, P., & Werner, C. Lonely losers: Stereotypes of single dwellers. *Personality and Social Psychology Bulletin*, 1978, *4*, 292–295. (a)

Parmelee, P., & Werner, C. M. Attributions to single and shared dwellers as a function of living status and preference. *Population*, 1978, *1*, 298–312.(b)

Parnes, S. J., & Meadow, A. Effects of "brainstorming" instructions on creative problem solving by trained and untrained subjects. *Journal of Educational Psychology*, 1959, *50*, 171–176.

Parsons, H. M. What happened at Hawthorne? *Science*, 1974, *183*, 922–932.

Parsons, H. M. Work environments. In I. Altman & J. F. Wohlwill (Eds.), *Human behavior and environment: Advances in theory and research. Volume I.* New York: Plenum Press, 1976. Pp. 163–209.

Pasamanick, B. A., & Knobloch, H. Early language behavior in Negro children and the testing of intelligence. *Journal of Abnormal and Social Psychology*, 1955, *50*, 401–402.

Pasamanick, B. A., & Knobloch, H. Brain damage and reproductive casualty. *American Journal of Orthopsychiatry*, 1960, *30*, 298–305.

Pastore, N. The role of arbitrariness in the frustration-aggression hypothesis. *Journal of Abnormal and Social Psychology*, 1952, *47*, 728–731.

Patterson, M. L. Compensation in nonverbal immediacy behaviors: A review. *Sociometry*, 1973, *36*, 237–252.

Patterson, M. L. An arousal model of interpersonal intimacy. *Psychological Review*, 1976, *83*, 235–245.

Patterson, M. L. An intimacy-arousal model of crowding. In P. Suedfeld, J. A. Russell, L. M. Ward, F. Szigelti, & G. David (Eds.), *The behavioral basis of design.* Stroudsberg, Pa.: Dowden, Hutchinson and Ross, 1977.

Patterson, M. L., Mullens, S., & Romano, J. Compensatory reactions to spatial intrusion. *Sociometry*, 1971, *34*, 114–121.

Paulson, F. L. Teaching cooperation on television: An evaluation of Sesame Street Social Goals Programs. *AV Communication Review*, 1974, *22*, 229–246.

Paulus, P. B., Annis, A. B., Seta, J., Schkade, J., & Mathews, R. Density does affect task performance. *Journal of Personality and Social Psychology*, 1976, *34*(2), 248–253.

Paulus, P., Cox, V., McCain, G., & Chandler, J. Some effects of crowding in a prison environment. *Journal of Applied Social Psychology*, 1975, *5*(1), 86–91.

Peck, R. F., & Havighurst, R. J. *The psychology of character development.* New York: Wiley, 1960.

Pellegrini, R. J., & Empey, J. Interpersonal spatial orientation in dyads. *Journal of Psychology*, 1970, *76*, 67–70.

Pennebaker, J. W., & Skelton, J. A. Psychological parameters of physical symptoms. *Personality and Social Psychology Bulletin*, 1978, *4*, 524–530.

Peplau, L. A., Rubin, Z., & Hill, C. T. Sexual intimacy in dating relationships. *Journal of Social Issues*, 1977, *33*(2), 86–109.

Peplau, L. A., Russell, D., & Heim, M. Loneliness: A bibliography of research and theory. *JSAS Catalog of Selected Documents in Psychology*, 1978, *8*(2), 38.

Perlman, D. The sexual standards of Canadian university students. In D. Koulack & D. Perlman (Eds.), *Readings in social psychology: Focus on Canada.* Toronto: Wiley, 1973. Pp. 139–160.

Pervin, L. A. Definitions, measurements, and classifications of stimuli, situations, and environments. *Human Ecology*, 1978, *6*, 71–105.

Peterson, J. H. *A disguised structured instrument for the assessment of attitudes toward the poor.* Unpublished doctoral dissertation, University of Oklahoma, 1967.

Peterson, M. Guidelines for psychologists in police consultation. Paper presented at the meeting of the American Psychological Association, New Orleans, September 1974.

Peterson, P. D., & Koulack, D. Attitude change as a function of latitudes of acceptance and rejection. *Journal of Personality and Social Psychology*, 1969, *11*, 309–311.

Pettigrew, T. F. Social psychology and desegregation research. *American Psychologist*, 1961, *16*, 105–112.

Pettigrew, T. F. *A profile of the Negro American.* Princeton, N.J.: Van Nostrand, 1964.

Petty, R. E., & Brock, T. C. Effects of responding or not responding to hecklers on audience agreement with a speaker. *Journal of Applied Social Psychology*, 1976, *6*, 1–17.

Petty, R. E., & Cacioppo, J. T. Forewarning, cognitive responding, and resistance to persuasion. *Journal of Personality and Social Psychology*, 1977, *35*, 645–655.

Petty, R. E., Wells, G. L., & Brock, T. C. Distraction can enhance or reduce yielding to propaganda: Thought disruption versus effort justification. *Journal of Personality and Social Psychology*, 1976, *34*, 874–884.

Pfeffer, J. The ambiguity of leadership. In M. W. McCall, Jr., & M. M. Lombardo (Eds.), *Leadership: Where else can we go?* Durham, N.C.: Duke University Press,

1978. Pp. 13–34.

Phares, E. J. *Locus of control in personality.* Morristown, N.J.: General Learning Press, 1976.

Phillips, D. P. *Dying as a form of social behavior* (Doctoral dissertation, Princeton University). Ann Arbor, Mich.: University Microfilms, 1970. No. 70-19, 799.

Phillips, D. P. Deathday and birthday: An unexpected connection. In J. M. Tanur (Ed.), *Statistics: A guide to the unknown.* San Francisco: Holden-Day, 1972.

Phillips, D. P. Airplane accident fatalities increase just after newspaper stories about murder and suicide. *Science*, 1978, *201*, 748–750.

Piaget, J. *The language and thought of the child.* New York: Harcourt-Brace, 1926.

Piaget, J. The general problems of the psychobiological development of the child. In J. M. Tanner & B. Inhelder (Eds.), *Discussion of child development: Proceedings of the World Health Organization study group on the psychobiological development of the child* (Vol. 4). New York: International Universities Press, 1960. Pp. 3–27.

Piaget, J. *The moral judgment of the child.* New York: Free Press, 1965. (Originally published, 1932)

Pile, J. *Open office planning: A handbook for interior designers and architects.* New York: Whitney Library of Design, 1978.

Piliavin, I. M., Rodin, J., & Piliavin, J. A. Good Samaritanism: An underground phenomenon? *Journal of Personality and Social Psychology*, 1969, *13*, 289–299.

Piliavin, J. A., & Piliavin, I. M. *The Good Samaritan: Why does he help?* Unpublished manuscript, University of Wisconsin, 1973.

Pilkonis, P. A. Shyness, public and private, and its relationship to other measures of social behavior. *Journal of Personality*, 1977, *45*, 585–595.

Pizer, S. A., & Travers, J. R. *Psychology and social change.* New York: McGraw-Hill, 1975.

Platt, J. Social traps. *American Psychologist*, 1973, *28*, 641–651.

Pliner, P., Hart, H., Kohl, J., & Saari, D. Compliance without pressure: Some further data on the foot-in-the-door technique. *Journal of Experimental Social Psychology*, 1974, *10*, 17–22.

Pocs, O., & Godow, A. G. Can students view parents as sexual beings? In D. Byrne & L. Byrne (Eds.), *Exploring human sexuality.* New York: Crowell, 1977.

Pollak, O. *Human behavior and the helping professions.* New York: Spectrum, 1976. (Distributed by Halsted)

Poor, D. *The social psychology of questionnaires.* Unpublished bachelor's thesis, Harvard University, 1967. (Cited in R. Rosenthal & R. L. Rosnow (Eds.), *Artifact in behavioral research.* New York: Academic Press, 1969.)

Poppen, P. J. *Sex differences in moral judgment.* Paper presented at the meeting of the American Psychological Association, New Orleans, September 1974.

Potter, D. A. Personalism and interpersonal attraction. *Journal of Personality and Social Psychology*, 1973, *28*, 192–198.

Powell, P. H., & Borden, R. J. *Sex, belief in technology and diffusion of environmental responsibility.* Paper presented at the meeting of the Midwestern Psychological Association, Chicago, 1978.

Prentice, N. M. The influence of live and symbolic modeling on promoting moral judgment of adolescent delinquents. *Journal of Abnormal Psychology*,

1972, *80*, 157–161.

Preston, M. Note on the reliability and validity of group judgment. *Journal of Experimental Psychology*, 1938, *22*, 462–471.

Price, C. R. Between cultures: The current crisis of transition. In W. Schmidt (Ed.), *Organizational frontiers and human values*. Belmont, Calif.: Wadsworth, 1970. Pp. 27–44.

Price, J. L. *The effects of crowding on the social behavior of children*. Unpublished doctoral dissertation, Columbia University, 1971.

Price, R. A., & Vandenberg, S. G. Matching for physical attractiveness in married couples. *Personality and Social Psychology Bulletin*, 1979, *5*, 398–400.

Proshansky, H., & Newton, P. The nature and meaning of Negro self-identity. In M. Deutsch, I. Katz, & A. R. Jensen (Eds.), *Social class, race, and psychological development*. New York: Holt, Rinehart & Winston, 1968. Pp. 178–218.

Pruitt, D. G. Choice shifts in group discussion: An introductory review. *Journal of Personality and Social Psychology*, 1971, *20*, 339–360. (a)

Pruitt, D. G. Conclusions: Toward an understanding of choice shifts in group discussion. *Journal of Personality and Social Psychology*, 1971, *20*, 495–510. (b)

Pruitt, D. G., & Kimmel, M. J. Twenty years of experimental gaming: Critique, synthesis, and suggestions for the future. In M. R. Rosenzweig & L. W. Porter (Eds.), *Annual Review of Psychology*, 1977, *28*, 363–392.

Pryor, J. B., & Kriss, M. The cognitive dynamics of salience in the attribution process. *Journal of Personality and Social Psychology*, 1977, *35*, 49–55.

Rabbie, J. M. Differential preference for companionship under threat. *Journal of Abnormal and Social Psychology*, 1963, *67*, 643–648.

Rabbie, J. M. *Effects of expected intergroup competition and cooperation*. Paper presented at the meeting of the American Psychological Association, New Orleans, August 1974.

Rabbie, J. M., & Wilkens, G. Intergroup competition and its effect on intragroup and intergroup relations. *European Journal of Social Psychology*, 1971, *1*, 215–234.

Rada, J. B., & Rogers, R. W. *Obedience to authority: Presence of authority and command strength*. Paper presented at the meeting of the Southeastern Psychological Association, New Orleans, April 1973.

Radloff, R. Opinion evaluation and affiliation. *Journal of Abnormal and Social Psychology*, 1961, *62*, 578–585.

Radloff, R., & Helmreich, R. *Groups under stress: Psychological research in SEALAB II*. New York: Irvington, 1968.

Ramirez, A. Chicano power and interracial group relations. In *Chicano psychology*. New York: Academic Press, 1977. Pp. 87–96.

Rands, M., & Levinger, G. Implicit theories of relationship: An intergenerational study. *Journal of Personality and Social Psychology*, 1979, *37*, 645–661.

Ransford, H. E. Isolation, powerlessness, and violence: A study of attitudes and participation in the Watts riot. *American Journal of Sociology*, 1968, *73*, 581–591.

Rapoport, A., & Chammah, A. *Prisoner's dilemma*. Ann Arbor: University of Michigan Press, 1965.

Rapoport, A., Guyer, M. J., & Gordon, D. G. *The 2 × 2 game*. Ann Arbor: University of Michigan Press, 1976.

Ratcliffe, J. M. (Ed.). *The Good Samaritan and the law*. Garden City, N.Y.: Doubleday Anchor, 1966.

Rather, D., & Gates, G. P. *The palace guard*. New York: Harper & Row, 1974.

Raven, B. H. Social influence and power. In I. D. Steiner & M. Fishbein (Eds.), *Current studies in social psychology*. New York: Holt, Rinehart & Winston, 1965. Pp. 371–382.

Raven, B. H. The comparative analysis of power and power preference. In J. T. Tedeschi (Ed.), *Perspectives on social power*. Chicago: Aldine, 1974. Pp. 172–198.

Raven, B. H., & Eachus, H. T. Cooperation and competition in means-interdependent triads. *Journal of Abnormal and Social Psychology*, 1963, *67*, 307–316.

Rawlings, E. I. Reactive guilt and anticipatory guilt in altruistic behavior. In J. Macaulay & L. Berkowitz (Eds.), *Altruism and helping behavior: Social psychological studies of some antecedents and consequences*. New York: Academic Press, 1970. Pp. 163–177.

Rayko, D. S. Does knowledge matter? Psychological information and bystander helping. *Canadian Journal of Behavioural Science*, 1977, *9*, 295–304.

Raynor, J. O. Future orientation and motivation of immediate activity: An elaboration of the theory of achievement motivation. *Psychological Review*, 1969, *76*, 606–610.

Raynor, J. O. Future orientation in the study of achievement motivation. In J. W. Atkinson & J. O. Raynor (Eds.), *Motivation and achievement*. Washington, D.C.: Winston, 1974. Pp. 121–154.

Reed, T. E. Caucasian genes in American Negroes. *Science*, 1969, *165*, 762–768.

Regan, D. T., & Fazio, R. H. On the consistency between attitudes and behavior: Look to the method of attitude formation. *Journal of Experimental Social Psychology*, 1977, *13*, 28–45.

Regan, D. T., Strauss, E., & Fazio, R. Liking and the attribution process. *Journal of Experimental Social Psychology*, 1974, *10*, 385–397.

Reichner, R. F. Differential responses to being ignored: The effects of architectural design and social density on interpersonal behavior. *Journal of Applied Social Psychology*, 1979, *9*(1), 13–26.

Reiss, I. *Premarital sexual standards in America*. New York: Free Press, 1960.

Reiss, I. *The social context of premarital sexual permissiveness*. New York: Holt, Rinehart & Winston, 1967.

Reuben, D. *Everything you always wanted to know about sex but were afraid to ask*. New York: David McKay, 1969.

Rice, R. W. Construct validity of the least preferred coworker score. *Psychological Bulletin*, 1978, *85*, 1199–1237.

Rice, R. W., Bender, L. R., & Vitters, A. G. *Organizational Behavior and Human Performance*, 1980, *25*, 46–78.

Richer, S., & Laporte, P. Culture, cognition, and English-French competition. In D. Koulack & D. Perlman (Eds.), *Readings in social psychology: Focus on Canada*. Toronto: Wiley, 1973. Pp. 49–58.

Rider, R. V., Taback, M., & Knobloch, H. Associations between premature birth and socio-economic status. *American Journal of Public Health*, 1955, *45*, 1022–1028.

Riesman, D. (in association with N. Glazer and R. Denney). *The lonely crowd: A study of the changing American character*. New Haven: Yale University

Press, 1950.

Ring, K. Experimental social psychology: Some sober questions about frivolous values. *Journal of Experimental Social Psychology*, 1967, *3*, 113–123.

Ring, K. *Let's get started: An appeal to what's left in psychology.* Unpublished manuscript, Department of Psychology, University of Connecticut, 1971.

Ring, K., Lipinski, C. E., & Braginsky, D. The relationship of birth order to self-evaluation, anxiety reduction, and susceptibility to emotional contagion. *Psychological Monographs*, 1965, *79*(10, Whole No. 603).

Ring, K., Wallston, K., & Corey, M. Mode of debriefing as a factor affecting subjective reactions to a Milgram-type obedience situation. *Representative Research in Social Psychology*, 1970, *1*, 67–85.

Ringer, R. J. *Looking out for number one.* New York: Fawcett, 1978.

Ringer, R. J. *Winning through intimidation.* New York: Fawcett, 1979.

Roberts, A. H., & Jessor, R. Authoritarianism, punitiveness, and perceived social status. *Journal of Abnormal and Social Psychology*, 1958, *56*, 311–314.

Rochester, S. R. The significance of pauses in spontaneous speech. *Journal of Psycholinguistic Research*, 1973, *2*, 51–81.

Rodin, J. Density, perceived choice, and response to controllable and uncontrollable outcomes. *Journal of Experimental Social Psychology*, 1976, *12*, 564–578.

Rodin, J. Somatopsychics and attribution. *Personality and Social Psychology Bulletin*, 1978, *4*, 531–540.

Rodin, J., & Janis, I. L. The social power of health-care practitioners as agents of change. *Journal of Social Issues*, 1979, *35*, 60–81.

Rodin, J., & Langer, E. J. Long-term effects of a control-relevant intervention with the institutionalized aged. *Journal of Personality and Social Psychology*, 1977, *35*, 897–902.

Rodin, J., Solomon, S. K., & Metcalf, J. Role of control in mediating perceptions of density. *Journal of Personality and Social Psychology*, 1978, *36*, 988–999.

Roethlisberger, F. J., & Dickson, W. J. *Management and the worker.* Cambridge, Mass.: Harvard University Press, 1939.

Rogers, C. R. A note on the "nature of man." *Journal of Counseling Psychology*, 1957, *4*, 199–203.

Rogers, C. R. *Freedom to learn.* Columbus, Ohio: Charles E. Merrill, 1969.

Rogers, L. E., & Farace, R. V. Analysis of relational communication in dyads: New measurement procedures. *Human Communication Research*, 1975, *1* (3), 222–239.

Rogers, R. W. A protection motivation theory of fear appeals and attitude change. *Journal of Psychology*, 1975, *91*, 93–114.

Rohe, W., & Patterson, A. H. The effects of varied levels of resources and density on behavior in a day care center. In D. H. Carson (Ed.), *EDRA 5: Man-environment interactions.* Milwaukee, Wis.: Environmental Design Research Association, 1974.

Rohner, R. P. *A worldwide study of sex differences in aggression: A universalist perspective.* Paper presented at the meeting of the Eastern Psychological Association, New York, April 1976.

Rokeach, M. *The open and closed mind.* New York: Basic Books, 1960.

Rokeach, M. *Beliefs, attitudes, and values.* San Francisco:

Jossey-Bass, 1968.

Rokeach, M. Faith, hope, bigotry. *Psychology Today*, 1970, *3*(11), 33–37ff.

Rokeach, M. *The nature of human values.* New York: Free Press, 1973.

Rokeach, M., & Mezei, L. Race and shared belief as factors in social choice. *Science*, 1966, *151*, 167–172.

Rokeach, M., Smith, P. W., & Evans, R. I. Two kinds of prejudice or one? In M. Rokeach, *The open and closed mind.* New York: Basic Books, 1960. Pp. 196–214.

Rollin, B. Everything Dr. Reuben doesn't know about sex. *Playboy*, 1972, *19*(11), 123–126 *ff.* (November issue)

Ronis, D. L., Baumgardner, M. H., Leippe, M. R., Cacioppo, J. T., & Greenwald, A. G. In search of reliable persuasion effects: I. A computer-controlled procedure for studying persuasion. *Journal of Personality and Social Psychology*, 1977, *35*, 548–569.

Rook, K. S., & Hammen, C. L. A cognitive perspective on the experience of sexual arousal. *Journal of Social Issues*, 1977, *33*(2), 7–29.

Rose, A. M. Anti-Semitism's root in city-hatred. *Commentary*, 1948, *6*, 374–378.

Rosen, B. C., & D'Andrade, R. The psychosocial origins of achievement motivation. *Sociometry*, 1959, *22*, 188–218.

Rosen, E. Differences between volunteers and non-volunteers for psychological studies. *Journal of Applied Psychology*, 1951, *35*, 185–193.

Rosen, S. Post-decision affinity for incompatible information. *Journal of Abnormal and Social Psychology*, 1961, *63*, 188–190.

Rosenbaum, R. Tales of the heartbreak biz. *Esquire*, 1974, *82*(1), 67–73; 155–158.

Rosenberg, L. A. Group size, prior experience, and conformity. *Journal of Abnormal and Social Psychology*, 1961, *63*, 436–437.

Rosenberg, M. J. When dissonance fails: On eliminating evaluation apprehension from attitude measurement. *Journal of Personality and Social Psychology*, 1965, *1*, 28–42.

Rosenberg, S., & Jones, R. A. A method for investigating and representing a person's implicit theory of personality: Theodore Dreiser's view of people. *Journal of Personality and Social Psychology*, 1972, *22*, 372–386.

Rosenberg, S., Nelson, C., & Vivekananthan, P. S. A multidimensional approach to the structure of personality impressions. *Journal of Personality and Social Psychology*, 1968, *9*, 283–294.

Rosenberg, S., & Sedlak, A. Structural representations of implicit personality theory. In L. Berkowitz (Ed.), *Advances in experimental social psychology* (Vol. 6). New York: Academic Press, 1972. Pp. 235–297.

Rosenblatt, P. C., & Stevenson, L. G. *Territoriality and privacy in married and unmarried cohabitating couples.* Unpublished manuscript, University of Minnesota, 1973.

Rosenfeld, H. M. Effect of an approval-seeking induction on interpersonal proximity. *Psychological Reports*, 1965, *17*, 120–122.

Rosenhan, D. The natural socialization of altruistic autonomy. In J. Macaulay & L. Berkowitz (Eds.), *Altruism and helping behavior: Social psychological studies of some antecedents and consequences.* New York: Academic Press, 1970. Pp. 251–268.

Rosenhan, D. L. Toward resolving the altruism paradox:

Affect, self-reinforcement, and cognition. In L. Wispé (Ed.), *Altruism, sympathy, and helping: Psychological and sociological principles.* New York: Academic Press, 1978. Pp. 101–113.

Rosenkoetter, L. I. Resistance to temptation: Inhibitory and disinhibitory effects of models. *Developmental Psychology,* 1973, *8,* 80–84.

Rosenkrantz, P. S., & Crockett, W. H. Some factors influencing the assimilation of disparate information in impression formation. *Journal of Personality and Social Psychology,* 1965, *2,* 397–402.

Rosenkrantz, P. S., Vogel, S. R., Bee, H., Broverman, I. K., & Broverman, D. M. Sex-role stereotypes and self-concepts in college students. *Journal of Consulting and Clinical Psychology,* 1968, *32,* 287–295.

Rosenthal, R. *Experimenter effects in behavioral research.* New York: Appleton-Century-Crofts, 1966.

Rosenthal, R., & DePaulo, B. M. Sex differences in eavesdropping on nonverbal cues. *Journal of Personality and Social Psychology,* 1979, *37,* 273–285.

Rosenthal, R., & Rosnow, R. L. *The volunteer subject.* New York: Wiley, 1975.

Rosnow, R. L. Whatever happened to the "Law of Primacy"? *Journal of Communication,* 1966, *16,* 10–31.

Rosnow, R. L., & Arms, R. L. Adding versus averaging as a stimulus-combination rule in forming impressions of groups. *Journal of Personality and Social Psychology,* 1968, *10,* 363–369.

Rosnow, R., & Robinson, E. (Eds.). *Experiments in persuasion.* New York: Academic Press, 1967.

Ross, A. S. Effect of increased responsibility on bystander intervention: The presence of children. *Journal of Personality and Social Psychology,* 1971, *19,* 306–310.

Ross, H. L., Campbell, D. T., & Glass, G. V. Determining the social effects of a legal reform: The British "Breathalyser" crackdown of 1967. *American Behavioral Scientist,* 1970, *13* (4), 493–509.

Ross, L. The intuitive psychologist and his shortcomings: Distortions in the attribution process. In L. Berkowitz (Ed.), *Advances in experimental social psychology* (Vol. 10). New York: Academic Press, 1977. Pp. 173–220.

Ross, L. D., Amabile, T. M., & Steinmetz, J. L. Social roles, social control, and biases in social-perception processes. *Journal of Personality and Social Psychology,* 1977, *35,* 485–494.

Ross, M., & DiTecco, D. An attributional analysis of moral judgments. *Journal of Social Issues,* 1975, *31*(3), 91–110.

Ross, M., & Shulman, R. F. Increasing the salience of initial attitudes: Dissonance versus self-perception theory. *Journal of Personality and Social Psychology,* 1973, *28,* 138–144.

Rossi, P. H., & Williams, W. (Eds.). *Evaluating social programs: Theory, practice, and politics.* New York: Seminar Press, 1972.

Rothbart, M., Fulero, S., Jensen, C., Howard, J., & Birrell, B. From individual to group impressions: Availability heuristics in stereotype formation. *Journal of Experimental Social Psychology,* 1978, *14,* 237–255.

Rotter, J. B. *Social learning and clinical psychology.* Englewood Cliffs, N.J.: Prentice-Hall, 1954.

Rotter, J. B. Generalized expectancies for internal versus external control of reinforcement. *Psychological Monographs,* 1966, *80*(1, Whole No. 609).

Rotter, J. B. Some problems and misconceptions related to the construct of internal versus external control of reinforcement. *Journal of Consulting and Clinical Psychology,* 1975, *43,* 56–67.

Rotter, J. B., Chance, J., & Phares, E. J. (Eds.). *Applications of a social learning theory of personality.* New York: Holt, Rinehart & Winston, 1972.

Rowland, K. F. Environmental events predicting death for the elderly. *Psychological Bulletin,* 1977, *84,* 349–372.

Rozelle, R. M., Evans, R. I., Lasater, T. M., Dembroski, T. M., & Allen, B. P. Need for approval as related to the effects of persuasive communications on actual, reported and intended behavior change—A viable predictor? *Psychological Reports,* 1973, *33,* 719–725.

Rubin, Z., Peplau, L. A., & Hill, C. T. *Loving and leaving: Sex differences in romantic attachments.* Unpublished manuscript, Brandeis University, 1978.

Rubin, Z. Measurement of romantic love. *Journal of Personality and Social Psychology,* 1970, *16,* 265–273.

Rubin, Z. *Liking and loving: An invitation to social psychology.* New York: Holt, Rinehart & Winston, 1973.

Rubin, Z., & Shenker, S. Friendship, proximity, and self-disclosure. *Journal of Personality,* 1978, *46,* 1–22.

Ruble, D. N., & Feldman, N. S. Order of consensus, distinctiveness and consistency information and causal attributions. *Journal of Personality and Social Psychology,* 1976, *34,* 930–937.

Rugg, E. A. *Social research practices opinion survey: Summary of results.* Unpublished paper, George Peabody College, May 1975.

Rule, B. G., & Ferguson, T. J. The attributional mediation of aggression. Paper presented at the meeting of the Society of Experimental Social Psychology, Princeton, N.J., November 1978.

Rule, B. G., & Hewitt, L. S. Effects of thwarting on cardiac response and physical aggression. *Journal of Personality and Social Psychology,* 1971, *19,* 181–187.

Rule, B. G., & Leger, G. J. Pain cues and differing functions of aggression. *Canadian Journal of Behavioural Science,* 1976, *8,* 213–222.

Rule, B. G., & Percival, E. The effects of frustration and attack on physical aggression. *Journal of Experimental Research in Personality,* 1971, *5,* 111–118.

Runkel, P. J., & McGrath, J. E. *Research on human behavior: A systematic guide to method.* New York: Holt, Rinehart & Winston, 1972.

Rush, M. C., Thomas, J. C., & Lord, R. G. Implicit leadership theory: A potential threat to the internal validity of leader behavior questionnaires. *Organizational Behavior and Human Performance,* 1977, *20,* 93–110.

Rushton, J. P. Generosity in children: Immediate and long-term effects of modeling, preaching, and moral judgment. *Journal of Personality and Social Psychology,* 1975, *31,* 459–466.

Rushton, J. P. Socialization and the altruistic behavior of children. *Psychological Bulletin,* 1976, *83,* 898–913.

Rushton, J. P., & Teachman, G. The effects of positive reinforcement, attributions, and punishment on model-induced altruism in children. *Personality and Social Psychology Bulletin,* 1978, *4,* 322–325.

Russell, D. *The politics of rape: The victim's perspective.* New York: Stein and Day, 1975.

Russell, J. A., & Mehrabian, A. Approach-avoidance and affiliation as functions of the emotion-eliciting quality of an environment. *Environment and Behavior,* 1978,

10(3), 355–387.

Russo, N. F. Eye contact, interpersonal distance, and the equilibrium theory. *Journal of Personality and Social Psychology*, 1975, *31*, 497–502.

Ryan, W. *Blaming the victim*. New York: Pantheon, 1971.

Rychlak, J. F. *Introduction to personality and psychotherapy: A theory-construction approach*. Boston: Houghton Mifflin, 1973.

Rychlak, J. F. Psychological science as a humanist views it. In W. J. Arnold & J. K. Cole (Eds.), *Nebraska Symposium on Motivation* (Vol. 22). Lincoln: University of Nebraska Press, 1975. Pp. 205–279.

Ryder, R. Husband-wife dyads versus married strangers. *Family Process*, 1968, *7*, 233–238.

Saarinin, T. F. Student views of the world. In R. Downs & D. Stea (Eds.), *Image and environment: Cognitive mapping and spatial behavior*. Chicago: Aldine, 1973. Pp. 148–161.

Sackeim, H. A., Gur, R. C., & Saucy, M. C. Emotions are expressed more intensely on the left side of the face. *Science*, 1978, *202*, 434–436.

Sadava, S. W. Teaching social psychology: A Canadian dilemma. *Canadian Psychological Review*, 1978, *19*, 145–151.

Saegert, S. C. *Effects of spatial and social density on arousal, mood, and social orientation*. Unpublished doctoral dissertation, University of Michigan, 1974.

Saegert, S., MacKintosh, B., & West, S. Two studies of crowding in urban public spaces. *Environment and Behavior*, 1974, *7*(2), 159–184.

Saegert, S. C., Swap, W., & Zajonc, R. B. Exposure, context, and interpersonal attraction. *Journal of Personality and Social Psychology*, 1973, *25*, 234–242.

Sahlein, W. J. *A neighborhood solution to the social services dilemma*. Lexington, Mass.: D.C. Heath, 1973.

Sahlins, M. *The use and abuse of biology*. Ann Arbor: University of Michigan Press, 1976.

Saks, M. J., & Ostrom, T. M. Jury size and consensus requirements: The laws of probability versus the laws of the land. *Journal of Contemporary Law*, 1975, *1*, 163–173.

Salancik, G. R., & Pfeffer, J. Constraints on administrator discretion: The limited influence of mayors on city budgets. *Urban Affairs Quarterly*, 1977, *12*, 475–496.

Salter, C. A., Dickey, M. J., & Gulas, D. L. Prosocial behavior as a function of location and cost of helping. *Journal of Social Psychology*, 1978, *106*, 133–134.

Sampson, E. E. Psychology and the American ideal. *Journal of Personality and Social Psychology*, 1977, *35*, 767–782.

Sanders, G. S., & Baron, R. S. The motivating effects of distraction on task performance. *Journal of Personality and Social Psychology*, 1975, *32*, 956–963.

Sanders, G. S., Baron, R. S., & Moore, D. L. Distraction and social comparison as mediators of social facilitation effects. *Journal of Experimental Social Psychology*, 1978, *14*, 291–303.

Sanford, F. H. *Authoritarianism and leadership*. Philadelphia: Institute for Research in Human Relations, 1950.

Sanford, N. The approach of the authoritarian personality. In J. L. McCary (Ed.), *Psychology of personality*. New York: Grove Press, 1956. Pp. 253–319.

Sanford, N. Whatever happened to action research? *Journal of Social Issues*, 1970, *26*(4), 3–23.

Sarbin, T. R., & Allen, V. L. Role theory. In G. Lindzey & E. Aronson (Eds.), *Handbook of social psychology* (Vol. 1) (2nd ed.). Reading, Mass.: Addison-Wesley, 1968. Pp. 488–567.

Sarnoff, I. R., & Zimbardo, P. G. Anxiety, fear, and social affiliation. *Journal of Abnormal and Social Psychology*, 1961, *62*, 356–363.

Sasfy, J., & Okun, M. Form of evaluation and audience expertness as joint determinants of audience effects. *Journal of Experimental Social Psychology*, 1974, *10*, 461–467.

Satow, K. L. *The role of social approval in altruistic behavior*. Paper presented at the meeting of the Eastern Psychological Association, Washington, D.C., April 1973.

Scarr, S., & Weinberg, R. A. IQ test performance of black children adopted by white families. *American Psychologist*, 1976, *31*, 726–739.

Scarr-Salapatek, S. Race, social class, and IQ. *Science*, 1971, *174*, 1285–1295. (a)

Scarr-Salapatek, S. Unknowns in the IQ equation. *Science*, 1971, *174*, 1223–1228. (b)

Schachter, S. Deviation, rejection, and communication. *Journal of Abnormal and Social Psychology*, 1951, *46*, 190–207.

Schachter, S. *The psychology of affiliation*. Stanford, Calif.: Stanford University Press, 1959.

Schachter, S. The interaction of cognitive and physiological determinants of emotional state. In L. Berkowitz (Ed.), *Advances in experimental social psychology* (Vol. 1). New York: Academic Press, 1964.

Schachter, S., Ellertson, N., McBride, D., & Gregory, D. An experimental study of cohesiveness and productivity. *Human Relations*, 1951, *4*, 229–238.

Schachter, S., & Singer, J. Cognitive, social, and physiological determinants of emotional state. *Psychological Review*, 1962, *69*, 379–399.

Schaps, E. Cost, dependency, and helping. *Journal of Personality and Social Psychology*, 1972, *21*, 74–78.

Scheflen, A. *Body language and the social order*. Englewood Cliffs, N.J.: Prentice-Hall, 1972.

Schein, E. H. Reaction patterns to severe chronic stress in American army prisoners of war of the Chinese. *Journal of Social Issues*, 1957, *13*(3), 21–30.

Schein, E. H. *Organizational psychology* (2nd ed.). Englewood Cliffs, N.J.: Prentice-Hall, 1971.

Schellenberg, J. A. *An introduction to social psychology* (2nd ed.). New York: Random House, 1974.

Schill, T., & Chapin, J. Sex guilt and males' preference for reading erotic literature. *Journal of Consulting and Clinical Psychology*, 1972, *39*, 516.

Schlenker, B. R. Social psychology and science. *Journal of Personality and Social Psychology*, 1974, *29*, 1–15.

Schlenker, B. R., & Forsyth, D. R. On the ethics of psychological research. *Journal of Experimental Social Psychology*, 1977, *13*, 369–396.

Schlosberg, H. Three dimensions of emotion. *Psychological Review*, 1954, *61*, 81–88.

Schmidt, G., & Sigusch, V. Sex differences in responses to psychosexual stimulation by film and slides. *Journal of Sex Research*, 1970, *6*, 268–283.

Schmidt, G., Sigusch, V., & Meyberg, V. Psychosexual stimulation in men: Emotional reactions, changes of sex behavior, and measures of conservative attitudes. *Journal of Sex Research*, 1969, *5*, 199–217.

Schneider, B., & Bartlett, C. J. Individual differences

and organizational climate. II: Measurement of organizational climate by the multitrait-multirater matrix. *Personnel Psychology*, 1970, *23*, 493–512.

Schneider, D. J. Tactical self-presentation after success and failure. *Journal of Personality and Social Psychology*, 1969, *13*, 262–268.

Schneider, D. J. Implicit personality theory: A review. *Psychological Bulletin*, 1973, *79*, 294–309.

Schneider, D. J., Hastorf, A. H., & Ellsworth, P. C. *Person perception* (2nd ed.). Reading, Mass.: Addison-Wesley, 1979.

Schneider, F. W. When will a stranger lend a helping hand? *Journal of Social Psychology*, 1973, *90*, 335–336.

Schneier, C. E. The contingency model of leadership: An extension to emergent leadership and leader's sex. *Organizational Behavior and Human Performance*, 1978, *21*, 220–239.

Schoenfeld, W. N. Notes on a bit of psychological nonsense: "Race differences in intelligence." *Psychological Record*, 1974, *24*, 17–32.

Schriesheim, C., & Kerr, S. Psychometric properties of the Ohio State leadership scales. *Psychological Bulletin*, 1974, *81*, 756–765.

Schulz, R., & Barefoot, J. Nonverbal responses and affiliative conflict theory. *British Journal of Social and Clinical Psychology*, 1974, *13*, 237–243.

Schwartz, G. E., Fair, P. L., Salt, P., Mandel, M. R., & Klerman, G. L. Facial muscle patterning to affective imagery in depressed and nondepressed subjects. *Science*, 1976, *192*, 489–491.

Schwartz, S. Effects of sex guilt and arousal on the retention of birth control information. *Journal of Consulting and Clinical Psychology*, 1973, *41*, 61–64.

Schwartz, S. H. Normative explanations of helping behavior: A critique, proposal, and empirical test. *Journal of Experimental Social Psychology*, 1973, *9*, 349–364.

Schwartz, S. H. Normative influences on altruism. In L. Berkowitz (Ed.), *Advances in experimental social psychology* (Vol. 10). New York: Academic Press, 1977. Pp. 222–279.

Schwartz, S. H. Temporal instability as a moderator of the attitude-behavior relationship. *Journal of Personality and Social Psychology*, 1978, *36*, 715–724.

Schwartz, S. H., & Clausen, G. T. Responsibility, norms, and helping in an emergency. *Journal of Personality and Social Psychology*, 1970, *16*, 299–310.

Schwartz, S. H., & Fleishman, J. A. Personal norms and the mediation of legitimacy effects on helping. *Social Psychology Quarterly*, 1978, *41*, 306–315.

Schweitzer, D., & Ginsburg, G. P. Factors in communication credibility. In C. W. Backman & P. F. Secord (Eds.), *Problems in social psychology*. New York: McGraw-Hill, 1966. Pp. 94–102.

Scott, F. G. Family group structure and patterns of social interaction. *American Journal of Sociology*, 1962, *68*, 214–228.

Scott, J. P. *Aggression*. Chicago: University of Chicago Press, 1958.

Scott, R. L. Communication as an intentional, social system. *Human Communication Research*, 1977, *3*, 258–267.

Sears, D. O. Political behavior. In G. Lindzey & E. Aronson (Eds.), *The handbook of social psychology* (2nd ed.) (Vol. 5). Reading, Mass.: Addison-Wesley, 1969. Pp. 315–458.

Sears, R., Maccoby, E., & Levin, H. *Patterns of child rearing*. Evanston, Ill.: Row, Peterson, 1957.

Selby, J. W., Calhoun, L. G., & Brock, T. A. Sex differences in the social perception of rape victims. *Personality and Social Psychology Bulletin*, 1977, *3*, 412–415.

Seligman, C., & Darley, J. M. Feedback as a means of decreasing residential energy consumption. *Journal of Applied Psychology*, 1977, *62*, 363–368.

Seligman, C., Kriss, M., Darley, J. M., Fazio, R. H., Becker, L. J., & Pryor, J. B. Predicting summer energy consumption from homeowners' attitudes. *Journal of Applied Social Psychology*, 1979, *9*, 70–90.

Seligman, M.E.P. *Helplessness: On depression, development, and death*. San Francisco: W. H. Freeman, 1975.

Selltiz, C., Wrightsman, L. S., & Cook, S. W. *Research methods in social relations* (3rd ed.). New York: Holt, Rinehart & Winston, 1976.

Selye, H. The evolution of the stress concept. In L. Levi (Ed.), *Society, stress, and disease* (Vol. I). London: Oxford University Press, 1971.

Severy, L. J., & Ashton, N. L. *Measuring differing prosocial tendencies*. Paper presented at the meeting of the Southeastern Psychological Association, New Orleans, April 1973.

Seyfried, B. A., & Hendrick, C. When do opposites attract? When they are opposite in sex and sex-role attitudes. *Journal of Personality and Social Psychology*, 1973, *25*, 15–20.

Shaffer, D. R. Some effects of consonant and dissonant attitudinal advocacy on initial attitude salience and attitude change. *Journal of Personality and Social Psychology*, 1975, *32*, 160–168.(a)

Shaffer, D. R. *Some effects of initial attitude importance on attitude change*. Paper presented at the meeting of the Southeastern Psychological Association, Atlanta, April 1975. (Also in *Journal of Social Psychology*, 1975, *97*, 279–288)(b)

Shaffer, D. R. Social psychology from a social-developmental perspective. In C. Hendrick (Ed.), *Perspectives on social psychology*. Potomac, Md.: Erlbaum, 1977.

Shannon, C., & Weaver, W. *The mathematical theory of communication*. Urbana: University of Illinois Press, 1949.

Shanteau, J., & Nagy, G. F. Probability of acceptance in dating choice. *Journal of Personality and Social Psychology*, 1979, *37*, 522–533.

Shantz, C. U. *Empathy in relation to social cognitive development*. Paper presented at the meeting of the American Psychological Association, New Orleans, September 1974.

Shapira, A., & Madsen, M. C. Cooperative and competitive behavior of kibbutz and urban children in Israel. *Child Development*, 1969, *40*, 609–617.

Sharp, G. *Exploring nonviolent alternatives*. Boston: Porter Sargent, 1970.

Sharp, G. *The politics of nonviolent action*. Philadelphia, Pa.: Pilgrim Press, 1971.

Shaver, K. G. *An introduction to attribution processes*. Cambridge, Mass.: Winthrop, 1973.

Shaver, P. European perspectives on the crisis in social psychology. *Contemporary Psychology*, 1974, *19*, 356–358.

Shaw, J. I., & Skolnick, P. An investigation of relative preference for consistency motivation. *European Journal of Social Psychology*, 1973, *3*, 271–280.

Shaw, M. E. A comparison of individuals and small groups in the rational solution of complex problems. *American Journal of Psychology*, 1932, *44*, 491–504.

Shaw, M. E. Some effects of unequal distribution of information upon group performance in various communication nets. *Journal of Abnormal and Social Psychology*, 1954, *49*, 547–553.

Shaw, M. E. *Scaling group tasks: A method for dimensional analysis.* Unpublished manuscript, Department of Psychology, University of Florida, 1963. (Mimeographed)

Shaw, M. E. Communication networks. In L. Berkowitz (Ed.), *Advances in experimental social psychology* (Vol. 1). New York: Academic Press, 1964. Pp. 111–147.

Shaw, M. E. *Group dynamics: The psychology of small group behavior.* New York: McGraw-Hill, 1976.

Shaw, M. E. Communication networks fourteen years later. In L. Berkowitz (Ed.), *Group processes.* New York: Academic Press, 1978. Pp. 351–361.

Shaw, M. E., & Costanzo, P. R. *Theories of social psychology.* New York: McGraw-Hill, 1970.

Shaw, M. E., & Gilchrist, J. C. Intragroup communication and leader choice. *Journal of Social Psychology*, 1956, *43*, 133–138.

Shaw, M. E., & Rothschild, G. H. Some effects of prolonged experience in communication nets. *Journal of Applied Psychology*, 1956, *40*, 281–286.

Sheehy, G. *Passages: Predictable crises of adult life.* New York: Dutton, 1976.

Shein, V. E. The relationship between sex-role stereotypes and requisite management characteristics. *Journal of Applied Psychology*, 1973, *57*, 95–100.

Shein, V. E. Relationships between sex-role stereotypes and requisite management characteristics among female managers. *Journal of Applied Psychology*, 1975, *60*, 340–344.

Sheldon, E. G., & Freeman, H. E. *Notes on social indicators: Promises and potential.* New York: American Elsevier, 1970.

Sherif, C. W., Sherif, M., & Nebergall, R. E. *Attitude and attitude change: The social judgment approach.* Philadelphia: Saunders, 1965.

Sherif, M. A study of some social factors in perception. *Archives of Psychology*, 1935, *27*, No. 187, 1–60.

Sherif, M. *In common predicament: Social psychology of intergroup conflict and cooperation.* Boston: Houghton Mifflin, 1966.

Sherif, M., Harvey, O. J., White, B. J., Hood, W. E., & Sherif, C. W. *Intergroup conflict and cooperation: The Robber's Cave experiment.* Norman: University of Oklahoma Book Exchange, 1961.

Sherif, M., & Hovland, C. *Social judgment.* New Haven, Conn.: Yale University Press, 1961.

Sherif, M., Taub, D., & Hovland, C. I. Assimilation and contrast effects of anchoring stimuli on judgments. *Journal of Experimental Psychology*, 1958, *55*, 150–155.

Sherman, J. A. *On the psychology of women.* Springfield, Ill.: Charles C Thomas, 1971.

Sherrod, D. R. Crowding, perceived control, and behavioral aftereffects. *Journal of Applied Social Psychology*, 1974, *4*(2), 171–186.

Sherrod, D., Armstrong, D., Hewitt, J., Madonia, B., Speno, S., & Teruya, D. Environmental attention, affect and altruism. *Journal of Applied Social Psychology*, 1977, *7*, 359–371.

Sherrod, D. R., & Downs, R. Environmental determinants of altruism: The effects of stimulus overload and perceived control on helping. *Journal of Experimental Social Psychology*, 1974, *10*, 468–479.

Sherwood, J. J. Authoritarianism, moral realism, and President Kennedy's death. *British Journal of Social and Clinical Psychology*, 1966, *5*, 264–269.

Sherwood, J. J., Barron, J. W., & Fitch, H. G. Cognitive dissonance: Theory and research. In R. V. Wagner & J. J. Sherwood (Eds.), *The study of attitude change.* Monterey, Calif.: Brooks/Cole, 1969. Pp. 56–86.

Shields, S. A. Functionalism, Darwinism, and the psychology of women. *American Psychologist*, 1975, *30*, 739–754.

Shiflett, S. Toward a general model of small group productivity. *Psychological Bulletin*, 1979, *86*, 67–79.

Shosteck, H. Respondent militancy as a control variable for interviewer effect. *Journal of Social Issues*, 1977, *33*(4), 36–45.

Shrum, R. Symbols of our times. *New Times*, February 18, 1977, p. 6.

Shuntich, R. J., & Taylor, S. P. The effects of alcohol on human physical aggression. *Journal of Experimental Research in Personality*, 1972, *6*, 34–38.

Siegel, J. M., & Loftus, E. F. Impact of anxiety and life stress upon eyewitness testimony. *Bulletin of the Psychonomic Society*, 1978, *12*, 479–480.

Siegman, A. W. A cross-cultural investigation of the relationship between ethnic prejudice, authoritarian ideology, and personality. *Journal of Abnormal and Social Psychology*, 1961, *63*, 654–655.

Sigall, H. E., Aronson, E., & Van Hoose, T. The cooperative subject: Myth or reality? *Journal of Experimental Social Psychology*, 1970, *6*, 1–10.

Sigall, H., & Landy, D. Radiating beauty: The effects of having a physically attractive partner on person perception. *Journal of Personality and Social Psychology*, 1973, *28*, 218–224.

Silverman, I. Physical attractiveness and courtship. *Sexual Behavior*, September 1971, pp. 22–25.

Silverman, I. Why social psychology fails. *Canadian Psychological Review*, 1977, *18*, 353–358.

Silverthorne, C. P., & Mazmanian, L. The effects of heckling and media of presentation on the impact of a persuasive communication. *Journal of Social Psychology*, 1975, *96*, 229–236.

Simon, L. M., & Leavitt, E. A. The relation between Wechsler-Bellevue IQ scores and occupational area. *Occupations*, 1950, *29*, 23–25.

Simonton, D. K. Multiple discovery and invention: Zeitgeist, genius, or chance? *Journal of Personality and Social Psychology*, 1979, *37*, 1603–1616.

Simpson, E. Moral development research: A case study of scientific cultural bias. *Human Development*, 1974, *17*(2), 81–106.

Singer, J. E. The use of manipulative strategies: Machiavellianism and attractiveness. *Sociometry*, 1964, *27*, 128–140.

Singer, J. E., & Glass, D. C. Some reflections upon losing our social psychological purity. In M. Deutsch & H. A. Hornstein (Eds.), *Applying social psychology: Implications for research, practice, and training.* Hillsdale, N.J.: Erlbaum, 1975. Pp. 15–31.

Singer, J. E., & Shockley, V. L. Ability and evaluation. *Journal of Personality and Social Psychology*, 1965, *1*, 95–100.

Sistrunk, F., & McDavid, J. W. Sex variables in conforming behavior. *Journal of Personality and Social Psychology*, 1971, *17*, 200–207.

Sizer, M. F., & Sizer, T. R. *Moral education*. Cambridge, Mass.: Harvard University Press, 1970.

Skinner, B. F. *Walden two*. New York: Macmillan, 1948.

Skinner, B. F. *Science and human behavior*. New York: Macmillan, 1953.

Skinner, B. F. *Beyond freedom and dignity*. New York: Knopf, 1971.

Skrypnek, B. J., & Snyder, M. *On the self-perpetuating nature of stereotypes about women and men*. Unpublished manuscript, University of Minnesota, 1979.

Slater, P. E. Contrasting correlates of group size. *Sociometry*, 1958, *25*, 129–139.

Sloan, L. R., Love, R. E., & Ostrom, T. M. Political heckling: Who really loses? *Journal of Personality and Social Psychology*, 1974, *30*, 518–525.

Slosnerick, M. *Social interaction by preschool children in conditions of crowding*. Paper presented at the meeting of the Midwestern Psychological Association, Chicago, May 1974.

Smedley, J. W., & Bayton, J. A. Evaluative race-class stereotypes by race and perceived class of subjects. *Journal of Personality and Social Psychology*, 1978, *36*, 530–535.

Smigel, E. O., & Seiden, R. The decline and fall of the double standard. *Annals of the American Academy of Political and Social Sciences*, 1968, *376*, 1–14.

Smith, M. B. Is experimental social psychology advancing? *Journal of Experimental Social Psychology*, 1972, *8*, 86–96.

Smith, M. B., Bruner, J. S., & White, R. W. *Opinions and personality*. New York: Wiley, 1956.

Smith, P. W., & Brigham, J. C. The functional approach to attitude change: An attempt at operationalization. *Representative Research in Social Psychology*, 1972, *3*, 73–80.

Smith, R. E., Keating, J. P., Hester, R. K., & Mitchell, H. E. Role and justice considerations in the attribution of responsibility to a rape victim. *Journal of Research in Personality*, 1976, *10*, 346–357.

Smith, R. G. Source credibility context effects. *Speech Monographs*, 1973, *40*, 303–309.

Snyder, C. R., & Fromkin, H. L. Abnormality as a positive characteristic: The development and validation of a scale measuring need for uniqueness. *Journal of Abnormal Psychology*, 1977, *86*, 518–527.

Snyder, C. R., & Fromkin, H. L. *Uniqueness: The human pursuit of difference*. New York: Plenum Press, 1980.

Snyder, M. The self-monitoring of expressive behavior. *Journal of Personality and Social Psychology*, 1974, *30*, 526–537.

Snyder, M. Self-monitoring processes. In L. Berkowitz (Ed.), *Advances in experimental social psychology* (Vol. 12). New York: Academic Press, 1979. Pp. 85–128.

Snyder, M., & Cunningham, M. R. To comply or not to comply: Testing the self-perception explanation of the "foot-in-the-door" phenomenon. *Journal of Personality and Social Psychology*, 1975, *31*, 64–67.

Snyder, M., & Ebbesen, E. B. Dissonance awareness: A test of dissonance theory versus self-perception theory. *Journal of Experimental Social Psychology*, 1972, *8*, 502–517.

Snyder, M., & Monson, T. C. Persons, situations, and the control of social behavior. *Journal of Personality and Social Psychology*, 1975, *32*, 637–644.

Snyder, M., & Rothbart, M. Communicator attractiveness and opinion change. *Canadian Journal of Behavioural Science*, 1971, *3*, 377–387.

Snyder, M., & Swann, W. B., Jr. When actions reflect attitudes: The politics of impression management. *Journal of Personality and Social Psychology*, 1976, *34*, 1034–1042.

Snyder, M., & Swann, W. B., Jr. Behavioral confirmation in social interaction: From social perception to social reality. *Journal of Experimental Social Psychology*, 1978, *14*, 148–162.

Snyder, M., & Tanke, E. D. Behavior and attitude: Some people are more consistent than others. *Journal of Personality*, 1976, *44*, 510–517.

Snyder, M., Tanke, E. D., & Berscheid, E. Social perception and interpersonal behavior: On the self-fulfilling nature of social stereotypes. *Journal of Personality and Social Psychology*, 1977, *35*, 656–666.

Snyder, M., & Uranowitz, S. W. Reconstructing the past: Some cognitive consequences of person perception. *Journal of Personality and Social Psychology*, 1978, *36*, 941–950.

Snyder, M. L., & Mentzer, S. Social perspectives on the physician's feelings and behavior. *Personality and Social Psychology Bulletin*, 1978, *4*, 541–547.

Snyder, M. L., & Wicklund, R. A. Prior exercise of freedom and reactance. *Journal of Experimental Social Psychology*, 1976, *12*, 120–130.

Sole, K., Marton, J., & Hornstein, H. A. Opinion similarity and helping: Three field experiments investigating the bases of promotive tension. *Journal of Experimental Social Psychology*, 1975, *11*, 1–13.

Solly, C. M. Effects of stress on perceptual attention. In B. P. Rourke (Ed.), *Explorations in the psychology of stress and anxiety*. Ontario: Longmans Canada Ltd., 1969. Pp. 1–14.

Solomon, L. Z., Solomon, H., & Stone, R. Helping as a function of number of bystanders and ambiguity of emergency. *Personality and Social Psychology Bulletin*, 1978, *4*, 318–321.

Solomon, S., & Saxe, L. What is intelligent, as well as attractive, is good. *Personality and Social Psychology Bulletin*, 1977, *3*, 670–673.

Sommer, R. Studies in personal space. *Sociometry*, 1959, *22*, 247–260.

Sommer, R. The distance for comfortable conversation: A further study. *Sociometry*, 1962, *25*, 111–116.

Sommer, R. The ecology of privacy. *The Library Quarterly*, 1966, *36*, 234–248.

Sommer, R. Classroom ecology. *The Journal of Applied Behavioral Science*, 1967, *3*(4), 489–503.

Sommer, R. *Personal space: The behavioral basis of design*. Englewood Cliffs, N.J.: Prentice-Hall, 1969.

Sommer, R. *Tight spaces*. Englewood Cliffs, N.J.: Prentice-Hall, 1974.

Sommer, R., & Becker, F. D. Territorial defense and the good neighbor. *Journal of Personality and Social Psychology*, 1969, *11*, 85–92.

Sommer, R., & Ross, H. Social interaction on a geriatrics ward. *International Journal of Social Psychiatry*, 1958, *4*, 128–133.

Sontag, S. *Illness as metaphor*. New York: Farrar, Straus and Giroux, 1978.

Sorenson, R. C. *Adolescent sexuality in contemporary America*. New York: World Publishing, 1973.

Sorrentino, R. M., & Boutilier, R. G. Evaluation of a victim as a function of fate similarity/dissimilarity. *Journal of Experimental Social Psychology*, 1974, *10*, 84–93.

Sorrentino, R. M., & Short, J.A.C. The case of the mysterious moderates: Why motives sometimes fail to predict behavior. *Journal of Personality and Social Psychology*, 1977, *35*, 478–484.

Southwick, C. H. The population dynamics of confined house mice supplied with unlimited food. *Ecology*, 1955, *36*, 212–225.

Spence, J. T., & Helmreich, R. Who likes competent women? Competence, sex-role congruence of interests, and subjects' attitudes toward women as determinants of interpersonal attraction. *Journal of Applied Social Psychology*, 1972, *3*, 197–213.

Spence, J. T., & Helmreich, R. L. *Masculinity and femininity: Their psychological dimensions, correlates, and antecedents.* Austin: University of Texas Press, 1978.

Spence, J. T., Helmreich, R. L., & Deaux, K. Sex roles and sex differences. In G. Lindzey & E. Aronson (Eds.), *Handbook of social psychology* (3rd ed.). Reading, Mass.: Addison-Wesley, 1981.

Spence, J. T., Helmreich, R., & Stapp, J. The Personal Attributes Questionnaire: A measure of sex-role stereotypes and masculinity-femininity. *JSAS Catalog of Selected Documents in Psychology*, 1974, *4*, 127.

Spence, J. T., Helmreich, R., & Stapp, J. Ratings of self and peers on sex-role attributes and their relation to self-esteem and conceptions of masculinity and femininity. *Journal of Personality and Social Psychology*, 1975, *32*, 29–39.

Sprafkin, J. N., Liebert, R. M., & Poulos, R. W. Effects of a prosocial televised example on children's helping. *Journal of Experimental Child Psychology*, 1975, *20*, 119–126.

Staats, A. W. An outline of an integrated learning theory of attitude formation and function. In M. Fishbein (Ed.), *Readings in attitude theory and measurement.* New York: Wiley, 1967. Pp. 373–376.

Staats, A. W. Social behaviorism and human motivation: Principles of the attitude-reinforcer-discriminative system. In A. G. Greenwald, T. C. Brock, & T. M. Ostrom (Eds.), *Psychological foundations of attitudes.* New York: Academic Press, 1968. Pp. 33–66.

Staats, A. W., & Staats, C. K. Attitudes established by classical conditioning. *Journal of Abnormal and Social Psychology*, 1958, *57*, 37–40.

Stang, D. J. Conformity, ability, and self-esteem. *Representative Research in Social Psychology*, 1972, *3*, 97–103.

Stang, D. J. Effect of interaction rate on ratings of leadership and liking. *Journal of Personality and Social Psychology*, 1973, *27*, 405–408.

Stang, D. J. Group size effects on conformity. *Journal of Social Psychology*, 1976, *98*, 175–181.

Staub, E. Helping a distressed person: Social, personality, and stimulus determinants. In L. Berkowitz (Ed.), *Advances in experimental social psychology* (Vol. 7). New York: Academic Press, 1974. Pp. 293–341.

Staub, E. (Ed.). *Positive social behavior and morality* (Vol. 1). *Social and personal influences.* New York: Academic Press, 1978.

Staub, E. (Ed.). *Positive social behavior and morality* (Vol. 2). *Socialization and development.* New York:

Academic Press, 1979.

Steele, F. I. Physical settings and organization development. In H. Hornstein, W. Burke, B. Benedict, R. Lewicki, & M. Hornstein (Eds.), *Strategies of social change: A behavioral science analysis.* Glencoe, Ill.: The Free Press, 1971.

Steigleder, M. K., Weiss, R. F., Cramer, R. E., & Feinberg, R. A. Motivating and reinforcing functions of competitive behavior. *Journal of Personality and Social Psychology*, 1978, *36*, 1291–1301.

Stein, A. H. A view through the electronic window. *Contemporary Psychology*, 1974, *19*, 438–439.

Stein, A. H., & Bailey, M. M. The socialization of achievement orientation in females. *Psychological Bulletin*, 1973, *80*, 345–366.

Stein, D. D., Hardyck, J. A., & Smith, M. B. Race and belief: An open and shut case. *Journal of Personality and Social Psychology*, 1965, *1*, 281–289.

Stein, R. T. Identifying emergent leaders from verbal and nonverbal communications. *Journal of Personality and Social Psychology*, 1975, *32*, 125–135.

Stein, R. T., Geis, F. L., & Damarin, F. The perception of emergent leadership hierarchies in task groups. *Journal of Personality and Social Psychology*, 1973, *28*, 77–87.

Steiner, I. D. *Group process and productivity.* New York: Academic Press, 1972.

Steiner, I. D. Whatever happened to the group in social psychology? *Journal of Experimental Social Psychology*, 1974, *10*, 94–108.

Steiner, I. D., & Johnson, H. Authoritarianism and "tolerance of trait inconsistency." *Journal of Abnormal and Social Psychology*, 1963, *67*, 388–391. (a)

Steiner, I. D., & Johnson, H. H. Authoritarianism and conformity. *Sociometry*, 1963, *26*, 21–34. (b)

Steinmetz, S. K., & Straus, M. A. The family as cradle of violence. *Society* (formerly *Transaction*), 1973, *10*, 50–56.

Steinmetz, S. K., & Straus, M. A. (Eds.). *Violence in the family.* New York: Dodd, Mead, 1974.

Steinzor, B. The spatial factor in face-to-face discussion groups. *Journal of Abnormal and Social Psychology*, 1950, *45*, 522–555.

Stephan, W. G. Parental relationships and early social experiences of activist male homosexuals and male heterosexuals. *Journal of Abnormal Psychology*, 1973, *82*, 506–513.

Stephan, W. C. School desegregation: An evaluation of predictions made in *Brown v. The Board of Education. Psychological Bulletin*, 1978, *85*, 217–238.

Stephan, W., Berscheid, E., & Walster, E. Sexual arousal and heterosexual perception. *Journal of Personality and Social Psychology*, 1971, *20*, 93–101.

Stephan, W. G., & Stephan, C. Role differentiation, empathy, and neurosis in urban migrants and lower-class residents of Santiago, Chile. *Journal of Personality and Social Psychology*, 1971, *19*, 1–6.

Stephenson, G. M., Ayling, K., & Rutter, D. R. The role of visual communication in social exchange. *British Journal of Social and Clinical Psychology*, 1976, *15*, 113–120.

Stewart, A. J., & Rubin, Z. The power motive in dating couples. *Journal of Personality and Social Psychology*, 1976, *34*, 305–309.

Stewart, N. AGCT scores of army personnel grouped by occupations. *Occupations*, 1947, *26*, 5–41.

Stires, L. K., & Jones, E. E. Modesty versus self-enhancement as alternative forms of ingratiation. *Journal of Experimental Social Psychology*, 1969, *5*, 172–188.

Stogdill, R. M. Personal factors associated with leadership. *Journal of Psychology*, 1948, *23*, 36–71.

Stogdill, R. M. Leadership, membership, and organization. *Psychological Bulletin*, 1950, *47*, 1–14.

Stogdill, R. M. *Manual for the Leader Behavior Description Questionnaire—Form XII*. Bureau of Business Research, Ohio State University, 1963.

Stogdill, R. M. Validity of leader behavior descriptions. *Personnel Psychology*, 1969, *22*, 153–158.

Stogdill, R. M. *Handbook of leadership: A survey of theory and research*. New York: Free Press, 1974.

Stogdill, R. M. *Leadership abstracts and bibliography 1904–1974*. Columbus: Ohio State University, 1977.

Stokols, D. On the distinction between density and crowding: Some implications for future research. *Psychological Review*, 1972, *79*, 275–277. (a)

Stokols, D. A social-psychological model of human crowding phenomena. *Journal of the American Institute of Planners*, 1972, *38*(2), 72–83. (b)

Stokols, D. The experience of crowding in primary and secondary environments. *Environment and Behavior*, 1976, *8*(1), 49–86.

Stokols, D. A typology of crowding experiences. In A. Baum & Y. Epstein (Eds.), *Human response to crowding*. Hillsdale, N.J.: Erlbaum, 1978. Pp. 219–255.

Stokols, D., Rall, M., Pinner, B., & Schopler, J. Physical, social, and personal determinants of the perception of crowding. *Environment and Behavior*, 1973, *5*, 87–115.

Stoller, R. J. Sexual excitement. *Archives of General Psychiatry*, 1976, *33*, 899–909.

Stone, G. C. Patient compliance and the role of the expert. *Journal of Social Issues*, 1979, *35*(1), 34–59.

Stoner, J.A.F. *A comparison of individual and group decisions involving risk*. Unpublished master's thesis, School of Industrial Management, M.I.T., 1961.

Storms, M. D. Videotape and the attribution process: Reversing actors' and observers' points of view. *Journal of Personality and Social Psychology*, 1973, *27*, 165–175.

Storms, M. D., & McCaul, K. D. Attribution processes and emotional exacerbation of dysfunctional behavior. In J. Harvey, W. Ickes, & R. Kidd (Eds.), *New directions in attribution research* (Vol. 1). Hillsdale, N.J.: Erlbaum, 1976. Pp. 143–164.

Stotland, E., Katz, D., & Patchen, M. The reduction of prejudice through the arousal of self-insight. *Journal of Personality*, 1959, *27*, 507–531.

Straus, M. Some social antecedents of physical punishment: A linkage theory interpretation. *Journal of Marriage and the Family*, 1971, *33*, 658–663.

Straus, M. A. A general systems theory approach to a theory of violence between family members. *Social Science Information*, 1973, *12*, 105–125.

Straus, M. A. *The marriage license as a hitting license: Social instigation of physical aggression in the family*. Paper presented at the meeting of the American Psychological Association, Chicago, September 1975.

Straus, M. A. *Normative and behavioral aspects of violence between spouses: Preliminary data on a nationally representative USA sample*. Paper presented at the Symposium on Violence in Canadian Society, Simon Fraser University, March 1977.

Streufert, S., Castore, C. H., & Kliger, S. C. *A tactical and negotiations game: Rationale, method, and analysis*. Technical Report No. 1, 1967, Purdue University, Office of Naval Research.

Strickland, B. R. Internal-external control of reinforcement. In T. Blass (Ed.), *Personality variables in social behaviors*. Hillsdale, N.J.: Erlbaum, 1977. Pp. 219–279.

Strodtbeck, F. L. Husband-wife interaction over revealed differences. *American Sociological Review*, 1951, *16*, 468–473.

Strodtbeck, F. L. Family interaction, values and achievement. In D. McClelland (Ed.), *Talent and society*. Princeton, N.J.: Van Nostrand, 1958. Pp. 135–191.

Strodtbeck, F., & Hook, H. The social dimensions of a 12-man jury table. *Sociometry*, 1961, *24*, 397–415.

Strodtbeck, F., James, R., & Hawkins, C. Social status in jury deliberations. *American Sociological Review*, 1957, *22*, 713–718.

Strodtbeck, F., & Mann, R. Sex role differentiation in jury deliberations. *Sociometry*, 1956, *19*, 3–11.

Stroop, J. R. Is the judgment of the group better than that of the average member of the group? *Journal of Experimental Psychology*, 1932, *15*, 550–562.

Struening, E. L., & Guttentag, M. (Eds.). *Handbook of evaluation research* (Vol. 1). Beverly Hills, Calif.: Sage, 1975.

Stuckert, R. P. Race mixture: The African ancestry of White Americans. In P. B. Hammond (Ed.), *Physical anthropology and archeology, selected readings*. New York: Macmillan, 1964. Pp. 192–197.

Suedfeld, P. Social isolation: A case for interdisciplinary research. *Canadian Psychologist*, 1974, *15*, 1–15.

Suedfeld, P., Bochner, S., & Wnek, D. Helper-sufferer similarity and a specific request for help: Bystander intervention during a peace demonstration. *Journal of Applied Social Psychology*, 1972, *2*, 17–23.

Suedfeld, P., & Rank, A. D. Revolutionary leaders: Long-term success as a function of changes in conceptual complexity. *Journal of Personality and Social Psychology*, 1976, *34*, 169–178.

Sullivan, H. S. *The interpersonal theory of psychiatry*. New York: Norton, 1953.

Suls, J., Gaes, G., & Gastorf, J. Evaluating a sex-related ability: Comparison with same-, opposite-, and combined-sex norms. *Journal of Research in Personality*, 1979, *13*, 294–304.

Suls, J., Gastorf, J., & Lawhon, J. Social comparison choices for evaluating a sex- and age-related ability. *Personality and Social Psychology Bulletin*, 1978, *4*, 102–105.

Suls, J. M., & Miller, R. L. (Eds.). *Social comparison processes: Theoretical and empirical perspectives*. Washington, D.C.: Halsted-Wiley, 1977.

Summers, D. A., Ashworth, C. D., & Feldman-Summers, S. Judgment processes and interpersonal conflict related to societal problem solutions. *Journal of Applied Social Psychology*, 1977, *7*, 163–174.

Sundstrom, E. Toward an interpersonal model of crowding. *Sociological Symposium*, 1975, *No. 14*, 124–144. (a)

Sundstrom, E. An experimental study of crowding: Effects of room-size, intrusion, and goal-blocking on nonverbal behavior, self-disclosure, and self-reported stress. *Journal of Personality and Social Psychology*, 1975, *32*(4), 645–654. (b)

Sundstrom, E. D. Crowding as a sequential process: Review of research on the effects of population density on humans. In A. Baum & Y. Epstein (Eds.), *Human response to crowding*. Hillsdale, N.J.: Erlbaum, 1978. Pp. 31–116.

Sundstrom, E., & Altman, I. Field study of territorial behavior and dominance. *Journal of Personality and Social Psychology*, 1974, *30*, 115–124.

Sundstrom, E., & Altman, I. Personal space and interpersonal relationships: Research review and theoretical model. *Human Ecology*, 1976, *4*(1), 47–67.

Sundstrom, E., & Sundstrom, M. G. *Workplaces: The psychology of the physical environment in organizations*. Monterey, Calif.: Brooks/Cole, in press.

Swenson, C. H. *Love, problems, and the development of the marriage relationship*. Unpublished manuscript, Purdue University, 1978.

Swift, J. *Gulliver's travels*. New York: New American Library, 1960.

Swingle, P. (Ed.). *The structure of conflict*. New York: Academic Press, 1970.

Swingle, P. G., & Santi, A. Communication in non-zero-sum-games. *Journal of Personality and Social Psychology*, 1972, *23*, 54–63.

Symonds, M. Victims of violence: Psychological effects and aftereffects. *The American Journal of Psychoanalysis*, 1975, *35*, 19–26.

Szent-Györgyi, A. Looking back. *Perspectives in Biology and Medicine*, 1971, *15*, 1–6.

Tajfel, H. Experiments in intergroup discrimination. *Scientific American*, 1970, *223*(2), 96–102.

Tannenbaum, A. S. *Social psychology of the work organization*. Belmont, Calif.: Wadsworth, 1966.

Tanner, K. L., & Catron, D. W. *The effects of examiner-subject variables (length of acquaintance and race of E) on WPPSI scores of preschool Negro boys*. Paper presented at the meeting of the Southeastern Psychological Association, Miami Beach, April 1971.

Tanser, H. A. *The settlement of Negroes in Kent County, Ontario, and the study of the mental capacity of their descendants*. Chatham, Ont.: Shepard, 1939.

Tanter, R., & Midlarsky, M. A theory of revolution. *Journal of Conflict Resolution*, 1967, *11*, 264–280.

Tapp, J. L. Psychology and the law: An overture. In M. R. Rosenzweig and L. W. Porter (Eds.), *Annual Review of Psychology*, 1976, *27*, 359–404.

Taylor, D. A., Altman, I., & Sorrentino, R. Interpersonal exchange as a function of rewards and costs and situational factors: Expectancy confirmation-disconfirmation. *Journal of Experimental Social Psychology*, 1969, *5*, 324–339.

Taylor, D. W., Berry, P. C., & Block, C. H. Does group participation when using brainstorming facilitate or inhibit creative thinking? *Administrative Science Quarterly*, 1958, *3*, 23–47.

Taylor, F. W. *Scientific management*. New York: Harper, 1911.

Taylor, R. B. *Human territoriality: A review and discussion of research needs*. Unpublished manuscript, Virginia Polytechnic Institute and State University, Blacksburg, Virginia, 1978.

Taylor, R. B., & Stough, R. R. Territorial cognition: Individual and group analysis of rep grid data. *Journal of Personality and Social Psychology*, 1978, *36*, 418–423.

Taylor, S. E. A developing role for social psychology in medicine and medical practice. *Personality and Social Psychology Bulletin*, 1978, *4*, 515–523.

Taylor, S. E. Hospital patient behavior: Reactance, helplessness, or control? *Journal of Social Issues*, 1979, *35*(1), 156–184.

Taylor, S. E., & Fiske, S. T. Point of view and perceptions of causality. *Journal of Personality and Social Psychology*, 1975, *32*, 439–445.

Taylor, S. E., Fiske, S. T., Etcoff, N. L., & Ruderman, A. J. Categorical and contextual bases of person memory and stereotyping. *Journal of Personality and Social Psychology*, 1978, *36*, 778–793.

Taylor, S. E., & Koivumaki, J. H. The perception of self and others: Acquaintanceship, affect, and actor-observer differences. *Journal of Personality and Social Psychology*, 1976, *33*, 403–408.

Taylor, S. E., & Levin, S. *The psychological impact of breast cancer: Theory and research*. San Francisco: West Coast Cancer Foundation, 1976.

Taylor, S. P. Aggressive behavior and physiological arousal as a function of provocation and the tendency to inhibit aggression. *Journal of Personality*, 1967, *35*, 297–310.

Taylor, S. P., & Epstein, S. Aggression as a function of the interaction of sex of the aggressor and the sex of the victim. *Journal of Personality*, 1967, *35*, 474–486.

Taylor, S. P., & Gammon, C. B. Effects of type and dose of alcohol on human physical aggression. *Journal of Personality and Social Psychology*, 1975, *32*, 169–175.

Taylor, S. P., & Gammon, C. B. Aggressive behavior of intoxicated subjects: The effect of third-party intervention. *Journal of Studies on Alcohol*, 1976, *37*, 917–930.

Taylor, S. P., Gammon, C. B., & Capasso, D. R. Aggression as a function of the interaction of alcohol and threat. *Journal of Personality and Social Psychology*, 1976, *34*, 938–941.

Taylor, S. P., & Pisano, R. Physical aggression as a function of frustration and physical attack. *Journal of Social Psychology*, 1971, *84*, 261–267.

Taylor, S. P., Schmutte, G. T., & Leonard, K. E., Jr. Physical aggression as a function of alcohol and frustration. *Bulletin of the Psychonomic Society*, 1977, *9*, 217–218.

Taylor, S. P., Vardaris, R. M., Rawtich, A. B., Gammon, C. B., Cranston, J. W., & Lubetkin, A. I. The effects of alcohol and delta-9-tetrahydrocan-nabinol on human physical aggression. *Aggressive Behavior*, 1976, *2*(2) 153–161.

Taynor, J., & Deaux, K. When women are more deserving than men: Equity, attribution, and perceived sex differences. *Journal of Personality and Social Psychology*, 1973, *28*, 360–367.

Teichman, Y. Emotional arousal and affiliation. *Journal of Experimental Social Psychology*, 1973, *9*, 591–605.

Terborg, J. R., & Ilgen, D. R. A theoretical approach to sex discrimination in traditionally masculine occupations. *Organizational Behavior and Human Performance*, 1975, *13*, 352–376.

Terhune, K. W. The effects of personality in cooperation and conflict. In P. Swingle (Ed.), *The structure of conflict*. New York: Academic Press, 1970. Pp. 193–234.

Terman, L. M., & Merrill, M. A. *Measuring intelligence*. Boston: Houghton Mifflin, 1937.

Tesser, A., Gatewood, R., & Driver, M. Some determinants of gratitude. *Journal of Personality and Social*

Psychology, 1968, *9*, 233–236.

Tesser, A., & Rosen, S. Similarity of objective fate as a determinant of the reluctance to transmit unpleasant information: The mum effect. *Journal of Personality and Social Psychology,* 1972, *23*, 46–53.

Tesser, A., & Rosen, S. The reluctance to transmit bad news. In L. Berkowitz (Ed.), *Advances in experimental social psychology* (Vol. 8). New York: Academic Press, 1975. Pp. 193–232.

Tetlock, P. E. Identifying victims of groupthink from public statements of decision makers. *Journal of Personality and Social Psychology,* 1979, *37*, 1314–1324.

Thibaut, J. W., & Kelley, H. H. *The social psychology of groups.* New York: Wiley, 1959.

Thibaut, J., & Walker, L. *Procedural justice: A psychological analysis.* Hillsdale, N.J.: Erlbaum, 1975.

Thomas, M. H., & Drabman, R. S. Toleration of real-life aggression as a function of exposure to televised violence and age of subject. *Merrill-Palmer Quarterly,* 1975, *21*, 227–232.

Thomas, M. H., & Drabman, R. S. *Effects of television violence on expectations of others' aggression.* Paper presented at the meeting of the American Psychological Association, San Francisco, August 1977.

Thorngate, W. *The analysis of variability in social psychology.* Unpublished manuscript, University of Alberta, 1974.

Thornton, B. Toward a linear prediction model of marital happiness. *Personality and Social Psychology Bulletin,* 1977, *3*, 674–676.

Thurstone, L. L. Attitudes can be measured. *American Journal of Sociology,* 1928, *33*, 529–554.

Tiger, L. *Men in groups.* New York: Random House, 1969.

Tilker, H. Socially responsible behavior as a function of observer responsibility and victim feedback. *Journal of Personality and Social Psychology,* 1970, *14*, 95–100.

Tillack, W. S., Tyler, C. W., Paquette, R., & Jones, P. H. A study of premarital pregnancies. *American Journal of Public Health,* 1972, *62*, 676–679.

Tilly, C. Collective violence in European perspective. In H. D. Graham & T. R. Gurr (Eds.), *Violence in America.* New York: New American Library, 1969. Pp. 4–42.

Time. The grueling life on the line. 1970, *96*(13), 70–71. (September 18, 1970 issue)

Time. Cutthroat pre-meds. 1974, *103*(21), 62. (May 20, 1974 issue)

Tinbergen, N. On war and peace in animals and man. *Science,* 1968, *196*, 1411–1418.

Titus, H. E., & Hollander, E. P. The California F scale in psychological research. *Psychological Bulletin,* 1957, *54*, 47–64.

Toda, M., Shinotsuka, H., McClintock, C. G., & Stech, F. J. Development of competitive behavior as a function of culture, age, and social comparison. *Journal of Personality and Social Psychology,* 1978, *36*, 825–839.

Toder, N. L., & Marcia, J. E. Ego identity status and response to conformity pressure in college women. *Journal of Personality and Social Psychology,* 1973, *26*, 287–294.

Toffler, A. *Future shock.* New York: Random House, 1970.

Touhey, J. C. Effects of additional women professionals on ratings of occupational prestige and desirability. *Journal of Personality and Social Psychology,* 1974, *29*, 86–89. (a)

Touhey, J. C. Effects of additional men on prestige and desirability of occupations typically performed by women. *Journal of Applied Social Psychology,* 1974, *4*, 330–335. (b)

Trager, G. L. Paralanguage: A first approximation. *Studies in Linguistics,* 1958, *13*, 1–12.

Triandis, H. C. A note on Rokeach's theory of prejudice. *Journal of Abnormal and Social Psychology,* 1961, *62*, 184–186.

Triandis, H. C. *Attitude and attitude change.* New York: Wiley, 1971.

Triandis, H. C. *Interpersonal behavior.* Monterey, Calif.: Brooks/Cole, 1977. (a)

Triandis, H. C. *Some universals of social behavior,* Address presented at the meeting of the American Psychological Association, San Francisco, August 1977. (b)

Triandis, H. C., & Davis, E. Race and belief as determinants of behavioral intention. *Journal of Personality and Social Psychology,* 1965, *2*, 715–725.

Triandis, H. C., & Vassiliou, V. Frequency of contact and stereotyping. *Journal of Personality and Social Psychology,* 1967, *7*, 316–328.

Triplett, N. The dynamogenic factors in pacemaking and competition. *American Journal of Psychology,* 1897, *9*, 507–533.

Trivers, R. L. The evolution of reciprocal altruism. *Quarterly Review of Biology,* 1971, *46*, 35–57.

Trivers, R. L., & Hare, H. Haplodiploidy and the evolution of the social insects. *Science,* 1976, *191*, 249–263.

Tunnell, G. B. Three dimensions of naturalness: An expanded definition of field research. *Psychological Bulletin,* 1977, *84*, 426–437.

Turiel, E., & Rothman, G. R. The influence of reasoning on behavioral choices at different stages of moral development. *Child Development,* 1972, *43*, 741–756.

Turner, C. F., & Martinez, D. C. Socio-economic achievement and the Machiavellian personality. *Sociometry,* 1977, *40*, 325–336.

Turner, C. W., Layton, J. F., & Simons, L. S. Naturalistic studies of aggressive behavior: Aggressive stimuli, victim visibility, and horn honking. *Journal of Personality and Social Psychology,* 1975, *31*, 1098–1107.

Turner, C. W., & Simons, L. S. Effects of subject sophistication and evaluation apprehension on aggressive responses to weapons. *Journal of Personality and Social Psychology,* 1974, *30*, 341–348.

Tversky, A., & Kahneman, D. Availability: A heuristic for judging frequency and probability. *Cognitive Psychology,* 1973, *5*, 207–232.

Tyler, L. E. *The psychology of human differences* (3rd ed.). New York: Appleton-Century-Crofts, 1965.

Tyler, L. *Individuality: Human possibilities and personal choice in the psychological development of men and women.* San Francisco: Jossey-Bass, 1978.

Tyler, T. R., & Sears, D. O. Coming to like obnoxious people when we must live with them. *Journal of Personality and Social Psychology,* 1977, *35*, 200–211.

Underwood, B., Froming, W. J., & Moore, B. S. Mood, attention, and altruism: A search for mediating variables. *Developmental Psychology,* 1977, *13*, 541–542.

Ungar, S. The effects of effort and stigma on helping. *Journal of Social Psychology,* 1979, *107*, 23–28.

U.S. Commission on Civil Rights. *Racism in America and how to combat it.* Washington, D.C.: U.S. Government Printing Office, 1969.

U.S. Riot Commission. *Report of the National Advisory Commission on Civil Disorders.* New York: Bantam Books, 1968.

Vacc, N. A., & Vacc, N. E. An adaptation for children of the Modified Role Repertory Test—A measure of cognitive complexity. *Psychological Reports*, 1973, *33*, 771–776.

Valle, V. A., & Frieze, I. H. Stability of causal attributions in changing expectations for success. *Journal of Personality and Social Psychology*, 1976, *33*, 579–587.

Varela, J. A. Aplicación de hallazgos provenientes de las ciencias sociales. *Revista Interamericana de Psicologia*, 1969, *3*, 45–52.

Varela, J. A. *Psychological solutions to social problems: An introduction to social technology.* New York: Academic Press, 1971.

Varela, J. A. Can social psychology be applied? In M. Deutsch & H. A. Hornstein (Eds.), *Applying social psychology: Implications for research, practice, and training.* Hillsdale, N.J.: Erlbaum, 1975. Pp. 157–173.

Varela, J. A. Social technology. *American Psychologist*, 1977, *32*, 914–923.

Varela, J. A. Solving human problems with human science. *Human Nature*, 1978, *1*, 84–90. (October 1978 issue)

Verbrugge, L., & Taylor, R. B. Consequences of population density and size. *Urban Affairs Quarterly*, in press.

Villaseñor, V. *Jury: The people vs. Juan Corona.* New York: Bantam Books, 1977.

Vinokur, A. A review and theoretical analysis of the effects of group processes upon individual and group decisions involving risk. *Psychological Bulletin*, 1971, *76*, 231–250.

Vollmer, H. M. Basic rules for applying social science to urban and social problems. *Urban and Social Change Review*, 1970, *3*(2), 32–33.

vonBaeyer, C. L. Sherk, D. L., & Zanna, M. P. *Impression management: Female job applicant, male (chauvinist) interviewer.* Paper presented at the meeting of the American Psychological Association, New York, September 1979.

von Cranach, M., & Ellgring, J. H. Problems in the recognition of gaze direction. In M. von Cranach and I. Vine (Eds.), *Social communication and movement.* New York: Academic Press, 1973. Pp. 419–442.

Vraa, C. W. Emotional climate as a function of group composition. *Small Group Behavior*, 1974, *5*, 105–120.

Vroom, V. H. *Some personality determinants of the effects of participation.* Englewood Cliffs, N.J.: Prentice-Hall, 1960.

Vroom, V. H., & Mann, F. C. Leader authoritarianism and employee attitudes. *Personnel Psychology*, 1960, *13*, 125–140.

Wall, P. M. *Eye-witness identification in criminal cases.* Springfield, Ill.: Charles C Thomas, 1971.

Waller, W. The rating and dating complex. *American Sociological Review*, 1937, *2*, 727–737.

Walster, E., Aronson, E., & Abrahams, D. On increasing the persuasiveness of a low prestige communicator. *Journal of Experimental Social Psychology*, 1966, *2*, 325–342.

Walster, E., Aronson, V., Abrahams, D., & Rottman, L. Importance of physical attractiveness in dating behavior. *Journal of Personality and Social Psychology*, 1966, *4*, 508–516.

Walster, E., & Berscheid, E. A little bit about love: A minor essay on a major topic. In T. L. Huston (Ed.), *Foundations of interpersonal attraction.* New York: Academic Press, 1974. Pp. 355–381.

Walster, E., Berscheid, E., & Walster, G. W. The exploited: Justice or justification? In J. Macaulay & L. Berkowitz (Eds.), *Altruism and helping behavior: Social psychological studies of some antecedents and consequences.* New York: Academic Press, 1970. Pp. 179–204.

Walster, E., Berscheid, E., & Walster, G. W. New directions in equity research. *Journal of Personality and Social Psychology*, 1973, *25*, 151–176.

Walster, E., Berscheid, E., & Walster, G. W. New directions in equity research. In L. Berkowitz (Ed.), *Advances in experimental social psychology* (Vol. 9). New York: Academic Press, 1976. Pp. 1–42.

Walster, E., & Piliavin, J. A. Equity and the innocent bystander. *Journal of Social Issues*, 1972, *28*(3), 165–189.

Walster, E., Piliavin, J. A., & Walster, G. W. The hard-to-get woman. *Psychology Today*, 1973, *7*(4), 80–83.

Walster, E., & Walster, G. W. *Love.* Reading, Mass.: Addison-Wesley, 1978.

Walster, E., Walster, G. W., & Berscheid, E. *Equity: Theory and research.* Boston: Allyn and Bacon, 1978.

Walster, E., Walster, G. W., Piliavin, J., & Schmidt, L. "Playing hard to get": Understanding an elusive phenomenon. *Journal of Personality and Social Psychology*, 1973, *26*, 113–121.

Walster, E., Walster, G. W., & Traupmann, J. Equity and premarital sex. *Journal of Personality and Social Psychology*, 1978, *36*, 82–92.

Walters, R. H., & Brown, M. Studies of reinforcement of aggression. III. Transfer of responses to an interpersonal situation. *Child Development*, 1963, *34*, 536–571.

Walters, R. H., Llewellyn-Thomas, E., & Acker, C. W. Enhancement of punitive behavior by audio-visual displays. *Science*, 1962, *135*, 872–873.

Walters, R., & Thomas, E. Enhancement of punitiveness by visual and audiovisual displays. *Canadian Journal of Psychology*, 1963, *17*, 244–255.

Warr, P. B., & Knapper, C. *The perception of people and events.* New York: Wiley, 1968.

Warriner, C. H. Groups are real: A reaffirmation. *American Sociological Review*, 1956, *21*, 549–554.

Washburn, S. L. The study of race. In M.F.A. Montagu (Ed.), *The concept of race.* New York: Free Press, 1964. Pp. 242–260.

Waters, H. F., & Malamud, P. "Drop that gun, Captain Video." *Newsweek*, 1975, *85*(10), 81–82. (March 10, 1975 issue)

Watson, G. *Action for unity.* New York: Harper, 1947.

Watson, J. B. *Behaviorism.* New York: Norton, 1930.

Watson, R. I., Jr. Investigation into deindividuation using a cross-cultural survey technique. *Journal of Personality and Social Psychology*, 1973, *25*, 342–345.

Waxler, N. E., & Mishler, E. G. Experimental studies of families. In L. Berkowitz (Ed.), *Group processes.* New York: Academic Press, 1978. Pp. 363–418.

Webb, E. J., Campbell, D. T., Schwartz, R. D., & Sechrest, L. *Unobtrusive measures: Nonreactive research in the social sciences.* Chicago: Rand McNally, 1966.

Wegner, D. M., & Vallacher, R. R. *Implicit psychology: An introduction to social cognition.* New York: Oxford

University Press, 1977.

Weick, K. E. The concept of equity in the perception of pay. *Administrative Science Quarterly*, 1966, *11*, 414–439.

Weick, K. The spines of leaders, In M. W. McCall, Jr., & M. M. Lombardo (Eds.), *Leadership: Where else can we go?* Durham, N.C.: Duke University Press, 1978. Pp. 37–61.

Weigel, R. H., Vernon, D.T.A., & Tognacci, L. N. Specificity of the attitude as a determinant of attitude-behavior congruence. *Journal of Personality and Social Psychology*, 1974, *30*, 724–728.

Weigel, R. H., Wiser, P. L., & Cook, S. W. The impact of cooperative learning experiences on cross-ethnic relations and attitudes. *Journal of Social Issues*, 1975, *31*(1), 219–244.

Weinberg, M. S., & Williams, C. J. *Male homosexuals: Their problems and their adaptations.* New York: Oxford University Press, 1974.

Weiner, B. (Ed.). *Achievement motivation and attribution theory.* Morristown, N.J.: General Learning Press, 1974.

Weiner, B., Frieze, I., Kukla, A., Reed, L., Rest, S., & Rosenbaum, R. M. Perceiving the causes of success and failure. In E. E. Jones, D. E. Kanouse, H. H. Kelley, R. E. Nisbett, S. Valins, & B. Weiner, *Attribution: Perceiving the causes of behavior.* Morristown, N.J.: General Learning Press, 1972. Pp. 95–120.

Weiss, C. H. *Evaluation research: Methods for assessing program effectiveness.* Englewood Cliffs, N.J.: Prentice-Hall, 1972.

Weiss, R. F. Persuasion and the acquisition of attitudes: Models from conditioning and selective learning. *Psychological Reports*, 1962, *11*, 709–732.

Weiss, R. F. An extension of Hullian learning theory to persuasive communication. In A. G. Greenwald, T. C. Brock, & T. M. Ostrom (Eds.), *Psychological foundations of attitudes.* New York: Academic Press, 1968. Pp. 109–145.

Weiss, R. F., Buchanan, W., Altstatt, L., & Lombardo, J. P. Altruism is rewarding. *Science*, 1971, *171*, 1262–1263.

Weiss, R. S. The emotional impact of marital separation. *Journal of Social Issues*, 1976, *32*(1), 135–145.

Weissbach, T. Racism and prejudice. In S. Oskamp, *Attitudes and opinions.* Englewood Cliffs, N.J.: Prentice-Hall, 1977. Pp. 318–338.

Weitz, S. Attitude, voice and behavior: A repressed affect model of interracial interaction. *Journal of Personality and Social Psychology*, 1972, *24*, 14–21.

Weitz, S. Sex differences in nonverbal communication. *Sex Roles*, 1976, *2*, 175–184.

Wellman, D. T. *Portraits of White racism.* New York: Cambridge University Press, 1977.

Wells, G. L., & Harvey, J. H. Do people use consensus information in making causal attributions? *Journal of Personality and Social Psychology*, 1977, *35*, 279–293.

Werner, C., & Latané, B. Responsiveness and communication medium in dyadic interactions. *Bulletin of the Psychonomic Society*, 1976, *8*, 569–571.

West, S. G., & Gunn, S. P. Some issues of ethics and social psychology. *American Psychologist*, 1978, *33*, 30–38.

West, S. G., Gunn, S. P., & Chernicky, P. Ubiquitous Watergate: An attributional analysis. *Journal of Personality and Social Psychology*, 1975, *32*, 55–65.

Westhues, K. *On marginality and its solutions in contemporary society.* Lecture presented at St. Francis Xavier University, Antigonish, Nova Scotia, February 1972.

Westie, F. R. A technique for the measurement of race attitudes. *American Sociological Review*, 1953, *18*, 73–78.

Westin, A. *Privacy and freedom.* New York: Atheneum, 1970.

Wetter, R. E. Levels of self-esteem associated with four sex role categories. In R. Bednar (Chair), *Sex roles: Masculine, feminine, androgynous, or none of the above?* Symposium presented at the meeting of the American Psychological Association, Chicago, 1975.

Wexler, M. The behavioral sciences in medical education: A view from psychology. *American Psychologist*, 1976, *31*, 275–283.

Weyant, J. M. Effects of mood states, costs, and benefits on helping. *Journal of Personality and Social Psychology*, 1978, *36*, 1169–1176.

Wheeler, L., & Nezlek, J. Sex differences in social participation. *Journal of Personality and Social Psychology*, 1977, *35*, 742–754.

Whitcher, S. J., & Fisher, J. D. Multidimensional reaction to therapeutic touch in a hospital setting. *Journal of Personality and Social Psychology*, 1979, *37*, 87–96.

White, G. M. Immediate and deferred effects of model observation and guided and unguided rehearsal on donating and stealing. *Journal of Personality and Social Psychology*, 1972, *21*, 139–148.

Whyte, W. H., Jr. *The organization man.* New York: Simon and Schuster, 1956.

Wicker, A. W. Undermanning, performances, and students' subjective experiences in behavior settings of large and small schools. *Journal of Personality and Social Psychology*, 1968, *10*, 255–261.

Wicker, A. W. Attitudes versus actions: The relationship of verbal and overt behavioral responses to attitude objects. *Journal of Social Issues*, 1969, *25*(4), 41–78. (a)

Wicker, A. W. Size of church membership and members' support of church behavior settings. *Journal of Personality and Social Psychology*, 1969, *13*, 278–288. (b)

Wicker, A. W. Undermanning theory and research: Implications for the study of psychological and behavioral effects of excess populations. *Representative Research in Social Psychology*, 1973, *4*, 185–206.

Wicker, A. W. *An introduction to ecological psychology.* Monterey, Calif.: Brooks/Cole, 1979.

Wicker, A. W., & Kirmeyer, S. From church to laboratory to national park: A program of research on excess and insufficient populations in behavior settings. In D. Stokols (Ed.), *Psychological perspectives on environment and behavior: Conceptual and empirical trends.* New York: Plenum Press, 1977.

Wicklund, R. A. *Freedom and reactance.* Potomac, Md.: Erlbaum, 1974.

Wicklund, R. A. Objective self-awareness. In L. Berkowitz (Ed.), *Advances in experimental social psychology* (Vol. 8). New York: Academic Press, 1975.

Wiemann, J. M., & Knapp, M. L. Turn-taking in conversations. *Journal of Communication*, 1975, *25*, 75–92.

Wiggins, J. S., & Holzmuller, A. Psychological androgyny and interpersonal behavior. *Journal of Consulting and Clinical Psychology*, 1978, *46*, 40–52.

Wilder, D. A. A theory of social entities: Effects of group membership on social perception and social influence. Unpublished doctoral dissertation, University of Wisconsin, Madison, 1975.

Wilder, D. A. Reduction of intergroup discrimination through individuation of the out-group. *Journal of Personality and Social Psychology*, 1978, *36*, 1361–1374.

Wilder, D. A., & Allen, V. L. *The effect of absent social support on conformity.* Paper presented at the meeting of the Midwestern Psychological Association, Chicago, May 1973.

Williams, E. Experimental comparisons of face-to-face and mediated communication: A review. *Psychological Bulletin*, 1977, *84*, 963–976.

Williams, E. Visual interaction and speech patterns: An extension of previous results. *British Journal of Social and Clinical Psychology*, 1978, *17*, 101–102.

Williams, W., & Evans, J. W. The politics of evaluation: The case of Head Start. In P. H. Rossi & W. Williams (Eds.), *Evaluating social programs: Theory, practice, and politics.* New York: Seminar Press, 1972. Pp. 247–264.

Willie, C. V. (Ed.). *Black/Brown/White relations: Race relations in the 1970's.* New Brunswick, N.J.: Transaction Books, 1977.

Willis, F. N., & Hoffman, G. E. Development of tactile patterns in relation to age, sex, and race. *Developmental Psychology*, 1975, *11*, 866.

Wilner, D. M., Walkley, R., & Cook, S. W. *Human relations in interracial housing: A study of the contact hypothesis.* Minneapolis, Minn.: University of Minnesota Press, 1955.

Wilson, D. W., & Donnerstein, E. Guilty or not guilty? A look at the "simulated" jury paradigm. *Journal of Applied Social Psychology*, 1977, *7*, 175–190.

Wilson, E. O. *Sociobiology: The new synthesis.* Cambridge, Mass.: Belknap Press of Harvard University Press, 1975.

Wilson, E. O. *On human nature.* Cambridge, Mass.: Harvard University Press, 1978.

Wilson, P. R. Perceptual distortion of height as a function of ascribed academic status. *Journal of Social Psychology*, 1968, *74*, 97–102.

Wilson, W. C. Pornography: The emergence of a social issue and the beginning of psychological study. *Journal of Social Issues*, 1973, *29*(3), 7–17.

Winch, R. F. *The modern family.* New York: Holt, 1952.

Winch, R. F., Ktsanes, I., & Ktsanes, V. The theory of complementary needs in mate selection: An analytic and descriptive study. *American Sociological Review*, 1954, *19*, 241–249.

Winsborough, H. The social consequences of high population density. *Law and Contemporary Problems*, 1965, *30*, 120–126.

Winterbottom, M. R. The relation of childhood training in independence to achievement motivation. Unpublished doctoral dissertation, University of Michigan, 1953. (Cited in D. C. McClelland et al., *The achievement motive.* New York: Appleton-Century, 1953.)

Wishner, J. Reanalysis of "impressions of personality." *Psychological Review*, 1960, *67*, 96–112.

Wispé, L. G. Positive forms of social behavior: An overview. *Journal of Social Issues*, 1972, *28*(3), 1–19.

Wispé, L. G. (Ed.). *Altruism, sympathy, and helping: Psychological and sociological principles.* New York: Academic Press, 1978.

Wispé, L. G., & Freshley, H. B. Race, sex, and sympathetic helping behavior: The broken bag caper. *Journal of Personality and Social Psy-*

chology, 1971, *17*, 59–65.

Witcover, J. *The resurrection of Richard Nixon.* New York: Putnam, 1970.

Witkin, H. A., Dyk, R. B., Faterson, H. F., Goodenough, D. R., & Karp, S. A. *Psychological differentiation.* New York: Wiley, 1962.

Wohlwill, J. F. Human adaptation to levels of environmental stimulation. *Human Ecology*, 1974, *2*(2), 127–147.

Wohlwill, J., & Kohn, I. The environment as experienced by the migrant: An adaptation-level view. *Representative Research in Social Psychology*, 1973, *4*, 135–164.

Wolfe, T. *The electric Kool-aid acid test.* New York: Farrar, Straus and Giroux, 1968.

Wolff, C. *Love between women.* New York: Harper & Row, 1971.

Wolff, L., & Taylor, S. E. Sex, sex-role identification, and awareness of sex-role stereotypes. *Sex Roles*, 1979, *5*, 177–184.

Wood, D. A. Effect of worker orientation differences on job attitude correlates. *Journal of Applied Psychology*, 1974, *59*, 54–60.

Wood, F. A. *The influence of monarchs.* New York: Macmillan, 1913.

Woodmansee, J., & Cook, S. W. Dimensions of verbal racial attitudes. *Journal of Personality and Social Psychology*, 1967, *7*, 240–250.

Wools, R., & Canter, D. The effect of the meaning of buildings on behavior. *Applied Ergonomics*, 1970, *1*(3), 144–150.

Worchel, S. The effect of three types of arbitrary thwarting on the instigation to aggression. *Journal of Personality*, 1974, *42*, 301–318.

Worchel, S., Arnold, S., & Baker, M. The effects of censorship on attitude change: The influence of censor and communication characteristics. *Journal of Applied Social Psychology*, 1975, *5*, 227–239.

Worchel, S., & Brehm, J. W. Direct and implied social restoration of freedom. *Journal of Personality and Social Psychology*, 1971, *18*, 294–304.

Worchel, S., & Esterson, C. *The effects of misattribution on the experience of crowding.* Paper presented at the meeting of the American Psychological Association, Washington, D.C., 1978.

Worthy, M. *Eye-color, sex, and race.* Anderson, S.C.: Droke House/Hallux, 1974.

Worthy, M., Gary, A. L., & Kahn, G. Self-disclosure as an exchange process. *Journal of Personality and Social Psychology*, 1969, *13*, 59–63.

Worthy, M., & Markle, A. Racial differences in self-paced versus reactive sports activities. *Journal of Personality and Social Psychology*, 1970, *16*, 439–443.

Wortman, C. B., & Brehm, J. W. Responses to uncontrollable outcomes: An integration of reactance theory and the learned helplessness model. In L. Berkowitz (Ed.), *Advances in experimental social psychology* (Vol. 8). New York: Academic Press, 1975. Pp. 277–336.

Wright, P. H., & Crawford, A. C. Agreement and friendship: A close look and some second thoughts. *Representative Research in Social Psychology*, 1971, *2*, 52–69.

Wrightsman, L. S. Effects of waiting with others on changes in level of felt anxiety. *Journal of Abnormal and Social Psychology*, 1960, *61*, 216–222.

Wrightsman, L. S. Measurement of philosophies of human nature. *Psychological Reports*, 1964, *14*, 743–751.

Wrightsman, L. S. *Attitudinal and personality correlates of presidential voting preferences.* Paper presented at the meeting of the American Psychological Association, Chicago, September 1965.

Wrightsman, L. S. *Assumptions about human nature: A social-psychological approach.* Monterey, Calif.: Brooks/Cole, 1974.

Wrightsman, L. S. The presence of others does make a difference—sometimes. *Psychological Bulletin,* 1975, *82,* 884–885.

Wrightsman, L. S. Personal documents as data in conceptualizing adult personality development. Presidential address, Division 8, American Psychological Association Convention, Montreal, September 1980.

Wrightsman, L. S., & Cook, S. W. *Factor analysis and attitude change.* Paper presented at the meeting of the Southeastern Psychological Association, Atlanta, April 1965.

Wrightsman, L. S., O'Connor, J., & Baker, N. J. (Eds.). *Cooperation and competition: Readings on mixed-motive games.* Monterey, Calif.: Brooks/Cole, 1972.

Wrightsman, L. S., & Satterfield, C. H. *Additional norms and standardization of the Philosophies of Human Nature scale—1967 revision.* George Peabody College for Teachers, 1967. (Mimeographed)

Wynne-Edwards, V. *Animal dispersion in relation to social behavior.* New York: Hafner Publishing Co., 1962.

Yancey, W. L. Architecture and social interaction: The case of a large-scale public housing project. *Environment and Behavior,* 1971, *3*(1), 3–21.

Yerkes, R. M. Psychological examining in the United States Army. *Memoirs of the National Academy of Science* (Vol. 15). Washington, D.C.: U.S. Government Printing Office, 1921.

Younger, J. C., & Doob, A. N. Attribution and aggression: The misattribution of anger. *Journal of Research in Personality,* 1978, *12,* 164–171.

Yukl, G. Toward a behavioral theory of leadership. *Organizational Behavior and Human Performance,* 1971, *6,* 414–440.

Zablocki, B. *The joyful community.* Baltimore, Md.: Penguin, 1971.

Zacker, J. Authoritarian avoidance of ambiguity. *Psychological Reports,* 1973, *33,* 901–902.

Zajonc, R. B. Social facilitation. *Science,* 1965, *149,* 269–274.

Zajonc, R. B. Attitudinal effects of mere exposure. *Journal of Personality and Social Psychology Monograph Supplement,* 1968, *9*(2, Part 2), 2–27. (a)

Zajonc, R. B. Cognitive theories in social psychology. In G. Lindzey & E. Aronson (Eds.), *Handbook of social psychology* (Vol. 1) (2nd ed.). Reading, Mass.: Addison-Wesley, 1968. Pp. 320–411. (b)

Zajonc, R. B., & Sales, S. Social facilitation of dominant subordinate responses. *Journal of Experimental Social Psychology,* 1966, *2,* 160–168.

Zander, A., & Armstrong, W. Working for group pride in a slipper factory. *Journal of Applied Social Psychology,* 1972, *2,* 293–307.

Zanna, M., Goethals, G., & Hill, J. Evaluating a sex-related ability: Social comparison with similar others and standard setters. *Journal of Experimental Social Psychology,* 1975, *11,* 86–93.

Zanna, M. P., & Pack, S. J. On the self-fulfilling nature of apparent sex differences in behavior. *Journal of Experimental Social Psychology,* 1975, *11,* 583–591.

Zillman, D., Bryant, J., Cantor, J. R., & Day, K. D. Irrelevance of mitigating circumstances in retaliatory behavior at high levels of excitation. *Journal of Research in Personality,* 1975, *9,* 282–293.

Zillman, D., & Cantor, J. R. Effect of timing of information about mitigating circumstances on emotional responses to provocation and retaliatory behavior. *Journal of Experimental Social Psychology,* 1976, *12,* 38–55.

Zillman, D., Katcher, A., & Milavsky, B. Excitation transfer from physical exercise to subsequent aggressive behavior. *Journal of Experimental Social Psychology,* 1972, *8,* 247–259.

Zimbardo, P. G. The human choice: Individuation, reason, and order versus deindividuation, impulse, and chaos. In W. J. Arnold & D. Levine (Eds.), *Nebraska Symposium on Motivation, 1969.* Lincoln: University of Nebraska Press, 1970.

Zimbardo, P. G., & Ebbesen, E. B. *Influencing attitudes and changing behavior.* Reading, Mass.: Addison-Wesley, 1969.

Zlutnick, S., & Altman, I. Crowding and human behavior. In J. Wohlwill & D. Carson (Eds.), *Environment and the social sciences.* Washington, D.C.: American Psychological Association, 1972. Pp. 44–60.

Zuckerman, M. Physiological measures of sexual arousal in the human. *Psychological Bulletin,* 1971, *75,* 297–329.

Zuckerman, M. Actions and occurrences in Kelley's cube. *Journal of Personality and Social Psychology,* 1978, *36,* 647–656. (a)

Zuckerman, M. Use of consensus information in prediction of behavior. *Journal of Experimental Social Psychology,* 1978, *14,* 163–171. (b)

Zuckerman, M., Lazzaro, M. M., & Waldgeir, D. Undermining effects of the foot-in-the-door technique with extrinsic rewards. *Journal of Applied Social Psychology,* 1979, *9,* 292–296.

Zuckerman, M., & Wheeler, L. To dispel fantasies about the fantasy-based measure of fear of success. *Psychological Bulletin,* 1975, *82,* 932–946.

Name Index

Abelson, H. I., 358, 361
Abelson, R. P., 22, 328, 340
Abrahams, D., 165, 359
Abramson, P. R., 72, 192, 193
Acker, C. W., 287
Acking, C. A., 512
Adams, J. S., 254
Adelberg, S., 556
Aderman, D., 85, 163, 248, 252
Adorno, T. W., 314, 431–434
Ahlering, R. F., 367
Aiello, J. R., 141, 144, 399, 527, 531, 537
Alexander, C. N., 96
Alexander, G. R., 74
Alexander, R. A., 489
Alioto, J. T., 287
Alkema, F., 131
Alker, H. A., 101
Alker, H. W., 101, 449
Allen, A., 450
Allen, B. P., 363, 369
Allen, J. G., 110, 111
Allen, V. L., 16, 381, 382, 383
Allgeier, E. R., 447
Allport, F., 458
Allport, G. W., 6, 68, 300, 310, 313, 316, 430
Alper, A., 77
Altman, I., 107, 141, 149, 157, 175, 513, 514, 515, 516, 517, 518, 519, 523, 532, 533
Altstatt, L., 237
Alvares, K., 494, 495, 498
Amabile, T. M., 85
Ames, L. B., 223
Amoroso, D. M., 203
Anastasi, A., 423
Anderson, C. A., 285
Anderson, N. H., 74, 75, 76, 167
Andrasik, F., 163
Andrews, F. M., 492, 552
Andrews, I. R., 466
Andrews, J. H. M., 492
Appelbaum, M. I., 417
Ard, B. N., Jr., 198
Ardrey, R., 268, 517
Argyle, M., 131, 143, 144, 145

Argyris, C., 504, 505
Arms, R. L., 74
Armstrong, D., 524
Armstrong, W., 503
Arnold, S., 397
Aron, A. P., 172, 174
Aronfreed, J., 221, 237, 248, 258
Aronson, E., 22, 42, 43, 46, 54, 59, 114, 165, 167, 230, 242, 328, 346, 359, 360, 371, 439
Arvey, R. D., 164
Asch, S., 22, 23, 73, 74, 380–382
Ashmore, R. D., 310, 313, 397
Ashton, N. L., 255
Ashworth, C. D., 555
Athanasiou, R., 189, 190, 200
Atkin, R. S., 468, 469, 473
Atkins, A., 71, 336
Atkinson, J. W., 410, 438, 440, 441, 442
Austin, W., 228, 229
Austin, W. T., 523
Ausubel, D., 22
Avellar, J., 244
Averill, J. R., 172, 524
Ayling, K., 151
Azjen, I., 317, 320, 323, 361, 367, 369
Azrin, N. H., 274

Bachy, V., 205
Back, K. W., 167, 472, 477, 529
Backman, C. W., 167
Baer, D. M., 223
Bailey, M. M., 410
Bakan, D., 445
Bakeman, R., 472
Baker, M., 397
Baker, N. J., 66, 240
Bales, R. F., 486, 487, 490, 492
Ball, R. L., 294
Ballachey, E., 382, 421
Balswick, J. O., 190, 191
Bandura, A., 19, 220, 221, 276, 277, 278, 284, 286, 412, 459, 474
Bane, A. L., 369
Banks, C., 52
Barach, J. A., 363

Barak, A., 505
Barash, D. P., 237
Barclay, A. M., 200
Bard, M., 558
Bardwick, J. M., 447
Barefoot, J., 144
Barker, R. G., 16, 26, 27, 49, 535
Barnes, P. J., 261
Barnes, R. D., 85, 103, 148, 448
Barnett, B., 241
Baron, R. A., 204, 270, 276, 278, 279, 284, 285, 287, 288, 293, 294
Baron, R. S., 458, 465
Barron, J. W., 344
Barron, N., 129
Barsaloux, J., 462
Bar-Tal, D., 165, 245, 255
Bartlett, C. J., 505
Bartlett, M. K., 548
Bass, B. M., 434, 489
Bassett, R., 387
Bates, F. L., 523
Batson, C. D., 247, 253, 258, 556
Battit, G. E., 548
Bauchner, J. E., 150
Bauer, R. A., 363, 552
Baughman, E., 417
Baum, A., 399, 530, 531, 536, 537
Baumeister, R., 101, 114
Baumgardner, M. H., 364
Baumrin, B. H., 542
Baumrind, D., 391, 434
Bayton, J. A., 302
Beach, F. A., 192, 194
Beaman, A. L., 261
Beane, W., 441
Beard, J. F., 103
Beattie, C., 310, 417
Beattie, M., 395
Becker, F. D., 520, 521
Becker, L. A., 359
Becker, L. J., 551
Becker, S. W., 230
Becker-Haven, J. F., 251
Bee, H., 305
Beecher, M. D., 257
Beekman, S., 408

Subject Index

To the owner of this book:

We hope that you have enjoyed *Social Psychology in the Eighties (Third Edition)* as much as we have enjoyed writing it. We'd like to know as much about your experiences with the book as you care to offer. Only through your comments and the comments of others can we learn how to make *Social Psychology in the Eighties* a better book for future readers.

School: _____ Your instructor's name: _____

1. What did you like most about *Social Psychology in the Eighties (Third Edition)?*
   _____
   _____

2. What did you like least about the book? _____
   _____

3. Were all of the chapters of the book assigned for you to read? _____
   If not, which ones weren't? _____

4. If you used the Glossary, how helpful was it as an aid in understanding psychological concepts and terms? _____
   _____

5. Did you use the Study Guide? _____
   If so, please tell us what component was most useful (terms, short-answer questions, multiple-choice items, or other components): _____
   _____

6. In the space below, or in a separate letter, please let us know what other comments about the book you'd like to make. (For example, were any chapters *or* concepts particularly difficult?) We'd be delighted to hear from you!

Optional:

Your name: _____ Date: _____

May Brooks/Cole quote you, either in promotion for *Social Psychology in the Eighties (Third Edition)* or in future publishing ventures?

Yes _____ No _____

Sincerely,

Lawrence S. Wrightsman

Kay Deaux

FOLD HERE

FOLD HERE

FIRST CLASS
Permit No. 84
Monterey, CA

BUSINESS REPLY MAIL
No Postage Necessary if Mailed in United States

Dr. Lawrence S. Wrightsman
Dr. Kay Deaux
Brooks/Cole Publishing Company
Monterey, CA 93940